T&T CLARK HANDBOOK OF THE EARLY CHURCH

T0414068

Forthcoming titles in this series include:

T&T Clark Handbook of Christology, *edited by Darren O. Sumner and Chris Tilling*

T&T Clark Handbook of Christian Prayer, *edited by Ashley Cocksworth and John C. McDowell*

T&T Clark Handbook of Public Theology, *edited by Christoph Hübenthal and Christiane Alpers*

T&T Clark Handbook of Election, *edited by Edwin Chr. van Driel*

T&T Clark Handbook of John Owen, *edited by Crawford Gribben and John W. Tweeddale*

T&T Clark Handbook of Anabaptism, *edited by Brian C. Brewer*

T&T Clark Handbook of Modern Theology, *edited by Philip G. Ziegler and R. David Nelson*

T&T Clark Handbook of the Doctrine of Creation, *edited by Jason Goroncy*

Titles already published include:

T&T Clark Handbook of Christian Theology and Climate Change, *edited by Ernst M. Conradie and Hilda P. Koster*

T&T Clark Handbook of Political Theology, *edited by Rubén Rosario Rodríguez*

T&T Clark Handbook of Pneumatology, *edited by Daniel Castelo and Kenneth M. Loyer*

T&T Clark Handbook of Ecclesiology, *edited by Kimlyn J. Bender and D. Stephen Long*

T&T Clark Handbook of Christian Theology and the Modern Sciences, *edited by John P. Slattery*

T&T Clark Handbook of Christian Ethics, *edited by Tobias Winright*

T&T Clark Handbook of Analytic Theology, *edited by James M. Arcadi and James T. Turner, Jr*

T&T Clark Handbook of Theological Anthropology, *edited by Mary Ann Hinsdale and Stephen Okey*

T&T CLARK HANDBOOK OF
THE EARLY CHURCH

Edited by
Ilaria L. E. Ramelli, John Anthony McGuckin
and Piotr Ashwin-Siejkowski

t&tclark

LONDON • NEW YORK • OXFORD • NEW DELHI • SYDNEY

T&T CLARK
Bloomsbury Publishing Plc
50 Bedford Square, London, WC1B 3DP, UK
1385 Broadway, New York, NY 10018, USA
29 Earlsfort Terrace, Dublin 2, Ireland

BLOOMSBURY, T&T CLARK and the T&T Clark logo are trademarks of
Bloomsbury Publishing Plc

First published in Great Britain 2022
Paperback edition published 2024

Cover image: *Christ the High Priest* by Eileen McGuckin.
The Icon Studio: eileenmcguckin1003@gmail.com

Library of Congress Cataloging-in-Publication Data
Names: Ashwin-Siejkowski, Piotr, 1964- editor. | McGuckin, John Anthony, editor. |
Ramelli, Ilaria, 1973- editor.
Title: T&T Clark handbook of the early church / edited by Piotr Ashwin-Siejkowski,
John Anthony McGuckin and Ilaria L.E. Ramelli.
Description: London ; New York : T&T Clark, 2021. | Series: T&T Clark handbooks |
Includes bibliographical references and index. | Identifiers: LCCN 2021011806 (print) |
LCCN 2021011807 (ebook) | ISBN 9780567680389 (hardback) |
ISBN 9780567700582 (paperback) | ISBN 9780567680402 (adobe pdf)
Subjects: LCSH: Church history—Primitive and early church, ca. 30-600.
Classification: LCC BR165 .T27 2021 (print) | LCC BR165 (ebook) | DDC 270.1—dc23
LC record available at https://lccn.loc.gov/2021011806
LC ebook record available at https://lccn.loc.gov/2021011807

ISBN: HB: 978-0-5676-8038-9
PB: 978-0-5677-0058-2
ePDF: 978-0-5676-8040-2
eBook: 978-0-5676-8039-6

Series: T&T Clark Handbooks

Typeset by Deanta Global Publishing Services, Chennai, India

To find out more about our authors and books visit www.bloomsbury.com and
sign up for our newsletters.

CONTENTS

FIGURES

CONTRIBUTORS

Piotr Ashwin-Siejkowski is a senior visiting research fellow in the Department of Theology and Religious Studies at King's College London. His research is focused on Christian origins and the formation of Christian doctrine in the period from the first to the later third century CE, particularly in the Alexandrian milieu. Among his recent publications are 'Clement of Alexandria' in *The Wiley Blackwell Companion to Patristics*, edited by K. Parry (2015), 84–97; 'Creeds, Councils and Doctrinal Development' in *The Christian Early World*, edited by Ph. F. Esler (2017), 631–46; 'Alexandria *ad Aegiptum*. The City That Inspired a Polyphony of Early Christian Theologies' in *The Urban World and the First Christians* (2017), 205–15; 'The Image of the Feminine in the Gospel of Philip: An Innovative Assimilation of Paul's Gender Legacy in the Valentinian Milieu', in *Patterns of Women's Leadership in Early Christianity*, edited by J. Taylor and I. Ramielli (2021), 96–108; and 'What Did Paul Hear in the Third Heaven? The Second-Century Christian Debate on Paul's Mystical Vision and Its Consequences', in *Interactions and Interpretations*, edited by J. Roskovec and V. Husek (2021), 37–49.

Paul M. Blowers (PhD, University of Notre Dame, 1988) is the Dean E. Walker Professor of Church History and Historical Theology in the Emmanuel Christian Seminary at Milligan University (Tennessee). A former president of the North American Patristics Society (2008–9), Blowers is a scholar especially of Greek and Byzantine patristics. Among his books are *Visions and Faces of the Tragic: The Mimesis of Tragedy and the Folly of Salvation in Early Christian Literature* (2020), *Maximus the Confessor: Jesus Christ and the Transfiguration of the World* (2016) and *Drama of the Divine Economy: Creator and Creation in Early Christian Theology and Piety* (2012). He is also the co-editor of *The Oxford Handbook of Early Christian Biblical Interpretation* (2019), and has edited and translated *Moral Formation and the Virtuous Life* (2019) and *The Cosmic Mystery of Jesus Christ: Selected Writings from Maximus the Confessor* (2003). Professor Blowers has published numerous essays in journals such as *Studia Patristica, Journal of Early Christian Studies, Vigiliae Christianae, Studies in Christian Ethics, International Journal of Systematic Theology* and *Modern Theology*.

Paul F. Bradshaw is Emeritus Professor of Liturgy at the University of Notre Dame, having taught there from 1985 to 2013. He received his BA and MA in theology from the University of Cambridge and his PhD in liturgical studies from the University of London, and in 1994 he was awarded the degree of Doctor of Divinity by the University of Oxford for his published works. He has also received an honorary

DD from the General Theological Seminary, New York. He has written or edited more than thirty books, together with over 130 essays or articles in periodicals. His major books include *The Search for the Origins of Christian Worship* (1992, 2nd ed. 2002 and translated into French, Italian, Japanese and Russian); (with Maxwell E. Johnson) *The Origins of Feasts, Fasts and Seasons in Early Christianity* (2011); and (with Anne McGowan) *The Pilgrimage of Egeria* (2018). He is a former president of the North American Academy of Liturgy and of the international *Societas Liturgica*, and from 1987 to 2005 he was the editor-in-chief of the scholarly journal *Studia Liturgica*.

Allen Brent (MA, DD, Cantab.) is former professor of Early Christian History and Iconography, King's College London, on a British Academy-funded (BARDA) project (with Markus Vinzent), 'Early "Christian" Art and Iconography after Dölger'. He was Visiting Professor, Augustinianum, Rome, and is a fellow of St Edmund's College, Cambridge. His published research focuses on the interface between early Christianity and classical culture, with a focus on the development of church order and non-literary epigraphic and iconographic sources for the transformation of classical culture. He is current joint editor of *Studia Patristica* and *Studia Patristica Supplements* with Markus Vinzent (King's College London). His earlier work focused on the development of church order in the Roman community in the late second century, in particular, in *Hippolytus and the Roman Church in the Third Century: Communities in Tension before the Emergence of a Monarch-Bishop* (*Supplements to Vigiliae Christianae*, 31: 1995). His most recent books are *Ignatius of Antioch and the Second Sophistic* (2006); *A Political History of Early Christianity* (2009); and *Cyprian and Roman Carthage* (2010).

Robert Daly S. J is Emeritus Professor of Early Christian Theology at Boston College, Massachusetts, and a world renowned expert in Early Christian thought. He is the author of classic and seminal studies on sacrifice (1978) and eschatology (2009) in the early Christian communities and numerous scholarly articles on wide-ranging matters of Catholic dogmatics. For many years he has contributed to the international research efforts on Origen of Alexandria, and as a board member, latterly Chair of the Board, of the Pappas Patristic Institute attached to Holy Cross College Brookline, he has helped in providing research support in early Christianity for many younger scholars. Among many of his publications are 'Robert Bellarmine and Post-Tridentine Eucharistic Theology' in *From Trent to Vatican II: Historical and Theological Investigations*, edited by Raymond F. Bulman and Frederick J. Parella (2006), 81–101; 'On the Biblical Concept of Creation' in *The Dialogue between Science and Religion: What We Have Learned from One Another*, edited by Patrick H. Byrne (2005), 85–112; and 'Eucharistic Origins: From the New Testament to the Liturgies of the Golden Age', in *Theological Studies* 66 (2005): 3–22.

Professor Mark Edwards completed his doctoral thesis (DPhil Literae Humaniores, Oxon), 'Plotinus and the Gnostics', at Corpus Christi College, Oxford, in 1988. He held a junior research fellowship in Classics at New College, Oxford, from 1989 to

1993, and since 1993 has been University Lecturer (now Associate Professor) in the Faculty of Theology (now Faculty of Theology and Religion) at the University of Oxford. During this period he has held concomitantly the post of Tutor in Theology at Christ Church, Oxford. Since 2014 he has also held the title Professor of Early Christian Studies. His books include *Neoplatonic Saints* (2000), *Origen against Plato* (2002), *John through the Centuries* (2003), *Culture and Philosophy in the Age of Plotinus* (2006), *Catholicity and Heresy in the Early Church* (2009), *Image, Word and God in the Early Christian Centuries* (2012), *Religions of the Constantinian Empire* (2015) and *Aristotle and Early Christian Thought* (2019).

Jaś Elsner FBA is Humfry Payne Senior Research Fellow in Classical Art and Archaeology at Corpus Christi College Oxford and Professor of Late Antique Art at the University of Oxford. He is also Visiting Professor of Art and Religion in the University of Chicago and External Scientific Member of the Kunsthistorisches Institut in Florenz. He was Senior Research Keeper at the British Museum from 2012 to 2018. He works on all areas of art and religion in antiquity and the early middle ages across Europe and Western Asia, including pilgrimage, travel-writing and the description of art in texts. His books include *Art and the Roman Viewer: The Transformation of Art from the Pagan World to Christianity* (1995), *Pilgrimage Past and Present* with Simon Coleman (1995), *Pilgrimage in Greco-Roman and Early Christian Antiquity: Seeing the Gods* edited with Ian Rutherford (2005), *Roman Eyes: Visuality and Subjectivity in Art and Text* (2007), *Saints: Faith at the Borders* edited with Françoise Meltzer (2011), *Imagining the Divine: Art and the Rise of World Religions* with Stefanie Lenk and others (2017), *The Art of the Roman Empire AD100–450* (2018). His most recent edited book, *Empires of Faith in Late Antiquity: Histories of Art and Religion from India to Ireland* (2020), is on the birth of the iconographies of the religions of late antiquity across Eurasia and the historiographic and methodological problems associated with the comparative study of this issue.

Saliba Er, born in Tur'Abdin (Southeast Turkey), earned his bachelor's (BA) at the University of Chichester (2011), master's at the University of Cardiff (2012) and PhD at the University of Vienna 2019. Since 2016 he has been Visiting Lecturer at the Department of Biblical Studies and Ecclesiological History, University of Salzburg. He teaches courses on the Syriac language, the Syriac liturgy and pastoral theology. He moved to Aleppo (Syria) in 2007, where he studied Arabic literature and served under the omophorion of Archbishop Gregorios Yuhanna Ibrahim (kidnapped since 2013), and after accomplishing his studies in the UK and in Vienna, he moved recently to Salzburg as a post-doctoral researcher at the University of Salzburg. He has published several articles about the Syriac liturgy and sacramental theology.

Paul van Geest is Professor of Church History and the History of Theology in Tilburg University (2007); Professor of Economy and Theology at Erasmus University, Rotterdam (2018); and Visiting Professor of Theology at Leuven's Catholic University (2019). He obtained his doctorate in philology at Leiden University (1986), his STL at the Pontifical Gregorian University (1991) and his PhD at

Utrecht (1996). After a senior research fellowship in the Netherlands (NWO), he was appointed to the endowed chair of Augustinian Studies at Utrecht (2001) and at VU University, Amsterdam (2006). In 2007 he became Full Professor at Tilburg University, and from 2008 to 2020 he was the director of the Centre for Patristic Studies (Tilburg and VU). In 2010 he was appointed *Pro-Decanus* of the Theological Faculty at Tilburg. He has been Visiting Professor at several universities and is a member of the Royal Dutch Society of Sciences and Humanities, as well as a member of the Pontifical Academy of Theology. He is the editor-in-chief of the *Brill Encyclopedia of Early Christianity* and *Brill Studies in Catholic Theology*. He has published and edited more than twenty books, including *The Incomprehensibility of God*: *Augustine as a Negative Theologian* (2010) and has numerous studies in such publications as *Journal of Early Christianity*, *Augustinian Studies*, *Augustinianum*, *Augustiniana*, *Gregorianum* and *Revue d'Etudes Augustiniennes*.

György Geréby is Associate Professor at the Medieval Studies Deparment in Central European University, Vienna-Budapest. He delivered the Isaiah Berlin lectures, Oxford, 2018, and has been a Keeley visiting fellow, Wadham College, Oxford, 2013/14 and a Fulbright teaching fellow at Rutgers University, 2004. Areas of specialization are the history of late antique and medieval philosophy and theology, including political theology. Recent articles include, 'The Nation, the Nations, and the Third Nation: The Political Essence of Early Christianity', in *Theology and World Politics Metaphysics, Genealogies, Political Theologies*, edited by Vassilios Paipais (2020), 181–210; 'The Angels of the Nations: Is National Christianity Possible?' in *Across the Mediterranean – Along the Nile: Studies in Egyptology, Nubiology and Late Antiquity Dedicated to László Török on the Occasion of His 75th Birthday*, 2 vols., edited by Tamás A. Bács, Ádám Bollók and Tivadar Vida (2019), 819–48; 'A Supremely Idle Question? Issues of the Beatific Vision Debate between 1331–1336', *Przegląd Tomistyczny* 24 (2018): 487–529; 'Hidden Themes in Fourteenth-Century Byzantine and Latin Theological Debates: Monarchianism and Crypto-Dyophysitism', in *Greeks, Latins, and Intellectual History 1204–1500*, edited by Martin Hinterberger and Chris Schabel (2011), 183–211; and 'Political Theology versus Theological Politics: Erik Peterson and Carl Schmitt', in *New German Critique* 105 (2008): 7–33.

Fr. Isidoros (Charalampos) Katsos, born in Athens, read Theology in Athens (BTh Hons) and Philosophy of Religion at Cambridge (MPhil), where he obtained his PhD (Cantab.) under the supervision of Rowan Williams. He is a Greek-Orthodox priest bearing the rank of Archimandrite. Prior to his ordination he studied extensively Law in Athens (LLB), Paris (LLM) and Berlin (PhD, Freie Universität) and worked as a lawyer (Athens Bar; European Commission). He is Postdoctoral Fellow at the Center for the Study of Christianity, Hebrew University (Jerusalem); Research Associate at the VHI, St Edmund's College (Cambridge); and Fellow of the Centre for the Study of Platonism (Cambridge). His research interests are on the intersection of philosophy and theology, with a focus on ancient sources (the theology of the early Church; late antique philosophy and hermeneutics; and Greek patristics). In addition, his research engages with contemporary debates pertaining to the analytic-continental divide, constructions of the person and the theological justification of human rights. He is currently preparing a monograph on 'The Metaphysics of Light in the Hexaemeral Literature'.

Bart J. Koet is ordinary professor of New Testament and extraordinary professor of Early Christian literature and Dean of Research at the Catholic Faculty of Theology at Tilburg University. He read theology and biblical exegesis in Amsterdam and Rome and philosophy in Amsterdam and has taught at several universities in the Netherlands and at the University of Duisburg-Essen in Germany. He is the chairman of the Dutch/Belgian *Studiosorum Novi Testamenti Conventus* and Director of the *Centre for the Study of Early Christianity* (Netherlands; Free University and Tilburg University). His research focuses on the interpretation of Scripture and the phenomenon of dreams; see, for example, Bart J. Koet, *Dreams and Scripture in Luke-Acts: Collected Essays* and Idem (ed.), *Dreams as Divine Communication in Christianity: From Hermas to Aquinas*. He also writes about leadership and ministry in the early church; see, for example, *The Go-Between: Augustine on Deacons* (2019), and Bart J. Koet, Edwina Murphy and Esko Ryökäs (eds), *Deacons and Diakonia in Early Christianity: The First Two Centuries* (2018).

Giulio Maspero is Full Professor at the Faculty of Theology of the Pontifical University of Holy Cross (Rome). He is member of the Association Internationale des Etudes Patristiques (AIEP) and a full member of the Pontifical Academy of Theology (PATH). He has published mainly on Gregory of Nyssa, Trinitarian theology and the relationship between philosophy and theology. In particular, he has published *Trinity and Man* (2007) and has directed, together with L. F. Mateo-Seco, *The Brill Dictionary of Gregory of Nyssa* (2009) and, together with R. Wozniak, *Re-thinking Trinitarian Theology* (2012). His most recent monographs are *Uno perché trino* (2011), *Essere e relazione* (2013) and *Dio trino perché vivo* (2018), the latter devoted to the pneumatology of the Greek Fathers. He also edited with Pierpaolo Donati and Antonio Malo the volume *Social Science, Philosophy and Theology in Dialogue* (2019).

The Very Revd. John A. McGuckin is currently a professor in the Faculty of Theology at the University of Oxford and the Nielsen Emeritus Professor of Church History at UTS and Columbia University, New York. He is an orthodox archpriest and rector of St Gregory's Chapel in St Anne's on Sea. He has taught in many universities, as Visiting Distinguished Professor or as Visiting Scholar, including Kiev, Sibiu, Bucharest, Oslo, Iasi, Cambridge, Belfast, Oxford, Yale, Sydney and Moscow. He was elected a fellow of the British Royal Society of Arts in 1986 and a fellow of the Royal Historical Society in 1996, and was the Luce Fellow in Early Christianity in 2006. In 2008 he was awarded the Order of St Stephen the Great, the Cross of Moldavia and Bukovina, by the Patriarch of the Romanian Orthodox Church. He is the recipient of Honorary Doctorates from St Vladimir's Orthodox School in New York (2013) and from the University of Sibiu in Romania (2014). He has written thirty-one books and over 150 research articles in scholarly journals. The central focus of his work has revolved around the thought of the Christian Fathers, the Byzantine mystical writers, and the culture of the Eastern Church.

Sarah Parkhouse is a British academy postdoctoral fellow at King's College London. She specializes in early Christianity and is particularly interested in Coptic apocrypha in the local contexts of Egypt and North Africa. She has held research posts at Australian Catholic University (ACU), Melbourne, and the Warburg Institute, London, after completing a PhD at Durham University in 2017. Her publications include articles and chapters on early Christian gospel texts, Coptic literature and gender in early Christian literature, and a monograph titled *Eschatology and the Saviour: The Gospel of Mary among Early Christian Dialogue Gospels* (2019).

Henryk Pietras SJ is Professor of Patrology at the Pontifical Gregorian University in Rome and at the Collegium Bobolanum in Warsaw. His recent publications include *Acta synodalia a. 553-600, Synodi et Collectiones Legum* XII (2020); *Escatologia patristica. Alcuni tratti*, PATH 18 (2019): 269–89; 'La speranza escatologica di Origene', in *Nadzieje upadającego świata. Nadzieja w chrześcijańskiej epistolografii łacińskiej IV i V wieku (Ambroży, Augustyn, Hieronim, Paulin z Noli)*, M. Wysocki et al. (eds), (2019), 199–216; 'Leone Magno retractavit? Il cambiamento del linguaggio cristologico del papa dopo il concilio di Calcedonia', *OCP* 84, no. 1 (2018): 82–97; 'La guerra di Costantinopoli. La posizione politico dottrinale dei vescovi alessandrini dopo il Concilio di Calcedonia', *OCP* 82 (2016): 307–51; *Council of Nicaea (325): Religious and Political Context, Documents, Commentaries*, trad. M. Fijak, 2016.

Professor Ilaria L. E. Ramelli, FRHistS, holds two MAs, a PhD, a doctorate h.c., a postdoctorate and various habilitations to Ordinarius. She has been Professor of Roman History, Senior Visiting Professor of Greek Thought at Harvard and Boston University, of Church History at Columbia and of Religion at Erfurt MWK, Full Professor of Theology and Endowed Chair at the Angelicum, and Senior Fellow at Durham University (twice), at Princeton (2017–), at Sacred Heart University and at both Corpus Christi and Christ Church in Oxford. She is also a senior member of the Centre for the Study of Platonism at the University of Cambridge a Humboldt Forschungspreis fellow at Erfurt, MWK, elected Senior Fellow at Bonn University and Professor of Theology (Durham University, hon.) and of Patristics and Church History (KUL). Her recent books include *The Christian Doctrine of Apokatastasis* (2013), *Evagrius' Kephalaia Gnostika* (2015), *The Role of Religion in Shaping Narrative Forms* (2015), *Social Justice and the Legitimacy of Slavery* (2016), *Evagrius, the Cappadocians, and Neoplatonism* (edited, 2017), *Bardaisan of Edessa* (2019), *Patterns of Women's Leadership in Ancient Christianity* with J. Taylor (2021), *Lovers of the Soul, Lovers of the Body* (co-edited, 2021) and *Eriugena's Christian Neoplatonism and Its Sources* (edited, forthcoming).

Nichlas Sagovsky is a visiting professor at King's College London. He has held professorial posts at the University of Roehampton, University of Liverpool

Hope, Newcastle University and Durham University, and taught Theology at the University of Cambridge where he was Dean of Clare College. From 2004 to 2011, he was Canon Theologian at Westminster Abbey. He is the author of a number of articles and books on ecumenism, ecclesiology and social justice, including *Christian Tradition and the Practice of Justice* (2009) and *Ecumenism, Christian Origins and the Practice of Communion* (2000). With Peter McGrail, he co-edited *Together for the Common Good* (2015). He has been a member of the Anglican-Roman Catholic International Commission (1991–2017) and the Inter-Anglican Theological and Doctrinal Commission (2001–8). He is a member of the Malines Conversations Group, an informal international Anglican-Roman Catholic Ecumenical Group.

Stefano Salemi (University of Oxford) read theology and biblical studies in Italy, Israel, the United States and the United Kingdom. He has been a postdoctoral fellow at Harvard and held visiting scholar and research fellow posts at Yale, Hebrew University of Jerusalem, Oxford, Sheffield and more. His interests lie broadly in biblical studies, biblical languages and also theology. He is particularly interested in intertextual studies, use-reception-transformation of the Hebrew Bible in the New Testament, biblical languages and semantics, biblical and systematic theology (esp. Christology), reception history, exegesis and Scriptural hermeneutics. In addition to various standing research grants and positions, he currently teaches in biblical and theological studies at the University of Oxford. He has taught also at King's College London, the University of London, the University of Chichester and elsewhere. Besides various articles and chapters, he authored a book on Christ's death and Passion narrative in John's Gospel and Early Christianity (2014), and on Hebrew semantics and theology in Ezekiel (2021). He has currently several contributions in contract in the field of biblical studies, early Christianity, theology, linguistic and textual studies.

The Revd. Professor Mark Sheridan, OSB, is a Benedictine monk. Born in Washington, DC, USA, he received the degree of AB in Philosophy from Georgetown University (1960), the Licentiate in Sacred Theology (STL) from the Catholic University of America (1966), the Licentiate in Sacred Scripture (SSL) from the Pontifical Biblical Institute (1971) and his PhD in Coptic Language and Literature from Catholic University of America (1990). In 1982 he took up residence in Rome and served there as the Prior of the Collegio S. Anselmo, Dean of the Faculty of Theology and Rector Magnificus of the Pontifical Athenaeum San Anselmo. He has been a member of the International Joint Commission for Theological Dialogue between the Roman Catholic Church and the Oriental Orthodox Churches since 2004. He first visited the Holy Land in 1971, but in 2010 he moved there to become a monk of the Jerusalem Dormition monastery and resident of Bethlehem. He is a world-leading expert in Monastic and Coptic culture, among his many publications are *Rufus of Shotep: Homilies on the Gospels of Matthew and Luke. Introduction, Text, Translation, Commentary* (1998) and *From the Nile to the Rhone and Beyond: Studies in Early Monastic Literature and Scriptural Interpretation. Studia Anselmiana*, 156 (2012).

Professor William Tabbernee, PhD, LittD, DD, was President and Stephen J. England Distinguished Professor of the History of Christianity at Phillips Theological Seminary in Tulsa, Oklahoma, until his retirement. Most recently he has taught in the Religious Studies Department of the University of Oklahoma. He is a fellow of the Melbourne College of Divinity and a past president of the North American Patristics Society. His scholarship and extensive publications focus on the history, archaeology and epigraphy of Montanism in Asia Minor and North Africa. His latest book is *Early Christianity in Contexts: An Exploration across Cultures and Continents* (2014).

Monica Tobon has a BA in Philosophy and an MA and PhD in Classics, all from University College London, where she holds an honorary research fellowship in the Department of Greek and Latin. She lectured in Philosophy and the History of Christian Spirituality at the Franciscan International Study Centre in Canterbury, UK, from 2010 until its closure in 2017, since when she has worked mainly on her first monograph, *Apatheia and Anthropology in Evagrius of Pontus* (2021). In addition to Evagrius her research interests include the Alexandrian and Cappadocian fathers, Plato, Cassian, Boethius, eco-theology, and philosophical and theological anthropology. As well as intersecting the latter domains, her interest in disability studies is motivated and informed by her own experience of disability. She has previously published on Evagrius, Dionysius the Areopagite, Bonaventure, and Daoism, and in addition to completing her monograph she is currently working on Evagrius and Dionysius and supervising a graduate student at the Polis Institute in Jerusalem. She lives with her cats as part of the extended family of the Benedictine Nuns of St Mildred's Priory, Minster Abbey, Kent.

Paula Tutty is a visiting research fellow at the Faculty of Theology at the University of Oslo where she works in collaboration with the ERC-funded project, 'Storyworlds in Transition: Coptic Apocrypha in Changing Contexts in the Byzantine and Early Islamic Periods (APOCRYPHA)'. She holds an MA in Coptic Studies from Macquarie University and a PhD in Early Christianity from UiO (Oslo). Working extensively with Greek and Coptic documentary papyri, she has researched fourth-century Egyptian monastic letter collections and the insights they can give into the embryonic monastic movement as it evolved in late antique Egypt. Her PhD thesis, entitled 'The Monks of Nag Hammadi: Contextualising a Fourth Century Monastic Community', explores one early monastic letter collection from Upper Egypt that was discovered within the covers of the Nag Hammadi Codices. Paula's recent work includes a study of the interconnections that exist between Coptic religious literature and various hagiographical writings. Her publications include *The Political and Philanthropic Role of Monastic Figures and Monasteries as Revealed in Fourth-Century Coptic and Greek Correspondence SP* XCI, vol. 17 (2017): 353–63 and 'Books of the Dead or Books with the Dead: Interpreting Book Depositions in Late Antique Egypt', in *The Nag Hammadi Codices and Late Antique Egypt* (STAC 110), edited by H. Lundhaug and L. Jenott (2018), 287–328.

Rowan Williams studied and taught theology at the University of Cambridge and the University of Oxford before becoming Bishop of Monmouth in 1992 and Archbishop of Canterbury from 2002 to 2012. He has recently retired from the Mastership of Magdalene College, Cambridge. He has written widely on early Christian thought and spiritual practice, including *Arius: Heresy and Tradition* (2002), as well as an edition of John Henry Newman's monograph: *The Arians of the Fourth Century*. He has also published a collection of essays on Augustine and several studies of early monastic writers.

Rev. Dr hab. Marcin Wysocki, is Professor in the University of Lublin (KUL) and a priest of the Archdiocese of Warmia. He graduated from John Paul II Catholic University of Lublin in Classics and Patrology (PhD in Theology-Patrology, MA in the Classics, Habilitation in the Classics), and after his doctorate has been a member of the Lublin faculty, becoming a full professor in 2018 in the Institute of Church History and Patrology. His research interests include Early Christian eschatology, relations between persecutions and the development of Christian doctrine, the aretology of the Church Fathers and fourth- to fifth-century Latin Christian epistolography. He is a member of the Polish Theological Society, the KUL Scientific Society, the North American Patristic Society, the Patristic Section of the Polish Episcopal Conference and the International Association of Patristic Studies (AIEP) He is the author of over 200 scientific articles and encyclopedia entries.

Markus Vinzent is Professor of Church History with a special focus on Early Christianity, Patristics and the Middle Ages at King's College London and is a fellow of the Max-Weber-Centre for Social and Cultural Studies at Erfurt University, Germany. He studied Philosophy, Theology, Jewish Studies, Ancient History and Archaeology at the Universities of Eichstaett, Paris, Munich and Heidelberg. He has worked and published for several years on the beginnings of Christianity, particularly on its development during the second century, but also on the creeds, the fourth and fifth-century theologies. He has researched the Neo-Platonic tradition from the fourth century to Friedrich Hölderlin in the nineteenth century: taking a special interest in Meister Eckhart (early fourteenth century). Among his many books and research articles is *Writing the History of Early Christianity* (2019), a critical reflection on historiographical methodology, applied to several case studies from the second century.

Tim Vivian is Professor Emeritus of Religious Studies at California State University Bakersfield and a retired priest in the Episcopal Church. He received a BA in English (UC Santa Barbara), an MA in American Literature (Cal Poly San Luis Obispo), an MA in Comparative Literature (Greek, Latin, German and Spanish) (UC Santa Barbara), an interdisciplinary PhD (History, Classics and Religious Studies) (UC Santa Barbara) and an MDiv (CDSP). For his scholarship and work for social justice, in 2018 he received a honorary Doctor of Divinity degree from the Church Divinity School of the Pacific (CDSP, Episcopal). Professor Vivian is the author of numerous books, articles and book reviews on early Christian monasticism; most recently he has published *Sayings and Stories of the Desert Fathers and Mothers* (2021) and, with Maged S. A. Mikhail, he is editor and translator of *The Life of Bishoi: The Greek, Arabic, Syriac, and Ge'ez (Ethiopic) Lives* (2021). He has published two books of poems: *Other Voices, Other Rooms: Reflections on Scripture* (2020) and *Poems Written in a Time of Plague: Further Reflections on Scripture* (2020).

Ville Vuolanto is Senior Lecturer in history and Latin language at Tampere University, Finland. He has specialized in the history of children, studying the social and cultural history of families in Roman, early Christian and late antique contexts. In many of his journal articles and book chapters he has integrated the perspectives of sociology (especially on agency, experience and life strategies) into the study of ancient history, paying special attention to issues of gender and age, social status, as well as the interplay of ideological changes and everyday life. Ascetics, grandparents and the city of Oxyrhynchos are also near to his heart professionally. His publications include *Children and Asceticism in Late Antiquity: Continuity, Family Dynamics and the Rise of Christianity* (2015).

ABBREVIATIONS

ANCIENT SOURCES

Acta Synodalia (ab anno 431 ad annum 504)
Acta Synodalia (ab anno 50 ad annum 381)

App. IX	Appendix IX: *Epistula Constantini imperatoris ad episcopos et plebem Africae, ut donatistas tolerant* (A.D. 321). (*The Emperor Constantine's letter to bishop and people of Africa on toleration to be granted to Donatists*)
App. X	Appendix X: *Rescriptum Constantini ad episcopos numidas ubi haeretici tulerunt basilicas a catholicis ut ad aliam basilicam faciendam sibi locum vel domum eis dent* (A.D. 330) (*Rescript of Constantine to the Bishops of Numidia*)
ATh	*Acta Theclae* (*Acts of Thecla*)

Ambrose of Milan

Com. Luc.	*Commentarium in Evangelium Lucae* (*Commentary on the Gospel of Luke*)
De ob	*De obitu Theodosii* (*the Funeral oration for Theodosius*)
Enn.Pss.	*Ennarationes in Psalmos.* (*Discourses on the Psalms*)
Ep.	*Epistulae* (*Letters*)
Ex.Luc	*Expositio in Lucam* (*Explanations on the Gospel of Luke*)
Exp. Ps.	*Explanatio Psalmi* (*Explanation of the Psalms*)
Exp.ps.118	*Expositio in Psalmum David CXVIII* (*Homilies of Saint Ambrose on Psalm 118 (119)*)
Fid	*De fide* (*On the faith*)
Hex	*Hexaemeron* (*Commentary on the six days of Creation*)
Sacr	*De Sacramentis* (*On the Sacraments*)
Spir	*De Spiritu Sancto* (*On the Holy Spirit*)

Ambrosiaster

QVNT	*Quaestiones Veteris et Noui Testamenti* (*Questions on the Old and New Testaments*)

Anastasius of Sinai

Hex	*Hexaemeron* (*Commentary on the six days of Creation*)

Anaxagoras

Ph	*Physica* (*Physics*)

Andrew of Caesarea
Com.Ap   *Commentarius In Apocalypsin* (*Commentary on the Apocalypse*)

Anonim
Haer   *De haeresibus* (*On Heresies*)
Praed   *Praedestinatus* (*Predestined*)
Apoph   *Apophthegmata Patrum* (*Apophthegms of the Fathers*)

Apuleius
Met   *Metamorphoses/Asinus Aureus* (*The Golden Ass*)

Aristeas
Ep.Arist   *Epistula Aristeas* (*Epistle of Aristeas*)

Aristotle
Metaph   *Metaphysica* (*Metaphysics*)
Ph   *Physica* (*Physics*)
Pol.   *Politica* (*Politics*)
Rhet   *Rhetorica* (*Rhetorics*)

Arnim, H. von (ed)
SVF   *Stoicorum Veterum Fragmenta*

Athanasius of Alexandria
Apol.sec.   *Apologia secunda contra Arianos* (*Second Apology against the Arians*)
decr.   *De decretis Nicaenae synodi* (*On the Decrees of the Synod of Nicaea*)
Ep. VIII   *Epistula VIII* (*Letter of Eusebius 8*)
Ep. Marc.   *Epistula ad Marcellinum* (*Letter to Marcellinus on the Psalms*)
Gent   *Contra Gentes* (*Against the Heathen*)
Inc   *De Incarnatione Verbi Dei* (*On the Incarnation of God the Word*)
Syn.   *De synodis Arimini in Italia et Seleuciae in Isauria* (*On the Synods of Arminium and Seleucia*)
Tom   *Tomus ad Antiochenos* (*Tome to the Antiochenes*)

Athenagoras of Athens
Leg   *Legatio pro Christianis* (*A Plea for the Christians*)

Augustine
Adv.Man   *De Genesi adversus Manicheos* (*On Genesis against Manichees*)
Brev. col.   *Breviculus collatio cum Donatistis* (*A Summary of the meeting with Donatists*)
Cath.   *Ad catholicos fratres* (*To Catholic Members of the Church*)
c. Adim   *Contra Adimantum Manichei discipulum* (*Against Adimantus, a Disciple of Mani*)
c. Cres.   *Contra Cresconium* (*Against Cresconius*)

c. litt. Pet	*Contra litteras Petiliani (Agains the Letters of Petilianus)*
c.sec.Iul.imp.	*Contra secundam Iuliani responsionem opus imperfectum. (Unfinished Work Against Julian's Second Response)*
Civ	*De Civitate Dei (The City of God)*
Conf	*Confessiones (Confessions)*
Cresc.	*Ad Cresconium grammaticum partis Donatis (to Cresconius, a Donatist Grammarian)*
Doc.	*De Doctrina Christiana (Concerning Christian Doctrine)*
Ench.	*Enchiridion (Handbook of Doctrine)*
En. Ps	*Enarrationes in Psalmos (Discourses on the Psalms)*
Ep. Cath.	*Epistula ad Catholicos (Letter to the Catholics)*
Ex. Prop. Rom	*Expositio quarundam propositionum ex epistula apostoli ad Romanos (Commentary on Statements in the Letter to Romans)*
Gn.litt	*De Genesi ad litteram (On the Literal Interpretation of Genesis)*
In Io.Ev.tr	*In Evangelium Joannis Tractatus (Tractates on the Gospel of John)*
Jo.Tr	*Joannis evangelium tractatus (Tractates on the Gospel of John)*
pecc. mer.	*De peccatorum meritis (On the Merits and Forgiveness of Sins)*
Serm	*Sermones (Sermons)*
Trin	*De Trinitate (On the Trinity)*

Barnabas
Barn.	*Epistle of Barnabas*

Basil the Great
Adv.Eunom.	*Adversus Eunomium (Against Eunomius)*
EpD	*Epistulae de decretis (Canonical Letters)*
Hom	*Homiliae (Homilies)*
Hom.Hex	*Homiliae in hexaemeron (Homilies on the Six days of Creation)*
Hom.Jul	*Homilia in martyrem Julittam (Homily on the Martyr Julitta)*
Hom. Ps.	*Homiliae in Psalmos (Homilies on the Psalms)*
Spir	*De Spiritu Sancto (On the Holy Spirit)*

Caesarius of Arles
Serm	*Sermones (Sermons)*

Cassiodorus
Chr.	*Chronica (Chronicles)*

Boetius
DeCon	*De consolatione philosophiae (The Consolation of Philosophy)*

Celsus
AL.	*Alêthês Logos (The True Doctrine)*
C-E.HET	*Cassiodori-Epiphanii Historia Ecclesiastica Tripartita (The Tripartite Ecclesiastical History of Cassiodorus-Epiphanius.)*

Cicero
DeLeg.	*De Legibus. (On the Laws)*
Flac.	*Pro Flacco (In defence of Flaccus)*

Clement of Alexandria

ExTh	*Excerpta ex Theodoto* (*Excerpts from Theodotus*)
Paed	*Paedagogus* (*the Instructor*)
Protrep	*Protrepticus* (*Exhortation to the Greeks*)
Strom	*Stromateis* (*Miscellanies*)
Quis Dives	*Quis Dives Salvetur* (*Who is the Rich Man that is being saved?*)
Cod. Thds.	*Codex Theodosianus* (*Theodosian Code*)
Const. Ap.	*Constitutiones Apostolorum* (*Apostolic Constitutions*)
Const. Ep.	*Constantine's Letter to Alexander the Bishop, and Arius the Presbyter*
Const. Ep. Eccl.	*Constantine's Letter to the Churches Respecting the Council at Nicaea*

Clement of Rome

1Clem	*First Letter to the Corinthians*

Cyprian of Carthage

Ep	*Epistulae* (*Letters*)
Laps	*De Lapsis* (*On the Lapsed*)
Unit. Eccl	*De unitate ecclesiae* (*On the Unity of the Church*)

Cyril of Alexandria

Com.Jo	*Commentarius in Joannis Evangelium* (*Commentary on John*)
Glaph.Ex	*Glaphyra in Exodum* (*Glaphyra – Elegant Comments – on Exodus*)

Cyril of Jerusalem

Catech.	*Catecheses* (*Catechetical Lectures*)
Decretum	*Decretum Gratiani* (*The Law Book of Gratian*)
Did	*Didache* (*The Teaching of the Twelve Apostles*)
Didas	*Didascalia Apostolorum* (*The Teachings of the Apostles*)

Diogenes Laertius

VP	*Vitae Philosophorum* (*Lives of the Philosophers*)
Nat	*De natura* (*On Nature*)

Egeria

It	*Itinerarium Egeriae* (*The Pilgrimage of Egeria*)

Ephrem the Syrian

ComGen	*Commentarius in Genesim* (*Commentary on Genesis*)
Hymn	*Hymnus contra haereses* (*The Song against heresies*)

Epictetus

Disc	*Epiktētou diatribai* (*Discourses*)

Epiphanius of Salamis

Pan.	*Panarion* (*Treasure Chest: Against Eighty Heresies*)

Eunomius
Ap.   *Apologiae (Apologies)*

Eusebius of Caesarea
ComPss.   *Commentarius in Psalmos (Commentary on Psalms)*
Con.Marc.   *Contra Marcellum (Against Marcellus)*
Dem.Ev.   *Demonstratio evangelica (Demonstration (Proof) of the Gospel)*
Ec.Th.   *De ecclesiae theologia (On Church Theology)*
Ep. Caes.   *Epistula Caesarianis (Letter to the Caesareans)*
HE.   *Historia ecclesiastica (Ecclesiastical History)*
LCons   *Laus Constantini (Oration in Praise of Constantine)*
Mart.Pal.   *De martyribus Palestinae (On the Martyrs of Palestine)*
Praep.Ev.   *Praeparatio evangelica (The Preparation of the Gospel)*
V.C.   *De vita Constantini (Life of Constantine)*

Eusebius of Emesa
ComGen   *Commentarius in Genesim (Commentary on Genesis)*

Evagrius of Pontus
Cap. grad.   *Capitula per gradus quosdam desposita consequential (Thirty Three Ordered Chapters)*
Cap. Orat.   *Capitula de Oratione (Chapters on Prayer)*
Eul.   *Ad Eulogium (To Eulogius on the Confession of Thoughts)*
Keph. Gn.   *Kephalaia Gnostica (Gnostic Chapters)*
Prakt.   *Praktikos (One Hundred Practical Chapters)*
Re.mon.rat.   *Rerum monachalium rationes (On Thoughts)*
Sent. virg.   *Sententiae ad virgines (Advice to Virgins)*

Evagrius Scholasticus
HE.   *Historia ecclesiastica (Ecclesiastical History)*

Galen
Diff. Puls.   *De Differentiis Pulsuum (On the variety of the pulses)*
Ord. libr.   *De ordine librorum proprio (On the Order of my own Books)*

Georgius Monachus
Chr.   *Chronicon (Chronicle)*

Gelasius of Cyzicus
HE.   *Historia ecclesiastica (Ecclesiastical History)*
Gnostikos   *Gnostic Treatise (Sources Chrétiennes, 356)*

Gregory of Nazianzus
Epig   *Epig. Epigrammata (Epigrams)*
Or   *Orationes (Orations)*

Gregory of Nyssa
Cant   *Commentarii in Canticum Canticorum (Commentary on the Song of Songs)*

Contra Eunom	*Contra Eunomium* (*Against Eunomius*)
De am. paup.	*De amore pauperorum* (*On the Love of the Poor*)
De hom opif	*De hominis opificio* (*On the creation of the human being*)
Ep	*Epistulae* (*Epistles*)
Exp.hex	*Explicatio apologetica in hexaemeron* (*The Apology on the Hexameron*)
Maced	*Adversus Macedonianos* (*Against Macedonians*)
Or. Catech	*Orationes Catecheticae* (*Catechetical Orations*)
VMos	*De vita Moysis* (*The Life of Moses*)

Gregory Thamamaturgus
Pan.	*Panegyris.* (*Panegyric Addressed to Origen*)

Hermas
Shep	*The Shepherd*

Hierocles
Prov	*De providentia* (*On Providence*)

Hilary of Poitiers
Syn.	*De synodis seu de fide orientalium* (*On the Councils*)
Frg. His.	*Fragmenta historica - Collectio antiariana Parisiana* (*Parisian Anti-Arian Collection*)
Trin.	*De Trinitate* (*On the Trinity*)

Hippolytus of Rome
Antichr.	*De Christo et antichristo* (*On Christ and Antichrist*)
Ben. Jac.	*De Benedictione Jacobi* (*On the Blessings of Isaac, Jacob, and Moses*)
Haer.	*Refutatio omnium haeresium* (*Refutation of All Heresies*)
Trad.Ap.	*Traditio Apostolica* (*Apostolic Tradition*)

Ignatius of Antioch
Eph	*Letter to the Ephesians*
Mag	*Letter to Magnesians*
Phil	*Lettter to the Philippians*
Rom	*Letter to the Romans*
Smyrn	*Letter to the Smyrnaeans*
Trall	*Letter to the Trallians*

Irenaeus of Lyons
Haer.	*Adversus Haereses* (*Against Heresies*)
Dem.	*Demonstratio apostolicae praedicationis* (*The Demonstration of the Apostolic Preaching*) (also known as *Epideixis*)

Jacob of Sarug
Hex	*Hexaemeron* (*Commentary on the six days of Creation*)

Jerome
De Vir. Ill.   *De Viris Illustribus (Lives of Illustrious men)*
Ep   *Epistulae (Letters)*

John Cassian
Conf   *Conferences*

John Chrysostom
Adv. Iud   *Adversus Iudaeos (Orations Against the Jews)*
Catech.   *Catecheses (Catechetical Homilies)*
Exp.Ps.   *Expositio in psalmum (Exposition of the Psalms)*
H. in 1 Tim.   *Homiliae in epistulam primam ad Timotheum (Homilies on 1ˢᵗ*
                        Timothy)
H.in Col.   *Homiliae in Colossenses (Homilies on the Epistle to the*
                        Colossians)
H.in Matth.   *Homilae in Matthaeum (Homilies on the Gospel of Matthew)*
H.in Rom.   *Homiliae in epistulam ad Romanos. (Homilies on the Epistle to*
                        the Romans)
Sac   *De sacerdotio (On the Priesthood)*

John of Damascus
Fide   *De fide orthodoxa (On the Orthodox Faith)*
Haer.   *De haeresibus (On Heresies)*

John Scotus Eriugena
Periph   *Periphyseon (On the Division of Nature)*

Josephus
AJ   *Antiquitates Judaicae (Jewish Antiquities)*
BJ   *De Bello Judaico (On the Jewish War)*

Julius Firmicus Maternus
Error   *On the Error of the Pagan Religions*

Justin Martyr
1 Apol.   *1 Apologia (1ˢᵗ Apology)*
2 Apol.   *2 Apologia (2ⁿᵈ Apology)*
Dial.   *Dialogue with Trypho*

Justinian
cod.   *Codex Iustinianus (The Codex of Justinian)*

Juvenal
Sat.   *Satires*

Lactantius
Epit.   *Epitoma (Epitome)*
Inst.   *Divinae Institutiones (Divine Institutes)*
Mort.   *De mortibus persecutorum (On the Deaths of the Persecutors)*

Leo I
Ep. XV   *Epistula XV ad Turribium (Letter to Turribius)*

Leontius of Byzantium
Nes   *Contra Nestorianos (Against Nestorians)*
Lib. Pont.   *Liber Pontificalis (Book of Pontiffs)*

Libellus sinodicus

Liberatus
Brev.   *Breviarium (Breviary)*

Lucretius
Rerum   *De rerum natura (On the Nature of Things)*
LXX   The Septuagint

Marcellinus Comes
Chr.   *Chronicon (Chronicle)*

Marcus Aurelius
Med.   *Meditationes (Meditations)*

Marius Victorinus
Ep.Eph   *In epistolam Pauli ad Ephesios (Commentary on the Letter to
                  the Ephesians)*

Maximus the Confessor
Ambig. Io.   *Ambigua ad Johannem (Exposition to John of Difficult Passages
                  in the Fathers)*
Ambig. Th.   *Ambigua ad Thomam (Exposition to Thomas of Difficult
                  Passages in the Fathers)*
ExOr   *Expositio orationis dominicae (Explanation of the Lord's
                  Prayer)*
Mystagog   *Mystagogia (Mystagogy)*
Schol.CH.   *Scholia in librum Dionysii Areopagiti de caelesti hierarchia .
                  (Scholia on Dionysius the Areopagite's Celestial Hierarchy)*
Schol. EH   *Scholia in librum Dionysii Areopagiti de ecclesiastica hierarchia .
                  (Scholia on Dionysius the Areopagite's Ecclesiastical Hierarchy)*
QTh   *Quaestiones ad Thalassium (Questions of Thalassius)*

Methodius of Olympus
Symp.   *Symposium eu Convivium Virginum (Symposium on Virginity)*

Minucius Felix
Oct.   *Octavius*

Musonius Rufus
Disc.   *Discourses*

Nag Hammadi Library
  The Holy Book of the Great Invisible Spirit, III, 2; IV, 2
  the *Gospel of Philip,* II, 3

Nestorius of Constantinople
Lib. Heracl.   *Liber Heraclidis (Book of Heracleides)*

Niceta of Remesiana
Psal.B   *De psalmodiae bono (On the Utility of Psalmody)*

Oecumenius
Com.Ap   *Commentarius In Apocalypsin (Commentary on the Apocalypse)*

Optatus
C. Parm.   *Contra Parmenianum Donatistam (Against Permenianus the Donatist)*

Origen
Cant   *Commentarii in Cantica Canticorum (Exposition of the Songs of Solomon)*
Cels.   *Contra Celsum (Against Celsus)*
Com. Gen   *Commentarii in Genesim (Commentary on Genesis)*
Com. Joh   *Commentarii in Ioannem (Commentary on the Gospel of John)*
Com. Matt.   *Commentarii in Matthaeum. (Commentary on the Gospel of Matthew)*
Com. Rom   *Commentarii in Epistulam ad Romanons (Commentary on the Letter to the Romans)*
Ex.M   *Exhortatio ad martyrium (Exhortation to Martyrdom)*
Frag.Luc   *Fragmenta in Lucam (Fragments of the Commentary on the Gospel of Luke)*
Heracl   *Dialogue with Heracleides*
Hom Ex   *Homiliae in Exodum (Homilies on Exodus)*
Hom.Ezek.   *Homiliae in Ezecheliem (Homilies on Ezekiel)*
Hom.Gen   *Homiliae in Genesim (Homilies on Genesis)*
Hom.Jer.   *Homiliae in Jeremiam (Homilies on Jeremiah)*
Hom. Jos   *Homiliae in Librum Jesu Nave. (Homilies on Joshua)*
Hom. Lev   *Homiliae in Leviticum (Homilies on Leviticius)*
Hom.Luc   *Homiliae in Evangelium Lucae (Homilies on The Gospel of Luke)*
Hom.Num   *Homiliae in Numeros (Homilies on Numbers)*
Hom.Ps   *Homiliae in Psalmos (Homilies on selected Psalms)*
Mart   *Exhortatio ad Martyrum (Exhortation to Martyrdom)*
PEuch   *Peri Euches (On Prayer)*
Princ   *De Principiis (On First Principles)*
Ser.Com.Matt   *Series commentariorum in matthaeum (Series of Commentaries on Matthew)*

Palladius of Helenopolis
Dial.   *Dialogus de vita Sancti Johannis Chrysostomi.* (*Dialogue on the Life of St. John Chrysostom*)

Pamphilus
Apol.   *Apologia* (*Apology*)
Passio Donati   *The Passion of Donatus*
Pass. Mar   *Passio Marculi* (*The Passion of Marculus*)
Pass. Max   *Passio Maximiani et Isaac* (*The Passion of Maximian and Isaac*)

Peter Chrysologus
Serm   *Sermones* (*Sermons*)

Philo of Alexandria
Congr   *De congressu quaerendae eruditionis gratia* (*On The Preliminary Studies*)
Decal   *De Decalogo* (*On the Decalogue*)
Heres   *Quis rerum divinarum heres sit?* (*Who Inherits Divine Blessings?*)
Prov.   *De providentia* (*On Providence*)
Vit. Cont   *De vita contemplativa* (*On the Contemplative Life*)

Plato
Cri   *Crito*
Gorg.   *Gorgias*
Philb   *Philebus*
Plt   *Politicus* (*The Statesman*)
Rep.   *Respublica* (*The Republic*)
Symp   *Symposium*
Ti   *Timaeus*

Pliny the Younger
Ep   *Epistulae* (*Letters*)

Polycarp
Frg.   *Fragmenta* (*Fragments*)
Phil   *Letter to the Philippians*

Porphyry
Abst.   *De abstinentia* (*On abstinence from animal food*)
Adv.Ch.   *Adversus Christianos* (*Against the Christians*)
VP   *Vita Plotini* (*Life of Plotinus*)

Proclus
ET   *Elementa Theologiae* (*The Elements of Theology*)
in Ti.   *Commentarii in Platonis Timaeum* (*The Commentary on Plato's Timaeus*)

Ps-Archelaeus
Acta   *Acta disputationis cum Manete* (*Records of the dispute with Mani*)

Pseudo-Clementines
  Recognitions

Ps-Dionysius the Areopagite,
DN   *De divinis nominibus (On the divine names)*

Ps-Tertullian
Haer   *Adversus Haereses (Against the Heresies)*

Seneca
Ben   *De beneficiis (On Benefits)*
Ep.   *Epistulae (Letters)*

Serapion of Thmuis
Euch.Serap.   *The Euchologion (Altar Book) of Serapion*

Sextus Empiricus
Pyr   *Pyrrhoneioi hypotyposeis (the Outlines of Pyrrhonism)*

Socrates Scholasticus
HE   *Historia ecclesiastica (Ecclesiastical History)*

Sozomen
HE   *Historia ecclesiastica (Ecclesiastical History)*

Suetonius
Domitian   *Lives of the Emperors: Domitian*
Nero   *Lives of the Emperors: Nero*

Sulpicius Severus
chronc.   *Chronicorum (Chronicles)*

Synodicon adversus Tragaediam Irenaei (Synodicon Against the Tragedy of Irenaeus)

Tacitus
Ann.   *Annales (Annals)*

Tatian
Or   *(Oratio ad Graecos) (Oration to the Greeks)*

Tertullian
An   *De Anima (On the Soul)*
Apol.   *Apologeticum (The Apology)*
Bapt.   *De Baptismo (On Baptism)*
Carn.   *De Carne Christi (On the Flesh of Christ)*
Cast.   *De exhortation castitatis (An Exhortation to Chastity)*
Cor.   *De Corona (On the Military Crown)*
Ecst.frg.   *(Fragment on Ecstasy)*
Fug.   *De Fuga (On Flight)*
Hermog.   *Adversus Hermogenem (Against Hermogenes)*
Idol.   *De Idolatria (On Idolatry)*

Jejun.	*De Jejunio* (*On Fasting*)
Jud.	*Adversus Judaeos* (*Against the Jews*)
Marc.	*Adversus Marcionem. Libri V* (*Against Marcion five books*)
Mart.	*Ad Martyras* (*To the Martyrs*)
Monog.	*De Monogamia* (*On Monogamy*)
Nat.	*Ad Nationes* (*Address to the Pagans*)
Orat.	*De Oratione* (*On Prayer*)
Prax.	*Adversus Praxean* (*Against Praxeas*)
Prescr.	*De Prescriptione Haereticorum* (*Against Heretics*)
Pud	*De Pudicitia* (*On Modesty*)
Scap.	*Ad Scapulam* (*To Scapula*)
Spect.	*De Spectaculis* (*On the games*)
Val	*Adversus Valentinianos* (*Against the Valentinians*)
Virg.	*De virginibus velandis* (*On the Veiling of Virgins*)

Theodore of Heraclea

Frag.M	*Fragmenta in Matthaeum* (*Fragements on Matthew*)

Theodore of Mopsuestia

Comm.Eph.	*Comentarii in Ephesios* (*Commentary on the Letter to Ephesians*)
Jo.	*Fragmenta in Iohannis* (*Commentary on the Gospel of John*)

Theodoret of Cyrrhus

Comm.Rom	*Commentarii in Epistulam Romanos* (*Commentary on the Epistle to Romans*)
HE	*Historia ecclesiastica* (*Ecclesiastical History*)

Theophanes

chron.	*Chronographia* (*Chronicle*)

Theophilus

Autol	(*To Autolycus*)
Diog.	(*The Letter to Diognetus – Anon*)

The Dead Sea Scrolls
   1QS iv.21-22
   Ritual A (4Q512), frg. 11
   Ritual B (4Q414), frg.2 ii.3-4

The Gospel of Thomas
   Saying

Victor of Vita

hist. pers.	*Historia persecutionis Africanae provinciae* (*History of persecution in the Provinces of Africa*)

Vigilius

Const.	*Constitutum* (*The Donation of Constantine*)

MODERN SOURCES

AARC	Atti dell'Accademia Romanistica Costantiniana
AB	The Art Bulletin
ABR	Australian Biblical Review
ACO	Acta Conciliorum Oecumenicorum
AH	Art History
AHP	Archivum Historiae Pontificiae
ANF	Nicene and Post-Nicene Fathers
ARAM	(Peeters Online Journal)
ARAW	Abhandlungen der Rheinisch-Westfälischen Akademie der Wissenschaften
AS	Augustinian Studies
ASKA	Arbeiten zum spatantiken und koptischen Agypten
Aug	Augustinianum

B	Babesch
Byz	Byzantion
BCNH.É	Bibliothèque copte de Nag Hammadi, section "Études"
BCNH.T	Bibliothèque copte de Nag Hammadi, section "Textes"
BEEC	The Brill Encyclopedia of Early Christianity
BETL	Bibliotheca Ephemeridum Theologicarum Lovaniensium
BibA	Biblical Archaeologist
BJRL	Bulletin of the John Rylands Library
BLE	Bulletin de la littérature ecclésiastique
BiblRev	Biblical Review
BMCR	Bryn Mawr Classical Review
BThB	Biblical Theology Bulletin
BSAC	Bulletin de la Société d'Archéologie Copte
BSR	Bulletin for the Study of Religion
BZ	Byzantinische Zeitschrift
BZNW	Beiheft zur Zeitschrift für die neustamentliche Wissenschaft und die Kunde der älteren Kirche

CAH	Cambridge Ancient History
CBR	Currents in Biblical Research
CCSL	Corpus Christianorum Series Latina
CCT	Christ in Christian Tradition
CGL	The Coptic Gnostic Library
CH	Church History
CHECL	Cambridge History of Early Christian Literature
CHRC	Church History and Religious Culture
CIL	Corpus Inscriptionum Latinarum
CnS	Cristianesimo nella Storia

CPG	*Clavis Patrum Graecorum*
CSCO	*Corpus Scriptorum Christianorum Orientalium*
CSEL	*Corpus Scriptorum Ecclesiasticorum Latinorum*
DECL	*Dictionary of Early Christian Literature*
DSP	*Dokumenty Soborów Powszechnych (Polish series)*
E	*Eirene*
EBR	*The Encyclopedia of the Bible and Its Reception*
ECS	*Eastern Christian Studies*
EO	*Ecclesia Orans*
EMC	*Échos du Monde Classique*
EpigAnat	*Epigraphia Anatolia*
EThL	*Ephemerides Theologicae Lovanienses*
ExClass	*Exemplaria Classica: Journal of Classical Philology*
Ex.Times	*Expository Times*
FHI	*Fides humanitas ius*
FTh	*Feminist Theology*
G	*Gregorianum*
GCS	*Griechischen Christlichen Schriftsteller*
GEDSH	*Gorgias Encyclopedic Dictionary of the Syriac Heritage*
GH	*Gender & History*
GJLS	*Grow Joint Liturgical Studies*
GNO	*Gregorii Nysseni Opera*
GRBS	*Greek, Roman, Byzantine Studies.*
Hermeneia	*Hermeneia: A Critical & Historical Commentary on the Bible*
HSCPh	*Harvard Studies in Classical Philology*
HTR	*Harvard Theological Review*
HTS	*Harvard Theological Studies*
ICCoptSt	*International Congress of Coptic Studies: Rome.*
IFAO	*Institut français d'archéologie orientale*
IJCT	*International Journal of the Classical Tradition*
IJPT	*International Journal of the Platonic Tradition*
IJSTh	*International Journal of Systematic Theology*
Inv.luc	*Invigilata lucernis*
JAAR	*Journal of American Academy of Religion*
JAAS	*Journal of Assyrian Academic Studies*
JAC	*Journal of Ancient Civilizations.*
JBL	*Journal of Biblical Literature*
JBNum	*Jahrbuch für Numismatik und Geldgeschichte*

JBR   *Journal of the Bible and Religion*
JCoptS   *Journal of Coptic Studies*
JDC   *Journal of Dialogue & Culture*
JECH   *Journal of Early Christian History*
JECS   *Journal of Early Christian Studies*
JECH   *Journal of Early Christian History*
JEH   *Journal of Ecclesiastical History*
JFSR   *Journal of Feminist Studies in Religion*
JLA   *Journal of Late Antiquity*
JLARC   *Journal for Late Antique Religion and Culture*
JHR   *Journal of Religious History*
JJP   *Journal of Juristic Papyrology*
JMS   *Journal of Mithraic Studies*
JRel   *Jahrbuch für Religionsphilosophie*
JPT   *Journal of Philosophy and Theology*
JR   *Japanese Religions*
JRS   *Journal of Religious Studies*
JSNT   *Journal for the Study of the New Testament*
JSP   *Journal for the Study of the Pseudepigrapha*
JSS   *Journal of Syriac Studies*
JTS   *Journal of Theological Studies*

LAA   *Late Antique Archaeology*
LAHR   *Late Antique History and Religion*

M   *Meander*
MAAR   *Memoirs of the American Academy in Rome*
MGH AA   *Monumenta Germaniae Historica. Auctores Antiquissimi*

NETS   *New English Translation of the Septuagint*
NHMS   *Nag Hammadi and Manichaean Studies*
NHS   *Nag Hammadi Studies*
NTS   *New Testament Studies*
NDPAC   *Nuovo dizionario patristico e di antichità cristiane, 3 vols.,*
                (Genova-Milano 2006–2010)
NICNT   *New International Commentary on the New Testament*
NIGTC   *The New International Greek Text Commentary*
NovT   *Novum Testamentum*
NPNF   *Nicene and Post-Nicene Fathers*
NRSV   *New Revised Standard Version*

OCA   *Orientalia Christiana Analecta*
OLA   *Orientalia Lovaniensia Analecta*
OLZ   *Orientalistische Literaturzeitung*
OS   *Ostkirchliche Studien*

P	*Philotheos*
PBSR	*Papers of the British School at Rome*
PG	*Patrologia Graeca*
PGM	*Papyri Graecae Magicae*
PhAnt	*Philosophie Antique*
PhilAnt	*Philologia Antiqua: An International Journal of Classics.*
PL	*Patrologia Latina*
PNH	*Przeglad Nauk Historycznych*
PP	*Past & Present*
QL	*Questions Liturgique/Studies in Liturgy*
RA	*Revue Archéologique*
RBL	*Review of the Biblical Literature*
REAug	*Revue des Études Augustiniennes*
RGRW	*Religions in the Graeco-Roman world*
RHE	*Revue d'histoire ecclésiastique*
RHEF	*Revue d'histoire de l'Eglise de France*
RhM	*Rheinisches Museum*
RIL	*Rendiconti dell'Instituto Lombardo, Classe di Lettere, Scenze morali e storiche*
RSCI	*Rivista di storia della chiesa in Italia*
RSR	*Revue de Sciences Religieuses*
RThL	*Revue Théologique de Louvain*
RUB	*Revue de l'Université de Bruxelles*
S	*Speculum*
SAC	*Studies in Antiquity and Christianity*
SC/JECS	*Second Century: A Journal of Early Christian Studies*
SCh	*Sources Chrétiennes*
SCI	*Scripta Classica Israelica*
SCJR	*Studies in Christian-Jewish Relations*
SCL	*Synodi et Collectiones Legum (Polish series)*
ScTh	*Scripta Theologica*
SDHI	*Studia et Documenta Historiae et Iuris*
SEA	*Studia Ephemeridis Augustinianum*
SEG	*Supplementum epigraphicum Graecum*
SGLLC	*Studies in German Literature, Linguistics and Culture*
SHR	*Studies in the History of Religions*
SNTW	*Studies of The New Testament and Its World*
SO	*Symbolae Osloenses*
Soph	*Sophia*
SP	*Studia Patristica*
SPCK	*Society for the Promotion of Christian Knowledge*
SPhiloA	*Studia Philonica Annual*

STAC	*Studien und Texte zu Antike und Christentum/Studies and Texts in Antiquity and Christianity*
STh	*Studia Theologica*
SupVCh	*Supplements to Vigiliae Christianae*
ThS	*Theological Studies*
TQ	*Theologisches Quartalschrift*
Traditio	*Traditio: Studies in Ancient and Medieval History, Thought, and Religion*
TSAJ	*Texte und Studien zum Antiken Judentum*
TUGAL	*Texte und Untersuchungen zur Geschichte der altchristlichen Literatur*
VChr	*Vigiliae Christianae*
VetChr	*Vetera Christianorum*
VP	*Vox Patrum*
WUNT	*Wissenschaftliche Untersuchungen zum Neuen Testament*
ŹMT	*Źródła Myśli Teologicznej (Polish series)*
ZAC	*Zeitschrift fur Antike und Christentum*
ZPE	*Zeitschrift für Papyrologie und Epigraphik*
ZPF	*Zeitschrift für philosophische Forschung*

CHAPTER 1

Introduction

On studying the early church

ROWAN WILLIAMS

Understanding any social reality involves understanding how it 'learns' – that is, how it develops a culture in which certain norms are settled, certain procedures for managing common life are developed and certain concepts defined, either tacitly or more explicitly. One of the most substantial challenges that can arise for an intelligent and critical social order – a community in which there is scrutiny of how authority is exercised and decisions made – is the drift towards a cultural mindset for which the processes of learning are uninteresting or unimportant, as if what currently obtains in speech and practice is so self-evident as not to need learning. And if we look at the history of Christian practice and discourse, we can see very easily how this assumption of a 'self-evident' and timeless system recurs. In challenging it, theologians are in effect saying that when we understand how the community learnt to say and do what it does, we *learn how to learn afresh*. We recover some crucial skills of discernment that have been buried by generations of uncritical repetition and so have in fact become something other than what they initially were.

This is why the study of patristic[1] texts *in extenso* and in their own terms is something that comes into focus in the Reformation era. It is not that this was the first time that Christians told a story of decline from early purity and simplicity; the 'apostolic' movements of monastic reform in the eleventh and twelfth centuries already appealed to a lost age of spiritual integrity. But the Reformation critique was a great deal more comprehensive and radical, arguing that both teaching and practice had been damagingly corrupted over the centuries. For the first time, it was important to break the tradition of quoting the Fathers piecemeal in the context of

---

[1]The use of the term is of course controversial to a degree: the very category of 'Fathers' of the Church encodes, it appears, a patriarchal assumption about what is generative or authoritative in Christian thinking. In its defence, it can only be said that it reflects an undeniable aspect of the self-understanding of the early Christian community, for whom authoritative teaching did indeed emanate from 'fathers', especially bishops, and of those in later Christian ages who looked to these sources. I have thought it best to leave the term unmodified but to note its problematic character for contemporary discourse.

expounding or defending an agreed system of doctrine. What mattered now was the question of whether that system itself could withstand the evidence of its own history. For the Reformers, this entailed showing that positions taken for granted in late medieval theology and liturgical practice – the 'treasury of merit' idea which provided the rationale for ecclesiastical indulgences, remissions of penance for the living and the dead, for example; or the developed cultus of the consecrated elements of the Eucharist – could not be traced in Scripture or in primitive Christian literature. The conclusion must be, so the Reformers argued, that these were created simply by compromised human decisions, that they were unjustified extrapolations from primitive doctrinal beliefs, and that their creation was designed to serve the interest of various power structures in the church (the Papacy and the clerical caste). And to establish such conclusions involved a new level of historical and philological interest in early Christian texts, with fresh editions being printed and a concern for the study of material in the original languages. It was, of course, an interest shared by Reformers and traditionalists: effective response to the Reformation critique required an equal level of historical and critical skill on the Catholic side, and the period from the sixteenth to the eighteenth century saw the production of a series of formidably encyclopedic church histories designed to support one or the other side in the controversies of the age. And within the spectrum of Reformed theology, another pressure rapidly developed: the need to resist some varieties of theological 'primitivism', which went beyond the critique of medieval theology to challenging the central credal formulae deriving from the early church. The denial of the doctrine of the Trinity by various groups in the sixteenth and seventeenth centuries prompted increasingly detailed argument over the interpretation of theological language from the period before the definitions of the Council of Nicaea and its successors, with more orthodox Protestant scholars seeking to establish that Trinitarian belief could be unambiguously discerned in such language.[2]

But this still remains largely in the realm of using patristic study to justify a position held in the present. There is undoubtedly, in this period, a new recognition that the texts of the Fathers need to be read as more than just a collection of useable quotations; but there was little interest in exactly how the Fathers themselves 'learn', how they arrive at their conclusions within a wider intellectual and social as well as theological context. For both sides in the Reformation debates, it is axiomatic that the authentic Christian faith is there to be discerned in the earliest ages. For the Protestant, trying to read the Fathers independently of the way they had been cited in medieval theology was a way of showing that later Christian thought had abandoned this early integrity; for the Catholic, deploying a fuller armoury of patristic scholarship showed that apparent discontinuities could in fact be understood in the light of a more extensive and theologically sophisticated reading of the early texts. But as the seventeenth-century discussions developed, two new and related perspectives came into play, whose effects still haunt contemporary

---

[2]For a lucid survey of anti-Trinitarian theologies in the post-Reformation period, see: M. Wiles, *Archetypal Heresy: Arianism Through the Centuries* (Oxford: Clarendon Press, 1996).

approaches to patristic thought. There was, first, a sharpened awareness on the part of some scholars that doctrinal language had actually undergone change. The great French Jesuit scholar Denis Petau (often referred to as Petavius; 1583–1652),[3] recognized that the actual formulations of doctrine in the early period were indeed ambiguous in the light of later orthodoxy and (in his view) unduly influenced by the philosophical ideas of the age: turns of phrase that would have been excluded by later orthodoxy were allowed to go unchallenged, and the key elements of the vocabulary of post-Nicene theology were not to be found in the primitive period. The historian of doctrine therefore had to undertake the task of showing something of how such vocabulary came into being; but for Petau this also had to do with the need for a clear decision-making authority in the church, sanctioning some interpretative developments and condemning others. The study of the Fathers thus became an element in the argument for a Catholic system of conciliar and papal government, since orthodoxy could not simply be read off from pre-Nicene texts; the diversity and ambiguity of these writings simply showed the need for some source of definitive clarity. It was an argument that rather shocked some orthodox Protestants, not least in the Church of England, where the encyclopedic learning of divines like Daniel Waterland, John Pearson and George Bull was used to confute the criticisms of 'Socinian' or 'Arian' dissidents, inside and outside the established Church of England, who had proposed that the classical creeds had no place in a rational and reformed Christian body.[4] The defenders of credal doctrine – like their predecessors in the sixteenth century – believed themselves bound to argue that this doctrine was present at least by clear implication in pre-Nicene theology – and that there was no need to appeal to anything except the texts themselves properly read and understood. Ironically enough, there were continental Catholics who seem to have been more comfortable with these Anglican savants than with Petau.

But second, the growing awareness of the philosophical literature available to early Christian writers and the impact of its vocabulary and thought-forms unsurprisingly led some to rather different conclusions. Interest in the intellectual climate of early Christianity became markedly stronger in some quarters by the early to mid-seventeenth century. In England, the Cambridge Platonists had developed a distinctive theological style, resuscitating the more overtly Platonic aspects of the Greek Fathers and focusing on some of the intellectual and spiritual techniques of contemplative enlightenment within this tradition, and on a metaphysical model of

---

[3]The best introduction to his life and work remains: P. Galtier, SJ, 'Petavius', in *Dictionnaire de théologie catholique* (Paris: Letouzay et Ane, 1933), vol. 12:1, cols 1313–1337.

[4]D. Levitin, *Ancient Wisdom in the Age of the New Science: Histories of Philosophy in England c.1640-1700* (Cambridge: Cambridge University Press, 2015), especially chapter 6, is now the authoritative guide to this. A. Middleton, *Fathers and Anglicans: The Limits of Orthodoxy* (Leominster: Gracewing, 2001) is a helpful but much more basic introduction. Some discussions of Newman's early work on the Arians also deal in passing with aspects of this tradition; see, for example (from the Bibliography): Williams (1990), Thomas (2003) and King (2009).

creation as imbued with divine agency, participating in divine life in some sense.[5] In some circles, this interest spilled over into a sympathy with 'hermetic' literature – the esoteric cosmology of late antique Mediterranean speculation, the Jewish Kabbala and other elements which could be regarded as 'Gnostic' in flavour or bordering on magic. None of this was entirely new; hermeticism and Kabbala had been studied by Renaissance writers and by faintly heterodox figures on both sides of the Reformation a century and more earlier than the Cambridge group. But in the context of a more critical and unsettled approach to the history of doctrine, and a growing rationalism in Protestant theology, this Platonic *ressourcement* prompted a fresh perspective on how doctrinal formulae were shaped – how the church had learnt, and, in this perspective, learnt the *wrong* things. The canonical Protestant idea that there had been a drastic falling-away from primitive purity was adapted to produce a narrative of the seduction of theology by alien philosophical and metaphysical styles of thought, turning the simplicities of biblical religion into an artificially systematized doctrinal pattern. The study of early Christian texts was thus important not as a positive but as a negative tool of argument and polemic, meant to show the process by which doctrine had been corrupted. Where Petau had seen the gradual emergence of a chastened Christian metaphysic under the providential guidance of a divinely sanctioned ecclesiastical authority that could sift the wheat from the chaff, some continental Protestant scholars saw a steady decline towards speculative excess and irrational myth.

The Lutheran theologian, Johann Lorenz von Mosheim (1693–1755), the most learned and influential German church historian of the eighteenth century, produced (in addition to some exhaustive critical commentary on the Cambridge Platonists) a major work on pre-Constantinian Christianity in which he traced the damaging effects of the Platonizing elements that found their way into patristic writing in the early centuries.[6] His narrative was to remain immensely powerful in German Protestant scholarship, reaching its climax in the monumental doctrinal history of Adolf von Harnack (1851–1930);[7] and the model of an early, unadorned proclamation compromised and diluted by myth and metaphysic persists in the 'demythologising' programme of Rudolf Bultmann (1884–1976), applied not only to patristic writers but to the New Testament texts themselves.[8]

---

[5]Further see: Levitin, *Ancient Wisdom*. For an introduction to the Cambridge Platonists, see S. Hutton, 'The Cambridge Platonists', *The Stanford Encyclopaedia of Philosophy*, ed. E. N. Zalta, at: https://plato.stanford.edu/archives/win2013/entries/cambridge-platonists/ (consulted October 2020); a helpful collection of recent studies is: D. Hedley and S. Hutton (eds), *Platonism at the Origins of Modernity: Studies in Platonism and Early Modern Philosophy* (New York: Springer 2008).

[6]See R. Williams, 'Newman's *Arians* and the Question of Method in Doctrinal History', in *Newman After a Hundred Years*, eds I. Ker and A. G. Hill (Oxford: Clarendon Press, 1990), pp. 279 ff., on Mosheim and his influence.

[7]Harnack's *Lehrbuch der Dogmengeschichte* appeared in three volumes between 1886 and 1889; an English translation in seven volumes (as *The History of Dogma*) followed in 1894-1899.

[8]R. Bultmann, *Jesus Christ and Mythology* (London: SCM Press, 1958), is a very brief introduction; see also G. Jones, *Bultmann: Towards a Critical Theology* (Cambridge: Polity Press, 1990).

As Bultmann's shrewder critics observed, the bare fact of putting convictions into intelligible shape and language entails some negotiation with the cultural milieu (and Bultmann was, of course, engaged in exactly that in his demythologizing programme, with its debt to Heidegger's existentialism). A belief which simply creates its own vocabulary and its own system of intelligibility is hard to imagine. Christian theology in fact begins as a radical commentary on the existing texts and practices of Jewish tradition, and so is already 'negotiating': it does not come from nowhere. And because that Jewish tradition itself is also already negotiating with Hellenistic ideas, and its Scriptures have already been translated into Greek, it is impossible to find some core primitive articulation of belief that can be lifted out of its context and 'purified' from alien elements. Thus the problem with most early modern approaches to patristic theology is that they work with a strongly territorial model of the relation between Christian reflection and the ambient culture. It is a picture in which there is an *essential* deposit, which may be corrupted by foreign invasion or preserved intact without change, or carefully nurtured by lawful authority to grow in the direction that is natural to it. What is positive in the Reformation and post-Reformation development of patristic study on a historical basis is the acknowledgement that the study of how communities learn their language can be a constructively critical tool in the present. What is less positive is the search for a simply 'given' language of belief, bestowed from heaven and recoverable by diligent research.

Yet this is not to say that the only thing historical study can produce is a primal soup of opinions and convictions. Any serious intellectual history will be looking for the ways in which beliefs develop a pattern of interrelation, the ways in which certain convictions are gradually seen (rightly or wrongly) to entail others. To trace the process by which a system of belief and practice is learnt, in the sense outlined already, we need to trace the development of what has been called the 'ecology' of the system – the interconnection of beliefs, the balance of perspectives and emphases, the reciprocal influence of practice and discourse. And in this context, what is distinctive about a system will come to light not by the uncovering of an essential core but in the discernment of a unifying or balancing ecology of this sort, emerging over time. This is as much a serious task for the 'detached' observer as for the scholar who is in some sense an inheritor and inhabitant of the history. One of the most teasing but necessary of intellectual tasks is to work out what *counts* as an instance of something. The temptation is indeed to look for an essential core; the creative agenda is to find some of the family likenesses which allow us to say that *this* phenomenon can illuminatingly be seen as a variant of *that*. The issues are familiar in the history of scientific taxonomy, but they are also part of the work of any humanities scholar. Is Dylan Thomas really a Modernist poet or a displaced Romantic? Is Edmund Burke a conservative political philosopher in the same sense as Carl Schmitt? The process will of course entail at some point bringing the classificatory schemes themselves into question in a fruitful way. The search for features that are mutually recognizable and mutually illuminating is certainly more complex and controversial than a mere measurement against an essential feature or group of features, but it does more adequate justice to the actuality of a historical process in which recognition and continuity are both real and contestable, non-obvious, coming into focus only with a certain passage of time and remaining fluid as particular phenomena are better understood.

What differentiates the uncommitted observer from the committed is not that the former will have no interest in the way norms and boundaries operate, but that the latter will have a stronger concern with some sorts of identifiable distinctiveness that allow for belief in a providential direction of the history of conflict such that we are able to speak of a continuing identity sustained and strengthened in the processes of argument. Alasdair MacIntyre famously defines a 'living tradition' as 'an historically extended, socially embodied argument', embodying 'continuities of conflict'.[9] A close study of the texts of the fourth Christian century will undoubtedly bring into focus the difficulties of identifying the boundaries between 'orthodoxy' and 'heresy' as the writers of that age understood the terms. What made certain thinkers recognize the same doctrine in each other, despite points of quite significant divergence, what allowed some theologians – notably Athanasius – to shift the way he defined the limits of acceptable variation in vocabulary at a certain historical point, what non-theological factors intensified or neutralized conflicts – all of this is the stuff of straightforward historical scholarship in quest of how conceptual 'ecologies' emerge and adjust. What makes the Athanasian settlement of language about the threefold God, or the Chalcedonian statement of the ingredients of acceptable language about Christ's two natures recognizable to the contemporary believer as an adequate (or at least not lethally inadequate) expression of what faith *must* say about God in Christ will not be determined by such scholarship. But without some attention to how and why ecologies developed and changed in the language of the Christian community, contemporary believers understand that much less about how they have learnt and are learning to live in a coherent spiritual narrative and world view. Thus it is possible in the fourth century to trace – for example – how anxieties rooted in controversies about Gnosticism steadily eroded what had earlier seemed a defensible conceptual structure in which a 'first' and 'second' God stood at the fountainhead of a hierarchically conceived flow of being that ran from active plenitude to passivity; or how, similarly, the insistence on the unqualified divine immutability of the Eternal Word steadily eroded the possibility of vaguely merging the subjecthood of the Eternal Word with the interior life of Jesus of Nazareth as a single member of the human race. What is more specifically the task of the theologically committed patrologist is to work at how and why moves like these contributed to a doctrinal ecology optimally 'habitable' by those who confess allegiance to Jesus of Nazareth as Saviour.

Patristics is inevitably the study of conceptual controversies, arguments over definitions, over the grammar of Christian belief, over limits and exclusions. This is – if the last few paragraphs have been at all on the right lines – not only a matter of historical clarification but necessarily an exercise for believers seeking to make sense

---

[9] A. MacIntyre, *After Virtue: A Study in Moral Theory* (London: Duckworth, 1981), pp. 206–7.

of their belonging in a community sustained through time by God's act, whatever disruptions may be at work. But, as the record of patristic scholarship over the last few decades amply shows, the study of conceptual controversy and definition is only one element in the exercise, whether historical or theological. Robert Wilken writes aptly that 'Christian thinking did not spring from an original idea, and it was not nourished by a seminal spiritual insight'.[10] The social reality of the Christian community came into being as the result of a specific set of events whose effect can be traced in a set of distinctive practices – not only what we might call spiritual disciplines, but patterns of relationship and decision-making and interaction with non-members. And it is not irrelevant to remember that the 'distinctiveness' of the early community was not a matter of defining some unique selling point for a particular ideology in a market of world views; it was the distinctiveness of a society proscribed by law. Defending what made the community its unique self was bound up with the necessity of knowing what you might be dying for; and while the copious literature of martyrdom in the early church is not simply an innocent record of innocent suffering but a sophisticated genre, with clear theological and often polemical aims, this hardly alters the fact that large numbers of Christian believers died in circumstances of extreme barbarity after refusing to compromise their faith.

So the identifying practices of Christian communities can be seen as including the practices of sacramental initiation and ritual eating (baptism and Eucharist), prayer to God as 'Father', debates over charismatic versus institutional authority, abstention from socially sanctioned behaviours around sex and military service; but also as frequently focused on the sharing of narratives of persecution and exemplary suffering, celebration of these exemplary deaths, and controversy over whether certain forms of life-saving compromise in the face of persecution invalidated claims to Christian identity.[11]

All of these contribute to a recognizable Christian profile at least as much as what was said and thought about 'doctrinal' questions. There is a fairly general acknowledgement that classical patristic study up to the later part of the twentieth century was characterized by an unbalanced stress on these latter questions; and the perennial issue in intellectual history arises of how far a history of ideas can be written that is consistently skewed in the direction of what a numerically tiny élite was arguing about. Evidence of practice outside élites is often hard to come by, but it is not completely inaccessible, and early Christian patristic archaeology has made significant and sometimes challenging contributions to the story of how a Christian ecology or grammar developed. Thus, for example, while our textual

---

[10]R. M. Wilken, *The Spirit of Early Christian Thought: Seeking the Face of God* (New Haven, CT and London: Yale University Press, 2003), p. 24. This is a particularly helpful and insightful overview of the central themes of early Christian self-understanding.

[11]These controversies were particularly fierce in North Africa in the third and fourth centuries; Augustine's struggle with the powerful group who claimed that compromises under persecution had in effect rendered void the authority of a whole generation of bishops, and their successors played a major role in his theological evolution.

evidence largely reinforces the picture of early Christianity as systematically opposed to military service, the presence of Christians in the Roman army in the pre-Constantinian period is borne out by archaeological evidence in the shape of military gravestones.[12] Or again: the excavated remains of large churches in North Africa provide evidence of activities not clearly evidenced in our textual sources.[13] A casual scrap of papyrus from Egypt, dated to 324 CE, tells us that the word *monachos* was used a good deal earlier than we might deduce from more formal literary evidence, and used to designate someone living within a village community, not in the isolation of the desert.[14]

These may not be facts that require a massive rewriting of doctrinal history; but they are a necessary reminder of what it is about the early communities that we cannot find in 'élite' texts. More positively, they remind us that the texts we have are grounded in various practices – the writing of philosophical 'open letters' to Roman authorities, the disciplines of rhetorical and philosophical education, the regular public reading and interpretation of sacred texts in the context of liturgical worship and so on. By the fourth Christian century, there was a complex symbiosis and interaction between discussions of doctrinal questions and the construction of – often very sophisticated – guidebooks for monastic meditation, which took for granted a specific model of human consciousness with diverse metaphysical roots.[15]

Christian 'anthropology' was the point at which theology and *paideia*, the practices of educational formation, intersected most decisively, and grasping some of the subtleties of this discipline of formation illuminates many difficult aspects of the theological debates. The relative ignoring of this overlap until the latter part of the twentieth century in much conventional scholarship about the early church left the doctrinal debates unduly opaque and abstract. To take an obvious example, any discussion of what it might mean to say that Christ enjoyed perfect human freedom entailed reference to what such freedom itself involved, what sort of freedom was assumed and/or cultivated in Christian practice, especially (by that date) in the ascetic world of monastic self-discipline, and how far spiritual freedom and stability

---

[12]See J. F. Shean, *Soldiering for God: Christianity and the Roman Army* (Leiden: E.J. Brill, 2010), for the archaeological evidence.

[13]R. MacMullen, *The Second Church: Popular Christianity A.D.200-400* (Atlanta, GA: SBL Press, 2009).

[14]E. A. Judge, 'The Earliest Use of *Monachos* for "Monk" and the Origins of Monasticism', in *Jahrbuch für Antike und Christentum*, vol. 20 (Munster: Aschedorff, 1977), pp. 72–89, is the seminal study.

[15]The works of Evagrius of Pontus and his follower John Cassian were among the most influential instances. Despite doctrinal anxieties over Evagrius' legacy, which resulted in some of his works circulating under other names and many surviving only in Syriac translation, his treatises provided a model for later spiritual writers. For examples, see G. Palmer, P. Sherrard and K. Ware (trans.), *The Philokalia*, vol. 1 (London: Faber and Faber, 1979); and on Evagrius himself, A. Casiday, *Evagrius Ponticus* (London: Routledge 2006), and Idem, A. Casiday, *Reconstructing the Theology of Evagrius Ponticus: Beyond Heresy* (Cambridge: Cambridge University Press, 2013); and I. L. E. Ramelli, *Evagrius Ponticus' Kephalaia Gnostika* (Leiden: E.J. Brill and Atlanta, GA: SBL, 2015), and I. L. E. Ramelli, 'Gregory Nyssen's and Evagrius's Biographical and Theological Relations: Origen's Heritage and Neoplatonism', in *Evagrius between Origen, the Cappadocians, and Neoplatonism, SP*, vol. 84, eds I. L. E. Ramelli et al. (Leuven: Peeters, 2017), pp. 165–231.

was compatible with the experience of 'trial', *peirasmos*, the unsettling awareness of options other than the practices of piety. The treatment of these questions by ascetical writers is part of the story of how the popular categorization of the 'seven deadly sins' evolved; but the original analysis of diverse forms of temptation or disruptions of the soul and intellect makes little sense outside the context of arguments over what it means for Christ to be fully human.[16]

But we can take this still further. The importance of clarifying what it meant to ascribe unqualified and undiminished human subjectivity to Christ rests on the broader and more primal sense that what Christ actually does is to restore humanity to where it should be – a theme given exceptionally vivid and coherent expression by Irenaeus in the second century.[17] Whatever is involved in the work of Christ, what we have to think of Christ as achieving in his life, death and resurrection if we are to make sense of the unique importance ascribed to him in worship must include this element of the restoration to humanity of a lost fullness or at least a lost horizon of possibility. And this lost horizon is in turn defined in relation to the calling of human subjects to share the divine life or divine nature – a form of words that occurs in precisely that rather general form in 2 Pet. 1.4, but is given a clearer relational definition in the Farewell Discourses of the Fourth Gospel with their talk about the mutual 'indwelling' of Father and Word and believing community. The implication is that the creation of human beings in the divine image, an image fully realized only in Christ, is the creation of finite subjects capable of living in filial relation to the source of all, in a way continuous with Christ's own intimacy with the Father in time and eternity.

The point is that the analysis of spiritual struggle, understood as the attempt to leave behind what blocks the possibility of this loving intimacy and contemplative beholding of the Father, is inextricably linked with (1) the exegesis of certain key scriptural texts, (2) the nascent doctrine of God as always 'beheld' by the co-eternal but derived reality that we call Logos and Son, (3) the conviction that Jesus of Nazareth restores human capacity to what God intends. It is bound up with the practices of the church as a community that reads and re-reads its sacred texts in public, and with what we would now call the doctrines of the Trinity and the Incarnation. Doctrine, in other words, is inseparable from what is *done* by Christians – both by those who have dedicated themselves to a certain style of Christian life as monastics and by those who routinely listen to expositions of scripture by authorized teachers. And in addition to this, we have the phenomenon of a further interweaving of practice and theology in the way in which sacramental ritual becomes both a site

---

[16]See, for example, Cassian's assimilation of the temptations of the ascetic to Christ's temptations in the desert, discussed in R. Williams, '"Tempted as we are": Christology and the Analysis of the Passions', in *Studia Patristica*, 45 (Leuven: Peeters, 2010), pp. 391–404.

[17]Especially in his treatise 'The Refutation and Overthrow of Knowledge Falsely So-called', normally referred to as *Adversus Haereses* (Against Heresies). Book 5 of this spells out the ways in which Christ restores what was lost to humanity in the fall of Adam and 'recapitulates' the story of Adam's failure so as to bring it to a new resolution. R. M. Grant, *Irenaeus of Lyons* (London: Routledge, 1996) is a good introduction to Irenaeus, with substantial extracts in translation.

for theological development and even polemic and a source to which appeal may be made in controversy.

It is Irenaeus, once again, who famously argues that a particular doctrinal point is reinforced by its congruity with the Eucharist.[18] What is done in the sacramental action makes sense only if certain things are clearly believed as regards the relation of flesh and spirit; the Eucharist is unintelligible if material reality is something alien to the divine purpose and incapable of manifesting the divine action. Later on, in the fourth-century controversies about the full divinity of the Holy Spirit, it is the practice of invoking the Spirit as the bearer of divine transformative agency in the sacraments that is appealed to by a controversialist like Basil of Caesarea as evidence for the doctrine – with the interesting refinement that inherited practice itself is indicative of a tacit consensus (*dogma*, an agreed position) before it becomes *kerygma*, something publicly articulated as an explicit *doctrine*.[19]

What we are studying in the literature and archaeology of the early Christian community is thus a complex interweaving of strictly textual argument with the evolution of practices, liturgical, ethical, ascetical, which responded to the generative story of Israel and Jesus. As is often stressed these days,[20] the fundamental task of interpreting the sacred text is what gives the context for everything in the history of doctrine; but to say this is simultaneously to say that the context in which Scripture was read is the context of doctrine – the assembly in which sacramental action is performed, the gathering which embodies what it is that the act of God in the life of Jesus is believed to have done, and what is promised for the future. 'The gathering which embodies': in the world of early Christian belief, this was an embodiment that was more than 'symbolic' in the modern sense, a deliberate pointer to or representation of something; it was a realization of divine agency at work in the shape of the gathered community and its common prayer, and what happened during the sacramental action was an authentic moment of restoration and of the experienced anticipation of the final fulfilment of the human calling. And in the light of this, we can say that what the early church thought of as its process of learning was in significant measure the experience of living in an environment that was grasped imaginatively as an actual new world – the court of heaven, the new Temple housing the sacrifice that restored the earth to its intended glory.[21]

---

[18]Irenaeus, *Haer*, 4.18.: 'Our opinion is in harmony with the eucharist, and the eucharist confirms our opinion.'

[19]Basil develops the argument about the Spirit's transformative role in his treatise 'On the Holy Spirit', especially *Spir*, 15; the distinction between *dogma* and *kerygma* is explained in *Spir*, 27. For a recent English translation, see S. M. Hildebrand (trans.), *St Basil the Great: On the Holy Spirit* (Yonkers, NY: St Vladimir's Seminary Press, 2011).

[20]The first three chapters of Wilken, *The Spirit of Early Christian Thought*, draw this out with great clarity.

[21]On the enormous and regularly underrated significance of Temple imagery in the formation of the early Christian mind, see the work of Margaret Barker, summarized in M. Barker, *Temple Theology: An Introduction* (London: SPCK, 2004). Barker's conclusions are not universally accepted, but the importance of the Temple is underlined even in a more 'mainstream' treatment of the theology of Christian Scripture

As we have already seen, tracing the story of how doctrinal terminology grows, wobbles, rebalances, moves forward with a cautious new vocabulary, consolidates further and gradually comes to regard certain issues as settled for practical purposes is a necessary exercise even for the student who finds the substance of the doctrine inaccessible. It is necessary simply because only this broadly 'ecological' understanding explains what doctrine *is*.

It is fatally easy for a modern intellect to assume that the system of Christian teaching which evolved through the first five or six centuries of Christian history can only be a series of theories about God developed on the slender basis of scriptural texts treated in a pre-critical fashion as simply inspired and infallible propositions. Such a perspective does not do a great deal to help us see why doctrinal controversy was so intense and bitter, sometimes over what seem to be minor matters of detail. It was not that salvation was thought to depend upon any kind of simple acceptance of some formula – a facile but still popular approach to early Christian doctrinal controversy, with its ultimate ancestry in Gibbon's dismissive accounts of these debates; rather that formulae were developed and refined precisely in order to encapsulate what was regarded as the core of the experienced reality of salvation.

In other words, the claim was not that if you failed to believe in the doctrine of the Trinity, you would be 'damned', but that without the doctrine of the Trinity, you would have no even partially adequate way of speaking about what it meant to be 'saved'. When the so-called Athanasian Creed (actually a Latin hymn, probably composed around 500 CE in Southern Gaul) declares that anyone not holding the Catholic faith will 'perish everlastingly' and goes on to specify the Catholic faith in terms of a series of increasingly detailed propositions about the Trinity, it is admittedly hard to read this as anything other than a requirement of verbal conformity. But even this severely abstract text begins by stating that the faith is first of all the fact that *we worship God in a certain way*, as Trinity. The recondite pattern of concepts that is set out in the text is still grounded in the fact that the church has learnt to encounter God liturgically in one way rather than another, and its 'damnatory' clause is a way of saying that the absence of this practice and the experience that accompanies it is spiritual death. We may dislike the absolutism of this; but it is more than an idolatry of formulae.

To recognize the inseparability of doctrine and liturgy in the early period and the close connections between essays in ascetical psychology and the fundamental structures of doctrine also allows us in fact to see how and why the *limits* of language are also of such interest in the literature of this period. Precisely as the language of theology became more fastidious, as definitions were more rigorously sharpened, theologians – often the same ones who were so concerned with this sharpening – felt the need to insist that no formulation would once and for all tell you all there was to know of the divine. Gregory of Nazianzus in the late fourth century, preaching to congregations in the imperial capital, is quite clearly speaking from a

---

like N. T. Wright, *Paul and the Faithfulness of God* (London: SPCK, 2013), especially pp. 355–8 on Paul's use of Temple imagery and conceptuality.

particular standpoint in the spectrum of bitter debate over the Trinitarian doctrine that overshadowed the entire century; but he insists on the paradoxical truth that the kind of precision he is defending is ultimately in the service of a recognition that the point of theology is not a full and exact verbal account of the divine, but a journey into the luminous darkness of divine life through contemplation and self-forgetfulness.[22]

In the same vein, his friend Gregory of Nyssa offers the gnomic comment that the *horos*, literally the 'defining limit', of a human life in proper relation with God is that it has no *horos*:[23] there is no final stage of spiritual growth in which we shall have 'mastered' the divine, because we are constantly moving deeper into an inexhaustible life. We are again reminded here of the close 'weave' of early Christian rhetoric: the effect of the events of revelation is to restore humanity to a liberty to behold God's generative mysteriousness in virtue of the relation created between the believing community and the Eternal Word; this beholding is something beyond any conceptual grasp, yet to locate it and understand it for what it is, we need such clarity as we can manage about the Trinitarian nature of God. What is rejected as heresy is what gives less than we need for this task, reducing the divine liberty of the Logos or the complete solidarity with us of the Logos made flesh. We cannot make truthful sense of the wordless contemplative intimacy to which we are called unless we can grasp it as the concrete realization of something that is possible *because* God is as God is, because God is Trinity.

But this underlines the importance of these early texts for understanding what the tradition of 'negative' or 'apophatic' theology is really about in the Christian context. Apophatic affirmations about God (statements that work by trying to define what God is not rather than what God is) are not, in the early church, generic admonitions about divine mysteriousness, though they will sometimes cite classical philosophical axioms on this; Gregory of Nazianzus is clear that Christian theologians are not just noting that it is *difficult* to talk about God, but asserting that the divine nature is necessarily incapable of conceptual definition and that it is known only by participation in the relation of the Word to the Father. There is no contradiction between the constant return to apophatic tropes and the confidence that Trinitarian and Christological formulae are making truth claims that cannot be compromised. On the contrary, the doctrinal definition is insisted upon so that the full sense of the apophatic/relational character of knowing God may be properly acknowledged. Thus, once again, doctrine is being clearly linked with a particular account of human capacity or human destiny: the definitions offered are ways of

---

[22]The texts of Gregory's 'Theological Orations' are translated in L. Wickham and F. Williams (eds and trans.), *Gregory of Nazianzus: On God and Christ: The Five Theological Orations and Two Letters to Cledonius* (Yonkers, NY: St Vladimir's Seminary Press, 2002); the second of these discourses contains Gregory's most developed thoughts on the ground and context of theological language.

[23]The quotation occurs at the beginning of Gregory's 'Life of Moses', *V.Mos.* (*Patrologia Graeca* 44. 300D). There is a good English translation by E. Ferguson and A. J. Malherbe (eds), *Gregory of Nyssa: The Life of Moses* (Mahwah, NJ: Paulist Press, 1978).

connecting what is said about God with what is said about human beings, and the practices of the community embody this connection, both in public liturgy and in personal self-knowledge and contemplative discipline.[24]

The study of early Christian literature does not uncover a theological Garden of Eden in which we can take refuge from the errors or forgetfulness of later ages; nor does it reveal a miraculously unchanging orthodoxy. What it does show us is the process by which a culture takes shape – a culture considerably more varied than many apologists of an earlier age would have liked, yet one that is undoubtedly preoccupied not only with truth but with the means by which truth can be recognized and securely transmitted in a complex historical environment where definitions do not stay passively unchanging while things change around them. Gradually, the Christian writers of the period formulate various tests of coherence and continuity; a fruitful study of the literature will clarify how this coherence took shape through the connecting of affirmations about God and God's action with affirmations about the human vocation or destiny – and thus about what authority human beings finally answered to (the issue centrally at stake in the accounts of Christians executed for refusing divine honours to the Roman emperor). As part of this, the development of apophatic strategies served to keep in focus the actual goal of theological argument and definition, the inhabiting of a new identity of filial intimacy with God the Father, lived out in non-conceptual contemplation and love.

As we noted earlier, this is an intellectual history that can to a large extent be traced even by a scholar not approaching it with a strictly theological interest; but for the theologian working within what considers itself a continuing community of belief, linked in 'communion' with earlier generations, however great the surface discontinuities, the study of the early church prompts some constructive reflection on theological method in general. It warns us against a facile assumption that the detail of doctrinal definition cannot be of practical significance; it clarifies the ways in which Christian speaking about God and Christian speaking about humanity intersect and illuminate each other; it suggests that the quest for doctrinal – let alone institutional – unity in the church is a more nuanced affair than some would suppose.[25]

In all these ways, it challenges the contemporary Christian community both to a more coherent and connected account of theology and practice *and* to a less monolithic and juridical picture of Christian unity. The often disconcerting detail that archaeology and social history provides, obliging us to acknowledge the gaps between elite and non-elite perceptions and priorities, may mean a better understanding of how the definition of Christian identity and indeed Christian unity lies not only in theological conformity but in what may be phenomenologically a very

---

[24]On the connection between language about God and language about the human, see, for example, M. C. Steenberg, *Of God and Man: Theology as Anthropology from Irenaeus to Athanasius* (London: T&T Clark, 2008).

[25]For some reflections on this, see R. Williams, *Why Study the Past? The Quest for the Historical Church* (London: Darton, Longman and Todd, 2005), especially ch. 2, pp. 52–3.

diverse network of affinities, 'family resemblances' and shared cultures of devotion and mutual support. Whether this study is undertaken ultimately for the sake of a more resourceful and imaginative grasp of the social reality of Christian identity – in a way that illuminates the present reality of Christian practice, especially in social contexts not wholly dominated by 'modern' preoccupations – or whether it is pursued as a necessary element in the self-understanding of Christian communities, it is an invitation to a far richer sense of the interconnectedness of language and practice, and a far more differentiated picture of unity and conflict in the Christian family than is offered by many other areas of theological specialization. It should not be surprising that so many theological programmes across the Christian world still regard it as foundational.

BIBLIOGRAPHY

Barker, M. *Temple Theology: An Introduction*. London: SPCK, 2004.

Bultmann, R. *Jesus Christ and Mythology*. London: SCM Press, 1958.

Casiday, A. *Evagrius Ponticus*. London: Routledge, 2006.

Casiday, A. *Reconstructing the Theology of Evagrius Ponticus: Beyond Heresy*. Cambridge: Cambridge University Press, 2013.

Ferguson, E. and Malherbe, A. J. (eds). *Gregory of Nyssa: The Life of Moses*. Mahwah, NJ: Paulist Press, 1978.

Galtier, P., SJ. 'Petavius', in *Dictionnaire de théologie catholique*, vol. 12:1, cols 1313–1337. Paris: Letouzay et Ane, 1933.

Grant, R. M. *Irenaeus of Lyons*. London: Routledge, 1996.

Harnack, A. Von. *History of Dogma*, trans. Neil Buchanan. Boston, MA: Little, Brown and Company, 1894–9.

Hedley, D. and Hutton, S. (eds). *Platonism at the Origins of Modernity: Studies in Platonism and Early Modern Philosophy*. New York: Springer, 2008.

Hildebrand, S. M. *St Basil the Great: On the Holy Spirit*. Yonkers, NY: St Vladimir's Seminary Press, 2011.

Hutton, S. 'The Cambridge Platonists', *The Stanford Encyclopaedia of Philosophy*, ed. E. N. Zalta. Consulted online October 2020, at: https://plato.stanford.edu/archives/win2013/entries/cambridge-platonists/

Jones, G. *Bultmann: Towards a Critical Theology*. Cambridge: Polity Press, 1990.

Judge, E. A. 'The Earliest Use of *Monachos* for "Monk" and the Origins of Monasticism', in *Jahrbuch fur Antike und Christentum*, vol. 20, 72–89. Munster: Aschedorf, 1977.

King, B. J. *Newman and the Alexandrian Fathers: Shaping Doctrine in Nineteenth Century England*. Oxford: Oxford University Press, 2009.

Levitin, D. *Ancient Wisdom in the Age of the New Science: Histories of Philosophy in England c.1640–1700*. Cambridge: Cambridge University Press, 2015.

MacIntyre, A. *After Virtue: A Study in Moral Theory*. London: Duckworth, 1981.

MacMullen, R. *The Second Church: Popular Christianity A.D.200–400*. Atlanta, GA: SBL Press, 2009.

Middleton, A. *Fathers and Anglicans: The Limits of Orthodoxy*. Leominster: Gracewing, 2001.

Palmer, G., Sherrard, P. and Ware, K. (trans.). *The Philokalia*, vol. 1. London: Faber and Faber, 1979.

Ramelli, I. L. E. *Evagrius' Kephalaia Gnostika*. Leiden: E.J. Brill, 2015.

Ramelli, I. L. E. 'Gregory Nyssen's and Evagrius's Biographical and Theological Relations: Origen's Heritage and Neoplatonism', in G. Maspero and I. L. E. Ramelli (eds), *Evagrius between Origen, the Cappadocians, and Neoplatonism*, *SP*, vol. 84, 165–231. Leuven: Peeters, 2017.

Shean, J. F. *Soldiering for God: Christianity and the Roman Army*. Leiden: E.J. Brill, 2010.

Steenberg, M. C. *Of God and Man: Theology as Anthropology from Irenaeus to Athanasius*. London: T&T Clark, 2008.

Thomas, S. *Newman and Heresy: The Anglican Years*. Cambridge: Cambridge University Press, 2003.

Wickham, L. and Williams, F. (eds and trans.). *Gregory of Nazianzus: On God and Christ: The Five Theological Orations and Two Letters to Cledonius*. Yonkers, NY: St Vladimir's Seminary Press, 2002.

Wiles, M. *Archetypal Heresy: Arianism Through the Centuries*. Oxford: Clarendon Press, 1996.

Wilken, R. M. *The Spirit of Early Christian Thought: Seeking the Face of God*. New Haven, CT and London: Yale University Press, 2003.

Williams, R. 'Newman's *Arians* and the Question of Method in Doctrinal History', in I. Ker and A. G. Hill (eds), *Newman After a Hundred Years*, 263–85. Oxford: Clarendon Press, 1990.

Williams, R. *Why Study the Past? The Quest for the Historical Church*. London: Darton, Longman and Todd, 2005.

Williams, R. '"Tempted as we are": Christology and the Analysis of the Passions', in *Studia Patristica* 45, 391–404. Leuven: Peeters, 2010.

Wright, N. T. *Paul and the Faithfulness of God*. London: SPCK, 2013.

PART I

Emerging Christian identity – First century CE

CHAPTER 2

Jewish-Christian relations

A *painful split*

MARKUS VINZENT

PROLEGOMENA

Before looking back into early Jewish-Christian relations, we need to note that as with all retrospective historiography,[1] so also in comparing entities and their links, it is 'the scholar's intellectual purpose – whether explanatory or interpretative, whether generic or specific – which highlights the principled postulation' of whatever is being claimed.[2] The field of research and the scholar's perspective are additionally impacted by the fact that, when speaking of 'Jewish' and 'Christian', the content of these terms is consciously or subconsciously filled by the existence and experience of two so-called world religions, which opens up a few potential pitfalls. The notion of 'religion' is highly problematic and so are the concepts of 'Jewish' or 'Judaism' and 'Christian' or 'Christianity'.

Following the more recent observations by D. Dubuisson,[3] B. Nongbri,[4] and C. A. Barton and D. Boyarin,[5] the terms 'religion' and 'religious' have come under scrutiny in the study of late antiquity. Given that a modern understanding of these terms too quickly contrasts 'secular' and 'religious', the terms themselves have no precise correspondence in ancient Greek, Latin or Hebrew. Instead, they reflect a modern understanding of religion being 'an individual's interior conviction

---

[1] M. Vinzent, *Writing the History of Early Christianity: From Reception to Retrospection* (Cambridge: Cambridge University Press, 2019).

[2] J. Z. Smith, *Drudgery Divine: On the Comparison of Early Christianity and the Religions of Late Antiquity* (Chicago: Chicago University Press, 1990); B. L. Mack, 'After "Drudgery Divine"', *Numen* 39 (1992): 225–33.

[3] D. Dubuisson, *The Western Construction of Religion: Myths, Knowledge, and Ideology* (Baltimore, MD: Johns Hopkins University Press, 2003).

[4] B. Nongbri, *Before Religion: A History of a Modern Concept* (New Haven, CT: Yale University Press, 2013).

[5] C. A. Barton and D. Boyarin, *Imagine No Religion: How Modern Abstractions Hide Ancient Realities* (New York: Fordham University Press, 2016).

and experience'.[6] In contrast, 'for Romans, Greeks, and others in antiquity cultic practices were anything but invisible, private, inconsequential'.[7] A related matter is the difference between a modern, mostly Christian, take on religion as privileging 'beliefs' instead of being primarily constituted of ritual and other practices. One could add the even more radical view that the Christ-movement post 135 CE – and this is also applicable to Jewish life of that time – 'should not be considered to be a religion at all', as it 'had no statues, temples, altars, priests, or bloody sacrifices'.[8] Edwin Judge rightly stated the difference between our knowledge and the perception of today's Christianity with what the historian can discover: 'It is hard to see, how anyone could seriously have related the phenomenon of Christianity' today to what has been lived and practised among Christ-followers during the first centuries, and, again, the same is equally true for the difference between contemporary Judaism and Jewish life in late antiquity. And even if we admitted that as an etic term one might rescue all three notions, 'religion', 'Judaism' and 'Christianity', given that Jews and Christ-followers engaged in 'prayer, ritualized eating', had 'an entrance ritual . . . and communal songs directed at their deity', I suggest that we follow John S. Kloppenborg's cautious approach to not employ the term 'religion' for cultic practices in late antiquity, in order not to run 'the risk of slipping into the tendency to think of "religion" as conceptually and practically separated from political, family, military, market, and other practices'.[9] Although the umbrella terms 'Judaism' and 'Christianity' are anachronistic and ought to be avoided in this context, the scholarly literature is replete with them as writers tend to look back at late antiquity from present-day experiences.

There is a legion of literature on the often painful relation between Christianity and Judaism,[10] on the (non-)parting of their ways,[11] on Christian supersessionism,[12] on anti-semitism within early Christianity[13] and less (but still existing) also on the philo-Judaism of early Christianity[14] – a body of scholarship which in this short contribution I cannot, and need not, rehearse.

---

[6]J. S. Kloppenborg, *Christ's Associations: Connecting and Belonging in the Ancient City* (New Haven, CT: Yale University Press, 2019), p. 11.

[7]Ibid., p. 14.

[8]Ibid.

[9]Ibid., p. 17.

[10]Further, see Bibliography for: Reed (2018); Alexis (2013); Schwartz (2011); Peck and Neusner (2009); Boyarin (1999) and (2004); Frederiksen (2003); Saldarini et al. (2004); Price (2002); Horst and Karrer (1995); Horst (1994); Hopkins (1999).

[11]See Bibliography for: Nicklas (2018); Hagner (2012); Robinson (2009); Gorsky (2009); Frederiksen (2003); Goodman (2003); Alexander (1992); Rowland (1992).

[12]See S. Heschel, 'Jews and Christianity', in *The Cambridge History of Judaism, vol. 8: The Modern World, 1815-2000*, eds M. Hart and T. Michels (Cambridge: Cambridge University Press, 2017).

[13]See Bibliography for: Strumzah (1996); Kahl (1985); Laqueur (2006); Berger (2010); Feldman (1996); Perry and Schweitzer (1994).

[14]See Bibliography for: Wertheim (2017); Karp and Sutcliffe (2011); Kinzig (2009) and idem also (1998, 1994c and 1994d).

I would like to start this chapter with John Chrysostom's *Orations against the Jews*, a set of texts that James Parkes (1896–1981)[15] in one of his later books called 'the most horrible and violent denunciations of Judaism to be found in the writings of a Christian theologian'.[16] Parkes had written almost all his life against anti-semitism and published, as early as 1930, the famous book *The Jew and His Neighbour*,[17] followed, in 1934, by his major study on the origins of anti-semitism, *The Conflict of the Church and Synagogue*.[18] Here he drew attention to the enormous impact that early Christian authors had on twentieth-century anti-semitism. With Chrysostom, as Parkes assumed, the pain of the split between Jews and Christians can be grasped by all, even though the ones who suffered from it were mostly Jews.

Christian against Jew

As Parkes already saw, Chrysostom's seven (plus one) homilies[19] are one of the most outspoken pieces of Christian rhetoric[20] on Jewish-Christian relations, voiced as homilies and written down during the late fourth century, when these relation had become a political issue.[21] Already during Chrysostom's lifetime they became famous and from that time until today are often 'quoted, discussed and contentious'.[22] More recently they were even used as anti-Jewish and anti-Zionist propaganda on a most 'horrific Catholic anti-Semitic website',[23] which indicates their continued presence in present-day religious politics.

In the standard edition of the *Patrologia Graeca* (Paris, 1862), these texts are entitled *Orations against the Jews*. We may note, however, that the title of the same work in Henry Savile's edition of Chrysostom (1610–13) was more specific. Even though it too started with *Orations against the Jews*, to this was added: '*pronounced against the Judaizers and those who fasted with those*'. As can be seen from the shortening of the title in *Patrologia Graeca*, the work has moved from being presented as a collection of in-group sermons[24] in the seventeenth century to being an out-

---

[15]H. Chertok, *He also Spoke as a Jew: The Life of James Parkes* (London: Vallentine Mitchell, 2006).

[16]J. Parkes, *Prelude to Dialogue: Jewish-Christian Relationships* (London: Vallentine Mitchell, 1969), p. 153.

[17]*The Jew and His Neighbour* (London: SCM Press, 1930).

[18]*The Conflict of the Church and the Synagogue: A Study in the Origins of Antisemitism* (London: Soncino Press, 1934).

[19]*Patrologia Graeca*, vol. 48, cols. 843–944.

[20]That Chrysostom sees it as a rhetorical battle is clear from the beginning of *Oration 5*.

[21]See G. Bady, 'L'antijudaïsme banalisé. Des homélies de Jean Chrysostome à leurs avatars: l'exemple du sermon inédit Sur le paralytique (CPG, 4857)', in *Les polémiques religieuses du Ier au IVe siècle de notre ère. Hommage à Bernard Pouderon*, eds G. Bady and D. Cuny (Paris: Beauchesne, 2019).

[22]See W. Mayer, 'Preaching Hatred? John Chrysostom, Neuroscience, and the Jews', in *Revisioning John Chrysostom: New Approaches, New Perspectives*, eds C. L. de Wet and W. Mayer (Leiden: Brill, 2019), p. 58: with further bibliography.

[23]See P. Halsall, 'Medieval Sourcebook: Notes on Reaction to the Posting of the Chrysostom Text on the Jews', 1996. https://sourcebooks.fordham.edu/source/chrysostom-jews6-react.asp (accessed 15 July 2020).

[24]On this social category see: H. Tajfel, 'Social Identity and Intergroup Behaviour', *Social Science Information* 13 (1974): 65–93. This shift should be taken into account when discussing whether these

group polemic in the eighteenth and nineteenth centuries. The background of this shifted emphasis would need to be studied in more detail but probably also reflects growing anti-semitic attitudes among French Catholics in the post-enlightenment of the eighteenth and the post-revolutionary period of the nineteenth centuries, when with Napoleon Jews were granted French citizenship, the first of its kind in Europe, and seemed to have 'generally felt secure in their rights and in their citizenship'.[25] Moreover, in the twentieth century Chrysostom is directly linked with Luther's anti-Jewish writings, when Arnold Ages writes: 'There is ample reason for Luther's unpopularity among Jews, for not since the exgressions of St. John Chrysostom had any Christian engaged in such vituperation against Jews and Judaism as had Martin Luther.'[26]

At a moment when Jews and Christians perceive themselves to be members of two different religions, it is difficult not to read this split into the sources of earlier centuries. Certainly, even if one took the most generous in-group reading of Chrysostom's *Orations*, his in-group criticism is dealing with members who according to Savile's title are called 'Judaizers' and who are taking part in fasting practices 'with those' others. How, then, if we are able to go beyond our contemporary anachronistic readings of these *Orations*, can we describe Chrysostom's view? And what might it reveal about the cultic practices of his time? Before answering these questions, we need to point out one further difficulty. Despite the importance of these *Orations* for the description of Jewish-Christian relations they offer, we still lack today a critical edition of Chrysostom's text. This is all the more problematic, as recent research by István Perczel shows that the text of Chrysostom's *Orations* had undergone considerable change and rewriting during the sixth century. As he argues, 'It was heavily manipulated – which, by the way, happened many times with other Chrysostomian texts as well, because of the great authority they enjoyed. This was done in order to shape them to the needs of a severe anti-Jewish turn in the sixth century, under Justinian, who revoked Jews' citizenship.'[27] The Greek text that we have in manuscripts at our disposal limits our knowledge so that Perczel further argues, 'We cannot go beyond the sixth-century redaction'.[28] Hence, when speaking about 'Chrysostom' in what follows, we might be looking into a sixth-century scenario under Justinian I. rather than into a fourth-century church situation.

---

homilies are primarily 'in-group texts' (See Bibliography for: Black (2014); Shepardson (2019, p. 101); Bibliowicz (2013, pp. 189–90); Drake (2013, p. 79); Côté (2012), 'out-group texts' (see especially Mayer, 'Preaching Hatred?'. I myself take them to reflect both groups. Yet I do not follow the difference, introduced by Wendy Mayer between the targeted audience (Judaizers) and those preached towards. Mayer overlooks that Chrysostom's 'us' is his rhetorical device, not so much reflecting an existing difference between his audience of 'Christians' and absent 'judaizers', but his attempt at creating exactly this divide in the minds of his audience, as we will see. Further see Bibliography for: Reed (2003) and Shepardson (2008).
[25]See: R. J. Golsan, 'Antisemitism in Modern France: Dreyfus, Vichy, and Beyond', in *Antisemitism: A History*, eds A. S. Lindemann and R. S. Levy (Oxford: Oxford University Press, 2010), p. 136.
[26]A. Ages, 'Luther and the Rabbis', *The Jewish Quarterly Review* 58 (1967): 63.
[27]From an email conversation with István Perczel, 16 July 2020.
[28]Ibid.

BLURRING BOUNDARIES

According to our modern interpreter and translator Robert Wilken, we are told that in Chrysostom's first *Oration* the targeted addressees are branded 'Judaizers' and seen as a 'disease' which is infectious:

> But if those who are sick with Judaism are not healed now when the Jewish festivals are 'near, at the very door' (Matt. 24:33), I am afraid that some, out of misguided habit and gross ignorance, will share in their transgressions, and sermons about such matters would be pointless.[29]

Infections, as the world in the twenty-first century has experienced again, are transmitted through contact, the closer the contact, the easier and more intense the transmission. The reason that Chrysostom (as he has stated shortly before this quote) was prepared to 'put off to another time' his discourses 'against the Anomoeans' and rather decided to engage with this form of disease was (he explains) because of the proximity of major Jewish festivals: the feast of Trumpets (i.e. New Year or Rosh Ha-Shanah, falling on the first of Tishri in Sept./Oct.); the feast of Tabernacles (falling on the fifteenth of Tishri, and lasting a week) and the Fasts (i.e. the Ten Days of Penitence between Rosh Ha-Shanah and Yom Kippur, the Day of Atonement).

As the end of the quote shows, the preacher seemed to have been anxious to miss the right time of warning from following a practice which he regarded as apocalyptically problematic. His reference to Matt. 24.33 points to the doomsday scenario, when the people will 'see the Son of Man coming on the clouds of heaven, with power and great glory' (Matt. 24.30), though this implies some cynicism when, instead of the Son of Man, Chrysostom refers to the Jewish festivals being 'near, at the very door'. Or did members of his audience not subscribe to the hope of the (imminent?) coming of the Lord? This would account for the 'gross ignorance' that he mentions. Or was it rather out of 'misguided habit', as ἀκαίρου συνηθείας has been translated?

Here, both the translation of Wilken and that of the other modern translator of the eight *Orations* who renders this expression by 'ill-suited association' seem to be inaccurate, reflecting the contemporary two-religions' split. The more literal translation of ἀκαίρου συνηθείας is an 'ill-timed' or 'unseasonable acquaintance' or association. Moreover, the Greek text puts this ill-timed relation first, before mentioning the 'gross ignorance'. If only 'ill-timed', Chrysostom is less radically set against any sharing of practices with those others mentioned here.[30] Nevertheless, he finds the timing of such association wrong, as it might give the impression that people had lost their hope in the coming of the Lord. In this, the second *Oration* differs, as now Chrysostom is also attacking the opinion of people in his congregation

---

[29]Chrysostom, *Adv. Iud.*, 1.1.5 (Wilken's translation, 1983, p. 117).

[30]Elsewhere the preacher is more radical and also rejects the many people attending a synagogue in Daphne where they used to sleep nearby, perhaps hoping to find healing from Jewish doctors, see: Chrysostom, *Adv. Iud.*, 6. Further on Daphne see W. Kinzig, 'Non-Separation: Closeness and Co-operation between Jews and Christians in the Fourth Century', *Vigiliae Christianae* 45 (1991): 37.

who questioned the criticism of circumcision, a sign that those whom Chrysostom had branded Judaizers did, indeed, follow the Jewish practice of circumcision.[31]

A second nuance of the above translation reveals the contemporary anachronistic reader when in the beginning of the quote the words τοὺς δὲ τὰ Ἰουδαϊκὰ νοσοῦντας are rendered as 'those who are sick with Judaism'. The abstract entity of an 'ism' is absent from the Greek (and even from its Latin translation: *Judaeorum autem morbo correptos*) as τὰ Ἰουδαϊκά rather refers to the Jewish festival and fasting practices that were mentioned before. In Chrysostom's *Discourses against Judaizing Christians* Paul W. Harkins translates: 'Those who are sick with the Judaizing disease', yet, the more literal rendering would be 'those who are sick with the Jewish practices'; hence, we have neither a reference to an abstract 'ism', or institution, nor does Chrysostom talk about a disease that is Jewish, but about members of his audience who he sees to be infected and attracted by what is Jewish, leading them to spreading their ill-timed practice of joining-in with Jewish festivals and fasting, and to displaying their gross ignorance.

Interestingly, in Chrysostom's further elaboration, he compares himself to a physician who has to first check the sick people which he deems more urgent and acute, though he admits that he sees the two cases of diseases, that of the Anomoeans and that of the Jews to be so closely related that he calls it a family relation (συγγένεια). The profile of the disease, however, has not primarily to do with ritual practice, but with the accusation that according to Anomoeans and Jews, Christ had 'made Himself equal to God'.[32] To this accusation Chrysostom later comes back, as he wants to make clear that he does not see himself (or those who like him had never been Jewish) in anyway linked to Jews, their history, their law, their practices or the belief in their God: 'The Jews say that they, too, adore God. God forbid that I say that. No Jew adores God! Who says so? The Son of God says so. For he said: "If you were to know my Father, you would also know me. But you neither know me nor do you know my Father."'[33]

For Chrysostom, the Jews fail to know God; hence, they cannot worship him in their cult practices. Later in the *Oration* they are even called Christ-murderers and their godless worship is put on equal par with that of the Greeks.[34] Even so, he knows that 'many'[35] of his associates have high regards towards 'the holy and great' (σεμνὰ καὶ μεγάλα) cult of the Jews,[36] they 'respect the Jews and think that their present way of life is a venerable one',[37] they also believe that 'the law has profited

---

[31] See Chrysostom, *Adv. Iud.*, 2. 1.

[32] Ibid., 1. 1.6.

[33] Chrysostom, *Adv. Iud.*, 1. 3.2.

[34] Ibid., 6. (PG. 48.852).

[35] Though, in another (perhaps unrelated) homily, Chrysostom downplays the numbers and speaks of 'most members' of his 'flock who are free' from the Jewish 'disease and that the sickness involves only a few', Chrysostom, *Adv. Iud.*, 3. 1. 4.

[36] Chrysostom, *Adv. Iud.*, 6.

[37] Ibid., 1. 3.1.

nature'[38] and that 'the Jews are more trustworthy teachers' and trust their 'account of Christ's passion and death' more than the Gospels that Chrysostom reads.[39] The word 'venerable' here means 'impressive on account of age or history' as Jewish life at Antioch had a long history, but it also highlights that not all Christians (according to Chrysostom even 'many') were in the position of Chrysostom, never having been a Jew, nor that they shared his criticism of living a Jewish life. These people seem to have lived out both: they were in a συνήθεια with Chrysostom which was seen as not excluding them from their apparently long-standing συνήθεια with Jews and their practices of observing Jewish festivals, attending synagogues and following the commandments of the Torah. Stating that his audience should not be surprised by him calling 'the Jews pitiful', he had carefully chosen his wording, as ἄθλιος ('pitiful') also carries the notion of 'being successful'. Apparently, many people in his audience were surprised that their bishop took offence at them, seeing them, defining and cornering them as 'Jews' so as to force them into a position of unfamiliar choice. In the ensuing tirade against the Jews, Chrysostom lists why he called them 'pitiful' and 'suffering'. He accuses them of having thrown aside the 'many blessings from heaven', the 'rays of the morning sun of justice' and by this sitting in 'darkness' they 'drew the light' to 'us'.[40] Using the 'us', Chrysostom claims for his own non-Jewish position the identity marker of the audience, excluding the Jewish history of those, for whom this was part of their upbringing and 'habit'. And by elaborating on the Jewish failures, he criticizes the position of those Jews who were part of his audience: 'From their childhood they read the prophets, but they crucified him whom the prophets had foretold' – admitting that these members of his congregation were brought up with the reading of the prophets, while excluding themselves from his own συνήθεια.

In the drastic style of an emphatic rhetorician, this is taken even further, by comparing the call of the Jews 'to the adoption of sons' and their following a 'kinship with dogs', with the irrational position of being dogs of the claimed 'us', which were able 'to rise to the honour of sons'.[41] In claiming that 'we became the children', while 'they became dogs', Chrysostom moves himself and his 'we' into replacing the Jews with a novel form of Jews, quoting *Phil.* 3.2-3. ('Beware of the dogs, beware of the evil workers, beware of the mutilation. For we are the circumcision.')[42] Placing himself beside Paul as 'the circumcision' is no rejection of Jewishness but an abrogation of the specific practice of Jewishness which is seen as a 'transgressing of the Law' and observing it at the wrong time, by claiming to 'keeping it'.[43] The reasons that Chrysostom then gives for the misleading interpretation of the Law

---

[38]See Chrysostom, *Adv. Iud.*, 2. 2.5. In *Oration 5*, Chrysostom states that he is sure that the temple after its destruction by Hadrian, and despite the attempts under Julian, will not be rebuilt again.

[39]See Chrysostom, *Adv. Iud.*, 3. 6.6. Apparently, even the fixing of the Easter date did not seem to have been accepted by all, see ibid., 3. 6.12-13.

[40]Chrysostom, *Adv. Iud.*, 1. 2.1.

[41]Ibid., 1. 2.1.

[42]Ibid., 1. 2.2.

[43]Ibid., 1. 2.3.

sound emphatic, but were they convincing at the time? He mentions 'gluttony' and 'drunkenness' and 'growing plump'.[44] Were the 'many' addressees members who were better off and enjoyed a higher social standing than the average member of the congregation? Chrysostom is still talking to people in front of him, not only to abstract people of the past: 'Now your fasting is untimely and an abomination', of course applying himself to prophets such as Isaiah and others.[45] He even mentions critical voices from his audience, which single himself out: 'I know that some suspect me of rashness because I said there is no difference between the theater and the synagogue.'[46] And though this might be a rhetorical device in this *Oration*, it seems to reflect some historical reality. In a first example, Chrysostom talks about 'a brutal, unfeeling man, who seemed to be a Christian (for I would not call a person who would dare to do such a thing a sincere Christian)', though it turns out that this man, indeed, was a Christian, who was 'forcing a woman to enter the place of the Hebrews'. The place is not named by Chrysostom into which the woman was supposedly dragged. Then, Chrysostom claims that the woman had 'come up' to him 'and asked for help', for, as he adds, 'it was forbidden to her, who had shared in the divine mysteries to go to that place'.[47] Indeed, in the 360s the synod of Laodicea in Phrygia 'had formulated important canons for the discipline of clergy and laity'. 'Canon 37 of that synod forbade anyone to take from Jews or heretics any gifts on feast days or to celebrate a feast with them,' and 'Canon 38 forbade anyone to accept unleavened bread from Jews or to participate in their sacrileges.'[48] Apparently, the narrative is based more on these legal sanctions (and the potential threat linked to them), which made her have to appear before the bishop, rather than a matter of her own reluctance to attend the meeting of Jews, as it might be read today.

Likewise, a little later in the same Oration, Chrysostom addresses his audience and calls them 'small children' who do not even realize what he himself perceives as fear instilled by Jews.[49] Hence, he suggests even the use of force to move people out of the synagogue and thereby reveals that his tale about the man dragging a woman was not a story about a Jew or a real situation that female members of his audience might have been exposed to but, rather, turns out to be an account of the way Chrysostom wants his audience to act with regard to Jews. As the further Orations demonstrate, Chrysostom does not seem to have been very successful in persuading his audience. Despite strong warnings in the first two *Orations before the Paschal fast*, *Oration* III speaks of the 'untimely obstinacy' of his listeners.[50]

As the Orations of Chrysostom, together with the Canons of Laodicea, confirm, the boundaries between locations, between congregations and within Chrysostom's

---

[44]Ibid., 1. 2.5; see also ibid., 1. 3.
[45]Ibid., 1. 2.7.
[46]Ibid., 1. 2.9.
[47]Ibid., 1. 3.4.
[48]P. W. Harkins, *St. John Chrysostom: Discourses Against Judaizing Christians* (Washington: Catholic University of America Press, 1979), p. 12, fn. 44.
[49]Chrysostom, *Adv. Iud.*, 1. 3.
[50]Ibid., 3. 1.1.

own audience, were anything but clear, and it was surely an endeavour of the bishops to create, firm up and regulate these matters, both in their homilies and synodal documents. Precisely because people saw little or no differences (knowing that Christ himself was a Jew and that Christians regularly observed the Jewish fasts and celebrated Pascha with the Jews[51] just as they did in the churches) and felt that the Jewish Pascha and the mystery of the cross were both reasons to fast and celebrate, then Chrysostom himself felt the need to 'build a fence', to 'dig ditches',[52] and label the Jewish members 'Half-Christians'[53] who 'walk upon two paths',[54] or live in two different 'folds'[55] who feel they should celebrate Pascha with 'cheerfulness and joy' because 'the cross has taken away sin'.[56]

Chrysostom compares Judaizing to the case of a soldier defecting to the enemies, giving up being a Roman,[57] and instead living and behaving like a Barbarian or Persian.[58] He claims that this choice means siding with another ethnicity (ἀλλοφύλος) and adds the opposition of -isms: Judaism and Christianity: 'If you hold Judaism to be true, why are you troubled with the Church? If Christianity is true (as it really is), remain and follow it.'[59] Even so, one notices the tension between these statements, as well as in what we read in a recently discovered addition to *Oration* II. Here Chrysostom still calls the 'Judaizers' 'our brothers' because of his 'hopes for their health'.[60] This is an indication that the received text of the Orations might not be the version that dates to the fourth century but, as we have previously mentioned, originates in the Justinianic era. It is a topic that we need to unfold in more detail.

HARDENING BOUNDARIES

Not only are today's clear boundaries being re-read into documents of the fourth century, but the 'presumed text' of the fourth century may itself even turn out to be already a reflection of the attempt at hardening boundaries in later times. Perczel's ongoing investigation argues that both the manuscript evidence and the comparisons of the *Orations Against the Jews* with other works of Chrysostom show that our

---

[51]Ibid., 3. 3.1 and 3.3.9. Chrysostom remarks on this, ibid., 3. 6.1.
[52]Chrysostom, *Adv. Iud.*, 4. 1.3.
[53]See Chrysostom, *Adv. Iud.*, 1. 3.
[54]Chrysostom, *Adv. Iud.*, 2 (supplement).
[55]Ibid., 3. 1.8.
[56]Ibid., 3. 4.7.
[57]Ibid., 4. 3.5.
[58]See also Chrysostom, *Adv. Iud.*, 4. 3.5.
[59]Chrysostom, *Adv. Iud.*, 4. 4.1. See D. Boyarin, *The Ways that Never Parted* (Tübingen: Mohr Siebeck, 2003) and Kinzig, 'Non-Separation', 27–53.
[60]Similarly, in *Oration*, 3. 1.2-3 Chrysostom talks about civil war 'amongst brothers' and *Oration*, 8, is more conciliary too, hoping for the brothers to come back and repent, Chrysostom, *Adv. Iud.*, 8. 4.5.

received text reflects the state of Jewish-Christian relations in the times of Justinian I.[61] In *Oration* 6, all the manuscripts state:

> Now nothing like this [the previous restorations of the Temple] has happened. There have elapsed a hundred years, and then twice as many, and then three times, and much more than four times as many, so that, counting from that time, we are reaching the five hundredth year, and still we do not see anywhere even a hidden sign foretelling such a change, but we see that their affairs have completely fallen down, and there is not even a dream inspiring some expectation similar to the previous ones.[62]

To this text, Perczel in recent unpublished researches[63] makes the following calculation and comments: '70 + 500 = 570. Thus, AD 570 is the *terminus ante quem* for the final redaction of the text, which is most conveniently placed to c. 550, the time of Justinian's anti-Jewish legislation.' More important than this calculation, however, are Perczel's comparisons between this version of the *Orations* and other work of Chrysostom, and the parallels he detects between the theological views about the Jews in these *Orations* and Pseudo-Caesarius' *Questions and Answers*, which he attributes to 'Theodore the Wine-Sack (*Askidas*), archbishop of Caesarea in Cappadocia, the all-powerful adviser of Justinian'.[64] Before I had read Perczel's studies, I had already wondered about the stark contrast between some of the theological statements about the Jews in the *Orations* and other works of Chrysostom and linked these to the different homiletic circumstances. Yet, Perczel's explanations make so much more sense.

A first example is the interpretation of Jesus' statement from Matt. 27.25 in *Oration*, 6.

> In fact, from our praises . . . their own glory [that of the martyrs] will not increase, but from the struggle against the Jews they are getting much pleasure and they would willingly listen to these discourses uttered in defence of God's glory. For the martyrs hate the Jews very much, because they loved so much the one whom the Jews have crucified. For the latter have said: 'His blood be on us and on our children!' (*Matt.* 27:25), while they have shed their own blood for the sake of the one whom they had murdered. For this reason, they would happily listen to these discourses.[65]

---

[61]See his *Novella* 146 (*On the Hebrews*), issued in 553; and I. Perczvel's note on it in his article: 'Universal Salvation as an Antidote to Apocalyptic Expectations: Origenism in the Service of Justinian's Religious Politics', in *Apocalypticism and Eschatology in Late Antiquity*, eds H. Amirav et al. (Leuven: Peeters, 2017), p. 131.

[62]Chrysostom, *Adv. Iud.*, 6. 2.3.

[63]Forthcoming but communicated to the author in an email correspondence, 16 July 2020.

[64]I. Perczel, Email to the author, 16 July 2020. See, on the attribution, several studies of Perczel dated to 2017, in the Bibliography.

[65]Chrysostom, *Adv. Iud.*, 4. 1.7.

Chrysostom makes the martyrs into authorities for his *Orations*; and here a strong support is perhaps needed, as the author knew about the drastic, perhaps even novel, interpretation that he was giving to this verse of *Matthew*. We know of similarly drastic readings of this verse (though without referring it to the martyrs), even before the time of Justinian I, but these occur only during the fourth century, whereas the verse is rarely used in the time before, and if at all, the self-cursing of the Jews is taken as an example of emphatic wickedness, something that should not be done and certainly not be imitated or followed up,[66] or, alternatively, that the destruction of the Temple, the Jews being driven into exile and their miseries are signs of God's punishment.[67] An example for a comparably emphatic reading is the *Fifth Sermon* on the *Resurrection* attributed to Gregory of Nyssa:

> When was he not honoured? When the dogs barked, and the Lord bore it patiently; when the wolves ravaged and the sheep stood still; when he was begged for life by a thief, and the Life of the World was drawn down to death; when they shouted with coarse and destructive voice, 'Away with him, away with him, crucify him! His blood be upon us and our children!' Hewers of the Lord, killers of the prophets, enemies of God; haters of God, unjust in law, enemies of grace, strangers to the faith of their fathers, patrons of the devil, a family of serpents, tale-bearers, babblers, minds stuck in darkness, the leaven of the Pharisees, the assembly of demons. Wicked men, wimps, stoners, haters of honesty. But justly they shout, 'Away with him, away with him, crucify him!' For the connection of divinity with flesh was serious to them; and, a blameworthy tradition, it was dangerous; for in death he was placed with sinners, and united and with those hated by the just.[68]

Given that Gregory's authorship is not secure, the text might be an indication of his or perhaps even a later author's derision of the Jews in these polemic words. Yet, one could also adduce the writings of Hilary of Poitiers who in his *Commentary on Matthew* stated the belief: 'Before the Law was given the Jews were possessed of an unclean devil, which the Law for a time drove out, but which returned immediately after their rejection of Christ.'[69] No surprise, therefore, that in his *Vita* we are told that 'he would not even answer the salutation of a Jew in the street', a fact which, however, 'amazed his biographer'. Indeed, one is reminded of harsh words that we find, for example, in Cyril of Alexandria, when in his tenth *Festal Letter* he writes:

> For concerning such folk the divine word says somewhere, 'May they be erased from the book of the living, and may they not be enrolled with the just!' But why

---

[66]See, for example, Eusebius, *Comm.Ps.*, 21.12-14.

[67]See, for example, Tertullian, *Marc.*, 2.15; *Jud.*, 8.18; Origen, *Hom.Jos.*, 3.5; ibid., 26.3; idem, *Comm. Matt.*, 14.19; Lactantius, *Inst.*, 7.1; Hilary, *Comm.Matt.*, 1.6; Ambrosiaster, *QVNT.*, 98.3.

[68]See, Gregory of Nyssa, *In luciferam sanctam Domini resurrectionem*, ed. E. Gebhardt, *Gregorii Nysseni Opera*, 9, Sermones (Leiden: Brill, 1967), p. 317.

[69]Hilary, *Comm.Matt.*, 13.22 . The passage in his *Vita* (*Patrologia Latina*, vol. 9, col.187), is translated in: Parkes, *The Conflict*, p. 160.

extend my discourse about matters so plain to view? For everyone knows the audacious deeds of the irreligious Jews. The wretches handed over for crucifixion the Master of all, inscribing the charge of impiety upon their own heads, and upon the whole race. For in their madness they dared to say, 'His blood be upon us and upon our children.' Not only that, but, looking at him nailed to the precious cross, they had the supreme insolence to deride him, and were persuaded by their own father, I mean Satan, to say, 'If you are God's Son, come down now from the cross, and we will believe you.' But the Lord Jesus Christ, seeing that the death which had long tyrannized over us was already trembling and falling (for it was to be completely destroyed by the death of the holy flesh), took no account of the reproaches of the Jews.[70]

So, it seems that later Christian preachers and apologists tried to harden the boundaries by rhetorically deepening the ditches, building higher walls and sharpening the theological knives to detach Jews not only from the present congregation, but even from eternal salvation in linking them to the companionship of Satan.

Nevertheless, one also has to note diverging voices who still during the fifth century held slightly different views to those of 'Gregory' and Cyril; such as when we read in *Sermon 35*, by Pope Leo I that, though he calls the Jews 'enemies', he 'desires and works for what belongs to true love . . . so that this same people who fell away from that spiritual nobility of their fathers might be "engrafted" back into the branches of their tree'.[71] Building on Paul (Romans 9–11), Leo sees his own Christian realm as the saving stem, yet he has not given up the hope for Jews, unlike 'Gregory' or Cyril. Likewise, we read in his *Sermons*:

> but to pardon them, saying, 'Father, forgive them, for they know not what they do.' Such was the power of his prayer that the preaching of Peter the apostle turned to repentance the hearts of many from among those who said: 'His blood be upon us and upon our children.' On a single day, 'almost three thousand' Jews 'were baptized', and all were made 'one in heart and soul', prepared now to die for him, the one for whom they had demanded crucifixion.[72]

Given these voices and what we read here and in *Oration 6 against the Jews*, Chrysostom's statement that we read in his *Commentary on Matthew* is even more clearly in stark contrast to these:

> What are [the Jews] doing? Since they had seen that the judge had washed his hands and said: 'I am innocent,' they shouted: 'His blood be on us and on our children!' (*Matt.* 27:25) Now at that time, when they condemned themselves, he allowed that all might happen [as it happened]. And see here as well the great folly. That much irrational impetus and evil desire does not allow one to see

---

[70]Cyril, *Festal Homily*, 10. 5.
[71]Leo, *Sermo*, 35 (trans. J. P. Freeland and A. J. Conway, *St. Leo the Great, Sermons*, Fathers of the Church 91 (Washington: Catholic University of America Press, 1996), p. 152).
[72]Leo, *Sermo*, 62 (trans. Freeland and Conway, *St. Leo the Great, Sermons*, p. 271).

anything that should be done. For let it be, curse yourselves. But why do you want to extend the curse also to your children? However, the Manloving (that is, Christ), although they had used so much rage both against themselves and against the children, not only did not confirm their condemnation of the children, but he did not accept it concerning themselves either. In fact, he accepted both from them and from their children those who repented and he deemed them worthy of innumerable benefits.[73]

Contrary to *Oration* 6, but also to 'Gregory' and Cyril, Chrysostom in his *Commentary on Matthew* explicitly rejects an interpretation, of which he seems to have known, according to which this verse excludes the Jews and their children from future salvation.[74] This interpretation does not minimize his attempt at creating a rift between what he sees as members of the church and those others who visit the synagogue, and much of what the *Orations* present seems to go back to him, but final separation and eternal segregation, and perhaps many of the invectives that link Jews to Satan, make them God-murderers and exclude them from the Christian congregation, seem to belong to theological rhetoric and synodal and state law-making of the fourth to the sixth centuries, rather than to Chrysostom himself.

This development, stretching into the sixth century however, only confirms what Wendy Mayer has shown[75] that Chrysostom's rhetoric is not just rhetoric, for while it may not really reflect ritual practice of the people at Antioch (and perhaps elsewhere in the Roman Empire of East and West),[76] it nevertheless instilled, prepared and spread the venom that more and more made those two 'isms' become a felt and for many (mostly Jews), a painful reality.

CHRISTIANS AND JEWS

An opposition of Judaism and Christianity?

For James Parkes it was already clear that neither Judaism nor Christianity 'were born' in the fourth century, though he points out that 'both are to this day, in many ways, fourth century religions'.[77] He points to the great Talmudic teachers and what in his view and older scholarships were called the schools or academies of Pumbedita and Sura (located close to today's Baghdad),[78] though more recent scholarship is cautioning us that the *Babylonian Talmud* 'never refers to "the academy of Sura" or of any other town' and proposes that the reference to these cities alludes to 'centres of Jewish population' with their locally 'important masters', 'but never

---

[73]*H. in Matth.*, 86.2.
[74]Similar views can be seen in his other works of his, for example, *H. in Rom.*, 19. 2-3.
[75]Mayer, 'Preaching Hatred'.
[76]See Kinzig, 'Non-Separation'.
[77]Parkes, *The Conflict*, p. 153.
[78]On these two centres of Jewish learning, see R. Brody, *The Geonim of Babylonia and the Shaping of Medieval Jewish Culture* (New Haven, CT: Yale University Press, 1998), pp. 35-6.

as the sites of academies'. In addition, we could add other places like Nehardea, Naresh, Meḥoza, Mata Meḥasya and others;[79] along with names such as Rabbah bar Nachmani, Joseph bar Hama, Abaye, their pupil, who taught at Pumbeditha, Raba bar Joseph bar Hama at Mahuza on the Tigris, and a generation later, Nahmani bar Isaac and Papa at Neres near Sura.[80] Equally, as we have already seen in the previous chapter, it was the golden age of Christian theologians with Eusebius of Caesarea (ca. 260–340) being one of the most important figures for the creation of the later understanding of the beginnings of Christianity.[81]

In his more systematic works, the *Preparatio Evangelica* and the *Demonstratio Evangelica*, Eusebius points to 'the superiority and greater antiquity of Christianity in comparison with all other religions', and in the second 'he proves the superiority of Christianity over Judaism and the uniqueness of the person of Christ'. This apparently clear distinction, however, is blurred by setting out from a difference that he makes between 'Hebrews' and 'Jews'. The latter are of little interest to him, while the former are to him 'the most ancient people in the world, and their religion is the basis of Greek philosophy'.[82] Wolfram Kinzig provided a graph of the complex relation that Eusebius had developed and which was refined by Jörg Ulrich:[83]

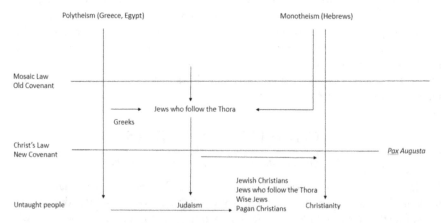

As we can see, Eusebius had a sophisticated and complex picture in mind. It seems as he thought first in terms of oppositions between Polytheism and Monotheism, between Greek/ Egyptian people and Hebrews, and between Judaism and

[79]Further on these see the Bibliography for Goodblatt (1977) and Gil (1990–1).

[80]See on this Parkes, *The Conflict*, p. 153.

[81]Further see M. Vinzent, *Offener Anfang. Die Anfänge des Christentums im 2. Jahrhundert* (Freiburg im Breslau: Herder, 2019a).

[82]Parkes, *The Conflict*, 1934.

[83]W. Kinzig, 'Novitas Christiana Elektronische Ressource Die Idee des Fortschritts in der Alten Kirche bis Eusebius', in 2 *Online-Ressource* (702 S.) (Göttingen: Vandenhoeck & Ruprecht, 1994). Ulrich's version (*Euseb von Caesarea und die Juden: Studien zur Rolle der Juden in der Theologie des Eusebius von Caesarea* (Berlin: de Gruyter, 1999)), I have here simplified and adapted.

Christianity. The Hebrews or 'friends of God' (φίλοι θεοῦ) he sees as having formed
already in olden times 'an entire people in fear of God'.[84] Eusebius reckons many
important people to belong to this great people of the Hebrews, for example, the
founding father Heber, Enoch, Noah, Melchisedek, Abraham, Isaac, Jacob, Job,
Joseph, Moses, then also the Prophets, as well as David and the Maccabees, and
the seventy translators of the Septuagint. But, according to Eusebius (unnoticed in
previous scholarship), there are still people who after the time of the incarnation
do not belong to the church, but who are still regarded as standing in continuity
with the old 'friends of God' and are therefore called 'Hebrews', such as Philo of
Alexandria and Josephus Flavius and even the dialogue partner of Justin Martyr,
namely Tryphon.[85]

Moreover, he also calls his local learned Jewish interlocutors,[86] more generally
Jews and those Jews who accept Jesus as the Messiah, 'Hebrews'.[87] Surely, Eusebius
maintains the difference between those 'Hebrews' who do accept Jesus and those
who do not, and sees the former as the only true 'Hebrews'; yet, given that all
are 'Hebrews', the apologetic boundary is not as sharp as has been pointed out in
previous scholarship.[88]

This is supported by the fact that 'Hebrews' and 'Christians' are often mutually
synonymous for Eusebius (though he also sees differences between them, Christians
are less interested in the procreation of offspring, nor do they practice animal
sacrifice),[89] so that the 'Hebrews' are forerunners of 'Christians'.[90] He clearly
differentiates Christianity from Hellenism (Ἑλληνισμός) and Judaism (Ἰουδαϊσμός),
but in both cases, there is no clear-cut opposition between these entities. Christianity
is 'something new and a true wisdom of God' (τις καινὴ καὶ θεοσοφία),[91] not 'new'
in the sense of 'new and strange',[92] but a true form of God-worship with its
own characters (οὔτε Ἑλληνισμός τίς ἐστιν οὔτε Ἰουδαϊσμός, οἰκεῖον δέ τινα φέρων
χαρακτῆρα θεοσεβείας),[93] but He admits that genealogically Christians derive from
the Greeks and think like Greeks, while at the same time they make use of the
Jewish books and have taken most of their teachings from their prophecies.[94] Such
dependence not only accounts for the Jewish Biblical books, but contrary to later
adoptions of Philo and Josephus, he clearly regards these as Jews whom he sees as

[84]Eusebius, *HE.*, 1.2. 22.
[85]Further see Ulrich, *Euseb von Caesarea*, pp. 63–7.
[86]Eusebius, *Dem.Ev.*, 4 1. 2.
[87]*Dem.Ev.*, 4. 11. 2.
[88]For this see Ulrich, *Euseb von Caesarea*, p. 68.
[89]Eusebius *Dem.Ev.*, 1. 9-10.
[90]Eusebius, *HE.*, 1. 4 .6.
[91]Eusebius, *Praep.Ev.*, 1. 5. 12.
[92]The difference from a positively seen novelty (καινότης) and a negatively seen newness (νεότης) has been
drawn out by Ulrich, *Euseb von Caesarea*, p. 112.
[93]Eusebius, *Dem.Ev.*, 1. 2. 1.
[94]Eusebius, *Praep.Ev.*, 1. 5. 10.

highly important reference authors.[95] Nevertheless, he develops an image of the Christians as the 'new' nation which outshines all other nations:

> When in recent times the appearance of our Saviour Jesus Christ had become known to all men there immediately made its appearance a new nation; a nation confessedly not small, and not dwelling in some corner of the earth, but the most numerous and pious of all nations, indestructible and unconquerable, because it always receives assistance from God. This nation, thus suddenly appearing at the time appointed by the inscrutable counsel of God, is the one which has been honored by all with the name of Christ.[96]

It is the continuity between this new nation and the 'Hebrews' that is at the basis of the super-eminence of Christians and Christianity. Hence, he thinks of one base line and two levels of fearing God, one is the people of polytheistic errors, the second is the people 'from the circumcision who through Mose have achieved the first level of fearing God' and those 'who thirdly thanks to the teaching of the Gospel have moved up'.[97] Christianity, therefore, is placed on the top for him, and all other forms of God-fearing are less. Like Justin Martyr in the second century, he calls Christianity *'verus Israel'*. In this 'true Israel', he sees not only those who have come from the Greeks but also those from 'Juda' and 'Israel' 'who have come through [Christ] to the fearing of God . . . who have kept the hidden Jew and the true Israel'.[98] As such Christians are no longer the same as these Jews; they are 'even better than them'.[99] Still, the most interesting element of the graphic portrayal above is the overlap between Judaism and Christianity in terms of membership, as seen by Eusebius. Christianity includes Jews who observe the Torah, whether or not they accept Jesus, while Judaism is the complementary entity that encompasses those who observe the Torah, but mainly do not accept Jesus as Messiah.

THE SPLIT BETWEEN JUDAISM AND CHRISTIANITY

How does Eusebius narrate this partial split/partial overlap between Christianity and Judaism as two entities he knows of? Eusebius has written several historical works, two of which are of paramount importance to our question. First, he created what he considered to be an innovative *Chronicle*,[100] which was soon followed by his *Church History*, developed in several stages and editions. For the latter Eusebius claims 'in its preface . . . to be the first in his field, founder of a new genus – an

[95]See Vinzent, *Offener Anfang*, pp. 59–111, and also Ulrich, *Euseb von Caesarea*, pp. 88–110.
[96]Eusebius, *HE.*, 1. 4. 2. (*Ante Nicene Fathers*, trans.).
[97]*Dem.Ev.*, 1. 6. 62.
[98]*Dem.Ev.*, 7. 3. 45.
[99]*Dem.Ev.*, 2. 2. 21.
[100]A. Mosshammer, *The Chronicle of Eusebius and Greek Chronographic Tradition* (Lewisburg: Bucknell University Press, 1979), p. 33.

undisputed claim to this day'.[101] Both works formed the basis for future generations of chroniclers and church historians, and 'what we know or know of the first three centuries of the Church rests almost entirely on one work, his church history'.[102] For this reason, until now, most of the answers to the question of Jewish-Christian relations are given on the basis of Eusebius.

The *Chronicle* is a 'highly labyrinthine and controversial'[103] work in two parts, the first of which, the *Chronographia*, deals with the basics on which the synchronistic tables and historical information of the second part rest. It suffers from its often problematic format. Wallace-Hadrill compares it to a screen that Eusebius wanted to show to his readership but could not stretch it out in one piece before their eyes because of the extensive comparison lists.[104] Moreover, it was probably intended more as a preparatory 'notebook', as 'the long source quotations' testify.[105] To add to the complexity for the modern reader, this work is no longer preserved in its original language but is most comprehensively only available in an Armenian translation, while the Latin translation produced and preserved by Jerome covers only the second part in a revised and partially extended format.[106] This second part was also extended by Jerome going beyond Eusebius' lifetime and leading up to the Roman–Gothic Battle of Hadrianopolis in the year 378.

'Part of Eusebius' purpose in writing his two-volume chronological work was to oppose what had become a popular eschatological view that the world would last 6,000 years from Creation and that Christ had been born in the year 5,500 (halfway through the metaphorical "sixth day" of Creation).'[107] The *Chronicle* is thus not an eschatological work that wants to predict or even calculate the years remaining until the end of the world, such as we find in the *Epistle of Barnabas*, Hippolytus, Justin, Theophilus of Antioch, Flavius Josephus and Philo.[108] In the first part of the *Chronicle* Eusebius gives a chronological overview of a number of cultures and peoples – Chaldeans, Assyrians, Hebrews, Egyptians, Greeks and Romans. To them he adds synchronistic tables that confront the events of pagan history with that narrated in the Bible. The second part of the *Chronicle* Eusebius called the 'Canons',

---

[101]M. Wallraff, *Der Kirchenhistoriker Sokrates. Untersuchungen zu Geschichts-darstellung, Methode und Person* (Göttingen: Vandenhoeck und Ruprecht, 1997), p. 136.

[102]As G. Fau put it, 'Ce que nou savons ou croyons savoir des trois premiers siècles de l'Eglise repose presque entièrement sur une œuvre: l'histoire ecclésiastique d'Eusèbe.' in 'Eusèbe de Césarée et son histoire de l'église', *Cahier du cercle Ernest-Renan* 24 (1976): 1.

[103]Mosshammer, *The Chronicle*, p. 30. Further on Eusebius's *Chronicle* see, from the Bibliography: Burgess (2002) and (2018); Barnes (1996, pp. 106–25); Grant (1980, pp. 3–9); Sirinelli (1961, pp. 31–63); and D. S. Wallace-Hadrill, *Eusebius of Caesarea* (London: Mowbray, 1960), pp. 157–67.

[104]Wallace-Hadrill, *Eusebius*, p. 155.

[105]'The impression made by the *Chronography* that it is an historian's note-book rather than a finished work is heightened by the lengthy quotation of sources,' Wallace-Hadrill, *Eusebius*, p. 155.

[106]R. M. Grant, *Eusebius as Church Historian* (Oxford: Clarendon Press, 1980), p. 4.

[107]R.W. Burgess, 'Jerome Explained: An Introduction to His Chronicle and a Guide to Its Use', *Ancient History Bulletin* 16 (2002): 8.

[108]This is pointed out by J. F. Sirinelli, *Les vues historiques d'Eusèbe de Césarée durant la période prénicéenne* (Dakar: University Press, 1961), pp. 38–9.

and it comprises chronological tables to merge the various and sometimes varying calendar data, in a comparative way, into a universal history. Unlike the chronicles of his predecessors Julius Africanus and Hippolytus of Rome, this combined history does not follow the prior apocalyptic tradition but counts from Abraham onwards and leads up to the days of Eusebius. In short, it is a history of the 'Hebrews'.

The second part of the *Chronicle* is structured year by year, beginning with the birth of Abraham, to which are added the Olympics from the year 1240 onwards. For each individual year, brief comments on the political, religious and cultural events of the listed data are added. The *Chronicle* served Eusebius not only as a 'skeleton' for 'the structure' of his own history of the church,[109] but it also had great importance for almost all further historiographers,[110] from the time of its composition in the early fourth century until the Reformation, and it 'formed the standard text of world chronology from the birth of Abraham (2016 BCE) to the Vicennalia of Constantine (325)'.[111]

Just as Eusebius with his *Chronicle* impacted immensely on later chroniclers and historians (especially as it was soon translated into different languages – Latin, Syrian, Armenian), so the literary librarian and later bishop of Caesarea had an enormous readership of his *Church History* with a tremendous heritage for coming generations. Doron Mendels calls this success a revolutionary 'media history' that has become an extremely powerful instrument bringing information to a wide-ranging audience.[112] Divided into ten books of almost equal length, which today would be called chapters,[113] Eusebius leads the readers from the past to his present, the year 324.[114] Book Six presents a special entity within his *Church History*, as it is dedicated almost exclusively to Origen (ca. 184–253), the teacher of his own idol Pamphilus.

Despite the weight of the two historical works, to which Eusebius added others, the verdict on their author has varied widely over the centuries. More recently, with reference to Herodotus, whom Cicero called 'the father of historiography',[115] he has been given the honorific name 'the father of church history'.[116] Indeed, Eusebius was even considered to be 'the greatest Christian scholar of his time.'[117] Others saw him merely as a man who was 'well-read, learned, and historically interested', 'a man of

---

[109]Grant, *Eusebius*, pp. 4, 22.

[110]See: W. Adler, 'Eusebius' Chronicle and Its Legacy', in *Eusebius, Christianity, and Judaism*, eds H. W. Attridge and G. Hata (Detroit, MI: Wayne State University Press, 1992).

[111]Mosshammer, *The Chronicle*, p. 15.

[112]D. Mendels, *The Media Revolution of Early Christianity. An Essay on Eusebius's Ecclesiastical History* (Grand Rapids, MI: Eerdmans, 1999), pp. 2–11.

[113]Only the last two books are a little shorter than the first eight.

[114]On this and the notion of time in Eusebius, see: F. Vittinghoff, 'Zum geschichtlichen Selbstverständnis der Spätantike', *Historische Zeitschrift* 198 (1964): 529–73.

[115]Cicero, *DeLeg.*, B. 1.1.5.

[116]See F. Winkelmann, *Euseb von Kaisareia. Der Vater der Kirchengeschichte* (Berlin: Verlags-Anst. Union, 1991).

[117]O. Bardenhewer, *Geschichte der altkirchlichen Literatur* (Freiburg im Breisgau: Herder, 1923), p. 243.

transition',[118] or 'the bishop of a provincial capital, who was gladly welcomed by the court', to whom 'something petty-bourgeois' clung,[119] or even more drastically the 'court-theological barber of the imperial wig' (Franz Overbeck).[120]

As a dependent, student, *famulus*, librarian and successor of Pamphilus[121] – he calls Pamphilus 'my lord', ὁ ἐμὸς δεσπότης[122] – Eusebius organized and managed the literary heritage of Origen, at a time when Origen became *the* 'father' and with him the beginnings of fatherly authority in Christianity began, or more precisely, when the signet 'Fathers of the Church' was formed by Eusebius,[123] using it for the first time in his claim for tradition and authority derived from his school background.[124] Eusebius counted himself among this class of church 'fathers' to equip himself, on the one hand, with the authority of the forefathers, on the other hand, however, to distance himself from his contemporary critics and to immunize himself against them.[125]

Although Eusebius was sometimes criticized for his theological views, condemned by many as Arian theology, even the sceptics and those who pointed out his historical 'fallacies, ignorance, and absurdities'[126] have acknowledged Eusebius' significance as a church historian.[127] In particular, scholars have recognized that Eusebius was an historian, interested in, and oriented towards, sources[128] so as to build his history of the beginnings of Christianity on as broad a base as possible. Eusebius was aware of his active choices, which he had to make in the light of the material: 'Having gathered therefore from the matters mentioned here and there by them whatever we consider important for the present work, and having plucked like flowers from a meadow the appropriate passages from ancient writers, we shall endeavor to embody the whole in an historical narrative.'[129] Eusebius relies heavily on written sources (often sources that are now called secondary sources, without him having made that distinction) and 'his description of the rapid spread of Christianity in *HE.* 2. 3, without any reference to a single source, is quite exceptional'.[130] And he was

---

[118]K. S. Frank and E. Grünbeck, *Lehrbuch der Geschichte der Alten Kirche* (Paderborn: Schöningh, 1997), p. 401.

[119]E. Schwartz (ed.), *Eusebios von Caesarea* (Berlin: Griechische Geschichtschreiber, 1959), p. 497.

[120]C. Schmitt, *Politische Theologie II. Die Legende von der Erledigung jeder Politischen Theologie* (Berlin: Duncker & Humbolt, 1970), p. 69.

[121]See Schwartz, *Eusebios von Caesarea*, pp. 496–7.

[122]Eusebius, *Mart. Pal.*, 11,1.

[123]Eusebius, *Con.Marc.*, 1. 4. 3; *Ec.Th.*, 1. 14.

[124]See T. Graumann, *Die Kirche der Väter. Vätertheologie und Väterbeweis in den Kirchen des Ostens bis zum Konzil von Ephesus (431)* (Tübingen: Mohr Siebeck, 2002), p. 17. This was an argument developed in the debate between Asterius, Marcellus of Ancyra and Eusebius of Caesarea. Further see M. Vinzent, 'Origenes als Postscriptum. Paulinus von Tyrus und die origenistische Diadoche', in *Origeniana Septima*, eds W. A. Bienert and U. Kühneweg (Leuven: Leuven University Press, 1999).

[125]Further see, in the Bibliography: Spiegel (1999); and also Bakhtin, Emerson and Holquist (1986).

[126]Particularly, Fau, 'Eusèbe de Césarée', p. 31.

[127]See Winkelmann, *Euseb von Kaisareia*, pp. 13–15.

[128]See Grant, *Eusebius*, pp. 60–83.

[129]Eusebius, *HE.*, 1. 1. 4.

[130]B. Gustafsson, 'Eusebius' Principles in Handling His Sources, as Found in His Church History, Books I-VII', *Studia Patristica* 4, no. 2 (1961): 429.

extremely reserved about non-literary or oral sources.[131] As becomes clear from the beginning and as the title states (as with his work on *On Church Theology*), Eusebius wanted to create an insider's product.[132] Hence, it starts with 'the very origin of Christ's dispensation',[133] 'the first historical-critical account of the life of Jesus'.[134]

In the very opening of the foreword to his *Church History* Eusebius explains that he wants to write a story of persons. With this approach, Eusebius joins the historiography of the imperial period, but with it he chose a literary form that 'during the Greek and Latin times up to late antiquity was regarded as a controversial . . . and less favourably judged historiographical form compared to a proper work of history'.[135]

Unlike the beginning of his *Chronicle* Eusebius starts his history of persons not with a sequence of the principal leaders, such as the apostles and their successors, but instead with a theological exposition of the divine life of the protagonist, Jesus Christ. He first connects this divine life with Jesus' earthly life, and then he follows the church's development up to his own lifetime. Church and political events, especially important ones, are linked with outstanding church leaders of 'the most prestigious communities.' But one particular topic, that Eusebius wanted to cover, was to report about the fate which the Jewish people had met immediately after its crime against the Saviour.

In the introduction to Book II of his *Church History*, according to which the whole of the first book could be understood as a preface,[136] Eusebius mentions that he wants above all to report 'the events which have taken place in connection with Christ's recent appearance', 'his Passion, and the selection of his apostles'.[137] It must have been a particularly big problem for Eusebius that in a world where age, antiquity and tradition carried more weight than novelty and where what was oldest was most venerable and every innovation suspicious, Jesus' rather recent appearance failed to convince, or had been seen as problematic. Consequently, Eusebius made every effort not to insist on the novelty of Christianity but to explain to his readers that Christianity is built on tradition, even though it represented an advance in the history of religion and culture. In doing so, he bypassed the alternative of 'old and new', and harnessed both into a dynamic that enabled him to explain both the long past and late appearance of Jesus Christ.[138] For him, 'this progress of Christianity in the world, which will continue even in the future (!), is not only numerical in nature, but also brings about practical consequences by providing a better life to mankind

---

[131]See, for example, his scepticism towards a Christ statue from Caesarea Philippi, *HE.*, 7.18.
[132]See Wallraff, *Der Kirchenhistoriker Sokrates*, p. 135.
[133]Eusebius, *HE.*, 1.1.8.
[134]So Winkelmann, *Euseb von Kaisareia*, p. 70.
[135]Winkelmann, *Euseb von Kaisareia*, p. 62.
[136]Eusebius, *HE.*, 1.1.1. Even though, only the first four chapters are probably meant and referred to as such. Further see, in the Bibliography: Brenenecke (2001, p. 84); Grant (1980, p. 34); Cameron (1994).
[137]Eusebius, *HE.*, 2. 1. 1.
[138]Well shown in W. Kinzig, *Novitas Christiana. Die Idee des Fortschritts in der Alten Kirche bis Eusebius* (Göttingen: Vandenhoeck und Ruprecht, 1994), pp. 517–66.

. . . political unity, . . . the worship of the highest God instead of idols . . . and a more just life.'[139]

One can see how the historian needs sophistic tricks to rectify the historical novelty and assert the idea of progress, in order to explain why the existence of Jesus Christ did not simply begin a few decades or even centuries ago with the birth of Mary, but predates even the beginning of humanity, indeed began in a divine generation from the Father, and thus happened even before the aeons of time and history began. God did not first set his work in action with the emergence of the world and the creation of Adam, as Flavius Josephus (Eusebius' much quoted author) had first reported in his *Jewish Antiquities*; rather, God laid the foundations through the One Word, which unfortunately was not recognized by all, as Greeks and other polytheists showed in their rejection of this one Word; but also as Israel demonstrates which, according to Eusebius, had corrupted this Word by only imperfectly preserving it. From the beginning of his *Church History*, therefore, the argument of the still-greater age of Christ and of Christianity compared to that of Israel, the Greeks and all other peoples is developed by Eusebius as an apologetic first guiding thought, based on age-proofing.[140]

Accordingly he paints 'the whole Jewish people', as causing self-harm 'in consequence of their plots against our Saviour'. This does not mean that Eusebius thought that 'the history of the Jewish people since Good Friday' would no longer needed to be part of his account,[141] but that the outcomes of the Jews' decision belonged to the history of errors, just like the pagan measures against the Christians with the making of martyrs.

Eusebius' *Church History* introduced a division of the beginnings of Christianity into the period before and the time after the ascension of Christ. This is followed by another, rather less marked structuring of the second post-ascension phase, divided between a time before and after the Bar Kokhba rebellion of the years 132 to 135. This division can best be seen from the drastic change from Eusebius' lively interest in Jewish matters prior to this rebellion and his marked disinterest for the time after it.

Until the time of Hadrian and the Bar Kokhba uprising, Eusebius followed mainly Josephus in his account[142] and Hegesippus; whereby he often addresses inner-Jewish developments. Up to this point in time and in contrast to separate developments of the many 'unconverted peoples' (the pagans), Eusebius describes the events among

---

[139]Kinzig, *Novitas Christiana. Die Idee,* pp. 521–2.

[140]See already: A. J. Droge, 'The Apologetic Dimensions of the Ecclesiastical History', in *Eusebius, Christianity, and Judaism,* eds Harold W. Attridge and G. Hata (Detroit, MI: Wayne State University Press, 1992).

[141]So H. C. Brennecke, 'Die Kirche als ΔΙΑΔΟΧΑΙ ΤΩΝ ΑΠΟΣΤΟΛΩΝ. Das Programm der HE. des Euseb von Caesarea', in *Wast ist ein Text?,* eds O. Wischmeyer and E. M. Becker (Tübingen: A. Francke, 2001), p. 86.

[142]See D. Mendels, 'The Sources of the Ecclesiastical History of Eusebius: The Case of Josephus', in *L'historiographie de l'église des premiers siècles,* eds B. Pouderon and Y.-M. Duval (Paris: Beauchesne, 2001).

Hebrews (who included Jews believing and not believing in Christ) as one single history. The Jews, who 'have only incompletely preserved monotheism' and have crucified Christ, and therefore have to bear the divine vengeance as their destiny, are still closely associated with the Christians who were predestined from preexistence 'to the full knowledge of God' and 'stay in direct continuity with the ancient Hebrews.'[143]

In contrast to this, for the time after Hadrian and the Second Jewish War, this picture of the one (albeit antithetical history of Jewish and Christian Hebrews) is abandoned by Eusebius. Martin Tetz has already pointed out that for the time after this revolt, 'the Jews in the portrayal of [Eusebius'] *Church History*, scarcely play any further role'.[144] In fact, Eusebius mentions that although from the beginning to the time of Emperor Hadrian, he 'nowhere found preserved in writing' anything about 'the chronology of the bishops of Jerusalem', he reports that he has 'learned this much from writings, that until the siege of the Jews, which took place under Hadrian', the entire ecclesial community consisted of 'Hebrew descent',[145] but that after the Roman conquest of the Jews, 'the bishops of the circumcision ceased at this time' in Jerusalem.[146] After the disastrous end of the Bar Kokhba uprising, not only the Jews were banished from the city of Aelia Capitolina (Jerusalem) but with them also the Jewish followers of Christ,[147] while the remaining uncircumcised Jews who believed in Christ were allowed to stay and chose a certain Mark to become the first uncircumcised bishop.

It is noteworthy that Eusebius has ostensibly given up his interest in Jews even so based most of his account of the beginnings of the Christian movement on Jewish writings and also makes extensive use of both Philo of Alexandria and Flavius Josephus. The latter especially serves him as a Jewish 'crown witness' against his own people in explaining the disasters that befell the Jews. Josephus had already warned the Jews not to act as the enemies of Rome, had blamed the Zelotes for the fall of Jerusalem and made out the Romans as God's tool to punish the whole Jewish people. Yet, Josephus also defended Jewish Torah observances (before and after Christ) against pagan criticisms,[148] and in many places where one is surprised that Eusebius does not refer to writings from the New Testament (e.g. the Gospels or the canonical *Acts of the Apostles*), it is actually Josephus who serves as a source for

---

[143]See Ulrich, *Euseb von Caesarea*, pp. 58–9, Kinzig, *Novitas Christiana. Die Idee*, p. 532.

[144]So the summary in Ulrich, *Euseb von Caesarea*, p. 51; see M. Tetz, 'Christenvolk und Abrahamsverheißung. Zum "kirchengeschichtlichen". Programm des Eusebius von Caesarea', in *Jenseitsvorstellungen in Antike und Christentum. Gedenkschrift für A. Stuiber*, ed. T. Klauser, *Jahrbüch für Antike u. Christentum*. Ergänzungsband, 9 (Münster: Aschendorf, 1982), p. 38.

[145]Eusebius, *HE.*, 4.5.1-2.

[146]Eusebius, *HE.*, 4.5.2.

[147]F. Blanchetière, 'De l'importance de l'an 135 dans l'évolution respective de la synagogue et du christianisme', in *L'historiographie de l'église des premiers siècles*, eds B. Pouderon and Y.-M. Duval (Paris: Beauchesne, 2001), p. 92.

[148]On both see Ulrich, *Euseb von Caesarea*, pp. 102–10.

his narrative of the early history of the church.[149] The early chapters of his *Church History* (which contain an astonishing epitome of the life of Jesus) especially are strongly inspired by Flavius Josephus, whose *Jewish Antiquities* and *Jewish War* are quoted more frequently than all the New Testament writings. In addition, fragments of a letter of Iulius Africanus to an otherwise unknown Aristides is given (only preserved by Eusebius), with which Eusebius emphasizes the harmonious agreement between the Gospels. Using these fragments, Eusebius fits Jesus' lifetime into the history of the various Jewish high priests. In his account of Jesus' birth under the rule of Herod, Eusebius draws primarily from Josephus, often supplemented only by a remark from *Matthew* or *Luke*.[150] Through Josephus he also tries to refute contemporary pseudonymous literature (such as the *Memoirs of Our Saviour*).[151] The continuous reliance on Josephus does not change with chapter ten of Book I, where Eusebius begins with his account of Jesus' appearance as a thirty-year-old. He is mainly concerned with placing Jesus' ministry into the history of the officiating High Priests which Josephus has reported, and it is important for him to emphasize that the Gospel accounts 'are not in conflict with the present [Josephus's] considerations'.[152] Nevertheless, Eusebius does not use the Gospels in these chapters as a comparable source, and so one learns nothing about Jesus' miraculous work, his parables or his actions, deeds and sufferings. In short, the only sources that Eusebius uses to record the earthly deeds of Jesus are the testimony of Josephus and an epistolary passage containing a letter from Jesus himself and a sermon on him.

From the eighteenth chapter of Josephus' *Jewish Antiquities* derives the famous so-called *Testamentum Flavianum*, in which it is reported about Jesus:

> And there lived at that time Jesus, a wise man, if indeed it be proper to call him a man. For he was a doer of wonderful works, and a teacher of such men as receive the truth in gladness. And he attached to himself many of the Jews, and many also of the Greeks. He was the Christ. When Pilate, on the accusation of our principal men, condemned him to the cross, those who had loved him in the beginning did not cease loving him. For he appeared unto them again alive on the third day, the divine prophets having told these and countless other wonderful things concerning him. Moreover, the race of Christians, named after him, continues down to the present day.[153]

Even though today this passage is perhaps one of the most talked-and-written-about texts of early Christianity, and it is considered by a number of researchers as a fake Christian interpolation in the work of Josephus,[154] by others as at best a minimally

---

[149]See Vinzent, *Offener Anfang*, pp. 76–111.
[150]See Eusebius, *HE.*, 1.8.16; 1.9.1.
[151]See Kraft, *Eusebius von Cäsarea, Kirchengeschichte* (Darmstadt: Wissenschaftliche Buchgesellschaft, 1989), p. 107.
[152]Eusebius, *HE.* 1.10.6.
[153]Eusebius, *HE.* 1.11.7-8.
[154]See S. Mason, *Flavius Josephus und das Neue Testament* (Tübingen: Francke, 2000).

revised passage,[155] it is for Eusebius the first text with which he summarizes the life, death and resurrection of Jesus and which forms the foundation of his historical account of the beginnings of Christianity. If the readership of Eusebius' *Church History* were only uncircumcized Christians, derived from Greek descendants, why would Eusebius need to make such extensive use of Josephus? Given his apparent own disinterest in the further history of non-Christian Jews, why does he give Josephus such an important place in his narration and the sources behind it?

Eusebius' reference to Josephus' giving this testimony on Christ and the Christians is all the more astonishing, as in the third century his teacher Origen had spoken clearly of the same work and precisely about this eighteenth book of the *Jewish Antiquities*, from which Eusebius claims to quote this text. But Origen writes that although Josephus 'in the eighteenth book of his *Jewish Antiquities* deals with John the Baptist, 'this same writer *did not* acknowledge Jesus as a Messiah, though he should have said in investigating the cause of the fall of Jerusalem and the destruction of the Temple, that it was the enmity against Jesus that brought this calamity upon the people; for they had killed the prophesied Messiah'.[156] Similarly, later in his treatise *Against Celsus* and again in his *Commentary on Matthew*, Origen repeated the same observation. Contrary to what Eusebius quotes in the above-cited *Testamentum Flavianum*, Origen claims to have read the opposite, namely that Josephus *did not* recognize that Jesus is the Christ.[157] Hence, Origen's testimony suggests that the passage in Josephus was originally either in the form in which the text was also known to Jerome, according to whom Josephus did not confess Jesus as the Christ, but that 'He was at best considered to be the Messiah';[158] or that Origen had even read in Josephus his explicit denial of Jesus being the Christ, which was later turned on its head by Christians; or (less convincingly), Origen knew the version of Eusebius, but thought it was a doubtful statement.

Whichever way one wishes to read the *Testamentum* and solve the complex textual problems, the important question needs to be raised again: Why did Eusebius orient himself almost exclusively using Josephus for his portrayal of the birth and life of Jesus up to His Ascension (the latter being not mentioned in the *Testamentum*)? Why refer to Josephus, so much more than the writings of the New Testament, above all the Gospels, about which Eusebius later in his *Church History* speaks at length and which he then evidently takes for testimonies that are historically reliable?[159] The further question may be added: Why did Eusebius add to Josephus' account only very few details from canonical *Acts* (Acts 1.23-26) and from Paul's *First Letter to the Corinthians* (1 Cor. 15.5-7), and then for the rest of his account

---

[155]See A. Whealey, 'Josephus, Eusebius of Caesarea, and the Testimonium Flavianum', in *Josephus und das Neue Testament*, eds C. Böttrich and J. Herzer (Tübingen: Mohr Siebeck, 2007).

[156]Origen, *Cels.*, 1.47.

[157]See *Cels.*, 2.13; *Com.Matt.*, 10. 17.

[158]Jerome, *De Vir. Ill.*, 13.

[159]Further see, from the Bibliography: Grant (1980, pp. 5, 40–1); Whealey (2007); Horn (2007); and Mason (2000).

of Jesus' life up to the Ascension and the beginnings of Christianity he makes use of one further testimony only, namely the letter exchange between King Abgar and Jesus, containing a Letter of Jesus to the King, in which Jesus promises the ruler of Edessa to send a disciple to heal him from a disease and at the same time to offer him and his family salvation.[160]

Eusebius is the first known early Christian author who makes such intensive and critical use of the works of Josephus, an author little valued by Latin and Greek church fathers before Eusebius.[161] Michael E. Hardwick even speaks of Eusebius as a 'turning point' in the reception of Josephus.[162] Heinz Schreckenberg writes that Eusebius 'belongs to the church fathers who regard Josephus as an authority in all questions of New Testament contemporary history and the history and religion of the Jewish people',[163] especially in his *Jewish Antiquities*. Moreover, Eusebius is the first to quote the *Testamentum Flavianum* – in three different works of his.[164] Likewise, he is the first to acquaint us with an 'original document' of Jesus Himself, the only one Eusebius obviously knew of. His explanation for using the quote from Josephus is:

> Since an historian, who is one of the Hebrews themselves, has recorded in his work these things concerning John the Baptist and our Saviour, what excuse is there left for not convicting them of being destitute of all shame, who have forged the Acts against them?[165]

Evidently Eusebius saw the so-called *Memories of our Saviour* (the 'Acts') as a major challenge and threat for him and his audience, so that in his representation of the life and work of Jesus he thought the testimony of Josephus – one of the few sources that his opponents may have accepted as reliable – needed to be given such a core standing. If so, however, it is still difficult to understand why Eusebius makes such intensive use of the correspondence between King Abgar and Jesus. Was this letter exchange more impressive for his opponents than the canonical Gospels and Acts? As Eusebius explained later, it was the civil servants of Emperor Maximinus Daia (308–313) who not only devoted themselves to the cult of the gods whose service he entrusted to them, but also to the task of killing Christians, always inventing new forms of sufferings, even 'forging *Acts of Pilate and our Saviour*, full of every kind of blasphemy against Christ', which

> they sent with the emperor's approval to the whole of the empire subject to him, with written commands that they should be openly posted to the view of

---

[160]Eusebius, *HE.*, 1. 13. 3.

[161]See M. E. Hardwick, *Josephus as an Historical Source in Patristic Literature through Eusebius* (Atlanta, GA: Scholars Press, 1989), p. 1; Mendels, 'The Sources', pp. 203–4.

[162]See Mendels, 'The Sources', pp. 202–3; Hardwick, *Josephus*, p. 121; H. Schreckenberg, *Die Flavius-Josephus-Tradition in Antike und Mittelalter* (Leiden: Brill, 1972).

[163]Schreckenberg, *Die Flavius-Josephus-Tradition*, p. 79.

[164]See Whealey, 'Josephus, Eusebius of Caesarea, and the Testimonium Flavianum', pp. 74–6.

[165]Eusebius, *HE.*, 1.11.9.

all in every place, both in country and city, and that the schoolmasters should give them to their scholars, instead of their customary lessons, to be studied and learned by heart.[166]

Hence, according to Eusebius, this piece of writing was also distributed for teaching pupils at school, so that 'the children in the schools had daily in their mouths the names of Jesus and Pilate, and the Acts which had been forged in wanton insolence'.[167]

With Eusebius' statement about Josephus, 'who is one of the Hebrews themselves', one must assume a Eusebian readership that was familiar with Josephus, perhaps one informed by Jewish education and also exposed to imperial propaganda. Therefore, Eusebius' readers were equally close to Judaism, the state and likewise to the church. This is why Eusebius built his edifice of the beginnings of Christianity on the pre-existent and time-born Saviour to satisfy the claim of antiquity of the Christian form of worship. On this foundation he makes the apostles succeed.

With the above-mentioned correspondence between King Abgar and Jesus, together with remarks on the healing of the king by Thaddaeus and his preaching to the citizens of Edessa, he appends 'perhaps the most extraordinary story about Jesus to survive from antiquity'.[168] One aspect of the Abgar history is the blaming of the Jews for the crucifixion of Jesus. Abgar says: 'So much have I believed in him that I wished to take an army and destroy those Jews who crucified him, had I not been deterred from it by reason of the dominion of the Romans.'[169] Here Rome is declared a protective power, preventing even the revenge on the Jews, a dubious statement and a hidden threat, when Abgar was promised that 'the petitions' of his heart 'shall be granted to him'.[170] As does Orosius later, Eusebius uses the argument that the divinity avenges misdeeds (including those of Christians[171]).

For Walter Bauer this made it obvious that Eusebius was systematically falsifying the evidence, albeit unintentionally (in this case being misled by a counterfeiter of the fourth century CE) and that he presented the 'heretical' beginnings of Christianity from this warped perspective, portraying Edessa as an early Christian fortress of orthodoxy, contrary to historical reality. In contrast to Bauer, Alexander Mirkovic claimed that Eusebius used this correspondence for apologetic and political reasons, in order to respond to the publication of the *Acts of Pilate* by Maximinus Daia, and to give Christianity value and credibility in the eyes of kings and those who had converted from Judaism or paganism to Christianity. This argument, as we saw, has some support in the text. However, the reflections of James Corke-Webster seem more appropriate when he reads, from this opening, the intention of Eusebius to propel Jesus as an educated letter writer who even corresponds with a prestigious

---

[166]Eusebius, *HE.*, 9.5.1.
[167]Eusebius, *HE.*, 9.7.1.
[168]See: J. Corke-Webster, 'A Man for the Times: Jesus and the Abgar Correspondence in Eusebius of Caesarea's Ecclesiastical History', *The Harvard Theological Review* 110 (2017): 563.
[169]Eusebius, *HE.*, 1.13.16.
[170]Eusebius, *HE.*, 1.13.15.
[171]See Eusebius, *HE.*, 7.30.21; 8.1.7-9; 9.8.15; 10.4.14, 33-34 and 59.

royal court outside the Roman Empire.[172] For Corke-Webster, Eusebius here shapes a stylized model for the interaction between Christianity and Rome. Accordingly, Eusebius gave his readership of the fourth century not 'the poor carpenter celebrated for his sacrificial suffering at the hands of misguided Roman principalities and powers', but 'a literate figure, the correspondent of kings who is aligned with the interests of Rome'.[173] Jesus became for Eusebius' 'fourth-century audience a man for their times, and us a key to his historical project'.[174] If one adds to Corke-Webster the sermon of Thaddaeus and the *Testamentum Flavianum*, one recognizes that Eusebius was even willing to present teaching contents at variance with his own theological ideas in order to bridge the gap not only between Christianity and Rome but also between Jewish readerships that were either interested in or averse to Christian matters.

Perhaps for this reason, Eusebius tried hard to downplay 'the Jews' and elevate 'the Christians'. The Jews meet the deserved fate of the persecution that reduces their political importance. In contrast, the persecution of believers in Christ and their martyrdoms lead to the significant ascent of the church. As we have seen, the eminent Jewish writers Josephus and Philo are made into witnesses to Christ, the learned letter writer and his church. Josephus' *testimonium* has already been cited, and Philo 'venerated and extolled, the apostolic men of his time, who were as it seems of the Hebrew race, and hence observed, after the manner of the Jews, most of the customs of the ancients'.[175] When Eusebius reviews the catalogue of Philo's writings, he praises him for being 'copious in language, comprehensive in thought, and sublimely elevated in his views of divine Scripture', because 'Philo has produced manifold and various expositions of the sacred books'.[176] At no point does Eusebius voice a critique against Philo for not commenting on the New Testament writings. Instead, Eusebius makes use of his work *On Contemplative Life* to testify that the *therapeutae* described in it were ascetics who had been converted to the preaching of the gospel by Mark.[177] What is more, Eusebius speculates that Philo's claim that the *therapeutae* 'read the holy Scriptures' and were obsessed 'with the writings of ancient men', meant, 'highly probably', that 'the works of the ancients, which he tells us they had, were the Gospels and the apostolic writings, and probably some expositions of the ancient prophets, such as are contained in the Epistle to the Hebrews, and in many others of Paul's Epistles'.[178]

According to David Runia, this passage in Eusebius forms the oldest surviving version of the legend of *Philo Christianus*, or (to stay closer to the wording of the text) of the notion that Philo is in close contact with the apostles and the first

---

[172]Corke-Webster, 'A Man for the Times', pp. 580–1.
[173]Ibid., p. 586.
[174]Ibid., p. 571.
[175]Eusebius, *HE.*, 2.17.2.
[176]Eusebius, *HE.*, 2.18.1.
[177]Eusebius, *HE.*, 2.16.2-2.17.2. Further See D. Runia, *Philo in Early Christian Literature: A Survey* (Minneapolis, MN: Fortress Press, 1993), pp. 217–18.
[178]Eusebius, *HE.*, 2.17.10-12.

Christian communities.[179] Does this suggest that though Eusebius apologetically and historically highlights the split between Jews and Christians, the lived reality of his audience still evidenced a much closer symbiosis and that there were a good number of Greek-speaking Jewish readers of Philo and Josephus who were both aligned and unaligned with the church?

As stated earlier, Eusebius' *Church History* was intended to develop a history of individual people, rather than that of communities or institutions. Perhaps for this reason, Eusebius does not provide an answer to our question, even though the presumption of a split community, at the latest from the end of the Bar Kokhba war onwards, has impacted later authors. Even so, what we do not find, yet, in Eusebius is any denigration or despising of 'the Jews'; instead, he values what he reads in Romans 9–11 and 'rejects an irreversible condemnation of the Jews', though salvation is bound up with becoming members of 'verus Israel'.[180]

Though some passages in Eusebius read as if the church has replaced the Synagogue, this was a fact of history which for Eusebius was a political and social result of the Bar Kokhba revolution and the banishing of the Jews from Jerusalem, so that pilgrims now visited and prayed at the Christian places of worship (the Mount of Olives and others).[181] As Jörg Ulrich has pointed out, the three eminent Jewish institutions of king, prophet and high priest were not adopted or integrated into the church but were concentrated in Christ, while the church, and in it all Christians, stood under the same threat of the final divine judgement as anybody else, Jews or non-Jew.[182]

As will have become clear, for Eusebius, Christianity was predominantly a Greek form of God-fearing. Its indebtedness to the Jewish past is theologically given through its relation to the 'Hebrews', along with its reliance on the Scriptures and the writings of many wise 'Hebrews' and Jews. Even though his explicit awareness of, or even interest in, Christians who simultaneously were Jews is very limited, Eusebius shows a high regard for those who follow the Torah, as one can see from his portrayal of Philo and Josephus and to these, one could add James, the brother of the Lord.[183]

THE JEWS

As we have seen, so far, it was chiefly Christian apologetic, political and legal endeavours that attempted to harden the boundaries and to define entities, create 'isms' and make people aware that they belonged to forms of worship and interpretations of the Torah that were incompatible with each other (something

---

[179]Runia, *Philo*, p. 218.
[180]Ulrich, *Euseb von Caesarea*, p. 212.
[181]Eusebius, *Dem.Ev.*, 6.18.22-23.
[182]Ulrich, *Euseb von Caesarea*, pp. 214–15.
[183]Eusebius, *HE.*, 3.27.1-6. See Ulrich, *Euseb von Caesarea*, p. 120.

often accepted uncritically today[184]), and yet, even during the fourth century, and outside the Roman and Byzantine empire for a much longer time, these boundaries were less distinct.

The parting of the ways in scholarship

Martin Goodman summarizes the state of research in this area:

> Historians both of early Christianity and of Judaism in late antiquity agree that at some point in the first four centuries CE the ways of the two religions parted. There is much less agreement about the date when this parting occurred and the extent of continued debate, rivalry and mutual influence between Jews and Christians after the separation. All depends on perspective. Viewed from the standpoint of Jews and Christians in the twenty-first century, the historical trajectories which mattered in late antiquity are those which were to create two distinct religious systems in due course, but the beginnings of those trajectories may have been almost unnoticed by those who followed them. Some Jews might have thought that some fellow Jews who believed in Christian doctrines were still Jews, while others, less tolerant, did not. The early Christian traditions that Jewish Christians were persecuted by their fellow Jews and expelled from synagogues are not reflected in the rabbinic sources, which is not to say that they are not true: the rabbis in fact had very little to say about Christians of any kind, treating Christians born as Jews within the general category of heresy and those born as gentiles simply as idolaters. Conversely, when ancient Christians described fellow believers as Jews or Judaizers they might be referring either to the ethnic origins of such Christians or to their continued practice of Jewish customs such as the circumcision of males, or simply to more scrupulous attention to the Old Testament than other Christians believed appropriate.[185]

One of the key phrases in this summary is: 'All depends on perspective', and the perspective that is used is 'the standpoint of Jews and Christians in the twenty-first century'; in other words one imported by scholarship already noting 'those trajectories' that point to a parting of ways and then only addressing the question of the dating its beginning. Here, interestingly, modern Jewish and Christian scholars differ significantly.

Christian scholarship had assumed for a long time that Christians existed ever since Jesus of Nazareth walked on earth, or at the latest from the times of Paul and that the movement grew out of the teachings and lives of these two protagonists.[186]

---

[184]See P. S. Alexander, 'The Parting of the Ways' from the Perspective of Rabbinic Judaism', in *Jews and Christians: The Parting of the Ways A.D.70 to 135*, ed. J. D. G. Dunn (Tübingen: Mohr Siebeck, 1992), p. 2.

[185]M. Goodman, *Rome and Jerusalem: The Clash of Ancient Civilizations* (London: Allen Lane, 2007), pp. 525–6. From the Bibliography see also Goodman (2003); Taylor (1995) and Lieu (1996).

[186]An example of scholarship that reads evidence back into our sources is P. Stulmacher, 'Das Christusbild der Paulus-Schule – eine Skizze', in Dunn (ed.), *Jews and Christians*. Here, the fact that Jesus' oracles

According to Peter Lampe,[187] the divide between Judaism and Christianity occurred at the latest in the year 49 CE, though others see it happening after the Roman destruction of the Temple of Jerusalem in 70 CE, or manifested at the beginning of the second century. The beginnings of Christian self-identity began during the mid-first century or at the latest in the decades after the first Jewish war in 70 CE.

Jewish scholars, however, differ from this view, opting for a later time and positing the separation between Judaism and Christianity as occurring after the second Jewish war in 132–135 CE. As Marcel Simon states in his famous *Verus Israel*, scholars often followed 'an unacknowledged assumption' that from early in the history of Christianity, 'the Church directed her attention exclusively to the gentiles, whilst Judaism became indifferent to everything outside herself, so that there was not the least occasion for contact between the two'.[188] Simon shows that one of the major proponents of this view was Adolf von Harnack, the towering twentieth-century scholar on Marcion:

> At the same time as he [Harnack] notes our almost total ignorance of the fortunes of Hellenistic Judaism after the destruction of the temple, he takes this event as the turning point: the diaspora itself would 'from this moment at the latest' have relaxed its ties with Greek culture, soon to break them altogether. As for Palestinian Judaism, it would already before A.D. 70, in condemning Greek culture, have repudiated the universalistic idea. Harnack can in consequence affirm elsewhere that by the end of the first century there was virtually no more contact between the gentile Church and the Synagogue.[189]

Harnack's theory was based on the assumption that 'Hellenistic Judaism' seemed to have disappeared with the destruction of the Temple of Jerusalem and that Palestinian Judaism was largely to be identified with a non- or anti-Hellenic form of Judaism as represented later in Rabbinic Judaism.

Today, however, the impact of the destruction of the Temple is sometimes questioned, especially with regard to the Western diaspora, since

> the vast majority of Jews had lived outside of the Land of Israel. . . . Generations of Jews spanning the centuries between the first and second destructions had never experienced living in the Jewish homeland at all, and evidently had accommodated themselves to this fact. Well before the year 70, the vast majority of Jews in the

---

and traditions cannot be found in 'any (!) of the New Testament epistles of apostles' (ibid., 163, my own trans.), but that Paul is displaying some of the Lord's oracles, makes Stuhlmacher conclude that Paul knew not only the (pre-)synoptic Jesus-traditions of Matthew, Mark and especially Luke, but even that his letters should be read as mirroring a Pauline missionary school of wisdom in which Paul himself has continuously taught and further developed these traditions.

[187] P. Lampe, *Die stadtrömischen Christen in den ersten beiden Jahrhunderten: Untersuchungen zur Sozialgeschichte* (Tübingen: Mohr, 1989), p. 16.

[188] M. Simon, *Verus Israel: A Study of the Relations between Christians and Jews in the Roman Empire (135 - 425)* (Oxford: Oxford University Press, 1986), (citation, ibid., p. x). See critiques of his "conflict theory" in the Bibliography: Taylor (1995) and Baumgarten (1999).

[189] Simon, *Verus Israel*, p. x.

Second Temple period had never gone on pilgrimage; thus (again, well before the year 70) the vast majority of Jews had never sacrificed at all. In brief, diaspora Jews were long accustomed to honoring their God without offerings and sacrifices. . . . In this respect, with the Temple's destruction, nothing changed. Instead, through the cycles of reading their scriptures, diaspora Jews could hear and learn about these sacrifices long before 70. They could and did continue to do so long after the Temple had ceased to exist.[190]

Against such an approach and its implied early divide and mutual ignorance between Judaism and Christianity, Simon outlined what had been achieved in research prior to him, a basis upon which he developed his own views in his book which, unsurprisingly, begins with the year 135 CE, the end of the Bar Kokhba war.[191]

Simon's early insights have been developed much further by more recent Jewish scholars, the most prominent being Daniel Boyarin. He sees that only the late second-century apologists started to make the divide between orthodoxy and heresy, providing the interlinked discourse that separated out Judaism from Christianity.[192] According to Boyarin, neither the notion of 'religion' existed nor that of 'Judaism' or 'Christianity' with the connotations we have of them today.[193] He argues that there were no 'preexistent different entities . . . that came (gradually or suddenly) to enact their difference in a "parting of the ways"', but it needed Christian heresiologists to be 'the anatomizers of heresy and heresies, and their Jewish counterparts, the Rabbis'.[194]

If Boyarin is right, how did the transition from a certain variety of Judaism to the existence of 'Christian heresiologists' on the one side, and 'Rabbis' on the other, actually come about? Against Boyarin some Christian and Jewish scholars have reinforced the older idea that Christianity, through its radical aspects concerning the interpretation of the Jewish Law, diverged from a normative Judaism; hence, its identity was given 'almost *ab ovo*' in contradistinction to a clearly defined Judaism, the essence of which was determined by 'retrojecting Rabbinic Judaism into first century Pharisaism'.[195] Boyarin has also been criticized as having created a 'contourless' Christianity and Judaism that both became 'peculiarly bloodless linguistic constructs'.[196] Like Boyarin's critics, Giorgio Jossa also moves back towards the approach of C. H. Dodd and sees already in Paul's letters (Gal. 3.28; cf. Rom. 10.12; 1 Cor. 12.13; Col. 3.11) Christianity as a *tertium genus*, alongside

---

[190]P. Frederiksen, 'How Later Contexts Affect Pauline Content, or: Retrospect Is the Mother of Anachronism', in *Jews and Christians in the First and Second Centuries: How to Write Their History*, eds P. J. Tomson and J. Schwartz (Leiden: Brill, 2014), p. 27.

[191]Simon, *Verus Israel*, p. xi.

[192]D. Boyarin, *Border Lines: The Partition of Judaeo-Christianity* (Philadelphia: University of Pennsylvania Press, 2004), p. 2.

[193]Barton and Boyarin, *Imagine No Religion*.

[194]Boyarin, *Border Lines*, p. 2.

[195]See: Alexander, 'The Parting of the Ways'.

[196]R. S. Boustan, 'Review of Border Lines', *Jewish Quarterly Review* 96 (2006): 441–6.

the traditional ones of the Jews and the Greeks.[197] Hence, the separation between Judaism and Christianity 'did not begin only with the destruction of Jerusalem by the Romans in 70, but already with the preaching of Paul (and even before him, by the Hellenists) to the Jews of the Diaspora and to the Gentiles',[198] especially, as '*Christian* communities (above all the Pauline ones) . . . had never been part of Judaism because they were born outside the synagogue. . . . In certain ways that history had really begun already with the birth of a Christian community after the death of Jesus, if not in the very preaching of the prophet of Nazareth.'[199] Jossa's results have been received with some reluctance.[200] In the title 'Christians' in Acts 11.26,[201] for example, Jossa takes as a self-designation of Christians, whereas Michael Bird contends that 'the term "Christians" seems to be predominantly an external derogatory title signifying "sycophants of Christ" and does not become an actual self-designation until the time of Ignatius of Antioch'.[202] Bird mentions three addenda and corrigenda to Jossa's conclusions: (1) The fact that Paul tried to 'win the Jew' (1 Cor. 9.20), that the gospel was for the 'Jew first' (Rom. 1.16, 2.9-10), and his experience of synagogue punishments (2 Cor. 11.24) would all suggest that Luke's portrait of Paul as missionizing among Jews and Gentiles is probably correct. That implies that his churches did include, in some locations, a mixture of Jewish and Gentile adherents. (2) That Paul rejected the imposition of the Torah upon his Gentile converts, even though it seems clear, from the collection that Paul took up for the saints in Jerusalem, that he wanted his converts to stay in a positive relationship with the Jerusalem church and thus with Jews. (3) It is difficult to see the social reality of the Pauline churches as entirely independent of Jews when their language, symbols, and scriptures remained firmly indebted to them.[203]

Accordingly, Bird queries 'whether there actually were Christian communities absolutely independent of Judaism prior to 70 C.E.', pointing to the fact that 'in the Pauline correspondence it is precisely issues related to Jewish law, Jewish identity, and Jewish theology that persistently arise'; topics that presuppose a Jewish audience or readers of a Jewish background.[204] Similarly, Jossa's reviewers found it 'questionable to speak of a Christianity of "exclusively Greek origin"' 'if it was Christian at all'.[205] Mimouni sharpens this position by stating that 'the entire Christian movement

---

[197]G. Jossa, *Jews or Christians? The Followers of Jesus in Search of their Own Identity* (Tübingen: Mohr Siebeck: 2006), p. 1.

[198]Ibid., p. 13.

[199]Ibid.

[200]See M. F. Bird, 'Review of Giorgio Jossa: Jews or Christians?', *Review of Biblical Literature* 4, no. 1 (16 February 2008): 76; S. C. Mimouni, 'Review of G. Jossa, Jews or Christians?', *Revue des Etudes Juives* 167 (2008): 594–7.

[201]See Jossa, *Jews or Christians?* pp. 126–7.

[202]Bird, 'Review of Giorgio Jossa', 76.

[203]Ibid.

[204]Ibid.

[205]C. W. Stenschke, 'Review of Giorgio Jossa, Jews or Christians? (2006)', *Vigiliae Christianae* 66 (2012): 105.

during the first and the second centuries was "Jewish", which does not exclude the 'Greek' presence that has become more and more dominant',[206] and that therefore 'all Christians until the years 100-150' were Jews, whether or not they were born Jewish. He sees the years 135–150, the aftermath of the Bar Kokhba war, as the epoch when the conflicts of identity and status between Christians of Jewish origin and those of non-Jewish origin broke out. This identity search, therefore, did not only happen between those who were born Jewish and those who were born non-Jewish, with the latter only wanting to be a 'third genus', but people, irrespective of how they were born, after the terrible outcome of the Bar Kokhba revolt against the Romans must have started to accept the earlier shame-name of 'Christians', with some (such as Marcion, Ignatius, some so-called apologists) not only maintaining links to Jews (as Justin demonstrates, despite all the differences, with his *Dialogue with Trypho*) but reflecting about their self-identity with the creation of names for the respective entities ('Judaism', 'Christianity'), while many others continued to observe the Torah either literally or spiritually and allegorically.

The diversity of Torah-adherence was often due to the individual agents of Torah-transmission.

Local judges, teachers, scribes, and so on, who were (as far as most Judaeans were concerned) the representatives of Torah. Whether or not they were intelligent men who had studied the Pentateuch and learned how to interpret it, they necessarily had to confront all sorts of traditional local practices, which some of them may have sometimes tried to reconcile with the Pentateuch. In addition, it was less the various local agents themselves who set out the Torah, as 'its authority rested not simply (and initially perhaps not at all) on the consensus of the Jews, but on the might of the imperial and native rulers of Palestine'.[207]

DIVERSE JEWISH STRATEGIES AFTER THE BAR KOKHBA REVOLT

If Christian scholarship dates the institutional separation 'to a very early stage', it must be one 'between strands of Judaism': between those 'which did not attach any importance to the person of Jesus and those which did'.[208] Taking into account the previous observations, even the entity of 'Judaism' is questionable, as too much of our present understanding of Judaism has been rejected into this label, as Goodman has demonstrated. That developments of identities took place is undeniable, just as it would be entirely normal if rivalry, estrangements and often mutual ignorance between the various Jewish strands during the first two or three centuries were to exist. A further complexity arises when assessing the first two centuries since

---

[206]Mimouni, 'Review of G. Jossa', p. 596.
[207]S. Schwartz, *Imperialism and Jewish Society: 200 B.C.E. to 640 C.E.* (Princeton, NJ: Princeton University Press, 2001), pp. 56, 68.
[208]Kinzig, 'Non-Separation', p. 29.

most of the writings from this time (including those of Jewish writers such as Philo and Josephus) have come down to us only through a long history of Christian transmission. They have been shaped through centuries of Christian rewritings and re-readings of their origins. And with this comes the issue of placing and dating these writings, for which external and internal evidence is mostly lacking. As a result, it is hardly possible to place most writings of the first two centuries precisely to a specific time or place.[209] If, for example, the traditional dating of the twenty-seven New Testament writings as being first century is correct (a premise on which the Christian narrative of the history of Jewish-Christian relations is often built), it would imply an earlier institutional split, but one would also expect to see a clearer self-identity of church versus synagogue. This, however, does not seem to be the case. If the destruction of the Temple of Jerusalem and the introduction of the *Fiscus Iudaicus*[210] led to a growing self-awareness of being Jewish[211] (because of the political obligation to declare by the payment of tax whether or not one counted oneself to be part of the Jewish community), we have no evidence that any Christ-follower rejected paying this tax. We only know of one Jewish tax avoider, and it is often stated that the Gospel saying seems to be related to this tax with the indication that Christ-followers ought to pay it (by giving to Caesar what is Caesar's).

Indeed, some inhabitants of Israel, and especially of the annexed provinces of Galilee, Samaria, Idumaea and Peraea, may only now, under the policing instituted by Vespasian (though how rigorous these measures were, is unclear), have had to decide whether or not they regarded themselves formally as Jews who needed to pay this tax.

'In contrast to the silence on the subject of proselytism in gentile texts before A.D. 96, there survives a series of comments, mostly very unfavourable, about such conversions in texts written in the early second century A.D.'[212] Proselytes who had joined the communities of 'Christians' may only now have had to declare themselves towards the Roman officials as belonging to Judaism, which would explain why, in texts of this period, we have the first discussions of the legal status of 'Christians', as we can see from the letter exchange between Pliny the Younger and the Emperor Trajan.

That 'Christians' were not asked to pay this tax, or that they did not pay it by apostatizing from Judaism or, in contrast, because they wanted to remain truthful to Judaism by not paying tax to a Roman emperor,[213] cannot be ascertained from our

---

[209]See Vinzent, 'Origenes als Postscriptum. Paulinus von Tyrus und die origenistische Diadoche'; M. Vinzent, *Christ's Resurrection in Early Christianity and the Making of the New Testament* (Farnham: Ashgate, 2011).

[210]See, Suetonius, *Domitian*, 12.1-2.

[211]So, M. Goodman, 'Nerva, the Fiscus Iudaicus and Jewish Identity', *Journal of Roman Studies* 79 (1989): 40–4. On the controversy surrounding discussion of the *Fiscus* see Bibliography for Heemstra (2010 and idem, 2014).

[212]Such as Epictetus, *Disc.*, 2.9.20; Juvenal, *Sat.*, 14.96-104; Tacitus, *Ann.*, 5.5.2. See, M. Goodman, 'Diaspora Reactions to the Destruction of the Temple', in Dunn (ed.), *Jews and Christians*, p. 33.

[213]So Jossa, *Jews or Christians?* pp. 138–44.

sources. From Suetonius it becomes clear that not only Jews by birth who 'concealed' their Jewish origin but also those who did not profess to be Jews (apparently not Jews by birth, but proselytes) were prosecuted for tax evasion. In addition, the story in Lk. 20.17-26 (also present in Marcion's Gospel), Mk. 12.10-7 and Matt. 21.42–22.22 about paying tax to the emperor rather points in the direction of 'Christians' having been encouraged to pay the *Fiscus Iudaicus*.[214] The Gospel story is not only set in the Temple, but it is also preceded by the quote from the (Temple) Psalm 118 and thus makes a direct connection between the Temple and tax payments. Hugh Montefiore seems right when he noted that the Gospel story, written after 70 CE, was not only a general remark about the Jewish payment of tax to the emperor but specifically about an indication, how to deal with the Temple tax that had become diverted to the Roman officials. It is certainly dubious to claim on such basis that 'Christians' 'did not pay the tax' and hence 'were clearly not Jews'.[215]

One more argument speaks for an increased need to self-define one's own belonging after the Bar Kokhba disaster, when it was opportune for those who wanted to live within the Roman Empire to distance themselves from Jewish revolutionaries and Jewishness. A good example of this are writings of Justin and those of the so-called apologists, particularly Aristides of Athens.

Aristides is (if one discounts his contemporary Quadratus, of whose *Apology* only fragments survive) the earliest of our apologists and most likely writes towards the end of the reign of Hadrian, or more likely during the early years of Antoninus Pius (138–161), hence after the Bar Kokhba war. If one follows the early datings of the New Testament, with strong views against Jews and the synagogue, as, for example, in John and in Acts, then why do we find our very first reflections on distinguishing Greeks, Jews and Christians only after the end of the Bar Kokhba war? It is noticeable that Aristides does not talk about Romans but only mentions three or four groups (depending on the surviving versions of his text that we can assess) that still do not carry the abstract names of 'Hellenismos', 'Judaismos' or 'Christianismos', and he reflects about their origin and nature.[216]

Likewise, Justin takes the Roman Empire for granted but endeavours to define Christians in contrast to Jews. The most radical and, as I have suggested, first attempt to coin the antithesis between 'Iudaismos' and 'Christianismos' is found in Marcion's *Preface* to the edition of his 'New Testament'. As Tertullian reports,

> Marcion lays it down that there is one Christ who in the time of Tiberius was revealed by a god formerly unknown, for the salvation of all the nations; and another Christ who is destined by God the Creator to come at some time still

---

[214]Astonishingly, these Gospel passages are not dealt with in Heemstra, *Fiscus Judaicus*, nor does he deal with the story in Matt. 27:24-7 according to which Peter and Jesus confirm that they are paying the Jewish temple tax.

[215]*Pace* Goodman, 'Diaspora Reactions', p. 33, following Heemstra, *Jews and Christians in the First and Second Centuries: How to Write Their History* (Leiden: Brill, 2014), p. 337.

[216]Further, see W. A. Simpson, 'Aristides' Apology and the Novel Barlaam and Ioasaph' (PhD. Diss., London: King's College, 2015).

future for the restitution of the Jewish status. Between these he sets up a great and absolute opposition, such as that between justice and kindness, between law and gospel, between Judaism and Christianity.[217]

In this first historical occurrence of the two joint labels of 'Judaism' and 'Christianity', they mark the difference not only between two sets of laws (law, gospel), or the interpretation of those laws (justice, kindness), but also between future political and theological outlooks (reestablishment of the Jewish kingdom, salvation of all the nations). Given that this Preface seems to have been written soon after the end of the Bar Kokhba war, it still reflects the issues of the day. And with its declared pacifism, Marcion seems to consciously distance himself and Christianity from a Judaism that is intending to reassert its former status. Yet, he neither claims, as Justin did after him, that Christianity disinherits Judaism nor did he claim that Judaism ceased to exist since the new condition of Christianity appeared, as Tertullian did.[218] To Marcion, Judaism was the contrasting mirror and the competitive environment in which Christianity was to flourish. The enormous reception that Marcion's distinction between 'Christianity' and 'Judaism', between 'Old' and 'New Testament', between 'law' and 'gospel', between universal salvation and 'restitution of the Jewish status' received, among almost all the writers and apologists of the late second century, was to close, or at least bridge, the drastic gap between the two entities that was created by Marcion, even among those who subsequently accepted the principle of a division, which was increasingly the post-Marcionite result. Even though the idea of Christianity as a new form of worship (*novitas Christiana*), with its own 'New Testament', can be found in the authors discussed here, in Eusebius, Chrysostom and others, for example, they all still attempted to reconnect this new entity with the old one of Judaism, perhaps out of recognition or even pressured by a lived reality that differed widely from the theoretical distinction Marcion had attempted to create.

NON-SEPARATION, AN AFTERWORD

In an important contribution to the question of Jewish-Christian relations in the early church, Wolfram Kinzig differentiated between four 'levels on which separation could and did take place, viz. the doctrinal, the theological, the institutional levels and the level of popular piety'.[219] Irrespective of which level we look at, we need to be aware that we approach these levels as a retrospective view and need to be cautious as to what extent our experience of different (often separated and in many ways distinct and often competing) world religions[220] such as those of contemporary

---

[217]*Marc.*, 4.6.3. (my trans. adapting that of Evans).

[218]*Marc.*, 4.33.8.

[219]Kinzig, 'Non-Separation', p. 27.

[220]On the problematic concept of 'world-religion' which by using it here, I do not subscribe to, see T. Masuzawa, *The Invention of World Religions or, How European Universalism was Preserved in the Language of Pluralism* (Chicago: University of Chicago Press, 2005).

Christianity and Judaism, cloud our reading of documents from the early church. To come back to Chrysostom's *Orations* in the light of Kinzig's statement that 'perhaps the most significant step towards Judaism was to actually get circumcised'.[221] Can this perspective be an anachronistical inversion? If those Christians, who are criticized by Chrysostom, habitually practiced circumcision while being also members of his church congregation, circumcision was not a question of a move 'towards Judaism', but Chrysostom's *Orations* highlight the problem of making people move away from a practice that he linked to an entity that only through his discourses were meant to become another 'ism', not because either this 'ism' or Chrysostom's own 'ism' existed. Part of apologetics is the very creation of boundaries and yet, as we can see through history, in the process that apologetics makes those 'isms' become a reality.

We mentioned James Parkes early on in this chapter, and I would like to close with him. In his introduction to the Eliot lectures, given in Chicago in the years 1946–7, Parkes said:

> I speak as a Christian, as one who believes in the essential truth of fundamental Christian doctrine, but in a sense I also speak as a Jew. That is, I speak on the basis of believing Judaism also to be true – as true as Christianity. . . . Both religions are true. Neither is simply an incomplete form of the other; and I do not desire to see either disappear, even by conversion to the other . . . Sinai and Calvary [are] two closely interlocked and complementary stages of a single divine plan. . . . In Judaism and Christianity together the 'I-Thou' relationship of a free creation is ultimately fulfilled. But in each is an essential part-fulfilment, and until there appears the way by which they can fulfil the two together without losing their own essential nature, each must fulfil its own part.[222]

'Even more than half a century later, for not a few thoughtful, mainstream Christians' these remain 'deeply disturbing notions', setting Christianity and Judaism on an equal footing, declaring both to be true and complementary of each other. They have been called 'problematic', 'pretentious' and 'awkward for a Jewish eye'.[223] Yet Parkes is also a witness that for anyone who has fought against anti-semitism as 'a pioneer, nay a revolutionary, in . . . recasting Christian and Jewish relations',[224] the long history of the creation of one 'ity' and another 'ism' made it possible to only think of an 'I-Thou' relationship of two different religions, Christianity and Judaism, that were separated already from the first century onwards.[225] The understanding and acceptance that these two entities had split had become too entrenched, even though a close retrospective reading, at least of the early centuries of our common

[221]Kinzig, 'Non-Separation', p. 37.

[222]Chertok, *He also Spoke as a Jew*, p. 368; J. Parkes, *Judaism and Christianity* (London: Victor Gollancz, 1948), pp. 18–19.

[223]So Jessica van't Westeinde in an Email to the author 26 August 2020.

[224]Irving Greenberg's Foreword in Chertok, *He also Spoke as a Jew*, p. ix.

[225]See Parkes, *The Conflict*, pp. 27–120.

era, reveals that on none of the levels, set out by Kinzig (except for what he called the 'theological' which I would rather term the 'apologetical'), did these separate entities exist.

Ever since the time Marcion coined the oppositional terms of 'Judaismos' and 'Christianismos', with 'Ignatius' and others following him, it took a long time, until they marked doctrinal differences and entered synodal canons, impacting the laws of the state. While it was Roman politics to exile Jews from Jerusalem and a cultural distinction was notable with regard to Hebrew/Aramaic-writing Jews (who required physical circumcision and reinterpreted the Jewish tradition in a non-sacrificial Torah-orientation), even so the predominantly Greek and Latin-speaking Jews had already opted for a spiritual interpretation of the Torah. In the light of this, following Marcion's collection of the New Testament around the middle of the second century, that second Testament within a few decades became perceived as an alternative, complementary and soon dominating collection of sacred Scriptures, through which lens the entire Jewish heritage started to be perceived. According to Guy Stroumsa,[226] the Jewish tradition (which had adhered more closely to its older sacrificial orientation) itself eventually adopted Marcion's terminological divide, a position that became pervasive, albeit only much later.

BIBLIOGRAPHY

Adler, W. 'Eusebius' Chronicle and Its Legacy', in H. W. Attridge and G. Hata (eds), *Eusebius, Christianity, and Judaism*. Detroit, MI: Wayne State University Press, 1992.

Ages, A. 'Luther and the Rabbis', *The Jewish Quarterly Review* 58 (1967): 63–8.

Alexander, P. S. '"The Parting of the Ways" from the Perspective of Rabbinic Judaism', in J. D. G. Dunn (ed.), *Jews and Christians: The Parting of the Ways. AD. 70 to 135*. Grand Rapids, MI: William B. Eerdmans, 1992.

Alexis, J. E. *Christianity and Rabbinic Judaism: A History of Conflict between Christianity and Rabbinic Judaism from the Early Church to Our Modern Time*. Bloomington, IN: WestBow Press, 2013.

Avery-Peck, A. J. and Neusner, J. *Judaism and Christianity: New Directions for Dialogue and Understanding*. Leiden: Brill, 2009.

Bady, G. 'L'antijudaïsme banalisé. Des homélies de Jean Chrysostom à leurs avatars: l'exemple du sermon inédit Sur le paralytique (CPG 4857)', in G. Bady and D. Cuny (eds), *Les polémiques religieuses du Ier au IVe siècle de notre ère. Hommage à Bernard Pouderon*. Paris: Beauchesne, 2019.

Bakhtin, M. M., Emerson, C. and Holquist, M. *Speech Genres and Other Late Essays*. Austin: University of Texas Press, 1986.

Bardenhewer, O. *Geschichte der altkirchlichen Literatur*. Freiburg im Breisgau: Herder, 1923.

---

[226]G. Stroumsa, 'The End of Sacrifice: Religious Mutations of Late Antiquity', in *Empsychoi Logoi: Religious Innovations in Antiquity: Studies in Honour of Pieter Willem van der Horst*, eds A. Houtman et al. (Leiden: Brill, 2008).

Barnes, T. D. *Constantine and Eusebius*. Cambridge, MA: Harvard University Press, 1996.

Barton, C. A. and Boyarin, D. *Imagine No Religion: How Modern Abstractions Hide Ancient Realities*. New York: Fordham University Press, 2016.

Baumgarten, A. I. 'Marcel Simon's "Verus Israel" as a Contribution to Jewish History', *The Harvard Theological Review* 92 (1999): 465–78.

Berger, D. *Persecution, Polemic, and Dialogue: Essays in Jewish-Christian Relations*. Boston, MA: Academic Studies Press, 2010.

Bibliowicz, A. M. *Jews and Gentiles in the Early Jesus Movement: An Unintended Journey*. New York: Palgrave, 2013.

Bienert, W. A. 'Marcion und der Antijudaismus', in G. May and K. Greschat (eds), *Marcion und seine kirchengeschichtliche Wirkung*. Berlin: DeGruyter, 2002.

Bird, M. F. 'Review of Giorgio Jossa: Jews or Christians? (2006)', *Review of Biblical Literature* 4, no. 1 (16 February 2008): 76.

Black, S. K. 'Ethnic Judeans and Christian Identity Formation in John Chrysostom's Adversus Judaeos', in S. K. Black (ed.), *To Set at Liberty: Essays on Early Christianity and Its Social World in Honor of John H. Elliott*. Sheffield: Sheffield Phoenix Press, 2014.

Blanchetière, F. 'De l'importance de l'an 135 dans l'évolution respective de la synagogue et du christianisme', in B. Pouderon and Y.-M. Duval (eds), *L'historiographie de l'église des premiers siècles*, 91–6. Paris: Beauchesne, 2001.

Boustan, R. S. 'Review of Border Lines', *Jewish Quarterly Review* 96 (2006): 441–6.

Boyarin, D. *Dying for God: Martyrdom and the Making of Christianity and Judaism*. Stanford, CA: Stanford University Press, 1999.

Boyarin, D. 'Semantic Differences; or, "Judaism" / "Christianity"', in A. H. Becker and D. Boyarin (eds), *The Ways that Never Parted: Jews and Christians in Late Antiquity and the Early Middle Ages*. Tübingen: Mohr Siebeck, 2003.

Boyarin, D. *Border Lines: The Partition of Judaeo-Christianity*. Philadelphia: University of Pennsylvania Press, 2004.

Boyarin, D. 'Why Ignatius Invented Judaism', in L. Baron (ed.), *The Ways that Often Parted: Essays in Honor of Joel Marcus*. Atlanta, GA: SBL Press, 2018.

Brändle, R., Heimgartner, M. and Pradels, W. 'Das bisher vermisste Textstück in Johannes Chrysostomus, Adversus Judaeos, Oratio 2"', *Zeitschrift für Antikes Christentum* 5 (2001): 23–49.

Breidenthal, T. 'Neighbor-Christology: Reconstructing Christianity before Supersessionism', *CrossCurrents* 49 (1999): 319–48.

Brennecke, H. C. 'Die Kirche als ΔΙΑΔΟΧΑΙ ΤΩΝ ΑΠΟΣΤΟΛΩΝ. Das Programm der ΕΚΚΛΗΣΙΑΣΤΙΚΗ ΙΣΤΟΡΙΑ des Euseb von Caesarea (Eus h.e. I.1)', in O. Wischmeyer and E. M. Becker (eds), *Wast ist ein Text?* Tübingen: A. Francke, 2001.

Brody, R. *The Geonim of Babylonia and the Shaping of Medieval Jewish Culture*. New Haven, CT: Yale University Press, 1998.

Burgess, R. W. 'Jerome Explained: An Introduction to His Chronicle and a Guide to Its Use', *Ancient History Bulletin* 16 (2002): 1–32.

Burgess, R. W. *Studies in Eusebian and Post-Eusebian Chronography*. vol. 1. *The Chronici Canones of Eusebius of Caesarea: Structure, Content, and Chronology*, AD 282–325. Stuttgart: Franz Steiner Verlag, 2018.

Burgess, R. W. *Studies in Eusebian and Post-Eusebian Chronography*. vol. 2. *The Continuatio Antiochiensis Eusebii: A Chronicle of Antioch and the Roman Near East during the Reigns of Constantine and Constantius II, AD 325–350*. Stuttgart: Franz Steiner Verlag, 2018.

Cameron, R. 'Alternate Beginnings - Different Ends: Eusebius, Thomas, and the Construction of Christian Origins', in L. Bormann K. Del Tredici and A. Standhartinger (eds), *Religious Propaganda and Missionary Competition in the New Testament World*. Leiden: Brill, 1994.

Carleton-Paget, J. 'Some Observations on Josephus and Christianity', *The Journal of Theological Studies* 52 (2001): 539–624.

Chertok, H. *He Also Spoke as a Jew: The Life of James Parkes*. London: Vallentine Mitchell, 2006.

Corke-Webster, J. 'A Man for the Times: Jesus and the Abgar Correspondence in Eusebius of Caesarea's Ecclesiastical History', *The Harvard Theological Review* 110 (2017): 563–87.

Côté, D. 'Le problème de l'identité religieuse dans la Syrie du IVe siècle', in S. C. Mimouni and B. Pouderon (eds), *La croisée des chemins revisitée*. Paris: Cerf, 2012.

Drake, S. *Slandering the Jew: Sexuality and Difference in Early Christian Texts*. Philadelphia: University of Pennsylvania Press, 2013.

Droge, A. J. 'The Apologetic Dimensions of the Ecclesiastical History', in H. W. Attridge and G. Hata (eds), *Eusebius, Christianity, and Judaism*. Detroit, MI: Wayne State University Press, 1992.

Dubuisson, D. *The Western Construction of Religion: Myths, Knowledge, and Ideology*. Baltimore, MD: Johns Hopkins University Press, 2003.

Dunn, G. D. (ed.). *Jews and Christians: The Parting of the Ways. AD. 70 to 135*. Grand Rapids, MI: William B. Eerdmans, 1992.

Fau, G. 'Eusèbe de Césarée et son histoire de l'église', *Cahier du cercle Ernest-Renan* 24 (1976): 1–32.

Feldman, L. H. *Josephus and Modern Scholarship (1937–1980)*. Berlin: de Gruyter, 1984.

Feldman, L. H. *Studies in Hellenistic Judaism*. Leiden: Brill, 1996.

Frank, K. S. and Grünbeck, E. *Lehrbuch der Geschichte der Alten Kirche*. Paderborn: Schöningh, 1997.

Frederiksen, P. 'What "Parting of the Ways"? Jews, Gentiles, and the Ancient Mediterranean City', in A. H. Becker and A. Y. Reed (eds), *The Ways that Never Parted: Jews and Christians in Late Antiquity and the Early Middle Ages*. Tübingen: Mohr-Siebeck, 2003.

Frederiksen, P. 'How Later Contexts Affect Pauline Content, or: Retrospect is the Mother of Anachronism', in P. J. Tomson and J. Schwartz (eds), *Jews and Christians in the First and Second Centuries: How to Write Their History*. Leiden: Brill, 2014.

Gerlach, E. *Die Weissagungen des Alten Testaments in die Schriften des Flavius Josephus und das angebliche Zeugniss von Christo*. Berlin: n.p., 1863.

Gil, M. 'The Babylonian Yeshivot and the Maghrib in the Early Middle Ages', *Proceedings of the American Academy for Jewish Research* 57 (1990–1991): 69–120.

Golsan, R. J. 'Antisemitism in Modern France: Dreyfus, Vichy, and Beyond', in A. S. Lindemann and R. S. Levy (eds), *Antisemitism: A History*. Oxford: Oxford University Press, 2010.

Goodblatt, D. 'Local Traditions in the Babylonian Talmud', *Hebrew Union College Annual* 48 (1977): 187–217.

Goodman, M. 'Nerva, the Fiscus Iudaicus and Jewish Identity', *Journal of Roman Studies* 79 (1989): 40–4.

Goodman, M. 'Diaspora Reactions to the Destruction of the Temple', in J. D. G. Dunn (ed.), *Jews and Christians: The Parting of the Ways. AD. 70 to 135*. Grand Rapids, MI: William B. Eerdmans, 1992.

Goodman, M. 'Modeling the "Parting of the Ways"', in A. H. Becker and A. Y. Reed (eds), *The Ways that Never Parted*. Tübingen: Mohr Siebeck, 2003.

Goodman, M. *Rome and Jerusalem: The Clash of Ancient Civilizations*. London: Allen Lane, 2007.

Gorsky, J. 'The Parting of the Ways: A Review Essay', *Heythrop Journal* 50 (2009): 996–8.

Grant, R. M. *Eusebius as Church Historian*. Oxford: Clarendon Press, 1980.

Graumann, T. *Die Kirche der Väter. Vätertheologie und Väterbeweis in den Kirchen des Ostens bis zum Konzil von Ephesus (431)*. Tübingen: Mohr Siebeck, 2002.

Gustafsson, B. 'Eusebius' Principles in Handling His Sources, as Found in His Church History, Books I-VII', *Studia Patristica* 4, no. 2 (1961): 429–41.

Hagner, D. A. 'Another Look at "The Parting of the Ways"', in M. F. Bird and J. Maston (eds), *Earliest Christian History. Festschrift: Martin Hengel*. Tübingen: Mohr Siebeck, 2012.

Halsall, P. 1996. 'Medieval Sourcebook: Notes on Reaction to the Posting of the Chrysostom Text on the Jews'. https://sourcebooks.fordham.edu/source/chrysostom-jews6-react.asp (accessed 15 July 2020).

Hardwick, M. E. *Josephus as an Historical Source in Patristic Literature through Eusebius*. Atlanta, GA: Scholars Press, 1989.

Harkins, P. W. *St. John Chrysostom: Discourses Against Judaizing Christians*. Washington: Catholic University of America Press, 1979.

Hayes, A. D. R. 'Defining Christianity: Justin's Contra-Marcionite Defence'. Ph.D. Diss, King's College, London, 2015.

Heemstra, M. *The Fiscus Judaicus and the Parting of the Ways*. Tubingen: Mohr Siebeck, 2010.

Heemstra, M. 'The Fiscus Judaicus: Its Social and Legal Impact and a Possible Relation with Josephus' Antiquities', in P. J. Tomson and J. Schwartz (eds), *Jews and Christians in the First and Second Centuries: How to Write Their History*. Leiden: Brill, 2014.

Heschel, S. 'Jews and Christianity', in M. Hart and T. Michels (eds), *The Cambridge History of Judaism, vol. 8: The Modern World, 1815–2000*. Cambridge: Cambridge University Press, 2017.

Hopkins, K. *A World Full of Gods: Pagans, Jews, and Christians in the Roman Empire*. London: Weidenfeld & Nicolson, 1999.

Horn, F. W. 'Das Testamentum Flavianum aus neutestamentlicher Perspektive', in C. Böttrich and J. Herzer (eds), *Josephus und das Neue Testament. Wechelseitige Wahrnehmungen*. Tübingen: Mohr Siebeck, 2007.

Horst, P. W. van der. *Hellenism, Judaism, Christianity: Essays on their Interaction*. Kampen: Kok Pharos, 1994.

Horst, P. W. van der and Karrer, M. 'Hellenism - Judaism - Christianity', *Theologische Literaturzeitung* 120 (1995): 428–9.

Jacobs, A. S. *Remains of the Jews: The Holy Land and Christian Empire in Late Antiquity*. Stanford, CA: Stanford University Press, 2004.

Jossa, G. *Jews or Christians? The Followers of Jesus in Search of their Own Identity*. Tübingen: Mohr Siebeck: 2006.

Kahl, H.-D. 'Die Vorprägung des Zusammenlebens von Christen und Juden in Deutschland durch die ältere Kirchengeschichte. Frühchristliche Wurzeln von Judenklischees und Antisemitismus', in J. Albertz (ed.), *"Judenklischees" und jüdische Wirklichkeit in unserer Gesellschaft*. Wiesbaden: Hochschul Verlag, 1985.

Karp, J. and Sutcliffe, A. *Philosemitism in History*. Cambridge: Cambridge University Press, 2011.

Kinzig, W. 'Non-Separation: Closeness and Co-operation between Jews and Christians in the Fourth Century', *Vigiliae Christianae* 45 (1991): 27–53.

Kinzig, W. 'Novitas Christiana Elektronische Ressource Die Idee des Fortschritts in der Alten Kirche bis Eusebius', in 2 *Online-Resource* (702 S.). Göttingen: Vandenhoeck & Ruprecht, 1994a.

Kinzig, W. *Novitas Christiana. Die Idee des Fortschritts in der Alten Kirche bis Eusebius*. Göttingen: Vandenhoeck und Ruprecht, 1994b.

Kinzig, W. 'Philosemitismus', Teil I: Zur Geschichte des Begriffs', *Zeitschrift für Kirchengeschichte* 105 (1994c): 202–28.

Kinzig, W. 'Philosemitismus', Teil II: Zur historiographischen Verwendung des Begriffs', *Zeitschrift für Kirchengeschichte* 105 (1994d): 361–83.

Kinzig, W. 'Philosemitismus angesichts des Endes? Bemerkungen zu einem vergessenen Kapitel jüdisch-christlicher Beziehungen in der Alten Kirche', in A. Lexutt and V. von Bülow (eds), *Kaum zu glauben. Von der Häresie und dem Umgang mit ihr*. Rheinbach: CMZ, 1998.

Kinzig, W. 'Philosemitismus – was ist das? Eine kritische Begriffsanalyse', in I. Diekmann and E. Kotowski (eds), *Geliebter Feind – gehasster Freund. Antisemitismus und Philosemitismus in Geschichte und Gegenwart. Festschrift zum 65. Geburtstag von Julius H. Schoeps*. Berlin: Verlag für Berlin Brandenburg, 2009.

Kloppenborg, J. S. *Christ's Associations: Connecting and Belonging in the Ancient City*. New Haven, CT: Yale University Press, 2019.

Kraft, H. (ed.). *Eusebius von Cäsarea, Kirchengeschichte*. Darmstadt: Wissenschaftliche Buchgesellschaft, 1989.

Laham-Cohen, R. *The Jews in Late Antiquity*. Amsterdam: Amsterdam University Press, 2018.

Lampe, P. *Die stadtrömischen Christen in den ersten beiden Jahrhunderten. Untersuchungen zur Sozialgeschichte*. Tübingen: Mohr, 1989.

Lampe, P. and Johnson, M. D. *From Paul to Valentinus: Christians at Rome in the First Two Centuries*. Minneapolis, MN: Fortress Press, 2003.

Laqueur, W. *The Changing Face of Antisemitism: From Ancient Times to the Present Day*. Oxford: Oxford University Press, 2006.

Lieu, J. *Image and Reality: The Jews in the World of the Christians in the Second Century*. Edinburgh: T&T Clark, 1996.

Maccoby, H. *The Mythmaker: Paul and the Invention of Christianity*. London: Weidenfeld & Nicolson, 1986.

Mack, B. L. 'After "Drudgery Divine"', *Numen* 39 (1992): 225–33.

Mason, S. *Flavius Josephus und das Neue Testament*. Tübingen: Francke, 2000.

Masuzawa, T. *The Invention of World Religions or, How European Universalism was Preserved in the Language of Pluralism*. Chicago: University of Chicago Press, 2005.

Mayer, W. 'Preaching Hatred? John Chrysostom, Neuroscience, and the Jews', in C. L. de Wet and W. Mayer (eds), *Revisioning John Chrysostom: New Approaches, New Perspectives*. Leiden: Brill, 2019.

Mendels, D. *The Media Revolution of Early Christianity: An Essay on Eusebius's Ecclesiastical History*. Grand Rapids, MI: Eerdmans, 1999.

Mendels, D. 'The Sources of the Ecclesiastical History of Eusebius: The Case of Josephus', in B. Pouderon and Y.-M. Duval (eds), *L'historiographie de l'église des premiers siècles*. Paris: Beauchesne, 2001.

Mimouni, S. C. 'Review of G. Jossa, Jews or Christians?', *Revue des Etudes Juives* 167 (2008): 594–7.

Momigliano, A. 'Heidnische und christliche Geschichtsschreibung im 4. Jh', in W. Nippel (ed.), *Ausgewählte Schriften zur Geschichte und Geschichtsschreibung*. Stuttgart: Weimar, 1963.

Montefiore, H. 'Jesus and the Temple Tax', *New Testament Studies* 11 (1964–1965): 60–71.

Mosshammer, A. *The Chronicle of Eusebius and Greek Chronographic Tradition*. Lewisburg: Bucknell University Press, 1979.

Nicklas, T. 'Parting of the Ways? Probleme eines Konzepts', in S. Roder (ed.), *Juden, Christen, Heiden? Religiöse Inklusion und Exklusion in Kleinasien bis Decius*. Tübingen: Mohr Siebeck, 2018.

Nongbri, B. *Before Religion: A History of a Modern Concept*. New Haven, CT: Yale University Press, 2013.

Olson, K. A. 'Eusebius and the Testamentum Flavianum', *Catholic Biblical Quarterly* 61 (1999): 305–22.

Overbeck, F. *Über die Anfänge der Kirchengeschichtsschreibung*. Basel: Reinhardt, 1892.

Parkes, J. *The Jew and His Neighbour*. London: SCM Press, 1930.

Parkes, J. *The Conflict of the Church and the Synagogue: A Study in the Origins of Antisemitism*. London: Soncino Press, 1934.

Parkes, J. *Judaism and Christianity*. London: Victor Gollancz, 1948.

Parkes, J. *Prelude to Dialogue: Jewish-Christian Relationships*. London: Vallentine Mitchell, 1969.

Perczel, I. 'Finding a Place for the Erotapokriseis of Pseudo-Caesarius: A New Document of Sixth-Century Palestinian Origenism', *ARAM* 18–19 (2006–2007): 49–83.

Perczel, I. 'Clandestine Heresy and Politics in Sixth-Century Constantinople: Theodore of Caesarea at the Court of Justinian', in H. Amirav and F. Celia (eds), *New Themes, New Styles in the Eastern Mediterranean: Christian, Jewish, and Islamic Encounters, 5th–8th Centuries*. Leuven: Peeters, 2017a.

Perczel, I. 'Universal Salvation as an Antidote to Apocalyptic Expectations: Origenism in the Service of Justinian's Religious Politics', in H. Amirav, E. Grypeou and G.

Stroumsa (eds), *Apocalypticism and Eschatology in Late Antiquity: Encounters in the Abrahamic Religions, 6th–8th Centuries*. Leuven: Peeters, 2017b.

Perczel, I. 'Is John Chrysostom the Father of Byzantine and Orthodox Christian Antisemitism? In Memoriam Zvetlana Michaela Tanasa (Mother Heruvina in the monastic orders)', in *The Byzantine Liturgy and the Jews*. (Papers of the Institute of Ecumenical Research, Lucian Blaga University, Sibiu, 9–11 July 2019), (publication forthcoming).

Perry, M. and Schweitzer, F. M. *Jewish-Christian Encounters over the Centuries: Symbiosis, Prejudice, Holocaust, Dialogue*. New York: Peter Lang, 1994.

Portnoff, S., Diamond, J. A. and Yaffe, M. D. *Emil L. Fackenheim: Philosopher, Theologian, Jew*. Leiden: Brill, 2008.

Pradels, W., Brändle, R. and Heimgartner, M. 'The Sequence and Dating of the Series of John Chrysostom's Eight Discourses Adversus Iudaeos', *Zeitschrift für Antikes Christentum* 6 (2002): 90–116.

Price, R. M. 'Christianity, Diaspora Judaism, and Roman Crisis', *The Review of Rabbinic Judaism* 5 (2002): 316–31.

Reed, A. Y. '"Jewish Christianity" after the "Parting of the Ways": Approaches to Historiography and Self-Definition in the Pseudo-Clementine Literature', in A. H. Becker and A. Y. Reed (eds), *The Ways that Never Parted: Jews and Christians in Late Antiquity and the Early Middle Ages*. Tübingen: Mohr Siebeck, 2003.

Reed, A. Y. *Jewish-Christianity and the History of Judaism: Collected Essays*. Tübingen: Mohr Siebeck, 2018.

Reichardt, W. (ed.). *Die Briefe des Sextus Julius Africanus an Aristides und Origenes*. Leipzig: Hinrichs, 1909.

Robinson, T. A. *Ignatius of Antioch and the Parting of the Ways: Early Jewish-Christian Relations*. Peabody, MA: Hendrickson, 2009.

Rowland, C. and Tuckett, C. 'The Parting of the Ways: The Evidence of Jewish and Christian Apocalyptic and Mystical Material', in J. D. G. Dunn (ed.), *Jews and Christians: The Parting of the Ways. AD. 70 to 135*. Grand Rapids, MI: William B. Eerdmans, 1992.

Ruether, R. R. *Faith and Fratricide: The Theological Roots of Anti-Semitism*. New York: Seabury Press, 1974.

Runia, D. T. *Philo in Early Christian Literature: A Survey*. Minneapolis, MN: Fortress Press, 1993.

Saldarini, A. J., Avery-Peck, A., Harrington, D. J. and Neusner, J. *When Judaism and Christianity began: Essays in Memory of Anthony J. Saldarini*. Leiden: Brill, 2004.

Scheck, T. P. [Eusebius of Caesarea's] *Apology for Origen*. Washington, DC: Catholic University of America Press, 2010.

Schiffman, L. H. *Who was a Jew?: Rabbinic and Halakhic Perspectives on the Jewish Christian Schism*. Hoboken, NJ: Ktav Publishing House, 1985.

Schmitt, C. *Politische Theologie II. Die Legende von der Erledigung jeder Politischen Theologie*. Berlin: Duncker & Humbolt, 1970.

Schreckenberg, H. *Die Flavius-Josephus-Tradition in Antike und Mittelalter*. Leiden: Brill, 1972.

Schwartz, E. (ed.). *Eusebios von Caesarea*. Berlin: Griechische Geschichtschreiber, 1959.

Schwartz, E. (ed.). 'Über Kirchengeschichte', in Idem, *Gesammelte Schriften*. Berlin: De Gruyter, 1963.

Schwartz, S. *Imperialism and Jewish Society, 200 B.C.E. to 640 C.E.* Princeton, NJ: Princeton University Press, 2001.

Schwartz, S. 'How Many Judaisms Were There? A Critique of Neusner and Smith on Definition and Mason and Boyarin on Categorization', *Journal of Ancient Judaism* 2 (2011): 208–38.

Shepardson, C. *Anti-Judaism and Christian Orthodoxy: Ephrem's Hymns in Fourth-Century Syria*. Washington, DC: Catholic University of America Press, 2008.

Shepardson, C. *Controlling Contested Places: Late Antique Antioch and the Spatial Politics of Religious Controversy*. Oakland: University of California Press, 2019.

Simon, M. *Verus Israel: A Study of the Relations between Christians and Jews in the Roman Empire (135 –425)*. Oxford: Oxford University Press - for the Littman Library, 1986.

Simpson, W. A. 'Aristides' Apology and the Novel Barlaam and Ioasaph', PhD. Diss. London: King's College, 2015.

Sirinelli, J.-F. *Les vues historiques d'Eusèbe de Césarée durant la période prénicéenne*. Dakar: University Press, 1961.

Smith, J. Z. *Drudgery Divine. On the Comparison of Early Christianity and the Religions of Late Antiquity*. Chicago: Chicago University Press, 1990.

Spiegel, G. M. *The Past as Text: The Theory and Practice of Medieval Historiography*. Baltimore, MD: Johns Hopkins University Press, 1999.

Spoerl, K. McC. and Vinzent, M. [Eusebius of Caesarea:] *Against Marcellus and On Ecclesiastical Theology*. Washington, DC: Catholic University of America Press, 2017.

Stenschke, C. W. 'Review of Giorgio Jossa, Jews or Christians? (2006)', *Vigiliae Christianae* 66 (2012): 103–5.

Stroumsa, G. 'The End of Sacrifice: Religious Mutations of Late Antiquity', in A. Houtman, P. Willemvan der Horst, A. de Jong and W. Wilhelmina Misset- van de Weg (eds), *Empsychoi Logoi: Religious Innovations in Antiquity: Studies in Honour of Pieter Willem van der Horst*. Leiden: Brill, 2008.

Strumzah, G. 'From Anti-judaism to Antisemitism in Early Christianity?' in O. Limor (ed.), *Contra Iudaeos*. Tübingen: Mohr-Siebeck, 1996.

Stuhlmacher, P. 'Das Christusbild der Paulus-Schule – eine Skizze', in J. D. G. Dunn (ed.), *Jews and Christians: The Parting of the Ways. AD. 70 to 135*. Grand Rapids, MI: William B. Eerdmans, 1992.

Tajfel, H. 'Social Identity and Intergroup Behaviour', *Social Science Information* 13 (1974): 65–93.

Taylor, M. S. *Anti-Judaism and Early Christian Identity: A Critique of the Scholarly Consensus*. Leiden: Brill, 1995.

Tetz, M. 'Christenvolk und Abrahamsverheißung. Zum "kirchengeschichtlichen" Programm des Eusebius von Caesarea', in T. Klauser (ed.), *Jenseitsvorstellungen in Antike und Christentum. Gedenkschrift für A. Stuiber. Jahrbüch für Antike u. Christentum*. Ergänzungsband, 9. Münster: Aschendorf, 1982.

Timpe, D. 'Was ist Kirchengeschichte? Zum Gattungscharakter der Historia Ecclesiastica des Eusebius', in W. Dahlheim (ed.), *Festschrift R. Werner*. Konstanz: Universitätsverlag, 1989.

Ulrich, J. *Euseb von Caesarea und die Juden: Studien zur Rolle der Juden in der Theologie des Eusebius von Caesarea*. Berlin: de Gruyter, 1999.

Vannier, M.-A. *Judaïsme et christianisme dans les commentaires patristiques de la Genèse*. Bern: P. Lang, 2014.

Vinzent, M. 'Origenes als Postscriptum. Paulinus von Tyrus und die origenistische Diadoche', in W. A. Bienert and U. Kühneweg (eds), *Origeniana Septima. Origenes in den Auseinandersetzungen des 4. Jahrhunderts*. Leuven: University Press, 1999.

Vinzent, M. *Christ's Resurrection in Early Christianity And the Making of the New Testament*. Farnham: Ashgate, 2011.

Vinzent, M. *Marcion and the Dating of the Synoptic Gospels*. Leuven: Peeters, 2013.

Vinzent, M. *Offener Anfang. Die Anfänge des Christentums im 2. Jahrhundert*. Freiburg im Breslau: Herder, 2019a.

Vinzent, M. *Writing the History of Early Christianity: From Reception to Retrospection*. Cambridge: Cambridge University Press, 2019b.

Vittinghoff, F. 'Zum geschichtlichen Selbstverständnis der Spätantike', *Historische Zeitschrift* 198 (1964): 529–73.

Wallace-Hadrill, D. S. *Eusebius of Caesarea*. London: Mowbray, 1960.

Wallraff, M. *Der Kirchenhistoriker Sokrates. Untersuchungen zu Geschichts- darstellung, Methode und Person*. Göttingen: Vandenhoeck und Ruprecht, 1997.

Wertheim, D. J. (ed.). *The Jew as Legitimation: Jewish-Gentile Relations Beyond Antisemitism and Philosemitism*. London: Palgrave Macmillan, 2017.

Whealey, A. 'Josephus, Eusebius of Caesarea, and the Testimonium Flavianum', in C. Böttrich and J. Herzer (eds), *Josephus und das Neue Testament. Wechelseitige Wahrnehmungen*. Tübingen: Mohr Siebeck, 2007.

Wilken, R. L. *John Chrysostom and the Jews: Rhetoric and Reality in the Late 4th Century*. Berkeley: University of California Press, 1983.

Winkelmann, F. *Euseb von Kaisareia. Der Vater der Kirchengeschichte*. Berlin: Verlags-Anst. Union, 1991.

CHAPTER 3

Graeco-Roman culture and Christians

Good neighbours?

PIOTR ASHWIN-SIEJKOWSKI

INTRODUCTION: THE ALEXAMENOS GRAFFITO – A LIMITED WINDOW ON THE LANDSCAPE

Discovered in 1857 in a house in the Imperial Palace of Emperor Caligula, the famous Alexamenos graffito depicts, as we know from the inscription, Alexamenos in front of a crucified man with the head of a donkey. One of Alexamenos' hands is raised which leads modern commentators to suggest that the graffito shows him in the act of worshipping the crucified man.[1] It is agreed that the graffito is a mocking description of a Christian who worshipped the crucified Christ. The relict seems to confirm the long-standing opinion that, for Graeco-Roman observers and critics, Christianity was a new cult, more precisely, a new superstition which combined irrational beliefs with a strong emotional attachment. But was that view widespread among Graeco-Roman neighbours during the first three centuries of the Common Era? Was the Roman Empire highly intolerant towards new religions? Were Christians spied on, chased, persecuted and killed by the Roman authorities in all provinces? And finally, was mockery the dominant attitude towards the followers of Jesus' teaching? This chapter investigates some details known to us from ancient sources, which challenge these and other assumptions.

---

[1]For the image, see E. Ferguson, *Background of Early Christianity*, 3rd edn (Grand Rapids, MI: William B. Eerdmans Publishing Company, 2003), p. 597. For the resent discussion, see Felicity Harley-McGowan, 'Alexamenos Graffito', in *The Reception of Jesus in the First Three Centuries*, eds Chris Keith, Helen K. Bond, Christine Jacobi and Jens Schröter, vol. 3 (New York and London: T&T Clark, 2019), pp. 105–40.

RELIGION AND THE MENTALITY OF
THE LATE ROMAN EMPIRE

A sketch of Roman religion and mentality should help us to understand better the growth and challenge of Christian communities emerging within this period. First, the vital notion of 'religion' calls for some additional comments. We should be aware of one of our notions 'at work' of a religion as a set of doctrines and rituals claiming to be a human response to a divine revelation.[2] For the ancient intellectuals, especially during the second century CE, *religio* referred to certain, distinguished opinions on gods combined with a commitment to a way of life (orthopraxy).[3] Another important correction comes from the observation that ancient Roman authors did not claim that one 'religion' was more true than another, while within a religious tradition there was no notion of 'heresy'. These later Christian additions shaped the understanding of religion in centuries to come.

Cicero famously said that each city has its own religion and that his metropolis, Rome, has one as well (*Flac.*, 69). In Rome, the Capitoline cult dedicated to Jupiter, Juno and Minerva encapsulated the Roman identity.[4] These three and other gods coexisted as one big divine family and were believed to respond to the different needs of people (travel/Mercury, healing and health/Hygeia, war/Mars, fertility/Juno) or to protect the local, geographical area (*genius loci*). Among those deities were some who came from other places such as the Greek hero Herakles, who in Latin was renamed as Hercules and the Etruscan Nethuns who became Neptune. The adaptation of other divinities and naming them in Latin show the inclusiveness of the Roman religious policy, their openness to new cults and rituals. We know that the Roman Senate had the power to authorize a new public divinity and his or her cult.[5] People were called to respect those divinities and to take part in celebrations under the guidance of the priestly college.[6] Those priests were not attached to a specific god but to all of them, and the priests' role was to conduct proper rituals. It should be added that they were not 'theologians', in the later Christian meaning, but 'liturgists'. Roman philosophers such as Cicero speculated about the nature of the gods, their existence and roles, while the priests were focused on the practical aspects of the cults. Alongside the priests were women who performed an active role in religion, such as, for instance, virgin priestesses. They served the goddess Vesta and safeguarded the Roman people by keeping alight the fire of the city (*ignis*

---

[2] I am fully aware that there are many definitions of 'religion'; however, I wish to highlight here one aspect of our modern perception, which is very different from what ancient Graeco-Roman authors understood as *religio*. See more in J. Hick, *An Interpretation of Religion: Human Responses to the Transcendent* (London: Macmillan, 1991), pp. 1–17.

[3] See, for example, Apuleius, *Met.*, 11.26.

[4] J. B. Rives, *Religion in the Roman Empire* (Oxford: Blackwell 2007), p. 84.

[5] For instance, it happened in 204 BCE when Cybele, a goddess originally from Anatolia, became a Roman deity.

[6] More in M. Horster, 'Living on Religion: Professionals and Personnel', in *A Companion to Roman Religion*, ed. J. Rüpke (Chichester: Wiley-Blackwell, 2011), pp. 331–41.

Vestae). Among the Roman gods, goddesses and their worshippers there was no tension or conflict. People could worship different divinities or combine public religion with a more esoteric cult (e.g. Mithraism). This image should not lead to the conclusion that the Roman Empire promoted religious tolerance and harmony in all provinces and cities. Rather, each city determined its own cults and religious celebrations; each city has different ethnic background and possible social tensions. The final aspect of that Roman religious mosaic, which ought to be mentioned in relation to the forthcoming emergence of Christian communities, is the cult of the emperor's *genius*. When Augustus received the title 'Father of the Fatherland' (*pater patriae*), his *genius*, that is his guardian spirit, became a cult object.[7]

In the Roman religious mentality vital importance was given to the order of the annual cycle of seasons. Every anomaly or unusual atmospheric phenomenon was treated as an expression of a forthcoming calamity and disturbance in the relations between the gods/divine and people/humans. Second, in the context of society, *pietas* was essential.[8] As such it endorsed the social, hierarchical and patriarchal order, the scrupulous observation of religious rituals. *Pietas* was in the centre of the relationship with the divine as well as with other people. Violation of this order was seen as an incitement of a cataclysm (*ira deorum*). Soon Christians in various parts of the empire would encounter these and other strong elements of the Roman traditional stance and would both challenge some of these elements and assimilate other borrowings from their Roman neighbours. Was that religious background fertile soil for the early Christian missionaries and house churches? Did it provide Christianity with space allowing its speedy advance, both socially and geographically? Let's look more carefully at that background, its values and challenges.

'NEWCOMERS': FEAR AND SUSPICION (SUETONIUS AND PLINY THE YOUNGER)

'Togetherness', although not a central Roman civic virtue, at least as a mindset and expectation, underpinned the style of life in the Roman Empire. People believed to live together in peace (*Pax Romana*), we speak the dominant language (majority Hellenistic Greek), we respect our emperor (*Dei Filius*), we attend the gladiatorial contests, we gossip in the baths and in the evenings we go to the theatre. Finally, together we worship the gods as our divine protectors in many temples and shrines. We offer them sacrifices bought from the local butcher and seller of incense. Indeed, the local butcher and incense seller enjoy economic profit from the religious activities in a city and busy liturgical calendar. When did the Romans notice that the followers of a certain Christ started to break out from that 'togetherness'? While the Romans

---

[7]Rives, *Religion*, p. 152.

[8]More in F. Berstein, 'Complex Rituals: Games and Processions in Republican Rome', in Rüpke (ed.), *A Companion*, p. 227.

acknowledged some room for Jewish religious particularities and absence from the public life, in the case of the followers of Jesus, who were not ethnically unanimous, their social withdrawal and secrecy prompted some questions. It is certain that Roman neighbours noticed some 'anti-social' behaviour among Christians in various places at various times.

The Roman historian Tacitus reported that the emperor Nero blamed Christians for the great fire of Rome (64) because they were 'hated for their atrocities' by the mob (*Ann.*, 15.44.).[9] If indeed autocratic Nero searched for excuse and the support of the opinion of the Roman mob, it must have been common to see people on the streets point out Christians as those who alienated themselves from the common life, shared passions, transgressions and joys as well as social ties. Suetonius, who also described Christianity as a 'new and vile superstition' (*Nero*, 16.2), highlights the esoteric character of the group. The term 'superstition' (*superstitio*) chosen by Suetonius denotes beliefs foreign and strange to the Roman taste and tradition.[10] They are allowed to be practised as barbarian, alien rites and beliefs, which recently came to the civilized Roman culture, but they do not have value in the eyes of the Roman (educated) citizen.

The renowned, early second-century letter of Pliny the Younger, governor of Bithynia (Asia Minor) to Emperor Trajan asked for some advice about the way of dealing with people denounced as Christians (*Ep.*, 10.96). The vital question for Pliny was: Should Christians be punished just for their attachment to the new cult or only when they committed a specific crime? Pliny's dilemma must have emerged in the context of Roman law, with the importance of an accusation and the role of accuser, even if anonymous.[11] In brief, the local people were aware of Christians' challenging and novel stance and asked the Roman authorities for action, correction and, if necessary, punishment. They accused Christians of antisocial behaviour. Trajan's response is also significant: the emperor approves Pliny's policy not to search for Christians, but, if they are found, that they should show their loyalty to Rome: 'worship our gods' (*Ep.*, 10.97). In the context of a very interconnected Roman social and religious life, this request calls for respect of traditional norms, religious rituals and political loyalties. It is important to remember that Trajan's policy did not encourage the deliberate hunt and persecution of Christians.[12] A similar policy would continue during the reign of Hadrian (117–138)[13] and Antonius Pius (138–161).[14] The change comes with Marcus Aurelius (161–180), when in various parts of

---

[9]B. Green, *Christianity in Ancient Rome: The First Three Centuries* (London: T&T Clark, 2010), pp. 50–1.

[10]R. L. Wilken, *The Christians as the Romans Saw Them* (New Haven, CT: Yale University Press, 1984), pp. 50–4.

[11]See T. B. Williams, 'Suffering from a Critical Oversight: The Persecution of 1 Peter within Modern Scholarship', *CBR* 10 (2012): 284–5.

[12]The case of Ignatius' martyrdom should be seen as an exception, rather than the expression of wider, state persecution.

[13]As it seems to be reported by Eusebius, *HE.*, 4.9.3.

[14]Again, Polycarp's execution was, as in the earlier case of Ignatius, an individual case magnified by Christian apologetic literature.

the empire (e.g. Rome, Lyons and north Africa) Christians were executed. The subsequent reign of Commodus (180–193) brought relative calm.

It is fair to conclude that during the first and second centuries Christians were perceived by their Roman neighbours as an antisocial, sometimes illicit and esoteric, sect. They were seen as people who rejected traditional religious values and stubbornly claimed that their founder, whom they recognized as the Son of God, was the ultimate Saviour of all. Apologetic Christian literature suggests that some Roman neighbours believed the gossip that Christians participated in 'Thyestean feasts and Oedipodean intercourse, and things which it is not possible to say aloud or to think'.[15] The power of common rumour combined with the strength of the mob was a significant factor, which prompted some local accusations and tensions. The Greeks and Romans seemed to believe that their new neighbours presented a threat to society and traditional values. They also feared the anger and reprisal of the gods (e.g. earthquakes, famine). Christian faith and their uncompromising ethos challenged the coherence of families (husbands, wives, daughters) and the social fabric (slaves and free men). This negative stereotype was still able to survive and prosper for more than one or two generations. However, the Christian lifestyle, which reinforced some New Testament exhortations, led to the false image that a coexistence between these groups was, if not impossible, certainly hard.

WERE CHRISTIANS SEPARATISTS? NEW TESTAMENT AND THE LETTER TO DIOGNETUS

Christianity, like Judaism before, was a religion of the scrolls (or books). As proven by Judith Lieu in both religions, there was a 'relationship' between identity and 'text*uality*'.[16] When early Christians first engaged with their Graeco-Roman neighbours, the political system, social order and family relationships during the first and at the beginning of the second century, they searched for inspiration and answers in the text of Scripture and memories (oral, Apostolic tradition), Pauline letters,[17] the Gospels and the emerging literature of the New Testament clearly highlighted Christian identity as opposed to the 'spirit of this world'.[18] The Apostle Paul, for instance, encouraged his congregations to be aware of the crucial difference between 'this age' (e.g. Rom. 12.2; 1 Cor. 1.20, 2.6, 2.8, 3.18; 2 Cor. 2.4; Eph. 1.21) and 'the coming age' (Eph. 2.7; Rom. 8.18-25). This distinction had its

---

[15]Eusebius, *HE.*, 5.1.14 and earlier, Athenagoras, *Leg.*, 3.

[16]J. M. Lieu, *Christian Identity in the Jewish and Graeco-Roman World* (Oxford: Oxford University Press, 2004), p. 27.

[17]In this context I shall ignore the division of the Pauline corpus into 'authentic' and 'deutero-Pauline' letters, as this distinction did not have an impact on Christians in our period.

[18]The notion of opposition between two ages originates in the Jewish apocalyptic tradition (e.g.4 Ezra) and was known to Paul and used by him in his didactic. As we see in the First Letter to the Corinthians, Paul identifies the present world as hostile to God and authentic believers. This world is governed by 'rulers of this age' opposed to God (1 Cor. 2.6 and 2.8). No doubt, Pauline notions were discussed by Christian missionaries and catechists in the next generation.

consequences in the life of Paul's disciples and in their view of the present affairs. Post-Pauline sources, such as the four Gospels, preserved the voice of Jesus calling his followers to 'take up the cross' and lead a life according to new values (e.g. the Sermon on the Mount), according to the Spirit (the Johannine tradition). The First Letter of Peter (1.13-21, 2.11-17, 4.12-19) witnesses to conflict in a Christian community between the new faith and social norms. It clearly calls for a separatist way of life in the light of a new Christian status. The book of Revelation clearly depicts the conflict between the divine realm and the realm of evil (e.g. 12), while calling its readers and listeners to undivided commitment (3.16). These and other texts were used commonly to teach and admonish in various communities in the formation of Christian identity. We may see further assimilation and development of that identity in the anonymous document from the later part of the second century, the *Letter to Diognetus*. The following passage is crucial:

> For Christians are not distinguished from the rest of humanity by country, language, or custom. For nowhere do they live in cities of their own, nor do they speak some unusual dialect, nor do they practice an eccentric life-style. This teaching of theirs has not been discovered by the thought and reflection of ingenious men, nor do they promote any human doctrine, as some do. But while they live in both Greek and barbarian cities, as each one's lot was cast, and follow the local customs in dress and food and other aspects of life, at the same time they demonstrate the remarkable and admittedly unusual character of their citizenship. They live in their own countries, but as aliens, they participate in everything as citizen, and endure everything as foreigners. Every foreign country is their fatherland, and every fatherland is foreign. [. . .] They live on earth, but their citizenship is in heaven.[19]

This romanticized picture of Christians portrays them as people on a journey, rather than entrenched in a particular place, city or province – as passers-by,[20] foreigners. These ideas of non-attachment to the current stage of the world, as noted by Lieu, are already present in the New Testament documents (1 Pet. 1.1, 1.17, 2.11; Eph. 2.19; Heb. 11.13).[21] These documents, while assimilating some Scriptural passages, reinforce Christian identity as citizens of another kingdom/realm. Yes, they are present here, but at the same time they remain untouched by the models/spirit of this world; they live in the cities but are aware of their true celestial homeland; in brief, they are a new 'race'.[22] With this notion we approach a more advanced, if not

---

[19]*The Letter to Diognetus*, 5.1-5 and 9. Trans. M. W. Holmes, *The Apostolic Fathers: Greek Texts and English Translations* (Grand Rapids, MI: Baker Books, 1999), p. 541. I discuss the emergence of Christian identity during the second century, including the *Letter to Diognetus*, in my forthcoming monograph: *Valentinus's Legacy and Polyphony of Voices* (London and New York: Routledge, 2021), Ch. 8.

[20]See the *Gospel of Thomas, Saying* 42.

[21]J. M. Lieu, *Neither Jew nor Greek? Constructing Early Christianity* (London: T&T Clark, 2002), p. 179.

[22]See more in E. S. Gruen, 'Christians as a "Third Race"', in *Christianity in the Second Century: Themes and Developments*, eds J. Carleton Paget and J. M. Lieu (Cambridge: Cambridge University Press, 2017), pp. 235–49.

philosophical, self-understanding. Did this self-perception encourage a change of opinion about Jesus' followers or, on the contrary, did it reflect only a fragmentary, apologetic picture?

GRAECO-ROMAN NEIGHBOURS INTRIGUED BY CHRISTIANS: THE CASE OF GALEN OF PERGAMON

The *Letter to Diognetus* also explains the relationship between Christians and their neighbours: Christians are like the soul, while the current world is the body; the soul, the metaphor continues, loves the body, while the body hates the soul (*Letter to Diognetus*, 6). This rather dualistic image echoes a philosophical, possibly Platonic, understanding of the relationship between spiritual and material elements.

The question is: At which stage of development of the Christian identity did Jesus' followers in the Graeco-Roman culture start to assimilate some philosophical concepts in order to explain better their self-understanding? As it has been pointed out before, for some non-Christian commentators, the new religion was a dangerous, antisocial cult. It did not have any similarities with any philosophical school. However, Galen of Pergamum (ca. 129/?–ca. 216/?), the great physician, eclectic thinker and polymath, saw Christianity, at least in its local form, as a philosophical school. Galen noted that the followers of Christ, like the followers of Moses, belonged to 'a school' (*diatribe*)[23] rather than to an irrational and dangerous sect (*superstitio*).[24] Following Richard Walzer's identification,[25] I wish to quote one remark of Galen, which is important to our discussion, and Galen's note shows an important change in the perception of Christianity among some intellectuals. In Galen's account:

> Most people are unable to follow any demonstrative argument consecutively; hence they need parables, and benefit from them . . . just as we now see the people called Christians drawing their faith from parables and miracles, and yet sometimes acting in the same way as those who philosophize. For their contempt of death and of its sequel is patent to us every day, and likewise their restraint in cohabitation. For they include not only men but also women who refrain from cohabiting all through their lives; and they also number individuals who, in self-discipline and self-control in matters of food and drink, and in their keen pursuit of justice, have attained a pitch not inferior to that of genuine philosophers.[26]

---

[23]Galen, *Diff.Puls.*, 3.3 and 2.4. Galen's note includes the important term διατριβή, diatribe, which in the context denoted a 'school', 'a rational way of life', including moral exhortation to a more noble life (e.g. self-control, the pursuit of virtues, the elimination of vice). 'Christians in Rome' appeared to Galen no longer as abominable cannibals or anarchists, but as students of a 'philosophical school'.

[24]Suetonius, *Nero.*, 16.2.

[25]R. Walzer's collection, translation and edition of Arabic sources in his *Galen on Jews and Christians* (London: Oxford University Press, 1949).

[26]For the source of this quote, see Wilken, *The Christians*, pp. 79–80 who refers to Walzer's edition, p. 15.

Although there was already a Christian community in Galen's native city of Pergamon (Asia Minor), it is possible to read Galen's observation as relating to his long period of time spent in Rome, where he practised medicine. Galen's remark, in the context of his other references to Christians, points out their philosophical life. As recently noted by Flemming,[27] Galen's view on Christians was not uncritical, as he found fault that primary value in their didactic is given to obedience to an authority, not to a logical examination of arguments. Still, they aimed for a noble life, and men as well as women were able to achieve virtue by practising asceticism and an ethical stance. Having said that, we do not know which exact group of Christians he had in mind, as Rome was a place where various teachers had settled. Among them were Justin Martyr, Tatian, Carpocratians, Ptolemy, the followers of Valentinus, Marcion of Synope, Hermas and the milieu which continued the theological legacy of the document known as *1 Clement*.[28] We do not have any evidence as to the social position of those Christian men and women mentioned in Galen's note. We can assume that the men and women who practised Christian *philosophy* were not exclusively 'the poorest' and 'the most vulnerable'. Each milieu adapted the meaning of Christian revelation to its local agenda, gender relations and philosophical background, even if that background was more general than academic. We should also add that each Christian school ('a way of life')[29] claimed that their model represented the true or genuine Christianity. This education approached the theme of salvation as a form of quest for wisdom and fullness of life. Galen's testimony, even if his observation comes through medical lenses with awareness of many, often opposite, practices,[30] provides us with a genuine effort to understand Christian neighbours as yet another group of people searching for wisdom and to live an ethical life. Galen's effort was not the dominant one among Graeco-Roman neighbours, while Celsus' derogatory critique continued the negative rhetorical discourse about Christians.

GRAECO-ROMAN NEIGHBOURS WHO RIDICULED CHRISTIANS (CELSUS)

Celsus, about whom we know almost nothing,[31] has been preserved for posterity thanks to Origen's work, in which the Christian scholar quotes and rebukes his

---

[27]R. Flemming, 'Galen and the Christians: Texts and Authority in the Second Century AD', in Carleton Paget and Lieu (eds), *Christianity in the Second Century*, p. 177.

[28]All these and more sources for Roman Christianity are discussed by Lampe, *Christians at Rome*, 206–358. In the case of *1 Clement*, as the document comes from the end of the first century, we can talk about the milieu which still existed in Rome in the first half of the second century.

[29]Hadot refers to the opinion of Sextus Empiricus (*Pyr.*, I.16 – 17) and defines 'school' as 'a way of life which follows a specific rational principle, in conformity with what appears to us', in *What is Ancient Philosophy?* p. 101. Christians soon presented their faith as a 'philosophy' and 'a school of life'. See Justin Martyr, *Dial.*, 8; Athenagoras, *Leg.*, 2; Melito in Eusebius, *HE.*, 4.26.7; Minutius Felix, *Oct.*, 4.4.

[30]Flemming, 'Galen and the Christians', p. 187.

[31]Little is known about Celsus himself; his work *True Doctrine* ('Αληθὴς λόγος) was written about 170 CE and survived only in Origen's treatise *Against Celsus* as a collection of selected passages.

critique of the Christian life and doctrine. It is evident that Celsus knew not only his Christian neighbours but also their Scriptures and teaching very well. From that acquaintance I wish to explore one aspect of Celsus' polemic: the role of women, as suggested by Celsus, in spreading the Christian message. According to Origen's account, Celsus reported that Christian women (e.g. Helena, Salome, Mariamne and Martha) were involved in leadership of their communities (Origen, *Cels.*, 5.62). These women, who represented different ecclesiastical groups, different theological traditions and lived in different geographical areas, were very efficient missionaries and teachers who introduced people to Christianity. Celsus has a specific polemical purpose in highlighting the activity of women as the main channels of communication and the source of its dangerous activity. If Christianity allowed women to teach and become leaders, in Celsus' argument, the new religion therefore unveiled itself as of low value and useless to educated men. One relevant passage from Celsus reports:

> In private houses also we see wool-workers, cobblers, laundry-workers, and the most illiterate and bucolic yokels, who would not dare to say anything at all in front of their elders and more intelligent masters. But whenever they get hold of children in private and some stupid women with them, they let out some astounding statements as, for example, that they must not pay any attention to their fathers and school-teachers, but must obey them; they say that these talk nonsense and have no understanding, and that in reality they neither know nor are able to do anything good, but are taken up with mere empty chatter. [. . .] They should leave their fathers and their schoolmasters, and go along with the women and little children who are their playfellows to the wooldresser's shop, or to the cobbler's or the washerwoman's shop, that they may learn perfection. And by saying this they persuade them.[32]

Celsus thus wished to over-emphasize, if not caricature, the involvement of women in Christianity with powerful gendered rhetoric. He aimed to depict the new religion as dominated by the feminine, which for his audience meant irrational, lower, weak and even worthless. Still, his critique and his use of arguments show that women in different churches attained the position of leaders, teachers and disciples. For Celsus, this fact, however, discredited the new religion. Celsus' comments aimed to show that Christian women played an active role in spreading the message to new people.[33] Not only were 'stupid women' (Celsus, according to Origen) and children thrilled by the new Christian religion;[34] other, in Celsus' view, uneducated individuals also aspired to perfection. In Celsus' rhetoric, Christianity, as he knew and wished to

---

[32]*Cels.*, 3.55, trans. H. Chadwick, *Origen: Contra Celsum* (Cambridge: Cambridge University Press, 1965), pp. 165–6.

[33]Yet another critic of Christianity, Lucian of Samosata, the author of the *Death of Peregrinus*, noted the role of widows and children (orphans) who waited near the local prison at the beginning of the day to pray for those who were imprisoned and in this way converted Peregrinus.

[34]See more in M. Y. MacDonald, *Early Christian Women and Pagan Opinion: The Power of Hysterical Women* (Cambridge: Cambridge University Press, 1996).

portray it, had nothing in common with the philosophical, valuable life. On the contrary, it attracted the most ignorant people from the lowest social stratum. Mona Tokarek LaFosse rightly points out that Celsus' ridicule reinforced the stereotype that women and children, in particular, 'were susceptible to superstition and easily duped'.[35] Celsus' intention, therefore, was to discredit Christians who, in his view, appealed to the most naive people in order to gain popularity and destabilize the traditional values of Graeco-Roman society. However, if we read between the lines of his critique, we may consider that, indeed, the role of women in various Christian groups was as important as that of male leaders and missionaries. In the highly gender-spaced Roman society, where women and men were attached to different public/private, visible/hidden spaces, women may have had greater opportunity to address other women and to share with them the core message of the new religion. That message, teaching and encouragement was not doomed to be irrational or naive, but it fulfilled women's expectations as well as their hopes.

CHRISTIANS WHO CELEBRATED THE GRAECO-ROMAN CULTURE (CLEMENT OF ALEXANDRIA)

Suetonius, Celsus and the author of the Alexamenos graffito, among others, expressed their highly critical views on the practices and beliefs of their Christian neighbours. In that highly rhetorical and negative perception, Christians were yet another group of 'barbarians' who brought disruption and undermined the classical Graeco-Roman values. Christians were treated more as 'aliens' than as 'some of us'. In that picture there was no room for the cultural coexistence of that new 'superstition' and the established classical legacy.

Clement of Alexandria (ca. 150–ca. 215) offers an example of the Christian connoisseur of Graeco-Roman culture, literature and philosophy. His works certainly provided a totally new outlook on the possible coexistence of the new religion with the rich and classical Graeco-Roman legacy. His project for the achievement of Christian perfection,[36] that is the ethical programme for a varied life, intellectual maturity and taking care of the soul,[37] encompassed the whole richness of the Graeco-Roman legacy. Let's look more carefully at Clement's stance.

Clement's own intellectual attitude has been called 'eclectic'; he carefully selected the best, in his view, elements of the Graeco-Roman philosophical doctrines, except Epicureanism,[38] as useful in his vision of Christian ethics and theology. Clement's fundamental conviction was that the Jewish people were brought to the truth through Moses and the Law, while the Greeks were through philosophy and, in both

---

[35]M. Tokare LaFosse, 'Women, Children and House Churches', in *The Early Christian World*, eds P. F. Esler, 2nd edn (London and New York: Routledge, 2017), p. 385.
[36]More in my *Clement of Alexandria: A Project of Christian Perfection* (London and New York T&T Clark, 2008).
[37]H. O. Meir, 'Clement of Alexandria and the Care of the Self', *JAAR* LXII, no. 3 (1994): 719–45.
[38]As Clement argued, this tradition was hedonistic and self-centred, *Strom.*, 6.8.67.1.-2.

cases, Jews and Barbarians were led towards the highest wisdom, recently revealed in the teachings of Jesus Christ.[39] Clement's positive assessment of various Graeco-Roman doctrines contrasted with his negative views on their religious traditions and heroes. These were of no use to Christians.[40] Consequently, Clement's works engaged with the great thinkers of antiquity, especially Plato, Pythagoras, the Stoics, while also preserving an impressive number of references to known and unknown authors. As pointed out by Annewies van den Hoek, Clement valued the authority of classical Greek authors such as Homer, Euripides, Hesiod and Herodotus.[41] Further that appreciation of the Graeco-Roman literary legacy is well illustrated by Stählin's index[42] with references identified by German editors to approximately 350 Graeco-Roman authors and sources. But we should not assess this immense literary evidence as Clement's own encyclopedic inclination. Clement lived and worked in Alexandria; his audience, as we may see from his rhetoric, logic and literary text, was sophisticated and well educated.[43] Those Alexandrians were surrounded by teachers and missionaries of all religions. It was an open market of ideas. If Clement wanted, and he certainly did, to attract their attention not just to Christianity but to his own expression of the Christian faith, he placed his ethos in a real fulfilment of the Jewish and Graeco-Roman sapiential traditions. By doing that, Clement competed not only with local Middle Platonists, Neopythagoreans, Stoics and Hermetists but also with other Christians such as the disciples of Valentinus, Theodotus, Basilides, Julius Cassianus, Carpocrates, Epiphanes and others. It was an inter-Christian struggle on many levels: hermeneutical with the attempt to interpret the Scriptures in a correct way; ethical with promoting an authentic Christian approach to, for example, marriage and procreation;[44] and theological with an intellectual effort to explain the notion of God that preserves some earlier philosophical (apophatic) intuition with the Christian revelation.[45] In Clement's contribution we can clearly see his engagement with the critical Graeco-Roman perception of Christianity as 'naive' or 'superstitious' and Clement's response that Christianity is highly philosophical or, using his language, 'scientific'.[46] We can also detect his ambition to show that Christian women are not those caricatured by

---

[39]See E. Osborn, *Clement of Alexandria* (Oxford: Oxford University Press, 2005), pp. 197–203.

[40]F. Jourdan, *Orphée et les Chrétiens, La réception du mythe d'Orphée dans la littérature chrétienne grecque des cinq premiers siècles, Tome I, Orphée du repoussoir au préfigurateur du Christ. Réécriture d'un mythe à des fins protreptiques chez Clément d'Alexandrie* (Paris: Les Belles Lettres, 2010).

[41]A. van den Hoek, 'Techniques of Quotation in Clement of Alexandria: A View of Ancient Literary Working Methods', *VChr* 50 (1996): 223–43.

[42]O. Stählin and U. Treu, *Clemens Alexandrinus: Register* (Berlin: Akademie-Verlag, 1980), pp. 30–59.

[43]D. Ridings, 'Clement of Alexandria and the Intended Audience of the *Stromateis*', *SP* XXXI (1996): 517–21.

[44]H. Fiskå Hägg, 'Continence and Marriage: the Concept of *Enkrateia* in Clement of Alexandria', *SO* 81 (2006): 126–43.

[45]H. Fiskå Hägg, *Clement of Alexandria and the Beginning of Christian Apophaticism* (Oxford: Oxford University Press, 2006).

[46]Osborn, *Clement of Alexandria*, pp. 203–5.

Celsus but are well trained in philosophy.[47] Our review of Clement must conclude that his inclusive, but conscientious, dialogue with non-Christian neighbours left an inspiring testimony of Christian education that brings out the best from the wisdom of the surrounding cultures. But his proposal was not the only one. Other Christian Apologists argued for a much more restricted stance. One of them was Tertullian of Carthage.

CHRISTIANS WHO REJECTED GRAECO-ROMAN VALUES (TERTULLIAN OF CARTHAGE)

Tertullian (ca. 160–ca. 225) and Clement of Alexandria lived under the same Roman Emperors on the same southern coast of the Mediterranean Sea. They both wished to promote their expression of Christianity as the most authentic and universal. However, Clement and Tertullian's approaches to Graeco-Roman culture were radically different. Their engagement in conversation with non-Christian neighbours, who cherished wisdom (*philosophy*), was very dissimilar. Looking at the Alexamenos graffito, if Clement only knew it, the Alexandrian apologists would argue the rationality of the Christian religion and message. Tertullian would explore a different stance: Christianity is true, because what it proclaims is impossible (*certum est, quia ineptum*).[48] The worshipper of the Crucified man is the embodiment of the genuine Christian believer, because to his Graeco-Roman or Jewish neighbours his faith is incomprehensible.[49] Tertullian was not afraid to offend his non-Christian fellow citizens (*Idol.*, 4), in a similar way as he would zealously argue against his fellow believers, whom he labelled as 'heretics' (e.g. *Prescr.*, 7.3). In a famous statement he explains that all heresies originate in 'Athens', that is, all come from philosophical speculation, while the genuine Christian faith and ethos dwells in 'Jerusalem' (*Praescr.*, 7.9). However, a more careful reading of Tertullian's works, or as Geoffrey D. Dunn proposes 'pamphlets',[50] certainly proves that Tertullian's own stance was based on a number of rational assumptions.

Our famous Latin orator stood up on many occasions to defend his religion and faith. Tertullian addressed the Roman authorities trying to convince them to abandon their persecution of his fellow Christians (e.g. *Scap.*). While, as we have seen previously, some critics accused Christians of antisocial and immoral behaviour, he emphasized their participation in the life of their communities. However, on another occasion, unlike in the *Letter to Diognetus*, Tertullian argued for the withdrawal of Christians from Graeco-Roman cultural life such as games and

---

[47]See more in J. Kovacs, 'Becoming the Perfect Man: Clement of Alexandria on the Philosophical Life of Women', in *Women and Gender in Ancient Religions: Interdisciplinary Approaches*, eds S. Ahearne-Kroll, P. Holloway and J. Kelhoffer (Tübingen: Mohr Siebeck, 2010), pp. 389–413.

[48]*Carn.*, 5.4.

[49]See valuable commentary in E. Osborn, *Tertullian First Theologian of the West* (Cambridge: Cambridge University, Press, 2003), pp. 48–64.

[50]G. D. Dunn, 'Tertullian', in Esler (ed.), *The Early Christian World*, p. 962.

theatres (e.g. *Spect.*, 1) and religion full of idols (e.g. *Idol.*). Sharing concerns with Celsus about the traditional position of women in Graeco-Roman private and public life, the orator from Carthage recognized the importance of various issues relating to women in a number of works. The way that Christian women were seen by non-Christian observers projected values on their communities. Women's visibility and veiling was one of his concerns (e.g. *Virg.*). Within the polemical inter-Christian context, Tertullian criticizes some, in his view, repugnant situations when women are allowed to baptize others, as in the well-known case of Thecla of Iconium (*Bapt.*, 17.4-5).[51] It is true that through his life and especially throughout his religious and spiritual journey, Tertullian's view developed in search of Christian perfection. His conversion from paganism to Christianity was the first stage, but later a second stage led Tertullian to move from 'Catholicism' to 'Montanism' or New Prophecy. Finally, the last phase reaffirmed what he believed was the core value of his Christianity and distinguished it from not only Graeco-Roman religious world but also other forms of Christianit*ies*: that is the uncompromised commitment to 'the rule of faith' (*regula fidei*) and its rigorous application in the context of married life, moral behaviour (forgiveness of sins), if necessary, martyrdom. He clearly wished to draw a line that distinguished his place from the neighbourhood. So, would Tertullian accept that, for the purity of the Christian faith, all bridges between his religion and the Roman Empire should be burned? Tertullian's interpretation of the role of Pontius Pilate in Jesus' death provides us with a surprising but important insight.

Tertullian's pamphlet, the *Apology*, presents an original portrait of Pontius Pilate. Tertullian showed a great deal of sympathy to the representative of the Roman order. Pontius is, according to Tertullian, under pressure from the Jews to sentence Jesus to crucifixion (*Apol.* 21.18). In his interpretation, Pontius is on Jesus' side and becomes the adversary of the Jews. Pontius is in favour of Jesus' teaching, but he is not strong enough to resist the intrigue of the Jews. In Tertullian's view, it was Pontius himself who told the story about Jesus to the emperor in Rome (*Apol.* 21.24). That colourful redecoration of Pontius' image by Tertullian hints at the possibility of a reconciliation between two neighbours: Christianity and the Roman Empire. In this setting Pontius Pilate represents the potential of accepting Jesus' teaching, which may lead to the end of animosity towards Christians and the end of persecution. We do not know how many representatives read or even heard about Tertullian's bold project, but if the idea was broadcast through the treatise, it may have reached the candidates who were to become converts among Roman upper classes, at least in Carthage. Tertullian, like many apologists before, tried to present the new system of belief as respectful and acceptable to a Roman audience. Tertullian illustrates very well the effort of some Christians expressed in the Apocrypha, to 'christen' Pontius Pilate and open the door to reconciliation with the Empire.

---

[51]See detailed discussion of Thecla and the review of resent hermeneutical approaches to this character in R. Shepard Kraemer, *Unreliable Witnesses: Religion, Gender and History in the Greco-Roman Mediterranean* (Oxford: Oxford University Press, 2011), pp. 117–52 and K. Cooper, *Band of Angels: The Forgotten Worlds of Early Christian Women* (Eusebius, NY: The Overlook Press, 2013), pp. 77–104.

CONCLUSIONS

The title of this chapter asks the following question: *Graeco-Roman Culture and Christians: good neighbours?* The selected documents and authors show that the beginning of that coexistence was not easy for either side. First, various Christian groups were trying to develop and reaffirm their identities on the basis of an uncompromised, strong belief that their founder, Jesus of Nazareth, was different from the heroes and gods of the Roman Pantheon. On this point there was no room for compromise. Christians also claimed that Jesus was different from Moses; however, here we may detect some voices (Judeo-Christians) which accepted a great deal of similarity between the Jewish lawgiver and Jesus of Nazareth. However, Christians needed the Graeco-Roman culture much more than vice versa. Christian Scriptures were written in *Koine*/Hellenistic Greek. Christians undertook missionary tasks around the Mediterranean with great success and speed thanks to Roman rule and security (*Pax Romana*) and the quality of roads along with well-organized sea transport. Some of those Christian leaders (e.g. Tertullian) used the existing social values and gender ideology to support the Christian order of life, both in the household and in public. The gradual assimilation of Stoic and Middle-Platonic ideas by various teachers, exegetes and commentators also showed the possibility of dialogue. But that possibility met strong Roman aversion to the new religion, as a foreign superstition, antisocial cult and esoteric sect. Apologists, such as Athenagoras of Athens, Justin Martyn and later Tertullian, wrote in defence of their religion and addressed either the local Roman authorities or even the emperors, but we do not know whether their literary products reached their intended recipients. The Graeco-Romans were not unanimous in their perception of the new religious movement. They were inclined to believe that followers of the crucified Jesus were not yet another philosophical school and were surprised to see that various members of that group preferred to suffer than to participate in the public act of acknowledgement of the *genius* of the emperor. Was the conflict between Graeco-Roman values and the Christian ethos inevitable? On one, religious, level, these traditions excluded each other. Yet on another level, where various issues are debated within a philosophical context, there was greater room for compromise and coexistence. But both sides needed to exclude ridicule and invective and to appeal to temperate language and arguments. However, both sides were also under pressure from other cultural, social and ideological factors and mentality, which made dialogue impossible. As in the previous case of Jesus of Nazareth and Pontius Pilate, they couldn't agree what or who is the truth.

BIBLIOGRAPHY

Ashwin-Siejkowski, P. *Clement of Alexandria: A Project of Christian Perfection.* London and New York: T&T Clark, 2008.

Berstein, F. 'Complex Rituals: Games and Processions in Republican Rome', in J. Rüpke (ed.), *A Companion to Roman Religion*, 222–34. Chichester: Wiley-Blackwell, 2011.

Cooper, K. *Band of Angels: The Forgotten Worlds of Early Christian Women.* New York: The Overlook Press, 2013.

Dunn, G. D. 'Tertullian', in P. F. Esler (ed.), *The Early Christian World*, 2nd edn, 959–75. London and New York: Routledge, 2017.

Ferguson, E. *Background of Early Christianity*, 3rd edn. Grand Rapids, MI: William B. Eerdmans Publishing Company, 2003.

Fiskå Hägg, H. 'Continence and Marriage: The Concept of Enkrateia in Clement of Alexandria', *SO* 81 (2006): 126–43.

Fiskå Hägg, H. *Clement of Alexandria and the Beginning of Christian Apophaticism*. Oxford: Oxford University Press, 2006.

Flemming, R. 'Galen and the Christians: Texts and Authority in the Second Century AD', in J. C. Paget and J. M. Lieu (eds), *Christianity in the Second Century: Themes and Developments*, 171–87. Cambridge: Cambridge University Press, 2017.

Green, B. *Christianity in Ancient Rome: The First Three Centuries*, 50–1. London: T&T Clark, 2010.

Gruen, E. S. 'Christians as a "Third Race"', in J. C.aget and J. M. Lieu (eds), *Christianity in the Second Century: Themes and Developments*, 235–49. Cambridge: Cambridge University Press, 2017.

Hadot, P. *What Is Ancient Philosophy?* Cambridge, MA: Harvard University Press, 2002.

Harley-McGowan, F. 'Alexamenos Graffito', in C. Keith, H. K. Bond, C. Jacobi and J. Schröter (eds), *The Reception of Jesus in the First Three Centuries*, vol. 3, 105–40. New York and London: T&T Clark, 2019.

Hick, J. *An Interpretation of Religion. Human Responses to the Transcendent*. London: Macmillan, 1991.

Hoek, van den A. 'Techniques of Quotation in Clement of Alexandria: A View of Ancient Literary Working Methods', *VChr* 50 (1996): 223–43.

Holmes, M. W. *The Apostolic Fathers: Greek Texts and English Translations*. Grand Rapids, MI: Baker Books, 1999.

Horster, M. 'Living on Religion: Professionals and Personnel', in J. Rüpke (ed.), *A Companion to Roman Religion*, 331–41. Chichester: Wiley-Blackwell, 2011.

Jourdan, F. *Orphée et l.es Chrétiens, La réception du mythe d'Orphée dans la littérature chrétienne grecque des cinq premiers siècles, Tome I, Orphée du repoussoir au préfigurateur du Christ. Réécriture d'un mythe à des fins protreptiques chez Clément d'Alexandrie*. Paris: Les Belles Lettres, 2010.

Kovacs, J. 'Becoming the Perfect Man: Clement of Alexandria on the Philosophical Life of Women', in S. Ahearne-Kroll, P. Holloway and J. Kelhoffer (eds), *Women and Gender in Ancient Religions: Interdisciplinary Approaches*, 389–413. Tübingen: Mohr Siebeck, 2010.

Lieu, J. M. *Neither Jew nor Greek? Constructing Early Christianity SNTW*. London: T&T Clark, 2002.

Lieu, J. M. *Christian Identity in the Jewish and Graeco-Roman World*. Oxford: Oxford University Press, 2004.

MacDonald, M. Y. *Early Christian Women and Pagan Opinion: The Power of Hysterical Women*. Cambridge: Cambridge University Press, 1996.

Meir, H. O. 'Clement of Alexandria and the Care of the Self', *JAAR* LXII, no. 3 (1994): 719–45.

Osborn, E. *Tertullian First Theologian of the West*. Cambridge: Cambridge University Press, 2003.

Osborn, E. *Clement of Alexandria*. Oxford: Oxford University Press, 2005.

Ridings, D. 'Clement of Alexandria and the Intended Audience of the Stromateis', *SP* XXXI (1996): 517–21.

Rives, J. B. *Religion in the Roman Empire*. Oxford: Blackwell, 2007.

Shepard Kraemer, R. *Unreliable Witnesses: Religion, Gender and History in the Greco-Roman Mediterranean*. Oxford: Oxford University Press, 2011.

Stählin, O. and Treu, U. *Clemens Alexandrinus: Register*. Berlin: Akademie-Verlag, 1980.

Tokare LaFosse, M. 'Women, Children and House Churches', in P. F. Esler (ed.), *The Early Christian World*, 2nd edn. London and New York: Routledge, 2017.

Walzer, R. *Collection, Translation and Edition of Arabic Sources in His Galen on Jews and Christians*. London: Oxford University Press, 1949.

Williams, T. B. 'Suffering from a Critical Oversight: The Persecution of 1 Peter within Modern Scholarship', *CBR* 10 (2012): 284–5.

Wilken, R. L. *The Christians as the Romans Saw Them*. New Haven, CT: Yale University Press, 1984.

CHAPTER 4

What was the role of women in the churches?

ILARIA L. E. RAMELLI

The issue of women in churches in early Christianity has to do with their behaviour in churches (such as in 1 Cor. 14.34-35, which several patristic thinkers did not deem a prohibition for women to hold ministries, as we shall see) and with that of women officeholders. There are important literary sources here, from Paul to patristic and conciliar sources, and the so-called Apocryphal Acts. Besides currents later labelled 'heretical', such as Montanists and Gnostics, who admitted of women officeholders, one prominent example from the mainstream church is Gregory Nazianzen's account of Theosebia, who was the colleague and sister of Gregory, bishop of Nyssa, and 'of equal dignity' with him. There is also significant iconographic and archaeological evidence, which, as far as is allowed by the word limit, will be brought to bear on this issue.

THE NEW TESTAMENT

The NT bristles with women active in churches. Most testimonies come from Paul, who states that he has given birth, with labour pains, as a mother, to those whom he has converted to Christ.[1] This notion was inspired by Isa. 42.14 on God as a woman in labour. Galatians 3.28 claims that there is 'no male and female' in Christ, but all are one. This declaration undermines ethnic, social and gender categories of inferiority, such as those theorized by Aristotle and the later Rabbinic prayer *Tefillat Shaḥrit*.[2] Paul calls Junia 'eminent among the apostles'.[3] Phoebe in Romans 16 is called a διάκονος in a church of Corinth and a προστάτις (president-patroness) of Paul himself and many followers of Jesus: she was the leader of a Corinthian

---

[1] Reidar Aasgaard, 'Children and Childhood in the Letters of the Apostle', *JBL* 126, no. 1 (2007): 129–59.

[2] See Ilaria Ramelli, 'Gal 3:28 and Aristotelian (and Jewish) Categories of Inferiority', *Eirene* 55 (2019): 275–310.

[3] See Eldon Epp, *Junia* (Minneapolis, MN: Fortress Press, 2005); Yii-Jan Lin, 'Junia: An Apostle before Paul', *JBL* 139, no. 1 (2020): 191–209; Carolyn Osiek, 'Diakonos and Prostatis', *Hevormde Teologiese Studies* 61 (2005): 347–70.

church, as Peregrinus was the revered leader of a Christian group, called προστάτης in Lucian *Per*. 11.

Romans 16 names many other women as συνεργοί (collaborators) in Paul's apostolic ministry: Phoebe, Prisca and Aquila,[4] Junia and Andronicus, Mary, Tryphaena and Tryphosa, and Persis. Prisca is often mentioned *before* her husband, which suggests that she was the leader of their house church. Besides these women apostles, others who hosted house churches seem to have been Mary the mother of John Mark in Acts 12.12, Lydia in Acts 16, Nympha in Col. 4.15, and the Elect Lady of 2 John.[5] Women presidents of house churches likely led the eucharistic prayer in their church.[6] Later biographies reflect this. The *Vita* of the Roman sisters Praxedes and Pudentiana portrays them as consecrated, preaching the Word of God and leading their house church.[7] Don Fioravante Martinelli (1655) and Dom Benigno Davanzati (1725) deemed Praxedes a *presbytera* who led a Christian house church.

In the NT, passages that could be considered misogynist and contrasting women's ecclesiastical ministries are in the so-called pastoral Epistles,[8] the domestic codes of Ephesians and Colossians and 1 Cor. 14.33b-35, which advise women to be silent in the assembly/church, ἐκκλησία.[9] Some scholars deem the last passage interpolated;[10] others maintain its authenticity but do not think that Paul forbade women to speak in public.[11] Several church fathers did not either, as we shall see.

---

[4]Acts 18.1-3, 18-26; Rom. 16.3; 1 Cor. 16.19; 2 Tim. 4.19. Prisca is usually the first to be named by Paul; Acts, or some scribes, tried to postpone her name or use a diminutive, Priscilla. Jerome Murphy O'Connor, 'Prisca and Aquila', *BiblRev* 8, no. 6 (1992): 40–62; Dominika Kurek, 'Is There an Anti-Priscan Tendency in the Manuscipts?', *JBL* 125 (2006): 107–28.

[5]On house churches: Carolyn Osiek and Margaret MacDonald, *A Woman's Place* (Minneapolis, MN: Fortress, 2006). Private churches could be compared, and sometimes were perceived as private associations (*thiasoi, collegia*): see Benedikt Eckhardt (ed.), *Private Associations and Jewish Communities in the Hellenistic and Roman Cities* (Leiden: E.J. Brill, 2019).

[6]Mary Schaefer, *Women in Pastoral Office* (Oxford: Oxford University Press, 2013), pp. 31, 375.

[7]Ibid., p. 16.

[8]Scholars mostly support their pseudo-epigraphic nature. I can offer no bibliography but indicate Adela Yarbro Collins, 'The Female Body as Social Space in 1 Timothy', *NTS* 57 (2011): 155–75, and Harry Maier, 'The Entrepreneurial Widows of 1 Timothy', in *Patterns of Women's Leadership in Ancient Christianity* (Oxford: Oxford University Press, 2021), pp. 59–73.

[9]See, for example, Margaret Y. MacDonald, 'Beyond Identification of the Topos of Household Management: Reading the Household Codes in Light of Recent Methodologies', *NTS* 57 (2010): 65–90. On the meaning of ἐκκλησία in Pauline communities, see Ralph Korner, *The Origin and Meaning of Ekklēsia in the Early Jesus Movement* (Leiden: E.J. Brill, 2017).

[10]For example, Hans Conzelmann, *1 Corinthians* (Philadelphia, PA: Fortress, 1975), p. 246; Gordon Fee, *The First Epistle to the Corinthians* (Grand Rapids, MI: Eerdmans, 1987), p. 699; Jouette Bassler, '1 Corinthians', in *Women's Bible Commentary* (Louisville, KY: Knox, 1998), pp. 418–19; Philip Payne, 'Ms. 88 as Evidence for a Text Without 1 Cor 14.34-5', *NTS* 44 (1998): 152–8; Idem and Paul Canart, 'The Originality of Text-Critical Symbols in Codex Vaticanus', *NT* 42 (2000): 105–13; Epp, *Junia*, pp. 15–20; Hans-Joseph Klauck, *Ancient Letters and the New Testament* (Waco, TX: Baylor University, 2006), pp. 307–8; my 'Prophecy in Origen: Between Scripture and Philosophy', *JECH* 7 (2017): 17–39.

[11]According to Elisabeth Schüssler Fiorenza, the verses refer only to the wives of Christians, since not all women in the community were married and not all were married to Christians (1 Corinthians 7): *Rhetoric and Ethics* (Augsburg: Fortress, 1999), pp. 230–3. Craig Keener, *Paul, Women, and Wives* (Peabody, MA:

Paul's reference in 1 Cor. 9.5 to 'bringing around with us an ἀδελφὴν γυναῖκα, as the other apostles, the brothers of the Lord, and Kephas do' refers to a female apostle, a γυνή (woman) and ἀδελφή, sister in the faith. Today it is usually assumed that Paul never married, because of 1 Corinthians 7, while some ancient interpreters, including Clement of Alexandria, thought that Paul was married, based on Phil. 4.3. Here Paul asks a 'faithful/noble colleague' (γνήσιε σύζυγε) to help the women apostles Euodia and Syntyche, because they have fought for the Gospel together with Paul himself. Besides Clement, a Syriac fragment ascribed to Epiphanius[12] names Persis as Paul's wife. Persis' name depends on Rom. 16.12, where Paul greets 'the beloved Persis, who has laboured [ἐκοπίασεν] so much in the Lord', meaning in Paul the apostolic mission. Persis was an apostle. The Origenian Palladius, an admirer of the ordained deacon Olympia, says that Persis 'laboured, just like Olympia'.[13]

Origen interpreted the 'noble colleague' of Paul in the apostolate as a woman, because he identifies this colleague with Persis mentioned in Rom. 16.12 as an apostle in *Com. Rom.* 10.29: 'This woman [Persis], whom Paul also calls "faithful/ genuine/noble colleague", has laboured a great deal in the Lord.' According to Origen, a woman, Persis, was a colleague of Paul as an apostle. Theodoret also claimed that in Phil. 4.3 Paul was not speaking of his wife but of a colleague in the faith (τῆς εὐσεβείας ζυγόν), on the grounds of 1 Cor. 7.8.[14]

Jesus not only inspired Paul, had women among his disciples like Mary Magdalene, addressed women such as the Samaritan and others may have sent Junia as an apostle (she was an eminent apostle, 'in Christ before' Paul, Rom. 16.7), and challenged societal norms with regard to women,[15] but also represented himself as a mother, a hen collecting her chicks under her wings (Matt. 23.37; Lk. 13.34[16]), and remembered that in Psalm 109 (110LXX), God's parenthood is represented as that of a mother: 'From the womb, before Morning-star, I brought you forth' (NETS).[17] Unlike other

---

Hendrickson, 1992), pp. 79–88, interprets vv. 34-35 circumstantially: for the sake of order in the church, some women should not be loud; Neal Flanagan and Edwina Snyder, 'Did Paul Put Down Women in 1 Cor 14:34-36?' *BThB* 11 (1981): 10–12: in vv. 34-35, Paul is quoting the words of the men he reproaches in v. 36. Jill Marshall, *Women Praying and Prophesying in Corinth* (Tübingen: Mohr Siebeck, 2017), neither maintains nor refutes the textual integrity of vv. 34-35.

[12]From the Mingana collection of the Library of the University of Birmingham, ms. 4, fol. 61a.

[13]*Dial.,* 17.

[14]*In Phil.*, 4:3, PG 82.585. Tertullian (*Monog.,* 8.4; *Cast.,* 8.3) and Jerome (*Ep.*, 22.20) agreed, based on 1 Cor. 7.8, that Paul was unmarried.

[15]See, for example, Lee A. Johnson and Robert C. Tannehill, 'Lilies Do Not Spin: A Challenge to Female Societal Norms', *NTS* 56 (2010): 475–90.

[16]This may be recalling of Deut. 32.11-12 on God as a mother eagle, and Hos. 13.8 on God as a mother bear.

[17]Discussion in my 'Paul on Apokatastasis: 1 Cor 15:24-28 and the Use of Scripture', in *Paul and Scripture*, eds Stanley Porter and Christopher Land (Leiden: E.J. Brill, 2019), pp. 212–32; M. Grohmann, 'Metaphors of God, Nature and Birth in Psalm 90.2 and 110.3', in *Metaphors in the Psalms*, eds P. van Hecke and A. Labahn (Leuven: Peeters, 2010), pp. 23–34; Jonathan Parker, 'My Mother, My God, Why Have You Forsaken Me?', *ExpTimes* 131 (2020): 199–204 offers a feminist, birth-sensitive interpretation of Ps. 22.9-11 and a feminist translation of Ps. 22.10b, accenting God's motherhood in the passage. On Jesus and women, see Ben Witherington III, *Women in the Ministry of Jesus* (New York: Cambridge University Press,

genealogies, Matthew's genealogy of Jesus remarkably includes five women.[18] The first Jesus followers in Jerusalem held everything in common and 'devoted themselves to prayer, together with the women and Mary the mother of Jesus, and his brothers' (Acts 1.14).[19] In *Life of the Virgin*, 96–9, Jesus' mother teaches the apostles and sends them forth. The women, called 'disciples', who studied with Jesus, were at the Last Supper (74), and both Mary and her son sacrificed as priests at that Supper: 'she sacrificed herself as a priest and was sacrificed, she offered and was offered.'[20] The notion of self-sacrifice as a priest will return with Macrina, as we shall see.

Women Apostles in some Apocryphal literature

Besides the prominence attached to Mary Magdalene in 'apocryphal' literature and in orthodox literature as 'apostle of the apostles',[21] both the *Acts of Philip* and those of *Paul and Thecla* feature a man and a woman apostles: Philip and Mariamme, and Paul and Thecla. Mariamme, Philip's sister, is depicted as a better apostle than Philip and is represented in the role of baptizing (14.9). An ancient redaction depicts an ascetic community in which women and men were deacons and presbyters and names male and female presbyters and 'eunuchs' or celibate men, deacons and virgins: πρεσβυτέρους, πρεσβυτίδας, εὐνούχους, διακόνους, διακονίσσας, παρθένους.[22] Likewise, in *Martyrdom of Matthew* 28, a converted king was ordained πρεσβύτερος, his wife πρεσβύτις, his son διάκονος and his wife διακόνισσα: the female titles indicate women officeholders, since they are included in ἱεροσύνη, 'the priestly dignity'.

In the *Acts of Thecla* (180–200 CE) Paul sends Thecla as an apostle and preacher (διδάσκειν) of the Word.[23] She taught women the Gospel in Seleucia (43.7), where a shrine was built in her honour. Thecla spent eight days teaching the women of Tryphaena's household (*ATh* 43.7 and 39). She spent her time in Seleucia teaching

---

1991); Sarah Parks, *Gender in the Rhetoric of Jesus: Women in Q* (Lanham, MD: Lexington-Fortress, 2019). Jesus held his mother in high regard: see my 'Τί ἐμοὶ καὶ σοὶ γύναι' (John 2.4): Philological, Contextual, and Exegetical Arguments for the Understanding: "What Does This Matter to Me and to You?"', *ExClass* 12 (2008): 103–33. A similar corrective should be applied to Luke 11.27–28.

[18]Peter-Ben Smit, 'Something about Mary? Remarks about the Five Women in the Matthean Genealogy', *NTS* 56 (2020): 191–207.

[19]Ilaria L. E. Ramelli, *Social Justice and the Legitimacy of Slavery* (Oxford: Oxford University Press, 2016), pp. 101–20; Christoph Stenschke, 'Enabling Conditions in the Conflicts of Acts 1–8:3', *JECH* 7 (2017): 54–86, 63–4.

[20]As recorded in the most ancient manuscript of this *Life* (eleventh-century Old Georgian Tbilisi A-40). See Ally Kateusz, 'She Sacrificed Herself as the Priest', *JFSR* 33 (2017): 45–67; *Mary and Early Christian Women: Hidden Leadership* (New York: Palgrave Macmillan, 2019).

[21]Antti Marjanen, *The Woman Jesus Loved* (Leiden: E.J. Brill, 1996); Ann Graham, *Mary Magdalene: The First Apostle* (Cambridge, MA: Harvard University Press, 2003); Karen King, 'Prophetic Power and Women's Authority: The Case of the Gospel of Mary Magdalene', in *Women Preachers and Prophets*, eds Beverly Kienzle and Pamela Walker (Berkeley: University of California, 1998), pp. 21–41.

[22]The Athos manuscript (Xenophontos 32) includes a longer, more ancient redaction than Vatican Codex V. See my 'Mansuetudine, grazia e salvezza negli *Acta Philippi*', *Inv.luc* 29 (2007): 215–28.

[23]δίδασκε τὸν λόγον τοῦ Θεοῦ, *ATh.*, 41.6.

noblewomen Christianity and healing (ms. G, *ATh* 45.6-14): Thecla is still called ἀπόστολος (ibid. 45.58). Similarly, Origen, who may have known the *Acts of Thecla*, described the task of women presbyters as teaching and announcing the Word of God, as we shall see. Thecla taught, baptized, and enlightened many people with the Word of God (43/4.18; *ATh* 4.15).

Thecla has been perceived as subversive, since she abandoned her fiancé to follow Paul and reconfigured binary concepts of gender identity.[24] Tertullian claimed that 'heretic women are impudent, since they dare teach, dispute, perform exorcisms and healings [*docere, contendere, exorcismos agere, curationes repromittere*], and perhaps even baptize' (*fortasse an et tingere, Praescr. haer.* 41.5). The *Acts of Thecla* and *Acts of Paul and Thecla*, and Tertullian's hysterical reaction above and in *Bapt.* 17,[25] indicate that women taught and baptized in early Christian communities.

WOMEN PROPHETS AND OFFICEHOLDERS BEFORE AND DURING ORIGEN'S TIME

Paul states that women 'pray and prophesy' in public meetings of the Corinthian church in 1 Cor. 11.2-16,[26] which some deem at odds with 1 Cor. 14.34-35. In Acts 13.1-2, prophets 'liturgize'. In *Didache* 10.7, prophets can celebrate the Eucharist (εὐχαριστεῖν, cf. 15.1). Now, prophets were both men and women (Acts 21.9, etc.). Male and female prophets are 'the high priests of the community' (*Didache* 13.1).

Pliny the Younger attests to women deacons or presbyters (*ministrae, Ep.* 10.96[97].7). Apuleius creates a parody of a Christian woman (*Metam.* 9.14-15), and

---

[24]Virginia Burrus, *Chastity as Autonomy: Women in the Stories of Apocryphal Acts* (Lewiston, ME: Mellen, 1987), pp. 102–3; passim; Kate Cooper, *Band of Angels* (London: Atlantic, 2013), pp. 92–4. On Thecla's relation with her mother and Tryphaena: Ross Kraemer, 'Jewish Mothers and Daughters in the Greco-Roman World', in *The Jewish Family in Antiquity*, ed. Shaye J. D. Cohen (Atlanta, GA: SBL, 2020), pp. 111–12; J. D. McLarty, *Thecla's Devotion: Narrative and Emotion in the Acts of Paul and Thecla* (Cambridge: Clarke, 2020), p. 226: the text remains 'a mixture of conventional and subversive elements'.
[25]On which see Laura Nasrallah, 'Out of Love for Paul', in *The Role of Religion in Shaping Narrative Forms*, eds Ilaria Ramelli and Judith Perkins (Tübingen: Mohr Siebeck, 2015), pp. 73–96; Emily Cain, 'Tertullian's Precarious Panopticon', *JECS* 27 (2019): 611–33.
[26]On 'veiling' in 11.2-16, see Shelly Matthew, 'A Feminist Analysis of the Veiling Passage', *Lectio difficilior*, 2015. http://www.lectio.unibe.ch/; Torsten Jantsch (ed.), *Frauen, Männer, Engel. Perspektiven zu 1Kor 11,2–16* (Neukirchen-Vluyn: Neukirchener, 2015), vets all the interpretations of 1 Cor. 11.2-16 about the head covering of women and men and its relation to respectability and self-control (ἐξουσία, v. 10); Lucy Peppiatt, *Unveiling Paul's Women: Making Sense of 1 Corinthians 11:2–16* (Eugene, OR: Wipf & Stock, 2018), thinks that Paul used a slogan followed by his counterresponse: these verses are a rhetorical interchange of the Corinthian ideas with Paul's corrective (26–41): Paul included and supported women in ministry and leadership. This passage promotes 'distinction without subordination' for Brian Robinson, *Paul's Rhetoric of Gender and Power in 1 Corinthians* (Lanham, MD: Lexington, 2019), p. 223. See also Jorunn Økland, *Women in Their Place* (London: T&T Clark, 2005). The veiling practice will endure for centuries, for instance in Byzantium: see Gabriel Radle, 'The Veiling of Women in Byzantium: Liturgy, Hair, and Identity in a Medieval Rite of Passage', *Speculum* 94, no. 4 (2019): 1070–115.

the old woman who visited her every day may have been a deacon who brought her the Eucharist.[27] Montanists and 'Gnostics' ordained women presbyters, following Gal. 3.27-28.[28] Montanists had 'women bishops, presbyters, and the rest; they say that none of this makes any difference because "In Christ Jesus there is neither male nor female"' (Epiphanius *Pan.*, 49.2.5).[29] Valentinians had women bishops;[30] Ambrosiaster criticized the ordination of women deacons by the Montanists (commenting on 1 Tim. 3.11). Epiphanius disapproved of female officeholders in his anti-Marcionite polemic[31] and attacked the Collyridians, whom he accused of worshipping Mary (*Pan.*,79).

In *The Shepherd of Hermas*, respected by Clement and Origen, the woman–church, the revealer of Visions 1–4, is a *presbytis* on a white cathedra, then a *presbytera* reading a book, whose message is sent to other churches and the local church's *presbyteroi*.[32] Grapte may be an *episcopa* of the Church of Rome. In the time of Origen, the *Didascalia Apostolorum* mentions πρεσβύτιδες with virgins and widows as ecclesiastical orders. Women deacons are an ecclesiastical order, ordained by the bishop by χειροτονία, like male deacons and presbyters, and included in the clergy. They are depicted in 2.26 as worthier of honour than presbyters and of equal worth as male deacons. The bishop is the type of God, a male deacon of Christ, a female deacon of the Spirit, the presbyters of the apostles and the widows of the altar. Tertullian attests that women presbyters taught, cured, baptized, offered the eucharistic sacrifice and in sum performed the 'office of a priest/bishop' (*sacerdotale officium*) while he deems all these 'manly tasks'.[33] In the first half of the third century, a presbyter (πρεσβυτέρα) Ammion lived in Phrygia; bishop Dioga dedicated her epitaph, indicating that she was a member of the clergy, not the wife of a presbyter. In Egypt, a second–third-century mummy mentions the parents of a 'presbyter' Artemidora, but not a spouse. Christian women authoritative in the church in the third century are attested by Porphyry: '*matronae* and other women constitute their ruling body, exercising authority in ecclesiastical congregations, and women's prejudice determines priestly rank'.[34] A prophetess in Cappadocia in 235

---

[27]See Ilaria Ramelli, *I Romanzi antichi e il Cristianesimo* (Madrid: Signifer; new edn, Eugene, OR: Cascade, 2011); 'Apuleius and Christianity', in *Echoes of Myth, Religion and Ritual in the Ancient Novel*, ed. Roger Beck (Berlin: De Gruyter, 2013), pp. 145–73.

[28]Ramelli, 'Gal 3:28'; Christine Trevett, *Montanism* (Cambridge: Cambridge University Press, 1996); John Turner, 'Feminine Principles in Platonic and Gnostic Texts', in *Women and Knowledge in Ancient Christianity*, eds Ulla Tervahauta et al. (Leiden: E.J. Brill, 2017), pp. 291–324; Nicola Denzey, 'Women in Gnosticism', in *Patterns of Women's Leadership*.

[29]On early criticism of women's authority in Montanism: Josef Lössl, 'Between Hipparchian Cynicism and Priscillian Montanism', *VChr* 74 (2020): 84–107.

[30]Tertullian, *Praescr.*, 41.5.

[31]*AH*, 42.4-5; *Anaceph.*, 42.3.

[32]Lora Walsh, 'The Lady as Elder in the Shepherd of Hermas', *JECS* 27, no. 4 (2019): 517–47, thinks that 'the Elder Lady's speech and action in the first three Visions renders visible a fuller range of her pastoral, prophetic, instructive, and inclusive model of presbyteral leadership'.

[33]*Virg.*, 9.1; cf. *Praescr.*, 41.5; *Bapt.*, 17.4.

[34]*Adv.Chr.* Frg. 97.

'sanctified the bread with a not unrespectable invocation, celebrated the Eucharist, offered the sacrifice to the Lord, not without reciting the customary eucharistic prayer, and baptized many, using the traditional, authentic words of inquiry, so that in no way did she appear to be in contradiction with ecclesiastical requirements'.[35]

ORIGEN ON ORDAINED WOMEN

Origen never criticized women's ecclesiastical ordination. He attacks the Montanists in *Princ.* 2.7.3, who assimilated the Holy Spirit to common spirits, but he does *not* attack them, or others, for ordaining women presbyters and bishops. He saw in 1 Timothy and Titus references to women presbyters. In his commentary on Rom. 10.17, Origen states that Phoebe was constituted *in ministerio Ecclesiae*:[36] her ministry was material and especially spiritual (*spiritalibus officiis*). Origen highlights her ecclesiastical ministry (*officium, ministerium*), which was extended to other women, called 'ecclesiastical ministers' (*ministrae in Ecclesia*). He declares the necessity of women ministers, taught by Paul with his 'apostolic authority'. Origen maintains that the women invested with material and spiritual ministry deserve to be honoured. Focusing again on Phoebe, Atto, the tenth-century bishop of Vercelli, asked by a priest about the nouns *presbytera* and *diacona* in the canons, recognized that women were regularly ordained deacons, presbyters and presidents of churches in the early church:

> In the primitive church, according to the word of the Lord, 'the harvest was great and the laborers few', religious women used also to be ordained as ministers of the cult [*cultrices ordinabantur*], as St Paul shows in the Letter to the Romans, when he says, 'I commend to you my sister Phoebe, who is in the ministry of the church at Cenchrae.' Here it is understood that not only men, but also women presided over the churches [*praeerant ecclesiis*], because of their great usefulness . . . those called *presbyterae* assumed the office of preaching, leading, and teaching, so female deacons had taken up the office of ministry and of baptizing.

In this and at least other two passages, Origen deemed the existence of women's ministries in the church, including presbyterate, based on the Bible. As did other copyists of uncial and minuscule manuscripts, Origen treated 1 Cor. 14.34-35 as a separate paragraph, possibly an interpolation,[37] but not as a prohibition of ordained ministry for women. Commenting on 1 Cor. 14.34-35,[38] he observes that, according to Paul, women prophesied, like Philip's daughters, and could speak to

---

[35]Firmilian of Caesarea, Letter 74, *ap.* Cyprian, CSEL 3.2.

[36]διάκονος according to Rom. 16.1 in Greek, the NT's and Origen's language; Rufinus' translation does not render *diaconus/diaconos*, but the phrase *in ministerio Ecclesiae*.

[37]See Philip Payne, 'Fuldensis, Sigla for Variants in Vaticanus, and 1 Cor 14.34-5', *NTS* 41 (1995): 250–62; Karin Neutel, 'The Problematic Origins of the Conjectural Emendation on 1Cor 14.33b–35', *NTS* 65, no. 4 (2019): 477–95.

[38]Fragment, *Catena in Corinthios* A74.

other Christians if they had a revelation, but not to men and women together in assemblies. Women can teach and say 'wonderful and holy things', better to other women. 1 Cor. 11.3-16, on the man as head, is also deemed an interpolation by some scholars.[39] Paul put forward 'a theology of mutuality in the context of relationships of people who are different'.[40] Women presbyters existed in Origen's time, as seen earlier, so he probably refers to women presbyters when he echoes Titus 2.3-4, on πρεσβύτιδες who are 'in a consecrated/ordained state' (ἐν καταστήματι ἱεροπρεπεῖ) and should teach other women – only, not in a public assembly, where men can announce God's word as well. Clement and Basil also read ἱεροπρεπεῖ in Titus 2.3 and thus assumed that it referred to women who were constituted 'in a consecrated state' of ecclesiastical ministry and viewed the parallel in Titus 2.2 as a reference to presbyters (not old men). Various manuscripts read πρεσβυτέρους ('presbyters') instead of πρεσβύτας ('old men') here; Origen read πρεσβυτέρους, as attested by a surely authentic, original Greek passage: *Com.Joh.* 32.12.132-133. Here, Origen refers to Titus 2.2-4 and parallels the prescriptions to πρεσβύτεροι and πρεσβύτιδες there, precisely on the task of *teaching*, common to both men and women presbyters. Πρεσβυτέρα/πρεσβύτις and *presbytera* are common in Greek and Latin, also in epigraphical attestations.[41] According to Origen, Titus 2.3-4 endorsed the existence of women presbyters in the church, and 1 Tim. 3.11 could be read as an endorsement of the existence of women deacons. In his commentary on Rom. 8.9, Origen calls ecclesiastical *ministerium* the episcopate, presbyterate, diaconate and the orders of widows and virgins, making no distinction between women's and men's orders.

Origen explained away potentially misogynist biblical passages. He interpreted symbolically the statement that women will be saved through 'childbirth' in 1 Tim. 2.15, interpreting childbirth as the production of Christ and virtue in one's heart.[42] Likewise, he referred the sin of Eve not to any real woman but to the woman of Canticles, namely the church from paganism.[43] Like Philo, Origen allegorized man as rationality, intellect and virtue, and woman as flesh, bodily matter, vice and pleasure.[44] The scriptural text refers to virtue and vice, not men and women.

In Origen's ecclesiology, all Christians are priests; a non-ordained person can be worthier of the priesthood than one ordained. Some deacons, presbyters and bishops in the earthly church, if unworthy, do not belong to the heavenly one; people not ordained on earth, but worthy, are presbyters and bishops in the heavenly church.[45] Only those who understand God are worthy of being called priests (*soli qui intelligent Deum et capaces sint scientiae Dei, Hom.Lev.* 1.5). One should be

---

[39]Christopher Mount, '1 Corinthians 11:3-16: Spirit Possession and Authority in a Non-Pauline Interpolation', *JBL* 124 (2005): 313–40.

[40]Kathy Ehrensperger, *That We May Be Mutually Encouraged* (London: T&T Clark, 2004), p. 194.

[41]See Madigan and Osiek, *Women*, pp. 163–202.

[42]*Com.Rom.*, 4.6.160; *Hom.Jer.*, 4.5; *Frag.Luc.*, 32 Rauer.

[43]*Cant.*, 2 (133 Baehrens).

[44]*Hom.Ex.*, 2.2-3, also *Hom.Gen.*, 4.4; 5.2.

[45]*Com.Matt.*, 16.20-23; *Com.Matt.Ser.*, 12.

called a presbyter/elder (*presbyteri et seniores*) owing to one's spiritual perfection of 'the inner human being' rather than an ordained office (*officio*).[46] Perfection is not conferred by an ecclesiastical ministry (*Hom.Jer.* 11.3). The true priest 'knows and understands one's own sins' and possesses eminence in all virtues.[47] Only the sage is priest (a Stoic paradox), having the worship that derives from the knowledge of God.[48] The true Levites and priests, independently of ordination, 'devote themselves to the divine Word and exist exclusively for the service of God'.[49] A minister on earth can have authority over a better gifted person, 'as Jesus was subject to Joseph'.[50] True teachers are not necessarily ordained; vice versa, some ecclesiastical ministers are not teachers, if they lack God's Logos and Wisdom (*Hom.Luc.* 18). A man or woman sent by Christ for the salvation of humans 'is an apostle of Christ': the Samaritan woman and other women are apostles.[51] The church rests on many Peters, who can be women;[52] Jesus gives 'the keys of the Kingdom' to Peter and these other Peters, irrespective of gender; an ordained bishop who judges unrighteously has 'the power of the keys'.[53] Based on Gal. 3.28, 'in Christ there is neither male nor female', and Origen proclaims that every soul is above gender[54] and the 'inner human' is neither male nor female.[55] The model is Christ, who is Bride and Bridegroom.[56]

CANONICAL, ARCHAEOLOGICAL, EPIGRAPHICAL AND OTHER SOURCES

Canon 11 of the Council of Laodicea attests to the existence of πρεσβύτιδες who presided over churches (προκαθημέναι). Canon 2 of the Synod of Nîmes (394) testifies to women presbyters, ordained *in ministerium leviticum*. A fifth-century sarcophagus in Hagia Sophia (Constantinople) represents a man and a woman,

---

[46]*Hom.4Ps.36.3.*

[47]*Hom.Lev.*, 2.1; 6.3.

[48]*Com.Joh.*, 2.16.112-113.

[49]*Com.Joh.*, 1.10-11.

[50]*Hom.Luc.*, 20. For the autobiographical overtones here see my 'Autobiographical Self-Fashioning in Origen', in *Self, Self-Fashioning and Individuality in Late Antiquity*, eds Maren Niehoff and Joshua Levinson (Tübingen: Mohr Siebeck, 2019), pp. 271–88.

[51]Respectively, *Com.Joh.*, 32.17.204; 13.28.169.

[52]'All those against whom the gates of hell will not prevail, who have in themselves a work called Peter, are also Peters' (*Com.Matt.*, 12.10-11; cf. *Com.Matt.*, 139).

[53]*Com.Matt.*, 12.14; see my 'Loosing and Binding: Greek and Latin Patristics', in *EBR* 16 (Berlin: de Gruyter, 2018).

[54]*Cant.*, 3.9.3-4. See Ramelli, 'Gal 3:28'.

[55]This notion comes from Paul and Philo. E.g. in *Cant.* prol. 2.4; 6.63; *Princ.*, 1.1.9. Clement had already adopted Philo's dichotomy (*Protrep.*, 10.98.4). See my 'The (Double) Creation of the Human Being and Philosophical Soteriology', in *Philo and Philosophical Discourse*, eds Michael Cover and Lutz Doering, forthcoming.

[56]*Cant.*, 1.6.14; *Hom.Gen.*, 14.1: 'Qua God's Logos he is called Bridegroom, qua God's Wisdom/Sophia is called Bride'.

perfectly parallel, celebrating at the altar.[57] Likewise, a fifth-century ivory casket coming from a Roman patriarchal basilica portrays the presbytery of Old St Peter's with two men and two women perfectly paired, who lead the prayer of the people.[58] A man and a woman face each other across the altar, inside the ciborium, and raise the eucharistic offerings. Female and male images are paralleled in the iconography of the early ninth-century church of Santa Prassede in Rome, expressing 'gender parity and church leadership'.[59] The two women in the Santa Pudenziana in early fifth-century apse are interpreted as two *presbyterae* who parallel the elders of the Apocalypse.[60] In the Zeno Chapel at Santa Prassede's, Mary Theotokos with Jesus is accompanied, as a bishop, by a deacon and a presbyter, and eight crowned women dressed in gold parallel the twelve apostles with Christ. In the chapel, three women saints, Agnes, Pudentiana and Praxedes, face the three male apostles Andrew, James and John. In the crypt under the high altar of Santa Prassede, iconographical evidence indicates Praxedes was attributed church ministry. In a painting, Praxedes and Pudentiana, flanking Mary, wear a priestly dalmatic and Praxedes has an ochre band of cloth similar to that of the sixth-century Christ icon in St Catharine's Sinai monastery. Likewise, in Santa Pudenziana, in a ninth-century fresco Praxedes, Peter and Pudentiana are dressed as Carolingian bishops.

A marble plaque in a chapel marks the tomb of the mother of Pope Paschal (the promoter of the Praxedes and Pudentiana cult), *domnae Theodorae episcopae*, 'the lady Theodora bishop';[61] in the mosaic, she also appears as *Theodo[ra] episcopa*, flanked by Praxedes, Mary (also represented as a bishop) and Pudentiana. Mary was indeed portrayed as *archiepiscopa* and intercessor, wearing a pallium with two or three crosses; popes and bishops wore *pallia* with one cross.[62] Fourth-century marble slabs in St-Maximin La-Sainte-Baume (Provence) depict Mary *orante* in a dalmatic robe with unveiled long hair as a 'minister in the Temple of Jerusalem'[63] – a tradition that goes back to the *Protoevangelium of James*. The *Gospel of Bartholomew* 2.15-20 described Mary as a priest, at the altar of the Temple, with the Great Angel, sharing a loaf and a cup of wine. Ancient authors portrayed Mary with religious authority, 'leading the apostles in prayer, serving in essence as their liturgical leader'.[64]

---

[57]Kateusz, 'She Sacrificed Herself as the Priest', 45–67, 54.

[58]Anna Angiolini, *La capsella eburnea di Pola* (Bologna: Pàtron, 1970), pp. 104–6; Margherita Guarducci, *La capsella di Samagher* (Trieste: Archeologia, 1978); Davide Longhi, *La capsella di Samagher* (Ravenna: Girasole, 2006).

[59]Schaefer, *Women*, p. 375.

[60]Ibid., p. 195.

[61]Her husband Bonosus, the father of Paschal, was neither bishop nor called *episcopus* owing to Paschal: Theodora cannot have had the title *episcopa* simply as a bishop's wife or mother.

[62]For example, in the Chapel of St Venantius in the Lateran Baptistery (640-642) and in the archiepiscopal chapel in Ravenna.

[63]*Maria virgo minester de tempulo Gerosale* [sic].

[64]Stephen Shoemaker, *Mary in Early Christian Faith and Devotion* (New Haven, CT: Yale, 2016).

Among ordinary humans, a *venerabilis femina episcopa Q* . . . is attested at Terni around 500,[65] and the Irish bishop Mel ordained the consecrated Brigid bishop.[66] Abbesses later had episcopal dignity.[67] Out of six *episcopae*, at least four were not wives of bishops in the Latin church;[68] many literary and epigraphic sources document *presbyterae*, who wore priestly attire. Ordination rituals of *presbyterae* were identical to those of *presbyteri*, by the imposition of hands. Liturgies were in the feminine form, but even when in the masculine, a rubric indicated that the rite was valid for both.[69]

The Vatican's Museo Pio Cristiano keeps fourth-century sarcophagi which depict women as teachers and philosophers; here, for instance, Crispina holds a Gospel. Women as ecclesiastical teachers are epigraphically and iconographically attested in Sant'Agnese and Santa Sabina in Rome, where the woman teacher in the mosaic, in the same teaching gesture as Christ's, seems to be a *presbytera*.[70] In the Domitilla Catacomb a woman's vestments and title *Veneranda* suggest an *episcopa*.[71] On a Roman fourth–fifth-century tombstone, Alexandra, an *orans* in a pastoral role between two sheep, can be an *episcopa*, parallel to male bishops. In the Priscilla Cemetery in Rome, a fresco in the Greek Chapel (early third century) shows women consecrating the Eucharist,[72] and in the cubiculum of the *velata*, two men flank a central female figure wearing a priestly 'chasuble' over an alb, with a Gospel scroll; the bishop's hand on her shoulder represents her teaching mission.[73] An enthroned bishop corresponds an enthroned woman, dressed alike: Mary *episcopa*.

In the fourth century, the liturgical prayers for the ordination of women by the laying of hands (χειροτονία) parallel those for the ordination of men in *Apostolic Constitutions* 8. Likewise, the rituals for men and women, including abbots and abbesses, are the same in the eighth-century Pontifical of Egbert of York and in the tenth-century Roman-Germanic Pontifical. Bishops impose their hands and invoke the Spirit for men and women; an abbess is given a pastoral staff and the *regimen animarum*, like a bishop.[74]

Ute Eisen offers rich epigraphical evidence on ordained women, presbyters, apostles, prophets, teachers, masters, ordained widows, deacons and bishops; Haye van der Meer, Ida Raming and John Wijngaards argued that the exclusion of women

---

[65]Schaefer, *Women*, p. 158.
[66]*Vita Brigidae* 17–19.
[67]Joan Morris, *The Lady Was a Bishop* (New York: Macmillan, 1973); Gary Macy, *The Hidden History of Women's Ordination: Female Clergy in the Medieval West* (Oxford: Oxford University Press, 2008).
[68]Hildeburga, the wife of bishop Segenfrid (tenth century), was *episcopissa*; *episcopiae* ('wives of bishops') differs from *episcopae* ('female bishops').
[69]Macy, *History*.
[70]Schaefer, *Women*, p. 205.
[71]Ibid., pp. 224–5.
[72]Ibid., p. 189; Ally Kateusz and Luca Badini, 'Women Church Leaders in and around Fifth-Century Rome', in *Patterns of Women's Leadership*.
[73]Schaefer, *Women*, pp. 191–2.
[74]Ibid., pp. 191–2, 254–5, 272–99; Macy, *History*.

from presbyterate and church hierarchy was due to historical circumstances and prejudice.[75] Kevin Madigan and Carolyn Osiek offered a nearly complete[76] collection of epigraphic, literary and canonical sources on ordained women in the Greek, Latin and partially Syriac churches in the first six–seven centuries.[77] Women administered baptism, preached, prayed, performed charitable works and participated in the eucharistic consecration, as still attested by Justinian and the *Testamentum Domini nostri*.

Many Eastern and Western sources describe women presbyters:[78] in the West, *presbyterae*, *sacerdotae* ('women presbyters/bishops') and the aforementioned *venerabilis episcopa*. Ordained women exercised the presbyterate with their bishops' approval in Southern Italy and other Italian regions in communion with Rome:[79] according to Pope Gelasius I's Letter 14 (494), Canon 26, they were 'encouraged and confirmed to exercise their ministry at the sacred altars and perform all the other tasks which would be assigned only to the service of men': liturgical, juridical and magisterial tasks of a presbyter. *Presbyterae*, who wore priestly garb, are epigraphically attested from Southern Italy to Greece to Egypt, Asia Minor, etc.[80] Rites for their ordination were identical to those for *presbyteri*, with the imposition of hands. On an inscription, Laeta *praesbytera* was not the wife of a presbyter, as her husband, the dedicator, was no presbyter.[81] Martia *presbyteria*, on another inscription, near Poitiers, made the oblations with Olybrius and Nepos, 'in the same way' as these did.[82]

NYSSEN AND WOMEN IN THE CHURCH

Gregory of Nyssa depicted symbolically his eldest sister Macrina, a consecrated virgin, as a presbyter: she taught the Christian doctrine (*Vita Macrinae*; *De Anima et Resurrectione*), participated in Christ's passion and offered herself as a sacrifice. Her final prayer in *Vita Macrinae* bristles with liturgical formulae, including the

---

[75]Haye van der Meer, *Priestertum der Frau?* (Freiburg: Herder, 1969); Ida Raming, *Der Ausschluss der Frau vom priesterlichen Amt* (Köln: Böhlau, 1973) and *Priesteramt der Frau* (Münster: Lit, 2002); Ute Eisen, *Women Officeholders in Early Christianity* (Collegeville, MN: Liturgical, 2000); John Wijngaards, *No Women in Holy Orders?* (London: Canterbury, 2002).
[76]For instance, Theosebia is missing.
[77]Kevin Madigan and Carolyn Osiek, *Ordained Women in the Early Church* (Baltimore, MD: Johns Hopkins, 2005); Ilaria Ramelli, 'Theosebia', *JFSR* 26 (2010): 79–102. See also Roger Gryson, *Le ministère des femmes dans l'église ancienne* (Gembloux: Duculot, 1972); Aimé George Martimort, *Les deaconesses* (Rome: Liturgiche, 1982).
[78]Madigan and Osiek, *Women*, pp. 163–202.
[79]Giorgio Otranto, 'Note sul sacerdozio femminile nell'antichità', *VetChr* 19 (1982): 341–60; MaryAnn Rossi, 'On Recovering the Women Priests in Early Christianity', *JFSR* 7 (1991): 73–94.
[80]Madigan and Osiek, *Women*; Ramelli, 'Theosebia'; Schaefer, *Women*, pp. 152–5.
[81]Fourth/fifth century, CIL 10.8079.
[82]*Pariter*: CIL 13.1183; Madigan and Osiek, *Women*, 196.

eucharistic anaphora.[83] Macrina was a *spiritual* presbyter for Nyssen, in the vein of Origen's spiritual ministers, as seen earlier.

Gregory, like Origen, did not regard 1 Cor. 14.34-35 as an interpolation (see above), nor as a prohibition against women teaching in churches. His exegesis of this passage in his homilies on the Book of Ecclesiastes (*In Eccl.* 7) is very reductionist[84] and omits verse 34b, the harshest against women: one should speak if one has something good to say for the edification of faith, but keep silent if one has something bad to say, or if some married women want to learn something: they should ask their husbands at home, not at church, where they would disturb the assembly. Paul's exhortation is not against women teaching or preaching as presbyters according to Gregory, who never cites vv. 34-35 anywhere else (and never cites 1 Tim. 2:11-15[85]).

Nyssen rejected both slavery[86] and discrimination against women in church: he uses ὁμότιμος to indicate both that God gave 'the same dignity' to masters and slaves and that Macrina and Emmelia made themselves 'of equal dignity' with their former slaves.[87] Now, Nyssen and Basil use ὁμότιμος also to designate the equal dignity of man and woman,[88] and Nazianzen to declare that Theosebia had the same ecclesiastical dignity as a priest/bishop, as we shall see.

Macrina led the female and male sections of her monastery as ἡγουμένη but was no deacon or presbyter, unlike Lampadion (or Theosebia: below). Lampadion was 'a woman in the diaconal order [ἐν τῷ τῆς διακονίας βαθμῷ], the director [προτεταγμένη] of the choir/group [χορός] of the virgins' at Annesi[89] in a liturgical ministry, for the Divine Office. Macrina 'had gathered a great χορός' of virgins around her, 'through her spiritual birth-pangs', like Saint Paul, 'and had brought them to perfection . . . psalmodies echoed at every hour, night and day' in the Annesi domestic monastery.[90] The same is the case for deacon Publia's monastery in Antioch under Julian.[91]

Nyssen took Gal. 3.27-28 seriously. Origen inspired him also in this respect, both with his own conception of the ministries of women in the church and of the spiritual and symbolical parallels to earthly liturgy and ordained ministries and with the orientation of the whole of his thought to eschatology.[92] For Gregory as well, Christian life and church practice must always draw their guidelines from the *telos*,

---

[83]Derek Krueger, 'Writing and the Liturgy of Memory in Gregory of Nyssa's *Life of Macrina*', JECS 8 (2000): 483–510, esp. 508–9.

[84]GNO 5.409.15-21.

[85]Only in *Contra Eunom.*, 3.10.16, GNO 2.295.9, Gregory of Nyssa refers to v. 14, not to criticize women's ministry but to argue that a woman had to be the first witness and apostle of the resurrection.

[86]Ramelli, *Social Justice*, pp. 172–211.

[87]Gregory of Nyssa, *VMacr.*, GNO 8/1.377.25-378.5; 381.22-27.

[88]Demonstration in Ramelli, 'Theosebia'.

[89]Gregory of Nyssa, *VMacr.*, 29.

[90]Gregory of Nyssa, *Ep.*, 19.7-8.

[91]Theodoret, *HE.*, 3.14.

[92]On this orientation: Ramelli, *The Christian Doctrine of Apokatastasis: A Critical Assessment from the New Testament to Eriugena*, SuppVCh, 120 (Leiden: E.J. Brill, 2013); *Social Justice*, Ch. 4.

which corresponds to God's eternal plan for humanity. This excludes slavery or discrimination against women.

Gregory Nazianzen, who according to tradition contributed to the redaction of Origen's *Philocalia*, is the most important source on Theosebia, the sister and colleague of Nyssen in the ecclesiastical ministry, σύζυγος of Nyssen according to Nazianzen's Letter 197.[93] This and Epigrams 161 and 164 indicate that she was one of the children of Emmelia (thus, a sister of Nyssen, Macrina and Basil), and the σύζυγος of a presbyter and bishop, Nyssen. Nazianzen speaks of her reverently: 'your holy [ἁγίας] and blessed sister [μακαρίας]' (*Ep.* 197.2), the daughter of Emmelia. Theosebia also lived at Nyssa and collaborated with Gregory (who 'lived together with such a woman' [τοιαύτῃ συζῆσαι], *Ep.* 197.4). Nazianzen extols 'my Theosebia' for her 'life consecrated to God' (*Ep.* 197.5) and her 'support of pious women' (ἕρμα γυναικῶν εὐσεβέων, *Epig.* 164) and τὴν γυναικῶν παρρησίαν ('women's confidence', *Ep.* 197.5). Theosebia supported and encouraged women in her church, inspiring them with confidence. As Nazianzen confesses, 'I exult even in the memory of this blessed woman' (*Ep.* 197.7).

What is more, in *Ep.* 197.5-6, Nazianzen celebrates Theosebia as

the glory of the Church [τὸ τῆς ἐκκλησίας καύχημα], the adornment of Christ, the benefit of our generation, the confidence and daring of women, the most wonderful and most outstanding [εὐπρεπεστάτην καὶ διαφανεστάτην] amidst such a great splendour of siblings, Theosebia, the *truly sacred* [τὴν ὄντως ἱεράν], *truly colleague of a priest-bishop, endowed with a dignity equal to his* [ἱερέως σύζυγον καὶ ὁμότιμον], and *worthy of the great Mysteries* [τῶν μεγάλων μυστηρίων ἀξίαν].

Nazianzen was a presbyter and bishop (ἱερεύς),[94] like Nyssen, Theosebia's brother and colleague. It is significant that he spoke in such reverent terms of Theosebia. Especially the description 'truly sacred and truly colleague of a priest-bishop, endowed with a dignity equal to his, and worthy of the great Mysteries' points to Theosebia's presbyterate. Theosebia is sacred/consecrated (ἱερά) and a colleague of a ἱερεύς, a priest-bishop. In *Epig.* 165.161, Nazianzen describes Theosebia likewise: ἱερήος σύζυγος, 'colleague of a priest-bishop', as Nazianzen repeats twice. Therefore, she must have been a priest herself. Ἱέρεια as 'female presbyter' is found in *Const. Ap.* 3.9.3 and Epiphanius, *Pan.* 79.7 and ἱέρισσαι in *Pan.* 79.4, where it is associated with πρεσβυτερίδες and may indicate women presbyters or bishops.

Two points confirm that σύζυγος in Nazianzen's words does not mean 'wife' (Theosebia was Nyssen's sister) but 'colleague' in the priestly office:

---

[93]Ramelli, 'Theosebia'; Silvas, *Letters*, 100 deems Theosebia the πρεσβυτέρα of the 'choir of virgins' of Nyssa.

[94]In a contemporary writer, Chrysostom, the word ἱερεύς is attested in the sense of 'bishop' (e.g. *Sac.*, 3.12), as in Gregory of Nazianzus' *Epig.*, 164 and *Ep.*, 16 PG 37.52A and other fourth/fifth-century authors, for example, Sozomen, *HE.*, 4.22.22. It designates both a bishop and a priest in *Const. Ap.*, 6.18.11 and 8.2.6; Epiphanius, *Pan.*, 80.5. In later texts, ἱερεύς is a synonym of 'presbyter' (e.g. Maximus the Confessor, *Schol. EH.*, 5.5; 5.6; and Ibid., *Schol.CH.*, 13.4.).

1. σύζυγος does not mean just 'spouse' but has many meanings in fourth-century Patristic Greek, some metaphorical, including 'colleague';[95]

2. Nazianzen, after calling Theosebia 'colleague of a priest-bishop', significantly insists that she was invested with a dignity and honour equal to that of a priest-bishop (ἱερέως ὁμότιμος). As anticipated, Basil, Nazianen's friend, frequently employs ὁμότιμος to indicate the equal dignity and honour between both genders, from the same human 'lump' (φύραμα), with the same honour and dignity (ὁμοτίμως), in perfect equality (ἐξ ἴσου); men are even inferior in piety.[96] Both genders have 'one and the same virtue', 'one and the same nature'; their creation was of equal honour and dignity (ὁμότιμος, as Basil insists), with the same capacity and activity (ἐνέργεια) and the same reward.[97]

Theosebia was a colleague and ὁμότιμος of a priest, according to Nazianzen: on account of her ecclesiastical office, she had such a dignity (ἀξία) as to be worthy to participate in the celebration of the 'great Mysteries', namely, from the time of Clement, the Mass.[98] As seen, the ancient church had women deacons, presbyters, presidents and perhaps bishops. Nazianzen, *Epig.* 164 and 161, exalts Emmelia and her children, among whom there were 'three illustrious priests' and one female 'colleague of a priest': 'three of her sons were illustrious priests-bishops [ἱερῆες]; a daughter of hers was a colleague of a priest [ἡ δ'ἱερῆος σύζυγος], and the rest of her children, like a host of saints.' The priests–bishops were Basil, Gregory and Peter; the colleague of a priest is, again, Theosebia, whom, in *Ep.* 197 as well, Nazianzen calls colleague and ὁμότιμος of a ἱερεύς. Significantly, in *Epig.* 164 Nazianzen, immediately after the three bishops, Basil, Peter and Gregory, does not mention other brothers of theirs, not even Naucratius, an exemplary ascetic, or their eldest sister, Macrina, revered by Nyssen, but Theosebia. This is probably because Theosebia was an ordained presbyter.

In strophe 163, Nazianzen extols 'the luminous virgin' Macrina, stressing her secluded life and glory; in 164–165, Nazianzen celebrates again Theosebia, then Nyssen, 'great ἱερεύς', and repeats for the third time that she was 'the colleague of a priest and bishop', and for the second time stresses her ministry to women: 'And you, Theosebia, daughter of the great Emmelia and *colleague* [σύζυγε] *of the great Gregory*, have descended under this sacred ground in all serenity and security, you *support of pious women* [ἕρμα γυναικῶν εὐσεβέων].' (s.164). Gregory Nyssen is praised by Nazianzen soon after her and in association with her (s.165), not as a mystic, ascetic, Christian author or theologian but as a 'great priest-bishop' (ἱερεὺς μέγας): only as an ordained ecclesiastical minister.

---

[95]Ramelli, 'Theosebia'.
[96]Basil the Great, *Hom Jul.*, 2. (PG. 31.241AB).
[97]*Hom.Ps.*, 1 PG 29.216-217.
[98]See Ilaria Ramelli, 'The Mysteries of Scripture', in *Clement's Biblical Exegesis*, eds. Judith Kovacs et al. (Leiden: E.J. Brill, 2016), pp. 80–110.

Theosebia's ministry, as described by Nazianzen, involved the celebration of the Mass, mentioned in his letter, and the spiritual (and perhaps material) support offered to pious women of her church, in addition to being for them a motive for pride, confidence and daring, as is said both in the letter and in the epigram. Remarkably, the functions of a presbyter–bishop (ἱερεύς) that Nazianzen indicates in *Carmina* 2.1.13.1-4, PG 37.1227A, namely the celebration of the Eucharist and the care of souls, are the same he ascribes to Theosebia.[99] Qua colleague of Nyssen, who was exiled by impulse of the '(Neo-)Arian' party, Theosebia was very probably 'anti-Arian' too.[100] During his exile, Theosebia might have taken up her brother's and colleague's tasks. Other ordained women in the Cappadocian church were active in the anti-'Arian' controversy, such as the three deacons, daughters of Terentius, governor of Cappadocia in the 370s. Basil of Caesarea, *Ep.* 105, in a letter on orthodoxy against 'neo-Arian' and Macedonian doctrines, *Ep.* 105, praised their orthodox (Nicene) faith as crucial.

Theosebia, depicted by Nazianzen as colleague of a ἱερεύς and of equal dignity, was ordained, celebrated the Mass, perhaps lead the Divine Office, and surely offered a spiritual, and maybe material, support of Christian women in Nyssa and a doctrinal direction (pivotal in a period of theological controversies) and lead the 'choir of virgins' in Nyssa. During her brother's and colleague's exile, she is probably a point of reference for the local church, and upon his return, she and her virgins welcomed him with lamps in the church. Nyssen's *Ep.* 6 describes how the people received him at his return to Nyssa (probably after his exile) with affection: he was also welcomed by 'the χορός of the virgins', with lanterns, at the entrance of the church of Nyssa (§10). Theosebia probably led the group of consecrated virgins of the church of Nyssa (and perhaps their monastic choir): they lived near the church, which they did not abandon to meet Gregory. Theosebia was their presbyter, colleague and ὁμότιμος of their bishop, who, as Nazianzen indicates, lived in Nyssa close to her.

OLYMPIA AS 'MOST HONOURABLE' AND HER ORDINATION

Deacon Olympia, the founder and leader of a city monastery in Constantinople (like Theosebia in Nyssa), was ordained by bishop Nectarius: 'he ordained [ἐχειροτόνησε] her deacon [διάκονον].'[101] She benefited bishops Nectarius, Gregory Nyssen or Nazianzen, Peter of Sebaste, Chrysostom and Epiphanius.[102] She received, and exhorted Chrysostom to protect, the Tall Brothers, Origenian monastic supporters of the doctrine of apokatastasis,[103] exiled by Theophilus of Alexandria.[104] Nyssen,

---

[99]The former function is also presented by Basil as a task of a presbyter in *Ep.*, 93 PG 32.485A.
[100]On these categories, see Lewis Ayres, *Nicaea and Its Legacy* (Oxford: Oxford University Press, 2004).
[101]Sozomen, *HE.*, 8.9.
[102]Palladius, *Dial.*, 17.
[103]Documentation on this doctrine in Ramelli, *Apokatastasis*.
[104]Palladius, *Dial.*, 16-17.

also an Origenian, dedicated to Olympia his exegesis of Canticles: in the preface, significantly, he calls Olympia σεμνοπρεπεστάτη, 'most honourable', using the superlative form of the address formula usually reserved for bishops.[105]

The anonymous fifth-century *Vita Olympiadis* narrates her ordination as a deacon and the construction of her monastery next to the cathedral (6), as that of the virgins led by Theosebia next to the cathedral at Nyssa. Olympia was aided by two other female deacons in her monastery in Constantinople.[106] Chrysostom ordained three women as deacons for Olympia's monastery (*V.Ol.* 7); he 'ordained [χειροτονεῖ] deacons [διακόνους] of the holy church three of her relatives, Elisanthia, Martyria, and Palladia, for the monastery; thus, by the four diaconal offices, the established procedure would have been accomplished by them uninterruptedly'.[107] Olympia, like Macrina, attracted her relatives and former slaves into her monastery. Olympia was also the superior and the monastery had four deacons.[108] Theosebia may also have guided her virgins in the divine office like Olympia's deacons, although this is unclear from the sources. What Nazianzen mentions is Theosebia's ministry, parallel and ὁμότιμος to that of a ἱερεύς, the celebration of the Mass and the support of pious women, to whom she offered motives for confidence and pride.

BIBLIOGRAPHY

Aasgaard, R. 'Paul as a Child: Children and Childhood in the Letters of the Apostle', *JBL* 126, no. 1 (2007): 129–59.

Angiolini, A. *La capsella eburnea di Pola*. Bologna: Pàtron, 1970.

Arbel, V. D. *Forming Femininity in Antiquity: Eve, Gender, and Ideologies in the Greek Life of Adam and Eve*. Oxford: Oxford University Press, 2012.

Aubineau, M. *Grégoire de Nysse: Traité de la virginité*. Paris: Cerf, 1966.

Aymer, M. 'Redaction, World Creation, and Resistance in the Acts of Paul and Thecla', *S* 75 (1997): 43–61.

Ayres, L. *Nicaea and Its Legacy*. Oxford: Oxford University Press, 2004.

Bain, K. *Women's Socioeconomic Status and Religious Leadership in Asia Minor*. Minneapolis: Fortress, 2014.

Barrier, J. *The Acts of Paul and Thecla*. Tübingen: Mohr Siebeck, 2009.

Barrier, J. W., Bremmer, J. N. and Nicklas, T. (eds). *Thecla: Paul's Disciple and Saint in the East and West*. Leuven: Peeters, 2015.

Batovici, D. 'Contrasting Ecclesial Function in the Second Century', *Aug* 51 (2011): 303–14.

Berger, T. *Gender Differences and the Making of Liturgical History*. Farnham: Ashgate, 2011.

---

[105]See my 'Apokatastasis and Epektasis in *Hom. in Cant.*', in *In Canticum Canticorum*, eds Giulio Maspero et al. (Leiden: E.J. Brill, 2018), pp. 312–39.

[106]Palladius, *Dial.*, 10.50.

[107]The fact that they had to be performed uninterruptedly and the parallel with deacon Lampadion, προτεταγμένη to the monastic choir at Annesi, suggests that here the reference is to the Divine Office.

[108]Subsequently, Pentadia and Procla took over the office of two of the previous deacons.

Bogdanović, J. *The Canopy and the Byzantine Church*. Oxford: Oxford University Press, 2017.

Bovon, F. 'Le privilège pascal de Marie-Madeleine', *NTS* 30 (1984): 50–62.

Bremmer, J. R. *Maidens, Magic and Martyrs in Early Christianity*. Tübingen: Mohr Siebeck, 2017.

Burrus, V. *Chastity as Autonomy: Women in the Stories of Apocryphal Acts*. Lewiston: Mellen, 1987.

Burrus, V. 'Mimicking Virgins', *Arethusa* 38 (2005): 49–88.

Burrus, V. 'Xanthippe, Polyxena, Rebecca', in S. R. Johnson, R. R. Dupertuis and C. Shea (eds), *Reading and Teaching Ancient Fiction: Jewish, Christian, and Greco-Roman Narratives*, 9–29. Atlanta, GA: SBL Press, 2018.

Cain, E. R. 'Tertullian's Precarious Panopticon: A Performance of Visual Piety', *JECS* 27 (2019): 611–33.

Calpino, T. J. *Women, Work, and Leadership in Acts*. WUNT 2.361. Tübingen: Mohr Siebeck, 2014.

Campbell, W. 'Consonance and Communal Membership in the *Didache*', *VC* 71 (2017): 469–94.

Chew, K. 'Passion and Conversion', in I. Ramelli and J. Perkins (eds), *Early Christian and Jewish Narrative: The Role of Religion in Shaping Narrative Forms*, 247–71. Tübingen: Mohr Siebeck, 2015.

Clark, E. *Jerome, Chrysostom, and Friends*. New York: Mellen, 1979.

Cloke, G. *This Female Man of God*. London: Routledge, 1995.

Coakley, S. *God, Sexuality, and the Self*. Cambridge: Cambridge University Press, 2013.

Cohick, L. and Hughes, A. *Christian Women in the Patristic World*. Grand Rapids, MI: Baker, 2016.

Collins, J. N. *Diakonia*. Oxford: Oxford University Press, 2009.

Collins, R. F. *Accompanied by a Believing Wife: Ministry and Celibacy in the Earliest Christian Communities*. Collegeville, MN: Liturgical, 2013.

Cooper, K. *Band of Angels*. London: Atlantic, 2013.

Corley, K. *Women and the Historical Jesus: Feminist Myths of Christian Origins*. Santa Rosa, CA: Polebridge, 2002.

D'Angelo, M. R. 'Women Partners in the New Testament', *JFSR* 6 (1990): 65–86.

Davis, S. J. 'From Women's Piety to Male Devotion: From Women's Piety to Male Devotion: Gender Studies, the Acts of Paul and Thecla, and the Evidence of an Arabic Manuscript', *HTR* 108 (2015): 579–93.

DeConick, A. *Holy Misogyny: Why the Sex and Gender Conflicts in the Early Church Still Matter*. New York: Bloomsbury T&T Clark, 2013.

den Dulk, M. 'I Permit No Woman to Teach Except for Thecla: The Curious Case of the Pastoral Epistles and the *Acts of Paul* Reconsidered', *NovT* 54 (2012): 176–203.

Denzey, N. 'Women as Independent Religious Specialists in Second-Century Rome', in U. Tervahauta, I. Miroshnikov, O. Lehtipuu and I. Dunderberg (eds), *Women and Knowledge in Early Christianity*, 21–38. Leiden: E.J. Brill, 2017.

Douglas, S. *Early Church Understandings of Jesus as the Female Divine: The Scandal of the Scandal of Particularity*. New York: Bloomsbury T&T Clark, 2016.

Draper, J. A. 'Prophets, Teachers, Bishops and Deacons', in C. Jefford (ed.), *The Didache in Context*, 284–312. Leiden: E.J. Brill, 1995.

Draper, J. A. (ed.). *The Didache in Modern Research*. Leiden: Brill, 1996.

Draper, J. A. '"Wandering Charismatics" in the Didache', *JECS* 6 (1998): 541–76.

Draper, J. A. and Jefford, C. N. (eds). *The Didache: A Missing Piece of the Puzzle in Early Christianity*. Atlanta, GA: SBL, 2015.

Eastman, D. '"Epiphanius" and Patristic Debates on the Marital Status of Peter and Paul', *VigChr* 67 (2013): 499–516.

Eckhardt, B. (ed.). *Private Associations and Jewish Communities in the Hellenistic and Roman Cities*. Leiden: E.J. Brill, 2019.

Edsall, B. 'Not Baptising Thecla: Early Interpretive Efforts on 1 Cor 1:17', *VChr* 71 (2017): 235–60.

Ehrensperger, K. *That We May Be Mutually Encouraged: Feminism and the New Perspective in Pauline Studies*. London: T&T Clark, 2004.

Eisen, U. *Amsträgerinnen in frühen Christentum*. Göttingen: Vandenhoeck & Ruprecht, 1996; *Women Officeholders in Early Christianity*. Collegeville, MN: Liturgical, 2000.

Elliott, J. K. 'Christian Apocrypha and the Developing Role of Mary', in A. Gregory and C. Tuckett (eds), *The Oxford Handbook of Early Christian Apocrypha*, 2nd edn, 269–88. Oxford: Oxford University Press, 2018.

Elm, S. *'Virgins of God': The Making of Asceticism in Late Antiquity*. Oxford: Oxford University Press, 1996.

Epp, E. J. *Junia*. Minneapolis, MN: Fortress, 2005.

Esbroeck, M. van. *Maxime le Confesseur: Vie de la Vierge*. CSCO 478–9. Louvain: Peeters, 1986.

Esch-Ermeling, E. *Thekla—Paulusschülerin wider Willen?* Münster: Aschendorff, 2008.

Estévez, E. *Las mujeres en los orígenes del cristianismo*. Estella: Verbo Divino, 2012.

Frey, J. and Rupschus, N. (eds). *Frauen im antiken Judentum und frühen Christentum*. Tübingen: Mohr Siebeck, 2019.

Gold, B. *Perpetua: Athlete of God*. Oxford: Oxford University Press, 2018.

Graham, A. *Mary Magdalene the First Apostle*. Cambridge, MA: Harvard University Press, 2003.

Greschat, K. *Gelehrte Frauen des frühen Christentums*. Stuttgart: Steiner, 2015.

Grohmann, M. 'Metaphors of God, Nature and Birth in Psalm 90.2 and 110.3', in P. van Hecke and A. Labahn (eds), *Metaphors in the Psalms*, 23–34. Leuven: Peeters, 2010.

Grundeken, M. 'Diakone in Rom', *VChr* 72 (2018): 93–101.

Gryson, R. *The Ministry of Women in the Early Church*. Collegeville, MN: Liturgical, 1976.

Guarducci, M. *La capsella di Samagher*. Trieste: Società di archeologia, 1978.

Haines-Eitzen, K. *The Gendered Palimpsest: Women, Writing, and Representation in Early Christianity*. Oxford: Oxford University Press, 2011.

Halvgaard, T. 'The Role of the Female Spiritual Principle and Epinoia', in U. Tervahauta, I. Miroshnikov, O. Lehtipuu and I. Dunderberg (eds) *Women and Knowledge in Early Christianity*, 237–52. SuppVCh, 144. Leiden: E.J. Brill, 2017.

Harrison, V. 'Male and Female in Cappadocian Theology', *JTS* 41 (1990): 441–71.

Hartenstein, J. 'Encratism, Asceticism, and the Construction of Gender', in A. Gregory and C. Tuckett (eds), *The Oxford Handbook of Early Christian Apocrypha*, 2nd edn, 389–406. Oxford: Oxford University Press, 2018.

Hemelrijk, E. *Women and Civic Life in the Roman West*. Oxford: Oxford University Press, 2015.

Hinsdale, M. A. 'St. Mary of Magdala Ecclesiological Provocations', *Catholic Theological Society of America Proceedings* 66 (2011): 67–90.

Hogan, P. 'Paul and Seneca on Women', in J. Dodson and D. Briones (eds), *Paul and Seneca in Dialogue: Ancient Theology and Religion Series*, 208–31. Leiden: E.J. Brill, 2017.

Hoklotubbe, C. *Civilized Piety: The Rhetoric of Pietas in the Pastoral Epistles and the Roman Empire*. Waco, TX: Baylor, 2017.

Hughes, A. 'The Legacy of the Feminine in the Christology of Origen, Methodius and Gregory of Nyssa', *VChr* 70 (2016): 51–76.

Hunter, D. 'Ambrosiaster on Women as Not God's Image', *JTS* 43 (1992): 447–69.

Hunter, D. 'Rivalry between Presbyters and Deacons in the Roman Church', *VChr* 71 (2017): 495–510.

Hylen, S. *A Modest Apostle: Thecla and the History of Women in the Early Church*. New York: Oxford University Press, 2015.

Hylen, S. *Women in the New Testament World*. Oxford: Oxford University Press, 2019.

Jantsch, T. (ed.). *Frauen, Männer, Engel. Perspektiven zu 1Kor 11,2–16*. Neukirchen-Vluyn: Neukirchener, 2015.

Jensen, A. *Thekla die Apostolin*. Freiburg: Herder, 1995.

Jensen, R. 'The Apocryphal Mary in Early Christian Art', in A. Gregory and C. Tuckett (eds), *The Oxford Handbook of Early Christian Apocrypha*, 2nd edn, 289–305. Oxford: Oxford University Press, 2018.

Johnson, L. 'In Search of the Voice of Women in the Churches', in E. MacCabe (ed.), *Women in the Biblical World*, 135–54. Lanham, MD: University Press of America, 2009.

Johnson, S. *The Life and Miracles of Thekla*. Washington, DC: Church History Society, 2006.

Kaestli, J.-D. and Rodorf, W. 'La fin de la vie de Thècle dans les *Actes de Paul et Thècle*', *Apocrypha* 25 (2014): 9–102.

Kartzow, M. B. 'Resurrection as Gossip: Representations of Women in Resurrection Stories of the Gospels', *Lectio Difficilior*, 2010. http://www.lectio.unibe.ch/

Kateusz, A. 'She Sacrificed Herself as the Priest', *JFSR* 33 (2017): 45–67.

Kateusz, A. *Mary and Early Christian Women: Hidden Leadership*. New York: Palgrave Macmillan, 2019.

Kateusz, A. and Badini, L. 'Women Church Leaders in and around Fifth-Century Rome', in J. E. Taylor and I. L.E. Ramelli (eds), *Patterns of Women's Leadership in Early Christianity*, 228–60. Oxford: Oxford University Press, 2021.

Keener, C. P. *Women, and Wives*. Peabody, MA: Hendrickson, 1992.

King, K. *Images of the Feminine in Gnosticism*. Philadelphia, PA: Fortress, 1988.

King, K. 'Prophetic Power and Women's Authority: The Case of the Gospel of Mary Magdalene', in B. M. Kienzle and P. J. Walker (eds), *Women Preachers and Prophets*, 21–41. Berkeley: University of California, 1998.

Kitzler, P. *From Passio Perpetuae to Acta Perpetuae*. Berlin: de Gruyter, 2015.

Korner, R. J. *The Origin and Meaning of Ekklēsia in the Early Jesus Movement*. Leiden: Brill, 2017.

Kraemer, R. *Unreliable Witnesses: Religion, Gender, and History in the Greco-Roman Mediterranean*. Oxford: Oxford University Press, 2011.

Kraemer, R. 'Jewish Mothers and Daughters in the Greco-Roman World', in S. J. D. Cohen (ed.), *The Jewish Family in Antiquity*, 89–112. Atlanta, GA: SBL, 2020.

Kristionat, J. *Die Rolle der Frau im frühen Manichäismus*. Heidelberg: Antike, 2013.

Krueger, D. 'Writing and the Liturgy of Memory in Gregory of Nyssa's *Life of Macrina*', *JECS* 8 (2000): 483–510.

Ledegang, F. 'Origen's View of the Apostolic Tradition', in A. Hilhorst (ed.), *The Apostolic Age in Patristic Thought*, 130–8. Leiden: E.J. Brill, 2004.

Lee, A. D. *Pagans and Christians in Late Antiquity: A Sourcebook*. London: Routledge, 2016.

Lehtipuu, O. and Dunderberg, I. 'Introduction', in U. Tervahauta et al. (eds), *Women and Knowledge in Early Christianity*, 1–19. Supplements to Vigiliae Christianae 144, Leiden: Brill, 2017.

Lin, Y.-J. 'Junia: An Apostle before Paul', *JBL* 139, no. 1 (2020): 191–209.

Lipsett, D. *Desiring Conversion: Hermas, Thecla, Aseneth*. Oxford: Oxford University Press, 2010.

Longhi, D. *La capsella di Samagher*. Ravenna: Girasole, 2006.

Lössl, J. 'Between Hipparchian Cynicism and Priscillian Montanism: Some Notes on Tatian, or 3.6', *VChr* 74 (2020): 84–107.

MacDonald, D. *The Legend and the Apostle: The Battle for Paul in Story and Canon*. Philadelphia, PA: Westminster, 1983.

Macy, G. 'The Ordination of Women in the Early Middle Ages', *ThS* 61 (2000): 481–507.

Macy, G. *The Hidden History of Women's Ordination: Female Clergy in the Medieval West*. Oxford: Oxford University Press, 2008.

Madigan, K. and Osiek, C. *Ordained Women in the Early Church*. Baltimore, MD: Johns Hopkins, 2005.

Marjanen, A. *The Woman Jesus Loved*. Leiden: E.J. Brill, 1996.

Marshall, J. E. *Women Praying and Prophesying in Corinth: Gender and Inspired Speech in First Corinthians*. Tübingen: Mohr Siebeck, 2017.

Martimort, G. *Les diaconesses*. Rome: Edizioni Liturgiche, 1982.

Matthew, S. 'A Feminist Analysis of the Veiling Passage: Who Really Cares that Paul was Not a Gender Egalitarian After All?', *Lectio Difficilior*, 2015. http://www.lectio.unibe.ch/

Matthews, A. *Gender Roles and the People of God*. Grand Rapids, MI: Zondervan, 2017.

Mayer, J. *Monumenta de viduis diaconissis virginibusque*. Bonn: Hanstein, 1938.

McCarthy, V. K. 'The Pure Eye of Her Soul', in J. McGuckin (ed.), *Orthodox Monasticism*. New York: Theotokos, 2014.

McLarty, J. D. *Thecla's Devotion: Narrative and Emotion in the Acts of Paul and Thecla*. Cambridge: James Clarke, 2020.

Meer, H. van der. *Priestertum der Frau?: Eine theologiegeschichtliche Untersuchung*. Freiburg: Herder, 1969.

Messmer, A. '¿Había pastoras en la Iglesia primitiva?', *Protestante Digital*, 20 August 2017. http://protestantedigital.com/

Militello, C. and Rigato, M.-L. (eds). *Paolo e le donne*. Assisi: Cittadella, 2006.

Morris, J. *The Lady Was a Bishop: The Hidden History of Women with Clerical Ordination and the Jurisdiction of Bishops*. New York: MacMillan, 1973.

Mount, C. '1 Corinthians 11:3-16: Spirit Possession and Authority in a Non-Pauline Interpolation', *JBL* 124 (2005): 313–40.

Murphy-O'Connor, J. 'Prisca and Aquila', *BiblRev* 8 (1992): 40–51.

Nasrallah, L. 'Out of Love for Paul', in I. Ramelli and J. Perkins (eds), *Early Christian and Jewish Narrative: The Role of Religion in Shaping Narrative Forms*, 73–96. Tübingen: Mohr Siebeck, 2015.

Nutzman, M. 'Mary in the *Protevangelium of James*?' *GRBS* 53 (2013): 551–78.

O'Donnell, K. 'Women and the Eucharist: Reflections on Private Eucharists in the Early Church', *FTh* 27, no. 2 (2019): 164–75.

Økland, J. *Women in Their Place: Paul and the Corinthian Discourse on Gender and Sanctuary Space*. London: T&T Clark, 2005.

van Oort, J. 'Manichaean Women in a Pseudo-Augustinian Testimony', *VChr* 71 (2017): 85–94.

Osiek, C. 'The Bride of Christ (5:22-23): A Problematic Wedding', *BThB* 32 (2002): 29–39.

Osiek, C. 'Diakonos and Prostatis', *Hevormde Teologiese Studies* 61 (2005): 347–70.

Osiek, C. and Balch, D. *Families in the New Testament World*. Louisville, KY: John Knox, 1997.

Osiek, C. and MacDonald, M. Y. with Tulloch, J. H. *A Woman's Place: House Churches in Earliest Christianity*. Minneapolis, MN: Fortress, 2006.

Otranto, G. 'Note sul sacerdozio femminile nell'antichità', *VetChr* 19 (1982): 341–60.

Parker, J. D. 'My Mother, My God, Why have You Fforsaken Me? An Exegetical Note on Psalm 22 as Christian Scripture', *Ex.Times* 131 (2020): 199–204.

Parks, S. *Gender in the Rhetoric of Jesus: Women in Q*. Lanham: Lexington-Fortress, 2019.

Payne, P. 'Fuldensis. Sigla for Variants in Vaticanus. And 1 Cor 14.34-5', *NTS* 41 (1995): 250–62.

Pentcheva, B. *Haghia Sophia*. University Park: Pennsylvania State University, 2017.

Peppiatt, L. *Unveiling Paul's Women: Making Sense of 1 Corinthians 11:2–16*. Eugene: Wipf & Stock, 2018.

Pihlava, K.-M. *Forgotten Women Leaders*. Helsinki: Finnish Exegetical Society, 2017.

Porter, S. 'What does it Mean to Be "Saved by Childbirth"?' *JSNT* 49 (1993): 87–102.

Ramelli, I. 'Il dossier di Perpetua: una rilettura storica e letteraria', *RIL* 139 (2005): 309–52.

Ramelli, I. 'Donne diacono', *Il Regno* 15 (2006): 171–5.

Ramelli, I. *Gregorio di Nissa: Sull'anima e la resurrezione*. Milan: Bompiani-Catholic University, 2007.

Ramelli, I. 'Mansuetudine, Grazia e salvezza negli *Acta Philippi* (ed. Bovon)', *Inv.luc* 29 (2007): 215–28.

Ramelli, I. 'Review of Madigan–Osiek 2005', *Orpheus* 28 (2007): 338–46.

Ramelli, I. 'Τί ἐμοὶ καὶ σοὶ γύναι; (John 2:4): Philological, Contextual, and Exegetical Arguments for the Understanding: "What Does This Matter to Me and to You?"', *ExClass* 12 (2008): 103–33.

Ramelli, I. *I Romanzi antichi e il Cristianesimo*. Madrid: Signifer, 2001; new edn, Eugene, OR: Cascade, 2011.

Ramelli, I. L. E. *Review of Morwenna Ludlow, Gregory of Nyssa: Ancient and Post Modern*. Oxford: Oxford University Press, 2007: *RBL* April 2008.

Ramelli, I. L. E. 'Origen, Patristic Philosophy, and Christian Platonism: Re-Thinking the Christianization of Hellenism', *VChr* 63 (2009): 217–63.

Ramelli, I. L. E. '1Tim 5:6 and the Notion and Terminology of Spiritual Death', *Aevum* 84 (2010): 3–16.

Ramelli, I. L. E. 'Theosebia: A Presbyter of the Catholic Church?', *JFSR* 26 (2010): 79–102.

Ramelli, I. L. E. 'The Pastoral Epistles and Hellenistic Philosophy', *CBQ* 73 (2011): 562–81.

Ramelli, I. L. E. 'Apuleius and Christianity', in Roger Beck (ed.), *Echoes of Myth. Religion and Ritual in the Ancient Novel*, 145–73. Berlin: De Gruyter, 2013.

Ramelli, I. L. E. *The Christian Doctrine of Apokatastasis: A Critical Assessment from the New Testament to Eriugena*. SuppVCh, 120. Leiden: E.J. Brill, 2013.

Ramelli, I. L. E. 'Lucian's *Peregrinus* as Holy Man and Charlatan, and the Construction of the Contrast between Holy Men and Charlatans in the *Acts of Mari*', in S. Panayotakis, G. Schmeling and M. Paschalis (eds), *Holy Men and Charlatans in the Ancient Novel*, 105–20. Groningen: Barkhuis/Groningen University Library, 2015.

Ramelli, I. L. E. 'The Mysteries of Scripture: Allegorical Exegesis and the Heritage of Stoicism, Philo, and Pantaenus', in V. Černuskova, J. Kovacs and J. Platova (eds), *Clement's Biblical Exegesis: Proceedings of the Second Colloquium on Clement of Alexandria, Prague-Olomouc 29–31 May 2014*, 80–110. SuppVCh, 139. Leiden: E.J. Brill, 2016.

Ramelli, I. L. E. *Social Justice and the Legitimacy of Slavery: The Role of Philosophical Asceticism from Ancient Judaism to Late Antiquity*. Oxford: Oxford University Press, 2016; US 2017.

Ramelli, I. L. E. 'Prophecy in Origen: Between Scripture and Philosophy', *JECH* 7 (2017): 17–39.

Ramelli, I. L. E. 'Apokatastasis and Epektasis in *Hom. In Cant.*: The Relation between Two Core Doctrines in Gregory and Roots in Origen', in G. Maspero, M. Brugarolas and I. Vigorelli (eds), *Gregory of Nyssa: In Canticum Canticorum*, 312–39. SuppVCh, 150. Leiden: E.J. Brill, 2018.

Ramelli, I. L. E. 'Creation, Double', in P. J. J. van Geest et al. (eds), *Brill Encyclopedia of Early Christianity*. Leiden: E.J. Brill, forthcoming; online November 2018.

Ramelli, I. L. E. 'Gregory of Nyssa on the Soul and the Restoration: From Plato to Origen', in A. Marmodoro and N. McLynn (eds), *Exploring Gregory of Nyssa: Philosophical, Theological, and Historical Studies*, 110–41. Oxford: Oxford University Press, 2018.

Ramelli, I. L. E. 'Autobiographical Self-Fashioning in Origen', in M. Niehoff and J. Levinson (eds), *Self, Self-Fashioning and Individuality in Late Antiquity: New Perspectives*, 271–88. Tübingen: Mohr Siebeck, 2019.

Ramelli, I. L. E. 'Gal 3:28 and Aristotelian and Jewish Categories of Inferiority', *Eirene* 55 (2019): 171–204.

Ramelli, I. L. E. 'Paul on Apokatastasis: 1 Cor 15:24-28 and the Use of Scripture', in S. Porter and C. Land (eds), *Paul and Scripture*, 212–32. Leiden: E.J. Brill, 2019.

Ramelli, I. L. E. 'The Father in the Son, the Son in the Father in the Gospel of John: Sources and Reception of Dynamic Unity in Middle and Neoplatonism, "Pagan" and Christian', *JBR* 7 (2020): 31–66.

Ramelli, I. L. E. 'Macrina. Life', in *Novel Saints*. ERC-funded database. University of Ghent. Print edition Turnhout: Brepols, forthcoming.

Ramelli, I. L. E. 'Patristic Anthropology, the Issue of Gender, and Its Relevance to Ecclesiastical Offices', in R. Franchi (ed.), *More than Female Disciples*. Turnhout: Brepols, forthcoming.

Ramelli, I. L. E. 'The Reception of Paul in Origen: Allegoresis of Scripture, Apokatastasis, and Women's Ministry', in S. Porter and D. Yoon (eds), *The Pauline Mind*. New York: Routledge, 2021.

Raming, I. *The Exclusion of Women from the Priesthood*. Metuchen, NJ: Scarecrow, 1976.

Raming, I. *Priesteramt der Frau*. Münster: Lit-Verlag, 2002.

Ratcliffe, R. 'The *Acts of Paul and Thecla*: Violating the Inviolate Body—Thecla Uncut', in J. E. Taylor (ed.), *The Body in Biblical, Christian and Jewish Texts*, 184–209. London: Bloomsbury T&T Clark, 2015.

Rea, J. and Clarke, L. *Perpetua's Journey: Faith, Gender, and Power in the Roman Empire*. Oxford: Oxford University Press, 2018.

Ricci, C. *Mary Magdalene and Many Others: Women Who Followed Jesus*. Minneapolis, MN: Fortress, 1994.

Robinson, B. J. *Paul's Rhetoric of Gender and Power in 1 Corinthians*. Lanham, MD: Lexington/Fortress Academic, 2019.

Rossi, M. 'On Recovering the Women Priests in Early Christianity', *JFSR* 7 (1991): 73–94.

Schaefer, M. *Women in Pastoral Office*. Oxford: Oxford University Press, 2013.

Schenk, C. *Crispina and Her Sisters: Women and Authority in Early Christianity*. Minneapolis, MN: Fortress, 2017.

Scopello, M. 'Julie, Manichéenne d'Antioche', *Antiquité Tardive* 5 (1997): 187–209.

Scopello, M. *Femme, gnose et manichéisme. De l'espace mythique au territoire réel*. Leiden: Brill, 2005.

Seabourne, C. 'New Directions in Redaction Criticism and Women', *Theology* 119 (2016): 335–41

Shoemaker, S. 'The Virgin Mary in the Ministry of Jesus and the Early Church According to the Earliest *Life of the Virgin*', *HTR* 98 (2005): 441–67.

Shoemaker, S. 'Mary the Apostle', in D. Bumazhnov et al. (eds), *Bibel. Byzanz und Christlicher Orient*, 203–29. Leuven: Peeters, 2011.

Shoemaker, S. *Mary in Early Christian Faith and Devotion*. New Haven, CT: Yale, 2016.

Silvas, A. *Gregory of Nyssa: The Letters*. Leiden: E.J. Brill, 2007.

Smit, P.-B. 'St Thecla: Remembering Paul and Being Remembered through Paul', *VChr* 68 (2014): 551–63.

Smit, P.-B. 'Something about Mary? Remarks about the Five Women in the Matthean Genealogy', *NTS* 56 (2020): 191–207.

Snyder, G. 'She Destroyed Multitudes', in U. Tervahauta, I. Miroshnikov, O. Lehtipuu and I. Dunderberg (eds), *Women and Knowledge in Early Christianity*, 39–61. SuppVCh 144. Leiden: E.J. Brill, 2017.

Solevag, A. R. 'Salvation. Gender and the Figure of Eve in 1 Timothy 2:9-15', *Lectio Difficilior*, 2012. http://www.lectio.unibe.ch/

Staniloae, D. 'The Mother of God as Intercessor', *Ortodoxia* 1 (1952): 79–129.

Stenschke, C. 'Enabling Conditions in the Conflicts of Acts 1–8:3', *JECH* 7 (2017): 54–86.

Stichele, C. V. and Penner, T. *Contextualizing Gender in Early Christian Discourse: Thinking Beyond Thecla*. London: Bloomsbury T&T Clark, 2009.

Stiefel, J. 'Women Deacons in 1 Timothy', *NTS* 41 (1995): 442–57.

Tabbernee, W. *Montanist Inscriptions and Testimonia*. Macon, GA: Mercer, 1997.

Taylor, J. and Ramelli, I. (eds). *Patterns of Women's Leadership in Ancient Christianity*. Oxford: Oxford University Press, 2021.

Tissot, Y. 'Encratism and the Apocryphal Acts', in A. Gregory and C. Tuckett (eds), *The Oxford Handbook of Early Christian Apocrypha*, 2nd edn, 407–23. Oxford: Oxford University Press, 2015.

Torjesen, K. J. *When Women Were Priests*. San Franscisco, CA: Harper, 1993.

Towers, S. *Constructions of Gender in Late Antique Manichaean Cosmological Narrative*. Turnhout: Brepols, 2020.

Trevett, C. *Montanism: Gender, Authority and the New Prophecy*. Cambridge: Cambridge University Press, 1996.

Tulloch, J. 'Women Leaders in Family Funerary Banquets', in C. Osiek and M. Y. MacDonald with J. Tulloch (eds), *A Woman's Place: House Churches in Earliest Christianity*, 273–313. Minneapolis, MN: Fortress, 2006.

Turner, J. 'Feminine Principles in Platonic and Gnostic Texts', in U. Tervahauta et al. (eds), *Women and Knowledge in Ancient Christianity*, 291–324. Leiden: Brill, 2017.

Vassiliadis, P., Papageorgiou, N. and Kasselouri-Hatzivassiliadi, E. (eds). *Deaconesses, the Ordination of Women, and Orthodox Theology*. Newcastle: Cambridge Scholars, 2017.

Walsh, L. 'The Lady as Elder in the Shepherd of Hermas', *JECS* 27, no. 4 (2019): 517–47.

Waters, K. 'Saved through Childbearing', *JBL* 123 (2004): 703–35.

Wehn, B. 'Selig die Körper der Jungfräulichen—Überlegungen zum Paulusbild der Thekla-Akten', in C. Janssen, L. Schottroff and B. When (eds), *Paulus: Umstrittene Traditionen - lebendige Theologie*, 182–98. Gütersloh: Kaiser, 2001.

Whelan, C. 'Amica Pauli: The Role of Phoebe', *JSNT* 49 (1993): 67–85.

Wijngaards, J. *No Holy Orders for Women? The Ancient Women Deacons*. London: Canterbury, 2002.

Williams, M. 'Wisdom: Our Innocent Sister', in U. Tervahauta, I. Miroshnikov, O. Lehtipuu and I. Dunderberg (eds), *Women and Knowledge in Early Christianity*, 253–90. Leiden: E.J. Brill, 2017.

Witherington III, B. *Women in the Ministry of Jesus*. New York: Cambridge University Press, 1991.

CHAPTER 5

To what extent were children and slaves welcomed in the early church?

VILLE VUOLANTO

INTRODUCTION

This chapter will discuss the cultural and social implications of the rise of Christianity for children and slaves, with a stress on actual and imagined relationships in households. The chronological span stretches from the late second to the early fifth century. This is the period in which the early church accommodated itself to the dominant cultural features of the Graeco-Roman cultural environment. Christian élites needed to enter into discussions over enculturation and differentiation, as to what would constitute a proper Christian way of life. Christian writers aimed to influence the socialization processes, which resulted in an unprecedented interest in all things pertaining to education, as well as in factors influencing individuals in their formation process towards becoming good Christians. It was this interest which also made household slaves visible in a new way. Children and slaves also became relevant for Christian discourse because of a linked factor: for these groups appear frequently in metaphors designed to explain complicated ethical, biblical and dogmatic points of argument in an easily palatable way.

In what follows, I begin with the position of children and slaves in the dominant Graeco-Roman household as a framework in which the early church developed. Next, I present early Christian teachings about children and childhood; and then do the same for slaves and slavery. I will then move on to show what can be said about the relevance of this ideological background for everyday life. Did Christianity change the way these groups were seen – and how they lived their everyday life in their now-Christianized environments? All these questions have been much discussed of late. I do not claim to be able to solve these difficult issues here, but I will aim to present a general perspective on the question.

THE FRAMEWORK: CHILDREN AND SLAVES IN THE GRAECO-ROMAN WORLD

To understand Christianity's relationship towards children and slaves, it is necessary to start with a short survey of slavery and childhood in the world in which Christianity developed. Christianity as such did not propose any revolution in ideas, attitudes and practices concerning children and slaves, and many social factors in fact did not change. First and foremost, throughout the whole period under scrutiny here, we need to remember that we are dealing with a strongly hierarchical society, which showed itself also in the basic power structures within the households: in the pairings of husband and wife, parents and children, and master and slave. These three relationships had already been used by Aristotle to show the natural base for a working *oikonomia* – the first mentioned 'head of the household', was always understood to be in the dominant position. In the Roman world, this ideology was summarized by the concept of *patria potestas*. If today we would be inclined to accept parental authority (up to a certain point) as natural, in the Graeco-Roman world the hierarchies based upon the man–woman and free–unfree juxtaposition also had the same degree of 'naturality' in them: shared gender and status distinctions lay deep in that discursive and social environment, which was also the context for the early church.[1]

It is important to keep in mind, of course, that 'children' in reality never formed a uniform group – there were huge differences in experiences between the children of the élites and those of the poor; between girls and boys and, indeed, between free and slave children. Likewise, slaves were in no way a unified group: some slaves would have had reasonable living conditions as teachers or stewards for élite households, and others might manage or even own slaves themselves. On the other hand, there were slaves overburdened in ploughing and harvesting on country estates (*latifundia*), those sent down the mines, working in bakeries, laundries or tanneries, or in brick and pottery production. Neither was the line between a slave and a free person always clear cut: a free person could become a slave, and a slave free, especially by kidnapping, or because of debts, or as a result of child abandonment. Nor was there any straightforward way to distinguish a slave – no particular ethnic background or clothing was characteristic only for slaves. Moreover, often slaves and free people lived and worked together, and they shared the same public and social spaces.[2]

Even so, slavery as an institution was a highly visible and characteristic feature of Roman society. During the early Roman Empire, in Italian urban areas, over one-

---

[1]Aristotle, *Pol*, book 1 (esp. 1.3). For the persistence of this idea in Roman culture, see: P. Saller, *Patriarchy, Property and Death in the Roman Family* (Cambridge: Cambridge University Press, 1994), pp. 74–101, 130–2.

[2]See K. R. Bradley, 'Images of Childhood in Classical Antiquity', in *The Routledge History of Childhood in the Western World*, ed. P. Fass (London and New York: Routledge, 2013), pp. 57–80; and S. E. Bond, *Trade and Taboo: Disreputable Professions in the Roman Mediterranean* (Ann Arbor: University of Michigan Press, 2016), for the variations in slave labour.

third of the population might have been slaves. In other parts of the empire slavery was less common, and overall perhaps some 10 to 15 per cent of the population was unfree. This would also mean that the ownership of slaves was not limited to the wealthiest élites. It has been estimated that perhaps 15 to 20 per cent of Roman households would have owned at least one slave. Slave ownership developed into a status-defining factor in the Roman world.[3]

If slaves were everywhere, the same was also the case for children. Approximately at least one-third of the population of the Roman Empire was under fifteen years of age. Ancient communities, which also include the early Christian congregations, were full of children taking part and being present in communal activities, roaming the streets, in fields, in different kinds of gatherings, both playing and working.[4] Modern research has shown that children were, in principle even if not always in practice, welcomed, valued and visible in all levels of Roman society. Children were seen as contributors to the family prosperity and survival. In the lower echelons of the society this was chiefly as a labour force and as guarantors of security in old age, while for the élites it was to carry on the family name, honour and fame. Emotional attachment to children was the norm, and childhood was recognized as a separate stage of human life, with widely recognized special needs for its well-being.[5]

However, children in the Roman world were often seen as inferior (comparable to slaves in this respect), in a low position in the social hierarchy and at the margins of civilized society, still needing to be socialized.[6] On the other hand, children were 'never marginal beings', as Keith Bradley writes. The Roman lawgivers, philosophers, letter writers, ecclesiastical authors and ordinary commemorators on tombstones wrote about, commented on, rejoiced and mourned over the lives and deaths of children on an unprecedented scale. The funerary epigraphical texts recognize the dead child as an individual and picture the hope of a future now lost, all of which reflect the central place of children in the lives of adult Romans. Children stood for a sense of continuity and hope for their parents and wider kin, and their worlds were in many ways less separate from the adult spheres of life (in work, education and sexuality) than they are today.[7]

---

[3]Further see: W. Scheidel, 'The Roman Slave Supply', in *The Cambridge World History of Slavery, vol. 1: The Ancient Mediterranean World*, eds K. Bradley and P. Cartledge (Cambridge: Cambridge University Press, 2011), pp. 287–310, and Idem, 'The Slave Population of Roman Italy: Speculation and Constraints', *Topoi* 9 (1999): 129–44.

[4]T. Parkin, 'The Demography of Infancy and Early Childhood in the Ancient World', in *The Oxford Handbook of Childhood and Education in the Classical World*, eds J. Evans Grubbs and T. Parkin, with R. Bell (Oxford and New York: Oxford University Press, 2013), pp. 41–2.

[5]B. Rawson, *Children and Childhood in Roman Italy* (Oxford: Oxford University Press, 2003), pp. 1, 59–70, 136–8; C. Laes, *Children in the Roman Empire: Outsiders Within* (Cambridge and New York: Cambridge University Press, 2011), pp. 101–4, 284. For the legislation, see T. A. J. McGinn, 'Roman Children and the Law', in Evans Grubbs and Parkin, with Bell (eds), *The Oxford Handbook of Childhood*, pp. 341–64.

[6]Laes, *Children in the Roman Empire*, pp. 282–5.

[7]Bradley, 'Images of Childhood', p. 34; Rawson, *Children and Childhood*, pp. 340, 352; V. Vuolanto, *Children and Asceticism in Late Antiquity: Continuity, Family Dynamics and the Rise of Christianity* (Farnham: Ashgate 2015), pp. 31–40, 192–203.

Slaves as a group shared some of these characteristics of children. But slaves also represented a group on the margins of the public life of the *polis*. In the case of children, however, this (partial) outsider position was temporary, whereas for slaves it was permanent. Ideologically, slaves would never become 'adults'. As a sign of this, regardless of their age, slaves were referred to by words such as *pais* (Greek), *puer*, *puella* (Latin), all being terms for 'a child'. A slave was always dependent. Discipline was harsh, violence was common and segregation cells, chains, collars, branding and whipping were always an impending threat. Even in a 'normal' situation, slaves often lived in their own crowded and dark quarters or barracks. There was no privacy; this was one part of the politics of subjugation.[8] In addition, slaves were always sexually available; even if this threat was not always carried out, the mere possibility tinged the everyday experience of every slave and gave the finishing touch to the view of slaves as people devoid of honour.[9]

Slaves did have de facto families; we have, for example, plenty of inscriptions with slaves calling each other spouses, but these relations had no legal footing. The slave owners were able to disperse a slave family whenever and wherever they wished.[10] In theory, the slaves were chattel, completely under the (even arbitrary) rule of the owners. The treatment of slaves was checked only by the customs and morals of the surrounding society.[11] If the ideologically normal emotion towards children was love, towards slaves it was fear. In the Roman imagination, there was a constant fear of slaves turning against their owners, pilfering, defying or resisting orders, and even threatening violence.[12]

Nevertheless, *pietas*, a virtue combining dutifulness, devotion and compassion, and reckoned widely as the guiding moral principle in family relationships, was seen to embrace also the slave families, not only Roman citizens. *Pietas* marked first and foremostly reciprocal duty and affection between parents and children, but also more widely between different household members, and ultimately between the individuals and the gods. Proper familial behaviour included nurture and support from the parents to their underage children and, in turn, *pietas* obligated children to take care of their ageing parents.[13]

---

[8]K. R. Bradley, *Slavery and Society at Rome* Cambridge: Cambridge University Press, 1994, pp. 84–5, 178; Laes, *Children in the Roman Empire*, pp. 163–5; J. Edmondson, 'Slavery and the Roman Family', in Bradley and Cartledge (eds), *The Cambridge World History of Slavery*, pp. 341–2, 346.

[9]Bradley, *Slavery and Society at Rome*, pp. 49–50; J. A. Glancy, *Slavery in Early Christianity* (Oxford: Oxford University Press, 2002), pp. 27, 50–3.

[10]H. Mouritsen, 'The Families of Roman Slaves and Freedmen', in *A Companion to Families in the Greek and Roman Worlds*, ed. B. Rawson (Oxford: Wiley-Blackwell, 2011), pp. 129–44.

[11]Edmondson, *Slavery and the Roman Family*, pp. 347–9; J. Gardner, 'Slavery and Roman Law', in Bradley and Cartledge (eds), *The Cambridge World History of Slavery*, pp. 414–37.

[12]S. Joshel and L. H. Petersen, *The Material Life of Roman Slaves* (Cambridge and New York: Cambridge University Press, 2014), pp. 13–17; Bradley, *Slavery and Society at Rome*, pp. 111–17, 123–5.

[13]Saller, *Patriarchy, Property and Death in the Roman Family*, pp. 105–14 (p. 112 on slaves and *pietas*).

EARLY CHRISTIAN TEACHING ABOUT CHILDREN

Early Christian writers extensively used family and childhood metaphors. In the 'Family of Christ', believers were children (imitating Christ himself as the Son of God – *Pais Theou*), connected to each other as brothers and sisters; the church itself was mother. On the other hand, the bishops and elders of the ascetic communities were 'fathers' and 'mothers' to those whose spiritual needs they took care of: there was a carefully forged conceptual link between the spiritual authority and paternity. *Pietas* should prevail both in Christian households and in congregations. Networks 'at every level of the Church hierarchy, from the ordinary parishes to the close-knit ascetic communities and from friendship relationships to episcopal entourages, were being shaped on the example of the family'.[14] Augustine, for example, reminds his friend and disciple Laetus how he had carried him ten months in his womb and suffered the pains of birth, of rearing and of nourishing him.[15] Because of this development, the vocabulary of childhood was ever-present in early Christian communities – this may have given new visibility to children, but it may have also served to hide the experience and lives of real children.

In associating childhood with purity, Christianity was no exception in the ancient world. The nature of exemplary children, such as those presented in Mk 10.13-16 where Jesus tells his disciples that the Kingdom of God belongs to children, seems to have caused uncertainty and different interpretations among his followers.[16] The earliest comments on the passage are vague, but in late antiquity the commentators generally refer to children as exemplary in their innocence, since children were not corrupted by passions or false worldly values. They were simple and humble, and inexperienced in regard to abilities, social skills or intentional wrongdoing. Children's true innocence consisted in that they were seen as not purposefully evil or envious. They also lacked ambition and sexual urges. As such they lived the angelic life and were suited as exemplary figures even for ascetics.[17]

---

[14]See, for example, B. Strawn, '"Israel, My Child": The Ethics of a Biblical Metaphor', in *The Child in the Bible*, ed. M. Bunge (Grand Rapids, MI: Eerdmans, 2008), pp. 103–40; C. Gerber, *Paulus and seine 'Kinder': Studien zur Beziehungsmetaphorik der paulinischen Briefe* (Berlin: De Gruyter, 2005); R. Aasgaard, *'My Beloved Brothers and Sisters!' Christian Siblingship in Paul* (London and New York: T&T Clark, 2004); J. Hellerman, *The Ancient Church as Family* (Minneapolis, MN: Fortress 2001). The quotation is from: Vuolanto, *Children and Asceticism*, p. 73 (and further, on Christian family metaphors and *pietas* in late antiquity, see Vuolanto, *Children and Asceticism*, pp. 65–79).

[15]Augustine, *Ep.*, 243. 3–7; with R. Krawiec, '"From the Womb of the Church": Monastic Families', *JECS* 11, no. 3 (2003): 289–92.

[16]See S. Betsworth, *Children in Early Christian Narratives* (London and New York: T&T Clark, 2015), pp. 65–8 – who promotes a reading of this passage as urging his disciples to accept the same position in the kingdom of heaven as that which children have in contemporary society, namely dominated, weak and vulnerable.

[17]G. Gould, 'Childhood in Eastern Patristic Thought: Some Problems of Theology and Theological Anthropology', in *The Church and Childhood*, ed. D. Wood (Oxford: The Ecclesiastical History Society, and Blackwell, 1994), pp. 41–4; V. Vuolanto, 'Faith and Religion', in *A Cultural History of Childhood and Family in Antiquity*, eds M. Harlow and R. Laurence (Oxford: Blackwell, 2014), pp. 148–9; B. Leyerle,

At the same time, children were connected with irrationality, unruliness, greediness, anger and lack of self-discipline. Augustine used these kinds of observations to press home the theological point that no one is sinless or pure, even at birth. The innocence of children would simply mean that they were not able to harm others (*in-nocentia*). This became the prevalent interpretation of the nature of children in the West until the sixth century. However, later writers, such as Isidore of Seville and Gregory the Great, returned to the earlier stress on the innocence and purity of children, at least before they could speak. This became the prevalent line of Christian thought into the high Middle Ages. Even for those who did not subscribe to Augustine's jaundiced view on childhood, children offered an ever-present and familiar set of warning examples to use in their rhetoric so as to direct their adult audience in moral virtues. What if there should be no control for the passions or no rationality for the good – 'look at the children and their behavior!' was their message.[18]

A prevailing view among Christian writers was that childhood was a transitory phase of life, which, after all, had no intrinsic value as such. Thus, child education and the socialization of the child to a proper (now Christian) way of life was a high priority. And because children lacked many 'adult' qualities, their guidance towards adult society was felt to be most effectively achieved by harsh discipline. Christian educational practices did not differ here much from those of their predecessors: control of passions would be achieved by using beatings and other punishments, even if the goal was no longer to bring up citizens for the earthly polis, but citizens for the heavenly Jerusalem. Moderation may have been the ideal but this clearly was not always the case.[19]

Indeed, children should obey their parents and other educators; the Old Testament commandments advocating the need for children to obey their parents were to be taken seriously. By the end of the fourth century, discussions took place on the need to obey God in preference to one's parents (e.g. if disagreements might arise in regard to an ascetic vocation), but the general discourse highlighted the need for correct social behaviour and a submissive role for children. Christians, after all, presented themselves as true Romans, with the Roman virtues: what parental authority and *pietas* required must be right.[20]

The Christian ascetic movement even put the blessing of having children under question. To have children was seen as an inferior goal, a seeking after psychological

---

'Children and "the Child" in Early Christianity', in Evans Grubbs and Parkin, with Bell (eds), *The Oxford Handbook of Childhood*, pp. 568–9.
[18]On Augustine, see: M. Stortz, '"Where or When Was Your Servant Innocent?": Augustine on Childhood', in *The Child in Christian Thought*, ed. M. Bunge (Grand Rapids, MI: Eerdmans, 2001), pp. 78–102; on later developments, see E. Abraham, *Anticipating Sin in Medieval Society: Childhood, Sexuality, and Violence in the Early Penitentials* (Amsterdam: Amsterdam University Press, 2017), pp. 47–54; and R. Meens, 'Children and Confession in the Early Middle Ages', in Wood (ed.), *The Church and Childhood*, p. 65.
[19]Leyerle, 'Children and "the Child"', pp. 570–2; Laes, *Children in the Roman Empire*, pp. 137–47.
[20]Vuolanto, *Children and Asceticism*, pp. 63–7.

and economical safety and an after-death commemoration and continuity. Better by far was to remain celibate and invest in heavenly treasures and a heavenly family. This was a true innovation in the context of Graeco-Roman antiquity. Having children here stood for earthly concerns. The negative rhetoric mentioned the pains of childbirth followed by the precarious health of children, the pain of childhood deaths or else the many problems of nursing, training and marrying off one's children, and the ultimate fate of the inheritance. Indeed, marriage itself was deemed a slavery. Children were visual reminders of sexual intercourse, which even if 'good' was widely seen by the ascetics as far from 'perfect'. Ecclesiastical writers regularly interpreted the Parable of the Sower's thirtyfold yield as for the married, whereas the hundredfold was for the celibate. Even if these opinions represented the minority view in terms of the number of people accepting this reasoning in the real world, the superiority of virginity over marriage and having children became a projected ideal for Christian life for centuries to come.[21]

Early Christian discussions on children and asceticism also demonstrate that there never was any unified Christian view on children and childhood. There was, rather, a rich variation of attitudes towards children; metaphors with references to childhood might even have opposite connotations; and the roles and functions of children depended on differences in status, gender, health, ethnicity and the cultural context in which people lived.

EARLY CHRISTIAN TEACHING ABOUT SLAVES

The Christian gaze, which gave new visibility to childhood, also brought slavery into the foreground, and early Christian writings abounded with metaphors and parables grounded on the social hierarchies at work between the free and the enslaved, and on the subjugated position of slaves. However, this was visibility for slavery in the abstract, not so much visibility for slaves in particular. The patristic Christian authors did not see physical slavery as so serious a matter as bondage of the mind and soul. Physical slavery was nothing but a label, a transitory condition and as such was an 'indifferent thing' (the Stoic category of *adiaphora*), whereas 'real slavery' was the bondage of sin and passions.[22]

If the values of the dominant Graeco-Roman culture dictated much of the attitudes and ideas about children and childhood in the early church, the same was true with slavery. As with the Stoic tradition, so too among the Christian writers

---

[21]Ibid., pp. 179–84.
[22]Glancy, *Slavery in Early Christianity*, pp. 34–8; C. de Wet, *Preaching Bondage: John Chrysostom and the Discourse of Slavery in Early Christianity* (Oakland: University of California Press, 2015), p. 272; J. A. Harrill, *Slaves in the New Testament: Literary, Social, and Moral Dimensions* (Minneapolis, MN: Fortress, 2006); I. L. E. Ramelli, *Social Justice, Social Justice and the Legitimacy of Slavery: The Role of Philosophical Asceticism from Ancient Judaism to Late Antiquity* (Oxford: Oxford University Press, 2016), pp. 147–51; but as she points out (pp. 113–14), Paul might have disagreed with this, seeing slavery as, in Stoic terms, 'non-preferable indifferent', something to be avoided.

there were discussions on how to treat slaves.[23] However, there was almost no discussion on the issue of the basic justification of slavery as such. Slavery as an institution was a self-evident and accepted fact both for the ideological and cultural landscape and for everyday life. In this, the Christian discourse mainly followed the Jewish tradition before it, which was itself well adjusted to the dominant Hellenistic cultural milieu.[24]

Christian writers widely shared the view that slavery was a result of original sin. As a consequence of sin, it was not something 'natural' and, ultimately, represented the prevalence of injustice. However, in God's eyes nobody was a slave, and any such distinctions would disappear in the afterlife. Slaves were useful, even necessary for the ordering of life; and, ultimately, slavery would be a beneficial state for those people for whom passions prevailed over reason. This Aristotelian view of the origins of slavery was de facto shared by most of the ecclesiastical writers, even by those who in general would see the enslavement of other persons as a sign of corruptness of the human nature. John Chrysostom, for example, held slaves generally to be wicked and prone to passions. Some writers went even further in sanctioning slavery. Augustine, for example, held slavery as divinely decreed, resulting not only from original sin but also arising as a punishment of individual sins. Thus, slavery, for him, was not an evil per se.[25]

Even so, there was discomfort with slavery among some Christians, and a few early Christian writers came near to demanding its abolition. Gregory of Nyssa perhaps went furthest in questioning slavery. According to him, since slaves are fellow human beings and images of God, they cannot be held as property; thus slavery was intrinsically unjust, even impious and certainly against God. Christians should not own any slaves, and those who do ought to emancipate all their slaves immediately. In addition Gregory of Nazianzus departs radically from the standard views (such as would later be promoted by Augustine), arguing that slavery was invented by Satan himself, and thus it certainly cannot be seen as divinely sanctioned.[26]

A Christian, as a slave of Christ, was in bondage and needed to be submissive to his new master, Jesus. For example, Mary is presented as a powerless slave (handmaid) of the Lord (and willing to bear His child). Likewise, in the early third-century *Acts of Thomas*, Jesus sells the apostle into slavery and later redeems him.[27] Rhetorical metaphors of slavery depended directly on institutional slavery and the cultural discourses on slaves in the Graeco-Roman world in which the early Christians lived. They were embedded in the slave system and took their part in normalizing and sustaining the discourses, and so also the practices, of slavery. Being

---

[23]Bradley, *Slavery and Society at Rome*, pp. 135–53.

[24]D. Martin, 'Slavery and the Ancient Jewish Family', in *The Jewish Family in Antiquity*, ed. S. Cohen (Atlanta, GA: SBL, 1993), pp. 113–19.

[25]Ramelli, *Social Justice*, pp. 152–71; de Wet, *Preaching Bondage*, pp. 51–61.

[26]Ramelli, *Social Justice*, pp. 171–217; See also de Wet, *Preaching Bondage*, p. 272 for Chrysostom.

[27]See especially Lk. 1.27 and *Acts of Thomas* 2, with M. Kartzow, *The Slave Metaphor and Gendered Enslavement in Early Christian Discourse: Double Trouble Embodied* (London and New York: Routledge, 2018), pp. 47–69, 125–43; and Glancy, *Slavery in Early Christianity*, pp. 96–7.

a slave demanded obedience and child like subordination; it amounted to (sexual) vulnerability and alienation from kin and inheritance; and it would result in the slave's body being liable to many different kinds of violations, brutality and even, ultimately, crucifixion and death. All these metaphorical connotations are present in the New Testament, and, subsequently, they were used by the most of the prominent Christian authors throughout the early Christian period.[28]

How these metaphors were understood in a cultural context in which slaves were ubiquitous, and how they were received by slaves themselves, we cannot know for sure. However, very little everyday authority was removed from Christian slaveholders: it was their right and indeed duty to educate, regulate, discipline and punish slaves and to teach their own sons to become just and efficient slave masters. In no way should the distance between the masters and the slaves be diminished in an ordinary household. Christian slaves should be even more obedient and hard-working, and they were to obey their masters 'with fear and trembling, in sincerity of heart, as to Christ'.[29] Following the example of Paul, who sent Onesimus back to his owner Philemon, the early church condemned any measures slaves might think of taking to liberate themselves against the wish of their masters.[30] As Chris de Wet summarized the viewpoint of John Chrysostom, it would be best to have no slaves, but not because of the injustice and oppressive nature of slavery but, rather, since all people should be self-sufficient and able to care for themselves. Life without slaves would keep arrogance and luxury at bay, and so ascetics should not possess slaves. Still, life without slaves was not for everyone, and so the others should make do with as small number of them as possible.[31]

CHILDREN AND SLAVES IN CHURCH LIFE

In early Christian culture infant baptism and its adjoining confirmation/chrismation was known as a practice already by the late second century, but it was not universal even in devoutly Christian families of the fourth century. Given the dominant view that the newborn was in no way impure, this is not surprising. Baptism was understood as a new (social) birth and, as such, infant baptism was a continuation of the Jewish and Graeco-Roman rituals of the acceptance of the child into the community, and to ensure divine protection. An important part of baptism was exorcism, and many parents considered baptism as a remedy for illnesses. Amulets, cross pendants and different kinds of apotropaic practices like incantations were

---

[28]See, for example, Gal. 5.1; 1 Cor. 7.23; 1 Cor. 6.20; Phil. 2.6-11; Jn 8.34–6; Lk. 16.13 (with parallels); with Kartzow, *The Slave Metaphor*; Glancy, *Slavery in Early Christianity*, esp. pp. 96–129; and de Wet, *Preaching Bondage*, esp. p. 272.

[29]Eph. 6.5; with de Wet, *Preaching Bondage*, pp. 273–6.

[30]Philemon.; see also 1 Tim. 6.1; Tit. 2.9-10; Synod of Gangra, *Canon* 3 (mid-fourth century); See also Council of Chalcedon (451), *Canon* 4, prohibiting slaves to become monks or to take ordination without the permission of their masters.

[31]de Wet, *Preaching Bondage*, p. 277.

used to heal children and to protect them from disease and demons in early Christian contexts. As a part of their families, children took part in church life and were acculturated to the proper ways of religious practices and to culturally valid beliefs early on. Children, therefore, were familiar with the liturgical routines. Families as a whole would have participated regularly in parish life. Already from Cyprian we know that the baptized babies received the Eucharist. Later, there were complaints of children causing disruptions by gaming and talking in churches during the mass, and stories refer to boys playing at being bishops and imitating the baptismal rite or liturgy word by word.[32]

There were no other public roles for girls except for singing hymns in the choirs. For boys the situation was different, as the actual assisting tasks in the liturgy were reserved for the male acolytes. Not only were the boy choirs a frequent phenomenon in churches around the Mediterranean, but at least by the fourth century many of the readers (*lectores*) in the liturgy were children or young men, starting most usually from the age of eight (but earlier ages are also recorded), with tasks to read the scriptures, to sing, to offer blessings over the offerings and to provide water for washing the officiating priest's hands. Among some Christian groups, there is also evidence for boys performing liturgical dances.[33] Children also attended religious festivals, taking part in the liturgical processions, for example, at the feasts of the martyrs, and they joined their parents when they visited local ascetic holy men or shrines of the saints to seek protection and recovery from illness.[34]

In Christian contexts, religious education depended on the everyday religious practices within individual families. There was some continuity of family celebration of rituals not associated with polytheistic practices. As Tertullian commented, it was not seen as a problem for Christians to attend celebrations of *toga virilis*, betrothals, marriage and the naming of children; these were seen as social events.[35] He does not mention birthdays, which in their Roman form were pointedly religious rituals. The church soon replaced the concept of birthday with that of 'saint's day'. As soon

---

[32]J. Martens, 'Children and the Church: The Ritual Entry of Children into Pauline Churches', in *Children in the Bible and the Ancient World: Comparative and Historical Methods in Reading Ancient Children*, ed. S. Flynn (London and New York: Routledge, 2019), pp. 94–114; E. Ferguson, *Baptism in the Early Church: History, Theology, and Liturgy in the First Five Centuries* (Grand Rapids, MI: Eerdmans, 2009); B. Caseau, 'Resistance and Agency in the Everyday life of Late Antique Children (3rd–8th century CE)', in *Children and Everyday Life in the Roman and Late Antique World*, eds C. Laes and V. Vuolanto (London and New York: Routledge, 2017), pp. 219–22; C. Horn and J. Martens (eds), *'Let the little children come to me': Childhood and Children in Early Christianity* (Washington, DC: Catholic University of America Press, 2009), pp. 268–94; O. M. Bakke, *When Children Became People: The Birth of Childhood in Early Christianity* (Minneapolis, MN: Fortress, 2005), pp. 246–51; and Vuolanto, 'Faith and Religion', pp. 134–7 for a comparison with earlier practices.

[33]Horn and Martens, *'Let the little children'*, pp. 296–300; Bakke, *When Children Became People*, pp. 251–6.

[34]S. R. Holman, 'Sick Children and Healing Saints: Medical Treatment of the Child in Christian Antiquity', in *Children in Late Ancient Christianity*, eds C. Horn and R. Phenix (Tübingen: Mohr Siebeck, 2009), pp. 143–70.

[35]Tertullian, *Idol.*, 16.1–2.

as children could reason, parents were expected to teach them the rudiments of faith. Christian families introduced their children early on to prayers, the singing of hymns and psalms, and the act of blessing themselves with the sign of cross. Both the hagiographic stories and the pedagogical treaties presuppose that a seven-year-old child could know the Creed in a way that it was understood as a proclamation of faith. Logically, the early penitentiaries presupposed that children made confessions. In early Christianity we begin to see the separation of secular schooling from spiritual upbringing. This is a quite distinct feature of Christianity when compared to polytheism or Jewish practices.[36] Socializing the child in the proper religious praxis was a family matter and prerogative of the child's parents.

All in all, children actively took part in the religious life of the church, in a similar way to other religions traditions in the contemporary Graeco-Roman world where children were presented to the gods right from birth, were considered to be protected by them and were included in all the major public and private rituals. They were equal to adults in receiving the divine gifts, sometimes even held to have a special relationship with the divine, but always having 'a rightful share in the service of the gods'.[37]

In the context of the Christian ascetic movement, there evolved a practice of dedicating children to God in the monastic life. Even if the sources highlight the free will of the children in making their decision (even depicting conflicts between parents and the child), in practice the decision for a minor to enter ascetic life was, almost without exception, taken by their parents. By means of child ascetics, families both forged a bond with God and amassed social capital in Christian congregations, securing both immanent and transcendental gains. Donating a child might have taken place already when the child was born (or even before), but most usually these child donations seem to have taken place when children were reaching their teens (and thus marriageable age). In the fourth century these children would have lived in the homes of their parents and received education there. For girls dedicated to virginity, their coming of age was marked by the public ceremony of taking the veil instead of by marriage. The number of such children must have been quite low during the centuries before the development of monasticism as an institution in the fifth century, when it then became possible for parents to take their children with them when they started their own ascetic careers or to give children to monastic communities to be brought up as ascetics. In West, the formation of the Benedictine order in the early sixth century systematized this kind of child oblation (*Oblati*). Monasteries would also have harboured other children: orphans and students, as well as workers (servants and slaves); their continual presence is highlighted in the

---

[36]Horn and Martens, '*Let the little children*', pp. 136–63; Gould, 'Childhood in Eastern Patristic Thought', pp. 43–8; Meens, 'Children and Confession', pp. 53, 61–3.

[37]Further see Vuolanto, 'Faith and Religion'. The citation is from J. Neils, 'Children and Greek Religion', in *Coming of Age in Ancient Greece: Images of Childhood from the Classical Past*, eds J. Neils and J. H. Oakley (New Haven, CT and London: Yale University Press, 2003), p. 159 (paraphrasing Melanippe).

monastic rules.[38] For these children, even if they were a small minority, Christianity certainly made a huge difference to their lives.

Orphans were a class of children profiting from the rise of Christianity. They had a pointed symbolic value as a group of people who need special protection (along with widows). Although this rhetoric was not absent from non-Christian discourse either, care of orphans and foundlings was highlighted as a major moral obligation for Christians.[39] The new 'fathers' of the church, bishops, had a special obligation to care for parentless children, leading to the establishment of ecclesiastical foundations, and ultimately to the founding of the *Orphanotropheion* in Constantinople.[40] There was a great need for such humanitarian measures: demographic conditions resulted in many parents dying prematurely, so there was a continuous supply of foundlings. Even if the Stoic moral condemnation of the abandonment of children was adopted by Christian writers, and thus preached to much wider audiences (even having some influence on legislation), the practice of abandonment continued without interruption and even remained common among the Christian population through the early Christian and medieval periods.[41]

As Jennifer Glancy already has pointed out,[42] slavery in the early Christian writings is pointedly urban in character: this was slavery of craftspeople and prostitutes, of domestic settings with janitors, nurses and educators and of financial agents and staff of public and private institutions. While the lot of urban slaves in docks, tanneries, laundries and bakeries was certainly not enviable, slavery as pondered by ecclesiastical writers seldom touched upon the lot of slaves in mines or on huge country *latifundia*, or of rowers in warships; and thus the most blatant abuses of slavery were out of their scope. In their rhetoric the ecclesiastical writers' main target was a wealthy urban (slave owning) *paterfamilias* running his household.

The tasks of the household heads also included the religious supervision of their slaves. It seems that just as slaves in non-Christian contexts took part in their household cult and visited the rituals in honour of Mithras and Isis with their free fellow devotees, so too Christian slaves were accepted as members in the Christian

---

[38]M. Giorda, 'Children in Monastic Families in Egypt at the End of Antiquity', in *Children and Everyday Life in the Roman and Late Antique World*, eds C. Laes and V. Vuolanto (London and New York: Routledge, 2017), pp. 232–46; Vuolanto, *Children and Asceticism*; B. Leyerle, 'Children and Disease in a Sixth Century Monastery', in *What Athens Has to do with Jerusalem: Essays on Classical, Jewish, and Early Christian Art and Archaeology in Honor of Gideon Foerster*, ed. L. V. Rutgers (Leuven: Peeters, 2002), pp. 349–72; C. Schroeder, 'Children in Early Egyptian Monasticism', in Horn and Phenix (eds), *Children in Late Ancient Christianity*, pp. 333–6 (also for child slaves).

[39]M. Sigismund, '"Without Father, Without Mother, Without Genealogy": Fatherlessness in the Old and the New Testament', in *Growing Up Fatherless in Antiquity*, eds S. R. Hübner and M. Ratzan (Cambridge: Cambridge University Press, 2009), pp. 83–101; J.-U. Krause, *Witwen und Waisen im Römischen Reich* IV: *Witwen und Waisen im frühen Christentum* (Stuttgart: Franz Steiner, 1995).

[40]Further see, T. Miller, *The Orphans of Byzantium: Child Welfare in the Christian Empire* (Washington, DC: Catholic University of America Press, 2003).

[41]J. Evans-Grubbs, 'Infant Exposure and Infanticide', in Evans Grubbs and Parkin, with Bell (eds), *The Oxford Handbook of Childhood*, pp. 83–107.

[42]Glancy, *Slavery in Early Christianity*, p. 40.

congregations.[43] Clearly slaves were included when 'whole households' were mentioned as having been baptized when the very first congregations were forming. These acts did not lead to any mass manumissions of slaves, and therefore, right from the beginning there were Christian households with Christian slaveholders. This reality comes forward in texts preserved to us in a more or less matter-of-fact manner. For example, in the second century, Athenagoras notes that among the Christian some have more slaves, some fewer; or when Justin Martyr writes how the torture of child slaves led to the arrest of their Christian masters.[44] In the fourth and fifth centuries, Christian senatorial households would have housed hundreds of slaves. A telling anecdote on the continuity of the practices connected to slavery is conveyed by a slave collar found from late antique Sicily with a text 'I am the slave of Felix the Archdeacon. Retain me lest I flee', thus underlining the master's total domination over the slave.[45] Very little seems to have changed.

Nevertheless, one of the results of the Christian transformation of sexual morality and its condemnation of any sexual experiences outside marriage was that the sexual exploitation of slaves was no longer tolerated. To abuse one's own slaves was strictly condemned and shamed, and even prostitution was frowned upon. This also led to a partial rehabilitation of the male slave's masculinity, and of the (sexual) dignity of slave women.[46] Here in the case of child slaves we come to a cross section between childhood and slavery: even if sexual abuse of children certainly did not stop, the raping of one's own child slaves was now seen as blatantly sinful. Still, among the Christians, to have child slaves was in no way more disapproved than any other form of slavery. Children outside the élites, both freeborn and slaves, Christian and non-Christian, were expected to work from the age of five or seven onwards, first with their parents or other household staff, then more independently and even outside the household.[47] On the other hand, there was nothing to hinder slave children from participating in everyday Christian church life.[48]

---

[43]See, however, the reservations voiced in Glancy, *Slavery in Early Christianity*, pp. 49–50, for the degree of slave participation in the early church (because of the sexual impurity of (some of) the slaves).

[44]Glancy, *Slavery in Early Christianity*, pp. 46–9, 131–3, 140–7, 151; Athenagoras, *Leg.*, 35.3; Justin Martyr, *2 Apol.*, 12.4.

[45]*Archaiologike Ephemeris,* 1975, p. 465; see also K. Harper, *Slavery in the Late Roman World,* AD 275–425 (Cambridge and New York: Cambridge University Press, 2011), p. 258; and Glancy, *Slavery in Early Christianity*, pp. 88–9.

[46]de Wet, *Preaching Bondage*, pp. 274, 276; On the new Christian sexual morality, see K. Harper, *From Shame to Sin: The Christian Transformation of Sexual Morality in Late Antiquity* (Cambridge, MA: Harvard University Press, 2013).

[47]K. Martens, '"Do Not Sexually Abuse Children": The Language of Early Christian Sexual Ethics', in Horn and Phenix (eds), *Children in Late Ancient Christianity*, pp. 227–54; Bakke, *When Children Became People*, pp. 142–9; Horn and Martens, *'Let the little children'*, pp. 225–39; Laes, *Children in the Roman Empire*, pp. 155–66, 268–75.

[48]Martens, 'Children and the Church'; M. Y. MacDonald, *The Power of Children: The Construction of Christian Families in the Greco-Roman World* (Waco, TX: Baylor University Press, 2014), pp. 33–66.

CONCLUSIONS

There was no all-embracing theology of childhood in early church, nor was there any overall theology of slavery. In this situation, the long continuity of old attitudes and practices comes as no surprise. The changes were slow and gradual, and changes in ideals, discourses, mentalities and social practices took place in different ways and at different speeds.[49] Similarly, instead of looking for one specific ideal or an attitude towards children or slaves, one has to be aware of potentially conflicting ideals and attitudes on various levels of discourse and social life.

And so, we need to reject claims that Christianity would have made a difference once and for all. As for children, we can see changes in practices connected with orphans and with the sexual abuse of children, but there seems to have been no clear changes in terms of religious participation in cult, with the practice of abandonment, or with the use violence at home or at school, for example. Certainly, Christianity neither invented childhood nor made children into people.[50]

Likewise, slavery was a self-evident and accepted fact for the early Christians, and people were kidnapped, sold and abandoned into slavery even within the Christian empire. Even if some of the ecclesiastical writers condemned slavery as utterly sinful, it was the notion of spiritual enslavement that dominated the Christian mind: exploitation of slaves and the slave system itself persisted regardless. Even if we have very little information on slave experiences, and still less on any cultural changes within it, given the rise of Christianity, nevertheless it is clear that hopes for freedom and fears of violence and sexual abuse still prevailed among slaves in late antiquity.[51]

However, even if the slave economy was very much present, there were definitely changes taking place in late antique slavery, as the line between free and unfree populations became more porous, and free labour became more common than in the earlier empire.[52] Here, as is often the case, the specific influence of Christianity cannot be fully extracted from among other intellectual and social developments taking place.

---

[49]Laes, *Children in the Roman Empire*, pp. 285–8; Evans Grubbs and Parkin, *The Oxford Handbook of Childhood*, pp. 8–9.

[50]Views for Christianity making radical difference, see especially Bakke, *When Children Became People*; T. M. Brenneman, 'Review of Horn and Martens, "Let the Little Children"', *CH* 80 (2011): 645–7; M. King, 'Children in Judaism and Christianity', in *The Routledge History of Childhood in the Western World*, ed. P. Fass (London and New York: Routledge, 2013), pp. 39–60; Horn and Martens, '*Let the little children*', pp. 346–51, are more cautious, stating that 'Christianity did not discover children or childhood', but still children became 'valuable in themselves', this leading to a change in child abandonment and in sexual violence. They also claim that children had more roles in Christian religious praxis than before.

[51]See Kartzow, *The Slave Metaphor*; Bradley, *Slavery and Society at Rome*, p. 92; K. Vlassopoulos, 'Hope and Slavery', in *Hope in Ancient Literature, History, and Art*, eds G. Kazantzidis and D. Spatharas (Berlin: De Gruyter, 2018), pp. 235–58.

[52]See: Bond, *Trade and Taboo*; Harper, *Slavery*; and also N. Lenski, 'Searching for Slave Teachers in Late Antiquity', in *ποιμένι λαῶν. Studies in Honor of Robert J. Penella*, ed. C. Sogno (RET Publishers, 2019), pp. 127–91, which offers a synthesis of the issue from the viewpoint of the slaves as teachers.

All that said, children and slaves in general were certainly welcomed in the early church – even if, pointedly, *as* slaves and *as* children, that is, with the social and cultural implications these designations carried in the matrix of the Graeco-Roman context. The presence of both children and slaves was pervasive in Christian communities, and the discursive visibility of both groups was clearly more pointed than ever before.

BIBLIOGRAPHY

Aasgaard, R. *'My Beloved Brothers and Sisters!' Christian Siblingship in Paul.* London and New York: T&T Clark, 2004.

Abraham, E. *Anticipating Sin in Medieval Society: Childhood, Sexuality, and Violence in the Early Penitentials.* Amsterdam: Amsterdam University Press, 2017.

Bakke, O. M. *When Children Became People: The Birth of Childhood in Early Christianity.* Minneapolis, MN: Fortress, 2005.

Betsworth, S. *Children in Early Christian Narratives.* London and New York: T&T Clark, 2015.

Bond, S. E. *Trade and Taboo: Disreputable Professions in the Roman Mediterranean.* Ann Arbor: University of Michigan Press, 2016.

Bradley, K. R. *Slavery and Society at Rome.* Cambridge: Cambridge University Press, 1994.

Bradley, K. R. 'Images of Childhood in Classical Antiquity', in P. Fass (ed.), *The Routledge History of Childhood in the Western World*, 17–38. London and New York: Routledge, 2013.

Brenneman, T. M. 'Review of Horn and Martens, "Let the Little Children"', *CH* 80 (2011): 645–7.

Caseau, B. 'Resistance and Agency in the Everyday Life of Late Antique Children (3rd–8th century CE)', in C. Laes and V. Vuolanto (eds), *Children and Everyday Life in the Roman and Late Antique World*, 217–31. London and New York: Routledge, 2017.

Edmondson, J. 'Slavery and the Roman Family', in K. Bradley and P. Cartledge (eds), *The Cambridge World History of Slavery, vol. 1: The Ancient Mediterranean World*, 337–61. Cambridge: Cambridge University Press, 2011.

Evans-Grubbs, J. 'Infant Exposure and Infanticide', in J. Evans Grubbs and T. Parkin, with R. Bell (eds), *The Oxford Handbook of Childhood and Education in the Classical World*, 83–107. Oxford and New York: Oxford University Press, 2013.

Evans-Grubbs, J. and Parkin, T. 'Introduction', in J. Evans Grubbs et al. (eds), *The Oxford Handbook of Childhood and Education in the Classical World*, 1–13. Oxford and New York: Oxford University Press, 2013.

Ferguson, E. *Baptism in the Early Church: History, Theology, and Liturgy in the First Five Centuries.* Grand Rapids, MI: Eerdmans, 2009.

Gardner, J. 'Slavery and Roman Law', in K. Bradley and P. Cartledge (eds), *The Cambridge World History of Slavery, vol. 1: The Ancient Mediterranean World*, 414–37. Cambridge: Cambridge University Press, 2011.

Gerber, C. *Paulus and seine 'Kinder': Studien zur Beziehungsmetaphorik der paulinischen Briefe.* Berlin: De Gruyter, 2005.

Giorda, M. 'Children in Monastic Families in Egypt at the End of Antiquity', in C. Laes and V. Vuolanto (eds), *Children and Everyday Life in the Roman and Late Antique World*, 232–46. London and New York: Routledge, 2017.

Glancy, J. A. *Slavery in Early Christianity*. Oxford: Oxford University Press, 2002.

Gould, G. 'Childhood in Eastern Patristic Thought: Some Problems of Theology and Theological Anthropology', in D. Wood (ed.), *The Church and Childhood*, 39–52. Oxford: The Ecclesiastical History Society, and Blackwell, 1994.

Harper, K. *Slavery in the Late Roman World*, AD *275–425*. Cambridge and New York: Cambridge University Press, 2011.

Harper, K. *From Shame to Sin*: *The Christian Transformation of Sexual Morality in Late Antiquity*. Cambridge, MA: Harvard University Press, 2013.

Harrill, J. A. *Slaves in the New Testament*: *Literary, Social, and Moral Dimensions*. Minneapolis, MN: Fortress, 2006.

Hellerman, J. *The Ancient Church as Family*. Minneapolis, MN: Fortress 2001.

Holman, S. R. 'Sick Children and Healing Saints: Medical Treatment of the Child in Christian Antiquity', in C. Horn and R. Phenix (eds), *Children in Late Ancient Christianity*, 143–70. Tübingen: Mohr Siebeck, 2009.

Horn, C. and Martens, J. *'Let the little children come to me'*: *Childhood and Children in Early Christianity*. Washington, DC: Catholic University of America Press, 2009.

Joshel, S and Petersen, L. H. *The Material Life of Roman Slaves*. Cambridge and New York: Cambridge University Press, 2014.

Kartzow, M. The *Slave Metaphor and Gendered Enslavement in Early Christian Discourse*: *Double Trouble Embodied*. London and New York: Routledge, 2018.

King, M. 'Children in Judaism and Christianity', in P. Fass (ed.), *The Routledge History of Childhood in the Western World*, 39–60. London and New York: Routledge, 2013.

Krause, J.-U. *Witwen und Waisen im Römischen Reich IV*: *Witwen und Waisen im frühen Christentum*. Stuttgart: Franz Steiner, 1995.

Krawiec, R. '"From the Womb of the Church": Monastic Families', *JECS* 11, no. 3 (2003): 283–307.

Laes, C. *Children in the Roman Empire*: *Outsiders Within*. Cambridge and New York: Cambridge University Press, 2011.

Lenski, N. 'Searching for Slave Teachers in Late Antiquity', in C. Sogno (ed.), ποιμένι λαῶν. *Studies in Honor of Robert J. Penella*, RET 12, supplément 8 (2019): 127–91.

Leyerle, B. 'Children and Disease in a Sixth Century Monastery', in L. V. Rutgers (ed.), *What Athens Has to do with Jerusalem: Essays on Classical, Jewish, and Early Christian Art and Archaeology in Honor of Gideon Foerster*, 349–72. Leuven: Peeters, 2002.

Leyerle, B. 'Children and "the Child" in Early Christianity', in J. Evans Grubbs and T. Parkin, with R. Bell (eds), *The Oxford Handbook of Childhood and Education in the Classical World*, 559–79. Oxford and New York: Oxford University Press, 2013.

MacDonald, M. Y. *The Power of Children*: *The Construction of Christian Families in the Greco-Roman World*. Waco, TX: Baylor University Press, 2014.

Martens, J. '"Do Not Sexually Abuse Children": The Language of Early Christian Sexual Ethics', in C. Horn and R. Phenix (eds), *Children in Late Ancient Christianity*, 227–54. Tübingen: Mohr Siebeck 2009.

Martens, J. 'Children and the Church: The Ritual Entry of Children into Pauline Churches', in S. Flynn (ed.), *Children in the Bible and the Ancient World: Comparative and Historical Methods in Reading Ancient Children*, 94–114. London and New York: Routledge, 2019.

Martin, D. 'Slavery and the Ancient Jewish Family', in S. Cohen (ed.), *The Jewish Family in Antiquity*, 113–19. Atlanta, GA: SBL, 1993.

McGinn, T. A. J. 'Roman Children and the Law', in J. Evans Grubbs and T. Parkin, with R. Bell (eds), *The Oxford Handbook of Childhood and Education in the Classical World*, 341–64. Oxford and New York: Oxford University Press, 2013.

Meens, R. 'Children and Confession in the Early Middle Ages', in D. Wood (ed.), *The Church and Childhood*, 53–65. Oxford: The Ecclesiastical History Society and Blackwell, 1994.

Miller, T. *The Orphans of Byzantium: Child Welfare in the Christian Empire*. Washington, DC: Catholic University of America Press, 2003.

Mouritsen, H. 'The Families of Roman Slaves and Freedmen', in B. Rawson (ed.), *A Companion to Families in the Greek and Roman Worlds*, 129–44. Oxford: Wiley-Blackwell, 2011.

Neils, J. 'Children and Greek Religion', in J. Neils and J. H. Oakley (eds), *Coming of Age in Ancient Greece: Images of Childhood from the Classical Past*, 139–61. New Haven, CT and London: Yale University Press, 2003.

Parkin, T. 'The Demography of Infancy and Early Childhood in the Ancient World', in J. Evans Grubbs and T. Parkin, with R. Bell (eds), *The Oxford Handbook of Childhood and Education in the Classical World*, 40–61. Oxford and New York: Oxford University Press, 2013.

Ramelli, I. *Social Justice and the Legitimacy of Slavery: The Role of Philosophical Asceticism from Ancient Judaism to Late Antiquity*. Oxford: Oxford University Press, 2016.

Rawson, B. *Children and Childhood in Roman Italy*. Oxford: Oxford University Press, 2003.

Saller, R. P. *Patriarchy, Property and Death in the Roman Family*. Cambridge: Cambridge University Press, 1994.

Scheidel, W. 'The Slave Population of Roman Italy: Speculation and Constraints', *Topoi* 9 (1999): 129–44.

Scheidel, W. 'The Roman Slave Supply', in K. Bradley and P. Cartledge (eds), *The Cambridge World History of Slavery, vol. 1: The Ancient Mediterranean World*, 287–310. Cambridge: Cambridge University Press, 2011.

Schroeder, C. 'Children in Early Egyptian Monasticism', in C. Horn and R. Phenix (eds), *Children in Late Ancient Christianity*, 317–38. Tübingen: Mohr Siebeck, 2009.

Sigismund, M. '"Without Father, Without Mother, Without Genealogy": Fatherlessness in the Old and the New Testament', in S. R. Hübner and M. Ratzan (eds), *Growing Up Fatherless in Antiquity*, 83–101. Cambridge: Cambridge University Press, 2009.

Stortz, M. '"Where or When Was Your Servant Innocent?": Augustine on Childhood', in M. Bunge (ed.), *The Child in Christian Thought*, 78–102. Grand Rapids, MI: Eerdmans, 2001.

Strawn, B. '"Israel, My Child": The Ethics of a Biblical Metaphor', in M. Bunge (ed.), *The Child in the Bible*, 103–40. Grand Rapids, MI: Eerdmans, 2008.

Vlassopoulos, K. 'Hope and Slavery', in G. Kazantzidis and D. Spatharas (eds), *Hope in Ancient Literature, History, and Art*, 235–58. Berlin: De Gruyter, 2018.

Vuolanto, V. 'Faith and Religion', in M. Harlow and R. Laurence (eds), *A Cultural History of Childhood and Family in Antiquity*, 133–51, 203–6. Oxford: Blackwell, 2014.

Vuolanto, V. *Children and Asceticism in Late Antiquity: Continuity, Family Dynamics and the Rise of Christianity*. Farnham: Ashgate 2015.

de Wet, C. *Preaching Bondage: John Chrysostom and the Discourse of Slavery in Early Christianity*. Oakland: University of California Press, 2015.

CHAPTER 6

Disability in the early church

MONICA TOBON

PROEM

This chapter considers attitudes to disability and disabled people in the early church.[1] A challenge for any such undertaking is that the category of disability is modern, rooted in a focus on a person's capacity for work, and has no equivalent in Graeco-Roman or Jewish antiquity. Laes proposes 'infirmity' as the more appropriate term in such contexts.[2] Given the familiarity of the term 'disability', however, I shall use both interchangeably. A related category is that of deformity, defined by Garland as deviation from normal appearance.[3] Deformity does not map straightforwardly onto disability since a person can be disabled without being deformed or vice versa. Again, scholars distinguish between impairment and disability, the former a person's physical or mental condition, the latter its impact upon their life given their social and cultural environment, but while important, this distinction is not directly relevant to the present discussion and I speak of impairment without intending a strong signal to it.

Insofar as disabling conditions were acknowledged in pre-modern societies, they could differ from those we recognize. In Byzantine society, for example, a woman's inability to conceive was stigmatized as a serious chronic illness and a curse,[4] while among ascetic Christians sexual desire and fecundity were considered impediments to salvation, the primary goal of human life.[5] We shall see that a common and catastrophic disability in antiquity was leprosy.[6]

---

[1] I wish to dedicate this chapter to Professor Ilaria L. E. Ramelli.
[2] C. Laes (ed.), *Disability in Antiquity* (London and New York: Routledge, 2016), p. 4.
[3] R. Garland, *The Eye of the Beholder: Deformity and Disability in the Graeco-Roman World* (London: Duckworth, 1995), p. 5.
[4] See S. Efthymiadis, 'The Disabled in the Byzantine Empire', in Laes (ed.), *Disability in Antiquity*, pp. 388–402, 389.
[5] J. W. Martens, 'The Disability within: Sexual Desire as Disability in Syriac Christianity', in Laes (ed.), *Disability in Antiquity*, pp. 376–87, focuses on late antique Syriac Christianity, but celibacy and virginity were highly prized by many Christian groups in antiquity; see, for example, P. Brown, *The Body and Society: Men, Women, and Sexual Renunciation in Early Christianity* (New York: Columbia University Press, 1988).
[6] H. Marx-Wolf and K. Upson-Saia, 'The State of the Question: Religion, Medicine, Disability, and Health in Late Antiquity', *Journal of Late Antiquity* 8, no. 2 (Fall 2015): 266–7 note that the term encompasses various skin diseases.

The present chapter does not attempt a comprehensive survey but rather to give a sense of how Christianity changed societal perceptions of, and responses to, disabled people and how disability was constructed by some of its most influential theologians. It will focus on the practical measures and theological perspectives that emerge in the fourth century from the dialogue between Egyptian desert monasticism and the Cappadocian Fathers Basil of Caesarea, Gregory of Nyssa, and Gregory Nazianzus, and the theological counterpoint provided by Augustine of Hippo. Since the early church has its cultural matrix in the Graeco-Roman world and its spiritual roots in scripture, I begin by outlining their attitudes to disability.[7]

DISABILITY IN THE GRAECO-ROMAN WORLD

Physical impairment would have been a familiar sight in the ancient world. Malnutrition, disease and interbreeding, all major causes of birth defects, were ubiquitous, and although infanticide was practised and both Plato and Aristotle proposed legal codes mandating the killing of deformed newborns,[8] its prevalence is unclear and it was in any case not confined to impaired infants, healthy newborns being exposed in order to limit family size and select for male children.[9] Whatever the incidence of congenital deformity, however, postnatally acquired infirmity would have been even more commonplace, its causes including accidents, combat wounds, penal mutilations, disease and old age.[10] While a few doctors offered their services free of charge,[11] medical attention was for the most part available only to those who could afford to pay, and incurable conditions were in any case beyond the remit of scientific medicine since its aim was to effect cures. The ability to distinguish between curable and incurable conditions was part of a physician's skill and to treat a patient he could not cure would damage his reputation.[12] Moreover, a person's perceived value was linked to their ability to contribute to society, an attitude to which Plato gives voice in having Socrates inveigh against treating chronic illness on the grounds that in a well-ordered society each person has work assigned to them and no one has leisure to spend their life undergoing medical treatment; he cites the example of a certain Herodicus who became a valetudinarian and used his medical knowledge to treat himself and as a result spent the rest of his days struggling against death yet unfit for life.[13]

---

[7]All translations are my own except for biblical words and quotations, for which I use the *NRSV*.
[8]See Plato, *Rep.*, 460c2-7; Aristotle, *Pol.*, 1335b20-1.
[9]See, for example, M. L. Rose, *The Staff of Oedipus: Transforming Disability in Ancient Greece* (Ann Arbor: University of Michigan Press, 2003), pp. 29–49. Aristotle, *Pol.*, 1335b22-5, prescribes exposure to limit family size, and if local customs forbid exposure, abortion before the child has developed sensation and life.
[10]See, for example, Rose, *The Staff of Oedipus*, pp. 9–28.
[11]A. T. Crislip, *From Monastery to Hospital: Christian Monasticism and the Transformation of Health Care in Late Antiquity* (Ann Arbor: University of Michigan Press, 2005), pp. 49–50, 124–5.
[12]Crislip, *From Monastery to Hospital*, p. 114; see also Rose, *The Staff of Oedipus*, p. 11.
[13]*Rep.*, 406b1-c6.

Cognitive function was evaluated in terms of a contrast between wisdom and folly, which does not map onto modern categories of mental ability or disability. Plato defines folly as a disease of the soul which can take the form of either madness or ignorance, the former due to a bad disposition of the body, the latter to bad education. Men are prone to madness due to the seed in the spinal marrow becoming too plentiful and overflowing, thereby destabilizing the body's elemental equilibrium and producing pleasures and pains whose intensity causes mental derangement.[14]

Despite Plato's advocacy of eugenic infanticide and objection to medical care in cases of chronic infirmity (if we take him at face value), his insistence that the soul is more valuable than the body and its condition not inferable from the body's appearance[15] favours those with physical infirmities, so too his observation that the mind (*dianoia*) begins to see clearly when the eyes grow dim,[16] and while he may not have made this connection, Christian thinkers did.

DISABILITY IN SCRIPTURE

The Hebrew Bible categorizes individuals according to their physical and mental state, appearance, alleged vulnerability and status as regards certain diseases[17] and attributes infirmity both to God and to natural causes.[18] Some impairments make a person ritually impure; Lev. 21.18-19 lists them as blindness, lameness, facial mutilation, an excessively long limb, a broken foot or hand, a hunched back, dwarfism, or damaged eyes, skin or testicles. A priest thus affected is prohibited from offering sacrifice. Leprosy is considered polluting and sufferers banished from the community,[19] and disabled people are associated with other disadvantaged groups including the oppressed, the hungry, prisoners, strangers, widows and orphans. But God's special regard for all marginalized persons is affirmed,[20] and the Levitical view of sacrifice and the ritual purity associated with it is challenged by Ps. 51.16-17, where God is said to prefer a broken and contrite heart to burnt offerings, and Hos. 6.6, where God desires steadfast love and knowledge of himself rather than sacrifice and burnt offerings. The spiritual priority of a person's interior state is affirmed at Joel 2.12-13, Ezek. 36.26 and Jer. 17.10, while according to Isa. 11.2-3 the one on whom the spirit of the Lord rests 'shall not judge by what his eyes see, or decide by what his ears hear'.

The New Testament builds on the Hebrew Bible's option for the marginalized, in part by re-envisioning its purity codes along the lines intimated by Psalm

---

[14]See *Tim.*, 86b3-d1.
[15]See, for example, *Gorg.*, 523c1-6. *Symp.*, 210b8-c1.
[16]See *Symp.*, 219a2-5.
[17]See S. M. Olyan, *Disability in the Hebrew Bible: Interpreting Mental and Physical Differences* (Cambridge: Cambridge University Press, 2008), pp. 1–2.
[18]See, for example, Exod. 4.1; 2 Chron. 26.16-21; 2 Sam. 4.4; 1 Kings 14.4.
[19]See Lev. 21.17-23, 13.45-46; Num. 5.1-4.
[20]See, for example, Ps. 146.7-9; also Job 29.12-16.

51 and Hosea in that Jesus likewise prioritizes a person's interior state over external considerations. At Matt. 15.1-20 he critiques the Pharisees' and scribes' preoccupation with external criteria of purity and declares that a person is defiled not by ritual impurity but by the evil thoughts that proceed from their heart,[21] and at Matt. 5.9 he declares a pure heart to be the requirement for seeing God. He also challenges purity codes by associating with infirm people, and at Matt. 9.13 he describes himself as a physician who has come to heal those who are sick. Some infirmities are associated with sin, but not all: at John 9.3 Jesus rebuts the suggestion that the man born blind was being punished for sins but at Matt. 9.1-8 he heals a paralytic by forgiving his sins.[22] Paul experienced the vulnerability of his flesh not only in its rebelliousness and the afflictions he endured but also in the 'thorn' that was given to him: when he prayed for deliverance from it, God refused, saying instead that his grace would sustain him, 'for power is made perfect in weakness'.[23]

INSTITUTIONAL CHARITY IN THE EARLY CHURCH

In the Graeco-Roman world the basic unit of social support, and thus of care for the disabled, was the family, and the church assumed this role from the outset by seeing itself as a family whose members supported each other, above all the neediest among them. Underlying its concern for vulnerable people was the belief, alien to Graeco-Roman paganism in any of its guises, that every human life has intrinsic value and marginalized people are to be seen not as burdens on a society to which they cannot contribute but as especially dear to God. Infanticide was condemned as part of a general prohibition against taking human life or shedding human blood, which also included abortion, gladiatorial contests, and brutal public executions, and sometimes extended to the killing of non-human animals.[24] Although no surviving condemnation of infanticide mentions impairment, Amundsen is surely correct in maintaining that the prohibition would have admitted of no exceptions.[25]

The initial model for the provision of social care by ecclesiastical charities was furnished as early as the first century by the idealized description at Acts 4.32–5 of the protochurch as a community whose members held all possessions in common,[26] and by Jewish charitable traditions. Further development came with the emergence in Egypt of monastic communities whose members renounced all links to secular society, including all family ties, meaning that it was incumbent upon the communities themselves to

---

[21]See also Mk 7.1-23.

[22]See also Mk 2.1-12; Lk. 5.17-26.

[23]Rom. 7.14-25; 2 Cor. 4.8-9, 11.23-30, 12.7-9-10.

[24]Almut Caspary, 'The Patristic Era: Early Christian Attitudes toward the Disfigured Outcast', in *Disability in the Christian Tradition: A Reader*, eds B. Brock and J. Swinton (Grand Rapids, MI and Cambridge: Wm. B. Eerdmans, 2012), pp. 24–64, 27, citing Lactantius, *Inst,* 20; Tertullian, *Apol.*, 9, and for the inclusion of non-human animals, Minucius Felix, *Oct.*, 30.

[25]D. W. Amundsen, *Medicine, Society, and Faith in the Ancient and Medieval Worlds* (Baltimore, MD and London: Johns Hopkins University Press, 1996), p. 64.

[26]Crislip, *From Monastery to Hospital*, pp. 50–5.

assume responsibility for their care. Crislip notes that the monastic healthcare system is apparent from the very beginnings of organized Christian monasticism in the fourth century and one of its defining characteristics.[27] It utilized medical healing comparable to what was available in the secular world, and while the divergent administrative structures of coenobitic and lavra communities determined the way healthcare was delivered in each,[28] sick and disabled monastics were consistently assured of social inclusion and support when needed, including care in their old age.[29] Illness was destigmatized: the sick were not to be blamed for their illness and monastics were forbidden to attribute a person's illness to their sins.[30] Non-medical healings were also a central feature of monastic life, performed by monks whose ascetic excellence had made them worthy to receive the charism of healing.[31]

The Egyptian monastic healthcare system served in turn as the template for the emergence of the hospital as its institutional extension, a development which coincided with the subordination of monasticism to the ecclesiastical hierarchy[32] and was pioneered by Basil of Caesarea. Basil toured the monastic settlements of Egypt and Palestine in 357, and following his elevation to the episcopate in 370 he constructed a hospital on the outskirts of Caesarea, which included apartments for himself as bishop and his guests along with accommodation for travellers in need, the poor and the sick, including a leprosarium. The poor who were able to work were either employed or trained in a trade, while the sick received both medical and hospice care.[33] Basil's hospital thus incorporated the monastic healthcare system and social services into the wider charitable mission of the church, and it formed the model upon which further hospitals were established throughout the Mediterranean and in Constantinople, Antioch, Jerusalem and elsewhere,[34] the Byzantine state in particular developing an elaborate system of institutional healthcare as part of a wider concern for social welfare.[35]

'A MYRIAD OF LAZARUSES'

Given the fear and stigma associated with leprosy, the most radical feature of Basil's foundation was undoubtedly the welcome he extended to those suffering from it. Their plight is vividly evoked by both Gregory of Nyssa and Gregory Nazianzus in orations devoted to the Christian imperative to show compassion for the poor

---

[27]Ibid., p. 9.
[28]Ibid., pp. 9–14.
[29]Ibid., pp. 39–40.
[30]Ibid., pp. 76–7.
[31]See Crislip, *From Monastery to Hospital*, pp. 21–8; C. Downer, 'The Coptic and Ethiopian Traditions', in Laes (ed.), *Disability in Antiquity*, pp. 357–75, 360–8, especially pp. 365–7.
[32]Crislip, *From Monastery to Hospital*, p. 100.
[33]S. R. Holman, *The Hungry Are Dying: Beggars and Bishops in Roman Cappadocia*. Oxford Studies in Historical Theology (Oxford: Oxford University Press, 2001), p. 74.
[34]Crislip, *From Monastery to Hospital*, pp. 141–2.
[35]See Efthymiadis, 'The Disabled in the Byzantine Empire', p. 393.

and infirm. Gregory of Nyssa's *On the Love of the Poor* 1 and 2 and Gregory Nazianzus' *Oration* 14 include graphic descriptions of leprosy's symptoms and the abuses it attracted. For Nazianzen it was the most loathsome and oppressive of evils,[36] devouring flesh, bone and marrow[37] and reducing its victims to a living death.[38] Such was the revulsion their condition aroused that they were regarded as abominations and subjected to complete social exclusion, shunned even by their own parents. They were driven from their homes, cities and all public gatherings and forbidden to drink or wash themselves at public fountains and streams for fear of pollution; should one happen to do so, the fountain or stream was condemned.[39] The stigma, says Nazianzen, weighed upon them even more heavily than their illness since they seemed to be hated for their misfortune.[40] For Gregory of Nyssa those suffering from leprosy were a 'myriad of Lazaruses' each of whom displayed terrible disfigurement: some appeared to have had their eyes gouged out, others to have had their feet amputated, while still others were mutilated in every limb.[41]

To the uniquely comprehensive loss endured by victims of leprosy, Basil responded with a compassion and respect denied them even by other Christians and even in churches.[42] Not only did he welcome them into his hospital, but he restored their human dignity by greeting them as his brethren, and whereas doctors were praised for their willingness merely to go near people suffering from other sicknesses, Basil himself worked in his leprosarium.[43] The Nyssen too practised hands-on care of the sick. Dismissing fears of contagion,[44] he enjoins his fellow Christians to embrace the wretched as if they were gold and care for them as if they were close family members.[45] Gregory Nazianzen stresses the imperative to attend to the physical needs of our neighbours, healthy or sick, no less than to our own needs, since we share with them both a common nature and, in consequence of the fall, a common infirmity. Whether rich or poor, slave or free, healthy or sick in body, we are all one in the Lord.[46] Both Gregories also adduce Christological grounds for ministering to the wretched. The Nyssen calls upon his listeners to recognize the presence of Christ in them. They 'bear Christ's countenance',[47] and whoever succours the hungry, the thirsty, the stranger, the prisoner, the naked and the sick succours the Lord himself.[48] Gregory Nazianzen urges his audience to heal, feed, clothe, welcome and

---

[36]*Or.*, 14.9.
[37]*Or.*, 14.6.
[38]*Or.*, 14.10.
[39]*De am. paup*, 2.479; *Or.*, 14.12.
[40]*Or.*, 14.9.
[41]*De am. paup*, 1.468, alluding to Lk. 16.19-31.
[42]Crislip, *From Monastery to Hospital*, p. 115.
[43]Gregory of Nazianzus, *Or.*, 43.63.
[44]*De am. paup*, 2.485.
[45]*De am. paup*, 1.459.
[46]*Or.*, 14.8, alluding to Col. 3.9; Gal. 3.27.
[47]*De am. paup*, 1.460.
[48]*De am. paup*, 2.474, alluding to Matt. 25.40.

honour Christ in the downtrodden and marginalized, thereby offering 'mercy and not sacrifice' to the Lord of all.[49]

In sum, leprosy disabled its victims not only physically but also socially and existentially, and the Cappadocian Fathers responded with the inclusiveness and compassion shown by Jesus in the Gospels. Defying and challenging the stigma associated with it, they not only cared for sufferers' physical needs but restored their human dignity, and by pointing to the presence of Christ in them, they showed that to succour them was to succour God himself. This would, in turn, have had positive implications for how other disabled and marginalized persons were viewed since if lepers could be shown to be icons of God, so too could they.[50]

INFIRMITY AS ASCETICISM

If the infirm could be seen as bearing the countenance of Christ, infirmity could in turn provide its sufferers with a route to conformity with Christ. It did so by functioning as a mode of asceticism, and it is accordingly in the context of asceticism – which includes the Cappadocian Fathers – that we see the Pauline themes of sustaining grace and power perfected in weakness most clearly and fully embodied. Towards the end of the fourth century Evagrius of Pontus (who prior to becoming a monk and retiring to the Egyptian desert was a protegé of Basil and Gregory Nazianzus, and whose thought also has strong affinities with Gregory of Nyssa), committed to writing a spiritual itinerary of the monastic life as conceived by the desert tradition he had embraced. Its underlying anthropology[51] presupposes an allegorical reading of the Adam and Eve narrative in the book of Genesis. In this Evagrius takes his lead from Origen, for whom the first three chapters of Genesis, like many other biblical narratives, makes little sense if interpreted literally.[52] Origen does not commit himself to any single understanding of them,[53] but among those he suggests is that since 'Adam' means *anthrōpos*, 'human', his sin and expulsion from Paradise represent those of all humankind.[54] For Evagrius Adam symbolizes Christ and Eve the rational creation for whose sake he left Paradise by assuming mortal nature.[55] In Paradise, which Evagrius refers to as the primary nature, the human person is a *nous* or intelligence bearing the image of God, perfectly united to God and perfectly unified in itself. The *nous* has a body which it enforms such that the body's elemental constitution (but not

---

[49]*Or.*, 14.40, citing Matt. 9.13.

[50]See J. A. McGuckin, *Saint Gregory of Nazianzus: An Intellectual Biography* (Crestwood, NY: St Vladimir's Seminary Press, 2001), p. 153.

[51]The following discussion of Evagrius' anthropology and asceticism is based on M. Tobon, *Apatheia and Anthropology in Evagrius of Pontus.* (London and New York: Routledge, forthcoming).

[52]*Princ*, 4.3.2–4.

[53]See, for example, P. W. Martens, 'Origen's Doctrine of Pre-Existence and the Opening Chapters of Genesis', *ZAC* 16 (2012): 516–49, especially pp. 520–1.

[54]*Cels.*, 4.40.

[55]*Keph. Gn.*, 5.1.

its appearance) reflects the spiritual state of the *nous*. In the primary nature all rational beings are equal in rank. In consequence of their perfect unity their bodies are incorruptible and immortal, and in consequence of their perfect equality their bodies are ungendered and free from all distinctions of race or status. In falling, however, the nous became a soul and its body became mortal and acquired gender and other differentiating characteristics. Our fallen state is the secondary nature. In it, moral corruptibility finds reflection in physical corruptibility. Our being currently spans both natures and will do so until we are fully restored to the primary nature. The aspect of us which exists in the primary nature is the inner or new self of Pauline doctrine, while the aspect which exists in the secondary nature is the outer or old self.[56] The primary nature is ontologically prior to space and time and compresent with, and accessible from, the secondary nature; in other words, we can access it during the present life. Being in principle accessible to us, it is already normative, meaning that we are called to live as far as possible by its standards. But we can only access it insofar as we are purified of the corruptibility we acquired in deflecting from God. Evagrius' scheme of the monastic life tells us how to undergo such purification. It involves a theory of our present state and how to remedy it, which utilizes the Greek philosophical category of pathos adapted by Evagrius to a Christian framework.

According to that theory, the mortality of our present body reflects the presence of pathos, the psychophysical disposition to sin which comes with alienation from God and is the hallmark of our fallen condition. The goal of asceticism is to attain apatheia, freedom from pathos. Apatheia is purity of heart[57] and the resurrection of the soul,[58] and its child is love (*agapē*),[59] which is to say that apatheia establishes love as the soul's stable disposition. Apatheia brings into being the new self, in whom there is neither 'male nor female', 'Greek nor Jew', 'circumcision nor uncircumcision, barbarian nor Scythian, slave nor free, but Christ all in all'.[60] Insofar as it is attained it conforms us to Christ and enables us to live from the perspective of the primary nature, and although none of our sources say as much, the Cappadocian Fathers demonstrate it with especial clarity in their attitude towards those suffering from leprosy. But attaining apatheia and stabilizing it in our soul and body involve courting infirmity since although pathos originate in the choice of the nous to turn away from God, it is rooted in the flesh, meaning that to attain apatheia it must be purged from the body and from the soul. Working from a reading of Paul informed by Greek medical and philosophical theories stressing the closeness of the soul–body relation, Evagrius supposed the best way of achieving this to be a regime of dietary restriction and fasting coupled with other ascetic disciplines such as sleep deprivation, manual labour, almsgiving, reading of scripture, chanting of psalms

---

[56]See Col. 3.9-10; 2 Cor. 4.16; Rom. 6.6.
[57]*Scholion* 199, Prov. 19.17 alluding to Matt. 5.8.
[58]*Keph. Gn.*, 5.22.
[59]*Prakt.*, Prologue 8.
[60]*Rer.mon.rat.*, 3.31-40, alluding to Col. 3.11 and Gal. 3.28.

and above all the unceasing prayer mandated by 1 Thess. 5.17.[61] Modelled on the Passion of Christ,[62] this regime was designed to mortify the old self and nourish the new self by subjecting the body to as much stress as it could bear in order to refine both it and the soul and thereby strengthen the nous. Although Evagrius insists that the body must be preserved and warns against pushing it beyond its limits,[63] he regards worries about its health as a demonic temptation to relax asceticism so that it loses its efficacy[64] and warns that to be overly concerned for its welfare is incompatible with the pursuit of apatheia.[65] Moreover, the sort of body which secular doctors regarded as healthy was from the perspective of the desert monks overfed and thus over-nourished, resulting in an excess of vital heat that burnt itself off as *pathe* whose turbulence and volatility reflected their fiery nature.[66] Such views were not confined to the desert and I take Gregory Nazianzus to be thinking along similar lines when he says that rather than simply admiring health and loathing infirmity, we should 'despise the health whose fruit is sin'.[67]

While we might baulk at the harshness of Evagrian asceticism,[68] it was a regime he inherited from his elders in the desert, and it would not have been observed and handed down had it not produced results. The combination of long-term bodily stress with intense devotional practices was, it would seem, spiritually efficacious along the lines described by Paul in relation to his thorn in the flesh, and this is the key to how infirmity could take its place alongside, or even instead of, the ascetic labours prescribed by Evagrius. Thus the desert mother Syncletica explains that we should not worry if the body's infirmity renders us incapable of standing in prayer or singing since bodily weakness, provided it is consecrated by prayer, can diminish the *pathe* as surely as fasting and sleeping on the ground. If our desires are blunted by sickness, then our ascetic labours become superfluous.[69] Again, I take Gregory Nazianzus to be thinking along these lines when he declares that victims of leprosy will be raised with Christ if only they suffer with him so that they might be glorified with him.[70] Syncletica also finds spiritual benefit in the loss of our bodily senses. To be deprived of our eyes is to have discarded organs of insatiable desire. It is with our inner eyes that we see the glory of the Lord. If we are deaf and dumb, we have cause for gratitude in our deliverance from vain sounds. If our bodily hands are

---

[61]See *Prakt.*, 49.
[62]See, for example, *Keph.Gn*, 6.40,
[63]See, for example, *Prakt.*, 29; *Rer.mon.rat*, 35.
[64]See, for example, *Prakt.*, 7.
[65]See, for example, *Sent. virg*, 51.
[66]For Evagrius the *pathe*, or more precisely the thoughts (*logismoi*) which are their cognitive correlate, can be divided into eight broad types, namely gluttony, fornication, avarice, distress, anger, acedia, vainglory and pride. See, for example, *Prakt.*, 6.
[67]*Or.*, 14.34.
[68]As did some of his contemporaries. Gregory of Nazianzus, for example, practised a less extreme form of asceticism than the Egyptian monks, and according to McGuckin, *Saint Gregory of Nazianzus*, p. 28, considered some of their practices uncouth.
[69]*Apophthegmat Patrum, Syncletica.*, 99.
[70]*Or.*, 14.14; Rom. 8.17.

afflicted, our inner hands are ready to fight the enemy.[71] Her reasoning recalls the doctrine of the spiritual senses, proposed by Origen and taken up by Evagrius.[72] The sense faculties of the inner self, that is the spiritual senses, discern spiritual realities. Analogous to the senses of the mortal body, they imply the compresence with it of the inner self's incorruptible body. For Evagrius the outer senses are heavily implicated in pathos[73] whereas to acquire apatheia is to acquire spiritual sensation.[74] It follows that to be deprived of our outer senses can be spiritually beneficial. In similar vein Gregory of Nyssa points out that however damaged that body might be, the soul remains intact. The mutilated hand remains sensitive to assistance, the gangrenous foot is able to run to God, and the missing eye can discern invisible goodness.[75] In facilitating our access to spiritual sensation, impairment becomes blessing.[76]

The contrast between outer and inner senses reflects the contrast between appearances and the realities which underly them and, in doing so, challenges the human tendency to view infirmity as a punishment or disabled people as somehow deficient. Gregory of Nazianzus reflects that we cannot tell from physical appearances whether one person is being punished and another rewarded, or whether, on the contrary, a virtuous person is being tested or a wicked person raised up in order that they might fall harder and their vice erupt like an abscess.[77] Lepers perhaps keep the image of God better than we do.[78] Syncletica's body was ravaged by illness in the final years of her life but her soul was healthy.[79]

In sum, whereas pathos binds us cognitively and affectively to appearances we cannot see beyond, apatheia enables us to engage with reality at a deeper level. Just as it is sometimes necessary to probe beneath the surface meaning of the biblical text in order to discover its deeper import, so there is more to human beings than meets the eye. From the perspective of the primary nature we are defined not by our physical characteristics and social circumstances but rather by our status as images of God, and this in turn is the key to the true significance of the visible dimension of our lives. But to attain apatheia it is necessary to undergo a process of purification analogous to crucifixion, and the sufferings associated with leprosy are a stark parody of the voluntary *agon* of the desert monk whereby he or she 'strips off the weight of the flesh'.[80]

---

[71]*Syncl.*, 99.

[72]See Origen, *Cant*, Prologue 2; *Heracl*, 16-20; Evagrius, *KephGn*, 1.37.

[73]See, for example, *Prakt.*, 4.

[74]*Keph. Gn.*, 1.37.

[75]*De am. paup*, 2.484.

[76]For a different argument against negative assumptions about disability, see S. T. Horne, 'Injury and Blessing: A Challenge to Current Readings of Biblical Discourse Concerning Impairment' (unpublished doctoral dissertation, University of Birmingham, 1999).

[77]*Or.*, 14.29-30.

[78]*Or.*, 14.14.

[79]*Apophthegmata Patrum, Syncletica*, 106-12.

[80]Evagrius, *Eul.*, Prologue 2.

CARE-GIVING AS ASCETICISM

While suffering infirmity could be a form of asceticism, so too could caring for the infirm. Evagrius' disciple Palladius tells of a certain Eulogius, a learned man from Alexandria who wished to pursue the monastic life but was unable to work and wished neither to enter a coenobium nor seek perfection in solitude. Having decided to remain in his own home, and in disposing of his property retaining enough to live on, he offered to take in a disabled man who was begging in the marketplace and care for him in his guest room so that each might be saved through the other. The disabled man accepted and Eulogius pledged to the Lord that in his name he would care for him until death. The man had neither hands nor feet and the only part of his body which was intact was his tongue. For fifteen years Eulogius attended to all his needs, but then a demon possessed him and he became abusive. When Eulogius could bear it no longer, he sought the advice of Antony, taking the disabled man with him. He explained to Antony that although he had pledged to nurse him so that they would be saved through each other, he was now tempted to cast him out. Antony rebuked them both sternly. First he asked Eulogius if he would cast out him when God who made him did not; if so, then God would raise up a better man to succour him. To the disabled man he said that since that he deserved neither earth nor heaven, would he not cease fighting against God? For it was Christ who was serving him and Christ whom he was abusing, it being for Christ's sake that Eulogius had made himself a slave to minister to him. Antony then sent them home, instructing them not to be separated from one another. For, he said, the temptation had come upon them because they were both near the end of their lives and 'about to be counted worthy of crowns'; the allusion is to 2 Tim. 2.5, 4.8. Within weeks both had died.[81]

A striking feature of this story is its portrayal of Eulogius and the disabled man as equals despite the latter's dependence and their differing social status. Eulogius' pledge was for the salvation of both, and although he was the active party in the sense of being the instigator and care provider, the disabled man was active in assenting to his ministry. In declaring that both been counted worthy of crowns Antony recognized both as mature ascetics. The disabled man was not just a passive recipient of Eulogius' charity but exercised equal agency and merited the same spiritual reward. I take it that the reason why Antony said he deserved nothing was not that his disability made him especially unworthy but that every human being is dependent on unmerited grace.

EVAGRIAN ANTHROPOLOGY AND BODILY IMPAIRMENT

Evagrian anthropology has radical implications for the notion of bodily normativity. Since every soul *qua* soul, and every mortal body *qua* mortal, is an impairment of

---

[81]Palladius, *LH*, 21.3-14.

our primary nature, no mortal body can be normative, not even the human body of Christ. God incarnated in the form best suited to his pedagogical–soteriological purposes, but his body in the primary nature is that which he revealed at the Transfiguration and it alone represents bodily normativity. It follows that all of the body's secondary characteristics, which include gender, race and social status, as well as the presence or absence of infirmity, are provisional: temporary features of temporary bodies best suited to the person's spiritual needs at a particular point in their journey of restoration to God. None implies that the person concerned is any more or less virtuous or sinful than anyone else. This does not mean that in the secondary nature a healthy soul never finds reflection in bodily well-being, only that such soul–body congruence cannot be presumed upon. Only in the primary nature does the body consistently reflect the state of the *nous* (i.e. of the soul in the primary nature). The only reliable bodily indicator of spiritual health is glorification.

EVAGRIUS ON INFIRMITY

The only infirmity which interests Evagrius is the spiritual infirmity of pathos, although he himself experienced serious illness at least twice, the first leading to his conversion to the monastic life and the second to his death in his mid-fifties, relatively young for a desert monk.[82] He stresses the importance of showing compassion to those unfortunate enough to be oppressed by illness[83] and warns that to hoard riches is to seize the food and shelter of those who are blind, lame or afflicted with leprosy.[84] Otherwise, his references to disability are purely symbolic. The monk should, for example, strive to have the *nous* 'stand deaf and mute at the time of prayer',[85] meaning that he or she should focus their attention and resist distractions, and Evagrius takes up a suggestion of Origen's to propose allegorical meanings for sixteen infirmities mentioned in scripture: blindness, he says, symbolizes noetic ignorance, and mutilation of the ear obduracy of the rational soul.[86] But these are not to be taken literally: Didymus, the Alexandrian exegete whom Evagrius revered as a gnostic, was physically blind,[87] and Ammonius, a monk of Evagrius' circle, mutilated his ear to avoid ordination.[88]

The Cappadocian and Egyptian monastic approaches: A summary

While none of the writers we have considered articulates a theology of infirmity and disability as such, the following points can be noted:

---

[82]Palladius, *LH*, 38.8-9; Coptic version 38.13.
[83]*Rer.mon.rat.*, 11.
[84]*Rer.mon.rat.*, 32.
[85]*Cap. Orat.*, 11.
[86]Evagrius, *Cap. grad.*, 4; 12; Lev. 21.18.
[87]Palladius, *LH*, 4.1.
[88]Palladius, *LH*, 11.2.

1. Christian charity should encompass even those most stigmatized, defusing the stigma with compassionate and respectful care and recognizing our essential kinship and the presence in them of Christ.

2. All of humankind suffers from the spiritual infirmity of pathos due to the fall.

3. Apatheia can to some extent be attained during the present life.

4. If infirmity is embraced as a form of asceticism, it can contribute to the attainment of apatheia.

5. Care-giving can be a form of asceticism.

6. The body's condition and appearance are no guide to a person's interior state.

7. No mortal body is normative, and gender, race and social status are as provisional as the presence or absence of impairment.

A DIFFERENT PERSPECTIVE: AUGUSTINE OF HIPPO

Augustine reflects upon the theological significance of bodily impairment and the plight of those affected, and also, unlike Evagrius or Greek philosophical tradition, on what we would class as intellectual impairment. There are key points of agreement between him and Evagrius but also deep differences.

In his polemic against the Pelagian Julian of Eclanum, Augustine responds to what he considers his over-optimistic view of human nature by charging him with insensitivity to the sufferings of

> the blind, the one-eyed, the myopic, the deaf, the mute, the lame, the deformed, the distorted, the worm-ridden, the leprous, the paralysed, the epileptic, or those who are deficient in whatever other way, some even looking monstrous because of their excessive ugliness and the horrible strangeness of their members.[89]

His own sensitivity to human suffering is evident in his discussion of how intellectually disabled people are used for amusement, even fetching higher prices in slave markets than their more able counterparts. The person who laughs at simpletons would not wish to be one, and if the father who delights in such things from his young child knew that he would grow up to be a fool, he would assuredly think him more to be mourned than if he were dead.[90] Augustine perhaps speaks from personal experience: his dialogue *The Teacher* pays tribute to his own son Adeodatus, who died at the age of seventeen.

The location of the image of God in the rational mind (*mens*) raises the question of whether slow-minded people are fully human, but Augustine insists they are:

---

[89]*c.sec.Iul.imp.*, 6.16.
[90]*pecc. mer.*, 66.

however small or even dormant the capacity for reason and understanding may seem, the human soul is always rational and intellectual.[91] Extreme bodily deformity raises the same question. In the *City of God* Augustine considers whether the monstrous races described in pagan histories are descended from Adam, that is, whether they are human. He argues that they are. No matter how unusual they might appear to our bodily senses, they are descended from the first human being.[92]

Both monstrous races and monstrous births deviate from the usual pattern of nature; it is, says Augustine, clear what the natural norm is.[93] For him that norm reflects divinely ordained human normativity as exemplified by Adam and Eve before the fall. In contrast to the Alexandrian tradition exemplified by Origen and Evagrius, Augustine understands them to be real human beings who existed in history and from whom we are physically descended. They had bodies like ours and were set in Paradise in order to populate it, with Adam ruling over his wife in obedience to God.[94] Because he failed to do so, he and Eve set themselves outside that order, and as their just punishment they were expelled from Paradise and afflicted with infirmity and suffering.[95] Just as the right ordering of creation is rooted in a hierarchy of obedience to God, so bodily beauty is to be found in suitably arranged parts together with pleasantness of colour.[96] Deformity is a defect consisting of improper arrangement and occurs only because of the penal condition under which we currently live.[97] It ruins a person's beauty just as loss of a limb undermines their soundness and sickness destroys their health.[98] As a curvature of the spine subverts all the body's beauty and grace, so if a person becomes blind, deaf, mad or demonically possessed, the beauty and grace of the mind are subverted.[99]

All the conditions Augustine cites in his polemic against Julian are therefore deficiencies relative to a norm of able-bodiedness and ideal proportion and as such wholly negative in their import. He makes no attempt to de-stigmatize impairment. Together with the other pains and privations we experience as a result of original sin, including moral failings and the pains associated with birth and death,[100] it is inconsistent with the happiness of the saints and will vanish when the body is resurrected. The only exception is impairment resulting from the wounds received by martyrs for the sake of Christ since they are not deformities but badges of honour.[101] Augustine also notes, however, that a person's character is more important than their physical appearance: we flee from a handsome man whom we know to be a

---

[91]*Trin.*, 14.2.6.
[92]*Civ.*, 16.8.
[93]Ibid.
[94]*Gn. litt*, 9.6-9.
[95]See, for example, *On Genesis: A Refutation of the Manichees*, 2.29-30; *Gn. litt.*, 11.50-5; *Civ.*, 22.22, 24.
[96]*Civ.*, 22.19.
[97]Ibid.
[98]*Civ.*, 19.4.
[99]Ibid.
[100]*c.sec.Iul.imp.*, 6.16.
[101]*Civ.*, 22.19.

thief and love a decrepit old man whom we know to be just, and we love the martyrs even though their limbs have been mangled by wild beasts since our love is guided not by the eyes of the flesh but by the eyes of the heart.[102]

Evagrius agrees that all privation and suffering are a consequence of our fallen state, that our present condition is one of spiritual infirmity reflected in both soul and body, and that the right ordering of creation depends on our obedience to God. He would agree too that no bodily or intellectual impairment diminishes the image of God within each of us. But in rejecting a literal reading of the Adam and Eve narrative he rejects the possibility of any gendered human body being normative, and whereas Augustine associates impairment primarily with divine punishment, Evagrius associates it primarily with spiritual opportunity. For both these reasons Augustine's unrelentingly negative view of impairment is alien to Evagrius. But Augustine's contrast between the eyes of the flesh and the eyes of the heart, the former seeing physical appearances, the latter inner realities, echoes Evagrius' understanding of spiritual sensation and sits uneasily with his (Augustine's) preoccupation with (outer) sense-perceptible indices of normativity. Similarly, Brock contrasts the minor strand of Augustine's thought which emphasises that knowing other people rightly means seeing beyond their apparent deficiencies and requires that our perception of them be sanctified or illuminated, with a more dominant tendency to situate them on a scale of perfection relative to an ideal.[103]

CONCLUSION

The early church revolutionized attitudes towards disabled people by insisting on the intrinsic value of every human being as an image of God and affirming inclusive health and social care to be a Christian imperative. Administered at first by ecclesiastical charities, such care was further developed by monastic communities in Egypt and then brought back within the purview of the institutional church and extended to the secular world by Basil of Caesarea. In Plato, the Hebrew Bible and Augustine a tension exists between exterior and interior criteria of value and purity. Jesus, however, emphasizes inner purity over external indices of value, an example followed by the Cappadocian Fathers and Egyptian monastics in their de-stigmatization of infirmity and emphasis on the unreliability of appearances as a guide to the underlying reality. Whereas for Augustine, Adam and Eve in Paradise represent bodily normativity, for Evagrius impairment is just one of the bodily variations found in the secondary nature, along with characteristics associated with gender, race and status. In contrast to Augustine's wholly negative evaluation of disability (excepting that incurred in martyrdom), monastic asceticism emphasizes its potential spiritual benefits for the sufferer, and where applicable their carer. From the ascetic perspective, pathos constrains us to judge by appearances and

---

[102]*Jo.Tr*, 3.20-1.
[103]B. Brock, 'Augustine's Hierarchies of Human Wholeness and Their Healing', in Brock and Swinton (eds), *Disability in the Christian Tradition*, pp. 65–100, 65–6.

consequently to see impairment as disability and deficiency, at best a problem to be solved, whereas the transfiguring gaze of apatheia enables us to see impairment as a deeper form of ability, the weakness in which God's power is perfected.

BIBLIOGRAPHY

Amundsen, D. W. *Medicine, Society, and Faith in the Ancient and Medieval Worlds.* Baltimore, MD and London: Johns Hopkins University Press, 1996.

Amundsen, D. W. and Ferngren, G. B. 'The Early Christian Tradition', in R. L. Numbers and D. W. Amundsen (eds), *Caring and Curing: Health and Medicine in the Western Religious Traditions*, 40–64. New York: Macmillan Publishing Company; London: Collier Macmillan Publishers, 1986.

Arbesmann, R., Daily, E. J. and Quain, E. A. (trans.). *Minucius Felix: Octavius.* Washington, DC: Catholic University of America Press, 1950.

Arbesmann, R., Daily, E. J. and Quain, E. A. (trans.). *Tertullian: Apologetical Works.* Washington, DC: Catholic University of America Press, 1950.

Avalos, H., Melcher, S. J. and Schipper, J. (eds). *This Abled Body: Rethinking Disabilities and Biblical Studies.* Atlanta, GA: Society of Biblical Literature, 2007.

Barnes, J. (ed.). *The Complete Works of Aristotle*, 2 vols. Princeton, NJ: Princeton University Press, 1984.

Brock, B. 'Augustine's Hierarchies of Human Wholeness and Their Healing', in B. Brock and J. Swinton (eds), *Disability in the Christian Tradition: A Reader*, 65–100. Grand Rapids, MI and Cambridge: Wm. B. Eerdmans, 2012.

Brown, P. *The Body and Society: Men, Women, and Sexual Renunciation in Early Christianity.* New York: Columbia University Press, 1988.

Burleigh, J. H. S. (trans.). *Augustine: Earlier Writings*, 69–101. Philadelphia, PA: The Westminster Press, 1953.

Caspary, A. 'The Patristic Era: Early Christian Attitudes toward the Disfigured Outcast', in B. Brock and J. Swinton, *Disability in the Christian Tradition: A Reader*, 24–64. Grand Rapids, MI and Cambridge: Wm. B. Eerdmans, 2012.

Castelli, E. A. (trans.). 'Pseudo-Athanasius's Life and Activity of the Holy and Blessed Teacher Syncletica', in V. L. Wimbush (ed.), *Ascetic Behaviour in Greco-Roman Antiquity: A Sourcebook*, 265–311. Minneapolis, MN: Fortress Press, 1990.

Chadwick, H. (trans.). *Origen, Contra Celsum: Against Celsus.* Cambridge: Cambridge University Press, 1980.

Crislip, A. T. *From Monastery to Hospital: Christian Monasticism and the Transformation of Health Care in Late Antiquity.* Ann Arbor: University of Michigan Press, 2005.

Daly, R. J. (trans.). *Treatise on the Passover and Dialogue of Origen with Heraclides and His Fellow Bishops on the Father, the Son, and the Soul.* New York: Paulist Press, 1992.

Downer, C. 'The Coptic and Ethiopian Traditions', in C. Laes (ed.), *Disability in Antiquity*, 357–75. London and New York: Routledge, 2016.

Dyson, R. W. (trans.). *St. Augustine: The City of God against the Pagans.* Cambridge: Cambridge University Press, 1998.

Efthymiadis, S. 'The Disabled in the Byzantine Empire', in C. Laes (ed.), *Disability in Antiquity*, 388–402. London and New York: Routledge, 2016.

Garland, R. *The Eye of the Beholder: Deformity and Disability in the Graeco-Roman World*. London: Duckworth, 1995.

Géhin, P. (ed.). *Évagre le Pontique: Scholies aux Proverbes*. SCh, vol. 340. Paris: Éditions du Cerf, 1987.

Grünstäudl, W. and Ferrari, M. F. (eds). *Gestörte Lektüre. Disability als hermeneutische Leitkategorie biblischer Exegese*. Stuttgart: Kohlhammer, 2012.

Hamilton, E. and Huntington, C. (eds). *The Collected Dialogues of Plato, Including the Letters*. Princeton, NJ: Princeton University Press, 1961.

Hill, E. (trans). *Saint Augustine: On the Trinity*. New York: New City Press, 1991.

Hill, E. (trans). *Saint Augustine: On Genesis*. New York: New City Press, 2002.

Holman, S. R. *The Hungry are Dying: Beggars and Bishops in Roman Cappadocia*. Oxford: Oxford University Press, 2001.

Horne, S. T. 'Injury and Blessing: A Challenge to Current Readings of Biblical Discourse Concerning Impairment'. Unpublished doctoral dissertation, University of Birmingham, 1999).

Kelley, N. 'Deformity and Disability in Greece and Rome', in H. Avalos et al. (eds), *This Abled Body: Rethinking Disabilities and Biblical Studies*, 31–45. Atlanta, GA: Society of Biblical Literature, 2007.

Laes, C., Goodey, C. F. and Rose, M. L. *Disabilities in Roman Antiquity: Disparate Bodies a capite ad calcem*. Leiden: E.J. Brill, 2013.

Laes, C. (ed.). *Disability in Antiquity*. London and New York: Routledge, 2016.

Lawson, R. P. (trans.). *The Song of Songs: Commentary and Homilies*. New York: Paulist Press, 1957.

McDonald, M. F. (trans.). *Lactantius: The Divine Institutes*. Books 1–7. Washington, DC: Catholic University of America Press, 1964.

McGuckin, J. A. *Saint Gregory of Nazianzus: An Intellectual Biography*. Crestwood, NY: St Vladimir's Seminary Press, 2001.

Martens, J. W. 'The Disability within: Sexual Desire as Disability in Syriac Christianity', in C. Laes (ed.), *Disability in Antiquity*, 376–87. London and New York: Routledge, 2016.

Martens, P. W. 'Origen's Doctrine of Pre-Existence and the Opening Chapters of Genesis', ZAC 16 (2012): 516–49.

Marx-Wolf, H. and Upson-Saia, K. 'The State of the Question: Religion, Medicine, Disability, and Health in Late Antiquity', *JLA* 8, no. 2 (Fall 2015): 257–72.

Meyer, R. (trans.). *Palladius: The Lausiac History*. New York: Paulist Press, 1964.

Olyan, S. M. *Disability in the Hebrew Bible: Interpreting Mental and Physical Differences*. Cambridge: Cambridge University Press, 2008.

Ramelli, I. L.E., 'Disability in Bardaisan and Origen. Between the Stoic Adiaphora and the Lord's Grace', in W. Grünstäudl (ed.), *Gestörte Lektüre. Disability als hermeneutische Leitkategorie biblischer Exegese*, 141–59. Stuttgart: Kohlhammer, 2012.

Ramelli, I. L. E. (trans.). *Evagrius' Kephalaia Gnostika: A New Translation of the Unreformed Text from the Syriac*. Atlanta, GA: SBL Press, 2015.

Rettig, J. (trans.). *St. Augustine: Tractates on the Gospel of John 1-10*. Washington, DC: Catholic University of America Press, 1998.

Rose, M. L. *The Staff of Oedipus: Transforming Disability in Ancient Greece*. Ann Arbor: University of Michigan Press, 2003.

Sinkewicz, R. L. (trans.). *Evagrius of Pontus: The Greek Ascetic Corpus*. Oxford: Oxford University Press, 2003.

Tobon, M. *Apatheia and Anthropology in Evagrius of Pontus*. London: Routledge, forthcoming 2021.

Vinson, M. (trans.). *Gregory of Nazianzus: Select Orations*. Washington, DC: Catholic University of America Press, 2003.

Vivian, T. (trans.). *Four Desert Fathers: Pambo, Evagrius, Macarius of Egypt, and Macarius of Alexandria: Coptic Texts Relating to the Lausiac History of Palladius*. Crestwood, NY: St. Vladimir's Seminary Press, 2004.

CHAPTER 7

Eschatology in the early Christian thought-world

JOHN A. MCGUCKIN

PROLEGOMENON

Eschatology derives from the Greek terms 'ἔσχατα' (last things) and 'λόγος' (rationale) and means the 'study of the last things'. It is a very modern terminology, first appearing and becoming commonplace in the theological literature of the nineteenth century,[1] but the idea behind it represents a very basic, widespread and indeed fundamental aspect of ancient Christian theology. In the scholastically dominated period of Christian thought, especially in Western school circles, the theme was often reduced to the 'four last things', namely, death, judgement, heaven and hell, and their respective relationships to each other and to wider Christian doctrine. This approach tended to dominate Christian thinking from early medieval times onward until the New Testament scholars of the nineteenth and early twentieth centuries (rediscovering the importance of intertestamental apocalypticism as a matrix of thought), demonstrated its hopelessly narrow approach and called for a holistic rethinking of the interpretive issues involved. This was something that tended to take place extensively in the mid- to latter part of the twentieth century. The discussions were so extensive at that time that the buzz term 'eschatology' took on so vast a range of meanings among authors that it ran the danger of obscuring more than it illuminated, as the New Testament scholar Carmignac warned at the time.[2]

We would be better defining Christian eschatology today as an overarching context of thinking that sees God as a saving force whose actions impress themselves upon and within the world's history and its ontological fabrics; acting upon the creation at every level from the point of creation, through the vicissitudes of the Fall and salvific restoration effected through the History of Israel, culminating in the ministry, Passion and Resurrection of Jesus the Incarnate Word of God, and

---

[1]Coined by K. G. Bretschneider in 1804 when he was discussing the 'four last things', then called *Res Novissimae*.

[2]J. Carmignac, 'Les dangers de l'eschatologie', *NTS* 17 (1971): 365–90.

pressing onwards as a renovative grace until the final consummation of God's justice in the Second Coming (Parousia) of the Lord, with its concomitant judgement and establishment of the Kingdom of God in all its fullness. If this seems a very large sweep (too broad for some) it is because eschatology is really a macro-conceptual framework rather than a single theory. In other words eschatology is a teleological structure in thought that guides and shapes all Christian reflection on the nature of God and the salvation he offers in creation and in its ongoing renovation, moving from historical considerations and evidences to metaphysical expressions of hope. As Michael Scanlon has noted, eschatology is, at core, a philosophical theology of history: 'Eschatology is the religious language of hope for the fulfilment of the divine promises. It necessarily entails an interpretation of time and history.'[3] This close relation that eschatology has with a philosophy of time is something we shall shortly consider in relation to the apocalyptic movement that, to a large extent, was the contextual 'bracket' that surrounded the originating Christian literature.

Eschatology, therefore, is something that impinges on most other correlated aspects of Christian teaching. It is fundamental, for example, to the very conception of the nature of God (theology), as well as to soteriology, Christology, ecclesiology, indeed most other significant Christian ideas that take their cue from the belief that God reaches out to the world he has made, in an ongoing and powerful sustenance that cannot be gainsaid. If it has rightly been said that most of the Old Testament theology celebrates the 'God who saves'; this is equally (and perhaps more focusedly) true of all Christian thought. It is certainly the case that not only the theology of the early church, most clearly the New Testament narratives, but also a great majority of the early Christian writings of the first 500 years are deeply eschatological in nature: the teleological 'drive' in the message (God's nearness and the demands this makes) giving much of the New Testament texts their extraordinary dynamism.

Unfortunately, the eschatological matrix can easily be lost sight of, precisely because it is such a macro context providing the general landscape to most of what is said in Christian antiquity. When this has happened, theology also has often lost the original dynamic pulse. One example of this is the manner in which scholastic approaches to Christian thought somewhat falsifyingly dismembered much of early theology by introducing their own subdivisions into theology, Christology, anthropology, soteriology, sacramentology and so forth: as if these were separate and discrete concepts, barely related to one another. The scholastic view was responsible for flattening out in a horizontal the steeply vertical thought-world of early eschatology. Another prime example of the 'flattening' of eschatological language is the manner in which Jesus' doctrine of the Kingdom of God (βασιλεία τοῦ θεοῦ), originally meaning the dynamics of divine dominion, moved so quickly in Christian consciousness from its original context of a teleological sense of God's inrush into human history, for judgement and renovation of the covenant, into a somewhat sedentary notion of the Kingdom as a restful place into which souls could enter after

---

[3]M. Scanlon, 'Eschatology', in *Augustine Through the Ages*, ed. A. D. Fitzgerald (Grand Rapids, MI: Eerdmans, 1999), pp. 316–18 (316 citation).

death. Here, as everywhere, the teleological sense (driven by the imperative of the
perceived end – or τέλος) is quintessentially the heart of the eschatological idiom
and, if diminished, eschatology quickly dissolves into something else; be it ethics,
cosmology or other forms of teaching.

In this chapter we shall be concerned with four important phases, or aspects, of
early eschatology: the first being the apocalyptic matrix of the scriptural texts that
led up to the New Testament; the second being the manner in which important
New Testament narratives took up the concept of the eschatological imperative and
adapted it creatively; the third being the manner in which the very early fathers
of the church thought about divine judgement. They began the patristic process
of reapplying the Semitic eschatological imagery in the thought-world of Greek
metaphysics to paint, in new colours, the doctrines of God's outreach to the world in
the structures of creation,[4] and his reshaping of the purposes of that creation towards
the final consummation. The fourth section divides out the patristic material across
the watershed of the great Origen of Alexandria. The post third-century patristic
era is clearly dominated by the impact of Origen's extensive thinking through the
biblical variegations. Almost all the fathers who came after him are dominated by his
agenda, even when they tried to refute him.

THE APOCALYPTIC REWRITING
OF PROPHETIC HOPES

A very broad theological overview of the Old Testament might reasonably conclude
that one of the dominant themes of Israel's relationship with its God was the
concept of future hope (e.g. Jer. 23.5-8). In all the many vicissitudes Israel suffered,
it persevered in looking to God as the one who promised deliverance and restoration
in times ahead, and who would remain faithful to the promise, despite present
circumstances that seemed to render it futile. It was in and by this future hope
that Israel came through catastrophic reversals (such as the exile). In many cases,
though not all, the future hope was attached to the notion of the Davidic messianic
promise. Belief in God as Israel's saviour and protector (something fundamental
to the very concept of the special covenant between God and Israel), being tested
by political and military troubles, was proven ('refined like gold in the fire' was a
common image) by Israel's enduring trust in God: a concept the New Testament
writers render by the word 'πίστις' which simultaneously means 'faith' as well as
trust and reliance.

The classic Hebrew prophets attempt to interpret why God has allowed sufferings
to befall Israel, and often characterize them as remedial punishments to bring an
erring people to their senses in repentance (e.g. Jer. 30.12-17). Named from the
Greek term for 'sin' this *hamartological* approach was a form of answer that was
becoming increasingly frayed in the post-exilic environment when the independent-

---

[4]The chapter by Professor Blowers on 'New Creation', in this volume, is highly recommended.

kingdom status of Israel was never realized, despite its hopes. The character of Job, in that eponymous book largely dedicated to the problem of suffering, doggedly resists it, without being able to supply a more viable alternative other than silence before the mystery. By the late third century before the Christian era, possibly as a result of Israel's own intellectual exposure to Babylonian and Persian ideas, a new theological ferment could be witnessed. It originated through a newly vitalized sense of history: or to be more precise, a theory of time.

Ancient societies hitherto had largely imagined time as a vastly cyclical affair: ages recurring, times of flourishing and times of decay. The notion of time as a great revolving wheel (turning, certainly, but not particularly going anywhere except 'round and round') exercised a dominant influence over the archaic imagination. The fixed cyclical model still predominates, to a large extent, in the metaphysical ideas of Asian religions such as Hinduism or Buddhism. However, this period in Semitic reflection witnessed a truly revolutionary intellectual movement. It now conceived of time as if the wheel rim of the great circle had been cut, and the time-line rolled out flat.[5] Now, horizontally positioned, time could be imagined as having had a beginning at one end and therefore a putative ending at another end. If the beginning (ἀρχή) was the past; this could be understood to be the creation. This would logically make the end-point (or τέλος) some form of consummation – the rolling up of the created order. If the beginning-creation was the place where God made his promises to Israel (setting up Israel as the 'purpose' of history) the end-point would presumably be where the promises were to be accounted for. This, then, made the τέλος or end, quintessentially a divine judgement upon all of history.

The theologians of Israel who worked with such a scheme of thought were now enabled to give an answer to the troubling question – Why had Israel's hopes been so often frustrated? It was not that God was careless of his promised word rather that historical forces (both earthly and *daimonic* powers) had deliberately frustrated God's design for his creation and arrogated to themselves power that had oppressed God's chosen people. At the end-judgement, God would redress all wrongs and show great might by making the end of history what the creation-beginning had promised it would be – the glorious election and glorification of Israel. The idea of God's decisive intervention to reorder history in judgement makes for a classic eschatological view of existence.

The scheme's powerful structures offered a dynamic way to think about creation, covenant and redemption for over 400 years, running on across the first Christian century where it has a clear impact on the New Testament. The sense of expectation in the earliest Christian communities of Jesus' return as universal judge (the Παρουσία or Second Coming) was a clear influence of apocalyptic, where the early church synthesized the notion of the coming judgement with the affirmation of Jesus' resurrectional glorification: namely, that a major aspect of his post-death exaltation was his appointment by God as Judge of the cosmos. In the Johannine tradition this

---

[5]Augustine in his *Civ* 12.20, contrasts this ('the vain and inept cycle of the impious [Greeks]') with the straight path of Christ who: 'has exploded their cycle'.

role of eschatological judge was to be shared with the Spirit-Paraclete: so named as a fundamental protagonist of the cosmic judicial trial demanded by the Judgement.[6] Even so, John's theology already argues throughout the Gospel that the Judgement (κρίςις) has in a real sense already come with Jesus' ministry and witness: in other words that classic (future oriented) apocalyptic understandings of the Judgement are too limited to convey the Christian reality. Nevertheless, apocalyptic imagery was very seductive in its vividness.

In the book of prophet Daniel, a classic apocalyptic text from the second century BCE, the eschatological matrix is sharpened even more than it is in, say, Jeremiah 31, and the writer there adopts a new technique to refresh his theology of judgement. The prophet is taken up for a revelation among the angels who direct world history; and from this heavenly perspective is able to look down on the story of the world, first looking at the long ages of the past (which he rehearses as a catalogue of fidelities and betrayals) but then being told to look upon the future, which he announces to his readers as a prophecy of the coming judgement. The future, of course, has to be 'unveiled' with more difficulty for the human prophet. The Greek term for unveiling is 'ἀποκάλυψις' (apocalypse – means literally 'taking the veil away'). The apocalyptic literary device gave a strong dynamic to Daniel's message: for as the prophet had accurately announced and interpreted the great events of the past – so too his hearers would be filled with awe by his ability to unveil what was imminently to happen in the future. In this way the apocalyptic genre sharpened history into a moral vehicle of urgent preaching. Like all other eschatologies, it became an acute philosophy of history. Partly because apocalyptic is so readily identifiable, some later commentators have (wrongly) identified it with eschatology as such; though the latter notion is more inclusive and broader in scope than simple apocalyptic.

ESCHATOLOGY IN THE EARLIEST CHRISTIAN LITERATURE

The apocalyptic movement was an inspiring contextual precedent for the New Testament era. Its tensively 'immediate' sense of impending judgement was a powerful rhetorical sharpening of the traditional, prophetic, adjudications of history: one that could be applied in diverse new situations. When taken literally as a model of history, as it often was, such texts even entered into the metaphysical domain, reshaping cosmology into a theology of retribution and vindication. In this scheme, history's apparent vicissitudes were now made clear in denouement as a punishment of the wicked and a glorification of the righteous.

It was nineteenth- and twentieth-century biblical scholarship that reclaimed this movement as a subtext of much New Testament thought; at the same time as recognizing the need to rehabilitate these modes of thought as 'authentically' ancient. But almost as soon as the recognition was made the need for accurate

---

[6]Jn 15.26-27.

classifications rose up as a problem of precision. It was Johannes Weiss (1816–1914) who began a deeper appreciation of this peculiar form of historiography. In turn he influenced Albert Schweitzer (1875–1965) who, in a perhaps more populist style, elevated the concept of the imminent doom of God's judgement to be the heart and soul of the message. This so-called futurist eschatology was taken by Schweitzer to be the main burden of Jesus' original preaching; and in this he profoundly marked the course of twentieth-century biblical criticism; many would now say 'misled' it. But Weiss's doctoral student Rudolf Bultmann (1884–1976) and the Welsh scholar C. H Dodd[7] (1884–1973) both countered that the evangelical eschatology was more 'existentialist' in character (here Bultmann was profoundly influenced by Heidegger) and they popularized the concept of 'realized eschatology': which was really another way of admitting that the apocalyptic 'coat' did not fit particularly well on the range of authentic Jesus materials: something, of course, seen as early as Paul and John.

Bultmann's important study on the various forms of eschatology available in this period[8] drew attention to the manner in which the early Christian writings increasingly turn to Christology (focus on the person and work of Jesus) to translate his prophetic message for the acceptance of future generations. This was certainly the road which the patristic literature, from the second century onwards, took as the main highway; but it is equally apparent in the apostolic writings of the first generation too. While some parts of Paul's earliest writings are decidedly eschatological, such as his discussion of the end of time in 1 Thessalonians, or the nature of the risen body in 1 Corinthians 15, the later Pauline thought clearly moves towards a more mature position seeing Christ as the universal cosmic mediator in whose person (ἐν χρίστῳ) the world coheres because of his divine work of reparation and redemption. It was Paul's Christology that ultimately supplanted the more 'eschatological' title of 'Son of Man'. This cosmic-Christological approach (especially the understanding of the Resurrection as a transcendence of time that did not apply simply to Jesus but was a prize won for his church) was taken up strongly by the Pauline school, as witnessed in Ephesians and Colossians; so that, already in the mid-first century, the early church had a much broader and more generous vision of the implications of the Christ-event than narrower apocalyptic categories could supply.

Although this cosmic-Christological understanding pointed the way to which the patristic era would reinterpret eschatology as a mystery of redemption (evidently so by the time of Clement and Origen of Alexandria in the third century, and reaching a climacteric in Maximus the Confessor in the seventh), there were, however, some archaizers among the very early Christian communities (especially in Asia Minor) who clung to a more literally apocalyptic hope. Chief among them were the Montanists[9] with their hope (in the second century) that soon Christ would return to establish

---

[7]*The Apostolic Preaching and Its Developments: Three Lectures with an Appendix on Eschatology and History* (New York: Harper, 1935).
[8]R. Bultmann, *History and Eschatology* (New York: Harper, 1955).
[9]See the chapter by W. Tabbernee in this volume.

an earthly Jerusalem. Similar were the Millenarists[10] (also known as Chiliasts) who taught that Christ would return to preside over a thousand-year earthly reign among his resurrected saints. Both were basing themselves on ideas taken from the book of Revelation. By the time of the fourth-century historian Eusebius of Caesarea, these movements were being classified, and dismissed, as archaic and ignorant, even in his most venerable sources (such as Papias of Hierapolis) whom otherwise he revered as witnesses. But as Baumgartner has shown[11] the seeds of this form of eschatology have, despite all criticism, kept on sprouting vigorously across the centuries, especially among marginal and disaffected groups.

EARLY PATRISTIC VIEWS OF THE ESCHATON

The insights of the late Pauline notion of the redemptive presence (Παρουςία) of the risen Christ were developed by the patristic writers as a way of bridging the tension between, on the one hand, the promise of Jesus that God's vindication was to be fully realized when the Kingdom came in all its fullness, a time of final judgement when evil would be decisively ended and the righteous would enter into their reward; and on the other hand, that in his Resurrection Jesus had somehow or other transcended time and entered into a permanent presence for, and to, his church. The prayer *Maranatha*, or 'Come Lord Jesus'[12] represents the first; the theology of the Fourth Gospel represents the second, where Jesus 'corrects' Martha's future-related conceptions at the tomb of Lazarus and asks her to believe in a resurrection already present in himself.[13]

By the end of the first century this disparate approach operative in the foundational texts had already started to be synthesized.[14] Pope Clement[15] is one of the first to speak of individual Christians (here Peter and Paul) having already entered into heaven (like the confessing thief[16]) as their reward for their martyrdom on earth: not for them the wait until the general resurrection of the dead and the final judgement. The idea of an immediate realization of vindication for all the martyrs was also strong in the early church. The elders of Smyrna confess that the martyred Polycarp has already received 'the crown of immortality'.[17] Hermas speaking about the destiny of the church in his book *The Shepherd* depicts it in the

---

[10]R. A. Landes, *Heaven on Earth: The Varieties of the Millennial Experience* (New York: Oxford University Press, 2011).

[11]F. J. Baumgartner, *Longing for the End: A History of Millennialism in Western Civilization* (New York: Palgrave, 1999).

[12]1 Cor. 16.22; *Did* 10.14.

[13]Jn 11.21-27.

[14]cf. J. N. D. Kelly, *Early Christian Doctrines*, 5th edn (London: Adam and Charles Black, 1980), pp. 439–89.

[15]Clement of Rome, *1Clem*, 5.

[16]Lk 23.43.

[17]*Martyrdom of Polycarp*, 17.1.

late first century as a tower almost nearing completion.[18] When it is finished the end will come. In the early second century Barnabas thinks the last days are already upon the church.[19] He takes clues from the six days of creation to argue that this is already late in the seventh age, and the eighth is the dawning of the 'New Age' of the Kingdom. From the symbolic Genesis chronology of 'seven days', several writers correlated that seven thousand years since the creation meant that the end of the first century would be the appointed end-time. This idea endured, in the West, even into the fourth-century writer Lactantius,[20] who adjusted it to fit Constantine's Golden Age. However, apart from the special dispensation offered to martyrs, who gain a speedy entry to paradise, most of the early church envisaged the general resurrection taking place as the immediate prelude to the Second Coming. In the *Didache* this is not for all (οὐ πάντων δέ)[21] seemingly only for the righteous. But the more accepted view was that all human souls would resurrect in the flesh to face the universal judgement. Like much else related to Christian thinking about the church in the earliest centuries, the stance taken was collective more than individual.

By the middle to end of the second century this simpler form of the Christian eschatology, turning around the poles of resurrection of the flesh and universal judgement, had come in for a good deal of serious criticism both from the Hellenistic philosophers such as Kelsos,[22] who mocked it as unbelievably crude compared with the Greek philosophical concept of the immortality of the soul, and from Christian Gnostics who used mythic schemes to advance similar ideas of the ascent of the purified soul. The temptation simply to replace biblical eschatology with Hellenistic metaphysics was resisted in the main. Justin Martyr, for example, is sure enough that the Platonic doctrine of immortality is incompatible with the Christian concept that God brought the soul into being by His word and will.[23] Conditional immortality might be as far along that road as the fathers were willing to go. The general insistence of the Apologists (especially Irenaeus, Tertullian and Hippolytus) in their struggle with gnostic-type 'spiritualisms' (the flesh is evil or at best irrelevant in terms of salvation which must be solely a matter of spirit) is that God created matter as a holy thing and, through the Incarnation of the Logos, has willed salvation to be a bodily as well as a spiritual matter (as such unavoidably historical): involving the resurrection and judgement of the soul in its own flesh.[24] Their core arguments are based primarily upon the testimony of the scriptures.[25]

---

[18]Hermas, *Shep: Vision,* 3.8.9.
[19]*Barn.,* 4.3; 4.9; 21.3.
[20]Lactantius, *Inst.,* 7.
[21]*Did* 16.6.
[22]In his treatise *True Word* which Origen would respond to, a generation later, in his *Cels.*
[23]Justin, *Tryph.,* 5.
[24]Irenaeus, *Haer.,* 5.14; Tertullian, *Carn.,* 5.11.
[25]Hippolytus, *Antichr.,* 65f.

ORIGEN'S IMPACT ON PATRISTIC ESCHATOLOGY

Origen of Alexandria (*c*.184–253) was the first internationally significant philosopher the Christian church produced. His razor sharp and deeply informed intellect was placed at the service of the exegesis of the Christian Scriptures; and it was one of his lifelong concerns to explain the apparent inconsistencies of teaching found there. In terms of eschatology, Origen represents the first thoroughgoing attempt to synthesize the various disparities of the biblical tradition. He does so, in one sense, by prioritizing the Johannine and Pauline traditions over the synoptics, and so he starts what will eventually become the wider patristic understanding of how all created intelligences (humans and angels) are blessed with the promise of communion with God: an intimate and growing union that gives to them an ever-increasing share in God's own ontological attributes (such as immortality and beatitude). This approach will eventually issue in the patristic doctrine of deification (θειοποίησις).[26] The approach is seen in the earliest patristic writers. Justin had already taught that the believer's salvation would consist in a share of God's own incorruptibility and impassibility.[27] As Irenaeus had also taught: 'Those who see God are within God, and share in his glory.'[28]

Origen was to make this approach mainstream, and in this he exercised a massive influence over the Christian fathers after him.[29] In the treatise on 'First Principles in Theology' he composed, he began by stating the church's core faith in: the doctrines of the creation and ending of the world, the resurrection, the final judgement, and the reward for the righteous but punishment for the wicked.[30] And then he goes on to explain what this all means in actuality. He takes an apologetic starting point, trying to steer a median course between the highly 'realized eschatology' of the Valentinian Gnostics (the final consummation as symbolized by terms of resurrection and eternal life, 'really' means the enlightenment of the immortal soul here and now) and the belief of the 'simpler souls' (*simpliciores*) that all of the apocalyptic details scripture talks about (fire and flood, new Jerusalems coming down from heaven, eternities of damnation and so on) are 'literally' going to take place.

For Origen, the exegesis of this rich and wildly poetical corpus that we call scripture has to be interpreted consistently: and that for him means to read it unfailingly as a set of deep spiritual symbols. An eternally enduring punishment in severities of flame for earthly sins is something that cannot possibly be educative or reformative: and as such, Origen argues, it is an idea 'unworthy of God', who

---

[26]Further see: N. Russell, *The Doctrine of Deification in the Greek Patristic Tradition* (Oxford: Oxford University Press, 2004); J. A. Wittung and M. J. Christensen (eds), *Partakers of the Divine Nature: The History and Development of Deification in the Christian Traditions* (Ada, MI: Baker Academic, 2008).

[27]Justin, *1Apol.*, 10 and 52; *Tryph.*, 124.

[28]Irenaeus, *Haer.*, 4.20.5.

[29]cf. B. E. Daley, 'Eschatology', in *The Westminster Handbook to Origen*, ed. J. A. McGuckin (Louisville: Westminster John Knox Press, 2004), pp. 95–6.

[30]Origen, *Princ.*, Preface, 5–7.

sends all suffering only to correct us temporarily.[31] All theology, he insists, has to be 'worthy of God' (θεοπρέπες). When scripture speaks of God being angry or jealous, it is clear we must not take this literally. It is a manner of speaking designed to tell us that God is ever seeking after our advancement and healing. So too when scripture speaks of 'eternal' flames of damnation, we ought to raise our intelligence beyond the literal idiom, to understand and realize that after the end of all time, there can be no such thing as 'eternal' meaning 'endless stretch of time'. Evangelical texts that speak of a vast punishment for the wicked,[32] for Origen, are meant as corrective warnings of the seriousness of the need to repent. If we are to think that there is something 'literal' in them, then it might be an indication that the souls of the wicked, even when they have been finally purified and restored by God's love, will still bear some distinguishing marks to show their peculiar resistance to God's love: a just recompense for their exceptional wickedness.[33]

Yet, Origen is not just a spiritualizing allegorist when it comes to biblical texts; he does not like to take literally: rather he consistently points out that scripture generally talks about logically impossible things as a spur to the intelligent to realize that *all* (without exception) of scripture's religious worth is contained in its spiritual meaning not in its 'letter'.[34] In dealing with the prophecies of the end-time in Matthew 24,[35] Origen shows that although the simpler souls often take this as meaning an imminent coming to relieve them of persecutions and sufferings, wiser Christian minds will understand that the bliss of the Kingdom will be the soul's entrance into cognitive communion with God in the perfection of love,[36] while the 'abomination of desolation' will be the falling away from God in heresy and immorality.

Origen insists that God has already brought about his Kingdom (his reign) in the souls of those who love him;[37] and this is the surest foretaste of the heavenly delight to come. But the Kingdom will truly and fully come only when all created souls come to acknowledge the dominion of God, and when Christ delivers up the Kingdom to God, so that the Father may be all in all.[38] The future form of the resurrected life is not going to be physical bodies such as we have now: but it will involve glorious 'spiritual bodies' (a line already taken by Paul in 1 Corinthians 15). As Paul had taught, such a form will be beyond our present imagining, but

---

[31]Origen, *Princ.*, 2.10. 4-6; *Hom.Ezek.*, 1.3.
[32]κόλασιν αἰώνιον. Mt. 25.46. Origen notes that it is an *aional* punishment spoken of here (not an earthly one but one appropriate to 'another age'). It clearly does not mean, he says, an 'endless time' of punishment.
[33]Origen, *Hom.Lev.,* 14.4; *Hom. Jer.,* 12. 5-6, and19.15.
[34]Further see J. A. McGuckin, 'The Exegetical Metaphysic of Origen of Alexandria', in *What Is the Bible? The Patristic Doctrine of Scripture,* eds M. Baker and M. Mourachian (Minneapolis, MN: Fortress Press, 2016), pp. 3–20.
[35]Origen, *Ser.Com.Matt.,* 32-60.
[36]Origen, *Mart.,* 47.
[37]Origen, *PEuch,* 25.1.
[38]Origen, *PEuch,* 25.2; citing 1 Cor. 15.24, 28, 53f.

it will certainly be an 'exceedingly refined and pure and splendid body.'[39] Against the literalists who taught a physical reconstitution, Origen argued that human bodies have been changing all the time into different forms even on earth, (baby, youth, geriatric for example) while the inner character remained the same. So too Jesus' body, though physical and real, was also capable of being 'changed' to the perception of his disciples or enemies,[40] sometimes even appearing old. The risen body will be, therefore, a distinctive form (τὸ χαρακτηρίζον ἐιδος) not simply a spirit, but one that is not restricted or cumbersome as earthly bodies are at present.[41] The state of final perfection will take place over an immense age of progressive purification the created souls still require.[42] In this, Origen marks the transition of classical Christian eschatology from the apocalyptic modality where the tension of the message entirely depends on the 'imminence' of the denouement. What his genius consisted in, however, was to keep the teleological driving principle at the core of his teaching, but to make it a progressive sense of purification, repentance and growth in holiness, that humans shared with angels in an advancement that took place over heavenly aeons: active through this lifetime but going on beyond it. At one and the same moment this is a thoroughly moral interpretation but one that is equally ontological. One of his later disciples, Gregory of Nyssa, would argue that this endless advancing (πρόκοπη)[43] is the one sure way the strictly limited creature, locked into its own ontological boundaries, can approximate to the infinite God – by endlessly and wondrously falling more and more deeply into the boundlessness of God throughout eternity (to this extent the time-bound creature experiences infinity directly).

For Origen the ultimate end is a communion of knowledge and love:

> And when it happens that one will gaze upon the Father, as now the Son alone sees the Father, one will be an eye-witness of the Father and of all that belongs to him, even as the Son is; no longer understanding his attributes out of which his own image [the Son] is formed, simply from that Image. And that, I think, is the End.[44]

---

[39]Origen, *Princ.*, 3.6.4.

[40]Further see: J. A. McGuckin, 'The Changing Forms of Jesus According to Origen', *Origeniana Quarta* (Innsbrucker Theologischen Studien) 19 (1986): 215–22.

[41]His later critics, Methodios of Olympos, Eustathius of Antioch and Jerome, all insisted that the risen body was not merely the 'form' but the substance of the earthly body, albeit endowed with greater characteristics appropriate to the human body before sin had marred its capacities. Gregory of Nyssa (in *On the Making of Man*, and *On the Soul and Resurrection*) would rehabilitate Origen's idea of the ἐιδος, with a compromise arguing that the soul was master in the risen life and could recognize the material elements it needed to recompose its own bodily identity. These were not stable fixed elements (for had not the material body changed many times in the course of a life?) but enough body-matter would be summoned and assembled around the soul to make for a true 'ensouled-body-resurrection' state. After the fifth century the church more or less ceased speculating on the issue.

[42]Origen, *Princ.*, 6.9.

[43]Gregory of Nyssa, *Cant.*, 4.

[44]Origen, *Com.Joh.*, 20.7; ibid., 1.16.

In other words – the final end (τέλος) to which we are moving. In this end comes the understanding of all God's providences and all the solutions for history.[45] If, after death, the soul is not sufficiently prepared by a life of virtue and asceticism, then there will be a remedial 'school for souls' as he calls it, located in a different part of creation to this present world-order, 'which the holy scripture calls Paradise' where souls will be specially purified and instructed so that they can be made ready for full union with God.[46]

Origen's custom, in his specifically theological works (as distinct from his preached homilies), was to raise a theological issue for his advanced students, and then to ask them to discuss it in a seminar-type situation. This would get him into trouble posthumously, as the bare text would be received in a less sympathetic doctrinal environment in the fourth century. In relation to his sense that God intended all creation to be fulfilled in love, one of the themes he raised for speculation and discussion was precisely whether 'all would be saved or not?' He proposes the idea of a universal restoration (ἀποκατάστασις) as no more than a speculation[47] which, as a hope at least, would not be contradictory to the beliefs of the church. His idea on the restoration was derived from Paul's hints about the Kingdom of God in 1 Cor. 15.4-28 ('God will be all in all'). Drawing also on Irenaeus, Origen insists that the final end of all created history must bear a strong relation to the foundational beginnings,[48] when God will be all things to all people: all that they see and think and are.[49] Even so, the notion would become one of the chief reasons for Origen's posthumous condemnation in later times, as early critics argued against him that this would logically imply the potential for endless falls and restorations, as well as the concept that even Satan would have to be saved before the end.[50]

Even so, Origen's extensive influence ran on to be the tone-setter for most of Christian thought on eschatology thereafter. Of course, most of the later fathers either jettisoned or heavily toned down the universalism of Origen's speculations on *Apokatastasis*[51] as well as all of his speculation on the pre-existence of souls (the end mirroring the beginning), but they followed his line on the endless progressive purification of souls towards ever more perfect union with God as being the whole point and purpose (τέλος) of the creation order (its divine entelechy).

The caucus of those most determined to rebuff Origen's influence (Methodios, Eustathios and Jerome) made the pulse of the argument about eschatology dwindle down to doctrines about the afterlife. Taking a stand against Origen's teleology of the spirit they tended to revert to the much earlier tradition which

---

[45]Origen, *Princ.*, 2.11.5.

[46]Origen, *Princ.*, 2.11.6-7; 3.6.8-9.

[47]Origen, *Princ.*, 1.6.3; *Com.Joh.*, 28.8.[7].

[48]Origen, *Princ.*, 1.6.2; 3.6.1 (3).

[49]Origen, *Princ.*, 3.6.3.

[50]Rufinus argued that Origen himself strongly protested that he ever taught the rehabilitation of demons.

[51]Augustine was a dominant influence on the West, and very happy to tell his congregation (pouring cold water on Ambrose and Jerome's milder views) that God did indeed intend to damn unrepentant sinners to an eternity of suffering (*Ench.*, 112).

had countered Hellenistic ridicule with the argument that although the concept of a material reconstitution of the same physical body of the believer in the resurrection sounded unbelievable – it ought to be taken on faith and with the assurance that God, who first created the body out of dust, can surely recreate it just as easily from dust. Jerome, intelligent though he was in most of his other exegesis, was led by a violently anti-Origenistic spirit to reassert the resurrection and judgement in highly literalist terms; whereas the Origenian school (in this instance led by Dionysios of Alexandria) advanced their position by a wholesale attack on the book of Revelation as not meriting canonical status. The Western church, however, was not so willing to let that book go; and both Jerome's and Augustine's own ideas on the judgement and the afterlife noticeably rooted the later Western Christian tradition in the kind of graphically physical imagery that appeared in many a doomsday painting on the walls of the medieval churches. Augustine is willing to admit that the 'worm which gnaws' might be a metaphor,[52] but he insists that what it symbolizes is dreadfully real – the bitter anguish of the damned which never ends through all eternity.[53]

All in all, the dynamic and forward-marching energy of patristic thought on the intervention of divine judgement as the end and goal of history surely made it as authentically eschatological in both spirit and form as the New Testament literature itself: to which it has remained a faithful but subtle witness.

Perhaps we can leave the last word on 'last things' in the Eastern patristic tradition to Cyril of Alexandria, an intelligent synthesizer of Origen, who presents the widely accepted view among the Greek theologians that the resurrectional state of the righteous will not be location in a place,[54] but will be rather a rootedness in God's own life. This is what he means by 'deification', and what he calls here the gift of 'a more blinding light of gnosis'. Freed from all limiting circumscription, Cyril says:

> 'Without needing any figure, or riddle, or parable, we shall contemplate, as if with unveiled faces (2 Cor. 3.18) and with an uncluttered mind, the whole beauty of the nature of our God and Father.'[55] And this perfect knowledge will be our complete fulfilment in eternal beatitude.[56]

---

[52] Isa. 66.24; Augustine, *Civ.*, 20.22; ibid., 21.9.2 and 21.10.1.

[53] Augustine, *Ench.*, 112.

[54] Though there was much speculation in many writers as to the varying departments of *Hades* to which most souls (other than martyrs or super-saints) would be sent to await the General Resurrection: with the righteous being in 'pleasant pastures' where they could look upon Paradise, and the sinners being held in a gloomy, smoke filled desolation. See Kelly, *Early Christian Doctrines*, pp. 482–3; and *The Departure of the Soul According to the Teaching of the Orthodox Church* (no author); (Florence, AZ: St. Anthony's Greek Orthodox Monastery, 2017). Origen prefers to think the righteous depart to be with Christ directly (*Hom. Luc.*, fr. 25.3; *Heracl.*, 23).

[55] Cyril of Alexandria, *Com.Jo.*, 16.25; *Glaph.Ex.*, 2.

[56] He echoes the teaching of Origen in his *Mart.*, 47.

BIBLIOGRAPHY

Bultmann, R. *History and Eschatology*. New York: Harper Torchbooks, 1955.

Carmignac, J. 'Les dangers de l'eschatologie', *NTS* 17 (1971): 365–90.

Daley, B. E. *The Hope of the Early Church*. Cambridge: Cambridge University Press, 1991.

Dodd, C. H. *The Apostolic Preaching and Its Development: Three Lectures with an Appendix on Eschatology and History*. New York: Harper, 1935.

Eger, E. *Die Eschatologie Augustins*. Greifswald: L. Bamberg, 1933.

Florovsky, G. 'Eschatology in the Patristic Age', *SP* 2 (1957): 235–50.

Gowan, D. E. *Eschatology in the Old Testament*, 2nd edn. London: T&T Clark, 1998.

Kelly, J. N. D. *Early Christian Doctrines*, 459–89. London: Adam and Charles Black, 1980.

Lincoln, A. T. *Paradise Now and Not Yet: Studies in the Role of the Heavenly Dimension in Paul's Thought, With Special Reference to his Eschatology*. Cambridge: Society for New Testament Studies: Monograph Series (vol. 43), 1981.

McGuckin, J. A. 'The Changing Forms of Jesus According to Origen', *Origeniana Quarta. Innsbrucker Theologischen Studien* 19 (1986): 215–22.

McGuckin, J. A. 'Martyr Devotion in the Alexandrian School (Origen to Athanasius)', *Studies in Church History*, vol. 30 (*Martyrs & Martyrologies*), 35–45. Oxford: Brewer, 1993.

McGuckin, J. A. 'The Exegetical Metaphysic of Origen of Alexandria', in M. Baker and M. Mourachian (eds), *What Is the Bible? The Patristic Doctrine of Scripture*, 3–20. Minneapolis, MN: Fortress Press, 2016.

Patterson, L. G. *God and History in Early Christian Thought*. New York: Seabury Press, 1967.

Perrin, N. *The Kingdom of God in the Teachings of Jesus*. London: SCM Press, 1963, 2012.

Pelikan, J. *The Mystery of Continuity: Time and History, Memory and Eternity in the Thought of St. Augustine*. Charlottesville: University Press of Virginia, 1986.

Scanlon, M. J. 'Eschatology', in A. D. Fitzgerald (ed.), *Augustine Through the Ages*, 316–18. Grand Rapids, MI: Eerdmans, 1999.

Tzamalikos, P. *Origen: Philosophy of History and Eschatology*. Leiden: Brill, 2007.

Visser, A. J. 'A Bird's-Eye View of Ancient Christian Eschatology', *N* 14 (1967): 4–22.

Wittung, A. and Christensen, M. J. (eds), *Partakers of the Divine Nature: The History and Development of Deification in the Christian Traditions*. Ada, MI: Baker Academic, 2008.

PART II

Diversity and unity in the second century

CHAPTER 8

Christianity and Christianities

MARK EDWARDS

INTRODUCTION

It is now becoming a fashion to maintain that 'Christianity' is a word that can be used only in the plural, as the phenomena which have fallen under that name possess no common denominator in a creed, a way of life, a canon of writings or a governing institution. This is all too easily said of the modern world, but some are prepared to say it even of the age that witnessed the promulgation of the Nicene and Chalcedonian formulae which their adherents still describe as oecumenical.[1] If this can be argued even for the fourth century, it must apply a fortiori to the second,[2] and of course it will follow that, as there was never a single Christianity, there can never have been one church. The thesis is already familiar to New Testament scholars, who have long distinguished not only a Pauline and a Petrine tendency in the texts that are yoked together by our canon, but Matthaean and Lukan improvisations upon a Marcan deposit, Johannine and Jacobian alternatives to Paul and, leavening all, a strong Jewish element which is especially conspicuous in the book of Revelation. Once we have added the Romanizing and Hellenizing tendencies of the Acts of the Apostles, together with lingering vestiges of Gnostic dissent in Paul and Mandaean influence in John, it is clear that there was no one patrimony to be defended, and hence no likelihood of concord between all groups who assumed the name Christian in the next few centuries.

If I, none the less, regard this transition from 'Christianity' to 'Christianities' with some misgiving, it is not because I wish to deny the plurality of early Christian teachings, even when they have a common basis in the exegesis of the New Testament. My reservations are philosophical rather than philological: to dispense

---

[1]See, for example, W. Braun, *Rhetoric and Reality in Early Christianities* (Waterloo, ON: Laurier University Press, 2005). T. F. X. Noble (ed.), *The Cambridge History of Christianity, vol. 3: Early Mediaeval Christianities* (Cambridge: Cambridge University Press, 2010).

[2]See B. D. Ehrman, *Lost Christianities: The Battles for Scripture and the Faiths We Never Knew* (New York: Oxford University Press, 2005).

altogether with general terms would leave us without a vocabulary, yet no general term can bear scrutiny if any and every difference between two members of a putative species sufficed to destroy the unity of that species. The modern biologist, no less than Aristotle, distinguishes those variations which are consistent with belonging to the same species from those which oblige us to recognize a new species where we had hitherto posited one. Because theology is not biology, it is unlikely that we shall ever arrive at consensus as to whether the disagreements between Athanasius and Didymus are taxonomically of a different order from those between Basil and Eunomius or (to widen the gulf) between Marcion and Tertullian. Rather than assume that there is one answer to this question, we ought perhaps to say that for certain purposes it is useful to attenuate the differences between Marcion and Tertullian, and for others to emphasize those between Athanasius and Didymus. In the following discussion I have chosen to accentuate the unity of the church as an institution and the efficacy of the measures which were taken to preserve that unity. I do not deny the legitimacy of a narrative that chooses instead to dwell upon the discordant elements which are subsidiary (though indispensable) to my own. I would, however, remind those who prefer the term 'Christianities' that this too is an abstraction which, if it has any meaning at all, must presuppose some diagnostic by which a particular school or movement is perceived to be one of the Christianities rather than, say, one of the equally numerous Judaisms or Platonisms.

A UNITED EPISCOPATE?

The alleged multiplicity of Christian sects in the second century need not detain us long, for while we are sure of the multiplicity of teachings, we are not sure how far it crystallized into sects or how many of these (if sects they were) would have called themselves Christian. The heresiologists intimate, by the mere act of writing against them, that the followers of Valentinus, Marcion and Basilides were apt to be taken for Christians – in their eyes erroneously. They also report that some groups, generally those without a named founder, described themselves as 'gnostics'. But is this a proper name comparable to Methodist or Baptist in the modern world, or merely a qualifier which might be used either by or of particular Christians without implying any breach of communion? Does the adjective 'Valentinian', in other words, suggest a distinct conventicle in the second century any more than 'Barthian' or 'Thomist' in our own time? If some of those impugned by the fathers professed to be pneumatic or spiritual, as they surely did, was this any more a secession from the main body than Clement's appropriation of the term 'gnostic'? Even if, as again is likely enough, the whole congregations assumed a pneumatic character and were shunned by those who did not profess the same gifts, does this constitute a division into two churches, any more than the appearance of charismatic congregations within the Anglican communion?

Serapion, bishop of Antioch, permitted the gospel of Peter to be read, then pronounced it heretical, but so far as we know neither ruling produced a schism (Eusebius, *HE* 6.12). It is possible that in other cases the bishops themselves created a paper sect by bringing together the aberrations of individuals under one opprobrious label: Were there in fact any Valentinians other than Valentinus, any Ptolemaeans other than Ptolemaeus?[3] Since 'Marcionite' appears as a self-designation in one inscription, we know that not all sects were constructs;[4] nevertheless, in our present state of knowledge, we can say how much of Christendom visibly lay outside the church of the bishops. And this, I shall argue, exhibited more unity than any episcopal regimen of more modern times, however diligently supported by the secular arm.

When the titles *episkopos* and *presbuteros* (overseer and elder) occur in the pastoral letters attributed to Paul, it can be argued that the *episkopos* is not the holder of a superior office but a presbyter to whom certain duties have been entrusted, perhaps in rotation rather than for the whole term of his life.[5] Not so in the letters of Ignatius, which if they were composed (as is widely held) in the first or second quarter of the second century, testify to the rapid emergence of a strict hierarchy in the churches on the west coast of Asia Minor. The *episkopos* is the guarantor of unity, but not by office a teacher. It is he, as a type of Christ or of God, who gives authority to the celebration of the Eucharist, and those who preach or celebrate in his absence sunder themselves from the body of Christ (whose incarnation some or all of them have denied); it is the presbyters, however, who take the place of the apostles (*Trallians* 3), whereas in bishops both youth and silence may be pardoned, or even praised (*Ephesians* 3; *Magnesians* 3). Ignatius has been suspected of creating the institutions which he assumes to be already extant,[6] but his own jibe at *Magnesians* 4 – 'they accept him in name, but do everything without him' – suggests that what was in dispute was not the legitimacy of the bishop's tenure but the scope of his jurisdiction. Of the constitution of the Roman Church Ignatius says nothing, whether through ignorance or by a calculated exercise of episcopal reticence. Irenaeus, the first author to quote him, uses presbyter and episcopus interchangeably for the president of the Roman Church, but certainly assumes, in his letter to Victor, that this church has only one president, and that Victor is not the first to hold this position (Eusebius, *HE.*, 5.24.16).

Indeed it is necessary to his argument that the Roman Church whose pre-eminence he extols should have had one head ever since the apostles Peter and Paul had set up Linus as their surrogate (*Haer* 3.3.3). The fidelity with which the successors of Linus have handed down the apostolic doctrine is mirrored in all other bishoprics, but the dignity and antiquity of Rome make it the paradigm, if not the arbiter, of orthodoxy. The Latin of *Against Heresies* 3.3.2 is obscure, but the Greek of Irenaeus' advice

---

[3]See the scholarship generated by C. Markschies, *Valentinus Gnosticus?* WUNT 65 (Tübingen: Mohr Siebeck 1992).

[4]See E. C. Blackman, *Marcion and His Influence* (London: SPCK 1948), p. 4. On heresy as construct, see Averil Cameron, 'How to Read Heresiology', in D. Martin and P. C. Miller, *The Cultural Turn in Late Antique Studies* (Durham, NC: Duke University Press, 2005), pp. 193–212.

[5]See especially the juxtaposition of elder and overseer in Tit. 1.5-9, and compare the portrait of the *episkopos* at 1 Tim. 3.2-12.

[6]W. Bauer, *Orthodoxy and Heresy in Earliest Christianity* (Philadelphia, PA: Fortress Press, 1971), esp. 63–75.

to Victor is clear enough when he urges him to follow his predecessors in granting the Asiatics in Rome the right to celebrate Easter according to their own calendar. Irenaeus thus seems to hold that uniformity in liturgical practice is not so essential to the unity of the church as agreement in doctrine. We do not know whether the outbreak of ecstatic prophecy in Asia Minor, which we now call Montanism, had already attained in his eyes the character of a schism or heresy, as it had in the eyes of some Greek commentators of his own and the next generation (Eusebius, *HE.*, 5.16-17). To his younger contemporary, the African Tertullian, the new prophecy (as he styled it) was neither schism nor heresy but a salutary reawakening of the Spirit, enabling the 'pneumatic' Christian not only to emulate but to excel the saints of the primitive church. While he appears to have shunned the assemblies of merely 'psychic' believers (*Pud.*, 1.10), Tertullian did not (so far as we know) set up his own clergy, as Montanus is said to have done (Eusebius, *HE.*, 5.18.2). Like the Asian supporters of the new prophecy, he acknowledges the charismatic gifts of women without approving the ordination of a female clergy.[7] His high regard for the episcopal office is evident from the ferocity with which he denounces its unworthy incumbents: the chief of offenders, because they have most power to do good, are the bishops of Rome, one of whom declines to bring peace to Asia by sanctioning the new prophecy, while another proclaims novel measures for the readmission of murderers, adulterers and apostates to the fellowship of the saints.[8]

Seditious as Tertullian was in some respects, he drew the bounds of orthodoxy almost exactly where Irenaeus drew them, never questioning the doctrinal unity of the episcopate and never proposing that other sects who boasted of their 'pneumatic' superiority should enjoy even toleration, let alone privilege, within the Catholic fold. In Alexandria Clement is more hospitable to Valentinian speculation,[9] but manifestly regards them as outsiders to the church. Origen too is prepared to learn from sectaries, but the true church for him is still the church of the bishops, notwithstanding his strictures on their laxity both in life and in legislation. Neither he nor Tertullian is prepared to tolerate pluralism in questions of morality, and neither will grant to any prelate, even the bishop of Rome, the authority to overrule existing canons. A sustained indictment of the transgressions of Bishop Callistus of Rome dominates Book 9 of the *Refutation of all Heresies*, sometimes ascribed to Hippolytus of Rome, who anciently had the reputation of a schismatic (Prudentius, *Peristephanon* 11). The author, however, does not profess to be a rival candidate for the Roman see; nor does he deny, as some modern commentators argue, that there is any Roman see to be contested.[10] He appears to recognize both the monarchic

---

[7]See further D. Rankin, *Tertullian and the Church* (Cambridge: Cambridge University Press 1995).
[8]*Prax.*, 1;5; *Pud.*, 1.6.
[9]See now P. Ashwin-Siejkowski, *Clement of Alexandria on Trial: The Evidence of Heresy from Photius' Bibliotheca*, SupVCh, 101 (Leiden: E.J. Brill, 2010).
[10]For the views that I reject here, see J. J. I. von Döllinger, *Hippolytus and Callistus* (London: T&T Clark, 1876); A. Brent, *Hippolytus and the Church of Rome at the End of the Second Century*, SupVCh, 31 (Leiden: E.J. Brill, 1995).

episcopate and the tenure of Callistus, desperately unworthy as he may be; as in the correspondence of Ignatius, the quarrel is not between monarchists and republicans but between an absolute and a constitutional notion of monarchy. Hippolytus subscribes, in the main, to the definitions of heresy which Tertullian and Irenaeus purport to derive from an unwritten rule of faith. He accuses Callistus of favouring heretics rather than devising or publishing a distinctive heresy,[11] and his diatribes thus bear witness to the continuing, if precarious, unity of the episcopate.

EPISCOPAL DIVISIONS

A generation later the Roman communion was torn apart by a contest for office between Cornelius and Novatian, the latter of whom accused his rival on being too indulgent to those who had lapsed during the Decian persecution. A similar party of rigorists opposed Cyprian in Carthage, but there was also a faction that advocated easier terms for the lapsed than were offered by either Cyprian or Novatian. United with Cornelius in his resistance to Novatian, Cyprian disputed his Roman brother's ruling that baptisms administered by Novatianists were orthodox in form, and therefore valid.[12] The same debate troubled the east, where some maintained that even those baptized in the Catholic Church must undergo a second immersion if they had defected and then returned (Eusebius, *HE* 7.7.4). The Novatianists, for their part, may have held that only their own baptisms were valid. Christendom was now divided with respect to the conditions for entrance into the Kingdom of God. At the same time, it can be said that the discord arose from one universal presupposition – that there is only one church and therefore only one proper order of ministers to perform the mandatory rite of initiation. In this period, it was only pagans who imagined that there is more than one species of Christian: it is Celsus, not Origen, who assumes that all Christians are accountable for the vagaries of the Ophites; it is only the persecutors of Pionius who ask which of the Christian sects he follows, and it is Porphyry who characterizes certain adversaries of his master Plotinus not only as heretics but as Christian heretics.[13]

In his controversy with Cyprian, Stephen of Rome, the successor to Cornelius, reminded him that he was also the successor to St Peter. His pretensions were denounced with some acrimony by Firmilian of Cappadocia (Cyprian, *Ep.*, 74), and we know of no Eastern Bishop in this period who was willing to accord a juridical primacy to Rome. The high esteem in which she was held as an arbiter, however, is illustrated by the appeal of a number of Libyan bishops to Rome against the teaching of Dionysius of Alexandria.[14] The latter, whose fame as teacher and confessor was

---

[11]See further R. E. Heine, 'The Christology of Callistus', *JTS* 49 (1998): 56–91.

[12]A. Brent, *Cyprian and Roman Carthage* (Cambridge: Cambridge University Press, 2010), pp. 59–68 and 295–311.

[13]Origen, *Cels.*, 6.24 and 29; *Martyrdom of Pionius* 9.6; Porphyry, *VP* 16.

[14]See Athanasius, *On the Opinion of Dionysius*, with M. J. Edwards, 'Dionysius of Alexandria In and Out of His Time', in *Crisi e cambiamento in età tardoantica*, eds A. Mazzanti and I. Vigorelli (Roma: Edusc, 2017), pp. 245–65.

unrivalled in his time, saw fit to reply to his Roman namesake and assure him that he did not intend, in asserting the Son's dependence on the Father and his instrumental role on earth, to rob him of his divinity or his community of nature with the Father. The correspondence reveals not so much a disparity of doctrine as an asymmetry of emphasis; the Romans were more fearful of tritheism, the easterners of a monarchian absorption of the Son into the Father.[15] It was this theological caveat, together with the overweening conduct of the bishop of Antioch, Paul of Samosata, that led to his deposition in 268 by a council of eighty bishops, including Firmilian. The unanimous rejection of psilanthropism, the doctrine that Christ was merely a man animated from above, attests once again the essential unity of the episcopate (Eusebius, *HE.*, 7.30.11). Its impotence as an executive body, however, was exposed by its inability to force Paul to quit his house. The eviction was accomplished by the Emperor Aurelian at the bishops' request; we do not know why this pagan and reputed persecutor took an interest in the conflict, or why he enjoined that Paul's successor should be appointed by the bishops of Italy, who would inevitably act as directed by the bishop of Rome (Eusebius, *HE.*, 7.30.19).

This event, the first recorded ousting of a bishop whose election was undisputed, is said to have engendered a dissident sect of Paulicians,[16] but caused no rupture between the east and west of the Roman Empire. Insofar, however, as it exemplified the tendency in the east to prize the divinity of Christ more than the unity of the Godhead,[17] it prefigured the dispute between a bishop and a presbyter which erupted in Alexandria on the eve of Constantine's union of the two realms. Hitherto the defence of orthodoxy had been the task of the presbyters, though the condemnation of heretics was the prerogative of the bishops who witnessed the interrogation. Origen had carried out a number of such prosecutions, while the confutation of Paul of Samosata had been entrusted to the presbyter Malchion.[18] Bishop Alexander of Alexandria, however, assumed the right to excommunicate his presbyter Arius, together with any presbyter or bishops who joined his cause, when Arius denied both the eternity of the Son and his community of nature with the Father (Theodoret, *HE* 1.5). Arius sued for protection to the powerful Eusebius of Nicomedia, whose see was the capital of the Eastern Empire. Under Constantine's auspices, the first oecumenical council, held at Nicaea, resolved to incorporate the word 'homoousion' into a creed which was signed by all but a handful of bishops. The signatories included the Roman legates; the few who were deposed included Arius and Eusebius of Nicomedia. In subsequent years the alliance between Alexandria and Rome was seldom broken. Even more significant in its effect on the future conduct debate was

---

[15]The prevalence of monarchianism in early Christian teaching, and especially at Rome, is maintained by R. M. Hübner and M. Vinzent, *Der Paradoxe Eine: Antignostischer Monarchianismus im zweiten Jahrhundert*, SupVCh, 50 (Leiden: E.J. Brill, 1999).

[16]F. C. Conybeare, *The Key of Truth: A Manual of the Paulician Church of Armenia* (Oxford: Clarendon Press, 1898).

[17]On the theological debate at Antioch, see D. A. Giulea, 'Antioch 268 and Its Legacy in the Fourth-Century Debates', *HTR* 111 (2018): 198–215.

[18]See U. M. Lang, 'The Christological Controversy at the Synod of Antioch in 268', *JTS* 51 (2000): 54–80.

the fact that the emperor, as a Christian, was now charged with the enforcement of its decrees. On the one hand, therefore, the power of the bishops was greatly enhanced; on the other hand, the council had set a precedent for division within the episcopate. As the division grew wider, the emperors adopted a policy of doctrinal reticence which was not easily reconciled with the intellectual severity of those bishops who, like Athanasius of Alexandria, stood in the tradition of Irenaeus and Hippolytus. Constantine himself enforced a uniform date for Easter – an issue of little moment to Irenaeus, as we have seen – while his measures to restore Arius and Eusebius to communion corroborate the judgement of the historian Socrates that in matters of doctrine he cared for nothing more than peace.[19]

THE NICENE WATERSHED

It is still not uncommon to represent the Nicene Council of 325 as a watershed between the loose discipline of the first three centuries and the era of oecumenical coercion under emperors and popes. As we have already said, one must be careful not to exaggerate the freedom of speculation even in the church's nonage; a number of modern studies have also heightened our awareness of the propensity of councils to multiply rather than heal divisions. Differences in philosophy, and even in exegesis, may be no bar to coexistence, but there can be no further sharing of communion when the subject of controversy is a synodical decree. Even formal acceptance of the decree is no guarantee of true consensus, for the typical aim of a council is to contrive a verbal remedy for discord that would need no remedy if they were purely verbal. The creeds which terminate council after council in the fourth century were not intended as timeless statements of belief – let alone as liturgical confessions for the laity, who were barely permitted to see them – but as recapitulations of the principles which had guided each assembly in its decisions. The wording was designed to accommodate as many parties as could be tolerated without admitting those whose exclusion had already been determined. Even when the creed of 325 began to be cited as a touchstone of orthodoxy, this studied indeterminacy of meaning was aggravated by discrepancies in the form of the text itself. In the time of Athanasius these were slight, though far from trivial, but both the version recited at Chalcedon in 451 and the version recited against Chalcedon in Armenia were so heavily augmented that they could hardly be recognized as the same formulary.[20]

It would not be good history to bisect the church after 325 into Arians and anti-Arians, or even into pro-Nicenes and non-Nicenes. If we mean by an Arian one who holds a position anathematized at Nicaea, we cannot be certain that anyone other than Arius maintained that the Son is out of nothing or that there was when he was not. According to Athanasius, anyone who maintains that the Son is created by the Father is an Arian, yet he and his transcribers are the only witnesses to the Nicene

---

[19]Eusebius, *V.C.*, 3.18; Socrates, *HE.*, 1.10; cf. 1.26027.
[20]See R. W. Thomson (ed.), *The Armenian History Attributed to Sebeos* (Liverpool: Liverpool University Press, 1999), 125–6.

anathema on this teaching. From the main text of the creed we might conclude that those who deny that the Son is from the Father's substance are anti-Nicenes, if not Arians; but shall we then argue that the expanded creed of 381, which omits this clause, is an Arian document, notwithstanding its subsequent adoption by the whole church as a liturgical confession? A refusal to accept the term 'homoousion' might be evidence of hostility to Nicaea, but it might also be evidence of a scruple regarding the use of unscriptural terms or of a desire to make allies of those who had such scruples, as Athanasius made common cause for a time with those who preferred the locution *homoios kat'ousian*, (a)like in essence. Even a common affirmation of the *homoousios* was no proof of doctrinal unanimity: the word 'us' undefined in the creed, and Eusebius of Caesarea states in a public letter that it signifies only the Son's superiority in nature to all other creatures. Athanasius hints that some of his views were aberrant, and modern scholars detect an Arian tendency in his writings against Marcellus; but does it make sense to deny that he is pro-Nicene when it was he, not Athanasius, who signed the Nicene Creed, and he who upholds against Marcellus the Nicene dogma of the pre-existent and unchanging Son?

Epiphanius' inventory of heresies in his Panarion includes, in addition to Arius, the semi-Arians (otherwise Homoiousians), the Anomaeans (otherwise Neo-Arians) and Marcellus of Ancyra, who is almost exonerated by his unbroken friendship with Athanasius. He makes no mention, however, of the Eusebians – that is, satellites of Eusebius of Nicomedia – whom Athanasius represents as clandestine allies of Arius. Eusebius of Caesarea occupies a different page in his atlas of errors, as does the sophist Asterius, whom he brands as an Arian notwithstanding the absence of any known association between the two men. At this rate of proliferation, we shall find ourselves positing as many heresies as there were bishops; yet it is salutary to remember that the distance between Athanasius and Eunomius the Neo-Arian was far smaller than the distance between the extremes of almost any large denomination today. Both believed in a personal God who creates and redeems the world by his sovereign will; both regarded the Word as a pre-existent being, miraculously incarnate of the Virgin Mary, crucified under Pilate and resurrected on the last day; both agreed that the matters on which they differed were to be settled by the collation and exegesis of all the relevant texts in the scriptural canon, the bounds of which were hardly in dispute.

The Arian controversy caused the deposition of a number of bishops, but it did not produce two rival institutions. Alexandria was indeed a contested bishopric so long as Athanasius remained in exile, but no schism was occasioned by the expulsion of Eusebius from Nicomedia or his return as bishop of Constantinople.[21] For decades Antioch lacked a clear successor to Eustathius, but the Roman opposition to Meletius did not prevent his subsequent elevation to the see of Constantinople. Nor did the supporters of Meletius break communion with the supporters of Paulinus.[22]

---

[21]On his career and the charge of Arianism, see D. Gwynn, *The Eusebians* (Oxford: Oxford University Press, 2006).
[22]See Athanasius, *Tom.*

The Luciferian schism, precipitated by Lucifer of Cagliari's objection to the return of bishops under Julian who were deemed Arian under Constantius, was neither universal nor enduring. In 343 a temporary bifurcation of Christendom took place at the Council of Sardica when the easterners retreated to Philippopolis rather than yield the seat for the bishop of Alexandria to Athanasius.[23] The Eastern assembly, whether by design or by inadvertence, wrote to Donatus as bishop of Carthage, thus endorsing an act of secession which had already created two distinct communions in Africa (Augustine, *c. Cres.*, 3.34.38). The Donatists had set up rival bishops because they held the consecration of Caecilian of Carthage to be invalid: the dispute at this time turned on a question of fact, and became theological only when their Catholic opponents began to argue that apostasy is more venial than schism, that the efficacy of the sacraments does not depend on the minister and that baptism is valid if administered in the right form and with true intent. At Sardica, by contrast, there was clearly some divergence between the Eastern and the Roman estimate both of the doctrine and of the clerical status of Athanasius; the fact that their recognition of Donatus did not give rise to further schism indicates that Christians of the Roman era had a sense of being one church that was not easily undermined.

ROME AS CANON

It is true that, when its canons were adduced to justify the deposition of John Chrysostom, it was judged to be heretical; Augustine used the same term when rejecting the appeal of the Donatists to its authority. If we believe Athanasius and Hilary, the synods of the 350s attested and reinforced the ascendancy of an Arianizing party, clearly distinguishable from the remnant which remained faithful to the creed of 325.[24] It is far from clear, however, that Nicaea had this function of a shibboleth in the eyes of its signatories: the Council of Antioch in 341, although it ratified the exile of Athanasius, republished the decision of the 'great and holy synod' regarding the calculation of a date for Easter.[25] Even the banished Athanasius did not at first contest the validity of the Antiochene synod. The blasphemy of Sirmium in 357, proscribing the very use of the term *'ousia'* as a heresy, was manifestly unpalatable to him, but not, it would seem, to Bishop Liberius of Rome or even to Hosius of Cordoba, whose name stands high in the list of those who endorsed the Nicene Creed.[26] As we have already said, conciliar statements are not so much articles of faith as protocols for coexistence: the plurality of opinions – which we cannot hope to quantify – is overwritten at every such assembly by the uncontested principle that there can be only one church.

---

[23]For narrative, see H. Hess, *The Canons of the Council of Sardica A.D. 343* (Oxford: Oxford University Press, 2002).

[24]See Hilary, *Syn*; Athanasius, *Syn*.

[25]See C. B. Stephens, *Canon Law and Episcopal Authority: The Canons of Antioch and Serdica* (Oxford: Oxford University Press, 2015), 67.

[26]Athanasius, *Syn.*, 8; *h. Ar.* 41.

Bishops of Rome assumed a prominence in these deliberations which was not readily accorded to them elsewhere. Even the Donatists were prepared to accept the arbitration of Bishop Miltiades until he gave judgement against them (Optatus, *Against Permenianus the Donatist* 1.24-26). It seems to have been in 341 that the bishop of Rome first claimed a prerogative which was challenged by the other churches: again rather than comply with a summons to answer for their conduct to Athanasius, the Eastern bishops sent Julius I a copy of a creed to which they had subscribed at the Council of Antioch.[27] As we have seen earlier, they obeyed the imperial summons to Sardica, where the withdrawal of the Easterners left the Western bishops free to augment the prerogatives of Rome. The addition of these canons to those of Nicaea was never authorized either in Africa or in the East;[28] nevertheless it was later to receive the tacit assent of Photius, patriarch of Constantinople and no friend to Papal primacy, when he wrote in a letter to Michael of Bulgaria that the Nicene council spanned the pontificates of Silvester and Julius.[29] Long before this the bishops of Rome had been lifted to absolute sovereignty in the west, and not only by their own thirst for power. It was Jerome the layman, who, having despaired of any consensual resolution of a schism at Antioch, declaimed in his letter to Pope Damasus, 'I know nothing of Vitalis, I repudiate Meletius, to me Paulinus is nothing: he who gathers not with you scatters' (*Ep.*, 15.2).

So far we have seen dissonance which does not yet amount to schism, let alone to a competition of Christianities. Yet Rome herself was divided from the third century to the fifth by the obstinacy of the Novatianists, whose founder had attempted to oust Cornelius, the candidate favoured in Carthage and the East, because the latter had offered terms of readmission to those who had lapsed under persecution. Novatianists all flourished in the east, where the adoption of the Roman date for Easter at Nicaea is said to have promoted them to revive the obsolescent, 'Quartodeciman' practice of making Easter coincide with the Jewish Passover (Socrates, *HE.*, 1.10). Although it had thus contravened an imperial edict, the sect became particularly strong in Constantinople, where its bishop, Sisinnius, admonished by his rival that there ought not to be two bishops in one city, replied that 'There are not' (Socrates, *HE.*, 6.22). Novatianists and Catholics therefore shared the conviction that there is only one church, but disagreed as to its topography. The same can be said of the Donatist schism, which planted in almost every see of North Africa a second bishop who held that he was the only one, just as he held that there was no baptism unless it was administered by his own church. The Donatists who set up their own episcopate in Rome were unmoved by the argument that if there is one church it cannot exist in only one corner of the world. Augustine himself forgot this argument when he heard that the acquittal Pelagius at Diospolis in 415 had been upheld by Zosimus, the

---

[27]See J. N. D. Kelly, *Early Christian Creeds* (London: SCM Press, 2006), 175–279.
[28]See further J. Merdinger, *Rome and the African Church in the Time of Augustine* (New Haven, CT: Yale University Press, 1997), 123–6.
[29]Photius, *Epistularum pars prima*, eds B. Laourdas and L. G. Westerink (Leipzig: Teubner, 1983), 4.

Greek-speaking successor of Peter.[30] Orthodoxy was now to be determined not by geography but by the truth as it emerged from one man's exegesis of scripture. The rupture was healed when Zosimus yielded, and under the pontificate of the Latin-speaking Celestine a Pelagian was a heretic as surely as a Donatist was a schismatic.

UNITY IN DISSENSION

Donatists and Novatianists, maintaining their own episcopate and spurning the Catholic sacraments, were evidently separated churches. Do they support the thesis of competing Christianities? None of the disputants named in the previous paragraph contributes to the ramification of Christian discourse after the Council of Nicaea concerning the Trinity and the nature of the Logos. Pelagius, as the mouthpiece of a ubiquitous ascetic movement, had as much as right as Arius to maintain that the church was of his mind and that those who opposed him were the sectaries; the putative disciples of both had no name for themselves but Christians. The Donatists, confessedly a minority in the Empire, invoked the oecumenical figure of Cyprian, not only a bishop but Papa (pope) of the African metropolis (Augustine, *Against Parmenian*, bks 6-7). The patriarchs were united against the Novatianists, and Celestine's contemporary Nestorius of Constantinople undertook to rid the Eastern capital of this distemper. On the other hand, he extended hospitality to fugitives who had been condemned as Pelagians in Rome, and imitated his predecessor John Chrysostom in presuming to review the case of a group of Egyptian monks who had been expelled from Alexandria.[31] Cyril of Alexandria and Celestine were therefore all the less disposed to wink when he offended half the Christian laity of Constantinople by suppressing the liturgical acclamation of Mary as Theotokos, the Mother of God.

This epithet was sanctioned by liturgical usage throughout the Christian world, and for a bishop at least the liturgy stood second only to scripture as a canon of orthodoxy. Athanasius had reasoned that if Christ is worshipped Christ is God, while Basil had urged that whether we name the Spirit 'with' or 'in' the Father and the Son we proclaim their equality (*Spir* 61-68). To Athanasius the appellation Theotokos was a proof against Arius of the Son's divinity (*C. Ar* 3.14, 29, 43); to Gregory Nazianzen it was a proof against Apollinarius that the flesh of Christ was derived from Mary (Letter 102). When Cyril denounced Nestorius, the latter appealed with overweening confidence to Celestine; but Rome and Alexandria had been allies before the foundation of Constantinople, and Celestine's legates at the Council of Ephesus were instructed to treat Cyril as their pope. They duly assented to the deposition of Nestorius by the prelates who assembled in time for the opening of the Council. The late arrival of John of Antioch with a posse of oriental bishops resulted in the mutual depositions of John and Cyril. The Emperor

---

[30]Merdinger, *Rome and the African Church*, 127–9.
[31]E. Schwartz, *Kyrill und der Mönch Victor* (Vienna: SBAW, 1928); D. Katos, *Palladius of Helenopolis* (Oxford: Oxford University Press, 2012).

Theodosius II, without annulling the judgement on Nestorius, required the other two patriarchs to make peace, and the Council terminated in 433 with a Formula of Reunion between Alexandria and Antioch. There is no other evidence of the inveterate rivalry between these two great centres that is so frequently alleged by modern scholars; nor does the history of the fifth-century councils suggest that Cyril and Nestorius each represented the doctrine of one half of the church.

When a new controversy erupted between Bishop Flavian of Constantinople and the archimandrite Eutyches, it was not because one was a partisan of Cyril and the other of Nestorius. At the Home Synod of 448 the one object of Flavian was to secure the assent of Eutyches to the Formula of Reunion, which he took to be the most considered version of Cyril's doctrine. When the Home Synod was countermanded in 449 by a council at Ephesus under Cyril's nephew Dioscorus of Alexandria, the latter imagined that he was upholding the true opinion of his uncle as expressed in his fiery letters to Nestorius before the first Council of Ephesus. When the Council of Chalcedon deposed Dioscorus in 451, it nonetheless repeated the condemnation of Nestorius and canonized at least two of Cyril's letters, including the one which commended and interpreted the Formula of Reunion. The formula also provided the nucleus of the Chalcedonian definition of the one person of Christ in two natures.[32] If additional matter was taken from the Tome which Leo of Rome had addressed to the second council at Ephesus, the purpose was not to amend a shortcoming in Cyril but to atone to the Apostolic see for Dioscorus' refusal to listen to its admonitions.[33] Chalcedon, as is well known, gave rise to schism after schism, but all were grounded in some existing notion of catholicity. Both the Armenian Church and the Syrian partisans of Nestorius held fast to the Nicene Creed, which the Chalcedonian fathers too had acclaimed as an irreplaceable canon, though one that admitted of further elucidation.[34] We now give the name miaphysites to those who adhered to the formula 'one nature of the Word enfleshed'; but even their Chalcedonian opponents conceded that, as it was Cyrilline, it must be reconcilable with their own belief.[35]

Certainly we have evidence of both dissonance and dissidence in late antique Christianity. If the phrase 'competing Christianities' signifies irresoluble conflicts of opinion and the severance of local congregations from the main body in the aftermath of these conflicts, we shall never be in want of illustration. We cannot say, however, that these phenomena are more endemic to the post-Nicene era than to the first three centuries, only that they have a different outcome in that they tend to give rise to new episcopal denominations. The survival of heresies which had been defined before Nicaea is sparsely documented, perhaps because they were also sparse in numbers or not so apt to be taken for Christians. The conventicles

---

[32]T. H. Bindley, *The Oecumenical Documents of the Faith* (London: Methuen, 1899), 229–35.
[33]See A. Halleux, 'La définition christologique à Chalcedoine', *RThL* 7 (1976): 155–70.
[34]See Bindley, *Oecumenical Documents*, 230–1, with Thomson (n. 15 above) and Leo, Letter 165.
[35]See Leontius of Jerusalem, *Against the Monophysites*, ed. P. Gray (Oxford: Oxford University Press 2006); M. J. Edwards, 'One Nature of the Word Enfleshed', *HTR* 108 (2015): 289–306.

described by Epiphanius are manifestly unlawful, and therefore secret, for otherwise there would be no need to unmask them.[36] When Julian intervenes to end a brawl between Valentinians and Arians (Letter 40), it is not clear whether either of these communities has a building or a bishop. Meanwhile, however the Catholic bishops quarrelled, they continued (as Optatus of Milevis notes) to exchange *formatae* or official letters (*Against the Donatists* 2.3). Leo's *Tome to Flavian* was a response to such a missive[37] – the purpose of which, however, was to inform him of a completed process rather than to solicit his approbation. The distinctive characteristic of the post-Nicene Church is not so much its propensity to discord as its ability to maintain cohesion in the face of discord. Of course this was not universally sustained, but the church which failed to contain the Donatists could at least avoid an Athanasian or a Pelagian schism.

Nowhere is this aspiration to unity more apparent than in the marshalling of witnesses which became an increasingly common feature of controversial literature. Athanasius cites Origen and Theognostus as harbingers of the Nicene faith not because they are Alexandrians like himself but on the contrary because they were widely held to have made Alexandria a seminary for Arius (*decr.*, 25-27). Basil's treatise *On the Holy Spirit* cites not only Origen but Bishop Dionysius of Alexandria, whose orthodoxy he himself had impugned in spite of Athanasius' efforts to vindicate him (*Spir.*, 72). On the same assumption that the suffrage of our enemies proves more than that of our allies, Theodoret takes care in the florilegia of his *Eranistes* not to appeal to Diodore and Theodore so frequently as to Cyril and his condemned precursor Apollinarius.[38] Augustine cites eclectically not only from Latin but from Greek precursors, lest it be said, by those who read that tongue more easily, that total depravity and original sin were the spawn of a Punic imagination. Sects had begun to emerge, but the sectarian mentality was exhibited only by those whose marginality was inescapable.

FURTHER REFLECTIONS

Doctrine and discipline have been the chief subjects of this study; but what if the deepest fissures in the early Christian world were those that separated not Arians and Nicenes, Augustinians and Pelagians, but Berbers and Romans, Syrians and Greeks? We know that today, in countries where indigenous cults still flourish, Christianity can take forms unrecognizable to the cultured European; we cannot, then, dismiss out of hand the theory that the Montanists, universally stigmatized as Cataphrygians, were predisposed by the native cult of Cybele to adopt an ecstatic mode of prophecy. On the other hand, we cannot take as evidence for this the invidious allegation of Jerome that Montanus had been a eunuch of Cybele (*Ep.*, 41.4), nor the comic tergiversation of a Phrygian in the *Martyrdom of Polycarp*, who

---

[36]See especially *Pan.*, 26 on the Borborites, of whom he professedly speaks from acquaintance.
[37]Bindley, *Oecumenical Documents*, 195.
[38]Theodoret, *Eranistes*, ed. G. Ettlinger (Oxford: Clarendon Press, 1975).

rushes forth to die but then repents and preserves himself by a hasty retreat into the crowd.[39] We must also ask why the new prophecy should have found a second home in Tertullian's Africa, where the orgies of Cybele were celebrated no more ardently than elsewhere.

It might be proposed that the Berbers of this region, fresh from slaking the altars of Saturn with human blood, embraced the new faith without giving up their old savagery: according to Frend, it was they who set up the Donatist Church in opposition to the effete 'Caecilianists' who enjoyed the favour of Rome.[40] While, however, our Catholic records of this schism do invite just such an inference, it is not supported either by archaeological research[41] or by a comparison of the literary and forensic skills of those who acted as spokesmen for either party. Arguments for the persistence of a Jewish Christianity which followed Christ without worshipping him, in strict adherence to the Mosaic law, are vitiated by the manifestly polemical tenor of Catholic references to the Ebionites and related sects.[42] The charge of Judaizing might be flung at those who were held to have denied the full divinity of Christ,[43] but it was never maintained that Arius was anything but a Greek, whether by birth or education. Abstinence from bloody or strangled meat was enjoined by the apostolic decree of Acts 15, which is treated as normative by authors who are manifestly not Jewish; the eating of pork was widely forbidden to Christians of every race. The romance known as the *Clementine Recognitions*, sometimes regarded today as a substantial relic of Jewish or Judaizing Christianity,[44] gave no offence in the fourth century to its Catholic and gentile translator Rufinus, whose Latin was as free from blemish as his orthodoxy.

Perhaps there was only one rival to the Catholic Church of this era whose profoundly alien system of belief could be traced to its origins outside the orbit of Greek or Roman culture. Mani, the founder of Manicheism, seems to have been raised among the Elchasaites, a Mesopotamian sect with at least some traits of Christianity.[45] He went on to propagate his own religion, which was sharply dualistic in its cosmogony and named Jesus only as one of his precursors, together with Zoroaster and the Buddha. Driven from Persia by the resurgent Zoroastrian priesthood, Manichaeism was persecuted first by Diocletian as a Persian virus, then

---

[39]*Martyrdom of Polycarp* 4. On the putative zealotry of the Montanists, see W. Tabernee, *Fake Prophecy and Polluted Sacraments: Ecclesiastical and Imperial Reactions to Montanism*, SupVCh, 84 (Leiden: E.J. Brill, 2007), pp. 201–42, esp. 226–7.

[40]W. H. C. Frend, *The Donatist Church: A Movement of Protest in Roman North Africa* (Oxford: Clarendon Press 1971).

[41]See E. Rebillard, 'William Hugh Clifford Frend', *SP* 53 (2013): 53–71.

[42]See further M. J. McCabe (ed.), *Jewish Christianity Reconsidered: Rethinking Ancient Groups and Texts* (Minneapolis, MN: Fortress Press, 2007).

[43]See R. Lorenz, *Arius Judaizans? Untersuchungen zur dogmengeschichtliche Einordnung des Arius* (Göttingen: Vandenhoeck and Ruprecht, 1979).

[44]See further M. Bockmuehl, *The Remembered Peter: In Ancient and Modern Debate*, WUNT 262 (Tübingen: Mohr Siebeck 2010), pp. 94–113.

[45]See A. Henrichs, 'The Cologne Mani-Codex Reconsidered', *HSCPh* 83 (1979): 339–67.

by Christian emperors and bishops as a heretical offshoot of their own religion. In this guise it was embraced and then rejected by Augustine, whose subsequent debates with its doctors Felix and Faustus suggest that they sought converts not by preaching the gospel of Mani but by rational criticism of the Old Testament. It would not be unfair to say that this recrudescent Marcionism and the theology of the Catholic Church were two distinct Christianities; since, however, Manichaeism originated in Persia as a distinct religion rather than a heresy, it cannot be cited as evidence of a tendency to fissiparation within the Catholic fold. As we have noted, new episcopates within the Roman Empire were typically born from quarrels regarding discipline, whereas heresies produced divisions followed by depositions, but not alternative hierarchies. And nowhere under episcopal rule do we find such a medley of disparate opinions as we have grown accustomed to see coexisting today within the bounds of a single church.

BIBLIOGRAPHY

Primary sources

Athanasius. *Werke*, antioch ed. H.-G. Optiz and others. Berlion: De Gruyter, 1934–.
   Works cited here can be found in the volume ed. by J. H. Newman and others, *Nicene and Post-Nicene Fathers*, Grand Rapids: Eerdmans, constantly reprinted.
Augustine. *Against Cresconius*, see *Scripta contra Donatistas*, pars 2, ed. M. Petschenig. Vienna: Tempsky, 1909.
Basil of Caesarea. *Sur le Saint-Esprit*, ed. and trans. B. Pruche. Paris: Cerf, 1968.
Cyprian. *Epistulae 58–81*, ed. G. F. Diercks. Turnhout: Brepols, 1960.
Epiphanius of Salamis. *Ancoratus und Panarion*, ed. K. Holl and others, 3 vols. Berlin: De Gruyter, 2013.
Eusebius of Caesarea. *Ecclesiastical History*, ed. and trans. K. Lake, 2 vols. Cambridge, MA: Harvard University Press, 1926.
Hilary of Poitiers. *De Synodis*, see L. Wickham (trans.). *Hilary of Poitiers: Conflicts of Conscience and Law in the Fourth-Century Church*. Liverpool: Liverpool University Press, 1997.
Hippolytus. *Refutation of all Heresies*, ed. and trans. D. Litwa. Atlanta, GA: Society of Biblical Literature, 2015.
Irenaeus of Lyons. *Contre les Hérésies, Livre III*, ed. and trans. A. Rousseau and L. Doutreleau. Paris: Cerf, 1974.
Jerome. *Epistulae 1–70*, ed. I. Hilberg. Vienna: Tempsky, 1910.
Leontius of Jerusalem. *Against the Monophysites*, ed. P. Gray. Oxford: Oxford University Press, 2006.
Martyrdom of Pionius, see H. Musurillo (ed. and trans.). *Acts of the Christian Martyrs*, 136–67. Oxford: Clarendon Press, 1972.
Nazianzen, G. *Lettres Théologiques*, ed. and trans. P. Gallay and M. Jourjon. Paris: Belles Lettres, 1974.
Optatus of Milevis. *Traité contre les Donatistes*, ed. and trans. M. Labrousse, 2 vols. Paris: Cerf, 1997.

Origen. *Gegen Celsus, etc.*, ed. P. Koetschau. Leipzig: Hinrichs, 1899.

Photius. *Epistularum pars prima*, ed. B. Laourdas and L. G. Westerink. Leipzig: Teubner 1983.

Porphyry. *Vie de Plotin*, ed. Luc Brisson and others, vol. 2. Paris: Vrin, 1992.

Prudentius with an English Translation, ed. and trans. H. J. Thomson. Cambridge, MA: Harvard University Press, 1949.

Socrates. *Kirchengeschichte*, ed. G. C. Hansen. Berlin: Akademie Verlag, 1995.

Tertullian. *Opera*, ed. A. Gerlo, 2 vols. Trunhout: Brepols, 1954.

Theodoret. *Eranistes*, ed. G. Ettlinger. Oxford: Clarendon Press, 1975.

Secondary sources

Ashwin-Siejkowski, P. *Clement of Alexandria on Trial: The Evidence of Heresy from Photius' Bibliotheca*. SupVCh, 101. Leiden: E.J. Brill, 2010.

Bauer, W. A. *Orthodoxy and Heresy in Earliest Christianity*. Philadelphia, PA: Fortress Press, 1971.

Bindley, T. H. *The Oecumenical Documents of the Faith*. London: Methuen, 1899.

Blackman, E. C. *Marcion and His Influence*. London: SPCK, 1948.

Bockmuehl, M. *The Remembered Peter: In Ancient and Modern Debate*, 94–113. WUNT, 262. Tübingen: Mohr Siebeck, 2010.

Braun, W. *Rhetoric and Reality in Early Christianities*. Waterloo: Ontario, 2005.

Brent, A. H. *Cyprian and Roman Carthage*. Cambridge: Cambridge University Press, 2010.

Brent, A. H. *Hippolytus and the Church of Rome at the End of the Second Century*. SupVCh, 31. Leiden: E.J. Brill, 1995.

Cameron, A. 'How to Read Heresiology', in D. Martin and P. C. Miller (eds), *The Cultural Turn in Late Antique Studies*, 193–212. Durham, NC: Duke University Press, 2005.

Conybeare, F. C. *The Key of Truth: A Manual of the Paulician Church of Armenia*. Oxford: Clarendon Press, 1898.

Döllinger, J. I. von. *Hippolytus and Callistus*. London: Hamilton, Adams and Co.; Edinburgh: T&T Clark, 1876.

Edwards, M. J. 'One Nature of the Word Enfleshed', *HTR* 108 (2015): 289–306.

Edwards, M. J. 'Dionysius of Alexandria In and Out of His Time', in A. Mazzanti and I. Vigorelli (eds), *Crisi e cambiamento in età tardoantica*, 245–65. Rome: Edusc, 2017.

Ehrman, B. D. *Lost Christianities: The Battles for Scripture and the Faiths We Never Knew*. New York: Oxford University Press, 2005.

Frend, W. H. C. *The Donatist Church: A Movement of Protest in Roman North Africa*. Oxford: Clarendon Press, 1971.

Giulea, D. A. 'Antioch 268 and Its Legacy in the Fourth-Century Debates', *HTR* 111 (2018): 198–215.

Gwynn, D. *The Eusebians*. Oxford: Oxford University Press, 2006.

Halleux, A. 'La définition christologique à Chalcedoine', *RThL* 7 (1976): 155–70.

Heine, R. E. 'The Christology of Callistus', *JTS* 49 (1998): 56–91.

Henrichs, A. 'The Cologne Mani-Codex Reconsidered', *HSCPh* 83 (1979): 339–67.

Hess, H. *The Canons of the Council of Sardica A.D. 343*. Oxford: Oxford University Press, 2002.

Hübner, R. M. and Vinzent, M. *Der Paradoxe Eine: Antignostischer Monarchianismus im zweiten Jahrhundert*. SuppVCh, 50. Leiden: E.J. Brill, 1999.

Katos, D. *Palladius of Helenopolis*. Oxford: Oxford University Press, 2012.

Kelly, J. N. D. *Early Christian Creeds*. London: Longman, 2006.

Lang, U. M. 'The Christological Controversy at the Synod of Antioch in 2689', *JTS* 51 (2000): 54–80.

Lorenz, R. *Arius Judaizans? Untersuchungen zur dogmengeschichtliche Einordnung des Arius*. Göttingen: Vandenhoeck and Ruprecht, 1979.

Markschies, C. *Valentinus Gnosticus?*. WUNT, 65. Tübingen: Mohr Siebeck, 1992.

McCabe M. J. (ed.). *Jewish Christianity Reconsidered: Rethinking Ancient Groups and Texts*. Minneapolis, MN: Fortress Press, 2007.

Merdinger, J. *Rome and the African Church in the Time of Augustine*. New Haven, CT: Yale University Press, 1997.

Noble, T. F. X. (ed.). *The Cambridge History of Christianity, vol. 3: Early Mediaeval Christianities*. Cambridge: Cambridge University Press, 2010.

Rankin, D. A. *Tertullian and the Church*. Cambridge: Cambridge University Press, 1995.

Rebillard, E. 'William Hugh Clifford Frend', *SP* 53 (2013): 53–71.

Schwartz, E. *Kyrill und der Mönch Victor*. Vienna: Sitzungberichte der Bayerischen Akademie der Wissenschaften, 1928.

Stephens, C. B. *Canon Law and Episcopal Authority: The Canons of Antioch and Serdica*. Oxford: Oxford University Press, 2015.

Tabernee, W. *Fake Prophecy and Polluted Sacraments: Ecclesiastical and Imperial Reactions to Montanism*. SuppVCh, 84. Leiden: E.J. Brill, 2007.

Thomson, R. W. (ed.). *The Armenian History Attributed to Sebeos*. Liverpool: Liverpool University Press, 1999.

CHAPTER 9

The church's unity around the bishop

Ignatius of Antioch and Irenaeus of Lyons

ALLEN BRENT

MODELS OF EARLY CHURCH ORDER

The historic ministerial ordering of Christendom, before the Western church experienced the Reformation, was characterized by a threefold order of bishops, presbyters (priests) and deacons. Previously, following the emergence of the concept of the unity of the church as something more than the unity of the local church congregation, church unity became with Cyprian of Carthage (c.200–258) the mutual recognition of bishops in an empire-wide network in a shared communion. To be a member of the body of Christ was to be in communion with a presbyter who was in communion with a bishop who in turn was in communion with every other (validly recognized) bishop throughout the Roman world.[1] But what was the basis of the unity of individual church congregations? And how had that unity developed before the concept of the church developed into this internationally organized system of mutually recognized bishops that determined (either by the exchange of letters or by meeting in councils) issues both of disputed theology or disputed church discipline, imposing their decrees by sanction of excommunication?

The two classic crown witnesses for such a legitimation of church order, and to a theology that determines both the validity of a church congregation and its unity, are Ignatius of Antioch (c. AD 135) and Irenaeus of Lyons (c. AD 180). Ignatius was on his way to martyrdom in Rome as a condemned prisoner, transported in chains across Asia Minor but, as he travelled, he addressed churches on route by letter. In these letters Ignatius represents the first unambiguous claim that in order to constitute a gathering of Christians as a church, one needs a single bishop with

---

[1] See, A. Brent, *Cyprian and Roman Carthage* (Cambridge: Cambridge University Press, 2010), pp. 55–68, 255–6.

a circle of presbyters and a number of deacons who preside over the Eucharist.[2] Irenaeus, on the other hand, claims that one needs a bishop whom he sometimes calls a 'presbyter' who occupies the authority of the teaching seat in succession to the apostles, by analogy with presidents of Greek philosophical schools. Irenaeus does not explicitly connect the bishop/presbyter with the Eucharist, which is the church's offering.[3] We shall see later the difficulty that was subsequently to be experienced in synthesizing these two distinct views of church order.

The development of both Ignatian and Irenaean views of church order was stimulated by the diversity of forms of Christianity that had emerged in the course of the second century, and the need for producing a church order that could produce sufficient unity to maintain a distinctive, Christian identity. We begin with a sketch of that early and increasingly expanding diversity that Ignatius and Irenaeus sought to address in their two distinct ways, each with a theology that made unity around a bishop essential to the nature of the church.

DIVERSITY IN THE EARLIEST FORMS OF MINISTRY SEEKING ECCLESIAL UNITY

The first century

The New Testament documents bear witness to a variety of church orders. We find a ministry of charismatic gift holders in 1 Cor. 12.4-10. In the pseudo Pauline letter to Eph. 4.11-12 we find that these charismatic gift holders have been given ministerial titles on the basis of their spiritual charisma, 'apostles (ἀποστόλοι)', 'prophets (προφῆται)', 'evangelists (εὐαγγελισταί)', 'shepherds (ποιμένες)' and 'teachers (διδασκ άλους)', each with an assigned function in salvation history (Eph. 4.12-13). We find a plurality of 'bishops and deacons (ἐπίσκοποι καὶ διακόνοι)' in Phil. 1.1, with no other reference to spiritual charisms, and we see leaders of various Roman house churches, with unnamed offices, in Rom. 16.3-15; though in 16.1 Phoebe, as bearer of the letter, is mentioned as 'deacon (διάκονος)' of the church of Cenchrea and 'patron (προστάτις)' of Paul and others.[4]

In the pseudo Pauline Pastoral epistles, we see first of all (a) that a figure called 'Timothy' is instructed to command and teach by virtue of an act of ordination by a presbyteral council that laid hands upon him (μετὰ ἐπιθέσεως τῶν χειρῶν τοῦ πρεσβυτερίου) as a result of the exercise of the charismatic gift (χάρισμα) of prophetic

---

[2]A. Brent, *Ignatius of Antioch and the Second Sophistic* (Tübingen: Mohr Siebeck, 2006), pp. 25–30; Idem, *Ignatius of Antioch: A Martyr Bishop and the Origin of Episcopacy* (London: Continuum, 2007), chap. 4.
[3]E. Molland, 'Irenaeus of Lugdunum and the Apostolic Tradition', *JEH* 1 (1950): 12–28. See also A. Brent, *Hippolytus and the Roman Church in the Third Century: Communities in Tension before the Emergence of a Monarch-Bishop*, *Vigiliae Christianae Supplementa*, 31 (Leiden: E.J. Brill, 1995), pp. 420–2, 446–53.
[4]For a discussion of the relationship between multi ἐπίσκοποι with διακόνοι, see A. C. Stewart, *The Original Bishops: Office and Order in the First Christian Communities* (Grand Rapids, MI: Baker Academic, 2014), pp. 11–31.

discernment (διὰ προφητείας).[5] But then (b) in 2 Timothy 1, the charismatic gift (χάρισμα) is no longer granted by the presbyteral council but by Paul himself who instructs Timothy to 'remember to stir up the charismatic gift (χάρισμα) that is in you through the imposition of *my* hands (my emphasis) (διὰ τῆς ἐπιθέσεως τῶν χειρῶν μου).' Thirdly (c) a figure called 'Titus' is commissioned by Paul as a bishop with the responsibility of ordaining others. Titus is 'to amend what is defective (ἵνα τὰ λείποντα ἐπιδιορθώσῃ) and appoint elders in every town (καὶ καταστήσῃς κατὰ πόλιν πρεσβυτέρους)'[6] and each of them has the title of 'bishop (ἐπίσκοπος).'[7] The different understandings of ministerial authority are thus (a) charismatic but with presbyteral sanction, (b) charismatic but with apostolic sanction, whose function is teaching, (c) episcopal with an ordaining function.[8] These features are not synthesized in the composite description of the life of the community drawn from the pseudonymous author's collecting together of these disparate elements. A unity is, however, claimed through the principle of apostolicity expressed in the pseudepigraphic literary form in which the pseudonymous writer claims that all comes from the direction and plan of 'Paul the apostle'.

A similar example of a literary and historiographic approach aimed at unifying disparate concepts of ministry by means of a narrative that brings them together into a single story without synthesizing them exists in the Acts of the Apostles. At the beginning of Luke's narrative we have 'the Twelve' constituted as the apostles whose standing is that they are eyewitnesses to the resurrection, with positions that need filling if any one of them is vacated. These are responsible for the ordination of the original deacons but there is no mention of them ordaining bishops as their successors.[9] Their role is to preside over the Jerusalem community and to adjudicate disputes between new Christian communities that have spread out from them into Judaea and even reached Asia Minor and that appealed to the original Jerusalem community in the cause of unity.[10] But we find other ministerial figures at Antioch-in-Syria, namely prophets and teachers and in the light of their charisma, after prayers and fasting had preceded a divine instruction, they laid hands in ordination on Barnabas and Paul and sent them off as missionaries. (Acts13.1-4) Only after, and in view of, this ordination are these two described as 'apostles' (Acts14.4 and 15.2) because, presumably, they are 'sent forth (ἀποστέλλειν),' even though this verb is not used of them.

Acts is an eirenic document composed with the intention of reconciling Petrine and Pauline communities in the late first or early second century. But its discourse of unity combines historical fragments referring to different ministerial forms, charismatic as well as presbyteral and apostolic without synthesizing them into a

---

[5]1 Tim. 4.11 and 14.
[6]Tit. 1.5.
[7]Tit. 1.7.
[8]Stewart, *Original Bishops*, pp. 38–40, 342–3.
[9]Acts 6.1-6.
[10]Acts 6.15.

coherent unitary structure. But we could say the same about the community of St Matthew's gospel with fragments describing charismatic and egalitarian groups and other presbyteral groups without any episcopal or apostolic ministry except that foreshadowed, but not concretely present, in the ministry of St Peter who represents the long-hoped bridge-builder between the conflicting communities.[11]

The second-century witnesses

We see continuing references to these offices in second-century literature. In the *Didache* we have references 'concerning apostles and prophets (περὶ ... τῶν ἀποστόλων καὶ προφητῶν)', who are in fact travelling missionaries requiring temporary accommodation on their travels.[12] Sometimes itinerant ministers are called a 'teacher (ὁ διδάσκων)'.[13] Instructions are given with examples of the kind of words to be used to celebrate the Eucharist[14] but apparently the preferred celebrant is a prophet who uses the words that his charism gives him.[15] Apparently the mainly itinerant prophets do not always settle (they need to do productive labour if they are genuine), and the implication was that the normal minister of the Eucharist was a prophet. In the absence of prophets and teachers they are instructed: 'elect [or ordain] (χειροτονήσατε) for yourselves, bishops and deacons . . . (ἑαυτοῖς ἐπισκόποις καὶ διακόνους).' These are to be honoured 'together with prophets and teachers (μετὰ τῶν προφητῶν καὶ διδασκάλων)' – a prescription necessarily addressed to a community who would, it is implied, otherwise despise them in favour of those with the prophetic charisma.[16] Raymond Brown, in his redaction criticism of the Matthaean community, detected a number of such divergent groups – egalitarian, presbyteral, charismatic – to which the author looked to the idealized figure of St Peter to provide a model of a bridge-builder, to be finally realized by an Ignatian style bishop in both Matthew's and the *Didache*'s Syria.[17]

We have observed in these previous documents various types of ministry, but other than perhaps in the case of 'Titus', there is a plurality of ministerial office holders, whether bishops, prophets and teachers, presbyters, apostles: there is no mention of one minister at the apex of a hierarchy. A plurality of presbyters (a name used interchangeably with bishops) is in evidence in the letter of Clement of Rome,[18] and it is at Rome that according to Hermas (*Shepherd: Visions* 2.2), a presbyterate who presides and not a single bishop. In the *Didache*, no theological justification is given for its stop-gap episcopal ministry, and no indication that such a ministry

---

[11]R. E. Brown and J. P. Meier, *Antioch and Rome: New Testament Cradles of Catholic Christianity* (New York: Paulist Press, 1982), pp. 57–72; Brent, *Ignatius: Martyr Bishop*, pp. 23–6.
[12]*Did.*, 11.3-8; 12-13.
[13]*Did.*, 11.1.
[14]*Did.*, 9-10.
[15]*Did.*, 11.1.
[16]*Did.*, 15.1-2.
[17]Brent, *Ignatius: Martyr Bishop*, pp. 26–30; Stewart, *Original Bishops*, pp. 60–4, 335–57.
[18]1 *Clem.*, 42.5; 44.5.

is needed to create unity but only to enable the Eucharist still to be offered in the absence of prophets. Clement does regard the plurality of bishops/presbyters as of dominical origin deriving their authority from an apostolic succession and as such intended to secure unity in particular in the divided Corinthian community that he addresses.[19]

The notion of a collective ministry of presiding presbyter-bishops raises a number of questions of the organization of a given community's liturgy. Did a number of presbyters concelebrate the Eucharist together? If eucharistic presidency was by a single presbyter, how did they decide on any given occasion which of them was to preside? Was there a collection of house churches, each with a single presbyter-bishop, who formed a single collective presbyterate supervising the city of Rome as a whole?[20] Each question in its own way raises issues about potential strife within the community.

Until the first quarter of the second century, therefore, there was no doctrine of ministry that synthesized considerable divergence of ministries into a single, unified concept. We shall now see how a distinctive theology of ministry remedying divisions both within early Christian communities and between such communities is presented in Ignatius of Antioch and Irenaeus of Lyons.

IGNATIUS OF ANTIOCH: THE SINGLE BISHOP AS A FOCUS OF UNITY

Ignatius introduces the issue of 'heresy' and 'false teaching' as a source of disunity in divided Christian congregations. In response he claims that in order for a Christian congregation to be valid as the gathered church (ἐκκλησία) there must exist a three-formed ministry that consists of a single bishop, with an encircling presbyterate, and a number of deacons. 'Without these (χωρὶς τούτων)', he claims, 'the gathered church cannot be summoned (ἐκκλησία οὐ καλεῖται).'[21]

Ignatian church order cannot be understood simply in terms of three different kinds of officials organizing a community. When he describes Christian ministers, his description is derived from their performance of their liturgical role at the Eucharist.[22] To the Magnesians he writes:

---

[19]*1 Clem.*, 44.1-5.

[20]M. Simonetti, 'Per un profilo dell' autore dell' Elenchos', in *Des évêques, des écoles et des hérétiques. Actes du colloque international sur la 'Réfutation de toutes les hérésies'*, eds G. Aragione and E. Norelli. Genève, 13-14 juin, 2008 (Lausanne: Editions du Zèbre, 2011), pp. 257–74, 267–71; and see A. Brent, 'The *Elenchos* and the Identification of Christian Communities in Second to Early Third Century Rome', in Aragione and Norelli (eds), *Des évêques, des écoles et des hérétiques*, pp. 275–314; Stewart, *Original Bishops*, pp. 300–9.

[21]Ignatius, *Trall.*, 3.1.

[22]S. Laeuchli, 'The Drama of Replay', in *Searching in the Syntax of Things*, eds M. Friedman, T. P. Burke and S. Laeuchli (Philadelphia, PA: Fortress, 1972); Brent, *Ignatius: Martyr Bishop*, pp. 23–30. See also Ignatius, *Trall.*, 3.1.

I exhort you to be anxious to do everything in God's harmony (ἐν ὁμονοίᾳ θεοῦ), with your bishop prominent (προκαθημένου τοῦ ἐπισκόπου) in creating an image of God (εἰς τύπον θεοῦ) and your presbyters an image of the council of the apostles, and the deacons . . . entrusted with the ministry of Jesus Christ (καὶ τῶν διακόνων . . . πεπιστευμένων διακονίαν Ἰησοῦ Χριστοῦ).[23]

Thus for Ignatius the three orders receive their significance and authority from the roles that they enact in the drama of redemption. The seated bishop is, as an icon or τύπος of God the Father, surrounded in a horseshoe by a seated presbyterate in the role of the apostles in the Upper Room of the Johannine tradition of which Ignatius is clearly aware. The laity, Ignatius says, gather for the Eucharist, along with their bishop and deacons, 'with the finely woven (ἀξιοπλόκου), spirit-endowed garland-crown (πνευματικοῦ στεφάνου) of your presbyterate (τοῦ πρεσβυτερίου ὑμῶν).'[24] In Jn 20.22 on the evening of the resurrection Christ 'breathed into (ἐνεφύσησεν)' the disciples and said: 'Receive the Holy Spirit.' Ignatius is well aware of this scene when he says to the Ephesians: 'For this reason he received oil upon his head (διὰ τοῦτο μύρον ἔλαβον ἐπὶ τῆς κεφαλῆς) in order that he might breath incorruption into the church (ἵνα πνέῃ τῇ ἐκκλησίᾳ ἀφθαρσίαν).'[25]

We should note that even if Ignatius incorporates a trace image of presiding presbyters bearing a prophetic charism from some forms of ministerial order before him, these presbyters are not like Clement's presbyter-bishops, heirs to a presbyteral succession coming down from the apostles.[26] There is no such succession running through secular history but rather at each Eucharist the image of the Johannine Pentecost in the Upper Room at the resurrection is realized afresh with barriers of time and space removed.[27] Here the presbyterate 'image' the apostles (εἰς τύπον συνεδρίου τῶν ἀποστόλων) just as the deacons 'image' Jesus Christ through imitating his ministry (πεπιστευμένων διακονίαν).[28]

In the timeless mystery drama in which *mimesis* thus leads to identification with that which is imitated, other divine persons are also associated with this mystical joining with the scene in the Upper Room. The liturgical scene in Ignatius is a cosmological one, setting the cosmic drama of redemption. The deacons are *in persona Christi*, they have the ministry (διακονία) of Jesus Christ, but the focus is not on the Christ who washed the disciples' feet in his earthly life but rather on the Christ 'who was before the ages with the Father and who appeared at the end of

---

[23]Ignatius, *Mag.*, 6.1.

[24]Ignatius, *Mag.*, 13.1.

[25]Ignatius, *Eph.*, 17.1. The 'anointing' is a reference to Mt. 26.7 and Mk 14.3, but the 'breathing incorruption' to Jn 20.21-22. See also Brent, *Ignatius: Martyr Bishop*, pp. 38–9 and Idem, *Ignatius: Second Sophistic*, p. 27.

[26]Further see Simonetti, 'Per un profilo'; Brent, 'The *Elenchos*'; Stewart, *Original Bishops*.

[27]A. Brent, 'History and Eschatological Mysticism in Ignatius of Antioch', *EThL*. 65, no. 4 (1989): 309–29.

[28]In Ignatius, *Mag.*, 6.1 the phrase εἰς τύπον is not directly used Ἰησοῦ Χριστοῦ but διακονίαν. Though a third repetition from the case of bishop and presbyters is avoided it is intended: see *Mag.*, 6.2: ἑνώθητε τῷ ἐπισκόπῳ καὶ τοῖς προκαθημένοις εἰς τύπον καὶ διδαχὴν ἀφθαρσίας.

time (ὅς πρὸ αἰώνων παρὰ πατρὶ ἦν καὶ ἐν τέλει ἐφάνη).'[29] The deacon is 'in persona' of the cosmological and eternal Christ, 'who proceeded from the one Father and is to him also as one who has returned (τὸν ἀφ' ἑνὸς πατρὸς προελθόντα καὶ εἰς ἕνα ὄντα καὶ χωρήσαντα).'[30]

Thus we have the liturgical scene that captures iconographically the eternal redemptive acts. The father bishop (for as Jn 6.32 says, 'it is my Father who gives you the bread from heaven to eat') is 'seated pre-eminently (προκαθημένος)', standing out before all, and consecrates the bread and wine and gives it to the deacons to take it to the people. In the early church the people themselves brought their own bread and wine, to be collected by the deacons to be taken to the father bishop and then returned to them consecrated. Thus, the deacons can be said to be like Jesus Christ, 'who proceeded from the one Father and is to him also as one who has returned.' Their liturgical role in the cosmic drama is to act as τύποι or icons of the cosmic Christ in his redemptive activity, while the presbyteral council prays in the spirit given to them at the insufflation at the Johannine Pentecost.

The laity come into union with the threefold hierarchy, one might say. But I would rather use here the word 'typology' to capture the sense of Ignatius; meaning a coming into union with the threefold typology. The bread and wine that we receive in this liturgical context are in his words: 'breaking the one bread which is the medicine of immortality, the antidote that we take in order not to die but the live forever in Jesus Christ (ἕνα ἄρτον κλῶντες, ὅς ἐστιν φάρμακον ἀθανασίας, ἀντίδοτος τοῦ μὴ ἀποθανεῖν, ἀλλὰ ζῆν ἐν Ἰησοῦ Χριστῷ διὰ παντός).'[31] The purpose of participating in the liturgy that requires the threefold order as icons or τύποι representing divine persons is to achieve 'incorruption (ἀφθαρσία).' In Letter to the Magnesians 6.2 we also read 'Be united with the bishop and with those who stand out as an image and a teaching of incorruption (ἑνώθητε τῷ ἐπισκόπῳ καὶ τοῖς προκαθημένοις εἰς τύπον καὶ διδαχὴν ἀφθαρσίας).'

The principle of Hellenistic ontology, that we become transformed into the object of our imitation, is primarily the principle of the Hellenistic mystery cult with its performance of its mystery drama. The role of episcopal presidency is that of a cult leader who through engagement with worshippers in the mystery-drama secures for them and himself union with the divine. Ignatius refers to 'those who are deacons of the mysteries of Jesus Christ (τοὺς διακόνους ὄντας μυστηρίων Ἰησοῦ Χριστοῦ).'[32]

The Ephesian Christians and all who join his procession are described as coming from and forming 'cult associations (σύνοδοι πάντες)', and are 'god-bearers (θεοφόροι)', 'temple bearers (ναοφόροι)', 'Christ bearers (χριστοφόροι)', 'bearers of holy objects (ἁγιοφόροι), in every way decked out in the commandments of Jesus Christ (κατὰ πάντα κεκοσμημένοι ἐντολαῖς Ἰησοῦ Χριστοῦ).'[33] They are, in other

---

[29]Ignatius, Mag., 6.1.
[30]Ignatius, Mag., 7.2.
[31]Ignatius, Eph., 20.2.
[32]Ignatius, Trall., 2.3.
[33]Ignatius, Eph., 9.2.

words, like the mystery procession of Isis described by Apuleius (*Metamorphoses* 11.10). Here 'the principal high priests of the sacred mysteries (*antistites sacrorum proceres*) . . . carried before them the distinctive attributes of the most powerful gods (*potentissimorum deorum proferebant insignes exuvias*).' But these θεοφόροι were also accompanied in the goddess's procession by a second group, with a priest who 'carried with both hands an altar (*manibus ambabus gerebat altaria*).' The altar in question clearly was miniature, and thus we have counterparts to Ignatius' ναοφόροι, or ἁγιοφόροι.'[34]

Ignatius could not make his role as an 'image bearer' or 'wearer' any clearer, since he uses this title (inaccurately identified as somehow constituting his personal name or *cognomen*), at the beginning of each letter. 'Theophoros (Θεοφόρος)' means not simply 'God bearer' but 'bearer of a divine image.' It is not a *cognomen*, which in any case is a term attested nowhere prosopographically. The leader (*agonothete*) of a cultic procession wore, often in their στέφανος or headdress, embossed images of the tutelary deities of their city or, if it involved the imperial cult, images of ancestral emperors. We have an inscription from Oinoanda in Lycia, a decree formalizing the benefaction of C. Iulius Demosthenes, who had founded a music festival and competition (ἄγων μουσικός) associated with the Imperial Cult (5 July AD 125).[35] The procession leader (ἀγωνοθέτης) is to wear 'a golden crown (στέφανος χρυσοῦς)' exhibiting images in relief (ἔχοντα ἔκτυπα πρόσωπα), of both the emperor Hadrian and of Apollo. In AD 96 Domitian presided at a festival at Rome in which the priests wore crowns with images of the Capitoline divine Triad but with his own image added to them, on the occasion of his being hailed as 'Lord and God (*Dominus et Deus*).'[36]

Ignatius too regards bishop, presbyters and deacons, in the Christian mysteries, as 'creating an image (εἰς τύπον)' of the Father, apostolic council and Jesus Christ respectively. His model of eucharistic celebration, with the bishop displaying the τύπος πατρός, just as in a civic celebration in any of the Greek city-states of Asia Minor, is a symbol of societal unity that both effects what it signifies and signifies what it effects. But that model of Eucharist as mystery play, the drama of recall, as it were, as festival and procession, is extended to include Ignatius' own progress as martyr-bishop to Rome and the future outpouring of his blood in the arena which replaces, in his vision, the church of Rome gathered for the Eucharist.[37] Ignatius says of the Ephesian representatives – deacons Burrhus and Croccus and bishop Onesimus[38] – that they were 'enflamed by the blood of God (ἀναζωπυρήσαντες ἐν αἵματι θεοῦ)' as mystery initiants (μιμηταὶ). Ignatius' language may here lead to

---

[34]Brent, *Ignatius: Second Sophistic,* pp. 124–80. See also P. Harland, 'Christ-Bearers and Fellow-Initiates: Local Cultural Life and Christian Identity in Ignatius' Letters', *JECS* 11 (2003): 481–99.

[35]*SEG* XXXVIII. 1462.C

[36]Suetonius, Domitian, 4.4. See also M. Wörrle, *Stadt und Fest im kaiserzeitlichen Kleinasien: Studien zu einer agonistischen Stiftung aus Oinoand*, Vestigia 39 (Munich: Beck, 1988), pp. 187–8.

[37]Ignatius, *Rom.*, 2 and 5.

[38]When they heard that he was chained and on the way to the wild beasts in the arena they hastened to see him and saw in Ignatius the τύπος (the impress in his flesh) of the suffering God. Ignatius, *Eph.*, 1.2-3.

a Patripassianism in which with a denial of distinct 'persons' in the godhead, it becomes possible to believe that 'the Father suffered in the Son.'

In the city-states of Asia Minor participation in the 'mysteries' was not the preoccupation of small groups of individuals but a collective celebration with wide participation leading to a sense of social identity iconographically represented by image bearers and image wearers; in many respects the festal gathering and its procession represented the unity of the pagan ἐκκλησία. So too for Ignatius, the congregation gathered as the Christian ἐκκλησία in festival and procession for the Eucharist. Mystery procession involved drama, and drama involved imitation in which one became what was imitated. Absorption into the divine meant 'incorruption (ἀφθαρσία)' replacing 'corruption (φθορά)' that is also a common Ignatian theme.[39] 'Unity (ἕνωσις or ἑνότης)' was the product of becoming 'mingled' with each other and with the risen Christ 'in order that everything may be in harmonious unity (ἵνα πάντα ἐν ἑνότητι σύμφωνα ᾖ).'[40]

Secondary to and a product of these metaphysical assumptions of the character of 'unity' was also the rhetorical concept of *Homonoia* that characterized the movement known as the Second Sophistic.[41] That rhetoric drew a distinction between the idea of groups within city-states, or in relations between city-states being at 'peace (εἰρήνη)' with one another and in 'harmony (ὁμόνοια)' with one another. The connotation of εἰρήνη was of a state resulting from conflicted persons or parties being pacified by force, by the exercise of the will of the conqueror over the conquered; whereas ὁμόνοια referred to the result of a mutual compact freely entered into, like joining a choir and freely following the musical rules in order to achieve a harmony desired by all. The operation of bodily organs functioned in this way in a healthy body. Such medical or choral metaphors, when applied to society, meant that the institutions of a healthy political constitution (aristocratic council, popular assembly, elected judges and so on) would act in a similarly harmonic way, following freely accepted rational principles; when one section forced εἰρήνη on the other, then society became dysfunctional: ὁμονοία was required for proper, natural functioning.

Ignatius calls upon the churches on his route to martyrdom to shun their divisions and to achieve ὁμόνοια. He instructs the Ephesians:

> every one of you to become a choir (καὶ οἱ κατ᾽ ἄνδρα δὲ χορὸς γίνεσθε), in order that in harmony on one note (ἵνα σύμφωνοι ὄντες ἐν ὁμονοίᾳ), taking your pitch from God (χρῶμα θεοῦ λαβόντες), you may sing in unity with one voice (ἐν ἑνότητι, ᾄδητε ἐν φωνῇ μιᾷ).[42]

---

[39]Ignatius, *Rom.*, 7.1-3; *Mag.*, 6.2. See also Brent, *Ignatius: Second Sophistic*, pp. 90 and 127.
[40]Ignatius, *Smyrn.*, 3.3; Ignatius, *Mag.*,1.2; *Eph.*, 5.1. See also Brent, *Ignatius: Second Sophistic*, pp. 88–91.
[41]S. Goldhill (ed.), *Being Greek under Rome: Cultural Identity, the Second Sophistic, and the Development of Empire* (Cambridge: Cambridge University Press 2001).
[42]Ignatius, *Eph.*, 4.2.

As in his contemporary city-states, so too in the Christian ἐκκλησία all sections of the constitution must exhibit in their functions the ὁμόνοια required even of individuals freely accepting rational principles of association. No one person or section of the constitution must compel the submission of the other.[43] Ignatius has almost universally been regarded as expounding a system in which a monarch bishop holds everyone in subjection under him, but this is the gross misrepresentation of the later *Didascalia Apostolorum*.[44] Ignatius never tells the presbyters and deacons that they must be subject to the bishop. After mentioning the bishop, in *Letter to the Ephesians* 4.1, he asserts this:

> For your worthily named presbyterate, worthy of God, are so united in harmony with the bishop, as a lyre is to its chords (τὸ γὰρ ἀξιονόμαστον ὑμῶν πρεσβυτέριον, τοῦ θεοῦ ἄξιον, οὕτως συνήρμοσται τῷ ἐπισκόπῳ, ὡς χορδαὶ κιθάρᾳ). On account of this, in your concord (διὰ τοῦτο ἐν τῇ ὁμονοίᾳ ὑμῶν) and harmonious love, Jesus Christ is sung (καὶ συμφώνῳ ἀγάπῃ Ἰησοῦς Χριστὸς ᾄδεται).

Ignatius does exhort the laity (in *Trall.*, 2.2) to 'do nothing without the bishop (ἄνευ τοῦ ἐπισκόπου μηδὲν πράσσειν)' but there is no monarch bishop standing alone in this text since he immediately adds: 'but be subject also to the presbyterate as to the apostles of Jesus Christ (ὑποτάσσεσθαι καὶ τῷ πρεσβυτερίῳ ὡς τοῖς ἀποστόλοις Ἰησοῦ Χριστοῦ)' and then 'please the deacons in every way (κατὰ πάντα τρόπον πᾶσιν ἀρέσκειν).' In other words, Ignatius exhorts the laity to be subject to all three orders, bishop, presbyter/priests and deacons, not simply to the one monarch bishop alone.[45]

Ignatius' view of the unity of the church is a radical enculturalization of the constitutions of the Greek city-states of Asia Minor in the second century, and Hellenistic metaphysical ideas that underlay that concept of unity. Ignatian church order reflects the image-bearing in civic cultic processions that both celebrate and cement such a unity. Ignatius' model is a unique and radical attempt to incorporate a variety of understandings of church order, charismatic, collectively presbyteral, and apostolic, such as we have seen to have existed before.[46] Ignatius' account was little understood in all its details by subsequent ecclesiastical commentators.

---

[43]J. P. Lotz, *Ignatius and Concord: The Background and Use of the Language of Concord in the Letters of Ignatius of Antioch*, Patristics Studies 8 (New York: Peter Lang, 2007). See also D. Kienast, 'Die Homonoia Verträge in der römischen Kaiserzeit', *JBNum* 14 (1964): 51–64; Idem, 'Zu den Homonoia-Vereinbarungen in der römischen Kaiserzeit', *ZPE* 109 (1995): 267–81; A. R. R. Sheppard, 'Homonoia in the Greek Cities of the Roman Empire', *Ancient Society* (1984–1986): 15–17 and 229–42.

[44]Brent, *Ignatius: Second Sophistic*, pp. 30–8.

[45]This non-monarchical character of Ignatian episcopacy has been long established but is largely ignored by R. Padberg, 'Das Amtsverständnis der Ignatiusbriefe', *Theologie und Glaube* 62 (1972): 47–54; Idem, 'Geordnete Liebe: Amt, Pneuma, und kirchliche Einheit bei Ignatius von Antiochien', in *Unio Christianorum, Festschrift für Erzbischof Dr Lorenz Jaeger* (Paderborn: Bonifacius, 1962), pp. 201–17; Idem, 'Vom gottesdienstlichen Leben in den Briefen des Ignatius von Antiochien', *Theologie und Glaube* 53 (1963): 337–47.

[46]Incidentally, my account refutes attempts to make the letters of the Middle Recension forgeries later than the death of Polycarp (23 February, 155), and reflective of a church order that only came into existence in the latter half of the second century.

After Irenaeus, the one bishop was a successor to the apostles, whereas for Ignatius presbyters represented the apostolic council. The classic view of eucharistic presidency is that the priest stands *in persona Christi* whereas for Ignatius it is the deacons. There is no legitimate place in the discussion for 'Ignatius' as a pseudepigraphic label justifying, at an earlier date, a later church order.[47] Let us now turn to the view of unity through apostolic succession in Irenaeus that was later to be synthesized with a distorted Ignatian view of church order.

IRENAEUS: UNITY IN A CONTINUING SCHOLASTIC SUCCESSION (ΔΙΑΔΟΧΗ)

Ignatius had sought to establish a distinctive Christian identity through the model of initiation into a mystery religion through the enactment of a sacred drama, with the bearing of sacred images, in which by imitating divine actions one became incorporated into the divine. Irenaeus sought originally the origins of the 'Gnostic' 'false teachers' in pagan mystery rites. Their leaders, as in the case of the Marcosans, were 'mystagogues (μυσταγωγοί)' who conducted mystery plays using images of Simon and Helena for representing Zeus and Athena.[48] Irenaeus may have, for this reason, marked his retreat from Ignatius' conception of church order as mystery play, and thus quoted him sparsely as 'one of our martyrs.'[49]

In dealing with the Valentinians and Basilideans, Irenaeus ignores this cultic origin of their aeonic systems and the derivation of their narratives of divine beings and their actions from liturgical performances. Instead he regards them not so much as cults but as philosophical schools with succession lists (διαδοχαί) of presiding teachers, and proceeds to construct 'family trees' that so link them in order to identify their true cultural and historical character as pagan and not Christian. The identity of a truly Christian group was in a common body of teaching, a *depositum fidei*, handed on by the apostles to their successors. Irenaeus claims that he can produce such a διαδοχή 'for all the churches',[50] nevertheless he can dispense with so long a procedure and instead, as an example, produce the succession list for Rome from its foundation by saints Peter and Paul until his own time under Pope Eleutherus (AD 174–189). In addition, he says, 'every church should form a compact with this church

[47]For most recent attempts at such an argument that start from a false position because they do not grasp that Ignatius does not share the later concept of apostolic succession found in Irenaeus and Hegesippus, see T. Lechner, *Ignatius adversus Valentinianos? Chronologische und theologiegeschichtliche Studien zu den Briefen des Ignatius von Antiochien. Supplementa Vigiliae Christianae,* 47 (Leiden: E. J. Brill 1999), pp. 73–4 and pp. 111–17; cf. Brent, *Ignatius: Second Sophistic,* p. 20 and pp. 122–9; R. Hübner, *Der paradox Eine: Antignostischer Monarchianismus im zweiten Jahrhundert. Mit einem Beitrag von Markus Vinzent. Supplementa Vigiliae Christianae 50.* (Leiden: E. J. Brill 1999), pp. 132–57, cf. Brent, *Ignatius: Second Sophistic,* p. 19. For a more detailed review of the principal recent attacks on authenticity, see Brent, *Ignatius: Martyr Bishop,* chap. 5.
[48]Irenaeus, *Haer.,* I. 23.4. 4-8 (81-88), see Brent, *Ignatius: Second Sophistic,* pp. 102–17, 111–18.
[49]Irenaeus, *Haer.,* 5.28.4 (83-89).
[50]Irenaeus, *Haer.,* 3.3.2 (15-22).

on account of its compelling first place (*propter potentiorem principalitatem*).' The pre-eminence of that position is indicated both by its foundation by two apostles, and from the fact that Rome stands at the junction of the world's highways and can be a witness to the universal tradition maintained by 'those who are Christians from all parts (*qui sunt undique fideles*) and where, by those who are from everywhere, the tradition that is from the apostles is preserved (*in qua semper ab his qui sunt undique conseruata est ea quae est ab apostolis traditio*).'[51]

Heretics can therefore be excluded from a society claiming to be Christian, on the basis of a body of doctrine handed down from the apostles. He constitutes the church as a teaching school with a presiding teacher occupying a place of authority, 'their own teaching position (*suum ipsorum locum magisteri*)' which the apostles have 'passed down (*tradentes*)'.[52] The bishops, therefore, teach by right of succession on the scholastic model in which the *locus magisterii* is regarded very much as an 'inheritance', as we see from Aristotle's will in which not simply literary archives, but mementos such as herms enter the successor's possession.[53] The position of president enables its holder to establish parameters of the discussion of the founding philosopher or philosophers' teaching within the school. Aristotle, for example, left the Academy and founded his own school when he could no longer defend any version of the theory of forms.

On such a model, Irenaeus could see a means of showing that the heretical Valentinians and Basilideans and those others whom his imagination converted into their associates were not members of the school of the apostles: the bishops had their *locus magisterii* and they could determine what was in the purview of their school and what was not, and which required as a result the creation of a quite separate school for its discussion and promulgation. Thus Irenaeus was to have, in contrast with Ignatius, a quite different concept of unity. Irenaeus' position was that though Christianity might have a variety of forms, not just anything could be regarded as a form of Christianity, and what could be so regarded was determined by the scholastic order of the Christian community with its presiding teacher with the right to determine the parameters of what was taught by virtue of his διαδοχή to their *locum magisteri*.

The problem with such a view of church order (securing a unity that functions on the model of the teaching succession of a philosophic school) was that broadly stated, and in its original form, it did not provide the exclusive concept of orthodoxy which Irenaeus was seeking. For Irenaeus, the heretics constituted philosophical schools that went back not to the apostles, but to Simon Magus, the implacable opponent of the apostles; that Simon 'from whom all heresies derive their foundation (*ex quo uniuersae haereses substiterunt*).'[54] But at this point we might conclude that there was no strict parallel between Irenaean orthodoxy and the preservation (within broad

---

[51]Irenaeus, *Haer.*, 3.3.2 (26-29).
[52]Irenaeus, *Haer.*, 3.3.1 (10-12).
[53]See: Diogenes Laertius, *VP,* 10.
[54]Irenaeus, *Haer.*, 1.23.2 (34-35).

parameters) of the teaching of a Hellenistic philosophical school. The Stoa, the Academy (Plato), the Lyceum (Aristotelians) and the Epicureans were admittedly in a critical dialogue with each other but one that did not involve mutual hostility and condemnation. Horace and indeed Justin Martyr were typical of young individuals who moved from one school to another with involvement in the discussion of their various ideas.[55] But Irenaeus hardly saw the quest for truth proceeding in this way.

Almost contemporary with Irenaeus, however, the concept of διαδοχή was to be used as a tool with which to construct a vision of Hellenistic philosophy as a completely Greek phenomenon, uncontaminated by either Latin, Egyptian or Indian influences. Diogenes Laertius, in his *Successions of the Philosophers*, is clear that several earlier writers had written on the subject and title of διαδοχαί φιλοσοφῶν. His thesis is that Sotion, as well as Aristotle in the *Magicus*, had been wrong in locating the origins of the διαδοχαί with Persian, Assyrian and Babylonian magicians, or with the Indian gymnosophists, or the Druids. Though writing circa AD 217, he ends his διαδοχαί with Epicurus (341–271 BC) and Chrysippus (282–206 BC): Latin writers such as Seneca and Lucretius are not included since Diogenes aims to show that philosophy is totally Greek in its origin.

Diogenes assures us that philosophy began in that golden age in which gods consorted with humans, when Linus wrote on creation and was born of Hermes and the Muse Ourania. Thus both philosophy and the human race began together, and it was Greek. In this context Diogenes developed the myth of the twelve wise men who wrote letters to each other that expressed their unity in a shared civilization. Two of these wise men, Pherekydes and Thales, each initiate a διαδοχή, whose first members are Anaximander and Pythagoras. In this way, and by means of this legend involving letter exchange, Diogenes expresses the unity of an uncontaminated, Hellenistic culture. For Irenaeus, there is only one and not two διαδοχαί ἀποστολῶν, but the later Pseudoclementines envisage Peter and James initiating two teaching successions but with an epistolary interchange indicating mutual recognition. It is in the context of such a scholastic historiography, therefore, that Irenaeus writes, and from which his concept of unity and cultural identity is derived.[56]

CONCLUSION: IGNATIUS AND IRENAEUS ON UNITY AROUND THE BISHOP

The classical Christian understanding of the unity of the church, and the order by which it is to be secured, has been forged from a synthesis between the Irenaean and Ignatian models of unity. According to that synthetic model, whose original advocate was Cyprian, the bishop stands in a position of monarch and supreme

[55]R. E. Wycherley, 'Peripatos: The Ancient Philosophical Scene', *Greece and Rome,* 8 (1961): 152–63 and 9 (1962): 1–21.
[56]A. Brent, 'Diogenes Laertius and the Apostolic Succession', *JEH* 44 (1993): 367–89; Brent, *Hippolytus and the Roman Church in the Third Century,* pp. 496–501.

teacher over a hierarchy in succession to the apostles.[57] The priest stands *in persona Christi*. Historically, Ignatius asserted that the presbyters were the apostles, and the deacons occupied Christ's position in the threefold typology that was realized liturgically. What was represented typologically existed in the timeless moment of mystery and sacrament: there was no procession through secular history in which the iconic ministers were appointed like relay-race runners handing on their batons. Neither in Irenaeus nor in Ignatius was the unity guaranteed by a monarch bishop. The monarchical nature of the bishop's office was to await its final confirmation at Rome at the time of the death of Pontianus (AD 235).[58]

BIBLIOGRAPHY

Brent, A. 'History and Eschatological Mysticism in Ignatius of Antioch', *EThL* 65, no. 4 (1989): 309–29.

Brent, A. 'Diogenes Laertius and the Apostolic Succession', *JEH* 44 (1993): 367–89.

Brent, A. *Hippolytus and the Roman Church in the Third Century: Communities in Tension before the Emergence of a Monarch-Bishop. Vigiliae Christianae Supplementa,* 31. Leiden: E.J. Brill, 1995.

Brent, A. *Ignatius of Antioch and the Second Sophistic*. Tübingen: Mohr Siebeck, 2006.

Brent, A. *Ignatius of Antioch: A Martyr Bishop and the Origin of Episcopacy*. London: Continuum, 2007.

Brent, A. *Cyprian and Roman Carthage*. Cambridge: Cambridge University Press, 2010.

Brent, A. 'The Elenchos and the Identification of Christian Communities in Second to Early Third Century Rome', in G. Aragione and E. Norelli (eds), *Des évêques, des écoles et des hérétiques. Actes du colloque international sur la 'Réfutation de toutes les hérésies'*. Genève, 13–14 juin, 2008. Lausanne: Editions du Zèbre, 2011.

Brent, A. 'How Irenaeus has Misled the Archaeologists', in S. Parvis and P. Foster (eds), *Irenaeus: Life, Scripture, Legacy*, 35–54. Philadelphia, PA: Fortress Press, 2012.

Brown, R. E. and Meier, J. P. *Antioch and Rome: New Testament Cradles of Catholic Christianity*. New York: Paulist Press, 1982.

Goldhill, S. (ed.). *Being Greek under Rome: Cultural Identity, the Second Sophistic, and the Development of Empire*. Cambridge: Cambridge University Press, 2001.

Harland, P. 'Christ-Bearers and Fellow-Initiates: Local Cultural Life and Christian Identity in Ignatius' Letters', *JECS* 11 (2003): 481–99.

Hübner, R. *Der paradox Eine: Antignostischer Monarchianismus im zweiten Jahrhundert. Mit einem Beitrag von Markus Vinzent*, 132–57. *Supplementa Vigiliae Christianae*, 50. Leiden: E. J. Brill, 1999.

Kienast, D. 'Die Homonoia Verträge in der römischen Kaiserzeit', *JBNum* 14 (1964): 51–64.

---

[57]Brent, *Cyprian and Roman Carthage*, pp. 15–17 and pp. 314–27.

[58]Brent, 'How Irenaeus has Misled the Archaeologists', in *Irenaeus: Life, Scripture, Legacy*, eds S. Parvis and P. Foster (Philadelphia, PA: Fortress Press, 2012), pp. 35–54; Brent, 'The *Elenchos*', pp. 300–2.

Kienast, D. 'Zu den Homonoia-Vereinbarungen in der römischen Kaiserzeit', *ZPE* 109 (1995): 267–81.

Laeuchli, S. 'The Drama of Replay', in M. Friedman, T. P. Burke and S. Laeuchli (eds), *Searching in the Syntax of Things*. Philadelphia, PA: Fortress, 1972.

Lechner, T. *Ignatius adversus Valentinianos? Chronologische und theologiegeschichtliche Studien zu den Briefen des Ignatius von Antiochien*, 73–4 and 111–17. *Supplementa Vigiliae Christianae*, 47. Leiden: E. J. Brill, 1999.

Lotz, J. P. *Ignatius and Concord: The Background and Use of the Language of Concord in the Letters of Ignatius of Antioch*. *Patristics Studies*, 8. New York: Peter Lang, 2007.

Molland, E. 'Irenaeus of Lugdunum and the Apostolic Tradition', *JEH* 1 (1950): 12–28.

Padberg, R. 'Geordnete Liebe: Amt, Pneuma, und kirchliche Einheit bei Ignatius von Antiochien', in O. Schilling und H. Zimmermann (eds), *Unio Christianorum, Festschrift für Erzbischof Dr. Lorenz Jaeger*, 201–17. Paderborn: Bonifacius, 1962.

Padberg, R. 'Vom gottesdienstlichen Leben in den Briefen des Ignatius von Antiochien', *Theologie und Glaube* 53 (1963): 337–47.

Padberg, R. 'Das Amtsverständnis der Ignatiusbriefe', *Theologie und Glaube* 62 (1972): 47–54.

Sheppard, A. R. 'Homonoia in the Greek Cities of the Roman Empire', *Ancient Society*, (1984–1986): 15–17 and 229–42.

Simonetti, M. 'Per un profilo dell' autore dell' Elenchos', in G. Aragione and E. Norelli (eds), *Des évêques, des écoles et des hérétiques. Actes du colloque international sur la 'Réfutation de toutes les hérésies'*. Genève, 13–14 juin 2008. Lausanne: Editions du Zèbre, 2011.

Stewart, A. C. *The Original Bishops: Office and Order in the First Christian Communities*. Grand Rapids, MI: Baker Academic, 2014.

Wörrle, M. *Stadt und Fest im kaiserzeitlichen Kleinasien: Studien zu einer agonistischen Stiftung aus Oinoanda*. *Vestigia* 39. Munich: Beck, 1988.

Wycherley, R. E. 'Peripatos: The Ancient Philosophical Scene', *Greece and Rome* 8 (1961): 152–63; and 9 (1962): 1–21.

CHAPTER 10

Unity around a teacher

Clement and Origen of Alexandria

ILARIA L. E. RAMELLI

In the period of the intellectual formation and expansion of early Christianity, in the late second century and the first half of the third, two prominent figures of Christian teachers emerged in Alexandria: Clement and Origen. Like Justin in Rome and Bardaisan, another Christian Platonist, in Edessa,[1] they founded their own schools, which became Christian universities.

Christianity at that time was accused of irrationality.[2] Thus, to claim that they adhered to reason, the *logos*, Christians had to ground their doctrines philosophically and develop a full theology of the Logos, which identified Christ with the pre-existent divine Logos. This move had started with the Johannine Gospel (its Prologue), and continued with Justin, most Valentinians, Clement and especially Origen and his followers. Some roots of the Logos/Memra theology go back to Philo and Jewish Hellenistic traditions, well known to Clement and Origen.[3] Thanks to Clement and Origen, 'teachers of the church' (Origen was called *magister ecclesiae* by Pamphilus[4] and was celebrated as such by his disciple Theodore/Gregory Thaumaturgus), Christianity could no longer be charged with being a religion for ignorant and irrational people (ἄλογοι).

CLEMENT

Titus Flavius Clement (*c.*150–215), who bore the Roman 'three names' (*tria nomina*), received an accurate education across the Mediterranean, both literary and philosophical, and in turn taught in Alexandria; he seems to have left this city

---

[1] See my *Bardaiṣan of Edessa* (Piscataway, NJ: Gorgias, 2009; DeGruyter, 2019); 'Bardaisan of Edessa, Origen, and Imperial Philosophy', *ARAM* (Peeters Journal) 30, nos. 1–2 (2018): 337–53.
[2] Examination in my 'Ethos and Logos', *VChr* 69, no. 2 (2015): 123–56.
[3] See Daniel Boyarin, 'The Gospel of the Memra', *HTR* 94 (2001): 243–84; my 'Philo as One of the Main Inspirers of Early Christian Hermeneutics and Apophatic Theology', *Adamantius* 4 (2018): 276–92.
[4] *Per tot annos magister Ecclesiae fuit* and *in Ecclesia catholica senuit* (*Apology for Origen*, 16).

in 202/203 on account of a persecution.[5] He spoke of the Church, ἐκκλησία, as a group of people who have πίστις[6] in Jesus as the incarnation of the Logos. He had a unifying function for the church in that he promoted unity around a teacher, as Origen did after him. His most important works are related to the notion of a teacher:

1. *Protrepticus*, an invitation to Christian philosophy for 'pagans', as Aristotle had composed an exhortation to turn to philosophy;

2. *Paedagogus*, the teacher, a work that shows to Christians how they should live and what virtues they should cultivate: Christ as 'Pedagogue strengthens the life of the soul . . . and directs the life of the patients with his humane precepts, as with gentle medications, to perfect the knowledge of the truth' (*Paed.* 1.1.3.1);

3. *Stromata/Stromateis*, where the image of the 'gnostic' or perfect Christian is delineated, in conversation with Greek philosophy and against 'heresies';

4. other works: a dialogue with, and a refutation of, the Valentinian Theodotus (*Excerpta ex Theodoto*); *Eclogae propheticae*, and the homily *Quid dives salvetur* ('Who Is the Rich Man Who Is Saved?'), from which Clement's position towards wealth emerges as more lenient and Stoicizing than that of the ascetic Origen.[7] The fragmentary *Hypotyposeis* are interpretive *scholia* on passages of Scripture, while a dubious *Letter to Theodore* refutes the Carpocratian interpretation of the Gospel of Mark and attests to a 'mystical Mark' for an audience of advanced readers in Alexandria.[8] Surely, Clement at his school had both less and more advanced students, like Origen shortly afterwards.

Clement knew both Philo and the Bible well, and, like Philo, was close to so-called Middle Platonism as a Christian Platonist.[9] He may have been a presbyter

---

[5]On Clement, see Alain Le Boulluec, 'Clément d'Alexandrie', in *Histoire de la littérature grecque chrétienne*, III, ed. Bernard Pouderon (Paris: Les Belles Lettres, 2017), pp. 56–169.

[6]Faith/Trust/Confidence: See Eric Osborn, 'Arguments for Faith in Clement of Alexandria', *VChr* 48 (1994): 1–24. On the notion of πίστις / *fides* as 'confidence', see my *Studi su Fides* (Madrid: Signifer, 2002); 'Alcune osservazioni su *credere*', *Maia* n.s. 51 (2000): 67–83. Teresa Morgan, *Roman Faith and Christian Faith* (Oxford: Oxford University Press, 2015); my review *JRS* 107 (2017): 368–70.

[7]See Ilaria L. E. Ramelli, *Social Justice and the Legitimacy of Slavery* (Oxford: Oxford University Press, 2016).

[8]Discussion in my 'The Birth of the Rome-Alexandria Connection', *SPhiloA* 23 (2011): 69–95; Michael Zeddies, 'An Origenian Background for the Letter to Theodore', *HTR* 112, no. 3 (2019): 376–406, who suggests Origen's authorship; 'Esoteric Interpretations of Scripture in Philo (and Hellenistic Judaism), Clement, and Origen', in *Esoteric Cultures of Scripture*, ed. Toby Mayer (Oxford: Oxford University Press, 2021).

[9]I limit myself to referring to Eric Osborn, 'Clement and Platonism', in *Origeniana VIII*, ed. Lorenzo Perrone (Leuven: Peeters, 2003), pp. 419–27; Henny Hägg, *Clement of Alexandria and the Beginning of Christian Apophaticism* (Oxford: Oxford University Press, 2006); Eric Osborn, *Clement of Alexandria* (Cambridge: Cambridge University Press, 2005).

in Alexandria, as a letter of Alexander of Jerusalem reported by Eusebius attests: Alexander, directly acquainted with Clement, wrote that letter from Alexandria and had Clement deliver it to the church in Antioch.[10] Photius at the beginning of his entry on Clement (*Bibliotheca*, 109) repeats that Clement was a presbyter: Ἀλεξανδρέως πρεσβυτέρου.[11] In any case, he was a masterful teacher.

A teacher of Christian philosophy,[12] Clement claimed that philosophy is a gift of Christ-Logos bestowed on the Greeks through good angels,[13] and criticized those Christians who rejected philosophy and only swore by Scripture.[14] Clement may, or may not, have taught Origen, who never mentions him in his extant works; however, as we shall see later, Origen certainly knew Clement's work and thought.

Clement was the disciple of Pantaenus, who taught in Alexandria under Commodus and in the early Severan age.[15] Eusebius calls him a 'Stoic philosopher' renowned for his learning.[16] Eusebius[17] identifies Pantaenus with the best of the Christian masters, mostly philosophers, cited by Clement in *Strom*. 1.1.11: Pantaenus, 'hiding in Egypt', was the last teacher found by Clement, 'but for capacity he was the first', the best among those who preserved 'the true tradition of the blessed teaching' through an oral transmission. Clement named Pantaenus as his teacher and exposed his Scriptural exegeses and traditions;[18] Clement himself presents his *Stromateis* as notes from his master's teaching.[19]

Pantaenus' teachings and exegesis, probably also allegorical,[20] were collected by Clement in the aforementioned *Hypotyposeis*, where he also mentioned Pantaenus by name as his teacher.[21] Clement's designation of Pantaenus as 'really a Sicilian

---

[10]*HE.*, 6.11.6, provided that the Clement mentioned by Alexander in his letter is our Clement.

[11]In Cod. 111.89b Bekker, Photius reports the full title he found in 'an old manuscript' of the *Stromateis*, which identifies him as a presbyter: Τίτου Φλαβίου Κλήμεντος πρεσβυτέρου Ἀλεξανδρείας τῶν κατὰ τὴν ἀληθῆ φιλοσοφίαν γνωστικῶν ὑπομνημάτων στρωματέων.

[12]Ulrich Neymeyr, *Die christlichen Lehrer im zweiten Jahrhundert* (Leiden: E.J. Brill, 1989), pp. 227–8, rightly argued that Christian teachers such as Justin or Clement were indistinguishable from contemporary 'pagan' teachers of philosophy.

[13]*Strom.*, 7.2.5.5; 2.6.4.

[14]*Strom.*, 7 prologue. On Clement's appreciation of philosophy, see also F. A. Sullivan, 'Clement of Alexandria on Justification through Philosophy', in *In Many and Diverse Ways*, eds D. Kendall and G. O'Collins (Maryknoll, NY: Orbis, 2003), pp. 101–13; C. Broc-Schmezer, 'La philosophie grecque comme propédeutique à l'évangile', *Foi et vie* 107 (2008): 77–87.

[15]Eusebius, *HE.*, 5.10.1-4.

[16]*HE.*, 5.10.1; 5.10.4.

[17]*HE.*, 5.11.2-5.

[18]Eusebius, *HE.*, 6.13.1-2.

[19]Clement, *Strom.*, 1.1.11.2.

[20]See A. Dinan, 'Αἴνγμα and αἰνίττομαι in the Works of Clement of Alexandria', *SP* 44 (2010): 175–81; Ilaria L. E. Ramelli, 'The Mysteries of Scripture', in *Clement's Biblical Exegesis*, eds Veronica Černuskova et al. (Leiden: E.J. Brill, 2016), pp. 80–110.

[21]Eusebius, *HE.*, 6.13.2. Photius, *Bibliotheca*. Cod. 109, summarizing Clement's *Hypotyposeis*, refers that Clement here attested that he was a disciple of Pantaenus.

bee'[22] alludes to his learning in Scripture, liberal arts and philosophy, as is confirmed by the use of the bee metaphor in *Strom.* 1.33.5-6, in reference to the indispensable education offered by philosophy, as a basis to theology (cf. 4.9.2). Origen praised Pantaenus in a letter reported by Eusebius,[23] where Origen defended his own interest in philosophy, because of charges;[24] while he was studying Scripture, he was approached by heretics, philosophers and experts in 'the Greek disciplines'. This is why he had 'to examine the opinions of the heretics as well as what the philosophers claimed to say concerning the truth'. Origen adduces the examples of Pantaenus and Heraclas, Alexandrine Christian philosophers. According to Origen here, Pantaenus had an excellent preparation in philosophy and Greek disciplines. Indeed, Alexander of Alexandria in a letter to Origen says that he had come to know Origen exactly through Pantaenus and Clement.[25] Eusebius states that Pantaenus was the founder of the Didaskaleion;[26] but this piece of information might be due to Eusebius' desire to trace an institutional continuity: the Pantaenus-Clement-Origen succession.[27]

Clement regards Plato as 'the philosopher taught by the Hebrews' (*Strom.* 1.1.10.2) and quotes Numenius – praised by Origen too – on Plato as 'Atticizing Moses'.[28] The same position was embraced by Numenius and Origen: the latter explained the striking convergences between Plato's ideas and Scripture – read through the lens of philosophical allegoresis – by hypothesizing that Plato was familiar with the 'Jewish philosophy' (*Cels* 4.39). Likewise, Clement deems Plato's metaphysics and philosophy dependent on 'the Mosaic philosophy', as already Philo named it:

> The Mosaic philosophy is divided into four: historical, legislative proper (both parts pertain to ethics), liturgical (already belonging to the theory of nature), and the fourth part, superior to all, the theological one: the contemplation, as Plato says, of the really venerable mysteries. Aristotle calls this 'metaphysics'. Thus, dialectics, according to Plato in his *Statesman*, is a science that aims at detecting the revelation of being . . . philosophical engagement applied to truth,

---

[22]*Strom.*, 1.11.2. Eusebius, *HE.*, 5.11.1 identifies this 'bee' with Pantaenus. He was right according to Theodor von Zahn, *Forschungen zur Geschichte des neutestamentlichen Kanons* 3 (Erlangen, 1884), p. 161; further arguments for this identification in my 'Annotazioni sulle origini del Cristianesimo in Sicilia', *RSCI* 53 (1999): 1–15.

[23]*HE.*, 6.19.12-14, who had direct access to Origen's letters, which he collected, ordered and kept in the Caesarea library (cf. 6.36.3).

[24]See my 'Origen, Patristic Philosophy, and Christian Platonism', *VChr* 63 (2009): 217–63.

[25]*HE.*, 6.14.9.

[26]*HE.*, 5.10.

[27]Then Eusebius reports that Pantaenus also became 'the announcer of the Gospel of Christ to Eastern peoples, sent as he was as far as the land of the Indians'. On this mission, see my 'Early Christian Missions from Alexandria to "India": Institutional Transformations and Geographical Identification', *Aug* 51 (2011): 221–31. Clement himself was very interested in the Indians.

[28]*Strom.*, 1.22.150.4.

genuine dialectics examines reality . . . and dares to advance toward the God of the universe.[29]

In *Strom.* 5.14.90, Clement lists examples of the dependence of Greek philosophy on the Mosaic philosophy. The importance of philosophy in the formation of Christians is emphasized in *Strom.* 1.5.31, on the basis of an allegorical interpretation of the story of Abraham, Hagar and Sarah, which reveals the hidden, symbolic meaning, μυστήριον, of this episode (as Origen will also argue)[30]: 'The passages I have quoted from Scripture can point to other symbolic meanings. From all this we can conclude that philosophy has as its specific task the investigation into the truth and the nature of reality. Now, truth is that about which the Lord himself said: "I am the Truth".'[31] Like Origen, Clement maintains that 'the culture that prepares for the rest in Christ trains the mind and awakens the intelligence, producing sagacity in research by means of the true philosophy. This is the philosophy that those initiated to the mysteries possess: they have discovered, or better received, it from the Truth itself', Christ. The 'divine mysteries' are learnt by the 'gnostic', the perfect Christian, from the Son of God.[32] The divine Logos was manifested partially before Christ, in Greek philosophy and the religions of several peoples:[33] 'all those who have spoken of God, barbarians and Greeks, have hidden [ἀπεκρύψαντο] the principles of reality and have communicated the truth by means of riddles, symbols, allegories, metaphors and the like, such as the oracles of the Greeks.'[34]

Justin used φιλοσοφία in reference to Christianity;[35] Clement describes Christianity as βάρβαρος φιλοσοφία[36] and true philosophy.[37] This position will be developed by Origen and his follower Eusebius.[38] Greek philosophy is a preparation for Christianity.[39] The Greeks received 'sparkles of the divine Logos';[40] Plato speaks 'as though he were inspired';[41] he and the other philosophers drew from 'Moses' the truths of their philosophy.[42] Clement invokes Philo and Aristobulus[43] to conclude that 'the whole Greek wisdom derived from barbarian philosophy'.[44] Greek

---

[29]*Strom.*, 1.28.176.1-3; reference to *Plt.*, 287A.
[30]As I show in 'The Reception of Paul in Origen: Allegoresis of Scripture, Apokatastasis, and Women's Ministry', in *The Pauline Mind*, ed. Stanley Porter (New York: Routledge, 2021).
[31]Jn 14.6.
[32]*Strom.*, 7.1.4.3.
[33]*Strom.*, 5.4.19.3-4.
[34]*Strom.*, 5.4.21.
[35]*Apol.*, 2.12.5; *Dial.*, 8.
[36]*Strom.*, 2.11.25.
[37]*Strom.*, 1.1.21; 28.156; 2.7.54.
[38]*Praep.Ev.*, 1.4.10.
[39]*Strom.*, 1.1-9; 1.21; 6.7-8.
[40]*Protrep.*, 7.74.7.
[41]*Strom.*, 1.8.42.1.
[42]*Strom.*, 2.1.1; 6.3.28.
[43]*Strom.*, 1.15.72.4; 5.14.97.7.
[44]*Strom.*, 5.14.140.2; 6.7.55.3-4.

philosophy is, 'in a way, providential'.[45] Greek philosophers had 'true doctrines' (ἀληθῆ, *Strom.* 1.19.91.1), and 'offered some parts of the true philosophy' (τινα τῆς ἀληθοῦς φιλοσοφίας, *Strom.* 1.19.94.1). Philosophy, 'on its own, did bring the Greeks to righteousness, although not to perfect righteousness' (*Strom.* 1.20. 99.3).

Philosophy can refute heresies:[46] the source of heresy is not philosophy, as many heresiologists claimed, but the wrong interpretation of Scripture.[47] Origen will agree.[48] Philosophy, for Clement, recognized God imperfectly and must progress, so as to participate in perfect 'gnosis',[49] brought about by Christ.[50] The Platonic ideal of assimilation to God and the Stoic ideal of behaving according to nature and eradicating passions are also found in Scripture.[51] Plato alluded to the Trinity, Empedocles to the resurrection;[52] Plato pointed to the knowledge of God and is in agreement with Paul.[53] Paul quotes Epimenides, because the latter 'expresses something of the truth'.[54] Christ and the apostles descended to hell for the salvation of the 'pagans'.[55]

The truth, contained in Moses's writings, has been dispersed in the various philosophical schools; Clement sought to re-gather it.[56] (A similar operation was done by contemporary Platonists with Platonic philosophy, and Atticus and Numenius viewed the history of philosophy in the same way.) For Clement, the unity of truth is anchored in the Word (*logos*); therefore, all true insights, including those of the 'pagans', constitute the truth. Clement described philosophy as 'not Stoicism, Platonism, Epicureanism, or Aristotelianism, but whatever has been well said by each of these schools [αἱρέσεων] . . . this eclectic whole [τοῦτο σύμπαν τὸ ἐκλεκτικόν]'.[57] Clement was no indifferentist, but had to counter scepticism – although, like Origen and other patristic philosophers, he also used sceptic arguments against the disagreements of 'pagan' philosophical and religious traditions, as well as of anti-

---

[45]*Strom.,* 1.1.18.4.

[46]*Strom.,* 1.19.95-96.

[47]*Strom.,* 7.16.97.4.

[48]See my 'Philo as Origen's Declared Model', *SCJR* 7 (2012): 1–17.

[49]*Strom.,* 6.39-70.

[50]*Strom.,* 1.18.90.1.

[51]Denis Bradley, 'The Transformation of Stoic Ethics in Clement', *Aug* 14 (1974): 41–66; my 'The Stoic Doctrine of *Oikeiōsis* and Its Transformation in Christian Platonism', *Apeiron* 47 (2014): 116–40.

[52]On Empedocles in Clement: I. Ramelli, 'La concezione delle religioni in Temistio ed il suo atteggiamento verso il Cristianesimo', *RIL* 139 (2005): 455–83.

[53]*Strom.,* 3.3.18. 1-2; 5.14.

[54]*Strom.,* 1.14.59.3.

[55]*Strom.,* 6.5-6. Clement indicates a number of doctrines that Greek philosophers shared with Scripture: for example, in Pythagoras (*Strom.,* 2.18.92.1; 5.5.27.7), Heraclitus (*Strom.,* 5.1.9.3), Plato (*Strom.,* 1.1.10.2; 2.19.92.3; 100.3; 5.11.67; *Paed.,* 1.8.67.1; 3.11.54.2); Antisthenes (*Strom.,* 5.14.108.4), Orpheus (ibid., 123.1), Aristotle (*Strom.,* 1.17.87.3), the Stoics (*Strom.,* 5.1.9.4: parallel between their conflagration theory and the resurrection; 3.17.6) and philosophers in general (*Strom.,* 5.5.29.3).

[56]So Raoul Mortley, *Connaissance religieuse et herméneutique chez Clément* (Leiden: E.J. Brill, 1973), pp. 167–70.

[57]*Strom.,* 1.37.6; cf. 1.29.1;1.57.1-6: truth is one, but different philosophical paths reached it.

Christian polemics.[58] Instead of being 'eclectic' himself (in the current meaning of the term), Clement clearly followed Platonism most, with aspects from Stoicism, especially in ethics.

He claimed that Plato mystically 'knew that the real principle is One', as esoterically indicated in *Tim.* 48C2-6.[59] This passage by Plato on apophaticism, along with *Seventh Letter* 341C, was authoritative for Clement[60] as for 'pagan' Middle Platonists. Clement therefore praised Plato's esotericism (*Strom.* 5.10.65.1-5). He argued that, since philosophy is true, it must come from God (*Strom.* 1.7). Already Clement, like Origen, regarded philosophy as 'the queen of the encyclopaedical disciplines [ἐγκύκλια μαθήματα]', and wisdom/theology as 'the queen of philosophy'.[61] Origen followed Philo, Aristobulus, Josephus and Clement[62] about Moses's anteriority to Homer and Plato, thereby demolishing Celsus' claim that biblical authors misunderstood Plato (*Cels.* 4.21; 6.7; 4.11). Similarities between Scripture and Plato depend on their common inspiration by the Logos or on Plato's encounter with 'Jewish philosophers'.

The Godhead expresses itself in Scripture: this should exhort Christians to research, making them 'zetetic', ζητητικοί – a key concept for Origen later. Human efforts induce God to communicate the Logos to us (*Strom.* 5.15-18): the truth, after being researched, is sweet (*Strom.* 1.2.21). For Clement, as for Origen, truth is expressed in symbols, so that deep, spiritual meanings may not be grasped by people unworthy of them, and exegetes may exert their minds in interpretation.[63] Not only Scripture, but many people 'expressed philosophical ideas symbolically' (συμβολικῶς φιλοσοφοῦντες, *Strom.* 5.9.56), for instance the Seven Sages uttered maxims, for which Clement finds Old Testament models.[64] Even 'the poets express symbolically many philosophical thoughts [δι' ὑπονοίας φιλοσοφοῦσι]: for instance, Linus, Musaeus, Homer, Hesiod, and the like'.[65]

The barbarians knew and used allegorical, symbolic expressions: the Hebrews in their 'Mosaic philosophy', the Egyptians in their hieroglyphics.[66] But especially the whole Bible – according to Clement just as to Philo and Origen – is symbolical, admittedly so.[67] Clement's indebtedness to Philo – like Origen's – with regard to the

---

[58]See, e.g., *Strom.*, 7.89.1; 7.89.3.

[59]So *Strom.*, 5.14.89.7.

[60]*Protrep.*, 6.67.2-68.1; *Strom.*, 5.12.78.1.

[61]*Strom.*, 1.5.30.1. On Clement's valuing of the liberal arts: Robert Edwards, 'Clement of Alexandria's "Gnostic" Exposition of the Decalogue', *JECS* 23 (2015): 501–28, 505–20.

[62]*Strom.*, 5.93-94; 5.89.1-2; 5.98.134; Aristobulus *ap.* Eusebius, *Praep.Ev.*, 13.1.

[63]*Strom.*, 5.4.24; 6.15.126.2.

[64]For example, Exod. 10.28; 34.12; Deut. 4.9 for *nosce te ipsum*, *Strom.* 2.15.70.5; cfr. 3.20.7. For this maxim as biblical and philosophical in Origen, see my '"Know Yourself" in Origen and Gregory of Nyssa: A Maxim of Greek Philosophy Found in Scripture', in *Know Yourself from Paul to Augustine* (Berlin: De Gruyter, forthcoming).

[65]*Strom.*, 5.4.24.

[66]*Strom.*, 5.4.20, with allegoreses drawn from Chaeremon: see my *Allegoristi dell'età classica* (Milan: Bompiani, 2007), pp. 671–707.

[67]Ps. 77.2; 1 Cor. 2.6-10, etc.

allegoresis of Scripture is difficult to overestimate. Just as Philo regarded Judaism as the true philosophy, so did also Clement deem Christianity the true philosophy, and they all interpret the Bible, their authoritative text, in the light of philosophy, through allegoresis. Clement actively used both allegory and allegoresis, as Philo and Origen did.[68] Allegory was a symbolic, covert expression in Clement's own writings, a strategy aimed at avoiding revealing the truth to those unworthy of it,[69] as Scripture does; allegoresis is allegorical exegesis, which Clement applied to Scripture in exegetical works such as the *Hypotyposeis* and everywhere, including the *Stromata*.

The end of exegesis and theology is the perfection of people and their ultimate salvation and restoration. Clement identifies the final apokatastasis ('restoration, reconstitution, reestablishment') with the state of perfection consisting of γνῶσις and ἀγάπη, as the end of an ascending process.[70] This will come after the necessary purification of one's sins through an instruction called 'salvific'; then, humans will enjoy 'the apokatastasis in eternal contemplation', which is deification, life with God in eternal contemplation, as Origen theorized in his eschatology.[71] Clement here, like Origen after him, characterizes the final apokatastasis as absolutely eternal (ἀΐδιος), not simply as αἰώνιος, pertaining to the other aeon.[72] As Origen will do, based on 1 Cor. 15.24-28, Clement connects the final apokatastasis to voluntary submission to the Lord, postulates a 'salvific passage' from incredulity to faith and from faith to gnosis. The latter brings about purification and finally yields to love, which is, for Clement as for Origen, the condition of apokatastasis and of stability in it.[73] Punishments are purificatory, and purification results from the illuminative action of knowledge. Their end is salvation. The noun ἀποκατάστασις is repeatedly attested in Clement, who connects it with the *telos* and the perfect Christian ('gnostic').[74]

Clement, in connection with his anti-Gnostic polemic, stressed individual freewill and accountability,[75] deeming it compatible with God's providence – like Origen,

---

[68]My 'Mysteries of Scripture', 'Philo as Inspirer' and 'The Philosophical Stance of Allegory in Stoicism and its Reception in Platonism, Pagan and Christian', *IJCT* 18 (2011): 335–71.

[69]*Strom.*, 1.1.15.1.

[70]*Strom.*, 7.10.56.2-6.

[71]See Ilaria L. E. Ramelli, 'Deification (*Theosis*)', in *Encyclopedia of the Bible and Its Reception* 6 (Berlin: De Gruyter, 2013), cols. 468-472.

[72]See my 'Αἰώνιος and Αἰών in Origen and Gregory of Nyssa', *SP* 47 (2010): 57–62; 'Time and Eternity', in *The Routledge Handbook of Early Christian Philosophy* (London: Routledge, 2021), pp. 41–54.

[73]See my 'Origen and Apokatastasis: A Reassessment', in *Origeniana X*, eds. Sylwia Kaczmarek and Henryk Pietras (Leuven: Peeters, 2011); *The Christian Doctrine of Apokatastasis: A Critical Assessment from the New Testament to Eriugena* (Leiden: E.J. Brill, 2013); 'Apokatastasis and Epektasis', in *Gregory of Nyssa: In Canticum Canticorum*, ed. Giulio Maspero (Leiden: E.J. Brill, 2018), pp. 312–39.

[74]In *Strom.*, 7.10.57.1-4 and more. See my 'Stromateis VII and Clement's Hints of the Theory of Apokatastasis', in *The Seventh Book of the Stromateis*, eds Matyaš Havrda et al. (Leiden: E.J. Brill, 2012), pp. 239–57.

[75]For example, in *Strom.*, 1.1.4.1; 2.14–15.60-71; 5.14.136; indeed, like Origen, he asserted this of every rational creature, including the devil, who was not forced by nature to choose evil (*Strom.*, 1.17.83–84). In 2.3 he maintains the freedom of human will against the Valentinians (also in 1.20.115–16) and Basilides.

whose doctrine of apokatastasis developed from his anti-Gnostic arguments.[76] Clement, whose main concern in his anti-Gnostic fight was theodicy, like Origen, quotes or echoes frequently *Resp.* 10.617E about virtue that 'has no master' (ἀρετὴ δὲ ἀδέσποτον) and is chosen or rejected by one's freewill; thus, 'the responsibility lies with the subject who chooses: God is not responsible [αἰτία ἑλομένου, θεὸς ἀναίτιος]'.[77] This thesis was hammered home by Plato elsewhere as well,[78] and will return in Porphyry, *Marc.* 12, *Corpus Hermeticum* 4.8, Maximus of Tyre, a 'Maximus' quoted by Eusebius, and inscriptions,[79] and very often in Clement, Origen and Gregory Nyssen. In *Strom.* 2.14-15, Clement debates at length the issue of responsibility with examples from Scripture and the classics: one's intention is what counts most in the assessment of one's responsibility (an idea that will still appear in the Christian Arabic works by Theodore Abū Qurra), and whatever is made out of ignorance or necessity is not responsible.[80] Clement emphasizes God's mercy even on voluntary faults, since God prefers the sinner's conversion to his death, and uses therapeutic metaphors, dear to him and Origen, with a view to the theory of apokatastasis.[81] In *Strom.* 1.17.83-84 Clement mentions Plato and Socrates and adduces many examples from Chrysippus' discussion of freewill.[82] Echoing the Johannine Prologue, Clement emphasises that 'we are not children of desire, but of freewill'.[83] Therefore, humans should not be governed by impulses, but by reason.[84] One's life is determined by one's voluntary choices.

Divine grace enables repentance and conversion, without detriment to human freewill – a synergy that Origen also will maintain: 'God wants us to save ourselves by ourselves' (*Strom.* 6.12.96.1-3). Some have very good innate qualities, but detach themselves from virtue and the Good (God) 'out of carelessness': Origen will repeatedly ascribe carelessness to those who neglect their spiritual improvement. Clement's view, like Origen's, is informed by his polemic against Valentinian predestinationism. Sin depends on one's free assent given to an impulse. Clement uses the Stoic and Platonic theory of assent;[85] this depends on the moral subject, who, for Clement (as for Origen) is helped by divine Providence by a 'therapy corresponding to the various passions', which must be cured by a will inspired by

---

[76]Argument in my 'Origen, Bardaisan, and the Origin of Universal Salvation', *HTR* 102 (2009): 135–68.

[77]*Paed.*, 1.8.69.1, *Strom.*, 1.1.4.1 (cf. 4.24.153.1-2); 1.17.84; 2.16.75; 4.23.150; 5.14.136.

[78]*Rep.*, 2.379BC; *Ti.*, 42DE; *Leg.*, 10.904C.

[79]See on him my '"Maximus" on Evil, Matter, and God', *Adamantius* 16 (2010): 230–55; 'The *Dialogue of Adamantius*: A Document of Origen's Thought?' *SP* 52 (2012): 71–98; 56, no. 4 (2013): 227–73; 'The *Dialogue of Adamantius*: Preparing the Critical Edition and a Reappraisal', *RhM* 163 (2020): 40–68.

[80]*Strom.*, 2.14.60-61; see also 2.15.62-64.

[81]*Strom.*, 2.15.66; 15.69-71.

[82]See my 'Baptism in Gregory of Nyssa's Theology and Its Orientation to Eschatology', in *Ablution, Initiation, and Baptism*, eds David Hellholm et al. (Berlin: De Gruyter, 2011), 2:1205–32; further in Ramelli, *Slavery*, chapter on Nyssen.

[83]*Strom.*, 3.7.58; cf. 1.1.4.

[84]*Strom.*, 3.9.65.

[85]*Strom.*, 1.17.83-84 and 2.12.54-55.

reason. Each one's salvation must be voluntary.[86] This is a core principle of Clement's and Origen's soteriology, eschatology and theology of freedom.

Clement inherits (Platonic-Socratic and Stoic) ethical intellectualism: evil things are chosen when they are deemed good, because of a wrong opinion, which the subject fails to correct out of foolishness and ignorance. In *Strom*. 1.17.84.2-4, Clement follows the Socratic principle that nobody chooses evil qua evil, but one chooses evil deeming it good.[87] Origen and Gregory Nyssen will retain many aspects of ethical intellectualism; Gregory Nyssen used it even to explain the so-called original sin: the protoplasts ate the forbidden fruit because, due to the snake's deception, they regarded it as good.[88] Clement himself, soon after the enunciation of the principle that nobody chooses evil qua evil, mentions the devil as the one who induces false impressions and thus makes evil look good.[89]

Errors due to deception, obfuscation and ignorance deserve punishment, but God's justice is 'salvific': Clement insists on the pedagogical, therapeutic value of all suffering inflicted by God:[90] 'everything, both in general and in the single cases, is ordered by the Lord of the universe with the aim of universal salvation', since 'God is good and from eternity and eternally saves through his Son' and 'the task of salvific Justice is to lead each being to what is better'.[91] This suggestion will be developed by Origen. Divine Providence operates through good deeds or punishment, but the end of both is salvation.[92] According to Clement (and Origen), salvific repentance/conversion is always possible, because God's goodness operates absolutely everywhere, 'both here on earth and on the other side'.[93]

Clement was a teacher, as seen, the author of the *Paedagogus* and the *Stromateis*, and wished to bring Christians to perfection. His pedagogical mentality had him lead a school in Alexandria to gather Christians in unity around a teacher, and caused him to ascribe to God a similar mentality, with momentous consequences on his eschatology. Origen will develop this train of thought and pedagogical metaphors into his doctrine of the eventual eviction of evil and apokatastasis. In Clement's opinion, the world is a school: 'This exterior appearance has been thrown upon us because of the entrance into this world, that we might enter this place of education [παιδευτήριον], common to all of us. But inside, hidden, the Father dwells, and his Son, who died for us and rose with us.' Consistently with this framework, Clement ascribes to the 'fire in the world to come', πῦρ αἰώνιον, a purifying and

---

[86]For example, in *Strom.*, 1.6.35.1; 2.3.11.2; 5.27.4; 4.26.170.4; 5.1.7.1-2; 13.83.1; 6.12.96.2; 7.2.6.3; 3.20.3.8; 12.1; 7.42.4.

[87]See, for example, *Strom.*, 2.6.26.5; 2.15.62.3; 4.26.168.2; 6.14.113.3.

[88]See my 'The Nous and the Will: Ethical Intellectualism', seminar, Loyola Marymount University, November 2019, forthcoming.

[89]*Strom.*, 1.17.84.6.

[90]E.g., in *Strom.*, 2.15.69–71; 7.16.102.1–3; 7.6.34.1–3 regarding the αἰώνιον fire, which is not 'eternal' but 'of the world to come'.

[91]*Strom.*, 7.2.12; cf. 1.17.86.1-2.

[92]*Strom.*, 1.17.173.

[93]*Strom.*, 4.6.37.7; cf. 6.6.45–47.

educative function; this is also why it is wise and endowed with discernment: 'the fire sanctifies, not the flesh of sacrificial offerings, but the souls of the sinners . . . a fire that is endowed with discernment [φρόνιμον], which spreads in the soul that passes through that fire.'[94]

Clement's therapeutic and pedagogical mindset, joined with his notion (shared by Origen) of a substantial continuity between the present and the future life, also explains how he hopes that 'the heretics' can be converted by God, even after death, thanks to God's parental care: 'we are corrected by divine Providence as kids are by their teacher or father. God does not *punish* [τιμωρεῖται], since punishment is the retribution of evil with further evil, but *corrects* [κολάζει] for the sake of those who are corrected, both in general and singularly.'[95] Clement is aware of Aristotle's distinction between retributive τιμωρία and educative κόλασις, and of the New Testament exclusive use of κόλασις/κολάζειν, decided by God here or in the other world (κόλασις αἰώνιος), never τιμωρία/τιμωρεῖσθαι. God's punishments are educative, not retributive but constructive, for the benefit of the sinner and of all. Christian believers are the first recipients of such instructive punishments; 'heretics' and non-Christians will be educated in this world, but in case they should die without having converted, God will educate them in the next, through paternal admonitions. Clement thereby leaves the path open to universal restoration.

Like Origen and Nyssen, Clement intimates that even demons can repent, convert and be saved.[96] Here, the πῦρ αἰώνιον sent by God the Logos against Sodom is called again 'full of discernment' (φρόνιμον), and the punishment of Sodom is for humans 'the image of their wise, or well calculated, salvation'.[97] Punishment aims at salvation. Clement also adds that threats and punishments are wanted by God to inspire a salutary fear, which keeps humans from sinning.[98]

According to Clement, just as later according to Origen, the *telos* is all humans' deification (θέωσις),[99] grounded in Christ's 'in-humanation',[100] a link that will be developed by Origen, Athanasius and the Gregories, Nazianzen and Nyssen. Salvific providence works through Christ-Logos, who always 'encourages, admonishes, saves'[101] and will bring about the harmonization of all beings.[102] Salvation must be freely chosen, but the Logos helps people to choose it, through purification and

---

[94]*Strom.*, 7.6.34.1-3.

[95]*Strom.*, 7.16.102.1-3. My emphasis.

[96]*Paed.*, 3.8.44-45 etc. On Origen and Gregory, see my *Apokatastasis*, the respective chapters. Further research on Origen is ongoing.

[97]Τῆς εὐλογίστου τοῖς ἀνθρώποις σωτηρίας εἰκών.

[98]Διὰ τοῦτο γὰρ αἱ κολάσεις καὶ αἱ ἀπειλαί, ἵνα δείσαντες τὰς δίκας τοῦ ἁμαρτάνειν ἀποσχώμεθα.

[99]*Protrep.*, 1.8.4.

[100]'In-humanation' translates ἐνανθρώπησις: the hyphen points to its etymology. Since ἐνανθρώπησις, preferred by Origen and his tradition, differs from ἐνσάρκωσις ('incarnation') from the philosophical and theological viewpoint, it is imprecise to translate them both 'incarnation'. The Latin translation of ἐνανθρώπησις, clear in Eriugena (e.g., *Periph.*, 5.24), is exactly *inhumanatio*, 'in-humanation'.

[101]*Protrep.*, 1.6.2; cf. 9.87.6.

[102]*Protrep.*, 1.5.2.

illumination; Christ thereby becomes a 'sting of salvation'. Thus, the Logos waits for unbelievers to believe, even after death, because it is the Lord of all and the Saviour of all,[103] and 'almost compels people to salvation, out of a superabundance of goodness'.[104] This is an application to soteriology of Plato's concept of the supreme Good as 'overflowing' in *Rep.* 508B.

CLEMENT AND ORIGEN

Clement's relation to Origen is problematic: we do not know whether he was the teacher of Origen, who never cites him in extant works. When Origen must adduce examples of Christian (presbyters) philosophers, he cites Pantaenus and Heraclas, but not Clement,[105] although Clement would have been an excellent example, all the more so if he had been Origen's teacher. Clement might have been a private teacher. He is reported by Eusebius to have been the head of the catechetical school of Alexandria before Origen; if he was, this was not the school described by Eusebius, which applied to the later institution controlled by the monarchic bishop of Alexandria.[106] Eusebius probably intended to draw an institutional succession: Pantaenus > Clement > Origen.[107]

Whatever their relation, Clement's thought was surely known to Origen, who in some respects developed it, including in soteriology, eschatology, protology and theology. Examples are the work *Stromateis* or *Miscellany* by Origen, the theory of apokatastasis, and the idea of Christ-Logos-Wisdom as noetic cosmos. Origen composed his *Stromateis*, now lost, after the example of Clement, who in *Strom.* 1.5.28 described philosophy as a gift from God and a preparation for Christian faith. In his own *Stromateis*, Origen compared the ancient philosophers' and the Christian ideas, and found them consistent: he confirmed the Christian beliefs by means of the doctrines of Greek philosophers.[108]

Christ as noetic cosmos emerges from *Strom.* 4.25.155.2–157.2, influenced by the first hypothesis of the *Parmenides*. Clement posits the couple of the One as

---

[103]*Strom.*, 6.6.46ff.; 7.2.7.6.

[104]*Strom.*, 7.14.86.6.

[105]In the aforementioned letter *ap.* Eusebius, *HE.*, 6.19.12-14.

[106]See at least Roelof van der Broek, 'The Christian School at Alexandria in the Second and Third Centuries', in *Centers of Learning*, eds Jan Willem Drijvers and A. MacDonald (Leiden: E.J. Brill, 1995), pp. 39–47; Clemens Scholten, 'Die alexandrinische Katechetenschule', *JAC* 38 (1995): 16–37; Annewies van den Hoek, 'The "Cathechetical School" of Early Christian Alexandria', *HTR* 90 (1997): 59–87; Alain Le Boulluec, 'Aux origines, encore, de l'école d'Alexandrie', *Adamantius* 5 (1999): 8–36; Attila Jakab, *Ecclesia Alexandrina* (Bern: Lang, 2004), pp. 91–106; Anthony Grafton and Megan Williams, *Christianity and the Transformation of the Book* (Cambridge, MA: Harvard's Belknap Press, 2006), with my review in *Adamantius* 14 (2008): 637–41; Osborn, *Clement*, ch. 1. Gilles Dorival and Alain Le Boulluec, *L'Abeille et l'Acier. Clément d'Alexandrie et Origène* (Paris: Les Belles Lettres 2019), after two long chapters, on Clement (Le Boulluec) and Origen (Dorival), a brief concluding chapter (347–51) compares Clement and Origen.

[107]*HE.*, 6.6.1.

[108]Jerome, *Ep.*, 70.4.

absolutely simple, transcending all existence and knowledge, and the One of the *Parmenides'* second hypothesis, One-Many as the complex unity containing all in itself, the Son-Logos-Wisdom, science and truth, all notions which in Philo were attributes of the Logos and in Origen will be *epinoiai* of Christ. These pertain to the epistemic field, related to Clement's idea of Christ-Logos as teacher and pedagogue, knowable and transmitter of knowledge (by being the noetic cosmos), as opposite to the Father, who is constructed on the *Parmenides'* first hypothesis and its transcendent One. The Son is the sum and unification of 'all the powers of the spirit taken together, transformed into one single thing; they end up into the same being: the Son'.[109] Christ-Logos unifies and transcends all in a superior unity, not simply One (the absolute, transcendent, ineffable God), not simply Many (the creatures, the Ideas/Forms, and the spiritual powers[110]), but One-Many. 'Indeed, the Son is not simply "one" as one thing; nor is he "many things" as parts of a sum, but is One as All things', the unity of multiplicity that transcends the many and makes them one.[111] The Son 'is the circle that embraces all the powers, encircled and *unified into one*' (my emphasis): the Logos is the principle of all things, as it embraces them all in a superior unity, and is the main agent of creation. 'For this reason, the Logos is said to be the Alpha and the Omega,[112] because only in his case *does the end coincide with the beginning*; the Logos "ends with the first principle", without admitting of any interruption at any point'.[113]

Clement's conception of Christ-Logos as the seat of the Ideas and the transcendent unity of all was adopted by Origen, against the backdrop, again, of Plato's *Parmenides*.[114] Origen posits the binary, God-One and God-One-Many, influenced by both the *Parmenides* and Clement. In his *Commentary on John*, Origen develops Clement's conception of the Logos being One-All by observing that, whereas God the Father is One and 'absolutely simply One', Christ the Logos is 'One through All' and 'One as All' (1.20.119). Christ is said to be 'the first and the last' in Revelation;[115] this confirms that Origen had in mind the previous passage by Clement, likewise referring to Rev. 22.13. Christ is the first, the last, and all that is in between, as Christ-Logos is 'all things'. This is also why Origen applies to Christ the concept of God as 'all in all' in the *eschaton*.[116] The dialectic between unity and multiplicity is clear in this initial section of Origen's *Commentary on John*, where he describes Christ as one, and yet having many *epinoiai*, which he lists and discusses: Christ-Logos-Wisdom is one, but also 'a multitude of goods'.

[109]*Strom.*, 4.25.156.1, examined in my 'The Logos/Nous One-Many between "Pagan" and Christian Platonism', *SP* 102 (2020): 175–204.

[110]See my 'Divine Power in Origen of Alexandria', in *Divine Powers in Late Antiquity*, eds Anna Marmodoro and Irini Fotini Viltanioti (Oxford: Oxford University Press, 2017), pp. 177–98.

[111]*Strom.*, 4.25.156.2; my 'Harmony between *arkhē* and *telos* in Patristic Platonism', *IJPT* 7 (2013): 1–49.

[112]Rev. 1.8; 22.13.

[113]*Strom.*, 4.25.157.1.

[114]This dialogue is present at least behind *Commentary on John*, *First Principles* and *Against Celsus*.

[115]*Com.Joh.*, 1.31.219.

[116]*Com.Joh.*, 1.31.225.

To indicate the dialectic of unity and multiplicity in the Logos and therefore the relation between the Logos and the Ideas-Logoi-paradigms of all creatures, in *C.Io.* 1.19.114-115 Origen uses the metaphor of the project in the mind of the architect (employed by Philo):

> A house or a ship are built according to architectonic models, so that one can say that the principle of the house or of the ship consists in the *paradigms and logoi that are found in the craftsman*. In the same way, I think, all things were made according to the *logoi of the future realities that God had already manifested beforehand in Wisdom*. It is necessary to maintain that God founded, so to say, a living Wisdom, and handed it the task of transmitting the structure and the forms, and, to my mind, also the substances, from the archetypes contained in it to beings and matter.

The living Wisdom of God, Christ-Logos, contains all the archetypes that are the paradigms of all creation. In *Com.Joh.* 1.34.39.243, Origen explains that the divine Logos, albeit being one, consists in many concepts/objects of contemplation/plans (θεωρήματα), which contain the *logoi* of all beings.

The *logoi* existed in God's Logos-Wisdom *ab aeterno*, before their creation as substances;[117] this theory is presented by Origen as a middle way between the coeternity of creatures with God and the notion of their creation in time, before which God was idle (a naïve idea of demiurgic creation). Origen claims in *Princ.* 1.2.2 that the Son-Logos-Wisdom contained in itself *ab aeterno* the 'principles, reasons, and forms' of the whole creation (*initia*, *rationes* and *species* in Rufinus' version). These are the Ideas in which, according to the Platonic category of 'participation', every existing being participates. For example, Christ-Logos is Justice itself, and every just creature is such insofar as it participates in Christ qua Idea of Justice: 'Our Saviour does not participate in Justice, but, being Justice itself [the Form/Idea of Justice], is participated in by the just.'[118] This depends on the Son's coeternity with the Father, a point that Origen supported vigorously.[119]

ORIGEN

Origen († *c*.255/6), perhaps the greatest Christian exegete and the first systematic theologian of the church, called by Pamphilus 'teacher of the Church', was still regarded as a venerated teacher by Rufinus, his admirer and translator. When Atarbius visited the Palestinian monasteries with anti-Origenian aims, Rufinus refused to disavow Origen – unlike Jerome – affirming: 'I neither accuse nor change my teachers,'[120] meaning Origen.

---

[117]*Princ.*, 1.4.5.
[118]*Cels.*, 6.64.
[119]See Ilaria L. E. Ramelli, 'Origen's Anti-Subordinationism and Its Heritage in the Nicene and Cappadocian Line', *VChr* 65 (2011): 21–49; 'Alexander of Aphrodisias', *PhilAnt* 13 (2013): 1–49; 'Sources and Reception of Dynamic Unity in Middle and Neoplatonism', *JBR* 7 (2020): 31–66.
[120]*Magistros meos nec accuso nec muto* (according to Jerome *Contra Rufinum*, 3.18).

Origen provided Christianity with a philosophico-theological foundation. He might have been the same as Origen the Neoplatonist (of whom Porphyry, Hierocles and Proclus speak)[121] as a close examination of all sources and a careful investigation of Origen's philosophical formation, readings and works suggest. His extensive reading of Plato, Numenius and other Middle Platonists/Neopythagoreans is similar to that of Plotinus.[122] His thought was informed by philosophy: Plato, Platonism, Stoicism and Aristotelianism.[123] Like Plotinus, he was a disciple of Ammonius Saccas, the Socrates of Neoplatonism. In his letters and works, Origen defended his identity of Christian philosopher, no less Christian for being a philosopher and no less of a philosopher for being Christian.

Origen was, like Clement, a teacher. His formation was sponsored by a patroness; he taught (as Stoics, Cynics, Pythagoreans and Platonists did) both men and women, and both Christians and 'pagans'. The instruction was delivered at the levels of liberal arts, philosophy and finally theology. Eusebius testifies that Origen was admired even among 'pagan' philosophers (*HE* 6.18). His school in Alexandria, then Caesarea, was the most important of the Christian institutions of his day.[124] Alexandria was a major cultural hub in Hellenistic, imperial and late antiquity. In Origen's time, it was home to 'Gnostic' and other Christian groups, and the cradle of Neoplatonism thanks to the school of Ammonius; it hosted a world-renowned library, which contained copies of virtually all Greek books from Homer to Roman imperial times, including the Septuagint. Copies of what became the New Testament, too, were possibly kept there. Jerome expressly described the library of Pamphilus, which consisted mainly in the Bible and in Origen's oeuvre, as emulating the Library of Alexandria, and depicted Origen's works as those of a genius.[125]

On First Principles (Περὶ ἀρχῶν) is Origen's philosophico-theological masterpiece, where he investigates God the Trinity, creation, philosophy of history, eschatology and exegesis, the first systematic work of Christian philosophical theology, equalled only by Eriugena's *Periphyseon*, which was inspired by Origen's *First Principles*,[126] and later, in Scholasticism, by Thomas Aquinas's *Summa Theologiae*.

Origen's exegetical works consist of:

---

[121]Discussion, also with literature, in 'Origen, Patristic Philosophy', 'Origen the Christian Middle/ Neoplatonist', *JECH* 1 (2011): 98–130; 'Origen and the Platonic Tradition', *Religions* 8, no. 2 (2017): 21; a work in preparation.

[122]See my 'Origen, Patristic Philosophy' and 'Autobiographical Self-Fashioning in Origen', in *Self, Self-Fashioning and Individuality in Late Antiquity*, eds Maren Niehoff and Joshua Levinson (Tübingen: Mohr Siebeck, 2019), pp. 273–92.

[123]My 'Alexander of Aphrodisias'; 'Origen's Critical Reception of Aristotle: Some Key Points and Aftermath in Christian Platonism', in *Aristotle in Byzantium*, ed. Mikonja Knežević (Alhambra, CA: Sebastian Press, 2020), pp. 1–43.

[124]On these: Christoph Markschies, *Christian Theology and Its Institutions in the Early Roman Empire* (Waco: Baylor, 2015); Josef Lössl, 'Theology as Academic Discourse', *JLARC* 10 (2016): 38–72, 64–71 on Origen's school.

[125]*Letter 34 to Marcella*, quoted by Rufinus, *Apologia contra Hieronymum*, 2.21.

[126]See my 'Origen, Patristic Philosophy'.

- commentaries on most biblical books, for the school;
- homilies, for church (he was a presbyter);[127]
- and scholia on specific, difficult scriptural points.

Unlike Clement, who wrote in a classicizing, highly rhetorical Greek language, Origen mostly used technical Koine Greek[128] and traditional forms of Greek scholarship, such as the critical edition (*Hexapla*), the scholarly treatise (*First Principles*, where he applied the philosophical genre περὶ ἀρχῶν[129]), and the scholarly commentary: he applied it to Scripture for the first time in a systematic way.[130] Origen's commentaries display special attention to philosophico-theological, philological and literary aspects of the texts commented on; for instance, in his *Commentary on the Song of Songs* he launches into a rhetorical and performance analysis. Jerome later translated and imitated Origen's scriptural commentaries, rich in grammatical and literary analysis, and also remarked upon the literary quality of various texts.

Against Celsus, a work of his advanced maturity, defends Christianity against a 'pagan' Middle Platonist, and maintains that philosophy is a search for truth that ennobles those who practice it (*Cels.* 7.6). Other works include *On Prayer* and *Exhortation to Martyrdom*. His (possibly spiritual) father Leonidas was a martyr, and Origen was a martyr or a confessor, who died after tortures. Eusebius speaks of the torments that Origen, already aged, endured under Decius (*HE* 6.39.5).

Origen's impact on subsequent exegesis and theology is staggering; his ideas enjoyed a wide reception in philosophy and theology, including in Syriac Christianity.[131] Origen built a grand theory of God's creation of rational beings, matter and the world, freewill (on which he insisted against 'Gnostic' predestinationism) in his theology of freedom,[132] fall and universal restoration or apokatastasis.[133] (Impressive parallels about the defence of freewill and apokatastasis have been detected between Origen and the Syriac philosophical theologian Bardaisan; they are the first supporters of apokatastasis within the context of the defence of freewill helped by divine grace.)[134] Apokatastasis depends on each creature's voluntary adhesion to God, the Good, and on Christ's incarnation and salvific cross and his being Logos,

---

[127]On their educative value, see for example John Solheid, 'Scripture and Christian Formation in Origen's Fourth Homily on Psalm 77(78)', *JECS* 27, no. 3 (2019): 417–42.

[128]Klaas Bentein, 'The Greek of the Fathers', in *The Wiley-Blackwell Companion to Patristics*, ed. Ken Parry (Oxford: Wiley-Blackwell, 2015), pp. 456–70, 460.

[129]Ramelli, 'Origen, Patristic Philosophy'; further work ongoing.

[130]Bernhard Neuschäfer, *Origenes als Philologe* (Basel: Reinhard, 1987).

[131]See my 'The Reception of Origen's Ideas in Western Theological and Philosophical Traditions', main lecture at *Origeniana Undecima*, ed. Anders-Christian Jacobsen (Leuven: Peeters, 2016), pp. 443–67; a work in progress on apokatastasis from ancient to late antique and medieval thought.

[132]Christian Hengstermann, *Origenes und der Ursprung der Freiheitsmetaphysik* (Münster: Aschendorff, 2015); Ramelli, *Social Justice*, pp. 172–211; an issue of *Modern Theology* in the works includes a chapter on Origen's theology of freedom.

[133]Ilaria L. E. Ramelli, 'Origen and Apokatastasis', in *Origeniana Decima*, ed. Henryk Pietras (Leuven: Peeters, 2011), pp. 649–70; *Apokatastasis*, pp. 137–215.

[134]See my 'Origen, Bardaisan, and the Origin'; 'Bardaisan . . . a Middle Platonic Context?'.

Physician and Teacher. This brings in a pedagogical conception of God already stressed by Clement. To come to perfection, a rational creature may need aeons; at the end of all aeons, apokatastasis will take place.[135] Then all will be perfected in love, and there will be no new fall from perfection, because 'love never falls'.[136] The theory of apokatastasis involves the restoration and return of fallen beings to their original condition and their adhesion to the supreme Good.

Origen's oeuvre exerted an enormous impact also on 'pagan' philosophy. Origen's footprint on Platonism is arguably more remarkable than usually assumed, for example with respect to the notion of hypostasis as individual substance, first bodies and apokatastasis.[137] Thus, a reassessment of his thought enables a reassessment of most patristic philosophical theology and exegesis, and even of ancient philosophy.[138] Origen was no pragmatist eclectic,[139] but aimed at the construction of an 'orthodox' Christian Platonism, against 'heresies' (Marcionism, 'Gnosticism', Monarchianism, proto-'Arianism'), against non-Platonist, wrong philosophies (such as Epicureanism) and against 'pagan' Platonism, rather than against Plato. Origen countered, not Platonism, but 'pagan' Platonism and 'Gnostic' Platonism,[140] because he intended to build an 'orthodox' Christian Platonism ('orthodox' in emic terms, as Origen speaks of 'heretics' and 'orthodox'; 'Christian Platonism' in etic terms). Of course, he rejected doctrines such as metensomatosis, which was incompatible with scripture and was supported by Plato himself in a mythical form.

Origen was a Christian philosopher, which his enemies considered to be a contradiction in terms. In a letter, Origen felt the need to defend himself for his interest in philosophy (ap. Eus. *HE* 6.19.12-14) because of the accusations levelled against him. He claims that, while he was studying Scripture, the Word of God, he was approached by heretics, philosophers and experts in 'Hellenic disciplines', and thus he had 'to examine both the heretics' opinions and what the philosophers

---

[135]Panayiotis Tzamalikos, *Origen: Philosophy of History and Eschatology* (Leiden: E.J. Brill, 2007); my 'Αἰώνιος and αἰών'; *Tempo ed eternità in età antica e patristica* (Assisi: Cittadella, 2015); 'Time and Eternity'.

[136]See my *Apokatastasis*, pp. 170–2; and 'Reception of Paul in Origen'.

[137]For Origen's notion of hypostasis and its influence on Porphyry's reading of Plotinus, see my 'Origen, Greek Philosophy, and the Birth of the Trinitarian Meaning of Hypostasis', *HTR* 105 (2012): 302–50; for the influence of Origen's theories of apokatastasis and first bodies on Proclus and later Neoplatonism, see my 'Proclus and Christian Neoplatonism', in *The Ways of Byzantine Philosophy*, ed. Mikonja Knežević (Alhambra, CA: Sebastian, 2015), pp. 37–70; further investigation will be devoted to both apokatastasis and the soul–body relation in late Platonism.

[138]Some suggestions are found, for example, in my 'Origen and the Platonic Tradition', and my conclusions to a book: 'The Study of Late Ancient Philosophy: Philosophy and Religion "Pagan" and Christian Platonism', in *Lovers of the Soul and Lovers of the Body: Philosophical and Religious Perspectives in Late Antiquity*, eds Svetla S. Griffin and Ilaria L. E. Ramelli (Cambridge, MA: Harvard University, 2021), pp. 397–403. Potential implications can be drawn in a fuller form.

[139]On the inadequacy of the label of eclecticism for early Christian philosophy, see also Troels Engberg-Pedersen, 'Introduction: A Historiographical Essay', in *From Stoicism to Platonism*, ed. Idem (Cambridge: Cambridge University Press, 2017), pp. 1–26.

[140]*Refutatio*, 6.21-22; 6.29; 6.37, preface.

claimed to say concerning the truth'. For the sake of self-defence, he adduces, as said earlier in the section 'Clement', the examples of Pantaenus and Heraclas, both Christian philosophers, whom he claims to be simply imitating. Pantaenus, Origen remarks in his letter, had an excellent preparation in philosophy and Greek disciplines, and Heraclas, 'who now sits among the presbyters of Alexandria', was first met by Origen 'at the school of the professor of philosophy' in Alexandria – probably Ammonius Saccas. Heraclas had been studying philosophy with Ammonius for five years before Origen himself began to attend Ammonius' classes. Heraclas was not only a Christian philosopher, but also dressed as a philosopher, and was still wearing philosophical garb and studying 'the books of the Greeks' when Origen wrote his letter of self-defence. Origen claimed there that it was perfectly possible to be a Christian philosopher, like Pantaenus and Heraclas: no less Christian qua philosopher, no less of a philosopher qua Christian.

Origen's adversaries were both Christians who viewed Greek philosophy with suspicion and 'pagan' philosophers such as Celsus and Porphyry, who saw Christianity as a non-culture and did not admit of an allegorical philosophical interpretation of the Christian Scriptures. Origen's formation as well as teaching centred on philosophy, and his masterpiece Περὶ ἀρχῶν in its structure and genre was inspired not by earlier Christian works but by 'pagan' philosophical works Περὶ ἀρχῶν stemming from the same thinkers as those read at Ammonius' and Plotinus' schools.[141]

In *First Principles*, in the preface, Origen pointed out that issues not clarified by Scripture or the apostolic tradition needed to be investigated rationally. Doctrinally, Origen was deemed a defender of 'orthodoxy' to the point that he was identified with Adamantius in the *Dialogue of Adamantius on the Orthodox Faith in God*; was 'copied' by Gregory of Nyssa to defend orthodoxy against 'Arian' tendencies,[142] and all the manuscripts of Book 1 of the 'anti-heretical' *Refutation of All Heresies* or *Philosophoumena* ascribe this work to Origen. In Book 10, the author puts forward 'the logos of truth' (ὁ τῆς ἀληθείας λόγος, 10.4), which may possibly reveal a polemic against Celsus' *True Logos*, ἀληθὴς λόγος, which was thoroughly refuted by Origen in *Against Celsus*. Like Origen, the author of the *Refutation* thinks that Greek philosophers held better opinions, 'more reverent towards the divine', than the 'heretics' who deformed their doctrines (*Refutatio* 1, preface. 8-9).

But to claim *logos* for themselves, while they were accused or irrationality (see the chapter, in this book 'Why Were Christians Obsessed by Dogmas?'), Christians had to develop a theology of the Logos, which identified Christ with God's Logos. This operation, anticipated to some extent by Philo and Hellenistic Judaism, started from the Johannine Prologue[143] and was continued by Justin, most Valentinians,

---

[141]Analysis in my 'Origen, Patristic Philosophy'.

[142]As I argued in 'Anti-Subordinationism' and 'The Father in the Son, the Son in the Father in the Gospel of John: Sources and Reception of Dynamic Unity in Middle and Neoplatonism, "Pagan" and Christian', *Journal of the Bible and Its Reception* 7 (2020): 31–66.

[143]Argument in my 'The Logos in the Johannine Prologue and Its Philosophical Reception', in *The Johannine Prologue and Its Resonances*, eds Stanley Porter and Andrew Pitts (Leiden: E.J. Brill, forthcoming).

Clement and especially Origen, and then by patristic philosophers influenced by Origen. Thanks to Origen, who was respected by 'pagan' philosophers, Christianity could no longer be labelled 'irrational'.

Origen, who 'was a Platonist' and used 'Platonic ways of thinking about God and the soul . . . to give an intelligent account of his Christian beliefs',[144] made the most in the process of making Christianity a philosophy. He depicted Christianity as philosophy *tout court* (like Justin and Clement), and built it through philosophical structures, categories and arguments. Origen shows the necessity of this operation in *Cels.* 4.9, after mentioning the end of the world and universal judgement: 'The [Christian] philosopher [φιλοσοφοῦντα] will need to prove the theories [τὰ τοῦ λόγου κατασκευάζειν] by means of demonstrations [ἀποδείξεων] of all sorts, taken from the divine Scriptures and the consequentiality of rational arguments [τῆς ἐν τοῖς λόγοις ἀκολουθίας]'.

This is what Origen did, basing his arguments on biblical foundations and philosophical reasoning. He maintained that Christianity without philosophy, based only on authority (αὐτὸς ἔφα), is for the 'simple-minded masses'. For the few – the philosophically minded – being Christian depends 'on a rigorous examination of the evidence' (βεβασανισμένως ἐξετασμένη, *Cels.* 3.38). Thus, Christianity for them was fully philosophy. Origen insists, in response to his opponents, that Christians cannot be separated from Christ by rational argument (*Cels.* pref. 3-4). Rational argument (philosophy) is not detrimental to Christians, against what Christians suspicious of philosophy intimated – they often claimed that philosophy brought about 'heresies'. According to Origen, Christians, who follow Christ-Logos, cannot do anything irrational: 'heresy' and what is opposite to Christ-Logos is irrational; Christianity accords with 'common notions', the Stoic *koinai ennoiai* (*Cels.* 4.4; 3.40; cf.1.4). One should not just believe, but provide reasons for belief: Origen urged the simple to merely believe, but provided the intelligent with 'rational arguments by questions and answers' (*Cels.* 6.10, quoting Plato's *Seventh Letter* 344B). Origen intended to construct a Christian philosophy for the philosophically demanding elites, as well as to spread the Christian faith among the 'simple'.

Philosophy is beneficial to life; no one who tries to act rightly can hate philosophy, not even among Christians; a good philosopher explores several schools of thought and follows the most convincing one (*Cels.* 3.12-13). This is what Justin and Clement did, before turning to Christian Platonism. Against charges that Christianity is for ignorant people, Origen declares:

- that Scripture rather wants people to be wise (*Cels.* 3.45);
- that he endeavoured to call philosophers to Christianity and blessedness (*Cels.* 3.57);

---

[144]Birger Pearson, 'Egypt', in *The Cambridge History of Christianity* 1, eds Margaret Mitchell and Frances Young (Cambridge: Cambridge University Press, 2006), pp. 331–50, 343; Henry Chadwick, *Early Christian Thought and the Classical Tradition* (Oxford: Clarendon, 1966), p. 123: 'Platonism was inside [Origen] *malgré lui*. I am skeptical only about 'malgré lui', all the more so if he was, as mentioned, a disciple of the 'Socrates of Neoplatonism', Ammonius Saccas, together with Plotinus.

- that education, study and intelligence are not a hindrance, but a help to know God (*Cels.* 3.49), since human *logos* has its principle (ἀρχή) in God's Logos, the Son. Therefore, no *logikon* can be alien to the Divinity (*Cels.* 4.25),[145] although some Christians have 'mere faith', others have *logos* and explore the Bible's meanings (*Cels.* 3.33);

- and that, if everyone could 'devote all their time to philosophy', this would be ideal; however, 'very few are keen on rational argument': hence the necessity of faith.[146]

Thus, 'it is the task of those who teach the true doctrines to help as many people as possible, and as far as it is in their power to win everyone over to the truth by their love of humanity – not only the intelligent, but also the obtuse' (*Cels.* 6.1). Origen would have been happy if all Christians had been philosophers and had practiced philosophy all the time through the exercise of rational argumentation. This is what he did in philosophical theology, exegesis, teaching, preaching and asceticism. He also passed on this ideal to a disciple, who in *Pan.* 79 agrees with Origen's words, which he reports, that 'perfect piety towards the Master of the Cosmos is impossible without philosophizing'. Thus, only Christian philosophers can practice perfect piety towards God. Origen opposed the binary between Greek philosophy and Christian faith, arguing that perfect Christianity was philosophy, and that for most philosophers adherence to a particular school was a matter of faith (*Cels.* 1.10). Origen was making the same point as Galen did in *Ord.libr.* 1. What Origen attacked is 'pagan' religion as polytheistic mythology (*Cels.* 1.23), not philosophy or henotheistic philosophical theology, on which he built. When Paul spoke against human wisdom (1 Cor. 1.18ff.), Origen claims that he was not attacking all philosophy but only materialistic philosophy, teaching that 'all ultimate realities are corporeal' (*Cels.* 3.47).

Even in his homilies, delivered before a non-philosophical public and numbering over 1,000 (Jerome, *Ep.* 84.8), Origen emphasises that philosophy has reached the truth in many cases and has many points of contact with Scripture and Christian doctrine. He acknowledges the philosophers' temperance and wisdom in *Hom. Jer.* 5.4. And in *Hom. Gen.* 14.3 Origen admits that 'the learned of this world thanks to the study of philosophy were able to grasp many truths': for instance,

> many philosophers write that God is one and created everything. In this respect they agree with God's Law. Some also add that God both made and governs all things by means of his Logos, and it is God's Logos that regulates all things. In this respect they write things that agree not only with the Law, but also with the Gospel. Moral and natural philosophy in almost all regards teaches the same as Christianity. It only disagrees when it claims that matter is coeternal with God,

---

[145]Indeed, all rational creatures are *oikeioi* or familiar with God, the opposite of alienated or *allotrioi*, being creatures of God and *logika* as Christ is Logos: see my 'The Stoic Doctrine of Oikeiosis and Its Transformation in Christian Platonism', *Apeiron* 47 (2014): 116–40.
[146]*Cels.*, 1.9. Cf. 8.22: 'the multitude of believers have not made such progress'.

or when it denies that God takes care of mortals, but limits divine providence to the superlunar realm. Philosophers disagree with us also when they have the lives of those who are born depend on the courses of stars, and when they claim that this world is eternal and is not to be closed up by any end.

The coeternity of matter with God and the eternity of the world were tenets of most Greek philosophical schools; the lack of providence in the sublunar sphere was an Aristotelian theory, which saw this sphere influenced by the stars,[147] and astral determinism was Stoic and 'Gnostic'. No specifically Platonic doctrine is mentioned here among those which collide with Christian teaching: Platonic doctrines are rather listed among those which *agree* with Christian tenets, particularly the 'Middle-Platonic' theory of the divine Logos as creator, besides more generic 'henotheism'. The former, Origen declares, is in accord not only with the Old Testament but also with the New: already the Johannine Prologue, extensively commented on by Origen (and by the 'pagan' Platonist Amelius), identified the Logos with Christ, explicitly characterized as creator.

Origen, in other passages as well, criticized false philosophical doctrines in Stoicism, Aristotelianism and Epicureanism, but, remarkably, *not in Platonism*. Origen supplied a philosophical foundation (mainly Platonic, with elements from Aristotelian, Stoicism etc.) to Christian tenets, including Christology, Trinitarian theology, creation, resurrection, restoration. He built, as suggested, an 'orthodox' Christian Platonism against 'pagan' and 'Gnostic' Platonisms, pantheistic Stoicism and 'atheistic' Epicureanism and Aristotelianism: Origen, like Porphyry,[148] included the philosophers who denied divine providence among the 'atheists'.

Origen studied, and had his best disciples' study, all philosophies apart from the atheistic ones (Gregory, *Pan*. 13-14) and 'became celebrated as a great philosopher even among the Greeks',[149] but mostly he followed Platonic tenets and even in *Against Celsus* he praised Plato. If Aristotle criticized Plato's doctrine of the Ideas and the soul's immortality, this is not because Plato was wrong: 'Plato was right', but Aristotle became ungrateful to his master.[150] References to Plato in Clement, known to Origen, and Eusebius, Origen's follower, are the most numerous after those to Scripture: Plato is the 'friend of truth' (*Strom*. 5.66.3), 'admirable/wonderful/amazing' (*Praep.Ev*. 11.21.7), Eusebius' 'best friend among the Greeks': Plato's thoughts are 'so dear and close' to those of Eusebius (*PE* 13.8). Eusebius, like Origen, praised Plato and criticized contemporary 'pagan' Platonists.

Origen's Platonism is *Christian*. For him, as for Clement, Plato was inspired by Scripture or Christ-Logos (one of whose 'incarnations' is Scripture). This is clear

---

[147]See Gad Freudenthal, 'The Astrologisation of the Aristotelian Cosmos', in *New Perspectives on Aristotle's De Coelo*, eds A. C. Bowen and Christian Wildberg (Leiden: E.J. Brill, 2009), pp. 239–81.

[148]'The atheists, who have abandoned ordinary human common sense and claim that *God* or *providence* do not exist': Gregory Thaumaturgus, *Pan*., 13; Origen, *PEuch*., 5.1; *Cels*., 8.38; Porphyry, *Commentary on the Timaeus*. F28 Sodano.

[149]Eusebius, *HE*., 6.18.

[150]*Cels*., 2.12.

from *C.Cant.* prol. 3.2-4, where Origen, after speaking of the division of philosophy into ethics, physics, epoptics and logic, posits epoptics (theology) as the summit of philosophy: theology is part and parcel of philosophy and cannot be studied without philosophical foundations. Then Origen states that Greek philosophers drew inspiration from Solomon's wisdom: hence the inevitable affinity between Scripture's and Plato's teachings. Origen found in the Bible many philosophical doctrines, primarily Platonic. The theory of apokatastasis is an excellent example: most of its premises are based on Scripture and Platonism,[151] but Origen adduces Scripture to buttress it, and corrects Plato on this point concerning some 'incurable' souls by having recourse to the (biblical) tenet of the omnipotence of God-Logos, Creator and Physician: 'Nothing is impossible for the Omnipotent, no being is incurable for the One who created it.' This supports universal apokatastasis.[152]

Origen often praised Plato for his metaphysics, dialectics, ethics, use of myths (which Origen appreciated methodologically and epistemologically)[153] and more. Plato 'taught such profound philosophy about the highest Good'.[154] In *Against Celsus*, aimed at 'pagans' and people 'weak in faith' (pr. 6), Origen is concerned with philosophical issues and is more eristic with Plato as interpreted by 'pagan' Platonists than with Plato himself. Christian Platonism does not oppose, but completes Plato, as Jesus fulfilled the Law instead of abolishing it; Origen, having posited God's incorruptibility and indivisibility as a Platonic principle against Epicurean and Stoic materialistic views of God, is quick to assure that God's 'in-humanation' did not entail a change from good to bad, since it was not a consequence of evil, as in a soul's fall, but of love.[155]

Like Clement, who adduced many parallels between Greek philosophy and Scripture, Origen explicitly states that Plato taught the same truths as the Bible,[156] perhaps because he came into contact with the 'Jewish philosophy', and ranks Plato as the best of philosophers, the closest to the scriptural doctrine (*Cels.* 1.10). Origen deeply respects Plato's style and noble philosophy,[157] appreciates Plato's criticism of 'pagan' mythology as unworthy of the divinities,[158] and agrees with Celsus that Plato's Socrates taught the same as Jesus did about turning one's cheek to offenders.[159] Origen explicitly agrees with Plato on the inexpressibility of the supreme Good in the Seventh Letter, and praises Plato as inspired by God.[160] Like most Neoplatonists,[161] Origen identifies Plato's Good with God, and insists that all

---

[151]As I argued in *Apokatastasis*.
[152]*Princ.*, 3.6.5.
[153]See my 'Philosophical Stance of Allegory' and 'Esoteric Interpretations of Scripture'.
[154]*Cels.*, 6.56.
[155]*Cels.*, 4.14-15.
[156]*Cels.*, 4.39 etc.
[157]*Cels.*, 6.2 and elsewhere.
[158]*Cels.*, 4.48, with reference to *Philb.*, 12B.
[159]*Cels.*, 7.58 and 61, with reference to *Cri.* 49BE.
[160]*Cels.*, 6.3.
[161]Lloyd Gerson, 'From Plato's Good to Platonic God', *IJPT* 2 (2008): 93–112.

good ideas in philosophy depend on inspiration by the Logos.[162] Origen applied Greek philosophy to Christian theology and exegesis in many ways. For instance, he imported the allegorical technique and the 'zetetic', heuristic method from philosophy to Christian exegesis and theology. Philo was the model for the transfer of allegoresis to biblical exegesis; the 'zetetic' method was shared by Plotinus.[163] Origen programmatically declares it in *Cels.* 1.11: a believer who uses reason/ argument (λόγῳ) in theology discovers proofs (ἀπόδειξις) 'through a thorough investigation' (τοῦ πάνυ ζητεῖν).

Origen's thought spanned most areas of philosophy, metaphysics, protology, anthropology, exegesis, ethics and so on. Origen's philosophical anthropology (and cosmology) differed from misrepresentations from the Origenistic controversy onwards. His real ideas concerning bodies, degrees of corporeality, souls, intellectual beings, the world, creation and God must be examined also in comparison with contemporary Platonism. It is pivotal to consider that Origen employed '(in) corporeal' and '(im)material' in a relative sense. Origen criticized metensomatosis and supported ensomatosis, the embodiment of soul from the beginning, without transmigrations.[164] Contrary to what is regularly assumed, Nyssen arguably did not attack Origen's anthropology.[165]

Origen is probably the first professional scholar of Christian Scripture. He polemicized against some 'pagan' intellectuals about the legitimacy of the allegoresis of Scripture and applied allegoresis to Scripture as a philosophical task (as it happened in Stoicism and 'Middle Platonism', but on other authoritative texts). This relates to the notion of Scripture as an embodiment of Christ-Logos.[166] Structural continuities must be pointed out between Origen and the Stoic allegorical tradition, as well as the struggle with Middle-Platonic allegorists for the definition of which authoritative traditions were to be allegorized. Origen's exegesis was philosophical and philosophy at that time was focusing more and more on commentaries, while Christian commentaries began to be produced in Origen's time. Commentaries in imperial and late antiquity became the predominant form of academic engagement with ancient, authoritative texts.[167] Even Plotinus' *Enneads*, which are formally

---

[162]*Cant.*, prol. 3.18-20.

[163]See my 'Philosophical Allegoresis of Scripture in Philo and Its Legacy', *StPhiloA* 20 (2008): 55–99.

[164]As I argue in 'Origen', in *A History of Mind and Body in Late Antiquity*, ed. Anna Marmodoro (Cambridge: Cambridge University Press, 2018), pp. 245–66; 'Origen on the Unity of Soul and Body in the Earthly Life and Afterwards', in *The Unity of Soul and Body in the Earthly Life and After*, eds Jörg Ulrich et al. (Leiden: E.J. Brill, 2021), pp. 38–77.

[165]As I argued in 'Gregory of Nyssa's Purported Criticism of Origen's Purported Doctrine of the Preexistence of Souls', in Griffin and Ramelli (eds), *Lovers of the Soul*, 397-40.

[166]See my 'Origen's Philosophical Exegesis', *SP* 103 (2021): 13–58.

[167]Philippe Hoffmann, 'What Was Commentary in Late Antiquity?' in *A Companion to Ancient Philosophy*, ed. Mary-Louise Gill (London: Wiley-Blackwell, 2006), pp. 597–622; my '"Revelation" for Christians and "Pagans" and their Philosophical Allegoresis', in *An Open Crossroad: Divination in Later Antiquity* (Cambridge: Cambridge University Press, forthcoming).

no commentary, were presented by him as an exegesis of Plato's dialogues.[168] Origen's *First Principles* is no formal commentary, but is structured as chunks of biblical commentaries throughout. The binary between (1) 'pagan' commentaries on poets, rhetoric and philosophy and (2) Christian commentaries of Scripture was in fact blurred:[169] 'pagan' philosophers such as Numenius and Amelius commented on Scripture, and Christians such as Origen and (if Christian) Calcidius on Plato. Scriptural allegoresis was a heritage of Philo, although 'pagan' Platonists such as Celsus and Porphyry failed – or refused – to recognize this, while Origen acknowledged his debt to Jewish Hellenistic allegorists.[170] Origen's attitude towards Jewish exegesis was less hostile than generally represented.[171] Pivotal instances of Origen's creative reception and transformation of Greek philosophy still have to be taken into account, such as the structure of *First Principles*, the cases of *hypostasis* and *oikeiōsis*, Atticus' influence on Origen, Origen's possible influence on 'pagan' Neoplatonism, the links with Alexander of Aphrodisias, let alone those with Ammonius Saccas, Plotinus, Amelius, Porphyry and so on.

Origen's 'anti-subordinationism' is theologically pivotal. As indicated in my chapter, in this volume, 'Why Were the Christians Obsessed by Dogmas?', Origen was arguably the (direct or indirect) inspirer of the Nicene formula of the Son's consubstantiality and coeternity with the Father (Nicaea), and of the Cappadocians' Trinitarian formula 'one common essence, three individual substances' (Constantinople), besides reflecting on the Theotokos epithet (Ephesus), and anticipating the Christological doctrine of Chalcedon. Origen 'imported' the formula 'there was a/no time when X was not' ([οὐκ] ἦν ποτε ὅτε οὐκ ἦν) from imperial Greek philosophical cosmological debates into Christology, where it became a catchphrase in the 'Arian' controversy.[172] Origen's true philosophy was received in the *Dialogue of Adamantius*[173] and absorbed by the Cappadocians, especially Nyssen. Gregory deeply understood and developed Origen's theology – in an 'orthodox', Nicene-Constantinopolitan way.

Remarkable aspects of Origen's ethical thought still need to be investigated (besides his theology of freedom, which has been examined recently). Origen transformed motifs of Greek moral philosophy, particularly Stoic ethics (often reproducing its very terminology), which was also well known to Plotinus, to the point that Porphyry even points out explicitly Stoic doctrines in Plotinus; some Aristotelian ethics, in the conviction that the Peripatetic was the most exact philosophical school about 'human goods' (probably in opposition to divine goods); and Platonic ethics,

---

[168]Plotinus is Plato's ἐξηγητής in Treatise 10(5.1)8, Περὶ τῶν τριῶν ἀρχικῶν ὑποστάσεων, probably entitled after Origen by Porphyry according to Ramelli, 'Hypostasis'.
[169]As I argue in 'Secular and Christian Commentaries in Late Antiquity', in *The Cambridge History of Later Latin Literature* (Cambridge: Cambridge University Press, forthcoming).
[170]See my 'Philosophical Stance of Allegory' and 'Philo as Origen's Declared Model'.
[171]As I argue in 'Origen's Philosophical Exegesis'.
[172]See my 'Alexander'.
[173]'The *Dialogue of Adamantius*: A Document of Origen's Thought?' 'The *Dialogue of Adamantius*: Preparing the Critical Edition and a Reappraisal'.

including the core ideal of the ascent towards the divine. This reception was made in light of Christianity, especially the Christian notion of grace, and humility, a virtue of Origen's and Christianity, but not of classical antiquity.[174] In this connection, one must also examine Origen's understanding of the church (and women's ministry therein[175]) and the Christian notions of Christ-Logos as subsuming all humanity, all *logika*, all creatures and all virtues, from Wisdom to Justice (a concept in turn based on the Platonic Logos/Nous One-Many), and of grace. This is applied, for example, to the theology of suffering, which finds its meaning in the theology of the Cross – the idea that suffering unjustly is a participation in Christ's Cross.[176] I have argued for Origen's rich Christian philosophical elaboration of the Middle-Platonic notion of the Logos as One-Many-All and as the seat of all Ideas,[177] including those of all virtues (Plato's Virtue-Forms): Justice, Truth and so on. Already the Middle Platonist Alcinous argued that the Stoic Logos – well known to Origen, and which had replaced Plato's Demiurge – was philosophically useful only within Platonism.[178] Origen seems to have thought that it was philosophico-theologically useful only within *Christian* Platonism. This had absorbed a great deal not only of the Stoic and the Platonic Logos, but also of the Philonic Logos and the Johannine Logos, the last of which had become human. This attracted the attention of 'pagan' Neoplatonists such as Amelius, who commented on John's Prologue, probably having Origen's *Commentary on John* in mind.[179]

Origen, who absorbed Stoic ethics, did not fight for the abolition of slavery as Nyssen to some extent did (although he was inspired by Origen in many of its premises).[180] But Origen's notion of grace, largely based on Paul, his ethically normative nature of the *telos*, and Platonic and Christian asceticism influenced respectively Origen's theology of the Cross, and his positions on richness as tantamount to theft, gender 'equality' in Christ, and women's spiritual authority, grounded in the Platonist notion of transcendence and in Paul (Gal. 3.28).[181]

Origen always fought what he perceived as 'Gnostic' (Valentinian) predestinationism and determinism[182] until his late ('Munich') homilies. He built his grand theory of rational creatures' creation, fall and apokatastasis against 'Gnostic' theories, attractive for intellectually demanding people. Ambrose, whom Origen later converted to the 'orthodox' faith, adhered to Valentinianism out of

---

[174]For example, my 'Humility', in *Encyclopedia of Ancient Christianity*, ed. Angelo Di Berardino, vol. 2 (Downers Grove, IL: InterVarsity, 2014), pp. 298–302.

[175]See here the chapter on 'What To Do With Women in Churches?'.

[176]See my 'Disability in Bardaisan and Origen', in *Gestörte Lektüre*, ed. Markus Schiefer Ferrari (Stuttgart: Kohlhammer, 2012), pp. 141–59, and the chapter by Monica Tobon in this volume.

[177]'The Logos/Nous One-Many' (see above).

[178]Franco Trabattoni, '*Logos* and *noēsis* in Alcinous, *Didaskalikos* 4', Ph 60 (2016): 60–81, 79.

[179]My 'Revelation'.

[180]Analysis in my: *Social Justice*, chs. 5–6. For the connection between Origen and Gregory in this respect, see n. 132.

[181]See my 'Gal 3.28 and Aristotelian (and Jewish) Categories of Inferiority', E 55 (2019): 275–310.

[182]As argued in my: *Apokatastasis*, pp. 773–815.

disgust for the 'irrational and vulgar faith' of the 'simple';[183] such 'heterodox' (ἑτεροδόξων), 'gluttonous souls' (λίχνοι), if they lack the salvific food, greedily approach 'prohibited foods',[184] symbolising 'heresies'. This metaphor appears again in Origen's late Munich homilies: in his youth, he remembers, heresies flourished, attracting many 'gluttons' (λίχνοι), 'hungry for Christ's teaching', who lacked 'adequate teachers in the Church'; thus, they became 'heretics'.[185] Consequently, it was necessary to provide the 'orthodox' faith with philosophical foundations. By applying philosophy to biblical exegesis and theology, Origen could win for the Church the rich Valentinian Ambrose and the most learned, culturally demanding and philosophically educated people.

Origen as a Christian philosopher (Platonist) was criticized, from inside the church and outside, during his life and afterward. Against such criticism Origen wrote the above-mentioned letter of self-defence and, after his death, Pamphilus, Eusebius, Nyssen and others defended his works and legacy. The presupposition of the incompatibility between Christianity and philosophy is still at work in modern theories of the 'Hellenization of Christianity'.[186] Hence also the purported necessity of distinguishing 'Origen the Platonist' from 'Origen the Christian'.

Origen was regarded as both interesting and problematic by Platonists and Christians alike. Porphyry recognized and respected Origen's knowledge of philosophical texts, but criticized his Christian practice and application of allegoresis to Hebrew texts – labelling this an 'absurdity' (ἀτοπία, F39). Dionysius, a Christian Platonist, criticized Porphyry, I suspect, claiming that 'uninitiated' deemed Scriptural allegoresis an 'outstanding absurdity' (ἀτοπίαν δεινήν, Letter 9). Here, as elsewhere, Dionysius was inspired by Origen and defended him, as Pamphilus, Eusebius, Didymus, Nyssen, Nazianzen, Rufinus, Socrates and others had done. In Origen's day, what it meant to be 'a Platonist' was still unclear[187] and not confined to 'pagan' institutional Platonism, as is intimated by Ammonius' debated identity, Heraclas' dressing as a philosopher while a presbyter, Origen himself, the Christians at Plotinus' school, Greek philosophers at Origen's school, Porphyry' study with Origen and Plotinus and more (down to Synesius' Neoplatonic beliefs while a bishop, Dionysius' ecclesiastical Neoplatonism and Eriugena' Christian Platonism).[188] Origen, Plotinus and Porphyry shared in 'internal quarrels about Platonism's true nature'[189] and endeavoured to appropriate Ammonius' legacy. Origen stands out as an inspired teacher and a gigantic intellectual figure primarily in the history not only of Christianity, theology, exegesis, but also in that of Platonism and philosophy.

---

[183]ἄλογος καὶ ἰδιωτικὴ πίστις.

[184]*Com.Joh.*, 5.8.

[185]*Hom.Ps.*, 77, fol. 233r.

[186]Argument in my 'Origen, Patristic Philosophy'; a work in preparation.

[187]Harold Tarrant, 'Platonism before Plotinus', in *Cambridge History of Philosophy in Late Antiquity*, ed. Lloyd Gerson (Cambridge: Cambridge University Press, 2010), vol. 1, pp. 63–99.

[188]See my: 'Origen and the Platonic Tradition'.

[189]Tarrant, 'Platonism', p. 70.

BIBLIOGRAPHY

Primary sources

Camelot, P.-T. and Mondésert, C. (eds). *Stromate II*. SCh 38. Paris: Cerf, 201; 1re éd., 1954.

Camelot, T. and Mondésert, C. (eds). *Clément d'Alexandrie. Les Stromates*. SCh 38. Paris: Cerf, 1954.

Blanc, C. (ed.). *Origène, Commentaire sur saint Jean*, tomes I-V. SCh 120 bis–385. Paris: Cerf, 1966–1992.

Borret, M. (ed.). *Origène, Contre Celse*, Livres I et II, tome I. SCh 132. Paris: Cerf, 2005: réimpr. de la 1re éd. rev; et corr., 1967.

Borret, M. (ed.). *Contre Celse*, Livres III et IV, tome II. SCh 136. Paris: Cerf, 2011, 2006, 1986; 1re éd., 1968.

Borret, M. (ed.). *Contre Celse*, Livres V et VI, tome III. SCh 147. Paris: Cerf, 1969.

Borret, M. (ed.). *Contre Celse*, Livres VII et VIII, tome IV. SCh 150. Paris: Cerf, 1969.

Borret, M. (ed.). *Origène. Homélies sur l'Exode*. SCh 321. Paris: Cerf, 1985.

Le Boulluec, A. and Voulet, P. (eds). *Stromate V*, tome I. SCh 278. Paris: Cerf, 2006.

Crouzel, H. and Brésard, L. (eds). *Origène. Comméntaire sur le Cantique*. SCh 375–376. Paris: Cerf, 1991–1992.

Crouzel, H. and Simonetti, M. (eds). *Origène. Les principes*, 5 vols. SCh 252–253, 268–269, 312. Paris: Cerf, 1978–1984.

Descourtieux, P. (ed.). *Stromate VI*. SCh 446. Paris: Cerf, 1999.

Hoeck, A. and Mondésert, C. (eds). *Stromate IV*. SCh 463. Paris: Cerf, 2001.

Junod, E. (ed.). *Origène. Philocalie*, sur le libre arbitre. SCh 226. Paris: Cerf, 1976.

Marrou, H. and Harl, M. (eds). *Le Pédagogue*, Livre I. SCh 70. Paris: Cerf, 1983; 1re éd., 1960.

Mondésert, C. and Marrou, H. (eds). *Le Pédagogue*, Livre II. SCh 108. Paris: Cerf, 1965.

Mondésert, C. (ed.). *Clément d'Alexandrie. Le pédagogue*, 3 vols. Sources chrétiennes 70, 108, 158. Paris: Cerf, 1.1960; 2.1965; 3.1970.

Mondésert, C. and Caster, M. (eds). *Stromate I*. SCh 30. Paris: Cerf, 2013.

Mondésert, C. and Matray, H. M. C. (eds.). *Le Pédagogue*, Livre III, SCh 158. Paris: Cerf, 1970.

Mondésert, C. and Plassart, A. (eds). *Protreptique*. SCh 2 bis. Paris: Cerf, 2013; 1re éd., 1941.

Harl, M. (ed.). *Origène. Philocalie, sules Ecritures. La lettre sur l'histoire de Suzanne*. SCh 302. Paris: Cerf, 1983.

Secondary sources

Bentein, K. 'The Greek of the Fathers', in K. Parry (ed.), *The Wiley-Blackwell Companion to Patristics*, 456–70. Oxford: Wiley-Blackwell, 2015.

Le Boulluec, A. 'Aux origines, encore, de l'école d'Alexandrie', *Adamantius* 5 (1999): 8–36.

Le Boulluec, A. 'Clément d'Alexandrie', in Bernard Pouderon (ed.), *Histoire de la littérature grecque chrétienne*, III, 56–169. Paris: Les Belles Lettres, 2017.

Boyarin, D. 'The Gospel of the Memra: Jewish Binitarianism and the Prologue to John', *HTR*, 94 (2001): 243–84.

Bradley, D. 'The Transformation of Stoic Ethics in Clement of Alexandria', *Aug*14 (1974): 41–66.

Broc-Schmezer, C. 'La philosophie grecque comme propédeutique à l'évangile: Clément d'Alexandrie', *Foi et vie* 107 (2008): 77–87.

van der Broek, R. 'The Christian School at Alexandria in the Second and Third Centuries', in J. W. Drijvers and A. MacDonald (eds), *Centers of Learning*, 39–47. Leiden: E.J. Brill, 1995.

Chadwick, H. *Early Christian Thought and the Classical Tradition*. Oxford: Clarendon, 1966.

Dinan, A. 'Αἴνιγμα and αἰνίττομαι in the Works of Clement of Alexandria', *SP* 44 (2010): 175–81.

Dorival, G. and Le Boulluec, A. *L'Abeille et l'Acier. Clément d'Alexandrie et Origène*. Paris: Les Belles Lettres, 2019.

Edwards, R. 'Clement of Alexandria's "Gnostic" Exposition of the Decalogue', *JECS* 23 (2015): 501–28.

Engberg-Pedersen, T. 'Introduction: A Historiographical Essay', in idem (ed.), *From Stoicism to Platonism: The Development of Philosophy, 100 BCE–100 CE*, 1–26. Cambridge: Cambridge University Press, 2017.

Freudenthal, G. 'The Astrologisation of the Aristotelian Cosmos: Celestial Influences on the Sublunar World in Aristotle, Alexander of Aphrodisias, and Averroes', in A. C. Bowen and C. Wildberg (eds), *New Perspectives on Aristotle's De Coelo*, 239–81, Philosophia Antiqua 117. Leiden: E.J. Brill, 2009.

Gerson, L. 'From Plato's Good to Platonic God', *IJPT* 2 (2008): 93–112.

Grafton, A. and Williams, M. *Christianity and the Transformation of the Book*. Cambridge, MA: Harvard's Belknap Press, 2006.

Hägg, H. F. *Clement of Alexandria and the Beginning of Christian Apophaticism*. Oxford: Oxford University Press, 2006.

Hengstermann, C. *Origenes und der Ursprung der Freiheitsmetaphysik*. Münster: Aschendorff, 2015.

van den Hoek, A. 'The "Cathechetical School" of Early Christian Alexandria and Its Philonic Heritage', *HTR* 90 (1997): 59–87.

Hoffmann, P. 'What Was Commentary in Late Antiquity?' in M.-L. Gill (ed.), *A Companion to Ancient Philosophy*, 597–62. London: Wiley-Blackwell, 2006.

Jaeger, W. *Early Christianity and Greek Paideia*. Cambridge, MA: Harvard University, 1961.

Jakab, A. *Ecclesia Alexandrina*. Bern: Lang, 2004.

Karfíková, L. 'Patristische Exegese: Origenes und Augustin', in Eadem, *Von Augustin zu Abaelard. Studien zum christlichen Denken*, 1–22. Fribourg: Paradosis, 2015.

Lössl, J. 'Theology as Academic Discourse in Greco-Roman Late Antiquity', *JLARC* 10 (2016): 38–72.

Markschies, C. 'Does It Make Sense to Speak about a "Hellenization of Christianity" Antiquity?', *CHRC* 92 (2012): 5–34.

Markschies, C. *Christian Theology and Its Institutions in the Early Roman Empire*. Waco: Baylor, 2015.

McGuckin, J. A. (ed.). *Westminster Handbook to Origen*. Louisville, KY: Westminster, 2004.

McGuckin, J. A. *The Eastern Orthodox Church: A New History*, 36–9. New Haven, CT: Yale, 2019.

Morgan, T. *Roman Faith and Christian Faith: Pistis and Fides in the Early Roman Empire and Early Churches*. Oxford: Oxford University Press, 2015.

Mortley, R. *Connaissance religieuse et herméneutique chez Clément*. Leiden: Brill, 1973.

Neuschäfer, B. *Origenes als Philologe*. Basel: Reinhard, 1987.

Neymeyr, U. *Die christlichen Lehrer im zweiten Jahrhundert. Ihre Lehrtätigkeit, ihr Selbstverständnis, und ihre Geschichte*. Leiden: E.J. Brill, 1989.

Osborn, E. 'Arguments for Faith in Clement of Alexandria', *VChr* 48 (1994): 1–24.

Osborn, E. 'Clement and Platonism', in L. Perrone (ed.), *Origeniana VIII*, 419–27. Leuven: Peeters, 2003.

Osborn, E. *Clement of Alexandria*. Cambridge: Cambridge University Press, 2005.

Pearson, B. 'Egypt', in M. Mitchell and F. Young (eds), *The Cambridge History of Christianity 1*, 331–50. Cambridge: Cambridge University Press, 2006.

Ramelli, I. L. E. 'Osservazioni sulle origini del Cristianesimo in Sicilia', *RSCI* 53 (1999): 1–15.

Ramelli, I. L. E. 'Alcune osservazioni su *credere*', *Maia* n.s. 51 (2000): 67–83.

Ramelli, I. L. E. 'La missione di Panteno in India: alcune osservazioni', in C. Baffioni (ed.), *La diffusione dell'eredità classica nell'età tardoantica e medievale. Filologia, Storia, Dottrina, Atti del Seminario Nazionale di Studio, Napoli-Sorrento 29–31 ottobre 1998*, 95–106. Alessandria: Edizioni Dell'Orso, 2000.

Ramelli, I. L. E. *Studi su Fides*, preface by Sabino Perea Yébenes, Graeco-Romanae Religionis Electa Collectio, 11. Madrid: Signifer Libros, 2002.

Ramelli, I. L. E. 'Vie diverse all'unico mistero: la concezione delle religioni in Temistio ed il suo atteggiamento verso il Cristianesimo', *RIL* 139 (2005): 455–83.

Ramelli, I. L. E. 'Philosophical Allegoresis of Scripture in Philo and Its Legacy', *StPhiloA* 20 (2008): 55–99.

Ramelli, I. L. E. *Bardaiṣan of Edessa: A Reassessment of the Evidence and a New Interpretation. Also in the Light of Origen and the Original Fragments from Porphyry*. Piscataway, NJ: Gorgias, 2009; Berlin: DeGruyter, 2019.

Ramelli, I. L. E. *Hierocles the Stoic*. Leiden: Brill; Atlanta: SBL, 2009.

Ramelli, I. L. E. 'Origen, Bardaisan, and the Origin of Universal Salvation', *HTR* 102 (2009): 135–68.

Ramelli, I. L. E. 'Origen, Patristic Philosophy, and Christian Platonism: Re-Thinking the Christianisation of Hellenism', *VChr* 63 (2009): 217–63.

Ramelli, I. L. E. 'Αἰώνιος and αἰών in Origen and Gregory of Nyssa', *SP* 47 (2010): 57–62.

Ramelli, I. L. E. '"Maximus" on Evil, Matter, and God: Arguments for the Identification of the Source of Eusebius PE VII 22', *Adamantius* 16 (2010): 230–55.

Ramelli, I. L. E. 'Atticus and Origen on the Soul of God the Creator: From the "Pagan" to the Christian Side of Middle Platonism', *Jahrbuch für Religionsphilosophie* 10 (2011): 13–35.

Ramelli, I. L. E. 'Baptism in Gregory of Nyssa's Theology and Its Orientation to Eschatology', in D. Hellholm, T. Vegge, O. Norderval and C. D. Hellholm (eds), *Ablution, Initiation, and Baptism: Late Antiquity, Early Judaism, and Early Christianity*, 3 vols, vol. 2, 1205–32. Beihefte zur Zeitschrift für die neutestamentliche Wissenschaft und die Kunde der älteren Kirche 176. Berlin: De Gruyter, 2011.

Ramelli, I. L. E. 'The Birth of the Rome-Alexandria Connection: The Early Sources on Mark and Philo, and the Petrine Tradition', *SPhiloA* 23 (2011): 69–95.

Ramelli, I. L. E. 'Early Christian Missions from Alexandria to "India": Institutional Transformations and Geographical Identification', *Aug* 51 (2011): 221–31.

Ramelli, I. L. E. 'Origen's Anti-Subordinationism and Its Heritage in the Nicene and Cappadocian Line', *VChr* 65 (2011): 21–49.

Ramelli, I. L. E. 'Origen and Apokatastasis: A Reassessment', in S. Kaczmarek and H. Pietras (eds), *Origeniana X*, 649–70. Leuven: Peeters, 2011.

Ramelli, I. L. E. 'Origen the Christian Middle/Neoplatonist', *JECH* 1 (2011): 98–130.

Ramelli, I. L. E. 'The Philosophical Stance of Allegory in Stoicism and Its Reception in Platonism, "Pagan" and Christian', *IJCT* 18 (2011): 335–71.

Ramelli, I. L. E. 'The *Dialogue of Adamantius*: A Document of Origen's Thought?' *SP* 52 (2012): 71–98; 56, no. 4 (2013): 227–73.

Ramelli, I. L. E. 'Disability in Bardaisan and Origen: Between the Stoic *Adiaphora* and the Lord's Grace', in W. Grünstäudl and M. S. Ferrari (eds), *Gestörte Lektüre. Disability als hermeneutische Leitkategorie biblischer Exegese*, 141–59. Stuttgart: Kohlhammer, 2012.

Ramelli, I. L. E. 'Origen, Greek Philosophy, and the Birth of the Trinitarian Meaning of Hypostasis', *HTR* 105 (2012): 302–50.

Ramelli, I. L. E. 'Philo as Origen's Declared Model. Allegorical and Historical Exegesis of Scripture', *SCJR* 7 (2012): 1–17. DOI: 10.6017/scjr.v7i1.2822

Ramelli, I. L. E. '*Stromateis* VII and Clement's Hints of the Theory of Apokatastasis', in M. Havrda, V. Hušek, and J. Plátová (eds), *The Seventh Book of the Stromateis*, 239–57. SupVCh. Leiden: E.J. Brill, 2012.

Ramelli, I. L. E. *The Christian Doctrine of Apokatastasis: A Critical Assessment from the New Testament to Eriugena*. SupVCh 120. Leiden: E.J. Brill, 2013.

Ramelli, I. L. E. 'Alexander of Aphrodisias: A Source of Origen's Philosophy?' *PhilAnt* 13 (2013): 1–49.

Ramelli, I. L. E. 'Harmony between *arkhē* and *telos* in Patristic Platonism', *IJPT* 7 (2013): 1–49.

Ramelli, I. L. E. 'Origen and Augustine: A Paradoxical Reception', *N* 60 (2013): 280–307.

Ramelli, I. L. E. 'Humility', in A. Di Berardino (ed.), *Encyclopedia of Ancient Christianity*, vol. 2, 298–302. Downers Grove: InterVarsity, 2014.

Ramelli, I. L. E. 'The Stoic Doctrine of *Oikeiōsis* and Its Transformation in Christian Platonism', *Apeiron* 47 (2014): 116–40. DOI: 10.1515/apeiron-2012-0063

Ramelli, I. L. E. '*Ethos* and *Logos*: A Second-Century Apologetic Debate between "Pagan" and Christian Philosophers', *VChr* 69, no. 2 (2015): 123–56.

Ramelli, I. L. E. 'Proclus and Christian Neoplatonism: A Case Study', in M. Knežević (ed.), *The Ways of Byzantine Philosophy*, 37–70. Alhambra, CA: Sebastian Press; Kosovska Mitrovica: Faculty of Philosophy, 2015.

Ramelli, I. L. E. *Tempo ed eternità in età antica e patristica: filosofia greca, ebraismo e cristianesimo*. Assisi: Cittadella, 2015.

Ramelli, I. L. E. 'The Mysteries of Scripture: Allegorical Exegesis and the Heritage of Stoicism, Philo, and Pantaenus', in V. Černuskova, J. Kovacs and J. Platova (eds), *Clement's Biblical Exegesis: Proceedings of the Second Colloquium on Clement of Alexandria, Prague-Olomouc 29–31 May 2014*, 80–110. SVCh 139. Leiden: E.J. Brill, 2016. DOI 63/9789004334_005

Ramelli, I. L. E. 'The Reception of Origen's Ideas in Western Theological and Philosophical Traditions', main lecture at *Origeniana Undecima: Origen and Origenism in the History of Western Thought, Aarhus University, August 2013*, ed. A.-C. Jacobsen, 443–67. BETL 279. Leuven: Peeters, 2016.

Ramelli, I. L. E. *Social Justice and the Legitimacy of Slavery: The Role of Philosophical Asceticism from Ancient Judaism to Late Antiquity*. Oxford: Oxford University Press, 2016.

Ramelli, I. L. E. 'Divine Power in Origen of Alexandria: Sources and Aftermath', in A. Marmodoro and I. F. Viltanioti (eds), *Divine Powers in Late Antiquity*, 177–98. Oxford: Oxford University Press, 2017.

Ramelli, I. L. E. 'Origen and the Platonic Tradition', in *Plato and Christ: Platonism in Early Christian Theology*, ed. J. Warren Smith = *Religions* 8, no. 2 (2017): 21. doi:10.3390/rel8020021

Ramelli, I. L. E. 'Apokatastasis and Epektasis in *Hom. in Cant.*: The Relation between Two Core Doctrines in Gregory and Roots in Origen', in G. Maspero, M. Brugarolas and I. Vigorelli (eds), *Gregory of Nyssa: In Canticum Canticorum. Commentary and Supporting Studies. Proceedings of the 13th International Colloquium on Gregory of Nyssa (Rome, 17–20 September 2014)*, 312–39. SupVCh 150. Leiden: E.J. Brill, 2018.

Ramelli, I. L. E. 'Bardaisan of Edessa, Origen, and Imperial Philosophy', *ARAM* 30, nos. 1–2 (2018): 337–53.

Ramelli, I. L. E. 'Origen', in A. Marmodoro and S. Cartwright (eds), *A History of Mind and Body in Late Antiquity*, 245–66. Cambridge: Cambridge University Press, 2018.

Ramelli, I. L. E. 'Philo as One of the Main Inspirers of Early Christian Hermeneutics and Apophatic Theology', *Adamantius* 24 (2018): 276–92.

Ramelli, I. L. E. 'Autobiographical Self-Fashioning in Origen', in M. Niehoff and J. Levinson (eds), *Self, Self-Fashioning and Individuality in Late Antiquity: New Perspectives*, 273–92. Tübingen: Mohr Siebeck, 2019.

Ramelli, I. L. E. 'Gal 3:28 and Aristotelian (and Jewish) Categories of Inferiority', *Eirene* 55 (2019): 275–310.

Ramelli, I. L. E. 'The *Dialogue of Adamantius*: Preparing the Critical Edition and a Reappraisal', *RhM* 163 (2020): 40–68.

Ramelli, I. L. E. 'The Father in the Son, the Son in the Father in the Gospel of John: Sources and Reception of Dynamic Unity in Middle and Neoplatonism, "Pagan" and Christian', *JBR* 7 (2020): 31–66. https://doi.org/10.1515/jbr-2019-0012

Ramelli, I. L. E. 'The Logos/Nous One-Many between "Pagan" and Christian Platonism', *SP* 102 (2020): 175–204.

Ramelli, I. L. E. 'Origen's Critical Reception of Aristotle: Some Key Points and Aftermath in Christian Platonism', in M. Knezevic (ed.), *Aristotle in Byzantium*, 1–43. Alhambra, CA: Sebastian Press, 2020.

Ramelli, I. L. E. 'Esoteric Interpretations of Scripture in Philo (and Hellenistic Judaism), Clement, and Origen', in T. Mayer (eds), *Esoteric Cultures of Scripture*. Oxford: Oxford University Press, 2021.

Ramelli, I. L. E. 'Gregory of Nyssa's Purported Criticism of Origen's Purported Doctrine of the Preexistence of Souls', in S. S. Griffin and I. L.E. Ramelli (eds), *Lovers of the Soul and Lovers of the Body: Philosophical and Religious Perspectives in Late Antiquity*, 397–40. Cambridge, MA: Harvard University Press, 2021.

Ramelli, I. L. E. 'Origen's Philosophical Exegesis of the Bible against the Backdrop of Ancient Philosophy (Stoicism, Platonism) and Hellenistic and Rabbinic Judaism', main lecture at the Conference, *The Bible: Its Translations and Interpretations in the Patristic Time*, 16–17 October 2019, in M. Szram and M. Wysocki (eds), *Studia Patristica CIII: The Bible in the Patristic Period*, 13–58. Leuven: Peeters, 2021.

Ramelli, I. L. E. 'Origen on the Unity of Soul and Body in the Earthly Life and Afterwards and His Impact', in J. Ulrich, A. Usacheva and S. Bhayro (eds), *The Unity of Soul and Body in the Earthly Life and After*, 38–77. Leiden: E.J. Brill, 2021.

Ramelli, I. L. E. 'The Reception of Paul in Origen: Allegoresis of Scripture, Apokatastasis, and Women's Ministry', in S. Porter and D. Yoon (eds), *The Pauline Mind*. New York: Routledge, 2021.

Ramelli, I. L. E. 'The Study of Late Ancient Philosophy: Philosophy and Religion – "Pagan" and Christian Platonism', in S. S. Griffin and I. L.E. Ramelli (eds), *Lovers of the Soul and Lovers of the Body: Philosophical and Religious Perspectives in Late Antiquity*, 397–403. Cambridge, MA: Harvard University Press, 2021.

Ramelli, I. L. E. 'Time and Eternity', in M. Edwards (ed.), *The Routledge Companion to Early Christian Philosophy*, 41–54. London: Routledge, 2021.

Ramelli, I. L. E. '"Know Yourself" in Origen and Gregory of Nyssa: A Maxim of Greek Philosophy Found in Scripture', in *Know Yourself from Paul to Augustine: Exploring the Delphic Maxim in Christian and Non-Christian Sources from the First Centuries*. Berlin: De Gruyter, forthcoming.

Ramelli, I. L. E. '"Revelation" for Christians and Pagans and their Philosophical Allegoresis: Intersections within Imperial Platonism', main lecture at the conference, *Ancient Revelation: Divination, Prophecy and Epiphany*, Durham University, 25–27 June 2019, forthcoming in E. Simonetti (ed.), *An Open Crossroad: Divination in Later Antiquity*. Cambridge: Cambridge University Press, forthcoming.

Ramelli, I. L. E. 'Secular and Christian Commentaries in Late Antiquity', in G. Kelly and A. Pelttari (eds), *The Cambridge History of Later Latin Literature*. Cambridge: Cambridge University Press, forthcoming.

Ramelli, I. L. E. 'Some Overlooked Sources of the Elements of Theology', in D. Calma (eds), *Reading Proclus and the Book of Causes, III, Sources of the Elements of Theology: Causality and the Noetic Triad*. Leiden: E.J. Brill, forthcoming.

Scholten, C. 'Die alexandrinische Katechetenschule', *JAC* 38 (1995): 16–37.

Solheid, J. 'Scripture and Christian Formation in Origen's Fourth Homily on Psalm 77(78)', *JECS* 27, no. 3 (2019): 417–42.

Strutwolf, H. *Gnosis als System: Zur Rezeption der valentinianischen Gnosis bei Origenes*. Göttingen: V&R, 1993.

Sullivan, F. A., 'Clement of Alexandria on Justification through Philosophy', in D. Kendall and G. O'Collins (eds), *In Many and Diverse Ways: FS J. Dupuis*, 101–13. Maryknoll, NY: Orbis, 2003.

Tarrant, H. 'Platonism before Plotinus', in L. Gerson (eds), *Cambridge History of Philosophy in Late Antiquity*, vol. 1, 63–99. Cambridge: Cambridge University Press, 2010.

Trabattoni, F. '*Logos* and *noēsis* in Alcinous, *Didaskalikos* 4', *Ph* 60 (2016): 60–81, 79.

Tzamalikos, P. *Origen: Philosophy of History and Eschatology*. Leiden: E.J. Brill, 2007.

von Zahn, T. *Forschungen zur Geschichte des neutestamentlichen Kanons* 3. Erlangen: Andreas Deichert Verlag, 1884.

Zeddies, M. 'An Origenian Background for the Letter to Theodore', *HTR* 112, no. 3 (2019): 376–406.

CHAPTER 11

Diversity around a prophet

The case of Montanism

WILLIAM TABBERNEE

INTRODUCTION

Around the middle of the second century CE, a prophet named Montanus founded
a new form of Christianity which, in later centuries, would come to bear his name.[1]
The earliest adherents of the movement simply called it the 'New Prophecy'. They
believed that they were living in the promised age of the Holy Spirit, or Paraclete (Jn
14.26) and that Montanus was the Paraclete's mouthpiece mandating higher than
traditional ethical standards for Christians in a new era of divine–human relations.
They also expected the imminent descent of the New Jerusalem out of heaven (Rev.
21.2–22.5), the location of which was revealed by the Spirit through Montanus
and subsequent New Prophets. The New Prophecy movement also differed from
contemporary 'mainstream' Christianity by incorporating women into the ranks of
the clergy, including the episcopate.

Montanus' new form of Christianity began in Phrygia, part of the Roman province
of Asia, in what is now Western Turkey, adding challenging diversity to the Christian
population of the region. It was not long before the proto-catholic bishops of the

---

[1]See, for example, Cyril of Jerusalem, *Catech.*, 16.8; On Montanism generally, see also C. Trevett,
Montanism: Gender, Authority and the New Prophecy (Cambridge: Cambridge University Press, 1996);
eadem, 'Montanism', in *The Early Christian World*, ed. P. S. Esler, 2nd edn (London: Routledge, 2017), pp.
867–84; W. Tabbernee, *Prophets and Gravestones: An Imaginative History of Montanists and Other Early
Christians* (Peabody, MA: Hendrickson; Grand Rapids, MI: Baker Academic, 2009). The major ancient
literary sources for Montanism are published in R. E. Heine, *The Montanist Oracles and Testimonia*,
PatrMS 14 (Macon, GA: Mercer University Press; Washington, DC: Catholic University of America Press,
1989). For material evidence, see W. Tabbernee, *Montanist Inscriptions and Testimonia: Epigraphic Sources
Illustrating the History of Montanism*, PatrMS 16 (Macon, GA: Mercer University Press; Washington, DC:
Catholic University of America Press, 1997), abbreviated as *IMont* when cited by inscription number. See
also idem, "The Montanist Oracles Reexamined," in *Hermeneuein in Global Contexts: Past and Present*,
vol. 2 of *Talking God in Society, Multidisciplinary (Re)constructions of Ancient (Con)texts, Festschrift
for Peter Lampe*, eds Ute E. Eisen and Heidrun E. Mader (Göttingen: Vandenhoeck & Ruprecht, 2020),
pp. 317–43.

area denounced the New Prophecy movement and excommunicated its members, leading to the establishment of separatist Montanist–Christian communities.

Despite (or perhaps partly because of) 'orthodox' opposition,[2] the movement spread from Phrygia to elsewhere in Asia Minor, to Thrace, Syria, Gaul and even to Rome itself by the end of the second century and to North Africa soon after that. In a few instances, such as in Thyatira, the whole, previously 'mainstream', church became Montanist.[3] The rapid expansion of 'Montanist Christianity' was aided not only by Montanus' strategy of appointing salaried emissaries ('apostles') to disseminate his teachings[4] but also to the circulation of written-down versions of his prophetic utterances.

THE PERSON OF MONTANUS

Montanus: A former priest of Apollo/Cybele?

If late-fourth-century anti-Montanist polemicists are to be believed, Montanus was a pagan priest before his conversion to Christianity. The so-called *Dialogue Between a Montanist and an Orthodox* calls Montanus 'the priest of Apollo'[5]. And Jerome (*c.*347–419) refers to him as 'the chopped-off and half-man Montanus'.[6] The Latin word '*semivir*' ('eunuch') was a commonplace synonym for the castrated priests of Cybele.[7]

The cult of Cybele, the mother goddess of Anatolia (Asia Minor, modern Turkey),[8] was particularly strong in Phrygia and had merged with the cults of Apollo and the local sun-god Lairbenos. A prominent temple to Apollo–Lairbenos was located near Ortaköy (Figure 11.1), only about 30 kilometers from where Montanus would later establish the centre of Montanism. Theoretically, therefore, the author of the *Dialogue* and Jerome could have been correct in their assumptions about Montanus' pre-Christian office. Similarities between aspects of Montanus' manner of ecstatic prophesying and that practised in the cult of Apollo–Cybele suggest that *Phrygian* Montanism was, indeed, affected by local pagan cultic practices.[9] There is

---

[2]For an analysis of early 'orthodox' charges against Montanist prophesying, see W. Tabbernee, *Fake Prophecy and Polluted Sacraments: Ecclesial and Imperial Reactions to Montanism*, Supplements to Vigiliae Christianae, 84 (Leiden: E. J. Brill, 2007), pp. 87–124.

[3]See, Epiphanius, *Pan.*, 51.33.4; also see Tabbernee, *Montanist Inscriptions*, pp. 136–8.

[4]See also S. Mitchell, 'An Apostle to Ankara from the New Jerusalem: Montanists and Jews in Late Roman Asia', *SCI* 25 (2005): 207–23.

[5]*Dialogue*, 4.5; and cf. 4.6.

[6]Jerome, *Ep.*, 41.4: *abscisus et semivirum*.

[7]See, Juvenal, *Sat.*, 6.513.

[8]See L. E. Roller, *In Search of God the Mother: The Cult of Anatolian Cybele* (Berkeley: University of California Press, 1999).

[9]See V. Hirschmann, *Horrenda Secta: Untersuchungungen zum fruhchristlichen Montanismus und seinen Verbindungen sur paganen religions Phrygiens*, Historia Einzelschriften 179 (Stuttgart: F. Steiner, 2005), pp. 88–92, 98–119, 139–45; W. Tabbernee, 'Review of Hirschmann, *Horrenda Secta*', *JECS* 14 (2006): 537–8.

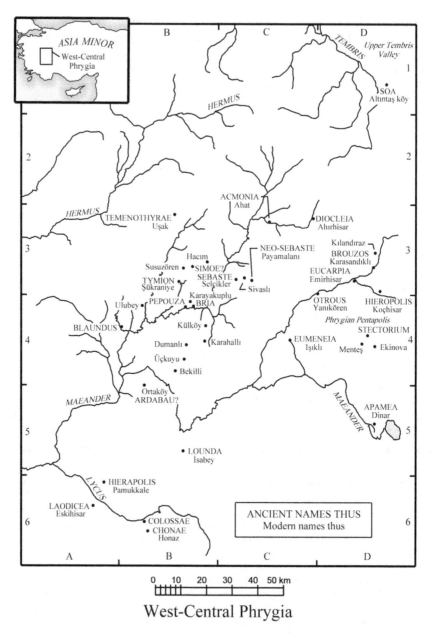

West-Central Phrygia

FIGURE 11.1 Map showing location of Pepouza, Tymion and related sites (map by Richard C. Engle; copyright by author).

no evidence, though, that such influences carried over into Montanism outside of Phrygia. While there were 'second-generation' Montanist prophetesses in Carthage during the first two decades of the third century,[10] their manner of prophesying exhibited none of the frenzied characteristics normative in the prophetic activity of Montanus.[11] *Phrygian* Montanism and Montanism in other parts of the world were very different expressions of the New Prophecy movement.

Since no early source calls Montanus a pagan priest, the late charge that Montanus had been a priest of Apollo–Cybele, therefore, may be nothing more than an example of the tendency by fourth-century (and later) 'catholic' authors to use Montanus as the embodiment of everything they deemed to be evil about the New Prophecy.[12]

Montanus: A recent convert

That Montanus was a relatively recent convert to Christianity from paganism when he began prophesying, as reported by a late-second-century author quoted by Eusebius of Caesarea (bishop 313–c.339),[13] need not be doubted. This author, commonly referred to as the 'Anonymous', was, almost certainly, a bishop in Phrygia who had made himself an expert on the New Prophecy through first-hand contact with members of the movement.[14] While not an exact contemporary, in that the events he describes occurred about thirty years before he wrote (c.193 CE), the Anonymous was at least much closer to the actual time when Montanus exercised his prophetic ministry than the fourth-century polemicists who portrayed him as a pagan priest.

EARLY ANTI-MONTANIST TREATISES

The Anonymous had been asked by the presbyters of the Christian community of Ancyra (modern Ankara, Turkey) to counter the influence of the New Prophecy in their city. Before he left, they asked him to put in writing the information he had shared with them orally about Montanus, the early history of the New Prophecy movement, and its dangers for 'orthodoxy'.[15] In addition to using the Anonymous's treatise as a source for his own account of Montanism,[16] Eusebius employed a synodical letter, composed and circulated by Apollinarius, bishop of Hierapolis, in the early 170s, as well as an anti-Montanist treatise by Apollonius, written c. 205.[17]

A fourth, also now anonymous, Christian author who wrote against the New Prophecy during the late second and early third centuries is referred to by scholars

---

[10]W. Tabbernee, '"Recognizing the Spirit": Second-generation Montanist Oracles', *SP* 40 (2006): 521–6.
[11]See Tertullian, *An.*, 9.4; *Virg.*, 17.3.
[12]Tabbernee, *Montanist Inscriptions*, pp. 17–18; idem, *Fake Prophecy*, pp. 342, 421.
[13]Eusebius, *HE*, 5.16.7.
[14]Tabbernee, *Fake Prophecy*, pp. 3–7.
[15]Anonymous, *Fragment*, in Eusebius, *HE*, 5.16.4-5.
[16]Eusebius, *HE*, 5.16-17.
[17]Eusebius, *HE*, 5.18.1-14.

as the 'Anti-Phrygian'.[18] The Anti-Phrygian's treatise was not drawn on by Eusebius, presumably because the great library at Caesarea Maritima[19] did not possess a copy of that particular work. Epiphanius of Salamis in Cyprus (bishop *c*.367–403) did, however, have access to the Anti-Phrygian's treatise, quoting it almost verbatim as the main source for the section of his *Panarion adversus haereses*[20] on the 'Cataphrygians'. 'Cataphrygians' is a late designation for Montanists, derived from the earlier and more accurate practice of referring to the adherents of the New Prophecy as those belong to 'the sect named *after the Phrygians*'.[21] The *'Phrygians'* in this context were Montanus as well as Maximilla and Priscilla, two 'high-born and wealthy women',[22] who soon joined the movement and prophesied in a manner similar to that of Montanus.[23]

Whereas the Anonymous denounces the prophesying of Montanus (and Maximilla and Priscilla) primarily on the grounds that its ecstatic nature is contrary to that of the more rational *manner* of prophesying demonstrated by the Hebrew prophets and by the prophets and prophetesses of the very early church,[24] the Anti-Phrygian claims that Montanist prophecy is illegitimate because genuine prophecy *had ceased with* the prophets of the very early church.[25] Moreover, he argues, the prophesying of the New Prophets is illegitimate because it occurs outside of the context of the true church.[26]

THE MONTANIST BEGINNINGS AT ARDABAU

Montanus began his prophesying in a village called Ardabau, located in a region of Phrygia bordering Mysia, when Gratus was proconsul of the province of Asia.[27] The exact location of Ardabau is not known but may have been at or near Ortaköy[28] in

---

[18]L. Nasrallah, *'An Ecstasy of Folly'*: *Prophecy and Authority in the Early Church*, HTS, 52 (Cambridge, MA: Harvard University Press, 2003), pp. 4, 167; Tabbernee, *Fake Prophecy*, pp. 50–3. Neither the Anti-Phrygian's provenance nor his date of writing is known – unless he can, indeed, be identified with the Apologist Miltiades as argued most recently by H. E. Mader, *Montanistische Orakel und kirchliche Opposition: Die frühe Streit zwischen den phrygischen 'neuen Propheten' und dem Autor der vorepiphanischen Quelle als biblische Wirkungsgeschichte des 2. Jh. n.Chr.* (Göttingen: Vandenhoeck & Ruprecht, 2012), pp. 114–44; cf. W. Tabbernee, 'Review of Mader, *Montanistische Orakel*', *JECS* 26 (2018): 495–7.

[19]On which, see A. J. Carriker, *The Library of Eusebius of Caesarea*, Vigilae Christianae Supplementa 67 (Leiden: E. J. Brill, 2003).

[20]Epiphanius, *Pan.*, 48.1.1–48.13.8.

[21]See Eusebius, *HE*, 5.16.1: τὴν λεγουμένη κατὰ Φρύγας. Later, the two originally separate words κατά ('after') and Φρύγας ('Phrygians') were combined by anti-Montanists to form the erroneous designation Κατάφρυγες or Καταφρυγασταί ('Cataphrygians'); cf. Latin: *Cataphrygas* and *Catafrigas*. See also A. Zisteren, 'Phrygier oder Kataphrygier?', *TQ* 74 (1892): 475–82.

[22]Jerome, *Ep.*, 133.4.

[23]Anonymous, *Fragment*, in Eusebius, *HE*, 5.16.9.

[24]Anonymous, *Fragment*, in Eusebius, *HE*, 5.16.7, 9; 5.17.2-4.

[25]Anti-Phrygian, *Fragment*, in Epiphanius, *Pan.*, 48.2.3.

[26]Anti-Phrygian, *Fragment*, in Epiphanius, *Pan.*, 48.1.5–48.2.1a.

[27]Anonymous, *Fragment*, in Eusebius, *HE*, 5.16.7.

[28]Tabbernee, *Montanist Inscriptions*, p. 18; idem, *Fake Prophecy*, p. 5, n. 8.

the vicinity of the Temple of Apollo–Lairbenos; especially if there is any credibility to the view that Montanus had been a priest of Apollo. More likely, Ardabau was further north, a little west or northwest of Temenothyrai (Uşak).[29]

The exact year when Montanus started prophesying is also unknown. Epiphanius gives 157 as the start of Montanism[30] whereas Eusebius places it in 171–172.[31] The year 171–172 CE is conceivably possible as the proconsul of Asia for that year has not yet been attested.[32] However, simply because Epiphanius was wrong about the year doesn't mean that Eusebius was correct; *both* Epiphanius *and* Eusebius may have been mistaken. Dating the beginning of Montanus' prophesying at Ardabau to around 165, halfway between the dates provided by Epiphanius and Eusebius, allows time for Maximilla and Priscilla to join Montanus soon afterwards, for the subsequent establishment of the Montanist centre at Pepouza,[33] and for the spread of the New Prophecy to some parts of Phrygia by the early 170s when 'orthodox' bishops first took official action against it. A mid-160s date also gives ample time for the New Prophecy to reach Lyons, in Gaul, before 177 when the then-still-presbyter Irenaeus (*c*.130–200; bishop from 177/8) delivered letters from the Christian community there to Eleutherus of Rome (bishop *c*.174–189) denouncing the movement.[34]

MONTANUS' ORACULAR PROPHESYING

Montanus, as noted, prophesied while in some kind of ecstatic trance, contrary to the traditional manner of prophesying deemed authentic within early Christian circles. As in the case of pagan oracles, such as those uttered by the priests, prophets and prophetesses of Apollo at Delphi and other shrines, Montanus' prophesying (at least on some occasions) was in the form of a response to questions. Despite the charges of unintelligible babbling,[35] the main content of Montanus' prophesying was communicated in understandable speech. The oracles themselves were produced by a 'stream-of-consciousness' interpretation of scriptural texts.[36] For example:

[Enquirer/Montanus]: Why do you call the one who has been saved more than a human being?

---

[29]So S. Mitchell, 'An Epigraphic Probe into the Origins of Montanism', in *Roman Phrygia: Culture and Society*, ed. Peter Thronemann (Cambridge: Cambridge University Press, 2013), pp. 168–97, 169–70.
[30]Epiphanius, *Pan.*, 48.1.2.
[31]Eusebius, *HE*, 4.27; *Chron.*, Olympiad 238.1.
[32]T. D. Barnes, 'The Chronology of Montanism', *JTS*, NS 21 (1970): 403–8, 403–4.
[33]On which, further later.
[34]Tabbernee, *Fake Prophecy*, pp. 28–36.
[35]See Anonymous, *Fragment,* in Eusebius, *HE*, 5.16.7, 9.
[36]D. E. Groh, 'Utterance and Exegesis: Biblical Interpretation in the Montanist Crisis', in *The Living Text: Essays in Honor of Ernest W. Sanders*, eds D. E. Groh and R. Jewett (Lanham, NY: University Press of America, 1985), pp. 73–95, 73–83.

> [The Paraclete/Montanus]: Because the righteous one shall shine a hundred times more than the sun and the little ones among you who have been saved shall shine a hundred times more than the moon.[37]

The primary underlying text of this oracle is Mt. 13.43: 'Then the righteous will shine like the sun in their Father's kingdom' but the oracle was also influenced by other scriptures such as Dan. 12.3 and Mk. 10.42. Loosely following Jesus' teaching (cf. Mt. 13:1–53), the Paraclete/Montanus 'revealed' that the righteous were destined for a radical new existence in heaven. They would inherit a transformed, angel-like, or more than human, 'body': a hundred times more radiant than the sun or, in the case of their 'saved' (baptized?) 'little ones',[38] a hundred times brighter than the *moon*.

Oracular introductory formulae

On most, if not all, occasions Montanist oracles or sayings were preceded by a formulaic introductory statement. The purpose of this introductory formula was to authenticate the prophet or prophetess as the mouthpiece of the divine speaker. Regrettably, the early 'mainstream' opponents who employed the written-down collections of the oracles of the New Prophets did not quote the oracles themselves in their own treatises. The alleged blasphemous content of the introductory formulae suited their anti-Montanist agendas even better than the oracles themselves. We have a material such as: 'Neither angel nor emissary, but, I, the Lord God the Father, have come';[39] or: 'I am the Word, the Bridegroom, the Paraclete, the Omnipotent One, I am All Things';[40] or: 'Behold a human being is like a lyre and I hover like a plectrum. The human being sleeps but I remain awake';[41] and: 'I, the Lord God Omnipotent, am the One dwelling in a human being. Come.'[42] Similarly, Maximilla implored: 'Hear not me, *but hear Christ*!'[43]

On these grounds, the New Prophecy's opponents claimed that Montanus was equating himself with God[44] but that charge is polemical and false.[45] Montanus' introductory formulae were no different in kind than those of Hebrew prophets proclaiming: 'Thus says the Lord' (Jer. 17.5) or Ignatius of Antioch (died *c*.115) who claimed to speak 'with the voice of God'.[46]

---

[37]Montanus, *Logion,* in Anti-Phrygian, *Fragment,* in Epiphanius, *Pan.,* 48.10.3.
[38]Which denotes children in Mk. 10.13-15; Mt. 19.13-15.
[39]Montanus, *Logion,* in Anti-Phrygian, *Fragment,* in Epiphanius, *Pan.,* 48.11.9.
[40]Montanus, *Logion,* in Theodore of Heraclea-Perinthus, *Frag.M.* See also A. M. Berruto Martone (ed.), *Dialogo tra un montanista e un ortodosso,* Biblioteca patristica 34 (Bologna: Edizioni Dehoniane Bologna, 1999), p. 98.
[41]Montanus, *Logion,* in Anti-Phrygian, *Fragment,* in Epiphanius, *Pan.,* 48.4.1a.
[42]Montanus, *Logion,* in Anti-Phrygian, *Fragment,* in Epiphanius, *Pan.,* 48.11.1.
[43]Montanus, *Logion,* in Anti-Phrygian, *Fragment,* in Epiphanius, *Pan.,* 48.12.4.
[44]For example: *Dialogue,* 3.1; 4.8.
[45]See Tabbernee, *Fake Prophecy,* pp. 380–3.
[46]Ignatius, *Magn.,* 7.1.

OPPOSITION TO THE NEW PROPHECY

The frenzied, and, at times, incomprehensible aspects of the prophesying of Montanus, Maximilla and Priscilla assured most who saw and heard them that they were inspired. For their supporters this proved that the New Prophets belonged to the authentic line of prophetic succession stretching back through Ammia of Philadelphia and Quadratus all the way to the daughters of Philip, to Silas and Agabus.[47] Their opponents, on the other hand, were convinced that the New Prophets were inspired by an evil spirit. For them, the New Prophecy was a *false*, rather than a *genuine new* prophecy, not only because of the *manner* of prophesying but also because of its *content*. This content was considered at best to have introduced into the church unwarranted novelties, such as additional fasts,[48] and at worst an erroneous understanding of the Holy Spirit. Maximilla was also accused of being a false prophet because her predictions about imminent wars, anarchy and the 'end of all things' did not come to pass.[49]

Attempts were made by local bishops, including Julian of Apamea and Sotas of Anchialus (both flourishing *c.*175), to exorcize Maximilla and Priscilla[50] Regional gatherings of church leaders met in Asia Minor condemning the New Prophets and excommunicating both them and their supporters.[51] Maximilla, who understandably, became frustrated by the attacks on her, complained: 'I am being banished as a wolf from sheep. I am not a wolf. I am Utterance and Spirit and Power.'[52]

In Rome, Victor (bishop *c.*189–*c.*198/99) had been on the point of officially endorsing the New Prophecy until persuaded to do otherwise.[53] Montanism, however, continued to exist in the capital city at least until the fifth century.[54] In the late second century there were two different groups (perhaps house churches) of adherents of the New Prophecy in Rome: one led by Aeschinus, the other by Proclus.[55] Pseudo-Tertullian accused Aeschinus' followers (but not those of Proclus) of equating Christ with God the Father, in other words of being proponents of Modalistic Monarchianism.[56] Around 200 CE, Proclus engaged in a public disputation with a Roman presbyter named Gaius about the validity of

---

[47]See Anonymous, *Fragment,* in Eusebius, *HE,* 5.17.2-4.
[48]On which, see below.
[49]Anonymous, *Fragment*, in Eusebius, *HE,* 5.16.18; Anti-Phrygian, *Fragment,* in Epiphanius, *Pan.,* 48.2.4.
[50]Anonymous, *Fragment*, in Eusebius, *HE,* 5.16.17; Apollonius, *Fragment*, in Eusebius, *HE,* 5.18.3; Eusebius, *HE,* 5.19.3.
[51]Eusebius, *HE,* 5.16.1-5.19.4. See Tabbernee, *Fake Prophecy,* pp. 15–24.
[52]*Logion,* in Anonymous, *Maximilla, Fragment,* in Eusebius, *HE,* 5.16.17.
[53]Tertullian, *Prax.,* 1.5.
[54]See Tabbernee, *Montanist Inscriptions,* pp. 452–9, 473, 544–50.
[55]Ps.Tertullian, *Haer.,* 7.1; cf. Tertullian, *Val.,* 5.1.
[56]Pseudo-Tertullian, *Haer.,* 7.2; cf. Pseudo-Hippolytus, *Ref.,* 8.19.2; and 10.26.1. See W. Tabbernee, '"Will the Real Paraclete Please Speak Forth!": The Catholic–Montanist Conflict over Pneumatology', in *Advents of the Spirit: An Introduction to the Current Study of Pneumatology,* eds B. F. Hinze and D. L. Dabney (Milwaukee, WI: Marquette University Press, 2001), pp. 97–118, 106–9.

the New Prophecy[57] where each protagonist appealed to their own community's possession of the tombs of their founders to support the authenticity and superiority of their form of Christianity.[58]

At about the same time, Serapion of Antioch-in-Syria (bishop c.199–211) wrote to some neighbouring churchmen condemning the New Prophecy, appending the synodical letter originally produced by Apollinarius, with supportive autographs and signatures of bishops as far away as Thrace.[59]

THE NEW PROPHECY'S PRACTICES AND TEACHINGS

As Montanist books were burned on the orders of Constantine I (ruled 306–37) and later emperors,[60] knowledge about what the New Prophets actually taught and what they encouraged their followers to practice is dependent upon reconstructing the fragmentary details preserved by the extant remnants of the earliest anti-Montanist treatises and the slightly later pro-Montanist works of Tertullian.

The Anonymous and the Anti-Phrygian each had access to previously compiled collections of the oracles of Montanus, Maximilla and Priscilla. The author of the *Refutation of All Heresies*, traditionally attributed to Hippolytus (c.170–237), states that the followers of Maximilla, Priscilla and Montanus possessed a countless number of their books.[61] That the New Prophets themselves wrote some of these books is implied, and can probably be presumed. Other early leaders of the New Prophecy certainly wrote books in defense of the movement, some of which incorporated the oracles of the founders. These leaders included Miltiades,[62] Themiso, who was accused of composing new 'catholic scriptures'[63] and Asterius Urbanus.[64]

In the early third century CE, a collection of the oracles of the New Prophets as well as a copy of Apollonius' anti-Montanist treatise fell into the hands of Tertullian (c.160–220), a lay theologian residing in Carthage in the Roman province of Africa proconsularis. Around 208 he became a strong defender of the New Prophecy movement, characterizing its opponents as *psychici* ('carnal Christians'),[65] the opposite of *pneumatici* ('spiritual Christians'), which was a Montanist self-designation.[66] There is, however, no evidence that bears the weight of scrutiny supporting the long-held but erroneous view that Tertullian left the proto-catholic

---

[57]Eusebius, *HE*, 2.25.5-7; 6.20.3.
[58]W. Tabbernee, "'Our Trophies are Better than your Trophies': The Appeal to Tombs and Reliquaries in Montanist–Orthodox Relations', *SP* 33 (1997): 206–17.
[59]Tabbernee, *Fake Prophecy*, pp. 16–18, 53–5.
[60]Eusebius, *V.C.*, 3.66; *Cod. Thds.*, 16.5.34.1.
[61]*Haer.*, 8.19.1; cf. *Dialogue*, 5.3-4.
[62]Anonymous, *Fragment*, in Eusebius, *HE*, 5.16.3.
[63]Apollonius, *Fragment*, in Eusebius, *HE*, 5.18.5; and see ibid., 6.20.3.
[64]Anonymous, *Fragment*, in Eusebius, *HE*, 5.16.1.
[65]Tertullian, *Marc.*, 4.22.5; *Jejun.* 1.1; *Pudic.*, 6.14.
[66]See Tabbernee, *Montanist Inscriptions*, pp. 401–6 (*IMont* 63), 544–6 (*IMont* 93), 550–2 (*IMont* 95).

church to form or join a separatist Montanist community. The New Prophecy in Carthage was an intra-church movement affecting some of the house churches there, especially the one of which Tertullian was a member and probably its patron. But this certainly *did not* amount to a schism.[67] Apollonius, whose anti-Montanist polemic was countered by Tertullian in a second edition of his *De ecstasi*, also appears to have used a collection of the oracles and other sayings of Montanus.[68]

ON THE END OF THE WORLD

One of Montanus' extant oracles is a prediction about what will ultimately happen to the cosmos: 'Fire will come and consume all the face of the earth.'[69] Tertullian probably alluded to this prediction by Montanus when he explained that the only difference between the adherents of the New Prophecy and other Carthaginian Christians was that the former 'do not permit second marriages, and *do not reject Montanus's prophecy concerning the impending judgment*'.[70]

Tertullian as a Millennialist believed in a literal 'one-thousand-year reign of Christ' on earth (Rev. 20.4-6) before the end of the world occurred (Rev. 21.1) and the subsequent 'Final Judgment' (Rev. 20.11-14). Whether or not Montanus and his Phrygian followers were Millennialists also is open to debate,[71] but they clearly believed that at the end of the age, fire would come down out of heaven to consume not only the enemies of Christ and his saints (cf. Rev. 20.9) but also the whole earth.

REJECTION OF SECOND MARRIAGES

The first oracle summarized by Tertullian in the previous quotation was cited by Tertullian as a corrective to Apollonius' claim that Montanus taught the dissolution of all marriages.[72] Tertullian, in an earlier work, had alluded to this same oracle as a decree of the Paraclete: 'Now, if at this present time, a limit of marrying is imposed, as for example, among us a spiritual reckoning decreed by the Paraclete is defended,

---

[67]See also C. Markschies, 'The *Passio Sanctarum Perpetuae et Felicitatis* and Montanism?' in *Perpetua's Passions: Multidisciplinary Approaches to the Passio Perpetuae et Felicitatis*, eds J. N. Bremmer and M. Formisano (Oxford: Oxford University Press, 2012), pp. 277–90 and W. Tabbernee, 'Montanism and the Cult of the Martyrs in Roman North Africa: Reassessing the Literary and Epigraphic Evidence', in *Text and the Material World: Essays in Honour of Graeme Clarke*, eds E. Minchin and H. Jackson (Uppsala: Astrom Editions, 2017), pp. 299–313, 302–3.

[68]Apollonius, *Fragment,* in Eusebius, *HE*, 5.18.2.

[69]Montanus, *Logion,* in Michael the Syrian, *Chron.*, 9.3.

[70]Tertullian, *Ecst. frg.,* in Praedestinatus, *Haer.*, 1.26.

[71]See C. E. Hill, *Regnum Caelorum: Patterns of Millennial Thought in Early Christianity*, 2nd edn (Grand Rapids, MI: Eerdmans, 2001), pp. 146–53; W. Tabbernee, 'The World to Come: Tertullian's Christian Eschatology', in *Tertullian and Paul*, eds T. D. Still and D. E. Wilhite, Pauline and Patristic Scholars in Debate 1 (New York: Bloomsbury, 2013), pp. 266–7.

[72]Apollonius, *Fragment,* in Eusebius, *HE*, 5.18.2.

prescribing a single matrimony in the faith, it will be his to tighten the limit who formerly had loosened it'[73]

Tertullian argues that the Holy Spirit, knowing that the people of God under the old and new covenants had not been capable of living up to the high ethical standards which had been God's ultimate will, had permitted a greater laxity about marriage than was permitted in the new age of Christian maturity now operative. The new revelations from the Paraclete made clear what was expected of mature Christians such as the adherents of the New Prophecy. In the changed context of a 'Christianity-come-of-age', it was the prerogative of the same Holy Spirit to insist on the stricter marital ethic which God had, in fact, always intended.

MONTANIST FASTING

Summarizing once again not only Montanus' (viz. the Paraclete's) oracle about marriage but also a different one concerning fasting, Tertullian complains that the Carthaginian 'psychics' 'reject the New Prophecy not because Montanus and Priscilla and Maximilla proclaim another God, nor because they evade Jesus Christ, nor because in some aspect of faith or hope they pervert the Rule of Faith, but simply because *they teach to fast more frequently than to marry*' (my emphasis).[74]

Tertullian, who had become totally convinced of the necessity of practising monogamy even after the death of one's spouse,[75] argues that even the New Prophecy's teaching on fasting was not unreasonably strict: 'For how little is the banishment of food among us? Two weeks in the year (not even complete ones – exclusive, of course, of Saturdays and Sundays) of eating dry foods only offered to God, abstaining from that which we are not rejecting but postponing.'[76]

PENANCE AMONG THE MONTANISTS

The New Prophecy also took a stronger position on penance than at least some mainstream Christian communities of the time. Tertullian, for example, complained that the earlier practice of protracted penance for serious sins such as adultery was being abandoned by the bishop of Carthage:[77] 'But, you [bishop] say, "The church has the power of forgiving sins". This I also acknowledge and prescribe to a greater extent for *I have the Paraclete himself declaring through New Prophets* (my emphasis): "The church has power to forgive sins, but I shall not, lest they should commit others also"'.[78] Tertullian does not identify the human instrument through

---

[73]Tertullian, *Marc.,* 1.29.4.
[74]Tertullian, *Jejun.,* 1.3; cf. 13.5; 15.2.
[75]Tertullian, *Castit.,* 9.1; *Monog.,* 4.3.
[76]Tertullian, *Jejun.,* 15.2.
[77]Tertullian, *Pudic.,* 1.6.
[78]Montanus, *Logion,* in Tertullian, *Pudic.,* 21.7.

whom this particular Montanist oracle was conveyed, but it is clear that the New Prophecy demanded life long penance for certain sins.[79]

Montanist worship services in Phrygia included not only ecstatic prophesying but an emotionally charged penitential rite. According to Epiphanius, during the liturgy:

> Seven lamp-bearing virgins[80] enter, undoubtedly arriving robed in white, in order to prophesy to the people. They exhibit a kind of enthusiasm to the people present, working a deception to make everyone weep; they pour forth tears as though in compassion, they are evoking repentance and by their demeanour are lamenting human existence.[81]

THE 'NEW JERUSALEM'

As well as charging Montanus with irregularities regarding marriage and fasting, Apollonius had complained about a third aspect of Montanus' teachings: 'He is the one having taught you to dissolve marriages; the one having enacted fasts; the one having named Pepouza and Tymion "Jerusalem" (these are small Phrygian cities), wishing people to gather there from everywhere'. [82] The designation 'Jerusalem' applied by Montanus to Pepouza and Tymion refers to the 'New Jerusalem' which, according to the book of Revelation, will descend out of heaven at the end of time (Rev. 3.12; 21.1–22.5). About thirty years before Montanus began his prophetic ministry, Jerusalem had been destroyed by the Romans after the Bar Kochba revolt. The emperor Hadrian (ruling 117–38) built a new city on the site, named Aelia Capitolina, which Jews (and, therefore, Jewish Christians) were forbidden to enter. Because of this and for other geographical and topographical considerations, Montanus taught that the 'Jerusalem out of heaven' would descend not, as may have been assumed, in Syria Palaestina, the location of the physical old Jerusalem, but in Phrygia, between Pepouza and Tymion.

The site of Pepouza is near Karayakuplu, Turkey.[83] The ancient city was located on either side of the river Sindros (Banaz Çayı) in a fertile valley protected on both sides by the edges of a canyon. An extensive plain stretches north from the top of the canyon towards and beyond the site of Tymion 9 kilometers distant. In Montanus' time, the plain comprised an agricultural estate owned by Roman emperors.[84] The

---

[79]See W. Tabbernee, 'To Pardon or not to Pardon?: North African Montanism and the Forgiveness of Sins', *SP* 36 (2001): 375–86.

[80]For the epitaph of a (later) Montanist lamp-bearing virgin at Ancyra, see Tabbernee, *Montanist Inscriptions,* pp. 518–25 [*IMont* 87].

[81]Epiphanius, *Pan.*, 49.2.3–4.

[82]Apollonius, *Fragment*, in Eusebius, *HE*, 5.18.2.

[83]W. Tabbernee and P. Lampe, *Pepouza and Tymion: The Discovery and Archaeological Exploration of a Lost Ancient City and an Imperial Estate in Phrygia* (Berlin: W. de Gruyter, 2008); W. Tabbernee, 'Pepouza', in *The Eerdmans Encyclopedia of Early Christian Art and Archaeology*, ed. P. C. Finney, 3 vols (Grand Rapids, MI: Eerdmans, 2017), vol. 2, pp. 314–15.

[84]Tabbernee and Lampe, *Pepouza and Tymion*, pp. 68–9, 72, 74.

plain and the sites of Pepouza and Tymion (Şukraniye) are clearly visible from the top of a nearby mountain now named Ömerçalı. Montanus undoubtedly equated this mountain with the mountain referred to in Rev. 21.10 from which the New Jerusalem could be seen descending out of heaven.

The plain between Pepouza and Tymion was large enough and level enough to accommodate (at least in Montanus' mind) the New Jerusalem. That Montanus considered Pepouza to be the site of the southern gate and Tymion that of the northern gate of the future heavenly city on earth explains why he called both Pepouza and Tymion 'Jerusalem'.[85]

Montanus' own oracle about the New Jerusalem is not extant but is presumably the basis of the following statement by Tertullian concerning it: 'This (is the city) with which Ezekiel was acquainted, the apostle John had seen, and for which the saying of the New Prophecy, which belongs to our faith, provides evidence'.[86] Priscilla, or, more likely, a later Montanist prophetess named Quintilla, had a dream in which Christ appeared to her in the form of a woman, confirming that Pepouza was, indeed, the locale of the expected New Jerusalem.[87]

The New Jerusalem did not descend on the plain between Pepouza and Tymion, but Pepouza, the larger of the two settlements became for the Montanists a kind of 'Vatican'. For almost four centuries Pepouza was the ecclesiastical, administrative centre of Montanism, eventually with its own patriarch supervising regional bishops called koinonoi.[88] After the death of the New Prophecy's founders, Pepouza also became a pilgrimage site where people from far afield came to visit the shrine which contained the bones of Montanus, Maximilla, and Priscilla, to partake of the Eucharist, or to be baptized.[89]

PROPHETS AND VISIONARIES

Maximilla was probably the last of the original New Prophets to die, most likely in 178–179. There is no credibility to the rumours that both she and Montanus had, on separate occasions, hanged themselves while under the influence of an evil

---

[85]W. Tabbernee, 'Portals of the Montanist New Jerusalem: The Discovery of Pepouza and Tymion', *JECS* 11 (2003): 87–94; idem, 'The Appearance of the New Jerusalem in the Interpretation of the Revelation of John', in *Die Johannesapokalypse: Kontexte – Konzepte – Rezeption*, eds Jörg Frey, James A. Kelhoffer and Franz Tóth, WUNT 287 (Tübingen: Mohr Siebeck, 2012), pp. 651–82; P. Lampe, 'Das Neue Jerusalem der Montanisten in Phrygien', in *Jerusalem und die Länder: Ikonographie – Topographie – Theologie*, eds G. Theißen et al. (Göttingen: Vandenhoeck & Ruprecht, 2009), pp. 253–70.

[86]Tertullian, *Marc.*, 1.29.4.

[87]Priscilla/Quintilla, *Logion*, Epiphanius, *Pan.*, 49.1.2-3.

[88]See Jerome, *Ep.*, 41.3; also see, W. Tabbernee, 'Montanist Regional Bishops: New Evidence from Ancient Inscriptions', *JECS* 1 (1993): 249–80, 254–7; idem, *Fake Prophecy*, 369–73.

[89]Epiphanius, *Pan.,* 48.14.1–2; 49.1.4. See, Tabbernee, *Fake Prophecy*, 350–64; idem, 'Initiation/Baptism in the Montanist Movement', in *Ablution, Initiation and Baptism: Late Antiquity, Early Judaism, and Early Christianity*, eds D. Hellholm et al., BZNW 176, 3 vols (Berlin: W. de Gruyter, 2011), vol. 2, pp. 917–45, 928–45.

spirit. Even the Anonymous, who reports these rumours, is skeptical about the gossip which circulated at the time of New Prophets' deaths.[90] No details, not even rumours, have survived about the circumstances of Priscilla's death.

Although Maximilla had predicted: 'After me, a prophet shall no longer exist – only the end!',[91] new generations of Montanist prophets and prophetesses arose in Phrygia and elsewhere and existed well into the fourth century and possibly later. They included the Carthaginian prophetesses in Carthage during the time of Tertullian; but presumably *not* Perpetua and Saturus who, while certainly being prophetic visionaries,[92] were martyred in 203, probably before the New Prophecy had reached Carthage.[93]

Firmilian, bishop of Caesarea in Cappadocia *c.*230–268, reports that there had been an ecstatic prophetess in his region around 235. She claimed to be filled with the Holy Spirit, performed baptisms and celebrated the Eucharist. She also frequently asserted that she was hurrying to Jerusalem,[94] which *may* have been a reference to the *New* Jerusalem at Pepouza. The Montanist prophetess Quintilla was operative at Pepouza most likely also in the third century. It was in relationship to the 'Quintillians', the sub-sect named after her, that the lamp-bearing virgin prophetesses are first attested.[95] The epitaph of a fourth-century Montanist prophetess named Nanas, who may even have functioned as a bishop,[96] has been discovered at Akoluk, 120 kilometers north-east of Pepouza in the Phrygian Highlands.[97]

MONTANIST WOMEN PRESBYTERS

Only about 30 kilometers due north of Pepouza and a little over 20 kilometers north of Tymion was an ancient city named Temenothyrai (modern Uşak) from which a fascinating group of Phrygian funerary monuments has survived.[98] These tombstones, in the shape of doors leading to the afterlife ('doorsteles'), commemorated prominent

---

[90]Anonymous, *Fragment*, in Eusebius, *HE*, 5.16.13-15.

[91]Maximilla, *Logion*, in Anti-Phrygian, *Fragment*, in Epiphanius, *Pan.,* 48.2.4.

[92]*Passio Perpetuae*, 1.5.

[93]For the view that Perpetua, her co-martyrs, and/or the author of the *Passio Sanctarum Perpetuae et Felicitas were* Montanists, see R. C. Butler, *The New Prophecy & 'New Visions': Evidence of Montanism in the Passion of Perpetua and Felicitas* (Washington, DC: Catholic University of America Press, 2006); T. J. Heffernan, *The Passion of Perpetua and Felicity* (Oxford: Oxford University Press, 2012), pp. 8–17, 171, 271, 295.

[94]Firmilian, *Ep.,* cited in Cyprian, *Ep.*, 75.10.1-5; 75.11.1.

[95]Epiphanius, *Pan.*, 49.1.1-2.4.

[96]So V. Hirschmann, '"Nach Art der Engel': Die phrygische Prophetin Nanas', *EpigAnat* 37 (2004): 160–8, 165–7.

[97]*IMont* 68; Tabbernee, *Montanist Inscriptions*, pp. 419–25; C. Trevett, '"Angelic Visitations and Speech She Had": Nanas of Kotiaeion', in *Prayer and Spirituality in the Early Church*, eds P. Allen, W. Mayer, and L. Cross, vol. 2 (Everton Park: Center for Early Christian Studies, 1999), pp. 259–77; J. C. Poirier, 'The Montanist Nature of the Nanas Inscription (Steinepigramme 16/41/15)', *EpigAnat* 37 (2004): 151–9.

[98]E. Gibson, 'Montanist Inscriptions at Uşak', *GRBS* 16 (1975): 433–42; Tabbernee, *Montanist Inscriptions*, pp. 60–90 (*IMont* 3–8); Mitchell, 'An Epigraphic Probe', pp. 168–97.

members of the community, two of whom are clearly identified as Christian clergy. Their epitaph inscriptions (*IMont* 3, 5) contain the title *episkopos* ('bishop') and the tombstones themselves display symbols such as eucharistic bread, Communion patens and portable Communion tables/altars. This series of doorsteles has recently been redated. Stephen Mitchell argues convincingly that the earlier of the two bishops, Artemidoros, was buried *c.*180 CE and not between 200 and 210 CE, as previously assumed, and that the tombstone of Artemidoros' episcopal successor, Diogas, should be dated between 210 and 215 CE.[99]

Diogas is also named on another doorstele inscription found at Uşak (*IMont* 4), where he is recorded as having commissioned a tomb 'for Ammion *presbytera*'. Since Diogas's wife's name was not Ammion but Aurelia Tatiane (*IMont* 5), the designation *presbytera* in *IMont* 4 cannot mean 'the wife of a presbyter (or bishop)' nor, in this context, can it simply mean 'elderly woman', especially as the term is used stylistically in the same way as Diogas is designated *episkopos*.[100] There is little doubt that *IMont* 4 provides evidence of a Christian *woman-presbyter* at Temenothyrai whose death occurred sometime after Diogas became bishop c.180 and before his death c.210 to 215. Consequently, Ammion lived and perhaps even died before the end of the second century.

Given the proximity of Temenothyrai to Pepouza and that the New Prophets were operative there during the 170s at presumably the same time that Artemidoros was bishop at Temenothyrai, Mitchell argues that Artemidoros, Diogas and other members of the Christian community at Temenothyrai 'would surely have been personally acquainted with Montanos [*sic*], Priscilla and Maximilla' and that they presumably belonged to the same social class.[101] Somewhat surprisingly, Mitchell does not assume Artemidoros, Diogas and Ammion to have been Montanist clergy.[102] However, as one of Epiphanius' strong complaints against the Montanists is that 'Among them women are bishops and women are presbyters and the like; as there is no difference, they say, "For in Christ Jesus there is neither male nor female"'[103] and because there is no independent evidence of women presbyters in mainline Christianity as early as 200 CE, it seems best to conclude that the Christian community to which Artemidoros, Diogas and Ammion belonged was at the very least influenced by the New Prophecy movement and had adopted its practice of enabling women as well as men to be ecclesiastical officeholders.

MARTYRDOM AND THE NEW PROPHECY

Some adherents of the New Prophecy suffered during times of persecution[104] but this does not necessarily mean that Montanists placed a greater emphasis on martyrdom

---

[99]Mitchell, 'An Epigraphic Probe', pp. 185–7; contrast the dating in Tabbernee, *Montanist Inscriptions*, p. 62.

[100]See Tabbernee, *Montanist Inscriptions*, pp. 66–76.

[101]Mitchell, 'An Epigraphic Probe', pp. 192–3.

[102]Ibid., p. 196.

[103]Epiphanius, *Pan.*, 49.2.5.

[104]Anonymous, *Fragment*, in Eusebius, *HE*, 5.16.20, 22.

than their proto-catholic counterparts, as has been assumed by some scholars. Two Montanist oracles are frequently cited in support of Montanist recklessness in the face of persecution and of the New Prophecy's alleged emphasis on voluntary martyrdom. The human instruments who uttered these oracles are not identified by Tertullian and are more likely to have been *Carthaginian* prophetesses than one of the founding New Prophets.[105]

The first of these two related oracles on martyrdom is quoted by Tertullian in his treatise *On Flight during Persecution*, written c.209–210:

> 'Are you publicly exposed?' he [the Spirit] says, 'That is good for you! For indeed, one who is not publicly exposed before human beings is being publicly exposed before the Lord. Do not be ashamed; moral integrity brings you forward into the public arena. Why be ashamed when you are producing glory? Authoritative power is being generated while you are being stared at by humankind.'[106]

Here Tertullian is exhorting Christians not to run away from persecution (cf. *Fug.*, 11.2). If arrested and condemned to fight wild animals in the arena, they should stand firm in the faith. Nor is the second oracle, which Tertullian quotes immediately after the first, intended to stand by itself as a call to voluntary martyrdom. It merely continues Tertullian's encouragement of Christians facing persecution: 'Choose to die not in comfortable beds nor in miscarriages and susceptible fevers but in martyrdoms, so that the one who suffered for you may be rendered honor.'[107]

That neither Tertullian nor the Montanist oracles he quotes are calling for irresponsible voluntary martyrdom by provoking one's own arrest is seen even more clearly from Tertullian's summary of the second oracle in his treatise *On the Soul*, written the following year: 'If you should die for God in the manner the Paraclete advises, not in susceptible fevers and in beds, but in martyrdoms, (and) if you take up your cross and follow the Lord, as he himself commands, your blood is the only key necessary for Paradise.'[108] When faced with persecution, the Christian's response should not be to run away but to obey the Lord's command to take up one's cross (cf. Mk 8.34), even if this leads to a martyr's death, thereby, according to Tertullian, attaining immediate entry into Paradise. While one may (and perhaps even should) desire to be a martyr, there is no evidence that Tertullian, or Montanists in general, taught *volunteering* for one's own martyrdom![109] Similarly, the traditional scholarly view that Phrygian 'Christians for Christians' inscriptions were provocative and exclusively Montanist[110] is not supported by a close examination of the extant evidence.[111]

---

[105]See Tabbernee, 'To Pardon or not to Pardon?', pp. 381–2.

[106]Tertullian, *Fug.*, 9.4a.

[107]Tertullian, *Fug.*, 9.4b.

[108]Tertullian, *An.*, 55.5.

[109]See William Tabbernee, 'Early Montanism and Voluntary Martyrdom', *Colloquium* 17 (1985): 3–44; idem, *Fake Prophecy*, pp. 214–16.

[110]For example, by William M. Calder, 'Philadelphia and Montanism', *BJRL* 7 (1922/3): 317–36.

[111]See William Tabbernee, 'Christian Inscriptions from Phrygia', in *New Documents Illustrating Early Christianity* ed. G. H. R. Horsley, vol. 3 (North Ryde, NSW: Macquarie University, 1983), pp. 128–39; idem, *Montanist Inscriptions*, pp. 143–50.

CONCLUSION

Montanus was a charismatic new prophet for a perceived new era of Christian moral and spiritual maturity. This new era was facilitated, according to the adherents of the New Prophecy movement, by the revelations poured out through Montanus, Maximilla and Priscilla on the church by the Holy Spirit/Paraclete. An able organizer as well as a prophet, Montanus established at Pepouza the administrative centre of the movement he had founded. From Pepouza, the New Prophecy with its strict ethics, full participation of women in the life and ministry of Christian communities, and belief in the imminent descent of the New Jerusalem spread rapidly throughout the Roman Empire.

Although in Rome there was one (but only one) group of adherents which had Modalist leanings, charges of heresy per se levelled at second-century Montanists were rare.[112] The diversity of the New Prophecy's alternate form of Christianity was centred on practice rather than doctrine. Nonetheless considered dangerous by the leaders of the mainstream and increasingly patriarchal church, the New Prophecy was formally condemned and gradually rooted out.

In 550 CE, the Montanist centre and pilgrimage site at Pepouza was demolished by the Monophysite bishop John of Ephesus (c.558–88), as agent of Emperor Justinian (ruling, 527–565). The shrine containing the bones of Montanus, Maximilla and Priscilla at Pepouza was destroyed and the bones themselves burned.[113] depriving the Montanists of their physical link to the New Prophets upon whose oracular utterances their alternate form of Christianity had been based. Montanism, which had long been eradicated elsewhere by ecclesiastical opposition and imperial legislation, ceased to exist also in Phrygia. The weeping and wailing which accompanied the burning of Montanus' bones was the death-knell of this particular type of Christian diversity centred around a prophet.

BIBLIOGRAPHY

Barnes, T. D. 'The Chronology of Montanism', *JTS*, NS 21 (1970): 403–4.

Butler, R. C. *The New Prophecy & 'New Visions': Evidence of Montanism in the Passion of Perpetua and Felicitas.* Washington, DC: Catholic University of America Press, 2006.

Berruto-Martone, A. M. (ed.). *Dialogo tra un montanista e un ortodosso.* Biblioteca patristica 34. Bologna: Edizioni Dehoniane Bologna, 1999.

Calder, W. M. 'Philadelphia and Montanism', *BJRL* 7 (1922/3): 317–36.

Carriker, A. J. *The Library of Eusebius of Caesarea.* SupVCh, 67, Leiden: E. J. Brill, 2003.

Gibson, E. 'Montanist Inscriptions at Uşak', *GRBS* 16 (1975): 433–42.

Groh, D. E. 'Utterance and Exegesis: Biblical Interpretation in the Montanist Crisis', in D. E. Groh and R. Jewett (eds), *The Living Text: Essays in Honor of Ernest W. Sanders*, 73–95. Lanham, NY: University Press of America, 1985.

---

[112]For post-second-century accusations of alleged Montanist heretical teaching, see Tabbernee, *Fake Prophecy*, pp. 376–88.

[113]Pseudo-Dionysius of Tell-Mahre, *Chronicon* (entry for year 861 of the Seleucid Era, viz. 550 CE); Michael the Syrian, *Chronicon.*, 9.33; Also see Tabbernee, *Montanist Inscriptions*, pp. 27–47; idem, 'Our Trophies are Better than your Trophies', pp. 213–17.

Heffernan, T. J. *The Passion of Perpetua and Felicity*. Oxford: Oxford University Press, 2012.

Heine, R. E. *The Montanist Oracles and Testimonia*. Macon, GA: Mercer University Press; Washington, DC: Catholic University of America Press, 1989.

Hill, C. E. *Regnum Caelorum: Patterns of Millennial Thought in Early Christianity*, 2nd edn. Grand Rapids, MI: Eerdmans, 2001.

Hirschmann, V. *Horrenda Secta: Untersuchungungen zum fruhchristlichen Montanismus und seinen Verbindungen sur paganen religions Phrygiens*. Historia Einzelschriften 179. Stuttgart: F. Steiner, 2005.

Hirschmann, V. '"Nach Art der Engel": Die phrygische Prophetin Nanas', *EpigAnat* 37 (2004): 160–8.

Lampe, P. 'Das Neue Jerusalem der Montanisten in Phrygien', in G. Theißen et al. (eds), *Jerusalem und die Länder: Ikonographie – Topographie – Theologi*, 253–70. Göttingen: Vandenhoeck & Ruprecht, 2009.

Mader, H. E. *Montanistische Orakel und kirchliche Opposition: Die frühe Streit zwischen den phrygischen 'neuen Propheten' und dem Autor der vorepiphanischen Quelle als biblische Wirkungsgeschichte des 2. Jh. n.Chr.* Göttingen: Vandenhoeck & Ruprecht, 2012.

Markschies, C. 'The *Passio Sanctarum Perpetuae et Felicitatis* and Montanism?' in J. N. Bremmer and M. Formisano (eds), *Perpetua's Passions: Multidisciplinary Approaches to the Passio Perpetuae et Felicitatis*, 277–90. Oxford: Oxford University Press, 2012.

Mitchell, S., 'An Apostle to Ankara from the New Jerusalem: Montanists and Jews in Late Roman Asia', *SCI* 25 (2005): 207–23.

Mitchell, S. 'An Epigraphic Probe into the Origins of Montanism', in P. Thronemann (ed.), *Roman Phrygia: Culture and Society*, 168–97. Cambridge: Cambridge University Press, 2013.

Nasrallah, L. *'An Ecstasy of Folly': Prophecy and Authority in the Early Church*. HTS 52. Cambridge, MA: Harvard University Press, 2003.

Poirier, J. C. 'The Montanist Nature of the Nanas Inscription (Steinepigramme 16/41/15)', *EpigAnat* 37 (2004): 151–9.

Roller, L. E. *In Search of God the Mother: The Cult of Anatolian Cybele*. Berkeley: University of California Press, 1999.

Tabbernee, W. 'Christian Inscriptions from Phrygia', in G. H. R. Horsley (ed.), *New Documents Illustrating Early Christianity*, vol. 3, 128–39. North Ryde: Macquarie University, 1983.

Tabbernee, W. 'Early Montanism and Voluntary Martyrdom', *Colloquium* 17 (1985): 3–44.

Tabbernee, W. 'Montanist Regional Bishops: New Evidence from Ancient Inscriptions', *JECS* 1 (1993): 249–80.

Tabbernee, W. *Montanist Inscriptions and Testimonia: Epigraphic Sources Illustrating the History of Montanism*. Macon, GA: Mercer University Press; Washington, DC: Catholic University of America Press, 1997 [abbreviated as *IMont* when cited by inscription number].

Tabbernee, W. '"Our Trophies are Better than Your Trophies": The Appeal to Tombs and Reliquaries in Montanist–Orthodox Relations', *SP* 33 (1997): 206–17.

Tabbernee, W. 'To Pardon or not to Pardon?: North African Montanism and the Forgiveness of Sins', *SP* 36 (2001): 375–86.

Tabbernee, W. '"Will the Real Paraclete Please Speak Forth!": The Catholic–Montanist Conflict over Pneumatology', in B. F. Hinze and D. L. Dabney (eds), *Advents of the*

Spirit: An Introduction to the Current Study of Pneumatology, 97–118. Milwaukee, WI: Marquette University Press, 2001.

Tabbernee, W. 'Portals of the Montanist New Jerusalem: The Discovery of Pepouza and Tymion', *JECS* 11 (2003): 87–94.

Tabbernee, W. '"Recognizing the Spirit": Second-generation Montanist Oracles', *StPatr* 40 (2006): 521–6.

Tabbernee, W. 'Review of Hirschmann, *Horrenda Secta*', *JECS* 14 (2006): 537–8.

Tabbernee, W. *Fake Prophecy and Polluted Sacraments: Ecclesial and Imperial Reactions to Montanism.* SupVCh, 84. Leiden: E. J. Brill, 2007.

Tabbernee, W. and Lampe, P. *Pepouza and Tymion: The Discovery and Archaeological Exploration of a Lost Ancient City and an Imperial Estate in Phrygia.* Berlin: W. de Gruyter, 2008.

Tabbernee, W. *Prophets and Gravestones: An Imaginative History of Montanists and Other Early Christians.* Peabody, MA: Hendrickson; Grand Rapids, MI: Baker Academic, 2009.

Tabbernee, W. 'Initiation/Baptism in the Montanist Movement', in D. Hellholm et al. (eds), *Ablution, Initiation and Baptism: Late Antiquity, Early Judaism, and Early Christianity*, 917–45. BZNW 176, 3 vols; vol. 2. Berlin: W. de Gruyter, 2011.

Tabbernee, W. 'The Appearance of the New Jerusalem in the Interpretation of the Revelation of John', in J. Frey, J. A. Kelhoffer and F. Tóth (eds), *Die Johannesapokalypse: Kontexte – Konzepte – Rezeption*, 651–82. WUNT 287. Tübingen: Mohr Siebeck, 2012.

Tabbernee, W. 'The Montanist Oracles Reexamined', in Ute E. Eisen and Heidrun E. Mader (eds), *Hermeneuein in Global Contexts: Past and Present*, Volume 2 of *Talking God in Society, Multidisciplinary (Re)constructions of Ancient (Con)texts, Festschrift for Peter Lampe*, 317–43. Göttingen: Vandenhoeck & Ruprecht, 2020.

Tabbernee, W. 'The World to Come: Tertullian's Christian Eschatology', in T. D. Still and D. E. Wilhite (eds), *Tertullian and Paul Pauline and Patristic Scholars in Debate*, vol. 1, 266–7. New York: Bloomsbury, 2013.

Tabbernee, W. 'Pepouza', in P. C. Finney (ed.), *The Eerdmans Encyclopedia of Early Christian Art and Archaeology*, 3 vols; vol. 2, 314–15. Grand Rapids, MI: Eerdmans, 2017.

Tabbernee, W. 'Montanism and the Cult of the Martyrs in Roman North Africa: Reassessing the Literary and Epigraphic Evidence', in E. Minchin and H. Jackson (eds), *Text and the Material World: Essays in Honour of Graeme Clarke*, 299–313. Uppsala: Astrom Editions, 2017.

Tabbernee, W. 'Review of Mader, *Montanistische Orakel*', *JECS* 26 (2018): 495–7.

Trevett, C. *Montanism: Gender, Authority and the New Prophec.* Cambridge: Cambridge University Press, 1996.

Trevett, C. '"Angelic Visitations and Speech She Had": Nanas of Kotiaeion', in P. Allen, W. Mayer and L. Cross (eds), *Prayer and Spirituality in the Early Church*, vol. 2, 259–77. Everton Park: Center for Early Christian Studies, 1999.

Trevett, C. 'Montanism', in P. S. Esler (ed.), *The Early Christian World*, 2nd edn, 867–84. London: Routledge, 2017.

Zisteren, A. 'Phrygier oder Kataphrygier?', *TQ* 74 (1892): 475–82.

CHAPTER 12

Unity around a martyr

Perpetua and Felicity

SARAH PARKHOUSE

INTRODUCTION

A number of things make *the Passion of Perpetua and Felicity* a valuable and striking text for the study of early Christianity. The third-century account of the martyrdom of a group of Christians in North Africa claims to include a first-person account of a high-born Roman woman in the lead up to her death. If this is true, then this is the first writing available to us from a Christian woman. Perpetua – or the author claiming to be Perpetua – narrates her feelings towards Christianity, her father and her infant son, and relates her rejection of the Roman status quo in favour of the God that forbids sacrifice to the emperor. The text also contains four of her visions and a vision of her companion and teacher Saturus, through which we gain a rare glimpse into local ideas of the Christian afterlife. An editor has written the extensive narrative surrounding Perpetua's and Saturus' first-hand accounts, which includes the labour of her pregnant companion Felicity and the group's sentencing and death by ferocious animals in the Carthaginian amphitheatre.[1]

There are many ways to approach the Passion, but here we will focus on four main themes that run throughout the narrative: (1) Perpetua as characterizing a rejection of Roman values, (2) ideas of heaven in the visions of Perpetua and Saturus, (3) the transference of the idea of the Christian mother from Perpetua to Felicity, and (4) death in the arena. I will also outline the consensus regarding the date of the Passion's events and the texts, the manuscripts, questions of historicity and the text's reception. But first we will start with a synopsis of the Passion.

---

[1]The Latin text of the Passion can be found in T. J. Heffernan, *The Passion of Perpetua and Felicity* (Oxford: Oxford University Press, 2012), pp. 100–24. Recent English translations can be found at Heffernan, *Passion*, pp. 125–35; J. Farrell and C. Williams, 'The Passion of Saints Perpetua and Felicity', in *Perpetua's Passions: Multidisciplinary Approaches to the Passio Perpetuae et Felicitatis*, eds J. N. Bremmer and M. Formisano (Oxford: Oxford University Press, 2012), pp. 14–23; B. K. Gold, *Perpetua: Athlete of God* (Oxford: Oxford University Press, 2018), pp. 165–74. The general scholarly consensus is that the amphitheatre referred to in the text was the main amphitheatre in the city of Carthage.

SYNOPSIS OF THE PASSION AND
NARRATIVE VOICES

It is generally agreed that the Passion has three authors: Perpetua, Saturus and a narrator or editor.[2] Whether the historical Perpetua and Saturus actually wrote the parts ascribed to them is a matter of contestation, but it is clear that they belong to a different authorial voice than the narrator. Chapters 3–10 are said to be Perpetua's first-hand account detailing arguments with her father, her imprisonment, her baby being taken away and her visions. Chapters 11–13, which narrate Saturus' vision, are likewise said to be his own account. The prison section, Felicity's delivery and the arena narrative are considered to be the work of a narrator, who also frames the work with a exhortatory introduction and conclusion.

The Passion has been split into twenty-one chapters:[3]

Author: Editor

    1 Scriptural Prolegomena
    2 Introduction of catechumens

Author: Perpetua

    3 Perpetua's first argument with her father, the baptism and imprisonment
    4 Perpetua's first vision: the ladder
    5 Perpetua's second argument with her father
    6 Trial before Hilarianus: Perpetua's third argument with her father
    7 Perpetua's second vision: her brother Dinocrates's suffering
    8 Perpetua's third vision: Dinocrates's refreshment
    9 Prison guard honours the Christians: Perpetua's fourth argument with her father
   10 Perpetua's fourth vision: the amphitheatre contest

Author: Saturus

   11 Saturus' vision: carried by angels with Perpetua
   12 Saturus' vision: blessing before the throne
   13 Saturus' vision: settling ecclesiastical disputes

Author: Editor

   14 Authenticity of visions
   15 Felicity's delivery

---

[2] The male pronoun is employed for the narrator or editor, as is common convention.
[3] This schema of chapters has been adapted from E. Ronsse, 'Rhetoric of Martyrs: Listening to Saints Perpetua and Felicitas', *JECS* 14 (2006): 283–327, 289.

16 Conversion of the guard: Perpetua's first persuasion of the tribune

17 Feast and prophesying to the masses

18 Parade to amphitheatre, Perpetua's second persuasion of the tribune and prophesying

19 Male contest with the beasts in the amphitheatre

20 Female contest with the beasts in the amphitheatre

21 Guard honoured by Saturus, the death of the Christians and the editor's final exhortations

PERPETUA: THE REJECTION OF ROMAN VALUES

The character of Perpetua – both her own account and what the editor tells us – is a fascinating insight into Roman values in early Christianity.[4] Perpetua chooses to die for her Christian faith instead of sacrificing to the emperor, and by doing so she is seen to reject both her infant son and her father, and thereby reject Roman familial values. She describes the love she feels for both her father and son, but the story narrates a role reversal between the traditional father and daughter relationship and a divine intervention that allows her to distance herself from her child physically, physiologically and emotionally.

Perpetua is introduced by the editor – who actually tells us relatively little. He writes that her name was Vibia Perpetua, she was about twenty-two years of age, well-born, well-educated and married in a respectable fashion. She had parents, two brothers, one who was a catechumen, and from Perpetua's vision we know that she had another brother who died in childhood. She also had an infant son, whom she was nursing.

Perpetua is the only character with a *nomen* 'Vibia' and a *cognomen* 'Perpetua', indicating that she was a member of the upper class, the *honestiores*. The gens Vibia belongs to a distinguished Roman family and Perpetua's family likely had local wealth and prestige.[5] As a recipient of a liberal education, Perpetua would be trained in Latin grammar and rhetoric; and in Saturus' vision we encounter Perpetua speaking in Greek.[6]

Perpetua's high-born status is immediately accentuated by the editor as he claims that she was married in a respectable fashion. In spite of this clear statement, Perpetua's marital status and her domestic situation has been the subject of intense

---

[4]The scholarly interest in the character of Perpetua may be seen through J. Salisbury, *Perpetua's Passion: The Death and Memory of a Young Roman Woman* (London: Routledge, 1997); W. Farina, *Perpetua of Carthage: Portrait of a Third Century Martyr* (Jefferson, NC: McFarland, 2009); Gold, *Perpetua*.

[5]See B. D. Shaw, 'The Passion of Perpetua', *PP* 139 (1993): 3–45, 11.

[6]On Perpetua's education, see Gold, *Perpetua*, pp. 115–19; Walter Ameling, '*Femina Liberaliter Instituta* – Some Thoughts on a Martyr's Liberal Education', in *Perpetua's Passions: Multidisciplinary Approaches to the Passio Perpetuae et Felicitatis*, eds J. N. Bremmer and M. Formisano (Oxford: Oxford University Press, 2012), pp. 78–102.

scholarly debate. When Perpetua is sentenced, her baby is held by her father; but by Roman law, it is likely that Perpetua's husband would have had ownership of their son – a husband that is never referred to in the Passion. It is possible that Perpetua was divorced or a widow, but this situation probably would have been mentioned in the text. Other explanations range from the possibility that Perpetua's husband was her co-martyr Saturus;[7] or that Perpetua was not a member of the *honestiores*, but a freedwoman or possible even a slave.[8] However, most agree that the description of Perpetua as well-born and honourably married is authentic, and the most likely explanation for her husband's absence is that he opposed her conversion to Christianity, rendering their relationship a standard type in early Christian conversion narratives.[9] Perhaps none of these are the case as, if Perpetua were still married, it is likely that the marriage was *sine manu*, through which her father would retain legal rights over her and her child – and thus her husband is completely irrelevant.[10]

Perpetua narrates her worry for her baby and her delight at being able to care for him and feed him. At one point, she entrusts him to her mother and brother, but then she is so fraught with worry that she requests that he be returned to her in the dark and crowded prison. Both Perpetua's father and the procurator Hilarianus use her son as a bargaining point in their failed attempts to persuade her to recant her Christian identity. Once the group are sentenced, Perpetua asks to nurse her baby, but the baby is now in the care of her father and he will not return him to her. At this point, God intervenes and the baby naturally self-weans with no negative consequences.

How Perpetua could choose death over her infant son has been the subject of much debate and discussion. Perpetua evidently cares deeply for her son – she nurses him,[11] she continuously worries about him, she misses him and she asks her mother and brother to care for him. She displays the ideal qualities of the Roman mother who wishes to care for the child herself, even when she is in prison. The emotional language that Perpetua uses to describe her overwhelming concern for her son has led scholars to see her not as abandoning her son through her death, but as entrusting him to her family.[12]

---

[7]C. Osiek, 'Perpetua's Husband', *JECS* 10 (2002): 287–90.

[8]K. Cooper, 'A Father, a Daughter and a Procurator: Authority and Resistance in the Prison Memoir of Perpetua of Carthage', *GH* 23 (2011): 685–702.

[9]R. Kraemer and S. Landar, 'Perpetua and Felicitas', in *The Early Christian World*, vol. 2, ed. P. F. Esler (London: Routledge, 2000), pp. 1048–68, 1059. A husband's opposition to their wife's conversion can be found in the Apocryphal Acts and Justin Martyr's account of the unnamed woman whose husband brings charges against her and her Christian teachers due to her sudden acceptance to asceticism (2 *Apol.* 2.4ff.).

[10]A. R. Solevåg, *Birthing Salvation: Gender and Class in Early Christian Childbearing Discourse*, Biblical Interpretation Series 121 (Leiden: Brill, 2013), p. 219; Heffernan, *Passion*, p. 165.

[11]On breastfeeding infants, see B. D. Shaw, 'The Family in Late Antiquity: The Experience of Augustine', *PP* 115 (1987): 3–51, 41–2.

[12]Solevåg, *Birthing Salvation*, p. 217; C. Moss, 'Blood Ties: Martyrdom, Motherhood, and Family in the Passion of Perpetua and Felicity', in *Women and Gender in Ancient Religions: Interdisciplinary Approaches*,

Perpetua's maternal angst is in conflict with her Christian identity. Her will is contrasted with the apparent needs of her son. Her father pleads: 'think about your son who will not be able to live without you' (5.3). She does not. At the hearing, her father appears with her son, asking her to 'Have pity on your baby' (6.2). Hilarianus, the procurator, reiterates this: 'spare your infant son. Offer the sacrifice for the health of the emperors' (6.3). Perpetua answers, 'I will not' (6.4). When her father refuses to return her son to her, this acts as the turning point at which Perpetua's worldly worries cease – 'And as God willed, the baby no longer desired my breasts, nor did they ache and become inflamed, so that I might not be tormented by worry for my child or by the pain in my breasts' (6.8) – and from this point on she is focused on heaven. Ultimately, Perpetua's desire for her baby is juxtaposed with God's desire for her. And once Perpetua's baby is removed from the situation, the role of the mother in the Passion is then transferred to Felicity.

As Perpetua's baby is physically and physiologically distanced from her, she also rejects her role as a traditional Roman daughter who submits to paternal authority. Perpetua's interactions with her father play a greater role in the narrative than her attachment and subsequent detachment from her child. The interactions between Perpetua and her father highlight issues of gender and authority. Her father has no fewer than four attempts at persuading her to renounce Christianity in order to spare her life. Perpetua begins with an account of her father visiting her and recounts their conversation through which she declares that she can be called nothing but a Christian.[13] Here, she describes her father becoming angry and throwing himself at her, which is in direct conflict with the expected behaviour of a Roman man. At his second visit, he pleads with her to have pity on her family. He throws himself at her feet, and calls her Lady *Domina* instead of daughter, further inversing the expected power dynamic.[14] Next, we see the Christians at the hearing. Perpetua's father, again, alongside the procurator Hilarianus, asks her to sacrifice to the emperor and thus avoid sedition, and to have pity on her family. But as Christians do not sacrifice, she does not and rather states that she is a Christian. Her father persists in his attempts, and Hilarianus has him beaten, in spite of his social ranking that would generally preclude this. Gold writes that the scene depicts a 'disturbing display of female intransigence and male loss of control over self and daughter'.[15] The group are moved to the military prison, and once again Perpetua's father visits, still worn with worry. Now he throws himself down before her, tears out his beard, a symbol of his masculinity, and once again fails to discourage her from martyrdom with heart-rending words.

Over the course of the four arguments, Perpetua's father is increasingly demasculinized, with an emphasis on his emotional instability, use of deceptive

---

eds S. P. Ahearne-Kroll, P. A. Holloway and J. A. Kelhoffer, WUNT 263 (Tübingen: Mohr Siebeck 2010), pp. 189–208, 205.

[13]Her philosophical argument is reminiscent of Platonic dialogue.

[14]On the connotations of *Domina*, see Shaw, 'The Passion of Perpetua', pp. 6–7.

[15]Gold, *Perpetua*, p. 108.

persuasion, loss of parental authority, his act of prostration before his daughter and a focus on his old age. Meanwhile Perpetua becomes ever stronger, taking on masculine characteristics that her father has lost: she is verbally and rhetorically persuasive, she is courageous and she has a connection to the divine.[16] During her fourth vision, to be discussed shortly, she must fight in the amphitheatre and she sees, 'I was stripped naked, and I became a man' (10.7). This gender-inversion is often seen as the final point within the trajectory of Perpetua's masculinization as she renounces her womanhood.[17] In the Roman world, the model of ideal athlete of God was male, and becoming a man may be seen as an affirmation of her ultimate victory.

In the text's depiction of Perpetua as a mother and a daughter, there are seemingly dissonant aspects of Perpetua's behaviour and description. The love she describes for her family are juxtaposed with seeming rejection and indifference. Her male courage is juxtaposed with her feminine concern for modesty as she is being mauled by a cow, as we shall discuss later. Her vision in which she becomes a man is, in actuality, 'a single, unique instance in a world of accentuated feminisation'.[18] Cobb argues that the feminized aspects are an editor's attempt to domesticate the masculine portrayal of a Roman woman.[19]

Rejection of Roman values in the Passion is further seen in the overturning of social classes. In the arena, when Felicity is knocked down, Perpetua raises her up and 'the two stood together, side by side' (20.7). The high-born Roman woman, a member of the *honestiores* class, is here equal with Felicity, a slave. Through the linking of the two women, the text makes a theological claim appropriate to Paul's phrase that there is neither slave nor free (Gal. 3.28). The women have become sisters in Christ, and therefore to live and die in the name of Christianity quashes the expectation of traditional Roman social structures.

VISIONS OF PERPETUA AND SATURUS

The editor begins the Passion with the claim that new revelation is superior to old revelation, that is, scripture. This opening claim gives credence to the account of five visions within the text: four from Perpetua and one from Saturus. These visions offer us a unique insight into vernacular ideas of the afterlife in third-century Carthage.

When the catechumens are first arrested, an anonymous brother asks Perpetua for a vision to see whether suffering or freedom is in store for them. Perpetua's unfazed response is telling: she accepts the request as she knows that she is able

---

[16]See L. S. Cobb, *Dying to Be Men: Gender and Language in Early Christian Martyr Texts* (New York: Columbia University Press, 2008), p. 102; Solevåg, *Birthing Salvation*, p. 220.
[17]Cobb, *Dying to Be Men*, pp. 105–7.
[18]See Sarah Parkhouse, 'The Fetishization of Female Exempla: Mary, Thecla, Perpetua and Felicitas', *NTS* 63 (2017): 567–87, 583.
[19]Cobb, *Dying to Be Men*, pp. 94–113.

to 'speak with the Lord' (2.2). In the vision, she sees a narrow, bronze ladder with iron weapons on either side that would mutilate anyone who lost footing. There is a giant serpent at the base, lying in wait for those who fall. Here we meet Saturus, the group's teacher who was not with them when they were arrested but handed himself in afterwards. In the vision, he climbs the ladder and calls Perpetua from the top. Perpetua knows that she will not be harmed and steps on the serpent's head, and it is said that the serpent fears her.[20] At the top, they reach a heavenly garden where they see a white-haired man who is wearing shepherd's clothing and milking sheep. There are thousands of people dressed in white. The shepherd is a God-figure who welcomes Perpetua and gives her cheese that he had milked. In a eucharistic fashion, she receives it in cupped hands and eats it. When she awakens from the vision, she recounts it to her brother and they know that they will suffer.

A few days later, Perpetua has another vision: she sees her brother Dinocrates who died in childhood trapped in a dark place with many others – a kind a proto-purgatory where the deceased dwell. He is dirty, pale and has the same wound on his face from when he died. He is unable to reach water and to take a drink. After Perpetua awakens, she spends days praying for his relief. She later sees a vision that her prayers have worked. Dinocrates is in the same dark place but he looks clean and refreshed, his wound has healed, and he is drinking and playing.

On the day before the games, Perpetua has a fourth and final vision, and this vision has roused the most scholarly interest. Here, Perpetua engages in physical combat with a foul-smelling Egyptian man who represents the devil.[21] Pomponius the deacon takes Perpetua on long, winding journey from the prison to the amphitheatre, where her supporters rub her in oil, preparing her for the fight, and the Egyptian rolls in the dust. Here, she writes: 'And I was stripped naked, and I became a man' (10.7) – which we will discuss in the following section. A Christ-like figure and gladiator-trainer, taller than the amphitheatre and wearing purple robes, adjudicates, and he is to give Perpetua a green branch with golden apples if she wins. Perpetua kicks the Egyptian man in the face, grabs his face and steps on his head. The crowd shouts and her supporters sing hymns. Perpetua receives the branch and walks to the Gate of Life. Perpetua wakes up and realizes that her fight is not with the beasts, but with the devil, and that she will be victorious. This is the end of Perpetua's account.

In this fourth vision, we find the common theme of martyrs as spiritual athletes enduring a cosmic battle.[22] Through her defeat of the devil-figure, both here as the Egyptian man and in her first vision by stepping on the snake, Solevåg sees Perpetua as an Eve-like character as her 'visionary and arena fights resemble Eve's struggle

---

[20]Her vision has literary antecedents: It is a conflation of Jacob's ladder, Jesus' remarks on the difficulty of attaining the path to eternal life, the dragon of Revelation, and the prophecy in Genesis that the woman will bruise the head of the serpent (Gen. 3.15, 28.12; Mt. 7.13; Rev. 12.3). See Heffernan, *Passion*, p. 168.

[21]There are many theories about why the author chose an Egyptian here. Some argue that the Egyptian god Serapis was important to the emperor, and so in the games to honour his son, an Egyptian is a logical opponent; others argue that the *topoi* of a male Egyptian, the devil and a mad cow are current in pagan belief at the time, and also appear in Apuleius. See Gold, *Perpetua*, pp. 26–7, 63.

[22]See also Tertullian, *Mart.*, 1.2.

with the snake in the Garden of Eden'. Thus, Perpetua 'can be seen as a kind of new Eve – a promise of resurrection'.[23]

The following three chapters comprise Saturus' vision. After the martyrs have departed from the flesh, four angels carry them to a nature-filled garden where they meet more angels and martyrs. Only Saturus and Perpetua are depicted, and it is not clear whether the rest of the group are intended to be there too. After passing through the garden, they enter a place that resembles a city of light where they meet an aged man with a youthful face, surrounded by elders. They all stand and offer each other the sign of peace, and then the elders tell the martyrs to go and play. They leave and meet Optatus the bishop and Aspasius the priest who have had a disagreement. Their argument appears to represent an argument on earth, perhaps between different Christian groups and the narrative may act as a reaction against the growth of the episcopacy in Carthage.[24] Perpetua speaks to them in Greek and then the angels admonish them and tell them to forgive one another.

The visions have often been interpreted as dreams, but the verb *video* (I see) is in the present tense and has a sense of vibrancy and immediacy.[25] Ronsse argues that through the use of the present tense, 'Perpetua's visions become less historical and more literary, more prophetic, performative even, and more participatory'.[26] Gold takes a more historical view, arguing that Perpetua's visions are 'a combination of her own experiences and imaginings that are deeply rooted in the Roman Africa and Carthage of the early third century'.[27]

The visions give us a glimpse of how the afterlife was imagined.[28] Whereas Dinocrates is held in a kind of non-Christian proto-purgatory, Perpetua and Saturus can expect immediate ascension to heaven after death. Perpetua ascends to a garden in her first vision, and Saturus' vision discloses that the garden that he sees is intended as a port-mortem dwelling place as he starts with the statement, 'we had departed from the flesh' (11.2), and it ends on the same note as Perpetua exclaims that she is happier now than when she was in the flesh (12.7). It is likely that heaven is made up of corporeal souls, as they can eat and drink, wear robes, sing, cup hands and meet God.[29] Contrary to the opinion of contemporary Christians such as Tertullian who argue that only martyrs can ascend directly to heaven without waiting for the final resurrection, in the Passion it looks as though these souls are

[23]Solevåg, *Birthing Salvation*, pp. 212–13.
[24]Heffernan, *Passion*, p. 12.
[25]Some refer to them as 'dream-visions', see Gold, *Perpetua*, p. 23.
[26]Ronsse, 'Rhetoric of Martyrs', p. 310.
[27]Gold, *Perpetua*, p. 24.
[28]For a recent monograph on this topic, see E. Gonzalez, *The Fate of the Dead in Early Third Century North African Christianity: The Passion of Perpetua and Felicitas and Tertullian*. WUNT (Tübingen: Mohr Siebeck, 2014).
[29]Gonzalez stresses the absence of a 'concept of a soul as separate from the body [and] of the notion of ascent of the martyrs to God', *Fate of the Dead*, pp. 54–8 and see pp. 197–208.

both martyrs and non-martyrs as Saturus writes that they recognized 'there many of our brothers, and martyrs also' (13.8).[30]

FELICITY: THE TRANSFER OF MOTHERHOOD

As Perpetua relinquishes the traditional roles of mother and daughter and assumes traditional Roman masculine traits, the role of the young, post-partum mother is transferred to Felicity. Felicity does not play so prominent a role as Perpetua, but she is important. The text came to be named after both women. Felicity is introduced by the editor (and we only know of her through the editor; Felicity is not mentioned in the accounts by Perpetua or Saturus) as the *conserua*, co-slave, of Revocatus, and later the editor narrates the delivery of her baby and her death. Felicity is in the eighth month of pregnancy and, as Roman law prohibits capital punishment of pregnant women, she is forlorn that she will not die in the arena with those whom she was arrested. The group prays for her to deliver her baby, and their prayers work. She delivers a premature baby in prison and has a unpleasant labour with a prison guard looking on. She delivers a baby girl, who a Christian sister brings up as her own daughter, and she rejoices that she can enter the arena with her companions and goes to her death with Perpetua.

Popular tradition suggests that Felicity was a slave in Perpetua's household, but this is not necessary. It is debated whether Felicity was a slave at all, as *conserua* could be a Christian metaphor for wife.[31] However, the labour scene reflects her low social standing: she is without midwives or assistants, and she is not shielded from the gaze of the male guard.[32] Furthermore, while we read that she suffered physically in labour, there is no reflection on the emotional strain of leaving her baby, and Solevåg argues that this reflects the typical 'disinterest in a slave's emotions'.[33]

The narration of her labour has theological overtones. Felicity's premature labour is excruciatingly painful, and one of the assistant jailors says to her, 'If you are suffering so much now, what will you do when you are thrown to the beasts which you scorned when you refused to sacrifice?' But Felicity replies, 'Now alone I suffer what I am suffering, but then there will be another inside me, who will suffer for me, because I am going to suffer for him' (15.5-6). As Felicity enters the arena, the editor describes her to be 'advancing from blood to blood, from the midwife to a net-bearing gladiator – now to be washed after childbirth in a second baptism' (18.4). Here, it is only the second blood that is likened to baptism, relegating the first blood (childbirth) to an inferior, secular and feminine position.[34]

---

[30]The question of whether martyrs – and only martyrs – are able to ascend straight to heaven without waiting for a final judgement is matter of contestation among contemporary Christian authors.

[31]M. Poirier, 'Note sur la Passio Sanctarum Perpetuae et Felicitatis: Félicité était-elle vraiment l'esclave de Perpétue?', *SP* 10, 1 (Berlin: Akademie Verlag, 1970), pp. 306–9.

[32]Solevåg, *Birthing Salvation*, p. 208.

[33]Ibid., p. 233.

[34]Parkhouse, 'Fetishization of Female Exempla', pp. 583–5.

Felicity is explicitly feminized – she is introduced with a male companion, she is pregnant and gives birth and in the arena her dripping breasts provoke horror from the crowd. The theological statement that she represents is that childbirth is inferior to martyrdom. The feminization of Felicitas serves as a foil to Perpetua. Perpetua is no longer the mother, but the martyr. Perpetua's child, which caused great anxiety in the prison narrative, is long forgotten by the arena scene. Perpetua's milk has been replaced by Felicity's milk.[35]

DEATH IN THE ARENA

During the lead up to the day of the arena, Perpetua uses the typically considered masculine skills of persuasion to convince the tribune to treat them more humanely. On the final day, the martyrs eat a love-feast or the agape, which may refer to a eucharistic meal but the description is terse. Several onlookers are converted to Christianity by witnessing how the martyrs rejoiced at their imminent death.

The account of the day of death continues the theme of the martyrs' triumph and the rejection of Roman values. The group joyously enter the amphitheatre. Here, the women are focused on: Perpetua is described as having a 'shining face and a calm step, as a wife of Christ and darling of God' (18.2). Her earthly husband is now replaced by a divine one, and although Perpetua's shining face may be reminiscent a divine transfiguration, this description reasserts her female place within a traditional husband–wife construct.[36] The female emphasis is then contrasted with her ability to reverse the voyeuristic gaze of the audience: 'the intensity of her stare caused the spectators to look away' (18.3).[37] Felicity rejoices that she will die with her friends. As we have seen, her recent childbirth allows the editor to make the theological claim that her death will be a second baptism. The martyrs are made to put on costumes; the men as priests of Saturn, the former Punic god Baal, and the women as priestesses of Ceres, who is associated with the local Tanit figure. Perpetua argues that this punishment is unjust as they are there willingly, and she wins her case.

Each martyr receives the death that they desire. Saturninus wishes to be thrown to several different beasts, and he and Revocatus are attacked by a leopard and a bear. Saturus wanted to die from the bite of a leopard, and when he is offered to a wild boar, the boar instead fatally wounds the hunter. Saturus is then offered to a bear, who will not leave his cage. Later, after a conversation with the soldier Pudens, whom he appears to convert, he dies by the bite of a leopard.

Perpetua and Felicity are more heavily focused on than the male martyrs, although the arena narrative is relatively short. The description is heavily focused on their flesh and gender. The women are to face a wild cow, matching their gender

---

[35]'She thus serves as a contrast or foil, fixed in her feminine, childbearing and lactating state, to Perpetua's transgender performances', Solevåg, *Birthing Salvation*, pp. 234-5.

[36]On the divine transfiguration, see Heffernan, *Passion*, p. 327; on the husband–wife construct, Parkhouse, 'Fetishization of Female Exempla', p. 586.

[37]On the gaze, see Cobb, *Dying to Be Men*, p. 98.

with the animal.[38] Cows were almost never used in the arena and this choice likely reflected the chastity of Christian women. Bulls were traditionally used, which signified sexual dishonour, but the cow could have been chosen due to its universal archetype of the nurturer. Thus, 'the choice of a cow is a parodic symbol of the women's unnatural responses to maternity'.[39]

Perpetua and Felicity are stripped naked and covered with nets, but the crowd recoil at Perpetua's delicate frame and Felicity's post-partem body, and so they must be redressed. In the arena, Perpetua is thrown to the floor and covers her thigh, 'more mindful of her modesty than her suffering' (20.4). She requests a pin for her dishevelled hair (20.5). The narrator's attention is on the gender and sexuality of the female martyrs. Felicity is crushed to the ground; Perpetua helps her. The crowd is sated so the women are taken to the Gate of Life, where Perpetua awakens from some kind of trance, not realizing that she has already been in the arena. She exhorts her brother and a catechumen to stand fast in faith (20.10).

Following Saturus' bite from the leopard, which is positioned around the narrative of Perpetua and Felicity's arena encounter, the crowd demands that the martyrs have their throats cut in the middle of the arena. The martyrs – the editor does not say who – have their throats cut 'in silence and without moving' (21.8), signifying an honourable Roman death, with the exception of Perpetua who is pierced incorrectly and screams in pain. This scenario allows her to have agency in her death as: 'And when the right hand of the novice gladiator wavered, she herself guided it to her throat. Perhaps such a woman, feared as she was by the unclean spirit, could not have been killed unless she herself had willed it' (21.9-10).

DATE, MANUSCRIPTS AND HISTORICITY

The traditional date given for the martyrdom of Perpetua and her companions is 7 March 203. This date is found in a late manuscript and at the end of the shorter and later retellings of Perpetua and her companions called the *Acta*, and the day and month are found in a Roman calendar from the mid-fourth century.[40] The Passion states that the martyrdom happened 'on the birthday of Geta Caesar' (7.9), one of the sons of the Emperor Septimius Severus.[41] Septimius and both his sons were in Africa from the late autumn of 202 until early June in 203, and it is possible that the Carthaginians would wish to honour the first African emperor and his family with a dedicatory celebration, especially if it were concurrent with their visit to

---

[38]The exact meaning of the phrase *ferocissimam vaccam* is ambiguous. Many translators choose to translate the phrase as 'mad heifier', but Heffernan argues that *ferocissimam* is a description of its natural state as a wild animal rather than a characteristic of the animal's disposition; Heffernan, *Passion*, p. 344.

[39]Heffernan, *Passion*, p. 339. See also Shaw, 'The Passion of Perpetua', pp. 7–8.

[40]The single Greek manuscript gives the date as the Nones of February, but this appears to be an erroneous date based on a different calendar. On the calendar and further evidence for the day and month, see Heffernan, *Passion*, p. 65.

[41]This is only found in the most complete manuscript.

Africa.[42] Further evidence for the year 203 is found in the mention of Hilarianus. Hilarianus had recently taken over as proconsul of Africa following the death of Minicius Timinianus, or more correctly, Opimianus (6.3), who had died earlier in 203.[43] The text of the Passion was probably in some form shortly after this date in 203. Tertullian knew a version of the Passion in 206/07, as he cites it in *De Anima*.[44]

We only know the Passion from manuscripts much later than the third century. We have nine Latin manuscripts and one Greek, dating from the ninth through the seventeenth centuries.[45] There is widespread agreement that the Latin was written before the Greek, though it is impossible to prove.[46] There are a number of variants in these manuscripts, and it has proven impossible to reconstruct an *ur*-text, a text that looks like the original.[47] As Gold writes, Perpetua's story is 'in flux from the beginning'.[48]

Of the nine Latin manuscripts, the most complete is Monte Cassino (Codex Casinensis), dated to the latter half of the eleventh century.[49] The earliest manuscript is St Gallen 577 (MS G) which is dated to the late ninth/early tenth century.[50] MS G lacks the prologue and ends with the words 'were threatened with a bear' at 19.3. We have a complete tenth-century Greek manuscript that contains significant variants, such as the event taking place during the reign of the emperors Valerian and Gallienus (253–260 CE).

There are ongoing questions regarding whether the narrator was one person, and if so, who;[51] and whether a high-born young woman really wrote any of Perpetua's account, or to what extent her words have been imagined or redacted by later, potentially male, authors. The editor's claim that Perpetua's words are her own does not mean that they are – as Kraemer and Landar point out: 'Writing something in someone else's name is a widespread practice in the ancient world.'[52] Martyr narratives, in particular, lie on the verge of history and fiction.

---

[42]Heffernan, *Passion*, p. 70. He notes: 'The imperial family need not have been present at the games for the honorific dedication to have retained its significance.'

[43]See Heffernan, *Passion*, pp. 62–4.

[44]*de Anima* is usually dated no later than 206/07, T. D. Barnes, *Tertullian: A Historical and Literary Study*, rev. edn (Oxford: Clarendon Press, 1985), p. 55. Heffernan argues that the Passion was most likely completed by the redactor before 209, see Heffernan, *Passion*, pp. 62–7.

[45]On manuscripts, see Heffernan, *Passion*, pp. 369–443. For a more succinct overview, see Gold, *Perpetua*, pp. 18–20, 96.

[46]The priority of the Latin version was established by P. Franchi de' Cavalieri, *Scritti agiografici* Vol. I (Rome: Tipografia Vaticana, 1962), pp. 41–155.

[47]For proposed stemma of the manuscripts, see J. Amat, *Passion de Perpétue et de Félicité suivi des Actes* (Paris: Les Éditions du Cerf, 1996); Heffernan, *Passion*, p. 375.

[48]Gold, *Perpetua*, p. 50.

[49]Heffernan dates it to the 'last third of the eleventh century', *Passion*, p. 371.

[50]A picture of this manuscript can be found in Heffernan, *Passion*, p. 386.

[51]There has been past speculation that the editor was Perpetua's contemporary in Carthage and prolific writer Tertullian. This theory has largely been disregarded.

[52]Kraemer and Landar, 'Perpetua and Felicitas', pp. 1054, 1059.

Many modern readers categorically accept the editor's claim that he has not amended any of the first-person text. Dodds pronounced that the Passion includes 'an authentic first-hand narrative of the last days of a gallant martyr',[53] and Dronke regards Perpetua's words to be thoroughly authentic due to the 'intimate and unselfconscious quality' of the literature.[54] Shaw, likewise, writes that there can be 'no reasonable question of their authenticity'.[55] He regards these chapters to have certain feminine qualities: Perpetua's 'composition . . . is more directly tied to the realities of actual face-to-face relationships than the abstractions and complexities of male literary production'.[56] Heffernan follows suit, writing that the 'language of Perpetua's diary in the *Passio* is unadorned and direct. . . . The lack of rhetorical conventions gives Perpetua's voice greater realism and tends to confirm our reception of it as autobiographical'.[57]

Others are more sceptical. The simple idea that Perpetua could have written this account in the squalid conditions of a North African prison raises the question: Where did she get the pen?[58] Perhaps Perpetua's account is a reconstruction of her words, which may have been edited.[59] Ronsse argues that the first-person account should be read as a part of the rhetorical composition of the whole text – much of which strays far from historical fact.[60] Kraemer and Perkins focus on the contemporary issues seen within the Passion and argue that the text should be read as a literary production that deals with such issues, whether that be an exemplary female martyr[61] or the female body.[62] Gold stresses the literary precedents for the Passion in Greek and Roman literature,[63] and Kraemer and Landar argue that the narrative is a dramatization of the text's citation of Joel 2:28-9/Acts 2:17–18.[64]

---

[53]E. R. Dodds, *Pagans and Christian in an Age of Anxiety* (Cambridge: Cambridge University Press, [1965] 2000), p. 52.

[54]P. Dronke, *Women Writers of the Middle Ages: A Critical Study of Texts from Perpetua (203) to Marguerite Porete (1310)* (Cambridge: Cambridge University Press, 1984), p. 6.

[55]Shaw, 'The Passion of Perpetua', p. 26.

[56]Ibid., pp. 19–20.

[57]T. J. Heffernan, *Sacred Biography: Saints and Their Biographers in the Middle Ages* (New York: Oxford University Press, 1988), pp. 185–230, 193–4. Heffernan later changed his mind, proposing instead that the prison narrative is a mediated account from one of Perpetua's visitors, T. J. Heffernan, 'Philology and Authorship in the *Passio Sanctarum Perpetuae et Felicitatis*', *Traditio: Studies in Ancient and Medieval History, Thought, and Religion* 50 (1995): 315–25, 323–4.

[58]Bremmer and Formisano note that letters from imprisoned Christians are well attested from Paul and Ignatius, 'Introduction', in *Perpetua's Passions: Multidisciplinary Approaches to the Passio Perpetuae et Felicitatis*, eds J. N. Bremmer and M. Formisano (Oxford: Oxford University Press, 2012), pp. 1–13, 5–6.

[59]Heffernan, 'Philology and Authorship', pp. 322–3.

[60]Ronsse, 'Rhetoric of Martyrs'.

[61]R. Kraemer, *Women's Religions in the Greco-Roman World: A Sourcebook* (New York and Oxford: Oxford University Press, 2004), pp. 5–6, 356–7.

[62]Judith Perkins, *Roman Imperial Identities in the Early Christian Era* (London: Routledge, 2009), p. 160.

[63]Gold, *Perpetua*, pp. 47–66, 114–15.

[64]Kraemer and Landar, 'Perpetua and Felicitas', p. 1056.

RECEPTION

From its beginnings to today, the Passion has enjoyed immense popularity.[65] By the fourth century, we see artefacts of Perpetua's martyrdom, text and commemoration; every year her words were recounted to various churches in North Africa and her vision reenacted.[66] The Passion functioned as a model for later martyrdom narratives such as Maxima, Donatilla and Secunda; Marianus and Jacobus; and Montanus and Lucius, whose stories share similarities to hers.[67]

In the fifth century, the story of Perpetua was rewritten into two shorter texts called the *Acta*. These Acts, roughly a quarter of the length of the Passion, became more popular than their precursor: forty-five Latin manuscripts of the Acta survive in two different recensions.[68] The rewriting of the story comprised serious editorial changes, and in the Acta Perpetua and her friends are arrested in Thuburbo Minus rather than Carthage, Saturus and Saturninus are said to be brothers and the women are interrogated separately from the men. Perpetua's vision of her brother and Saturus' vision are not included. The women are reimagined as less radical – Perpetua's husband is not only mentioned but is present, and Felicity is also given a plebeian husband, whom she publicly rejects which mitigates the scandal of her circumstances. In some versions, Perpetua's son is not mentioned, and Perpetua does not draw the sword to her own throat, but is killed by a lion.[69]

CONCLUSION

There is so much more to say about the Passion than has been said here. Through the summary of the main themes and issues both within the text and surrounding it, I have attempted to give a cursory description of the narrative arc and the contemporary issues contained within it, and to offer an introduction to the question of why it has been of such great interest to both Christians and to scholars since it was first written. Any comprehensive discussion of the Passion will deal with theology, eschatology and prophecy; death and martyrdom; gender, motherhood

---

[65]The text was often thought to have connections to Montanism, although this possibility is generally now disregarded. See C. Markschies, 'The Passio Sanctarum Perpetuae et Felicitatis and Montanism?', in *Perpetua's Passions: Multidisciplinary Approaches to the Passio Perpetuae et Felicitatis*, eds J. N. Bremmer and M. Formisano (Oxford: Oxford University Press, 2012), pp. 277–90. *Contra*, Heffernan, *Passion*.

[66]On the reception of the Passion including the *Acta* see, P. Kitzler, *From 'Passio Perpetuae' to 'Acta Perpetuae': Recontextualizing a Martyr Story in the Literature of the Early Church*. Arbeiten zur Kirchengeschichte 127 (Berlin: De Gruyter, 2015).

[67]See Shaw, 'Passion of Perpetua', pp. 14–16; Kitzler, *From 'Passio'*, pp. 65–72.

[68]On the popularity of the *Acta*, see Heffernan, *Passion*, pp. 442–3. The brevity 'suggests they may have been composed for public recitation rather than private reading', Kraemer and Landar, 'Perpetua and Felicitas', p. 1051.

[69]Cobb argues that Perpetua's agency in death is one of the aspects of the Passion that the author of the Acta edited in order to put its theology in line with the Augustinian perspective and to deny the Donatists' claim to the martyrs. L. Stephanie Cobb, 'Suicide by Gladiator? The Acts of Perpetua and Felicitas in its North African Context', *CH* 88 (2019): 597–628, 597.

and sexuality; Roman family and values, its reception and so much more, and the Passion offers a unique insight into the milieu of early-third-century Christianity in North Africa.

BIBLIOGRAPHY

Amat, J. *Passion de Perpétue et de Félicité suivi des Actes*. Paris: Les Éditions du Cerf, 1996.

Ameling, W. 'Femina Liberaliter Instituta – Some Thoughts on a Martyr's Liberal Education', in J. N. Bremmer and M. Formisano (eds), *Perpetua's Passions: Multidisciplinary Approaches to the Passio Perpetuae et Felicitatis*, 78–102. Oxford: Oxford University Press, 2012.

Barnes, T. D. *Tertullian: A Historical and Literary Study*, rev. edn. Oxford: Clarendon Press, 1985.

Bremmer, J. N. and Formisano, M. 'Introduction', in J. N. Bremmer and M. Formisano (eds), *Perpetua's Passions: Multidisciplinary Approaches to the Passio Perpetuae et Felicitatis*, 1–13. Oxford: Oxford University Press, 2012.

de' Cavalieri, P. F. *Scritti agiografici*, vol. I, 41–155. Rome: Tipografia Vaticana, 1962.

Cobb, L. S. *Dying to Be Men: Gender and Language in Early Christian Martyr Texts*. New York: Columbia University Press, 2008.

Cobb, L. S. 'Suicide by Gladiator? The Acts of Perpetua and Felicitas in its North African Context', *CH* 88 (2019): 597–628.

Cooper, K. 'A Father, a Daughter and a Procurator: Authority and Resistance in the Prison Memoir of Perpetua of Carthage', *GH* 23, no. 3 (2011): 685–702.

Dodds, E. R. *Pagans and Christian in an Age of Anxiety*. Cambridge: Cambridge University Press, [1965] 2000.

Dronke, P. *Women Writers of the Middle Ages: A Critical Study of Texts from Perpetua (203) to Marguerite Porete (1310)*. Cambridge: Cambridge University Press, 1984.

Farina, W. *Perpetua of Carthage: Portrait of a Third Century Martyr*. Jeffersen, NC: McFarland, 2009.

Farrell, J. and Williams, C. 'The Passion of Saints Perpetua and Felicity', in J. N. Bremmer and M. Formisano (eds), *Perpetua's Passions: Multidisciplinary Approaches to the Passio Perpetuae et Felicitatis*, 14–23. Oxford: Oxford University Press, 2012.

Gold, B. K. *Perpetua: Athlete of God*. Oxford: Oxford University Press, 2018.

Gonzalez, E. *The Fate of the Dead in Early Third Century North African Christianity: The Passion of Perpetua and Felicitas and Tertullian*. Tübingen: Mohr Siebeck, 2014.

Heffernan, T. J. *Sacred Biography: Saints and Their Biographers in the Middle Ages*. New York: Oxford University Press, 1988.

Heffernan, T. J. 'Philology and Authorship in the *Passio Sanctarum Perpetuae et Felicitatis*', *Traditio: Studies in Ancient and Medieval History, Thought, and Religion* 50 (1995): 315–25.

Heffernan, T. J. *The Passion of Perpetua and Felicity*. Oxford: Oxford University Press, 2012.

Kitzler, P. *From 'Passio Perpetuae' to 'Acta Perpetuae': Recontextualizing a Martyr Story in the Literature of the Early Church 'Arbeiten zur Kirchengeschichte'*, vol. 127. Berlin: De Gruyter, 2015.

Kraemer, R. and Landar, S. 'Perpetua and Felicitas', in P. F. Esler (ed.), *The Early Christian World*, vol. 2, 1048–68. London: Routledge, 2000.

Kraemer, R. *Women's Religions in the Greco-Roman World: A Sourcebook*. New York: Oxford University Press, 2004.

Markschies, C. 'The Passio Sanctarum Perpetuae et Felicitatis and Montanism?' in J. N. Bremmer and M. Formisano (eds), *Perpetua's Passions: Multidisciplinary Approaches to the Passio Perpetuae et Felicitatis*, 277–90. Oxford: Oxford University Press, 2012.

Moss, C. 'Blood Ties: Martyrdom, Motherhood, and Family in the Passion of Perpetua and Felicity', in S. P. Ahearne-Kroll, P. A. Holloway and J. A. Kelhoffer (eds), *Women and Gender in Ancient Religions: Interdisciplinary Approaches*, 189–208. WUNT 263. Tübingen: Mohr Siebeck, 2010.

Osiek, C. 'Perpetua's Husband', *JECS* 10 (2002): 287–90.

Parkhouse, S. 'The Fetishization of Female Exempla: Mary, Thecla, Perpetua and Felicitas', *NTS* 63 (2017): 567–87

Perkins, J. *Roman Imperial Identities in the Early Christian Era*. London: Routledge, 2009.

Poirier, M. 'Note sur la Passio Sanctarum Perpetuae et Felicitatis: Félicité était-elle vraiment l'esclave de Perpétue?' *SP* 10, no. 1 (1970): 306–9. Berlin: Akademie Verlag.

Ronsse, E. 'Rhetoric of Martyrs: Listening to Saints Perpetua and Felicitas', *JECS* 14 (2006): 283–327.

Salisbury, J. *Perpetua's Passion: The Death and Memory of a Young Roman Woman*. London: Routledge, 1997.

Shaw, B. D. 'The Family in Late Antiquity: The Experience of Augustine', *PP* 115 (1987): 3–51

Shaw, B. D. 'The Passion of Perpetua', *PP* 139 (1993): 3–45.

Solevåg, A. R. *Birthing Salvation: Gender and Class in Early Christian Childbearing Discourse 'Biblical Interpretation Series'*, vol. 121. Leiden: Brill, 2013.

PART III

Worship and faith

CHAPTER 13

Community and liturgy

Emerging of the Trinitarian formula baptism

PIOTR ASHWIN-SIEJKOWSKI

INTRODUCTION

The well-known ending of the Gospel of Matthew (28.19) suggests that the Christian ritual of baptism started with a clear, Trinitarian formula pronounced by Jesus himself.[1] More analytical, critical research into the practice of baptism within the scope of the New Testament and early Christianity shows a much more complex picture. This chapter will not only explore the development of a specific liturgical and Trinitarian trajectory, which later became orthopraxy, but also sketch the essential background with some alternative traditions, which appeared in early Christian communities in the pre-Nicaean period around the Mediterranean Sea.

The early followers of Jesus did not invent the rite of baptism as a form of purification.[2] At the beginning of Jesus' ministry, we encounter a certain Jewish, charismatic prophet known as John the Immerser/Baptist. Joan Taylor, who has offered an extensive analysis of John's practice, has argued that the originality of John's baptism was not related to the act of immersing people in the water of the Jordan, but in his emphasis on the important connection between the ritual and an inner disposition towards righteousness.[3] This connection between 'outer', public rite and 'inner' disposition is very important to the origin of Christian baptism. Another scholar, Everett Ferguson, has provided many examples of immersing

---

[1]Historicity of the pericope is rather widely dismissed by scholars, see, for instance, Jack Dean Kingsbury, 'The Composition and Christology of Matt. 28:16-20', *JBL* 93 (1974): 573–84, more recently similar view in K. M. Hartvigsen, 'Matthew 28:9-20 and Mark 16:9-20', in *Ablution, Initiation, and Baptism: Late Antiquity, Early Judaism, and Early Christianity*, eds D. Hellholm, T. Vegge, Ø. Norderval and Ch. Hellholm (Berlin: W. de Gruyter, 2011), pp. 655–62.
[2]Already noted by J. Daniélou, *The Theology of Jewish Christianity* (London: Darton, Longman & Todd, 1964), p. 316.
[3]J. E. Taylor, *The Immerser: John the Baptist within Second Temple Judaism* (Grand Rapids, MI: William B. Eerdmans Publishing Company, 1997), pp. 99–100.

as a purification in the Graeco-Roman Pagan culture,[4] as well as during Second Temple Judaism.[5] These examples include self-purification[6] as well as purification by an agent (e.g., Lev. 14.6-8; 15-16).[7] In the Dead Sea Scrolls we find important information that bathing, not just the cleansing of the body, but rather as a religious act, is understood as a medium which God uses to purify the inner life of members of the community.[8] We don't have much information whether the Qumran rituals were accompanied by any words of confession of sins, hymns or prayer,[9] however it is possible to assume from the Jewish context that the members of the community said some form of blessing while performing the rite of purification with water.[10] John the Baptist appears as the one who binds together the physical act with spiritual or religious transformation, or a proper piety towards God.[11] However, unlike other Jewish religious ablutions, John's act was directly linked to his belief in the forthcoming judgement of God. This apocalyptic, original dimension highlighted the emergency of repentance and return to God (e.g., Mk 1.4; Lk. 3.3). It also points to the role of the one who is performing this act as God's mediator. These aspects will become important in the new context of Jesus' movement.

JESUS' BAPTISM AND THE QUESTION ABOUT JESUS' PRACTICE OF BAPTISM OF HIS FOLLOWERS

All four canonical Gospels explore different aspects of Jesus' baptism. Mark (1.9-11) places it as the opening event in Jesus' life as the confirmation of Jesus' selection by God with a 'voice' which declares Jesus' special status (Mk 1.11). Matthew (3.13-17) and Luke (3.21-22) expound the story with different theological agendas.[12] Matthew points out the resistance of John the Baptist to baptize Jesus, while Luke omits the role of John, while reaffirming Markian tradition of the voice from heaven which declares Jesus' unique status. The Gospel of John does not mention the baptism of Jesus, but its theological focus is on the identification of Jesus as 'the lamb of God who takes away the sin of the world' (Jn 1.29). John also highlights the mission of Jesus who will practise the true 'baptism by the Holy Spirit', not just ablution with water (Jn 1.33). The imminent question is: 'why was Jesus baptised?'

---

[4]Everett Ferguson, *Baptism in the Early Church: History, Theology, and Liturgy in the First Five Centuries* (Grand Rapids, MI: William B. Eerdmans Publishing Company, 2009), pp. 25–37.

[5]Ferguson, *Baptism*, pp. 60–82.

[6]For example, Juvenal, *Sat.*, 6.552-25 in Ferguson, *Baptism*, p. 31.

[7]Ferguson, *Baptism*, p. 62.

[8]1QS iv.21-22, Ferguson, *Baptism*, p. 62.

[9]For instance, the *Damascus Document* does not mention any prayer during ablution. See *The Complete Dead Sea Scrolls in English*, trans. Geza Vermes (London: Penguin Books, 2004), p. 141.

[10]See, for example, the Purification Ritual A (4Q512), frg. 11, in *The Complete Dead Sea Scrolls*, p. 397 and the Purification Ritual B (4Q414), frg.2 ii.3-4 in *The Complete Dead Sea Scrolls*, p. 398.

[11]Josephus, *AJ.*, 18.116-117 (5.2), Ferguson, *Baptism*, p. 84.

[12]In this place it is not my aim to establish the direct interdependence among the Synoptic Gospels, while describing this episode.

and no doubt the Synoptic sources will give three different reasons: Matthew 'to fulfil righteousness', Mark and Luke to facilitate the appointment as God's 'beloved son'. This identification is especially important to Mark, as he does not have the nativity story, so we lack the Lukian report on the conversation between angel Gabriel and Mary (1.26-38). We may conclude, both historically and theologically, that Jesus encountered John the Baptist and that that encounter was a changing point in Jesus' life.

Did Jesus continue John's mission and baptize his followers? Unlike the Synoptics, the Fourth Gospel preserves some short but slightly confusing references to that kind of activity (Jn 3.22 and 26, then later 4.1-2). Let's look more carefully. The first reference states:

> After this Jesus and his disciples went into the Judean countryside, and he spent some time there with them and baptized. [. . .] They came to John and said to him, 'Rabbi, the one who was with you across the Jordan, to whom you testified, here he is baptizing, and all are going to him.'[13]

The text, without any alternative readings,[14] clearly states that Jesus was (the Greek uses here the imperfect tense) baptizing for some time. Brown suggests that this was a baptism similar to John the Baptist and not a later Christian ritual.[15] Beasley-Murray argues for the historicity of Jesus' role as the one who was baptizing and who authorized his followers to perform this act.[16] This Scriptural testimony is later contradicted in Jn 4.1-2:

> Now when Jesus learned that the Pharisees had heard, 'Jesus is making and baptizing more disciples than John' – although it was not Jesus himself but his disciples who baptized.

Again, the manuscripts are unanimous about v 2 and the noticeable editorial intervention and explanation of the previous statement in Jn 3.22. Still, we see that the followers of Jesus practised some form of ablution as a possible sign of repentance and then acted as having become members of the earliest community around Jesus. It is clearer from the Acts of the Apostles (2.38-42) that catechumens were introduced to Christian fellowship by baptism 'in the name of Jesus Christ' (2.38).[17] However, as we know from the note in the Acts of the Apostles, a certain Apollos from Alexandria 'knew only the baptism of John' (18.25). Similarly, in Paul's teaching (1 Cor. 1.13 and 15), the ritual happened with different wording ('in the name of . . .). Ferguson highlights that the baptism 'in the name of Jesus's' was:

---

[13]The English translation follows NRSV.
[14]See Nestle-Aland 28 apparatus.
[15]R. E. Brown, *The Gospel According to John I-XII* (New Haven, CT: Yale University, 2008), p. 151.
[16]G. R. Beasley-Murray, *Baptism in the New Testament* (Grand Rapids, MI: William B. Eerdmans Publishing Company, 1973), p. 69.
[17]See also Acts 8.16; 10.48 and 19.5.

an expression of faith in him and in worship towards him.[18]

Concluding the limited evidence from the emerging authority of the canonical Gospels and Pauline teaching, it is correct to say that baptism was an initiatory ritual offered to adults. It was seen in relation to John's practice; however, after Jesus' death and resurrection, Christians understood it as the fundamental relationship between the believer and Christ. That vital link was expressed by the idiom 'in the name of Jesus Christ'. Baptism, as understood by the early followers of Jesus, brought forgiveness of previous sins, endowed the gifts of the Holy Spirit and led to salvation. Personal faith and commitment to a new way of life were crucial. Further, direct link with other members of the community expounds the social, not private or esoteric, character of baptism.[19]

EARLY CHRISTIAN LITERATURE: BAPTISM AND THE TRINITARIAN FORMULA

Among early-second-century writings, one document in particular, is highly relevant to our subject. The anonymous collection of rules, known under its short title as the *Didache*, contains very significant chapter. Chapter 7 states a number of guidelines about the correct way of baptism and the invocations which accompany the rite:

> Now, concerning baptism, baptize as follows: after you have reviewed all these things, baptize 'in the name of the Father and of the Son and the Holy Spirit' in running water. But if you have no running water, then baptize in cold water, then do so in warm. But if you have neither, then pour water over the head three times 'in the name of Father and Son and Holy Spirit'.[20]

The Trinitarian formula is clearly pronounced here, echoing the wording from Mt. 28.19.[21] In another section of the *Didache* (9.5) we find the familiar idiom of 'being baptized into the name of the Lord'. Some commentators, such as Aaron Milavec, argue that the reference to the three divine names was a description of the rite, but was not reflecting the Trinitarian formula.[22] However other scholars

---

[18]Ferguson, *Baptism*, p. 183.
[19]It is important to state that our knowledge of further details of baptism during the first century is very limited. We really don't know whether men and women were baptised by full immersion or just by sprinkling of water. Equally, we can only speculate whether it was possible to baptise people who were arrested and awaiting trial accused of pro-Christian sympathies. Was anointing with oil a part of the ritual of baptism? More evidence comes from second century sources.
[20]The English translation follows M. W. Holmes, *The Apostolic Fathers: Greek Texts and English Translations* (Grand Rapids, MI: Baker Books, 1999), pp. 250–69.
[21]It is not my aim to discuss the relationship between Matthew and the *Didache*: for more information about the possible relation, see Ch. M. Tuckett, 'The Didache and the Synoptics Once More: A Response to Aaron Milavec', *JECS* 13, no 4 (Winter 2005): 509–18.
[22]See Aaron Milavec, *The Didache: Faith, Hope & Love of the Earliest Christian Communities, 50-70 C.E* (New York: Newman, 2003), pp. 264–8.

(e.g., Simonetti) contest that and argue for the direct Trinitarian aspect of baptism.[23] Ferguson suggests triple immersion, once for each of the three divine names.[24] I would like to place the Trinitarian formula found in the *Didache* alongside another important trajectory: the development of the faith in the Trinity. It is vital, in my view, to recognize that the *Didache* affirms not only the exact act of performing baptism, but also clearly the theological notion of God as three distinct persons. This doctrinal statement appeared in the context of and during the conflict with at least three theological alternatives related to the Christian notion of God and the practice of baptism.

First, another theology known under the tag 'Monarchianism' ('a single principle of authority') claimed that there was one God, but he has shown himself in three different appearances as the Father (in Jewish history), the Son (recently) and the Holy Spirit (now).[25] Secondly, some early Jewish Christians (called 'Ebionites' as 'those who were poor') proclaimed strict monotheism with one God – the Father and the divinity of Jesus was rejected.[26] Finally, those Christians, labelled as 'Sethians', endorsed some exegetical speculation believed in different characters of the Trinity: the Father (Invisible Spirit), the Mother (Barbelo) and the Child (Autogenes).[27] Each of these groups used an initiation ritual, possible ablution, and their theologies were reflected in prayers during those rituals. Let's sketch all three alternatives in order to understand better the context of the guidelines given in the *Didache*. First, in the case of the 'Monarchian' tradition, which highlighted unity and strict monotheism, Tertullian of Carthage's criticism allows us to see what for him was an erroneous theology and liturgical practice. In his work *Against Praxeas* Tertullian states:

> and, lastly, [Christ – P.A-S] commands them to baptize unto the Father and the Son and the Holy Spirit, not unto one <only>: for not once, but thrice, are we baptized, unto each several Person at each several name.[28]

From this condemnation we can assume that Tertullian's opponents practised baptism in one, not three, names as they believed in one divine being. Secondly, another Christian group, the 'Ebionites', this time according to Epiphanius of Salamis, in a very Jewish manner had not only daily ablutions with water (*Pan.*, 30.15.3.), but also baptism as the rite of initiation (*Pan.*, 30.16.1). However, we don't have any reports about their prayers or invocations during the baptism. Still, if we look at similar, Jewish Christian practices of baptism, the immersion in water

---

[23]M. Simonetti, *Seguendo Gesù. Testi Cristiani Delle Origini*, vol. I (Milan: Fondazione Lorenzo Valla/ Arnoldo Mondadori Editore), p. 435; see also earlier pp. 28–31.

[24]Ferguson, *Baptism*, p. 203.

[25]That would be the view of Noetus, Praxeas and Sabellius. I will discuss their theology further in the next section while introducing Tertullian's theology of baptism.

[26]Eusebius, *HE.*, 3, 27. More in S. Häkkinen, 'Ebionites', in *A Companion to Second-Century Christian 'Heretics'*, eds A. Marjanen and P. Luomanen, VCSup 76 (Leiden: E.J. Brill, 2008), pp. 247–8.

[27]See J. D. Turner, 'The Sethian School of Gnostic Thought', in *The Nag Hammadi Scriptures: The Revised and Updated Translation of Sacred Gnostic Texts,* ed. M. Meyer (New York: HaperOne, 2009), p. 785.

[28]*Prax.*, 26. The English translation follows Evans.

is accompanied by special prayer.[29] The 'Ebionites' baptism reflected what they found in their scriptures as the report of Jesus' baptism and adoption as God's Son. Thirdly, among 'Sethian' Christians, baptism was accompanied by a prayer, possibly a hymn to some divine spirit ('attendant') Yesseus Mazareus Yessedekeus[30] and ended with a recitation of some vowel sounds.[31] The 'Sethians' theology of baptism is rather complex as different documents ascribed to this tradition by modern scholars differ in details; still, baptism was practised as an initiation into Christian faith and accompanied by various prayers.

These three sketched examples, among many others,[32] illustrate the diversity of beliefs and baptismal rituals during the second century and possibly even during the first century. The recommendations found in the *Didache* should be assessed against that diverse background. The author of the *Didache* recommends to his or her milieu the exact manner of baptizing new members of the community, as, in his or her mind, that way was the most genuine and apostolic. The protection of the Trinitarian formula against any innovation, omission or error led to the detailed account of baptism, leaving its theological explanation to other sources and occasions. For our modern research it is important to read the testimony of the *Didache* as a significant contribution to the emerging proto-orthodox creation of the Christian identity by the correct theology and reflected in the appropriate liturgy.

IMPORTANT GREEK AND LATIN APOLOGISTS AND THEIR VOICES

The next stage of clarification comes from the Greek and Latin Apologists who were not only engaged in inter-Christian polemic but were also aware of Graeco-Roman anti-Christian stance and polemic. Among them two authors are important to our research: Justin Martyr who was active in Rome around the middle of the second century and the already mentioned Latin orator, Tertullian of Carthage (*c.* 160–*c.* 220). Both of them not only addressed their followers but also defended the Christian faith in the triune God against other Christian theologies as well as Graeco-Roman and Jewish critics.

Justin Martyr addressed his *1 Apology* to three consecutive Roman emperors: Antoninus Pius, Verissimus and Lucius,[33] however, we do not know whether any

---

[29]For instance, in Pseudo-Clementines, we have a testimony that baptism was supplemented by an invocation of 'the thrice blessed name' (*Recognitions*, 3.67-68). We can assume that it was the holy name of God, see *Recognitions*, 7.29.

[30]*The Holy Book of the Great Invisible Spirit*, 64 in *The Nag Hammadi Scriptures*, p. 265. Mayer suggests that this name is another version of Jesus Nazarene, the righteous, see note 71.

[31]*The Holy Book of the Great Invisible Spirit*, 66.8-68.1

[32]I will talk in detail about the baptism in the *Gospel of Philip* in section '*Significant voice and theology: The Gospel According to Philip II, 3*'.

[33]Verissimus was the nickname of Marcus Aurelius, while Lucius' full name was Lucius Aurelius Verus Commodus. Antoninus Pius ruled from 138 to 161, Marcus Aurelius from 161 to 180, Commodus from 180 to 192, see more in D. Minns and P. Parvis (eds), *Justin, Philosopher and Martyr. Apologies* (Oxford:

of them actually read or heard of Justin's work. The following excerpt from the *1 Apology* is significant to our discussion. The passage retells the procedures of baptism.

> Then they are led by us to where there is water and they are reborn in the kind of rebirth [ἀναγεννήσεως] in which we ourselves were also reborn [αὐτοὶ ἀναγεννήθημεν ἀναγεννῶνται]. For at the name of the Father of all and Lord God and of our saviour Jesus Christ and of the holy Spirit they then wash in water.[34]

We need to add a number of observations. First, the terminology. As Justin had in mind Roman readers who were not familiar with Christian idioms, he avoided the term 'baptism'[35] and talked about 'washing in water' (ἐν τῷ ὕδατι τότε λυτρὸν ποιοῦνται).[36] We shall also highlight the use of terms such as 'rebirth', 'being reborn' and 'regeneration'. For the Christian audience, especially one familiar with the episode preserved by the Gospel of John about Jesus' conversation with Nicodemus (Jn 3.1-15) the terminology sounded familiar. However, as Justin, the Christian philosopher, is addressing as well as the other two emperors, Marcus Aurelius, the Stoic Sage, we can detect an effort to show an important difference between natural birth and regeneration through the act of will. With Seneca, Roman Stoicism rediscovered the value of will (*voluntas*) as the important factor of the noble, ethical and sapiential life.[37] Freedom of choice was advocated by Justin on various occasions in his *Apologies* (*1 Apol.*, 8.1; 10.3; .12.2 and *2 Apol.*, 6.5).[38] Justin clearly aimed to present Christianity as a new philosophy, which shared some values with Roman Stoicism, and therefore should not be despised, rejected or persecuted.

The second observation is related to the clear Trinitarian formula of baptism. Although Justin claimed the ineffable nature of God (*1 Apol.*, 61.11), with the ecclesiastical tradition he retained the belief that baptism should be done in the name of 'the Father, Son and the Holy Spirit'. Does this specification worry or surprise a Stoic mind? We know that Marcus Aurelius' philosophy combined elements of religiosity, personal devotion to God, while avoiding metaphysical speculation about

---

Oxford University Press, 2009), pp. 36–41. This study will provide all English translations to Justin's works in my discussion.

[34]*1 Apol.*, 61.3. And further: 'And the one being enlightened washes himself at the name of Jesus Christ who was crucified under Pontius Pilate and at the name of holy Spirit who proclaimed through the prophets beforehand everything concerning Jesus', *1 Apol.*, 61.13.

[35]However, in his other treatise, the *Dialogue with Trypho*, while facing this time a Jewish opponent, Justin uses the term and explains its meaning, see Chapter 16.

[36]Minns and Parvis raised a question on the basis of the grammar, whether the candidate baptiszd himself or herself, but this question is not relevant to our discussion. More important is their note that Justin's report suggests 'baptism by threefold formula', not threefold interrogation as found in the *Apostolic Tradition*. See *Justin*, p. 239, the note 2. I shall discuss the *Apostolic Tradition* in the next section.

[37]See M. Pohlenz, *Die Stoa: Geschichte einer Geistigen Bewegung* (Gottingen: Vandenhoeck & Ruprecht, 1964), p. 89. See also Seneca, *Ep.*, 80.4. Closer to Marcus Aurelius' own stance, see Epictetus and his emphasis on moral choice (*proairesis*) which reflects the act of reason in *Disc.*, I.17.25, more II.23.5-19; III.1.40; IV.5.32.

[38]See also *1 Apol.*, 28.3; 43.8-44.1

the divine being.[39] The fact that Justin highlighted the axiom of his religious and philosophical tradition does not need to be seen in the Stoic context as preposterous. Instead it reinforced what was the original Christian understanding of God as the Father, Son and the Holy Spirit. For the trained Stoic mind, the notion of God as the Father was not surprising; Seneca,[40] Musonius Rufus[41] and Epictetus acknowledged that God is the Father who watched over his children.[42] Equally Stoics such as Epictetus accepted that the natural goodness of the human being/sage or virtuous man or woman had a divine origin.[43] Finally, the notion of the cosmic spirit (πνεῦμα) identified with God was cherished by their theology.[44] Justin, therefore, was talking in a language which resonated with Stoic imagination and theology.

Thirdly, reading all the references to baptism in Justin's works leads us to see that his knowledge about this ritual, as well as his understanding, showed a new stage of development from, for example, the *Didache*. There are many reasons why this is possible. First, although Christians in Rome during the second century differed in theology and rituals,[45] the practice of baptism in the Roman milieu strongly emphasized the Trinitarian character of the formula as opposed to those Christians who advocated alternative notions of God and then of the invocations. Secondly, Justin himself had some intellectual aspirations to treat his religion as a philosophy. Therefore, his commentary, observations and insights were different from those one found in the *Didache*, or even from those common among other early Christian leaders and writers, later called the 'Apostolic Fathers'.[46] Thirdly, Justin's aim to explain and justify the Christian religion to the Romans and Jews called for another level of debate, language and exegetical arguments. He remains an important witness to the development of the theology of baptism in his milieu.

Moving to Tertullian of Carthage and his contribution to our debate, we shall consider his work which is most important to our discussion: *On Baptism*. We do not know when this treatise was written; some commentators such as Barnes[47] claim

---

[39]See, for instance, *Med.*, II.3; V.27; VI.7; VI.23 and especially IX.40.

[40]*Ep.*, 110.10.

[41]Musonius 8.64.14-15; 16.104.31.

[42]*Disc.*, 1.14.1, 9; 1.30.1; 3.26.28.

[43]*Disc.*, 1.1.12; 1.3.1; 1.9.4-5, 13.

[44]Diogenes Laertius, *VP.*, VII, 147; Aetius in *SVF.*, II.1027, Alexander of Aphrodiasias on Chrysippus, in *SVF.*, II, frg. 473. More in D. Frede, 'Stoic Determinism', in *The Cambridge Companion to the Stoics*, ed. B. Inwood (Cambridge: Cambridge University Press, 2003), pp. 185–6; D. Baltzly, 'Stoic Pantheism', *Soph.* 34 (2003): 3–33.

[45]For instance, Marcion and his milieu, which I will not discuss in this chapter. See more Ferguson, *Baptism*, pp. 276–8.

[46]Commonly Jean-Baptiste Cotelier is seen as the author of this term in his work *Patres, qui temporibus Apostolicis floruerunt* (1672); however earlier it was William Wake (1657–1737), the Archbishop of Canterbury, who used this term. More in H. J. De Jonge, 'The Origin of the Term "Apostolic Fathers"', *JTS*, n. s. 29 (1978): 503–5.

[47]T. D. Barnes, *Tertullian: A Historical and Literary Study* (Oxford: Clarendon Press, 1985), p. 55. Tertullian went through three stages of his life with first conversion from paganism to Christianity, later with another transition, this time from Christianity to its more radical, sectarian expression: Montanism.

that it was composed in Tertullian's pre-Montanist stage.[48] His apologetic work argues for the uniqueness of the Christian baptism in comparison with some pagan washing rituals (*Bapt.*, 5.1-3 and 15.3) and reaffirms the necessary preparations (e.g., fasting in *Bapt.*, 20.1), as well as the exact procedure of baptism with the evident invocation of the three divine names: Father, Son and the Holy Spirit (*Bapt.*, 6.1.). Tertullian is very familiar with the formula of baptism found at the end of the Gospel of Matthew (28.19) and uses it as the affirmation of correct practice in his Christian milieu (*Bapt.*, 13.3). In the context of Tertullian's ongoing polemic against various Jewish, Pagan and Christians groups, the Trinitarian formula found in his treatise calls for additional comments.

Tertullian not only reports or advocates the exact manner of baptizing candidates. Together with his effort to defend and explain the mystery of the Holy Trinity, the baptismal formula is the climax of the profession of the Christian faith in one God, but as the Father, Son and the Holy Spirit (*Prax.*, 31). That faith was seen by Tertullian's contemporaries as both tri-theism and undermining monotheism, the latter of which being long established by Judaism. Tertullian claimed that Jews were not monotheists, but idolaters who worshipped the golden calf (*Jud.*, 1). This accusation leads Tertullian to propose in his work *Against Jews* that the new Christian covenant with God has replaced the previous, deficient Jewish one. Through Christ, his followers have new access to God and God's mystery. But Tertullian's criticism of Judaism does not share any common ground with Marcion. In another work, this time under the title *Against Marcion*, Tertullian explains that his Christian opponent's idea that there are two gods: one the God of the Jews and the Old Testament (the righteous one) and the second the Father of Jesus (the merciful one) is erroneous. Tertullian boldly states that God the Creator is both righteous and merciful, the God revealed in the Old and New Testament (*Marc.*, II.29). In brief, there is one God. The Unity of God is preserved. However, that Unity of God was also emphasized by other Christians, such as Praxeas who proposed that One God revealed himself in three different ways in history: as the Father (Old Testament), the Son (New Testament) and the Holy Spirit (recently). This way of thinking led to some surprising, but logical, conclusions undermined the distinction between each divine person claimed that the Father suffered on the cross in the same manner as the Son (*Prax.*, 1). This theology produced confusion and opened Christians to accusations of absurdity, incomprehensibility and contradiction.

Tertullian's contribution was not the only original one but also combined faith and rational argument. God is one, however, the ways in which God interacts with

---

His apologetic writings reflect gradually changing theology, which moved from Catholic (198–203) to later Montanist stance. I follow here Barnes and Dunn, see his *Tertullian* (London and New York: Routledge, 2004). The main reason why I point out the importance of these stages in Tertullian's life is to explain his theology of baptism in the context of his own beliefs, which had changed.

[48]On Montanism, including very interesting comments on Tertullian's links with this charismatic (prophetic) movement, see C. Trevett, *Montanism: Gender, Authority and the New Prophecy* (Cambridge: Cambridge University Press, 2002).

human history and salvation reveals that there are three divine beings who share the same nature. Using a number of metaphors (e.g., the root, the tree and the fruit or the fountain, the river and the stream, *Prax*, 8), Tertullian is able to illuminate the mystery of God who is One, yet still exists as the Trinity. Tertullian's contribution to the development of the Christian theology of God remains vital. It also serves to explain the Christian faith to candidates who wished to change their life, repent of their sins and receive absolution while being washed by the water of baptism. This ritual introduced them not only into a new personal relationship with the Father, the Son and the Holy Spirit but also into a community where that faith was shared.

BAPTISMAL INTERROGATION IN THE NAME OF THE FATHER, THE SON AND THE HOLY SPIRIT

Our next important document concerned with the church order is known as the *Apostolic Tradition*. Although it is ascribed by some scholars to Hippolytus of Rome,[49] others argue that the document reflected a more Alexandrian (Egyptian) tradition,[50] than the one found in Rome.[51] Dating of this document is problematic and embraces the spectrum from mid-second century (early material) to the mid-fourth century.[52] Debate around this work proposes that its content reflects many Christian traditions while its redaction did not come from a single author.[53] All this initial information is significant in discussion of the motif of the baptismal interrogation witnessed by this document. Chapter 21 is central to our investigation. First, it starts with a renunciation of Satan, his servants and his works, followed by the anointment with the oil of exorcism. Then, while the candidate is baptized, three questions are asked and after each, the candidate answers: 'I believe'.[54]

The first question is 'Do you believe in God, the Father Almighty?' The second question is much longer and shows particular Christology: 'Do you believe in Christ Jesus, the Son of God, who was born by the Holy Spirit of the Virgin Mary, and was crucified under Pontius Pilate, and was dead and buried, and rose again the third day, alive from the dead, and ascended into heaven, and sat at the right hand of the Father, and will come to judge the quick and the dead?' The closing question

---

[49]For a summary of the discussion, see a valuable paper by J. F. Baldovin, 'Hippolytus and the *Apostolic Tradition*: Recent Research and Commentary', *ThS* 64 (2003): 520–42.

[50]For example, M. J. Hanssens, *La liturgie d'Hippolyte: Ses documents – son titulaire – ses origines et son caractère*, 2nd edn, OCA, 155 (Roma: Pontificum Institutum Orientalium Studiorum, 1965), pp. 506–11.

[51]More in A. Brent, *Hippolytus and the Roman Church in the Third Century: Communities in Tension before the Emergence of a Monarch-Bishop*, SupVCh 31 (Leiden: E.J. Brill, 1995).

[52]*The Apostolic Tradition: A Commentary* by P. F. Bradshaw, M. Johnson, L. E. Phillips and H. W. Attridge, *Hermeneia* (Minneapolis, MN: Fortress 2002), p. 14. This dating is also confirmed by Ferguson, *Baptism*, p. 327.

[53]C. Markschies, 'War schrieb die sogennante *Traditio Apostolica?*', in *Tauffragen und Bekenntnis*, eds W. Kinzig, C. Markschies and M. Vinzent (Berlin: W. de Gruyter, 1999), pp. 21–38.

[54]My translation of the forthcoming interrogation.

is about the Holy Spirit: 'Do you believe in the Holy Spirit, in the holy Church and the resurrection of the flesh?'

It is evident from this passage that the Christological section is the longest one and reflects some debates around the nature of Jesus (human and divine) and his relationship with the Father. It also highlights the role of Pontius Pilate, his real death, resurrection, ascension and forthcoming judgement. This profession reflects some theological concerns and correctness of Christian belief. Finally, the third part briefly mentions the Holy Spirit, alongside the church and the resurrection of the flesh. No further information is given about the nature of the Holy Spirit.

As in previous cases, I would like to offer some comments on the excerpt. First, the interrogation has a clear Trinitarian structure. The structure reaffirms the personal faith of the candidate and gives him or her[55] the possibility to answer to each question. The second Christological part of this passage is, as I have mentioned, quite long, but it is correct to think that the original version might have been shorter.[56] Secondly, the ritual provided the candidate with a new Christian identity combined with a declaration of a new allegiance to the Trinitarian God as well as the Christian community (here: church). I think that it is correct to see some similarity between this baptismal declaration and Roman legal practice. Stewart refers to Harrill's observation that the Roman way of forming a legal contract (*stipulatio*) was based on a series of questions and answers which repeat the verb in question.[57] My third observation follows Ferguson[58] as it is worth pointing out that the wording of the three statements echoes the structure of the Old Roman Creed. The question about the chronological priority of either the interrogatory confessions or the declaratory formula of the earliest creed is a subject of ongoing debate.[59] Still, we can affirm that the *Apostolic Tradition* reaffirms the direct connection between receiving a new Christian identity through baptism and its essential Trinitarian character.

SIGNIFICANT VOICE AND THEOLOGY: THE GOSPEL ACCORDING TO PHILIP II, 3

Among fifty-two tractates discovered near Nag Hammadi in Upper Egypt in 1945 there is one with the title at the end of the last page: the *Gospel According to*

---

[55]I assume that the same questions were given to men and women, however the details from the text witness that the candidate received baptism naked (21.3 and 11). It happened in the presence of a deacon, a presbyter and a bishop who officiated the ritual. It can be assumed that, in the case of a woman, other women members of the congregation would assist the immersion of the female candidate.

[56]As the preserved wording reflects an anti-Arian theology, the earlier version might have been focused on the reality of incarnation, death and resurrection.

[57]A. C. Stewart, 'The Early Alexandrian Baptismal Creed. Declaratory, Interrogatory... or Both?', *QL* 95 (2014): 237–53 and J. A. Harill, 'The Influence of Roman Contract Law on Early Baptismal Formulae (Tertullian, Ad martyras 3)', *SP* 36 [M. F. Wiles and E. J. Yarnold (eds), (Leuven: Peeters, 2001)]: 275–82.

[58]Ferguson, *Baptism*, p. 332.

[59]L. H. Westra, *The Apostles' Creed: Origin, History, and Some Early Commentaries* (Turnhout: Brepolis, 2002), pp. 30–68.

Philip (86.19). Although in the Coptic title we find the noun 'gospel', this collection of parables, aphorisms and exhortations does not share the characteristics of the four canonical Gospels.[60] Still, it is a Christian reflection on the meaning of Jesus' revelation and salvation. It is a well-preserved Coptic document, but scholars agree that it is a later translation of an earlier and original Greek anthology.[61] Dating it is problematic; we know that the collection of documents found near Nag Hammadi can be dated to the early fourth century CE. Scholars[62] proposed that the original, Greek anthology was written earlier in various stages[63] and was a product of the Christian academic milieu identified with the followers of Valentinus.[64] I wish to add one short comment on that theological allocation. Even if the *Gospel According to Philip* emerged within a theological legacy of Valentinus' thought, we should not think that it represents this tradition in its purest form.[65] The value of this document for our reflections is related to the importance of baptism as advocated in the *Gospel According to Philip* and its original, Trinitarian explanation. This anthology can be placed alongside our proto-orthodox documents and authors (the *Didache*, Justin Martyr, Tertullian), not entirely agreeing with their theology, but pronouncing some new interpretation both the Holy Trinity and of the meaning of baptism. In my view the *Gospel According to Philip* expresses a polemical character, adds some insightful comments on the nature of the Holy Trinity and its relationship with baptism. As such it should be included in our research.

The significance of baptism in the context of salvation is one of the subjects discussed in our Coptic documents. Baptism is debated together with the proposed/corrected understanding of the Holy Trinity; therefore, we should approach the subject in the following two phases. First, I would like to explore the doctrine of the Holy Trinity as pronounced by the document. Secondly, I wish to explore the meaning of baptism directly linked with Jesus' baptism. I shall also, although briefly, mention the value of baptism among other rituals (or sacraments) proposed by the Coptic Gospel. Let's begin with the first aspect.

---

[60]Briefly, all four canonical Gospels are 'narrative', which provides their readers with information about the context of Jesus' teaching and redemptive acts. The Coptic Gospel does not share these features.

[61]See W. W. Isenberg, 'Introduction', in *Nag Hammadi Codex II, 2, CGL*, ed. B. Layton (Leiden: E.J. Brill, 1989), pp. 134–5. A different view, dating and context is suggested by H. Lundhaug, 'Begotten, Not Made, to Arise in This Flesh: The Post-Nicene Soteriology of the Gospel of Philip', in *Beyond the Gnostic Gospels: Studies Building on the Work of Elaine Pagels*, eds E. Iricinschi, L. Jenott, N. Denzey Lewis and Ph. Townsend, STAC 82 (Tübingen: Mohr Siebeck, 2013), pp. 235–71.

[62]Isenberg, 'Introduction', pp. 134–5.

[63]M. Lee Turner, *The Gospel According to Philip*, NHMS, 38 (Leiden: E.J. Brill, 1996), pp. 40–59.

[64]For instance, see B. Layton, *The Gnostic Scriptures: A New Translation with Annotations and Introductions* (London: SCM Press, 1987), p. 325. E. Thomassen, 'How Valentinian Is the *Gospel of Philip*?', in *The Nag Hammadi Library After Fifty Years: Proceedings of the 1995 Society of Biblical Literature Commemoration*, eds J. D. Turner and A. McGuire, NHMS 44 (Leiden: E.J. Brill, 1997), pp. 251–9.

[65]To be more specific, as we shall see, this Coptic document postulates the feminine nature of the Holy Spirit.

The theology of the three divine persons presented in our document has a clearly polemical character with other Christian views.[66] The vital relationship between the divine Father and the Son is affirmed (*ExTh.*, 54.5-13;). One important Trinitarian statement in openly declared in the context of the clarification about the meaning of names:

> 'Father' and 'son' are simple names, 'holy spirit' is a double name. They are everywhere, above and below, in the hidden and in the visible. The Holy Spirit is in the visible, and then it is below, and the Holy Spirit is in the hidden, and then it is above.[67]

The passage affirms both the apophatic nature of each person ('hidden') as well as their appearance in the current world.[68] It is the name of the Holy Spirit, which is placed apart from the other two names. What is so special about the name of the Holy Spirit? The original understanding of the Holy Spirit is hinted at in the following passage and further expounded in another one. Next short passage concludes with exhortation:

> So a disciple once asked the master for something from the world, and he said, 'Ask your mother, and she will give you something from another realm.'[69]

Indeed, the *Gospel According to Philip* advocates the view of the Holy Spirit as female. Although this opinion was not very popular among theologians of the Great Church,[70] here we find an echo of an earlier Jewish reflection about the nature of divine Wisdom.[71] The strongest confirmation of this theology is found in the following section:

---

[66]See, for instance, 53.23-54: 'The names of worldly things are utterly deceptive, for they turn the heart from what is real to what is unreal. Whoever hears the word god thinks not of what is real but rather of what is unreal. So also with the words father, son, holy spirit, life, light, resurrection, church, and all the rest, people do not think of what is real but of what is unreal, [though] the words refer to what is real. The words [that are] heard belong to this world.' English translation follows Meyer's text.

[67]59.11-18. I discuss this and other baptismal fragments from the *Gospel*, in my forthcoming forthcoming monograph: *Valentinus and Polyphony of Voices* (London and New York: Routledge, 2021), ch. 9.4.2.

[68]Earlier, for instance, the author highlights that double aspect of the divine names hidden and revealed: 53.23-54.5; 54.5-13; 56.3-13 in the latter section we find a discussion of the hidden name of Jesus, while Jesus' revealed name is interpreted in 62.6-17. A similar didactic is seen in the section dedicated to the name of 'Christian' in 62.26-35. The author proposes the real meaning (name) of the Eucharist is found in 63.21-24. The process of revelation of what is hidden is mentioned in 67.30-68.17; while the value of knowledge is emphasized in 77.15-35 and 83.30-84.14. See more in J. Jacobsen Buckley, '"The Holy Spirit is a Double Name": Holy Spirit, Mary, and Sophia in the *Gospel of Philip*', in *Images of the Feminine in Gnosticism*, ed. K. L. King (Harrisburg, PA: Trinity Press International, 2000), pp. 211–27.

[69]For the context and the quote, see 59.18-27.

[70]Clement of Alexandria was yet another one who attributed female characteristics to God, but not to the Holy Spirit, see *Quis Dives*, 37. See more in H. M. Schenke, *Das Philippus-Evangelium. Neu herausgegeben, übersetzt und erklärt* (Berlin: Akademie Verlag, 1997), p. 215.

[71]Proverb 8.22, more in G. von Rad, *Wisdom in Israel* (London: SCM Press LTD, 1972), pp. 151–7 and a different approach by A. DeConick, *Holy Misogyny: Why the Sex and Gender Conflicts in the Early Church Still Matter* (London: Bloomsbury, 2013), pp. 1–12.

Some said Mary became pregnant by the Holy Spirit. They are wrong and do not know what they are saying. When did a woman ever get pregnant by a woman?[72]

The Coptic Gospel goes back to the Jewish intuition that God's 'gift of life', 'life-giving breath', and later personification and his companion 'Wisdom', were all one female character. In the Coptic Gospel the Holy Spirit, as the mother, continues giving life to the believers[73] as she previously gave life to the Hebrews (52.15-24). Functions such as begetting, enlivening and animating are ascribed in our document not to God, the Father, but to the Holy Spirit. In another statement we see this commentary on baptism:

We are born again through the Holy Spirit, and we are conceived through Christ in baptism with two elements. We are anointed through the Spirit, and when we were conceived, we were united. No one can see oneself in the water or in a mirror without light, nor can you see yourself in the light without water or a mirror. So it is necessary to baptize with two elements, light and water, and light is chrism.[74]

This important explanation places baptism as the necessary initiation into the process of salvation.[75] At this point it is necessary to refer to two short passages which connect Jesus' baptism with the baptism proposed by the Coptic Gospel. It is evident that the author of the Gospel was familiar with the Scriptural testimonies of Jesus' baptism, however, our Coptic document does not mention the role of John the Baptist. In the first instance, we find the note:

Jesus revealed himself [at the] Jordan River as the fullness of heaven's kingdom. The one [conceived] before all was conceived again; the one anointed before was anointed again; the one redeemed redeemed others.[76]

Although the passage is partially reconstructed, the theology of Jesus' baptism in the Jordan emphases the crucial moment of revelation which started the process of salvation. In a quite Markian style, the story about Jesus' salvific work omits the nativity stories (Matthew and Luke) and, similarly, omits the role of John the Baptist in the Gospel of John. Jesus' baptism in the *Gospel According to Philip* confirms his pre-election to salvation, which starts with this important episode. The second fragment connects Jesus' baptism with that of the believers:

---

[72]And the context: 55.23-33.

[73]64.22-31. See K. Rudolph, 'A Response to the "The Holy Spirit is a Double Name"', in King (ed.), *Images*, pp. 233–4.

[74]69.4-14.

[75]On that connection and theology of salvation in relation to the sacraments, see A. D. DeConick, 'The True Mysteries: Sacramentalism in the *Gospel of Philip*', *VCh* 55 (2001): 225–61.

[76]70.34-71.3. Schenke suggests that this passage reflects the liturgy of baptism, *Das Philippus-Evangelium*, p. 418.

[It] was [necessary for Jesus] to go down into the water [in order to perfect] and purify it. [So also] those who are [baptized] in his name [are perfected]. For he said, '[Thus] shall we perfect all righteousness.'[77]

Even with some reconstruction of the text which fills the lacunae, the message is quite clear. The baptism of the believer leads to the achievement of perfection in all righteousness.[78] Again, the crucial role of Jesus' baptism and the role of the Holy Spirit as the giver of life are declared in the following excerpt:

As Jesus perfected the water of baptism, he poured death out. For this reason we go down into the water but not into death, that we may not be poured out into the spirit of the world. When it blows, winter comes. When the Holy Spirit blows, summer comes.[79]

Baptism, in theology of the Coptic Gospel, allows current life to be left behind as foretaste of life after death.[80] Finally, it is important to place baptism, as seen in our Coptic Gospel, with the other two important rituals: 'chrism' and 'the Eucharist'.[81] This short fragment explains the relationship between chrism and baptism:

Chrism is superior to baptism. We are called Christians from the word 'chrism', not from the word 'baptism'. Christ also has his name from chrism, for the Father anointed the Son, the Son anointed the apostles, and the apostles anointed us. Whoever is anointed has everything: resurrection, light, cross, Holy Spirit. The Father gave all this to the person in the bridal chamber, and the person accepted it. The Father was in the son and the son was in the Father. This is heaven's kingdom.[82]

Baptism is, thus, the initial stage in the process of salvation, which then leads to the next phases of transformation on the spiritual path. I agree with DeConick that baptism stands for a ritual performed with water, while chrism represents a type of baptism of (heavenly) fire.[83] Still, as we can see from all the evidence, baptism is vital

---

[77]72.29-73.1.
[78]See Mt. 3.13-17. On the contrary, D. A. Bertrand argues that the passage reflects the theology of baptism from the Gospel of the Ebionites, in *Le Baptême de Jésus, Histoire de l'exégèse aux deux première siècles* (Tübingen: Mohr Siebeck, 1973), p. 48.
[79]77.7-15.
[80]73.1-8: 'People who say they will first die and then arise are wrong. If they do not receive the resurrection first, while they are alive, they will receive nothing when they die. So it is said of baptism, "Great is baptism," for if people receive it, they will live.' Again, I see in this statement an echo of the polemic with other Christian interpretations of baptism.
[81]The *Gospel According to Philip* places baptism within the sequence of other sacraments, but as they don't have an analogy with our proto-orthodox teaching, I will not discuss them in this chapter. See 67.27-30: 'The master [did] everything in a mystery: baptism, chrism, eucharist, redemption, and bridal chamber.' More on the sequence in Einar Thomassen, *The Spiritual Seed: The Church of the 'Valentinians'*, NHMS, vol. 60 (Leiden: E.J. Brill, 2006), p. 341.
[82]74.12-24.
[83]DeConick, 'True Mysteries . . .', pp. 231–3.

and irreplaceable. In a similar way the connection between baptism (offered once) and the Eucharist (celebrated many times) is reaffirmed by our document:

> The cup of prayer contains wine and water, for it represents the blood for which thanksgiving is offered. It is full of the Holy Spirit and it belongs to the completely perfect human. When we drink it, we take to ourselves the perfect human. The living water is a body, and we must put on the living human. Thus, when one is about to go down into the water, one strips in order to put on the living human.[84]

What starts with the ritual of baptism is thus strengthened, nourished and supported by the Eucharist; and this understanding does not differ from the proto-orthodox theology of the Apologists.

In this section, I have given some limited attention to the *Gospel According to Philip*. It is an important witness of later development, the alternative trajectory of the theology of baptism. It is evident that the Trinitarian context of baptism plays a vital role in this didactic. The original understanding of the Holy Trinity, especially the gender of the Holy Spirit, does not add something new, but instead goes back to the earlier, Jewish intuition about the nature and role of Wisdom. Jesus' earthly baptism is confirmed and provides Christians with the certainty that their baptism begins the process of transformation which leads, together with the other sacraments, to salvation. As an alternative trajectory, this theology helps us to better assess the earlier apostolic documents and theologies.

CONCLUSION

In the world of the early Christians, as well as in the surrounding Graeco-Roman culture and religions, rituals were ubiquitous. As we have seen, neither the followers of Jesus nor Jesus himself invented immersion or baptism as a public rite with a special meaning. On the contrary, Christians adapted and developed the act practised by a charismatic preacher, John the Immerser/Baptist. This ritual allowed the candidate to enter into a new relationship with God and his or her new community. It put an emphasis on the inner transformation, repentance, conversion and trust (faith) in Jesus, God's Messiah (Christ). The ritual of baptism also had an important emotional aspect as it attached the believer to the Saviour and allowed the believer to take part in the life of Christ (in his death and resurrection) and also led to the participation in the sacred meal (the Eucharist). In its ultimate meaning, it promised salvation and eternal life. Baptism provided the candidate with a new identity. He or she became a member of a new religious family with new brothers and sisters; some elders became their fathers and mothers. The didactic aspect of baptism as a stage in the quest for greater knowledge about God's plan of salvation was an important characteristic of the ritual. It distinguished this act from magic, while also expecting moral progress. Baptism was never seen as a sudden, surprising illumination, but

---

[84]75.14-25.

rather as an outcome of a thoughtful choice, a long catechetical preparation and an ascetic dedication to new values. Unlike other rituals, such as, for instance, the Eucharist, it was not repeated in the life of the believer.

As we have seen, during the first and second centuries Christians practised baptism in various forms as their understanding of God's mystery and nature was a subject of ongoing debate. Faith and practice, or beliefs and rituals, are interconnected; therefore various Christians postulated different way of carrying out baptisms. Theological debate raised some criticism, rejection and affirmation of what Apologists believed to be 'orthopraxy'. In all that development the faith of the individual was central. Throughout all stages of development, the correct, as postulated by the Apologists, understanding of the Holy Trinity was essential. As various theologians speculated about the relationship within the divine, other forms (or rather wording) of baptisms echoed that enquiry.

The final aspect of early Christian baptism belongs to the crucial relationship between the community and the liturgy. The candidates were baptized by already-committed Christians; and self-baptism was rather a rare case. That social aspect was very important as it allowed cross-communal boundaries to be broken. Slaves became brothers and sisters 'in Christ' of Christians who were more affluent. Liturgy, which gathered the local groups of Christians, endorsed that original and profound intuition. As the belief in God, as the Father, the Son and the Holy Spirit became more dominant and mainstream, human society aimed to reflect that coexistence of many members, united in one, spiritual body: the church.

BIBLIOGRAPHY

The Apostolic Tradition: A Commentary, by P. F. Bradshaw, M. Johnson, L. Edward Phillips and H. W. Attridge, *Hermeneia*. Minneapolis, MN: Fortress, 2002.

The Complete Dead Sea Scrolls in English, trans. Geza Vermes. London: Penguin Books, 2004.

Baldovin, J. F. 'Hippolytus and the *Apostolic Tradition*: Recent Research and Commentary', *ThS* 64 (2003): 520–42.

Baltzly, D. 'Stoic Pantheism', *Soph* 34 (2003): 3–33.

Barnes, T. D. *Tertullian: A Historical and Literary Study*. Oxford: Clarendon Press, 1985.

Beasley-Murray, G. R. *Baptism in the New Testament*, 2nd edn. Grand Rapids, MI: William B. Eerdmans Publishing Company, 1973.

Bertrand, D. A. *Le Baptême de Jésus, Histoire de l'exégèse aux deux première siècles*. Tübingen: Mohr Siebeck, 1973.

Brent, A. *Hippolytus and the Roman Church in the Third Century: Communities in Tension before the Emergence of a Monarch-Bishop*. SupVCh 31. Leiden: E.J. Brill, 1995.

Brown, R. E. *The Gospel According to John I-XII*. New Haven, CT: Yale University, 2008.

Buckley, J. '"The Holy Spirit is a Double Name": Holy Spirit, Mary, and Sophia in the *Gospel of Philip*"', in K. L. King (ed.), *Images of the Feminine in Gnosticism*, 211–27. Harrisburg, PA: Trinity Press International, 2000.

Danielou, J. *The Theology of Jewish Christianity*. London: Darton, Longman & Todd, 1964.

DeConick, A. D. 'The True Mysteries: Sacramentalism in the *Gospel of Philip*', *VCh* 55 (2001): 225–61.

DeConick, A. D. *Holy Misogyny: Why the Sex and Gender Conflicts in the Early Church Still Matter*. London: Bloomsbury, 2013.

De Jonge, H. J. 'The Origin of the Term "Apostolic Fathers"', *JTS*, n. s. 29 (1978): 503–5.

Dunn, G. D. *Tertullian*. London and New York: Routledge, 2004.

Ferguson, E. *Baptism in the Early Church. History, Theology, and Liturgy in the First Five Centuries*. Grand Rapids, MI: William B. Eerdmans Publishing Company, 2009.

Frede, D. 'Stoic Determinism', in B. Inwood (ed.), *The Cambridge Companion to the Stoics*, 185–6. Cambridge: Cambridge University Press, 2003.

Häkkinen, S. 'Ebionites', in A. Marjanen and P. Luomanen (eds), *A Companion to Second-Century Christian 'Heretics'*, 247–78. VCSup 76. Leiden: E.J. Brill, 2005.

Hanssens, J. M. *La liturgie d'Hippolyte: Ses documents — son titulaire — ses origines et son caractère* 2ed, OCA, 155, 2nd edn, 506–11. Roma: Pontificum Institutum Orientalium Studiorum, 1965.

Harill, J. A. 'The Influence of Roman Contract Law on Early Baptismal Formulae (Tertullian, Ad martyras 3)', *SP* 36 (2001): 275–82.

Hartvigsen, K. M. 'Matthew 28:9-20 and Mark 16:9-20', in D. Hellholm, T. Vegge, Ø. Norderval and Ch. Hellholm (eds), *Ablution, Initiation, and Baptism: Late Antiquity, Early Judaism, and Early Christianity*, 655–62. Berlin: W. de Gruyter, 2011.

Holmes, M. W. *The Apostolic Fathers: Greek Texts and English Translations*. Grand Rapids, MI: Baker Books, 1999.

Isenberg, W. W. 'Introduction', in B. Layton (ed.), *Nag Hammadi Codex II, 2, CGL*, 134–5. Leiden: E.J. Brill, 1989.

Justin, Philosopher and Martyr: Apologies, edited with commentary by D. Minns and P. Parvis. Oxford: Oxford University Press, 2009.

Kingsbury, J. D. 'The Composition and Christology of Matt. 28:16-20', *JBL* 93 (1974): 573–84.

Layton, B. *The Gnostic Scriptures. A New Translation with Annotations and Introductions*. London: SCM Press, 1987.

Lundhaug, H. 'Begotten, Not Made, to Arise in This Flesh: The Post-Nicene Soteriology of the Gospel of Philip', in E. Iricinschi, L. Jenott, N. Denzey Lewis and Ph. Townsend (eds), *Beyond the Gnostic Gospels: Studies Building on the Work of Elaine Pagels*, 235–71. STAC 82. Tübingen: Mohr Siebeck, 2013.

Markschies, Ch. 'War schrieb die sogenannte *Traditio Apostolica*?', in W. Kinzig, Ch. Markschies and M. Vinzent (eds), *Tauffragen und Bekenntnis*, 21–38. Berlin: W. de Gruyter, 1999.

Milavec, A. *The Didache: Faith, Hope & Love of the Earliest Christian Communities, 50–70 C.E.* New York: Newman, 2003.

Pohlenz, M. *Die Stoa: Geschichte einer Geistigen Bewegung*. Gottingen: Vandenhoeck & Ruprecht, 1964.

Rad, von G. *Wisdom in Israel*. London: SCM Press LTD, 1972.

Rudolph, K. 'A Response to the "The Holy Spirit is a Double Name"', in K. L. King (ed.), *Images of the Feminine in Gnosticism*, 233–4. Harrisburg, PA: Trinity Press International, 2000.

Simonetti, M. *Seguendo Gesù. Testi Cristiani Delle Origini*, vol. I. Milan: Fondazione Lorenzo Valla/Arnoldo Mondadori Editore, 2010.

Stewart, A. C. 'The Early Alexandrian Baptismal Creed: Declaratory, Interrogatory… or Both?', *QL* 95 (2014): 237–53.

Taylor, J. E. *The Immerser: John the Baptist within Second Temple Judaism*. Grand Rapids, MI: William B. Eerdmans Publishing Company, 1997.

Thomassen, E. 'How Valentinian Is the *Gospel of Philip*?', in J. D. Turner and A. McGuire (eds), *The Nag Hammadi Library After Fifty Years: Proceedings of the 1995 Society of Biblical Literature Commemoration*, 251–79. NHMS 44. Leiden: E.J. Brill, 1997.

Thomassen, E. *The Spiritual Seed: The Church of the 'Valentinians'*, NHMS, vol. 60. Leiden: E.J. Brill, 2006.

Trevett, Ch. *Montanism. Gender, Authority and the New Prophecy*. Cambridge: Cambridge University Press, 2002.

Tuckett, Ch. M. 'The Didache and the Synoptics Once More: A Response to Aaron Milavec', *JECS* 13, no. 4 (Winter 2005): 509–18.

Turner, J. D. 'The Sethian School of Gnostic Thought', in M. Meyer (ed.), *The Nag Hammadi Scriptures: The Revised and Updated Translation of Sacred Gnostic Texts*, 784–9. New York: HaperOne, 2009.

Turner, M. L. *The Gospel According to Philip*. NHMS, 38. Leiden: E.J. Brill, 1996.

Schenke, H. M. *Das Philippus-Evangelium. Neu herausgegeben, übersetzt und erklärt*. Berlin: Akademie Verlag, 1997.

Westra, L. H. *The Apostles' Creed: Origin, History, and Some Early Commentaries*, 30–68. Turnhout: Brepolis, 2002.

CHAPTER 14

The community's commemoration of Jesus in the Eucharist

JOHN A. MCGUCKIN

THE EARLIEST EVIDENCES

Thanksgiving and blessing

The very first designations for what the church would later commonly call the 'Eucharist' were the 'breaking of the bread' (*Klasis tou artou*)[1] and the 'Lord's Supper' (*Deipnos Kyriou*).[2] But 'Eucharist' (*eucharistia* or thanksgiving) soon became the common term to signify the great prayer of thanksgiving that the Church continued to offer in memory of Jesus and at his command ('Do this in memory (*anamnesis*) of me'[3]) when he celebrated his last meal with the disciples before his arrest and execution. This prayer and ritual of thanksgiving was also one of solemn consecration since the early church tended to follow the Jewish pattern of prayer, in which blessings were chiefly in the form of thanksgivings which gratefully lauded the name of God for the various elements of Creation given by Him as benefits to humankind. The Jewish rite of blessing a thing or person was neither indicative ('I bless this thing') nor precative ('May God bless this thing') but rather an invocation by blessing the holy name of God and thanking God over the thing, and for the thing itself. The single Hebrew word '*berakah*' means blessing and thanksgiving whereas Greek requires two terms, '*eulogia*' and '*eucharistia*'. The blessing of bread at the beginning of a Jewish meal is preserved in the *Mishnah* tractate *Berakoth*: 'Blessed are You O Lord our God, eternal King, who bring forth bread from the earth.' And the Mishnah goes on to give several other blessing forms for various occasions. For solemn occasions the formal prayer of thanksgiving was to be delivered over a cup of wine. These solemn *Mishnah* blessings tend to recite the greatest source for

---

[1] Lk. 24.35; Acts 2.42; and later – *Acts of Paul and Thecla*, 5; *Euch.Serap.*, 14.15.
[2] 1 Cor. 11.19.
[3] Lk. 22.19.

giving God thanks – namely the redemptive acts he has done for his people Israel, drawing them out of bondage and establishing them in his kingdom on earth. The Christians likewise, from earliest times, tended to make the narrative of redemption history (*Heilgeschichte*) the central burden of their own great eucharistic prayers of thanksgiving, but always the sacrificial self-offering of Jesus is made the pivotal point of this new salvation testament: the event that brings together a new covenant people in the body broken and the blood outpoured. The Church's great prayers of, thanksgiving always culminated also in the ritual of offering, breaking and sharing the 'holy gifts' of bread and wine; and from this latter aspect, the term 'Holy Communion' also became widespread in the Western traditions.

The controversy whether the Last Supper (known in the Eastern church as the 'Mystical Supper') in the synoptic Gospel accounts was an anticipated Passover meal, a simpler *kiddush* blessing, a *chaburah* meal, or something else, took up much of the discussion on the Eucharist in the last century, but the point is not really a central one, in so far as the Christian Eucharist clearly became something almost sui generis from the outset. The synoptic accounts are surely the foundational reason why this rite became so early and so widely established in all the ancient Christian communities. The Fourth Gospel, however, does not have an institution rite in its narrative though John does interpret the Last Supper as a *kenosis* rite (Jesus' washing of the apostles' feet in the guise of a slave).

Dom Gregory Dix in a widely influential study[4] broke down the ritual aspect of the New Testament accounts of the Eucharist into a heptagrammatic form. The seven aspects in turn broken down into four concerned with the bread at the beginning of the meal, and three concerned with the cup at the end. The bread ritual emerges as: (a) He took, (b) He blessed, (c) He broke and (d) He gave. Dix noted that the ritual for the cup was not entirely symmetrical as it lacked (c). But in fact, it would surely be better to say that the original and most ancient ritual has a clear and absolute mirror parallelism in octagonal form since the (c) and (d) of the bread rite (breaking and giving) are just as clearly symbolized in the rite of the cup where (c) and (d) are both present yet fused, since the cup has to be tilted in order to give it, and the tilting is the equivalent of 'poured out'; the comparable symbol of the bread/body being broken, being reflected in the wine/blood being outpoured or shed. And so, already by the time the New Testament narratives of the Last Supper were formulated, the ritual or proto-liturgical aspect of the Christians' Eucharist, clearly influenced the form of the written account. The separation of the blessing of the bread from that of the cup in the New Testament narrative may also have been influenced by the apparent (and very early) practice of holding the *Agape*[5] common meal around, within, or alongside the Eucharist proper.

By the end of the first century, the discussions of the Eucharist, both in terms of its ritual practice, and its theological significance (synopsized in the potent symbolic form of the bread broken and the blood-red wine outpoured), became predominantly

---

[4]G. Dix, *The Shape of the Liturgy* (London: Dacre Press, 1945).
[5]So named as a 'Love-Feast'.

understood through the lens of the Pauline literature of the middle of that century, and this perspective starts to become constitutive of the actual liturgies of the church communities, which we begin to hear of more commonly from the second century onwards.

Controversies over the Agape

These earliest Eucharists seem at first to have involved a communal meal, in the ordinary understanding of that term, as the controversies over public order and decorum mentioned in Paul's first Letter to the Corinthians[6] and the Letter of James[7] suggest. Even so, the Eucharist proper was set apart from the meal by the solemn prayer of thanksgiving and consecration that contextualized it as the memorialization of the Lord's Passion. Already in these very early instances involving the *Agape*, the close juxtaposition of the meal and the eucharistic commemoration caused friction. We know from both Paul and James that some people, eating in an unfitting manner (particularly the rich frustrating the sense of communality by insisting on their privileges), have disturbed the apostles' sense of that unity which the Eucharist was meant to symbolize in the church. The solemn commemoration of the death of the Lord must always have sat at an acute angle to the conviviality of a community meal, one suspects. Many ancient societies in the Graeco-Roman empire embraced the rituals of a meal together, but the Christian Eucharist's explicit *anamnesis* of the death of the Lord clearly prevented this rite from ever becoming a simple breakfast book club.

In writing to complain about the Corinthians, Paul himself makes an explicit distinction between the *Agape* and the Eucharist proper, demanding that the believers should stop and realize that in the 'Lord's Supper' they are commemorating his death, repeating Jesus own actions and therein marking a definite break with their fellowship meals. He concludes that if any are too hungry to be 'properly reflective' (*dokimazéto*) before the eucharistic ritual is celebrated (another reference to the Eucharist as *anamnesis*) then they should eat at home beforehand, otherwise the eating of the eucharistic bread and wine turns into a blasphemy that God will correct by punishing them, since they eat and drink judgement instead of salvation.

This very early epistolary evidence prefigures how the sense of unity around Christ and a certain entrance (*eisagoge*) this brought into the redemptive mystery of the Lord's Passion and Resurrection shall become the twin poles around which all early Christian eucharistic theology will revolve. Tertullian (*c*.155–240) still mentions the *Agape* as a noble part of Christian practice but he is addressing pagan emperors and so passes over mention of the Eucharist per se in his *Apology*; probably as part of the *disciplina arcani* whereby the early Christians fiercely protected their eucharistic rites from the sight of the unbaptized. But in spite of the prominence the *Didache* gives to the *Agape* (and we need to remember here that this text is an

---

[6] 1 Cor.11.17-34.
[7] Jas. 2.1-4.

archaizing one) the close juxtaposition of *Agape* and Eucharist was relatively quickly to become a thing of the past. The problems the apostles had noted, as well as the pressures attendant on any communal meal in a growing community, pushed aside the *Agape* and left it, where it did survive (as in the *antidoron* distribution of the Byzantine rite), after, and separate from, the eucharistic ritual.

Jesus' doctrine of meals

Although Paul may be the theologian par excellence who underlines the connection between the redemptive Passion of Jesus and the Church's continuing ritual of *anamnesis*[8] or memorializing meal, nevertheless that formulaic symbolism of the death of Jesus so tightly attached to the ritual recorded in the context of the Last Supper 'on the night before he died', certainly did not arise from him. It was already to be found in the ministry of Jesus during his lifetime; for Jesus appeared to have used a practical 'doctrine of meals' as a central pillar of his teaching about the coming Kingdom of God, and what this demanded from its willing responders. To share food with another human being is so archetypal and profound a gesture that it tends to create reconciliation and forge kinship bonds in its very process. If two people are in conflict and one offers a hand containing the gift of some food meant to be eaten together, there are only two outcomes that are possible: either the food is accepted, communion is created in some degree, and reconciliation of difference is effected; or, the gift is rejected and the rift between the protagonists is underlined.

The typical 'sign of the prophet' chosen by Jesus to be his archetypal symbol of his preaching of the Kingdom, which can be seen in so many of the prophets (Jeremiah's shattered pots, Isaiah's oddly named children, or John's river baptisms, to take three examples), was always exactly shaped to the core message the prophet wished to deliver. In Jeremiah's case the breaking of the earthenware pots signified the destruction drawing near to Jerusalem. In John's case the washings (*mikvehs*) he instituted in the river Jordan signified the need for the Temple pilgrims to seek urgent purification. In turn, Jesus' message of the Kingdom of God centred often on the notion of the joyous feast there would be when God's *Basileia* dawned on Israel, and how this might be anticipated by the active seeking of reconciliation of mutual forgiveness – the kind of reconciliation God himself would freely offer to Israel if it turned again in repentance (*shub*). The outline of this theology is simply encapsulated in the terms of the Lord's Prayer: 'Forgive us as we forgive others.'[9] That Jesus used the apostles to arrange such meals of reconciliation in the villages

---

[8] *Anamnesis* is a rich and complex term. In the Christian usage it means more than simply 'remembering' (*mneme*) but connotes a more volitional memorializing, a highly conscious and solemn matter (Hebrews 10.3 refers it to the recollection witnessed at *Yom Kippur*) involving a sense that the bringing to mind renders the matter real. 1 Corinthians 11.24 and Lk. 22.19 use the word to evoke the sense of 'making present once again' what the Lord once did. Cf. O. Behm, 'Anamnesis', in *Theological Dictionary of the New Testament*, ed. G. Kittel (Grand Rapids, MI: Eerdmans, 1978), pp. 348–9.

[9] "May Your Kingdom come . . . give us this day our daily bread and forgive us our debts as we forgive those who are indebted to us' (Mt. 6.12).

where he gave his parables (the immediate context of his preaching), well explains the clashes between opposing characters that we find in the Gospel stories; the purist Pharisees and the many sinners whom, they complained, ate and drank with Jesus.[10] Clearly the appeal to reconciliation could easily be interpreted by some as a scandalously loose doctrine of forgiveness: especially if the moment was brought to a crisis by the deliberate seating next to each other of those most mutually opposed.

For Jesus symbolically eating and drinking together at a Messianic banquet seemed to be a matter not of inviting only the pure and observant, but rather any repentant Israelite who had been reconciled gratuitously by God. This forcing of conflicted relationships to a resolution around the fact and symbol of a shared meal can also explain why, when Jesus sensed the apostolic band was slipping into disarray and conflict in the last week in Jerusalem, he used the 'sitting at a meal' tactic on his own disciples, just as they had used it on Galilean villagers. Luke's account of the Last Supper remembers how puzzling it was to the disciples that the seating and other arrangements had mysteriously been prepared in advance for them.[11] On that occasion the reconciliation Jesus hoped to bring about with Judas clearly failed, and it was the latter's act of betrayal (his departure to provide the High Priest's police force with the group's address in Bethany[12]) that made Jesus' thoughts turn to his imminent danger.[13] Ever since, the eucharistic words of institution have been introduced by the phrase: 'On the night on which he was betrayed.'

The Christian Eucharist, however, following Jesus' original intention that the meal should be one of joyful celebration of the Kingdom achieved, before it became a quintessential memorial of his Passion, never lost sight of the two mysteries as harmonized notes, and always understood the sacred meal as a reconciling sacrament of both the Death and Resurrection of the Lord: the Cross being the door to the radiant Kingdom 'for the many'[14] who thereby received the forgiveness of sins.

THE EUCHARIST IN THE EARLIEST FATHERS

Ignatius of Antioch

This profoundly rich mix of eucharistic theology emerging from the foundational New Testament accounts was not lost on the first generation of the Fathers. A mere fifty years after Paul, we find that the Asian bishop, Ignatius of Antioch (c.35–107), is a pioneer in the use of Eucharist as a technical term for the liturgy

---

[10]Mt. 9.10.

[11]Lk. 22.10.

[12]The Garden of Gethsemane is sited at the last crossroads exiting Jerusalem to the East and South, a ready means of escape should Jesus have intuited this was God's will: the question behind his extended prayer, which effectively took away his window of opportunity to escape, since the disciples had not obeyed his command to 'keep watch' (precisely – keep a look out down the Kidron valley).

[13]For a fuller account of this argument, see 'The Sign of the Prophet: The Significance of Meals in the Doctrine of Jesus' (in McGuckin, *Witnessing the Kingdom* (New York: SVS Press, 2017), pp. 11–28).

[14]Mt. 26.28.

(*leitourgia*, or public prayer) of the church, teaching that the Eucharist makes the risen Christ present to it, and re-actualizes within the church the redemptive force of the incarnation, which in the here and now brings unity to the Christian assembly. Ignatius' iteration of these twin cardinal aspects of eucharistic thought (the resurrectional presence, and the force of unity this brings to constitute the Church) are widely influential in most patristic writing afterwards.

The Eucharist occupies a central place in Ignatius' theology of Christ, church and sacrifice.[15] He stresses that the Eucharist must be presided over by a single bishop in a highly structured presidential clerical order[16] that symbolizes and realizes the unity of the Church. Christ's regenerative life-force he sees as becoming truly present within and through that unity: 'The one bread that is the medicine of immortality, the antidote for death, so that we might live forever in Christ Jesus.'[17] The perfectly strong link between the Eucharist and the Passion of the Lord is demonstrated in a graphically realist way for Ignatius, when he says: 'The eucharist is the flesh of our saviour Jesus Christ who suffered for our sins, and is that very flesh which the Father raised up in his goodness.'[18] Only that rite is valid, he insists, which confesses this foundation in the Lord's ongoing redemptive work and which observes the unity of church order. He makes a statement that is observed by the entire patristic tradition thereafter: 'Let only that be considered a valid eucharist which is celebrated by the bishop and those whom he appoints.'[19] This focal point of unity meant, for the classical tradition, that there ought only to be one altar with one bishop presiding. Even when demographics meant this simple city-unitary model of the church could not be sustained, the single episcopal presidency was remembered through the sending out of individual presbyters to country churches with the office of representing the bishop. In Rome the popes commanded the deacons to bring eucharistic particles from other city altars and he would combine them in his own chalice, to signify this unifying presidency.

Throughout all the ancient era this is why the liturgical celebration of the Eucharist bore a markedly corporate, more than individual, character of devotion. From earliest times, as can be already observed in Justin Martyr and the *Didache*, the image of how the eucharistic bread and wine are baked and fermented out of many elements combined into one (grains and grapes transfigured into a new and richer wholeness) becomes a widespread trope among the Fathers, underlining how the Eucharist is the primary symbol of the unity of the Church. Incorporation into the mystical body of Christ within the sacred elements is thus a social as well as a heavenly mystery. Hilary of Poitiers, Cyril of Alexandria and Pseudo Dionysius are

---

[15]Ignatius, *Eph.*, 5.2; 13.1; 20.2; *Mag.*, 7.1-2; *Phil.*, 4; *Smyrn.*, 7.1; 8.1-2.

[16]This was often referred to as the 'monarchical episcopacy', but in Ignatius' time it was not near the undisputed sense of distinct authority the single bishop would have (as separate from the council of presbyters). This would only evolve more completely by the mid-third century. Further, see the chapter, in this volume, by Allen Brent

[17]Ignatius, *Eph.*, 20.2.

[18]Ignatius, *Smyrn.*, 7.1.

[19]Ignatius, *Smyrn.*, 8.1.

especially insistent on the notion of the grace-filled deification (*theiopoiesis kata charin*) of believers which the Eucharist achieves, and this will become a dominant theme of Byzantine eucharistic theology ever afterwards.

Ignatius sees his own possible martyrdom in eucharistic terms – he will be like wheat ground in the teeth of lions. The martyr himself becomes a liturgical offering, reflecting the total gift of self that Christ first modelled. This theme of the martyr dying like wheat to rise again, and that this act of self-immolation is eucharistic in character, is found in several martyr texts from the earliest ages. An underlying reason for this is the widespread belief among the Christians in how the power of resurrection belonging to Christ, is shared out with those who partake of his mystery.[20] For Ignatius this is why the Eucharist is par excellence 'The medicine of immortality' (*pharmakia tes athanasias*).

The Eucharist in Justin Martyr

The first extended written notice of the Eucharist, however, has to wait until the second century and comes from the pen of Justin Martyr (d. circa 165), a native of Nablus in Palestine. He studied the various philosophical schools of the Hellenistic world, and converted to Christianity sometime before 132. As a Christian philosopher he taught first in Ephesus and then after 150 in Rome where he was denounced by a rival teacher and died as a martyr in 165. In his *Dialogue* with the Jewish protagonist Trypho, Justin describes the Eucharist as: 'A pure oblation and a spiritual sacrifice.'[21] His *First Apology*,[22] written about ten years before he died, was addressed to Emperor Marcus Aurelius and his sons. Here he says that the Christians call their central prayer ritual 'The Eucharist', and he explains how the ritual was commanded: 'In memory of Jesus, in those memoirs which are called the Gospels.' Justin first describes the baptismal rite of initiation followed by a Eucharist as follows:

> At the conclusion of the [baptismal] prayers, we greet one another with a kiss.[23] Then bread and a cup containing wine and water are presented to the one presiding over the brethren. He then accepts them and offers praise and glory to the Father of All through the name of the Son and the Holy Spirit, making a long prayer of thanksgiving to God who has counted us worthy of such favours. At the end of these prayers and thanksgiving, all express their agreement by saying Amen. . . . And those whom we call deacons call out each one there to partake of

---

[20]Ignatius is one of the earliest post New Testament writers positively to develop the symbolism of Eucharist as a mystery, entered into by the *mimesis* of the worshipper. See Ignatius, *Trall.*, 2.3; also compare his account of the eucharistic mystery rite in *Eph.*, 9.2 with the account of the rite in Apuleius', *Met.*, 11.10; Further see A. Brent, *Ignatius of Antioch and the Second Sophistic* (Tübingen: Mohr Siebeck, 2006), pp. 124–80.

[21]Justin, *Tryph.*, 41 & 117.

[22]Justin, *1Apol.*, 65-66.

[23]1 Peter. 5.14.

the bread and wine and water over which the thanksgiving has been pronounced. They also carry it to members who are absent.[24]

Following on from this description Justin speaks also of the more regular Sunday eucharistic assembly, where he describes the rite as beginning with readings from the 'memoirs of the apostles' (that is, the New Testament) 'or the writings of the prophets . . . as much as there is time for'. According to Justin, the readings were followed by a homiletic explanation of the texts and a moral encouragement given by the president of the assembly, then standing prayers, followed by the presentation of bread and wine, a presidential eucharistic prayer made 'to the best of his ability', and then the distribution of the elements to those present and absent, and finally a collection sponsored by the wealthy members for the relief of the poor.[25]

This seminal account in Justin's *First Apology* also gives us one of the earliest post scriptural theological explanations of the Eucharist; albeit one simplified and designed to make a pagan outsider understand:

> We call this food the Eucharist. Only they are permitted to share in it who believe our teachings to be true, and who have been washed in that bath for the forgiveness of sins, and who live as Christ commanded. We do not regard these elements as common bread or common drink but, as we have been taught, just as through the word of God Our Saviour Jesus Christ was incarnate assuming flesh and blood for our salvation, just so the food over which thanksgiving has been offered by the prayer of his word, that food which by assimilation nourishes our flesh and blood, is both the flesh and the blood of that same incarnate Jesus. The apostles in their memoirs, which are called Gospels, have handed down that they were commanded to do this; for Jesus took bread and after having given thanks he said: 'Do this in memory of me; this is my body.' Likewise he also took the cup, gave thanks, and said: 'This is my blood.' And to the apostles alone did he communicate this.[26]

In explaining the ritual to the emperor, Justin wishes to distance the Eucharist from any echoes it might have for the pagans, of the Mithraic mysteries. He complains that the apparent similarities between the Eucharist and the pagan mysteries were a mockery saying that this was a tactic the demons had arranged in order to lead humans astray from the truth.[27] This anxiety to distance the Christian rite from the Greek mysteries endured for some time in the church. Even into the mid-fourth century Julius Firmicus Maternus, among others, goes to some length to distance the Eucharist from the rites of Attis, which involved the initiate in 'eating from the timbrel and drinking from the cymbal'.[28] Paul himself had first used the analogy of

---

[24]Justin, *1Apol.*, 65.

[25]Justin, *1Apol.*, 67.

[26]Justin, *1Apol.*, 66.

[27]Justin, *1Apol.*, 66; text in: D. Sheerin, *The Eucharist* (Wilmington, DE: Michael Glazier, 1986), p. 36.

[28]Julius Firmicus Maternus. *Error.*18. It is interesting to note how he tells his readers that the Christian eucharistic ritual derives by Christ's own command as given in the Johannine teachings. cf. Jn 6.35; Jn 7.37-38; Jn 6.54.

the pagan mysteries to speak about the salvific mystery of Christ; often subverting the very sense of the pagan mystery (a word meaning 'to keep strict silence'), such as in his renowned witticism: 'Behold! I will speak out to you a mystery.'[29]

Once the age of the Apologists had passed, the fourth-century Greek Fathers are not so worried about absorbing Paul's language of mystery and pushing his point that the mystery of Christ fulfils all that the ancient mysteries had merely foreshadowed. Among them Gregory the Theologian stands out in his homilies delivered in the great cathedral at Constantinople.[30] The Latin Fathers of the fourth century simply transliterated the Greek Christian language of *ta mysteria* into Latin as *mysteria*,[31] or transcribed it into *sacramenta*.[32]

Justin also calls the Eucharist the '*Anamnesis*' which is a very particular and charged word for 'memorialization' when used in this sense. For him the Eucharist as memorial eschatologically recalls to the church's mind and synopsizes all of God's salvific action from the beginning of creation to the future end-times. The eschatological imperative of the Eucharist is, for Justin, the strongest encouragement for the disciples to express their remembrance of the Saviour: 'in a life in conformity with the Lord's precepts'.[33]

The later church continued this usage sporadically. The substitutionary term 'the *Anamnesis*' still appears in the third-century Apostolic Tradition,[34] as well as in the fifth-century liturgy of St John Chrysostom; but by and large the favoured patristic technical terms for the eucharistic liturgy as a whole, or the specifically sacramental aspect of holy communion were: the *Anaphora* (the prayer of consecration – or what would be called in the Latin church the *Canon*), or *To Mysterion* (the eucharistic mystery).[35]

THE ERA OF THE APOLOGISTS

The age of the Apologists was dominated by the fact and fear of persecution. One of the charges that surfaced against the church in this context was cannibalism, surely representing a half-heard report of the eucharistic practice of consuming the body and blood of Christ, but perhaps also a kind of witness to reports heard from Christians themselves that their Eucharist was 'truly the body and blood', for this

---

[29]1 Cor. 15.51, echoed in Eph. 5.32; see also Rom. 11.25; Rom. 16.25; Eph. 1.9; Eph. 3.9 and passim in Colossians.

[30]See especially *Orat.* 39. 1-2. ('*On the Holy Lights*').

[31]Ambrose, *Com.Luc*, 7.11; Pope Innocent. *Epistle.*, 25.

[32]Tertullian, *Cor.*, 3; Cyprian. *Epistle.*, 74.4. Hilary, Ambrose and Augustine follow them in this usage. 'Mass' as a Latin church connotation of the Eucharist starts to come into common usage from the later fourth century – deriving from the dismissal rite concluding the liturgy (*ite missa est*). cf. *Itinerary of Egeria*, 25.10; Ambrose, *Epistle.*, 76.4.

[33]Justin, *1Apol.*, 66.1.

[34]Hippolytus, *Ap. Trad.*, 4.10.

[35]In modern times the term '*synaxis*' has also become prevalent. In antiquity this referred only to the service of readings, homiletic and intercessions that preceded the eucharistic ritual.

realist strand is very pronounced from the outset. The charge appears in the *Acts of the Martyrs of Lyons*, from the persecution of 177[36]:

> Some pagan household slaves of our people were arrested . . . and charged us falsely as the soldiers had prompted them, with Thyestean[37] banquets . . . when the report of these things was spread abroad, everyone became savage towards us.[38]

The charges of incest, cannibalism and eating blood-soaked bread are also mocked by Tertullian twenty years later in 197.[39] Minucius Felix[40] notes how they had been revived by Marcus Cornelius Fronto, tutor to Marcus Aurelius, in his rabid anti-Christian propaganda. Pliny the Younger, making a report on Christian practices sometime between 110 and 113 for the Emperor Trajan, seems at pains to lay these calumnies to rest, which would have been deeply disturbing to the wider Roman society. He investigates names which an informer has given to him, for people who claim they had given up Christian practice some years back, and have now renounced Christ. They told him that:

> It was their practice to meet on appointed day before sunrise, to sing together a hymn to Christ as if to a god and to bind themselves by an oath . . . [not commit malpractices] . . . upon the completion of these activities their practice was to separate but assemble again later to take food, though of an ordinary and harmless kind.[41]

Pliny goes on to say that he confirmed this report by torturing two active Christian deaconesses and found only 'perverse superstition', nothing criminal.

IRENAEUS' THEOLOGY OF THE EUCHARIST

Like Justin, the Asian bishop of Lyons, Irenaeus (died *c*.200), also sees the Eucharist eschatologically and soteriologically. For him it stands, as the heart of the Christ-event, poised in the middle of history recapitulating all the offerings which the just have made to God throughout all creation. The immense glory which transfigures the sacrifice that Christ makes of himself turns the Eucharist into that offering which anticipates the final harvest God will make of all the righteous of the earth. Irenaeus stresses the reality of this sacred material offering as a weapon against

---

[36]cf. H. Musurillo, *The Acts of the Christian Martyrs* (Oxford: Oxford University Press, 1972), pp. 64–6.

[37]Thyestes was the son of Pelops and king of Olympia, whose brother Atreus, taking the throne from him took revenge for personal offences by murdering his sons and serving them to him as roasted meat which he unwittingly ate.

[38]*Acts of the Martyrs of Lyons,* 14-15. Cited from Sheerin, *The Eucharist,* p. 26.

[39]Tertullian, *Apol.,* 8.7.

[40]Minucius Felix, *Oct.,* 8.4; 9. 5-6.

[41]Pliny the Younger. *Ep.* 10. 96-98.

extra-ecclesial (gnosticizing) 'spiritualities' which cannot see the flesh as having any divine potency at all.

> He instructed his disciples to offer God the first-fruits of his own creation; not because he stood in any need of them, rather so that they might not be unfruitful or ungrateful themselves. He took bread, a created material thing, and gave thanks, saying: 'This is my body.' And the cup (which is also a part of the creation to which we belong) he pronounced to be his own blood. In this way he taught us the new oblation of a New Covenant. The church has received all this from the apostles and throughout the whole world it offers this to God, the one who gives us the first-fruits of his own gifts in the New Covenant so that we might live by them.[42]

Irenaeus' understanding of the Eucharist as sacrificially potent becomes widely influential in later patristic thought:

> The oblation of the Church which God has commanded to be offered throughout the whole world, has been accepted by God as a pure sacrifice. He stands in no need of any sacrifice from us; but he who makes the offering is himself glorified through what he offers if his gift is acceptable; since by offering gifts our honour and love to the king are made known.[43]

Much of later patristic writing uses this term of oblation, or 'offering', to connote the eucharistic rites (Latin *oblatio,* Greek *prosphora*) which clearly derives from its liturgical character in the churches – that is the offering of the great prayer of thanksgiving at the centre of the eucharistic celebration. The term just as strongly connotes the sense that the early church had of the offering of the elements of bread and wine as the body of Christ, being a sacrificial mystery: the bread broken, the wine outpoured, to remind the church that Christ's offering of himself to the Father, and gift of himself to the church, was achieved through the sufferings of the cross and consummated in the glory of the resurrection. These are two mysteries which cannot be separated and in fact are as one: as the Fourth Evangelist underlines in his teaching that the Passion is the Glory of the Lord.[44] To underline the point, the Eucharist is often referred to in both the Latin and Greek churches as 'the bloodless sacrifice'. Tertullian simply refers to the Eucharist on one occasion as: 'The sacrificial prayers'.[45]

LATIN EUCHARISTIC THOUGHT: CYPRIAN OF CARTHAGE

The third-century African aristocrat and bishop Cyprian (*c.*200–258) offers us the first specifically designed Christian essay on eucharistic theology that attempts to think through the mystery (as distinct from earlier narratives that celebrate it in

[42]Irenaeus, *Haer.,* 4. 17.5.
[43]Irenaeus, *Haer.,* 4.18.1.
[44]Jn 13.31.
[45]Tertullian, *Orat.,* 19.

mystic forms and symbols more than syllogistic reflection). Cyprian was a pagan city magistrate whose rapid elevation as a Christian bishop in a very fraught time made it necessary for him to write extensively, so as to educate himself in the Christian doctrines before serving as a theological master whose duty was to teach others.

In his sixty-second epistle,[46] Cyprian is initially motivated to speak against certain groups that have begun to offer only water, rather than wine mixed with water at the Eucharists. He forbids this practice since it does not 'follow that which Jesus Christ, our Lord and God, the founder and teacher of this sacrifice, himself did and taught'. The faithful servant, he says, must obey 'Whatever is prescribed by the inspiration and command of God'. Showing he is closely aware of Paul,[47] Cyprian speaks of the church having to observe what was 'handed on' (traditio, paradosis) from the Lord himself. Wine is the sacred symbol of the Lord's blood and is fundamentally necessary for the sacramental shaping of this sacrifice, he argues:

> For when Christ says, 'I am the true vine' (Jn 15.1) the blood of Christ is assuredly not water, but wine; neither can His blood by which we are redeemed and made alive appear to be in the cup, if in that cup there is no wine whereby the blood of Christ is manifested, a thing which is declared by the sacrament and testimony of all the Scriptures.[48]

Cyprian demonstrates from the example of Noah and Melchizedek (heading up a whole series of biblical types) the necessity of the offering of wine for the consecration. For him the core of the eucharistic action is the implicit sacrifice offered (a theme which after him dominates much of Latin theological thought):

> For who is more a priest of the most high God than our Lord Jesus Christ, who offered a sacrifice to God the Father, offering the very same thing which Melchizedek once offered, namely bread and wine, that is, His body and blood?[49]

For Cyprian, the Eucharist of the churches must of necessity be aligned with the Passion of the Lord, in order to make the sacrifice not only possible, but legitimate:

> The cup which the Lord offered was mixed, and this was the wine which He called His blood. From this it follows that the blood of Christ is not offered if there is no wine in the cup, neither is the Lord's sacrifice being celebrated with a legitimate consecration unless our oblation and sacrifice respond to His Passion.[50]

The anamnesis of the Passion is, in Cyprian's hands, made secure within the church chiefly by mimesis of the Lord's own actions:

> For if our Lord and God Jesus Christ is Himself the High Priest of God the Father, and has first offered Himself as a sacrifice to the Father, commanding this

---

[46]Cyprian. Ep., 62: [To Caecilius on the Sacrament of the Lord's Cup].
[47]1 Cor. 11.23.
[48]Cyprian. Ep., 62.2.
[49]Cyprian. Ep., 62.4.
[50]Cyprian. Ep., 62.9.

to be done in memory of Himself, then there can be no doubt that only the priest who imitates what Christ Himself did, truly stands in Christ's place and thus offers a true and complete sacrifice in the Church to God the Father.[51]

Cyprian's authority gave birth in the Latin church to the long mimetic tradition of the priest as the *alter Christus* and underlined the major approach to the Eucharist as sacrifice within Latin ecclesiology.

BOOKS OF CHURCH ORDER

In the late nineteenth century an important and early 'Church Order' book was discovered in the library of the Patriarch of Jerusalem. Its full title was *The Teaching of the Lord through the Twelve Apostles to the Nations*. It is more commonly known today as the *Didache*. Its publication caused a sensation with some even believing it dated from the first generation of the Church (circa AD 60) and gave a snapshot of how liturgy was actually conducted in that era. Now the dust has settled on numerous arguments it is more generally accepted that the work is from the end of the first century or early second, and represents an archaizing picture of a Syrian community out of the run of the mainstream (something that applied to many such communities there). Many of the later Church order books (produced well into the fourth century[52]) similarly try to achieve a high status by pseudepigraphically claiming the apostles' authority for their desire to influence their neighbour's practices or defend their own.

Chapters seven to ten of the *Didache* give instructions about baptism, prayer and fasting and how the *Agape* ought to be celebrated. Chapters nine to ten of the book seem to be (though it is not entirely clear) more of a reference to the actual ritual of the Eucharist held after a baptism. The prayers offered here echo Jewish prayers of blessing but reworked to contain a clearer Christian spirit. The context of common prayer giving thanks to God (*eucharistia*) is more pronounced in chapter fourteen of the *Didache* which again seems to connote a Eucharist separate from baptism, and perhaps the more regular Sunday form.

The *Didache* tells how on each Lord's day the church should come together and 'break bread and give thanks, after confessing your transgressions so that your sacrifice may be pure. . . . And so, elect for yourselves bishops and deacons who are worthy of the Lord, men who are approved.' What is most noticeably and strangely missing in *Didache* chapters nine and ten is any reference to words of institution or any focus on the Passion of the Lord.

The Apostolic Tradition is another important church order book, deriving this time from Rome. It was composed by the theologian-philosopher Hippolytus (*c.*176–236) in the early third century and gives an example of what the author thinks is a good model for a eucharistic presidential prayer. The text is not an archival account of what was actually happening in the Roman liturgy of its time, but it does give a picture of how the eucharistic prayers, which earlier had been said extempore, are

---

[51]Cyprian. *Ep.*, 63.14.
[52]The *Didascalia Apostolorum* from the third century, the *Apostolic Church Order* from the early fourth, and the *Apostolic Constitutions* from the late fourth.

now passing into more settled forms. By the fourth century the days of personal extemporization by the president would be more or less over; though even those earlier free-flowing prayers were most likely modelled on the baptismal creeds and the recitation of the great works of God that have saved and gathered his people, culminating in the Passion of the Lord and the sending of the Spirit.

The Roman Apostolic Tradition and the Egyptian Anaphora of Serapion are two of the earliest written eucharistic *anaphora* prayers surviving – but are quite different from each other, and neither of them can claim to represent a standard form that may be presumed to operate universally. Serapion was a country bishop from Thmuis in Egypt in the mid-fourth century, under the governance of Athanasius. Serapion's *anaphora* mentions the taking, breaking and giving of the blessed bread, but strangely omits the form of the blessing itself. The Hippolytan Apostolic Tradition refers to the taking and blessing of the bread and cup but not to the breaking and giving. Both of these aspects demonstrate at what an early date the insertion of the mini-narrative of the Last Supper made its way into the eucharistic prayers before they assumed a more extensive (and balanced) form later.

The great eucharistic prayer of the Apostolic Tradition is entirely Christocentric and turns constantly around the universal redemption effected in Christ's life. The concept of thanksgiving for creation's benefits, which is so noticeable in ancient Jewish prayers of blessing, as well as in the Syrian *anaphora* contained in the *Apostolic Constitutions* (the so-called *Clementine Liturgy*), is missing here, but the Apostolic Tradition does include the words of institution, gives thanks in the form of an *anamnesis* of the events, and calls down the grace of the Holy Spirit on the gifts in an explicit prayer of *epiclesis*: all things which will become standard.

In turn, the *Apostolic Constitutions* offers a form of *anaphora*, dating from the late fourth to early fifth century, and gives us the connecting bridge between the ancient forms of the great eucharistic prayers and what emerges out of the patristic era. Here the 'classical' form of the great prayer emerges as a thanksgiving for all the gifts of God's creation, his election of humankind, and the faithfulness of God throughout salvation history. This recitation leads up to the chanting of the Sanctus hymn, and then there follows the solemn prayer of thanks, the words of institution, the specific recalling (*anamnesis*) of the Lord ('Do this in memory of Me'), an *epiclesis* or invocation of the Holy Spirit over the elements, and a great prayer of intercession for all the church, past and present.

In all the classical patristic forms of Greek and Latin liturgies there is a clear sense (later sometimes obliterated) that the reception of the sacred elements (or communion), symbolically moves the focus of the eucharistic drama from the sufferings of the Passion into the glorious presence (*parousia*) of the Resurrection.

THE PATRISTIC GOLDEN AGE OF LITURGICAL FORMULATION

The classical patristic era of the fourth and fifth centuries witnessed an extensive consolidation of the church's liturgical prayers. Various styles of liturgy, with differing eucharistic *anaphora* prayers, rose up in the geographical centrifuges of the influence of the great churches; Antioch, Alexandria, Jerusalem, Cappadocian Caesarea, Rome, Milan and Aquileia. Constantinople adopted the Syrian tradition from Antioch which had originally been its mother church. Once Byzantium itself rose to major prominence in the eastern Christian world, its liturgical style served as a force of major dissemination and consolidation throughout the East. The Byzantine liturgical family laid great stress on the *epiclesis* to the Holy Spirit as a cardinal consecratory moment, and both here and in Alexandria the *Sanctus* hymn was introduced after the fourth century; marking a certain dislocation between the flow of the *anaphora* leading up to the words of institution.

Jerusalem's pilgrim practice of having long series of intercessions (*litanies*) spread widely in the East, and was observed even at Rome with the original Greek laity responses (*kyrie eleison*). Rome's great prominence in the West also served to standardize its liturgical forms widely there, especially after the Carolingian era. A notable aspect of the Western rite was the increasing disconnection between the preface and the core of the eucharistic prayer which became known as the *Canon*, the word meaning 'standard rule' and which showed the fixity that had already become a feature of the previously creative liturgical eras. The seventh-century Pope Gregory the Great became credited with giving the Roman liturgy a definitive form, and future change (until the modern era) would be glacially slow.

It is interesting to note that the classical patristic age used the awareness of the real presence of Christ in the elements (the original sense of the ecclesial sense of 'Mystical Body' until it became a term that started to designate the church itself) to argue, by extension, for the reality of the Incarnation of the divine Word. It was not the other way round. After the Reformation era the question whether the fathers supported a realist or a symbolist eucharistic theology became a hot topic and quotes were amassed from the ancients supporting either side, mainly along a Catholic/Protestant divide. The fact is that in antiquity neither opinion was seen to preclude the other.

Origen wished to play down the 'material' aspect of union with the Logos through the Eucharist, but not to deny a realist doctrine, rather in an attempt to make the faithful appreciate that the scriptures were also vehicles of the divine presence. He wanted the faithful to have the same reverence towards hearing the words of scripture in church as they showed towards holding and consuming the sacred eucharistic elements.[53] Remember, he says, that eating the body of Christ and drinking his blood 'does not only happen in the manner of the mysteries, but also when we receive his words, which contain life as Christ himself told us.'[54]

The same approach can be observed in Tertullian,[55] Ambrose,[56] Augustine[57] and Caesarius of Arles,[58] and in none of these cases does it serve as a denial of

---

[53]Origen, *Hom. Ex.*, 13.3; *Com.Matt.*, 11.14; Further see L. Lies, *Wort und Eucharistie bei Origenes. Zur Spiritualisierungstenden des Eucharistieversstandnisses* (Innsbruck: Tyrolia-Verlag, 1978).
[54]Origen, *Hom.Num.*, 16.9.
[55]Tertullian consistently shows a realist approach to the Eucharist in: *Pudic.*, 9; *Carn.*, 8; *Orat.*, 6; *Cor.*, 3; *Idol.*, 7; and a symbolist approach in: *Carn.*, 37; *Marc.*, 4.40.
[56]Ambrose, *Enn.Pss.*, 1.33.
[57]Augustine, *Serm.*, 78.2; *En.Ps.*, 31.
[58]Caesarius, *Serm.*, 78.2.

the argument for real presence: a doctrine which Augustine, for example, sustains strongly[59] and which he delivers to his catechumens as a basic matter of belief,[60] even while at the same time[61] insisting that Christians do not venerate the eucharistic sacrament 'in carnal slavery, but rather in a spiritual liberty'.

Cyril of Alexandria also shows how a profoundly concrete and realist understanding of eucharistic presence applied throughout his theology; using the Church's universal belief in the divine grace of Christ inherent in the eucharistic gifts so as to demonstrate how quintessentially ontological (hypostatic) was the union between Godhead and Manhood in the One Christ.[62] After him his arguments became standard throughout the East. In the West the prevailing realist sense of eucharistic theology was not challenged until the Carolingian period and again, much later, in the Reformation era.

For most of the classical patristic period, the devotional sense of the church reflecting on the eucharistic mystery is one of high exaltation, deeply Christocentric and set within the overall theme of the divine incarnation redeeming the faithful and through the forgiveness of sins, lifting them into sacred communion with the deity. Latin and Greek liturgical hymns begin to accumulate in the early medieval period, and by the later medieval era they turn more personalistically around the theme of eucharistic joy that the presence of the Lord brings to the believer's heart. Latin eucharistic hymnology focuses, in the main, around the praises of the Lord considered as triumphant Victor, while (similarly) those of the Greek tradition celebrate the saving deeds of God in history:[63] a form of the wider tradition of victory chants. The following Byzantine *Koinonikon,* or communion hymn, for Wednesday of Holy Week can give the sense:

Melchizidek the priest blessed Abraham,
With gifts of bread and wine (Gen. 14.18-19);
But you O Lamb of God have saved us
Giving your own body and blood.
Praise God in his holy ones.
Praise him in the firmament of his might. (Ps. 150.1)[64]

THE MYSTERIUM FIDEI

In all the voluminous literature that the Church produced on its eucharistic experience, it is abundantly clear that the sacramental, ritual, aspect is always seen

---

[59]Augustine, *En.Ps.*, 33.1.

[60]Augustine, *Serm.*, 228B.2.

[61]Augustine, *Doc.*, 3.9.

[62]Further see: E. Gebremedhin, *Life-Giving Blessing: An Inquiry into the Eucharistic Doctrine of Cyril of Alexandria* (Uppsala: Uppsala University Press, 1977); and H. Chadwick, 'Eucharist and Christology in the Nestorian Controversy', *Journal of Theological Studies* (New Series) 2 (1951): 145–64.

[63]See, for example, the *Odes of Kosmas Melodos*, in W. Christ and M. Paranikas, *Anthologia Graeca carminum christianorum* (Leipzig: Tuebner, 1871), pp. 190–3.

[64]Anonymous, in: A. Papadopoulos-Kerameus, *Analekta Hierosolymitikes Stachyologias*, vol. 2 (Petrograd: Typographeion V. Kirsvaoum, 1894), p. 82; cited in Sheerin, *The Eucharist*, p. 374.

as one of the most profound and central mysteries of the Christian faith; a synopsis which is at the same time a practical 'entering in' to the mystery of salvation that Christ has effected for his Church once and for all, but one which the Spirit renews for the access of his faithful from age to age across the generations. By and through the Eucharist the Church is incorporated into Christ. In this sense the eucharistic celebration, in the understanding of the ancients, truly 'makes' the church.

BIBLIOGRAPHY

Chadwick, H. 'Eucharist and Christology in the Nestorian Controversy', *JTS*, New Series, 2 (1951): 145–64.

Christ, W. and Paranikas, M. *Anthologia Graeca carminum christianorum*. Leipzig: Tuebner, 1871.

Dix, D. G. *The Shape of the Liturgy*. London: Dacre Press, 1947.

Gebremedhin, E. *Life-Giving Blessing: An Inquiry into the Eucharistic Doctrine of Cyril of Alexandria*. Uppsala: Uppsala University Press, 1977.

Hamman, A. *Prières eucharistiques des premiers siècles*. Paris: Desclée de Brouwer, 1957.

Hamman, A. *L'Eucharistie dans l'antiquité chrétienne*. Paris: Desclée de Brouwer, 1981.

Heinrichs, A. 'Pagan Ritual and the Alleged Crimes of the Early Christians', in *Kyriakon: Festschrift J. Quasten*, 18–35. Munster: Aschendrof, 1970.

LaVerdiere, E. *The Eucharist in the New Testament and in the Early Church*. Collegeville, MN: Liturgical Press, 1996.

Lies, L. *Wort und Eucharistie bei Origenes. Zur Spiritualisierungstenden des Eucharistieverssstandnisses*. Innsbruck: Tyrolia-Verlag, 1978.

Mascall, E. *Corpus Christi: Essays on the Church and the Eucharist*. London: Longmans Green and Co., 1957.

McGuckin, J. A. *Witnessing the Kingdom: Studies in New Testament History and Theology*. New York: St. Vladimir's Seminary Press, 2017.

Musurillo, H. *The Acts of the Christian Martyrs*. Oxford: Oxford University Press, 1972.

Mynors, R. A. B. *The Letters of Pliny the Younger*. Oxford: Oxford University Press, 1963.

Papadopoulos-Kerameus, A. *Analekta Hierosolymitikes Stachyologias*, vol. 2, 82. Petrograd: Typographeion V. Kirsvaoum, 1894.

Sheerin, D. J. (ed.). *The Eucharist*. Wilmington, DE: Michael Glazier, 1986. (A *wide selection of Greek and Latin patristic texts, in English translation, about the Eucharist*).

CHAPTER 15

Prayer and poetry in the early Christian community

PAUL F. BRADSHAW

PRAY WITHOUT CEASING

Unlike rabbinic Judaism, which was developing alongside it, early Christianity did not attempt to impose normative forms of praying on its adherents. Even St Paul's injunction to 'pray without ceasing' (1 Thess. 5.17), which was described by some early Christian authors as the only absolute rule, was at first understood to mean treating one's whole life as an act of prayer, as an offering to God, punctuated by specific times of actual praying each day.[1] Only later did it begin to be taken more literally by certain perfectionist and ascetic Christians, as we shall see.

The earliest recommended pattern of prayer appears to have been three times each day (an arrangement that seems to have some Jewish precedent[2]) with prayer again in the middle of the night. The three times seem to have been morning, noon and evening in rural areas and the third, sixth and ninth hours of the day (approximately 9 am, 12 noon and 3 pm) in city locations, where these hours would be announced publicly by the civic authorities. Some later Christian authors encouraged even more frequent occasions of daily prayer by proposing the combination of the two arrangements into five times of prayer in the day and once again in the night. Each of these times was justified by reference to various biblical precedents for them. The use of the Lord's Prayer was also commended, at least as a basis or outline for one's own prayers, and in the fourth century those preparing for baptism were required to be able to recite that prayer from memory, and presumably expected to use it regularly. How far the advice was followed with regard to either the hours of prayer or their content, however, is impossible to know. Nevertheless, though the night hour might seem challenging to modern eyes, it needs to be remembered how little

---

[1] See, for example, Tertullian, *Orat.*, 23-25; Origen, *PEuch.*, 12.2; cf. Rom. 12.1. On the times of prayer, see P. F. Bradshaw, *Reconstructing Early Christian Worship* (London: SPCK, 2009 and Collegeville, MN: Liturgical Press, 2010), Chapter 7.

[2] See R. S. Sarason, 'Communal Prayer at Qumran and Among the Rabbis: Certainties and Uncertainties', in *Liturgical Perspectives: Prayer and Poetry in Light of the Dead Sea Scrolls*, ed. E.G. Chazon (Leiden: Brill, 2003), pp. 151–72 (also 157 fn. 24; and 167 fns. 64, 65).

could be done between dusk and dawn in pre-modern times, and as all those hours would not be needed for sleep, it was not unusual for people in pre-modern times to break their rest into two parts.

Christians were instructed to face East when praying, whether alone at home or in gatherings of believers, a practice that seems to have some pagan and Jewish (particularly Essene) antecedents.[3] Washing ones hands on rising and before praying, as a symbol of purification, was also a well-attested Jewish practice (see *Ep. Arist.* 304-6), and is prescribed for Christians in the *Ap. Trad,* 41.1, 11 (but cf. ibid. 41.13). Clement of Alexandria (*c.*150–*c.*215) and Tertullian (*c.*155–*c.*240), however, discourage this practice, Tertullian denouncing it as 'superstitious' on the grounds that Christians had been cleansed from all ritual defilement by baptism.[4] On the other hand, to attract this criticism suggests that it was something that at least some Christians were doing. Tertullian and Origen (*c.*185–*c.*253) also encouraged a modification of the original practice of lifting up the hands in prayer to stretching them out instead in symbolic representation of the crucifixion, although they disagreed as to whether the eyes also should be raised to heaven in the traditional manner (see Lk. 18.13) or instead lowered, like the arms, as a sign of modesty and humility.[5] Other early Christian writers confirm the widespread nature of these traditions.[6] Following St Paul's instructions, men prayed with their heads uncovered, but women with heads covered (1 Cor. 11.3-7). Both standing and kneeling for prayer are attested. Tertullian described both postures, noting that kneeling was customary on days of fasting as a mark of humility and also on ordinary days at least for the very first prayer of the day, but that standing was the rule on Sundays, and was adopted by some Christians on Saturdays too, although he disagreed with the latter custom.[7]

THE EARLIEST PRAYER FORMS

Because prayers were usually improvised on the spot or else transmitted orally, there is an almost total absence of prayer texts as such in the first three centuries, and we have to wait until well into the fourth century before written prayers in any numbers are found. The earliest indications of Christian prayer forms, on the other hand, not surprisingly suggest a family resemblance to their Jewish counterparts, albeit with an apparent growing preference for the active thanksgiving form of introduction ('we give thanks for/that . . .')[8] over the passive blessing formula ('Blessed be the God of . . .

---

[3]Tertullian, *Apol.,* 16; *Nat.,* 1.13; Clement of Alexandria, *Strom.,* 7.7; Origen, *P.Euch.,* 32. For Jewish precedents, see Josephus, *War,* 2.128; Philo, *Vit. Cont.,* 27, 89.

[4]Clement, *Strom.,* 4.22; Tertullian, *Orat.,* 13.

[5]Tertullian, *Orat.,* 14, 17; *Apol.,* 30; Origen, *P.Euch.,* 31.2; *Hom. Ex.,* 3.3.

[6]See, for example, Minucius Felix, *Oct.,* 29; Ambrose, *Sacr.,* 6.4.18; John Chrysostom, *H. in I Tim.,* 14.4; Augustine, *En. Ps.,* 62.13.

[7]Tertullian, *Orat.,* 23; *Cor.,* 3.4.

[8]See, for example, Mt. 11.25//Lk. 10.21; Rom. 1.8; Col. 1.3; 3.17; *Did.,* 9-10. The same preference was seemingly shared by the community behind the Dead Sea Scrolls: see in particular the *Hodayot* scroll.

who . . .')[9] that was being promoted and developed within rabbinic Judaism, perhaps even in conscious reaction to the Christian tendency. In the earliest examples, Jesus would be mentioned in them either as God's servant who was the revealer of divine knowledge, or as Christ the high priest through whom the offering of worship was being made, or in a fusion of the two concepts. As time went by, 'servant' language declined, the title 'Son of God' increased, and mention of the Holy Spirit began to appear in association with him in the first steps that would lead in the fourth century to various Trinitarian formulations in prayers amid the doctrinal debates of the time. Similar developments also occurred in the doxological conclusions to prayers, from the simple 'Glory to you for evermore', to a full Trinitarian formula.[10]

Former generations of liturgical historians insisted that from the beginning public prayer would always have been made to God the Father through the Son, and any prayers addressed directly to Christ would only have occurred in private prayer. Such a precise category division is not only anachronistic but flies in the face of the evidence from the third-century theologian Origen, the Apocryphal Acts and other sources. Origen, in particular, while being a strong advocate of the use of a Trinitarian form by others not only thereby revealed that at least some of them were praying to Christ alone but also that he even thought it legitimate for him to do the same because he was one of those 'capable of a clear understanding of the absolute and the relative sense of prayer',[11] namely, understanding praying to Christ as actually praying through Christ to God.[12] Moreover, the fact that North African ecclesiastical legislation at the end of the fourth century found it necessary to stipulate, 'let no one in prayers name either the Father instead of the Son, or the Son instead of the Father; and when one stands at the altar, let prayer always be directed to the Father',[13] indicates that the propensity still continued. The Holy Spirit seems to have been mentioned less often in prayer in the first few centuries, not least because there was not then as completely clear a differentiation between what later orthodoxy would regard as the Second and Third persons of the Holy Trinity. The Spirit could be thought of as the Spirit of God or of Christ, and hence to speak of Christ was the same as to speak of his spirit, and vice versa.

In addition to the expression of praise and thanksgiving for what God had done in Christ, early Christian praying could also include petition for Christ's return and the consummation of God's kingdom: see, for example, 'Come, Lord Jesus' (Rev. 22.20; see also 1 Cor. 16.22; *Didache* 10.6). Even intercession for others, including the civil authorities, which Christians were instructed to make (see 1 Tim. 2.1-2),

---

[9]But cf. 2 Cor. 1.3; Eph. 1.3; 1 Pet. 1.3; Ignatius, *Eph.*, 1.3; *Barn.*, 6.10.

[10]See P. F. Bradshaw, 'The Status of Jesus in Early Christian Prayer Texts', in *Portraits of Jesus: Studies in Christology*, ed. S. E. Myers, WUNT 2. Reihe 321 (Tübingen: Mohr Siebeck, 2012), pp. 249–60.

[11]Origen, *Cels.*, 5.4.

[12]See P. F. Bradshaw, 'God, Christ, and the Holy Spirit in Early Christian Praying', in *The Place of Christ in Liturgical Prayer: Christology, Trinity, and Liturgical Theology*, ed. B. D. Spinks (Collegeville, MN: Liturgical Press, 2008), pp. 51–64.

[13]Canon 21 of the Council of Hippo Regius (393), repeated as canon 34 of the Third Council of Carthage (397).

seems to have been related to this objective. Tertullian in North Africa at the end of the second century adds to the mention of the civil authorities prayer for 'the peace of the world and the delay of the end', presumably the conditions necessary so that the gospel might be preached to all peoples before the final coming of God's kingdom.[14]

PRAYER AS SACRIFICE

'Through him [Jesus] therefore let us offer a sacrifice of praise continually to God, that is, the fruit of the lips that confess his name' (Heb. 13.15-16). The expression, 'the fruit of the lips', meaning what comes out of the mouth, and here specifically the verbalization of praise, is drawn from Isa. 57.19 and Hos. 14.2 and had already been taken up by the Jewish community at Qumran. Finding themselves unable to perform the requisite sacrifices in the temple because they regarded it as corrupt and defiled, they were forced to turn to the offering of verbal praise as a temporary substitute for that activity. However, what they regarded as merely temporary became for Christians the permanent replacement for those sacrifices and a major feature of their discourse about prayer. Thus, the second-century apologist Athenagoras spoke of 'the bloodless sacrifice and spiritual worship' offered by Christians (*Plea for the Christians* 13), employing an expression already current in Greek thought and echoing in part Rom. 12.1.[15] Justin Martyr (*c.*100–*c.*165) similarly averred that 'prayers and thanksgivings that are made by the worthy are the only perfect and pleasing sacrifices to God' (*Dialogue with Trypho* 117.2); and Tertullian argued that Christians did 'sacrifice for the emperor's safety, but to our God and his, and in the way God commanded, by pure prayer' (*Scap.*, 2.8). He described their offering as 'the ascription of glory and blessing and praise and hymns' (*Marc.*, 3.22.6) and 'simple prayer from a pure conscience' (ibid. 4.1.8). For him, prayer was:

> a spiritual victim (*hostia*) which has abolished the former sacrifices. . . .[W]e sacrifice, in spirit, prayer – (a victim) proper and acceptable to God, which indeed he has required, which he has provided for himself. This (victim), devoted from the whole heart, fed on faith, tended by truth, entire in innocence, pure in chastity, garlanded with love, we ought to escort with a procession of good works, amid psalms and hymns, to God's altar, to obtain for us all things from God. (*Orat.*, 28)

This understanding of prayer also fed into the polemic between Jews and Christians. Citing the Septuagint text of Mal. 1.11 rather loosely along the lines of, 'My

---

[14]Tertullian, *Apol.*, 39. See also ibid., 30–2; Polycarp, *Phil.*, 12; John Chrysostom, *H.in I Tim.*, 6; and the extensive intercessory prayer in *1 Clem.* 59–61, including for rulers in 60.4–61.1.

[15]See B. Eckhardt, '" Bloodless Sacrifice": A Note on Greek Cultic Language in the Imperial Era', *GRBS* 54 (2014): 255–73; and for its use among Christians, K. W. Stevenson, '"The Unbloody Sacrifice": The Origins and Development of a Description of the Eucharist', in *Fountain of Life*, ed. G. Austin (Washington, DC: Pastoral Press, 1991), pp. 103–30.

name shall be glorified among the Gentiles, and in every place a sacrifice offered to my name, and a pure sacrifice', the Christians argued that God had rejected the sacrifices of the Jews that had been offered in only one place, the Jerusalem temple, and accepted instead the pure offering of prayer made by Christians in every place.[16] Origen even claimed that the daily 'perpetual' sacrifices of the Old Testament (the *Tamid*; see Exod. 29.38; Num. 28.3) had found their true fulfilment in the unceasing, that is 'perpetual', prayer of Christians.[17]

THE USE OF THE BIBLE

No mention has been made so far of any reading of Scripture in connection with prayer. That is because, in antiquity, the possession of a copy of the text of even a part of the Bible would have been so expensive that it would only have been possible for a very few wealthy Christians to have read it at home,[18] and the low levels of literacy among many other converts would in any case have been a barrier to the practice. Thus, Bible reading generally belonged to communal gatherings – to the weekly Eucharist and to services of the word – when those present might listen to it being read aloud. Services of the word appear to have been held regularly in many places on Wednesdays and Fridays at the conclusion of the fasting usually observed by Christians on those days, at the ninth hour (around 3 pm), the end of the normal working day. There is no sign of a fixed lectionary at this stage, but the books of the Old Testament, and later also of the New, seem usually to have been read in a continuous fashion, passage by passage on each occasion. On the other hand, what prayer texts we have suggest that brief allusions to and quotations from scripture were a standard feature of Christian praying, indicating a culture steeped in the biblical world, again something mirrored in the few Jewish prayers extant from the period.

LATER DEVELOPMENTS

Apart from this continuing use of biblical language, close resemblance to Jewish forms and styles of prayer did not last long. Except for a few fourth-century works that consciously reproduce the vocabulary of earlier texts and the incorporation of some prayers of a decidedly Jewish character in the *Apostolic Constitutions*,[19] only

---

[16]See *Did.*, 14; Justin Martyr, *Dial.*, 28.5; 41.2; Irenaeus, *Haer.*, 4.17.5-6. Clement of Alexandria, *Strom.*, 5.14.136.

[17]Origen, *Hom. Num.*, 23.3.

[18]It was this minority, presumably, to whom instructions like 'if there is a day when there is no catechesis, when each one is at home, let them take the holy book and read in it' (*Ap. Trad.*, 41.4) were addressed.

[19]See D. A. Fiensy, *Prayers Alleged to be Jewish: An Examination of the Constitutiones Apostolorum*, 'Brown Judaic Studies', 65 (Chico, CA: Scholars Press, 1985); P. W. Van der Horst, 'The Greek Synagogue Prayers in the Apostolic Constitutions, Book VII', in *From Qumran to Cairo: Studies in the History of Prayer*, ed. J. Tabory (Jerusalem: Hotsa'at Orhot, 1999), pp. 32–6; E. G. Chazon, 'A "Prayer Alleged to be Jewish" in

East Syrian Christianity preserved a strongly Semitic character in its liturgical forms, no doubt occasioned by its comparative geographic, linguistic, cultural and political isolation, straggling as it did the eastern frontier of the Roman Empire.[20] Elsewhere quite different prayer forms and styles emerged in the cultural environment of the Graeco-Roman world. While the element of praise or thanksgiving in one form or another continued to constitute the beginning of major prayers, it was much abbreviated in other cases, with emphasis falling more on petition. Many prayer texts seem to have been formed by combining together shorter units. The later Roman tradition used tightly compressed language in the Classical Latin style; other traditions tended to be more prolix to a greater or lesser extent, with intercessions commonly being expressed in the form of a litany – a series of short petitions with a communal response, usually 'Lord, have mercy', to each one.

With the emergence of the Church from sporadic persecution into a legitimate place in the society of the Roman Empire in the early fourth century, Christians attracted more to join their numbers and were able to hold public assemblies for worship, not only the celebration of the eucharistic liturgy on Sundays and other holy days, the twice-weekly services of the word on Wednesdays and Fridays, but also daily prayer services led by the clergy. The pattern of multiple times of prayer during the day, and prayer again in the night that had been recommended to earlier generations of believers, now began to fall more on the deaf ears of less committed members, and were retained only by the especially devout in households and small groups. Public daily worship was usually held only twice a day, morning and evening, times when (at least in large cities) a sizable number of people would be free to attend. These assemblies came to be thought of as the spiritual fulfilment of the morning and evening sacrifices of the Old Testament, and were composed primarily of praise and intercession. This arrangement has been termed the 'cathedral office' by modern scholars, about which more will be said later.

NEARLY CEASELESS PRAYER

At the beginning of the third century come the first signs of those wanting to take St Paul's injunction to 'pray without ceasing' much more literally. Clement of Alexandria, while recommending fixed times of prayer for 'ordinary' Christians, describes perfect Christians (or 'Gnostics' as he calls them) as praying throughout their whole life: 'We cultivate our fields, praising; we sail the sea, hymning' (*Strom.*, 7.7). This spirituality was adopted by the desert ascetics who began to flourish in the early fourth century. Taking themselves off into solitude, they spent the whole of their days in prayer, even as they worked at manual tasks, its duration only being punctuated by minimal interruptions for food and sleep. The same pattern was

---

the Apostolic Constitutions', in *Things Revealed: Studies in Early Jewish and Christian Literature in Honor of Michael E. Stone*, eds E. G. Chazon et al. (Leiden: E.J. Brill, 2004), pp. 261–77.
[20]For examples, see *Prayers of the Eucharist: Early and Reformed*, 4th edn, eds P. F. Bradshaw and M. E. Johnson, Alcuin Club Collections, 94 (Collegeville, MN: Liturgical Press, 2019), pp. 63–84.

maintained when small communities of these desert dwellers began to be formed. Some of these prayed alone in their cells during the week and only assembled for communal worship on Saturdays and Sundays; other communities established formal times of communal prayer each day, but still expected their members to continue the prayer alone throughout the rest of the day.

What was most significant about this prayer was that it was of a quite different kind than before – primarily meditation and petition for personal salvation rather than praise or intercession for others. The ascetic reflected on God's word, usually focusing on the canonical psalms, as we shall see later, and then prayed for spiritual growth towards perfection. In time, this practice and its spirituality also began to influence those devout individuals and small household groups elsewhere who were mentioned earlier as still observing various hours of prayer each day, and they tended to convert their traditional time of prayer in the middle of the night into an extended vigil of meditation on the Psalms lasting until early morning.

'PSALMS AND HYMNS AND SPIRITUAL SONGS'

The twenty-six Puritan signatories to the preface of the 1673 London edition of the *Scottish Metrical Psalter*, like many other Reformed Christians, believed that 'David's Psalms seems plainly intended' by the phrase '*Psalms and hymns and spiritual songs*' occurring in both Eph. 5.19 and Col. 3.16, and it has often been used to forbid or at least discourage the singing of non-canonical compositions in certain Protestant churches. Some have claimed that the terms 'psalms' (*psalmoi*), 'hymns' (*hymnoi*) and 'songs' (*odai*) are intended to refer specifically to headings used in the book of Psalms. Even those who would not define the phrase so narrowly have commonly thought that the canonical psalms would have been the primary songs heard at the meetings of the earliest Christian communities. This is not an altogether surprising conclusion, as the book of Psalms is cited more frequently in the New Testament than any other Old Testament scripture.

Psalms in a Jewish background

Traditionally, this view of the use of the Psalms in early Christian worship was often been predicated on the conviction that they were sung in the synagogue services of the first century CE, and sometimes consequently on the romantic belief that the boy Jesus would have known them by heart and sung them to himself as he went about his daily labours. But more recent research has led to the conclusion that a Sabbath synagogue liturgy as such did not exist until after that century was over, and so, *a priori*, as the musicologist James McKinnon observed, a regular cycle of psalmody cannot have been known at the time.[21] Indeed, in the later synagogue

---

[21]J. McKinnon, 'On the Question of Psalmody in the Ancient Synagogue', *Early Music History* 6 (1986): 159–91, especially 170–80. On the absence of a synagogue liturgy in the first century, see, for example, D. Falk, 'Jewish Prayer Literature and the Jerusalem Church in Acts', in *The Book of Acts in its Palestinian*

liturgies only a handful of the Psalms have ever been used, and according to the *Mishnah* only a single psalm was sung in the Temple by the Levites to accompany the sacrifices on each of the seven days of the week.[22]

This is not to say that other psalms were never used by Jews in the first century, but only that they do not seem to have occupied a particularly privileged position. In his description of the common life of an ascetic Jewish community called the Therapeutae that resided near Lake Mareotis in Egypt, Philo of Alexandria (*c.*20 BCE–*c.*50 CE) says that the members 'compose psalms (*asmata*) and hymns (*hymnous*) to God in all sorts of metres and melodies which they write down', and he spoke of their singing at their festal meals thus:

> [T]he President rises and sings a hymn (*hymnon*) composed as an address to God, either a new one of his own composition or an old one by poets of an earlier day who have left behind them [hymns in] many measures and melodies, hexagon and iambic, lyrics suitable for processions or in libations and at the altars, or for the chorus whilst standing or dancing, with careful metrical arrangements to fit the various evolutions. After him all the others take their turn as they are arranged and all in the proper order while all the rest listen in complete silence except when they have to chant the closing lines or refrains, for then they all lift up their voices, men and women alike. . . .
>
> After the supper they hold the sacred vigil which is conducted in the following way. They rise up all together and standing in the middle of the refectory form themselves first into two choirs, one of men and one of women, the leader and precentor chosen for each being the most honoured amongst them and also the most musical. Then they sing hymns to God composed of many measures and set to many melodies, sometimes chanting together, sometimes taking up the harmony antiphonally, hands and feet keeping time in accompaniment, and rapt with enthusiasm reproduce sometimes the lyrics of the procession, sometimes of the halt and of the wheeling and counter-wheeling of a choric dance. Then when each choir has separately done its own part in the feast, having drunk as in the Bacchic rites of the strong wine of God's love they mix and both together become a single choir, a copy of the choir set up of old beside the Red Sea in honour of the wonders there wrought.[23]

Setting, ed. R. Bauckham (Grand Rapids, MI: Eerdmans, 1995), pp. 267–301, 277–85; L. I. Levine, *The Ancient Synagogue* (New Haven and London: Yale University Press, 2000), pp. 134–59; H. A. McKay, *Sabbath and Synagogue: The Question of Sabbath Worship in Ancient Judaism* (Leiden: E.J. Brill, 1994); but see also P. W. Van der Horst, 'Was the Synagogue a Place of Sabbath Worship before 70 C.E.?', in *Jews, Christians and Polytheists in the Ancient Synagogue*, ed. S. Fine (London and New York: Routledge, 1999), pp. 18–43.

[22]*Tamid* 7.4; these seven psalms were 24, 48, 82, 94, 81, 93 and 92.

[23]Philo, *Vit. Cont.*, 29, 80, 83-85; English translation from F. H. Colson, *Philo IX* (Loeb Classical Library; London: Heinemann; Cambridge, MA: Harvard University Press, 1941), pp. 129–31, 163–5. See further J. E. Taylor and P. R. Davies, 'The So-Called Therapeutae of *De Vita Contemplativa*: Identity and Character', *HTR* 91 (1998): 3–24.

While the canonical psalms may have been intended by – or at least included among – the hymns 'by poets of an earlier day', it is obvious that they did not have a pre-eminent place over other compositions in this community, and we have no evidence to suggest that things were significantly different more generally in the Judaism of the time. Certainly, among the Dead Sea scrolls from the community at Qumran there are a large collection of poetical compositions (*Hodayot*), though we do not know exactly to what use they were put.[24]

The New Testament era

The earliest Christians, therefore, appear to have been distinctive in their apparent preference for the Psalms. Yet when we examine the New Testament citations, they tend to be of individual verses used as messianic prophecy. Indeed, we could say that the book of Psalms was treated as the primary prophetic text of the scriptures. Jesus himself appears to have initiated this approach:

> While Jesus was teaching in the Temple, he said 'How do the scribes say that the Messiah is the son of David? David himself, by the Holy Spirit, said, 'The Lord said to my Lord, "Sit at my right hand, until I put your enemies under your feet."' David himself calls him Lord; and how is he his son?[25]

Among examples of psalm verses being used in this way by the first Christians, we may point in particular to Acts 2.25-31, where Ps. 16.8-11 is cited as a prophecy of Jesus' resurrection; Acts 4.24-30, where Ps. 2.1-2 is cited within a prayer; and Acts 13.33-37, where both Ps. 2.7 and Ps. 16.10 are quoted as prophesying the resurrection. But there is no firm evidence that whole psalms were sung in their worship. Apart from such references to particular verses as prophecy, the Greek word '*psalmos*' occurs only three times in the New Testament, in the two instances cited at the beginning of this section (Eph. 5.19 and Col. 3.16), and once in 1 Cor. 14.26, where it is included in a list of verbal contributions individuals might bring to a Christian assembly ('when you come together, each one has a psalm, a teaching, a revelation, a tongue, an interpretation'). The related verb '*psalleto*' occurs in Jas 5.13.

All these instances could refer to the canonical psalms, but not necessarily so, or not exclusively so. The reference in 1 Cor. 14.26 to an individual contributing a 'psalm' in the same way as others brought a teaching or revelation to the assembly might be thought to imply that it was the person's own composition, but in any case suggests that whatever it was, it was read or sung by that person while the rest listened in silence or responded with some sort of acclamation or refrain, as do the expressions in Eph. 5.19 to 'speaking to one another in psalms' and in Col. 3.16 to 'teaching and admonishing one another in psalms.' That the earliest Christians do

---

[24]E. M. Schuller, 'Some Reflections on the Function and Use of Poetical Texts among the Dead Sea Scrolls', in Chazon (ed.), *Liturgical Perspectives*, pp. 173–89.
[25]Mk. 12.35-37a, citing Ps. 110.1.

appear to have been composing their own songs may be supported by the numerous claims that have been made to discern poetic or hymnic fragments within the New Testament texts themselves, and by the existence of such material in other Christian works of the period, most notably in the *Odes of Solomon*.[26]

Psalmody in the third century

The same combination of both canonical psalms and Christian hymnic compositions at meal gatherings is found more than a century later in the account by Tertullian of a Christian supper: 'After the washing of hands and [the bringing in of] lights, each one is invited into the midst to sing to God, as they are able, either from the holy scriptures or of their own composition.'[27] What the contemporary songs might have been we cannot say, as nothing has survived. Nor can we be certain from this account whether the canonical psalms were all being chosen on the basis of their clear messianic content or for some other reason.

However, another work by Tertullian reveals what seems to be a new development. He says: 'Those who are more diligent in praying are accustomed to include in their prayers Alleluia and this type of psalms, with the ending of which those who are present may respond.'[28] What we learn from this is that psalms did not form a normal part of the daily prayers but their inclusion was an innovation by the more pious; that this was done when other people were present rather than by individuals praying on their own; and that the elements chosen for this purpose were psalms of praise, so that the others might respond to the verses with an Alleluia refrain. This responsorial method was probably how psalms and other songs had been sung at the community meals from which the rest of this practice seems to have been derived.

This does not mean that the messianic or Christological interpretation of psalms ceased, even if it were not so popular for liturgical use. On the contrary, it had continued in the second century – an example is in Justin Martyr's *Dialogue with Trypho* 97–106, which features an extensive treatment of Psalm 22 – and it flourished even more in the third century, gradually extending from selected verses to encompass virtually the whole Psalter, apparently under the influence of the exegetical method adopted by Origen from classical literature.[29] The words of the psalms were understood either as addressed by the Church to Christ, or as speaking about Christ, or as the voice of the Christ himself. Indeed, even those texts that

---

[26]See H. Löhr, 'What Can We Know about the Beginnings of Christian Hymnody?', in *Literature or Liturgy?*, eds L. Clemens and H. Löhr (Tübingen: Mohr Siebeck, 2014), pp. 157–74; J. H. Charlesworth, *The Earliest Christian Hymnbook: The Odes of Solomon* (Cambridge: James Clarke; Eugene, OR: Cascade Books, 2009).

[27]*Apologeticum* 39. This expression is strikingly similar to Philo's language about the Therapeutae's practice mentioned earlier. See also P. Jeffery, 'Philo's Impact on Christian Psalmody', in *Psalms in Community*, eds H. W. Attridge and M. E. Fassler (Atlanta, GA: SBL, 2003), pp. 147–87.

[28]Tertullian. *Orat.*, 27.

[29]See M. J. Rondeau, *Les commentaires patristiques du Psautier (IIIe-Ve siècles)*, II OCA, 220 (Rome: Pontificium Institutum Studiorum Orientalium, 1985), pp. 39ff.

referred explicitly to God were commonly interpreted as really meaning the divine Christ.

Psalms in the monastic tradition

It was in the fourth century, however, that this Christological interpretation of the Psalter was more widely adopted. Among ascetics and early monastic communities, especially those in the Egyptian desert, the canonical psalms came to occupy a prominent place. The desert fathers in general singled out the Psalter from the rest of the scriptures and encouraged their followers to commit its contents to memory and to recite it constantly throughout their waking hours. Several of their sayings tell of individuals completing the whole Psalter in the course of a single night.[30] While such stories certainly go far beyond normal practice, they clearly illustrate the ideal towards which the serious Christian ascetic was expected to strive. Because Origen's ideas exercised a strong influence over the spirituality of the desert fathers, it is easy to see why his Christological exegesis of the psalms would have commended itself to the early ascetics, whose fundamental aim was to conform their lives to the pattern of Christ.

However, even more was claimed for the Psalter. It was thought to encapsulate the whole of what the Old Testament had to teach, and thus the desert monk was expected to apply its words to his life and view them as fulfilled in him.[31] This idea spread outside monastic circles. Because virtually every leading Christian figure of the period had lived as a monk at one time or another, this was the spiritual practice that they also advocated to ordinary lay people. Basil of Caesarea (*c*.330–379) typifies the attitudes of his contemporaries:

> Now the Prophets teach some things, the Historians other things, the Law still other things, and the form of advice of the Proverbs something else, but the Book of Psalms encompasses what is valuable from them all. It prophesies what is to come; it recalls history; it legislates for life; it gives practical advice; and it is in general a common treasury of good teachings, carefully finding what is suitable for each person. For it heals the old wounds of souls; it brings swift recovery to the recently wounded; it treats what is diseased; it preserves what is pure; and as far as possible it takes away the passions that in many ways dominate souls in the life of human beings. And it does this with a certain diligent persuasion and sweetness that engender a moderate disposition.[32]

Those who viewed the psalms from this perspective did not lose sight of the fact that they were also hymnic in form, but they argued that the teaching function was

---

[30]See, for example, *Apoph*: Epiphanius 3; Serapion 1; Anonymous 150.
[31]See John Cassian, *Conf.,* 10.11; Athanasius, *Ep.Marc.,* 11.
[32]Basil of Caesarea, *Hom. Ps.,* 1.1. For other examples, see Ambrose, *Exp.Ps.,* 1.7, 9; Athanasius, *Ep. Marc*; John Chrysostom, *Exp.Ps.,* 41.1; Niceta of Remesiana, Psal.B., 5. See also B. Daley, 'Finding the Right key: The Aims and Strategies of Early Christian Interpretation of the Psalms', in Attridge and Fassler (eds), *Psalms in Community*, pp. 189–205.

primary, and that God had deliberately arranged matters in this way in order to make learning more pleasurable for human beings:

> When the Holy Spirit saw that the human race was with difficulty led toward virtue, and that because of our inclination toward pleasure we neglected an upright life, what did he do? He mixed sweetness of melody with the teachings so that by the pleasantness and softness of the sound heard we might receive without realizing it the benefit of the words, just like wise physicians, who often smear the cup with honey when giving the fastidious rather bitter medicines to drink. Therefore he devised these harmonious melodies of the psalms for us, so that those who are children in age or even those who are young in their ways might appear to be singing but in reality be training their souls.[33]

It is often said that the individual ascetics and early monastic communities 'prayed the psalms', but this was not the case. The sources frequently speak of prayer *and* psalmody, and reveal that the characteristic way of using the psalms in this tradition was to alternate the saying or singing of a psalm with a period of silent prayer. When two or more people prayed together, only one of them recited the psalm and the other(s) listened to it. Then all prayed in silence, and after that came another psalm, and so on. Thus the psalm was functioning not as prayer itself, but as a reading, as the source of inspiration for the silent meditative prayer that was to follow it.[34] The psalms were almost always recited in their biblical order, as many of them being used as would fill the time available.

Psalms in the 'cathedral' tradition

Outside this milieu things were different. Although lay people were encouraged to adopt the monastic spirituality, that did not – at least at first – influence the daily public services of the Church that began to be held after the cessation of persecution in the fourth century.[35] Here, only a very few psalms began to be used to precede the intercessions, and most of these were repeated every day. Continuing the practice of Tertullian's 'more pious', psalms of praise or psalms appropriate to the hour of the day were chosen. Thus, Pss 148–50 ('Alleluia' psalms) eventually became a universal component of the morning service, in some places preceded by Ps. 63, its first verse in Greek containing the verb '*orthrizō*', 'I call before dawn'. The evening service varied rather more from place to place, but very often included Ps. 141, with its request in v 2 for prayer to be as incense, and the lifting up of hands as the evening sacrifice.

---

[33]Basil, *Hom.Ps.*, 1.1. See also John Chrysostom, *Exp.Ps.*, 41.1; *Hom. Col.*, 9.2; Niceta of Remesiana, *Psal.B.*, 5.

[34]See further A. De Vogüé, 'Psalmodier n'est pas prier', *EO* 6 (1989): 7–32.

[35]For more on the daily church services and their designation as 'cathedral' worship, see P. F. Bradshaw, *Daily Prayer in the Early Church*, Alcuin Club Collections, 63 (London: SPCK, 1981; New York: Oxford University Press, 1982; reprint: Eugene, OR: Wipf & Stock, 2008), Chapters 4 and 6; R. F. Taft, *The Liturgy of the Hours in East and West* (Collegeville, MN: Liturgical Press, 1986; 2nd edn, 1993), Chapters 3 and 8.

Out of what must have been a wealth of non-scriptural hymnic compositions in previous ages, however, almost nothing survived into these daily services, no doubt partly because of the high spiritual value now attached to the canonical psalms but also because of the fear of unwittingly adopting songs with heretical content in a church that was now determined to define its orthodoxy over against other Christian groupings. The *Doxologia* ('Glory to God in the Highest') and the hymn at lamp-lighting, the 'Gladsome Light' (*Phos hilaron*), found a permanent home in the morning and evening services respectively in many Eastern churches, but they were exceptions.

Although we may reasonably presume that some sort of informal service of the word continued to accompany the Eucharist after it became detached from the meal, just as it had done before, we do not have any details of its contents, and especially whether it would regularly (or sometimes?) have included a psalm or psalms. It appears that the inclusion of a psalm after the first reading as a standard practice may only date from the late fourth century,[36] and that its relation in theme to that reading governed which psalm was chosen. Even though it was sung, the use of the responsorial method, both here and in the daily services, is probably an indication that it was thought of as a reading, with the congregational response as an act of assent. John Chrysostom (*c*.349–407) describes its meaning thus:

> Do not then think that you have come here simply to say the words, but when you make the response, consider that response to be a covenant. For when you say, 'As the deer longs for running water, so my soul longs for you, O God', you make a covenant with God. You have signed a contract without paper or ink; you have confessed with your voice that you love him more than all, that you prefer nothing to him, and that you burn with love for him.[37]

Somewhat clearer is the role of psalms in connection with the annual celebration of Easter. The late-third/early-fourth-century Syrian *Didascalia Apostolorum*[38] speaks of the paschal vigil taking place 'with readings from the prophets, and with the Gospels and with psalms'. Although the function of the psalms here is not made explicit, it is defined in the account of Good Friday at Jerusalem by the late-fourth-century traveller Egeria:

> From the sixth to the ninth hour nothing else is done except that readings are read thus, that is, first there are readings from the Psalms, wherever they speak of the passion; there are also readings from the Apostle, either from the letters of the Apostles or from the Acts, wherever they speak of the Lord's passion; and also passages from the gospels where he suffered are read; so they read from the prophets where they say that the Lord will suffer and then they read from the gospels where he speaks of his passion.[39]

---

[36]See J. W. McKinnon, 'The Fourth-Century Origin of the Gradual', *Early Music History* 7 (1987): 91–106.

[37]*Exp. Ps.,* 41.5.

[38]*Didasc.,* 5.19.1.

[39]Egeria, *It.,* 37.5; English translation from A. McGowan and P. F. Bradshaw, *The Pilgrimage of Egeria: A New Translation of the Itinerarium Egeriae with Introduction and Commentary,* Alcuin Club Collections, 93 (Collegeville, MN: Liturgical Press, 2018), p. 177.

In all these various ways, therefore, the ancient prophetic and Christological understanding of the psalms was kept alive alongside their later function as hymns of praise, and both approaches would persist into the later life of the church.

BIBLIOGRAPHY

Bradshaw, P. F. *Daily Prayer in the Early Church*. Alcuin Club Collections, 63. London: SPCK, 1981; New York: Oxford University Press, 1982 = Eugene, OR: Wipf & Stock, 2008.

Bradshaw, P. F. 'God, Christ, and the Holy Spirit in Early Christian Praying', in B. D. Spinks (ed.), *The Place of Christ in Liturgical Prayer: Christology, Trinity, and Liturgical Theology*, 51–64. Collegeville, MN: Liturgical Press, 2008.

Bradshaw, P. F. *Reconstructing Early Christian Worship*. London: SPCK, 2009; Collegeville, MN: Liturgical Press, 2010.

Bradshaw, P. F. 'The Status of Jesus in Early Christian Prayer Texts', in S. E. Myers (ed.), *Portraits of Jesus: Studies in Christology*, 249–60. WUNT 2. Reihe 321. Tübingen: Mohr Siebeck, 2012.

Bradshaw, P. F. and Johnson, M. E. (eds). *Prayers of the Eucharist: Early and Reformed*, 4th edn. Alcuin Club Collections, 94. Collegeville, MN: Liturgical Press, 2019.

Charlesworth, J. H. *The Earliest Christian Hymnbook: The Odes of Solomon*. Cambridge: James Clarke; Eugene, OR: Cascade Books, 2009.

Chazon, E. G. 'A "Prayer Alleged to be Jewish" in the Apostolic Constitutions', in E. G. Chazon, D. Satran and R. E Cements (eds), *Things Revealed: Studies in Early Jewish and Christian Literature in Honor of Michael E. Stone*, 261–77. Leiden: E.J. Brill, 2004.

Colson, F. H. *Philo IX*. Loeb Classical Library. London: Heinemann; Cambridge, MA: Harvard University Press, 1941.

Daley, B. 'Finding the Right Key: The Aims and Strategies of Early Christian Interpretation of the Psalms', in H. W. Attridge and M. E. Fassler (eds), *Psalms in Community*, 189–205. Atlanta, GA: SBL, 2003.

Eckhardt, B. '"Bloodless Sacrifice": A Note on Greek Cultic Language in the Imperial Era', *GRBS* 54 (2014): 255–73.

Falk, D. 'Jewish Prayer Literature and the Jerusalem Church in Acts', in R. Bauckham (ed.), *The Book of Acts in Its Palestinian Setting*, 267–301. Grand Rapids, MI: Eerdmans, 1995.

Fiensy, D. A. *Prayers Alleged to be Jewish: An Examination of the Constitutiones Apostolorum*. Brown Judaic Studies, 65. Chico, CA: Scholars Press, 1985.

Van der Horst, P. W. 'The Greek Synagogue Prayers in the Apostolic Constitutions, Book VII', in J. Tabory (ed.), *From Qumran to Cairo: Studies in the History of Prayer*, 32–6. Jerusalem: Hotsa'at Orhot, 1999.

Van der Horst, P. W. 'Was the Synagogue a Place of Sabbath Worship before 70 C.E.?', in S. Fine (ed.), *Jews, Christians and Polytheists in the Ancient Synagogue*, 18–43. London and New York: Routledge, 1999.

Jeffery, P. 'Philo's Impact on Christian Psalmody', in H. W. Attridge and M. E. Fassler (eds), *Psalms in Community*, 147–87. Atlanta, GA: SBL, 2003.

Levine, L. I. *The Ancient Synagogue*. New Haven, CT and London: Yale University Press, 2000.

Löhr, H. 'What Can We Know about the Beginnings of Christian Hymnody?', in L. Clemens and H. Löhr (eds), *Literature or Liturgy?* 157–74 Tübingen: Mohr Siebeck, 2014.

McGowan, A. and Bradshaw, P. F. *The Pilgrimage of Egeria: A New Translation of the Itinerarium Egeriae with Introduction and Commentary*. Alcuin Club Collections, 93. Collegeville, MN: Liturgical Press, 2018.

McKay, H. A. *Sabbath and Synagogue: The Question of Sabbath Worship in Ancient Judaism*. Leiden: E.J. Brill, 1994.

McKinnon, J. 'On the Question of Psalmody in the Ancient Synagogue', *Early Music History* 6 (1986): 159–91.

McKinnon, J. 'The Fourth-Century Origin of the Gradual', *Early Music History* 7 (1987): 91–106.

Rondeau, M. J. *Les commentaires patristiques du Psautier (IIIe-Ve siècles)*, II OCA, vol. 220. Rome: Pontificium Institutum Studiorum Orientalium, 1985.

Sarason, R. S. 'Communal Prayer at Qumran and Among the Rabbis: Certainties and Uncertainties', in E. G. Chazon (ed.), *Liturgical Perspectives: Prayer and Poetry in Light of the Dead Sea Scrolls*, 151–7. Leiden: E.J. Brill, 2003.

Schuller, E. M. 'Some Reflections on the Function and Use of Poetical Texts among the Dead Sea Scrolls', in E. G. Chazon (ed.), *Liturgical Perspectives: Prayer and Poetry in Light of the Dead Sea Scrolls*, 173–89. Leiden: E.J. Brill, 2003.

Stevenson, K. W. '"The Unbloody Sacrifice": The Origins and Development of a Description of the Eucharist', in Gerard Austin (ed.), *Fountain of Life*, 103–30. Washington, DC: Pastoral Press, 1991.

Taft, R. F. *The Liturgy of the Hours in East and West*. Collegeville, MN: Liturgical Press, 1986; 2nd edn, 1993.

Taylor, J. E. and Davies, P. R. 'The So-Called Therapeutae of *De Vita Contemplativa*: Identity and Character', *HTR* 91 (1998): 3–24.

Vogüé, A. de. 'Psalmodier n'est pas prier', *EO* 6 (1989): 7–32.

CHAPTER 16

The Christian community and its structure

Deacons, priests and bishops

PAUL VAN GEEST AND BART J. KOET

INTRODUCTION

It seems possible at first sight to distill a clear picture of the organization of the early Christian communities from the synoptic Gospels, Luke's Acts and the letters of Paul. And so, the men called by Christ himself to accompany him and who are named by the synoptics, appear to be the most authoritative organized group around his person.[1] Luke mentions Jesus' appointment of seventy two ('The 70') itinerant missionaries.[2] It also seems clear that there was a caesura in the Christian community after Jesus' death, which did not last long due to Easter and Pentecost.[3] Paul and Luke suggest that the first Christian communities in Jerusalem, Antioch, Alexandria, Rome and other places were small house communities, like those founded by the Christian couple Aquila and Prisca, who had fled from Rome.[4] Paul records many names of places where Christians gathered in an *oikos* (a 'house' or 'extended family') but at the same time speaks of *ekklesia*,[5] a term which meant both the small domestic community[6] and the community of all Christian communities, which was simultaneously represented in the house community.[7]

But Luke is vague about the relationship between the 'seventy' disciples and 'the first Christian community'. Moreover, Paul is one of the few sources that we have

---

[1]Mk 3.14; cf. Mt. 10.1; Lk 6.13.
[2]Lk. 10.1-9.
[3]See 1 Cor. 15.5-7; E. Dassmann, *Kirchengeschichte. Vol. 1. Ausbreitung, Leben und Lehre der Kirche in den ersten drei Jahrhunderten, Kohlhammer Studienbücher Theologie,* vol. 10 (Stuttgart: Kohlhammer, 1991), pp. 4–5.
[4]cf. Acts 18.2-4.
[5]Rom. 16.1; 1 Corinthians 16.
[6]1 Cor. 1–2; 16.1.
[7]1 Cor. 15.9; Gal. 1.13.

for the organization of early Christian communities. As a result, Faivre has observed that we know nothing about the organizational structure of communities that Paul did not describe.[8] In addition, Faivre has noted, the history of the organization and the ministries it included has often been written with the purpose of showing that ministries that arose in later periods could be traced back to clearly defined ministries in the early church. In Faivre's view, this procedure fails to do justice to the versatility of the various ecclesial traditions in the early centuries: a tendency enhanced by the limited number of sources. Moreover, in parallel with the idea that Hellenization caused Christianity to deviate from its origins, German Protestant scholars suggested that there was no continuity between the early church and the first followers of Jesus, because the first Christians primarily thought in terms of charisms and therefore did not have tightly organized structures. Every subsequent form of organization in later Catholicism was thus a deviation from the norm set by the free communities. Luke already mentions this aberration in his Acts. The deviation was negatively described as *Frühkatholizismus*.[9]

Taking into account the scarcity of sources and the existence of bias which, through our familiarity with the later hierarchy of ministry, is liable to affect our view of the organization of the first Christian communities, we will attempt to describe both discontinuities and continuities in the development of ministries and ecclesiastical organization, as well as in the (moral) requirements which ministers were expected to meet.

FIRST DEVELOPMENTS IN THE ORGANIZATION OF COMMUNITIES

It can be seen from Paul's letters that communities gathered in a particular place[10] and usually ate together.[11] However, this form of organization cannot be associated with a description of the precise organizational structure of the earliest followers of Jesus. Although no such description has been handed down in any other source, Paul's letters contain some indications as to how the community of the followers of Jesus was organized. In his first letter to the saints of Corinth, as he calls the fellowship at the start of his epistle,[12] Paul uses particular terms that refer to

---

[8] Cf. A. Faivre, 'La question des ministères à l'époque paléochrétienne. Problématique et enjeux d'une périodiastion', in A. Faivre, *Chrétiens et Églises: des identités en construction. Acteurs, structures, frontières du champ religieux chrétien* (Paris: Les Éditions du Cerf, 2011), pp. 117–50, at 117; cf. H. von Campenhausen, *Kirchliches Amt und geistliche Vollmacht in den ersten Jahrhunderten* (Tübingen: Mohr Siebeck, 1953), p. 59.

[9] Cf. E. Käsemann, 'Amt und Gemeinde im Neuen Testament', in *Exegetische Versuche und Besinnungen*, vol. 1 (Göttingen: VandenHoeck & Ruprecht, 1960), pp. 109–34, esp. p. 130; U. Luz, 'Erwägungen zur Entstehung des "Frühkatholizismus". Eine Skizze', *ZNWKÄK* 65, nos. 1–2 (2009): 88–111.

[10] 1 Cor. 14.23.

[11] 1 Cor. 11.17- 20; cf. 1 Cor. 11.33; Acts 1.13; Acts 2.46.

[12] 1 Cor. 1.2.

leadership roles and leadership functions to denote himself and Apollos, namely: *oikonomos*,[13] *sunergos*[14] and *diakonoi*.[15]

In 1 Cor. 12.28, Paul even ranks a number of offices in hierarchical order: first, the apostles; second, the prophets;[16] and third, the teachers. Most of the terms he uses in this letter derive from more general roles rather than from sacred functions. Paul has no hesitations in also calling himself an apostle,[17] possibly also because the term is reminiscent of the Hebrew word '*shaliah*' – authorized representative – and of the notion of 'being sent'. Yet there is no reference in his work to 'twelve apostles'. Nor is there any indication that 'The Twelve' became leaders in separate Christian communities after the death of Jesus. Of the Twelve, Paul regards James, the brother of the Lord, Peter (Cephas), and John as occupying pivotal positions in the *ekklesia*.[18] He mentions that he has permission from these three to go to the Gentiles.[19]

Paul calls Stephanas and Epainetos '*aparche*' (firstlings of the offerings).[20] Perhaps this expression indicates a certain position of pre-eminence within the community. This is how Clement of Rome understood the word when he used it to say that the apostles had appointed these 'firstlings' as bishops and deacons.[21] Later, in his letter to the Philippians, Paul mentions *episkopoi* and *diakonoi* for the first time.[22] Although some scholars have argued that 'kai' (and) in this phrase must be read as an *explicativum*, it is generally accepted that Paul is, in fact, addressing two groups of people who have a special role in the community; perhaps this is an early form of 'feste Amtsbezeichnung' or even a title.[23]

The fact that Paul uses titles that later became technical terms for particular types of office does not mean that they already had a definite meaning for him. For example, a term like '*diakonos*' (the masculine form) is used to describe the role Phoebe fulfills.[24] She is a woman with a leadership role who does what deacons were instructed to do in later centuries: to act as a go-between between different groups of christian leaders.[25]

The Gospels and the Acts of the Apostles were written some decades after Paul's epistles. Here, the terms 'apostle' or 'prophet', which Paul uses to designate certain

---

[13]1 Cor. 4.1-2.
[14]1 Cor. 3.9.
[15]1 Cor. 3.5.
[16]See also 1 Cor. 14.29, 32 and 31.
[17]Rom. 1.1, 1 Cor. 1.1; 4.9; 9.1-2.
[18]cf. Gal. 1.18-19.
[19]Gal. 2.9.
[20]1 Cor. 16.15; Rom. 16.5; see Numbers 18; Deut. 12.6.
[21]1 *Clem.*, 42.4.
[22]Phil. 1.1; cf. 1 Timothy 3; *episkopoi* are further mentioned in Tit 1.7; 1 Pet. 2.25; Acts 20.28.
[23]See already Von Campenhausen, *Kirchliches Amt*, p. 74.
[24]Rom. 16.1.
[25]In critical editions of the Greek New Testament between 1930 and 1998, Junias (Rom. 16.7) is regarded as a man; later editions once again present Junias as a woman. There is discussion about what her task was.

tasks and offices, are still in use.[26] However, the word '*apostolos*', in particular, has taken on a more definite meaning. It has also gained in importance. Each of the synoptic gospels mentions the twelve apostles (analogous to the twelve tribes of Israel) and Mark gives a story of how they were chosen and a description of the mission they were given (to proclaim, heal the sick and exorcise devils).[27]

Luke gives the most precise description of the *apostolos*. He mentions explicitly that Jesus chooses them from among his disciples.[28] In the Acts he describes what exactly makes an apostle an apostle: namely, an apostle is a disciple who has followed Jesus from the day he was baptized by John until the day he was taken away from them.[29] Luke is the first to describe the task of the apostle as a *diakonia* (a service, or ministry).[30] Their *diakonia* is to become witnesses of the resurrection.[31]

But it soon turns out that *diakonia* also involves a different role of (assistant) leadership. Although he does not use the word '*diakonos*' in the description of the appointment of 'The Seven',[32] Luke describes their task and that of the apostles with the same word: *diakonia*. It is not surprising, therefore, that, in the spirit of a casual remark by Irenaeus of Lyons,[33] the Seven have often been characterized as the prototypes of later deacons.[34] After all, there is reference to an official appointment, and to dual leadership (Apostles and the 'Seven'). The way Luke speaks about this has striking parallels in the earliest sources which mention *episkopoi* and *diakonoi*. The Seven were given the task by the apostles of 'taking care of the tables'.[35] However, in the remainder of Acts, some of the Seven also appear to act as independent preachers of the gospel.[36]

In addition to the apostles and 'their' Seven, there is mention of teachers and prophets, in Acts 13.1, as well as in the works of Paul. But these are not described in any detail. Luke, however, comparatively has a lot to say about *presbuteroi* in his double work. Like the other gospels and the Septuagint, he always presents them as a collective group of experienced, older[37] and wise men. In the Gospels and in the beginning of Acts, just as in Jewish sources, they are a group of leaders who are found in Jewish communities. Luke actually introduces one such group, which

---

[26]cf. 1 Cor. 12.28-29; Acts 13.1; Acts 11.30.

[27]Mk 3.14; see also Mt. 10.1; Mt. 10.2-4; Mk 3.16-19; Lk. 6.14-16.

[28]Lk. 6.14-16.

[29]Acts 1.21-22; see also Lk. 22.28.

[30]Acts 1.17.25.

[31]Luke 24.48; Acts 1.10.

[32]Acts 6.1-7.

[33]Irenaeus, *Haer.*, 3.12.10.

[34]B. J. Koet, *The Go-Between: Augustine on Deacons*, in: *Brill Studies in Catholic Theology*, vol. 6 (Leiden: E.J. Brill, 2019), pp. 28–9.

[35]cf. Acts 6. 1-7; cf. Acts 2. 44-45.

[36]Stephen in Acts 6.8-7.53; and Philip in Acts 8.5-40, see also Acts 21.8.

[37]We note that *presbyteros* is a comparative form of *presbus* (old person).

initially led the communities of followers of Jesus alongside the apostles.[38] Later they are also mentioned as leaders without the presence of apostles.[39]

At a meeting later called the 'Apostolic Council', the apostles and *presbyteroi* made a pronouncement about the conditions that non-Jews who wish to follow Jesus Christ must observe.[40] Their authority is also evidenced by the fact that Paul asks the *presbyteroi* of the *ekklesia* of Ephesus to come and visit him.[41] The fact that Luke uses both *episkopos* and *presbyteros* in Acts 20.17-38 was the reason Ysebaert concluded that these terms were synonymous.[42] But this view is not shared by everyone.[43]

Another source for organization in the early church is the *Didachè*. This is a short Greek work that was written in the milieu around Matthew and Luke at the beginning of the second century, and was intended for Christians who were familiar with Jewish customs, prayers and forms of organization.[44] It clearly defines the offices of apostle, prophet, teacher,[45] bishop and deacon,[46] as they were developing in the earliest Christian communities. The teacher (*didaskalos*) is expected to teach.[47] The prophets teach, like the teachers, but it is explicitly said of them that they accomplish their teaching under the inspiration of the Spirit.[48] Like the apostles, they too are

---

[38]Acts 11.30; 14.23; 15.2-6; 22-23.

[39]Acts 20.17; 21.18. This is one of the reasons why John N. Collins, *Diakonia. Re-interpreting the Ancient Sources* (Oxford: Oxford University Press, 2009) has argued that *diakonia* is not the same as 'humble service', as German Protestants circles have argued since the nineteenth century. Dieter Georgi had already shown that *diakonoi* cannot simply be translated as 'servant'. See D. Georgi, *The Opponents of Paul in Second Corinthians: A Study on Religious Propaganda in Antiquity* (Philadelphia, PA: Fortress, 1986; English translation and greatly expanded edition of the German original from 1964). A. Hentschel, *Diakonia im Neuen Testament* (Tübingen: Mohr, 2007), confirms Collins's findings and states that the interpretation of *diakonia* and 'diaconal' as indicating social or charitable activity by the churches is not based on the use of this word and its cognates in the New Testament. See also B. Koet, 'Like a Royal Wedding: On the Significance of *diakonos* in John 2,1-11', in *Diakonia, diaconiae, diaconato: semantica e storia nei Padri della Chiesa. XXXVIII incontro di studiosi dell' antichità cristiana. Roma, 7-9 maggio 2009*, eds V. Grossi, B. Koet and P. van Geest (Rome: Augustinianum, 2010), pp. 39–52 (SEA 117); id., 'Whatever became of the Diaconia of the Word', *New Diaconal Review*, (IDC-NEC) Issue 1 (November 2008): 22–31.

[40]Acts. 15. 6-21.

[41]Acts 20.17-38.

[42]J. Ysebaert, *Die Amtsterminologie im Neuen Testament und in der Alten Kirche* (Breda: Eureia, 1994), p. 60; see also Dassmann, *Kirchengeschichte*.

[43]See Ysebaert, *Die Amtsterminologie*, p. 60; See also A. Stewart, *The Original Bishops: Office and Order in the First Christian Communities* (Grand Rapids, MI: Baker, 2014), pp. 48–9; P. M. Gy, 'Rémarques sur le vocabulaire antique du sacerdoce chrétien', in *Études sur le sacrement de l'ordre*. [Lex Orandi vol. 22] (Paris: Les Éditions du Cerf, 1957), pp. 125–45.

[44]For the historiography of the research on the *Didachè*, see J. Draper (ed.), *The Didache in Modern Research* (Leiden: E.J. Brill, 1996).

[45]*Did.*, 11-13.

[46]*Did.*, 15.

[47]*Did.*, 11.

[48]*Did.*, 11.

described as itinerant ministers of the gospel,[49] but it appears that prophets were also sometimes attached to a particular community for a longer term, allowing them to preside over the eucharistic meal, like the Jewish high priests.[50] Their model are the prophets of old,[51] but the discontinuity with the Jewish tradition lies in the fact that they take the place of the high priest, so that it is no longer necessary to attend the temple as Jewish Christians did.[52] The Didachist also mentions the ministry of the *episcopos*.[53] This ministry developed in the Greek Christian communities that consisted mainly of former pagans. More so than the *presbyteros*, the *episkopos* developed into the primary leader of Christian communities, at the expense of the prophets and teachers.[54] Thus the *Didache* also appears to reflect something of the early Christian shift to a more international context in emphasizing the fact that *episkopoi* and *diakonoi* can perform the same services as the prophets and teachers who had been present for some time,[55] although they should not be given the same honor.[56] In a certain sense, the *Didache* provides insight into two traditions, in one of which *episkopoi* and *diakonoi* were the leaders of the congregation; this latter tradition clearly became the dominant one.

Incidentally, it should be noted that just before the composition of the *Didache*, Ignatius mentioned a distinction between ministers and lay people. Tertullian, Cyprian and later Jerome also distinguished: '*inter ordinem et plebem*'.[57] In Classical Latin, *ordo* has the connotation of 'sequence', 'rank', 'degree', and after the fall of the Roman monarchy, the word designated any well-organized group.[58] Both meanings are present in the writings of the first Christians.

In summary, it can be said that Paul uses different terms to describe the positions of prominence in the early Christian community. But because their meaning varies on occasion and because he does not provide explicit job descriptions, it is difficult to draw the organigram of a Pauline *ekklesia*. Moreover, it is important to realize that

---

[49]*Did.*, 11.

[50]*Did.*, 13; cf. 11.

[51]*Did.*, 11.

[52]*Did.*, 13.

[53]*Did.*, 15.

[54]W. Rordorf and A. Tuilier, 'Introduction', in *La doctrine des douze Apôtres (Didachè)*. SCh, 248 (Paris: Les Éditions du Cerf, 1978), pp. 75–6.

[55]*Did.*, 15.1.

[56]*Did.*, 15; cf. Acts 6.1-7.

[57]Ignatius of Antioch, *Eph.*, 2.4.20; Tertullian, *Castit.*, 7.3; cf. also: John Chrysostom, *Sac.*, l. III, n. 5-6; Cyril of Alexandria, *Com.Jo* .XX, 22-23; Jerome, *Lucif.* 11. This distinction was adopted in imperial law (see, for instance, *Cod. Thds*, 4.3.1 *De clericorum et monachorum*). Cf. G. Dix, *Le ministère dans l'église ancienne* (Paris: Neuchatel, 1955), pp. 74, 77; A. Nocent, 'Ordine-ordinazione', *Dizionario patristico e di antichità cristiane* 2 (1983): 2496–501; Ch. Pietri, *Roma Christiana. Recherches sur l'Église de Rome, son organization, sa politique, son idéologie de Miltiade à Sixte III (311-440)* (Rome: École française de Rome, 1976), passim.

[58]P. van Beneden, *Aux origines d'une terminologie sacramentelle 'ordo', 'ordinare', 'ordinatio' dans la littérature chrétienn avant 313* (Louvain: Spicilegium sacrum Lovaniense, 1974), pp. 2–4 . In the word group 'ordo sacerdotum' the word 'ordo' meant the 'college' as well as the 'hierarchy' that was at the service of the deity represented.

there were also non-Pauline communities that may have had a different structure. Much is uncertain, therefore, with regard to the way the first Christian communities were organized.

The Didachist shows that the boundaries between the offices as they had developed in the Jewish Christian and Greek Christian communities may well have been fluid. In other sources (Phil. 1.1 and the *Didache* are among the earliest) *episkopos*, *diakonos* and *presbyteros* have in a sense become technical terms for specific offices of leadership. The Acts of the Apostles, the letters of Peter, James and Paul, as well as letters attributed to Peter, show that these words were already in use before AD 100 and that there was probably already a distinction between them.[59] The plural *presbyteroi* in Acts refers to collective leadership, which was based on a Jewish leadership model. Like *ecclesia*[60] they have remained untranslated in Latin and in later modern languages ('église').

There are certainly arguments to be found for the thesis that there was a twofold model of ministry of *episkopoi* and *diakonoi* in the early church; texts from a somewhat later date are important in this context.[61] In the letter written by Clement, the bishop of Rome, the twofold leadership of bishops and deacons as their assistants (the latter are compared to the Old Testament Levites) still seems clearly present.[62] It is a model that can be typified as episcopal. There are a number of scholars who believe that a fundamentally presbyteral form of organization also existed.[63] There has been much discussion about how these models related to each other, but most scholars now follow H. Lietzmann's suggestion that two systems merged together into a threefold order (*episkopos-presbyteros-diakonos*).[64]

Ignatius is usually seen as the first witness to a threefold form of leadership, as he describes the bishop and deacons as individuals and the priests as collective.[65] The

---

[59]Cf. for ἐπίσκοπος: Act 20.28; Phil. 1.1; 1 Tim. 3.2; Tit. 1.7; 1 Pt. 2.25; for πρεσβύτερος: Act 14.22sq.; 15.2-23; 16.4; 20.17; 21.18; 1 Tim. 4.14; 5.17-19; Tit. 1.5; Iac 5.14; 1 Pt. 5.1.5; 2 Io 1.1; 3 Io 1.1; for διάκονος: Rom. 16.1; 1 Cor. 3.5; Eph. 6.21; Phil. 1.1; Col. 1.7; 4.7; 1 Thess. 3.2; 1 Tim. 3.8.12; 4.6.

[60]Signifying 'people of Israel in the LXX and 'first collection of Jesus'' disciples' in the NT.

[61]See already, A. Hatch, *The Organisation of the Early Christian Churches* (London: Rivingtons, 1881), passim.

[62]1 *Clem.* 42.5. According to Ysebaert, 1 *Clement* contains echoes of the meaning that is given to *presbuteroi* in the New Testament. He regards it as a word that encompasses all forms of leadership in the Christian community. Cf. Ysebaert, *Die Amtsterminologie*, 90. Cf. B. J. Koet, 'Isaiah 60.17 as a Key for Understanding the Two-fold Ministry of ἐπισκόποι and διάκονοι according to 1 Clement (1 Clem. 42.5)', in *The Scriptures of Israel in Jewish and Christian Tradition: Essays in Honour of Maarten J. J. Menken*, eds B. Koet, S. Moyise and J. Verheyden. SNT, 148 (Leiden: E.J. Brill, 2013), pp. 345–62.

[63]For an outline of this problem, see, for instance, A. Stewart-Sykes, 'Deacons in the Syrian Church Order Tradition: A Search for Origins', in *Διακονία, Diaconiae and the Diaconate: semantics, history, ecclesiology. XXXVIII Incontro di Studiosi dell'Antichità Cristiana 2009. Roma, 7-9 maggio 2009.* SEA, 117 (Roma: Institutum Patristicum Augustinianum, 2010), pp. 111–19.

[64]H. Lietzmann, 'Zur altchristlichen Verfassungsgeschichte', *ZWT* 55 (1914): 97–153.

[65]E. Junod, 'Les diacres d'Ignace', in *Histoire et herméneutique. Mélanges offerts à G. Hammann*, ed. M. Rose (Genève: Labor et fides, 2002), pp. 177–206, and B. Koet, 'The Bishop and His Deacons. Ignatius of Antioch's View on Ministry: Two-fold or Three-fold?', in *Deacons and Diakonia in Early Christianity: The First Two Centuries*, eds B. J. Koet, E. Murphy and E. Ryokas, WUNT II, 479 (Tübingen: Mohr Siebeck, 2018), pp. 149–64.

presbyterium is related to the *episkopos* as the strings are to a harp.[66] For Ignatius it is the bishop who leads the Eucharist, but because he could delegate this task, this subsequently also became a privilege of the presbyterate.[67] The *presbuteroi* were not permitted to baptize or celebrate the Eucharist (*agape*) without authorization from the *episcopos*.[68] The deacons had a special bond with the *episcopos*.[69]

SUBSEQUENT DEVELOPMENTS IN THE ORGANIZATION OF THE COMMUNITIES

There must have been important regional differences, and an urban diocese like Rome was certainly organized differently than small rural dioceses.[70] It is impossible, therefore, to give an exhaustive description of the way organizational structures developed, all the less so because the oldest data are certainly not complete. Nevertheless, one of the greatest common denominators between the communities of the East and the West was the fact that the office of bishop assumed a more fixed form from the end of the second century onward.[71] The rise of monepiscopacy was thus complete, and the *episkopos* (*episcopus*) became the sole leader. Ignatius was an important early witness to this development. He even compares the bishop to God the Father, indicating that the bishop's leadership in the Christian community had become undisputed.[72] In the *Traditio Apostolica*, too, an anonymous collection of texts from the third century (or a little earlier) which contains echoes of several early Christian traditions, the bishop is presented as the person who offers bread and wine,[73] baptizes catechumens,[74] cares for the poor and sick[75] and takes cares for the burial of the dead.[76]

The writings of Cyprian of Carthage seem to indicate that the central role of the bishop had been definitively established around 250. Cyprian, in fact, describes

---

[66]Ignatius, *Eph.*, 4; *Trall chs.*, 2, 3, 7, 12, and 13.

[67]Ignatius, *Smyrn.*, 8.1.

[68]Ignatius, *Trall.*, 2.3.

[69]Ignatius, *Eph.*, 2; *Trall.*, 3.

[70]Missionary journeys and circular letters, the formulation of a common creed, meetings of bishops, ordination ceremonies and the (hierarchical and territorial) division of dioceses (cf. Nicaea canon 6) are the ways in which *koinonia* was achieved during the first centuries. See, pp. 240–5; 248–56; 256–71.

[71]The studies by A. Faivre, *Naissance d' une hiérarchie. Les premières étapes du cursus clérical.* 'Théologie historique' 40 (Paris: Éditions Beauchesne, 1977) and J. Gibaut, *The Cursus Honorum: A Study of the Origins and Evolution of Sequential Ordination.* 'Patristic Studies', 3 (New York: Peter Lang Publishing, 2000) are both considered standard works. See also: F. Sullivan, *From Apostles to Bishops: The Development of the Episcopacy in the Early Church* (New York and Mahwah: Newman Press, 2002) and A. Di Berardino, *Istituzioni della Chiesa Antica* (Venezia: Marcianum Press, 2019), pp. 143–5, 145–55. For the legal requirements for admission to the clerical state, see Di Berardino, *Istituzioni*, pp. 169–72.

[72]Ignatius, *Trall.*, 6.1.

[73]*Trad.Ap.*, 4.

[74]*Trad.Ap.*, 7-8.

[75]*Trad.Ap.*, 34.

[76]*Trad.Ap.*, 40.

how the bishop was assisted in all kinds of activities by his deacons, a council of presbyters, and other clerical assistants.[77] Cyprian calls the bishop alone the first *sacerdos*[78] but also describes him as a member of the *collegium episcoporum*.[79] The use of the word '*sacerdos*' represents the introduction of a cultic term in reference to Christian leadership, which the earliest followers of Jesus had avoided. Later it became the standard word for bishop, *in vice Christi* and is used as such in the *Traditio Apostolica*. Cyprian mostly used the term '*sacerdos*' to denote the bishop but he sometimes applies it to the presbyters as well.[80] In *Ep.* 61.3 he describes presbyters as – 'cum episcopo presbyteri sacerdotali honore coniuncti' – joined in sacerdotal honour with the bishop.[81]

It is not clear from the *Traditio Apostolica* whether the priests joined in with the bishop saying the eucharistic prayer.[82] But Ignatius had mentioned earlier that the bishop could delegate a priest to preside at the Eucharist.[83] Tertullian also states that the presbyters share in the bishop's *ordo sacerdotalis*,[84] although his work contains no reference to presbyters celebrating the Eucharist on their own.[85] Nevertheless, priests were increasingly delegated to celebrate the Eucharist once the church began to spread to rural areas (from the third century onward). It should be noted, however, that in the third century priests 'only' celebrated the Eucharist in the absence of the bishop.[86] The bishop presided at the offering of the eucharistic gifts. He also administered baptism and regulated penitential practice.[87] If necessary, he delegated the management of church property to a priest or a deacon.[88]

During the third century, the term '*sacerdos*' slowly began to be applied more widely to priests.[89] During that century, the already existing division between λαϊκός and κλῆρος became not only more liturgical but also acquired a social nature. In

---

[77]R. Seagraves, *Pascentes cum disciplina: A Lexical Study of the Clergy in the Cyprianic Correspondence* (Fribourg: Éditions Universitaires, 1993).

[78]Cyprian, *Ep.*, 59 and 66.

[79]Cyprian, *Ep.*, 55.21.2. 'actum suum disponit et dirigit unusquisque episcopus, rationem sui domino redditurus'; see also *Ep.*, 72.3; and *Ep.*, 55.8 on the infallibility of the bishops together.

[80]For the bishop, see *Ep.*, 63; as applied to the *presbyteri*, see *Epp.*, 40.2; 67.4; 72.2.

[81] Cf. H. Bakker, P. van Geest and H. van Loon, 'Introduction: Cyprians' Stature and Influence', in *Cyprian Studies in His Life, Language and Thought*, eds H. Bakker, P. van Geest and H. van Loon. 'Late Antique History and Religion' 4. (Leuven-Dudley: Peeters, 2010), pp. 1–27, esp. pp. 15–22; Bakker, Van Geest, Van Loon, 'Introduction', 15-22 (on the collegium); M. Bévenot, '"Sacerdos" as Understood by Cyprian', *JTS*, n.s. 30 (1979): 416, 421–3 (on the term 'sacerdos').

[82]*Ap. Trad.*, 4; Cf. A. Stewart-(Sykes), *The Didascalia Apostolorum. An English version with Introduction and Annotation*. 'Studia Traditionis Theologiae 1' (Turnhout: Brepolis Publishers, 2009).

[83]Ignatius, *Smyrn.*, 8.1.

[84]Tertullian. *Castit.*, 7.

[85]A. Vilela, *La condition collegiale des prêtres au 3e siècle*. 'Théologie Historique', n 14 (Paris: Beauchesne, 1971), p. 251.

[86]Tertullian, *Coron.*, 3; Cyprian, *Ep.*, 13, 2 and *Ep.*, 5,12 and 16.

[87]Tertullian, *Bapt.*, 17 (baptism); *Coron.*, 3.5 (Eucharist); *Pudic.*, 21 (penance).

[88]Cyprian, *Ep.*, 5,12,16 and 52.

[89]A. Blaise, *Le vocabulaire latin des principaux thèmes liturgiques* (Turnhout: Brepols Publications, 1966), pp. 500–1.

Rome and North Africa, the deacon, presbyter and bishop are clearly distinguished at the time as the higher *ordines*.[90] The 'ordo episcoporum' means that the bishops are regarded as successors of the apostles.[91] The distinctions between the ordained ministers and the so-called *confessores* remain vague.[92]

Jerome is one of the first authors who tried to minimize the distinction between the *ordines* of bishop and priest. In a sarcastic epistle about Roman deacons he says that the *sacerdotes* (meaning both bishops and priests) receive a power at their ordination that deacons do not have, particularly the power to preside at the Eucharist.[93] He draws a sharp caesura between priests and deacons,[94] but much less so between priests and bishops. He speaks contemptuously of the fact that priests are not allowed to preach.[95] It is clear from the same letter, however, that he is aware of the difference between bishops and priests. He says the priest must be subservient to his bishop even though he ultimately emphasizes the unity between priest and bishop by comparing them to Aaron and his sons, who were one in ministry.[96] In the same spirit, the *Canones Hippolyti*, canonical guidelines probably written around 340 in Egypt, stipulate that the presbyter is the equal of the bishop, except with respect to the episcopal see and ordination, as the priest did not have the power to ordain.[97] In the *Sacramentarium Veronense* they are called *sacerdotes*, although *secundi meriti*.

From the third century onward, the minor orders of *subdiaconus, lector, acolythus and exorcista* were distinguished.[98] The hierarchical relationship between them is not exactly clear, nor whether (or, if so, how) the lector was ordained or instituted. In the *Constitutiones Apostolicae* the laying on of hands is mentioned in connection with subdeacons and lectors.[99] The *De traditione Apostolica* presents lectors, subdeacons, virgins and widows as being part of the people (laity).[100] Many hypotheses are plausible with respect to the relationship between lectors and

---

[90]Tertullian, *Praescr.,* 41; *Bapt.,* 17; cf. Cyprian, *Ep.,* 40.

[91]Tertullian, *Praescr.,* 32.1; *Marc.,* 5.2; Van Beneden, *Aux origines d'une terminologie,* pp. 18–2.

[92]Cf. A. Faivre, *Chrétiens et Églises: des identités en construction. Acteurs, structures, frontières du champ religieux chrétien* (Paris: Les Éditions du Cerf , 2011), p. 143sq. See also Di Berardino, *Istituzioni,* pp. 177–202 for a description of the offices of bishop (177–84); *presbyteri* (including in the East) pp. 185–9; deacons (pp. 189–93); the lower orders (pp. 193–200) and for the status of the *confessor* (the Christian who had remained faithful to his or her religion during the persecutions (200–2).

[93]Jerome, *Ep.,* 146.

[94]I. Bodrozic, 'Girolamo e la disputa sulla superiorità tra il sacerdozio e il diaconato', in *Diakonia, diaconiae, diaconato: semantica e storia nei Padri della Chiesa. XXXVIII incontro di studiosi dell' antichità cristiana. Roma, 7-9 maggio 2009,* ed. V. Grossi, B. Koet and P. van Geest. SEA 117 (Rome: Augustinianum, 2010), pp. 399–412.

[95]Jerome, *Ep.,* 52.7; cf. 52.4; 52.8.

[96]Jerome, *Ep.,* 52.7.

[97]Ibid., *Canon.,* 4.

[98]Cf. V. Saxer, *Vie liturgique et quotidienne à Carthage vers le milieu du 3e siècle* (Città del Vaticano: Libreria Editrice Vaticana, 1969), pp. 76–88; Gibaut, *The Cursus Honorum,* pp. 59–157.

[99]*Const.Ap.,* 3.11.1; 3.11.3; and 8.21.

[100]*Trad.Ap.,* 9; cf. Cyprian, *Ep.,* 8.1; 9.1; 29; and 34.4.

subdeacons. Around AD 400, the subdiaconate was the highest of the minor orders; and it was moving in the direction of the 'real' clergy, although the subdeacon's liturgical function was modest. Subdeacons functioned as messengers between local churches, and had acolytes as attendants.[101]

Finally, in the fifth century, the Imperial Law recognized the following *ordo*: *episcopus, presbyter, diaconus, diaconissa, subdiaconus, cuiuslibet alterius loci clericus, monachus, mulier* (here to be interpreted as nun).[102] It was established at the Council of Serdica (343) that only men who had been ordained lector, deacon and priest could be consecrated a bishop. But not until the end of the fifth century, or perhaps even the beginning of the sixth, can we truly speak of a *cursus completus per gradum*.[103] It had already been established at the Council of Nicaea[104] that baptism was a requirement for admission to an ordination.

AUGUSTINE'S VISION OF THE ORGANIZATION OF THE ECCLESIAS AND OF ECCLESIASTICAL MINISTRIES

At a time when the organization of the ecclesial communities in the East, the West and Africa had taken definite shape, Augustine from the start of his ministry as bishop in Hippo regularly referred explicitly the 'state of affairs' in respect of ecclesiastical offices. He also made a clear distinction between *ordo clericorum*[105] and the *congregatio laicorum*[106] When Augustine spoke of 'ministerium', or 'ministerium dominici corporis',[107] he referred exclusively to the *ordines* of bishop and priest and their exclusive tasks of administering the sacraments and proclaiming the Word.[108] In pastoral and spiritual terms, however, the bishop and the priest were defined as servants under the servant Christ. In addition, Augustine distinguished a superior and an inferior rank in the *ordines*. The first consisted of the bishops, priests and deacons.[109] Only the bishops were regarded as successors of the apostles.[110] Each bishop was also a member of a leading 'collegium' in the universal church.[111] It was in this context that letters of communion were exchanged.[112] Within the 'ordo' of bishops, Augustine distinguished the ranks of metropolitan, primate and bishop

---

[101]cf. Cyprian, *Ep.*, 47, 65, 77, 78 and 79.

[102]Cf. *Cod. Thds.*, 5,3,1; cf. Faivre, *Naissance*, pp. 279–87, 313–438.

[103]Faivre, *Naissance*, p. 255; see Gibaut, *The Cursus Honorum*, passim.

[104]*Canon.*, 19.

[105]Augustine, *Parm.*, 2.24; *Jo.Tr.*, 41.10; *Ep.*, 60.11.

[106]Augustine, *En. Ps.*, 8,13 ('plebs/laici' - 'ministri'); *Ep.*, 67.34; 60.1; 228.5.

[107]See Augustine, *Ep.*, 228.6.

[108]Augustine, *Conf.*, 11.2; *Civ.*, 8.27; 22.8.10; *En. Ps.*, 109.1; 113.2.6; *Ep.*, 69.1.

[109]Augustine, *Ep.*, 43.3.7.

[110]Augustine, *En Ps.*, 44.32. 'Pro apostolis filii nati sunt tibi, constituti sunt episcopi'. Cf. *Jo.Tr.*, 47.3.

[111]cf. P. Zmire, 'Recherches sur la collegialité épiscopale dans l'église d'Afrique', *RechAug* 7 (1971): 1–72, esp. 24–31.

[112]Augustine, *Ep.*, 43.1.7sq.; 182.2.

'simpliciter'[113] and he spoke of 'praepositura', 'gubernatio' or 'praeesse', 'regere', 'superintendere'[114] only in relation to the duties of a bishop. It must be added that there were many bishops at the time; the ratio of bishops to priests must have been 1:10 in North Africa; hence Episcopal consecrations took place quite frequently.

In agreement with the opinion prevailing at the time, Augustine thus regarded the episcopacy as something higher than the priesthood.[115] But he emphasized unity in diversity. Thus as a bishop, Augustine addressed priests as co-presbyter, just as Jerome did for instance.[116] And unlike Cyprian, he addressed deacons as *condiaconus*.[117] There are no similar references to the *clerici inferioris ordinis* although he does mention these orders. This strict distinction between the higher and lower clergy is rather surprising, because, according to Augustine, reception into the rank of subdeacon was an ordination rather than an institution[118]; moreover, unlike in other dioceses, he regarded the subdeacon as a cleric who must embrace celibacy, just like the bishop, the priests and the deacons.[119]

In spite of his caesura between the higher and lower clergy, the inclusive aspect appears to predominate in Augustine's thinking about ministries within the ecclesial communities. He believed the collegiality of the bishops was not limited to that of the Catholic bishops among themselves, as Cyprian thought, who considered that leaving the church meant losing the Holy Spirit. Augustine compared ordination into one of the *ordines* to baptism.[120] Consequently, a minister, once validly ordained, could validly administer ordination, even outside church communion.[121] This position on rebaptism or reordination, which possibly derived from Ambrose, created scope for, and recognition of, ordination to the *ordines* outside the Catholic Church.[122] In addition to his conviction that the Donatist bishops had been ordained in the apostolic tradition, Augustine's conviction regarding the sacraments explains why, unlike Cyprian, he regarded apostate bishops (and at his time that meant Donatists) as bishops in the full sense, and why he was prepared to concelebrate with them.[123]

He consistently called both Catholic and Donatist bishops (co-)*episcopi*, *fratres* and *consacerdotes*.[124] Augustine's comment in a sermon on the anniversary of his

---

[113]Augustine, *Emer.*, 1; for primates: cf., for example, *Ep.*, 209.

[114]cf. Augustine, *Civ.*, 19.19.

[115]Augustine, *Ep.*, 82.4.33. '*episcopatus presbyterio maior sit*'. Cf. *Jo.Tr.*, 47.3; *Haer.*, 53.

[116]Augustine, *Epp.*, 36; 67; 71; 73; 74; 82; and Jerome, *Ep.*, 40. Further references in: L. F. Bacchi, *The Theology of the Ordained Ministry in the Letters of Augustine of Hippo* (San Francisco, CA: International Scholars Publications, 1998), p. 93.

[117]Augustine, *Ep.*, 101.4.

[118]Augustine, *Ep.*, 63.1. '*Nam ordinatus est . . . subdiaconus Timotheus*'.

[119]Augustine, *Serm.*, 356.3. Augustine is unclear about the offices of the acolyte-messenger, 'ostiarius' and 'lector'.

[120]Augustine, *Parm.*, II, 13.28-14, 32.

[121]Augustine, *b. coniug.*, 32.

[122]Augustine, *Parm.*, 2.13.28.

[123]Augustine, *Ep.*, 128.3.

[124]Augustine, *c. Gaud.*, 2.14. Further, see Bacchi, *The Theology of the Ordained Ministry*, p. 87.

consecration, that he was a bishop for his faithful, but a Christian with them[125] proves, moreover, that his inclusiveness in relation to Christian fellowship was of a spiritual rather than an organizational nature.[126]

ASPECTS OF ECCLESIASTICAL LEADERSHIP

The bishop as a leader in society

The Emperor Constantine's recognition of Christianity as a *religio licita* in 312 had consequences for the way in which the church and its leaders were anchored in the society. Although Late Antique society was firmly rooted in paganism, Christianity increasingly emerged as what it had already become: a social factor of importance. Many bishops came from the upper classes, were well educated and self-confident. Many, like Ambrose, Paulinus of Nola and Augustine in the West, or the Cappadocian Fathers in the East, were able to adapt their sermons to the social and cultural context of their audiences. The ability to do this was regarded as a virtue and was listed as one of the most important responsibilities recommended in treatises on correct episcopal behavior.[127] But in late antique society, institutions were also adapted to the church, which was becoming increasingly powerful. Imperial legislation, which unified local and provincial customs by subjecting them to the guidance of a single supreme authority, entrusted judicial authority to the bishops. The episcopal court became 'an institution characteristic of the life of the early church'.[128] Episcopal arbitration commonly took precedence over that of the civil courts. This gave bishops a special relationship with the emperor. Both were connected to the divine and the sacred, as well as to earthly structures.[129] The fact that Pope Damasus was given the honorary title of *Pontifex Maximus* by the Emperor Gratian in 375 (formerly the title of the pagan chief priest of Rome, which the emperor had borne since the time of Augustus) is an indication of how powerful the bishop of Rome had become. Together with emperors such as Constantine II and Constantius, for example, he was able to enforce the decisions of ecumenical councils.

Even though he was a judge himself, Augustine was alive to the dangers of giving social power to ecclesiastical dignitaries. He was not alone in this. Augustine was one of many authors who warned against the pride of the clergy and who criticized the social and economic privileges and the relatively high incomes of the higher clergy.[130]

---

[125]Augustine, *Serm.,* 340.1.

[126]See section 6 and: G. Lawless, 'Augustine's Burden of Ministry', *A* 61 (1984): 295–315.

[127]L. Testa, 'The Late Antique Bishop: Image and Reality', in Philip Rousseau, *A Companion to Late Antiquity* (Chichester: Willey-Blackwell, 2012), pp. 523–38, esp. 531.

[128]W. K. Boyd, *The Ecclesiastical Edicts of the Theodosian Code* (New York: Columbia University Press, 1905), pp. 88–91 [repr. 2001].

[129]Testa, 'The Late Antique Bishop', p. 526.

[130]cf. Augustine, *Ep.*, 10.2; 21.1; 77; 78.3; 85; 209; 213.1; 250.2. Further cf. J. Gaudemet, *L'Église dans l'empire romain* (Paris: Sirey, 1958), pp. 174f., 213f., 316, and 319; E. Elm, *Die Macht der Weisheit. Das Bild des Bischofs in der Vita Augustini des Possidius und andere spätantiken und frühmittelalterlichen*

His remedy for these dangers was to encourage clerics to live as much as possible as monks. According to Possidius he himself lived according to this counsel.[131] Other examples of well-educated and self-confident bishops from the highest classes who chose to live as monks are Gregory of Nazianzus, Gregory of Nyssa, Basil of Caesarea, Ambrose and Martin of Tours.[132] Similarly, Gregory the Great, a member of one of the most important families of Rome and thus well acquainted with the customs in those circles, founded a monastery on the Caelian hill, and eventually became bishop of Rome. The bishop thus became a social and political leader, a judge, teacher and pastor. Many bishops primarily wanted to be monks, but had to find a balance between their secular and their religious tasks. These two worlds, the secular and the religious, had become more closely intertwined by the fourth century. Holiness remained the basis of all the competences of a bishop. Just as Moses prepared himself through his stay in the desert to lead the Jewish people, so apprenticeship as a monk could prepare a bishop for his religious and secular duties.[133]

Celibacy as the identity marker of the leaders

An important change in the criteria for the function of *episcopus* occurred at the beginning of the fourth century. Up to that time, there was no ecclesiastical provision for celibacy, even though many bishops advocated the observance of the biblical laws of purity (which had originally been prescribed to make priests in the Old Testament eligible 'only' for temple service) for the sake of a life lived entirely in abstinence.[134]

A first step towards compulsory celibacy was taken with *canon* 33 of the regional synod of Elvira (306) (Denzinger 119).[135] The Council of Nicaea adopted this provision in 325 in its canon 3. However, the Egyptian bishop Paphnutius feared

---

Bischofsviten. 'Studies in the History of Christian Thought' 109 (Leiden: E.J Brill, 2003); P. van Geest, '*Quid dicam de vindicando vel non vindicando*? (*Ep.*, 95.3). Augustine's Legitimation of Coercion in the Light of his Role of Mediator, Judge, Teacher and Mystagogue', in *Violence in Ancient Christianity: Victims and Perpetrators*, eds A. Geljon and R. Roukema, SupVCh no 125 (Leiden: Brill, 2014), pp. 151–84

[131]Possidius, *VA.*, 11.

[132]Cf. E. Rébillard and C. Sotinel (eds), *L'évêque dans la cité du IVe au Ve siècle: image et autorité. Actes de la table ronde organisée par l'Instituto patristico Augustinianum et l'Ecole française de Rome 1995* (Rome: École française de Rome, 1998).

[133]For the comparison of a monk's sojourn in the desert to that of Moses, see C. Rapp, *Holy Bishops in Late Antiquity: The Nature of Christian Leadership in an Age of Transition.* 'The Transformation of the Classical Heritage' 37 (Berkeley and Los Angeles, CA and London: University of California Press, 2005), pp. 107–8.

[134]This is the thesis of R. Gryson, *Les origines presentes du célibat ecclésiastique du premier au septième siècle* (Gembloux: Duculot, 1970). For the abstinence of the High Priest, see Lev. 21.13-14; for that of the priests (though note that this refers to the *cohanim*, and not to the elders), see Ezek. 44.22. Di Berardino, *Istituzioni*, pp. 335–7 (proof of ritual purity).

[135]Text in Denziger. 119. See also: Chr. Cochini, *The Apostolic Origins of Priestly Celibacy* (San Francisco, CA: Ignatius Press, 1990) which is a treasure trove for evidence from the New Testament, the works of church fathers and council documents up to the seventh century used to defend or impose celibacy, including for deacons.

that this measure would lead to fornication,[136] and it is clear that the rule was not accepted by all. Even at the time of Jerome and Augustine the issue was still subject to fundamental debate. In *De bono coniugali* (400) and *De sancta uirginitate* (401) Augustine refuses to present the choice between marriage and virginity as a choice between good and evil. He describes it as a choice between two 'goods' (*bona*). Yet he presents the spiritual state of life as the higher good.[137] Augustine proposed this idea in response to the dispute between Jerome and Jovinian on this issue.[138] Jovinian had suggested before 389 that the life of consecrated virgins or male religious, for whom abstinence was compulsory, was no more meritorious than that of married couples. Baptism established the equality of all Christians: the choice to lead an ascetic life did not alter this.[139] Jerome reacted furiously to Jovinian's views in 393. Thus he characterized marriage as vomit to which no widow would wish to return, all the less so because this state of life had supposedly only arisen after the Fall,[140] and he also called marriage a bad state of life,[141] whose only redeeming feature was that virgins were born from it.[142] Jerome attacked Jovinian because the latter's ideas did not correspond with Jerome's struggle to introduce the ideal of the priest-monk. He proposed his own form of life as the best way to lead a Christian life; not only was it better than marriage, it was also better than simply being a cleric.[143]

In the polemic between Jovinian and Jerome, Augustine thus occupied a middle position. But as has been seen, he preferred a celibate clergy. And even though he formulated this choice less polemically than Jerome, he too saw the monastic life as the basis for life as a cleric. As co-episcopus of his own bishop Valerius, he therefore founded a *monasterium clericorum* for the formation of celibate clerics. This formation, including that of future bishops, was based on a deliberate strategy. The clerics he formed were sent out to other areas, and Augustine always managed to have reliable friends appointed bishops to neighboring sees. Thus Alypius became

---

[136]cf. Socrates Scholasticus, *HE.*, 1.23.

[137]Augustine, *Serm.*, 132.3: 'diverse lucebunt: sed omnes ibi erunt. Splendor dispar, coelum commune'; cf. *b.coniug.* 3.3 and passim, *Virg.*, 10.9; 12.12; 18.18; 21.21; *retr.*, 2.48. However, see D. Hunter, 'Augustine, sermon 354A: Its Place in His Thought on Marriage and Sexuality', *AS* 33 (2002): 39–60. See also P. van Geest, 'Nuptiae', in *Augustinus-Lexikon*, eds C. Mayer, K.-H. Chelius and A. Grote (Basel: Zentrum fur Augistinus Forschung, 1986+), vol. 4, fasc.1-2 (Basel: Zentrum fur Augistinus Forschung, 2012), col. 243-261; A. Dupont, P. van Geest, M. Lamberigts and W. François, 'Sex', in *The Oxford Historical Guide of the Reception of Augustine*, eds K. Pollmann et al. (Oxford: Oxford University Press, 2013), vol. 3, col. 1726–1737; P. van Geest, 'Asceticism', in *The Oxford Historical Guide of the Reception of Augustine*, eds K. Pollmann et al. (Oxford: Oxford University Press, 2013), vol. 2, pp. 572–9.

[138]See D. Hunter, *Marriage, Celibacy, and Heresy in Ancient Christianity: The Jovinianist Controversy. Oxford Early Christian Studies* (Oxford and New York: Oxford University Press, 2007).

[139]Augustine, *retr.*, 2.22-23.

[140]Jerome, *Jovin.*, 1.47.

[141]Ibid., 1.4; and 16.

[142]Jerome, *Ep.*, 22.20; and cf. 22.

[143]In Jerome's estimation, being a cleric was good, but ultimately being a monk was better, even for a cleric. He expressed this view in all manner of variations, for example, in many of his letters, and it has the ring of propaganda. For such letters, see *Ep.*, 14, *To Heliodorus, bishop of Altinum*, and *Ep.*, 52, *To Nepotian*, and *Ep.*, 58, the letter *To Paulinus of Nola*.

bishop of Thagaste and Severus bishop of Mileve. Possidius applied the same strategy once he became bishop of Calama.[144]

Although married clergy continued to exist in the Western church, the ideal of the priest-monk that Jerome and Augustine had propagated became predominant. The ideal of priestly celibacy was stimulated by Popes Leo the Great and Gregory the Great, who themselves were devoted to the monastic form of life, and ultimately it was made almost obligatory as, for example, in Leo's *Epistle* 167.3.

Women as leaders

Women played a leading role in the communities that the Apostle Paul founded. As has been seen, Phoebe was called a *diakonos* in Rom. 16.1-2. She became the prototype of the later deaconesses. Paul's letter to Timothy also shows that widows held leadership positions; they were not only objects of care, but – once they had passed the age of sixty – also subjects of leadership.[145]

Female deacons were not the only women to hold formal positions of leadership: this was also true for widows, as can be deduced from the origin of the *ordo viduarum*. Widows who belonged to this group were allowed (with the bishop's permission) to perform tasks such as visiting the sick and even the laying on of hands during prayer, as for example in *Didaskalia apostolorum* 3.1.3. Gryson has argued that these women nevertheless remained lay people. By contrast, Thurston believes that they were widely considered to belong to the clerical state.[146] Elm has concluded on the basis of Gregory Nyssen's *Life of Macrina*, the *Traditio Apostolica* and the *Constitutiones Apostolicae* (ibid. 8.25.1), that the widows' 'only' task was to persevere in prayer, be calm and meek, not to give catechetical instruction, and to refer people who asked questions about doctrine to the bishop.[147]

At the same time, however, Tertullian mentioned widows as 'other ministers'.[148] Moreover, he taught that it was not entirely clear what the position of widows was because he indicated that if there were not enough widows, virgins could also be included in the *ordo viduarum*.[149] His *De virginibus velandis* also teaches that the *ordo viduarum* had been the more important group in the early church, and that the emphasis had shifted over time to the virgins. The rise of deaconesses similarly contributed to the declining status of the widows.[150]

---

[144]Possidius, *VA.*, 11. See: P. van Geest, 'Medium tenebat, neque in dexteram, neque in sinistram declinans' (*VA* 22.1). Possidius' relationship to Augustine and Augustine's embodiment of the *Praeceptum* in the *Vita Augustini*', *REA* 63 (2017): 99–122.

[145]1 Tim 5.1-14. See also: S. Elm, *Virgins of God: The Making of Asceticism in Late Antiquity* (Oxford: Clarendon Press, 1994), pp. 6–7, 25–9 and 137–83.

[146]R. Gryson, *The Ministry of Women in the Early Church* (Collegeville, MN: Liturgical Press, 1976), pp. 110–11; B. Bowman Thurston, *The Widows: A Women's Ministry in the Early Church* (Minneapolis, MN: Fortress Press, 1989), 104–5.

[147]*Const.Ap.* 8.25.1; See also: Elm, *Virgins of God*, pp. 169–70.

[148]Tertullian, *Praescr.*, 3.

[149]Tertullian, *Virg.*, 9.2.

[150]Elm, *Virgins of God*, pp. 170–8, esp. 172–3; cf. Di Berardino, *Istituzioni*, pp. 329–31.

Be that as it may: the various states of female ascetics were frequently discussed by ecclesiastical authors such as Ambrose and Jerome. Jerome suggested that (certain) widows had a clear role to play in the community, but that virgins should mainly keep far away[151] from the 'world' and that they must study scripture and fast (the same criteria that he had applied to 'clerics'.[152] His injunction that virgins should fast and renounce their inheritance because otherwise they would not partake of Christ's inheritance, also corresponds with his injunction against male clerics inheriting.[153] Thus, for Jerome, clerics and virgins were similar in the way their lives were oriented.

The task of the deaconess was to assist the bishop in the baptism of women and to administer the anointing to women; they also judged strangers in the community and were active in dispensing charity.[154] The question whether women, like *diakonoi* or presbyters, could also become part of the hierarchy has only seriously come to scholarly attention in recent decades. Madigan and Osiek have collected the source material, which shows that there were female deacons. In Canon 19 of the Council of Nicaea, the female form of 'deacon' is mentioned for the first time. Female deacons were often recruited from among the widows or virgins.[155] The overwhelming majority of the evidence for female deacons (or deaconesses) comes from the Greek East.[156] A well-known example is Olympias, who became deaconess of Constantinople as a widow.[157] It can be deduced from her life that the word 'deaconess' was regarded as an honorific, and that the order of deaconesses had absorbed the qualities of the widow and, as Elm says: 'merged them with its own attributes and those of the virgin to form a concept that applied to a vast variety of women: hence the virgin-widow-deaconess as leader of ascetic communities'.[158]

Although research into the role of women in the early church has progressed in recent decades, further study will be needed to determine their position more precisely.[159] Archaeological material, such as epitaphs and other inscriptions, will help to deepen our understanding of the structure of church organizations and the role of women within them, since literary sources deal mainly and 'only' with the position of the higher and male clergy. In inscriptions in Asia Minor, for example, thirty-two deaconesses are mentioned by name. It is necessary to examine these further to see what can be deduced about their ecclesiastical status.

---

[151]Jerome, *Ep.*, 22.

[152]Jerome, *Ep.*, 22, 16; cf. *Ep.*, 52, 7; *Ep.*, 52, 12.

[153]Jerome, *Ep.*, 22.17; cf. *Ep.*, 52.5; *Ep.*, 22.17; *Ep.*, 52.12.

[154]For these tasks of deacons and deaconesses, see P. Pylvänäinen, *Agents in Liturgy, Charity and Communication: The Tasks of Female Deacons in the Apostolic Constitutions*. STT 37 (Turnhout: Brepols Publications, 2020).

[155]*Const.Ap.*, 3.11; 8.12.

[156]K. Madigan and C. Osiek (eds), *Ordained Women in the Early Church: A Documentary History* (Baltimore, MD: The John Hopkins University Press, 2005), p. 204.

[157]See: *Vita Olympiadis*. Sch, vol. 13.

[158]Elm, *Virgins of God*, pp. 178–83.

[159]For a survey of the role of deacons in first two centuries, see B. J. Koet, E. Murphy and E. Ryökäs (eds), *Deacons and Diakonia in Early Christianity: The First Two Centuries* (Tübingen: Mohr Siebeck, 2018).

> *'Oportet . . . sacerdotes . . . integros atque immaculatos esse'*
> *(Cyprian, ep. 72.11.2)*

The morality and integrity of those who belong to an 'ordo'

The New Testament, the writings of the Apostolic Fathers and the church fathers, and the *Didaskalia* pay much attention to the moral qualities required of those who belong to an *ordo*, much more so than to descriptions of competencies and formal relations. In his letter to his disciple Timothy, Paul gives a first 'profile' of an *episkopos*, in which he emphasizes that the *episkopos* should be the husband of one wife and should be sober, prudent, moderate, hospitable, accommodating, peaceful and not adrift or avaricious. Moreover, he must show that he is able to manage his household well, because this is the litmus test for how he will lead the community.[160] Thus Paul makes no distinction between how an *episkopos* functions in the private domain and in the public domain. He mentions only one competency in the strict sense of the term for the *episkopos*: he must be *didaktikos*, apt to teach, something that should apply to every assistant (*doulos*) of God as outlined in 2 Tim. 2.24. Paul also emphasizes in 1 Tim. 1.3 that deacons must not be greedy or drunk.

In writing this passage, Paul set the tone for a long time to come. Several church fathers copied and commented on the profiles of ministers in 1 Timothy. Ignatius of Antioch, in addition to speaking about the organizational structure of the church in Asia Minor[161] and about obedience to the bishop and the priests and respect for the deacons,[162] also held up the bishop of Philadelphia's temperance (*epikeia*), selflessness and discretion as an example.[163] He also praised his virtue (*énarètos*), peace (*ákinètos*) and indulgence (*áorgètos*).[164] Polycarp required deacons to be irreproachable as servants of God and Christ and not to blaspheme or speak ambiguous words. Nor must they be guided by greed. They must be temperate, merciful and truthful in everything.[165] For *presbyteroi*, clemency and mercy are the main characteristics; they must put this last virtue into practice in their care for those who have gone astray, the sick, widows, the poor and orphans. They should also refrain from anger, unjust judgements, greed, gullibility or severity in judgement.[166] *The Shepherd of Hermas* expresses similar ideas when the author condemns deacons who rob widows and orphans[167] and praises bishops – and possibly also priests – who open their own houses to the needy and to widows.[168]

---

[160]1 Tim. 1, 3.1-7; cf. Tit. 1.5-8.
[161]Ignatius, *Trall.*, 2.1-3; 3.1; *Phil.*, prologue.
[162]Ignatius, *Smyrn.*, 8.1; *Trall.*, 2.1-3; 3.1; cf. *Magn.*, 3.1; cf. *Eph.*, 3.1.
[163]Ignatius, *Phil.*, 1.1.
[164]Ignatius, *Phil.*, 1.2.
[165]Polycarp, *Phil.*, 5.2.
[166]Polycarp, *Phil.*, 6.1.
[167]Hermas, *Sim.*, 9.26.2.
[168]Hermas, *Sim.*, 27.2.

The *Didache* says that the bishop must be kind, not keen on money, honest and of proven character.[169] It is striking that the community has the authority to judge pastors on whether they observe the Christian 'codes of conduct'.[170] To prevent idleness, the Didachist states that apostles and prophets may stay at any given place for a maximum of three days, unless, in the case of prophets, he is able to provide for himself (*Did.*, 13). If Christ is proclaimed out of personal gain (*Did.*, 12), then the integrity and authenticity of the prophet must be questioned (*Did.*, 11). Thus, the community is expected to judge not so much the orthodoxy of its leaders as their authenticity as Christians, the purity of their intentions and motives (cf. *Did.*, 2 and 10). For the Didachist, holiness is not a quality that can be achieved through ritual or participation in cultic actions.

The *Didache* as it has been handed down to us can be understood as a 'snapshot' in a process of writing and editing.[171] The text must have circulated in several versions in several communities and therefore does not have a single author. The guidelines it gives for the liturgy, organization and good order of life must therefore have been widely supported. An echo of the guidelines of 1 Tim. 1.3 is also visible in the *Didaskalia apostolorum*[172] and the *Constitutiones Apostolorum*, a collection of writings on the liturgy of the ordination of bishops, priests and deacons as it then existed, parts of which were written at the beginning of the third century.[173] The fourth to eighth chapters of the *Didaskalia* tersely highlight the discretionary and, especially, the moral qualities of the bishop, as head of the priests. As if they were a commentary on Mt. 5.5-9, 1 Tim. 3.2 and Tit. 1.7, these chapters point out that the pastor-bishop must be impeccable in body and spirit and free of blame; he must be merciful, peaceful and free from evil and unrest.[174] Moreover, he must judge without regard to persons,[175] not for personal gain or luxury, and must be patient in admonitions and ardent in preaching and in the refutation of errors.[176] His essence and activity should be equally marked by a clear conscience, mercy for those who are repentant[177] and care for widows and orphans. The second book of the *Apostolic Constitutions* (whose first to sixth books are a somewhat loose paraphrase of the *Didaskalia*) pays attention mostly to the morality and authenticity of the bishop. He must be learned and eloquent, and there should be no anger or profligacy in

---

[169]*Did.*, 15.2.

[170]*Did.*, 11; cf. *Mtt.*, 7.5; Hermas, *Mand.*, 11,7.

[171]J. Zangenberg, 'Reconstructing the Social and Religious Milieu of the Didache: Observations and Possible Results', in *Matthew, James, and Didache. Three Related Documents in Their Jewish and Christian Settings*, eds H. van de Sandt and J. K. Zangenberg, SBL no 45 (Atlanta, GA: Society of Biblical Literature, 2008), pp. 43–69.

[172]G. Schöllgen, *Die Anfänge der Professionalisierung des Klerus und das Kirchliche Amt in der syrischen Didaskalie*, JAC Ergänzungsband, 26 (Münster: Aschendorffsche Verlagsbuchhandlung, 1998); Stewart-Sykes, *The Didascalia apostolorum*.

[173]cf. Stewart, *The Original Bishops*.

[174]*Didas.*, 4.2.1 and 8.

[175]*Didas.*, 4.2.5.

[176]Arianism in particular caused bishops much trouble between 260 and 380, cf. *Didas.*, 5.2.8.

[177]*Didas.*, 6.2.12.

him. He should flee laziness and lethargy, as well as greed, indulgence and corrupt judgement. He must encourage good people, strengthen the weak, reform the fallen. It is striking that the *Apostolic Constitutions* mentions the obedience that deacons and priests owe to their bishop and that lay people owe to the clergy only after this has been said.[178]

Church fathers in the East and West also strove to emphasize the moral qualities of the ideal priest. In his treatise *On The Priesthood* Chrysostom tells his audience that the *sacerdos* must have devotion, have a good understanding of Catholic doctrine, be skillful in dealing with different kinds of people and, above all, show exemplary behavior that would encourage the congregation to follow his teachings and pagans to recognize him a worthy advocate.[179] Jerome sounded a characteristically radical note when he told clerics or priests that they were not allowed to keep their material inheritance because they could not otherwise become an heirloom of the Lord. The poor and strangers must know that their table is austere and they must visit the sick and get to know families; they must not accept gifts, respond to flattery or compliments; they must continue to study, be subservient to the bishop, call for repentance in their sermons, refrain from slandering others and dress soberly. Bishops should marry virgin brides only and no clerics should attend fashionable dinners but they should fast as much as possible.[180]

Augustine constantly emphasizes that bishops and priests should follow Christ.[181] Both in the private and the public domain, he demands honesty and transparency from his clergy.[182] Because he speaks of the *ministerium caritatis et humilitatis*, it is evident that clerics should embody these virtues in their attitude to life.[183] And although Augustine uses a formal distinction between the clergy and the 'plebs', he uses inclusive language when he reminds the shepherd that he himself also belongs to the flock (cf. *Sermo.*, 47, 2), and that he should listen to Christ more than the faithful should listen to him *sermo Guelf.* 32,2. In *Sermo.*, 46, he criticizes pleasers of the people who love praise and abdicate their responsibility to point out the faults of the sheep because it might make them unpopular. In *Sermo.*, 46,12 Augustine summarizes what is required of a good shepherd: he must reprove and encourage, frighten and console, strike and, ultimately and above all, heal.[184]

---

[178]*Const. Ap.*, 2.1.1-7; 2.11.1-10; 4.1-7; 5.1-7; 6.1-17 and passim.

[179]Sozomen, *HE.* 8.3. See also: Testa, 'The late Antique Bishop', 533.

[180]Jerome, *Ep.*, 52, 5-16.

[181]Augustine, *Civ.*, 10.6 ('forma serui').

[182]Augustine, *Sermo.*, 355–6.

[183]Augustine, *Sermo.*, 340; see also *Jo.Tr.*, 58.5. See also: L. F. Bacchi, 'A Ministry Characterized by and Exercized in Humility: The Theology of Ordained Ministry in the Letters of Augustine of Hippo', in *Augustine: Presbyter Factus Sum*, eds J. Lienhard et al. (New York: Peter Lang, 1993), pp. 405–15.

[184]P. van Geest, '"We shepherd you, we are shepherded with you": St. Augustine about the Motives of a Good Shepherd', in *The Recruiting Power of Christianity in Three Perspectives*, eds S. de Blaauw, E. Moorman (Rome: Edizioni Qasar Papers of the Royal Netherlands Institute in Rome, 2021).

Epilogue

Although it might appear that the offices of deacon, deaconess, priest and bishop – the organization of early Christian communities – had assumed their final shape within a century, much is still uncertain. Comments by evangelists and church fathers on the tasks these ministers exercised, as well as on the organization and structure of these communities, are often inconclusive, and it is also unclear to what extent there were regional differences in organization. It is therefore impossible to draw up a definitive chart of the forms of organization in the earliest church.

Nevertheless, it soon became clear that there would be a single office of leadership in these Christian communities: the *episkopos*. In the Greek Hellenistic world this word referred to the secular function of a supervisor. In the New Testament it also refers to the pastoral figures of the Old Testament and to God as shepherd (cf. Ezek. 34). *Episkopos* became the official title of the most important leader of a Christian community, both in the East and in the West.

From the oldest sources onward, this function is often mentioned together with deacons, the assistants of the bishop. In Rome and Constantinople, deacons remained important because they assisted the bishop in various ways and often went on to become bishops themselves well into the Middle Ages. But the *presbyteroi*, who appear in the earliest Christian sources as a leadership collective, as they were in Judaism, were gaining in influence. The figure of the presbyter emerged from this collective in the course of the third century, eventually presiding at the Eucharist on behalf of the bishop, and also in many other ways becoming the face of the Christian communities. Both in the West and in the East, a *cursus honorum* emerged. In the East, in addition to the seven ordinations that this *cursus* encompassed (doorkeeper, acolyte, lector, subdeacon, deacon, priest and bishop), deaconesses were also mentioned as members of the clergy. Soon after the edict of Milan, bishops were increasingly given secular tasks, for instance that of magistrate-judges. The bishop's court became a social, religious and political factor in society, and in this way the organizational structure of the first Christian communities, which is difficult to reconstruct completely, resulted in an ecclesiastical organization that was recognizable and increasingly intertwined (while retaining its own individuality) with the agrarian-feudal society of the Middle Ages.

Although remarks about the offices and the organization of the communities are ambivalent, there is nothing but clarity in the New Testament, the works of church fathers or treatises such as the *Didaskalia* when it comes to the moral qualities that those must have who belong to an *ordo*.

The author of the First letter to Timothy and the Didachist appear to have had prophetic foresight when they stressed that the *episkopos* should not be driven by lust for prestige, luxury, power or money. After the edict of toleration, when bishops began to look more and more like city governors and acquired extensive civil and judicial powers, the danger that this tendency would ruin them became greater than ever. From the beginning, all ecclesiastical authors knew that this would be disastrous for the ecclesiastical organization because this would lose one of its greatest assets: its credibility in proclaiming the values that Christ represented. This is why Augustine said that ecclesiastical leaders such as bishops should lead the flock conscientiously and in an authentically Christian way. But above all, they should be aware that believers must listen to Christ rather than to them. This capacity for self-reflection was perhaps the most important characteristic of the leaders of the church in early Christianity.

BIBLIOGRAPHY

Bacchi, L. F. *The Theology of the Ordained Ministry in the letters of Augustine of Hippo.* San Francisco, CA: International Scholars Publications, 1998.

Bacchi, L. F. 'A Ministry Characterized by and Exercized in Humility: The Theology of Ordained Ministry in the Letters of Augustine of Hippo', in J. Lienhard et al. (eds), *Augustine: Presbyter Factus Sum*, 405–15. New York: Peter Lang, 1993.

Bakker, H., van Geest, P. and van Loon, H. 'Introduction: Cyprian's Stature and Influence', in H. Bakker, P. van Geest and H. van Loon (eds), *Cyprian: Studies in His Life, Language and Thought*, 1–27. Leuven: Peeters, 2010.

van Beneden, P. *Aux origines d'une terminologie sacramentelle 'ordo', 'ordinare', 'ordinatio' dans la littérature chrétienn avant 313.* Louvain: Spicilegium sacrum Lovaniense, 1974.

di Berardino, A. *Istituzioni della Chiesa Antica.* Venezia: Marcianum Press, 2019.

Bévenot, M. '"Sacerdos'" as Understood by Cyprian', *Journal of Theological Studies, n.s.* 30 (1979): 416, 421–3.

Blaise, A. *Le vocabulaire latin des principaux thèmes liturgiques*, 500–1. Turnhout: Brepols, 1966.

Bodrozic, I. 'Girolamo e la disputa sulla superiorità tra il sacerdozio e il diaconato', in V. Grossi, B. Koet and P. van Geest (eds), *Diakonia, diaconiae, diaconato: semantica e storia nei Padri della Chiesa. XXXVIII incontro di studiosi dell' antichità cristiana. Roma, 7–9 maggio 2009*, 399–412. SEA 117. Rome: Augustinianum, 2010.

Bowman-Thurston,B. *The Widows: A Women's Ministry in the Early Church.* Minneapolis, MN: Fortress Press, 1989.

Boyd, W. K. *The Ecclesiastical Edicts of the Theodosian Code.* New York: Columbia University Press, 1905.

Campenhausen, H. von. *Kirchliches Amt und geistliche Vollmacht in den ersten Jahrhunderten.* Tübingen: Mohr Siebeck, 1953.

Cochini, C. *The Apostolic Origins of Priestly Celibacy.* San Francisco: Ignatius Press, 1990.

Collins, J. N. *Diakonia: Re-interpreting the Ancient Sources.* New York and Oxford: Oxford University Press, 2009.

Dassmann, E. *Kirchengeschichte.* Vol. 1. *Ausbreitung, Leben und Lehre der Kirche in den ersten drei Jahrhunderten. Kohlhammer Studienbücher Theologie 10.* Stuttgart: Kohlhammer, 1991.

Dix, G. *Le ministère dans l'église ancienne.* Paris: Neuchatel, 1955.

Draper, J. (ed.). *The Didache in Modern Research.* Leiden: E.J. Brill, 1996.

Elm, E. *Die Macht der Weisheit. Das Bild des Bischofs in der Vita Augustini des Possidius und andere spätantiken und frühmittelalterlichen Bischofsviten.* Studies in the History of Christian Thought, vol. 109. Leiden: E.J. Brill, 2003.

Elm, S. *Virgins of God: The Making of Asceticism in Late Antiquity*. Oxford: Clarendon Press, 1994.

Faivre, A. *Naissance d' une hiérarchie. Les premières étapes du cursus clérical*. Théologie historique, vol. 40. Paris: Éditions Beauchesne, 1977.

Faivre, A. *Chrétiens et Églises: des identités en construction. Acteurs, structures, frontières du champ religieux chrétien*. Paris: Les Éditions du Cerf, 2011.

Faivre, A. 'La question des ministères à l'époque paléochrétienne. Problématique et enjeux d'une périodiastion', in A. Faivre, *Chrétiens et Églises: des identités en construction. Acteurs, structures, frontières du champ religieux chrétien*. Paris: Les Éditions du Cerf, 2011.

Gaudemet, J. *L'Église dans l'empire romain*. Paris: Sirey, 1958.

van Geest, P. 'Nuptiae', in C. Mayer, K. H. Chelius and A. Grote (eds), *Augustinus-Lexikon*, vol. 4, fasc.1–2, cols. 243–261. Basel: Zentrum fur Augistinus Forschung, 2012.

van Geest, P. '*Quid dicam de vindicando vel non vindicando? (ep. 95.3)*. Augustine's Legitimation of Coercion in the Light of His Role of Mediator, Judge, Teacher and Mystagogue', in A. Geljon and R. Roukema (eds), *Violence in Ancient Christianity: Victims and Perpetrators*, 151–84. Leiden: E.J. Brill, 2014.

van Geest, P. "Medium tenebat, neque in dexteram, neque in sinistram declinans" (*Vita Augustini* 22.1). Possidius' relationship to Augustine and Augustine's embodiment of the *Praeceptum* in the *Vita Augustini*', *REAug* 63 (2017): 99–122.

van Geest, P. '"We Shepherd You, We Are Shepherded with You": St. Augustine on the motives of a Good Shepherd', in S. de Blaauw and E. Moorman (eds), *The Recruiting Power of Christianity in Three Perspectives*. Rome: Edizioni Qasar Papers of the Royal Netherlands Institute in Rome, 2021.

Georgi, D. *The Opponents of Paul in Second Corinthians: A Study on Religious Propaganda in Antiquity*. Philadephia, PA: Fortress, 1986.

Gibaut, J. *The Cursus Honorum: A Study of the Origins and Evolution of Sequential Ordination*. 'Patristic Studies', 3. New York: Peter Lang Publishing, 2000.

Gryson, R. *Les origines presentes du célibat ecclésiastique du premier au septième siècle*. Gembloux: Duculot, 1970.

Gryson, R. *The Ministry of Women in the Early Church*. Collegeville, MN: Liturgical Press, 1976.

Gy, P. M. 'Rémarques sur le vocabulaire antique du sacerdoce chrétien', in *Études sur le sacrement de l'ordre. Lex Orandi*, vol. 22, 125–45. Paris: Les Éditions du Cerf, 1957.

Hatch, A. *The Organisation of the Early Christian Churches*. London: Rivingtons, 1881.

Hentschel, A. *Diakonia im Neuen Testament*. Tübingen: Mohr, 2007.

Hunter, D. 'Augustine, sermon 354A: Its Place in His Thought on Marriage and Sexuality', *AS* 33 (2002): 39–60.

Hunter, D. *Marriage, Celibacy, and Heresy in Ancient Christianity: The Jovinianist Controversy. Oxford Early Christian Studies*. Oxford: Oxford University Press, 2007.

Käsemann, E. 'Amt und Gemeinde im Neuen Testament', in *Exegetische Versuche und Besinnungen*, vol. 1. Göttingen: VandenHoeck & Ruprecht, 1960.

Koet, B. J. 'Whatever became of the Diaconia of the Word', *New Diaconal Review*, (IDC-NEC) Issue 1 (November 2008): 22–31.

Koet, B. J. 'Like a Royal Wedding: On the Significance of *diakonos* in John 2,1–11', in V. Grossi, B. Koet and P. van Geest (eds), *Diakonia, diaconiae, diaconato: semantica e storia nei Padri della Chiesa. XXXVIII incontro di studiosi dell' antichità cristiana. Roma, 7–9 maggio 2009*, 39–52. SEA, 117. Rome: Augustinianum, 2010.

Koet, B. J. *The Go-Between: Augustine on Deacons. Brill Studies in Catholic Theology* vol. 6. Leiden: E.J. Brill, 2019.

Koet, B. J., Moyise, S. and Verheyden, J. (eds). *The Scriptures of Israel in Jewish and Christian Tradition: Essays in Honour of Maarten J. J. Menken*, 345–62. SNT, no 148. Leiden: E.J. Brill, 2013.

Koet, B. J., Murphy, E. and Ryökäs, E. (eds). *Deacons and Diakonia in Early Christianity: The First Two Centuries*. Tübingen: Mohr Siebeck, 2018.

Lietzmann, H. 'Zur altchristlichen Verfassungsgeschichte', *ZWT* 55 (1914): 97–153.

Luz, U. 'Erwägungen zur Entstehung des "Frühkatholizismus". Eine Skizze', *Zeitschrift für die Neutestamentliche Wissenschaft und die Kunde der Älteren Kirche* 65, nos. 1–2 (2009): 88–111.

Madigan, K. and Osiek, C. (eds). *Ordained Women in the Early Church: A Documentary History*. Baltimore, MD: The John Hopkins University Press, 2005.

Pylvänäinen, P. *Agents in Liturgy, Charity and Communication: The Tasks of Female Deacons in the Apostolic Constitutions*. Turnhout: Brepols, 2020.

Rapp, C. *Holy Bishops in Late Antiquity: The Nature of Christian Leadership in an Age of Transition. The Transformation of the Classical Heritage,* series vol. 37. Los Angeles: University of California Press, 2005.

Rébillard, E. and Sotinel, C. (eds). *L'évêque dans la cité du IVe au Ve siècle: image et autorité. Actes de la table ronde organisée par l'Instituto patristico Augustinianum et l'Ecole française de Rome 1995*. Rome: École française de Rome, 1998.

Rordorf, W. and Tuilier, A. 'Introduction', in *La doctrine des douze Apôtres* (Didache). *Sources Chrétiennes* vol. 248. Paris: Les Éditions du Cerf, 1978.

Saxer, V. *Vie liturgique et quotidienne à Carthage vers le milieu du 3e siècle*. Città del Vaticano: Libreria Editrice Vaticana, 1969.

Schöllgen, G. *Die Anfänge der Professionalisierung des Klerus und das Kirchliche Amt in der syrischen Didaskalie*. JAC Ergänzungsband. 26'. Münster: Aschendorffsche Verlagsbuchhandlung, 1998.

Seagraves, R. *Pascentes cum disciplina: A Lexical Study of the Clergy in the Cyprianic Correspondence*. Fribourg: Éditions Universitaires, 1993.

Stewart-Sykes, A. *The Didascalia Apostolorum: An English version with Introduction and Annotation*. Turnhout: [*Studia Traditionis Theologiae*, vol. 1], 2009.

Stewart-Sykes, A. 'Deacons in the Syrian Church Order Tradition: A Search for Origins', in Διακονία, *Diaconiae and the Diaconate: Semantics, History, Ecclesiology. XXXVIII Incontro di Studiosi dell'Antichità Cristiana 2009. Roma, 7-9 maggio 2009*. Rome: *Studia Ephemeridis Augustinianum*, vol. 117, 2010.

Stewart-Sykes, A. *The Original Bishops: Office and Order in the First Christian Communities*. Grand Rapids, MI: Baker, 2014.

Sullivan, F. *From Apostles to Bishops: The Development of the Episcopacy in the Early Church*. New York: Newman Press, 2002.

Testa, L. 'The Late Antique Bishop: Image and Reality', in P. Rousseau (ed.), *A Companion to Late Antiquity*, 523–38. Chichester: Willey-Blackwell, 2009.

Ysebaert, J. *Die Amtsterminologie im Neuen Testament und in der Alten Kirche*. Breda: Eureia, 1994.

Zangenberg, J. 'Reconstructing the Social and Religious Milieu of the Didache: Observations and Possible Results', in H. van de Sandt and J. K. Zangenberg (eds), *Matthew, James, and Didache: Three Related Documents in their Jewish and Christian Settings*, 43–69. SBL. no 45. Atlanta, GA: Society of Biblical Literature, 2008.

Zmire, P. 'Recherches sur la collegialité épiscopale dans l'église d'Afrique', *Recherches Augustiniennes* 7 (1971): 1–72.

CHAPTER 17

Dismissal from the clerical state and its consequences in the early church[1]

HENRYK PIETRAS

INTRODUCTION

The present topic shall be discussed on the basis of the legislation of the early church, as enshrined in the synodal canons as well as in the canons of the church fathers affirmed by synods. I would like to begin with a few introductory comments of a more general nature.

From the beginning, the church had been appointing individuals known as presbyters and bishops to preside over each Christian community and deacons to assist them in the performance of their duties.[2] Nonetheless, soon in the next generations the realities of daily life made it necessary to establish some other 'auxiliaries' for ecclesiastical functions such as proclaiming the scripture reading to the faithful, administering the Holy Communion to the ill and infirm, assisting at baptism and funeral ceremonies, maintaining order. Some were called 'elders' or 'clergy' even though they were subject to various church regulations. They are all mentioned in synodal documents beginning from the fourth century onwards. There is no doubt that they had been active in the earlier period, but we have very few extant documents from the earlier synods.

In the Judeo-Christian milieu, they were appointed by the laying on of hands, following the Jewish tradition.[3] In Graeco-Roman communities, where offices

---

[1]This chapter was previous published in its original Polish version in K. Dyrek (ed.), *Laicization Among the Clergy: A Historical and Psychological Study* (Kraków: WAM, 2010), pp. 7–19.
[2]See Acts 6.1-7. Among many studies, see H. Von Campenhausen, *Ecclesiastical Authority and Spiritual Power* (London: SCM Press, 1919), E. Schillebeeckx, *The Church with a Human Face: A New and Expanded Theology of Ministry* (London: Xpress Reprints, 1988); more recently J. T. Burtchaell, *From Synagogue to Church: Public Services and Offices in the Earliest Christian Communities* (Cambridge: Cambridge University Press, 2004).
[3]See Num. 27.15-23; Deut. 34.9. This ritual is seen in Acts 8.17-19.

were assigned by nomination or election, hands would be raised (resembling the voting practice known as 'show of hands'), instead of the laying on of hands. The appointing was therefore technically referred to as 'appointment by show of hands' (χειροτονία), as in office appointments. For instance, a deutero-Pauline exhortation determined the moral qualifications that candidates were to fulfil: they were to be morally upright people, respectable, not given to excessive drinking, with well-mannered children, married to one wife only and, of course, orthodox, which was not easy to define precisely.[4] Such were the criteria for allowing a member of the clergy to remain in the clerical state or for having them expelled.

Clergymen of all ranks would be removed for any mortal sin according to the contemporary nomenclature, namely idolatry, sexual immorality, murder, consumption of animal blood, in accordance with the Apostolic decree,[5] as ordered by the Council of Nicaea in 325[6] and reaffirmed by Basil the Great in the canons that would be later incorporated in the body of the legislation adopted at the Council in Trullo (692). The canon in question also states that the expulsion from clergy should not be combined with excommunication, as two penalties cannot be imposed for one and the same offence.[7] The very sentence of deposition issued by a bishop or a synod did not have to take effect immediately, as the incriminated person could appeal to the provincial metropolitan or synod, or even the metropolitan of a neighbouring province, or, in the West, to the bishop of Rome, as decided at Sardica.[8] Let us first proceed to discussing expulsions as a consequence of doctrinal violations.

DISMISSAL FOR DOCTRINAL REASONS

In times of persecution, the most common reason was the abandoning of faith for fear of torture and death, and the offering made to idols, as attested in a synodal letter from the time of St Cyprian of Carthage,[9] as well as one of the Nicaean canons referring to those who deserted their faith and were subsequently ordained as priests, apparently failing to inform other members of the church of that previous circumstance.[10] In later periods, penalties would be applied to embracing heretical beliefs. An example of such a verdict may be a ruling passed at the Council of Ephesus (431) that effectively dismissed those who adhered to the Messalian group,

---

[4]See 1 Tim. 3.2.
[5]Acts 15.22-29.
[6]The First Council of Nicaea (325), canon 2, (DSP 1, pp. 27–8). More on this Council in H. Pietras, *Council of Nicaea (325): Religious and Political Context, Documents, Commentaries*, trans. M. Fijak (Rome: Gregorian & Biblical Press, 2016).
[7]Basil the Great, *EpD.*, 32.51: 'Clerics who are guilty of the sin unto death are degraded from their order, but not excluded from the communion of the laity' (SCL 3, p. 47* and p. 52*), (trans. ANF).
[8]The Synod of Sardica (343-344), canons 4, 5 and 13. (SCL 1, p. 149* and p. 154*). More in L. W. Bernard, *The Council of Sardica 343 A.D* (Sofia: Synodal Pub. House, 1983).
[9]The Synod of Carthage (254) I, 1 (SCL 1, p. 16*). More in Geoffrey D. Dunn, 'Cyprian of Carthage and the Episcopal Synod of Late 254', *REAug* 48 (2002): 229–47.
[10]The First Council of Nicaea (325), canon 10 (DSP 1, p. 37).

fairly extreme in their approach to fasting practices and sexuality. As the sentence reads:

> Those who refuse and do not want to renounce heresy, should they be presbyters, deacons, or perform some other function in the Church, shall be divested of their clerical rank, function, and community (ἐκπίπτειν καὶ κλήρου καὶ βαθμοῦ καὶ κοινωνίας), whereas laymen shall be excluded from the communion of the Church. Those who are proven to have taken part in heresy, are prohibited from having a monastery so that this weed would not disseminate and grow any further.[11]

As can be seen, Basil's caveat to the effect that there should be one penalty for one offence is not employed in this case, as the sentence provides for stripping heretical clergymen of their rank and post as well as for removing them from the church communion, which is tantamount to excommunication. Lay people were confronted by the penalty of an anathema (a higher degree of excommunication) for committing the same offence. Unfortunately, we do not have sufficient evidence to determine how, when and who understood and interpreted the difference between anathema and exclusion from the communion of the church. It could only be presumed that such penalties would have allowed a person to accept penance and to return to the church, unless otherwise indicated, as we shall see further on. Conversely, divesting someone of clerical rank would lead inevitably and ultimately to their laicization, if decided so, immediately or following the appeals procedure, as specified in the statements of Basil the Great.[12] As a result, in the case of the previous verdict of the Council of Ephesus, a cleric is removed from his office for all time, while the punishment of excluding a person from the communion of the church shall be terminated when they show signs of true conversion.

The same council imposed, in a very solemn phrasing, similar penal measures for violations of the Nicene Creed. It reads as follows:

> No one is allowed to espouse, write down, or formulate any faith other than that specified by the holy Fathers assembled at Nicaea in communion with the Holy Spirit. Those who shall dare to formulate, disseminate, and teach any other faith to those who wish to convert from paganism, Judaism, or any heresy, and to turn to the true faith, should be dismissed from their office (ἀλλοτρίους εἶναι), if they are bishops or clergymen: bishops from their episcopate, clergymen from priesthood; if they are lay people, they shall be excluded from the communion of the Church (ἀναθεματίζεσθαι).[13]

---

[11]The Council of Ephesus (431), *The definition against the Impious Mesallians*, 5. ACO., part 1, I, 7, pp. 117–118. (DSP vol. 1, p. 171), (trans. ANF).

[12]Basil the Great, *EpD.*, 3 (SCL 3, p. 35*).

[13]The Council of Ephesus (431), canon 7, (DSP 1, pp. 167–8), ACO., part 1, I, 7, pp. 89–106. (trans. ANF).

It is perplexing why the same council Fathers punish clergymen of all ranks with 'only' laicization for formulating any new creed, yet they do not compound this sanction with excommunication, as was done in the case of the Messalian group. It would seem that this particular offence was mainly disciplinary, and only partly doctrinal in nature. The key point here is not the faith itself, but the necessity of putting a stop to formulating new creeds to serve the emperor's purposes. It was significant first to Constantine the Great, and thereafter to his successors, that the visible sign of the unity of the church in their state was one *credo* subscribed to and endorsed by everybody. He was only slightly concerned about whether anybody would use it in liturgy; there was a complete freedom in this regard. It is also worth recalling that the use of the so-called Apostolic Creed in liturgy had never been discontinued in Rome, in spite of the endorsement of the Nicene one. The text also appears to imply that the bishops congregated there would not have heard of a creed reportedly established in Constantinople in 381.

In the same spirit, and with almost exactly the same words, the Third Council of Constantinople[14] states its position on the teachings of all the previous general councils, while the Second Nicene Council reiterates the penal consequences awaiting those who would dare to keep heretical books.[15]

Another doctrine-related issue debated over the centuries was how to determine the date of Easter. A number of synods attempted to resolve this question, in view of the existence of the Judeo-Christian tradition where it was celebrated according to the lunar calendar, that is, at the same time as the Jews, regardless of the given day of the week, and the 'rest of the world' that celebrated Easter on the Sunday following that date, a combination of the lunar and solar calendars. The problem was actually of doctrinal importance, as the fact of celebrating anything along with the Jews would amount to nothing less than a heresy. Moreover, considering the presence of multiple calendars in use, adhering to the lunar calendar could possibly result in having years with two Easter Sundays or, on the contrary, in years without an Easter date, as the accepted principle was to celebrate Easter after the spring equinox. However, the said calendar relied on computation, not observation, in determining the equinox date. Although the Council of Nicaea decided that all the Christians should celebrate Easter at the same time, it was not specified when the celebration should take place, as stated in the *Letter of Emperor Constantine to All the Churches*.[16] Apparently, the call to celebrate together was not very effective, as the synod of Antioch (341) threatened that the clergymen who celebrated Easter on the Jewish Passover date would be not only dismissed from their rank and office, but also expelled from the church.[17]

An example of deposition and laicization par excellence was the Council of Ephesus's (431) verdict on Nestorius:

---

[14]The Third Council of Constantinople (680-681), *Definition of Faith* 20 (DSP 1, p. 323).
[15]The Second Council of Nicaea (787), canon 9, (DSP 1, p. 359).
[16]See in Eusebius of Caesarea, V.C., III, 18.
[17]The Synod of Antioch (341), II/B, canon 1, (SCL 1, p. 135*).

The holy synod said: As, in addition to all else, the excellent Nestorius has declined to obey our summons and has not received the holy and God-fearing bishops we sent to him, we have of necessity started upon an investigation of his impieties. We have found him out thinking and speaking in an impious fashion, from his letters, from his writings that have been read out, and from the things that he has recently said in this metropolis which have been witnessed to be others; and as a result we have been compelled of necessity both by the canons and by the letter of our most holy father and fellow servant Celestine, bishop of the church of the Romans, to issue this sad condemnation against him, though we do so with many tears. Our lord Jesus Christ, who has been blasphemed by him, has determined through this most holy synod that the same Nestorius should be stripped of his episcopal dignity and removed from the college of priests (ἀλλότριον εἶναι τὸν αὐτὸν Νεστόριον τοῦ τε ἐπισκοπικοῦ ἀξιώματος καὶ παντὸς συλλόγου ἱερατικοῦ).[18]

This statement calls for a few words of commentary. For the first time, it can be seen that the bishops convened at a synod state that Christ Himself utters a ruling through them. Out of respect for Nestorius's office of Bishop of Constantinople, they refer to him as τιμιώτατος, which was rendered into Latin, by a contemporary author, as 'excellent' (honoratissimus). They believe that the deposition is a sad affair, a necessary evil caused by the recalcitrant attitude of the incriminated bishop, who espoused the view that Jesus Christ was a human being miraculously born of the Virgin, whereas the deity was somehow imparted to Him later. In consequence, since the Virgin Mary had not given birth to God, the title 'Mother of God' (Θεοτόκος) should not be attributed to her. Expelled definitively from the priesthood, Nestorius should nonetheless remain as a member of the church. Indeed, as he had been a monk in Antioch prior to his elevation to Bishop of Constantinople, he continued to be a monk and returned to his monastery, whence the Emperor Theodosius II would later banish him to a monastery in the Upper Egypt. He died there in 451 as an ordinary member of his monastic community.

DISMISSAL FOR DISCIPLINARY REASONS

Although orthodoxy was always regarded in the church as more important than orthopraxis, abuses and violations of the latter domain would also very frequently lead to expulsions from the clerical state. As noted earlier in this chapter, this should have taken place as a consequence of each mortal sin committed by a clergyman. Let us now have a look at what transgressions would be perceived as a cardinal sin.

---

[18]The Council of Ephesus (431), *Decree of the Council against Nestorius ACO*, part 1, I, 2, 54 (DSP 1, p. 159). N. P. Tanner (ed.), *Decrees of the Ecumenical Councils*, vol. I (Washington, DC: Georgetown University Press, 1990), pp. 61–2. More in M. Starowieyski (in Polish) 'Sobór Efeski i sprawa Nestoriusza – problem źródeł', *M* 50 (1995): 23–35.

Violation of the law

Even though every sin constitutes some sort of violation of the law, we are concerned here with only such transgressions as disrespecting the law, disregarding and defying the rules and regulations and so on. Therefore, it was seen as necessary to divest a clergyman of his clerical rank or excommunicate a lay person, should they happen to disregard any decision of a synod.[19] If a synod deposed a bishop, or a bishop stripped a presbyter or a deacon of their rank, but they would dare to continue performing any liturgical function:

> If any bishop who has been deposed by a synod, or any presbyter or deacon who has been deposed by his bishop shall presume to execute any part of the ministry, whether it be a bishop according to his former custom, or a presbyter, or a deacon, he shall no longer have any prospect of restoration in another Synod; nor any opportunity of making his defense; but they who communicate with him shall all be cast out of the Church (ἀποβάλλεσθαι τῆς ἐκκλησίας), and particularly if they have presumed to communicate with the persons aforementioned, knowing the sentence pronounced against them.[20]

It could be inferred from the above passage that such a deposition was not yet final, as there was still a possibility to appeal against the verdict. A cleric would lose such an option, however, if he failed to submit to the initial sentence. The same censure was ruled by the synod of Antioch for making an appeal to the emperor, instead of to a synod:

> If any presbyter or deacon deposed by his own bishop, or any bishop deposed by a synod, shall dare to trouble the ears of the Emperor, when it is his duty to submit his case to a greater synod of bishops, and to refer to more bishops the things which he thinks right, and to abide by the examination and decision made by them; if, despising these, he shall trouble the Emperor, he shall be entitled to no pardon, neither shall he have an opportunity of defence, nor any hope of future restoration.[21]

It was only when a provincial synod decided in favour of the deposition unanimously, the verdict would become irrevocable.[22] Such a provision was determined in Antioch (341), becoming a law used more and more frequently and finally entering the *Law Book of Gratian (Decretum Gratiani)*,[23] the main body of ecclesiastical law in the West, beginning from the Middle Ages until as late as the Code of Canonical Law of 1917.

The issue of appealing from hastily passed deposition verdicts became a problem of major concern to the bishops assembled at the synod of Sardica in 343. As the

---

[19]The Synod of Carthage (348), canon 14, (SCL 1, p. 199*).
[20]The Synod of Antioch (341), II, canon 4 (SCL 1, p. 136*).
[21]The Synod of Antioch (341), II, canon 12 (SCL 1, p. 138*). (Transl. ANF)
[22]The Synod of Antioch (341), II, canon 15 (SCL 1, p. 139*).
[23]*Decretum*, c. VI, quest. 4, canon 5, (564).

emperors Constantius II and Constans intended, the synod was to be a general council, yet it was soon split into the Eastern and Western synods for reasons that remain beyond the subject of this chapter. The bishops of the West decided to stay at Sardica and established, for the first time, the rules of appealing to the bishop of Rome.[24] The same synod also determined that clergymen of all ranks who abandoned the churches for which they had been assigned, and refused to return there,[25] should be laicized irrevocably, thus making the earlier Nicene article (providing for the penalty of excommunication) more precise. It was decided that they could return to the church as lay members. At this point, it is also worth noting that in the early centuries of Christianity priests would not be ordained to be at a local bishop's 'disposal', but all of them were always assigned to a specific church, which they were not permitted to leave, for example, to choose a 'better' parish or diocese. At least in theory, of course, as many synods would reiterate the pronouncement of the Council of Nicaea that the clergy, especially bishops, were prohibited from moving from church to church,[26] with apparently very poor results, as the practice of transferring to a 'better' diocese would keep flourishing and continues to this day.

The Council of Ephesus, which carried through the irrevocable deposition of Nestorius, bishop of Constantinople, for doctrinal reasons,[27] ordered that all bishops who would oppose the council's decision should be stripped of their office, rank and title.[28] Still, with no punishment of excommunication being applied, they could remain in the church as secular members.

The practice of simony was another legal problem. If ordination or appointment of a person to any office or administrative position in the church was achieved in exchange for monetary benefits, the accountable bishop was to be deposed from his office, along with all the individuals concerned, and all the laymen involved should be excommunicated.[29] It was decided by the greatest synod of the ancient church, the Council of Chalcedon in 451,[30] followed by other synods and general councils.[31] Nonetheless, let us take note of the fact that making specific payments for the ordination of the sacred orders was sanctioned by law in Armenia: a presbyter was obliged to pay four 'gold coins' (*thaler*) to the bishop, a deacon – three, if he was a free man, or two, if not. Members of a princely family were to offer a horse with a

---

[24]The Synod of Sardica (343-344), canon 5.13 (SCL 1, p. 149* and p. 154*).
[25]The Synod of Sardica (343-344), canon 5.19 (SCL 1, p. 149* and p. 156*); The First Council of Nicaea (325), canon 16 (DSP 1, p. 41).
[26]The First Council of Nicaea (325), canon 15 (DSP 1, p. 41).
[27]The Council of Ephesus (431), *Decree of the Council against Nestorius* (DSP 1, p. 159).
[28]The Council of Ephesus (431), canons 1-2 (DSP 1, p. 163).
[29]E. Wipszycka, "Fonctionnement de l'église égyptienne aux IVᵉ-VIIIᵉ siècles (sur quelques aspect)", in *Études sur le christianisme dans l'Égypte de l'antiquité tardive*. SEA 52 (Roma: Augustinianum, 1996), pp. 195–212.
[30]The Council of Chalcedon (451), canon 2 (DSP 1, pp. 225–7).
[31]The Second Council of Nicaea (787), canon 19 (DSP 1, pp. 373–5).

harness, and should they fail to do so, this duty would fall on their families.[32] If the appointment of a new bishop was actually not encumbered with any payment, but involved support from a secular authority, he would have to be deposed as well, as the Second Council of Nicaea determined.[33]

Another legal ground for the laicization procedure related to the office of 'rural bishop' (Χωρεπίσκοπος), whose scope of powers was restricted, and dependent on the nearest bishop of the city. They were authorized to appoint, *sua sponte*, subdeacons, lectors and exorcists. If they ordained a presbyter or a deacon without the urban bishop's consent, they would lose their office and rank.[34]

Expulsion for cardinal (mortal) sins

As mentioned at the beginning of this chapter, the case in point would be first of all the main four 'commandments' from the decree of the so-called apostolic synod. Besides, the penalty of unconditional expulsion from office was applied to those clergymen who practised usury, which was the term used to refer to any lending of money at interest, believed to be a particularly grave harm done to the poor, as written in the documents of the Council of Nicaea (325), and the synods of Elvira (306), Arles (314), Carthage (348).[35]

Sexual transgressions were seen as possible grounds for the loss of a church office and rank. In accordance with Paul's instruction, married men could be ordained as priests, but since then on they would have been forbidden from having intercourse with their wives or even from co-habiting with them, on penalty of laicization.

> Considering this a dignified, decent, and noble thing, we advise brethren that priests and deacons refrain from having a sexual relation with their spouses, as they perform their daily [God's] service. Whoever acts in contravention of this precept, [he] shall be divested of his clerical rank (*Quicumque contra hanc constitutionem fecerit, a clericatus honore deponatur*).[36]

It can be seen very clearly that this provision is underpinned by the need to preserve ritual purity. As sexual contact was deemed as impure, it was prohibited to those who were to perform liturgical services.

The relevant canon issued by the synod of Elvira (306) is noteworthy because of the fact that it seems its content does not correspond with the title. This canon,

---

[32]The Synod in Artashat (after 373), canon 2 (SCL 1, p. 278*). More on this Synod in Armenia, see E. Boré, 'Histoire des Aghovans et leur conversion au Christianisme', *L'Université Catholique, Recueil religieux, philosophique, scientifique et littéraire* 22, no. II/7 (Paris 1846): 137–52.

[33]The Second Council of Nicaea (787), canon 3 (DSP 1, p. 347).

[34]The Synod of Antioch (341), II/B, canon 10 (SCL 1, pp. 137*–8*).

[35]The First Council of Nicaea (325), canon 17 (DSP 1, p. 43); The Synod of Elvira (306), canon 20 (SCL 1, p. 53*); The Synod of Arles (314), II/A, canon 13 (SCL 1, p. 72*); The Synod of Carthage (348), canon 13 (SCL 1, p. 199*). More on the Synod of Elvira in M. Meigne, 'Concile ou collection d'Elvire', *RHE* 70 (1975): 361–87; J. Vilella Masana, 'Colecciones falsamente atribuidas a un concilio', *CnS* 39 (2018): 137–241.

[36]The Synod of Arles (314), II/B, canon 29 (SCL 1, pp. 74*–75*). My translation.

entitled *On Bishops and Presbyters, to Abstain from Intercourse with Their Wives* reads as follows:

> It is forbidden to bishops, presbyters, and deacons, 'or to all clergymen', performing liturgical services, to abstain from intercourse with their wives and [from] begetting offspring. Whoever shall do so, should be excluded from the honour of priesthood (*quicunque vero fecerit, ab honore clericatus exterminetur*).[37]

It is possible that this particular canon might have been 'distorted' by copyists or added to the collection in the second half of the fourth century, when the Priscillians, who were very strict in this regard, condemned all sexuality, including marital sex. As it is, it looks as though a cleric could be expelled from the priesthood if he refused to have children. Since canon titles were usually added by the editors of the entire canon collections, it is no wonder the above-mentioned title is different and does not match the contents. At any rate, clergymen in Spain would live together with their wives, as another canon provided for expelling a priest whose wife committed adultery and he failed to dismiss her.[38] For adultery, the same synod laid down the penalty of deposition in conjunction with absolute excommunication, which meant that the delinquent would not be given the Holy Communion even on his deathbed.[39] Still, the synod of Elvira is not necessarily representative of the whole church, as it prohibits dispensing the Communion in the extremity of death also in the cases such as killing a person with a spell (6), relapsing to prostitution after completing penance (7), deserting one's husband and living with another man until death (8.11), procuring (12), marrying one's daughter off to a pagan priest (17), incest (66), paedophilia (71) and giving a false testimony against a clergyman (75). It comes as no surprise, as Spain was known for introducing a number of strict measures, both in a positive and a negative way.

In the church as a whole, nevertheless, a clergyman was not allowed to remarry after the death of his wife.[40] Remarrying by widows and widowers was considered as permissible at the most, but generally not recommended, as it involved the necessity of doing penance.[41] Clergymen were meant to be free from this imperfection. This precept remains valid in the Orthodox churches, where widowed priests are not permitted to remarry.

---

[37]The Synod of Elvira (306), canon 33 (SCL 1, p. 55*). My translation. This canon caused various interpretations by modern scholars, for instance, M. Meigne, 'Concile ou collection d'Elvire' argued that it was later canon against Priscillians. A different view was presented by E. Griffe, 'Le Concile d'Elvire et les origines du célibat ecclésiastique', *BLE* 77 (1976): 123–7. More on the Synod in M. J. Lázaro Sánchez, 'L'état actuel de la recherche sur le concile d'Elvire', *RSR* 82, no. 4 (2008): 517–46.

[38]The Synod of Elvira (306), canon 65 (SCL 1, p. 59*).

[39]The Synod of Elvira (306), canon 18 (SCL 1, p. 52*).

[40]The Synod of Neo-Caesarea (314-319), canon 1 (SCL 1, p. 75*); Basil, *EpD.*, 12 (SCL 3, p. 40*). Cf. E. Wipszycka, 'Les ordres mineurs dans l'Église d'Égypte', in her *Études sur le christianisme dans l'Égypte de l'antiquité tardive*, SEA 52 (Roma: Augustinianum, 1996), pp. 243–5.

[41]See Basil, *EpD.*, 4.24 (SCL 3, p. 36* and p. 45*).

Let us also add that the practice of excessive fasting was also regarded as a grave sin. As the synod of Ancyra (present-day Ankara) pronounced in 314:

> A priest who is an abstainer from flesh, let him merely taste it and so let him abstain. But if he will not taste even the vegetables cooked with the meat let him be deposed (πεπαῦσθαι αὐτοὺς τῆς τάξεως).[42]

The cause of this particular synodal decision was the existence of many Christian groups in Asia, who would push some ascetic practices to the extreme, on the verge of showing scorn to all material elements. For this reason, it was strictly forbidden to abstain from consuming meat or wine beyond periods of fasting.

The synods convoked in the Graeco-Roman world until the late fourth century did not concentrate on such issues more thoroughly. Unlike in Syria, where the so-called *Apostolic Constitutions* were created at the end of the fourth century,[43] part of which are the Apostolic Canons (Book VIII, chapter 47). The *Constitutions* had not been approved by the whole of the church, but they became popular in the East and even now they remain in force in the Ethiopian Church. On the contrary, the *Apostolic Canons* would have a life of their own, exerting tremendous influence on the later legislation, as they soon became recognized as the genuine teaching of the apostles.

These canons provide for deposing clergymen for transgressions such as, to name just a few: beating sinners (27); adultery, perjury, theft (25); playing dice and inebriation (42-43); consuming meat with blood or carrion (63); abstaining from consuming meat or from drinking wine on Sunday (53); not fasting during Lent (69); fasting on Saturdays and Sundays (64); eating a meal at a tavern when not travelling (54); showing neglect towards clergymen of a lower rank or the people (58); refusing to accept a converted sinner (52); performing baptism in a faulty manner (49–50); recognizing baptism of heretics (46–47); repeatedly receiving or giving ordination (68); joining the army (83); repeatedly receiving baptism (47); celebrating together with Jews (70); entering a synagogue or a heretical church (65); injuring or killing a person (66); heresy (60); insulting a bishop (54); insulting the emperor or his official (84).

The authority of the above canons was so great that the same or even more meticulous precepts can also be found later on in the West in the *Penitential Books*. For instance, in the *Penitentiary* attributed to Jerome, but actually dating from the eighth or ninth century, it is determined how many years of fasting, and for which offences, a cleric must endure. Besides, they should be dismissed from office for transgressions such as drunkenness, adultery, self-castration, homosexuality and zoophilia. In other relevant sources, such lists are even longer.

It is also worth taking note of the provision of the *Apostolic Canon* that calls for deposing a clergyman who received the holy orders or administered the ordination to another (68). This is associated with the so-called (later) character of the

---

[42] The Synod of Ancyra (314), canon 14 (SCL 1, p. 66*). (trans. ANF)
[43] *Const. Ap*, SCL 2.

ordination. In antiquity, this particular term was not used, but, according to Basil's account,[44] the act of deposition was irrevocable, and the ordination could not be administered for a second time. The oft-cited phrase that the deposed clergyman should participate in the life of the church as a layman bears testimony to the fact that the earliest tradition had no knowledge of the teaching later established at the Council of Trident:

> If anyone says the holy Spirit is not given through holy ordination, and so bishops say *Receive the holy Spirit* in vain; or that no character is imprinted by it; or that someone who was once a priest can became a layman again: let him be anathema.[45]

CONCLUSION

In conclusion, it can be observed that the early church made it easier to stop being a priest than to become one. The heaviest punishment was laicization combined with excommunication, while the excommunication alone was less harsh to the incriminated as it was brought to termination upon completion of a penance. It was possible to appeal from the verdict of deposition to a higher instance: the metropolitan, a provincial synod, or to a metropolitan from one of the neighbouring dioceses, while in the West to the bishop of Rome. When the verdict was passed ultimately and definitively, it was irrevocable. On the next day, the deposed clergyman could take part in the life of the church as a lay person.

BIBLIOGRAPHY

Acta Synodalia, (ab anno 50 ad annum 381) 'Synodi et Collectiones Legum' (=SCL) 1, in A. Baron and H. Pietras (eds), *ŻMT 37*. Kraków: Wydawnictwo WAM, 2006.

Baron, A. and Pietras, H. (eds). *Dokumenty Synodów od 50 do 381 roku*, vol. 1. ŻMT. Kraków: WAM, 2006.

Bernard, L. W. *The Council of Sardica 343 A.D.* Sofia: Synodal Pub. House, 1983.

Boré, E. 'Histoire des Aghovans et leur conversion au Christianisme', *L'Université Catholique, Recueil religieux, philosophique, scientifique et littéraire* 22, no. II/7 (1846): 137–52.

Canones Patrum Graecorum, 'Synodi et Collectiones Legum' (=SCL) 3, in A. Baron and H. Pietras (eds), ŻMT 49. Kraków: Wydawnictwo WAM, 2009.

Campenhausen, H. Von. *Ecclesiastical Authority and Spiritual Power*. London: SCM Press, 1919.

---

[44]Basil, *EpD.*, 3 (SCL 3, p. 35*).

[45]The Council of Trident, Session 23: Canons on the sacrament of order, can. 4; trans. in Tanner (ed.), *Decrees*, p. 744*. Cf. C. Vogel, 'Laica communione contentus. Le retour du presbytre au rang des laïcs', *RSR* 47 (1973): 56–122 and 64–75.

Dunn, G. D. 'Cyprian of Carthage and the Episcopal Synod of Late 254', *REAug* 48 (2002): 229–47.

Eusebius Caesariensis, Vita Constantini, in F. Winkelmann, *Eusebius Werke* I/1 (*GCS* VII/1, 1975).

Friedberg, A. (ed.). *Decretum Gratianis – Corpus Iuris Canonici*. Editio Lipsiensis seconda, vol. 1 (1879) reprint. Graz: Akademische Druck – U. Verlagsanstalt, 1959.

Griffe, E. 'Le Concile d'Elvire et les origines du célibat ecclésiastique', *BLE* 77 (1976): 123–7.

Lázaro Sánchez, M. J. 'L'état actuel de la recherche sur le concile d'Elvire', *RSR* 82, no. 4 (2008): 517–46.

Meigne M. 'Concile ou collection d'Elvire', *RHE* 70 (1975): 361–87.

Pietras H. *Council of Nicaea (325). Religious and Political Context, Documents, Commentaries*, trans. M. Fijak. Rome: Gregorian & Biblical Press, 2016.

Tanner N. P. (ed.). *Decrees of the Ecumenical Councils*, vol. I. Washington, DC: Georgetown University Press, 1990.

Schillebeeckx, E. *The Church with a Human Face: A New and Expanded Theology of Ministry*. London: Xpress Reprints, 1988.

Schwartz, E. *Acta Concilium Oecumenicorum*. (=ACO). Berolini et Lipsiae, 1927–1932.

Starowieyski, M. 'Sobór Efeski i sprawa Nestoriusza – problem źródeł', *M* 50 (1995): 23–35.

Vilella Masana, J. 'Colecciones falsamente atribuidas a un concilio', *CnS* 39 (2018): 137–241.

Vogel, C. 'Laica communione contentus. Le retour du presbytre au rang des laïcs', *RSR* 47 (1973): 56–122.

Wipszycka, E. 'Fonctionnement de l'église égyptienne aux IVe-VIIIe siècles (sur quelques aspect)', in *Études sur le christianisme dans l'Égypte de l'antiquité tardive*, 195–224. SEA 52. Roma: Augustinianum, 1996.

Wipszycka, E. 'Les ordres mineurs dans l'Église d'Égypte', in *Études sur le christianisme dans l'Égypte de l'antiquité tardive*, 225–55. SEA 52. Roma: Augustinianum, 1996.

CHAPTER 18

Graeco-Roman and Christian art in late antiquity

JAŚ ELSNER

INTRODUCTION: SOME WORKING ASSUMPTIONS

Let us begin with some propositions, not universally shared in the history of the study of early Christian art, but which will form the basis of the argument put forward here.

1. Early Christian art is just one among the religious arts generated within the glory-period of religious creativity and multiplicity of the Roman Empire from the second to the fourth century AD. It is thus not a unique or special development, but intrinsically related to a broad competitive context of parallel religious affiliations, identities and self-assertions (from ancient civic cults like the worship of Artemis of Ephesus, ancient mystery religions like the initiations at Eleusis and ancient tribal or local cults like Judaism via modern revivals and adaptations of foreign cults like that of Isis or Dionysus or Cybele and Attis to what appear to be new religions like Mithraism and Christianity), many of them more or less semi-detached from official state or civic religion.[1]

---

[1]See on art, for example, J. Elsner, *The Art of the Roman Empire AD 100 – 450* (Oxford: Oxford University Press, 2018), pp. 185–219; R. M. Jensen, *Face to Face: Portraits of the Divine in Early Christianity* (Minneapolis, MN: Fortress Press, 2005), pp. 35–68; J. Huskinson, 'Art and Architecture, AD 193-337', in *CAH*, eds A. K. Bowman, P. Garnsey and A. Cameron, vol. 12, 2nd edn (Cambridge: Cambridge University Press, 2005), pp. 672–703 – an integrated survey of art from AD 193–337; R. M. Jensen and M. D. Ellison (eds), *The Routledge Handbook of Early Christian Art* (Abingdon: Routledge, 2018) – an up-to-date general handbook; on religion J. North, 'The Development of Religious Pluralism', in J. Lieu, J. North and T. Rajak (eds), *The Jews among Pagans and Christians in the Roman Empire* (London: Routledge, 1992), pp. 174–93 and M. Beard, J. North and S. Price, *Religions of Rome*, vol. 1 (Cambridge: Cambridge University Press, 1998), pp. 245–312.

2. Christianity is not unique in any special way among these religions (any more than each of the others is exceptional),[2] but it has certain special features which are fundamental to the development of its art. These include the fact that (along with Judaism) Christianity possessed a set of written scriptures, of which certain elements rapidly became canonical, while others were established as less significant but nonetheless broadly acceptable (a wide range of items from the Old and New Testament apocrypha to such texts as the *Protoevangelium* of James and the various saints' lives and martyr-acts whose literary level and market seem connected to the ancient novel)[3] and still others became 'heretical'. Clearly the existence of scripture meant that visual imagery could be related to a canonical set of texts (though whether the manner of that relation was didactic, illustrative, commentarial or exegetic was a complex and in some corners a charged point). We need to beware exaggeration. It is not certain that some of the other cults did not have parallel 'scriptural' traditions preserved orally and through memorization (this would certainly explain the stereotypical – or at least repeated – nature of some complex Mithraic imagery): there is no evidence for this, but there would not be in a lost religion (like Mithraism) whose sacred lore was oral – Buddhism, which preserved a very large number of very early scriptures in an oral memorized form only wrote those down after several centuries, and had the religion been entirely lost after say two centuries (like Mithraism or the cult of Jupiter Dolichenus) we would be wrong in our (methodologically correct but reductivist) assumption that it had no scriptures because none were preserved.

3. 'Christianity' in the early period is a dangerous generalization, since there were numerous local and regional varieties, multiple theologies, a complex culture of dispute and disagreement (partly the product of that very literacy which made Christianity special).[4] The very genesis of Christian art has in one argument been attributed to this competitive pluralism of views and establishments within the broad spectrum of 'Christians',[5] among whom one might include such outright 'heretics' as the Manichees from the third century onwards as well as numerous sectarian varieties through the fourth and fifth centuries (such as Arians, Nestorians, Monophysites and so forth). It has, however, proved next to impossible to attribute

---

[2]See esp. J. Z. Smith, *Drudgery Divine: On the Comparison of Early Christianities and the Religions of Late Antiquity* (Chicago: University of Chicago Press, 1990), pp. 36–46 for this argument.

[3]See D. R. Cartlidge and J. K. Elliott, *Art and the Christian Apocrypha* (London: Routledge, 2001) for a useful and lively introduction to uses of the Christian Apocrypha in art.

[4]For a lively account, see K. Hopkins, *World Full of Gods: Pagans, Jews and Christians in the Roman World* (London: Weidenfeld and Nicolson, 1999).

[5]See J. Elsner, 'Inventing Christian Rome: The Role of Early Christian Art', in *Rome the Cosmopolis*, eds C. Edwards and G. Woolf (Cambridge: Cambridge University Press, 2003a), pp. 73–5.

particular iconographies to particular sectarian tendencies with any degree of assurance.[6] Moreover, within even mainstream 'Christianity', we must expect significant experimentation and variety as iconographies and forms for different themes were developed, discarded, transformed and re-invented over several centuries.

4. Few disciplines have been more marked by repeated, competitive ideological investments from generations of Roman Catholic and Protestant scholars than the study of the early Church.[7] In the case of ancient Christian art, the excessive Protestantism which determined the pure faith of both late ancient Judaism and early Christianity to have been aniconic, probably anti-iconic, even iconoclastic before the third century AD has been rightly corrected.[8] But the current consensus on the enthusiasm of early Christians for art is probably also excessive. Despite the uses made of images by some third-century Christians – especially in Rome, to judge by our surviving archaeological evidence – Christianity never raised images to the level of scripture itself. This is in specific contrast to the stance taken by Mani (216–76) whose *Picture-Book* appears to have had canonical status in a universalizing salvific and scriptural religion that deliberately borrowed from, and adapted many features of, Christianity and was designed to be in direct opposition to it.[9] Moreover, the strand of opposition to images within Christianity – an opposition on the one hand to pagan practice as well as some of ancient polytheism's more complex intellectual discussions of art (such as Dio Chrysostom's *Olympian Oration*, for example) and on the other to Manichaean visual scripture – remains a feature of some theological attitudes to art up to

[6]See D. Gwynn, 'Archaeology and the "Arian Controversy" in the Fourth Century', in *Religious Diversity in Late Antiquity*, eds D. Gwynn and S. Bangert. LAA, vol. 6 (Leiden: E.J. Brill, 2010), pp. 229–63 and B. Ward-Perkins, 'Where Is the Archaeology and Iconography of Germanic Arianism', in Gwynn and Bangert (eds), *Religious Diversity in Late Antiquity*, pp. 265–89.
[7]The classic account is Smith, *Drudgery Divine*. For the historiography of art, see J. Elsner, 'The Viennese Invention of Late Antiquity: Between Politics and Religion in the Forms of Late Roman Art', in *Empires of Faith: Antiquity: Histories of Art and Religion from India to Ireland*, ed. J. Elsner (Cambridge: Cambridge University Press, 2020), pp. 110–27.
[8]See esp. S. C. Murray, 'Art and the Early Church', *JTS* 28 (1977): 305–45 and *Rebirth and Afterlife: A Study in the Transmutation of Some Pagan Imagery in Early Christian Funerary Art* (Oxford: BAR Publishing, 1981); P. C. Finney, *The Invisible God: The Earliest Christians on Art* (Oxford: Oxford University Press, 1994), pp. 15–68.
[9]On Mani's *Picture-Book*, see, for example, H.-J. Klimkeit, 'On the Nature of Manichaean Art', in *Studies in Manichaean Literature and Art*, eds M. Heuser and H-J. Klimkeit. NHMS, vol. 46 (Leiden: E.J. Brill, 1998), pp. 270–5 and S. Gulácsi, *Mani's Pictures: The Didactic Images of the Manichaeans from Sasanian Mesopotamia to Uygur Central Asia and Tang-Ming China*. NHMS, vol. 90 (Leiden: E.J. Brill, 2015) at length. The key texts include *Kephalaion 92* (234.24-236.6) in I. Gardner, *The Kephalaia of the Teacher*. NHMS, vol. 37 (Leiden: E.J. Brill, 1995), pp. 241–2 and Gulácsi, *Mani's Pictures*, pp. 29–32, and *Kephalaion 151* (371.25-30) in I. Gardner and S. Lieu, *Manichaean Texts from the Roman Empire* (Cambridge: Cambridge University Press, 2004), p. 266 and Gulácsi, *Mani's Pictures*, pp. 26–9.

and including the period of Byzantine Iconoclasm in the eighth and ninth centuries.[10] We may say that within the range of early Christianities, the use of art (largely to support burial, liturgy and scripture – never to replace any of them) represents one option, an option which remained predominant (though occasionally challenged) within the forms of Christianity that won out after the Edict of Toleration.

5. Christianity as a religion, like its cousin Manichaeism, spread rapidly east into Persia and thence as far as India and China,[11] as well as west into the Roman world. Even in the context of an essay discussing the visual aspects of the traditional topic of the religion's take-over of Rome, we should not forget Christianity's life as a non-hegemonic faith of choice and conversion in numerous contexts which necessitated material-cultural creativity (for instance in adapting the image of the Cross to local forms of visual culture) or the spectacular learning that enabled the translation of the gospels into pretty well every language in Eurasia and their writing on codices easily transported by road or sea.

RELIGIOUS ART IN THE GRAECO-ROMAN ENVIRONMENT

Christian art, or rather imagery with recognizably Christian themes, emerged around AD 200 within a complex of religions and religious arts in Graeco-Roman antiquity. Exactly how much weight to put on the term 'religion' in this context is a charged and disputed question, as is the issue of whether an iconography evoking a particular religious affiliation designates a strong adherence to that religion on the part of maker, owner or viewers.

Take the example of Isis. There are numerous images with reference to ancient Egyptian subjects, styles, deities and potentially to the Isiac mysteries in the wall paintings and mosaics of Rome and Pompeii in the first centuries BC and AD.[12] Were these religious, or did they only allude to religion? Were they a kind of exotic 'chinoiserie' evoking distant lands recently conquered? Were they the equivalent of a postmodern stylistic addition to the already hectic and creative eclecticism

---

[10]See within a huge literature, for example, J. Elsner, 'Iconoclasm as Discourse: From Antiquity to Byzantium', *AB* 94 (2012): 368–94.

[11]See, for example, N. Andrade, *The Journey of Christianity to India in Late Antiquity* (Cambridge: Cambridge University Press, 2018) on Persia and India; N. Standaert (ed.), *Handbook of Christianity in China. Volume One: 635-1800* (Leiden: E.J. Brill, 2001), pp. 1–42 and M. Deeg, 'The "Brilliant Teaching": The Rise and Fall of "Nestorianism" (Jingjiao) in Tang China', *JR* 31 (2006): 91–110. On art: Elsner, *The Art*, pp. 221–42.

[12]See, for example, M. de Vos, *L'egittomania in pitture e mosaici Romano-Campani della prima età imperiale*. Études préliminaires aux Religions Orientales dans l'Empire Romain, vol. 84 (Leiden: E. J. Brill, 1980) and on the Villa Farnesina in Rome, S. Wyler, 'Roman Replications of Greek art at the Villa della Farnesina', *AH* 29 (2006): 215–354.

that characterizes Roman art in this period?[13] Different scholars have answered 'yes' to each of these propositions and in the absence of documentary clarification of the visual evidence we can only decide on the basis of our own prejudices.[14] Clearly, Isiac images in domestic settings – like the Villa Farnesina in Rome or the Casa dei Cubicoli floreali in Pompeii (I.9.5) (Figure 18.1) – went side by side with mythological imagery including themes that potentially evoked other initiatory deities like Dionysus and with painted cult images (such as the Penates). Again, we cannot tell the extent of 'belief', veneration or awe accorded to such images.[15] But what of Isiac and other Egyptian imagery (whether originals imported from Egypt or modern versions made in Pharaonic styles in Italy) from the temples of Isis – say at Pompeii or in the Campus Martius in Rome (Figure 18.2)? Were these images imbued with the sacred power of cult, initiation and salvific conviction, or were they also a form of religious chic writ large?[16] It does not help in attempting to find an answer that our most interesting and subtle Roman text on the cult of Isis – the *Golden Ass* of Apuleius, perhaps written between AD 170 and 180 – is a brilliant piece of fiction, with a spectacularly ironic play on matters of conversion and salvation, and has proved almost impossible to read in recent years without a sense of the author's aporetic agnosticism or at least unwillingness to come clean as to whether his novel is a spoof.[17] It has to be said that before these questions –

[13]On the stylistic languages of Roman eclecticism (focusing on Greek models), see T. Hölscher, *The Language of Images in Roman Art* (Cambridge: Cambridge University Press, 2004), further, for example, E. Perry, *The Aesthetics of Emulation in the Visual Arts of Ancient Rome* (Cambridge: Cambridge University Press, 2005) and E. Varner, 'Reading Replications: Roman Rhetoric and Greek Quotations', *AH* 29 (2006): 282–305.

[14]For a repertoire of responses with earlier bibliography, see M. J. Versluys, *Aegyptiaca Romana: Nilotic Scenes and the Roman Views of Egypt*. RGRW, vol. 144 (Leiden: E.J. Brill, 2002), pp. 308–12, 322–4, 329–35, 374–6.

[15]Belief is a notoriously difficult concept to deal with in antiquity, not least because the advent of Christianity changed the basic meanings and even grammatical structures of the words 'credo' and 'pisteuô' (meaning 'I believe' in Latin and Greek and each the first word of the Creed in the two respective languages): see T. Morgan, *Roman Faith and Christian Faith: Pistis and Fides in the Early Roman Empire and Early Churches* (Oxford: Oxford University Press, 2015) at length; also still P. Veyne, *Did the Greeks Believe in Their Myths?* (Chicago: University of Chicago Press, 1988).

[16]On the Isaeum in Rome, see K. Lembke, *Das Isaeum Campense in Rom. Studie über den Isiskult unter Domitian* (Heidelberg: Verlag Archäologie und Geschichte, 1994) stressing religion pp. 84–132 against, for example, M. J. Versluys, 'The Sanctuary of Isis on the Campus Martius in Rome', *B* 72 (1997): 163 and 165 stressing exoticism; now M. J. Versluys, K. B. Clausen and G. C. Vittozzi (eds), *The Isaeum Campense: From the Roman Empire to the Modern Age* (Roma: Scienze e Lettere, 2018). On the Isaeum in Pompeii, see U. Egelhaaf-Gaiser, *Kulträume im römischen Alltag* (Stuttgart: Steiner, 2000), pp. 185–99 with bibliography.

[17]For a classic statement (over sixty years old now) of belief in Apuleius' good faith and the sincerity of the hero Lucius' conversion, see A.-J. Festugière, *Personal Religion among the Greeks* (Berkeley: California University Press, 1954), pp. 68–84. For a strong statement of the parodic and satiric intent of the *Golden Ass* (its laughter at sincerity), see S. J. Harrison, *Apuleius: A Latin Sophist* (Oxford: Oxford University Press, 2000), pp. 235–52, esp. p. 244, pp. 248–9. For the classic statement of deliberate ambivalence on Apuleius' part, see J. Winkler, *Auctor and Actor* (Berkeley: University of California Press, 1985), pp. 123–32, esp. p. 124 and pp. 226–7. For a long and balanced review, see Egelhaaf-Gaiser, *Kulträume im*

FIGURE 18.1 Casa dei Cubicoli floreali, Pompeii (1.9.5). Cubiculum 8, west wall.
Note the Egyptianizing ('Isiac') panels in the upper half and the Egyptian figure in the
shrubbery to the lower left which are mixed in with theatrical and natural motifs as well
as a Dionysiac panel inset in the centre. About AD 40–50. Photograph: DAI Inst Neg:
64.2262.

FIGURE 18.2 Two sides of a marble altar dedicated to Isis from the Isaeum Campense in Rome. Anubis carrying cult attributes. First half of the second century AD. Capitoline Museum, Rome. Photograph: DAI Inst. Neg. 2001.2209.

effectively issues of belief, seriousness of religious conviction, the nature of cult identity – scholarship finds itself responding with the limitations of the dominant views of its time. A hundred years ago there would have been far fewer voices of doubt than there have been in the last thirty years about the seriousness of the religion in ancient art and texts, and in another century that may be true again. Indeed modern scholarship on ancient religion has rightly been characterized as excessively secularist.[18]

The very confrontation with questions of religion in antiquity raises the problematic of our ancestral relations to the rise of Christianity in the Graeco-Roman environment and of our own affiliations and ambivalences, as individuals and as a collective culture, with that past – including its rejection.[19] This is an arena in which scholarship, guided one hopes by certain agreed principles and rules, cannot hope to be objective (and is usually least so when it claims to be!). The very fact that the bulk of our evidence for ancient religion rests not on documents, which can at least be philologically interpreted even if they are not always fully understandable, but on images – many of them more or less symbolic and referring to myths or rituals of which we have no knowledge beyond the findings of archaeology – serves to heighten the stakes of subjective interpretation, since all arguments are founded on the importation of any given scholar's axiomatic presuppositions about an arena so charged as religious conviction. For example, Richard Gordon, perhaps the premier student of Mithraism in the last thirty years and certainly the most impressive interpreter of its art, writes as follows:

> The history of religion is the history of taller and taller stories being claimed more and more true, until no one bothered to understand or interpret: the symbols and discourse lose their evocative power; the institution which tells the stories becomes just one of several, with no outstanding claim upon attention, upon the desire to interpret afresh. Its claims are just ideology, merely mad, an affront to good sense, or irrelevant to 'real' problems.[20]

Now, whatever one thinks of this position, it stands very much outside any religious system it may attempt to assess. It is hard to imagine any Mithraist in antiquity or a believing Christian at any time finding much to agree with here. It is not clear

römischen Alltag, pp. 29–106, 116–63; also J. Elsner, *Roman Eyes: Visuality and Subjectivity in Art and Text* (Princeton, NJ: Princeton University Press, 2007), pp. 289–302.

[18]P. Horden and N. Purcell, *The Corrupting Sea: A Study of Mediterranean History* (Oxford: Blackwell Publishers, 2000), p. 447; J. Elsner and I. Rutherford, 'Introduction', in *Pilgrimage in Greco-Roman and Early Christian Antiquity: Seeing the Gods*, eds J. Elsner and I. Rutherford (Oxford: Oxford University Press, 2005), p. 8.

[19]For some reflections on ancestralism, see Smith, *Drudgery Divine*, pp. 1–35; J. Elsner 'Archaeologies and Agendas: Jewish and Early Christian Art in Late Antiquity', *JRS* 83 (2003b): 119–24, 128.

[20]R. L. Gordon, 'Reality, Evocation and Boundary in the Mysteries of Mithras', *JMS* 3 (1980): 21 = idem, *Image and Value in the Graeco-Roman World: Studies in Mithraism and Religious Art* (Aldershot: Ashgate Publishing Limited, 1996), p. 21.

to me that this kind of 'outsider's' view offers a *better* picture of the meanings of cult-adherence and the arts of a given religion than the kinds of 'insider' views held by adherents, and it is obvious that starting from a strongly secularist position of this kind leads to a very different kind of picture of the workings of religious art from one that begins from a religious internalist's standpoint. One might argue that religious images are so difficult to pin down as positive evidence (for anything) *because* they were designed to have multiple meanings – especially to signify quite different things to religious insiders and outsiders, or in the context of mystery cults to initiates and the excluded.[21] A lamb is just a sheep to a pagan, but it may be the Sacrificed Lord to a Christian believer.[22]

As implied by my switch from Isis to Mithras, the problematic I have illustrated here by reference to Isis can be extended equally to the arts produced by all the other cults. My own view is that in each case we should expect within any cult a range of responses from very strong and committed faith, instantiated in the case of Christians by the martyrs or by bishops, for instance, to far weaker forms of affiliation and affirmation in addition to all the potential meanings such cult-specific images may have generated in outsiders. In some cases, especially among Jews and Christians, religious affiliation sometimes meant an oppositional stance to alternatives (including in the visual sphere – hence the long-term move away from statues in the round in Christian art) while in others (including most of the polytheistic cults) religious affiliation was not necessarily exclusive. All this implies that in the study of art generally – but especially in the history of religious art where the key issues lie in the *affect* of image upon worshipper – we need to move away from a patronage-based model of art history based on artists and owners or commissioners to a more audience-related model based on viewers, collectors and recipients. This effectively spans a much longer time-period than the initial moment of creation or commission – a moment traditionally privileged by art history – to include not only varieties of spectators at any one time but also the changing history and circumstances of reception over time.

Nor, in the ancient Christian period, can we ever be sure at what level to interpret any given image. Take a picture of Jonah beneath the gourd-vine, the episode which follows his encounter with the whale, from an unprovenanced gold glass in Rome, probably made in the fourth century AD (Figure 18.3).[23] To one viewer, it might have Jewish connotations – referring to the story of a prophet in something like the way the cycle of paintings in the Dura Europos synagogue from Syria (of about AD

---

[21] See Elsner, *Roman Eyes*, pp. 253–8 for the general proposition.

[22] See J. Elsner, *Art and the Roman Viewer: The Transformation of Art from the Pagan World to Christianity* (Cambridge: Cambridge University Press, 1995), pp. 1–3, 191, 222.

[23] C. R. Morey, *The Gold-Glass Collection of the Vatican Library* (Vatican City: Biblioteca Apostolica Vaticana, 1959), no. 46, p. 22. On the category of late antique gold glasses, see D. Howells, *A Catalogue of the Late Antique Gold Glass in the British Museum* (London: British Museum Press, 2015) and S. Walker, 'Gold Glass in Late Antiquity', in Jensen and Ellison (eds), *The Routledge Handbook of Early Christian Art*, pp. 124–40.

FIGURE 18.3 Gold glass medallion depicting Jonah resting beneath the gourd-vine. Fourth century AD, from Rome or Cologne. British Museum. Photograph: by courtesy of the Museum.

240) narrates the biblical histories of heroes such as David, Moses and Ezekiel.[24] To another, it might be no more than an alternative mythology to put beside the rich mix of mythological variation typical of ancient polytheism – the repose after a trial not ultimately very different in kind from the labours of Heracles or Odysseus or Theseus. To another, it might have Christian connotations – either historically as an allusion to the Old Testament narratives that underlie Christian Scripture, or exegetically following the typological method evidenced in both literary texts (sermons and commentaries as well as oral tradition, one assumes) and in numerous

[24]The literature on the Dura synagogue is vast. Fundamental is C. Kraeling, *The Excavation sat Dura-Europos: Final Report VIII.2. The Christian Building* (New Haven, CT: Dura Europos Publications, 1967). Accessible modern account with bibliography: S. Fine, *Art and Judaism in the Greco-Roman World* (Cambridge: Cambridge University Press, 2005), pp. 172–83; L. I. Levine, *Visual Judaism in Late Antiquity* (New Haven, CT: Yale University Press, 2012), pp. 69–118.

visual juxtapositions where Jonah being swallowed and vomited by the whale and resting beneath the gourd-vine thereafter becomes a type of Christ's own death, resurrection and entry into paradise. The context of use, to which we have no archaeological access in this case, makes a substantial difference to the resonances carried by such an image. Was it just another ornament, or a specially selected *ex voto* to put by the grave of a loved one, or an iconic image to be dedicated at an altar, even perhaps designed to receive prayer? None of the meanings given here are certainly right or can be wholly ruled out – for we depend on a series of unknowns, from the maker and different owners such an object may have had to the variety of contexts (domestic, liturgical, funerary) in which it might have found itself over say half a century. Indeed an object like this may have passed through the entirety of this range of readings as it fell into the hands of a series of different owners holding different religious convictions between say AD 300 and 350.

What we can say is that in the early period – say, from the first inception of Christian art in the archaeological record (about AD 200)[25] to the triumph of Constantine and the official sanction of Christianity as an imperially favoured religion (312) – Christian art, alongside that of the other cults, served to define religious identity for its users and commissioners. Images from all these cults, whether worn as amulets, displayed in a domestic setting or placed in a more 'charged' religions context such as a shrine or burial site, were deliberately amenable to a set of cult-specific viewings but also to a different series of ('lay'?) viewings to outsiders. The levels of cult-investment made in any given image – from being seen as no more than wall-paper, to being an object of religious reflection, to receiving fully fledged worship, even sacrifice – were varied and multiple, with perhaps even the same image receiving different responses from different viewers. By extension, religious, including Christian, art came to adorn spaces special to religion. Images defined an environment – most particularly liturgical and funerary space – as specific to a particular religious affiliation, that is to a group of people sharing a common identity, and excluding others who would not have understood the esoteric meanings or references of those images in the same way as initiates.

This function of establishing sacred space is as true of the spectacular accumulative symbolism of a mithraeum and the relatively stereotypical form of its sacred icon, the tauroctony (Figure 18.4), as it is of synagogues from Dura Europos to Ostia and of Christian cult buildings – at least, of the one that certainly survives from the pre-Constantinian period, the house church at Dura Europos (Figure 18.5).[26] The Christian paintings at Dura – from only one room of a house converted to a church in the 230s or 240s – survive only in a fragmentary state. They were crude – far less sophisticated in execution and design than other murals from the same period in

---

[25]See the discussion of Finney, *The Invisible God*, pp. 99–274.

[26]For a convenient guide to religious architectural space in this period (focussing on Judaism, Mithraism and Christianity), see L. M. White, *Building God's House in the Roman World* (Baltimore, MD: Johns Hopkins University Press, 1990), idem, *The Social Origins of Christian Architecture*, vol. 2 (Valley Forge, PA: Trinity Press, 1997).

FIGURE 18.4 White marble relief of Mithras killing the bull with a dog and snake licking the blood, a scorpion at the bull's testicles, the sun, moon and a raven at the top, and other accompanying figures and scenes from Mithraic mythology to the sides. From Nersae in central Italy. About AD 170. National Museum, Rome. Photograph: Faraglia, DAI Inst Neg: 36.949.

the Dura synagogue or some of the pagan temples. The subject matter of a number of scenes is controversial, but the west wall above what appears to have been the baptismal font likely depicted the Good Shepherd and his sheep juxtaposed against an image of Adam and Eve. Other imagery includes some miracles of Jesus, such as the healing of the paralytic and Christ walking on water, and Old Testament scenes such as David and Goliath (probably impossible to identify had it not been for the names of the protagonists being inscribed in the plaster).[27] The feature of religious imagery that demarcates liturgically charged space relates to art on a series of levels: from 'decorative' materials, for instance mosaics or wall paintings like those at Dura, to the range of votive offerings (paintings, sculptures) sited around a given sanctuary and to more specifically cult images to which worship was offered like the tauroctony. The frequent use of inscriptions to name a dedicator both recorded such

---

[27]See Kraeling, *The Excavation*, pp. 45–88 for the standard account (but note that many identifications made there are contestable) and M. Peppard, *The World's Oldest Church: Bible, Art and Ritual at Dura-Europos, Syria* (New Haven, CT: Yale University Press, 2016).

FIGURE 18.5 Dura Europos in Syria. Christian building, about AD 240, as reconstructed at Yale University Art Gallery in the second half of the twentieth century. Photograph: Yale University Art Gallery, Dura Europos Collection.

patrons of the shrine in perpetuity and added the direct affirmation of an individual – a real person who lived in real time, like you or me or any worshipper – into a highly symbolic scheme often with extravagant and general salvific or cosmological connotations.

Just as images demarcated liturgical space so they helped to define funerary space – claiming it for the adherents of specific cults. Here, in the summoning of a definitive religious ideology into the private sphere of death, Christianity acts a little differently from other ancient religions, both the mystery cults and the civic or local or state cults. The majority of pagan religions in the Roman Empire give evidence of funerary altars for their adherents, as well as stelae and other memorials – some carved in elaborate detail (e.g., Figure 18.2, which is an Isiac funerary altar, or Figure 18.6, a second-century tomb portrait of a priest of Magna Mater).[28] Christianity, on the other hand, rejected pagan sacrificial rituals in any form and in general subsumed personal memorials such as portraits in favour of identification with its chosen, scriptural, myth-histories as represented by visual narratives and

---

[28]See Beard, North and Price, *Religions of Rome*, vol. 2, p. 211 and M. Vermaseren, *Corpus Cultus Cybelae Attidisque III*. Études préliminaires aux religions orientales dans l'Empire romain, vol. 50 (Leiden: E.J. Brill, 1977), no. 466, pp. 152–3.

FIGURE 18.6 Marble tomb portrait of a gallus, a priest of Cybele, in female dress and with various cult accoutrements. From near Rome. Mid-second century AD. Capitoline Museum, Rome. Photograph: Faraglia, DAI Inst Neg: 5877.

juxtapositions. Instead of the altar or funerary relief (which in pagan contexts *may* have cited religious affiliations, but may equally have featured portraits, imagery drawn deceased's real or ideal biography, references either to this past life or to an Elysian future, or figuration involving mythological allusions), Christianity

FIGURE 18.7 Marble sarcophagus from Rome, showing Dionysus between nude male personifications of the seasons and figures of Tellus and Oceanus. Much restored. About AD 260. Vatican Museum. Photograph: DAI Inst Neg: 37.772 A.

– at any rate, in Rome – favoured sarcophagi. These individual coffins were a traditional form of burial largely for the inhumation of whole bodies rather than cremated ashes, going back to archaic, Hellenistic and Etruscan times. But the use of sarcophagi had become popular from about AD 100.[29] The majority were decorated with abstract patterns such as stripes (or 'strigillation') but many were historiated. What can be said of the variety of subjects portrayed (many mythological, many 'biographic' illustrating idealising scenes from public and private life, many with portraits, many with stock scenes such as lions, garlands or hunting)[30] is that any reference to the mystery or religious cults is extremely rare. The only exceptions to this are Christianity, the odd Jewish example and the wonderful wealth of Dionysiac sarcophagi (e.g., Figure 18.7) which may have had religious connotations but may equally have evoked a sense of liberating festivity in an ideal mythological world of love, wine, dance and music after death.[31]

Effectively, Christianity appropriated for its own cult-specific imagery a form of monument not otherwise used by the mystery cults. Even if we assume religious meanings for the Dionysiac sarcophagi, these were to be read into a standard mythological repertoire to be viewed alongside the myths of Endymion, Meleager, Phaedra and so on. Part of the effect was to elevate (or, depending on one's viewpoint, to reduce) Christian mythology – that is, scriptural narrative from the

---

[29]For a general picture, see Elsner, *The Art of the Roman Empire*, pp. 135–43.

[30]Good modern introductions: J. Elsner and J. Huskinson (eds), *Life, Death and Representation: Some New Work on Roman Sarcophagi* (Berlin: W. de Gruyter, 2011); P. Zanker and B. Ewald, *Living with Myths: The Imagery of Roman Sarcophagi* (Oxford: Oxford University Press, 2012); M. Koortbojian, 'Roman Sarcophagi', in *A Companion to Roman Art*, ed. B. Borg (Chichester: Wiley-Blackwell 2015), pp. 286–300.

[31]For some reflections on these issues, see J. Elsner, 'Some Observations on Dionysiac Sarcophagi', in *Visual Histories of the Classical World: Essays in Honour of R.R.R. Smith*, eds C. Draycott, R. Raja, K. Welch and W. T. Wootton (Turnhout: Brepols Publisher, 2019), pp. 425–46.

FIGURE 18.8 Marble sarcophagus from Sta Maria Antiqua, Rome, showing Jonah and the whale, a female Orant, a reading philosopher figure, the good shepherd, the baptism of Christ. About AD 300. Photograph: Boehringer, DAI Inst Neg: 52.421.

Old and New Testaments – to the same level as the normative range of polytheistic mythologies. This had the effect of mounting a substantive cultural argument through art about the place of Christianity, of specifically Christian narratives, within the then dominant pagan culture. This intervention within a living visual tradition of workshops carving coffins – some commissioned by specific patrons but many bought ready-made from stock – was of huge importance for the development of Christian iconography as such. For it was under the sculptors' chisels, adapting such themes as the sleeping Endymion or Ariadne to the reclining Jonah, that a repertoire of what were to become standard Christian themes and visual types was established.

For instance, in the pre-Constantinian sarcophagus from Sta Maria Antiqua in the Roman Forum, the iconography shows from left to right Jonah's ship, the sea monster, Jonah resting beneath the gourd-vine above which are three sheep, a female Orant, a philosopher with a scroll, the good shepherd and the baptism of Jesus (Figure 18.8).[32] Many of these image-types appear in pagan contexts such as the philosopher, or the shepherd carrying his sheep.[33] Others, like Jonah, are directly adapted from pagan mythological iconography, such as the common type of sleeping Endymion.[34] Still others, notably the baptism, are constructed out of a

---

[32]See G. Bovini and H. Brandenburg, *Repertorium der Christlich-Antiken Sarkophage I Rom und Ostia* (Wiesbaden: Franz Steiner Verlag, 1967), no. 747, pp. 306–7. The date given there, third quarter of the third century (i.e., 250–75), is now thought too early. N. Himmelmann, *Über Hirten-Genre in der antiken Kunst*. ARAW, vol. 65 (Opladen: Westdeutscher Verlag, 1980), pp. 133–6, 157 argues for about 300; G. Koch, *Frühchristliche Sarkophage* (München: C.H. Beck 2000), pp. 4, 237 for about 270–80.

[33]On the philosopher, see B. Ewald, *Der Philosoph als Leitbild* (Mainz: Ph. Von Zabern, 1999); on the shepherd, see Himmelmann, *Über Hirten-Genre* and J. Awes Freeman, 'The Good Shepherd and the Enthroned Ruler', in *The Art of Empire: Christian Art in Its Imperial Context*, eds L. Jefferson and R. Jensen (Minneapolis, MN: Augsburg Fortress, 2015), pp. 159–96.

[34]See Elsner, *The Art of the Roman Empire*, pp. 141–5.

repertoire of pre-existing figures to create a new scriptural image.[35] There is no doubt of the Christian thematics, however, created by the juxtaposition of these themes. If one wishes, one can tell a typological story whereby the Old Testament narrative of Jonah on the left prefigures and is fulfilled in the Incarnation, as represented by Christ the Shepherd and His baptism. Interestingly the heads of the central figures of the Orant and the philosopher are unfinished and appear to have been left for the carving of funerary portraits of the deceased – a typical feature of sarcophagus manufacture.[36] Although those portraits were never carved, the intent to affirm a certain personal and individual identity within the scriptural frame may even imply the theological entailment that the two scriptural halves of the sarcophagus are to be fulfilled or unified in the present tense, as it were, of a good Christian life.

Whereas most pagan mythological sarcophagi render a specific narrative or scene, Christian art in this context works by typological juxtaposition, effectively imposing a new (or at least hitherto very rare) interpretative model on the viewing of images. We find typology – whether borrowed by artistic practice from sermons and theological commentaries or a simultaneous development in both art and text – not only on sarcophagi but also in painting. It may be said to go back at least to the juxtaposition of the Good Shepherd with Adam and Eve (that is, an image figuring Redemption with one figuring in the lunette of the niche the Fall) on the west wall of the house church at Dura in the 240s (Figure 18.5).[37] In developed form – taking almost at random a well-preserved and beautifully decorated cubiculum from the large and well published catacomb of Marcellinus and Peter in Rome – typological juxtaposition can use images in a highly sophisticated way to show the process of Christian salvific development, its theological implications spelled out entirely in pictures.[38] In room 51 of the catacomb, whose decoration is dated to about AD 320,[39] there is an arcosolium with Susanna caught between the elders in the lunette (Figure 18.9). This is an Old Testament image that might stand for the soul of the good Christian in distress. Above this image on the arcosolium's vault are three scenes: to the left, Moses or Peter striking the rock to produce water, to the right, Adam and Eve with the serpent and apple, and in the centre Noah in the Ark with the dove bringing a flowering spray. Here symbols not only of the

---

[35]See R. M. Jensen, *Baptismal Imagery in Early Christianity* (Grand Rapids, MI: Baker Academic, 2012) in general and pp. 14–16 on the earliest images.

[36]On blank heads, see J. Huskinson, '"Unfinished Portrait Heads" on Later Roman Sarcophagi', *Papers of the British School at Rome* 64 (1998): 129–58; S. Birk, *Depicting the Dead: Self-Representation and Commemoration on Roman sarcophagi with Portraits*. Aarhus Studies in Mediterranean Antiquity 11 (Aarhus: Aarhus University Press, 2013), pp. 55–8; V. Platt, 'Framing the Dead on Roman Sarcophagi', in *The Frame in Classical Art: A Cultural History*, eds V. Platt and M. Squire (Cambridge: Cambridge University Press, 2017), pp. 356–7.

[37]See Kraeling, *The Excavation*, pp. 50–7.

[38]On typology, see A. Grabar, *Christian Iconography: A Study of Its Origins* (Princeton, NJ: Princeton University Press, 1968), pp. 109–46; Elsner, *Art and the Roman Viewer*, pp. 271–87.

[39]On cubiculum 51 and its pictures, see J. G. Deckers, H. R. Seeliger and G. Mietke, *Die Katakombe 'Santi Marcellino e Pietro': Repertorium der Malereien*. Roma sotterranea cristiana, 6,2 (Vatican City: Pontificio Istituto di Archeologia Cristiana, 1987), pp. 281–4.

FIGURE 18.9 Catacomb of Marcellinus and Peter, Rome. Cubiculum 51, back wall of the arcosolium showing a fresco of Susanna and the Elders. About AD 320. Photograph: PCAS Foto Lau G 22.

Fall but also of the hope for Redemption, most from the Old Testament, extend the imagery's ramifications beyond the personal crisis of Susanna to a broader theological sphere of sin and the potential for its atonement. In the vault over the whole room (Figure 18.10), the Good Shepherd stands in the centre surrounded by four images from the narrative of Jonah (being flung to the whale, being spewed out by the whale, and beneath the gourd-vine, twice), as well as four Orants – two male and two female. Here the Old Testament narratives of Jonah as a symbol for distress and freedom may both be said to figure the hope for individual souls buried in the cubiculum (themselves perhaps reflected in the image of Susanna in the Orant pose or the Orants in the main vault, both male and female) and at the same time to represent the death and resurrection of the Redeemer, as also symbolized by the Good Shepherd. In the shaft above the vault, which serves as both a light well and an air vent, are an image of Christ raising Lazarus from the dead – the first and only scene unambiguously from the New Testament, which explicitly signals the salvation of the dead. Above this is Daniel in the Lions' den, which may be said to figure Christ's own triumph over adversity and death.

Such imagery, only a few years after the Peace of the church, shows an explicit and theological form of thought governing the production of decoration. The relative heights of the groupings of images are carefully used to produce an exegetic hierarchy with images of redemption mainly from the New Testament at

FIGURE 18.10 Catacomb of Marcellinus and Peter, Rome. Cubiculum 51, vault with the good shepherd surrounded by a cycle of scenes from the story of Jonah and Four Orants. About AD 320. Photograph: PCAS Foto Lau G 16.

the top and Old Testament images of trial – Susanna, Noah, Jonah – mainly at the lower and middle levels. Clearly there is an implicit movement from the Fall to the unambiguous salvific implications of the resurrection of Lazarus, from the crisis of Susanna to the divine protection of Daniel among the lions, with Daniel being the wise judge who proves Susanna's innocence in the scriptural narrative. The potential of such typology to create rigid hierarchies – as when Old Testament scenes appear in the nave and New Testament images in the apse and triumphal arch at Sta Maria Maggiore in the 430s – is already apparent,[40] but has not yet become a dogmatic insistence on the priority of the New Testament over the Old. Images may have more than one function, so that Jonah can prefigure Christ and represent the process of trial and salvation through which any Christian soul must pass. The personal, especially in the image of Susanna and the praying Orants, combines with the general – the imagery's theological call to, or recapitulation of, a salvific system.

The variety of possible models for representing any one of these Christian scenes may be examined by comparing the Susanna from Cubiculum 51 of the Marcellinus and Peter Catacomb with a mid- to late-fourth-century image of the same theme

---

[40]On Sta Maria Maggiore, see M. Miles, 'Sta Maria Maggiore's Fifth Century Mosaics: Triumphal Christianity and the Jews', *HTR* 86 (1993): 155–75.

FIGURE 18.11 Praetextatus Catacomb, Rome. Wall below the arcosolium of Celerina with a fresco of Susanna and the Elders as a lamb between wolves. Late fourth century. Photograph: PCAS Foto Pre C 20.

from the wall below an arcosolium in the Praetextatus Catacomb (Figure 18.11). Here Susanna (labelled, so as to avoid ambiguities) is represented symbolically as a sheep between the elders (also labelled) who are figured as wolves. This image itself is made to resonate with the now damaged painting in the lunette of the arcosolium above and behind that of Susanna, which shows Christ as a sheep between two sheep. Here – apart from the numerous scriptural intertexts of sheep and wolves which such a rendition must surely have been designed to evoke, we have a very different more deliberately allegorical, model for telling the story. The practice of using sheep instead of humans as actors in scriptural or theologically resonant narratives is not the dominant one but is certainly frequent – attested for instance in the spandrels of the arches of the lower tier of carvings on the Sarcophagus of Junius Bassus (the grandest of all fourth-century sarcophagi, Figure 18.12), the Cubiculum Leonis of the Commodilla Catacomb, numerous paintings and mosaics from fourth- to sixth-century churches,[41] and in the *tituli* composed by Paulinus of Nola to accompany and interpret the now lost decorations of the basilica he built in Nola dedicated to St Felix in the late fourth century. This iconographic variety, which we ought perhaps to expect in an evolving canon of imagery, is rooted in aesthetic variation and different kinds of models borrowed from different traditions (pagan and Jewish, visual and textual) which were ancestral to the establishment of Christianity. But it also reflects on potentially different theological or exegetic purposes – that is to say different kinds of functions – expected from images in different contexts or by different patrons.

---

[41]On the substitution of lambs for persons in early Christian art, see E. S. Malbon, *The Iconography of the Sarcophagus of Junius Bassus* (Princeton, NJ: Princeton University Press, 1990), pp. 72–6.

FIGURE 18.12 Sarcophagus of Junius Bassus, from the Vatican, Rome. The scenes between the columns show: Top: the sacrifice of Isaac, the arrest of Peter, Christ between Peter and Paul, the arrest of Christ, Pilate washing his hands; bottom: Job, the Fall, the entry into Jerusalem, Daniel in the Lions' den, the arrest of Paul. AD 359. Photograph: Anger, DAI Inst Neg: 88.4.

AFTER CONSTANTINE

Clearly, the triumph of an avowedly Christian emperor in 313 and his willingness to foster Christianity as a public, imperially sponsored, religion had implications for Christian art that are impossible to over-estimate.[42] Suddenly a cult whose practices had been small-scale, largely private, even secret, was not only public but mainstream – the chosen religion of the reigning emperor and his family (which ultimately and crucially meant all his successors with the single and brief exception of Julian). This is not the place to rehearse the full extent of this transformation – the result of a happenstance of politics – save in its ramifications for the visual arts.[43] But one may say that it is only from this point that the terminology of 'Christian art' (meaning the official arts of the principal – by the end of the fourth century, the

---

[42]See, for example, the essays in N. Lenski (ed.), *The Cambridge Companion to the Age of Constantine* (Cambridge: Cambridge University Press, 2005), with bibliography; also J. Bardill, *Constantine, Divine Emperor of the Christian Golden Age* (Cambridge: Cambridge University Press, 2012).

[43]For an introduction with bibliography, see Elsner, 'Perspectives in Art in the Age of Constantine', in Lenski (ed.), *The Cambridge Companion*, pp. 255–77.

only legally sanctioned – religious cult of the Roman state) can begin to be used to mean the equivalent of 'Roman' or 'Greek' art rather than of 'Mithraic' or 'Isiac' art.

With Constantine's dominance over the city of Rome came a restructuring of urban topography whereby huge public basilicas – effectively the architectural and decorative equivalent of prestige pagan temple foundations in earlier reigns – surrounded the city's periphery, as also in Milan.[44] That is, not only was the state's support of religion directed to an entirely new end, but the kind of buildings (churches without exterior altars for animal sacrifice) and the placing of those buildings (outside the traditional city walls) were all new. What was created was a novel liturgical topography celebrating the sites where a new kind of religious hero, the Christian saint or martyr, had been buried. If we are to believe the sixth-century entry in the *Liber Pontificalis* under Constantine (*Lib. Pont.* 36. ix-x), Christian images – equivalent in size, disposition and abundance of precious materials to pagan cult statues – were created for such churches as the Lateran basilica. With this kind of spectacular up-grading of scale, materials, patronage and prestige for Christian art (which included the establishment of imperially sponsored churches in other major cities such as Antioch, Constantinople and Jerusalem in addition to the buildings erected by bishops and other Christian aristocrats) went the depredation of various pagan images – including, one supposes, cult statues – to serve the decorative (rather than religious) purpose of adorning Constantinople as an antiquarian collection of the proudest baubles of the past.[45] Whether such images passed wholly from a religious viewing to the realm of aesthetic esteem, or preserved an element of pagan sanctity in their new contexts is perhaps a moot point.

While Christian art preserved and developed some aspects of its pre-Constantinian heritage (notably typology), it necessarily had to go through a rapid process of adapting earlier models of state art to create its new spaces and their decoration. The basilica form was borrowed from that of the ancient audience hall, and the range of variations on Christian church design (including octagons or circles, such as the Octagon in Antioch, the Anastasis Rotunda in Jerusalem, Santa Costanza in Rome, San Lorenzo in Milan or San Vitale in Ravenna, and centralized crosses,

---

[44]See R. Krautheimer, *Three Christian Capitals: Topography and Politics* (Berkeley: University of California Press, 1983), idem, 'The Ecclesiastical Building Policy of Constantine', in *Costantino il Grande dall'antichità all' umanesimo*, eds G. Bonamente and F. Fusco, 2 vols (Macerata: Università degli studi di Macerata, 1993), pp. 509–52. More recently H. Dey, *The Afterlife of the Roman City: Architecture and Ceremony in Late Antiquity and the Early Middle Ages* (Cambridge: Cambridge University Press, 2015), pp. 68–84. On Rome, see, for example, J. Curran, *Pagan City and Christian Capital: Rome in the Fourth Century* (Oxford: Clarendon, 2000), pp. 70–157; R. Ross Holloway, *Constantine and Rome* (New Haven, CT: Yale University Press, 2004), pp. 57–117. On Jerusalem, see, for example, E. D. Hunt, 'Constantine and Jerusalem', *JEH* 48 (1997): 405–24.

[45]On the collection of pagan statuary in Constantinople, see S. Bassett, *The Urban Image of Late Antique Constantinople* (Cambridge: Cambridge University Press, 2004) and U. Gehn and B. Ward-Perkins, 'Constantinople', in *The Last Statues of Antiquity*, eds R. R. R. Smith and B. Ward-Perkins (Oxford: Oxford University Press, 2016), pp. 136–44.

such as the so-called Mausoleum of Galla Placidia in Ravenna)[46] again reflects the creativity of an evolving and unfixed tradition. The need to cover large interior spaces with decoration led to the rapid development of impressive programmes of mosaics. Special attention was paid to the sacred space over the apse in basilica churches – with several spectacular surviving examples in Sta Pudenziana and the two apses at Sta Costanza in Rome, all from the later fourth century, Hosios David in Thessalonika and Sant' Aquilino in Milan from the mid fifth (e.g., Figure 18.13).[47] Likewise, the flat walls above the arcades of the main nave of a basilica could be adorned with long and complex programmes of mosaics, as in Sta Maria Maggiore in Rome in the second quarter of the fifth century or Sant' Apollonare Nuovo in Ravenna in the early part of the sixth century.[48] Again the vaults and walls of round buildings from the mausolea of Centcelles and Sta Costanza in the mid-fourth century to the baptisteries at Ravenna and Naples in the early to mid-fifth century came to boast exquisite decorative programmes in which Christian scriptural themes were combined with numerous motifs (patterns, animals, vines and vintagers)

FIGURE 18.13 Apse mosaic from the church of Hosios David in Thessalonike, representing Ezekiel's vision with Christ as its apogee (Ez. 1.4-28). Perhaps fifth century AD, perhaps early sixth century. Photograph: DAI Inst. Neg. 35.1941.

---

[46]On centralized churches, see now M. Johnson, *San Vitale in Ravenna and Octagonal Churches in Late Antiquity* (Wiesbaden: Reichert Verlag, 2018).

[47]On apses, see, fr example, B. Brenk, *The Apse, the Image and the Icon: An Historical Perspective of the Apse as a Space for Images*. Spätantike – Frühes Christentum – Byzanz 26 (Wiesbaden: Reichert Verlag, 2010) with bibliography.

[48]For Christian wall mosaics from the fourth to the sixth century, see now L. James, *Mosaics in the Medieval World* (Cambridge: Cambridge University Press, 2017), pp. 155–253 with bibliography.

borrowed from the pre-existing visual repertoire. These prestige sites of imperially sanctioned cult were lavishly adorned in all their fitments. The carved fifth-century wooden doors from the church of Sta Sabina in Rome (with a typologically arranged mix of Old and New Testament scenes whose original order is now unfortunately impossible to recover Figure 18.14),[49] the range of high-quality carved ivory boxes (of which perhaps the most outstanding is the late-fourth-century casket now in Brescia, maybe originally a pyxis for the eucharistic bread or a reliquary),[50] the lavish marble inlays in such fifth-century churches as Sta Sabina or the Lateran baptistery in Rome, the Orthodox baptistery in Ravenna and above all in the sixth-century church of St Sophia in Constantinople, the elaborate fourth-century floor mosaics surviving in the cathedral at Aquileia, all these examples give disparate evidence of an immense wealth of luxurious church furnishings. We have no top

FIGURE 18.14 Detail of a relief panel from the wooden doors of the church of St Sabina in Rome, showing one of the earliest representations of the Crucifixion. Second quarter of the fifth century AD. Photograph: Bartl, DAI Inst Neg: 61.2535.

---

[49]See, for example, I. Foletti and M. Gianandrea, *Zona liminare. Il nartece di Santa Sabina a Roma, la sua porta e l'iniziazione cristiana* (Roma: Viella - Liberia Editrice, 2015) with bibliography.
[50]On the Brescia Casket, see C. B. Tkacz, *The Key to the Brescia Casket: Typology and the Early Christian Imagination* (Paris: Institut d' Études Augustéennes, 2002); and on the Pola Casket, see J. Elsner, 'Closure and Penetration: Reflections on the Pola Casket', *Acta ad archaeologiam et artium historiam pertinentia* 26 (2013): 183–227.

quality survivals from this period of elite liturgical silverware, processional crosses, woven vestments and hanging tapestries, or painted icons,[51] although the late-fourth-century painted cloth from Egypt, now in Riggisberg, with scenes from Genesis and Exodus is an extremely impressive example of a luxury fitment.[52] But some impression of what once was may be gleaned by looking at later examples of these genres – the great gem encrusted crosses now in Brescia and Aachen, the jewelled cross pictured in mosaic in the sixth-century apse of Sant Apollinare in Class near Ravenna, the few remaining sixth-century icons of which the best survivals are now in Sinai. All these elements of church art, while they were new in the context of public buildings of Christian worship and their iconography was specifically adapted to Christian subjects, can be paralleled in earlier public, domestic and religious imagery in the Roman world.

One of the more controversial interventions in recent discussion of early Christian art has proposed that the borrowing of earlier models to articulate Christian imagery after the Edict of Toleration was resistant to specifically imperial forms.[53] It is surely right that before Constantine there can have been little temptation for Christians to appropriate imperial imagery, given that this alluded to an often persecutory and certainly pagan authority. But the evidence of the portrayal of Christ enthroned and in the dress of an emperor or magistrate, seated over the earth or its personification, in such images as the central scene from the upper tier on the main face of the Junius Bassus Sarcophagus (made in the 350s for the urban prefect of the city of Rome, Figure 18.12) or in the sixth-century mosaics of the apse in the presbytery at San Vitale in Ravenna, is hard to reject. Likewise in the Quedlinburg Itala – a fifth-century Latin manuscript with illustrations from the Old Testament books of Samuel and Kings, surely produced in Italy – the imperial dress used for a figure like King Saul and the landmarks deposited in his urban environment (including a tomb and triumphal arch) seems to speak of a specific desire to translate ancient scriptural narrative into the contemporary context of imperial representation.

It is in the context of the elite visual impact of Christian religion specifically fostered by the post-Constantinian state that special mention should be made of the book.[54] Graeco-Roman culture had favoured the papyrus roll as its privileged

---

[51]See the range of excellent contributions on various media in early Christian art in R. M. Jensen and M. D. Ellison (eds), *The Routledge Handbook of Early Christian Art* (Abingdon: Routledge, 2018).

[52]See L. Kötzsche, *Der Bemalte Behang in der Abegg-Stiftung in Riggisberg* (Riggisberg: Abegg-Stiftung, 2004).

[53]The resistance to imperial imagery in T. F. Mathews, *The Clash of Gods: A Reinterpretation of Early Christian Art* (Princeton, NJ: Princeton University Press, 1993) has been much criticised, it may be said. See also now the essays in Jefferson and Jensen (eds), *The Art of Empire*.

[54]On the early codex, see, for example, E. Turner, *The Typology of the Early Codex* (Philadelphia: University of Philadelphia Press, 1977), C. Roberts and T. Skeat, *The Birth of the Codex* (London: The British Academy, 1983) and G. Boudelis, *The Codex and Crafts in Late Antiquity* (New York: Bard Graduate Center, 2018). For early illuminated manuscripts, see J. Lowden, 'The Beginnings of Biblical Illustration', in *Imaging the Early Medieval Bible*, ed. J. Williams (University Park: The Pennsylvania State University Press, 1999), pp. 9–58 and H. Kessler, 'The Word Made Flesh in Early Decorated Bibles', in J. Spier, *Picturing the Bible: The Earliest Christian Art* (New Haven, CT: Yale University Press, 2007), pp. 141–68.

means of preserving written texts, as had Judaism (at any rate for its scriptures). But Christianity consistently preferred the codex, which certainly came to facilitate its liturgical need to flip across biblical texts between the Old and New Testaments, into the psalms and the epistles, and to intersplice these readings with other more recent or more dogmatic writings (like the Creed or particular prayers). The codex is a book of pages sewn together like our own books in form, but with the texts hand-copied with great care and at great length on a vellum-ground, much more durable than papyrus, and of great expense since it was made from the cured skins of cattle or sheep. Some of the most lavish examples of the genre – the parchment dyed purple and written over with gold or silver ink – were illuminated with pictures which might serve to illustrate the text (as in Figure 18.15 from the sixth-century Sinope gospels) or to extend its meanings through visual exegesis – as in the miniature of the Good Samaritan from the sixth-century Rossano Gospels where the Samaritan is clearly presented as a figure for Jesus himself. Illustrated bibles of this kind – again showing the characteristics of an emerging genre, with experiments in marginal illustration, the accumulation of all the images at the front as a kind of visual frontispiece, the parallel placement of images and text side by side, the use of full page illuminations interspersed among full pages of text and so forth – were surely made for the grandest patrons, members of the court or bishops. They may have been made available to others by being carried in processions or displayed on holy days. Parallel with such biblical illumination (our very earliest surviving illuminated codex is the few surviving pages of the Quedlinburg Bible of the second quarter of the fifth century) other elite illuminated books – literary like texts of Homer, Vergil and Terence, scientific like the Astronomy of Aratus or the Vienna Dioscorides, or antiquarian like the Codex Calendar of AD 354 – are attested.

The fourth century in particular, prior to the Theodosian legislation that made pagan practices illegal, is a period of great artistic innovation that comprised deep conservatism with significant change. Certain of the earliest Christian visual forms – including the use of catacomb paintings and sarcophagi – continued, with many of the most complex and impressive examples produced in the mid- to late fourth century. But by the early fifth century, both catacomb paintings and sarcophagi went out of fashion and – except in very few, exceptional instances – were rarely repeated. The domestic arts – silverware, some ivories, some small–scale marble sculpture, tapestries (to judge by the Egyptian evidence), floor-mosaics – are most marked in their conservatism, preserving mythological, 'secular' and pagan subject-matter, as well as antique classicising styles well into the seventh and eighth centuries. One presumes that objects with this kind of imagery were not for ecclesiastical use, and the paucity of surviving non-religious art from medieval Byzantium makes it hard to judge how long this tradition of what has been called 'Hellenism' continued in the private sphere.[55] But certainly until the sixth century we have plenty of evidence from the East of the empire for public honorific statuary and bases carved to very

---

[55]On Hellenism, see G. Bowersock, *Hellenism in Late Antiquity* (Cambridge: Cambridge University Press, 1990).

FIGURE 18.15 Detail from an illumination in the Sinope Gospels (BN Suppl. Gr. 1286), fol. 29r. The text of this page (written in gold uncials on purple parchment) is Mt. 20.32–21.2, where Christ heals the blind as illustrated in the painting. Bibliothèque nationale, Paris. Sixth century AD. Photograph: Bibliothèque nationale de France.

high quality in both two and three dimensions in continuance of pre-Constantinian Roman traditions of public sculpture.[56] The cases where pagan subject-matter or

---

[56]On the range of evidence and materials here, see J. Elsner, 'Late Antique Art: The Problem of the Concept and the Cumulative Aesthetic', in *Approaching Late Antiquity: The Transformation from Early to Late Empire*, eds S. Swain and M. Edwards (Oxford: Oxford University Press, 2004), pp. 277–86 with bibliography.

FIGURE 18.15 (Continued)

myth coincide with or were juxtaposed against Christian iconography (in silverware on Sevso's hunting plate, for instance, or the casket of Projecta; in mosaic on the Hinton St Mary floor for example) seem largely confined to the fourth century.[57]

One significant development of fourth-century art was the rise in the use of *spolia* – objects deliberately borrowed from earlier (in the early period inevitably pre-Christian) contexts, and reused in new cumulative works of art. The Arch of Constantine in Rome is the most famous example, but the Constantinian and later basilicas are no less so.[58] The enthusiasm for spoliation – including the use of ancient gems and ivories in church treasures like crosses and ambos – lasted well into the Middle Ages. It might be argued that the cult of relics was its Christian development.[59] These material pieces of bone or earth were sometimes displayed, encased in a lavish frame, or preserved hidden in an often elaborate box or casket. The relic contained or displayed was the raison d'être for the work of art (its container), but was, like a *spolium*, something from elsewhere and before. The importance of relics in Christian art (not only in visible reliquaries but also buried beneath altars or in the foundations of buildings, or inserted into crosses and icons) is that their employment carried the ontological significance of moving Christian images from the sphere of (mere) representation into a discourse of actual, tangible contact with (indeed the inclusion of) material that was itself holy and capable of miraculous effects. Whereas the principle functions of ancient

---

[57]See, for example, J. Engemann, 'The Christianization of Late Antique Art', in *The Seventeenth Annual Byzantine Congress: Major Papers* (New Rochelle, NY: Aristide D. Carateas Publishers, 1986), pp. 83–103; J. Elsner, 'Art and Architecture, 337-425', in *CAH*, eds A. Cameron and P. Garnsey, vol. 13, 2nd edn (Cambridge: Cambridge University Press, 1998), pp. 744–8.

[58]On spolia in English, see, for example, D. Kinney, 'Spolia, Damnatio and Renovatio Memoriae', *MAAR* 42 (1997): 138–61 and idem, 'Roman Architectural Spolia', *Proceedings of the American Philosophical Society* 145 (2001): 138–61.

[59]See J. Elsner, 'From the Culture of Spolia to the Cult of Relics: The Arch of Constantine and the Genesis of Late Antique Forms', *PBSR* 68 (2000): 149–84 for this argument.

Christian images might be described as exegetic, illustrative or commentarial (that is secondary to scripture) as well as decorative in the sense of defining spaces or objects as connected with a religious purpose, the inclusion of relics into the materiality of images from the later fourth century allowed Christian art to fulfil some of the direct functions of mediation which had been characteristic of pagan cult images or of holy men and women. The potential access to the sacred by means of relics was ultimately transferred to other forms of sanctified matter including sacred images such as icons and the eucharistic host. It is through its association with relics that Christian art was to reclaim that direct priority of sacred intervention in the world which those most opposed to pagan idolatry had specifically feared.

CONCLUSION

It is worth pressing a currently unfashionable, but fundamental, 'Protestant' question: Why was there a Christian art at all? This cannot be wholly separated from the question of what roles did Christian art play and how did these relate to the roles of images in the other religions of late antiquity. There clearly were cross-overs of function as well as form, style and iconography (especially in the rise of the icon and the use of relics as holy objects) which exercised those within Christianity who worried about 'idolatry'. Clearly also there were specific problems associated with the use of art in the 'scriptural' religions (Judaism, Christianity, Manichaeism, and later Islam) which promoted not only the visual as a commentary on the scriptural but also the generation of texts to explain images. Interestingly, in Judaism and Christianity, there was a certain resistance to the visual (more or less pronounced at different periods), expressed both in texts and in actual or reported acts of iconoclasm, while in Manichaeism art was elevated into the scriptural canon. The problems here press beyond an easy narrative of the development and genesis of Christian art (such as all chapters like this one are necessarily expected to create) and tease at the pleasant teleological assumptions that such an evolutionary story fails to test. Another way of worrying about this is to ask why we think of Christianity as something separate from Christian art – which is to say, why we nominate Christian art as a specific item in its own right (something on which there should be a separate chapter in a book like this).[60] To speak of 'Christian art' is implicitly to deny that 'Christianity' per se is simply the sum of all its expressions (textual, liturgical, institutional and artistic) and implicitly to affirm a priority of the scriptural (whereby the true Christianity lies in a set of texts), which is in itself a strongly 'Protestant' position. One might say that art within any of the late antique religions, including Christianity, is one set of expressions – a group of gestures leading to the definition and affirmation of personal and group identities, an instrumental construct that helps to orientate the worshipper whether in liturgical space or ritual action or

---

[60]For some of the problems in this issue, see J. Elsner, 'Archaeologies and Agendas: Jewish and Early Christian Art in Late Antiquity', *JRS* 83 (2003b): 114–28.

in relation to theological meanings or to scriptural histories. The role of art as a mediator between the individual and that model of religious superstructure to which he or she turned in late antiquity – one of as many competing and structurally interrelated models as postmodern and multicultural religious culture in the West offers today – is perhaps crucial, embodying a universal and cosmological religious significance in a directly accessible material form, tangible equally to the physical senses and to the imagination.

BIBLIOGRAPHIC NOTE

I have attempted in the notes – given that this chapter is in the first instance designed for student use – to refer primarily to English language sources, not very successfully in a field whose scholarship is gloriously international. Here I cite a few introductory accounts which may be useful for further reading. My generation was brought up on Grabar's *The Beginnings of Christian Art* and *Christian Iconography* – still important accounts, the former beautifully illustrated – and the important exhibition catalogue of Weitzmann's *Age of Spirituality*. The modern revisionism of early Christian art includes articles in volumes 12, 13 and 14 of the revised *Cambridge Ancient History* (CAH) – respectively Huskinson's 'Art and Architecture', Elsner's 'Art and Architecture' and Cormack's 'The Visual Art', as well as the following books: Lowden's *Early Christian and Byzantine Art*, Jensen's *Understanding Early Christian Art*, Cormack's *Byzantine Ark*, Elsner's *The Art of the Roman Empire* AD 100 – 450. Two crucial exhibition catalogues are Ensoli and La Rocca's *Aurea Roma: dalla città pagana alla città Cristiana* and Spier's *Picturing the Bible: The Earliest Christian Art*. Among handbooks, Koch's *Early Christian Art and Architecture* is poorly illustrated but comprehensive in its coverage of the range of materials; the most recent is Jensen and Ellison's *The Routledge Handbook of Early Christian Art*. Mathew's *The Clash of Gods: A Reinterpretation of Early Christian Art*, revised and expanded in 2003, remains very controversial but visually acute. For a historiographic review of the major trends in the scholarly accounts, see Elsner's 'Late Antique Art: The Problem of the Concept and the Cumulative Aesthetic' in S. Swain and M. Edwards (eds), *Approaching Late Antiquity*, pp. 271–77, and most recently Elsner, 'The Viennese Invention of Late Antiquity: Between Politics and Religion in the Forms of Late Roman Art' in Elsner (ed), *Empires of Faith in Late Antiquity*, pp. 110–127 and Lidova, 'The Rise of Byzantine Art and Archaeology in Late Imperial Russia' ibid., 128-60. Finally, a note of thanks: I am most grateful to Margaret M. Mitchell, Robert S. Nelson and the editors for their comments.

BIBLIOGRAPHY

Andrade, N. *The Journey of Christianity to India in Late Antiquity*. Cambridge: Cambridge University Press, 2018.

Awes Freeman, J. 'The Good Shepherd and the Enthroned Ruler', in L. Jefferson and R. Jensen (eds), *The Art of Empire: Christian Art in Its Imperial Context*, 159–96. Minneapolis, MN: Augsburg Fortress, 2015.

Bardill, J. *Constantine, Divine Emperor of the Christian Golden Age*. Cambridge: Cambridge University Press, 2012.

Bassett, S. *The Urban Image of Late Antique Constantinople*. Cambridge: Cambridge University Press, 2004.

Beard, M., North, J. and Price, S. *Religions of Rome*, 2 vols. Cambridge: Cambridge University Press, 1998.

Birk, S. *Depicting the Dead: Self-Representation and Commemoration on Roman sarcophagi with Portraits*. Aarhus Studies in Mediterranean Antiquity 11. Aarhus: Aarhus University Press, 2013.

Bonamente, G. and Fusco, F. (eds). *Costantino il Grande dall'antichità all' umanesimo*, 2 vols. Colloquio sul Cristianesimo nel mondo antico, Macerata 18-20 dicembre 1990, I–II, Macerata 1992-93. Macerata: Università degli studi di Macerata, 1993.

Boudelis, G. *The Codex and Crafts in Late Antiquity*. New York: Bard Graduate Center, 2018.

Bovini, G. and Brandenburg, H. *Repertorium der Christlich-Antiken Sarkophage I Rom und Ostia*. Wiesbaden: Franz Steiner Verlag, 1967.

Bowersock, G. *Hellenism in Late Antiquity*. Cambridge: Cambridge University Press, 1990.

Brenk, B. *The Apse, the Image and the Icon: An Historical Perspective of the Apse as a Space for Images*. Spätantike – Frühes Christentum – Byzanz 26. Wiesbaden: Reichert Verlag, 2010.

Cartlidge D. R. and Elliott, K. J. *Art and the Christian Apocrypha*. London: Routledge, 2001.

Cormack, R. 'The Visual Arts', in A. Cameron and P. Garnsey (eds), *CAH*, vol. 14, 2nd edn, 884–917. Cambridge: Cambridge University Press, 2000.

Cormack, R. *Byzantine Art*. Oxford: Oxford University Press, 2018.

Curran, J. *Pagan City and Christian Capital: Rome in the Fourth Century*. Oxford: Clarendon, 2000.

Deckers, J. G., Seeliger R. H. and Mietke, G. *Die Katakombe 'Santi Marcellino e Pietro': Repertorium der Malereien*. Roma sotterranea cristiana, 6,2. Vatican City: Pontificio Istituto di Archeologia Cristiana, 1987.

Deeg, M. 'The "Brilliant Teaching": The Rise and Fall of "Nestorianism" (Jingjiao) in Tang China', *JR* 31 (2006): 91–110.

Dey, H. *The Afterlife of the Roman City: Architecture and Ceremony in Late Antiquity and the Early Middle Ages*. Cambridge: Cambridge University Press, 2015.

Egelhaaf-Gaiser, U. *Kulträume im römischen Alltag*. Stuttgart: Steiner, 2000.

Elsner, J. *Art and the Roman Viewer: The Transformation of Art from the Pagan World to Christianity*. Cambridge: Cambridge University Press, 1995.

Elsner, J. 'Art and Architecture, pp. 337–425', in A. Cameron and P. Garnsey (eds), *CAH*, vol. 13, 2nd edn, 736–61. Cambridge: Cambridge University Press, 1998.

Elsner, J. 'From the Culture of Spolia to the Cult of Relics: The Arch of Constantine and the Genesis of Late Antique Forms', *PBSR* 68 (2000): 149–84.

Elsner, J. 'Inventing Christian Rome: The Role of Early Christian Art', in C. Edwards and G. Woolf (eds), *Rome the Cosmopolis*, 71–99. Cambridge: Cambridge University Press, 2003a.

Elsner, J. 'Archaeologies and Agendas: Jewish and Early Christian Art in Late Antiquity', *JRS* 83 (2003b): 114–28.

Elsner, J. 'Late Antique Art: The Problem of the Concept and the Cumulative Aesthetic', in S. Swain and M. Edwards (eds), *Approaching Late Antiquity: The Transformation from Early to Late Empire*, 271–309. Oxford: Oxford University Press, 2004.

Elsner, J. 'Perspectives in Art in the Age of Constantine', in N. Lenski (ed.), *The Cambridge Companion to Constantine*, 255–77. Cambridge: Cambridge University Press, 2005.

Elsner, J. *Roman Eyes: Visuality and Subjectivity in Art and Text*. Princeton: Princeton University Press, 2007.

Elsner, J. 'Iconoclasm as Discourse: From Antiquity to Byzantium', *AB* 94 (2012): 368–94.

Elsner, J. 'Closure and Penetration: Reflections on the Pola Casket', *Acta ad archaeologiam et artium historiam pertinentia* 26 (2013): 183–227.

Elsner, J. *The Art of the Roman Empire* AD *100 – 450*. Oxford: Oxford University Press, 2018.

Elsner, J. 'Some Observations on Dionysiac Sarcophagi', in C. Draycott, R. Raja, K. Welch and W. T. Wootton (eds), *Visual Histories of the Classical World: Essays in Honour of R.R.R. Smith*, 425–46. Turnhout: Brepols Publisher, 2019.

Elsner, J. 'The Viennese Invention of Late Antiquity: Between Politics and Religion in the Forms of Late Roman Art', in J. Elsner (ed.), *Empires of Faith in Late Antiquity: Histories of Art and Religion from India to Ireland*, 110–27. Cambridge: Cambridge University Press, 2020.

Elsner, J. and Huskinson, J. (eds). *Life, Death and Representation: Some New Work on Roman Sarcophagi*. Berlin: W. de Gruyter, 2011.

Elsner, J. and Rutherford, I. 'Introduction', in J. Elsner and I. Rutherford (eds), *Pilgrimage in Greco-Roman and Early Christian Antiquity: Seeing the Gods*, 1–38. Oxford: Oxford University Press, 2005.

Engemann, J. 'The Christianization of Late Antique Art', in *The Seventeenth Annual Byzantine Congress: Major Papers*, 83–103. New Rochelle, NY: Aristide D. Carateas Publishers, 1986.

Ensoli, E. and La Rocca E. (eds). *Aurea Roma: dalla città pagana alla città Cristiana*. Rome: L'Erma Di Bretschneider, 2000.

Ewald, B. *Der Philosoph als Leitbild*. Mainz: Ph. Von Zabern, 1999.

Festugière, A.-J. *Personal Religion Among the Greeks*. Berkeley: California University Press, 1954.

Fine, S. *Art and Judaism in the Greco-Roman World*. Cambridge: Cambridge University Press, 2005.

Finney, C. P. *The Invisible God: The Earliest Christians on Art*. Oxford: Oxford University Press, 1994.

Foletti, I and Gianandrea, M. *Zona liminare. Il nartece di Santa Sabina a Roma, la sua porta e l'iniziazione cristiana*. Roma: Viella – Liberia Editrice, 2015.

Gardner, I. *The Kephalaia of the Teacher*. NHMS vol. 37. Leiden: E.J. Brill, 1995.

Gardner, I. and Lieu, S. *Manichaean Texts from the Roman Empire*. Cambridge: Cambridge University Press, 2004.

Gehn, U. and Ward-Perkins, B. 'Constantinople', in R. R. R. Smith and B. Ward-Perkins (eds), *The Last Statues of Antiquity*, 136–44. Oxford: Oxford University Press, 2016.

Gordon, L. R. 'Reality, Evocation and Boundary in the Mysteries of Mithras', *JMS* 3 (1980): 19–99.

Gordon, L. R. *Image and Value in the Graeco-Roman World: Studies in Mithraism and Religious Art*. Aldershot: Ashgate Publishing Limited, 1996.

Gulácsi, S. *Mani's Pictures: The Didactic Images of the Manichaeans from Sasanian Mesopotamia to Uygur Central Asia and Tang-Ming China*. NHMS, vol. 90. Leiden: E.J. Brill, 2015.

Grabar, A. *The Beginnings of Christian Art*. London: Thames & Hudson Ltd, 1967.

Grabar, A. *Christian Iconography: A Study of Its Origins*. Princeton, NJ: Princeton University Press, 1968.

Gwynn, D. 'Archaeology and the "Arian Controversy" in the Fourth Century', in D. Gwynn and S. Bangert (eds), *Religious Diversity in Late Antiquity*, 229–63. LAA, vol. 6. Leiden: E.J. Brill, 2010.

Harrison, J. S. *Apuleius: A Latin Sophist*. Oxford: Oxford University Press, 2000.

Himmelmann, N. *Über Hirten-Genre in der antiken Kunst*. ARAW, vol. 65. Opladen: Westdeutscher Verlag, 1980.

Hölscher, T. *The Language of Images in Roman Art*. Cambridge: Cambridge University Press, 2004.

Hopkins, K. *World Full of Gods: Pagans, Jews and Christians in the Roman World*. London: Weidenfeld and Nicolson, 1999.

Horden, P. and Purcell, N. *The Corrupting Sea: A Study of Mediterranean History*. Oxford: Blackwell Publishers, 2000.

Howells, D. *A Catalogue of the Late Antique Gold Glass in the British Museum*. London: British Museum Press, 2015.

Hunt, D. E. 'Constantine and Jerusalem', *JEH* 48 (1997): 405–24.

Huskinson, J. '"Unfinished Portrait Heads" on Later Roman Sarcophagi', *Papers of the British School at Rome* 64 (1998): 129–58.

Huskinson, J. 'Art and Architecture, AD 193–337', in A. K. Bowman, P. Garnsey and A. Cameron (eds), *CAH*, vol. 12, 2nd edn, 672–703. Cambridge: Cambridge University Press, 2005.

James, L. *Mosaics in the Medieval World*. Cambridge: Cambridge University Press, 2017.

Jefferson, L. and Jensen, R. (eds). *The Art of Empire: Christian Art in Its Imperial Context*. Minneapolis, MN: Fortress Press, 2015.

Jensen, M. R. *Understanding Early Christian Art*. London: Routledge, 2000.

Jensen, M. R. *Face to Face: Portraits of the Divine in Early Christianity*. Minneapolis, MN: Fortress Press, 2005.

Jensen, M. R. *Baptismal Imagery in Early Christianity*. Grand Rapids, MI: Baker Academic, 2012.

Jensen, M. R. and Ellison, D. M. (eds). *The Routledge Handbook of Early Christian Art*. Abingdon: Routledge, 2018.

Johnson, M. *San Vitale in Ravenna and Octagonal Churches in Late Antiquity*. Wiesbaden: Reichert Verlag, 2018.

Kessler, H. 'The Word Made Flesh in Early Decorated Bibles', in J. Spier, *Picturing the Bible: The Earliest Christian Art*, 141–68. New Haven, CT: Yale University Press, 2007.

Kinney, D. 'Spolia, Damnatio and Renovatio Memoriae', *MAAR* 42 (1997): 117–48.

Kinney, D. 'Roman Architectural *Spolia*', *Proceedings of the American Philosophical Society* 145 (2001): 138–61.

Klimkeit, H.-J. 'On the Nature of Manichaean Art', in M. Heuser and H.-J. Klimkeit (eds), *Studies in Manichaean Literature and Art*, 270–90. NHMS, vol. 46. Leiden: E.J. Brill, 1998.

Koch, G. *Early Christian Art and Architecture*. London: SCM Press, 1996.

Koch, G. *Frühchristliche Sarkophage*. München: C.H. Beck, 2000.

Koortbojian, M. 'Roman Sarcophagi', in B. Borg (ed.), *A Companion to Roman Art*, 286–300. Chichester: Wiley-Blackwell, 2015.

Kötzsche, L. *Der Bemalte Behang in der Abegg-Stiftung in Riggisberg*. Riggisberg: Abegg-Stiftung, 2004.

Kraeling, C. *The Excavation sat Dura-Europos: Final Report VIII.2. The Christian Building*. New Haven, CT: Dura Europos Publications, 1967.

Krautheimer, R. *Three Christian Capitals: Topography and Politics*. Berkeley: University of California Press, 1983.

Krautheimer, R. 'The Ecclesiastical Building Policy of Constantine', in G. Bonamente and F. Fusco (eds), *Costantino il Grande dall'antichità all' umanesimo*, 2 vols, 509–52. Macerata: Università degli studi di Macerata, 1993.

Lembke, K. *Das Isaeum Campense in Rom. Studie über den Isiskult unter Domitian*. Heidelberg: Verlag Archäologie und Geschichte, 1994.

Lenski N. (ed.). *The Cambridge Companion to the Age of Constantine*. Cambridge: Cambridge University Press, 2005.

Levine, I. L. *Visual Judaism in Late Antiquity*. New Haven, CT: Yale University Press, 2012.

Lidova, M. 'The Rise of Byzantine Art and Archaeology in Late Imperial Russia', in Elsner (ed.), *Empires of Faith in Late Antiquity*, 128–60. Cambridge: Cambridge University Press, 2020.

Lowden, J. *Early Christian and Byzantine Art*. London: Phaidon Press Ltd, 1997.

Lowden, J. 'The Beginnings of Biblical Illustration', in J. Williams (ed.), *Imaging the Early Medieval Bible*, 9–58. University Park: The Pennsylvania State University Press, 1999.

Malbon, S. E. *The Iconography of the Sarcophagus of Junius Bassus*. Princeton, NJ: Princeton University, Press, 1990.

Mathews, F. T. *The Clash of Gods: A Reinterpretation of Early Christian Art*. Princeton, NJ: Princeton University Press, 1993.

Miles, M. 'Sta Maria Maggiore's Fifth Century Mosaics: Triumphal Christianity and the Jews', *HTR* 86 (1993): 155–75.

Morey, R. C. *The Gold-Glass Collection of the Vatican Library*. Vatican City: Biblioteca Apostolica Vaticana, 1959.

Morgan, T. *Roman Faith and Christian Faith: Pistis and Fides in the Early Roman Empire and Early Churches*. Oxford: Oxford University Press, 2015.

Murray, C. 'Art and the Early Church', *JTS* 28 (1977): 303–45.

Murray, C. *Rebirth and Afterlife: A Study in the Transmutation of Some Pagan Imagery in Early Christian Funerary Art*. Oxford: BAR Publishing, 1981.

North, J. 'The Development of Religious Pluralism', in J. Lieu, J. North and T. Rajak (eds), *The Jews among Pagans and Christians in the Roman Empire*, 174–93. London: Routledge, 1992.

Peppard, M. *The World's Oldest Church: Bible, Art and Ritual at Dura-Europos, Syria*. New Haven, CT: Yale University Press, 2016.

Perry, E. *The Aesthetics of Emulation in the Visual Arts of Ancient Rome*. Cambridge: Cambridge University Press, 2005.

Platt, V. 'Framing the Dead on Roman Sarcophagi', in V. Platt and M. Squire (eds), *The Frame in Classical Art: A Cultural History*, 331–58. Cambridge: Cambridge University Press, 2017.

Roberts, C. and Skeat, T. *The Birth of the Codex*. London: The British Academy, 1983.

Ross Holloway, R. *Constantine and Rome*. New Haven, CT: Yale University Press, 2004.

Smith, Z. J. *Drudgery Divine: On the Comparison of Early Christianities and the Religions of Late Antiquity*. Chicago: University of Chicago Press, 1990.

Spier, J. *Picturing the Bible: The Earliest Christian Art*. New Haven, CT: Yale University Press, 2007.

Standaert, N. (ed.). *Handbook of Christianity in China. Volume One: 635-1800*. Leiden: E.J. Brill, 2001.

Tkacz, B. C. *The Key to the Brescia Casket: Typology and the Early Christian Imagination*. Paris: Institut d' Études Augustéennes, 2002.

Turner, E. *The Typology of the Early Codex*. Philadelphia: University of Philadelphia Press, 1977.

Varner, E. 'Reading Replications: Roman Rhetoric and Greek Quotations', *AH* 29 (2006): 282–305.

Vermaseren, M. *Corpus Cultus Cybelae Attidisque III* Études préliminaires aux religions orientales dans l'Empire romain, vol. 50. Leiden: E.J. Brill, 1977.

Versluys, M. J. 'The Sanctuary of Isis on the Campus Martius in Rome', *B* 72 (1997): 159–69.

Versluys, M. J. *Aegyptiaca Romana: Nilotic Scenes and the Roman Views of Egypt*. RGRW, vol. 144. Leiden: E.J. Brill, 2002.

Versluys, M. J, Clausen, B. K. and Vittozzi, C. G. (eds). *The Isaeum Campense: From the Roman Empire to the Modern Age*. Roma: Scienze e Lettere, 2018.

Veyne, P. *Did the Greeks Believe in Their Myths?*. Chicago: University of Chicago Press, 1988.

Vos, de M. *L'egittomania in pitture e mosaici Romano-Campani della prima età imperiale*. Études préliminaires aux religions orientales dans l'empire romain, vol. 84. Leiden: E.J. Brill, 1980.

Walker, S. 'Gold Glass in Late Antiquity', in R. M. Jensen and M. D. Ellison (eds), *The Routledge Handbook of Early Christian Art*, 124–40. Abingdon: Routledge, 2018.

Ward-Perkins, B. 'Where Is the Archaeology and Iconography of Germanic Arianism', in D. Gwynn and S. Bangert (eds), *Religious Diversity in Late Antiquity*, 265–89. LAA, vol. 6. Leiden: E.J. Brill, 2010.

Weitzmann, K. (ed.). *Age of Sprituality: Late Antique and Early Christian Art, Third to Seventh Century*. New York: Metropolitan Museum of Art, 1979.

White, M. L. *Building God's House in the Roman World*. Baltimore, MD: Johns Hopkins University Press, 1990.

White, M. L. *The Social Origins of Christian Architecture*, vol. 2. Valley Forge, PA: Trinity Press, 1997.

Winkler, J. *Auctor and Actor*. Berkeley: University of California Press, 1985.

Wyler, S. 'Roman Replications of Greek art at the Villa della Farnesina', *AH* 29, no. 2 (2006): 215–354.

Zanker, P. and Ewald, B. *Living with Myths: The Imagery of Roman Sarcophagi*. Oxford: Oxford University Press, 2012.

CHAPTER 19

The community's hope

Soteriology in the early church

ROBERT J. DALY, SJ

FOREWORD

Soteriology, the study of the saving work of Jesus Christ, as we now commonly define it, is our subject. We focus on the period between St Paul, the beginning of Christian soteriology, and the mature theological position reached by Maximus the Confessor (d. 662)[1] at the end of the patristic period. Unable to compete with, or even do justice to Hans Urs von Balthasar's account of Maximus,[2] my effort will be both to outline what led to that achievement and, in so doing, to attend to its theological significance. That combination of the genetic and the thematic characterizes my attempt to deal with the fact that, except for Athanasius, Gregory of Nyssa, and Augustine, the fathers usually did not devote specific attention to what we define as the dogma of soteriology. If our goal were to impose a clear definition of soteriology on the teaching of the fathers, and had no space limitations, we could end up producing a whole series of books with varying chapter and subheading titles such as: (1) illumination, victory, divinization, sacrifice of atonement; and/or: (2) liturgy, exposition of scripture, instruction, spirituality and devotion, art; and/or: (3) defending the true faith, the true divinity of the Son and the Spirit, the unity of Christ, the necessity of grace; and/or: (4) the soteriological principles of patristics, the necessity of divine theophany, the principles of satisfaction, the incarnation as presupposition, mediation: bridging God and creation, education/example/model,

---

[1]Although John of Damascus (c.655–c.750) is usually thought of as marking the end of the patristic age, I follow here those who with Studer note that, in Christology, the best of John of Damascus is copied from Maximus – see Michael Schmaus, Alois Grillmeier, Leo Scheffczyk und Michael Seybold (eds), *Handbuch der Dogmengeschichte* [especially: Band III, Faszikel 2a: Basil Studer unter Mitarbeit von Brian Daly, *Soteriologie In der Schrift und Patristik*] (Freiburg, Basel und Wien: Herder, 1978), p. 223; See also Mariyan Stoyadinov, 'The Soteriological Argument in the Context of the Iconoclastic Controversy: St John Damascene and St Theodore the Studite', in *Für Uns und für Unser Heil: Soteriologie in Ost und West*, eds Theresia Hainthaler et al. (Innsbruck and Wien: Tyrolia-Verlag, 2014), pp. 303–11.

[2]Hans Urs von Balthasar, *Cosmic Liturgy: The Universe According to Maximus the Confessor*, trans. Brian E Daly, S.J. (San Francisco, CA: Ignatius Press, 2003).

solidarity and so forth. And all the while, coursing through and around these themes would be the omnipresent question: *cur Deus homo?* and its answer : *for us and for our salvation.*[3]

Instead, we will try to present a readable brief summary of the development of early Christian soteriology that attends to chronological and historical location, but does not presume that there is, or even always should be, a linear or cause-and-effect relationship between what comes before and what comes after.

AN ORIENTATION

It was only when the medieval scholastics began to ask systematizing questions about Jesus' identity and mission that distinctions were consistently made between the person of Christ, thus Christology, and the saving work of Christ, thus soteriology. But the Pauline letters of the early New Testament already contain at least ten different conceptual images with which Paul attempted to express both the fact of and the implications of the saving Christ-event: justification, salvation, reconciliation, expiation, redemption, freedom, sanctification, transformation, new creation, glorification. No one of these, however, nor any particular selection of them, can begin to express for us the breadth and depth of Paul's sense of Christ's saving mission.

In our own day, contemporary theologians, influenced as they usually have been by the philosophical turn to the subject and the various hermeneutical movements of postmodernity, are generally aware that the soteriology of the fathers of the church was an attempt to explain the unfolding of an integral continuous mystery that began, as we now know, with the beginning of our universe some 13 or 14 billion years ago, intensified with the beginning of life billions of years later, and then, with the advent of *homo sapiens*, moved towards its pivotal high points in the formation of the covenantal people of God and the unique historical event of the Incarnation, and that continues now in the multifarious ways in which Christians have expressed and tried to explain this mystery, of which they themselves are a part, as something that is still moving towards its consummation in the *Eschaton* when Christ will finally bring all things into glorious subjection to the Father.

---

[3]*Cur Deus homo?/Why Did God become Man?* is, of course, the name of the pivotal work in which Anselm of Canterbury (*c.*1033–1109) tried to answer this question for his monks; and *propter nos homines et propter nostram salutem/for us humans and for our salvation* has (as already formulated at Nicaea in 325 and Constantinople in 381) long been the presumed beginning of every Christian answer. But before proceeding, two background notes: (1) For a rich recent treatment by twenty seven Catholic and Orthodox scholars, see Hainthaler et al. (eds), *Für Uns und für Unser Heil* (above, f.n. 1). (2) Stepping back even farther, our overview of patristic soteriology, undertaken from the purview of a traditional Christian theologian, presumes awareness of the enormous complexity that stands behind (or ahead of) it. See, for example, my recent book: *Sacrifice in Pagan and Christian Antiquity* (London and New York: T&T Clark, 2019) and Aisle Eikrem, *God as Sacrificial Love: A Systematic Exploration of a Controversial Notion* (London and New York: Bloomsbury Academic, 2018).

Here, in my own attempt to make sense of all this, or at least to outline the 'facts' of the matter, I rely on Basil Studer's magisterial outline of patristic soteriology in the *Handbuch der Dogmengeschichte*,[4] and also presume my own summary of the biblical background in that volume: since we must never forget that the church fathers were consistently and dedicatedly biblical in their theology.

THE EARLY CENTURIES

At the beginning of the Christian era there was general sense that human beings were in a situation characterized by a kind of world-pessimism from which they needed to be freed. The unfolding of this into a Christian doctrine of salvation involved the challenging task of bringing belief in creation into conformity with the new Christian teaching on salvation. And then, as early Christianity, along with its gradual Hellenization, became less dominated by its Jewish heritage, it became increasingly susceptible to radical solutions. This developed in an extreme form as the Gnosticism of Marcion (d. *c*.160). But the orthodox Christian response not only remained abidingly loyal to the Bible but also, as time went on, characterized by a deepening sense of divinization – especially among the Alexandrians – and, as key to everything authentically Christian, a growing awareness of and commitment to the fact of the Incarnation and to all its implications.

The early works and writers known as the Apostolic Fathers – the early-second-century *Didache,* Clement of Rome (fl. *c*.96) and Ignatius of Antioch (d. *c*.107), and the mid-second-century *Shepherd of Hermas* and *Letter of Barnabas* – taught much that eventually found its place in the early Christian 'Rule of Faith' and classical creeds, especially the belief that the source of salvation is God the Creator as made manifest in the sending of the Son, Jesus Christ.[5] Although much remained vague and undefined, especially regarding the *what* and the *how* and the *why* of Trinity and Incarnation, anti-docetism and the soteriological *pro nobis* motif remained strong throughout. The lines leading from a strong Jewish heritage through a pervasive Hellenistic milieu to Christian theology's eventual appropriation of a Neoplatonic intellectual toolbox were already visible.

The second century[6] saw the development of a soteriology heavily influenced by the mythological and cosmological categories of Jewish apocalyptic as found in the Christian apocryphal and Greek apologetic writings of the time. This generated a religiosity emphasizing mystery, the irrational, and the transcendence of the divine, along with an anti-world, anti-flesh dualism to which Christians, as in their struggles with Marcion's Gnosticism, were particularly susceptible. Christianity, seeing itself as the kingdom of the Logos, and paganism as the kingdom of Satan, identified pagan divinities with the demons. In this context, the Christian macro-narrative focused on the kenotic descent and triumphal, all-conquering ascent of Jesus, the

---

[4]Studer, *Soteriologie In der Schrift und Patristik* (see f.n. 1).
[5]See, Studer, *Soteriologie In der Schrift und Patristik*, pp. 59–65.
[6]Further, see Studer, *Soteriologie In der Schrift und Patristik*, pp. 65–73.

heavenly Logos, freeing those enslaved by death (namely, Satan) in order to bring them back triumphantly with him to heaven. This story then developed to include the theme of the 'just' treatment of the devil and even, as later with Gregory of Nyssa (c.330–c.395) and others, the popular theory of the deception of the unjust devil and his minions. The more 'gross' or sensational aspects of this theory, such as the 'fish-hook', 'bait' and mouse-trap' images did encounter serious criticism from other Christians such as Gregory of Nazianzus (c.329–c.389). Overall, however the theme of the victory of Christ remained dominant, while in the later Latin Fathers, that of the devil's abuse of power contributed to the legalism that unhappily passed through them to the later Western tradition.

But still back in the second century, we find Irenaeus of Lyons (c.130–c.200)[7] and after him Tertullian in Africa (c.160–225) leading Christianity's defense against Gnosticism's insistence on self-salvation and the unsaveability of the flesh.[8] They emphasized the unity of the creating and redeeming God and along with that the unity of the spiritual *and* material unity of the human being, in other words, the *salus carnis* (salvation of the flesh) and the actual fact and implications of the Incarnation. Irenaeus, who could be described as a 'Christian gnostic', was actually the first to develop a consequent, carefully thought-out soteriology. He begins with human beings being formed in the image and likeness of God (Gen. 1:26) and placed on a path to grow from childlike and innocent immortality to the maturity of being a son of God and his progeny being children of God. Adam's sin, according to Irenaeus, did not ruin that plan, but it did result in the Incarnation becoming not the perfection of the human being, but rather his restoration, his salvation. Irenaeus emphasizes, as the fathers generally did, that only a mediator who was both divine and human could have set in motion this 'history' of an all-encompassing economy of salvation in Christ's making-up for Adam's delinquency.

THIRD-CENTURY DEVELOPMENTS

Then Tertullian in the early third century, in general following Irenaeus, emphasizes even more the unity of creation and Incarnation. But he imagines the *sacramentum salutis* as beginning in God even *before* creation, and thus the 'subsequent' Incarnation of the Word as a kind of 'second step' in this 'process' of the divine economy coming to be. There is a strong emphasis here on restoration, requital and judgement, and that expressed in magnificent Latin prose that marks the beginning of a long (and largely sad) tradition of juridical language and thinking about these matters in the Western church.

Moving into the third century, we encounter the first of the great Alexandrians, Clement (c.150–c.215) and Origen (185–c.254) self-confidently taking their place in the thought-world of Middle Platonism. Offering a Christian answer to the

---

[7]See Ysabel de Andia, '"Opus Spiritus salus carnis": Le salut de la chair selon Irénée de Lyon', in Hainthaler et al. (eds), *Für uns und für Unser Heil*, pp. 53–65.
[8]Further see Studer, *Soteriologie In der Schrift und Patristik*, pp. 73–85.

Greek philosophical question of the One and the Many, they saw Christ, in virtue of his constitution as divine Logos, as the mediating revelation of the *mysteria*, the sacramentality of all things. All created beings, precisely in virtue of their reality as creatures, were understood as simultaneously revealing and concealing the transcendence of God. And beyond that, in Origen's mind, all intelligent creatures of God, precisely in virtue of their reality as both spiritual and bodily creatures, have the capacity to be open to and educatable into that divine transcendence. Both Clement and Origen, as profoundly committed Christians, were careful to emphasize the historical human life and example of the Word, Jesus, his actual teaching, suffering, death, resurrection, return to the Father, and sending of the Spirit. But most students of Origen have felt that these physical, material, historical and this-worldly aspects of the Christ-event have remained too far in the background, and that it is to later fathers like Athanasius and Augustine that we must turn to find a more balanced patristic soteriology.

By the mid-third century, the church of Cyprian of Carthage in North Africa, strongly centralized around its bishop, was struggling to deal with the problem of persecution-caused apostates seeking reconciliation.[9] In the course of developing a strong penance-oriented devotional life, Cyprian's Church developed a highly Romanized ecclesial soteriology with its principle that outside this church with its sacraments of baptism and Eucharist there is no salvation (*extra ecclesiam nulla salus*). While continuing to insist that merciful forgiveness is a gift from God, there was a stronger emphasis on what human beings must contribute to their own salvation, and on conceiving that contribution in legalistic terms as a just satisfaction for sins committed.

In this highly 'Roman' type of soteriology, the necessary salvific activity of Christ is strongly conceived under the concepts of Christ the master teacher and saving model and, no longer silent as in his own suffering, the final judge now handing out rewards and punishments. We should emphasize, however, that Cyprian's institutionalized legalism is tempered by a strongly positive, even warm, sense of the ongoing saving presence of Christ in the saving institutions of his one true church actively bringing about the *salus generis humani*.

With Lactantius (*c.*250–*c.*325) we encounter the deeply apologetic and, by then highly traditional (even archaic) soteriology of a Latin rhetorician standing in the line of the Roman-influenced Cyprian.[10] For him, a deep bipolar antagonism in the visible world: fire and water, active and passive elements, earth and heaven, darkness and light and so forth dominates his view of human life. But he manages to escape an explicit dualism by seeing everything as being under the will of the Creator. Definitely subordinationist, as was common before Nicaea, Lactantius sees the unity of Father and Son as primarily moral, and leaves no place for the Holy Spirit. He does emphasize the Incarnation and the soteriological necessity that Christ, the mediator, be both human and divine. But it is God and not Christ who

---

[9]Ibid., pp. 96–106.
[10]Ibid., pp. 106–16.

is most often spoken of as *Dominus* and *Imperator* (Lord and Master). He prefers to speak of the justice of God rather than of Christ the judge, and emphasizes the divine side of the mediatorship of Christ. There are indeed places where Lactantius speaks in great detail about the suffering and death of Christ, and he follows Hippolytus in repeating the erroneous 'pascha-passion' etymological identification; but in key places the soteriological effect is attributed to God and not to Christ, and the definitive restoration of life at the end of the thousand-year reign is brought about not by Christ but by God.

THE COUNCIL OF NICAEA AND ITS AFTERMATH

After the 325 Council of Nicaea the anti-Arian struggles were largely an argument about the heritage of the Middle Platonism-influenced Logos Christology of Origen.[11] While there was little danger of Origen placing the Logos outside of the divine sphere, that was not the case when, with Arius (d. 336) and his followers, the emphasis was no longer on the salvific functions of the Son and the Spirit but more on the inner life of the Trinity, and thus on seeing the Son as a creature of the will of the Father, decidedly on the side of being a creature. In response, the Nicene *homoousion* placed the Son decidedly on the divine side, thus requiring new theological thinking about the Son as unchangeably God in a (theologically) new relationship to his assumed humanity. Athanasius of Alexandria (*c*.296–373) and Hilary of Poitiers (*c*.315–67/8), for example, understood *homoousios* to signify a kind of generation *within* the divine life and nature of God. Thus, the saving work of the Son was the work of someone fully divine as well as fully human.[12]

In Eusebius of Caesarea, the first church historian (*c*.260–*c*.340), this new Nicaea-inspired image of Christ became prominent. Christ the Logos (the archetype) battles the invisible enemies, just as the Emperor Constantine (d. 337) (the copy/image of the archetype) and his successors battle visible enemies.[13] This, what we would now call 'political soteriology', became enormously successful both in the East with Cyril of Jerusalem (*c*.315–87) and Athanasius of Alexandria (*c*.296–373), and in the West with Ambrose of Milan (*c*.339–97). Typically imperial titles like *Dominus Salvator* (Lord and Saviour) were attributed to Christ (for example, by Athanasius) and typically Christological terms like '*conservator dominus noster*' (Our Lord and Protector) were given to the emperor (for example, by Ambrose). Phrases from Roman salutology (court acclamations) such as *salus aeterna* and *salus generis humani* (eternal salvation, salvation of the human race) found their way into preaching, liturgy and hymnody. A classic example of this is the *Te Deum*. This *rex gloriae* theme (King of glory) had actually begun back in the New Testament and

---

[11]Ibid., pp. 116–21.
[12]Apart from the Arians, many theologians at the time of Nicaea considered the Word, the Logos, to replace the human soul of Christ. No one, however, paid much attention to this or, in general, to the interior life of Jesus. That neglect, even to this day, remains relatively undeveloped in Christian theology.
[13]Further see Studer, *Soteriologie In der Schrift und Patristik*, pp. 121–5.

had found a further life in the early *Acts of the Martyrs* before becoming popular in the preaching of the fourth and fifth centuries when even Christ's Way of the Cross was seen as a kind of triumphal parade. That time also saw the development of special devotion to the Holy Cross and its relics, and the custom of thinking of, and referring to, Christ simply as God (*theos*).

Athanasius in the East and Hilary of Poitiers in the West played major roles in defending and deepening the faith of Nicaea. For Athanasius, it was an incarnational Logos Christology in which the pre-existing Logos makes our body his own, a shift away from the (by-then traditional) gnostic-leaning cosmo-soteriological orientation towards a focusing on the Word becoming one with humans not just to save them but also to begin their divinization in the Spirit. This position, while continuing to emphasize the absolutely full Incarnation in the flesh of the absolutely full divinity of the Word, goes significantly beyond Irenaeus in considering this 'work' to be a *new creation* that, had there been no sin, would not have come about at all. But note that Athanasius does not explicitly formulate either *that* or *how* this de facto double consubstantiality of the Incarnate Word constitutes the actual foundation of redemption.

Meanwhile, Hilary focused on the revelatory glorification of the human being that was taking place in the *oikonomia* of the Incarnation. In doing so he was careful not to present the body as evil (for it is, after all, the earthly mode of existence of the soul), but he may actually have been thinking more of the human soul than of the body as that which is being transformed from its slave existence (*forma servilis*) and from its lowly corruptibility (*humilitas, infirmitas, corruptio* and *corruptio mortis*) in order to be brought to the glory in which alone it possesses its ultimate destiny, namely, the eternal life of God. The seeming dualism of this somewhat Origen-influenced view is subject to the same theological criticism customarily levelled against that tradition.

Be that as it may, Hilary sees three stages or 'births' in Christ's existence: (1) the eternal begetting by the Father of the Son, (2) Jesus, born of Mary, becoming fully human while remaining fully divine, (3) his resurrection and return to full divine glory. The transition from (1) to (3) takes place in the *kenosis* of (2) which is the 'location' of the traditional themes of death as victory over the devil, over death and sin, and particularly of the theme of the death of Christ as a sacrifice of atonement. Finally, the moral (and so-to-speak 'natural') union with Christ that takes place in the Church becomes the principle of the glorification of humanity.

By the end of the fourth century, especially with Gregory of Nyssa (*c.*330–95) and the other Cappadocians, Christian thinking had become largely a dialogue with Neoplatonism.[14] Philosophical categories and models were now being used to teach about the ideal human goal, namely, divinization (*theiopoiesis*).[15] Even for the philosophers that ultimate goal for humanity was their understanding of

---

[14]Ibid., pp. 136–43.
[15]Further see: N. Russell, *The Doctrine of Deification in the Greek Patristic Tradition*. Oxford Early Christian Studies (Oxford: Oxford University Press, 2006).

divinization. For Gregory and the Christian thinkers the Incarnation was not the ultimate principle of salvation, but it did open up for us the absolutely necessary path to that final goal of all human striving: the glorifying vision of the divine beauty. On this point, Stoic ideas regarding the organic unity of the whole body of humanity may also have played a role in shaping Gregory's sense of the unifying universality of Christ's saving work. But while he reminds us that full attainment of the divine vision is impossible for us (it would imply a Trinity-like equality with God) he continues to insist that baptism marks the beginning of our never-ending and never-completable process of becoming one with God. It is to be a stretching forth (*epektasis*) into an endless progress (*prokope*) into God.

Throughout the patristic period, and certainly by the end of the fourth century, the liturgy (*lex orandi*) had come to play a major role in the Church's theology (*lex credendi*) especially in the soteriology involved with the practices and teaching regarding baptism, penance and Eucharist. Never far from the consciousness of Christians was their living relationship to the mysteries of the life of Christ, with martyrdom and ascetical practices understood to be radical realizations of baptism, penitential practices as activating the merciful intercession of their heavenly redeemer, and the Eucharist as making present to them the sacrificial death and resurrection of Jesus. Monasticism only intensified these developments.[16]

Probably most important of all were the effects of the mystagogical catecheses preached by, among others, Cyril of Jerusalem (*c*.315–87), Asterius (d. after 301), John Chrysostom (*c*.347–407), Theodore of Mopsuestia (*c*.350–428), Ambrose of Milan (*c*.339–97), Augustine of Hippo (354–430) and Niceta of Remesiana (d. *c*.414). Common to these popular sermons, preached normally to new Christians after their initiation rites, was the conviction that salvation depended upon – and (as Cyril insisted) had already begun to take place in – the baptismal bath and anointing, with the past saving events of Jesus' death and resurrection being the originating type of what the baptizands had just experienced, in a kind of cultic *mimesis*. A similar approach can be seen in Theodore of Mopsuestia's teaching that the becoming-present of the sacrifice of the cross in the Eucharist was enabling actual participation in the heavenly liturgy; or, for example with Ambrose's teaching that Jesus' saving actions became present and actively salvific in the lives of his hearers by this liturgical *anamnesis*. By the end of the fourth century, theological summaries of these developments were being expressed (and then commented on) in the baptismal symbols, or creeds, namely, that salvation was the work of Christ. In other words, Jesus, by working with the Father and the Spirit and 'making present' the principal events of his earthly existence, especially his death and resurrection, was bringing about in us the forgiveness of sins and everlasting life.

Greatly contributing to this development and its influence on later Christianity (especially in the East) was the radical Christocentricity of the monks.[17] This can be seen in the *Life of Anthony*, traditionally attributed to Athanasius, as well as in his

---

[16]Further see Studer, *Soteriologie In der Schrift und Patristik*, pp. 144–53.
[17]Ibid., pp. 153–4.

Christological reading of the Psalms; as exemplified in his *Ad Marcellinum*. It was a thematic approach later perfected by Augustine. Another figure of great influence was the Origen-influenced spiritual writer, Evagrius Ponticus (346–99), especially in the East but also in the West by way of John Cassian (*c.*480–*c.*550). However, the most influential figure for later developments was probably Ambrose of Milan, the most prominent Latin bishop of the fourth century, and especially his incomparably brilliant disciple, Augustine of Hippo (354–430), whose towering figure stands out at the end of the Nicene age.[18]

AUGUSTINE'S CONTRIBUTION

Although no particular work of Augustine directly addresses soteriology as such, the rich variety of Christological themes spread across the full range of his successive struggles, first with Manicheism and Neoplatonism, and then with Donatism, and finally with Pelagianism, along with his awareness of what was also going on in the East, make him the primary source for the soteriology of his age. Ever attentive both to local details and to the 'big picture', his theology in general and his Christology/soteriology in particular was so wide-ranging (comparable to the scope of his earlier fellow-giant, Origen) as to evade all attempts at synthesizing. Here we attempt only to point out some of the major themes.[19]

At the outset, the mediatorship of Christ is pervasive. As, for example, gathered in the relatively early work, *Enchiridion*, under the general theme of *reconciliatio per sacrificium mediatoris* (reconciliation through the mediator's sacrifice) we find the notions of: the healing of pride, the call to return to proximity with God, an example of obedience, a model of grace, proof of the resurrection, victory over the devil and, of course, Christ doing all of this in virtue of his being both divine and human.[20]

The Incarnation of the Word, understood in the full sense as being from Jesus' conception in Mary's womb to his final glorification, is, for Augustine, the highest grace, the highest truth, the foundation for all his teaching on the divine missions and the heart of his spirituality. As the highest revelation of the love of God, this salvific work will ultimately lead to consummation in the vision of God.

Augustine sees this as unfolding in the teaching and, above all, in the empowering example of Christ, wisdom incarnate that (beginning with the prophets and including even the wise men of the pagans!) was not just teaching us, but effectively showing

---

[18] Ibid., pp. 155–74; see also the following articles in Hainthaler et al., *Für Uns und für Unser Heil*: Michel Stavrou, 'Liberté et salut chez saint Augustin et saint Jean Cassien: un débat sotériologique entre Occident et Orient chrétiens', pp. 161–79; Dominique Gonnet, SJ, 'Sacrifice et salut selon saint Augustin', pp. 197–206; Vittorino Grossi, 'Augustine's Soteriology Regarding Original Sin: Ancient Questions and Research Orientations', pp. 221–43.

[19] See also, F. G. Clancy, 'Redemption', in *Augustine Through the Ages*, eds A. D. Fitzgerald et al. (Grand Rapids, MI: Eerdmans, 1999), pp. 702–4.

[20] Augustine, *Ench.*, 108.

us, how not to fear death. This teaching was then significantly deepened in the later anti-Pelagian writings emphasizing the effectiveness of inner grace over against mere external example.

Under the general concept of *sacramentum passionis* Augustine presents a bewildering wealth of mostly traditional soteriological themes and images, but often without going into or explaining them. He has, for example, frequent mentions in *De Civitate Dei* of both the positive and negative (and sometimes even popular) aspects of Christ's victory over the devil, sin and death. Then, under his general theme of 'sacrifice of reconciliation', we find frequent political, military and cultic forms of expression, and ultimately a very spiritualized concept of the sacrificial death of Christ, especially in the famous 'definition' he offers in *De Civitate Dei* 10.6 that seems to locate the essence of sacrifice (both Christ's and ours) not precisely in suffering but in the love with which the soul in suffering unites itself with God. And finally, despite apparent reservations about seeing Christ's abasement as a humbling of God, Augustine sees the death of Christ, the just one, as the beginning of our own becoming just.

The ecclesiological aspect of soteriology is particularly strong in Augustine, and that not solely under the aspect of the mediatorship of Christ as head of the Church, but also under the aspect of the universal mediatorship of Christ. As head of the Church, Christ is constantly present and active as author and priest of the sacraments. Then, depicting Christ as universal mediator, although Augustine shows he is still within the African tradition of 'no salvation outside the Church', he is, perhaps paradoxically, constantly reminding us of the universalist implications of the fact that the Word became incarnate, suffered, died, rose and sent his Spirit among us for the salvation of *all* humankind. Overall, Augustine, far more perhaps than the other fathers, allows, and indeed insists, that his theology is inspired by, grounded on, and shaped by the Bible and by the apostolic teaching mediated to him in the Christian Church.

CHALCEDON (451) AND ITS AFTERMATH

Leading up to the Council of Chalcedon (451), the denial of a human soul in Jesus by Apollinarius of Laodicea (*c*.310–*c*.90) had precipitated, soteriologically, a vigorous defence of the full human nature of Jesus; one that emphasized the traditional axiom:[21] *What was not assumed was not redeemed.* After the ensuing massive Christological dispute over the 'monophysite question',[22] begun by the conflict between Nestorius (after 351–after 451) and Cyril of Alexandria (the eventual winner) over the issue of the unity of Christ, a key outcome was actually Nestorius' insight that questions of unity and duality in Christ were not on the same level.

---

[21]First argued by Origen (see *Heracl.,* 7; *Com.Matt,* 12. 29; *Cels.,* 4.19); and then explicated by Gregory of Nazianzus in his *Epistle 101 to Cledonius.*
[22]After the Word 'became one' with his flesh did one speak of 'one nature after the union'? or two? (human and divine-intimately joined but not with one subsumed in the other).

This set up the complex question of the unity of Christ to be thrashed out by the three major antique theological traditions, the Alexandrian, the Antiochian and the Latin; with their respective champions: Cyril of Alexandria (d. 444), Theodore of Mopsuestia (c.350–428) and Pope Leo the Great (d. 461).[23]

Theodore's soteriology, while flowing from a wide variety of sources, is clearly centered in Christ, the 'Assumed Man' (*homo assumptus*), in whom the divinity of the Word and the humanity of Jesus, both clearly distinct and forever one, is where God brings together all creation in a union that will be complete only in the final universal resurrection.[24] But here and now, the Easter mystery, the *transitus* of Christians to their destined fulfillment is already anticipated; for here Christ has already become both the model and the guarantee of eternal fulfillment – the *homo assumptus* now being the living model of all loving union with God, having actually been, in his earthly life, the head and renewer of all Christians and indeed of all creation.

Then, with Cyril of Alexandria (d. 444) appropriating the rich tradition behind him and sharpening his own position in argument with the Antiochians, especially Nestorius, we see him developing a soteriology of the real union of God with humanity that brought him beyond all that had gone before.[25] A summary of his position could read:

> In order to renew all things in himself the Word did not enter into an already constituted human being, but instead, the Word itself became human while neither mixing or confusing the divine and the human nor ceasing to be God.

This indicates Cyril's preference for an ontic concept of the mediatorship of Christ as well as his concern to express the union of Christ (both with the Father and with us) in realistic terms. In blunt language, God himself died for us. An explicitly Trinitarian summary of this might read:

> In that the Incarnate Word itself communicates the Holy Spirit, that Word becomes the priest who, by means of the Holy Spirit, leads human beings to the Father.

Leo the Great (pope 440–61) marks the end (at least in the West where his teaching served as a kind of completion) of the formal Christological debates.[26] His theology, acclaimed as orthodox in 451 at Chalcedon (it had actually been quite traditional since before the time of Augustine) condemns the Monophysitism of Eutyches (c.

---

[23]Further, see Studer, *Soteriologie In der Schrift und Patristik*, pp. 175–6.

[24]See Studer, *Soteriologie In der Schrift und Patristik*, pp. 181–90; see also in Hainthaler et al., *Für Uns und für Unser Heil*: Daniel Buda, 'Die soteriologischen Aspekte der anti-apollinaristischen Polemik in den Katechetischen Homilien Theodors von Mopsuestia und in den Taufkatechesen des Johannes Chrysostomos', pp. 113–25.

[25]See Studer, *Soteriologie In der Schrift und Patristik*, pp. 190–200.

[26]Ibid., pp. 200–12; see also in Hainthaler et al., *Für Uns und für Unser Heil*: Daria Morozova, 'Theodoret of Cyrus and Leo the Great: 'In Different Languages' on the Same Salvation', pp. 245–55; and Theresia Hainthaler, 'Soteriologie in der Definition von Chalcedon und im Tomus Leonis', pp. 257–67.

378 – 454) and emphasizes Christ's unity of person as well as his consubstantiality with *both* his heavenly Father *and* his earthly mother. The union and distinction of these two substantialities have since then been generally considered to be central to orthodoxy.

Many claim that Leo's crowning achievement and influence lay in his liturgical preaching where, in line with the wide tradition of mystagogical catecheses before him, he demonstrates how the mystery of Jesus' active, personal, saving presence, transcending ordinary time-space differences, remains continuously present in the liturgy and sacraments of the Church. Thus, what Jesus used to teach and do while living bodily among us, he now does through his sacramental bodily presence in the Church.

A BYZANTINE SYNTHESIS

The final, culminating figure in our survey of patristic soteriology, Maximus the Confessor (580–662), appropriated with remarkable depth and breadth what had been developing in both East and West and addressed what still needed to be thrashed out in the centuries following the Council of Chalcedon.[27] That 'thrashing out' set various defenders of Chalcedon (usually those in line with Cyril of Alexandria) against those with dyo-physite tendencies (usually those in line with Nestorius). What helped ultimately to bring about a mostly happy ending was the common faith of all concerned. On the one hand, those on the Chalcedonian side could not resist the charm of theopaschite-sounding formulae like 'One of the Trinity suffered'; and on the other hand, those siding with the Monophysites really couldn't reject the doctrine of twofold consubstantiality since even they saw that only someone who was true God *and* who had actually become one of us, could bring us to salvation. That enabled a teacher and exemplifier of a mystical theology of the cross, such as Maximus, to push all oppositions towards ultimate unity in a cosmic vision of a suffering and glorified Christ.

In addition, because of his connection to the monastic traditions of his time, Maximus's view of Christian life was, from the outset, completely centered on the Incarnation, most specifically on the insight that Christ, in his whole human-historical existence, has lived out in advance, for us, what Christian life means, such that all are called to participate in the death, burial and resurrection of Christ. In other words, Christ's 'going home' to the Father has already, in an enabling way, anticipated our doing the same.

Grounding that calling/destiny is the fact that Christ is the summation/consummation of all being, a 'fact' that Urs von Balthasar summarizes with the pregnant phrase: 'cosmic liturgy'. This is a theological vision that has now become possible because of the maturation of Chalcedonian theology and faith that had

---

[27]See Studer, *Soteriologie In der Schrift und Patristik*, pp. 212–23; See also in Hainthaler et al., *Für Uns und für Unser Heil*: T. Tollefsen, 'St Maximus the Confessor's Doctrine of Deification', pp. 297–301.

taken place in the two centuries since that Council was first held in 451. That 'matured' view thinks of all created reality as being involved in one or more of the following five distinctions: (a) the entirety of created being as distinct from uncreated being; (b) the thinkable as distinct from the sense-perceptible; (c) heaven as distinct from the earth; (d) paradise as distinct from the inhabited earth; (e) man as distinct from woman.

The nexus of these all-encompassing distinctions, which Maximus apparently owes to Gregory of Nazianzen, seems to be the theological key with which Maximus at least begins to unlock for us the mystery of soteriology.[28] Because humanity, indeed the human being precisely *qua human*, finds itself in the midst of and ultimately involved with all this created reality, it thus has the potential capacity to unite it all in itself. This situation is at the heart of the 'work' of Maximus, namely, opening up the *why* of the Incarnation. For the whole meaning of creation as being united in God is included and disclosed in the Incarnation where this unifying 'work' has already begun to take place, namely, on the Cross and in the Ascension. But what has already taken place in Christ now needs to be completed in us. This is the 'work' of the Body of Christ, the soteriology of a cosmic liturgy being performed in heaven and on earth, in and with Christ, by all those called to take part in Christ's death and resurrection.

CONCLUDING REMARKS

Rather than summarize a text that is already a summary, let me first acknowledge how traditional this is. For there is nothing radically new in my work here except perhaps, as we fervently hope, its usefulness as a platform that encourages us to look ahead. Indeed, what the pessimist sees may well be only vagueness and uncertainty, but what the optimist may see is excitingly open-ended. This is largely because commonly available information technology enables even the ordinary scholar to accomplish in relatively few years feats of research and synthesis to which the scholarly giants of former times (on whose shoulders we gratefully stand) had to devote a lifetime of work.

BIBLIOGRAPHY

de Andia, Y. '"Opus Spiritus salus carnis": Le salut de la chair selon Irénée de Lyon', in T. Hainthaler, F. Mali, G. Emmenegger and M. L. Ostermann (eds), *Für Uns und für Unser Heil: Soteriologie in Ost und West*, 53–65. Innsbruck and Wien: Tyrolia-Verlag, 2014.

Balthasar, H. Urs von. *Cosmic Liturgy: The Universe According to Maximus the Confessor*, trans. Brian E. Daley, SJ. San Francisco, CA: Ignatius Press, 2003.

---

[28]See Studer, *Soteriologie In der Schrift und Patristik*, p. 219; and Daniel Munteanu, 'Theosis and Perichoresis in den Theologien von Gregor von Nazianz und Maximus Confessor', in Hainthaler et al., *Für Uns und für Unser Heil*, pp. 389–403.

Buda, D. 'Die soteriologischen Aspekte der anti-apollinaristischen Polemik in den Katechetischen Homilien Theodors von Mopsuestia und in den Taufkatechesen des Johannes Chrysostomos', in T. Hainthaler et al. (eds), *Für Uns und für Unser Heil: Soteriologie in Ost und West*, 113–25. Innsbruck and Wien: Tyrolia-Verlag, 2014.

Clancy, F. G. 'Redemption', in A. D. Fitzgerald et al. (eds), *Augustine Through the Ages*, 702–4. Grand Rapids, MI: Eerdmans, 1999.

Daly, R. J. *Sacrifice in Pagan and Christian Antiquity*. London and New York: T&TClark, 2019.

Eikrem, A. *God as Sacrificial Love: A Systematic Exploration of a Controversial Notion*. London and New York: Bloomsbury Academic, 2018.

Hainthaler, T. 'Soteriologie in der Definition von Chalcedon und im Tomus Leonis', in T. Hainthaler, F. Mali, G. Emmenegger and M. L. Ostermann (eds), *Für Uns und für Unser Heil: Soteriologie in Ost und West*, 257–67. Innsbruck and Wien: Tyrolia-Verlag, 2014.

Morozova, D. 'Theodoret of Cyrus and Leo the Great: "In Different Languages" on the Same Salvation', in T. Hainthaler et al. (eds), *Für Uns und für Unser Heil: Soteriologie in Ost und West*, 245–55. Innsbruck/Wien: Tyrolia-Verlag, 2014.

Munteanu, D. 'Theosis and Perichoresis in den Theologien von Gregor von Nazianz und Maximus Confessor', in T. Hainthaler et al. (eds), *Für Uns und für Unser Heil: Soteriologie in Ost und West*, 389–403. Innsbruck and Wien: Tyrolia-Verlag, 2014.

Russell, N. *The Doctrine of Deification in the Greek Patristic Tradition. Oxford Early Christian Studies*. Oxford: Oxford University Press, 2006.

Schmaus, M., Grillmeier, A., Scheffczyk, L. and Seybold, M. (eds). *Handbuch der Dogmengeschichte* [especially: Band III, Faszikel 2a: Studer, B., (with the cooperation of Brian Daley) *Soteriologie In der Schrift und Patristik*]. Freiburg, Basel and Wien: Herder and Co., 1978.

Stoyadinov, M. 'The Soteriological Argument in the Context of the Iconoclastic Controversy: St John Damascene and St Theodore the Studite', in T. Hainthaler et al. (eds), *Für Uns und für Unser Heil: Soteriologie in Ost und West*, 303–11. Innsbruck and Wien: Tyrolia-Verlag, 2014.

Studer, B., 'Soteriologie In der Schrift und Patristik', in M. Schmaus, A. Grillmeier, L. Scheffczyk, M. Seybold and E. Naab (eds), *Handbuch der Dogmengeschichte*, Vol. 3. Part 2a. Freiburg, Basel and Wien: Herder and Co., 1978.

Tollefsen, T. 'St Maximus the Confessor's Doctrine of Deification', in T. Hainthaler et al. (eds), *Für Uns und für Unser Heil: Soteriologie in Ost und West*, 297–301. Innsbruck and Wien: Tyrolia-Verlag, 2014.

PART IV

Under Christian emperors

CHAPTER 20

From the community of martyrs to the church of the empire

GIULIO MASPERO

INTRODUCTION

The relationship between the early Christian communities, exposed to the danger of martyrdom, and the imperial church, can be approached in sociological and dialectical terms, following the trend of modern studies linked to colonialism. Some common points are undeniably present, such as the existence of a collective memory, forged constructively in different historical situations, including political ones, therefore with reference to the empire,[1] but the risk of anachronism is also very high. Thus, when speaking of early Christianity, it may be useful to try to assume the epistemological perspective of the fathers of the church themselves, who tried to relate and recognize the relationships between the different moments of history and the different truths found in it, starting from faith in the presence and authority of God over history itself.[2] In this way, both the historical and the theological approaches will be used. This will lead us, first, to try to show how the relationship between martyrdom and Roman Empire is already inherent in Scripture, since it reflects a fundamental element introduced by the narrative of creation and the criticism of the idols in the self-awareness of the people of Israel with respect to the conception of power that characterized the pagan religions (a). Then, we shall present the phenomenon of persecution and martyrdom in the first centuries AD from the stated perspective as a form of coherent development with respect to the foundation of Christian identity, in an attempt to avoid any sociological reductionism or hermeneutical anachronism (b). Next, we shall try to show how the development of theological understanding changed the relationship with the

---

[1]See the discussion on memory and Empire in D. Joslyn-Siemiatkoski, *Christian Memories of the Maccabean Martyrs* (New York: Palgrave-Macmillan, 2009), p. 3.

[2]See Ch. Gnilka, *Chrêsis: die Methode der Kirchenväter im Umgang mit der antiken Kultur: Der Begriff des "rechten Gebrauchs"* (Basel: Schwabe Verlag, 2012).

empire in late antiquity, in particular with regard to the new position on religious and personal freedom (c), together with the complex historical events that followed until the emergence of a real ambivalence in developments post-Constantine (d). Finally, we shall try to show how the relationship between the first community of martyrs and the imperial church of the following centuries can be read from the perspective of the *use* (*chrêsis*) developed in the Christian sphere of the universalism inherent in the very idea of the Roman Empire to express the universality of the salvific proposal of the faith itself.[3]

SCRIPTURE AND VICTIMS: BIBLICAL CONTEXT

René Girard pointed out how the Judeo-Christian revelation has revealed the mimetic mechanism inherent in the structure of the human being who is constantly trying to resolve, through sacrifice, the social conflicts caused by converging on the same (limited) objects of the (infinite) desire of human beings who are always thirsty for life.[4] This calls into question three fundamental dimensions of power, each of which refers to an aspect of the religious phenomenon: the cosmic dimension, the social dimension and the properly supernatural dimension of the divine. In primitive thought, these elements were interconnected in a profound and somehow inextricable way. One thinks of the connection introduced by Marcus Terentius Varro in the first century BC between the mythical theology of the poets, the natural theology of the philosophers and the civil theology of the peoples (*mythicon appellant, quomaxime utuntur poetae; physicon, quo philosophi; civil, quo populi*).[5] The gods were divided into the Olympic gods and the gods most directly linked to the earth, but, in both cases, they were symbols of cosmic forces. Thus, the existence of a city or community was linked to the favour of their divinities which then appeared as the foundation of social life. This was not without conflicts, which the Greek genius had the courage and intellectual strength to represent, as in the case of the tragedies. Here the laws of the cosmos and the gods, as well as those of the *polis* and the family, collide, generating victims of which Oedipus and Antigone, with their homonymous tragedies, are shining examples. The extreme value of Girard's contribution was to show how, in the Bible, this confusion of powers is definitively resolved, revealing the innocence of the victim in the face of the society which, to solve the internal tension, lynches the scapegoat.[6] The point is that infinite human desire always clashes with the limit of the individual's own life and existence. This puts in crisis the relationship between

---

[3]Cf. E. von Ivánka, *Rhomäerreich und Gottesvolk. Das Glaubens-, Staats- und Volksbewusstsein der Byzantiner und seine Auswirkung auf die ostkirchlich-europäische Geisteshaltung* (Freiburg im Breisgau: Alber, 1968).

[4]See, among other works, R. Girard, *The Scapegoat* (Baltimore, MD: Johns Hopkins University Press, 1989).

[5]Cf. Varro, *Frag.*, 7, in Augustine, *Civ.*, VI, 5.

[6]Cf. R. Girard, *Wissenschaft und christlicher Glaube* (Tübingen: Mohr Siebeck, 2007).

the one and the many that afflicts human thought and life from the confrontation between Parmenides and Plato which was formulated in a masterful way in the *Sophist*. As Girard has shown, the religious act itself presents itself as an attempt to manage the limit of the finite life of the whole by sacrificing the individual. There is an evident relevance in all this for martyrdom and for its relationship with the empire which, in its absolutism and universalism, always clashes with the life of the individual.

This confrontation runs through the entire biblical text, from the conflict between Cain and Abel onwards, with the sign imposed by God on the former to stop the victimization mechanism (Gen. 4.15), to the Acts of the Apostles with the proto-martyr Stephen (Acts 7.54–8.1) and the conversion of Saul into Paul (Acts 9.1-8). Starting from the narrative of original sin, the confrontation is always with the monarchy of God, even when it is understood as an imposition. The case of Adam and Eve's children is extremely significant because Cain was a farmer while Abel was a shepherd, roles that imply a mutual relationship and therefore a first form of sociality. The comparison with the different reaction of the Creator, who, as such, is the divine power at the absolute origin of the cosmos, puts the fraternal relationship in crisis, leading to the first innocent victim in history, sacrificed to solve the social tension. From the theological-political point of view, this is an essential step, because the scriptural text already highlights a principle of separation of the political monarchy from the religious one.

Abram's first confrontation with the Egyptian Pharaoh (Gen. 12.10-19) is also significant because the spousal relationship with Sarai is sacrificed by the patriarch to save his own life. Once again, however, the text shows how the divine monarchy is superior to the political one, unmasking, through a process marked again by some element of tragic mythology, the injustice of the solution implemented by the patriarch.

The confrontation between Pharaoh and God was evidently to reach a highly dramatic moment with the Mosaic Exodus and the events that led to it. The killing of the male sons of the Jews can be considered a form of proto-martyrdom in combination with the death of the firstborn of the Egyptians (Exod. 12.29-30), later read in the patristic period as a prophetic sign of the Cross of the Only Begotten Son of God. The ambivalence of the monarchic principle with Saul and David is so evident as to present the scriptural narrative as a literary and historical *unicum*, inasmuch as the sins of a king are presented not only to justify a dynastic change but to relativize it, pointing again to fidelity to monotheism as the only foundation of the political principle. Both historically and theologically, this passage is essential because the political monarchy is founded on the religious one, but not identified with it.

The second Babylonian exile is a further moment of confrontation with the absolutist claim of an empire. This proves ambivalent, however, because the initial political oppression was to be followed by the awareness on the part of Israel that even the foreign and pagan sovereign can become an instrument of the one God. Therefore, with the Maccabees and their confrontation with the Seleucid Antiochus IV Epiphanes, martyrdom was to be placed at the centre of the political theology of the Old Testament.[7] It can be said that the universalism achieved by the enterprise of Alexander the Macedonian leaves as a legacy a cultural universalism that introduces into the political monarchy a dialectical principle towards the religious one. The Hellenized sovereign thus enters into conflict with the faithful Jew, since the former has lost the distinction between divine and political power which had been gained laboriously by the people of Israel.[8] The clash comes to an intensity that would be tragic without faith in the resurrection that, precisely at this moment, is fully formulated as a theological consequence of creation from nothing (2 Macc. 7.28). The episode of the three young men in the furnace in the book of Daniel 3 is part of the same context, even though it is characterized by a non-martyrial outcome. In the path thus outlined, one can notice a growing religious universalism which, precisely in the clash with the political one, leads to a spiritualisation of the messianic claim, an immediate narrative preparation for the New Testament.

The contribution of the Old Testament is essential, therefore, for understanding the relationship between martyrdom and empire. This will reach its most significant moment with the Cross of Christ, where the claim of universalism that arises from the theological element was to be confronted directly, not with Roman universalism but with the religious authorities of the time and their conception of the relationship between politics and messianism. Jesus' attitude towards the tax-collectors reveals, in fact, that the monarchy of his Father is always superior to the collaborationism and corruption of those who deal with imperial power and its representatives. Instead, it is the way of the cross that makes the disciples run away, that is, the mismatch between political expectations and the concrete realization of the kingship of Christ. This is confirmed paradoxically by the crucifixion itself; it is the outcome of Pilate's judgement which stands as a definitive solution to the *crisis*, in the etymological sense of *judgement*, thanks to the revelation of the Father's monarchy through the Cross of Jesus, who voluntarily surrenders himself to reveal his own eternal filiation and, in this way, defeat death. The claim of power is thus based on the authority of the universalism of the salvation offered to everybody, that is, the foundation of the Christian community and its mission to baptize all nations (cf. Mt. 28.16-20).

The Easter event is also intentionally presented as a paradigm in the narrative of the first martyrdom in Acts 7.[9] Stephen, in fact, at a time between 33 and 35, retraces the steps of the Master. Finally, with Saul's conversion on the road to Damascus, we are witnessing the transformation of the persecutor into an apostle. Paul's own appeal to Caesar, in the name of his Roman citizenship (cf. Acts 25:1-12), plays a fundamental role, at the same time theological and historical, because

---

[7]On the related texts and their time of composition, see R. Ziadé, *Les martyrs Maccabées: de l'histoire juive au culte chrétien. Les homélies de Grégoire de Nazianze et de Jean Chrysostome*, SupVCh, vol. 80 (Leiden: E.J. Brill, 2007), pp. 29–48.

[8]On Jewish martyrs and the difference from Christianity, see: S. Shepkaru, *Jewish Martyrs in the Pagan and Christian Worlds* (Cambridge: Cambridge University Press, 2005).

[9]C. R. Moss, *The Other Christs: Imitating Jesus in Ancient Christian Ideologies of Martyrdom* (Oxford: Oxford University Press, 2010), p. 34.

it marks the definitive meeting of Christian religious universalism with imperial political universalism.

The doctrine of creation, which made it possible to distinguish divine power from cosmic and social power, is summarized in the salvific claim of the Risen One which spreads through the streets of the Roman Empire, between the light and dark of spiritual transformation and persecution which intertwine in the early centuries.[10]

CHRISTIANITY AND PERSECUTION

It would be erroneous either to think of the first three centuries of the Christian era as one of continuous persecution or to deny the phenomenon.[11] As Marta Sordi has shown, in fact, moments of crisis alternated with long periods of relative stability.[12] It would be equally reductive to identify the moments of conflict with those of political crisis. Actually, as had already happened in both the Greek and Roman spheres, the phenomena of persecution could emerge just when a form of government was stronger,[13] such as in democratic Athens, which, within less than a hundred years, between 415 and 324 BC, tried both Socrates and Aristotle after Protagoras, or in republican Rome, with the repression of the Bacchanalia in 186 BC.

The point, as seen in the previous section, is that from the pagan perspective it was impossible to separate the political and religious dimensions, unlike today.[14] However, initially, the Christians did not represent a danger to the stability of the Roman Empire. Indeed, Tiberius' policy of toleration, who, like Claudius later, refused the imperial cult,[15] was intended to treat the 'new Jewish' sect (i.e., Christians) in the same way as previously. The emperor presented the senate with a proposal to that effect. It was rejected, however, and, in fact, this resulted in the declaration of Christianity as an unlawful superstition (superstitio illicita).[16]

The 'it is not lawful to be Christian' (non licet esse christianos) began to play a role for the safety of Christians in 62. In this year James, the brother of the Lord, was put to death in Jerusalem, but only in a moment of vacatio of the Roman

---

[10]The Trinitarian dimension of the Christian confession is evident from the beginning in this context, see P. Prete, 'Confessioni Trinitarie in alcuni Atti di martiri dei sec. II (Giustino, Apollonio, Policarpo)', Aug 13 (1973): 469–82.

[11]For a comparative approach, see G. Filoramo, Il martirio cristiano: una prospettiva comparata (Pisa: Fabrizio Serra, 2010).

[12]Cf. M. Sordi, I Cristiani e l'impero romano (Milan: Jaca Book, 2011), p. 11.

[13]See M.-F. Baslez, Les persécutions dans l'Antiquité. Victimes, héros, martyrs (Paris: Fayard, 2007), p. 392.

[14]On this period and the related texts, see D. Boyarin, Dying for God: Martyrdom and the Making of Christianity and Judaism (Stanford, CA: Stanford University Press, 1999) and M. Lapidge, The Roman Martyrs: Introduction, Translations and Commentary (Oxford: Oxford University Press, 2018). For a synthesis, see J. A. McGuckin, The Path of Christianity: The First Thousand Years (Downers Grove, IL: IVP Academic, 2017), pp. 117–34.

[15]See Tacitus, Ann., 4, 38.

[16]M. Sordi is in favour of the authenticity of Tertullian's news, see her I Cristiani e l'Impero romano, pp. 27–9.

governor.[17] Nero had recourse to a decree of the senate (*senatus consultum*) and started the ferocious persecution linked to the fire in Rome in 64,[18] followed by the martyrdom of Peter and Paul. Later, under Domitian, who reigned between 81 and 96 and demanded divinization for himself, Christians continued to be persecuted along with the Stoics, especially at the level of the aristocracy. This ended only with Nerva's reign, which began in 96.

Under Trajan, however, the persecutions resumed, and extended to those who did not offer religious sacrifices. Extremely significant is the testimony of Pliny the Younger, who, from Bithynia, where he was governor at the beginning of the second century, asked the emperor for instructions on the repression of Christians. He wrote that he had never had to deal with such accusations before and that he did not know how to treat the variety of ages and situations. In particular, he said that he did not know whether crimes linked to being Christian or simply bearing the name of a Christian should be condemned.[19] The judge seemed uncertain because he saw in the new religion nothing more than 'a debased and boundless superstition' (*superstitionem pravam et immodicam*).[20] Thus, after having ordered the accused to recant three times, he condemned to death those who resisted, for the simple act of disobedience and obstinacy (*obstinationem*).[21] Pliny's inquisitorial technique was very simple and consisted in demanding that Christians 'worshipped your statues and images of the gods, and blasphemed Christ' (*et imaginem tuam deorumque simulacra venerati sunt et Christo male dixerunt*).[22] The words of the governor reveal an astonishment that can also account for the doubt and the request to Rome:

> They maintained, however, that all that their guilt or error involved was that they were accustomed to assemble at dawn on a fixed day, to sing a hymn antiphonally to Christ as God (*carmenque Christo quasi deo dicere secum invicem*), and to bind themselves by an oath (*sacramento*), not for the commission of some crime, but to avoid acts of theft, brigandage, and adultery, not to break their word, and not to keep money deposited with them when asked for it. When these rites were completed, it was their custom to depart, and then to assemble again to take food, which was however common and harmless. They had ceased, they said, to do this following my edict, by which, in accordance with your instructions, I had outlawed the existence of secret brotherhoods.[23]

Pliny reported how the measures had been effective until then, because the phenomenon, which had been extending from the cities to the countryside, was

---

[17]Ibid., p. 22.
[18]See Tacitus, *Ann.,* 15, 44.
[19]Pliny, *Ep.,* 10, 96.2.
[20]Ibid., 96.8.
[21]Ibid., 96.4.
[22]Ibid., 96.6.
[23]Ibid., 96.7.

now receding, so much so that the temples were filling up again and the meat of idols was being sold.[24]

The social and political value that emerges from the lives of the first Christians is evident. The simultaneous reference to the statue of the emperor and those of the idols, although not necessarily implying the divinization of Trajan, demonstrates the inseparability of the worship of the gods and loyalty to the empire. We should also note the importance of the name of a Christian around which the whole question seems to revolve, so much so that blaspheming the name of Christ is the definitive criterion for absolution. It is also interesting how Trajan, in his reply, states that Pliny had proceeded correctly and that there could be no univocal procedure for the case of Christians. They should not be sought, but only punished if accused and found guilty, encouraging the possibility of repentance and leaving aside anonymous accusations.[25] This response reveals the public and social dimension of the problem posed by Christians. The problem is not their crimes or their names but the crisis they cause socially by their obstinacy to renounce civic religion in the name of personal religion. It is the confrontation with imperial absolutism and universalism which has begun. However, Christians are not yet opposed as an unlawful church (*collegium illicitum*), that is, at the institutional level.

This happened with Marcus Aurelius who allowed the search for Christians. It seems that another reason for the position of the philosopher emperor was the anti-Roman attitude of the Montanists.[26] Thus, between 175 and 177, Athenagoras, Melito, Apollinarius of Hierapolis and Miltiades composed their apologies, inaugurating a kind of theological thought aimed at justifying the possibility of the existence of Christians on the basis of universal reasons that could be shared with philosophy, that is, on the common ground of natural religion. In 177, in fact, persecutions had taken place in Vienne and Lyon, together with the deportation of the Christians of Rome to the mines in Sardinia. The persecutions then spread to Africa and Cappadocia until, in the last years of his reign, Marcus Aurelius softened and introduced rules aimed at getting Christians out of hiding as well as penalties for those who accused them unjustly, a stratagem commonly used to eliminate personal enemies. With Commodus and next with the Severan dynasty, the places of worship were returned, and a situation of de facto toleration was disturbed only by small-scale, local persecutions. At this juncture the spread of Christianity reached the court to such a degree that, in 235, on the death of Alexander Severus, Maximinus the Thracian began a real purge.

Eusebius states that Philip the Arab, emperor from 244 to 249, became a Christian,[27] although the information is doubtful. Certainly the possibility of living one's faith undisturbed during his reign was remarkable and totally different from what happened with his successor Decius. Between 249 and 250, the latter was

---

[24]Ibid., 96.10.
[25]Ibid., 97.
[26]Sordi, *I Cristiani e l'Impero romano*, pp. 111–12.
[27]Eusebius, *HE.*, 6.34.

the author of an edict that made the sacrifice to the gods mandatory for everybody along with a booklet certifying it. This gave rise to the phenomenon of the *lapsi*, that is, Christians who asked to return to the church after having given in during the persecution.

With Valerian, in August 257, the attack on Christians at the institutional level began through the requirement for bishops and priests to sacrifice to the gods, under the threat of forced labour, and the prohibition of access to cemeteries and meetings on pain of death. The following year, an imperial rescript, ratified by a decree of the senate (*senatus consultum*), ordered the execution of bishops, priests and deacons, along with that of Christian senators and notables, together with the confiscation of property. In August, the clergy of Rome were decimated. The quantitative and qualitative level of the persecution also reveals that Christianity had spread to the highest social levels.

In 260, the drama of events led to Gallienus' edict of tolerance, with the restitution of property confiscated from the church and the declaration of Christianity as an unlawful religion (*religio licita*),[28] followed by forty years of peace.

During the reign of Diocletian, however, persecution resumed from the direction of the military:[29] in fact, the Christians seemed to be endangering the peace of the gods (*pax deorum*) in a historical context where the war effort had increased.[30] Thus, at the turn of the third and fourth centuries, the purge of Christians from the army took place. The first edict of persecution bears the date of 24 February 303 and ordered the demolition of churches, one of which was built directly in front of the imperial palace of Nicomedia, the destruction of sacred books and the confiscation of properties, along with the prohibition of meetings. In the summer of 303, a second edict ordered the imprisonment of the clergy. The popular dimension of persecution is witnessed by the introduction of the Apocryphal Acts of Pilate as a compulsory text in schools. In the autumn, because of the overcrowding of prisons, a third edict proclaimed an amnesty for those who sacrificed to the gods. Finally, at the beginning of 304, a fourth edict was issued which triggered the general persecution, imposing the test of sacrifice on everyone. This universal obligation was reiterated in the East in 306 and 309 by Maximinus and Galerius.

In April 311, on his deathbed, with the edict of Serdica, Galerius granted toleration and returned the places of worship. The following year Maximinus granted an amnesty until the edict of Milan in 313. This was the law with which Constantine, who had defeated Maxentius and reunited the empire after the period of the tetrarchies, introduced freedom of worship.

Historical data suggest that Christians cannot be defined as a foreign body in the empire,[31] nor that we can understand the aversion to them as a consequence of their

---

[28]Ibid., 7,13.

[29]See J. Leoni, 'Martiri e soldati in Eusebio di Cesarea', *RHE* 110 (2015): 5–30.

[30]On the role of pagan oracles in promoting persecution, see C. Addey, *Divination and Theurgy in Neoplatonism: Oracles of the Gods* (Farnham: Ashgate, 2014), pp. 89–90.

[31]A thesis that seems to be supported by the classical E. Gibbon, *The History of the Decline and Fall of the Roman Empire*. Penguin Classics (London: Abridged Ed edition, 2000).

rejection of the state, a phenomenon that characterized only the Montanists, but not the great church. Before converting to this heresy, Tertullian himself reported that Christians used to pray to obtain from God 'a safe Empire, strong armies and a world at peace' (*imperium securum, exercitus fortes, orbem quietum*).[32]

Yet it is a fact that martyrs are concentrated in the first three centuries, when Christianity was still considered an unlawful religion (*religio illicita*).[33] They are a completely new phenomenon that surprised contemporaries, who recognized the difference between the self-sacrifice of Christians, who did not agree to renounce their faith at the cost of their lives, and the death of Socrates or other similar cases. The Athenian philosopher is mentioned in some texts related to the martyrs but only in an apologetic key to defend the reasonableness of the act.[34] In fact, Tacitus despised the behaviour of those Christians who suffered death on account of their faith because, in his view, they loathed life.[35] From a Stoic perspective, the emperor and philosopher, Marcus Aurelius, did not understand them.[36] Justin, on the other hand, claimed to have converted precisely because he was struck by their testimony.[37]

The novelty is also revealed by the semantic shift of the term 'martyr' itself which, in the second half of the second century, acquired a new meaning with respect to its original sense of 'witness'.[38] The core of the question and its specificity is that the choice of Christians was framed in a well-developed theology of the Resurrection. Martyrdom was, therefore, interpreted as a manifestation of Christ's power over death of which the martyrs themselves were recognized as witnesses. Thus, they began to be considered as intercessors.

This was the foundation of a Christian universalism that broke the intimate connection between civil and mythical religion, marking an absolute novelty and discontinuity in the history of human thought.

THEOLOGICAL SIGNIFICANCE

In order to understand the historical events linking the community of martyrs with their final outcome, it is essential also to keep in mind the historical-theological fact of the existence of a true spiritual rebirth in the pagan world itself between the second and third centuries. The spread of Christianity in both the popular and the higher classes had a profound influence, demonstrated by the persecutions themselves. Between the end of 302 and 303, the presence in the Council of Nicomedia of Neoplatonic scholars, such as Hierocles, philosopher and

---

[32]Tertullian, *Apol.*, 30,4.
[33]See W. Rordorf's article 'Martyr-Martyrdom', in *Encyclopedia of Ancient Christianity*, ed. A. Di Berardino, II (Downers Grove, IL: IVP Academic, 2014), pp. 700–1.
[34]See *Martyrium Pionii* 17 and *Acta Apollonii*, 41.
[35]See Tacitus, *Ann.*, 15, 44,6.
[36]Marcus Aurelius, *Med.*, XI, 3,3.
[37]See Justin, *2 Apol.*, 12.
[38]See G. Bowersock, *Martyrdom and Rome* (Cambridge: Cambridge University Press, 1998), p. 5.

governor of Bithynia[39] and probably Porphyry,[40] who asked Diocletian to unleash the persecution, is evidence of a confrontation that now assumed the tones of a clash over the danger of a real influence of the 'new' Christian ideas on the religiosity of the people. The gods' peace (*pax deorum*) was perceived, in fact, as intimately linked to the preservation of the custom of the ancients (*mos maiorum*), but political theology had to deal with the influence of a faith like the Christian one according to which God was personal and, therefore, close and capable of being addressed. Inevitably, from a classical perspective in which the supreme divinity was anonymous and devoid of any relationship with human beings, unlike the lowest steps of the hierarchical ladder of the gods, where the emperors themselves, like the heroes, could find a place, we have moved on to a conception in which the relationship with the supreme god was the exclusive prerogative of the emperor himself, while the people had access to the lower divinities. It seems that this is precisely what happened with Diocletian. The emperors did not identify themselves with the gods, therefore, but based their absolute power on an exclusive relationship with them, being called Jupiter's (*Iovius*) or Hercules's (*Herculeus*).

In the case of Constantine, the link between history and theology is particularly evident because Maximian's suicide created a problem of legitimacy over the succession, something which put in crisis precisely the tetrarchy's connection with Jupiter and Hercules. The imperial genealogy required a new principle, one which appeared in Trier, in 310, in the pagan panegyric of an anonymous rhetorician from Autun.[41] This is Panegyric VII from the Budé collection of Latin Panegyrics published by Édouard Galletier in 1952.[42] The text links Constantine, and, therefore, his father, Constantius Chlorus, to the emperor Claudius Gothicus, who had reigned for a short time and was remembered almost exclusively for a victory over the Goths near Naissun, Constantine's birthplace. The latter could thus have boasted of a more illustrious birth than any of the other claimants to the throne, although it seems that he used this argument only against Licinius after 316.[43] This panegyric is the only source that narrates the pagan vision that Constantine is supposed to have had during his visit to a famous sanctuary of Apollo, probably

---

[39]M. B. Simmons, *Arnobius of Sicca. Religious Conflict and Competition in the Age of Diocletian* (Oxford: Clarendon, 1995), pp. 25–6.

[40]Lactantius refers to the participation of two philosophers, the first of whom is mentioned explicitly while the second is defined as 'high priest of philosophy' (cf. Lactantius, *Inst.*, 5,2), a term used by Porphyry himself to define the philosopher in *Absti.*, II, 49,1. See R. L. Wilken, *The Christians as the Romans Saw Them* (New Haven, CT: Yale Univ. Press, 2003), pp. 134–5.

[41]See S. N. C. Lieu and D. Montserrat (eds), *From Constantine to Julian Pagan and Byzantine Views: A Source History* (London and New York: Routledge, 1996), p. 66.

[42]É. Balletier, *Panégyriques latins*, vol. II (Paris: Les Belles Lettres, 1952). About the panegyricus of 310, see: B. Müller-Rettig, *Der Panegyricus des Jahres 310 auf Konstantin den Grossen: Übersetzung und historisch-philologischer Kommentar* (Stuttgart: F. Steiner Verlag, 1990).

[43]See T. Grünewald, *Constantinus Maximus Augustus: Heerschaftspropaganda in der zeitgenössischen Überlieferung* (Stuttgart: F. Steiner, 1990), p. 50.

in Grand (Vosges), on the border between Belgica and Germania Superior.[44] There, Apollo himself and the goddess Victoria were said to have appeared to the future emperor, congratulating him on his successes. The most probable reason for the appearance of this vision was the need to find a dynastic alternative to the patronage of Hercules after the annihilation of Maximianus Herculius. Beyond the question as to whether this apparition was real or a simple rhetorical artifice, a question that escapes the possibilities of investigation by historical science, one can certainly deduce from everything that, in the context of Roman religiosity, the path to the imperial purple had an inescapable theological dimension, which led Constantine to set out in search of the true God.

It has been denied that this search was then fulfilled in the encounter with the Cross shortly before the battle of the Milvian Bridge so that, for some, the pagan vision would have been Constantine's only vision.[45] Marta Sordi has challenged these readings through the analysis of two other pagan panegyrics, that of 313 and 321, defending the authenticity of the emperor's conversion to Christianity.[46] In this case, too, it is not a question of demonstrating the authenticity of a person's conversion but of proving a real discontinuity in the position of the emperor, whose actions manifested a new attitude towards the divinity and towards Christians in particular. Extremely important is the historiographical contribution of Lactantius. Probably writing before 315, he relates Constantine's Christian vision before the battle of the Milvian Bridge. Unlike in Eusebius,[47] Maxentius is not presented as a persecutor, so much so that Chapter 43, dedicated to his clash with Constantine, begins with a reference to Maximinus, as Marta Sordi rightly notes, because he is considered a true enemy of the Christian religion.[48] The clash in Rome, on the other hand, was considered the epilogue of a civil war.[49]

On the eve of the anniversary of Maxentius' assumption of power, on 28 October 313, Constantine received in a dream the instruction to prepare the shields by drawing on them a heavenly sign (*caeleste signum*), described in the transverse expression 'refers to Christ by means of a letter X circumflexed at the top' (*X littera, summo capite circumflexo, Christum in scutis notat*).[50] This can be interpreted as the superimposition of the X with a P, forming the monogram of Christ, or as a cross whose vertical axis has been closed on the right at the top, giving rise again to a P which is superimposed on a horizontal bar that, precisely, forms a cross. Marta Sordi prefers this second possibility, referring also to the testimony of Jerome.[51] This sign cannot be confused with a star or a solar symbol in any way. It should be

[44]On the relation of Constantine with the cult of the sun, see I. Tantillo, 'L'impero della luce. Riflessioni su Costantino e il sole', *Mélanges de l'école française de Rome* 115 (2003): 985–1048.

[45]See H. Grégoire, 'La "conversion" de Constantin', *RUB* 36 (1930-31): 231–72.

[46]See M. Sordi, *Il cristianesimo e Roma* (Bologna: Licinio Cappelli Editore, 1965), pp. 377–404.

[47]Eusebius, *HE.*, 9, 9.

[48]See Sordi, *Il cristianesimo e Roma*, p. 386.

[49]Lactantius, *Mort.*, 44.1.

[50]Ibid., 44.5.

[51]See Sordi, *Il cristianesimo e Roma*, p. 387.

noted that, unlike Eusebius, Lactantius concentrates divine intervention in support of Constantine wholly on the time of the battle of the Milvian Bridge and does not extend it to the entire campaign, as in Eusebius. Lactantius tells how, during the first fierce clash, Maxentius was not present but was participating in Rome in the games for his anniversary. The indignation of the people led him to consult the Sybilline Books (*Libri Sibillini*), from which he was supposed to have received the answer that that day the enemy of the Romans would perish. Going down into battle, Maxentius fell into the Tiber and was definitively overwhelmed. Upon entering Rome, Constantine was proclaimed the first Augustus by the senate, arousing the wrath of Maximinus who claimed that title for himself and who was even more outraged by the wedding between Constance, Constantine's stepsister, and Licinius in Milan.

It seems important to note that Lactantius, not at all enthusiastic about Licinius, seems to give more importance and supernatural value to the victory of the latter over Maximinus, narrating the dream of an angel to the sovereign of the East with the revelation of the prayer to the highest god (*summus deus*) that his soldiers were to recite before the battle. From the point of view of persecution, in fact, the eastern provinces were those most populated by Christians and the ones which had suffered most severely. This seems to give even greater value to the testimony about the conversion of Constantine who was to enter a Rome that was pagan at both the popular and senatorial levels. Unlike Licinius, Constantius Chlorus's son had no political advantage in taking his religious position.

In chapter 45 of *On the Deaths of the Persecutors* (*De mortibus persecutorum*), Lactantius also recounts the marriage in Milan, without, however, explaining the significance of the event for what would later be called, improperly, the Edict of Milan. In chapter 48, he reports the rescript, addressed to the governor of Bithynia and issued by Licinius in Nicomedia on 13 June 313, after the victory over Maximinus, presenting the measures in favour of Christians. The text is made to go back, originally, to 'the meeting in Milan' (*cum . . . apud Mediolanum convenissemus*).[52] This writing overturns the logic of Serdica's edict because Christianity is no longer only tolerated, but also there is an affirmation of the right to choose one's own religion for Christians and for all: 'to grant Christians and everyone the free right to follow whatever religion everyone wants in reference to whatever divine element is in heaven' (*ut daremus et Christianis et omnibus liberam potestatem sequendi religionem quam quisque voluisset, quod quicquid est divinitatis in sede caelesti*).

These are expressions that mark a turning point in human life because they recognize the freedom of choice of religion, 'whatever religion everyone wants' (*quam quisque voluisset*), clearly distinguishing the civil religion from the personal one. In this way, the inviolability of a space of conscience? is affirmed which is absolutely beyond the reach of the state. The distinction between what is Caesar's and what is God's is affirmed here not as a moral principle or as a spiritual teaching but as a principle of government deriving from the political choice of an emperor.

---

[52]Lactanctius, *Mort.*, 48,2.

This new situation allowed a new development of Christianity. However, this cannot be translated into an opposition between a golden and heroic pre-Constantinian era contrasted with a relaxation of the imperial church. As we have seen, in fact, the persecutions were interspersed with periods of peace already characterized by a cooling of fervour, just as the martyrs themselves had been accompanied by the phenomenon of the *lapsi*, which had brought out the element of mercy in the Christian message. Jean Daniélou writes:

> The only truth is that in the first centuries the expansion of Christianity to a huge number of people – and its expansion is part of the very essence of Christianity – was hindered by the fact that its development took place within a society whose social frameworks and cultural structures were hostile to it. Belonging to Christianity therefore required a strength of character of which most men were not capable. Constantine's conversion, by removing these obstacles, made the Gospel accessible to the poor, that is to say, to those who were not part of the elite, to the man in the street. Far from distorting Christianity, this conversion enabled it to fulfil itself in its nature as a people.[53]

IMPERIAL AMBIVALENCE

Constantine had overcome the incompatibility between *Romanus* and *Christianus* but remained fully within the syncretistic tradition of the empire. This explains how the confusion between state and church remains, once the latter has been allowed to exist. The concessions to the Christian clergy were, in fact, an extension of those to pagan priests.[54] The difference from the relationship with the state in the church in Armenia, the first nation to convert, is clear evidence of the Roman ambivalence towards the relationship between church and empire that was to characterize the years after 313.

Eusebius' political theology is an example of this. The fundamental principle of its construction is that, as the Father is the only God, so the emperor must be one and only one.[55] In this process, which makes the earthly kingdom the image of the heavenly kingdom, the *Logos* is the efficient cause,[56] because, just as Christ is the vicar of the Father, so the emperor is of Christ.[57] Some authors even went so far as to affirm that it was precisely this conception of the empire that dictated Eusebius' Trinitarian theology.[58] Later, in the *City of God* (*De civitate Dei*), Augustine was to

---

[53]J. Daniélou, *L'oraison, problème politique*. Bibliothèque du Cerf (Paris: Fayard, 1965), p. 12.

[54]See Sordi, *Il cristianesimo e Roma*, p. 407.

[55]See Eusebius, *LCons.*, 7, 12, 68.

[56]See R. Farina, *L'impero e l'imperatore cristiano in Eusebio di Cesarea. La prima teologia politica del cristianesimo* (Zurich: Pas Verlag, 1966), p. 117.

[57]See Eusebius, *LConst.*, 3, 6, 11-12.

[58]See J. M. Sansterre, 'Eusèbe de Césarée et la naissance de la théorie "césaropapiste"', *Byz* 42 (1972): 131–95, here p. 152.

develop a very different position, considering the empire only 'at the most tolerable' (*maxime tolerabile*).

In the Arian crisis, the ambivalence inherent in this political theology emerges strongly because, after the death of Constantine, in 337, his sons Constantius and Constans made Arianism itself the force of the empire's cohesion, while Pope Liberius, Athanasius, Osius of Cordoba and Hilary of Poitiers were exiled. Paradoxically, it was only with the emperor Julian, restorer of the pagan cult that the church returned to the enjoyment of autonomy and freedom. This highlights precisely the principle of distinction between the theological monarchy of the Father and civil monarchies, with the consequent distinction of areas of authority. In fact, in the years of the great Apologies, between 176 and 178, Celsus wrote the *True Doctrine* (*Alêthês logos*), invoking the *mos patrum* as the fundamental criterion of the religion (*religio*) from a conservative position of a Middle Platonist matrix. At the end of Book VII, he writes:

> I mean, if it is accepted that all of nature – everything in the world – operates according to the will of God and that nothing works contrary to his purposes, then it must also be accepted that the angels, the demons, heroes – everything in the universe – are subject to the will of the great God who rules over all. Over each sphere there is a being charged with the task of governance and worthy to have power, at least the power allotted it for carrying out its task. This being the case, it would be appropriate for each man who worships God also to honor the being who exercises his allotted responsibilities at God's pleasure, since that being must have been licensed to do what he does by God. Your Jesus says 'It is impossible for the same man to serve many masters. (Mt. 6.24)[59]

The strength of the evangelical precept and its theological-political value are evident. In fact, the question is not merely linked to Cicero's ideal of religious fidelity to 'the custom of the ancients' (*mos patrum*), an element clearly present in both Celsus and Porphyry after him, but it is precisely the uniqueness of the monarchy revealed by Christ that is at stake, as well as the foundation of its universality which goes beyond the confines of the empire itself. In the face of this, Porphyry's ironic observations are useless:

> Let us explore completely this matter of the monarchy of the only God and the manifold rule [polyarchy] of those who are revered as gods. Your idea of the single rule [monarchy] is amiss, for a monarch is not the only man alive but the only man who rules. He rules, obviously, over his kinsmen and those like himself. Take for example the emperor Hadrian: he was a monarch because he ruled over those who were like him by race and nature – not because he existed alone somewhere or lorded it over oxen and sheep, as some poor shepherd might do. In the same way: the supreme God would not be supreme unless he ruled over

---

[59]Origen, *Cels.*, VII, 70. My translation follows R. J. Hoffmann, *Celsus, On the True Doctrine: A Discourse against the Christians* (Oxford: Oxford University Press, 1987), p. 115.

other gods. Only this sort of power would do justice to the greatness of God and redound to his honor.[60]

It is important to note the parallelism between the emperor and the divinity, a parallelism which the Christian faith could not accept. Indeed, the course of history shows that the ambiguity of the civil monarchy requires the intervention of those in the church who have the task of reaffirming the divine monarchy and its absolute and universal scope even when the emperor is orthodox, as in the case of Theodosius.

A particularly beautiful and important example is *The Funeral Oration for Theodosius* (*De obitu Theodosii*), pronounced by Ambrose on 25 February 395 during the funeral of the emperor who died on 17 January of the same year. The relationship between justice and mercy is present at a very deep level in this homily which was dedicated to a believer who was the civil monarch, readmitted to communion after being excommunicated by the same bishop only five years earlier for having ordered the Roman legions to massacre thousands of innocent citizens in Thessaloniki where an uprising against the Goths had broken out. Ambrose's line of argument is totally centred on gift and gratuitousness as fundamental elements of human reality. Thus, in commenting on the 'in all things give thanks' of 1 Thess. 5.18, he writes:

> Indeed, when do you have something that you do not owe to God or when are you deprived of the gift of God, you to whom every day the possibility of living is given by the Lord? In fact, 'What do you own that you have not received?' (1 Cor. 4.7) Therefore, as long as you always receive it, always invoke it, and since what you possess is from God, acknowledge that you are always in debt.[61]

The bishop affirms that it is right to have forgiven the emperor because justice and mercy coincide (*misericordia ipsa iustitia est*)[62] from God's point of view because all we have is his gift, as demonstrated by the very birth of man on account of which Ambrose rereads the condition of creaturely indigence in a filial key.[63]

This text unites poetic expression with speculative vigour, going as far as to examine the heart of the Ambrosian identification of justice and mercy. This is not a denial of reality, but a recognition that the 'one's own' (*suum*) that justice must recognize 'to each' (*cuique*) is indeed always a gift from another, is always 'from someone else' (*alterius*). In this way, filiation reconfigures our gaze on the world, allowing us to recognize mercy towards those in need and to declare their need as an authentic measure in which the freedom and dignity of every person are founded. It was a fundamental moment in the confrontation between the church and the empire because the superiority of the former was brought back to this new vision of the

---

[60]Porphyry, *Adv.Ch.*, Fr. 75, Apocrit. IV.20-IV.23. My translation follows R. J. Hoffmann, *Porphyry's against the Christians: The Literary Remains* (Amherst, NY: Prometheus Books, 1994), pp. 83–4.
[61]Ambrose, *De ob.*, 22, 7-11: CSEL 73, 382.
[62]Ibid., 25.5-26.2: CSEL 73, 383-4.
[63]Ibid., 26.7-14: CSEL 73, 384.

world and history that made it possible to make a judgement even on the emperor himself.

This judgement had also prompted the fathers of the fourth century to promote the cult of the martyrs precisely to remember this primacy of theological monarchy over the civil one.[64] It was not a question of imposing the faith on anyone, but of making visible how Christian revelation implied a primacy of personal conscience of universal scope which could not be suppressed by any political absolutism.

The Cappadocian Fathers distinguished themselves particularly in this work,[65] and monasticism itself can be read along these lines.[66] Certainly, the new political situation allowed the development of charitable institutions so humane that not even Julian, in his work of restoring paganism, could eliminate them, as in the case of the Basiliad[67] and hospital-like institutions. With its link with both ascetical circles and Cappadocian theology, the condemnation of slavery is a clear example of this.[68]

However, the ambiguity in the relationship with the imperial power, even in its perfectly Christian expression, emerged once again in the sixth century in the discussions over Theodore of Mopsuestia, and Theodoret of Cyrrhus. On 14 May 553, in the first *Constitutum*, Pope Vigilius had ruled out the possibility of condemning the dead.[69] However, Justinian had already expressed an opposite position to that of the pope, first in the Edict of 551 on the Orthodox faith, then in the letter of the spring of 553 to the Holy Synod on Origen and his followers.[70] Thus, practically half of the proceedings of the fifth session of the Second Council of Constantinople were devoted to this question, sealed by the conclusion of Patriarch Euthychius who rejected what had been said previously by Pope Vigilius.[71] This made it possible to add Origen explicitly at the end of the sequence of heretics, 'Arius, Eunomius, Apollinaris, Nestorius, and Eutyches', in the eleventh canon of the Council.[72] The emperor forced the pope to accept this, after having held him prisoner for a long time.

---

[64]See J. Leemans et al. (eds), *Let us Die that We May Live: Greek Homilies on Christian Martyrs from Asia Minor, Palestine, and Syria, c. 350 – c. 450 AD* (London and New York: Routledge, 2003).

[65]See V. M. Limberis, *Architects of Piety: The Cappadocian Fathers and the Cult of the Martyrs* (Oxford: Oxford University Press, 2011).

[66]See M. Girardi, *Basilio di Cesarea e il culto dei martiri nel IV secolo: scrittura e tradizione*, Vol. 21 (Bari: Istituto di studi classici e cristiani, 1990).

[67]The Basiliad was an episcopal complex conceived as a city where ill and poor people could find a place and be taken care of, see L. D. M. Driver, *Christ at the Center: The Early Christian Era* (Louisville, KY: Westminster John Knox Press, 2009), p. 199.

[68]See I. Ramelli, *Social Justice and the Legitimacy of Slavery: The Role of Philosophical Asceticism from Ancient Judaism to Late Antiquity* (Oxford: Oxford University Press, 2016).

[69]Vigilius, *Const.*, I, in: CSEL 35 [83] 292, 16-26.

[70]Georgius Monachus, *Chr.*, II, 630-3 in C. De Boor, *Georgii monachi chronicon* (Lipsiae: B.G. Teubneri, 1904).

[71]*Concilium Constantinopolitanum II, Acta*, Sessio V, n. 93, in E. Schwartz (ed.), *Acta Conciliorum Oecumenicorum*, IV.1 (Berlin: W. De Gruyter, 1971), p. 130. For an English translation, see R. Price, *The Acts of the Council of Constantinople of 553* (Liverpool: Liverpool University Press, 2009).

[72]See Schwartz, *Acta Conciliorum Oecumenicorum*, IV.1, 218.

The ambivalence of imperial theology emerges in all its depth from this episode, the scope of which should be further explored because, in a certain sense, it marks a new path that will lead to the changes of the medieval and Byzantine eras.

CONCLUSION

In short, to trace the relationship between the community of martyrs that characterized the first centuries of the Christian era and the ensuing centuries marked by a peaceful relationship with the empire, it seems necessary to take an epistemological position that allows us to avoid two fundamental reductionisms that dialectically oppose the situation in the two periods or disregard any real difference between them. The strength of the relational approach is precisely that of being able to respect the historical data as much as possible, considering both the divergences and the points of contact at the same time. For this reason, we have tried to have recourse to an epistemology that is both historical and theological. In fact, the historical value of persecution cannot be grasped if the confrontation between empire and Christianity is reduced to a political conflict and then resolved in an alliance that was to corrupt the purity of the early Christian spirit. In the same way, one cannot ignore the fact that the historical path itself shows a progressive deepening of a theological understanding which, intersecting with the light and dark of political and social events, led to a formulation of the relationship between church and empire which was marked by ties that, however complex, were and are inescapable. Subsequent historical developments are somehow contained at embryonic level in the ambivalence highlighted in the fourth century. Therefore, rather than political, the confrontation is theological because the question at stake is the use (*chrêsis*)[73] of imperial universalism as a form, instrument or even unacceptable ballast from the perspective of the universalism of personal dignity recognized by Christian thought, thanks to the revelation of the New Testament. This judgement may have oscillated at different times, but its existence, and therefore the perspective that this entails, remain an essential key to understanding the events.

BIBLIOGRAPHY

Addey, C. *Divination and Theurgy in Neoplatonism: Oracles of the Gods*. Ashgate Studies in Philosophy and Theology in Late Antiquity. Farnham: Ashgate, 2014.

Allen, P., Dehandschutter, B., Leemans J., and Mayer, W. (eds). *Let us Die that We May Live: Greek Homilies on Christian Martyrs from Asia Minor, Palestine, and Syria c.* AD *350 – c.* AD *450*. London and New York: Routledge, 2003.

Baslez, M.-F. *Les persécutions dans l'Antiquité. Victimes, héros, martyrs*. Paris: Fayard, 2007.

---

[73]On the Patristic *chrêsis* as method, see A. M. Mazzanti (ed.), *Un metodo per il dialogo fra le culture. La chrêsis patritsica* (Brescia: Morcelliana, 2019).

Boor, C. De. *Georgii monachi chronicon*. Lipsiae: B.G. Teubneri, 1904.

Boyarin, D. *Dying for God: Martyrdom and the Making of Christianity and Judaism*. Stanford, CA: Stanford University Press, 1999.

Bowersock, G. *Martyrdom and Rome*. Cambridge: Cambridge University Press, 1998.

Daniélou, J. *L'oraison, problème politique*. Bibliothèque du Cerf. Paris: Fayard, 1965.

Di Berardino, A. (ed.). *Encyclopedia of Ancient Christianity*. Downers Grove, IL: IVP Academic, 2014.

Driver, L. D. M. *Christ at the Center: The Early Christian Era*. Louisville, KY: Westminster John Knox Press, 2009.

Farina, R. *L'impero e l'imperatore cristiano in Eusebio di Cesarea. La prima teologia politica del cristianesimo*. Zurich: Pas Verlag, 1966.

Filoramo, G. *Il martirio cristiano: una prospettiva comparata*. Pisa: Fabrizio Serra, 2010.

Galletier, É. *Panégyriques latins*, vol. II. Paris: Les Belles Lettres, 1952.

Gibbon, E. *The History of the Decline and fall of the Roman Empire*. Penguin Classics. London: Abridged Ed edition, 2000.

Girard, R. *The Scapegoat*. Baltimore, MD: Johns Hopkins University Press, 1989.

Girard, R. *Wissenschaft und christlicher Glaube*. Tübingen: Mohr Siebeck, 2007.

Girardi, M. *Basilio di Cesarea e il culto dei martiri nel IV secolo: scrittura e tradizione*, vol. 21. Bari: Istituto di studi classici e cristiani, 1990.

Gnilka, Ch. *Chrêsis: die Methode der Kirchenväter im Umgang mit der antiken Kultur: Der Begriff des 'rechten Gebrauchs'*. Basel: Schwabe Verlag, 2012.

Grégoire, H. 'La "conversion" de Constantin', *RUB* 36 (1930–31): 231–72.

Grünewald, T. *Constantinus Maximus Augustus: Herrschafts-Propaganda in der zeitgenössischen Überlieferung Heerschaftspropaganda in der zeitgenössischen Überlieferung*. Stuttgart: Steiner, 1990.

Hoffmann, R. J. *Celsus, On the True Doctrine: A Discourse against the Christians*. Oxford: Oxford University Press, 1987.

Hoffmann, R. J. *Porphyry's Against the Christians: The Literary Remains*. Amherst, NY: Prometheus Books, 1994.

Ivánka, von E. *Rhomäerreich und Gottesvolk. Das Glaubens-, Staats- und Volksbewusstsein der Byzantiner und seine Auswirkung auf die ostkirchlich-europäische Geisteshaltung*. Freiburg and Munich: Karl Alber, 1968.

Joslyn-Siemiatkoski, D. *Christian Memories of the Maccabean Martyrs*. New York: Palgrave Macmillan, 2009.

Lapidge, M. *The Roman Martyrs: Introduction, Translations and Commentary*. Oxford Early Christian Studies. Oxford: Oxford University Press, 2018.

Leoni, J. 'Martiri e soldati in Eusebio di Cesarea', *RHE* 110 (2015): 5–30.

Lieu, S. N. C. and Montserrat, D. (eds). *From Constantine to Julian pagan and Byzantine Views: A Source History*. London and New York: Routledge, 1996.

Limberis, V. M. *Architects of Piety: The Cappadocian Fathers and the Cult of the Martyrs*. Oxford: Oxford University Press, 2011.

Mazzanti, A. M. (ed.). Un metodo per il dialogo fra le culture. La *chrêsis* patritsica. Brescia: Morcelliana, 2019.

McGuckin, J. A. *The Path of Christianity: The First Thousand Years*. Downers Grove, IL: IVP Academic, 2017.

Moss, C. R. *The Other Christs: Imitating Jesus in Ancient Christian Ideologies of Martyrdom*. Oxford: Oxford University Press, 2010.

Müller-Rettig, B. *Der Panegyricus des Jahres 310 auf Konstantin den Grossen. Übersetzung und* historisch-philologischer Kommentar. Stuttgart: F. Steiner Verlag, 1990.

Prete, S. 'Confessioni Trinitarie in alcuni Atti di martiri dei sec. II (Giustino, Apollonio, Policarpo)', *Aug* 13 (1973): 469–82.

Price, R. *The Acts of the Council of Constantinople of 553*. Liverpool: Liverpool University Press, 2009.

Ramelli, I. *Social Justice and the Legitimacy of Slavery: The Role of Philosophical Asceticism from Ancient Judaism to Late Antiquity*. Oxford: Oxford University Press, 2016.

Sansterre, J.-M. 'Eusèbe de Césarée et la naissance de la théorie "césaropapiste"', *Byzantion* 42 (1972): 131–95.

Schwartz, E. *Acta Conciliorum Oecumenicorum, IV.1*. Berlin: W. de Gruyter, 1971.

Shepkaru, S. *Jewish Martyrs in the Pagan and Christian Worlds*. Cambridge: Cambridge University Press, 2005.

Simmons, M. B. *Arnobius of Sicca. Religious Conflict and Competition in the Age of Diocletian*. Oxford: Clarendon, 1995.

Sordi, M. *Il cristianesimo e Roma*. Bologna: Licinio Cappelli Editore, 1965.

Sordi, M. *I Cristiani e l'Impero romano*. Milan: Jaca Book, 2011.

Tantillo, I. 'L'impero della luce. Riflessioni su Costantino e il sole', *Mélanges de l'école française de Rome* 115 (2003): 985–1048.

Wilken, R. L. *The Christians as the Romans saw Them*. New Haven, CT: Yale University Press, 2003.

Ziadé. *Les martyrs Maccabées: de l'histoire juive au culte chrétien. Les homélies de Grégoire de Nazianze et de Jean Chrysostome*. VCSup, vol. 80. Leiden: E.J. Brill, 2007.

CHAPTER 21

Doctrine

Why were Christians obsessed with dogmas?

ILARIA L. E. RAMELLI

THE QUESTION AT STAKE

Christians were somehow 'obsessed with dogmas' and built the dogmatics of Christianity in the first ecumenical councils, which discussed Trinitarian theology and Christology (particularly Nicaea, Constantinople, Ephesus and Chalcedon, but also later councils, especially concerning mono- and dyotheletism in reference to Maximus the Confessor's doctrines), because they had to structure their message philosophically. This was imperative, since Christ is the Logos and is the centre of all Christianity. So, Christianity must be logical/rational and informed philosophically. The philosophical structure of Christian theology mainly rested on Platonism,[1] along with Stoic and Aristotelian elements. Later on, with medieval Scholasticism, it would be mainly Aristotle's thought that would buttress Christian theology.

Christians also needed dogmas for practical reasons: Keith Hopkins observed that faith statements became important for Christians in the first centuries, because Christians formed small, scattered cells, with few literate members but absorbed many outsiders as new members. Therefore, dogmas and creeds were an efficient way of summarizing the tenets of Christianity.[2] This helped to define group membership.[3] Hopkins's thesis is plausible; however, the definitions of dogmas went beyond their

---

[1]Werner Beierwaltes, 'Wie plantonisierten Christen?' *VChr* 28 (1974): 15–28; *Platonismus in Christentum* (Frankfurt: Klostermann, 1998); 'Zur Geschichte des Platonismus, I', *Philosophisches Jahrbuch* 100 (1993): 194–9; I. L. E Ramelli, 'Origen, Patristic Philosophy, and Christian Platonism', *VChr* 63 (2009): 217–63; eadem, '"Revelation" for Christians and Pagans and their Philosophical Allegoresis', in *Divination in Later Antiquity* (Cambridge: Cambridge University Press, forthcoming). This project has benefited from a Research Professorship in Patristics and Church History, KUL, that I have been awarded. This chapter has been supported by the Polish Ministry of Science and Higher Education within the 2019–22 'Initiative of Excellence' program # 028/RID/2018/19.
[2]Keith Hopkins, 'Christian Number and Its Implications', *JECS* 6 (1998): 185–226.
[3]This opinion is confirmed by Outi Lehtipuu, *Debates over the Resurrection of the Dead* (Oxford: Oxford University Press, 2015), p. 14.

crystallization in creedal statements that not many Christians could grasp fully[4] and resulted from profound philosophico-theological knowledge and discussion.[5]

THE ROLE OF THE CHRISTIANIZATION OF PHILOSOPHY

The main role in the process which gave rise to the dogmas that structurally define Christian theology was played by Origen, the Cappadocian Fathers, Cyril of Alexandria, Maximus the Confessor and others. Origen's authentic philosophical theology was very probably received in the *Dialogue of Adamantius on the Orthodox Faith in God*[6] and absorbed by the Cappadocians, especially Gregory Nyssen.[7] Gregory intimately understood and developed Origen's theology in an 'orthodox', Nicene-Constantinopolitan direction. Accurate historico-theological research yields that Origen, far from being the precursor of 'Arianism', was the main inspirer of the Nicene-Constantinopolitan 'orthodoxy' and of the dogmas of Ephesus and Chalcedon, as I shall argue. This is the outcome of informed and rigorous historical investigation and challenges the *communis opinio* concerning Origen, which sometimes proves questionable and is influenced more by the Origenistic controversy and old handbooks and preconceptions than by any meticulous reading of Origen and his most insightful followers.

By Origen's day Christianity was beginning to represent itself as philosophy, as can be seen with Justin, Clement and Origen himself. Even the third century martyr Pionius is portrayed as assimilating Christians to philosophers, 'who practiced philosophy, justice, and steadfastness' (*M.Pion.* 17.3). The Seneca-Paul correspondence, possibly roughly coeval, speaks of Christianity as a philosophy instead of a religion:[8] Letter 9, attributed to Seneca and addressing Paul, names some member of the Jesus Movement in Rome 'followers of your philosophical orientation', *disciplinarum tuarum comites*: Christianity is not called *religio* or *superstitio*, but

---

[4]Ramsay MacMullen, *The Second Church: Popular Christianity A.D. 200-400* (Atlanta GA: SBL, 2009), with my review in *BMCR* 2009.

[5]For the case of the discussions at Nicaea, see my 'Origen, Patristic Philosophy', 'Origen's Anti-Subordinationism and Its Heritage in the Nicene and Cappadocian Line', *VChr* 65 (2011): 21–49; 'Sources and Reception of Dynamic Unity in Middle and Neoplatonism', *JBR* 7 (2020): 31–66.

[6]Argued by I. L. E. Ramelli, 'The *Dialogue of Adamantius*', *SP* 52 (2012): 71–98; 56, no. 4 (2013): 227–73; 'The *Dialogue of Adamantius*: Preparing the Critical Edition and a Reappraisal', *RhM* 163 (2020): 40–68.

[7]Arguments in my 'Origen, Gregory of Nyssa, and the Biblical and Philosophical Basis of the Doctrine of Apokatastasis', *VChr* 61 (2007): 313–56; 'Origen's Anti-Subordinationism'; 'Divine Power in Origen of Alexandria: Sources and Aftermath', in *Divine Powers in Late Antiquity*, eds Anna Marmodoro and Irini Fotini Viltanioti (Oxford: Oxford University Press, 2017), pp. 177–98: 'Apokatastasis and Epektasis in *Hom. in Cant.*: The Relation between Two Core Doctrines in Gregory and Roots in Origen', in *Gregory of Nyssa: In Canticum Canticorum*, ed. Giulio Maspero (Leiden: Brill, 2018), pp. 312–39, and 'Sources and Reception'.

[8]On this correspondence see my 'A Pseudepigraphon Inside a Pseudepigraphon?', *JSP* 23 (2014): 259–89; 'Paul's Problematic Relation to Judaism in the Seneca-Paul Original Correspondence', in *The Early Reception of Paul the Jew,* ed. Gabriele Boccaccini (London: T&T Clark, 2018), pp. 220–35.

disciplinae, which, like *secta*,[9] designates the teachings of a philosophical school. In the second century, 'there existed no intellectual discipline equivalent to the modern academic discipline of "theology,"' as Winrich Löhr notes.[10] Eusebius, an admirer of Origen, called Christianity 'divine, true philosophy'.[11] Socrates and Sozomen often depicted monasticism as true philosophy.[12] Schools and 'universities', such as that of Origen, and 'catechetical' schools were the principal, but not the only, form of Christian education.[13]

Qua philosophy, Christianity was also beginning to respond to hostile charges of irrationalism, behaviour according to habit (ethos vs. logos) and fideism. The Syriac apology to 'Antoninus Caesar' – probably the emperor-philosopher Marcus Aurelius – ascribed to Melito reacted to accusations of irrationality by ascribing logos to Christianity but behaviour based on a bad ethos to 'paganism'; and so did Clement of Alexandria, one of the Christian intellectuals most committed to demonstrating Christianity's rationality.[14] Justin Martyr (*Dial.* 1), after attending several philosophical schools, which he left, finally found the Platonic school, which he does not criticize like the others, and described his conversion to Christianity (Christian Platonism) as a conversion to a 'divine philosophy'.[15] He continued to wear philosophical garb after this (just as Heraclas continued to wear philosophical garb even when he was an Alexandrian presbyter, according to Origen[16]) and described philosophy as 'the greatest and most honourable possession before God, to whom it leads us' (*Dial.* 2.1). Justin recognized that the Christians 'say the same things as the Greeks say' (*1 Apol.* 24) and appreciates Plato for his theology, his rejection of polytheism and his psychology: 'the aim of Plato's philosophy is the contemplation of God' (*Dial.* 2.6), he argues. Philosophy, particularly Platonism, cannot but be excellent for Christians, since it leads to God. This was also the goal of Origen's own philosophical theology. According to Justin, Christ is a philosopher, not a sophist (*1 Apol.* 14.5), as Lucian had styled him.[17] This move of presenting Christianity

---

[9]Corresponding to αἵρεσις (Letter 5).

[10]*Christianity in the Second Century*, eds Judith Lieu and James Carleton-Paget (Cambridge: Cambridge University Press, 2017), p. 152.

[11]ἔνθεον καὶ ἀληθῆ φιλοσοφίαν, *Mart.Pal.* 4.1-15 short recension.

[12]Socrates 4.27.4; Sozomen 1.12, etc. See A. M. Malingrey, *'Philosophia'* (Paris: Klincksieck, 1961); Andreas Westergren, 'Emperors and Monks in Socrates' Church History', in *Monastic Education in Late Antiquity*, eds Lillian Larsen and Samuel Rubenson (Cambridge: Cambridge University Press, 2018), pp. 53–72, and the whole book, which argues for a continuity of monastic instruction with classical paideia.

[13]See *Teachers in Late Antique Christianity*, ed. Peter Gemeinhardt (Tübingen: Mohr Siebeck, 2018).

[14]Arguments from Justin, Bardaisan, Ps.Melito, Clement, Origen, Epictetus, Musonius, Marcus Aurelius, Celsus, Galen and Lucian in my 'Ethos and Logos: A Second-Century Apologetical Debate between "Pagan" and Christian Philosophers', *VChr* 69 (2015): 123–56.

[15]Φιλοσοφία θεία (*Apol.* 2.12.5). On the *Dialogue*, see Matthijs DenDulk, *Refiguring Justin Martyr's Dialogue with Trypho* (London: Routledge, 2018).

[16]*Ap.* Eusebius *HE* 6.19.12-14.

[17]See my 'Lucian's Peregrinus as Holy Man and Charlatan', in *Holy Men/Women and Charlatans in the Ancient Novel*, eds Michael Paschalis et al. (Groningen: Barkhuis, 2015), pp. 105–20.

as a philosophy was shared by Galen,[18] who called Judaism and Christianity 'the philosophical school [διατριβή] of Moses and Christ' (*Diff. Puls.* 2.4).

To offer philosophical foundations to Christian theology, Christians developed a theology of the Logos, which identified Christ with God's Logos. This operation, anticipated by Philo and Hellenistic Judaism, started from the Johannine Prologue and was continued by Justin, most of the Valentinians, Clement and especially Origen and by those patristic philosophers influenced by Origen. Christianity could no longer be labelled 'irrational' largely thanks to Origen, who was deeply respected by 'pagan' philosophers too, as Eusebius remarked. Origen used 'Platonic ways of thinking about God and the soul . . . to give an intelligent account of his Christian beliefs'.[19] Like Justin and Clement, he depicted Christianity as philosophy *tout court* and built it through philosophical structures, categories and arguments. Origen shows the necessity of this operation in *Cels.* 4.9, after mentioning the end of the world and universal judgement: 'The [Christian] philosopher [φιλοσοφοῦντα] will need to prove the theories by means of demonstrations of all sorts, taken from the divine Scriptures and the consequentiality of rational arguments.'

Origen grounded his theology and dogmatic constructions in Scripture, his main authority, which he read in Platonic terms, and also interpreted Plato, mirroring the exegesis of contemporary Platonists. Origen imported the formula 'there was no time when *x* was not' – never used by Christians beforehand – from the cosmological debates of Greek philosophy into Christology, where it entered anti-'Arian' polemics and became standard in Nicene theologians.[20] Origen was inspired by imperial philosophical and medical literature, Scripture, and Philo for his innovative Trinitarian notion of hypostasis (ὑπόστασις) as individual substance of each divine Person versus their common divine essence (οὐσία). He thereby anticipated the dogmatic formula 'one common essence, three individual substances' (μία οὐσία τρεῖς ὑποστάσεις), associated with the Council of Constantinople and Cappadocian theology, as we shall see. With his innovative notion of hypostasis, Origen may even have impacted 'pagan' Platonism.[21]

Origen planned *First Principles* (Περὶ ἀρχῶν) as a philosopher to 'confirm by reason our faith' (*Princ.* 4.1.1); its antecedents are in the Greek philosophical tradition of treatises Περὶ ἀρχῶν. Only Eriugena's *Periphyseon* will be a comparable comprehensive exposition of systematic theology and theoretical philosophy,

---

[18]See Ilaria Ramelli, 'Galeno e i Cristiani', *InvLuc* 25 (2003): 199–220; 'Ethos and Logos'; 'Galen (doctor)', in BEEC (Leiden: Brill, forthcoming; online 2018: http://dx.doi.org/10.1163/2589-7993_EECO_SIM_00001368).

[19]Henry Chadwick, *Early Christian Thought and the Classical Tradition* (Oxford: Clarendon, 1966), 123 – I only doubt that 'Platonism was inside [Origen] *malgré lui*'. See my 'Origen's Philosophical Theology', in *Hellenism, Early Judaism and Early Christianity*, ed. Jiri Hoblik (Berlin: de Gruyter, 2021).

[20]As I argue in 'Alexander of Aphrodisias: A Source of Origen?', *PhAnt* 14 (2014): 237–90.

[21]Demonstration in: Ilaria L. E. Ramelli, 'Origen, Greek Philosophy, and the Birth of the Trinitarian Meaning of Hypostasis', *HTR* 105 (2012): 302–50 (henceforth 'Hypostasis').

inspired by Origen's Περὶ ἀρχῶν: the only available model.[22] The ἀρχαί in Origen's title are primarily the Trinity's three hypostases, which open the whole of *First Principles* and appear again in the phrase *archike Trinitas* in *Princ.* 1.4.3 (Rufinus transliterated ἀρχική) and as 'three principal hypostases' (τρεῖς ἀρχικαὶ ὑποστάσεις) in Eusebius and in Porphyry's titles of Plotinus' treatises.[23] For Origen, the triune God, who creates matter and thinks all Forms/Ideas, replaces the three ἀρχαί of 'Middle Platonism':[24] God, matter and forms. Origen rejected μοναρχία, that is, the positing of one hypostasis, the Father, as one ἀρχή instead of three (*Heracl.* 3.20–4.9). Indeed, Origen and Plotinus lived 'before a priestly and consciously polytheistic brand of Platonism became the norm'.[25]

NICAEA

A good part of the dogmatic discussion and definition at the Council of Nicaea (325) depends on previous theologians, among whom Origen is paramount. His 'anti-subordinationism' is connected with his discourse on the Son as divine Principle (ἀρχή) and divine hypostasis. He was so convinced of the Son's divinity and coeternity with the Father that he first applied to him the formula 'there was no time when he was not', which later became a cornerstone of anti-'Arian' apologetic.[26] Origen was arguably the main inspirer of the Nicene dogmatic definition of the consubstantiality of the Son with the Father, deriving from their coeternity and common divinity, which he supported, and of the Cappadocians' Trinitarian formula 'one essence, three individual substances' (μία οὐσία τρεῖς ὑποστάσεις), which developed the Nicene formula at the Council of Constantinople (381).[27] Mark Edwards, Panayiotis

---

[22]Robert Crouse, 'Origen in the Philosophical Tradition of the Latin West', in *Origeniana V,* ed. Robert Daly (Leuven: Peeters, 1992), pp. 565–9; Ilaria L. E. Ramelli, *The Christian Doctrine of Apokatastasis: A Critical Assessment from the New Testament to Eriugena*, Supplements to Vigiliae Christianae 120 (Leiden: Brill, 2013), pp. 773–815 and 'Eriugena's Protology and Eschatology against the Backdrop of His Platonic Patristic Sources', in *Eriugena's Christian Neoplatonism and Its Sources in Patristic Philosophy*, ed. Eadem (Leuven: Peeters, 2021), pp. 1–26.

[23]Porphyry was arguably influenced by his knowledge of Origen's notion of hypostasis in the choice of the title of Plotinus' treatise on the three ἀρχικαὶ ὑποστάσεις, as Eusebius was likely aware. Argument in my 'Hypostasis'.

[24]This umbrella term was coined by Karl Praechter, *Hierokles der Stoiker* (Leipzig: Dieterich, 1901), p. 93.

[25]Harold Tarrant, 'Forgetting Procline Theology', in *Proclus and His Legacy*, eds David Butorac and Danielle Layne (Berlin: de Gruyter, 2017), pp. 33–44, 34.

[26]As argued in Ilaria L. E. Ramelli, 'Alexander of Aphrodisias: A Source of Origen's Philosophy?', *PhAnt* 14 (2014): 237–90 (henceforth 'Alexander').

[27]As I argued in 'Origen's Anti-Subordinationism' and 'Hypostasis'. Dragos Giulea, 'Basil of Caesarea's Authorship of Epistle 361', *VChr* 72 (2018): 41–70, 55 and 'Antioch 268 and Its Legacy in the Fourth-Century Theological Debates', *HTR* 111, no. 2 (2018): 192–215, n. 22, Mark Edwards, 'Did Origen Apply the Word *Homoousios* to the Son?', *JTS* 49 (1998): 658–70, PierFranco Beatrice, 'The Word *Homoousios* from Hellenism to Christianity', *Church History* 71 (2002): 243–72, 250–1, and Panayiotis Tzamalikos, *Anaxagoras, Origen, and Neoplatonism* (Berlin: DeGruyter, 2016), pp. 1567–68 (with my review in *Gnomon* 92, no. 2 (2020): 109–13) also surmise Origen used *homoousios*. Lewis Ayres, *Nicaea and Its Legacy* (Oxford: Oxford University Press, 2004), pp. 20–30 and 236–40, rightly lists Origen among

Tzamalikos, Alfons Fürst, Henryk Pietras and others agree with me about Origen's essential anti-subordinationism.[28]

Gregory Nyssen's Nicene anti-subordinationistic argument in *In Illud* depends on Origen, in scriptural and verbal echoes and in its general theory, namely, that the Son's submission to the Father in 1 Cor. 15.28 does not denote the divine Son's inferiority, but the submission and salvation of the body of Christ, that is, humanity.[29] Gregory followed Origen's *Princ.* 3.5.6-7, which already contrasted a 'heretical' subordinationistic interpretation of 1 Cor. 15.28. The same anti-subordinationistic argument was in Origen's *Hom. Lev.* 7.2 and *Com. Rom.* 7.3.60-68. Both Origen and Gregory interpreted 1 Cor. 15.28 as a declaration, not of the Son's subordination but of universal restoration.

Christ 'has nobody over him', not even the Father: 'for he is not after [*post*] the Father, but from [*de*] Him'; 'heretics' state that Father and Son have 'different natures', while for Origen they have the same 'essence' (*substantia vel natura*) but different 'properties' (*proprietates*), which explains their different hypostases (*Com. Rom.* 7.12.146-147). The determinative article distinguishes the Father (ὁ θεός) from the Son (θεός), but it does not imply subordinationism, being an explanation of John 1.1-3, in which θεός without article depends on its being a predicate (*Com. Joh.* 2.14-15). The Father is the source (πηγή) of divinity and the Son (*Autologos*) of the *logos* in all rational creatures (*Com. Joh.* 2.20.1-9). Father and Son have the same honour (*Com. Rom.* 8.4.25-26).

The accuracy of Rufinus' above-mentioned translation on the sameness of honour (ὁμοτιμία) in the case of the Father and the Son in Origen is confirmed by the following texts:

- Nyssen's *In Illud*;
- a fragment by Marcellus of Ancyra;[30]
- a scholion attributed to Origen, which quotes the Nicene and Constantinopolitan dogmatic formulae (*homoousios* and *mia ousia treis hypostaseis*),[31] either by Origen or by someone who read such formulae in Origen's Greek, since τρεῖς ὑποστάσεις is attested in Origen's *Com. Joh.* 2.10.75 in Greek;
- and especially *Com. Joh.* 32.324-325: 'The Logos who was God was not susceptible of being raised', because it is already God, like the Father, so it cannot become loftier;

---

the 'Nicene'; Anders-Christian Jacobsen, *Christ the Teacher of Salvation* (Münster: Aschendorff, 2015), recognizes that Origen's theology paved the way for Nicaea and Chalcedon; Tzamalikos, *Anaxagoras*, also concurs that Origen inspired Nicaea, Athanasius and the Cappadocians.

[28]*Origenes: Grieche und Christ* (Stuttgart: Hiersemann, 2017), pp. 139, 152. He calls the Nicene dogma, and other conciliar dogmata, 'language regulations' ('Sprachregelungen', pp. 152, 160).

[29]Demonstration in 'Gregory's Trinitarian Theology'; on the notion of Christ's body my 'Soma (Σῶμα)', in *Das Reallexikon für Antike und Christentum* 30 (Stuttgart: Hiersemann, 2021), pp. 814–47.

[30]Fragment 31 *ap.* Eusebius, *C.Marc.*, 1.34.

[31]*Schol.Matth.* PG 17.309.47.

- *Com. Joh.* 2.10.74;23.149, where Father and Son are defined as one in their essence (οὐσίᾳ) and substratum (ὑποκειμένῳ),
- and *Cels.* 8.12, which details that God's essence (οὐσία) is one, but Father and Son are distinct in their individual substances (τῇ ὑποστάσει). Here Origen is speaking of Christ's divine nature. God-Logos assumed body and soul (*C.Cant.* 2.6.8); the Saviour is 'a compound' (σύνθετος).32 Christ is not God in his human body or soul, but in the divine Logos, God's Son (*Cels.* 2.9); this is why Paul taught a higher Christology to the perfect, revealing Christ as God's Wisdom, and a lower one to the imperfect, preaching Christ crucified (*Hom. Ex.* 12.4). The Son-Logos-Wisdom is only God, while Christ is a compound of God and creature, but Origen sometimes calls Christ the Son, divine Logos and divine Wisdom (e.g. *Com. Rom.* 7.5.41-51), availing himself *ante litteram* of the *communicatio idiomatum*. In reference to Christ's divine nature, in *Com. Matth.* 17.14 and *Com. Joh.* 10.37.246, Origen criticizes those who do not distinguish Father and Son according to their individual substance (κατὰ ὑπόστασιν), although they are right in deeming them one in their common essence (ἓν οὐσίᾳ).

This terminology entails the concept and perhaps lexicon of ὁμοούσιος. Origen employed the term in *Com. Joh.* 13.25.149-150 to criticize the Valentinian view that 'spiritual' humans are consubstantial (ὁμοούσιοι) with the divine, whose nature-*ousia* is rather 'non-generated and supremely blessed': humans are not consubstantial with God; only the Trinity's hypostases are. Already Clement, also attacking some 'Gnostics', rejected the hypothesis that 'we are a part of God and consubstantial with God' (μέρος αὐτοῦ καὶ ὁμοουσίους τῷ θεῷ).[33]

Perhaps Origen used ὁμοούσιος in *Fr.Ps.* 54.3-4 in reference to the Son. Commenting on Heb. 1.3, Origen described Christ-emanation-vapour (ἀπόρροια) as ὁμοούσιος, a noun kept by Rufinus and glossed 'of the same essence' (*unius substantiae*): the vapour must come from the same substance as its origin, the Father.[34] Christ as ἀπόρροια from the Father is close to Plotinus' model of derivation of the hypostasis Nous from the hypostasis One (e.g. *Enn.* 5.2.1).

Rufinus, who read and translated Origen's Greek, in *Adult.* 1 states that Origen applied ὁμοούσιος to the Father and Son (*unius substantiae, quod graece homoousion dicitur, designavit*). If this be the case, in *Apol.* 99 Rufinus was not inserting a term that Origen did not use. Here Origen used ὁμοούσιος within the exegesis of Heb. 1.3 and Wis. 7.25-26, the same passages he quotes in *Princ.* 1.2.6, stating that they expressed the 'unity of nature and essence' between Father and Son: *naturae ac substantiae . . . unitatem*. In *Dial. Adam.* 1.2, which reflects Origen's ideas, the

---

[32]*H1Ps.15*.3 (77.22 Perrone).
[33] *Strom.*, 2.16.73.4–74.3.1, SC 38.92. Cf. 2.16.75.1, SC 38.93: 'we are neither parts of God [μορίων αὐτοῦ] nor children of God by nature [φύσει τέκνων]'.
[34]Pamphilus, *Apol.*, 99. Pamphilus' conclusion (100) summarizes: 'Origen declared the Son born of God's substance, that is, ὁμοούσιον – of the same substance as the Father', Rufinus glosses.

Greek includes ὁμοούσιος in Adamantius' words: 'God the Logos, consubstantial with the Father' (τὸν ἐξ αὐτοῦ Θεὸν Λόγον ὁμοούσιον). Rufinus renders ὁμοούσιον as *consubstantivum*, attributing again this catchword to Origen. Plotinus and Porphyry, who both knew Origen's work, used ὁμοούσιος as 'sharing the same substance/nature'.[35]

Athanasius read Origen in Greek and in *Decr.* 27.1-2 represented him as a supporter of the Son's coeternity (ἀϊδίως συνεῖναι) and consubstantiality (μὴ ἑτέρας οὐσίας) with the Father and a critic of subordinationists.[36] Athanasius also praised Theognostus, Origen's follower, for declaring the Son born 'from the Father's essence' (ἐκ τῆς οὐσίας, *Decr.* 25.1). The anonymous apologist preserved by Photius (*Bibl.*117.91b-92a) and Socrates (*HE* 6.13) also read Origen in Greek and defended him from accusations of forerunning 'Arianism'.

Eusebius' *Letter to His Church*[37] reports that Constantine at Nicaea promoted the introduction of 'consubstantial' (ὁμοούσιος) into the profession of faith (§7). Nicaea added that the Son arose 'from the Father's essence' (ἐκ τῆς οὐσίας), 'begotten not made, consubstantial with the Father' (ὁμοούσιον τῷ Πατρί), and anathematized (§8) those who claimed that 'there was a time when the Son was not [ἦν ποτε ὅτε οὐκ ἦν]; before being born he was not; he arose from nonbeing,[38] or is from another substance,[39] or created [κτιστόν], or mutable [τρεπτόν], or alterable [ἀλλοιωτόν]'. Origen did not reserve the terms κτίζω and κτιστόν to creatures, but also used it for God's 'foundation' of Wisdom/Son (*Com. Joh.* 1.19.114-115); however, he definitely separated the Son – divine, immutable, coeternal and consubstantial with God – from creatures and thereby grounded the Nicene dogma.

Constantine's addition of ὁμοούσιον, as Eusebius' letter reports, was 'thoroughly debated in questions and answers and put to the test' by the Nicene fathers (§9). As Origen had done, the Nicene participants clarified that 'from the substance' (ἐκ τῆς οὐσίας) did not indicate that the Son is a part/fragment of the Father's essence, materially (μέρος αὐτοῦ τῆς οὐσίας, §§10-11). This concern was already expressed by Origen twice: the Son is not a part/fragment of the Father's substance that has been divided or diminished (διαίρετος); his generation is not 'similar to the birth of animals'.[40] Against a materialistic notion of the Son's eternal generation,

> if the Son was born from the Father's substance [ἐκ τῆς οὐσίας] as though God were diminished and deprived of a part of his substance [μειουμένου καὶ λείποντος τῇ οὐσίᾳ] after his birth . . . then one should deem Father and Son corporeal [σῶμα] and the Father divided . . . they will reduce the Father to a body.[41]

---

[35]*Enn.*, 4.4.28.56;4.7.10.19; *Abst.*, 1.19; *Sent.*, 33.
[36]Analysed in my 'Anti-Subordinationism' and 'Dynamic Unity'.
[37]Socrates, *HE.*, 1.8; Athanasius, *Decr.*, 33.
[38]Ἐξ οὐκ ὄντων, like a creature.
[39]Ἐξ ἑτέρας ὑποστάσεως ἢ οὐσίας: Origen's distinction between *ousia* and *hypostasis* is not yet received.
[40]*Princ.*, 4.4.1 in Greek = Marcellus F31 (Eusebius, *C.Marc.*, 1.4).
[41]*Com. Joh.*, 20.18.157.

Origen countered contemporary 'heretics' who deemed 'a part of God's essence transformed into the Son' (*partem aliquam substantiae Dei in Filium versam*), or the Son 'created from no substance' (*ex nullis substantibus*) and outside God.[42]

At Nicaea, in the conciliar fathers' discussion about the insertion of *homoousion* in the dogma, Origen's argument emerged clearly. The Nicene fathers, according to Eusebius' letter, raised the same objection as Origen, which Eusebius emphasized also in *DE* 4.3.13, 5.1.4-14: the Son's generation is unlike any physical generation by separation of a part of a substance (*ousia*). He is consubstantial and coeternal with the Father; therefore, as Eusebius claims with Origen, it is impossible to state that 'there was a time in which He was not' (4.3.3, 5.1.15). The Son was generated by the Father 'without deprivation, diminution, severance, or division' (οὔτι πω κατὰ στέρησιν ἢ μείωσιν ἢ τομὴν ἢ διαίρεσιν, 4.3.11). This is what both Origen and the Nicene fathers stressed too. Eusebius of Nicomedia reported the same concern when he observed that if the Son derives 'from the Father, in the sense that the Son is a part of the Father or an emanation of the Father's essence/substance [μέρος αὐτοῦ ἢ ἐξ ἀπορροίας τῆς οὐσίας], it could not be claimed that he was created or established' (κτιστόν, θεμελιωτόν).[43] That the Son is a part or fragment (μέρος) of the Father was denied by Origen and the Nicene fathers, who ruled out that *homoousios* could be understood materialistically, in defining the Nicene dogma.

Once established that *homoousios* – a non-biblical word[44] – did not entail a corporeal generation – through Origen's assurance that the Son 'is not a part/fragment of the Father's essence' (οὐ μὴν μέρος αὐτοῦ τῆς οὐσίας) – Eusebius gave his assent to the creedal formula with ὁμοούσιος, adhering to its 'correct meaning' (τῆς ὀρθῆς διανοίας, §10): the same meaning defended by Origen. This cleared away misunderstandings of *homoousios* as implying the Son's material separation from the Father: Origen had already contested such misunderstandings. Eusebius seems to think with Origen's definition of 'ἐκ τῆς οὐσίας' in mind, describing the Son's generation not 'by division of material substance' (κατὰ διαίρεσιν τῆς οὐσίας), nor 'by alteration of the Father's substance' (κατ'ἀλλοίωσιν τῆς τοῦ Πατρὸς οὐσίας); the Son is not 'from another substance [ἐξ ἑτέρας οὐσίας], but from that of the Father [ἐκ τοῦ Πατρός]'.

In Eusebius' report, the Nicene fathers declared that the noun ὁμοούσιος is found, if not in Scripture, in the oeuvre of 'learned and illustrious [λογίους καὶ ἐπιφανεῖς] ancient bishops and writers'. Eusebius probably refers to 'bishops' such as Irenaeus and to the 'writer' Origen, who had rejected the dogmatic formulae later anathematized at Nicaea: the Son was generated 'from non-being' (ἐξ οὐκ ὄντων, perceived as reducing the Son to a creature) and 'there was a time when (the Son) did not exist' (ἦν ποτε ὅτε οὐκ ἦν, later used by Arius, whose subordinationism

---

[42]*Princ.*, 4.4.1 in Latin.
[43]*Letter to Paulinus of Tyre, ap.* Theodoret, *HE.*, 1.5.
[44]Eusebius, *Ep.Caes.*, 8.

was condemned at Nicaea).[45] From Origen, such a rejection passed on to Nicaea's dogmatic definitions, formally through Constantine, who was no learned theologian, knew very little Greek and required a translator (even at Nicaea) to have his speech rendered into Greek (*V.C.* 3.13.1), and who read Eusebius' works in Latin translation (*V.C.* 4.35.2-3). Thus, he had to rely on theological advisers for *homoousios* and the relevant literature: primarily Origen, probably through Eusebius. Eusebius *V.C.* 2.48 reports Constantine's letter to Alexander of Alexandria and Arius, where he states that their division was of no importance: 'I find the cause to be really insignificant, really unworthy of such a fierce contention.' Constantine emerges as having little perception of the theological issues at stake with *homoousios* and its corollaries and could hardly have introduced it by himself at Nicaea.[46] Arianism, moreover, was not the cause of the convocation of Nicaea by Constantine.[47]

Eusebius in his late *Theophany* seems to have fully espoused the Nicene Christological dogma: 'God from God', 'unique image of the light of the Father's essence', 'one in essence' (ὁμοούσιος). Constantine's argument for the introduction of *homoousios* is also explained in the *Oration to the Saints* (*Oratio ad sanctorum coetum*, appended to Eusebius' *Vita Constantini* in the manuscripts) 9, where the Nicene faith is claimed consistent with Plato's theology as understood by 'Middle Platonism' and early Neoplatonism: a God above every essence, and a second God – two, but possessing one perfection; the second comes from the first and is the agent of creation. God-Logos ordered everything and is God and God's Son. Constantine was inspired by Eusebius in all the *Oration*. The *Oration* expresses Eusebius' Origenian convictions on Plato's and Christianity's agreements and its reasons, on anti-fatalism, anti-casualism, the valuing of free will against the objection that God could create humans docile (the same to which Origen and Bardaisan responded[48]), the use of 'second God' (δεύτερος θεός) but in reference to Plato, Christ as Physician and his anti-materialistic generation, and more. If Constantine famously described himself as 'bishop of those outside' (ἐπίσκοπος τῶν ἐκτός),[49] this was Eusebius' definition: he viewed Constantine as 'bishop', teaching virtue and faith to his

---

[45]In an Athanasian fragment, in *Princ.*, 4.4.1, and elsewhere. Argument on ἦν ποτε ὅτε οὐκ ἦν in my 'Alexander of Aphrodisias'. Arius' dogmatic statements are reported by his opponents, especially Athanasius and the historians Socrates and Sozomen.

[46]That there is someone else before Constantine's *homoousios* is hypothesized by Mark Edwards as well, who thinks of Alexander of Alexandria: 'Alexander of Alexandria and the Homoousion', *VChr* 66, no. 5 (2012): 482–502. Even Alexander, I note, was influenced by Origen; however, Alexander never used *homoousios* in any extant writing (Henryk Pietras, *Council of Nicaea* (Rome: GBP, 2016), p. 184).

[47]Constantine's post-synodal letters to the Church of Alexandria and of the Council to the Alexandrian Church were forged: Pietras, *Nicaea*; see also Ayres, *Nicaea*; Mark Smith, *The Idea of Nicaea in the Early Church Councils* (Oxford: Oxford University Press, 2018), and also on the complex legacy of Nicaea, Carlos Galvão Sobrinho, *Theological Controversy and Christian Leadership in the Late Roman Empire* (Oakland: University of California, 2013).

[48]See my 'Origen, Bardaisan, and the Origin of Universal Salvation', *HTR* 102 (2009): 135–68.

[49]*V.C.* 4.24.1; cf.1.44.1.

subjects and liberating them from demons; Eusebius used ἐπισκοπή/ἐπισκοπέω in reference to Christ's government.[50]

Constantine's emphasis upon the Son as the Father's consubstantial 'will' (βουλή/ βούλησις)[51] and creator of all reminds me of Origen and his teachers, Pantaenus and Ammonius, who posited the Logos as God's βουλή which established all creation.[52] Eusebius may also have transmitted this idea: according to him, the Son-Logos subsisted by the Father's βούλησις and God's will created the universe.[53] Eusebius depends on Origen, who assimilated God's Logos-Nous-Wisdom to God's Will[54] and deemed the world created by God's will (1.2.6: 'the Father's will is sufficient to the subsistence of what the Father wants', *sufficere voluntas Patris ad subsistendum hoc quod vult Pater*). For Origen, the unity between Father and the Son is a sharing of both essence-*ousia* and will: 'God's will [θέλημα] is in the Son's will, which is indistinguishable from that of the Father, so they are not two wills [δύο θελήματα], but one.'[55] Origen is speaking of the Son's divine will (different from Jesus' human will according to later dyotheletism). God's Wisdom is 'the immaculate mirror of God's activity [ἐνεργείας = *inoperationis*), and the Son's operation does not differ from that of the Father, and their act of will [*motus*] is the same in all . . . without any dissimilarity between Son and Father' (*Princ.* 1.2.12). Gregory Nyssen built on this, arguing that from their equality of essence (οὐσία) comes their equality of power (δύναμις) and operation (ἐνέργεια); he was also drawing on Origen when establishing Christ's two wills, depending on his two natures,[56] as later Maximus did: and his dyotheletism built the dogma concerning Christ's two wills later on.[57] Notably, Origen established the identity of substance between Father and Son (ὁμοουσιότης) also through their shared essence as 'charity-love': since the Father is ἀγάπη and the Son is ἀγάπη, they have the same nature (*C.Cant.* prol. 2.26).

Origen first imported the formula 'there was a/no time when X did not exist', (οὐκ) ἦν ποτε ὅτε οὐκ ἦν, crucial to the Nicene dogma, from imperial Greek philosophical cosmological debates ('pagan', but also Philonic[58]) into Christology.

---

[50]Hazel Johannessen, *The Demonic in the Political Thought of Eusebius* (Oxford: Oxford University Press, 2016), 163–7.

[51]Opitz 27.1.

[52]Pantaenus of Alexandria, *Frag.* 2, in *Reliquiae sacrae*, vol. 1, ed. M. J. Routh, Oxford (E Typographei Academico) 1846 = Clement of Alexandria *Frag.* 48 Stahlin apud Maximus the Confesssor, *De variis difficilibus locis Dionysii et Gregorii*, 60–1 Oehler (PG 91.1085). Ammonius *ap.* Photius, *Bibl.*, 251.461b-462; see my 'Divine Power'.

[53]Eusebius, *Con. Marc.*, 95-96 Logan.

[54]*Princ.*, 4.4.1: 'will from the mind', *voluntas a mente*; 1.2.6=1.2.9: *voluntas ex mente*.

[55]*Com.Joh.*, 13.36.228; cf.13.36.231.

[56]*Antirrh.* GNO III/1.181.18–23.

[57]Excellent overview from Nicaea to the dyotheletism controversy in John McGuckin, *The Eastern Orthodox Church* (New Haven, CT: Yale University Press, 2020), pp. 89–121; also Sergey Trostyanskiy (ed.), *Seven Icons of Christ: An Introduction to the Oikoumenical Councils* (Piscataway, NJ: Gorgias Press, 2016).

[58]Philo, *Decal.*, 58: 'There was a time when the world was not'; *Prov.*, 1.7: 'There was never a time when God did not create.'

His defence of the dogmatic formula 'there was no time when Christ did not exist' further supports his anti-subordinationism. Origen and Alexander of Aphrodisias both have this formula; Origen didn't take it from Christian texts. In Origen, 'there was a time when [Christ] did not exist' (ἦν ποτε ὅτε οὐκ ἦν) describes his adversaries' Christologically subordinationist position, later attributed to Arius.[59] The idea of eternity was a central concern in Origen's philosophy and theology:[60] he attached absolute eternity, transcending time (all times and all aeons), exclusively to God, so that the Son's coeternity with the Father[61] implied the Son's divinity. Origen warns that the formula (οὐκ) ἦν ποτε ὅτε οὐκ ἦν, 'there was no time when he did not exist', must be understood correctly, since the meanings of 'when' and 'no time' refers to time, while the statements concerning the Father, the Son, and the Holy Spirit[62] must be understood as transcending all time, aeons and eternity. For the Trinity alone surpasses the comprehension not only of temporal, but even of eternal intelligence, whereas all other beings, not included in it, are measured by times and aeons.[63]

Only God is absolutely eternal, adiastematic or adimensional, therefore transcending time.

Anticipating the Nicene dogma, Origen used οὐκ ἦν ποτε ὅτε οὐκ ἦν twice in *Princ.* 4.4.1 (cited earlier), a tenet which Origen defended against 'heretics'. Rufinus translated *fuerit aliquando quando non fuerit* ('there was a time when the Son was not', in the positive, referred to 'heretics') and *Numquam fuit quando non fuit*, 'there was no time when the Son was not' – Origen's position. The polemic against those who posited the Son's temporal beginning is still reflected in *Com. Rom.* 1.7.15-19: 'This we said against those who express impiety against God's only-begotten Son, who always was, like the Father [*semper fuit sicut et Pater*].' In *Com. Rom.* 1.7.4-5, *non erat quando non erat*, and in *Princ.* 1.2.9, *non est quando non fuerit*, both in reference to the Son, translate οὐκ ἦν ποτε ὅτε οὐκ ἦν. The former is also reported by Pamphilus, and Rufinus' translation is the same: 'in spirit, the Son was before (Jesus' birth) and there was no time when He was not' (*non erat quando non erat, Apol.* 52). *Princ.* 1.2.9, too, is reproduced by Pamphilus and rendered by Rufinus likewise: *non est autem quando non fuerit* (*Apol.* 58).

---

[59]Its presence in Nicaea's anathemas, for Mark Edwards, either is 'a caricature' of Arius' thought or addressed someone else ('The First Council of Nicaea', in *Cambridge History of Christianity 1*, eds Margaret Mitchell and Frances Young (Cambridge: Cambridge University Press, 2006), pp. 552–67, 563. I note that it is not only ascribed to Arius by Alexander and other hostile sources who report his thought (such as Athanasius and Socrates), but it is also the formula that Origen already attributed to the subordinationists of his day. It is impossible to establish whether they used it or it is Origen's own formulation. Arius may have turned Origen's Christological formula upon its head.

[60]See Ilaria L. E. Ramelli and David Konstan, *Terms for Eternity* (Piscataway, NJ: Gorgias, 2007; 2013, new ed.), pp. 126–38.

[61]Supported in *Com. Joh.*, 2.19.130, *Hom. Jer.*, 9.4, *Princ.*, 1.2.2; 1.2.11, the Athanasian fragment, and elsewhere.

[62]For Origen's and his followers' reception of the Holy Spirit, especially Johannine, see my 'The Spirit as Paraclete', in *Receptions of the Fourth Gospel in Antiquity*, ed. Jörg Frey (Tübingen: Mohr Siebeck, 2021).

[63]*Princ.*, 4.1.28.

Origen's eternity formula is not Rufinus' forgery, there being at least three Greek attestations, the first from direct textual transmission and not fragmentary:

1. *Com. Joh.* 2.19.130, of the Logos' coeternity with the Father: 'there was no time when the First Principle was without Logos/irrational' (οὐκ ἦν γὰρ ὅτε ἡ ἀρχὴ ἄλογος ἦν);

2. F31 from Marcellus (*ap.* Eusebius *Con. Marc.* 1.34) and

3. Origen's fragment quoted by Athanasius, *Decr.* 27.1-2, on the Son:

> If it is an image [εἰκών] of the invisible God, it is an invisible image. I would even dare add that, being also the Father's likeness [ὁμοιότης], *there is no time when it was not* [οὐκ ἔστιν ὅτε οὐκ ἦν]. For *when is it that* [πότε] the Godhead . . . had not the effulgence of its own glory [ἀπαύγασμα τῆς ἰδίας δόξης], so that one could dare ascribe a beginning [ἀρχήν] to the Son, who *purportedly earlier was not* [πρότερον οὐκ ὄντος]? *When is it that* the image of the Father's individual substance [ὑποστάσεως], the expression, the Logos that knows the Father, *was not* [πότε . . . οὐκ ἦν]? Whoever dares say, 'There was a time when the Son was not' [ἦν ποτε ὅτε οὐκ ἦν] should consider that he will also say: 'At a certain time *Wisdom was not* [ποτὲ οὐκ ἦν], *the Logos was not* [οὐκ ἦν], *Life was not* [οὐκ ἦν].'

Here the (*ante litteram*) dogmatic formula is attested repeatedly, within the affirmation of the Son's coeternity with the Father, as in *Com. Joh.* 2.19.130. The coeternity of Christ-Logos-Wisdom with God, affirmed by Origen at the end of the passage quoted by Athanasius, is probably the source of Alexander of Alexandria's *Letter to All Bishops* 13: 'How is it possible that there was a time when the Son of God, Logos and Wisdom, was not [ἦν ποτε ὅτε οὐκ ἦν]? For this is tantamount to stating that *God was at some point without Logos and Wisdom*', irrational and stupid (ἄλογον καὶ ἄσοφον ποτέ).[64] Origen had already warned that 'There was a time when the Son was not' is tantamount to declaring: '*At some point Wisdom was not, the Logos was not.*' Alexander affirms the same, inspired by Origen, in his *Letter to Alexander of Constantinople*:

> Is it not impious to state that *there was a time when God's Wisdom did not exist* [μὴ εἶναί ποτε τὴν σοφίαν τοῦ Θεοῦ] . . . God's power was not [τὴν δύναμιν τοῦ Θεοῦ ποτε μὴ ὑπάρχειν], God's Logos was missing? . . . If the image of God had not existed eternally [ἀεί], clearly God, whose image is the Son, would not exist eternally.[65]

In the history of dogmas, 'there was no time when the Son was not' (οὐκ ἦν ποτε ὅτε οὐκ ἦν) became a catchphrase of Nicene 'orthodoxy' against the 'Arian' slogan 'there was a time when [the Son] was not' (ἦν ποτε ὅτε οὐκ ἦν). Alexander of Alexandria

---

[64]*Ap.* Socrates, *HE.*, 1.6.
[65]*Ap.* Theodoret, *HE.*, 1.3.

ascribed to Arius the sentence ἦν ποτε ὅτε οὐκ ἦν.[66] These opposite sentences are largely attested in Christianity from the Arian controversy onwards. But before Origen, these formulae are never found in Christian authors, only in two 'pagan' philosophers who lived immediately before him:

1. The Middle Platonist Alcinous, who argued that the cosmos has a cause, but not a temporal beginning: 'When it is said that the cosmos is originated [γενητόν], it should not be understood that *there was a time when the cosmos was not*' (ἐν ᾧ οὐκ ἦν κόσμος),[67] and

2. Alexander of Aphrodisias, who alone repeatedly used the same expression as Origen (and Nicaea), ἦν ποτε ὅτε οὐκ ἦν, within his reflection on eternity/ perpetuity (ἀϊδιότης).[68]

This expression arose within philosophical discussions of eternity, about the definition of what is perpetual (ἀΐδιον), as is clear from Alcinous and Alexander. The 'Middle Platonist' Calvenus Taurus also discussed the world's eternity (*Com. Tim.* 28AC); the same problem was debated by Atticus, known to Origen,[69] who thought – based on his exegesis of Plato – that the world was created 'in time' (κατὰ χρόνον). This was a widely discussed issue in 'Middle Platonism': what Plato meant by saying that the cosmos γέγονεν (*Tim.* 28B7).[70] Establishing whether the cosmos began in time and 'there was a time when it was not' was pivotal in relation to the 'perishability axiom': whatever had a temporal beginning must also have a temporal end. If 'there was a time when [the cosmos] was not' (ἦν ποτε ὅτε οὐκ ἦν), then 'there will be a time when it will no longer be' (ἔσται ὅτε οὐκ ἔσται).

Origen (possibly through Eusebius, Constantine and maybe Alexander) is probably the principal, if not immediate, inspirer of the Nicene notion of the Son's coeternity and consubstantiality with the Father, both (1) by positing the identity of *ousia* between Father and Son and (2) through his formula, 'there was no time when the Son was not', as Athanasius, Nyssen and other theologians were aware. Moreover, by claiming that the Trinity has one common *ousia* but three individual substances or 'hypostases', he inspired the dogmatic definition *mia ousia treis hypostaseis* through Nyssen and (from a certain point onwards) Basil and Nazianzen.[71] Origen's assertion of the Son's divinity, coeternity with the Father and consubstantiality (through the sharing of the same *ousia*), along with his anti-subordinationistic reading of 1 Cor. 15.28, taken up by Nyssen, confirm Origen's role in anticipating the Nicene and

---

[66]Socrates, *HE.*, 1.16.15.

[67]*Didaskalikos*, 14.3.

[68]Argument in my 'Alexander of Aphrodisias'. Ramelli-Konstan, *Terms for Eternity*, pp. 29–30 on Alexander's concept and terminology of eternity; 28–35 on Aristotle and Hellenistic philosophy; 12–28 on eternity in Plato and Platonism.

[69]See Ramelli, 'Atticus and Origen on the Soul of God the Creator', *JahRel* 10 (2011): 13–35.

[70]On this Platonic interpretive controversy concerning the *Timaeus*, see George Boys-Stones, *Platonist Philosophy 80BC to AD250* (Cambridge: Cambridge University Press, 2018), Chs 6–7; Christina Hoenig, *Plato's Timaeus and the Latin Tradition* (Cambridge: Cambridge University Press, 2018), pp. 22–9.

[71]On this definition in Nyssen and later theologians, literature in Ramelli, 'Hypostasis'.

Constantinopolitan dogmatic lines. Even Origen's supposed exhortation to pray to God but not to Christ, usually deemed a proof of 'subordinationism', is countered by his assertion that both God and God's Logos must be prayed.[72]

THE COUNCIL OF CONSTANTINOPLE

The Nicene and Constantinopolitan dogmatic line was prepared by the theology of Origen and the Cappadocians, especially Gregory Nyssen. The Cappadocians developed and emphasized the notion of equality, bringing the Trinitarian hypostases to the level of Plotinus' One, but the premises were in Origen's theology and his concept of the divinity and coeternity of the three hypostases:[73] Nyssen (like Athanasius in *Decr.* 27) used Origen's arguments in his own anti-Arian polemic. Origen impacted the Nicene-Cappadocian line. This line, which was represented above all by Nyssen, is that God is 'one and the same nature or essence [μία οὐσία] in three individual substances [τρεῖς ὑποστάσεις]' and the Son is consubstantial (ὁμοούσιος) with the Father. The three hypostases of the Trinity share in the same divine nature (οὐσία). Origen maintained that they have the same divine, eternal nature but are three different individual substances (ὑποστάσεις): Nyssen followed him.

Origen's thought arguably represented a novel, foundational theory with respect to the individuality of the Trinity's ὑποστάσεις, whom he conceived as three different individual substances within the common divine essence of one God.[74] On the basis of early Imperial philosophical and medical debates, Origen maintains that the Father is endowed with his own hypostasis or individual substance and the Son with his own, different from the Father's. For instance, in *Cels.* 8.12, Origen criticizes those who denied that the Father and the Son were 'two different hypostases' (δύο ὑποστάσεις). Origen was closely influenced by philosophical and medical authors of the early Imperial age, and by Scripture, especially Heb. 1.3.[75] Mainly under the impact of the Cappadocians, the Trinitarian terminology was clarified through the aforementioned formula 'one common essence, three individual substances' (μία οὐσία, τρεῖς ὑποστάσεις), which continued to be used and was still ascribed to them by the Origenian Eriugena (*Periph.* 2.34).[76] Now, the Cappadocians, and especially Nyssen, depended on Origen. The role of Origen in the construction of the Trinitarian notion of hypostasis was so remarkable that he may have influenced the interpretation of the Neoplatonic Triad (against Plotinus' own use)

---

[72]*Cels.*, 8.26.

[73]Demonstration in my 'Dynamic Unity'.

[74]In 'Hypostasis' (2012); further in 'Dynamic Unity'.

[75]As I extensively argued in 'Hypostasis' and further 'Hebrews and Philo on Hypostasis: Intersecting Trajectories?', in *Pascha nostrum Christus*, eds PierFranco Beatrice and Bernard Pouderon (Paris: Beauchesne, 2016), pp. 27–49.

[76]See my 'From God to God: Eriugena's Protology and Eschatology against the Backdrop of His Platonic Patristic Sources', in *Eriugena's Christian Neoplatonism and Its Sources in Patristic Philosophy and Ancient Philosophy*, dir. Ilaria L. E. Ramelli (Oxford University, August 2019), forthcoming in *SP* [1–25].

as three hypostases: αἱ τρεῖς ἀρχικαὶ ὑποστάσεις, 'the three hypostases that are the first principles' (ἀρχαί) of all, precisely as the three divine hypostases theorized by Origen, which were conceived as the first principles (ἀρχαί) of all.[77]

Gregory of Nyssa through his anti-subordinationistic argument in *In Illud: Tunc et Ipse Filius* interpreted 1 Cor. 15.28, which buttressed Origen's theory of apokatastasis, in an anti-subordinationistic way. Gregory claimed that the Son is not subordinate to the Father in his divinity but in his body, which corresponds to all humanity. Gregory's anti-subordinationistic demonstration derives from Origen. Origen's influence is clear everywhere, from the main arguments to the finest exegetical details.[78] Gregory closely took up Origen's argument against subordinationism and its connection to the doctrine of apokatastasis (the link between anti-subordinationism and apokatastasis in Gregory's argument was established already by Origen, in *Princ.* 3.5.6-7 and elsewhere). Gregory's dependence on Origen in his polemic against subordinationism, within his stance against 'Arianism', confirms that Origen was not seen as a precursor of Arianism by theologians such as Gregory, Athanasius, the Cappadocians and Eusebius – who subscribed to the Nicene Creed –, but as a forerunner of their own Nicene-Constantinopolitan dogmatic line. Athanasius, who construed himself as the champion of anti-Arianism, cited Origen as an authority on the Son as coeternal with the Father, against the 'Arians', being aware that the Son's coeternity entailed the sharing of the same divine nature with the Father (as pointed out earlier).

Gregory of Nyssa in *Against Eunomius* refuted the argument of Eunomius, who entertained a subordinationistic view of the Son. Gregory here used σχέσις often, to describe the equality of the Father–Son relationship. Eunomius denied the egalitarian relation between these two hypostases. Relying on Origen's innovative notion of hypostasis as individual substance within the common Trinitarian *ousia*, Gregory claimed that the Father and the Son are in a reciprocal relation, on a par. For Gregory, all the three hypostases of the Trinity (not only the Father) correspond to the first principle, Plotinus' One, as is clear, for instance, from *Ad Graecos*. From the ontological equality of the three hypostases derived the equality of their powers and activities: Nyssen made this point on the basis of Origen's premises.[79] On the same basis, Gregory's doctrine of 'social analogy' maintained that the same egalitarian relationship that obtains within the Trinity also obtains within all

---

[77]Argument in Ramelli, 'Hypostasis'.

[78]I comprehensively demonstrated this in 'Origen's Anti-Subordinationism'; 'Gregory of Nyssa's Trinitarian Theology in *In Illud*: His Polemic against "Arian" Subordinationism and Apokatastasis', in *Gregory of Nyssa: The Minor Treatises on Trinitarian Theology and Apollinarism,* eds Volker Drecoll and Margitta Berghaus (Leiden: Brill, 2011), pp. 445–78.

[79]See Ramelli, 'Divine Power' and 'La triade Ousia-Energeia-Dynamis in Gregorio di Nissa', in *La Triade nel Neoplatonismo*, eds Giulio D'Onofrio, Renato De Filiippis and Ernesto Sergio Mainoldi (Turnhout: Brepols, forthcoming).

humanity; Gregory also applied this equation, which stressed the equal dignity of all human beings, to the rejection of social injustice and slavery.[80]

THE COUNCIL OF EPHESUS

Earlier Christian theology, including that by Origen, proved seminal not only for the dogmatic definitions at Nicaea and Constantinople (in the latter case, Origen through the Cappadocians) but even for Ephesus and Chalcedon. Origen was among the very first to use Theotokos ('Mother of God', established dogmatically at Ephesus) of Mary, and the first to explain its meaning theologically. In *C.Rom.* 1 he 'extensively examined how/in what sense Mary is called Theotokos' or 'what is the meaning of "Theotokos"'.[81] Origen's Greek fragments also feature Θεοτόκος in reference to Mary,[82] a term used by Origen's admirers Eusebius,[83] Nyssen,[84] Nazianzen[85] and Athanasius, who quoted Origen as a model of Nicene orthodoxy *ante litteram*. Furthermore, that Origen was the precursor of the Ephesian dogma is supported by the fact that Pierius, a close, immediate follower of Origen, wrote *On the Theotokos*, indicating that this was a theological concern of Origen. This is confirmed by the De Boor fragments attributed to Philip of Side, but probably coming from scholia to Eusebius' *Church History* and an epitome:[86] Pierius, besides composing a *Pascha* (Περὶ Πάσχα) like Origen, wrote 'many other needed works, especially that *On the Theotokos* [καὶ μάλιστα τὸ Περὶ τῆς Θεοτόκου]'.[87]

Origen seems to witness the use of Θεοτόκος well before Ephesus. That there was a rich devotion to Mary in the second–third century is well documented.[88] Origen already applied the doctrine of *communicatio idiomatum* in *Princ.* 2.6.3 – a tenet that was developed at length in subsequent theological discussions – so he could both affirm the Son of God's death and declare Mary 'God's Mother' (*Theotokos*), not merely 'mother of Jesus' or 'of Christ' (as Nestorius preferred), thus anticipating both Ephesus' *Theotokos* dogma, and Chalcedon's definition of Christ's two natures and their interrelation. Origen insisted on Christ's two distinct natures, in *Princ.* 2.6.2, *Com. Joh.* 10.23 (which describes Christ as 'human', because he died, and 'not human', *qua* more divine than human), *Com. Matth.* 12.37 (and everywhere), on the divine nature, 'in the form of God', which appeared to the disciples at the

---

[80]See my *Social Justice*, 172-210 and 'Christian Slavery in Theology and Practice: Its Relation to God, Sin, and Justice', in *The Cambridge History of Ancient Christianity*, eds Bruce Longenecker and David Wilhite (Cambridge: Cambridge University Press, 2021).

[81]Πῶς Θεοτόκος λέγεται πλατέως ἐξήτασεν, Socrates, *HE.*, 7.32.17.

[82]*Fr.Luc.*, 41b.1; 80.4; *Schol.Luc.* PG 17.321; *Fr.Ps.* 21:21; *Fr.Deut.* PG 12.813.

[83]*V.C.* 3.43.2; *Con. Marc.*, 2.1.4; *C.Ps.* PG 23.1344.11, etc.

[84]*Ep.*, 3.24.3; *Virg.*, 14.1; 19.1, etc.

[85]*Or.*, 29 De Filio 4; 23 occurrences in *Christus patiens*, of dubious attribution.

[86]See Luke Stevens, 'The Origin of the de Boor Fragments', *JECS* 26, no. 4 (2018): 631–57.

[87]Fragment around *HE.*, 7.32.26.

[88]Stephen Shoemaker, *Mary in Early Christian Faith and Devotion* (New Haven, CT: Yale University Press, 2016).

Transfiguration on the mountain, and the human nature, 'in the form of a servant', visible to those who waited at the foot of the mountain, which symbolizes closeness to God. But the human and the divine nature belong to one hypostasis. Origen inspired Nyssen's and Evagrius' Christology, Cyril of Alexandria, Ephesus and Chalcedon.

THE COUNCIL OF CHALCEDON

The Chalcedonian dogmatic definition, indeed, rests on Origen, the Cappadocians, Evagrius and other theologians, including Cyril of Alexandria. It has, as mentioned, close relations to Ephesus, since the choice between *Theotokos* and *Khristotokos* for Mary (the object of Cyril's and Nestorius' dogmatic clash) depends on how Christ is conceived: one hypostasis with two natures or two hypostases.

The Council of Chalcedon is the third ecumenical council after Nicaea (325), Constantinople (381) and Ephesus (431).[89] Its confession (451) focused on the crucial issue of the relationship between the human and the divine nature of Christ, in continuity with the earlier councils:

> We, then, following the holy Fathers, all with one consent, teach people to confess *one and the same Son*, our Lord Jesus Christ, the same perfect in Godhead and also perfect in humanhood; truly God and truly man, of a rational soul and body; consubstantial with the Father according to *Divinity*, and consubstantial with us according to *Humanity*; in all things like us, but without sin; begotten before all ages of the Father according to Divinity, and in these latter days, for us and for our salvation, born of the Virgin Mary, the Theotokos, according to Humanity – *one and the same* Christ, Son, Lord, only begotten, to be acknowledged *in two natures, without confusion, change, division or separation* (ἐν δύο φύσεσιν ἀσυγχύτως, ἀτρέπτως, ἀδιαιρέτως, ἀχωρίστως) the *distinction* of natures being by no means taken away by the *union*, but rather the property of each nature being preserved, and concurring in one Person and one Individual Substance (Hypostasis), not parted or divided into two Persons, but one and the same Son, the only begotten God the Logos, the Lord Jesus Christ; as the prophets from the beginning [have declared] concerning Him, and the Lord Jesus Christ Himself has taught us, and the Creed of the holy Fathers has handed down to us.

Even Evagrius, who followed the Cappadocians and especially Nyssen, notwithstanding accusations of subordinationism and dichotomic Christology, anticipated Chalcedon's adverbs on the unconfused unity of the two natures in Christ. My reading of the first sentence of KG 6.14[90] confirms that Christ is

---

[89] On Chalcedon, see Brian E. Daley, *God Visible: Patristic Christology Reconsidered* (Oxford: Oxford University Press 2018); ch. 1 includes a presentation of scholarship on the Christology of Chalcedon.
[90] See my commentary in *Evagrius' Kephalaia Gnostika* (Leiden: Brill; Atlanta: SBL, 2015); further arguments in 'Gregory Nyssen's and Evagrius' Biographical and Theological Relations', in *Evagrius between Origen, the Cappadocians, and Neoplatonism*, ed. Eadem (Leuven: Peeters, 2017), pp. 165–231.

homoousios with the Father, as is supported by KG 3.1. In *Skemmata* 1, Evagrius treats Christ as a compound of creatural and divine nature: he claims that Christ *qua* Christ possesses 'the essential knowledge', that is, God, who constitutes his own divine nature. Consistently, Palladius in his biography of Evagrius depicts him as supporting, against 'heretics' such as 'Arians' and Eunomians, the full divinity of Christ-Logos, the Son of God, who also assumed a human body, soul and intellect. Therefore, Christ is both God and a rational creature.

Evagrius' alleged dichotomic Christology is charged with failing to point in the direction of Chalcedon. However, apart from the issue of judging Evagrius from the perspective of posterior theological developments, it must be noted that in KG 6.14 Christ is said to possess 'inseparably' the 'substantial knowledge' that is God. This adverb at Chalcedon describes the inseparability of the two natures of Christ (ἀχωρίστως, ἀδιαιρέτως). Here, Evagrius uses 'inseparable' to describe the union of the divine and human natures in Christ (as Chalcedon would do): 'Christ is the only one who *always and inseparably* possesses substantial knowledge in himself.' 'Always' also anticipates Chalcedon's ἀτρέπτως. Christ is both God and human; he is a rational creature (a *logikon*), *and* divine, 'always and inseparably'.

Cyril of Alexandria (the aforementioned supporter of the Theotokos dogma against Nestorius, on the basis of the Christology that would be expressed at Chalcedon)[91] applied the future Chalcedonian adverb ἀχωρίστως to the Trinity: it is consubstantial (ὁμοούσιος), 'a clear and unconfused individuality [ἀσύγχυτον ἰδιότητα] of the three Hypostases [τῶν τριῶν ὑποστάσεων], each in its own existence [ἐν ὑπάρξεσιν ἰδικαῖς]'.[92] In 'pagan' Platonism, shortly after Chalcedon, the same adjective will occur especially in Syrianus and Proclus – the latter, a great inspirer of Dionysius along with Origen[93] – in reference to the Ideas/Forms. Syrianus speaks of the 'divine and noeric Ideas [θεῖα εἴδη καὶ νοερά]' that can 'unite with one another and be separated from one another purely and non-confusedly [καθαρῶς καὶ ἀσυγχύτως]'.[94] Similarly, Proclus states that each Form/Idea 'preserves its own property pure, and at the same time it participates in the others non-confusedly [μετέχειν δὲ καὶ τῶν ἄλλων ἀσυγχύτως], not becoming the other, but participating in the property of the other and offering to the other its own in participation' (*In Parm.* 755.5-14). The Chalcedonian definition made use of adverbs that were used in philosophico-theological debates at that time.

Chalcedon precipitated a schism in the Eastern churches. For some, the acceptance of two *physeis* in Christ was tantamount to Nestorianism. Churches that

---

[91]John McGuckin, *St. Cyril of Alexandria and the Christological Controversy* (Leiden: Brill, 1994); Idem, 'Theotokos: The Mother of God in the Later Patristic Period', in *The Cambridge Companion to the Virgin Mary* (Cambridge: Cambridge University Press, 2008), pp. 115–20.
[92]*Trinit.*, 423.4-11.
[93]See my 'Origen, Evagrios, and Dionysios', in *The Oxford Handbook to Dionysius the Areopagite* (Oxford: Oxford University Press, forthcoming); '"Pagan" and Christian Platonism in Dionysius: The Double-Reference Scheme and Its Meaning', in *Byzantine Platonists 284-1453*, eds Frederick Lauritzen and Sarah Klitenic Wear (Steubenville: Franciscan University, 2021).
[94]*In Metaph.*, 1179b33-35, p. 119.28.

rejected Chalcedon ended up with becoming schismatic. Division and confusion sometimes were one of the effects of a dogmatic definition; the same had happened after Nicaea.[95] The monotheletism/dyotheletism controversy, which we have no room to address here, even yielded exiles and tortures: the main victim was Maximus, who died and became a Confessor of the dogmatic orthodoxy (namely, dyotheletism).

CONCLUDING REMARKS: NOT ONLY CHRISTIANS OBSESSED WITH DOGMAS

As pointed out, Christians were somehow 'obsessed with dogmas' because they had to ground philosophically their theology, to claim that Christianity was not irrational, according to widespread charges, but was rational and philosophical, founded on the Logos. It must be acknowledged that 'pagan' Neoplatonists were also 'obsessed with dogmas', especially in late antiquity, when Platonism tended to become a religion – no less than Christianity became a philosophy. Emperor Julian, for example, who studied the theurgic Neoplatonist Iamblichus, was a Christian formerly, but became a 'pagan' Neoplatonist. In his final prayer in *To the Mother of the Gods*, 179D-180C, he invokes the Mother of the 'intellectual gods', 'Wisdom, Providence, and Creator of our souls', to grant 'to all humans happiness [εὐδαιμονία], whose main element is the knowledge of the gods [ἡ τῶν θεῶν γνῶσις]'. Now, for himself too, Julian asks first of all 'truth in the dogmas–convictions concerning the gods', ἀλήθειαν ἐν τοῖς περὶ θεῶν δόγμασιν. Indeed, already Seneca stated that 'the first cult offered to the deities is to believe that there are deities': *Primus est deorum cultus deos credere*.[96]

BIBLIOGRAPHY

Primary texts

Kinzig, W. *Faith in Formulae: A Collection of Early Christian Creeds and Creed-Related Texts*, 4 vols. Oxford: Oxford University Press, 2017.

Mansi, D. (ed.). *Sacrorum conciliorum nova et amplissima collection*. Graz: Akademische Druck u. Verlagsanstalt, 1960 reprint.

Munier, C. (ed.). *Les Statuta Ecclesiae Antiqua*. Édition-Études critiques. Paris: Presses universitaires de France, 1960.

Tanner, N. *Conciliorum oecumenicorum decreta. Decrees of the Ecumenical Councils*, vol. 1: *Nicea to Lateran V*. Washington, DC: Georgetown University Press, 1990.

---

[95]Ayres, *Nicaea*; Pietras, *Nicaea*.

[96]See my 'Alcune osservazioni su *credere*', *Maia* n.s. 51 (2000): 67–83; *Studi su Fides* (Madrid: Signifer, 2002); Teresa Morgan, *Roman Faith and Christian Faith: Pistis and Fides in the Early Roman Empire and Early Churches* (Oxford: Oxford University Press, 2015); my review *JRS* 107 (2017): 368–70.

Secondary sources

Ayres, L. *Nicaea and Its Legacy*. Oxford: Oxford University Press, 2004.

Beatrice, P. 'The Word *Homoousios* from Hellenism to Christianity', *CH* 71 (2002): 243–72.

Beierwaltes, W. 'Wie plantonisierten Christen?' *VChr* 28 (1974): 15–28.

Beierwaltes, W. 'Zur Geschichte des Platonismus, I', *Philosophisches Jahrbuch* 100 (1993): 194–9.

Beierwaltes, W. *Platonismus in Christentum*. Frankfurt: Klostermann, 1998.

Boys-Stones, G. *Platonist Philosophy 80BC to AD250: An Introduction and Collection of Sources in Translation*. Cambridge: Cambridge University Press, 2018.

Broc-Schmezer, C. 'La philosophie grecque comme propédeutique à l'évangile: Clément d'Alexandrie', *Foi et vie* 107 (2008): 77–87.

Broek, R. van der. 'The Christian School at Alexandria in the Second and Third Centuries', in Jan Willem Drijvers and Anthony MacDonald (eds), *Centers of Learning*, 39–47. Leiden: Brill, 1995.

Chadwick, H. *Early Christian Thought and the Classical Tradition*. Oxford: Clarendon, 1966.

Crouse, R. 'Origen in the Philosophical Tradition of the Latin West', in Robert Daly (ed.), *Origeniana V*, 565–9. Leuven: Peeters, 1992.

DenDulk, M. *Between Jews and Heretics: Refiguring Justin Martyr's Dialogue with Trypho*. London: Routledge, 2018.

Daley, Brian E. *God Visible: Patristic Christology Reconsidered*. Oxford: Oxford University Press, 2018.

Dinan, A. 'Αἴνιγμα and αἰνίττομαι in the Works of Clement of Alexandria', *SP* 44 (2010): 175–81.

Dorival, G. and Le Boulluec, A. *L'Abeille et l'Acier. Clément d'Alexandrie et Origène*. Paris: Les Belles Lettres, 2019.

Edwards, M. 'Did Origen Apply the Word *Homoousios* to the Son?', *JTS* 49 (1998): 658–70.

Edwards, M. 'The First Council of Nicaea', in Margaret Mitchell and Frances Young (eds), *The Cambridge History of Christianity 1*, 552–67. Cambridge: Cambridge University Press, 2006.

Edwards, M. 'Alexander of Alexandria and the Homoousion', *VChr* 66, no. 5 (2012): 482–502.

Edwards, R. 'Clement of Alexandria's "Gnostic" Exposition of the Decalogue', *JECS* 23 (2015): 501–28.

Engberg-Pedersen, T. 'Introduction: A Historiographical Essay', in *From Stoicism to Platonism: The Development of Philosophy, 100 BCE–100 CE*, 1–26. Cambridge: Cambridge University Press, 2017.

Freudenthal, G. 'The Astrologisation of the Aristotelian Cosmos: Celestial Influences on the Sublunar World in Aristotle, Alexander of Aphrodisias, and Averroes', in A. C. Bowen and Christian Wildberg (eds), *New Perspectives on Aristotle's De Coelo*, 239–28. Philosophia Antiqua 117. Leiden: Brill, 2009.

Gerson, L. 'From Plato's Good to Platonic God', *JPT* 2 (2008): 93–112.

Giulea, D. 'Antioch 268 and Its Legacy in the Fourth-Century Theological Debates', *HTR* 111, no. 2 (2018): 192–215.

Giulea, D. 'Basil of Caesarea's Authorship of Epistle 361', *VChr* 72 (2018): 41–70.

Grafton, A. and Williams, M. *Christianity and the Transformation of the Book.* Cambridge, MA: The Belknap Press of Harvard University Press, 2006.

Hengstermann, C. *Origenes und der Ursprung der Freiheitsmetaphysik.* Münster: Aschendorff, 2015.

Hoek, A. van den. 'The "Catechetical School" of Early Christian Alexandria and Its Philonic Heritage', *HTR* 90 (1997): 59–87.

Hoenig, C. *Plato's Timaeus and the Latin Tradition.* Cambridge: Cambridge University Press, 2018.

Hoffmann, P. 'What Was Commentary in Late Antiquity?' in Mary-Louise Gill (ed.), *Companion to Ancient Philosophy*, 597–62A. London: Wiley-Blackwell, 2006.

Hopkins, K. 'Christian Number and Its Implications', *JECS* 6 (1998): 185–226.

Jaeger, W. *Early Christianity and Greek Paideia.* Cambridge, MA: Harvard University, 1961.

Jacobsen, A.-C. *Christ the Teacher of Salvation.* Münster: Aschendorff, 2015.

Jakab, A. *Ecclesia Alexandrina.* Bern: Lang, 2004.

Johannessen, H. *The Demonic in the Political Thought of Eusebius.* Oxford: Oxford University Press, 2016.

Karfíková, L. 'Patristische Exegese: Origenes und Augustin', in *Von Augustin zu Abaelard. Studien zum christlichen Denken*, 1–22. Fribourg: Paradosis, 2015.

Lehtipuu, O. *Debates over the Resurrection of the Dead.* Oxford: Oxford University Press, 2015.

Lieu, J., and Carleton-Paget, J. (eds). *Christianity in the Second Century: Themes and Developments.* Cambridge: Cambridge University Press, 2017.

Lössl, J. 'Theology as Academic Discourse in Greco-Roman Late Antiquity', *JLARC* 10 (2016): 38–72.

MacMullen, R. *The Second Church: Popular Christianity A.D. 200–400.* Writings from the Greco-Roman World Supplements 1. Atlanta, GA: Society of Biblical Literature, 2009.

Malingrey, A. M. *'Philosophia' Étude d'un groupe de mots dans la littérature grecque des présocratiques au IVe siècle après J.-C.* Paris: Klincksieck, 1961.

Markschies, C. *Christian Theology and Its Institutions in the Early Roman Empire.* Waco: Baylor, 2015.

McGuckin, J. A. *St. Cyril of Alexandria and the Christological Controversy: Its History, Theology, and Texts.* Leiden: Brill, 1994; New York: St Vladimir Seminary Press, 2004.

McGuckin, J. A. 'Theotokos: The Mother of God in the Later Patristic Period', in S. Boss (ed.), *The Cambridge Companion to the Virgin Mary*, 115–20. Cambridge: Cambridge University Press, 2008.

McGuckin, J. A. *I Believe in One Lord Jesus Christ: Ancient Christian Doctrines.* Downers Grove, IL: InterVarsity Press, 2009.

McGuckin, J. A. *The Eastern Orthodox Church: A New History.* New Haven, CT; London: Yale University Press, 2020.

Morgan, T. *Roman Faith and Christian Faith: Pistis and Fides in the Early Roman Empire and Early Churches*. Oxford: Oxford University Press, 2015.

Mortley, R. *Connaissance religieuse et herméneutique chez Clément*. Leiden: Brill, 1973.

Neuschäfer, B. *Origenes als Philologe*. Basel: Reinhard, 1987.

Neymeyr, U. *Die christlichen Lehrer im zweiten Jahrhundert. Ihre Lehrtätigkeit, ihr Selbstverständnis, und ihre Geschichte*. Leiden: Brill, 1989.

Osborn, E. 'Arguments for Faith in Clement of Alexandria', *VChr* 48 (1994): 1–24.

Osborn, E. 'Clement and Platonism', in Lorenzo Perrone (ed.), *Origeniana VIII*, 419–27. Leuven: Peeters, 2003.

Osborn, E. *Clement of Alexandria*, Cambridge: Cambridge University Press, 2005.

Pearson, B. 'Egypt', in Margaret Mitchell and Frances Young (eds), *The Cambridge History of Christianity 1*, 331–50. Cambridge: Cambridge University Press, 2006.

Praechter, K. *Hierokles der Stoiker*. Leipzig: Dieterich, 1901.

Ramelli, I. L. E. 'Alcune osservazioni su *credere*', *Maia* n.s. 51 (2000): 67–83.

Ramelli, I. L. E. *Studi su Fides*, preface by Sabino Perea Yébenes. Graeco-Romanae Religionis Electa Collectio, 11. Madrid: Signifer Libros, 2002.

Ramelli, I. L. E. 'Galeno e i Cristiani: una messa a punto', *InvLuc* 25 (2003): 199–220.

Ramelli, I. L. E. 'Christian Soteriology and Christian Platonism: Origen, Gregory of Nyssa, and the Biblical and Philosophical Basis of the Doctrine of Apokatastasis', *VChr* 61 (2007): 313–56.

Ramelli, I. L. E. 'Philosophical Allegoresis of Scripture in Philo and Its Legacy', *StPhiloA* 20 (2008): 55–99.

Ramelli, I. L. E. 'Origen, Patristic Philosophy, and Christian Platonism: Re-Thinking the Christianisation of Hellenism', *VChr* 63 (2009): 217–63.

Ramelli, I. L. E. *Bardaiṣan of Edessa: A Reassessment of the Evidence and a New Interpretation: Also in the Light of Origen and the Original Fragments from Porphyry*. Piscataway, NJ: Gorgias, 2009; DeGruyter, 2019.

Ramelli, I. L. E. *Hierocles the Stoic*. Leiden: Brill; Atlanta, GA: SBL, 2009.

Ramelli, I. L. E. 'Origen, Bardaisan, and the Origin of Universal Salvation', *HTR* 102 (2009): 135–68.

Ramelli, I. L. E. 'Αἰώνιος and Αἰών in Origen and Gregory of Nyssa', *Studia Patristica* 47 (2010): 57–62.

Ramelli, I. L. E. '"Maximus" on Evil, Matter, and God: Arguments for the Identification of the Source of Eusebius *PE* VII 22', *Adamantius* 16 (2010): 230–55.

Ramelli, I. L. E. 'Atticus and Origen on the Soul of God the Creator: From the "Pagan"' to the Christian Side of Middle Platonism', *JRel* 10 (2011): 13–35.

Ramelli, I. L. E. 'Baptism in Gregory of Nyssa's Theology and Its Orientation to Eschatology', in David Hellholm, Tor Vegge, Oyvind Norderval and Christer David Hellholm (eds), *Ablution, Initiation, and Baptism: Late Antiquity, Early Judaism, and Early Christianity*, 3 vols, vol. 2, 1205–32. Beihefte zur Zeitschrift für die neutestamentliche Wissenschaft und die Kunde der älteren Kirche 176. Berlin: De Gruyter, 2011.

Ramelli, I. L. E. 'Gregory of Nyssa's Trinitarian Theology in *In Illud*: *Tunc et ipse Filius*: His Polemic against "Arian" Subordinationism and Apokatastasis', in Volker Drecoll and Margitta Berghaus (eds), *Gregory of Nyssa: The Minor Treatises on Trinitarian Theology and Apollinarism*, 445–78. Leiden: Brill, 2011.

Ramelli, I. L. E. 'Origen's Anti-Subordinationism and Its Heritage in the Nicene and Cappadocian Line', *VChr* 65 (2011): 21–49.

Ramelli, I. L. E. 'Origen and Apokatastasis: A Reassessment', in Sylwia Kaczmarek and Henryk Pietras (eds), *Origeniana X*, 649–70. Leuven: Peeters, 2011.

Ramelli, I. L. E. 'Origen the Christian Middle/Neoplatonist', *JECH* 1 (2011): 98–130.

Ramelli, I. L. E. 'The Philosophical Stance of Allegory in Stoicism and Its Reception in Platonism, "Pagan" and Christian', *IJCT* 18 (2011): 335–71.

Ramelli, I. L. E. 'The *Dialogue of Adamantius*: A Document of Origen's Thought?' *SP* 52 (2012): 71–98; 56, no. 4 (2013): 227–73.

Ramelli, I. L. E. 'Disability in Bardaisan and Origen: Between the Stoic *Adiaphora* and the Lord's Grace', in Wolfgang Grünstäudl and Markus Schiefer Ferrari (eds), *Gestörte Lektüre. Disability als hermeneutische Leitkategorie biblischer Exegese*, 141–59. Stuttgart: Kohlhammer, 2012.

Ramelli, I. L. E. 'Origen, Greek Philosophy, and the Birth of the Trinitarian Meaning of Hypostasis', *HTR* 105 (2012): 302–50.

Ramelli, I. L. E. 'Philo as Origen's Declared Model: Allegorical and Historical Exegesis of Scripture', *Studies in Christian-Jewish Relations* 7 (2012): 1–17. DOI: 10.6017/scjr. v7i1.2822

Ramelli, I. L. E. '*Stromateis* VII and Clement's Hints of the Theory of Apokatastasis', in Matyaš Havrda, Vit Hušek and Jana Plátová (eds), *The Seventh Book of the Stromateis*, 239–57. Supplements to Vigiliae Christianae; Leiden: Brill, 2012.

Ramelli, I. L. E. *The Christian Doctrine of Apokatastasis: A Critical Assessment from the New Testament to Eriugena*. SupVCh, 120. Leiden: Brill, 2013.

Ramelli, I. L. E. 'Harmony between *arkhē* and *telos* in Patristic Platonism', *IJPT* 7 (2013): 1–49.

Ramelli, I. L. E. "Origen and Augustine: A Paradoxical Reception', *Numen* 60 (2013): 280–307.

Ramelli, I. L. E. 'Alexander of Aphrodisias: A Source of Origen's Philosophy?', *Philosophie Antique* 14 (2014): 237–90.

Ramelli, I. L. E. 'A Pseudepigraphon inside a Pseudepigraphon? The Seneca-Paul Correspondence and the Letters Added Afterwards', *JSPs* 23, no. 4 (2014): 259–89.

Ramelli, I. L. E. 'The Stoic Doctrine of *Oikeiōsis* and Its Transformation in Christian Platonism', *Apeiron* 47 (2014): 116–40. DOI: 10.1515/apeiron-2012- 0063

Ramelli, I. L. E. '*Ethos* and *Logos*: A Second-Century Apologetical Debate between "Pagan" and Christian Philosophers', *VChr* 69, no. 2 (2015): 123–56.

Ramelli, I. L. E. *Evagrius' Kephalaia Gnostika*. Writings from the Greco-Roman World 38. Leiden: Brill; Atlanta: SBL, 2015.

Ramelli, I. L. E., 'Lucian's Peregrinus as Holy Man and Charlatan, and the Construction of the Contrast between Holy Men and Charlatans in the *Acts of Mari*', in Michael Paschalis, Gareth Schmeling and Stelios Panayotakis (eds), *Holy Men/Women and Charlatans in the Ancient Novel, Proceedings of RICAN 6, Sixth Rethymno International Conference on the Ancient Novel, University of Crete, 30-31 May 2011*,

105–20, Ancient Narrative Supplementum, 19. Groningen: Barkhuis-Groningen University Library, 2015.

Ramelli, I. L. E. 'Proclus and Christian Neoplatonism: A Case Study', in Mikonja Knežević (ed.), *The Ways of Byzantine Philosophy*, 37–70. Alhambra, CA: Sebastian Press; Kosovska Mitrovica: Faculty of Philosophy, 2015.

Ramelli, I. L. E. *Tempo ed eternità in età antica e patristica: filosofia greca, ebraismo e cristianesimo*. Assisi: Cittadella, 2015.

Ramelli, I. L. E. 'Hebrews and Philo on Hypostasis: Intersecting Trajectories?', in Pier Franco Beatrice and Bernard Pouderon (eds), *Pascha nostrum Christus: Essays in Honour of Fr Raniero Cantalamessa*, 27–49. Paris: Beauchesne, 2016.

Ramelli, I. L. E. 'The Mysteries of Scripture: Allegorical Exegesis and the Heritage of Stoicism, Philo, and Pantaenus', in Veronica Černuskova, Judith Kovacs and Jana Platova (eds), *Clement's Biblical Exegesis: Proceedings of the Second Colloquium on Clement of Alexandria, Prague- Olomouc 29-31 May 2014*, 80–110. Supplements to Vigiliae Christianae 139. Leiden: Brill, 2016. DOI 63/9789004334_005

Ramelli, I. L. E. 'The Reception of Origen's Ideas in Western Theological and Philosophical Traditions', main lecture at *Origeniana Undecima: Origen and Origenism in the History of* Western *Thought, Aarhus University, August 2013*, ed. Anders-Christian Jacobsen, 443–67. Bibliotheca Ephemeridum Theologicarum Lovaniensium 279. Leuven: Peeters, 2016.

Ramelli, I. L. E. *Social Justice and the Legitimacy of Slavery: The Role of Philosophical Asceticism from Ancient Judaism to Late Antiquity*. Oxford: Oxford University Press, 2016.

Ramelli, I. L. E. 'Divine Power in Origen of Alexandria: Sources and Aftermath', in Anna Marmodoro and Irini Fotini Viltanioti (eds), *Divine Powers in Late Antiquity*, 177–98. Oxford: Oxford University Press, 2017.

Ramelli, I. L. E. 'Gregory Nyssen's and Evagrius' Biographical and Theological Relations: Origen's Heritage and Neoplatonism', in *Evagrius between Origen, the Cappadocians, and Neoplatonism*, editor Eadem, in collaboration with Kevin Corrigan, Giulio Maspero and Monica Tobon, 165–23. *SP* LXXXIV. Leuven: Peeters, 2017.

Ramelli, I. L. E. 'Origen and the Platonic Tradition', in *Plato and Christ: Platonism in Early Christian Theology*, ed. J. Warren Smith = *Religions* 8, no. 2 (2017): 21. doi:10.3390/rel8020021

Ramelli, I. L. E. 'Philo as One of the Main Inspirers of Early Christian Hermeneutics and Apophatic Theology', *Adamantius* 24 (2018): 276–92.

Ramelli, I. L. E. 'Galen' (doctor), in Paul J. J. van Geest, David Hunter and Angelo Di Berardino (eds), *BEEC: Brill Encyclopedia of Early Christianity*. Leiden: Brill, forthcoming; online 2018: http://dx.doi.org/10.1163/2589-7993_EECO_SIM _00001368

Ramelli, I. L. E. 'Apokatastasis and Epektasis in Hom. in *Cant.*: The Relation between Two Core Doctrines in Gregory and Roots in Origen', in Giulio Maspero, Miguel Brugarolas and Ilaria Vigorelli (eds), *Gregory of Nyssa: In Canticum Canticorum. Commentary and Supporting Studies: Proceedings of the 13th International Colloquium on Gregory of Nyssa (Rome, 17–20 September 2014)*, 312–39. Supplements to Vigiliae Christianae 150. Leiden: Brill, 2018.

Ramelli, I. L. E. 'Bardaisan of Edessa, Origen, and Imperial Philosophy', *ARAM* 30, nos. 1–2 (2018): 337–53.

Ramelli, I. L. E. 'Origen', in Anna Marmodoro and Sophie Cartwright (eds), *A History of Mind and Body in Late Antiquity*, 245–66. Cambridge: Cambridge University Press, 2018.

Ramelli, I. L. E. 'Paul's Problematic Relation to Judaism in the Seneca-Paul Original Correspondence', in Gabriele Boccaccini and Isaac Oliver (eds), *The Early Reception of Paul the Jew*, 220–35. London: Bloosmbury T&T Clark, 2018.

Ramelli, I. L. E. 'Autobiographical Self-Fashioning in Origen', in Maren Niehoff and Joshua Levinson (eds), *Self, Self-Fashioning and Individuality in Late Antiquity: New Perspectives*, 273–92. Tübingen: Mohr Siebeck, 2019.

Ramelli, I. L. E. 'Gal 3:28 and Aristotelian (and Jewish) Categories of Inferiority', *Eirene* 55 (2019): 275–310.

Ramelli, I. L. E. 'The *Dialogue of Adamantius*: Preparing the Critical Edition and a Reappraisal', *RhM* 163 (2020): 40–68.

Ramelli, I. L. E. 'Christian Slavery in Theology and Practice: Its Relation to God, Sin, and Justice', in Bruce Longenecker and David Wilhite (eds), *The Cambridge History of Ancient Christianity*. Cambridge: Cambridge University Press, 2021.

Ramelli, I. L. E. 'Esoteric Interpretations of Scripture in Philo (and Hellenistic Judaism), Clement, and Origen', in Toby Mayer (ed.), *Esoteric Cultures of Scripture*. Oxford: Oxford University Press, 2021.

Ramelli, I. L. E. 'The Father in the Son, the Son in the Father in the Gospel of John: Sources and Reception of Dynamic Unity in Middle and Neoplatonism, "Pagan" and Christian', *JBR* 7 (2020): 31–66. https://doi.org/10.1515/jbr-2019-0012

Ramelli, I. L. E. '"From God to God": Eriugena's Protology and Eschatology against the Backdrop of His Platonic Patristic Sources', lecture, Oxford workshop, *Eriugena's Christian Neoplatonism and Its Sources in Patristic Philosophy and Ancient Philosophy*, dir. Ilaria Ramelli, Oxford University, August 2019, SP, 1–26. Leuven: Peeters, 2021.

Ramelli, I. L. E. 'Gregory of Nyssa's Purported Criticism of Origen's Purported Doctrine of the Preexistence of Souls', in Svetla S. Griffin and Ilaria L. E. Ramelli (eds), *Lovers of the Soul and Lovers of the Body: Philosophical and Religious Perspectives in Late Antiquity*. Cambridge, MA: Harvard University Press, 2021.

Ramelli, I. L. E. 'The Logos/Nous One-Many between "Pagan" and Christian Platonism', *Studia Patristica* 102 (2020): 175–204.

Ramelli, I. L. E. 'Origen's Critical Reception of Aristotle: Some Key Points and Aftermath in Christian Platonism', in Mikonja Knežević (ed.), *Aristotle in Byzantium*, 43–86. Alhambra, CA: Sebastian Press, 2020.

Ramelli, I. L. E. 'Jesus of Nazareth', in Sander Goldberg, Elizabeth DePalma Digeser and Tim Whitmarsh (eds), *The Oxford Classical Dictionary*, digital edition. Oxford: Oxford University Press, 2021.

Ramelli, I. L. E. 'Origen's Philosophical Exegesis of the Bible against the Backdrop of Ancient Philosophy (Stoicism, Platonism) and Hellenistic and Rabbinic Judaism', main lecture at the conference, *The Bible: Its Translations and Interpretations in the Patristic Time*, 16–17 October 2019, in Mariusz Szram and Marcin Wysocki (ed.), *Studia Patristica CIII: The Bible in the Patristic Period*, 13–58. Leuven: Peeters, 2021.

Ramelli, I. L. E. 'Origen's Philosophical Theology, Allegoresis, and Connections to Platonism', main lecture, international conference, *Hellenism, Early Judaism and Early Christianity: Transmission and Transformation of Ideas*, Academy of Sciences, Prague, 12–13 September 2019, eds Radka Fialova, Jiri Hoblik and Petr Kitzler. Berlin: de Gruyter, 2021.

Ramelli, I. L. E. 'Origen on the Unity of Soul and Body in the Earthly Life and Afterwards and His Impact', in Jörg Ulrich, Anna Usacheva and Siam Bhayro (eds), *The Unity of Soul and Body in the Earthly Life and After*, 38–77. Leiden: Brill, 2021.

Ramelli, I. L. E. '"Pagan" and Christian Platonism in Dionysius: The Double-Reference Scheme and Its Meaning', in Frederick Lauritzen and Sarah Klitenic Wear (eds), *Byzantine Platonists 284–1453*. Theandrites: Studies in Byzantine Platonism and Christian Philosophy; Steubenville: Franciscan University Press, 2021.

Ramelli, I. L. E. 'The Reception of Paul in Origen: Allegoresis of Scripture, Apokatastasis, and Women's Ministry', in Stanley Porter and David Yoon (eds), *The Pauline Mind*. New York: Routledge, 2021.

Ramelli, I. L. E. 'Soma (Σῶμα)', in *RAC: Das Reallexikon für Antike und Christentum* 30. Stuttgart: Hiersemann Verlag, 2021, 814–847.

Ramelli, I. L. E. 'The Spirit as Paraclete in 3rd to 5th-Century Debates and the Use of John 14-17 in the Pneumatology of That Time', in Jörg Frey and Tobias Nicklas (eds), *Antik-christliche Johannesrezeption - Receptions of the Fourth Gospel in Antiquity* Tübingen: Mohr Siebeck, 2021.

Ramelli, I. L. E. 'The Study of Late Ancient Philosophy: Philosophy and Religion – "Pagan" and Christian Platonism', in Svetla S. Griffin and Ilaria L. E. Ramelli (eds), *Lovers of the Soul and Lovers of the Body: Philosophical and Religious Perspectives in Late Antiquity*, 397–402. Cambridge, MA: Harvard University Press, 2021.

Ramelli, I. L. E. 'Time and Eternity', in Mark Edwards (ed.), *The Routledge Companion to Early Christian Philosophy*, 41–54. London: Routledge, 2021.

Ramelli, I. L. E. 'The Construction of the Professional Identity of Origen of Alexandria and the Question of Which Origen', in E. DePalma Digeser, H. Marx and I. L. E. Ramelli (eds), *Problems in Ancient Biography: The Construction of Professional Identity in Late Antiquity*. Cambridge: Cambridge University Press, forthcoming.

Ramelli, I. L. E. '"Know Yourself" in Origen and Gregory of Nyssa: A Maxim of Greek Philosophy Found in Scripture', in Jens Schröter and Ole Jakob Fitveld (eds), *Know Yourself from Paul to Augustine: Exploring the Delphic Maxim in Christian and Non-Christian Sources from the First Centuries*. Berlin: De Gruyter, forthcoming.

Ramelli, I. L. E. 'Origen, Evagrios, and Dionysios', in Mark Edwards (ed.), *Oxford Handbook to Dionysius the Areopagite*, Ch. 5. Oxford: Oxford University Press, forthcoming.

Ramelli, I. L. E. '"Revelation" for Christians and Pagans and their Philosophical Allegoresis: Intersections within Imperial Platonism', main lecture at the conference, *Ancient Revelation: Divination, Prophecy and Epiphany*, Durham University, 25–27 June 2019, forthcoming in Elsa Simonetti (ed.), *An Open Crossroad: Divination in Later Antiquity*. Cambridge: Cambridge University Press, forthcoming.

Ramelli, I. L. E. 'Secular and Christian Commentaries in Late Antiquity', in Gavin Kelly and Aaron Pelttari (eds), *The Cambridge History of Later Latin Literature*. Cambridge: Cambridge University Press, forthcoming.

Ramelli, I. L. E. 'Some Overlooked Sources of the Elements of Theology', in Dragos
 Calma (ed.), *Reading Proclus and the Book of Causes*. Leiden: Brill, forthcoming.

Ramelli, I. L. E. and Konstan, D. *Terms for Eternity: Αἰώνιος and ἀίδιος in Classical and
 Christian Authors*. Piscataway, NJ: Gorgias, 2007; new edn, 2013.

Shoemaker, S. *Mary in Early Christian Faith and Devotion*. New Haven, CT: Yale
 University Press, 2016.

Smith, M. *The Idea of Nicaea in the Early Church Councils, AD 431–451*. Oxford: Oxford
 University Press, 2018.

Sobrinho, C. G. *Doctrine and Power: Theological Controversy and Christian Leadership in
 the Late Roman Empire*. Oakland: University of California, 2013.

Solheid, J. 'Scripture and Christian Formation in Origen's Fourth Homily on Psalm
 77(78)', *JECS* 27, no. 3 (2019): 417–42.

Strutwolf, H. *Gnosis als System: Zur Rezeption der valentinianischen Gnosis bei Origenes*.
 Göttingen: V&R, 1993.

Sullivan, F. A. 'Clement of Alexandria on Justification through Philosophy', in D. Kendall
 and G. O'Collins (eds), *In Many and Diverse Ways: FS J. Dupuis*, 101–13. Maryknoll,
 NY: Orbis, 2003.

Tarrant, H. 'Platonism before Plotinus', in Lloyd Gerson (ed.), *Cambridge History of
 Philosophy in Late Antiquity*, vol. 1, 63–99. Cambridge: Cambridge University Press,
 2010.

Tarrant, H. 'Forgetting Procline Theology', in David Butorac and Danielle Layne (eds),
 Proclus and His Legacy, 33–44. Berlin: de Gruyter, 2017.

Tobon, M. *Apatheia and Anthropology in Evagrius of Pontus: Restoring the Image of God*.
 London: Routledge, 2021.

Trabattoni, F. '*Logos* and *noēsis* in Alcinous, *Didaskalikos* 4', *Phronesis* 60 (2016): 60–81,
 79.

Trostyanskiy, S. (ed.). *Seven Icons of Christ: An Introduction to the Oikoumenical
 Councils*. Piscataway, NJ: Gorgias Press, 2016.

Tzamalikos, P. *Origen: Philosophy of History and Eschatology*. Leiden: Brill, 2007.

Tzamalikos, P. *Anaxagoras, Origen, and Neoplatonism: The Legacy of Anaxagoras to
 Classical and Late Antiquity*, vols. 1–2. Berlin: DeGruyter, 2016.

Westergren, A. 'Paideia, Piety, and Power: Emperors and Monks in Socrates' Church
 History', in Lillian Larsen and Samuel Rubenson (eds), *Monastic Education in Late
 Antiquity: The Transformation of Classical 'Paideia'*, 53–72. Cambridge: Cambridge
 University Press, 2018.

CHAPTER 22

Councils

The path towards an agreement in faith

HENRYK PIETRAS

INTRODUCTION

From the beginning, the synods in the church have become a permanent element in the normal management and running of the community of believers. They dealt with current affairs, among which the question of faith and its expression occupied a prominent place. Until the time of Constantine the Great, we do not see that there was any need in the church to unify the confession of faith. Each local church had its confession of faith, passed on to the catechumens and used at baptism, and no one minded this. It was generally accepted that biblical language was used in these confessions without care for additional precision. The point of reference in judging some views as heretical was *regula fidei*, understood in the sense of the transmitted deposit of faith. Unified formulae were avoided, also during the eucharistic celebration, which was probably caused by fears of suspicion of using magical formulae.

THE BEGINNINGS OF SYNODS

The first synods dealing with matters of faith and seeking to reject views regarded as heterodox are already recorded in the second century, although information on this subject is quite uncertain. And so at that time a synod against Gnostic Heracleon,[1] in Rome against the adoptionist Theodor of Byzantium,[2] in Pergamum in 152 against the Gnostic named Colarbus,[3] and about 160 in Hierapolis against the Montanists,[4]

---

[1] Anonim, *Haer.*, frag., in G. D. Mansi, *Sacrorum Conciliorum nova et amplissima collection*, vol. I (Venezia 1759–98; reprint: Paris, 1901–27), p. 647.
[2] See *Libellus sinodicus* Mansi I, 662; SCL 1, p. 2.
[3] Anonim, *Praed.*, 15 Mansi I, 669; PL 53, 591; SCL 1, p. 2.
[4] See Eusebius, *HE.*, 5, 16.

would take place in Sicily. In the third century, the synod in Asia Minor condemned Noetus' Monarchianism.[5]

The first synod well documented, dealing with the expression of faith, took place in Rome around 263, and it concerned the first misunderstanding of terminology between East and West, or rather between Greek and Latin theologians. The idea was to examine the allegations made by some believers in the Alexandrian church against their Bishop Dionysius. (It was submitted for consideration of charges by some of the faithful of the Church of Alexandria against their Bishop Dionysius.) There were many accusations, but the most serious one seems to be talking about the three hypostases in the Trinity. The accusers were apparently Monarchians, the proponents of talking about 'one being' *ousia* or 'individual substance' *hypostasis* of God. Dionysius of Rome, together with the synod, responded to the allegations in a letter to Alexandria agreeing with the accusers. In Rome, in the Latin-speaking theological circles, the Greek term *hypostasis* was evidently translated into Latin as *substantia*, so three substances, which meant three Gods, were made of three hypostases as suggested by the Greek term.[6] The synod interpreted the statements of Dionysius of Alexandria exactly in this manner, although his style of speaking was widely accepted in the East, rejected only by the Sabelians. We can point out that such polarization of positions, along with conferring the Greek terms *ousia* and *hypostasis* (Lat. *essentia* and *substantia*) a generic meaning in the West, and at the same time maintaining the possibility of their use to identify an individual in the East, will lead to monophysite and duophysite disputes in the fifth century.

TOWARDS THE ARIAN CRISIS AND NICAEA

Paul of Samosata proclamation in Antioch with views that denied the eternity of the Son of God and treating Jesus Christ as a human person, the son of the Virgin Mary, with whom the non-personal Word of God merged, prompted bishops to speak on three synods in the 360s in Antioch. A synodal letter of the third of them, from the turn of 268/269, announces Paul's deposition only in general terms, showing the relationship of his views with the little known Artemas, a third-century Adoptionist, focusing instead on moral claims.[7] Paul of Samosata's fragments of writings, which have survived to our times, indicate that his Christology was indeed dangerous from the point of view of the church's faith; it simplified the mystery of the Incarnation

---

[5]Epiphanius of Salamis, *Pan.*, 57 in *GCS*, 31, 345, v. 5-10.

[6]Athanasius, *decr.* in Opitz II/1, 22–3; See more in H. Pietras, 'La difesa della monarchia divina da parte del papa Dionigi (+268)', *AHP* 28 (1990): 335–42. Idem, 'L'unità di Dio in Dionigi di Alessandria', *G* 72 (1991): 459–90.

[7]Eusebius, *HE.*, 7, 29-30, see more in H. De Riedmatten, *Les actes du procès de Paul de Samosate, Étude sur la cristologie du IIIe au IVe siècle* (Fribourg en Suisse: Edition St. Paul, 1952); P. De Navascués, *Pablo de Samosata y sus adversarios. Estudio histórico-teológico del cristianismo antioqueno en el s. III*, SEA 87 (Roma: Institutum Patristicum Augustinianum, 2004), pp. 78–87; U. M. Lange, 'Cristological Controversy at the Synod of Antioch in 268/9', *JTS* 51 (2000): 54–80.

and it is no wonder that its ever new followers were still a problem in the church throughout the fourth century and were often condemned in many synods.

The first synod known to us that took place during the reign of peace in the church, although only in the Western church, gathers in Elvira, perhaps after Diocletian's abdication and the takeover of power by Constantine in 306,[8] yet it is difficult to state this precisely. This synod deals with many disciplinary matters, including the treatment of heretics. Although the synod does not deal with any specific heresy, nor does it establish a new formula of faith, equating heresy with adultery is of interest to our study. This manifests itself in determining the length of penance necessary for a heretic who wishes to return to the church community,[9] for an adulterer who promises improvement,[10] for an apostate,[11] and also for the one assisting in offering sacrifices.[12] It follows that not only is a departure from the faith treated as a theoretical problem concerning orthodoxy, but it also belongs to orthopraxis, and heresy is not only a mistake but a sin to be repented of. This is probably related to the biblical comparison of infidelity to God with adultery;[13] interesting, however, that such an understanding gradually disappears in the next decades. Still, in the canons of the Council of Nicaea of 325, certain forms of penance are imposed on heretics returning to the church. However, at the end of the fourth century, the opinion that departing from error is necessary starts to predominate, without imposing any additional conditions, for example, in the form of ten years of penance, as in Elvira.

The synod of Arles in 314, dealing with Donatists at the behest of the Emperor Constantine, distinguished between heretics who were baptized in the name of the Father, Son and Holy Spirit, and those who did not mention the Trinity on this occasion.[14] The disciplinary issue raised by Cyprian in Africa regarding the non-acceptance of the baptism of 'heretics', whoever they may be, has been by that means determined doctrinally: the validity of baptism depends on the faith in the Trinity, and not on belonging to one community or another. Even though Africans did not accept this, from now on, this argument will be more and more often reiterated.

The questions of faith become more present in many synods, starting with the proclamation of Arius.[15] Probably in 323, there was a dispute in Alexandria between

---

[8]G. Martínez and F. Rodríguez, *La Colección Canónica Hispana*, vol. IV, ed. F. Rodríguez (Madrid: Ediciones Aldecoa, 1984), pp. 233–68. The bibliography on this synod is extensive. I confine myself to mentioning two works: M. Meigne, 'Concile ou collection d'Elvire', *RHE* 70 (1975): 361–87 (I propose to treat the set of synodal canons as a collection created throughout the whole fourth century) oraz J. Vilella Masana, 'Collectiones falsamente atribuidas a un concilio', *CnS* 19/1 (2018): 137–75 (proves that some canons could not have been created before the end of the fifth century).
[9]The Synod of Elvira (after 306?), canon 22, SCL 1, p. 53.
[10]The Synod of Elvira (after 306?), canon 64. 72, SCL 1, pp. 59–60.
[11]The Synod of Elvira (after 306?), canon 46, SCL 1, p. 57.
[12]Elvira (after 306?), canon 59, SCL 1, p. 58.
[13]Jer. 3.6-10.
[14]The Synod of Arles (314), canon 9(8), SCL 1, p. 70.
[15]See H. Pietras, *Council of Nicaea (325): Religious and Political Context, Documents, Commentaries*, trans. M. Fijak (Rome: Gregorian and Biblical Press, 2016).

Bishop Alexander and presbyter Arius over the person of the Son of God. It seems that Arius' problem was an inability to reconcile Christ's obedience and being unchanging God. Obedience is merit only if disobedience is possible – even theoretically – and in God such a possibility of changeability is impossible.[16] Alexander judged that this was contrary to the church's faith in the Son's deity and ordered Arius to submit a profession of faith. He did this and in a clear manner presented his theory about the Son, the highest and greatest creation, who, however, cannot be God equal to the Father.[17] Alexander and the synod responded with a circular letter to all bishops, in which he systematically criticizes Arius' position and announces his condemnation together with other signatories of the letter.[18] Arius appealed to his friends, among whom the most important was Eusebius of Nicomedia; apparently, in Bithynia, a synod was held in his defence[19] and many letters were written.[20] At this time, in this place, the Emperor Constantine intervened, and immediately after the victory over Licinius in September 324 convened the bishops for the great synod to Ancyra (later moved it to Nicaea), to celebrate the commencement of the jubilee of the twenty years of rule and to declare peace and unity of the empire and the church under his rule.[21] Only then could he find out about the dispute between Alexander and Arius who was introducing a new confusion and disrupting imperial plans. The emperor wrote to both opponents calling for agreement in the dispute, which in his view was insignificant and not worthy of attention.[22] Bishop Hosius, who delivered the letter and – as I suppose – the invitation to the synod, remained in Alexandria, where during the winter he took part in the synod dedicated to the Melitians[23] because Constantine also wanted to reconcile them to the church. Then he went to another synod, this time to Antioch, just after Easter 325.[24] This was the first known synod which drew up a confession of faith,[25] expressing indignation over Arius' proclamation and solidarity with Bishop Alexander and even proclaiming that the submitted creed was a paraphrase of his statements against Arius.

One can ask about the reason for drawing up the confession of faith at this synod, probably for the first time in the history of the church, assuming that the post-synodal letter preserved only in Syrian is authentic. We know that Hosius was sent

[16]Arius, *Thalia* in Athanasius, *A Letter to African Bishops* 12 in PG 25, 564–5.

[17]Arius, *Letter to Alexander of Alexandria* Athanasius, *Syn.*, 16, ed. Opitz II/1, pp. 243–4.

[18]Socrates, *HE.*, I, 6; SCL 1, 78-82 and Pietras, *Council of Nicaea (325)*, pp. 39–51.

[19]See Sozomen, *HE.*, 1, 15.

[20]Pietras, *Council of Nicaea (325)*, pp. 39–99.

[21]See H. Pietras, 'Le ragioni della convocazione del Concilio Niceno da parte di Costantino il Grande. Un'investigazione storico-teologica', G 82/1 (2001): 5–35.

[22]*Const. Ep.*, in Eusebius, *v.C.* II, 64-72; see more in Pietras, *Council of Nicaea (325)*, pp. 101–27.

[23]See Athanasius, *Apol.sec.*, 76, Opitz II/1, 4, pp. 155–6.

[24]See Opitz, *Athanasius Werke* III/1, 36-41; SCL 1, pp. 83–90 and Pietras, *Council of Nicaea (325)*, pp. 138–42; L. Abramowski, 'The Synod of Antioch 324/25 and Its Creed', in *Formula and Context: Studies in Early Christian thought* (London: Variorum, 1992), p. 3.

[25]'The Synod of Antioch', in *A New Eusebius: Documents Illustrating the History of the Church to* AD 337, ed. J. Stevenson (Lodnon: SPCK, 1990), pp. 335–6.

on a mission to the East,[26] and not just to Alexandria. Since the expedition preceded the convening of the synod, we may surmise that it was related to the synod; that is, the synod would deal with concerns which lay upon the emperor's heart and which he intended to carry out in the synod. He presents this intention, inter alia, in the aforementioned letter to Alexander and Arius:

> My design then was, first, to bring the diverse judgments formed by all nations respecting the Deity to a condition, as it were, of settled uniformity; and, secondly, to restore to health the system of the world, then suffering under the malignant power of a grievous distemper.[27]

The second goal was to be achieved by the strength of the army, while the first by reaching an agreement between the servants of the church. Delivering the letter to Alexander and Arius was part of this goal, but Hosius was too important a person to only deliver letters. So he probably negotiated with them and took part in the synod on Melitians, and went to Antioch. We do not know whether he tried to form a unified formula of faith in Alexandria, perhaps the environment was too much at odds for such an opus, so he tried it in Antioch. As the document states, three bishops did not want to agree to the proposed wording of the text, among them Eusebius of Caesarea, and they downplayed the problem; however, it is not known what this exactly means. At all events, the three dissidents were criticized and were later to be tried in the great synod to be held. This confession of faith, however, was then forgotten; there is no mention of it either in Eusebius' letter to his parishioners shortly after the council, nor in any place at Athanasius of Alexandria, though it could have been useful to him in his later anti-Arian polemic. Eusebius of Caesarea mysteriously disappears, and no more is said of subjecting him to any judgement. We should not attach too much attention to him, for the Council of Nicaea will soon begin, in which the confession of faith will be drawn up beyond any doubt. It will be the subject of dispute for the next several dozen years, so let us quote its content.

> We believe in One God, the Father Almighty, Maker of all things visible and invisible. And in One Lord Jesus Christ, the Son of God, begotten of the Father, Onlybegotten, that is, from the essence of the Father; God from God, Light from Light, Very God from Very God, begotten not made, One in essence with the Father, by Whom all things were made, both things in heaven and things in earth; Who for us men and for our salvation came down and was made flesh, was made man, suffered, and rose again the third day, ascended into heaven, and cometh to judge quick and dead. And in the Holy Ghost.
>   And those who say, 'Once He was not', and 'Before His generation He was not', and 'He came to be from nothing', or those who pretend that the Son of

---

[26]Cf. Sozomen, *HE.*, 1, 16 (trans. NPNF).
[27]Eusebius, *Vit. Const.*, II, 65.

God is 'Of other subsistence or essence', or 'created' or 'alterable', or 'mutable', the Catholic Church anathematizes.[28]

I cite the text of the creed according to the version given by Eusebius of Caesarea, which Athanasius quoted in *On the Decrets of the Synod of Nicaea* (*De decretis Nicaenae synodi*). This text was signed and fell immediately into oblivion – for at least the next twenty-five years, no one refers to it, nobody quotes it and nobody speaks a good word about it. At least this can be concluded from all the preserved documents from the epoch. The bishops signed the text because the emperor ordered so, and the only voice trying to justify the emperor is precisely the letter of Eusebius, from which the quoted text comes. Why did this happen?

First, this is probably the first time there is a discrepancy between what the emperor wanted and what the bishops wanted. The emperor revealed his goals in the above-mentioned letter to Alexander and Arius and repeated it in the letter to all churches after the council:

I have judged that it ought to be the first object of my endeavors, that unity of faith, sincerity of love, and community of feeling in regard to the worship of Almighty God, might be preserved among the highly favored multitude who compose the Catholic Church.[29]

However, it seems that the emperor understood this primarily in the sense of unity of public worship, and not in the sense of orthodoxy. He accused Arius and Alexander of dealing with insignificant matters, comparable to disputes between philosophical schools, something that should not have any impact on peaceful coexistence and cooperation. He could not understand that differences of opinion on matters of faith could violate the unity of worship in the church. While the bishops thought differently, as is clear from earlier synodal documents, differences in faith were the reason for exclusion from the church, as in the case of the condemnation of Arius in Alexandria. The emperor demanded the signing of a unified creed for the sake of maintaining order in the state, and not because he was concerned about removing anyone from the church. We will see the consequences of such a policy below, in relation to Arius' supporters. Thus, Constantine's approach to heretics or schismatics was quite different from the one used hitherto in the church. When one's views were considered heretical, the heretic was condemned, that is, excluded from the church until further notice. The synod led by Constantine did not formulate any condemnation, it did not exclude anyone from the church, and in relation to those separated from the church, it took up the matter of accepting them back, and not excluding them. Thus, canon 8 tries to regulate the issue of accepting 'the pure' *katharoi* returning to the church, and canon 19 – of accepting the returning followers of Paul of Samosata. The anathema was only used as a threat to those who thereafter

---

[28]Athanasius, *Ep. VIII* (trans. NPNF); Socrates, *HE.*, 1, 8; Theodoret, *HE.*, 1, 12. See more in Pietras, *Council of Nicaea (325)*, pp. 191–202.

[29]*Const. Ep.* in Eusebius, *V. C.*, III, 17 (trans. NPNF).

would use the phrases indicated in anathematism found at the end of the Symbol of Faith. This lack of condemnation of no one is perhaps the most characteristic feature of the Council of Nicaea. This was in line with the policy of the emperor, who wanted peace in the state and in the church, but rather incomprehensible to the bishops prone to pruning the dry branches, obviously out of concern for the truth. Therefore, their comments on the Symbol will usually be directed against someone.

Second, the bishops did not seem to share the emperor's view that the creed should be unified. In each church, a confession of faith was used in baptism, and previously, it had been taught to catechumens, but there were differences between these confessions and this was not a problem for anyone. There was no demand in the church for a unified confession of faith. It was needed by the emperor, who as Pontifex Maximus was the head of all religions in the empire, and after 'adopting' Christianity, he considered himself (and was considered) the superior of the church. He required unity of worship, and to achieve this, in accordance with Roman customs, one formula was needed for all.

Third, the text, signed under duress, contained wordings which many bishops, if not all, did not like because, contrary to tradition, they were not of biblical origin. This concerned above all the concept of 'one substance' (Gr. *homoousios*), which for some was associated with matter, for others with heresy, as it was used by Gnostics, and probably likewise by Paul of Samosata. The bishops were also not pleased with the phrasing that 'the Son derived from the Father's *ousia*'.

The above-mentioned canon 8 regulated the issue of receiving all 'Cathars', including Melitians. At least, this seems to be the result of Athanasius' words, who, without concealing his discontent, later wrote that 'they were received in a certain way, and there is no need now to explain why'.[30] He himself sought to eliminate them rather than to accept them and was criticized for it by others[31] and later exiled. The Eastern bishops, when carrying out the will of the emperor to reconcile apostates, which was expressed in handwriting, at the synod of Jerusalem[32] accepted some followers of Arius to the church when they presented a satisfying confession of faith; they could not accept Arius himself, for he was condemned in Alexandria and could only be rehabilitated there, in accordance with the fifth canon of the Council of Nicaea.

We can conclude from this that Athanasius was probably banished from Alexandria for failing to comply with the will of the emperor expressed in the eighth canon of Nicaea and did not want to apply it to the Melitians. This was not a great claim to fame, so Athanasius tried to show that the real reason for his exile had been doctrinal, and his critics – both altogether and each individually – are Arians or crypto-Arians. In this spirit, the synod in Alexandria spoke,[33] and Athanasius

---

[30]Athanasius, *Apol.sec.*, 59 Opitz II/ 1, pp. 139–40.
[31]See the First Synod of Tyre (335) Socrates, *HE.*, 1, 28-32; SCL 1, p. 91.
[32]See the Synod of Jerusalem (335); Athanasius, *Syn.*, 21, 3-4; Opitz, II/1, pp. 102–3; SCL 1, 92.
[33]The Synod of Alexandria (338/339), *Epistula synodalis* in Athanasius, *Apol. sec.*, 3-19; Opitz II/1, pp. 88–101; SCL 1, pp. 93–109.

imposed this interpretation on the synod of fifty bishops together with Pope Julius in Rome.[34] That is how the expulsion of Athanasius became a doctrinal issue and the subject of the synods, and the interpretation of events presented in Julius's letter became binding in the West, while in the East it was propagated after a hundred years by historians Socrates and Sozomen. In Rome Athanasius was believed immediately, because none of the members of the synod were in Nicaea, and in the East later, when all died. Although this letter contains a lot of information previously unknown: that in Nicaea everyone condemned Arius' supporters (so why did they not write so?), that 300 bishops took part in the council (250 is mentioned earlier), that the council condemned Bishop Secundus for Arianism (he was condemned together with Arius, so in Nicaea he could neither have participated in the deliberations, nor could he have signed the confession of faith, even if he wanted). This letter also confirms the orthodoxy of Marcellus of Ancyra. L. Ayres claimed that just then, around 340, Arianism arose,[35] paradoxically not in connection with the proclamation of Arius, who was already dead, but in connection with the polarization of positions brought about by Athanasius.

BEYOND NICAEA

Among these problems and misunderstandings, the church continued to seek a better formula of faith. The synod in Antioch in 341 proposed four different formulae,[36] the synod of Western bishops in Sardica in 343/344 proposed their own version,[37] and of Eastern bishops their own.[38] It is no use to say that the term *homoousios* does not appear in either of those versions, which can only mean that none of the persons present was interested in it. And there was also Athanasius, who would strongly deny drawing up any formula of faith in Sardica, but apparently, it was being circulated in churches, since at the end of his life he forbade reading it as a counterfeit.[39]

A year later in Antioch, a new *creed* of extraordinary length, called 'the Creed of the Long Lines' (*Ekthesis macrostichos*),[40] was drawn up, the next one in Sirmium in

---

[34]The Synod of Rome (340/341), *Epistula ad Antiochenos* in Athanasius, *Apol. sec.*, 12-35; Opitz II/1, pp. 102–13; SCL 1, pp. 110–23.

[35]See more in L. Ayres, *Nicaea and Its Legacy, an Approach to Fourth-Century Trinitarian Theology* (Oxford: Oxford University Press, 2004), pp. 105–30.

[36]The Synod of Antiochia (341); Socrates, *HE.*, 2, 10; Sozomen, *HE.*, 3, 5; Athanasius, *Syn.*, 22-25; More in P.-P. Joannou (ed.), *Les canons des synodes particuliers* ('Pontificia commissione per la redazione del codice di diritto canonico orientale'; Fonti, Fasc. IX, t. I/2, SCL 1; Roma/Grottaferrata, 1962), pp. 129–34.

[37]Theodoret, *HE.*, 2, 8, pp. 39–52; see *Théodoret de Cyr, Histoire ecclésiastique, Livres I-II*, in J. Bouffartique et al. (eds), SCh 501 (Paris: Les Éditions du Cerf, 2006), pp. 368–74; SCL 1, pp. 143–5.

[38]Hilary, *Syn.*, 34 in PL 10, 507-509 and *Frg. His.*, in A. L Feder (ed.), *CSEL* 65 (Vindebonae, 1916), pp. 69–73.

[39]Athanasius, *Tom.*, 5 in *Athanasius Werke* III/1, 596-597; SCL 1, p. 251.

[40]Athanasius, *Syn.*, 26, in Opitz II/1, pp. 251–4.

351,[41] known as the *first formula*, and in 357 the next, that is, the *Second Formula of Sirmium*,[42] and then the third (358)[43] and fourth (359),[44] which were approved in Rimini and in Nike in Thrace (359), respectively. Athanasius quotes all these confessions of faith, noting that they were established by the decision of the bishops, in contrast to the Nicene Creed, which was not the arbitrary decision of the Fathers, but their profession of the authentic apostolic faith.[45] These synods have been recorded, but as regards the format of the meetings of the bishops of other dioceses on this matter, the sources remain silent on this subject.

After the year 350, Athanasius decided to defend the Nicene Creed by writing *On the Decrets of the Synod of Nicaea*. It would have been a long time before people read this. Perhaps under its influence at the synod in Paris in 360/361, it was agreed to accept the Nicene Creed, especially since the synod was presided over by Hilary of Poitiers who had returned from exile.[46] So that the true facts are recorded, let us add that the second synod, which officially adopted the Nicene Creed, took place in Sicily in 366.[47] However, in 360, a synod at Constantinople also took place, which confession of faith played a significant role and in the future will be recognized by Theodosius the Great as equivalent to that of Nicaea:

> We believe in One God, Father Almighty, from whom are all things; And in the Only-begotten Son of God, begotten from God before all ages and before every beginning, by whom all things were made, visible and invisible, and begotten as Only-begotten, only from the Father only, God from God, like to the Father that begat Him according to the Scriptures; whose origin no one knows, except the Father alone who begat Him. He as we acknowledge, the Only-begotten Son of God, the Father sending Him, came hither from the heavens, as it is written, for the undoing of sin and death, and was born of the Holy Ghost, of Mary the Virgin according to the flesh, as it is written, and convened with the disciples, and having fulfilled the whole Economy according to the Father's will, was crucified and dead and buried and descended to the parts below the earth; at whom hades itself shuddered: who also rose from the dead on the third day, and abode with the disciples, and, forty days being fulfilled, was taken up into the heavens, and sitteth on the right hand of the Father, to come in the last day of the resurrection in the Father's glory, that He may render to every man according to his works. And in the Holy Ghost, whom the Only-begotten Son of God Himself, Christ, our Lord and God, promised to send to the race of man, as Paraclete, as it is

---

[41]Athanasius, *Syn.*, 27 in Opitz II/1, pp. 254–6; Hilary, *Syn.*, 38 in PL 10, 509-512; SCL 1, pp. 200–1.

[42]Hilary, *Syn.*, 11 in PL 10; 487-489; Athanasius, *Syn.*, 28 in Opitz II/1, pp. 256–7; SCL 1, pp. 208–9.

[43]Hilary, *Syn.*, 81 in PL 10, 534.

[44]Athanasius, *Syn.*, 8, in Opitz II/1, pp. 235–6; SCL 1, pp. 225–6.

[45]Athanasius, *Syn.*, 5, Opitz II/1, p. 234; see also S. Fernandez, 'Criterios para interpretar los textos sinodales según el "De synodis" de Atanasio', *ScTh* 49 (2017): 9–30, esp. 13.

[46]Cf. Hilary, *Frag.Hist.*, 11, in A. L. Ferder (ed.), CSEL 65, 43-6 = SCh 241, 92-9; SCL 1, pp. 246–9.

[47]C-E.*HET* VII, 25, 13; Socrates, *HE.*, 4, 12, 38; Sozomenos, *HE.*, 6, 11, 3-12, 3.

written, 'the Spirit of truth' (Joh. 16. 13), which He sent unto them when He had ascended into the heavens.[48]

We may note that it was not original, because the formula already known from Sirmium, Rimini and Nike in Thrace was adopted and approved, as I have mentioned earlier. However, a statement categorically rejecting the philosophical terms *ousia* and *hypostasis* was added to it, and it declared the simple similarity of the Father and the Son. Ulfilas, bishop of the Goths, took part in the synod, signed this text and took it to his people. The Goths accepted it as their own and learnt the faith based on it. It is difficult to say how well they were aware that at the same time Athanasius, in defence of the Nicene symbol, and of himself as well, called all his opponents Ariomaniacs (*ariomaniakoi*). The situation had become a stalemate. On the one hand, there was Athanasius' anti-Arian offensive, with many *pro vita sua* apologies, against the enemies he systematically identified with the Arians and the growing support of the monks whom he managed to convince, and on the other hand, the constant resistance of the definite majority of bishops rejecting the Nicene formula. It could not have been without imperial intervention that followed the decrees of the emperors Gratian, Valentinian and Theodosius issued in Thessaloniki on 27 February 380, and in Heraclea on 30 July 381.[49] In both, the Unity of God in the Trinity is emphasized, and it is made a determinant of belonging to the church. The second decree explicitly speaks of the inviolability of the Nicene Confession of Faith. It probably did not much impress the Western bishops, because – as we have seen – they had long believed in the interpretation of Athanasius. It was different in the East, where the numbers of proponents of the Nicene consubstantiality – for example, the Cappadocian Fathers – were also growing, but it was far from unanimity. Thus imperial decrees tried to extort this unanimity. By writing down the names of the three Augusti exercising the office, the law was made binding throughout the empire, although it is generally accepted that the main author of these constitutions was Theodosius the Great, the emperor of the East from 379. However, it was not enough for him to declare the law, and he also wanted it to be approved by the bishops. Note that a considerable amount of time elapsed between the promulgation of both constitutions so that the bishops could decide on the universal recognition of Nicaea, which the emperor subsequently confirmed. Theodosius, therefore, called the Eastern bishops to Constantinople to vote down first of all on two important issues: ending the disputes over the confession of faith and, in the process, the primacy of Constantinople over the Eastern church. Two established canons read as follows:

1. The profession of faith of the holy Fathers who gathered in Nicaea in Bithynia is not to be abrogated, but it is to remain in force. Every heresy is to be anathematized, and in particular that of the Eunomians or Anomæans, that

---

[48]The Synod of Constantinople (360), see Athanasius, *Syn.*, 30, 2-10, Opitz II/1, pp. 258–9; SCL 1, pp. 243–4 (trans. NPNF).
[49]*Cod. Thds.* XVI, 1, 2-3; SCL 7, 2-3.

of the Arians or Eudoxians, that of the Semi-Arians or Pneumatomachi, that of the Sabellians, that of the Marcellians, that of the Photinians, and that of the Apollinarians.

3 Because it is new Rome, the bishop of Constantinople is to enjoy the privileges of honour after the bishop of Rome.[50]

The first canon confirmed the Nicene Creed but added what Constantine in Nicaea did not want, that is, the condemnation of various heretics, ideological followers of heresiarchs, each of whom was condemned in his own time. At the same time, let us mention that no heretic was ever excommunicated twice unless he was rehabilitated after his first condemnation, as it happened later in the case of Eutyches: he was condemned in Constantinople in 448, rehabilitated in Ephesus in 449 and again condemned in Chalcedon in 451. This is why Arius could not be condemned in Nicaea, because his excommunication from Alexandria remained effective. *Nolens volens*, Constantinople's first position in the Eastern church, was also voted down, which would become a bone of contention between the capital and Alexandria for the next decades.

The Roman church did not accept this synod until 519 and the end of the Acacian schism, although the approval of the Nicene Creed was fully accepted there. There is a widespread opinion[51] that in Constantinople a new confession of faith was drawn up, complementing that which might have been lacking in the Nicene about the Holy Spirit. Rather, this became a legend because, first, this would be contrary to the established first canon, and second, because until the Council of Chalcedon no one had heard of such a creed – neither the Fathers of the Ephesus Council in 341 nor the bishops gathered to examine the case of Eutyches in 449, nor even the participants of the 'Robber Council' in 449.[52] This creed appears unexpected in Chalcedon, and there were good reasons for this, from the point of view of Constantinople. We will come to that, but for now, let us return to the political consequences of the first canon of 381 and the imperial constitution of Heraclea. They proved to be much more than just doctrinal; the bishops might not have been interested, but it must have interested the Emperor Theodosius. As a result of these decisions, all those using the confession of faith other than the Nicene found themselves outside the church, their churches were taken away and they were called heretics and were subject to penalties announced by the emperors. There is no reason to believe that staunch anti-Niceans have been convinced, but it is difficult to estimate how large this group was and what influences it could have

---

[50]The Council of Constantinople (381), canon 1. 3; more in N. P. Tanner (ed.), *Decrees of the ecumenical Councils*, vol. 1 (Washington, DC: Georgtown University Press, 1990), pp. 31–2.

[51]See B. Degórski, 'Il Primo Concilio di Costantinopoli (381). Uno schizzo storico e teologico', *VP* 36 (2016), vol. 65, pp. 156–70, esp. 166.

[52]See documents of individual synods, for example, Constantinople (448), 225 (SCL 6, p. 63). The fathers declare that they are basing their pronouncements only on the results of Nicaea and Ephesus – repeated twelve times; Constantinople (449) SCL 6, p. 118 and next – repeated five times; Ephesus (449 – 'Latrocinium'), SCL 6, p. 145 and next – repeated eighteen times).

had. Undoubtedly, this also concerned the Goths, who took the creed accepted in Constantinople in 360 as their own. Theodosius had a huge problem with the Goths, inherited from the Emperor Valens and his unfortunate battle of Adrianople in August 378. They were a crowd of millions difficult to control, negotiating with them and finding a place for them was one of the most important internal problems of the empire. The only thing they had in common with the Romans was Christianity, and they had to keep to this. Therefore, the emperors had to revise their position and, for political reasons, soften their previous position and, in addition to the followers of the Nicene Creed, also recognize the right of existence of the supporters of Rimini/Nike in Thrace/Constantinople Creed from 360. On 23 January 386, the emperors issued an appropriate constitution, granting them the right to assemble and to have churches, also threatening all who would oppose this with the death penalty.[53] It can be assumed that this was a voice of common sense, without any threat to orthodoxy, because this confession of faith was also orthodox, except that it did not use the terms *ousia*, *hypostasis* and *homoousios*. However, it weakened the position of the uncompromising supporters of Nicaea, who were increasing. Among historians of the fifth century, there also appears the term 'Arians' to describe the Goths. They believed Athanasius, who called them all anti-Niceans, but this rather suited them; they began to define themselves as such and Arianism became their national religion.[54]

It is also worth paying attention to the list of heretics condemned in the first canon of 381, and then compare it with the canon of Gennadius, bishop of Constantinople (458–471), which is traditionally published as the seventh canon of this synod. Let us note that all heresies appear to be treated equally in the first canon, from Eunomians to Apolinarists. The first ones are juxtaposed in pairs, for greater clarity: Eunomians are Anomean, Arians are Eudoxians and Half-Arians are 'opponents against (divinity) of the Spirit' (*pneumatomachoi*). Eunomius did indeed proclaim that the Son is unlike the Father.[55] Eudoxius was a supporter of the confession of faith from Nike in Thrace/Constantinople.[56] The semi-Arians accepted the deity of the Son but not of the Holy Spirit. Can this be considered in descending order, from the most serious to the less serious heresies? It would mean that the perception of Arianism has changed since Athanasius painted it in demonic colours. Gennadius' canon, formed after over a dozen years, when coexistence with the Goths was still a burden in the Eastern part of the empire, gives us more clarity; it was not until 489 that the Emperor Zeno managed to send Theodoric and his people to Italy.[57]

---

[53]*Cod. Thds.*, XVI, 1, 4; SCL 7, 4-5.

[54]See M. Ożóg, *Inter duas potestates*: *The Religius Policy of Theoderic the Great* (Frankfurt am Main: Peter Lang 2016), pp. 23–43.

[55]Eunomius, *Ap.*, in L. Doutreleau (ed.), SCh 305 (Paris: Les Éditions du Cerf 1983).

[56]See M. Simonetti, 'Eudossio', in A. di Berardino (ed.), *Nuovo dizionario patristico e di antichità cristiane*, 1 vols (Genova-Milano: Marietti, 2006-2010), pp. 1823–4.

[57]Marcellinus Comes, *Chr.*, A. D. 489, *MGH AA* XI, 93; Cassiodorus, *Chr.*, A. D. 489, MGH AA XI, 159.

The canon deals with the conditions for reception of heretics into the church and sets forth the following:

> Those who embrace orthodoxy and join the number of those who are being saved from the heretics, we receive in the following regular and customery manner: Arians, Macedonians, Sabbatians, Novatians, those who call themselves Cathars and Aristeri, Quartodecimans or Tetradites, Apollinarians – these we receive when they hand in statements and anathematise every heresy which is not of the same mind as the holy, catholic, and apostolic church of God. They are first sealed or anointed with holy chrism on the forehead, eyes, nostrils, mouth and ears. As we seal them we say, 'Seal of the gift of the holy Spirit.' But Eunomians, who are baptized in a single immersion, Montanists (called Phrygians here), Sabellians, who teach the identity of Father and Son, and make certain other difficulties, and all other sects – since there are many here, not least those who originate in the country of the Galatians – we receive all who wish to leave them and embrace orthodoxy, as we do Greeks. On the first day we make Christians of them; on the second catechumens; on the third we exorcise them by breathing thrice into their face and their ears; and thus we catechise them and make them spend time in the church and listen to the scriptures; and then we baptize them.[58]

We can see that the Arians are among those who do not need to be baptized when they come to the church, and this means that their Trinitarian faith is considered to be orthodox. So they are not simply the followers of Arius, because he undoubtedly did not recognize the Son of God as true God, but rather the so-called Arians, orthodox Christians but ones creating a separate community; in modern language, we would call them schismatics, not heretics.

FURTHER DEVELOPMENTS

Synods continued to take place from 381 until the crisis related to Nestorius' proclamation; however, the situation seems calmer. The church is struggling with its own affairs, setting forth disciplinary canons on synods, acting against Pelagians, Priscillianists, Messalians or Donatists, not to mention the old heresies that were being revived. Nonetheless, we can say that it was normal administration. The situation changes with Nestorius and the Council of Ephesus of 431. This assembly is considered to be the Third General Council, but it is worth remembering that its course was highly irregular, and its conclusion even more scandalous – with the condemnation of supporters of Cyril of Alexandria by bishops led by John of Antioch, and vice versa, and with the deposition from the office of the major players of the drama, that is, Nestorius, Cyril and Memnon of Ephesus, by order of the Emperor Theodosius II.[59] From a theological point of view, Cyril was closer to

---

[58]The Council of Constantinople (381), canon 7; more in Tanner (ed.), *Decrees*, p. 35.
[59]See Ch.-J. Hefele and H. Leclercq, *Histoire des conciles d'après les documents originaux* (Paris: Letouzey et Ané 1907), p. 347.

the truth; nonetheless, in the background of the dispute, there were also problems unrelated to the issue itself. The bishop of Alexandria was hostile out of principle to the bishop of Constantinople since the synod of 381; it would be so until the split in the church after the Council of Chalcedon. In addition, Nestorius had enemies in his city, because within a few years he would apparently manage to antagonize everyone by his stubbornness and extreme rigour.[60] Even before taking over the capital of Constantinople, Theodor of Mopsuestia warned him in a friendly manner to restrain his enthusiasm in fighting people who had a different opinion from him, but to no avail.[61] This was overlapped with the friendship between Nestorius and John of Antioch who did not want to accept the condemnation of his friend. So when the council was over, or rather when it was interrupted by imperial decision, on his way to Antioch John organized synods at which Cyril was condemned. We have information about such gatherings in Tarsus, Ancyra, Antioch and Anazarbus in Cilicia.[62] In the latter, bishops swore that even if they were at risk of torture and death, they would not recognize Cyril as orthodox.[63] It turned out again that the emperor was more concerned with resolving disputes than the bishops. It was his envoy, Aristolaos, who led to an agreement and the signing of a document of union.[64] The same bishops who previously did not want to hear about consent now rushed to accept this act, as evidenced by the preserved testimonies of the synods at Zeugma (433),[65] Tarsus (434)[66] and Antioch (435).[67] Such a political compromise on matters of faith could hardly be permanent.

This became clear after over a dozen years in the circumstances of Eutyches' proclamation. In Constantinople, the Endemousa Synod gathered several times in 448 and 449 addressing this problem, where due consideration was given.[68] Eutyches' Christology was found to be erroneous, negating Christ's consubstantiality with humans, contrary to the *Formula of Union* of 343. However, the condemnation of Eutyches was, in fact, the condemnation of the whole of the *Logos-sarx* theology, which the Alexandrian followers did not abandon by any means.

---

[60]See Nestorius, *Lib. Heracl.* 'Introduction', p. VII.

[61]The text cited in Nestorius, *Lib. Heracl.*, 'Introduction', p. VI.

[62]See Ch.-J. Hefele and H. Leclercq, *Histoire des conciles*, p. 382.

[63]The Synod of Anazarbus in Cilicia (431–432), see the Latin text *Synodicon adversus Tragaediam Irenaei* in PG 84, 531–864, ca. 113 (pp. 724–5); SCL 6, p. 2.

[64]The Council of Ephesus (431), *Formula of Union*, more in Tanner (ed.), *Decrees*, pp. 69–70; see also Ch., Fraisse-Coué, 'Le débat théologique au temps de Théodose II: Nestorius', in *Histoire du christianisme : des origines à nos jours. II, Naissance d'une chrétienté (250-430)*, eds J. M. Mayeur et al. (Paris: Desclée 1995), pp. 449–50 and pp. 542–9.

[65]*Synodicon adversus Tragaediam Irenaei* in PG 84, 531-864, c. 126. 129. 137, pp. 741, 743–4, 753; Mansi V, 1061-62; SCL 6, p. 3.

[66]*Synodicon adversus Tragaediam Irenaei* in PG 84, 531-864, c. 192, pp. 804–5; Mansi V, 1061-62; SCL 6, p. 3.

[67]See *Synodicon adversus Tragaediam Irenaei* in PG 84, 531-864, canon 190, pp. 803–4; SCL 6, pp. 3–4.

[68]The Synond of Constantinople (448), ACO II/1, 1, pp. 100 and next. SCL 6, pp. 62–105; (449) ACO II/1, 1, p. 148. SCL 6, 105-143; See V. Vranić, 'The Christology of Eutyches at the Council of Constantinople 448', *P* 8 (2008): 208–21.

According to historians of the sixth century, it would be the mighty of this world who are to blame, those who would interfere in doctrinal matters for their own interests. Liberatus writes that Eutyches was the godfather of Chrysaphius, an influential eunuch at the imperial court,[69] and Evagrius adds that Chrysaphius was also annoyed with Bishop Flavian because he did not receive rich enough gifts from him.[70] It seems, however, that Bevan and Gray are right in supposing that a sufficient driving force behind a new dispute was a, merely dormant after 433, conflict between Antioch and Alexandria, that is, between supporters of the *Logos-sarx* theology and followers of the *Logos-anthropos* theology, along with – let us add – ambitious animosity between the bishops of Alexandria and Constantinople in the background. So the Nestorian and Eutychian controversy are de facto two battles of the same war, with victims on both sides and with such a dramatic episode as the 'Robber Council' in 449.

The Council of Chalcedon did not bring peace. As John of Damascus wrote years later, 'the Egyptians – Schismatics or Monophysites – under the pretext of Chalcedon's decisions, separated from the Orthodox Church, although they were orthodox.'[71] In the West, there was duophysitism, in the East, monophysitism produced monothelitism and monoenergetism, which will be dealt with by the Council of Constantinople III in 861. Then the most important Christological problems of the ancient church were solved, among those the problem of Arius, who could not understand the obedience of Jesus Christ.

BIBLIOGRAPHY

Abramowski, L. 'The Synod of Antioch 324/25 and Its Creed', in *Formula and Context: Studies in Early Christian thought*. London: Variorum, 1992.

Anonim. *De haeresibus*, frag., in G. D. Mansi, *Sacrorum Conciliorum nova et amplissima collection*, vol. I, 647. Venezia 1759–1798, reprint: Paris, 1901–1927.

Anonim. *Praedestinatus 15*; in G. D. Mansi, *Sacrorum Conciliorum nova et amplissima collection*, vol. I, p. 669; PL 53, 591; SCL 1, p. 2. Venezia 1759-1798, reprint: Paris 1901-1927.

Acta Synodalia (ab anno 50 ad annum 381) 'Synodi et Collectiones Legum' 1, in A. Baron and H. Pietras (eds), ŻMT 37. Kraków: Wydawnictwo WAM, 2006.

Acta Synodalia (ab anno 431 ad annum 504) SCL 6, in A. Baron and H. Pietras (eds), ŻMT 62. Kraków: Wydawnictwo WAM, 2011.

Athanasius. *De decretis Nicaenae synodi*, in H. G. Opitz (ed.), *Athanasius Werke* II,1,1, pp. 1–45. Berlin: W. de Gruyter, 1935.

---

[69]Liberatus, *Brev.*, 11, E. Schwartz (ed.), *Concilium universale Chalcedonense*, vol. 5 ('Collectio Sangermanensis', ACO II/5; Berlin/Leipzig, 1936), pp. 98–141, esp. 114.

[70]See Evagrius, *HE.*, 2, 2.

[71]John of Damascus, *Haer.*, 83 in PG 94, 677-780 (741); in B. Kottler (ed.), *Die Schriften des Johannes von Damaskos IV* (Berlin: W. de Gruyter 1981).

Athanasius. *Letter of Eusebius 8* (NPNF 2,4); in H. G. Opitz (ed.), *Athanasius Werke* II,1,1, pp. 42–7. Berlin: W. de Gruyter, 1935.

Athanasius. *Apologia contra Arianos (Apologia secunda)*, in H. G. Opitz (ed.), *Athanasius Werke* II,1,3-5, pp. 87–168. Berlin: W. de Gruyter, 1938–1940.

Athanasius. *De synodis Arimini in Italia et Seleuciae in Isauria*, in H. G. Opitz (ed.), *Athanasius Werke* II,1,6–7, pp. 231–78. Berlin: W. de Gruyter, 1940–41.

Athanasius. *Tomus ad Antiochenos*, Tomus ad Antiochenos PG 26, 796–809; 'Synodi et Collectiones Legum' 1, 249–25. Hanns Christof Brennecke, Annette von Stockhausen, Christian Müller, Uta Heil, Angelika Wintjes (Hrsg.), *Athanasius Werke. Dritter Band, erster Teil. Dokumente zur Geschichte des arianischen Streites. 4. Lieferung: Bis zur Synode von Alexandrien 362*, 592–603. Berlin and Bosonn: W. de Gruyter, 2014.

Ayres L. *Nicaea and Its Legacy, an Approach to Fourth-Century Trinitarian Theology.* Oxford: Oxford University Press, 2004.

Bevan, G. A. and Gray, P. T. R. 'The Trial of Eutyches: A New Interpretation', *BZ* 101, no. 2 (2008): 617–57.

Cassiodori-Epiphanii Historia Ecclesiastica Tripartita. CSEL 71, in W. Jacob (ed.). Vindobonae: Holder-Pichler-Tempsky, 1952.

Cassiodorus. *Chronica, MGH AA*, XI, in Th. Mommsen (ed.), 120–61, Berolini, 1894.

Codex Theodosianus XVI, texte latin. T. Mommsen (SCh 497), Synodi et Collectiones Legum' 7. Paris: Les Éditions du Cerf; Paris: Cerf, 2005. Polish edition in M. Ożóg and M. Wójcik (eds). Kraków: Wydawnictwo WAM, 2014.

Constantine's Letter to Alexander the Bishop, and Arius the Presbyter in Eusebius of Caesarea, *Vita Constantini* II, 64–72.

Constantine's Letter to the Churches Respecting the Council at Nicaea in Eusebius of Caesarea, *Vita Constantini* III, 17.

'The Council of Antioch, 325: Letter of the Council', in J. Stevenson (ed.), *A New Eusebius: Documents Illustrating the History of the Church to* AD 337. London: SPCK 1990.

John of Damascus, *De haeresibus* in PG 94, 677–780.

Degórski B. 'Il Primo Concilio di Costantinopoli (381). Uno schizzo storico e teologico', *VP 36 65* (2016): 156–70.

De Navascués, P. *Pablo de Samosata y sus adversarios. Estudio histórico-teológico del cristianismo antioqueno en el s. III* SEA 87. Roma: Institutum Patristicum Augustinianum, 2004.

De Riedmatten, H. *Les actes du procès de Paul de Samosate, Étude sur la cristologie du IIIe au IVe siècle.* Fribourg en Suisse: Edition St. Paul, 1952.

Eunomius. *Apologie* in L. Doutreleau (ed.), SCh 305. Paris: Les Éditions du Cerf, 1983.

Eusebius Caesariensis, Vita Constantini, in F. Winkelmann, *Eusebius Werke* I/1. GCS VII/1, 1975.

Eusebius. *Historia Ecclesiastica*, in E. Schwartz, *Eusebius Werke: Die Kirchengeschichte.* GCS IX/1–3. Leipzig, 1903–1909.

Evagrius Scholasticus. *Historia Ecclesiae, The Ecclesiastical History of Evagrius with the Scholia*, eds J. Bidez and L. Parmentier. London, 1898; repr. 1979.

Fernandez S. 'Criterios para interpretar los textos sinodales según el "De synodis" de Atanasio', *ScTh* 49 (2017): 9–30.

Fraisse-Coué, Ch. 'Le débat théologique au temps de Théodose II: Nestorius', in J.–M. Mayeur et al. (eds), *Histoire du christianisme: des origins à nos jours. II, Naissance d'une chrétienté (250-430)*, 449–550. Paris: Desclée, 1995.

Hefele, Ch.-J. and Leclercq, H. *Histoire des conciles d'après les documents originaux.* Paris: Letouzey et Ané, 1907.

Hilary of Poitiers, De synodis seu de fide orientalium, PL 10, 479–546.

Hilary of Poitiers, Fragmenta historica 11, in A. L. Feder (ed.), *CSEL* 65. Vindebonae, 1916.

Joannou, P.-P. (ed.). *Les canons des synodes particuliers*, SCL 12, pp. 129–34. 'Pontificia commissione per la redazione del codice di diritto canonico orientale'. Fonti, Fasc. IX, vol. I/2; Roma/Grottaferrata, 1962.

Kottler B. (ed.). *Die Schriften des Johannes von Damaskos IV*. Berlin: W. de Gruyter 1981.

Lange, U. M. 'Cristological Controversy at the Synod of Antioch in 268/9', *JTS* 51 (2000): 54–80.

Libellus sinodicus Mansi I., 662; SCL 1, p. 2.

Liberatus, *Breviarium*, in E. Schwartz (ed.), *Concilium universale Chalcedonense*, vol. 5, 98–141, 'Collectio Sangermanensis' (ACO, II/5), Berlin/Leipzig, 1936.

Mansi, G. D. *Sacrorum Conciliorum nova et amplissima collection* (= Mansi) Venezia 1759-1798. Reprint: Paris, 1901–1927.

Marcellinus Comes, *Chronicon*, MGH AA XI, in Th. Mommsen (ed.), 60–104. Berolini, 1894.

Martínez, G. and Rodríguez, F. (eds). *La Colección Canónica Hispana* vol. IV: Concilios galos, Concilios hispanos, primera parte. Madrid: CSIC. Instituto Enrique Flórez, 1984.

Meigne M. 'Concile ou collection d'Elvire', *RHE* 70 (1975): 361–87.

Nestorius. *Le livre d'Héraclide*, in F. Nau (trans.). Paris: Letouzey et Ané, 1907.

Ożóg, M. *Inter duas potestates: The Religious Policy of Theoderic the Great*. Frankfurt am Main: Peter Lang, 2016.

The Panarion of St. Epiphanius, Bishop of Salamis, trans. P. Amidon. New York and Oxford: Oxford University Press, 1990.

Pietras, H. 'La difesa della monarchia divina da parte del papa Dionigi (+268)', *AHP* 28 (1990): 335–42.

Pietras, H. 'L'unità di Dio in Dionigi di Alessandria', *G* 72 (1991): 459–90.

Pietras, H. 'Le ragioni della convocazione del Concilio Niceno da parte di Costantino il Grande. Un'investigazione storico-teologica', *G* 82, no. 1 (2001): 5–35.

Pietras, H. *Council of Nicaea (325): Religious and Political Context, Documents, Commentaries*, trans. M. Fijak. Rome: Gregorian & Biblical Press, 2016.

Schwartz E. (ed.). *Concilium universale Chalcedonense*, vol. 5. 'Collectio Sangermanensis' ACO, II/5. Berlin and Leipzig, 1936.

Simonetti, M. 'Eudossio', in A. di Berardino (ed.), *Nuovo dizionario patristico e di antichità cristiane*, 1 vols, 1823–4. Genova-Milano: Marietti, 2006–2010.

Socrates Scholasticus, *Histoire Ecclesiastique*, vol. I, introduction and edition P. Maraval. SCh 477, Paris 2004

Sozomène: *Histoire ecclésiastique, Livres I-II*, in G. Grillet, G. Sabbah amd A.-J. Festugiere (eds), SCh 306. Paris: Les Éditions du Cerf, 1993. The English translation in NPNF Second Series, vol. 2. Peabody, MA: Hendrickson Publishers, 1994.

Synodicon adversus Tragaediam Irenaei, PG 84, 531–864.

Tanner, N. P. (ed.). *Decrees of the Ecumenical Councils*, vol. 1. Washington, DC: Georgtown University Press, 1990.

Théodoret de Cyr, Histoire ecclésiastique, Livres I-II, in J. Bouffartique et al. (eds), SCh 501. Paris: Les Éditions du Cerf, 2006.

Vilella Masana, J. 'Collectiones falsamente atribuidas a un concilio', *CnS* 19, no. 1 (2018): 137–75.

Vranić, V. 'The Christology of Eutyches at the Council of Constantinople 448', *P* 8 (2008): 208–21.

CHAPTER 23

'Light from light'

The metaphysics of light of the early church[1]

ISIDOROS CHARALAMPOS KATSOS

APPROACHING THE 'LIGHT'

The Gospel of John opens with a reflection on the divinity of the Word:

> In the beginning was the Word, and the Word was with God, and the Word was God. He was in the beginning with God. All things were made through him, and without him nothing was made that was made. In him was life, and the life was the light of men. And the light shines in the darkness, and the darkness did not comprehend it. (Jn 1.1-5)

The Christian creed advances from this to explain the relation of the Word to God as an *X from X* causal relation, like begetting and light: 'Light from Light, true God from true God, begotten not made, consubstantial with the Father; through him all things were made.' The relation 'God from God' and the demiurgic attribute 'through him all things were made' make it abundantly clear that the third verse of the creed is a brief 'midrash', or exegetical commentary, on the opening verses of John. The celebrated formula 'light from light' also belongs to this midrash: the Word is light and his sonship and divinity entail that God the Father is also light.[2]

Amidst a vast number of studies devoted to the Nicene Creed, it is often forgotten that the celebrated formula 'light from light' is itself an interpretation of Scripture. According to a fundamental tenet of ancient hermeneutics, one should 'interpret scripture by scripture'. This means that early Christians did not think of light as a

---

[1]This study was composed under the auspices of the Center for the Study of Christianity at the Hebrew University of Jerusalem.

[2]On 'light from light' as an '*X from X*' causal relation, see M. R. Barnes, *The Power of God:* Δύναμις *in Gregory of Nyssa's Trinitarian Theology* (Washington, DC: The Catholic University of America Press, 2001), pp. 119–21.

chance metaphor but as an illustration derived directly from Scripture itself.[3] The passages that they mostly had in mind are the following:

- 'God is light and in him is no darkness' (1 Jn 1.5);
- 'In thy light we shall see light' (Ps. 35.10 [LXX]);
- Wisdom is 'the radiance of the eternal light and an unspotted mirror of the working of God and an image of his goodness' (Wis. 7.26);
- The Son is 'the radiance of the glory of God and the express image of his substance' (Heb. 1.3);
- The Word 'was the true Light, which lights every man that comes into the world' (Jn 1.9);
- 'I am the light of the world: he that follows me shall not walk in darkness, but shall have the light of life' (Jn 8.12).

All these passages are grouped together and discussed in the opening chapters of Origen's *De Principiis* (1.1-2, 6 and 2.4-5, 6-9, 11). That means that by the mid-third century, Christian thinkers had already developed a unified and coherent exegesis of God as light based on a systematic reading of Scripture. This exegesis was based on the model of the sun and its ray, already ubiquitous in early Christian literature. According to Justin, the Word 'is indivisible and inseparable from the Father, just as they say that the light of the sun on earth is indivisible and inseparable from the sun in the heavens'.[4] 'God', Tertullian wrote, 'produced the Word [. . .] as a root produces the shoot, a spring the river, the sun a ray.'[5] Origen in the *De Principiis* combined the sun/ray model with the biblical language of light/radiance:

> Our eyes frequently cannot look at the nature of the light itself, that is, upon the substance of the sun; but when we see its radiance and rays pouring in through windows, perhaps, or any small opening for light, we can reflect about how great is the source and fountain of bodily light' (1.1.6). '"God is light", according to John. The only-begotten Son, therefore, is the radiance of this light, proceeding from him inseparably, as does radiance from light, and enlightening the whole creation' (1.2.7). '. . . Wisdom is said to be the radiance of eternal light; the force of this expression we have explained in the preceding pages, when we introduced the illustration of the sun and the radiance of its rays' (1.2.11). Such, therefore, is the saying, 'In your light shall we see light', that is, in your Word and Wisdom, who is your Son, in him we shall see you, the Father. (1.1.1)[6]

Origen's interpretation is crucial for our understanding of the early Christian language of light. First, the sun/ray model echoes the celebrated 'sun simile' at the

---

[3]For a hermeneutically sensitive history of the Nicene Creed, see J. Behr, *The Nicene Faith*, 2 vols (New York: St Vladimir's Seminary Press, 2004).

[4]Justin Martyr, *Dial.*, 128.3.

[5]Tertullian, *Prax.*, 8.

[6]Translation Behr (Oxford University Press, 2017), slightly amended.

end of the sixth book of Plato's *Republic*, which entered biblical reflection through the medium of Hellenistic Judaism, as we know through the writings of Philo of Alexandria. Second, all the parties involved in the fourth-century trinitarian debates agreed with Origen's interpretation, though each of them understood it in differing ways. Let us take, for example, the talk of God as 'light'. Today we would almost intuitively identify 'light' with the light-ray. That is not, however, always the meaning of the term in the aforementioned biblical passages. Strange as it may sound to modern readers, Origen, following Scripture, following the Greek language, understood 'light' equivocally, as either the light-source, namely the sun, or its illuminative power, that is, the ray. To say, 'God is light', then, means that God is like the sun; and 'in thy light we shall see light' means that in the Son we perceive the nature of Father just as in the brightness of the sunbeam we perceive the intensity of the light-source that generates it. The example is indicative: just as today we might debate over which sense of 'light' is applicable in each Scriptural passage, just so did the early Christian authors. And since the creed is a midrash on Scripture, the credal light language is the result of a certain interpretation of Scripture.[7]

Once we try to understand this language, we stumble upon difficulties. On the one hand, Origen regards the sun/ray image as an explanatory model, a metaphor or analogy[8] taken from the sensible world and applied to the divine. On the other hand, he adds two claims which seem incongruous with metaphorical language: he claims that Christ is light properly speaking, since he is 'the true light', according to Jn 1.9; and that the true light 'has nothing in common with the light of this sun'.[9] The latter claim is easy to understand. It demarcates the limits of the analogy of the sun/ray to God/Word, warning against a merely material interpretation of its light language.[10] The former claim, however, is more difficult to process. For how is it possible to speak of God as light both in a proper and in a metaphorical sense while maintaining that Scripture is a coherent and consistent text?

In what follows, I will explain what that means. It should be noted at the outset, however, that this chapter does not intend to enquire into the meaning of the light language of the early church. Instead, its aim is to enquire into the conditions of meaning. The aim of this chapter, therefore, is cathartic. It aims to show that until we learn how to think properly about the use of the scriptural light language, it is rather pointless to enquire into its meaning. This suggests that many contemporary attempts to decipher the early Christian language of light have failed to address properly the question of meaning. To show why this is the case, I first need to explain what lies beneath the strange term 'metaphysics of light'.

---

[7]The synonymous use of πῦρ (fire) and φάος (light) in Greek language goes at least as far back as Parmenides and Empedocles. It is recorded by Plato in *Timaeus* (39b4-5), and reprised by Basil of Caesarea in *Hom. Hex.*, 6.2. The double sense of 'light' as either the light-ray or the light-source is essential part of the fourth-century trinitarian debates, see Athanasius, *Decr.*, 5.24.
[8]Origen, *Princ.*, 1.1.6: '*similitudine*'.
[9]Origen, *Princ.*, 1.2.6.
[10]Origen, *Princ.*, 1.1.1-2, 1.2.6.

WHAT IS THE 'METAPHYSICS OF LIGHT'?

'Metaphysics' is a term unknown to ancient writers; but its subject matter is. In the collection of treatises handed down under the title *Metaphysics*, Aristotle describes the subject matter of his enquiry in three different ways: it is the study of 'being qua being';[11] the study of 'first causes and principles';[12] and the study of what is 'changeless and separate'.[13] One way of making sense of all three claims as part of a unified project is the following: in studying being *qua being*, Aristotle enquires into the nature of being in general, that is, in universal terms. To do so, Aristotle turns to the study of the primary instance of being, namely substance. The primary kind of substance is the 'unmoved mover', Aristotle's God.[14] Aristotle's enquiry, then, leads to the study of God as a first principle or cause of all beings, *qua* beings. In this interpretation, the subject matter of Aristotle's project in the *Metaphysics* is the study of the divine being, or God, as the primary and most exemplary being, upon which all beings depend. It is in this sense that Aristotle calls the subject matter of his enquiry 'first philosophy' or 'theology'.[15]

Late antique thinkers followed Aristotle in this regard. The church fathers were no exception. Starting with Philo, who for a long time was considered as 'a Church Father honoris causa',[16] the philosophically educated readers of Scripture saw in the self-disclosure of God to Moses as the truly existent the subject matter of Aristotle's enquiry in the *Metaphysics*: 'I am the one who is' (ἐγώ εἰμι ὁ ὤν) of Exod. 3.14 exhibits a striking lexical similarity to Aristotle's formula 'being qua being' (ὄν ᾗ ὄν).[17] Once the connection was established, it was no surprise that the church fathers understood themselves as 'first philosophers' and 'theologians' in the sense of the *Metaphysics*. That is not to say that they identified Aristotle's divine being with the God of the Bible. Instead, they understood the God of the Bible as fulfilling all of Aristotle's requirements of *being qua being*. The Christian God was subsequently understood as primary being and first principle and cause of all beings.[18]

---

[11]Aristotle, *Metaph.*, 6.1 1003a.21–22.

[12]Aristotle, *Metaph.*, 1.1 981b28.

[13]Aristotle, *Metaph.*, 6.1 1026a.16.

[14]Aristotle, *Metaph.*, 12.7.

[15]Aristotle, *Metaph.*, 6.1 1026a.18-32; see C. Shields, 'Being Qua Being', in C. Shields (ed.), *The Oxford Handbook of Aristotle* (Oxford: Oxford University Press, 2012), pp. 344–71.

[16]See D. Runia, *Philo in Early Christian Literature: A Survey* (Assen: Van Gorcum, 1993), pp. 3–33.

[17]On the ancient reception of Aristotle, see A. Falcon (ed.), *The Brill Companion to the Reception of Aristotle* (Leiden: Brill, 2016); and also: M. Edwards, *Aristotle and Early Christian Thought* (London: Routledge, 2019).

[18]On Christian theology as philosophy, see characteristically Gregory Nazianzen, *Orat.*, 27.3. Gregory's *Orat.* 28.1 calls theology 'first philosophy'. *Orat.*, 28.4.2 calls Plato a theologian and thus Plato's *Ti* 28e is philosophical theology. In *Orat.*, 28.3.7: God is the first and pure nature. In *Orat.*, 28.9: the task of the theologian is to enquire into the nature of being, both cataphatically and apophatically. See also G. Karamanolis, *The Philosophy of Early Christianity* (Durham: Acumen Press, 2013), pp. 17–18; I. Ramelli, 'Origen, Patristic Philosophy, and Christian Platonism: Re-Thinking the Christianisation of Hellenism', *VChr* 63 (2009): 217–63.

470 T&T CLARK HANDBOOK OF THE EARLY CHURCH

In considering God as exemplary being and the principle and cause of all beings, Aristotle was following his teacher Plato. In the *Republic* (509b), Plato theorized the Good as the ontological foundation of intelligible beings, that is, of the 'forms' – the Platonic equivalent to Aristotle's 'beings in so far as they are beings'. In the *Timaeus* (37d5-6), the *Philebus* (28e3) and the *Laws* (967b5-6), Plato identified the cause of order in the world with a divine intellect (νοῦς). Aristotle's notion of God as intellect and the good can be regarded as one possible way of unifying Plato's two accounts of primary being and divine causality. Later Platonists either followed Aristotle's solution or opted for hierarchical systems. The trinitarian theology of the early church developed in this context.[19]

A striking point in Plato's discussion of the Good in the *Republic* 6 is his reluctance to speak of it directly. Instead, he offers an elaborate analogy between, on the one side, the Good, knowledge and being, and on the other side, the sun and its double power, illuminative and generative: 'whatever the Good is in the intelligible realm, in relation to the intellect and intelligible things, the same is the sun in the visible realm, in relation to sight and visible things' (*Rep*, 508b13-c2); 'not only do the objects of knowledge owe their being known to the Good, but their being is also due to it, although the Good is not being, but superior to it in rank and power' (*Rep*, 509b5-9). The analogy is further developed into a simile (509a1-5: ὥσπερ – οὕτω) grounded on the insight that the sun is the image (509a9: εἰκόνα) and likeness (509c6: ὁμοιότητα) of the Good. Aristotle, in the *De Anima* 3, also uses an analogy from light (οἷον) to illustrate the relation of the so-called 'active' intellect to the objects of knowledge (ibid. 430a14–7). Interestingly, the attributes of the active intellect in the *De Anima* 3 are very similar to the attributes of God in the *Metaphysics* 12, who is also pure intellect: thought thinking itself. This resemblance prompted Alexander of Aphrodisias, Aristotle's most brilliant ancient commentator, to identify the active intellect with God. As a result, two of the most influential ancient schools of philosophy, the Platonic and the Peripatetic, increasingly had recourse to light imagery in their attempt to speak of the divine as cause of being.[20]

The reason for the extended use of this light imagery was already hinted at by Plato and further explained by the commentators of Aristotle's logical works:

---

[19]On Aristotle's synthesis of Plato's views, see S. Menn, 'Aristotle and Plato on God as Nous and as the Good', *The Review of Metaphysics* 45 (1992): 543–73. On the late antique reception, see L. P. Gerson, *Aristotle and Other Platonists* (Ithaca, NY: Cornell University Press, 2005); G. Karamanolis, *Plato and Aristotle in Agreement? Platonists on Aristotle from Antiochus to Porphyry* (Oxford: Clarendon Press, 2006).

[20]For Aristotle's divine attributes, see *An.*, 3.5 and *Metaph.*, 12.7 and 9: eternal, unmovable, separate, without parts, indivisible, impassible, unalterable, whose very essence is actuality. We note that most of the attributes are negative. Though it is often forgotten, negative theology is integral part of Aristotle's project in the *Metaphysics*. For Alexander's divine interpretation of the active intellect, see C. Shields, *Aristotle: De Anima* (Oxford: Clarendon Press, 2016), pp. 312–29. For the Stoics, pure fire/light is not an image of the divine but its very substance, see P. Boyancé, *Études sur le songe de Scipion: Essais d'histoire et de psychologie religieuses* (Bordeaux: Feret et Fils, 1936), pp. 65–78; and C. Stead, *Philosophy in Christian Antiquity* (Cambridge: Cambridge University Press, 1994), pp. 46–7. The three approaches, Stoic, Aristotelian and Platonic, became schematic in modern scholarship giving rise to three different theoretical models of 'metaphysics of light', as we will note.

definitions rely on some simple and primary notions, which must remain undefinable on pain of infinite regress. Substance is such a primary notion. If we now regard the divine being as pure substance, as the *Metaphysics* suggest, then this being cannot be defined. Yet, the impossibility of defining substance does not result in complete agnosticism. Ancient commentators suggested that undefinable things can still be described through their properties or illustrated by examples.[21] Light is precisely such an example. It is an interesting and far-reaching question why light should be chosen as an appropriate example of being. Assuming the suitability, the term metaphysics of light denotes the use of light as an illustration of the subject matter of metaphysics, that is of *being qua being*.

Here, there has been a shift from speaking of Aristotle's *Metaphysics* to speaking of 'metaphysics' in general. This is because Aristotle's project in the *Metaphysics* became so influential that it gradually gave rise to a discipline with the same name and the same subject matter. It is what we call today 'traditional metaphysics' (not to be confused with contemporary metaphysics). The 'metaphysics of light', therefore, denotes light as the most powerful illustration of the divine being in traditional metaphysics: light as a privileged symbol (analogy or metaphor) of *being qua being* or of being as such.

One can already sense a tension. In order to use light as an illustration of being qua being, one must first have a clear grasp of what light is. How can we use light to speak of substance if we do not first know whether (and in what sense) light is itself a substance? Or, how can we use light to speak of the first cause, if we do not first know whether (and in what sense) light is itself a cause? In short, how can we use light to speak of being as such, if we do not first know what is light as such? We thus have two enquiries and an analogy that connects them: the subject matter of traditional metaphysics (*being qua being*); light as a particular field of application of general metaphysics (*light qua being*); and an analogy from the particular to the general (*being qua light*). In the next section, we will see that the three are often confused, generating mistakes in the process.

RIGHT REASONING ABOUT LIGHT REASONING

A tripartite classification: Origins, development and reception

The term 'metaphysics of light' (*Lichtmetaphysik*) was coined by the German medievalist Clemens Baeumker, who distinguished between three ontological-cum-linguistic versions of it:

1. A physicalist model corresponding to a univocal use of light language in which the divine is the most refined form of physical light or fire, like the

---

[21]On the difference between 'definition' and 'description', see Porphyry *In Cat.*, 60.15-20, 72.30-73.14, 87.16-22, 88.8-12; J. Barnes, *Porphyry: An Introduction* (Oxford: Clarendon Press, 2003), pp. 57–62; S. Strange, *Porphyry On Aristotle's Categories* (London: Bloomsbury, 1992), p. 38, n. 40.

Heraclitean/Stoic cosmic fire, Manichean light or the astral deities of the Hellenistic cosmic religion;

2. A transcendental model corresponding to a non-literal use of light language, in which the divine is 'light' only metaphorically speaking due to its ontological difference from all beings, in the sense of Plato's discussion of the Good in the *Republic* 6;

3. A participatory model corresponding to an analogical use of light language, in which the divine is light, properly speaking, as the intelligible archetype of all light. Conversely, intellectual (e.g. angelic) light and sensible (e.g. the sun's) light are also 'light' properly speaking but this time derivatively so, in virtue of their participation in the intelligible archetype. According to Baeumker, this model was introduced by Philo and was fully developed in later Platonism, especially in the works of Plotinus and Proclus, before it acquired its highest pitch in medieval scholastic philosophy.[22]

Baeumker's tripartite classification has had a long trajectory in Western scholarship. Throughout the twentieth century continental scholars heatedly debated the use of light language in the Platonic tradition, most notably in Philo and Plotinus.[23] While the physicalist model was easily dismissed, it was already unclear to Baeumker which of the other two models characterizes a specific text. The ambivalence remains. The reason for the uncertainty has to do with the insight, first expressed by Hans Blumenberg, that the metaphysics of light (*Lichtmetaphysik*) is grounded on light metaphors (*Lichtmetaphorik*). What Blumenberg meant was that the reflection on light, incited by a metaphor, reveals something true about the nature of being: being reveals itself through its self-communication.[24] Werner Beierwaltes further expanded Blumenberg's thesis by showing that when light metaphors collapse into light metaphysics, they generate a participatory ontology which can only be expressed through analogical language. From then onwards, it was an issue of the history of ideas to show that the collapse of light metaphors to metaphysics, which was first intuited by Plato, acquired its fullest expression in Proclus. And since Proclus was the intellectual great grandchild of Plotinus and the unknown forefather of medieval Neoplatonism (through the tremendous influence of the *Liber de causis*),

---

[22]C. Baeumker, *Witelo: Ein Philosoph und Naturforscher des XIII. Jahrhunderts* (Münster: Aschendorf, 1908), pp. 357–433 (see p. 360 for the tripartite classification).

[23]For notorious controversies, see (1) as regards the Hellenistic metaphysics of light, especially Philo: G. Wetter, *Phōs: Eine Untersuchung über hellenistische Frömmigkeit zugleich ein Beitrag zum Verständnis des Manichäismus* (Uppsala: Akademiska Bokhandeln, 1915); and F. N. Klein, *Die Lichtterminologie bei Philon von Alexandrien und in den hermetischen Schriften* (Leiden: Brill, 1962); (2) as regards Plotinus, W. Beierwaltes, 'Die Metaphysik des Lichtes in der Philosophie Plotins', *ZPF* 15 (1961): 334–62; and R. Ferwerda, *La signification des images et des metaphors dans la pensée de Plotin* (Groningen: Wolters, 1965).

[24]H. Blumenberg, 'Licht als Metapher der Wahrheit: Im Vorfeld der philosophischen Begriffsbildung', in *Ästhetische und metaphorologische Schriften*, ed. H. Blumenberg (Frankfurt: Suhrkamp, 2001), pp. 139–76, especially, 142–3.

the metaphysics of light became the secret thread that gave a sense of unity and continuity to the history of Western metaphysics. This kind of historiography brought a slight change of meanings: *Lichtmetaphysik* was no longer a term open to three different interpretations but was identified itself with one interpretation, namely Baeumker's participatory/analogical model. Conversely, *Lichtmetaphorik* became the signpost for Baeumker's transcendental/metaphorical model. Thus, the problem of ambiguity in the sources (analogy or metaphor) became the history of the passage from metaphor to the analogy of being in Western metaphysics.[25]

The term 'metaphysics of light' was introduced into English scholarship through medieval studies, especially in the field of Grosseteste, to denote a cluster of meanings. In the words of David Lindberg:

> There has been much discussion of Grosseteste's 'metaphysics of light' (for which I prefer to substitute the expression 'philosophy of light', since much of it has nothing to do with metaphysics), but this discussion has frequently suffered from a failure to make several indispensable distinctions among differing bodies of ideas. Within Grosseteste's philosophy of light, there are at least four distinct strands, each employing optical analogies and metaphors: (1) the epistemology of light, in which the process of acquiring knowledge of unchanging Platonic forms is considered analogous to corporeal vision through the eye; (2) the metaphysics or cosmogony of light, in which light is regarded as the first corporeal form and the material world as the product of the self-propagation of a primeval point of light; (3) the etiology or physics of light, according to which all causation in the material world operates on the analogy of the radiation of light; and (4) the theology of light, which employs light metaphors to elucidate theological truths.[26]

Lindberg's classification is valuable for several reasons: First, it shows the proliferation of the term 'metaphysics of light' in English literature, so that almost any subject that involves light imagery can be clustered under that term. Second, it is an attempt to distinguish between different senses of 'metaphysics of light', very much in the direction suggested at the end of our previous section. Third, it is a testimony to several misconceptions that have grown over time. It is clear from

---

[25]For the expansion of Blumenberg's thesis into a participatory model, see Beierwaltes, 'Die Metaphysik des Lichtes'; idem, 'Lichtmetaphysik', in J. Ritter and K. Gründer, *Historisches Wörterbuch der Philosophie*, vol. 5 (Darmstadt: Wissenschaftliche Buchgesellschaft, 1980), col. 289. For the identification of the participatory model with Proclean analogy, see W. Beierwaltes, *Proklos: Grunzüge seiner Metaphysik* (Frankfurt: Klostermann, 2014), pp. 153–8, and 329–38. For light metaphysics as connecting thread in Western intellectual history, see W. Beierwaltes, 'Lichtmetaphysik', cols 282–6. Implicit in Beierwaltes' thesis is the equivocal use of 'analogy' for both language (symbol or metaphor) and being (ontology). Through the metaphysics of light Beierwaltes aimed to capture the passage from analogy of language to analogy of being. Yet, he never spelled out the equivocation, resulting in the conflation of analogy with participation.

[26]D. Lindberg, *Theories of Vision from Al-Kindi to Kepler* (Chicago: The University of Chicago Press, 1976), p. 95.

Baeumker's discussion (and our foregoing analysis) that what Lindberg classifies under two different senses, namely (1) the epistemology of light and (4) the theology of light, are in fact two complementary aspects (epistemological and ontological) of one and the same analogy or metaphor of *being qua light*. Lindberg's sense (2) is the study of light qua substance (*light qua being*). Sense (3) is the study of *light qua first principle* or cause, grounding the analogy of being and light. Thus, what Lindberg regards as a coincidental cluster of meanings, much of which 'has nothing to do with metaphysics' is, in fact, the unified subject matter of the metaphysics of light as it consolidated in high scholasticism.[27] Clearly, much has happened since the time Baeumker introduced the term in Western scholarship in order for Lindberg to miss the unity of the underlying subject matter. I want to argue that what happened was a systemic error: from its very beginning, the modern discussion on the metaphysics of light laboured under false premises.

From metaphor to metaphysics (and back again)

The first and most questionable assumption was the alleged opposition between metaphorical and analogical use of light language. As already mentioned, the distinction is not present in Plato's sun simile, the foundational text of the metaphysics of light. In the *Republic* 6, the sun functions as analogous (ἀνάλογον) to the Good and a simile (ὁμοιότης) at the same time. Aristotle, who laid out the foundations of the classical theory of metaphor, distinguishes in the *Poetics* 21 between four types of metaphors, three types of transference of property between species and genus and a fourth type of transference of property between things that come under the same genus, identified with analogical or proportional metaphor (1457b6-33). In the *Rhetoric* 3, Aristotle argues that analogical metaphors are the most popular, appropriate, vivid and elegant metaphors (1411a1–b23). The claim is informative: given that similarity is the ground of metaphor (*Poet.* 1459a7–8; *Top.* 140a10–11), the supremacy of analogical metaphors implies that proportionality is the best exemplification of similarity. That makes proportional metaphors the focal point of the classical theory of metaphor.[28] It is now easy to perceive that Baeumker's division between the metaphorical and the analogical use of light language is based on a false assumption. According to the classical theory, from Plato's celebrated 'sun simile' and Aristotle's 'active intellect' to Plotinus' generation of intellect from the One as the light from the sun (*Enn.* 5.1.6.28-30), we stand in front of clear-cut cases of analogical metaphors. Baeumker's tripartite classification and the subsequent narrative of the passage from *Lichtmetaphorik* to *Lichtmetaphysik* obfuscate the

---

[27]For a unified account of the medieval metaphysics of light, see J. McEvoy, 'The Metaphysics of Light in the Middle Ages', *PhS* 26 (1978): 126–45; idem, *Robert Grosseteste* (Oxford: Oxford University Press, 2000), pp. 87–95 (dedicated to Beierwaltes).

[28]For Aristotles, see S. R. Levin, 'Aristotle's Theory of Metaphor', *Philosophy & Rhetoric* 15 (1982): 24–46; for later writers, see D. Innes, 'Metaphor, Simile, and Allegory', in *Metaphor, Allegory, and the Classical Tradition: Ancient Thought and Modern Revisions*, ed. G. R. Boys-Stones. (Oxford: Oxford University Press, 2003), pp. 7–27, especially, pp. 15–16.

unity of metaphor and analogy in the pre-modern mindset. Ancient talk of *being qua light* is analogical *and* metaphorical: the best onto-theological images of light are construed as proportional metaphors. The distinction between a metaphorical and an analogical use of light language, so fundamental to the modern debate on the metaphysics of light, is simply a false dichotomy.[29]

The second questionable assumption builds upon the first. It has to do with a remarkable lack of interest in examining the meaning of ancient metaphors of light through a pre-modern perspective. According to the classical theory, the structure of a metaphor consists of the transfer of meaning (i.e. of a semantic property) from a source domain to a target domain, establishing a relation of similarity between the two. In the case of light metaphors, the source domain is physical light and the target domain is the core of being (identified with the divine being). In order to understand the meaning of an ancient author predicating 'light' of the divine, we need to know which properties of light the author had in mind in a particular context. This, in turn, requires an investigation into the nature of light that grounds these properties. To date, the debate on the metaphysics of light has still not touched upon the physical theories that grounded analogical metaphors of God talk as light. The latter charge requires a qualification. It does not mean that the scholars involved in the debate were not aware of the physical theories of light present in the sources; rather that, with very few exceptions, scholars did not integrate physical theories into the discussion of the metaphysics of light because of a remarkable reluctance to approach ancient metaphors from within their own proper context, namely as linguistic transference mechanisms.[30] One of the obvious consequences is a failure to recognize the unbreakable continuity between the physics and the metaphysics of light in pre-modern thought, already visible in Lindberg's remarks. Another consequence is that until we start taking seriously the physics that grounds the metaphysics of light, the meaning of analogical metaphors (that is, the exact properties transferred from physical light to pure being) will remain elusive. As a result, much of the current discussion on the ancient metaphysics of light is, at best, speculative.[31]

---

[29]For the Platonic light imagery, see G. E. R. Lloyd, *Polarity and Analogy: Two Types of Argumentation in Early Greek Thought* (Cambridge: Cambridge University Press, 1966), p. 402. Aristotle includes in his examples of (analogical) metaphors in *Rhet*. 3.10 (1411b12-3) the imagery of intellect as light, borrowing from Plato's poetic description of the creation of the sun in *Tim*. 39b4-5. The image generates a powerful proportional metaphor of the intellect as the sun (and of the soul as heaven), which, through the mediation of Philo (e.g. *Heres.*, 263, *Congr.*, 47), becomes the ground of the Christian imagery of Christ as the sun, see Origen, *Hom.Gen.*, 1.5-7.

[30]The transfer of a physical property to pure being was emphatically denied by Beierwaltes, 'Lichtmetaphysik', 289.

[31]For the missing discussion on the physics of light, see Pierre Boyancé's review of Klein, *Lichtterminologie*, in *Latomus* 22 (1963): 115–16; and Christopher Stead's review of Pelikan's Gifford Lectures in *JTS* 45 (1994): 725–7. There are notable exceptions such as (for Plotinus) F. M. Schroeder, *Form and Transformation: A Study in the Philosophy of Plotinus* (Montreal: McGill-Queen's University Press, 1992), pp. 24–39; (for patristics) Stead, *Philosophy in Christian Antiquity*, pp. 140–3; and in general: M. Wallraff,

The third questionable assumption concerns the reception history of the metaphysics of light which still forgoes a serious engagement with patristic sources. From the preceding discussion it is quite clear that the trinitarian theology of the early church was articulated in the philosophical context of Hellenistic and late antique metaphysics of light. Baeumker already included Philo, Gregory Nazianzen, Augustine and the fifth-century author known under the literary name of Dionysius the Areopagite among the great metaphysicians of light. Blumenberg and Beierwaltes also looked to the Greek patristic tradition for early Christian versions of the metaphysics of light. When the discussion reached English-speaking scholarship, through medieval studies, it was already preoccupied with innerdisciplinary tensions and dynamics between the Augustinian *Lichtmetaphysik* and the Thomistic *Lichtmetaphorik* – a juxtaposition of which, by now, the reader should rightly suspect.[32] And so, while it is not possible to study Grosseteste's metaphysics of light without at least some engagement with the Greek patristic tradition, there is a surprising dearth of studies on the metaphysics of light in patristic scholarship. One suspects language barriers and disciplinary limits as the cause of such silence. Be it as it may, the term 'metaphysics of light' remains almost unknown in English-speaking patristic literature.

This might have been a blessing in disguise. The continental discussion was for decades trapped in the 'analogy or metaphor' dichotomy, a pseudo-dilemma, as already mentioned, from which English patristics might have been spared by ignorance. Alas, it was not so. The best study that we still have on the language of light of the early church is a short monograph by Jaroslav Pelikan, in which Athanasius plays the role of the early Christian hero of the language of light.[33] In his analysis, Pelikan speaks interchangeably of light as 'symbolic statement' (pp. 21, 31), a 'figure of speech' (p. 21), a 'metaphor' (p. 44) or an 'analogy' (pp. 24, 84–5). And yet, Pelikan denies that light was for Athanasius *merely* a figure of speech or a symbolic statement. Instead, it was a παράδειγμα (pp. 26–31) in the sense of a Platonic paradigm:

> At one level of discourse it was accurate to say that the statement 'God is light' is symbolic. *Yet this did not mean that one already knew, from some source or other apart from God, what light was, and that one then attributed some quality of this light to God.* On the contrary, God was uncreated light, the light that illuminated every other light, himself the ultimate source of every illumination in his universe. (pp. 33–4; my italics)

To avoid a blunt identification with metaphor, Pelikan's favourite term throughout the book, present already in the subtitle, was 'the image of light', which was never clarified,

---

'Licht', in *Reallexikon für Antike und Christentum*, eds. G. Schöllgen et al., vol. 23 (Stuttgart: Anton Hiersemann, 2010), cols. 100–37.

[32] For the juxtaposition, see indicatively: McEvoy, 'Metaphysics of Light', pp. 139–41. McEvoy in the end recognizes in analogy of proportion the unitary aspect of the two traditions. McEvoy's conclusion clarifies what is already known in other fields, namely that schematic dichotomies of Platonic/Augustinian *Lichtmetaphysik* and Aristotelian/Thomistic *Lichtmetaphorik* belong to an older style of historiography but are too simplistic.

[33] J. Pelikan, *The Light of the World: A Basic Image in Early Christian Thought* (New York: Harper, 1962).

but which was clearly understood in the sense of Plato's sun simile in the *Republic* 6.[34] Pelikan's study is remarkable in that it avoids a false antinomy between metaphor and analogy. And yet in denying that God was called 'light' in virtue of some physical property of light attributed to God, he denied the application of the transference theory, which means that he denied that talk of God as light was metaphorical. As a result, he reiterated the exact same ambivalence (metaphor or not?) that we found in continental scholarship. In addition, Pelikan's Platonic interpretation of Athanasius made it abundantly clear that the Christian notion of God was the equivalent to the notion of the divine being in traditional metaphysics, that is, as perfect being and cause of beings. Thus, even though Pelikan never once mentioned the term 'metaphysics of light' in his study, he treated the question of *being qua light* in exactly the same way as Baeumker and Beierwaltes did, this time applied to Christian sources.[35]

As a result, Pelikan repeated the errors of his continental colleagues. In conflating the question of language with the participatory model of light, he failed to distinguish between 'light' as the subject matter of philosophy of language (proportional metaphor) and light as a field of application of general ontology (*light qua being*). Moreover, and astonishingly so, in a book devoted exclusively to the image of light in early Christian literature, he found no reason to reflect on the physical theories that ground the meaning of early Christian images of light. This was deliberate. He did not just think that such reflection was unnecessary; he believed it was mistaken. Just like Beierwaltes, Pelikan denied 'that one already knew, from some source or other apart from God, what light was, and that one then attributed some quality of this light to God'. The subsequent discussion contributed very little to make things better.

CONCLUDING THOUGHTS

To recapitulate: The term 'metaphysics of light' was introduced in twentieth-century continental scholarship to denote three different ontological-cum-linguistic models of light in pre-modern thought. The three models were based on an artificial division between metaphor and analogy, which does not exist in the pre-modern ('classical') theory of metaphor. From Plato to Platonism, light images function as analogical metaphors of the subject matter of metaphysics, namely of *being qua being*. The patristic corpus was born in this philosophical context. There is no evidence that early Christian thinkers ever wanted (or needed) to deviate from the general rule.[36] Analogical metaphors, however,

---

[34]Pelikan, *Light of the World*: *paradeigmata* as Platonic ideas (p. 26); images of 'light' and 'radiance' as Platonic *paradeigmata* (p 26); with a Platonic conclusion (p. 31); and a Platonic confession (p. 33).

[35]See Schroeder, *Form and Transformation*, p. 33. n. 29. Tellingly, in his *Gifford Lectures*, thirty years later, Pelikan mentioned the term 'metaphysics of light' summarizing (without citing) the position of Beierwaltes, 'Lichtmetaphysik', see J. Pelikan, *Christianity and Classical Culture: The Metamorphosis of Natural Theology in the Christian Encounter with Hellenism* (New Haven, CT: Yale University Press, 1993), pp. 103–4, and 236–7.

[36]See Origen, *Com.Joh.*, 1.157-66 (analogy); Gregory Nazianzen, *Orat.*, 28.31, 30.25-8, 31.32 (analogy and its limits); Gregory of Nyssa: *Contra Eunom.*, 3.1.126-36, 3.8.10 (metaphorical meaning). In all these passages the tenor of the metaphor is light's capacity to reveal, just as in Plato's sun simile. Blumenberg, 'Licht

generate meaning by the transfer of some property from one part of the analogy to the other. We can only know what properties are available in the case of light by studying the early Christian physics of light. Yet, the reflection on early Christian light metaphors through the prism of the physics of light is still pending.[37]

Once the question of the *use* of light language has been settled, there is much worth in the discussion of the metaphysics of light which remains. All authors seem to agree that Philo, Athanasius, Gregory Nazianzen, Augustine and Dionysius are working within a participatory ontology, in which God is pure being and the cause of all beings. As pure being, God is separate from the world – an intuition already present in Plato's Good and Aristotle's divine intellect. In Christian jargon, this is the realm of 'theology'. As the cause of beings, God is present in the world – as is Plato's form of the Good (*Rep.* 505a) and Aristotle's God as final cause (*Metaph.* 12.7). In Christian jargon, it is the realm of creation or 'economy', which corresponds to the realm of change or physics in Aristotelian taxonomy. This double aspect of being, transcendent and immanent, seems to be the fundamental axiom of ancient participatory metaphysics, captured eloquently by Plotinus in the famous dictum that the One is 'everywhere and nowhere' (*Enneads.* 3.9.4; 6.8.16). Once we decide to leave the past behind and disentangle the question of language from the question of ontology, we can thus make a lot of sense of the early Christian metaphysics of light.

THE INEXPRESSIBLE 'LIGHT'

We can now return to the question asked at the beginning of this chapter: is it possible to speak of God as light both properly and metaphorically? So far, we have seen that the early Christian light language is metaphorical in the tradition of the great

---

als Metapher', p. 142, was right in claiming that the metaphor of light entailed the revelatory nature of being, and so was Baeumker, *Witelo*, p. 364, n. 4, who claimed that the Nicene formula 'light from light', just as all early Christian light language, starting with the *Gospel of John*, is metaphorical. But Baeumker was wrong in assuming that the tenor of a metaphor excluded the proper use of language (see next section).

[37]For a critical discussion of the current state of knowledge on ancient theories of light, see I. Katsos, 'Chasing the Light: What Happened to the Ancient Theories?', *Isis* 110 (2019): 270–82. For the early Christian physics of light and their philosophical context, see I. C. Katsos, 'The Metaphysics of Light in the Hexaemeral Literature: From Philo to Ambrose of Milan' (PhD diss., Pembroke College, University of Cambridge, 2018) electronically accessible at https://www.repository.cam.ac.uk/handle/1810/293894 [last accessed: 19 June 2021]. Currently, the pioneer paper of G. van Kooten, 'The "True Light which Enlightens Everyone" (John 1:9): John, Genesis, the Platonic Notion of the "True, Noetic Light", and the Allegory of the Cave in Plato's Republic', in G. van Kooten (ed.), *The Creation of Heaven and Earth: Re-interpretations of Genesis 1 in the Context of Judaism, Ancient Philosophy, Christianity, and Modern Physics* (Leiden: Brill, 2005), pp. 149–94 of M. DelCogliano, *Basil of Caesarea's Anti-Eunomian Theory of Names: Christian Theology and Late-Antique Philosophy in the Fourth Century Trinitarian Controversy*. SupVCh, vol. 103 (Leiden: Brill, 2010), pp. 224–34; and A. Radde-Gallwitz, *Basil of Caesarea, Gregory of Nyssa, and the Transformation of Divine Simplicity* (Oxford: Oxford University Press, 2009), pp. 154–69, 200–7; and the two articles by G. O'Collins, S.J., '"Light from Light": The Divine Light Reflected in and by the Son and the Holy Spirit', pp. 103–21, esp. 114–16 and K. E. Tanner, 'The Use of Perceived Properties of Light as a Theological Analogy', pp. 122–30, esp. 122–6, both appearing in: G. O'Collins and M. A. Meyers (eds), *Light from Light: Scientists and Theologians in Dialogue* (Grand Rapids, MI: Eerdmans, 2012).

analogical metaphors of Plato's 'sun simile', Aristotle's illuminating 'active intellect' and Plotinus' super-luminous 'One'. We have also seen that the metaphysics that undergirds early Christian light metaphors is participatory because, according to the doctrine of creation, God is primary being and the cause of all beings, including light. This does not mean that we can talk of God as light in the same sense that we speak of physical light. The use of light language is here, by necessity, equivocal since the *transcended* cause and the visible effect do not 'shine' or 'illuminate' in the same way. To reprise an analogy from *imminent* causation, pure whiteness is a quality that is neither tangible nor visible. A white thing, however, is both tangible and visible. Whiteness as an abstract quality (assuming with early Christian authors the existence of such universals) is not 'white' in the same sense that each visible white thing is. But it would be very strange indeed to claim that whiteness is not itself 'white'. To solve this ancient philosophical conundrum, one must distinguish between different senses of 'white'. Pure whiteness and a white thing are therefore both 'white' but they are equivocally so. The exact same solution holds for the relation between pure luminosity and physical light.[38]

Early Christian authors used several terms to denote the equivocity of light. Origen who was closer to the rhetorical tradition than is often acknowledged used the technical term 'allegory'. Gregory of Nyssa who together with Basil were forced by Eunomius to engage closely with Porphyry's commentary on Aristotle's *Categories* preferred the term 'homonymy'. But they also spoke of τροπολογία in the same sense as Origen's 'allegory', that is, of sustained (analogical) metaphor as a figure of speech. Similarly, Athanasius' preferred term of Platonic παραδείγματα denoted merely model building in the sense of sustained or extended analogies. Gregory Nazianzen in his turn spoke of εἰκόνα (image) and ὑπόδειγμα (example) to also denote analogical reasoning (ἀναλόγως). So too did the author of the celebrated *Letter* 38.[39] Thus, different technical terms were introduced to denote

---

[38]For this parallel, see Basil, *Hom.Hex.*, 6.3. The predicative relation of imminent universals (like luminosity) to their sensible instances (like physical light) is a typical case of equivocation *by deriving from and being relative to a single source* (ἀφ' ἑνὸς καὶ πρὸς ἕν), see Porphyry, *Categories*, 66.2-21. The predicative relation of universals to the divine transcendent cause is a case of equivocation *by analogy*, see Porphyry, *Categories*, 65.31-66.2. Analogical reasoning is indispensable for our cognition of imminent and transcendent causes, since it is from the sensible particulars that we intuit both universals and the divine demiurgic cause, see Gregory Nyssen, *Contra Eunom.*, 2.13. Consequently, light analogies should not be regarded as fallacious but as necessary cognitive devices, even if the insights they grant do not amount to full knowledge of the intelligible causes, see Nyssen, *Contra Eunom.*, 3.6.12-4; cf. L. Ayres, *Nicaea and Its Legacy: An Approach to Fourth-Century Trinitarian Theology* (Oxford: Oxford University Press, 2004), pp. 284–5; J. A. McGuckin, '"Perceiving Light from Light in Light" (*Oration* 31.3) The Trinitarian Theology of Saint Gregory the Theologian', *The Greek Orthodox Theological Review* 39 (1994): 7–32, especially p. 11.

[39]See Origen, *Com. Joh.*, 1.157-81: 'anagogy and allegory' (180) in the sense of extended analogical metaphor (163); Basil, *Adv. Eun.*, 1.14.22 (tropology and allegory); Gregory Nyssen, *Apology*, 19 (GNO, 32.7: homonymy), 21 (GNO, 33.1: tropology); *Contra Eunom.*, 3.6.77-80 and 3.10.20 (homonymy); Gregory Nazianzen, *Orat.*, 28.30.1-4 (Plato's sun simile); *Orat.*, 31.31 (image, example, analogy); Basil (?), *Letter* 38.5 (e.g. analogy). For allegory as a version or subtype of metaphor (extended metaphor), see Aristotle, *Poetics.*, 1458a22-30: 'riddling metaphor'; for the ancient theory of tropes, see Innes, 'Metaphor', pp. 19–20.

the common insight that 'light' was predicated properly, but differently: (1) of God as the first principle and cause of being; (2) of the universal substance (form or *logos*) of light; and (3) of physical light as a contingent instantiation of one kind of being. These are all proper senses of 'light' but different senses nonetheless: God is pure intellective substance; intelligible light is one instance, though universal, of intellective substance; the different kinds of physical light are hylomorphic instances of this universal substance. And since God is the transcendent cause of both intelligible and physical light, 'God is light' is a mere application of the ancient metaphysical axiom that the cause is greater than its effect.[40] It is precisely this ability of equivocal language to capture the multiple causal layers of ancient participatory ontology that so evidently escaped Baeumker's 'metaphysics of light' and the subsequent discussions.[41]

Analogy becomes the antidote to equivocity: it helps us see the cause through its effects without conflating causal roles. Metaphor thus transforms language into a mirroring device: it helps us talk meaningfully of what we do not perceive (viz. intelligible causes) through what we perceive (viz. physical manifestations). The latter possibility of generating new meaning from existing words is precisely the deeper and most precious function of analogical metaphors according to the classical theory. If we are now willing to accept, with the ancients, that light, as the special object of sight, guarantees immediate access to the world of the senses, light becomes the most powerful perceptual metaphor that human language can produce. To the possible objection that the advanced can dispense with metaphor once they have acquired direct knowledge of intelligible causes, early Christian thinkers would side with Platonic transcendentalism by quoting Paul: universal substances, that is, beings as such, are 'inexpressible words', impossible to be captured in human language (2 Cor. 12.4). So much so for the divine being, the apophatic first principle of every universal substance. It is the very nature of human language which necessitates that all God talk as light is equivocal; and that the only way to make sense of this equivocity from within human language is through analogical metaphors from physical light.[42] Theological metaphors of light are, therefore, and to conclude, indispensable for naming what is beyond naming: the God of Exod. 3.14 as pure, unqualified being.[43]

---

[40]See A. C. Lloyd, 'The Principle That the Cause Is Greater than Its Effect', *Ph* 21 (1976): 146–56.

[41]Echoing the scholastic tradition, Bauemker's tripartite model builds on the *contrast* of analogy with equivocity. But the early Christian metaphysics of light build on the different modes of *integration* of analogy to equivocity, see Gregory Nyssen, *Contra Eunom.*, 2.302-8, 3.1.126-38, 3.10.20; T. Dolidge, 'The Cognitive Function of Epinoia in Contra Eunomium II and Its Meaning for Gregory of Nyssa's Theory of Theological Language', in *Gregory of Nyssa: Contra Eunomium II*, eds L. Karfíková, S. Douglass and J. Zachhuber, SupVCh, 82 (Leiden: E.J. Brill, 2007), pp. 445–59, 453–7; R. Williams, *Arius: Heresy and Tradition* (Grand Rapids, MI: William B. Eerdmans, 2002), pp. 215–29.

[42]For the ability of proportional metaphors to name things which have no name see Aristotle, *Poetics.*, 3 (1457b25-30); *Rhet.*, 3.2.12 (1405a33-b3).

[43]See Basil, *Adv. Eun.*, 1.13.25-14.48; Nyssen, *Contra Eunom.*, 3.1.103-9, 135.

BIBLIOGRAPHY

Ayres, L. *Nicaea and Its Legacy: An Approach to Fourth-Century Trinitarian Theology*. Oxford: Oxford University Press, 2004.

Baeumker, C. *Witelo: Ein Philosoph und Naturforscher des XIII. Jahrhunderts*. Münster: Aschendorf, 1908.

Barnes, J. *Porphyry: An Introduction*. Oxford: Clarendon Press, 2003.

Barnes, M. R. *The Power of God: Δύναμις in Gregory of Nyssa's Trinitarian Theology*. Washington, DC: The Catholic University of America Press, 2001.

Behr, J. *The Nicene Faith*, 2 vols. New York: St Vladimir's Seminary Press, 2004.

Beierwaltes, W. 'Die Metaphysik des Lichtes in der Philosophie Plotins', *ZPF* 15 (1961): 334–62.

Beierwaltes, W. 'Lichtmetaphysik', in J. Ritter and K. Gründer (eds), *Historisches Wörterbuch der Philosophie*, vol. 5. Darmstadt: Wissenschaftliche Buchgesellschaft, 1980.

Beierwaltes, W. *Proklos: Grunzüge seiner Metaphysik*. Frankfurt: Klostermann, 2014.

Blumenberg, H. 'Licht als Metapher der Wahrheit: Im Vorfeld der philosophischen Begriffsbildung', in H. Blumenberg (ed.), *Ästhetische und metaphorologische Schriften*. Frankfurt a.M.: Suhrkamp, 2001.

DelCogliano, M. *Basil of Caesarea's Anti-Eunomian Theory of Names: Christian Theology and Late-Antique Philosophy in the Fourth Century Trinitarian Controversy*. SupVCh, vol. 103. Leiden: E.J. Brill, 2010.

Dolidge, T. 'The Cognitive Function of Epinoia in Contra Eunomium II and Its Meaning for Gregory of Nyssa's Theory of Theological Language', in L. Karfíková, S. Douglass and J. Zachhuber (eds), *Gregory of Nyssa: Contra Eunomium II*, 445–59. SupVCh, 82. Leiden: E.J. Brill, 2007.

Edwards, M. *Aristotle and Early Christian Thought*. London: Routledge, 2019.

Falcon, A. (ed.). *The Brill Companion to the Reception of Aristotle*. 'Brill Companions to Classical Reception', vol.7. Leiden: E.J. Brill, 2016.

Ferwerda, R. *La signification des images et des metaphors dans la pensée de Plotin*. Groningen: Wolters, 1965.

Gerson, L. P. *Aristotle and Other Platonists*. Ithaca, NY: Cornell University Press, 2005.

Innes, D. 'Metaphor, Simile, and Allegory', in G. R. Boys-Stones (ed.), *Metaphor, Allegory, and the Classical Tradition: Ancient Thought and Modern Revisions*, 7–27. Oxford: Oxford University Press, 2003.

Karamanolis, G. *Plato and Aristotle in Agreement? Platonists on Aristotle from Antiochus to Porphyry*. Oxford: Clarendon Press, 2006.

Karamanolis, G. *The Philosophy of Early Christianity*. Durham: Acumen Press, 2013.

Katsos, I. 'The Metaphysics of Light in the Hexaemeral Literature: From Philo to Ambrose of Milan'. PhD diss., Pembroke College, University of Cambridge, 2018 (https://www.repository.cam.ac.uk/handle/1810/293894, last accessed: 19 June 2021).

Katsos, I. 'Chasing the Light: What Happened to the Ancient Theories?', *Isis* 110 (2019): 270–82.

Klein, F. N. *Die Lichtterminologie bei Philon von Alexandrien und in den hermetischen Schriften*. Leiden: E.J. Brill, 1962.

Levin, S. R. 'Aristotle's Theory of Metaphor', *Philosophy & Rhetoric* 15 (1982): 24–46.

Lindberg, D. *Theories of Vision from Al-Kindi to Kepler*. Chicago: The University of
    Chicago Press, 1976.
Lloyd, A. C. 'The Principle That the Cause Is Greater than Its Effect', *Ph* 21 (1976): 146–56.
Lloyd, G. E. R. *Polarity and Analogy: Two Types of Argumentation in Early Greek
    Thought*. Cambridge: Cambridge University Press, 1966.
McEvoy, J. 'The Metaphysics of Light in the Middle Ages', *Philosophical Studies* 26
    (1978): 126–45.
McEvoy, J. *Robert Grosseteste*. Oxford: Oxford University Press, 2000.
McGuckin, J. A. '"Perceiving Light from Light in Light" (*Oration* 31.3) The Trinitarian Theology
    of Saint Gregory the Theologian', *The Greek Orthodox Theological Review* 39 (1994): 7–32.
Menn, S. 'Aristotle and Plato on God as Nous and as the Good', *The Review of
    Metaphysics* 45 (1992): 543–73.
O'Collins, G. '"Light from Light": The Divine Light Reflected in and by the Son and the
    Holy Spirit', in G. O'Collins and M. A. Meyers (eds), *Light from Light: Scientists and
    Theologians in Dialogue*, 103–21. Grand Rapids, MI: Eerdmans, 2012.
Pelikan, J. *The Light of the World: A Basic Image in Early Christian Thought*. New York:
    Harper, 1962.
Pelikan, J. *Christianity and Classical Culture: The Metamorphosis of Natural Theology in
    the Christian Encounter with Hellenism*. New Haven, CT: Yale University Press, 1993.
Radde-Gallwitz, A. *Basil of Caesarea, Gregory of Nyssa, and the Transformation of Divine
    Simplicity*. Oxford: Oxford University Press, 2009.
Ramelli, I. 'Origen, Patristic Philosophy, and Christian Platonism: Re- Thinking the
    Christianisation of Hellenism', *VChr* 63 (2009): 217–63.
Runia, D. *Philo in Early Christian Literature: A Survey*. Assen: Van Gorcum, 1993.
Schroeder, F. M. *Form and Transformation: A Study in the Philosophy of Plotinus*.
    Montreal: McGill-Queen's University Press, 1992.
Shields, C. 'Being Qua Being', in C. Shields (ed.), *The Oxford Handbook of Aristotle*,
    344–71. Oxford: Oxford University Press, 2012.
Stead, C. *Philosophy in Christian Antiquity*. Cambridge: Cambridge University Press, 1994.
Strange, S. *Porphyry On Aristotle's Categories*. London: Bloomsbury, 1992.
Tanner, K. E. 'The Use of Perceived Properties of Light as a Theological Analogy', in G.
    O'Collins and M. A. Meyers (eds), *Light from Light: Scientists and Theologians in
    Dialogue*, 122–30. Grand Rapids, MI: Eerdmans, 2012.
Van Kooten, G. 'The "True Light which Enlightens Everyone" (John 1:9): John,
    Genesis, the Platonic Notion of the "True, Noetic Light", and the Allegory of the
    Cave in Plato's Republic', in G. van Kooten (ed.), *The Creation of Heaven and
    Earth: Re-interpretations of Genesis 1 in the Context of Judaism, Ancient Philosophy,
    Christianity, and Modern Physics*, 149–94. Leiden: Brill, 2005.
Wallraff, M. 'Licht', in E. Dassmann, F. J. Dolger, T. Klauser, H. Lietzmann, G. Schöllgen
    and J. H. Waszink. (eds), *Reallexikon für Antike und Christentum*, vol. 23. Stuttgart:
    Anton Hiersemann, 2010.
Wetter, G. *Phōs: Eine Untersuchung über hellenistische Frömmigkeit zugleich ein Beitrag
    zum Verständnis des Manichäismus*. Uppsala: Akademiska Bokhandeln, 1915.
Williams, R. *Arius: Heresy and Tradition*. Grand Rapids, MI: William B. Eerdmans, 2002.

CHAPTER 24

The origins of monasticism

TIM VIVIAN

The emergence of monasticism in the East, its rapid development in the fourth and fifth centuries, and its establishment as a major institution in Christianity are among the most significant phenomena in the history of Christianity.[1] What is the cosmogenesis of early Christian monasticism? Was there a 'Big Bang'? Or was its cosmology a 'Steady State', a slow development from earlier Judeo-Christian asceticism? We can safely rule out *creatio ex nihilo*: something cannot come out of nothing, at least sublunary. Was Egypt 'the homeland of monks'? Or Syria? Or Palestine? Or Asia Minor? As is the case with virtually everything in Western antiquity and late antiquity, what we do not know exceeds, sometimes far exceeds, what we do know. But each year what we know increases. Many scholars of Judaism and Christianity use the terms 'Judaisms' and 'Christianities'. These are valid coinages, emphasizing that these religions, like every other religion, have never been monolithic, even in the beginning. It is better to speak, therefore, of the origins, not the origin, of early monasticism.

In the beginning, so to speak, was the first church historian Eusebius (ca. 260–340), who, in his *Ecclesiastical History*, describes the origin of asceticism in Egypt. He reports ('they say') that Mark first preached in Egypt 'and was the first to establish churches in Alexandria itself'. Eusebius then connects asceticism with the very beginning of Christianity in Egypt in the first century. For Eusebius, monasticism burst on the scene already a legend:

> The élite ascetic life, a life above nature and beyond common human living, is so central to his understanding of Christianity that it pushes itself back into his recovery of Christianity's formative years. In joining together the powers of Christianity and Rome, he presented Christianity as the new philosophy which demanded among its elite practitioners an ascetic life.[2]

[1] S. Rubenson, 'Asceticism and Monasticism, I: Eastern', in *The Cambridge History of Christianity*, vol. 2, *Constantine to c. 600*, eds A. Casiday and F. Norris (Cambridge: Cambridge University Press, 2007), pp. 637–68 (637).

[2] J. A. Goehring, *Ascetics, Society, and the Desert: Studies in Early Egyptian Monasticism* (Harrisburg, PA: Trinity, 1999), pp. 14–18, esp. 15, 17.

Eusebius, like Clement (ca. 150–ca. 215) and Origen (ca. 185–ca. 254) before him, sees a life of asceticism and study as a 'philosophic' life. There is no doubt that Origen was ascetic, and some philosophical schools followed ascetic practices, but we will not find a single-pointed origin of Christianity either in Graeco-Roman philosophy or, as Eusebius did, in Judaism. Eusebius' beginning can no longer be ours.

THE ASCETIC IMPULSE (EVEN IMPERATIVE): THE NEW TESTAMENT

Long before Eusebius, one – the primeval – origin of early monasticism must lie in the asceticism of Jesus, and then Paul, and then the Christian writings in the second and third centuries.[3] The *Life of Paul and Thecla* (second–third century), some 200 years before the 'rise of monasticism', already emphasizes not just asceticism but asceticism as salvific; this *Life*, thus, demonstrates the strong ascetic impulse, even imperative, in early Christianity. As Elizabeth Clark notes, 'The Apocryphal Acts, probably composed largely in the third century (although in all likelihood based on earlier oral traditions), present the message of apostolic Christianity as one of asceticism, pure and simple.'[4] 'Ascetic' and 'asceticism' (*askētēs, askētikós*) derive from Greek *áskēsis* (noun) and *askéō* (verb). *áskēsis* means 'training', 'exertion', 'practice', 'exercise' (for war), then, by the time of Clement, 'spiritual practice', 'discipline', 'way of life' (of philosophers and 'philosophical' Christians), then 'asceticism'; *askéō* means 'to work', then 'practice, pursue' 'exert oneself, strive, seek'. The noun originally meant 'one who practices an art or profession, practitioner, professional'. By the time of Aristophanes (ca. 257–180 BCE) it could mean 'athlete'; and then in Christianity an athlete for Christ, 'ascetic, hermit, monk'.

The New Testament origins of asceticism and monasticism, however, are not linguistic: *áskēsis*, and *askētikós* occur not at all. If we start with the definition of 'asceticism' as 'the renunciation of physical pleasures, with other forms of bodily self-denial, as a means of spiritual development',[5] then the behaviour described in the New Testament is certainly ascetic. This is especially true if one adds this sociological insight: 'An ascetic life, whether practiced alone or in common with like-minded individuals, involved *withdrawal from certain social patterns of human existence* (family and sex).'[6] The SBL Group on Ascetic Behavior in Graeco-Roman antiquity, after much debate, focused on 'observed practices': 'ascetic behavior represents a range of responses to social, political, and physical worlds often

---

[3]'Primeval origin' does not mean that there is a direct line or link from N.T. asceticism to early monasticism; rather, it means that the early monks looked back at the asceticism of the N.T. as source, model and inspiration.

[4]E. A. Clark, *Reading Renunciation: Asceticism and Scripture in Early Christianity* (Princeton, NJ: Princeton University Press, 1999), p. 26.

[5]'Asceticism', in *The Harper Collins Dictionary of Religion*, ed. J. Z. Smith (San Francisco, CA: Harper-San Francisco, 1995), pp. 77–82 (77).

[6]Goehring, *Ascetics*, 21; emphasis mine.

perceived as oppressive or unfriendly, or as stumbling blocks to the pursuit of heroic personal or communal goals, lifetimes, and commitments.'[7]

A select list of quotations from the New Testament shows that it is ascetic (but not monastic), at least if we use the definitions above:

- Jesus: 'Do not be afraid, little flock, for it is your Father's good pleasure to give you the kingdom. Sell your possessions, and give alms' (Lk. 12.33).

- Paul: 'Do not be conformed to this world, but be transformed by the renewing of your minds' (Rom. 12.2).

- Acts: 'Now the whole group of those who believed were of one heart and soul, and no one claimed private ownership of any possessions, but everything they owned was held in common' (Acts 4.32).[8]

ONLY CONNECT: SOURCES AND EPISTEMOLOGY

'Only connect! Only connect the prose and the passion, and both will be exalted. . . . Live in fragments no longer.'[9]

Samuel Rubenson makes this important observation: 'The history of early Egyptian monasticism has been intensely debated in the last decades because of both the discovery and presentation of new sources and the conscious reinterpretation of the history based on new methods and new theoretical insights.'[10] Before we proceed, we need first to look at the recent discussions about monastic epistemology. This scholarship has revived and reassessed both the literary sources for early monasticism, upon which most studies have depended, and now other sources such as letters, papyri, art and architecture.

Malcolm Choat has emphasized the importance of letters: 'As with Christianity itself, our earliest literary texts from a monastic milieu are letters, preceding the written lives of their composers. Focusing on letters thus provides an excellent insight into the historical development of monasticism.'[11] Choat makes four major points:[12]

1. The letters highlight the 'translocal nature of many monastic communities'.

2. '[F]or those who wish to withdraw from the world metaphorically, the letters preserve that separation.'

---

[7]Clark, *Reading Renunciation*, p. 1. One notes that the 'pursuit' here lacks the terms 'spiritual' and 'religious'.

[8]See also Lk. 9.23, 12.33, 14.26, 33; 1 Cor. 1.28; 1 Cor. 7.8; Gal. 4.3.

[9]E. M. Forster, *Howards End* (London: Arnold, 1910), ch. 22.

[10]S. Rubenson, 'To Tell the Truth: Fact and Fiction in Early Monastic Sources', *CSQ* 48, no. 3 (2013): 317–24. See further M. Sheridan, 'Early Egyptian Monasticism: Ideals and Reality, or, The Shaping of the Monastic Ideal', *JCSCopS* 7 (2015): 9–24.

[11]M. Choat, 'The Epistolary Culture of Monasticism between Literature and Papyri', *CSQ* 48, no. 2 (2013): 227–37 (228).

[12]Ibid., pp. 233–5.

3. There is a 'readily observable difference in the types of letters. . . . The manuscripts are full of long letters dispensing spiritual advice, while papyri . . . tell us much, and in many cases more, about everyday life.'

4. 'Among the papyri, we have many letters between monks, but a great number also to and from the secular world.'

Choat concludes by saying that we need 'to create a dialogue between the literary and documentary sources reading papyrus and manuscript letters alongside one another actually enhances one's appreciation of the usefulness of the latter in reconstructing early monasticism in Egypt'.[13]

Reconstruction requires caution and humility. David Brakke offers this salutary advice: 'As long as we keep our focus relatively broad – on the monks' culture, spirituality, and lifestyle, rather than on details concerning any particular monk or event – then the *Apophthegmata* are no more or less reliable than most ancient sources.'[14] Rubenson agrees and adds that the texts 'illustrate a shared reality' and that we should 'try to recover the memories' of the early monks in later sources. He then puts up a 'Proceed with Caution' sign: he draws attention to our own biases and assumptions and asks, 'In what sense can we speak about sources being reliable, and how do we know?'[15]

Rubenson cautions that history and hagiography, especially 'pure' history and hagiography, are 'our own mental constructs'.[16] With regard to our various monastic sources, he asks: 'Aren't all stories, all artifacts, created? Is there any history that is not created? Can we distinguish between "authentic memory" and interpretation and elaboration? I do not think so.' He concludes with a vital observation: 'All our stories and letters are interpretations, attempts to create meaning within the circumstances in which they were produced' – and within our present circumstances. He advises us to 'look more at the story as communication and ask *why* the story has been transmitted to us in its various versions'.[17] In other words, what do the early monks *continue* to say to us today?[18]

In looking at the earliest uses of *monachós* (monk), Mark Sheridan suggests that it was a 'self-designation' for 'those who had freely chosen celibacy in the context of the Christian community'; he points toward 'celibacy in the New Testament and the "pre-monastic" practice of celibacy in the early Church.'[19] The term 'ascetic'

---

[13]Ibid., p. 237.

[14]D. Brakke, 'Macarius's Quest and Ours: Literary Sources for Early Egyptian Monasticism', CSQ 48, no. 2 (2013): 239–51, esp. 240.

[15]Rubenson, 'To Tell the Truth', pp. 318, and 319.

[16]Ibid., p. 320.

[17]Ibid., p. 23; emphasis added. See further Sheridan, 'Early Egyptian Monasticism', esp. pp. 14–17.

[18]Such reflections on what the early monastics mean today are numerous and encouraging; for a recent example, see the Introduction to T. Vivian (trans.), *The Saying and Stories of the Desert Fathers and Mothers: The Greek Alphabetical Sayings of the Apophthegmata Patrum*, vol. 1, (Collegeville, MN: Cistercian Publications, 2021).

[19]Sheridan, 'Early Egyptian Monasticism', pp. 11–12.

later could mean both a solitary monk and a cenobite. Although anchorites, semi-anchorites and apotactic 'renunciants' (discussed below) continued, the last term disappeared and cenobitism became the rule (discussed below with Pachomius). In fact, the Sahidic Coptic *Life of Pachomius* makes the remarkable declaration that cenobitism 'was revealed' as 'the path of the apostles'.[20] Sheridan points out that the assertions in the *Life* 'relegate earlier forms of monasticism to a past dispensation. Something new and better had been revealed. This passage then is not merely theology, but rather ideology, for it is designed to assert the superiority of a particular development in the varied Egyptian monastic landscape and to delegitimize the others.'[21] In general, the later literary sources were responsible for such 'delegitimizing', and without the papyri the earliest monastics, the apotactics, might have disappeared almost entirely, mirages on a receding desert road.

PALESTINE AND ASIA MINOR[22]

In 314, the Council of Ancyra takes as a given that there are men and women 'who have proclaimed virginity', and it forbids women to live together with men 'like sisters'.[23] Around 340, the Council of Gangra in Asia Minor anathematized women who left their husbands for lives of asceticism.[24] By 350 monasticism was clearly established in Palestine, Asia Minor, Syria and Egypt. As Antoine Guillaumont says, 'Within Christianity, monasticism appeared in numerous places in an independent and almost simultaneous fashion.'[25] We will discuss them in the order above, with the emphasis on Egypt. Yizhar Hirschfeld sees 'four chronological stages . . . in the development of monasticism in the Judean desert'; the first stage, the fourth century, will concern us here.[26] The 'lavra' was unique to Palestine; Hirschfeld defines it as 'a community of recluses. It offered the advantages of living in solitude in individual cells most of the time, but of meeting for communal prayer and Mass on the weekends.'[27]

Scholars commonly refer to the above as 'semi-anchoritism', and we will see it below with the monks of the Wadi Natrun in Egypt. The other main form was

---

[20]*Pachomian Koinonia*, vol. 1, *The Life of Saint Pachomius*, trans. Armand Veilleux, 'Cistercian Studies' 45 (Kalamazoo, MI: Cistercian, 1980), pp. 183–4.

[21]Sheridan, 'Early Egyptian Monasticism', p. 18.

[22]Palestine: see J. Binns, *Ascetics and Ambassadors of Christ: The Monasteries of Palestine, 314-631* (Oxford: Clarendon Press, 1994), esp. pp. 154–61; Y. Hirschfeld, *The Judean Desert Monasteries in the Byzantine Period* (New Haven, CT: Yale University Press, 1992), esp. pp. 10–17; and, for a concise overview, Rubenson, 'Asceticism and Monasticism', pp. 652–5.

[23]S. Elm, *Virgins of God: The Making of Asceticism in Late Antiquity* (Oxford: Oxford University Press, 1996), p. 25.

[24]*Canon 14*, Synod of Gangra (fourth Century).

[25]Antoine Guillaumont, *Aux origins du monachisme chrétien: pour une phénoménologie du monachisme*, Spiritualité orientale 30 (Bégrolles-en-Mauges: Abbaye de Bellefontaine, 1979), p. 217 (translation mine).

[26]Y. Hirschfeld, *The Judean Desert Monasteries in the Byzantine Period* (New Haven, CT: Yale University Press, 1992), p. 10.

[27]Ibid.

cenobitism, from Greek *koinòs bíos*, 'communal life'; we will see this below with Pachomius and Shenoute in Egypt. The first two figures we have in Palestine are Chariton (late third century–ca. 350) and Hilarion (ca. 291–371) whom, according to literary sources, were in Palestine at the turn of the fourth century – a slightly later figure is Epiphanius (ca. 315–403), later bishop of Salamis. Hirschfeld notes: 'The monastic presence in the Judean desert grew considerably in the fifth century under the leadership of Euthymius the Great. Between the death of Chariton ca. 350 and that of Euthymius in 473, the number of monasteries increased from three to fifteen.'[28]

North in Asia Minor (present-day Turkey), Eustathius of Sebaste, later a bishop, is the first key figure by the 360s; he 'radicalized' the gospel, condemning marriage, wealth and manual work and did not think well of clergy. His followers were itinerant, open-air ascetics. Eustathius influenced Basil of Caesarea (ca. 330–379), but the latter, with his brother Gregory of Nyssa (ca. 330–ca. 395), and his sister Macrina (ca. 327–379), reconfigured Eustathius' asceticism. Later, Basil, as bishop in Caesarea, founded a monastery and wrote his 'rules', the *Asketikon*.[29] Nilus of Ancyra (*fl*. ca. 390–430) seems to have established urban monasticism in Asia Minor in the late-fourth-early-fifth centuries; Palladius reports that there were 2,000 or more virgins in Ancyra.[30]

SYRIA: 'THE ASCETIC SLANT'[31]

Some parents in Antioch in the 380s complained when their sons 'left home' and went 'off to join a lot of dirty vagrants', that is, monks. And John Chrysostom (ca. 347–407), sometime between 383 and 386, wrote 'Against the Detractors of the Monastic Life'.[32] Where we can see the smoke of anti-monastic detractors, there is monastic fire. Sebastian Brock observes that fourth- and fifth-century ascetics in Syria 'were heirs to a remarkable native ascetic tradition that went back to the very beginnings of Christianity'.[33] He points out that in Syria and Mesopotamia such an early figure as Tatian (second century) and groups like the Marcionites altered Gospel accounts to make them more rigorously ascetic; he argues that Luke's Gospel, vis-à-vis parallels in Matthew, has much more of an 'ascetic slant'.

In the early Syriac-speaking church, both *parthénos*, 'virgin', and the Syriac equivalent *bathula* applied to men as well as women, and Tatian condemned marriage: 'In some communities in the East views like these were held with such

---

[28]Ibid., p. 12.

[29]Rubenson, 'Asceticism and Monasticism', p. 660; on Basil, see Elm, *Virgins of God*, pp. 60–77.

[30]Palladius, *Lausiac History* 67, trans. J.Wortley (Kalamazoo, MI: Cistercian Studies vol 252, 2015), p. 136.

[31]This section relies on S. P. Brock, 'Early Syrian Asceticism', N 20, no. 1 (April 1973): 1–19; see also Rubenson, 'Asceticism and Monasticism', pp. 655–8.

[32]Brock, 'Early Syrian Asceticism', p. 1.

[33]Ibid., p. 3.

seriousness that celibacy was regarded as an essential condition for baptism.'[34] Brock points out that the *Acts of Thomas*, 'very much the product of early Syriac-speaking Christianity', was popular among the Marcionites and Manicheans, guaranteeing its ascetic character.[35] In the *Acts*, as with *Paul and Thecla*, the 'ascetic life thus becomes an essential step on the road to salvation'. These apocryphal works also emphasize that Christians in the world are 'strangers' and 'foreigners'. As Brock points out, 'an ascetic understanding of Christianity in the Syrian Orient was fundamental from its earliest times, even in that sphere of the Syriac church that would emerge as "orthodox" Syriac spirituality called for a life of renunciation and above all of celibacy, not simply for its elect but for all its faithful.'[36]

Such eminent 'orthodox' writers of the fourth century as Aphrahat (or Aphraates) and Ephrem continue these emphases. In Syriac, the root *qdš* 'has the basic connotation of separateness', so the holy man or woman, *qaddīshā*, 'is someone apart' from his or her surroundings, someone who has alienated him- or herself from, and 'is untouched by', 'the world'. Aphrahat's 'monks' 'are ascetics living either individually or in small groups'. (We will see this theme later in the discussion of Egyptian monasticism.)[37] Brock emphasizes that Aphrahat 'represents Syriac Christianity completely untouched by western influences', which implicitly indicates that fourth-century monasticism in Syria was independent of monastic impulses and movements elsewhere. Brock and Susan Ashbrook Harvey point out that 'Christianity first emerged in the Syrian Orient out of the Jewish communities, largely independent of the Graeco-Latin churches to the west, and with a powerful spirituality born of Semitic tradition rather than that of Classical Greece and Rome'.[38]

EGYPT:[39] VILLAGE ASCETICS – THE APOTACTITES (APOTAKTIKOÍ)[40]

For a very long time, Antony grabbed the page-one headlines for early Egyptian monasticism, with a sidebar on Pachomius, and monastics who did not fit into the Antonian or Pachomian paradigm found themselves on page fifteen dwarfed by ads. Sources in Egypt, especially, the papyri, show that women (see the next section) and men in the third to fifth centuries lived ascetic lives per the definitions at the beginning of this article. The names for these women and men survive in the papyri

---

[34]Ibid., p. 7.

[35]Ibid., p. 8.

[36]S. P. Brock and S. A. Harvey, *Holy Women of the Syrian Orient* (Berkeley: University of California Press, 1987), p. 7.

[37]Ibid., p. 11.

[38]Ibid., p. 6.

[39]On earliest Christianity in Egypt, see B. A. Pearson and J. E. Goehring (eds), *The Roots of Egyptian Christianity* (Philadelphia, PA: Fortress Press, 1986), esp. ibid., pp. 132–60.

[40]See especially Goehring, *Ascetics*, pp. 53–72.

(which are becoming increasingly, even exponentially, important for the study of early Christianity and monasticism in Egypt): *apotaktikoí* and *apotaktikaí*, male and female apotactics or 'renunciants'. Goehring has shown that 'a simplified bi-polar understanding of Egyptian monasticism' – that is, of anchorites and cenobites – 'rapidly overshadowed the apotactic movement in the middle to latter half of the fourth century'.[41] This was due largely to (1) the rise of Antonian anchoritic monasticism and Pachomian cenobitic monasticism and (2) later monastic writers like Jerome (ca. 342–420) and Cassian (ca. 360–435), who misunderstood and, ex post facto, pilloried the apotactics.[42]

E. A. Judge sees a link (how direct we cannot say) between the ajpotaktikoiv of Egypt with the ascetic Christian past: 'men followed the pattern long set for virgins and widows, and set up houses of their own in town, in which the life of personal renunciation and service in the church would be practiced.'[43] In Mk 6.46 Jesus 'takes leave of' or 'withdraws' (*apotaxámenos*) from the disciples in order to go up the mountain to pray; in Lk. 14.25-33 Jesus bluntly declares the cost of discipleship, including 'none of you can become my disciple if you do not give up [or "renounce": *apotássetai*] all your possessions'.

Goehring provides a succinct summary:

> From the papyri, one learns that *apotaktikós* was a church rank . . . , that the *apotaktikós* could own land . . . , that he might retain family ties . . . , that the title later came to include women . . . , and that it served to indicate an ascetic's more active position within the civil community in distinction from the less active role of the *anachōrētē* [anchorite].[44]

Such an ascetic, as noted earlier, withdrew from certain social patterns of human existence; as Goehring emphasizes, early on 'withdrawal to the desert was not central'.[45] The first extant use of 'monk' in a technical sense applies not to an Antony who, his *Life* says, ultimately withdrew from society around 285 (*Life* 11–13), then around 313 to 'the interior desert' (*Life* 49).[46] In fact, the *Life* itself acknowledges that 'no monk at all knew the remote desert; each one who wished to watch over himself spiritually would practice ascetic discipline [a[skhsiV] by himself not far from his own village'. Antony apprentices himself to an old man (or elder) who from 'his youth had practiced the solitary life of an ascetic' (*Life* 3.1-3).

One such ascetic was Isaac of Karanis. In a petition for redress dated 6 June 324, Isidorus Ptolemaius claims that two assailants attacked and beat him and 'would have finished me off completely' if 'the deacon Antoninus and the monk

[41]Goehring, *Ascetics*, p. 55.
[42]Ibid.
[43]E. A. Judge, 'The Earliest Use of Monachos for "Monk" (P. Coll. Youtie 77) and the Origins of Monasticism', *JAC* 10 (1977): 72–89; esp. p. 85.
[44]Goehring, *Ascetics*, p. 56.
[45]Ibid., p. 21.
[46]Athanasius of Alexandria, *The Life of Antony: The Coptic Life and the Greek Life*, trans. T. Vivian and N. A. Athanassakis, Cistercian Studies 202 (Kalamazoo, MI: Cistercian Press, 2003).

[*monachós*] Isaac' had not 'chanced' to pass by and help out. This is the first extant use of *monachós*. This in and of itself is important but the occurrence turns out to be very important because Isaac is not the monk we probably assume: the petition takes it 'for granted that he can be identified by the public authorities. He is no remote hermit. On the other hand, his association with the deacon suggests that he is in some way church-related and not a monk from a coenobitic monastery. Since no further details are given, it can be assumed that he belongs to the village of Karanis.'[47]

As Goehring points out, 'Isaac represents a type of ascetic termed elsewhere an *apotaktikós* [apotactic].'[48] The *Life of Antony* 14 vividly tells us, most likely accurately, that before the holy man left for the far desert, he attracted numbers of people who 'yearned for his way of life and wished seriously to follow his ascetic practice'.[49] The *Life* adds that he performed healings and offered counsel to the villagers. Goehring's insight about Antony may well apply also to Isaac. That persons from his village followed Antony to his desert retreats and sought his presence might be interpreted to mean not that they wished to emulate him but that they felt cheated by his departure. In seeking solitude in the desert away from the village, he was taking with him *the power of God made available to the village through his presence.* The ascetic had a function in the village, and Antony's innovative departure called this function into question.[50]

EGYPT: VIRGINS OF GOD – EARLY FEMALE MONASTICS[51]

In his *Lausiac History* 41, written around 420, Palladius says that he 'must also commemorate some courageous women whom God granted equality in prizes with men so as not to allege that they are less vigorous in the quest for virtue'.[52] The *Historia Monachorum in Aegypto*, chapter 5, written ca. 400, tells us that Oxyrhynchus in Middle Egypt 'is so full of monasteries that the very walls resound with the voices of monks' and that 'there are said to be five thousand monks within the walls and as many again outside'. The bishop 'had under his jurisdiction ten thousand monks [*monachoús*] and twenty thousand virgins [*parthénous*]'.[53] Numbers in antiquity and late antique sources are often suspect, and the figures here are most likely hyperbole, but they nevertheless offer some important evidence: (1)

---

[47]Judge, 'The Earliest Use of Monachos', pp. 73–4.

[48]Goehring, *Ascetics*, p. 22.

[49]Vivian and Athanassakis, *The Life of Antony*, p. 91.

[50]Goehring, *Ascetics*, p. 21 (emphasis mine).

[51]See Elm, *Virgins of God,* pp. 253–82; Further see E. A. Mathieson, *Christian Women in the Greek Papyri of Egypt to 400* CE (Turnhout: Brepols, 2014).

[52]Palladius, *Lausiac History*, ed. W. K. Lowther Clarke (London: Macmillan, 1918), p. 102.

[53]*Historia Monachorum* 5.1, 5.4 and 5.6; *The Lives of the Desert Fathers*, trans. Norman Russell (London: Mowbray and Kalamazoo, MI: Cistercian Publications, 1980), p. 67, has altered 'nuns' to 'virgins'.

as with the *apotaktikoí*, male renunciants like Isaac, living within the city, there were also in Oxyrhynchus *apotaktikaí*, female ascetics, as we will shortly discuss. (2) If it is not an anachronistic statement, and by 400 it probably is not, the monks, male and female were under the jurisdiction of the local bishop (in the *Apophthegmata*, however, bishops are fairly rare – and always far, far away). (3) There are twice as many female monks as male.

The *Historia Monachorum* is both later and literary. What about documentary evidence? Here we are fortunate. In two letters probably from the early fourth century, Didyme ('and the sisters (*adelphaí*)') writes to a 'lady sister', Atienateia, about some business matters. In another letter, Didyme, with the sisters, writes to Sophias, 'my beloved sister [*agapētê(i)/: adelphê(i)/:*]'. She concludes with 'Farewell in the Lord' and 'The Lord preserve you'.[54] David Brakke notes that '[t]here were virgins in several of the cities and towns of Egypt in the 4th century'; with regard to Antony's sister, he says, 'How organized these women were is not clear. It is possible that this is not a historical fact, but merely Athanasius' [anachronistic] depiction of what he thought Antony should have done with his sister.'[55] Probably the first thing that strikes us today is Antony's sister's agency – or, rather, lack thereof. But it is also very significant that Athanasius says that there were women – a group of women – practising the ascetic life.

Alanna Emmett states: 'There is no doubt that Didyme is a Christian' and is writing on behalf of the 'sisters', 'an association of some kind on behalf of which she acts and writes'. It is likely that Atienateia lived in Oxyrhynchus which, we have seen, had perhaps thousands of monastics by 400. As Emmett concludes, 'Didyme and the sisters have not withdrawn from the world but are aware of and catering for worldly and practical items. . . . Didyme is running an entrepôt.'[56] If this is in fact the case, are Didyme and the sisters female apotactics? And, if Didyme is writing around 300, is her community like the 'well-known and faithful virgins' whom, Athanasius says, Antony gave his sisters to?[57] The *Alphabetical Apophthegmata* contains sayings of and stories about some 125 men with hundreds of sayings. There are three women with forty-six sayings.[58] As Susanna Elm bluntly states, 'Women were in the desert, not only as apparitions in the minds of tormented Fathers, but as real human beings.'[59]

As with the terms *apotaktikoí* and *apotaktikaí*, the term *monachē*, '(female) monk', can give us insights. A writer greets two 'beloved fathers', three 'brothers',

---

[54]A. M. Emmett, 'An Early Fourth-Century Female Monastic Community in Egypt?' in *Maistor: Classical, Byzantine, and Renaissance Studies for Robert Browning*, ed. A. Moffatt, Byzantina Australiensia 5 (Canberra: The Australian Association for Byzantine Studies, 1984), pp. 77–83, esp.79–80.

[55]D. Brakke, *Athanasius and the Politics of Asceticism* (Oxford: Clarendon Press, 1995), p. 24.

[56]Ibid., p. 83.

[57]*Life of Antony* 3.1; Vivian and Athanassakis version, p. 61.

[58]On women in the *Apophthegmata*, see S. Elm, *Virgins of God*, pp. 253–82, and T. Vivian, 'Courageous Women: Three Desert Ammas – Theodora, Sarah, and Syncletica' CSQ 71:1 (March 2020): 75–107.

[59]Elm, *Virgins of God*, p. 271.

three women 'and all the brothers in the monastery'.[60] An ostracon dating from the fourth to the early fifth centuries uses the term *monachē*, as does a papyrus fragment from Oxyrhynchus on 25 January 392; Annis, the apotactite, lives on property she inherited.[61]

A fourth-century papyrus addresses Aurelia Theodora and Aurelia Tauris, 'apotactic monks', along with their father.[62] Mathieson states that '*parthénos*, "virgin", unqualified, is the most frequent designation of ascetic women in Christian literature. *parthénoi* are not ordained but dedicate themselves to a vow.'[63] The term 'ever-virgin' (*aeipárthenos*) occurs frequently: a fourth-century papyrus is addressed 'To Nonna and her ever-virgin daughter'; a papyrus dated before 371 speaks of Didyme, ever-virgin, whose status 'is recognized administratively and socially'.[64] A particularly interesting papyrus from Lycopolis around 350 shows Bishop Plousianos in the forecourt of the catholic church (*k[ath]olikês ekklēsías*) adjudicating a dispute between Thaesis, ever-virgin and some heirs. Mathieson concludes that 'the texts reflect an early form of asceticism located in ordinary village and family life'.[65] Susanna Elm agrees: 'As in Asia Minor, women in Egypt pursued their ascetic life within the confines of their own home and their own family . . . or else in community with others, whether men or women. Again, as in Asia Minor (and seemingly more frequently), women broke these confines; they, as well as men, withdrew into the desert.'[66]

EGYPT: ANCHORITES, SEMI-ANCHORITES AND CENOBITES

One of the key transformative monks was Antony the Great (ca. 251–356). A long-standing epithet for Antony is 'the father of monasticism'. Antony could well be the 'father' of eremitism ('desert asceticism', from Greek *erēmos*, 'wilderness, desert'). But, as we have seen with the apotactites, there were village ascetics before him. Some of the earliest sources tell us also about a 'schismatic' Melitian monastic community at Hathor, a village near the Nile delta.[67] Another papyrus shows that 'virgins of God' (*parthénoi toû theoû*) were there; Mathieson comments: 'This text then provides evidence for groups, perhaps organised communities, of consecrated Melitian women.' Goehring summarizes that we may 'have here a Melitian organization

---

[60]Mathieson, *Christian Women*, pp. 236–7.
[61]Ibid., pp. 236, 243.
[62]Ibid., pp. 242–3.
[63]Ibid., p. 246.
[64]Ibid., pp. 243, 240.
[65]Ibid., p. 246.
[66]Elm, *Virgins of God*, p. 281.
[67]See H. I. Bell, *Jews and Christians in Egypt: The Jewish Troubles in Alexandria and the Athanasian Controversy* (Oxford: Oxford University Press, 1924), pp. 58–63.

which parallels closely the Pachomian *koinonia* or "community of monasteries" and thus challenges the usual assumption of such a system as a Pachomian innovation'.[68]

The first monastic biography–hagiography (the doublet is very significant), Athanasius' *Life of Antony*, raises a serious question – or set of questions. Although it is very difficult to know how much and what portions of Athanasius' *Life of Antony* are historical, two very important statements by the bishop of Alexandria early on deserve our attention and seem very plausible.[69] As we saw earlier, when Antony embraces a life of asceticism, he learns from an old man in the neighbouring village and entrusts his sister 'to well-known and faithful virgins, giving her to them to be raised in virginity'.[70]

As Goehring has emphasized, Antony's early significance is not that he 'founded' the ascetic life but that 'he withdrew from village life into remoter and remoter places – the desert'.[71] When Antony decided to become an ascetic, there were already men – and women – living as Christian ascetics in towns and villages, the apotactics. According to tradition, around 340 Antony 'one time paid a visit to Abba Amoun at the monastic settlement of Nitria'.[72] Later that day, they walk out into the desert, plant a cross and found a monastic settlement, depending on the sources, 5–12 miles from Nitria; perhaps eventually 600 anchorites lived in this area, with its own church. Its name was Kellia, 'Cells'. The settlements of Nitria, Kellia and Scetis became the most important in Lower Egypt, the Wadi Natrun.[73]

It is best to describe the monks of the Wadi Natrun as 'semi-anchorites'. At least early on, the monks lived alone or with another monk, often with a disciple, in scattered cells of two to three rooms where they would pray and do handiwork. The monks would come to the main area of the settlement, where the church was, on Saturday and Sunday for the *synaxis* (communal prayer), a common meal and the Eucharist on Sunday. If one stands now atop a sand-commandeered wall of the long-abandoned Monastery of John the Little and looks out over the desert, he or she sees dozens of circular areas where the sand is darker. These are *manshubia*, Arabic for Coptic *manshōpe*, 'place of being/living'. These are where the semi-anchorites lived.

Some of the great figures of early Egyptian monasticism were at the Wadi Natrun, where most of the Greek *Apophthegmata* originated: Arsenius, Evagrius, John the Little (Colobos), Macarius the Great, Moses, Poemen and others. Evagrius (d. 399)

---

[68]Goehring, *Ascetics*, p. 193.

[69]See Brakke, *Athanasius and the Politics of Asceticism*, pp. 21–57, and idem, *Athanasius and Asceticism* (Baltimore, MD: Johns Hopkins University Press, 1998).

[70]*Life of Antony* 3.1; Vivian and Athanassakis version, p. 61. In early monasticism, the usual word for a female monk is 'virgin'.

[71]Goehring, *Ascetics*, pp. 13–35 (24). The quotation marks around 'founded' are mine, not Goehring's.

[72]*Alphabetical Apophthegmata: Antony*, 34.

[73]See Goehring, *Ascetics*; also, D. Chitty, *The Desert a City* (Crestwood, NY: St Vladimir's, 1966); and Hugh Evelyn-White (ed. W. Hauser), *The Monasteries of the Wâdi 'N Watrun*, Volume II, *The History of the Monasteries of Nitria and Scetis* (New York: Metropolitan Museum, 1932; repr. Arno Press, 1973) available online.

was the first great monastic theologian and one of the great patristic writers on spirituality. His statement on prayer may be the most quoted aphorism from early monasticism: 'If you are a theologian you truly pray. If you truly pray you are a theologian.'[74] With his 'Against the Eight Passionate Thoughts', Evagrius, through John Cassian,[75] is the forefather of the 'Seven Deadly Sins'. Two key ideas in Evagrius' writings are 'thoughts' (*logismoî*) and the 'passions' (*páthos/páthē*) – and, through training (ascesis), living without them: apatheia (*apátheia*).

Connected with thoughts and passions is Evagrius' demonology: the demons influence us through our thoughts, causing undesirable passions.[76] What Evagrius says about the monk in his or her ascetic practices applies to each person, then and now: let them 'keep careful watch' over their thoughts. Let them observe 'their intensity, their periods of decline, and follow them as they rise and fall'. Then 'let them ask from Christ the explanations of these data they have observed'.[77] David Brakke gives a good summary of Evagrius' teaching on the ascetic (i.e. the reflective, spiritual life).

He divided the monk's career into two broad stages. As a *Praktikos* or 'ascetic practitioner', the monk gained practical knowledge of himself, the vices and virtues, and the demons' tactics, in order to reach a state of 'freedom from the passions' (*apatheia*). For Evagrius, apatheia comprises not only the external self-control (*enkrateia*) that prevents one from committing sins actively but also the interior serenity that prevents one from having 'impassioned thoughts in one's thinking'.

Apatheia can then blossom 'into the other-directed love of *agápē* where the person, now a *gnōstikós*, a gnostic, one who knows and understands', gains 'true knowledge of things that exist'.[78] The twentieth-century Cistercian monk Thomas Merton calls this 'gnostic' understanding knowledge of 'the true self'.

Evagrius shows that a collection of *Apophthegmata* or sayings existed before 400, and monks in Palestine most likely edited them in the fifth to sixth century. Translations/versions exist, among many, in Coptic, Syriac, Latin, Ethiopic, Armenian and Arabic; thus, the sayings (and stories) saw very wide diffusion in the Roman world, and beyond.[79] Some key concepts in the *Sayings* are: love (*agápē*), peace (*eirēnē*), discernment (*diákrisis*), self-control-moderation (*enkráteia*), patient endurance (*hypomonē*), the passions (*páthos*, pl. *páthē*), contemplative quiet (*hēsychia*), inward stillness (*anápausis*), and hope and joy (*elpís* and *chará*). Some key

---

[74]Evagrius, *Cap. Orat.* 60.

[75]Evagrius, *Prakt.*, cited in J. E. Bamberger (trans.), *The Praktikos and Chapters on Prayer* (Kalamazoo, MI: Cistercian Publications, 1981), pp. 20–6; See also Cassian, *Conf*, Books 5–12.

[76]See especially D. Brakke, *Demons and the Making of the Monk: Spiritual Combat in Early Christianity* (Cambridge, MA: Harvard University Press, 2006) and I. Graiver, *Asceticism of the Mind: Forms of Attention and Self-Transformation in Late Antique Monasticism* (Toronto: Pontifical Institute of Mediaeval Studies, 2018).

[77]Evagrius, *Prakt.,* 50; idem, *Prakt.*, 29–30. (My version has inclusivized the language.)

[78]Brakke, *Demons*, p. 51.

[79]See J. Wortley (ed.), *More Sayings of the Desert Fathers: An English Translation and Notes* (Cambridge: Cambridge University Press, 2019).

themes are: community, mutuality, neighbour and stranger; discernment, judging and compassion; and ego and humility (*tapeinosophrūnē*).[80] Eastern monasticism, as in Syria and Palestine, became very important in the Byzantine Empire, especially through the *Philokalia*, and later writers such as John Cassian (ca. 360–435), *The Conferences* and *The Institutes*; Palladius (fifth century), *The Lausiac History*; Jerome (ca. 342–420), *De Viris illustribus*; and Rufinus (ca. 345–410), *The Ecclesiastical History*, and translations; all helped spread its history, ideals and practices to the West and on to Benedict, the chief architect of European monasticism.

The four early monasteries of the Wadi Natrun – Macarius, Bishoy, Syrian and John the Little – eventually evolved (except John's monastery, which was later abandoned) from semi-anchoritic communities into the cenobitic monasteries today. As we saw earlier, the Pachomian koinonia used 'apotactic' for its members, showing that the term could mean what we call 'cenobite'. As with Antony as the 'father of monasticism', we now know that it is simplistic to restrict 'monasticism' to the desert regions. James Goehring prefers that we call the communities founded by Pachomius 'urban asceticism'; Pachomius (ca. 290–346) founded his first two communities (seven more were added during his lifetime; eventually there were two monasteries for women) 'in the fertile valley in or near villages whose names they bore'. At the time of his death in 346, the communities for men numbered some 5,000 monks. 'Properly understood', Armand Veilleux adds, 'Pachomian monasticism is not a product of the desert, but a form of village asceticism'.[81] According to the Pachomian sources, Pachomius first founded a monastic community in Tabennese.[82]

Pachomius later founded a second community at Pbow, a short distance away. Ascetic withdrawal here and probably at the later communities was within the village, eventually behind a gated wall. It is likely that the subsequent communities followed the same pattern. Goehring makes the following important assessment about the koinonia: 'As the papyrus evidence of the urban *apotaktikoi/ai* illustrates their legal and social connection with the wider community, so too the Pachomian evidence reveals [the Pachomians'] legal and social integration within Roman Egypt.' Again, like the apotactites, Pachomian communities owned land and paid taxes; the eventual creation of a steward at each monastery and a 'great steward' for the koinonia as a whole shows these communities' social and commercial involvement.[83]

Armand Veilleux argues that, according to the sources, Pachomius did not think 'of founding a new form of monasticism but sought to establish a cooperative brotherhood'. He sees the 'ideal of mutual service' lying 'at the root of the nascent Pachomian *koinonia* (community)' and constituting 'the essence of his spirituality'.

---

[80]See Vivian, *Saying and Stories*, pp. 19–85, 261–318.
[81]Veilleux, 'Pachomius, Saint', in *Coptic Encyclopedia* (London: Macmillan Reference Library, 1991), pp. 1859a–1864b (Used online – the electronic edition does not have page numbers). See Goehring, *Ascetics*, p. 91. For extensive discussion, see P. Rousseau, *Pachomius: The Making of a Community in Fourth-Century Egypt* (Chicago: University of Chicago Press, 1985).
[82]Goehring, *Ascetics*, pp. 93–4.
[83]Ibid., pp. 100–8.

Pachomius and his communities have left us with numerous literary works.[84] These include *Lives* in Coptic, Greek and Arabic; *Rules* 'that he took from the scriptures' that were 'not a set text' but constantly evolved with the evolution of the *koinonia*, during the lifetime of Pachomius as well as under his successors'; *Catecheses* on scripture that the heads of 'houses' taught with twice a week; and *Letters* that are either Pachomius' or have their provenance in 'a Pachomian milieu'. According to Veilleux, the 'living community that he left behind him taught many generations of [male and female monastics] much more than all the books of spirituality he could have written. His disciples left a very detailed description of his spiritual journey and of his activity as a founder.'[85]

Shenoute the Great (or 'the Archimandrite') (ca. 347–465), although unknown in the West until the late seventeenth century, is, as Brakke and Crislip argue,[86] one of the greatest native writers of Coptic in history. The Pachomian model directly inspired Shenoute, and he viewed Pachomius as a forefather. By 372 he became a monk at the White Monastery in Atripe in Upper (southern) Egypt led by his uncle Pcol. He became the leader of the monastery around 396 and eventually 'consolidated and directed a federation of three monasteries (two for men and one for women in and near Atripe)' and became the most important Christian leader in the region. At least one thousand men and women joined the federation, which he led as a desert hermit until close to his death.[87] Although his influence eventually extended into Lower Egypt (since the ninth century three Coptic popes have borne his name), Shenoute has been a controversial figure, partly because of his polemics and partly because he used violence at least several times against non-Christian opponents.

Shenoute saw himself 'as a voice crying out in the wilderness' (Mt. 3.3); he wanted to create 'an ascetic culture separate from "the world", within which the monk could seek his salvation', and sought 'to bring his message of repentance, moral purity, and fidelity to Christ and his Church to the larger Christian community and the region of Panopolis'.[88] He became a very important civic leader, something new in monasticism, and his goals and methods led to conflict, especially with lay élites in Panopolis and with non-Christians; he led an attack on a temple, travelled to other cities to defend Christians who had attacked temples and led raids on the homes of wealthy non-Christians.

---

[84]On the literary works of the Pachomian Koinonia, see A. Veilluex, *Pachomian Koinonia*, vol. 1, *The Life of Saint Pachomius*; vol. 2, *Pachomian Chronicles and Rules*; vol. 3, *Instructions, Letters, and Other Writings of Saint Pachomius and His Disciples* (Kalamazoo, MI: Cistercian Press, 1980–2).

[85]Veilleux, 'Pachomius, Saint'.

[86]D. Brakke and A. Crislip (trans.), *Selected Discourses of Shenoute the Great: Community, Theology, and Social Conflict in Late Antique Egypt* (Cambridge: Cambridge University Press, 2015).

[87]Veilleux, 'Pachomius, Saint', p. 1. For Shenoute's relationships, often testy, with the female monastics see R. Krawiec, *Shenoute and the Women of the White Monastery: Egyptian Monasticism in Late Antiquity* (Oxford: Oxford University Press, 2002).

[88]Krawiec, *Shenoute*, p. 5.

But Shenoute was not merely local; he also saw himself as an advocate for Alexandrian theology and patriarchal rule, even accompanying Archbishop Cyril to the Council of Ephesus in 431. Shenoute was not just about preaching and politics, though; what we now call 'social justice' inspired part of his vision: he attacked a 'former governor's alleged paganism, but also his and other wealthy men's oppressive actions against the poor'.[89] After 'barbarian' invasions in the 440s, thousands of people (Shenoute says 20,000) fled to the White Monastery, which provided them with shelter, food and medical care for three months.[90]

From his desert habitation Shenoute was a prolific writer. Although much of his work has disappeared or lies in tatters, recent efforts have restored much of it and thus have provided a far better picture of his life and times. He 'compiled his own letters into a set of nine volumes of "canons" which served as a set of rules for the monastery during Shenoute's lifetime and then for centuries afterwards'.[91] His *Discourses* (*Logoi*) set him apart from Antony and Pachomius because they 'reflect the increasing engagements of monastic institutions with the outside world', with 'some intended for mixed audiences of monastics, laypeople, and even non-Christians'. Thus, they reveal 'the changing cultural landscape of late ancient Egypt, in particular the rise of monastic institutions as economic and patronal forces in the changing agricultural and spiritual economics of the fourth and fifth centuries and the emergence of monasteries as centers of popular piety, pilgrimage, and instruction'.[92]

Since the sixth to seventh centuries almost all Coptic popes, as with bishops in the Orthodox Churches, have come from the monasteries, and monasteries today in Egypt, and throughout the orthodox world, remain centres of popular piety, pilgrimage and instruction. Thus, as we have seen, early monasticism in Palestine, Syria, Asia Minor and Egypt evolved greatly from the late third century to the fifth. The apotactites, semi-anchorites, anchorites, cenobites, and male and female figures such as Antony, Evagrius, Pachomius and Shenoute in Egypt and Basil in Asia Minor created what evolved into a worldwide phenomenon in many varieties. Monasticism is no longer a phenomenon (but perhaps in our secularized, monetized world, it is); it has, though, remained spiritually important for a great many people, both monastic and non-monastic.

BIBLIOGRAPHY

Athanasius of Alexandria. *The Life of Antony: The Coptic Life and the Greek Life*, trans. T. Vivian and A. N. Athanassakis. Kalamazoo, MI: Cistercian, 2003.
Bell, H. I. *Jews and Christians in Egypt: The Jewish Troubles in Alexandria and the Athanasian Controversy*. Oxford: Oxford University Press, 1924.

---

[89] Ibid., p. 8.
[90] Ibid.
[91] S. Emmel, 'Shenoute', in *Encyclopedia of Religion*, ed. L. Jones (New York: Macmillan Reference USA, 2004), pp. 8318a–20a (8319a).
[92] Brakke and Crislip (trans.), *Selected Discourses*, p. 15.

Binns, J. *Ascetics and Ambassadors of Christ: The Monasteries of Palestine*, 314–631. Oxford: Clarendon, 1994.

Brakke, D. *Athanasius and the Politics of Asceticism*. Oxford: Clarendon, 1995.

Brakke, D. *Athanasius and Asceticism*. Baltimore, MD: Johns Hopkins University Press, 1998.

Brakke, D. *Demons and the Making of the Monk: Spiritual Combat in Early Christianity*. Cambridge, MA: Harvard Johns Hopkins University Press, 2006.

Brakke, D. 'Macarius's Quest and Ours: Literary Sources for Early Egyptian Monasticism', *CSQ* 48, no. 2 (2013): 239–51.

Brock, S. P. 'Early Syrian Asceticism', *N* 20, no. 1 (April 1973): 1–19.

Brock, S. P. and Ashbrook Harvey, S. *Holy Women of the Syrian Orient*. Berkeley: University of California Press, 1987.

Cassian, J. (trans.), Ramsey, B. *The Conferences*. New York: Paulist Press, 1997.

Chitty, D. *The Desert a City*. Crestwood, NY: St Vladimir's, 1966.

Choat, M. 'The Epistolary Culture of Monasticism between Literature and Papyri', *CSQ* 48, no. 2 (2013): 227–37.

Clark, E. A. *Reading Renunciation: Asceticism and Scripture in Early Christianity*. Princeton, NJ: Princeton University Press, 1999.

Elm, S. *Virgins of God: The Making of Asceticism in Late Antiquity*. Oxford: Oxford University Press, 1996.

Emmett, A. M. 'An Early Fourth-Century Female Monastic Community in Egypt?' in A. Moffatt (ed.), *Maistor: Classical, Byzantine, and Renaissance Studies for Robert Browning*, 77–83. Byzantina Australiensia 5. Canberra: The Australian Association for Byzantine Studies, 1984.

Evagrius Ponticus. *The Praktikos and Chapters on Prayer*, trans. J. E. Bamberger. Kalamazoo, MI: Cistercian Publications, 1981.

Evelyn-White, H. G. (ed. Walter Hauser). *The Monasteries of the Wâdi 'N Watrun*, Volume II, *The History of the Monasteries of Nitria and Scetis*. New York: Metropolitan Museum, 1932 (repr. Arno Press, 1973), available online.

Goehring, J. A. *Ascetics, Society, and the Desert: Studies in Early Egyptian Monasticism*, 13–35. Harrisburg, PA: Trinity, 1999.

Guillaumont, A. *Aux origins du monachisme chrétien: pour une phénoménologie du monachisme*. Spiritualité orientale 30. Bégrolles-en-Mauges: Abbaye de Bellefontaine, 1979.

Hirschfeld, Y. *The Judean Desert Monasteries in the Byzantine Period*. New Haven, CT and London: Yale University Press, 1992.

Historia Monachorum in Aegypto. Translated by N. Russell, as: *The Lives of the Desert Fathers*. Kalamazoo, MI: Cistercian Publications, 1980.

Judge, E. A. 'The Earliest Use of Monachos for "Monk" (P. Coll. Youtie 77) and the Origins of Monasticism', *JAC* 10 (1977): 72–89.

The Lives of the Desert Fathers, trans. N. Russell. Kalamazoo, MI: Cistercian Publications, 1980.

Mathieson, E. A. *Christian Women in the Greek Papyri of Egypt to 400 CE*. Turnhout: Brepols, 2014.

Palladius of Aspuma. *The Lausiac History*, trans. John Wortley. Collegeville, MN: Cistercian Publications, 2015.

Pearson, B. A. and Goehring, J. E. *The Roots of Egyptian Christianity*. Philadelphia, PA: Fortress Press, 1986.

Rubenson, S. *The Letters of St. Antony: Monasticism and the Making of a Saint*. Minneapolis, MN: Fortress, 1995.

Rubenson, S. 'Asceticism and Monasticism, I: Eastern', in A. Augustine Casiday and F. Norris (eds), *The Cambridge History of Christianity*, vol. 2, *Constantine to c. 600*, 637–68. Cambridge: Cambridge University Press, 2007.

Rubenson, S. 'To Tell the Truth: Fact and Fiction in Early Monastic Sources', *CSQ* 48, no. 3 (2013): 317–24.

Smith, J. Z. (ed.). *The HarperCollins Dictionary of Religion*. San Francisco, CA: HarperSanFrancisco, 1995.

Veilleux, A. (ed. and trans.). *Pachomian Koinonia*, vol. 1, *The Life of Saint Pachomius*; vol. 2, *Pachomian Chronicles and Rules*; vol. 3, *Instructions, Letters, and Other Writings of Saint Pachomius and His Disciples*. Kalamazoo, MI: Cistercian, 1980–1982.

Veilleux, A. 'Pachomius, Saint', in A. S. Atiya (ed.), *Coptic Encyclopedia*, 1859a–1864b. London: Macmillan Reference Library, 1991.

Vivian, T. (trans.). *The Saying and Stories of the Desert Fathers and Mothers: The Greek Alphabetical Sayings of the Apophthegmata Patrum*, vol. 1. Collegeville, MN: Cistercian Publications, (2021).

Wipszycka, E. *The Second Gift of the Nile: Monks and Monasteries in Late Antique Egypt*, trans. D. Jasiński, *JJP* Supplements. Warsaw: The University of Warsaw, 2018.

Wortley, J. (trans.). *Palladius of Aspuma: The Lausiac History*. Collegeville, MN: Cistercian Publications, 2015.

Wortley, J. *More Sayings of the Desert Fathers: An English Translation and Notes*. Cambridge: Cambridge University Press, 2019.

CHAPTER 25

Persecution of heretics[1]

MARCIN WYSOCKI

INTRODUCTION

The so-called Edict of Milan (AD 313) and the victory of Constantine over Licinius (AD 324) triggered a number of changes in the perception of Christianity by others and by itself.[2] The attitude of Roman authorities changed, which gave Christians religious freedom, but also the involvement of state authorities in the functioning of the church. The church herself could also focus more on her internal structure and core elements, rather than defending herself against attacks of pagans and imperial authorities. This is why the period following AD 313 is called the golden period in the development of theology. At that time, having gained insight into herself, the church was able to better define what orthodoxy was and give it a more specific shape. This took place at the great councils of that period and was manifested in the works of eminent theologians such as Athanasius, Augustine and the Cappadocian Fathers. Until then, the essence of orthodoxy and heresy had not yet been specified.[3] Despite the lack of such certainty, there were disputes and conflicts around the basic truths of faith, ways of interpreting the Holy Scriptures, views on morality and church punishment within Christianity. It ended, however, with an exchange of acrimonious attacks on one another, leading to polemical and anti-heretical works. When Christianity gained the status of *religio licita* (AD 313) and subsequently *religio regalis* (AD 384), its situation changed considerably. Church people turned from the persecuted into the persecutors.[4] More importantly, the state apparatus was

---

[1]This chapter was partly sponsored by the Polish Ministry of Science and Higher Education within the programme titled 'Regional Initiative of Excellence', 2019–22, project number: 028/RID/2018/19.
[2]See N. Lenski, 'The Significance of the Edict of Milan', in *Constantine: Religious Faith and Imperial Policy*, eds Edward Siecienski (London: Routledge, 2017), pp. 27–56.
[3]See M. Edwards, *Catholicity and Heresy in the Early Church* (Farnham: Routledge, 2009).
[4]Generally, about persecution and the epoch see W. H. C. Frend, *Martyrdom and Persecution in the Early Church: A Study of a Conflict from the Maccabees to Donatus* (New York: Anchor Books, 1967); H. A. Drake, *Constantine and the Bishops: The Politics of Intolerance* (Baltimore, MD: Johns Hopkins University Press, 2000); C. M. Odahl, *Constantine and the Christian Empire* (New York: Routledge, 2004); M. Gaddis, *There Is No Crime for Those Who Have Christ: Religious Violence in the Christian Roman Empire* (Berkeley: University of California Press, 2005); T. D. Barnes, *Constantine: Dynasty, Religion and Power in the Later Roman Empire* (Chichester: Wiley-Blackwell, 2011); P. Maraval, *Constantin le Grand. Empereur*

involved in purging the church of the heretics because it had the necessary means and experience for such operations.[5] The Roman Empire officially recognized only the faith established by the Council of Nicaea[6] and considered as 'heretics' anyone who departed 'even in a minor point of doctrine, from the tenets and the path of the Catholic religion'.[7] So we see two authorities – secular and ecclesiastical – who had motives and means to persecute heretics. For this reason, we should take a look at the way the Roman state, on the one hand, and the bishops, on the other, responded to heresy in the early Christian period to gain a better understanding of this fascinating time.

IMPERIAL POWERS

Edward A. Ryan is certainly right in saying: 'The history of the Christian emperors is largely that of the state struggle for religious unity in the interests of political unity.'[8] The persecution of heretics was a natural consequence of the combination of religious and civil duties and rights, the confusion of the civil and the ecclesiastical, the judicial and the moral – which all came to pass from the time of Constantine. It comes from the state and from the emperors, who in this respect styled themselves as the successors of the *Pontifices Maximi,* with their attitude to the church reversed.[9] But there were other, more serious reasons for the persecution of heretics as well, known from the earlier periods of persecution of Christians. Together with emperors, they generally shared the views of their pagan contemporaries, feeling that religious individual misconduct might bring punishment not merely upon individuals but at least upon their immediate environment, or even perhaps the whole empire. The role of the emperor was to save and protect the empire against 'all the others whose sects it disgusts us to insert in our most pious sanctions, all of which have different names but a single perfidy' as it was said in one of the edicts.[10] Therefore, almost immediately after his conversion and declaration of religious tolerance,[11] striving for unity and inner peace of the empire, Emperor Constantine became involved in the internal conflicts among Christians, including those caused by wrong teachings.

romain, empereur chrétien (306-337) (Paris: Tallandier, 2011); B. D. Shaw, *Sacred Violence: African Christians and Sectarian Hatred in the Age of Augustine* (Cambridge: Cambridge University Press, 2011).
[5]P. Brown, *Power and Persuasion in Late Antiquity: Towards a Christian Empire* (Madison: University of Wisconsin Press, 1992).
[6]*Cod. Thds.*, XVI 1, 2; XVI 5, 6.
[7]Ibid., XVI 5, 28. See V. Escribano Paño, 'La construction de l'image de l'hérétique dans le Code Théodosien XVI', in *Empire chrétien et Église aux IVe et Ve siècles: intégration ou «concordat»? Le témoignage du Code Théodosien,* eds J.-N. Guinot and F. Richard (Paris: Éditions du Cerf, 2008), pp. 389–412.
[8]E. A. Ryan, 'The Problem of Persecution in the Early Church', *ThS* 3 (1944): 310–39, 329.
[9]See P. Maraval, 'Le devoir religieux des empereurs: de la tolérance à la répression', in *Chrétiens persécuteurs. Destructions, exclusions, violences religieuses au IVe siècle,* ed. M.-F. Baslez (Paris: Albin Michel, 2014), pp. 37–62.
[10]See *Cod. Thds.*, XVI 5, 60.
[11]See T. D. Barnes, 'The Conversion of Constantine', *EMC* 4 (1985): 371–91.

During his reign, he laid the foundations for legislation against heretics for the future, and it was his legislative activity that led to the isolation of 'heretics and schismatics' as a separate category of religious communities alongside pagans, Jews and orthodox Christians.[12] As early as in AD 313, Constantine deprived priests who were outside the Catholic Church of all privileges granted to the clergy,[13] and later obliged them to carry the appropriate burden for the state, so-called *munera*.[14] In the spring of AD 317 he issued a decree in which he demanded that all Christians return to unity, announcing that severe sanctions would be imposed on Donatists.[15] The churches they occupied were to be taken away and their leaders sentenced to exile.[16] The legislation and actions against the Donatus' party were the first manifestations of persecution against heretics and schismatics.[17] Another group opposed by Constantine was Arius and his followers.[18] Shortly after the Council of Nicaea (AD 325), he was to issue an extremely harsh edict ordering that Arius' writings be burnt and all those who dared to preserve them punished by death.[19] In the edict, quoted later by Socrates of Constantinople, Constantine stated that 'Arius has imitated wicked and impious persons' and he compared him to Porphyry, 'that enemy of piety'.[20] That showed that the emperor took the Arians to be enemies of the Christian faith similar to pagans attacking the church. The credibility of Socrates' message remains problematic, because it is known that such an edict was issued not immediately after the Council but in AD 333. Nevertheless, it demonstrates the authorities' attitude towards heretics. Sometime after the Council of Nicaea, Constantine issued another edict directed against heretics, in which he ordered the repression of the Novatians, Valentinians, Marcionites, Paulians, Phrygians and

---

[12]T. D. Barnes, 'From Toleration to Repression: The Evolution of Constantine's Religious Policies', *SCI* 21 (2002): 189–207; S. Bralewski, 'Uwagi na temat antyheretyckiego ustawodawstwa cesarza Konstantyna Wielkiego' ['Comments on the Anti-heretic Legislation of Emperor Constantine the Great'], *PNH* 1 (2002): 7–20.

[13]*Cod. Thds.*, XVI 2, 1; *The Copy of the Imperial Letter Commanding the Heads of the Churches to be exempted from all public duties* in Eusebius, *HE.*, X 7; J. Gaudemet, 'La législation religieuse de Constantin', *RHEF* 122 (1947): 25–61.

[14]*Cod. Thds.*, XVI 5, l.

[15]See C. Alexander, 'Rethinking Constantine's Interaction with the North African "Donatist" Schism', in *Rethinking Constantine: History, Theology, and Legacy*, ed. E. L. Smither (Eugene, OR: Pickwick Publications, 2014), pp. 37–90.

[16]*Cod. Thds.*, XVI 6, 2.

[17]Cf. P. Marone, 'Some Observations on the Anti-Donatist Legislation', in *The Uniquely African Controversy: Studies on Donatist Christianity*, eds A. Dupont, M. A. Gaumer and M. Lamberigts, LAHR 9 (Leuven, Paris and Bristol: Peeters, 2015), pp. 71–84.

[18]See O. Norderval, 'The Emperor Constantine and Arius: Unity in the Church and Unity in the Empire', *STh* 42 (1988): 113–50.

[19]See Socrates, *HE.*, I 9; Athanasius, *decr.*, 39; Gelasius of Cyzicus, *HE.*, II 36; more S. Bralewski, 'Polityka Konstantyna Wielkiego wobec arian po soborze w Nicei: nagły zwrot czy kontynuacja?' ['Policy of Constantine the Great towards the Arians after the Council of Nicaea: a sudden turn or continuation?'], *VP* 34–5 (1998): 347–8.

[20]Socrates, *HE.*, I 9.

other heretics and ordered to confiscate their houses of prayer and forbade them to hold religious meetings both in public places and in private.[21]

Decrees could demonstrate the emperor's determination to fight heretics in the name of defending the unity of the church, but at the same time, it must be remembered that the edict issued against Donatists was revoked by the emperor after four years, and Arius was soon removed from exile.[22] The document did not mention the heretics who caused the most problems, that is, Arians, Melitians and Donatists, as well as Manicheans. In addition, the emperor allowed exceptions to its application, as it is evidenced by the edict of Spoleto of 326, allowing Novatians to retain churches and cemeteries with the exception of those that had belonged to the Catholic Church. Such various treatments of heretics by the authorities did not result from legal chaos but, rather, from the influence of heretics on the emperor, who, if they had access to him to convincingly present their arguments, could improve their situation. Certainly, the emperor, drawing on the past events, and having his own experience, recognized the ineffectiveness of power solutions and began to look for other effective means to put an end to heresies, and above all the schism of Donatists. Later, he was more committed to compromise, seeing in it the key to resolving the heresy issues. In the face of heretics, such as Arians, he did not demand a total renunciation of his views, but only to keep them for themselves and to stop accusing others of doctrinal errors. In the actions of the emperor, efficiency was the most important thing, so Constantine made concessions to the powerful and did not shy away from the use of force against the weak, as is evidenced by his legislation directed against the destroyers of the unity of the church.[23] And we have to remember that he himself was baptized shortly before his death by an Arian bishop. His son Constantius was a fanatical persecutor both of idolatry and the Nicene orthodoxy and endeavoured with all his might to establish Arianism alone in the empire. It wasn't until the reign of Emperor Theodosius (347–96), who proclaimed the exclusive authority of the Nicene Creed, that brought new laws against heretics. Soon after his baptism, in 380, the emperor, whose ruling principle of public life was the unity of the empire and of the Orthodox Church, issued, in connection with his co-emperors Gratian and Valentinian II, an edict which confirmed the only true faith. It was the faith taught by St Peter to the Romans and which was faithfully preserved by tradition, and which was professed by Pope Damasus and Peter, bishop of Alexandria, and only the adherents of this faith could have been called Catholic Christians. In addition, the emperors stated that they would brand all the senseless followers of other religions with the infamous name of heretics and forbid their converts to assume the name 'church', and also managed that besides the condemnation of divine justice, they must expect the heavy penalties which their authority, guided by heavenly wisdom, shall think

---

[21]Cf. Eusebius, V. C., III 64-65; Sozomen, HE., II 32.
[22]Socrates, HE., I 25-26.
[23]See Bralewski, 'Comments on the Anti-heretic Legislation', pp. 11–13.

proper to inflict.[24] In the course of fifteen years this emperor issued at least fifteen penal laws against heretics,[25] whereby he gradually deprived them of all rights to exercise their religion, excluded them from all civil offices and threatened them with fines, confiscation, banishment and, in some cases, as with the Manichaeans, Audians, and even Quartodecimanians, with death. A series of edicts of 381 laid down different kinds of punishment for heretics. The edict of 10 January 381 gave all churches into the hands of Homouzians and forbade heretics to worship in towns and refused to call them Christians. The edict of 8 May, in turn, was aimed at the Manichaeans, and, most unusually, it had a retrospective effect. Further attacks on heretics of all kinds followed in 382 and 383, with a final decree of 21 January 384, followed by a break for several years. From the time of Theodosius, therefore, dates the state–church theory of the persecution of heretics, and its embodiment in legislation. His primary design was rather to terrify them and convert than to punish – the unruly subjects.[26] There was, however, a small step from theory to practice, taken by his rival and colleague, Maximus, who, inspired by the unworthy bishop Ithacius, had the Spanish bishop, Priscillian and six respectable adherents of his Manichaean-like sect (two presbyters, two deacons, the poet Latronian and Euchrocia, a noble matron of Bordeaux) tortured and beheaded with a sword at Treves in 385. This was when the first heretic blood was shed on account of religious convictions by a Christian prince. When the government of Theodosius II, under the influence of Nestorius, made a vigorous effort to sweep heresy from the world, the Manichaeans were stigmatized as men who had 'descended to the lowest depths of wickedness', and were condemned anew to be expelled from towns and perhaps to be put to death (428).[27] Arcadius, at the beginning of his reign, reaffirmed all the pains and prohibitions which his predecessors had enacted against heretics. In most cases, this meant the suppression of their services and assemblies and ordinations. The Eunomians, an extreme branch of the Arians, who held that the Son was unlike the Father, were singled out for more severe treatment and deprived of the right of executing testaments. In the following decades, the internal problems of the Western empire, and above all the invasions of Barbarians and ultimately the fall of the Western empire in 476, weakened the anti-heretical actions of the Imperial authorities. However, the Justinian revival in the eastern part of the empire caused the new wave of repressions of heretics and schismatics. Emperor Justinian issued severe laws against heretics in 527 and 528. For this reason, those who dissented from the authorized line were debarred from public offices, forbidden to practice certain professions, prohibited from holding meetings and denied the civil rights of Roman citizens. For them, as Justinian said, 'to exist is sufficient' – for the time being. In several of his laws, Justinian demonstrates that he expected divine punishment of a collective nature to

---

[24]*Cod. Thds.*, XVI 1,2.
[25]Ibid., XVI 6-33.
[26]See Sozomen, *HE.*, I 7,12.
[27]See *Cod. Thds.*, XVI 5,7.

follow the commission of certain religious offences. For example, in a novel of 535 against blasphemy and taking the name of God in vain when taking an oath, he declares that such crimes lead directly to 'famine, earthquakes and plagues',[28] and in a novel of 536 he provided that the writings of Severus the Monophysite were to be burnt and that anyone who copied them was to have his hand cut off.[29] Later, the persecution of heretics took place in connection with the iconoclastic dispute. Theophanes mentions attempts in 721/2 made by Emperor Leo III (717–741) to bring about the conversion of Jews and 'Montanists'. Under the year 725/6, he records mass unrest at Constantinople over the iconoclastic doctrines favoured by the emperor and the punishment of many people, especially men from noble families and men of learning, by mutilation, whipping, exile or fines, and for 728/9 (or the following year) he and Nicephorus note the first punishments and mutilations of image worshippers in 811/2. The pious emperor Michael I (811–813), acting on the advice of the patriarch of Constantinople, Nicephorus and others, decreed a death penalty against them but was later persuaded 'by other evil-minded advisers', who were the monks of the Constantinopolitan monastery of Studios led by their famous abbot Theodore (759–826).[30] When the Iconoclastic Controversy came to an end in 843, the government of Empress Theodora did not adopt a tolerant attitude towards the iconoclastic clergy, which had been taken in 787 by Irene, but when pressured by a monastic party carried out a thorough purge of the clergy. Other than that, there is no evidence that after the 'restoration of orthodoxy' the victorious iconophiles started to persecute their opponents. Thus, the persecution of heretics by the imperial authorities in the early Christian period ended.

In the history of persecution of heretics outlined earlier, of special importance and scale was the persecution of Donatists in Africa, in which the secular authorities were involved almost from the beginning and in a unique way. In 317, Constantine directed his two commissioners, Ursacius and Leontius, to try to win over the Donatist Church. This strategy was used only to exasperate Donatist bishops: they stirred up their communities to very determined resistance. More forcible measures soon followed, such as Constantine's promulgation of an edict of union which compelled followers of Majorinus to go into exile and to abandon their basilicas.[31] As Optatus of Milevis mentions, the Donatists were attacked by armed troops when assembled for divine worship, but does not provide any particulars, and even recognizes Donatists as guilty of these actions.[32] Nonetheless, Constantine realized

---

[28]Justnian, *cod.*, Novella 77,1,1.

[29]See ibid., 42,1,2.

[30]See Theophanes, *chron.*, Annus Mundi 6303; P. J. Alexander, 'Religious Persecution and Resistance in the Byzantine Empire of the Eighth and Ninth Centuries: Methods and Justifications', *S* 2 (1977): 238–64.

[31]See *Cod. Thds.*, XVI 6,2; Marone, 'Some Observations on the Anti-Donatist Legislation', pp. 72–7; S. Gherro, 'Stato e Chiesa di fronte alla controversia donatista nei primi anni dell'età costantiniana', *SDHI* 36 (1970): 359–409; T. Spagnuolo Vigorita, 'Legislazione antidonatista e cronologia agostiniana', *FHI* 8 (2007): 351–70.

[32]See Optatus, *C. Parm.*, III 1,1.

soon afterwards that the use of violence to resolve issues concerning Christians in Africa was counterproductive and in 321 repealed his edict of union. In a letter addressed to Verinus, the Imperial Vicar of North Africa, he granted Donatists full liberty to act according to their own convictions, declaring that this was a matter which was judged by God.[33] In 347, in order to reunite the divided African church, the emperor Constans decided to intervene more directly, though initially he had avoided the use of force. The imperial commissioners, Paul and Macarius, entered Northern Africa, distributed money to the poor in the name of the emperor, presented costly church utensils to individual communities and, at the same time, exhorted all to offer no resistance to the unity of the church. Bishop Donatus Magnus of Carthage repelled the advances of the imperial officer with the remark: 'What has the emperor to do with the Church?'[34] He sent admonitions to all the Donatist Churches, charging them to accept none of the money. So Constans published an edict of union which assigned the property of the Donatist community to the Catholics and sent those who refused to cooperate into exile.[35] The Donatists rose in revolt and found themselves being persecuted more harshly than they had been thirty years before. In this instance, the religious furore of the Donatists combined with the resistance put forth by the Roman soldiers resulted in considerable bloodshed. The imperial commissioners Paul and Macarius failed to secure ecclesial unity in North Africa, but the coercive measures taken at this time sealed the Donatists' reputation as a church of martyrs.[36] Later, in the second half of the fourth century, the Roman Empire returned once again to indirect fighting against Donatism through laws concerning public order. In the case in point, Constans II reintroduced Constantine's laws on anonymous libellous pamphlets,[37] and in order to keep a check on the cult of relics practised by the Donatists, he prohibited the desecration of funereal buildings. Nevertheless, during the early decades of the fourth century, there were still no explicit sanctions against the Donatist doctrine. Only after the Council of Carthage, presided over by Gratus (345–8), do we have the two laws of Valentinian which prohibited rebaptism as being in conflict with the teachings of the Apostles.[38] During the reign of Valentinian, the 'dissident' church, assisted by the anti-government faction of the Circumcellions, is reported to have started committing acts of violence against the official Catholic clergy. When this state of affairs continued for almost twenty years, the imperium resolved to confiscate the financial resources of the Donatist Church. Thus, in 392, Theodosius issued a law which imposed a fine of ten gold pounds on all 'heretical' clerics responsible

---

[33]See idem, *App.*, IX.

[34]Idem, *C. Parm.*, III 3,3.

[35]See *Cod. Thds.*, XVI 6,2; *Passio Marculi*, PL 8, 761.764.

[36]See Optatus, *C. Parm.*, III 3,2; III 4,1; III 12,2; M. Tilley, *Donatist Martyr Stories: The Church in Conflict in Roman North Africa* (Liverpool: Liverpool University Press, 1996); Marone, 'Some Observations on the Anti-Donatist Legislation', pp. 73–4.

[37]See *Cod. Thds.*, IX 34,5.

[38]See ibid., XVI 6,1-2; also P. G. Caron, 'Ne sanctum baptisma iteretur (CTh. 16.6; CI. 1.6)', *AARC* 6 (1986): 107–80; P. Marone, 'Some Observations on the Anti-Donatist Legislation', p. 74.

for attacks against the Catholic clergy.[39] Furthermore, between 399 and 409, Honorius put forward a series of regulations concerning the seizure of Gildo's estates, who was the count of Africa and protected and encouraged Donatism. Honorius, just like Valentinian, was preoccupied with a second baptism. Not only did he prohibit the practice of a second baptism but also identified the Donatists as 'heretics'.[40] Under his imperial rule, the Donatists were neither allowed to leave wills nor collect inheritances.[41] Instead, they were obliged to leave their belongings to their nearest Catholic relatives.[42] Furthermore, they were also forbidden from undersigning sales contracts and business transactions.[43] Additionally, so long as they refused to convert to the Catholic Church, they were forced to pay fines in silver and gold and risked having their properties seized.[44] So Honorius' legislation penalized both those confessing the Donatist faith and more generally those who supported the Donatist movement. Between 408 and 409, he even made provision for the death penalty for Donatists disrupting Catholic services[45] and decreed that organizers of illegal congregations were to be exiled or deported to far off islands or provinces. But in 410 he sent a letter to governor of Africa Eraclianus, granting freedom of worship to all.[46] Then a delegation of Catholic bishops persuaded Honorius to revoke the edict of toleration and to summon the followers of Cecilianus and the followers of Majorinus to a public debate. Marcellinus arranged and presided over the Council of Carthage in 411,[47] at the end of which he stated that the Donatists had been refuted *omnium documentorum manifestatione*[48] by the Catholics. In this way, between 412 and 414, while the Catholic Church continued to enjoy a collection of privileges (exemption from compulsory public service or tax payments, etc.),[49] Donatist clerics were forced to abandon their churches and go into exile,[50] whereas Donatist laymen were obliged to pay fines, ranging from fifty gold pounds for high-ranking officials to five gold pounds for ordinary citizens.[51] None of the laws mentioned here were easy to enforce and, in particular, enforcing the seizure of buildings used for worship was especially problematic. In fact, Constantine had a new basilica built for the Catholics in Cirta rather than force the Donatists to

---

[39]See *Cod. Thds.*, XVI 5,21.
[40]Ibid., XVI 6,3.4.
[41]See ibid., XVI 6,5.
[42]See ibid., XVI 5,54.
[43]See ibid., XVI 5,65.
[44]See ibid., XVI 5,52.54.
[45]See ibid., XVI 2,31.
[46]See Council of Carthage. (418), canon 108; Augustine, *Ep.*, 108,6,19.
[47]See *Cod. Thds.*, XVI 11,3.
[48]Augustine, *Brev. coll.*, 3,43.
[49]See *Cod. Thds.*, XVI 2,1; XVI 5,1; XVI 2,14; XVI 2,34; Eusebius, *HE.*, X 7,1-2; R. Lizzi Testa, 'Privilegi economici e definizione di status: il caso del vescovo tardoantico', *Atti dell'Accademia nazionale dei Lincei. Classe di scienze morali, storiche e filologiche* (Rendiconti serie 9) 11 (2000): 55–103; R. Lizzi Testa, 'Te Bishop Vir Venerabilis: Fiscal Privileges and Status Definition in Late Antiquity', *SP* 34 (2001): 125–44.
[50]See *Cod. Thds.*, XVI 5,52.
[51]See ibid., XVI 5,45.46.

abandon their basilica.[52] While it is true that some places of worship were actually seized,[53] it can also be said that, in the earliest times, legislation concerning the Donatists, either directly or indirectly, encountered a series of obstacles. As Paula Marone states, although various *passiones*, such as the *Passio Maximiani et Isaac*, contain both a record of judicial interrogations and accounts of deaths during the time of Constans,[54] it is not easy to ascertain whether the Donatists, who were put to death in the mid-fourth century, had been condemned by a specific law, had been the victims of the harshness of a particular imperial official or had suffered on account of the intolerance of other religious groups.[55] Edicts often resulted in exiles, and at this point we should recall at least the expatriation of Donatus the Great from Africa and Claudianus from Rome.[56] But the persecution also had less extreme forms and beatings with clubs and rods were the normal means of coercion. For example, during the Conference of Carthage in 411, Flavius Marcellinus had a special *ius gladii* and thwarted acts of aggression. It was a form of punitive violence that was found in all basic units of social discipline: 'A form of restraint that is customarily used by the teacher of liberal arts, by parents themselves, and by bishops in their courts.'[57]

For many years, *Passio Donati* was held as an example of cruel persecution of Donatists; it was supposed to serve as the evidence for persecutions of heretics during the time of Emperor Constantine.[58] However, recent research indicates that this is not a traditional martyr narrative but a sermon delivered on the anniversary of the incident it recounts, which arose much later than probable events of which we know little. Those who would see in the *Passio Donati* evidence for massive open imperial violence must content themselves not just with its disappointing circumstantial case for large-scale slaughter but also with several indications in the same text that Constantine made every effort to avoid conflict and bloodshed. The *Passio Donati* constitutes a very weak platform on which to build a case for a massive and sustained application of violent force by the agents of Constantine from 317 to 321.[59] So we do not have direct evidence regarding the persecution of heretics and their victims, and we can draw conclusions only from the preserved legal acts only concerning possible oppressions and actions of the state apparatus,

---

[52]See Optatus, *App.,* X.

[53]See Augustine, *C. litt. Pet.,* I 18,20.

[54]See *Pass. Max.,* PL 8, 766–73.

[55]See Augustine, *Ep.,* 93,11,49; *Cath.,* 14,36; *c. Cres.,* III 56,62; IV 4,5; IV 7,9.

[56]See Optatus, *C. Parm.,* III 3.

[57]Augustine, *Ep.,* 133,2; 134,2; *Cod. Thds.,* XVI 5,55.

[58]See F. Dolbeau, 'La *Passio Sancti Donati* (BHL 2303b). Une tentative d'édition critique', in *Memoriam Sanctorum Venerantes: Miscellanea in onore di Monsignor Victor Saxer* (Roma: Pontificio Istituto di Archeologia Cristiana, 1992), pp. 251–67.

[59]N. Lenski, 'Constantine and the Donatists: Exploring the Limits of Religious Toleration', in *Religiöse Toleranz. 1700 Jahre nach dem Edikt von Mailand,* ed. M. Wallraff (Berlin: W. de Gruyter, 2016), pp. 111–12.

which, most often, apart from issuing the laws *contra haereticos*, did not go about their strict enforcement.

THE CHURCH POWERS

The second group that somehow participated and was interested in ending the case of the heretics were the shepherds of the church and the ecclesial community itself. Of course, since the beginning of the church there was concern for the purity of the doctrine. Eradication of doctrinal errors was part of the process. In the ante-Nicene age, heresy and schism were as much hated and abhorred indeed, as afterwards, yet were met only in a moral way, by word and writing, and were punished with excommunication from the rights of the church. Justin the Martyr, Tertullian and even Lactantius were the first advocates of the principle of freedom of conscience and maintained, against the heathen, that religion was essentially a matter of free will and could be promoted only by instruction and persuasion not by outward force.[60] However, there was enormous resentment against those who distorted Christian faith. For example, Polycarp of Smyrna, a disciple of the Apostles, told how Apostle John, when entering the baths at Ephesus, saw the notable heretic Cerinthus inside and immediately rushed out shouting: 'Away, lest the very baths collapse, for within is Cerinthus, the enemy of the truth' and refused even to remain under the same roof because it was dangerous.[61] Polycarp also, when accosted by the heresiarch Marcion with the question 'Do you recognise me?', replied: 'I recognise, I recognise the first-born of Satan.'[62] Eusebius mentioned, too, that the early Montanists complained that they were driven away from the faithful as wolves from the fold.[63] Irenaeus, in his *Against Heresies*, shows his detestation of heretics. To him they appear blasphemous and impudent sophists, blind men led by the blind, who deservedly fall into the ditch of ignorance.[64] Alluding to this attitude, Celsus charged that the Christians hated each other with perfect hatred. Eusebius also mentions that not only state and church forces but also heavenly ones were involved in punishing heretics. He recalls the story of Natalis, the Roman confessor, who (ca. 200) was hired by the Adoptionists for 150 denarii per month to be their bishop. Warned in visions of the error of his ways, he paid no heed, and his pre-eminence was too sweet. Then he 'was scourged by holy angels and punished severely through the entire night'. Natalis was cured of his desire for pre-eminence: 'He put on sackcloth and covered himself with ashes and with great haste and in tears fell down before Zephyrinus the bishop, rolling at the feet not only of the clergy but also of the laity.'[65] It would be one of the first examples of the use of corporal punishment for heresy.

---

[60]Justin, *1 Apol.*, 2,4,12; Tertullian, *Apol.*, 24,28; *Scap.*, 2; Lactantius, *Inst.*, 19,20; *Epit.*, 54.
[61]Irenaeus, *Haer.*, III 3,4; Eusebius, *HE.*, III 28,6; IV 14,6.
[62]Eusebius, *HE.*, IV 15,7.
[63]Ibid., V 16,17.
[64]Irenaeus, *Haer.*, V 20.
[65]Eusebius, *HE.*, V 28,10-12.

But similar behaviours towards heretics were also shown by ordinary people who did not want to deal with heretics. Theodoret of Cyrus recalls the story of an Arian bishop Eunomius. In about 374, the eastern emperor Valens, who had Arian sympathies, exiled the orthodox anti-Arian bishop Eusebius of Samosata. He was replaced by Eunomius. When it happened that Eunomius went down to the public baths and his attendants shut everyone else out, he graciously ordered that the doors be opened and everyone who wanted to come in be admitted. Eunomius urged them to come into water with him, but they all held back, which he attributed to the respect for himself as bishop. When he went off, the others refused to enter the bath until the water had been drained and replaced, feeling that it had been subject to pollution by the presence of the heretic.[66] Certainly, the majority of the early Christians thought, with St Hilary, that they were obstinate men who misunderstood the Holy Scriptures, and then pertinaciously refused to listen to the corrections of the church.[67] It was also clear that in some cases their intransigence was motivated more by greed, ambition and spite than by sincere religious conviction.[68]

At that time, bishops manifested various attitudes towards heretics. In 381, the Council of Constantinople declared that every heresy would be anathematized,[69] and Pope Leo the Great, in a letter to his bishops, urged them to be watchful in apprehending heretics in order that such offenders might not pollute the holy flock by their contagion but might rather be banished into perpetual exile.[70] Many pastors, who were against the application of the death sentence for heresy, were outspoken adherents of the employment of other temporal penalties. The suppression of heretical assemblies was urged by St Ambrose[71] and St John Chrysostom seems to have deprived the heretics in Lydia of their churches. Chrysostom expresses his views on the repression of heretics in his *Homilies on Matthew*, where he comments on the Parable of the Tares and says that they should be silenced but not put to death.[72] In AD 428, in his first homily after his election to the patriarchate of Constantinople, Nestorius said to Emperor Theodosius II very important and well-known words: 'Give me the earth purged of heretics and I will give you heaven in return. Destroy the heretics with me, and I will destroy the Persians with you.'[73] Many welcomed these words, but many listeners pointed out the recklessness of the words spoken and the impetus and boastfulness of the new bishop of the capital of the empire. He would soon put these words into action wanting to tear down the Arian temple, but his plans caused such great panic among the Arians that they themselves set fire to their temple, which caused a fire in nearby buildings, and because of that Nestorius

---

[66]Theodoret of Cyrrhus, *HE.*, IV 15,2-3.

[67]Hilary of Poitier, *Trin.*, II 3.

[68]See Ryan, 'The Problem of Persecution in the Early Church', p. 316.

[69]See the Council of Constantinople (381) canon I.

[70]Leo, *Ep.*, 17.

[71]See Ambrose, *Ep.*, 4 extra coll. (10), 11.

[72]See John Chrysostom, *H. in Math.*, 46.

[73]Socrates, *HE.*, VII 29,5.

was given the nickname 'Arsonist'. So he bothered other heretics as well, disrupting the order in the city, but soon he himself joined them.

In disputes with heretics and schismatics, bishops often had the final word. For example, in a dispute with the Donatists' deeds of the Council of Carthage (418) illustrate the crucial position occupied by the Catholic bishop. He appeared as directly responsible for summoning the imperial executors to suppress heresy in his town, and he was the only one who could know who had communicated with the Catholic Church and who was still on what must have been a list of heretics. The authoritarian action of the Roman government would be ineffective without the zealous application of the Catholic Church.

There is an opinion that Augustine of Hippo was one of the main theorists of the persecution of heretics. During his episcopate he struggled with, among others, the problem of Donatists and Pelegians.[74] Augustine, who himself belonged to the Manichaean sect for nine years, and was miraculously converted by the grace of God to the Catholic Church, without the slightest external pressure, held at first the truly evangelical view that heretics and schismatics should not be violently dealt with, but won by instruction and conviction; but after the year 400 he turned and retracted this view, in consequence of his experience with the Donatists, whom he endeavoured in vain to convert by disputation and writing, while many submitted to the imperial laws.[75] From then on he was led to advocate the persecution of heretics, partly by his doctrine of the Christian state, partly by the seditious excesses of the fanatical Circumcelliones, partly by the hope of a wholesome effect of temporal punishments and partly by a false interpretation of the famous words: *cogite intrare*, from the Parable of the Great Supper (Lk. 14.23). He says,

> It is, indeed, better that men should be brought to serve God by instruction than by fear of punishment or by pain. But because the former means are better, the latter must not therefore be neglected. [. . .] Many must often be brought back to their Lord, like wicked servants, by the rod of temporal suffering, before they attain the highest grade of religious development. [. . .] The Lord himself orders that the guests be first invited, then compelled, to his great supper.[76]

Augustine thinks that if the state is denied the right to punish for religious errors, neither should it punish any other crime, like murder or adultery, as Paul (Gal. 5.19) attributes divisions and sects to the same source in the flesh. He charges his Donatist opponents with inconsistency in approving the emperors' bans on idolatry but condemning their persecution of Christian heretics. It is to the honour of Augustine's heart, indeed, that in actual cases he earnestly urged the magistrates to show clemency and humanity, and thus in practice he remained true to his noble maxim: 'Nothing conquers but truth, the victory of truth is love.'[77] But his

---

[74]See P. R. L. Brown, 'St. Augustine's Attitude to Religious Coercion', *JRS* 54 (1964): 107–16.
[75]See Augustine, *Ep.*, 93,17.
[76]Augustine, *Ep.*, 185,21.24.
[77]Idem, *Serm.*, 358,1.

theory contains the germ of the whole system of spiritual despotism, intolerance and persecution, even to the court of the Inquisition. The great authority of his name was often afterward made to justify cruelties from which he himself would have shrunk with horror. Soon after him, Leo the Great, the first representative of consistent, exclusive, universal papacy, advocated even the penalty of death for heresy.[78]

At the same time, however, many bishops defended heretics who suffered from too severe persecution by the imperial authorities. It was so in the case of the Spaniard Priscillian, who was accused of magic, immorality and rigorist teaching and was condemned by councils and rebuffed by the pope and the leading bishops before he was put to death by the civil power. It is thought that Maximus, the usurper, who ordered the execution, hoped that his act would conciliate the orthodox.[79] But the event proved the exact opposite. St Ambrose refused to hold communion with the bishops who had approved the death of Priscillian.[80] St Martin of Tours reprobated both the shedding of the blood of the heretic and the persecution of his followers.[81]

It should also be remembered that, especially in the case of the Arian dispute, both parties triumphed in turns becoming persecutors of each other and considering each other heretical. A special case of persecution of Catholics as heretics is St Athanasius of Alexandria. When in 326 he assumed the Alexandrian bishopric, so great was strife and intolerance from the site of the Arian majority that Athanasius was driven into exile five times during his forty-six years of service as bishop. Under Emperor Constantius, the civil authority was so strongly involved to protect the Arian church that many Orthodox clerics sought refuge in Rome. In 355, at the Synod of Milan, Constantius submitted the Arian creed with the order that those who did not sign should be exiled. By an edict against the Orthodox Catholics, those who refused to communicate with the Arian bishops were deprived of the immunities of ecclesiastics and of the right of Christians. Patriarch Macedonius of Constantinople (fourth century), who was later banished by radical Arians, forcibly opened the mouths of Catholics, forcing them to receive his communion. During the reign of Valens, who became emperor of the East in AD 367 and was at first tolerant, under the influence of radical Arian leaders, the Arian candidates to the bishoprics received the support of civil authorities, and the death of Athanasius was a signal for persecutions in Egypt, in which Valens' ecclesiastical ministers often exceeded the orders, or even the intentions, of the emperor. During this period, depending on the advisers and favour of the ruler, not only were Arians deprived of their places of worship, but Catholics were also forced to give their temples to the Arians, as was the case even in Milan. The next phase of persecution of Catholics as heretics was the barbarian invasion of the fifth century, when the Orthodox, or Latin church, suffered another period of Arian persecution, especially under the

---

[78]See Leo, *Ep.*, XV.
[79]See A. R. Birley, 'Magnus Maximus and the Persecution of Heresy', *BJRL* 1 (1983): 13–43.
[80]See Ambrose, *Ep.*, 30 (24), 12.
[81]See Sulpicius Severus, *chron.*, II 5.

Vandals in Africa.[82] In his persecution of the Catholics, the Vandal leader Hunneric remarked that he was merely following the Imperial Roman edicts against heresy,[83] and indeed they were strongly inspired from anti-Donatist legal measures enacted by the court of Honorius.

CONCLUSION

Various types of persecution of heretics, undertaken with greater or lesser force, only partially fulfilled their task as a means of purifying Christianity of errors and the empire from enemies of public order. Donatism and Arianism were finally overcome, but Nestorianism, Monophysitism, Monothelitism and other heresies replaced them. Nestorianism was stamped out in the empire, but it established itself in Persia and became a great missionary church. Monophysitism, by allying itself in Syria and Egypt with nationalistic opposition to Byzantine domination, survived the empire and exists till this day. Monothelitism was apparently long cherished by the Maronites. Achieving religious unity – which the emperors and bishops strove for – proved to be an extremely difficult task in the first centuries of Christianity. It simply could not be established by force. Sentences of exile, confiscation of property, heavy fines, harassment, the suppression of the right of assembly and even corporal punishment proved ineffective.

BIBLIOGRAPHY

Alexander, C. 'Rethinking Constantine's Interaction with the North African "Donatist" Schism', in E. L. Smither (ed.), *Rethinking Constantine: History, Theology, and Legacy*, 37–90. Eugene, OR: Pickwick Publications, 2014.

Alexander, P. J. 'Religious Persecution and Resistance in the Byzantine Empire of the Eighth and Ninth Centuries: Methods and Justifications', *S* 2 (1977): 238–64.

Barnes, T. D. 'The Conversion of Constantine', *EMC* 4 (1985): 371–91.

Barnes, T. D. 'From Toleration to Repression: The Evolution of Constantine's Religious Policies', *SCI* 21 (2002): 189–207.

Barnes, T. D. *Constantine: Dynasty, Religion and Power in the Later Roman Empire*. Chichester: Wiley-Blackwell, 2011.

Birley, A. R. 'Magnus Maximus and the Persecution of Heresy', *BJRL* 1 (1983): 13–43.

Bralewski, S. 'Polityka Konstantyna Wielkiego wobec arian po soborze w Nicei: nagły zwrot czy kontynuacja?' ['Policy of Constantine the Great towards the Arians after the Council of Nicaea: a sudden turn or continuation?'], *VP* 34–5 (1998): 347–8.

---

[82]See E. Fournier, 'Persecuting Heretics in Late Antique North Africa: Tolerant Vandals and Intolerant Bishops', in *Inclusion and Exclusion in Mediterranean Christianities, 400-800*, eds E. Buchberger and Y. Fox, Cultural Encounters in Late Antiquity and the Middle Ages 25 (Turnhout: Brepols, 2019), pp. 147–66.

[83]See Victor of Vita, *hist. pers.*, III 8-11.

Bralewski, S. 'Uwagi na temat antyheretyckiego ustawodawstwa cesarza Konstantyna Wielkiego' ['Comments on the Anti-heretic Legislation of Emperor Constantine the Great'], *PNH* 1 (2002): 7–20.

Brown, P. *Power and Persuasion in Late Antiquity: Towards a Christian Empire*. Madison: University of Wisconsin Press, 1992.

Brown, P. R. L. 'St. Augustine's Attitude to Religious Coercion', *JRS* 54 (1964): 107–16.

Caron, P. G. 'Ne sanctum baptisma iteretur (CTh. 16.6; CI. 1.6)', *AARC* 6 (1986): 107–80.

Dolbeau, F. 'La *Passio Sancti Donati* (BHL 2303b). Une tentative d'édition critique', in *Memoriam Sanctorum Venerantes: Miscellanea in onore di Monsignor Victor Saxer*, 251–67. Roma: Pontificio Istituto di Archeologia Cristiana, 1992.

Drake, H. A. *Constantine and the Bishops: The Politics of Intolerance*. Baltimore, MD: Johns Hopkins University Press, 2000.

Edwards, M. *Catholicity and Heresy in the Early Church*. Farnham: Routledge, 2009.

Escribano Paño, V. 'La construction de l'image de l'hérétique dans le Code Théodosien XVI', in N. Guinot and F. Richard (eds), *JEmpire chrétien et Église aux IVe et Ve siècles: intégration ou «concordat»? Le témoignage du Code Théodosien*, 389–412. Paris: Éditions du Cerf, 2008.

Fournier, E. 'Persecuting Heretics in Late Antique North Africa: Tolerant Vandals and Intolerant Bishops', in E. Buchberger and Y. Fox (eds), *Inclusion and Exclusion in Mediterranean Christianities*, 400–800. 'Cultural Encounters in Late Antiquity and the Middle Ages' 25. Turnhout: Brepols, 2019.

Frend, W. H. C. *Martyrdom and Persecution in the Early Church: A Study of a Conflict from the Maccabees to Donatus*. New York: Anchor Books, 1967.

Gaddis, M. *There Is No Crime for Those Who Have Christ: Religious Violence in the Christian Roman Empire*. Berkeley: University of California Press, 2005.

Gaudemet, J. 'La législation religieuse de Constantin', *RHEF* 122 (1947): 25–61.

Gherro, S. 'Stato e Chiesa di fronte alla controversia donatista nei primi anni dell'età costantiniana', *SDHI* 36 (1970): 359–409.

Lenski, N. 'Constantine and the Donatists: Exploring the Limits of Religious Toleration', in M. Wallraff (ed.), *Religiöse Toleranz. 1700 Jahre nach dem Edikt von Mailand*, 101–39. Berlin: W. de Gruyter, 2016.

Lenski, N. 'The Significance of the Edict of Milan', in Edward Siecienski (ed.), *Constantine: Religious Faith and Imperial Policy*, 27–56. London: Routledge, 2017.

Lizzi Testa, R. 'Privilegi economici e definizione di status: il caso del vescovo tardoantico', *Atti dell'Accademia nazionale dei Lincei. Classe di scienze morali, storiche e filologiche* (Rendiconti serie 9) 11 (2000): 55–103.

Lizzi Testa, R. 'Te Bishop Vir Venerabilis: Fiscal Privileges and Status Definition in Late Antiquity', *SP* 34 (2001): 125–44.

Maraval, P. *Constantin le Grand. Empereur romain, empereur chrétien (306–337)*. Paris: Tallandier, 2011.

Maraval, P. 'Le devoir religieux des empereurs: de la tolérance à la répression', in M.-F. Baslez (ed.), *Chrétiens persécuteurs. Destructions, exclusions, violences religieuses au IVe sièclei*, 37–62. Paris: Albin Michel, 2014.

Marone, P. 'Some Observations on the Anti-Donatist Legislation', in A. Dupont, M.
    A. Gaumer and M. Lamberigts (eds), *The Uniquely African Controversy: Studies on
    Donatist Christianity*, 71–84. LAHR 9. Leuven, Paris and Bristol: Peeters, 2015.
Norderval, O. 'The Emperor Constantine and Arius: Unity in the Church and Unity in the
    Empire', *STh* 42 (1988): 113–50.
Odahl, C. M. *Constantine and the Christian Empire*. New York: Routledge, 2004.
Ryan, E. A. 'The Problem of Persecution in the Early Church', *ThS* 3 (1944): 310–39.
Shaw, B. D. *Sacred Violence. African Christians and Sectarian Hatred in the Age of
    Augustine*. Cambridge: Cambridge University Press, 2011.
Spagnuolo Vigorita, T. 'Legislazione antidonatista e cronologia agostiniana', *FHI* 8
    (2007): 351–70.
Tilley, M. *Donatist Martyr Stories: The Church in Conflict in Roman North Africa*.
    Liverpool: Liverpool University Press, 1996.

CHAPTER 26

The Western church and its thought-world (major Latin Fathers)

JOHN A. MCGUCKIN

PROEM

This chapter forms a pair with the one that follows. It attempts to provide a generic overview of the intellectual culture, and some of the more salient points of development, of the western, that is, the predominantly Latin-speaking, Christian Churches. Many detailed aspects of life in Western Christianity will have already been noticed more concentratedly in the works of other specialists in this book; and in this respect it would be useful to consider especially Chapter 3 by Piotr Ashwin-Siejkowski on the relations between the church and Graeco-Roman culture in general; Chapters 4 and 5 by Hilaria Ramelli and Ville Vuolanto, respectively, on the place of women in the church and the importance afforded to children and slaves; Chapter 11 by William Tabbernee on the Montanist movement, which, though it began in Phrygia, enjoyed a fertile second wave in Latin North Africa; Chapter 12 on the great North African martyrs Perpetua and Felicitas, who, in a real sense, synopsize that often savage era of persecutions that so marked early Latin Christianity; many of the chapters in Part Three of the book draw out themes common to early Christianity in most of its provinces; and also Chapter 22 on the great councils which, though predominantly held in the church's eastern provinces were, from the outset, adopted by the Western churches as fundamental structures guiding its intellectual heritage.

The present chapter will be chiefly prosopographical and set out to sketch the main features of some of the greatest thinkers writing in Latin, whose work accumulated over the late antique and Early Medieval centuries, to make up the distinctive theological character of the church in the western provinces. The chief figures considered in this chapter were, it can be argued, extraordinary writers and intellectual forces that marked the 'mindset' (what the Greeks would call the *phronema*) of Latin Christianity. The most notable were: the second- to third-century lawyer, Quintus Septimus Florens, commonly known by his moniker 'Tertullian'; a third- to fourth-century writer who formed Constantine's Christian sensibility and was the master-rhetorician of the age, that is, Lactantius; in addition, the West's fifth-century towering spiritual and systematic theologian Augustine; and lastly the massively influential Pope Gregory I in the late sixth century, known to history as Gregory the Great.[1] Three of the four were from Africa which, together with Rome itself, formed the real epicentres of early Latin Christianity.

To attempt to portray a coherent picture, as we survey such a large period of time and over such a vast territory (that stretches, in the east, from the regions of Scythia by the Black Sea, or the Adriatic countries facing the eastern shores of Italy, even to Ireland's western coast; and in the North from the chill monasteries of Scotland and Scandinavia, to the burning sands of Morocco), it shall be inevitable that this treatment will leave much out and can treat its main characters only in an introductory fashion. The suggested reading in the notes and bibliography will indicate supplemental reading for those, perhaps, who would like to go further and deeper.

LATIN NORTH AFRICA

The Apologists

The state persecutions of Christianity affected the North African church in particularly savage forms. From an early stage they marked the African ecclesial sensibility as a 'church of martyrs'. The renowned story of the deaths of Perpetua and Felicity, in the early third century, gives a vivid sense of this in highly dramatic form, as (more intellectually) does the *Address to the Martyrs* by Tertullian.[2] The shock of this experience of both state and mob violence against the new religion produced a series of skilled Christian intellectuals writing across several generations, who collectively have come to be known as the 'Apologists'.[3] Several major writers in this category were Greek,[4] of course, but the North African littoral produced more than its fair share, and these writers shaped Latin Christianity internationally, giving it a very practical character, not to say legal cast, being some of the first theologians to reflect at length about the new faith and its relation to society: writers such as Tertullian of Carthage (ca. 155–240), the Berber lawyer Minucius Felix (d. 250), the

---

[1]And in the East (where he spent the years 579–85 as papal ambassador (*apocrisarios*) to Constantinople) known as Gregory the Dialogist, from the title of one of his most popular books.

[2]T. J. Heffernan, *The Passion of Perpetua and Felicity* (Oxford: Oxford University Press, 2012); discussed further in T. D. Barnes, *Tertullian: An Historical and Literal Study* (Oxford: Oxford University Press, 1973).

[3]See, R. M. Grant, *The Greek Apologists of the Second Century* (London: SCM Press, 1988); N. L. Thomas, *Defending Christ: The Latin Apologists before Augustine* (Turnhout: Brepols, 2011); J. Engberg, A. C. Jacobsen and J. Ulrich (eds), *Defence of Christianity: Early Christian Apologists* (New York: Peter Lang, 2014).

[4]In the third century Clement and Origen of Alexandria are among the greatest, already exceeding the category of simple apologists, but there are also Aristides, Athenagoras, Justin, Tatian and Theophilus of Antioch.

professor of rhetoric Arnobius (ca. 255–330) and the philosopher and litterateur Lactantius (ca. 250–325). The tradition of apologia reaches a zenith in the opening books of Augustine's *De Civitate Dei*, published in 426, where he summarizes his predecessors' sharp satires on the cruelty and narrow self-centredness of Roman imperial ambitions. The fact that almost all the Latin Apologists were lawyers by training and profession sets a tone for much of Latin systematics (the redemption, often cast in legal terms of justification and penalty), ethics (as conceived as part of the social contract) and political validity (Christ's pastoral dominion contrasted with the claims of earthly powers who have so often proved to be predatory).

Tertullian

Tertullian did not just write but composed a veritable library of theological and apologetic works, and, as he went, he forged a new Christian vocabulary for terms and concepts that did not exist in previous Latin (pagan) literature.[5] He has rightly been called 'the first theologian' of the Western church. He is a strong and relentless opponent of injustice and learnt the pugnacity, which often appears in his texts when writing against those he considers dangerous perverters of the Christian tradition, from his career as prosecutor (and defender) in the Roman law-courts. His sharpening of the idea of 'heresy'[6] in early Christianity had a long-lasting influence on the attitudes of the Latin church. As an adult convert trying to make sense of the whole body of Christian belief once he had entered the church, Tertullian realized that he was faced with numerous internal dissonances. This made it difficult for him, in terms of the establishment of a coherent and recognizable body of Christian teaching (its presentation to others as a distinctive and attractive 'school of thought').

As a result he applied the concept of 'Prescription'. This is a technical legal argument that only allows people to appear in a legal case if they are legitimate representatives of the corporations who are presently in dispute. 'Christian dissidents', Tertullian maintained, had so departed from the evangelical and ecclesial tradition that they no longer had the right to designate themselves as Christian representatives at all. So, while he could quickly describe the heretical position for his readers, he did not need to take it deeply into account since de facto it had lost the right to be considered part of the Christian fabric of teaching. He applied this concept of the 'prescription of heresy'[7] like a chisel, not simply to present a closed mind to opponents (as some have suggested) but rather to carve out of the lump of plaster the strong lineaments of a discrete school of statements that could be

---

[5]A very readable introduction is that by Eric Osborn, *Tertullian: First Theologian of the West* (Cambridge: Cambridge University Press, 1997).

[6]*Haeresis* in pre-Christian Greek thought had meant originally a divergence of opinion between philosophical schools: something that stimulated further enquiries to establish a normative position. Beginning in the Johannine Epistles, the concept of internal divisions progressively took on a darker aspect in the church as a morally reprehensible departure from the truth.

[7]Most fully set out in his treatise of that title: *De Praescriptione Haereticorum: On the Prescription of Heretics.*

identified as the core Christian response to all manner of questions on which there were no explicit Gospel *dicta*.

This argument shaped many centuries of later exegesis of the Latin scriptures. In arguing the case, Tertullian implicitly appealed to the law that allowed an injunction to be taken out against those who illegitimately took to themselves the rights or property of others. Tertullian's contention was that the heretics had stolen the scriptures that rightly belonged only to the church and then twisted them (stolen copyright we might even say) in order to make up a spurious product of their own from out of the mix and then had set out to 'pretend' (by false representation) this was Christian in order to attract buyers. Tertullian's very sharp lawyer's mind placed an order (a taxonomy) over so much of the earliest forms of Latin Christian systematic thinking, that the legal cast endured for generations to follow.

His writings were so encyclopedic in scope, and so valued by his successors in the Latin church, that his reputation remained unusually high for many centuries, until eventually Augustine superseded him. Even so, his long influence over the phrasing of Latin theology can still be seen in the aftermath of Augustine's era, when Pope Leo the Great fuses much of his work together with that of Augustine, so as to make up the definitive statement of fifth-century Roman Christology which he published as *Leo's Tome*.

Tertullian was the son of a pagan centurion and, before his conversion, knew the pagan traditions intimately. He entered the church probably in middle age, and some accounts (Jerome's *De Viris Illlustribus* 53 is the source of them) say that he became a presbyter of the church. His facility in both Greek and Latin made Tertullian one of the first thinkers to be able to have a grasp of the international shape of Christian thought, and, in the process, he became an important proponent of the ascendant Logos theology (which would distinguish the persons of the Trinity within the Unity of God) that was pitting itself against the more archaic Monarchian tradition (a monist view of God) then prevalent in Rome under Pope Callixtus (pope 218–22).

One of Tertullian's major works, which sets down the terms of Logos theology and sketches out the Trinitarian theology, is titled *Against Praxeas*. Rather than being the name of an individual, it is probably a reference to Pope Callixtus himself (the word means 'Busybody'), whose confused thinking about the Father's relation to the Son, Tertullian characterizes as 'Patripassianism'. (He accused him of making the Father suffer on the cross, thus caricaturing him as a ridiculous thinker.)

Many of Tertullian's modern readers (especially women, to whom in his writings he represents the stern face of the Christian *paterfamilias*) find his sarcastic and withering style very off-putting. He was a practitioner of that common ancient style of apologetics that decided that any ridiculous implication that one could feasibly draw from an opponent's position could legitimately be attributed to them: and so, much caution is needed when reading his attacks, so as not to imagine that he actually describes faithfully what they originally said on any controverted point. When he is not engaged in full-scale assault, he shows himself a very reflective and considered thinker, possessed of a highly refined intelligence.

As a writer, Tertullian was the master of the terse aphorism, and many of his *sententiae* have been passed down with admiration even into the modern church. Warning the authorities that their persecution policy was futile, he said:[8] 'The blood of Christians is seed' for the church. Speaking of the mystery of 'why on earth?' God would reveal himself in the crucified and resurrected Christ, he argued:[9] 'I am more inclined to believe it precisely because it is so inappropriate' (*prorsus credibile est, quia ineptum est*). This was repackaged by Renaissance apologists in the more familiar form of: 'I believe because it is absurd' (*Credo quia absurdum est*). Tertullian here not only answered the mockery of the Resurrection in the Roman world but also underlined how often human cleverness is distanced from the mysterious humility of God's revelation. Scornfully dismissing the ridicule of contemporary philosophers for the Christian movement, he replied: 'What has Athens to do with Jerusalem?'[10] And in an appendix to his *Apologeticus* (chapter 17) where he considers the best of pagan instinctive reactions to the thought of God, he argued that the human heart is, in itself, an instinctual witness to the divine presence, and so he makes the bold apologetic statement:[11] 'The Soul is naturally Christian.'

From around 205 onwards his writings[12] show an increasing respect for so-called 'Montanist' ideas:[13] their liveliness of spirituality and vivid sense of the inner workings of the Holy Spirit in the day-to-day life of believers; a more vivid sense of eschatology; and a decidedly rigorist attitude in dealing with sinful lapses in the body of the faithful.[14] There has been a long-running controversy as to whether he did, or did not, join the dissident Montanist movement in later life, with Jerome claiming in *De Viris Illustribus* 53, that he 'lapsed' to the Montanists and recent studies tending to suggest this is anachronistically mistaken.

The style of Montanism as it was then influential in North Africa was a very moderated form of the original Asia-Minor movement, and certainly, there is no evidence that Tertullian ever broke away from the catholic community whose integrity he had always defended so acutely, and whose unity he had always valued as a priority. His so-called Montanist works simply record the rigorist condition of the North African church in his own age, which later generations looked back on as too severe.

---

[8]Tertullian. *Apol.*, 13. *Plures efficimur, quitiens metimur a vobis: semen est sanguis Christianorum.*

[9]Tertullian. *Carn.*, 10.

[10]Tertullian, *Prescr.*, 7.9.

[11]Tertullian, *Apol.*, 17.6; literally: *O testimonium animae naturaliter christianae.*

[12](*On Monogamy, Exhortation to Chastity, On Fasting, On Modesty*).

[13]Further, see Chapter 11 in this book, by William Tabbernee.

[14]His *On Modesty* (*De Pudicitia*) was written in a state of furious disbelief that the Roman Pope Callixtus had decided to allow the reconciliation of believers convicted of serious sexual offences: and worse, that the bishop of Carthage was presently considering allowing the same process. In his treatise *De Paenitentia* 7, & 9–10 Tertullian had, with great reluctance, acknowledged that one 'second repentance' is possible (he means after the remission of sins given in baptism) if it was supported by the adoption of a life of severe penance involving long prayers, fasting, prostration before the presbyters in the churches and finally a special prayer of intercession before God from the church community.

Tertullian's *Apologeticus* is perhaps his major work, written ca. 197, where he makes a passionate appeal for legal toleration of Christianity and argues that Roman state's claim that its hostility to the church is a religious position is totally deluded, since religion without morality is a blasphemy. In this work (and conscious that Roman law made any crime against religion high treason not needing a formal trial to initiate the death sentence) Tertullian makes an eloquent defence of the inalienable principles of freedom of conscience and generous toleration of religious observances. It was always remembered in the church, but unfortunately not always observed once the political power balance had been redressed.

The *De Praescriptione*, which we have already noticed, is also a major treatise. But Tertullian also wrote numerous other short studies on moral themes addressed to a Christian audience, and almost each of them (*On Attending the Theatre, On Military Service, On Idolatry, On Penance*) had the impact of a 'first consideration of the problem', which established a long-lasting set of traditions in the church. In these moral works he consistently warns believers about the dangers of cultural assimilation with a pagan society, which is profoundly, and often unconsciously, immersed in idolatrous and immoral attitudes. He particularly stands opposed to Christians entering the military as a career choice: largely because of the requirement, attendant on any Roman soldier, so often to worship the imperial *genius*,[15] though he argues also from a genuine conviction that such a life is contrary to the Gospel of peace.

Christian Gnostics at Rome, who formed a lively and variegated school, were a consistent object of his attack, and Tertullian produced a series of books against Gnostics and Marcionites, whom he considered the greatest dissident threat to Christianity in his day (*Against Marcion, Against Hermogenes, On the Resurrection of the Dead, On the Flesh of Christ*). In these works his dominant idea is to stand against spiritualizing the Gospel into abstractions. Christ's incarnation, he argues, was a true material reality and a movement from the part of God to the world which vindicated the essential goodness of the material world and gave the promise of true resurrection to believers.

Tertullian's writings on Christ, set in the overall context of his Logos theology (he knew Hippolytus at Rome and admired him), not only established the foundations of what would be the long-term Latin theology of the Trinity but also set Latin Christological thinking on a very long and specific trajectory, for Tertullian applied legal categories to the central Christological problem of the nature of the Incarnate Lord as both human and divine. His approach described the 'two natures' in the sense of legal possessions. Christ's single person is the legal owner of both sets of attributes: they are equally his but his single possession does not make him twofold as a subject. This way of setting out the issues of Christological personalism would come into crisis in the fifth century when *Leo's Tome* placed it in dialogue with the Christology of the Alexandrian Church. Even so, all of the major Latin writers

---

[15]On payday each Roman soldier was expected to offer grain of incense to the Imperial *genius* after he collected his *peculium*.

who followed him, particularly Cyprian, Lactantius and Augustine, venerated the memory of Tertullian, even when they set out to adapt and reconfigure his work.

Cyprian

Cyprian of Carthage (ca. 200–58) was another figure of the early Latin tradition who exercised a shaping and long-lasting influence: this time chiefly on the church's polity more than its doctrine. His advent to the church came when he was forty-five years old. He had been one of the high ranking and most successful lawyers in the North African capital of Carthage, and he had taken notice of the vilification endured by the Christians in his town and exercised sufficient independence of mind to conclude that it was unjustified. He had friendly relations with the Carthaginian presbyter Caecilius, who eventually persuaded him that, to fulfil his monotheistic philosophy, he ought to convert: and so he was duly baptized.

On his conversion, Cyprian gave away the large part of his considerable fortune for the service of the poor and was soon enrolled as a presbyter himself. Only three years later the office of the metropolitan bishop of Carthage became vacant and widespread popular acclaim shouted for Cyprian to be consecrated. His political astuteness made the faithful feel secure in an atmosphere of increasing hostility against them. However, several members of the bench of presbyters looked on his election unfavourably, regarding him as insufficiently proven, and not well enough instructed in the Christian faith. In fact, most of his writings on theology and polity are exercises in informing himself as to correct procedure, assisted by the counsel of Caecilius. He also approaches the scriptures as a new reader, intent on applying traditional Roman methods of exegesis to draw out moral lessons for his audience.[16] Cyprian taught the entire Latin church after him how to approach the homily.

His infant administration was overturned in 250 by the crisis of the persecution of the emperor Decius, who insisted on making all citizens offer sacrifice to the gods. Reading that Jesus himself had advised withdrawal in times of persecution,[17] Cyprian went into hiding, knowing that he was a marked man as far as the authorities were concerned, but keeping in touch with the church from his seclusion. The North African church, however, had a fierce tradition from generations beforehand that martyrdom was a gift from God that, if offered, ought never to be spurned, and many in the Christian community judged him harshly because of his flight. After emerging in the time of peace, he composed an apologia to justify himself; but his authority had been shaken and several of his critic presbyters made things difficult for him.

When the church settled down once more, many of those who had either offered sacrifice, either under duress or because they were simply afraid (the *sacrificati*), or craftily bought the certificate to pretend they had sacrificed (the *libellatici*) wanted

---

[16]Further, see M. A. Fahey, *Cyprian and the Bible: A Study in 3rd Century Exegesis* (Tubingen: Mohr, 1971).
[17]Matt. 10.23.

to come back and resume Christian community life. The bishop, being primarily in charge of all liturgical matters, was faced with the question of whether they could be admitted. At the time, as Tertullian's attitude in the earlier generation had shown,[18] the view was prevalent that the church was quintessentially a community of the saints worshipping God in purity: and that the presence of serious sin in its midst was impossible. Therefore, if a member sinned greatly (murder, adultery and apostasy were regarded as the three greatest sins), he or she had definitively ended their baptismal consecration and could not be re-baptized.

It was a question that went to the heart of Christian belonging in an age when structures of penance had not yet been clearly elaborated. Hearing that the Roman Pope was inclined to judge those who had lapsed in the persecution in varying degrees of severity, according to the pressures they were under, he canvassed opinion in Carthage and found that some renowned faithful believers who had suffered in the troubles but survived (known as 'Confessors') were prophetically claiming the God-given right to readmit penitents to communion in worship. Cyprian vetoed the confessors' judgement (causing more murmurs against himself) and decreed that the lapsed had to observe many years of penance before thinking of taking communion again. The threat of a new persecution under Gallus, the following year, made him change his mind on this and he allowed a general reconciliation. That threat never materialized, but soon the dissension among the ranks of his clergy focused on the matter of who had higher authority in the community: the institutional episcopal administrator or the charismatic confessors? In the aftermath of the Decian persecution the Roman church too was caught up in dissensions over how, if at all, the lapsed ought to be readmitted. The rigorist anti-pope Novatian stood against the more lenient pope Cornelius and initiated a great controversy over how valid were the sacraments administered by heretical or schismatic clergy. Cyprian and his African church were drawn into the fight between 255 and 257, and a war of letters opened up between Cyprian and Pope Stephen, on this issue and over the question of the rights of their mutual sees. Cyprian's dissident clergy broke out into open revolt and declared they had elected a new bishop, Fortunatus, to replace him.

This partly explains why Cyprian contradicted the more lenient view of Stephen[19] (schismatic clergy might be in the wrong but the validity of the sacraments was so powerful in and of themselves that they were nevertheless valid at their hands) and instead declared that anyone lapsing from the unity of the church, proven by a personal union with the local bishop, had lost all claim to Christianity, had lost the gift of the Spirit and (if they were clergy) could in no way communicate grace through the sacraments. Schismatic ordinations were thus entirely null and void. Rome censured him for this view, and, indeed, though his position was later to be greatly diluted by Augustine (who had to consider the issue once more in the context of the Donatist crisis), his views had a more long-lasting influence on the eastern

---

[18]Tertullian, *De Paenitentia*.
[19]In a treatise entitled *On the Lapsed* (*De Lapsis*).

church. Cyprian's treatise on this topic, *On the Unity of the Church*,[20] became one of the most-read Latin patristic writings outside the corpus of Augustine, becoming a foundation of Latin ecclesiology.

In 257 the emperor Valerian issued a new edict demanding sacrifice from citizens, and this time Cyprian stayed put in Carthage. He was arrested, sent into exile, and a year later (since he refused to cooperate with the authorities) he was brought for a hearing in Carthage and in 258 was ordered to be beheaded by the Proconsul Galerius Maximus. His martyr's death sealed his authoritative standing.

Cyprian's literary skill is very evident in his most valuable collection of *Letters* (*Epistulae*), which are one of the most precious historical resources about life in the third-century church. In a real sense his coming late to the church, and being thrust so soon afterwards into the spotlight as episcopal teacher and administrator, meant that his theology was 'learned on the job', as it were. He composed some general treatises pleading for toleration of the Christian faith;[21] and also some interesting short works for internal consumption: *On the Lord's Prayer*, *On Almsgiving* and *On the Veiling of Virgins*. The treatise *To Quirinus*, was listed among his works but in reality is a surviving, and very antique, book of scriptural testimonies that he must have used to construct his sermons. It is a precious resource showing us the Christian approaches to oracular scripture from at least the second century.

Lactantius

Lucius Caecilius Firmianus was a native of North Africa from near the town of Cirta. He was known by his *cognomen*, or nickname, as Lactantius ('milky') though what this once referred to is no longer obvious. He has been designated in later Christian history as the 'Christian Cicero' not only because he absorbed, Christianized and made many aspects of Cicero's thought capable of wide reception in the later church but also because, of all the ecclesiastical figures writing in Latin, his is the purest style and bears comparison with the ancient greats. It was his work that paved the way for Augustine's concept in his *De Civitate Dei*, of baptizing Roman culture rather than anathematizing it out of hand. In the Renaissance Lactantius' works were among the first to be printed in Europe[22] and were widely appreciated for their style. His account of Constantine's 'dream' before the battle of the Milvian Bridge became immensely famous in Christian literature and was regularly depicted in art.

Lactantius trained as a highly successful rhetorician and lawyer and was so renowned for his literary skill that he drew the attention of Diocletian's imperial court and, in 300, was invited to fill the professorship of rhetoric at Nicomedia. There he made it known that he was a Christian and attracted the enmity (as he had earlier the bitter rivalry) of another rhetor, Sossianus Hierocles, who would

---

[20]*De Unitate Ecclesiae Catholicae*. Further see: P. B. Hinchcliff, *Cyprian of Carthage and the Unity of the Christian Church* (London: Chapman, 1974); also: M. M. Sage, *Cyprian*, Patristic Monograph Series, 1 (Cambridge, MA: Philadelphia Patristic Foundation, 1975).

[21]*To Donatus*, and *To Demetrianus*.

[22]Aldo Manutius brought out an edition in 1535, and Claude Garamont followed suit in 1545.

eventually denounce him when Diocletian began his persecution by purging the court of Christians. In 303, Diocletian burned down the church building there, and it was this time that Lactantius fled westwards. He did this in the company of his chief student: no less than Constantine who had been held hostage in Nicomedia and who, with the hostilities announced by Diocletian and fomented by Galerius, realized that his own hopes to succeed his father, the Caesar Constantius Chlorus, were not to be permitted.

Constantine and Lactantius moved first to Trier, and then the younger man joined his father in York and was present when Constantius' troops mourned his death. They then elevated his son on the shield, claiming for him the purple, and thus initiating the Roman Civil War that would eventually leave Constantine the monarchical ruler of the empire. At Trier, the emperor again chose Lactantius to be the tutor of his son the Caesar Crispus. Many of the legal and philosophical reflections of Lactantius appear to have influenced Constantine: not least his notion of a Golden Age that God's Christ has opened up in the rule of the enlightened philosopher emperor.[23] It is something that Eusebius of Caesarea, a new court rhetor for a new age, would develop more fulsomely.

Lactantius also has speculations on how the aspirations of all world religions towards moral improvement and intellectual sophistication were met and elevated in the Christian faith. He draws in testimonies to Christ from the Hermetic literature, the Sibyllines and the myth of the Phoenix, whose story he retells in elegant poetic form as a symbol of the resurrection of Christ.[24] His sense that Christ is the refiner of Roman culture, not its destroyer, appealed to the emperor and in many senses became a code by which the latter lived as self-styled 'bishop of those outside the church'.

Lactantius is a major historical source for the fourth-century persecutions, and in his work *On the Deaths of the Persecutors*, he organizes his account of world history around the notion that God's providential plan always stirs up wicked rulers, as agents of Satan, who will always try to suppress the spread of the Kingdom of God but can never prevail. His literary plan is taken from the books of Kings, and his role as a propagandist for Constantine is obvious, but there is considerable theological talent at work here: for he is one of the first, in the West, who understood the scriptures not simply to be a scattered library of religious texts but, as Origen had seen, rather as an interrelated set of mystical oracles (like the Roman Sibyllines) giving insight into histories past and things destined to come. His is a highly eschatological vision of culture.

---

[23]See further: E. De Palma-Digeser, *The Making of a Christian Empire: Lactantius and Rome* (Ithaca, NY: Cornell University Press, 2000). There is an extensive online Lactantius – bibliography available at: https ://www.carleton.edu/classics/overview/history/lactantius/

[24]Text in E. Flintoff (trans.), *The Phoenix* (with introduction by J. A. McGuckin) (Bath: Old School Press, 1995); M. Roberts, 'Lactantius's Phoenix and Late Latin Poetics', in *The Poetics of Late Latin Literature*, eds J. Elsner and J. H. Lobato (Oxford: Oxford University Press, 2017).

He is also arguably the first of the Latin theologians to compose a systematic theology. This he does in his magnum opus, the seven books of *The Divine Institutes*. These are a curious and enigmatic set of arguments. Although written on the eve of the Council of Nicaea, they hardly seem to reference the real life of the churches at all. There is little to no mention of the realities of church organization, offices or sacraments. This is probably explicable in that they were surely addressed to the rather narrow audience he had in mind: the educated class of Roman pagan nobility, outside the church. His writing was, in a sense, both a robust *apologia* for Christianity which had been attacked by an imperial administration that he saw as corrupt and illegitimate, and also a presentation of that same religion as the 'natural' next step for those who were attracted by the newly emergent monotheistic cults of the Sun-God, Hermes Trismegistus and the like: but also ready for a faith that had a vital social programme in mind.

Lactantius presents a picture of the ancient world trapped in two systems of inquiry that had become paralysed and inert. The first was religion; the second was philosophy. Both systems had tried, in different ways, to make a pathway to the truth and to find the universal answer to human existence by its ascent. One had walked the road of *pietas*, that central Roman virtue which literary society placed at the core of all civilization. But, though beginning with reverence for the divine, Lactantius says, Roman religion degenerated into the cults of warlords (he relies on Euhemerus' deconstruction of the cult of the gods) and eventually became not merely polytheistic but also bloody and degenerative. *Pietas* was lost in the loss of religious simplicity, and the worst state of all was when bloodthirsty demons (posing as gods) stimulated the cupidity of Romans to enslave the world and call it peace.

There were those who turned from this road of false cults and tried to find the truth by reason. The philosophers, he argues, have also lost the path to truth by becoming so relativistic that no school of philosophy can claim any certainty and all conflict among themselves. He has a memorable axiom to illustrate this: 'Plato did not know God, he only had vague dreams about him.'[25] For Lactantius Christ came to earth as the supreme High-Priest-Philosopher, to make the reconciliation of the failed aspirations of both religion and philosophy, now reconciled in his own person. He who is the Eternal Wisdom offers himself as a priestly sacrifice to the *Summus Deus*, to atone and heal the fragmentations of ancient society and to set it on the road to a renovation leading to the Golden Age. Since Christ, he argues, is the supreme *Doctor* and *Sacerdos*, the High Priest and Teacher of ethics, the worship of this God is 'full and perfect prudence'.[26] Such worship is entirely a service of the mind[27] and synonymous with moral behaviour, since 'To serve God means nothing

---

[25]'Plato, indeed, spoke many things respecting the one God, by whom he said that the world was framed; but he spoke nothing respecting religion: for he only dreamed of God, but he had never known Him': *non cognovit deum solum somniavit de eo*; Lactantius, *Divine Institutes*. 5.15; see too, A. Kurfess, 'Lactantius und Plato', *Philologus* 78 (1923): 381–92.

[26]D.I. 2.5.3; also D.I. 2.8.71.

[27]D.I. 6.9.1.

else than to fulfil good works and observe just lifestyles'.[28] At the same time as Christ teaches humans to live justly, so he is instructing them in the true worship of God, showing that He is at one and the same moment Priest and Philosopher.[29]

It is both an unusual and vastly capacious model: the style of apologetics perhaps designed to appeal to a large contingent of educated and capable men and women outside the church who now knew which way the wind was blowing after Constantine made Christianity his 'most favoured' religion.[30] At the same time, this perhaps made Lactantius' thought, and appeal, quite limited to his own generation. After his death, sometime before the Council of Nicaea, the church definitively left his theology, and his inclusivist attitudes, far behind,[31] even as later Latin writers reproduced his works as examples of good apologetic from someone Augustine had called 'one of our old good men of faith'.

Augustine

When, in the year 386, Augustine (354–430) re-converted to the Catholic faith,[32] after a youthful dalliance with Manicheism[33] two spurs had brought him back; the first was relief that a scholar such as Ambrose of Milan (ca. 340–97)[34] could show the scriptures to be capable of serious philosophical exegesis (Augustine had been ashamed of them as a young professor); the second was the closeness, as he saw, of many aspects of Christianity's metaphysics to Neoplatonic ideas, yet improving on the latter in terms of its sense of divine nearness and its social compassion. These early insights of his work as a theologian marked him for all the rest of his life. He is at one and the same time a profoundly scripture-based thinker (offering deep commentaries as well as wealth of homiletic material) and a highly grounded pastor-bishop.

---

[28]D.I. 3.9.14-15.
[29]V. Loi, *Lattanzio nella storia del linguaggio e del pensiero teologico pre-niceno* (Rome: Citta Nuova, 1970), pp. 259–60. 'La redenzione operata dal Cristo e, per Lattanzio, essenzialmente un "magisterium": il Figlio di Dio si e incarnato per essere maestro dell' umanita mediante la rivelazione dei misteri divini e per illuminare le menti umane con la luce della sapienza divina.'
[30]See: J. A. McGuckin, 'The Problem of Lactantius the Theologian', in *The Classical or Christian Lactantius?* eds M. Vinzent and O. Nicholson (Studia Patristica. LXXX – vol. 6: Papers presented at the Seventeenth International Conference on Patristic Studies, Oxford, 2015; Leuven: Peeters, 2018), pp. 17–34.
[31]He has, what seemed to the Nicene generation, 'antiquarian' remnants of thought; such as a binitarian theology, Chiliasm and Angel-Christology. Further, see: J. A. McGuckin, 'The Christology of Lactantius', *SP* 17 (Oxford, 1982): 813–20; idem, 'The Non-Cyprianic Scripture Texts in Lactantius' Divine Institutes', *VCh* 36 (1982) 145–63; idem, 'Spirit Christology: Lactantius and His Sources', *HeyJ* 24 (1983): 141–8; idem, *Lactantius as Theologian: An Angelic Christology on the Eve of Nicaea. Rivista di Storia e Letteratura Religiosa* (Firenze) 22, no. 3 (1986): 492–7.
[32]Further see: J. A. McGuckin, 'The Enigma of Augustine's Conversion: Sept. AD 386', *Clergy Review* 72, no. 8 (September 1986): 315–25.
[33]Between 377 and 386.
[34]Ambrose's priest Simplicianus was also an important mentor, as too was the example of the sensational conversion (ca. 355) of the renowned Neo-Platonist Gaius Marius Victorinus.

Augustine was unquestionably the greatest intelligence the Western church had yet seen, but he also brought into his capacious writings a deep sense of compassionate humanity,[35] and this too marked much of Latin theology after him. His intelligence is all the more impressive when one considers the limited libraries that were available to him in his North African see. In the Western church he occupies the towering position of influence that Origen commanded in the East. He knows the major writers of the Latin church's past but is also aware that they are now an archaic corpus that needs radical refurbishment. His own work (much of it 'occasional' in the sense that a busy provincial bishop had to respond to many local and some international crises) was consciously designed to offer a definitive and practical set of responses to that problem of *renovatio*.

Augustine's life story, presented with great literary skill as an individual example of salvation history, is one of the most well known in all ancient history because of the *Confessions* that he wrote.[36] In modern times his own *vita* has been matched by three equally fine studies contextualizing him and his thought.[37] After leaving Milan, where he was baptized by Ambrose, and spending some time in Rome, where his mother Monnica died, Augustine returned to North Africa in 388 and set up residence in a villa at Thagaste[38] with his son Adeodatus[39] gathering round him a small collegium of friends, several of whom remained with him for years, as his religious community. His plans to live a retired scholarly life were overthrown when, entering the local seaport of Hippo Regius one day, the local Christians seized him and forcibly held him down while he was ordained presbyter by Bishop Valerius. He accepted this initiation into the clergy gracefully and so began a long career as a preacher and exegete. In 395 he was consecrated auxiliary bishop and soon after became Valerius' successor.

Several North African bishops held his promotion in suspicion. (He was known to have fathered a child, and he had renounced his catholic faith in Carthage and joined the Manichees, and even decided to be baptized elsewhere – thus avoiding the strict programme of life-scrutinies traditional in African baptismal preparation). His elevation seemed to them to weaken catholic credibility in the face of the rigorist schismatic group of Donatist bishops that divided them. So, his early work was largely determined to establish himself. He composed treatises against the

---

[35]The Medieval church adopted the burning heart as his saintly, symbolic, device.

[36]See F. van Fleteren, 'Confessiones', in *Augustine through the Ages: An Encyclopedia*, ed. A. D. Fitzgerald (Grand Rapids, MI: Eerdmans, 1999), pp. 227–32.

[37]P. Brown, *Augustine of Hippo: A Biography* (Berkeley: University of California Press, 1967); G. Bonner, *St Augustine of Hippo: Life and Controversies* (London: SCM Press, 1963); and Fitzgerald (ed.), *Augustine through the Ages*.

[38]Soukh Ahras in modern-day Algeria. It was a Romano-Berber town, Augustine's birthplace, inland from Hippo.

[39]He never mentions the name of the child's mother, a concubine with whom he had lived for fifteen years (and was persuaded to send back to Africa before his baptism) but spoke of her kindly in later life as a bishop, noting (wistfully?) that she never loved or married another after him.

Manichees, wrote his own scrutinies (in the brilliant form of the *Confessions*) and then set to meet the Donatist schism head on.

These were a group of arch-conservatives who, emerging from the disruption of the third-century persecutions, held fast to the old Cyprianic view that a schismatic or unworthy minister could not be regarded as conveying any sacramental grace at all. One of the implications of this was the way they pointed the finger at bishops they thought had 'wobbled' during the times of pressure, and so they refused to accept any of their subsequent ordinations. This brought chaos into the hierarchical structure of the North African Church. Augustine's work on these lines would soon form the basic substructure of all western catholic ideas of sacramentality and ecclesial legitimacy. Against the narrow rigorism of the Donatist 'pure church' position, he argued the church was both a heavenly and earthly body (a synthesis like Christ himself of spirit and flesh). It could, therefore, contain good and bad elements, but its essential core was indefectible in that it would never be abandoned by its Lord and even when erring, would be brought back to salvation. Unworthy ministers, he concluded, could be sinners and yet still indefectibly convey the inherent power and grace of the sacraments.

Augustine was opposed, at first, to the application of legal strictures against dissident bishops and laity (there was much opposition to the Catholics in the rural regions), but after acts of violence against him and his clergy, he reluctantly admitted the utility of appealing for help to the emperor's military. He applied to this end the parable statement: 'Compel them to come in' (Lk. 14.23). It would be an example, sadly appealed to far too often, in later ages when it developed into the theory of the church's 'secular arm'. Even so, his general thinking about the Donatist issues led to his elaboration of a profound theology of grace and its effects which not only dominated all his later thought but became constitutive of one of the most fundamental themes of wider Latin theology.[40]

Augustine regarded humanity as having nothing at all on which it could base its salvation: all was a free gift of God. Left to itself, Humanity could only slip into the slavery of sin and corruption. These ideas were set out by Augustine as a theology of praise for God's merciful providence, but in later, more negative, readings of his legacy, the pessimistic tone predominated in an unbalanced way. In this sense, Augustine underlined a certain pessimistic tendency in Latin theology to focus on the notions of Original Sin, the corruption of the material world and humanity's ever-present tendency to depravity.

His greatest works, standing alongside his *Confessions* as classics of world literature, were his *City of God* and *On The Trinity*. He wrote the first between 412 and 427 in the aftermath of Alaric's sack of Rome (410), which many pagan critics laid to the door of Christian weakness in governance. In the work he begins with a radical critique of pagan Rome's political cruelty and then moves on to consider what Christian polity might be: and how the religion of Christ considers

---

[40]Further, see J. Patout Burns, 'Grace', in Fitzgerald (ed.), *Augustine Through the Ages*, pp. 391–8.

the concept of civilization. Two 'cities' that of the world, and that of God, are contrasted: moral corruption and ethical purity. The church stands in the world as the witness to mercy and reconciliation, given the destiny to guide civilization to its heavenly destiny: a goal which earthly greed and ambition will always try to subvert.

He composed the monumental *De Trinitate* between 399 and 419. Here Augustine constructs a major anti-Arian apologetic around the Nicene faith in Christology and Pneumatology. He demonstrates, from a wide variety of triadic cosmic and psychological[41] patterns, the reasonableness of the doctrine of three divine persons subsisting in one single nature. In his spiritual writings Augustine demonstrates a very attractive heart-centred affectivity that captivated many disciples in later history. Here, only a few of his large number of compositions can be noticed individually, but some of those which had the most far-reaching effects were the following: the *De Doctrina Christiana* laid out his philosophy of exegesis; the *De Bono Conjugali* argued (somewhat reluctantly) for the intrinsic holiness of sexuality in marriage but even so lukewarm a defence served, importantly, to de-fuse Jerome's deeply hostile opinions; the *De Peccatorum Meritis et Remissione* and the *De Natura et Gratia* both demonstrate the reliance on God at the heart of his theology of grace, and why Pelagianism is so corrupting a theory; the *Enchiridion* is a short reference handbook of theology that soon became a clerical 'ready-reckoner'. His greatest exegetical works are perhaps his *124 Tractates on the Gospel of John* and his *Commentary on the Text of Genesis*. His eloquent *Commentary on the Psalms* (*Enarrationes in Psalmos*) demonstrates his deep love for them as prayers. When he lay dying, he instructed his friend Possidius to inscribe Psaltic verses in large letters on his bedroom wall.

By the time of his death, on 28 August 430, his literary corpus was seen as so authoritative and so all-encompassing that it more or less took the oxygen out of most other theological writings for centuries to come. This was a tendency that would be accelerated by one of his most fervent later disciples: Pope Gregory the Great.

The Irish monks

Although Christianity came to Ireland before the fifth century,[42] it was the mission of Palladius and then Patrick that initiates the real history of the church in Erin. According to Prosper of Aquitaine,[43] in 431 Pope Celestine sent one of his deacons (thought to be Palladius) to be a bishop 'for the Irish [*Scoti*] believing in Christ', but further hard knowledge of Palladius and his activity is lost. The most renowned Apostle of Ireland was indisputably Patrick, a British Christian who had been abducted as a slave by Irish pirates and set to work as a shepherd. After several years

---

[41]On the basic premise that the human soul is made in the image and likeness of God.
[42]There are scattered archaeological finds from the fourth century; further see: J. F. Kenny, *The Sources for the Early History of Ireland*. vol. 1. *Ecclesiastical*, *Records of Civilisation*, vol. 11 (New York: Octagon Press, 1966).
[43]*Chronicon* (for the year 431).

he escaped and entered the monastic life, finally returning to evangelize in Northern Ireland as a missionary bishop, travelling for more than thirty years among the violent pagan lords of the North. His apostolate was attacked by British clergy who felt he had infringed their rights. He composed his famed *Confessions* to justify himself. His *Letter to Coroticus*, a British king, bravely threatened the Christian warlord with excommunication for having enslaved Irish Christians during a raid. Both writings are the earliest known documents written in Ireland, and they present a vivid picture of a man filled with the sense of his apostolic destiny.

After him, Irish sources are quiet until the later sixth century, when a series of monastic saints (Columba (521–97), Brigid[44] (ca. 451–525), Brendan[45] (ca. 484–577) and Columbanus (540–615)) demonstrate the highly ascetical and penitential character of the Irish church, which became very characteristic of it for many centuries afterwards. Columba was known as *Colm Cille* (the dove of the church) in Irish. His style of monasticism was based around his rank as royal lord. His monks were very tightly bound to him, in obedience and kinship, like servants in a new clan. Disobedience brought the swift retribution of an appointed system of beatings. The stories of his life revolve around clashing conflicts, self-appointed exiles,[46] and show how greatly the copying of manuscripts was prized in his communities. Taking a gift of land from the Pictish king Bride, he founded the renowned monastery on Iona. Later came the monastery of Durrow. In 574 he anointed the King of the Scots of Dalriada, Aedan MacGabrain. His monastics proved to be effective and much-travelled missionaries.

Columbanus left the abbey of St Comgal in Bangor around 590 and travelled to Gaul founding monasteries of very strict observance in the Vosges region. He brought a spirit of mourning and penance to the fore in his monastic rule, as well as insisting on his monks' regular opening of all the secrets of the heart to the superior. This eventually grew into the foundation of the sacramental celebration of Confession in the Latin churches. The Gallic bishops, alarmed by his severity, challenged him at a synod in 603, and when he fell foul of the local king, he was expelled from Gaul in 620, eventually settling in a new foundation at Bobbio in Italy.[47]

The seventh century saw the proliferation of Irish Christian colleges which led over the next 200 years to numerous Irish scholars, manuscript copyists, illuminators and missionaries, wandering far and wide in Gaul, Germany and Italy, taking their literary and artistic skills with them. Writers such as Sedulius Scotus[48] (flourished 840–60) would take the Celtic influence into the heart of the Carolingian court and

---

[44]Further, see N. Kissane, *St. Brigid of Kildare: Life, Legend and Cult* (Dublin: Four Courts Press, 2017); K. McCone, 'Brigit in the 7th Century: A Saint With Three Lives', *Peritia* 1 (1982): 107–45.

[45]Abbot of Clonfert; popularly known as Brendan the Navigator from the legend of his voyage by coracle to America.

[46]Regarded by the Irish monks as one of the most bitter penances to be endured – *Xeniteia*, the leaving of home and kin.

[47]A short extract of his Monastic Rule is given in: J. A. McGuckin, *The Path of Christianity: The First Thousand Years* (Downers Grove, IL: IVP Academic, 2017), p. 422.

[48]*Scotus* (Scot) is the Latin term for 'Irish'.

empire. It was Irish monastic copyists who preserved the works of the Latin Fathers for western Europe in a period when the infrastructure of the western Roman Empire had effectively collapsed. Irish Christian poetry remains one of the jewels of all early medieval literature.

ITALY AND THE PAPACY

Pope Gregory the Great

Italy, and eventually Rome at its heart, was destined to become the powerhouse that gave the core characteristics to Latin theology and ecclesiastical life. At first things were not so heavily centralized. Church centres such as Aquileia and Milan, or the monastic communities of Gaul, were both independent and lively. The great figure of Ambrose of Milan (ca. 340–397) gave to the West one of the rare examples of a Latin theologian versed enough in Greek to make adaptations of Greek originals[49] – Origen in his case, whose ideas he moderated to Latin consciousness, even at a time when the scholar, exegete and biblical translator Jerome (ca. 347–420) was attacking his reputation (while simultaneously heavily using his texts). John Cassian, a Scythian from the Black Sea, brought the monastic traditions of Egypt to Gaul, at Marseilles, and as a renowned abbot there produced the highly influential *Institutes* and *Conferences* for his monks, and for generations that followed. But it was the great see and martyr shrine of Rome that was destined to rise as an irradiating star in the fortunes of the Western church

Here, Gregory I (ca. 540–604) was one of the most important of all the early popes. A wealthy aristocrat from a ruling family, and Prefect of Rome before he decided to embrace the life of a retired ascetic, he was called back as a brilliant administrator of the church soon after when Pope Pelagius II commanded him to serve the church. He transformed his villa[50] into a monastery, and his subsequent propelling of ascetical attitudes to the centre of his thought and polity brought monasticism from the fringes of the Latin church into the very centre of operations for centuries to come. From 579 to 586 Gregory served as the papal representative (*apocrisarios*) in Constantinople and brought many Byzantine ideas back to Rome with him, which enlivened the liturgy and musical life of the church.[51]

He also learnt that little practical help would emanate from the emperor in Constantinople and made decisive moves to make Rome (politically and ecclesiastically) stand on its own feet. The Great Plague of 590 saw Gregory acting vigorously to administer aid, and on the occasion of Pelagius' death, Gregory was elected as pope. In the face of inactivity from the emperor's agents in Ravenna,

---

[49]In later centuries the papacy also elevated him as a paradigm of a bishop who could excommunicate an emperor (as when he forbade Theodosius I to attend the liturgy in Milan because of recent killings he had ordered).

[50]On the Caelian hill in Rome, now the important basilica and monastery of St Andrew.

[51]From his liturgical work he became an exemplar of how later popes adapted and developed the liturgy over time: many of which changes were retrospectively fathered onto him.

Gregory negotiated a separate peace with the Lombard invaders, giving a striking paradigm of how popes would begin to combine priesthood with kingship in their own office: however much the emperor protested.

Gregory brought pastoral and hagiographical matters to the fore in his theological writing and set a tone for much of what would follow in the medieval period. His dogmatics are a simplified form of Augustine's writings, and in making that simpler digest of the master, he popularized him immensely and, more than any other Latin thinker (save perhaps Prosper of Aquitaine) he championed and secured Augustine's stature as the chief spokesman of the Western church. Gregory gave pre-eminence in his thought to the doctrine of grace, adding in his own views of the soul's purgatorial cleansing after death: adding immense weight to this notion. Shortly after becoming Pope he composed the *Pastoral Rule* – originally meant as a guide to himself for governing the church. It became one of the most-read works of the Latin church and served across generations as the 'go-to' manual for bishops: and beyond them for clergy, on how to preach scripture.

The work standardized western exegetical method as ideally being composed of three stages (like building a house he said): 'foundations' as the literal historical sense of a text; 'roof and walls' as the allegorical exposition of hidden depths in a passage; and lastly 'interior decorations', in the shape of moral counsels designed to elevate the lives of the listeners. In four books of *Dialogues* Gregory gave the lives and miracles of Italian saints, setting the tone of hagiography for almost all the later Western churches. In book 2 of this, he so praised Benedict of Nursia that Benedictine forms of monastic life were soon destined to predominate. The Carolingian rulers made this a certainty, by legal intervention.

CHRISTIAN CAROLINGIANS

The lamentable failure of the imperial exarch at Ravenna during the Lombard invasion of Italy in the mid-eighth century confirmed, in his successors, Gregory's opinion that Byzantium was no longer the natural protector of the Christian West; and while this would lead to an increasing centralization of power in the papal office itself, at first that had no element of armed force about it. So it was natural the popes should look elsewhere for military protection. They turned to the one rising kingdom that had shown devotion to the successor of Peter: the court of Charles Martel. His Christian name gives the dynasty its title: the Carolingians. Martel's grandson, Charlemagne, would be the most famous king in the line. His aspirations to be Holy Roman Emperor of the West (equal to, no longer subordinate to, Constantinople) were advanced by Pope Leo III who, in gratitude to this king of the Franks for clearing out of the last remnant of the Lombards from Italy, placed the crown upon his head in a ceremony in St Peter's on Christmas day 800. From this time onwards, aided by (what is now known as the forgery of) the *Donation of Constantine*,[52] it was not only the fortunes

---

[52]Documents that purported to be edicts of Constantine the Great giving his contemporary pope Sylvester a parallel right to his own, to political dominion in the western territories. See: McGuckin, *The Path of Christianity*, pp. 666–90.

of the Carolingians that grew apace, but also the papacy that assumed more and more powers to itself, becoming the single major factor in the shaping of early medieval Christendom. In this it replaced other, earlier, independent centres of Latin church life, such as Milan and Aquileia, or even the monastic communities of Gaul – though the latter were to find a more enduring successor in the traditions of Irish monasticism. Because of papal encouragement, and a very strong Carolingian endorsement, it was Benedictinism (revolving around a Roman centre of focus) that predominated massively in the West from this time on.

The Carolingian court encouraged the scholarly aspect of Benedictine houses (copying of manuscripts, gathering of libraries) and for a brief but brilliant period, the Christian scholars of Charlemagne's dynasty became world leaders. Alcuin (735–804) came from York to be Charlemagne's adviser and tutor to the royal family. His advice persuaded Charlemagne to remove the death penalty attached to religious dissidence. He is also reputed to be the author of the phrase *vox populi vox dei*,[53] which gave weight to popular opinion in political reasoning: a startling thought in an era which saw might as (divinely given) right. Sedulius Scotus was a literary critic and poet[54] at the itinerant Carolingian court. His treatise on how a kingly ruler ought to govern[55] shows *in nuce* how closely the Latin church had inserted itself into the political fabrics of the West by this era. Theodulf of Orleans (ca. 750–821) was also a renowned scholar of the court. They saw to it, using legislative means, that each monastery was to have a library and to encourage scholarly labours, not least the provision of schools for the children of the nobility. From this time onwards Latin ecclesiastical establishments were rarely divorced from the enterprise of learning. Through the Dark Ages and beyond, the Western church became a lighthouse of the traditions of Roman culture.

BIBLIOGRAPHY

Barnes, T. D. *Tertullian: An Historical and Literal Study*. Oxford: Oxford University Press, 1973.

Brown, P. *Augustine of Hippo: A Biography*. Berkeley: University of California Press, 1967.

Chadwick, H. *Augustine*. Oxford: Oxford University Press, 1986.

Croinin, D. O. *Early Medieval Ireland: 400–1200*. London: Longman, 1995.

Dyson, R. W. (trans.). *Sedulius Scottus: De Rectoribus Christianis: On Christian Rulers*. London: Boydell & Brewer, 2010.

Engberg, J., Jacobsen, A. C. and Ulrich, J. (eds). *Defence of Christianity: Early Christian Apologists*. New York: Peter Lang, 2014.

---

[53]'The voice of the people is the voice of God.'

[54]Ably sketched in the renowned books of Helen Waddell, *The Wandering Scholars* (London: Constable, 1927) and *Medieval Latin Lyrics* (London: Constable, 1929).

[55]See R. W. Dyson (trans.), *Sedulius Scottus: De Rectoribus Christianis: On Christian Rulers* (London: Boydell & Brewer, 2010).

Evans, G. *The Thought of Gregory the Great*. Cambridge: Cambridge University Press, 1986.

Fahey, M. A. *Cyprian and the Bible: A Study in 3rd Century Exegesis*. Tubingen: Mohr, 1971.

Fitzgerald, A. D. (ed.). *Augustine Through The Ages: An Encyclopedia*. Grand Rapids, MI: Eerdmans, 1999.

Flintoff, E. (trans). and McGuckin, J. A. (intro). *The Phoenix*. Bath: Old School Press, 1995.

Grant, R. M. *The Greek Apologists of the Second Century*. London: SCM Press, 1988.

Heffernan, T. J. *The Passion of Perpetua and Felicity*. Oxford: Oxford University Press, 2012.

Hinchcliff, P. B. *Cyprian of Carthage and the Unity of the Christian Church*. London: Chapman, 1974.

Kenny, J. F. *The Sources for the Early History of Ireland*. vol. 1: *Ecclesiastical. Records of Civilisation,* vol. 11. New York: Octagon Press, 1966.

Kurfess, A. 'Lactantius und Plato', *Philologus* 78 (1923): 381–92.

Loi, V. *Lattanzio nella storia del linguaggio e del pensiero teologico pre-niceno*. Bibliotheca Theologica Salesiana. series 1. fontes 5; Rome: Citta Nuova, 1970.

McDonald, M. F. *Lactantius: The Divine Institutes*. Fathers of the Church Series vol. 49; Washington, DC: Catholic University of America, 1964.

McDonald, M. F. *Lactantius; The Minor Works*. Fathers of the Church Series vol. 54; Washington, DC: Catholic University of America, 1965.

McGuckin, J. A. *The Theology of Lucius Firmianus Caecilius Lactantius*. Unpublished PhD. Diss. University of Durham, UK, 1980.

McGuckin, J. A. 'The Non-Cyprianic Scripture Texts in Lactantius' Divine Institutes'. *VChr* 36 (1982): 145–63.

McGuckin, J. A. 'Spirit Christology: Lactantius and His Sources', *HeyJ* 24 (1983): 141–8.

McGuckin, J. A. 'Lactantius as Theologian: An Angelic Christology on the Eve of Nicaea', *Rivista di Storia e Letteratura Religiosa* 22, no. 3 (1986): 492–7.

McGuckin, J. A. *The Path of Christianity: The First Thousand Years*. Downers Grove, IL: IVP Academic, 2017.

Markus, R. A. *From Augustine to Gregory the Great*. London: Variorum, 1983.

van der Meer, F. *Augustine the Bishop*. London: Sheed and Ward, 1961.

Morgan, J. *The Importance of Tertullian in the Development of Christian Dogma*. London: Kegan Paul, 1928.

Osborn, E. *Tertullian: First Theologian of the West*. Cambridge: Cambridge University Press, 1997.

de Paor, L. *St. Patrick's World: The Christian Culture of Ireland's Apostolic Age*. Dublin: Four Courts Press, 1996.

Richards, J. *Consul of God: The Life and Times of Gregory the Great*. London: Routledge and Kegan Paul, 1980.

Roberts, M. 'Lactantius' Phoenix and Late Latin Poetics', in J. Elsner and J. H. Lobato (eds). *The Poetics of Late Latin Literature*. Oxford: Oxford University Press, 2017.

Roberts, R. E. *The Theology of Tertullian*. London: Epworth Press, 1924.

Sage, M. M. *Cyprian*. Patristic Monograph Series, 1. Cambridge, MA: Philadelphia Patristic Foundation, 1975.

Straw, C. *Gregory the Great: Perfection in Imperfection*. Berkeley: University of California Press, 1988.

Thomas, N. L. *Defending Christ: The Latin Apologists before Augustine*. Turnhout: Brepols, 2011.

CHAPTER 27

The Eastern church and its thought-world (major Greek Fathers)

JOHN A. MCGUCKIN

PROLEGOMENA

The theological and philosophical contexts of the world of the early Greek Christians have been the important focus of several other key chapters in this book. Piotr Ashwin-Siejkowski chapter 3 and György Gereby chapter 30 have both discussed the relations of the Christians to their wider ambient Greek culture. Mark Sheridan chapter 28 and Saliba Er Akhsenoyo chapter 29 have looked respectively at the affairs of the Coptic and Syriac-speaking churches. Isidoros Katsos chapter 23 has delved into how significantly Christian theorists have been influenced by the Greek metaphysics of light, while Henryk Pietras chapter 22 has given us an insight into how the church councils served to coalesce many aspects of Christian teaching over several formative generations and to establish international ecclesial norms. Allen Brent, with his study of the life and times of Ignatius of Antioch and Irenaeus of Lyons (3.2), and Hilaria Ramelli (3.3) who throws light on two of the most important early Christian philosopher-theologians, Clement and Origen of Alexandria, have equally illuminated the intellectual culture of the Greek church. Origen's influence was extraordinarily deep and long-lasting in both the Eastern and Western forms of Christianity, despite several attempts by less intellectual churchmen over the ages, to suffocate his fire. Lastly, all the chapters turning around the liturgical and devotional life of the church, that together comprise Part 3 of this book, serve also to give the reader a very spacious window on the thought-world and cultural presuppositions of the early Christians.

This being the case, the present chapter, in attempting to give a favour of the thought-world of the Greek Christian writers, will look more precisely at a period between the fourth and eighth centuries, and particularly at a shortlist of some of the most influential philosopher-theologians and policymakers of the eastern church in its classical formation. These are they whom later Christian tradition has identified as the major 'Greek Fathers',[1] retrospectively elevating them in the historical record as constituent markers of the path of ecclesial Orthodoxy. The churches of catholic tradition still to this day regard the 'Fathers' as teachers of high authority – even as *pneumatophoroi*, Spirit-bearing saints: prophetically important. The Protestant traditions, generally speaking, tend either to ignore them or to regard them chiefly as of passing historical interest, although some of the Reformers (Luther and Calvin are chief examples) held them in high regard and used their writings.

This chapter will focus on three clusters of what has been, since the eighteenth century, called the patristic[2] tradition. First, it will consider Athanasius and Cyril both theologian-bishops of the great Church of Alexandria; the latter being the first in honour of all the eastern sees until the rise of the city of Constantinople overshadowed it ecclesiastically, after the late fourth century. Both of them were theologians who emerged at a moment of high crisis in the Christian tradition and both offered long-lasting solutions that formed a major school of theological and spiritual thinking. These are arguably the two most important minds for the Christological and soteriological traditions of world Christianity.

Second, it will introduce the so-called Cappadocian Fathers. Three of them[3] were very significant: Gregory the Theologian (*Nazianzenos*), his friend Basil of Caesarea and the latter's brother (and the other Gregory's student) Gregory of Nyssa. All three were in the thick of the great crises of the late fourth century, offering theological teaching that became the cornerstone of the church's monastic spirituality, its exegetical tradition and its Trinitarian confession. I am allowing Gregory the Theologian to have the main voice on behalf of them.

Third, the chapter will consider two representative later Fathers of the church from the Byzantine era: Maximus the Confessor and John Damascene. Both men consciously look back from their historical vantage points and both try to assimilate, make fresh and coherent, the long spread of the earlier core traditions. These seven great saints are not merely intellectual giants of the theological past but, in a real sense, stand themselves as windows onto the thought-world of the Greek church: an ascetical and mystical ethos that took seriously, but not uncritically, the achievements of their Hellenistic literary and philosophical cultures, but sought

---

[1] The title 'father' for a senior cleric probably originated in early fourth-century circles to designate a spiritual guide of high worth. *Abba* is the monastic word for such a guide. The female form is *Amma*. By the end of that century, however, the clerical elite adopted the concept as a title for the ordained – at first bishops, then spreading later to priests also. It became so closely tied to 'authoritative teaching bishops' (who were all male) that it is only in recent times that the concept of 'Mothers of the Church' has been investigated, by extension. The paucity of the writings of ancient female theologians is an abiding difficulty of this genre of study, but works such as Susanna Elm's *Virgins of God: The Making of Asceticism in Late Antiquity* (Oxford: Oxford University Press, 1996) show how a percipient historian can reveal hidden things.

[2] The adjective deriving from the Latin term for 'Father' (*pater*).

[3] One might enumerate three others from the same family nexus: Macrina, Basil's sister and monastic leader, and bishops Amphilokios of Iconium and Peter of Sebaste.

always to subordinate them to the moral imperatives of the Kingdom of God as revealed in Scripture.

In preserving the works of these seven, to whom it ascribed high sainthood and profound wisdom, the Greek church set up for itself a compendium of archetypes to which it aspired, and to which it could come back century after century, in good times and in bad, to renew its sense of purposes, and to repristinate its concept of excellence in theology, churchmanship and pastoral care. If we were to say anyone was missing from this mini 'Library of the Fathers', it would have to be Origen himself[4] (never himself afforded patristic status but always read as a grand master among the intelligentsia) and also John Chrysostom.[5] The Greek Christians always looked to Chrysostom as their own evangelical Demosthenes. He gave them paradigms of biblical interpretation and homiletic in his extensive writings. To him they also attributed the eucharistic liturgy that became standard in the churches: probably because of some reforms he introduced into the church of Constantinople during his short but turbulent incumbency as archbishop there (398–404), based upon the rite of Antioch and abbreviating the forms that have been preserved elsewhere in the liturgy attributed to the name of St Basil. Unlike Origen, whose intellectual heritage was extensively digested and disseminated along a chain of later authors, Chrysostom is not so much an original thinker as a pastoral and homiletic master. The Greek Christians, from his own time even into modernity, valued and learned by heart much of his writing as high examples of Christian erudition, and across many centuries where education was occluded by oppressive regimes, the homilies of Chrysostom were repeated by bishops and priests to both village and town congregations, thus keeping the patristic mentality (*phronema*), as well as Greek Letters, alive in the ongoing culture of the Eastern church.

THE ALEXANDRIAN FATHERS: ATHANASIUS AND CYRIL

Alexandria was, until about the sixth century, one of the greatest of all university cities of the Late Roman world. It boasted of its schools and teachers of rhetoric and philosophy. It was the centre of the world-renowned experiment in learning known as the Great Library. Every ship or camel caravan that came into the city was searched for copies of literature, and every text not already possessed by the library was taken to be copied. The original was retained and the copy restored to the owners. The body of scholars associated with the library was world-renowned for being careful commentators and exegetes on the ancient traditions of Greek

---

[4]Further, see Hilaria Ramelli's chapter in this volume; also J. A. McGuckin (ed.), *The Westminster Handbook to Origen* (Louisville, KY: WJK Press, 2004), with extensive bibliography; H. Crouzel, *Origen*, trans. A. Worrall (Edinburgh: T&T Clark, 1989).
[5]Further, see J. N. D. Kelly, *Golden Mouth: The Story of John Chrysostom: Ascetic, Preacher, Bishop* (London: Duckworth, 1996); J. Pelikan (ed.), *The Preaching of Chrysostom (Homilies on the Sermon on the Mount)* (Philadelphia, PA: Fortress Press, 1967).

literature and thought. It was in the Alexandrian church that we find some of the earliest examples of leading churchmen expected to be influential and intellectual theologians. Indeed, a school of Alexandrian theology arose that exercised immense influence over international Christianity up until the rise of Constantinople (with its more Syrian traditions) overshadowed it to some degree. Two of the most illustrious examples of these great Alexandrian thinkers were its chief bishops in the fourth and fifth centuries, respectively: Athanasius (ca. 292–373) and Cyril (ca. 376–444). They were both caught up in major theological crises that roiled the international Christian Oecumene of their day, and the solutions they offered became constituent of what later generations regarded as quintessential orthodoxy.

Athanasius was the chief spokesman of anti-Arian resistance throughout the fourth-century Christological crisis, and Cyril developed on this Athanasian Christology to take it further into the realms of mystical metaphysics and show how it permeated every aspect of Christian spirituality. Both men were regarded, ever after, as among the greatest of all the Greek patristic theologians. Athanasius was called the 'Pillar of the Church' and Cyril gained the title of the 'Seal of the Fathers'.[6] Athanasius' reputation was equally high in the Latin Christian world, though that of Cyril, though venerable enough, was an intellectual heritage that was overshadowed by the West's much greater reliance on Augustine. While the works of Athanasius were translated into English in the nineteenth century and had a wide readership among the clergy, those of Cyril were excluded from the popular translation series of the time, and his importance did not begin to re-emerge in the English-speaking world until the late twentieth century.

Athanasius' great contribution was twofold. He solidified, by his personality and his extensive teachings, the Eastern church's commitment to the Nicene Creed at a time when it underwent a generation of imperial pressure to adopt a more Arian-leaning set of compromises. In his early works, such as the *De Incarnatione* and his exegeses of the Psalms, he had already made the point, which became more and more central to all his thought, that the kenotic[7] Incarnation of the divine Word as man entailed the reverse of that same dynamic of grace: namely, the elevation of the adopted humanity into the divine ambit. This concept of 'deification by grace' (how the Word healed, reconciled and glorified fallen humanity in the act of Incarnation) became critically important for him and for all the major fathers who followed his lead – not least Cyril of Alexandria. After Athanasius the Eastern church never lost sight of the notion that Christology is fundamentally an account of soteriology: namely that the act of Incarnation is the dynamic of atonement that not merely reconciles but restores the human race to a new profundity of union with God.

---

[6]In the sense that he set a signet seal (*sphragis*) on all their work, summing them up and rounding them off.
[7]See Phil. 2.5-11. *Kenosis*, or the divine self-emptying of the divine Word to become a human, is reversed in the divine glory, wherein the Word is lifted up again after his sacrifice and carries all humanity along with him in his triumph. The scheme is strong in Paul, but in this Philippians hymn Paul quotes a hymn already sung in the church before his date.

The second great contribution Athanasius made to the whole of eastern Christian theology was his strong defence of the divinity of the Holy Spirit. He saw from an early date that the implication of the *homoousion* (the full and consubstantive divinity of the Son) entailed the necessity of placing Christology not only into the nexus of thought about salvation but also into the context of a new semantic for Trinitarian thought. His ideas were to be taken to a refined pitch by the Cappadocian Fathers, especially Gregory the Theologian who supplied the actual semantics of three *hypostases* and the single divine *ousia* of the Father, which the Father gifts to the Son and the Spirit as their own. But Athanasius fought for the issue against many conservatives of his own day, fearful of abandoning a more primitive monism in speaking about God. The Arian parties were especially strong in resisting him.

Just as, they argued, it was not necessary to raise the Son of God to fully divine status (albeit he could be assigned honorific glory), it was even more unnecessary to speculate about the divinity of the Spirit of God. For the Arians He ought to be classified strictly as a servant and creature. Athanasius[8] turned to the liturgical tradition of the church and demonstrated that its ethos consistently approached, and acclaimed, the Spirit as divine. This was surely more truly the voice of the church's core faith than any speculative theologian could systematize. If, Athanasius argued, the Spirit's task in Baptism was to deify the believer by his consecration, how could He not be God who supplied such a gift? After Athanasius, the Cappadocian Fathers would once more refine the thinking and characterize the roles of the three hypostases of the Trinity. (Gregory the Theologian's *Five Theological Orations* are the classic examples of this together with Basil of Caesarea's treatise *On the Holy Spirit*.) While these two authors marked major advances, in turn they both depended on Athanasius for having given all the earlier indications of the future path to follow, and not least for having so tenaciously defended the theology while such oppressive measures were raised against him throughout his career.

Cyril was Athanasius' fifth-century successor as Archbishop of Alexandria. He had been trained in administration from his youth by his uncle Theophilus, the present archbishop, and had used his time to study both the philosophers and the Christian biblical and theological tradition. The archival library of the Alexandrian church was unrivalled, and in this way Cyril came to know the primary writings of Origen, Athanasius, Dionysios of Alexandria, Gregory of Nazianzen, Didymus and John Chrysostom: all of whom leave traces in his own work. Athanasius was especially his mentor. From him he learnt that the act of Incarnation by the Word was the decisive moment in the history of salvation. It was this exchange of dynamism: the infinite power and mercy of God entering into weak and debilitated humanity's condition that raised up the creature into the presence of God the creator.

Cyril added two distinct and refining aspects to the Athanasian vision of the dynamics of Incarnation. The first was a closer interest in the manner of the dynamic interchange between God and Man in the Christ-event. He propelled the concept of

---

[8]Particularly in his Letters to Serapion. See C. R. B. Shapland (ed. and trans.), *The Letters of St. Athanasius Concerning the Holy Spirit to Bishop Serapion* (London: Epworth Press, 1951).

Henosis to the fore. The word means literally the 'Union' or the 'making one'. Cyril saw the manner in which the Eternal Word made himself 'One with his flesh' to be the key to understanding the process of salvation. After this *Henosis* there could be no separation spoken of or implied between the divinity and the humanity of the Incarnate Lord. It was certainly not the case that one could speak of the Eternal Word (the Logos) and then also of an earthly man (Jesus), and maybe also a figure that showed both aspects of power and vulnerability (the Christ).

Nestorius, the new Archbishop of Constantinople, seemed to Cyril to be speaking in this way, and it disturbed him greatly. Nestorius wanted 'more exactitude' (*akribeia*) in how Christians spoke. He did not want sloppy thoughts. He believed God statements had to be kept clean and pure: never, on any account, miring them in the affairs of this world. So, commonly heard pieties such as 'God died for us on the cross' and 'Mary is the Mother of God' (*Theotokos*) had to be banned. When Cyril questioned why Nestorius had forbidden his faithful from using the title *Theotokos* for Mary, he received the answer that God has no mother, being eternal; and so, 'strictly speaking', Mary cannot be the Mother of God. Cyril replied: 'If Mary is not, strictly speaking, the Mother of God, then, strictly speaking, the one who is born from her is not God.' The great Christological argument of the fifth century thus opened on that account.

More than simply arguing over niceties of expression, however, Cyril thought that what was really at stake was the church's real belief in the power of the *Henosis*. Did the Word really unite himself to his human life? Or did he just appear to be a human? Or stay at arm's length from the created (historically embodied) existence he had assumed at birth? Cyril felt Nestorius' all-too-pure and distant God was not the God of the Bible as much as that of the Greek philosophers and their transcendently distant Absolute.

Cyril therefore posed sets of *aporia*, intellectual puzzles demanding a certain answer. Two of the most famous were: 'Christ as God suffered and died on the cross impassibly' (*Apathos epathen*); and 'Mary is the Mother of God' (*Theotokos*). Nestorius thought he was speaking nonsense by using such paradoxes and could never quite grasp his point that these pieties conveyed the full force of the church's belief that Christ was God, simply said; one of the eternal Trinity, though (when it concerned statements about his earthly life) now working through the medium of the earthly existence and material (created) body. So, for Cyril it was co-terminously true to say that God died on a cross and that God is impassible and immortal. Simultaneously it is true to say that God, in Christ, is at once untouched by the vagaries of the world and yet fully immersed in human suffering and pain – so as to heal it.

The apparent contradiction is resolved when it is understood we are talking about the Incarnate word – who died in his humanity but, with the Father, raised that humanity to life once more in his divinity and in his Eternal Godhead, since one of the Trinity could never, and never did, die 'as Logos'. Likewise, Mary is truly the Mother of God for she gave birth to God himself, in human form. Christ is not just a title for the Man whom the Word is supposed to have assumed (or borrowed).

Christ is the name given to the God-Man, whose person is the Eternal Word of God. In short Cyril laid all his stress on the single subjectival unity of the Incarnate Lord. One person, one force of intelligence and action. He summed this up in an equally dense axiom: 'One concrete reality of God the Word Incarnated' (*Mia physis tou theou logou sesarkomene*).

His vision of this powerful *Henosis* not only secured the idea of the single subjectivity of the Incarnate Christ, however, and thus secured the church's logic in acclaiming Christ as God; it went further. The dynamic of the *Henosis* was explained by Cyril as an exchange: divine gift (grace) for human weakness. Just as it was in the case of Christ, divine power entered into the fabric of the human creatureliness (we can take the example of the spittle of Jesus restoring sight to the blind man, or the human voice of Jesus calling Lazarus back to life); so too God's energy was passed over into the fallen human race. The gifts of restoration were given to all of humanity because the Word made his own body, his own life on earth, the model and first exemplar of the new restoration. Christ personally became the New Adam promised in scripture, so that his disciples might profit from the New Humanity he had instituted.

The old humanity was defined by alienation from God, and by the mortal fallibility and sinfulness that followed from that. The New Humanity (being 'in Christ' as Paul expressed it) was defined by ontological reunion with God, and the immortality and grace that followed from that. After Cyril's exposition of the powerful dynamic of the Union-*Henosis*, all the major Greek theologians understood the Incarnation as the mystical restoration of the entire human race and the way God engineered the making of a new divine-humanity. The shorthand for this whole Christological soteriology was 'deification by grace' (*theiopoiesis kata charin*) and its centrality, now assured by Cyril's work, made the whole subsequent history of eastern Christian thought into a deeply mystical, spiritually intuitive tradition, quite distinct in character from the much more syllogistical and formulaic approach of the Western church: one that laid its central stress on the Incarnation as a preparation for Christ's offering of a legal sacrifice of atonement to an offended Godhead.

Cyril's second great contribution to the thought-world of the Eastern church was the manner in which he pointed to the actuality of how this exchange from Old Adam to New Adam was accomplished. In Christ's own body it was a dynamic energized by his own indwelling person, as Eternal Word. In the Christian believer, Cyril said, it was energized by the indwelling gift of the presence of the Holy Spirit: whose role in the history of the church was to 'make Christ' in the temple of the believer. The Spirit forms the presence of the holy in the faithful, makes them into Christs as God the Father sees them and thus lifts them up into the life-giving presence of the Holy Trinity. This Cyril saw as practically accomplished in the sacramental life of the church which the Spirit also energized (especially the Eucharist and Baptism), also in the life of virtue which He inspired, and the ongoing mystical life of prayer undertaken by believers. All the transformative power of the Christian life was supplied by the Spirit to keep the fire of the Christ-transformation (the process of salvation ongoing in history) alive in the church. Because of Athanasius and Cyril all subsequent Eastern Christianity has had this view of the mystical process of ongoing deification as central to its theological life and its common spiritual and liturgical traditions. Not all the faithful had ever read their works, but almost all had heard of them; heard them preached; and their vision of the divine Christ transfiguring all his believers most certainly became the common heritage of simple piety and of the learned scholars.

THE CAPPADOCIAN FATHERS: BASIL AND THE TWO GREGORIES

Cappadocia had traditionally been evangelized by the great student of Origen, Gregory Thaumaturgos. It was an area that held strategic importance in the Roman Empire, a major supply base of agricultural goods and military-grade horses, for the troops who guarded Rome's eastern borderlands. By the mid-fourth century we begin to see important Cappadocian families, rich landed gentry, who are not only Christian but have been rooted in the faith for several generations. Two of those families were near neighbours. One was that of Gregory the bishop and his wife Nonna, with their hillside estate of Arianzum, and their townhouse at Nazianzus. Multimillionaires, and owners of vast acreages, it was only right that they would assume the status of *honestiores*, and that Gregory should occupy the position of the local magistrate. Once Constantine had allowed Christian bishops to assume magisterial rank and duties (making the office respectable for the first time) and granted generous tax exemptions to Christian clergy (making the office highly desirable to the upper classes), it followed fairly quickly that instead of rural poor being the local bishop, the upper-class gentry tend to appear in the posts.

Gregory and Nonna made sure that their sons, Gregory and Caesarius, would receive the best education possible, and both of them spent over a decade in their youths studying in Caesarea, Alexandria and Athens. The son Gregory would become possibly the most cultured man of his age, would adopt the Christian ascetical life and eventually become bishop, succeeding his father at Nazianzus, before being invited to Constantinople to give a set of Orations against the Arians,[9] and assuming the role of the chief Nicene bishop there under the patronage of the new emperor Theodosios I; even chairing the Oecumenical Council of Constantinople in 381, until, despairing of the inter-episcopal wrangling, he handed in his resignation and retired back to the relative tranquillity of life on his estates. His brother Caesarios pursued a medical career and became a doctor in the imperial entourage of Julian, before being killed prematurely in an earthquake.

---

[9]His major work is this series of Orations (numbers 27–31) delivered just before the Council of 381 opened, setting out the elements of the Nicene Trinitarian faith. They are known today as the 'Five Theological Orations' (see F. W. Norris, *Faith Gives Fullness to Reasoning: The Five Theological Orations of Gregory Nazianzen* (Leiden: E.J. Brill, 2015). The Council of Chalcedon in 451 gave Gregory the honorific title of 'The Theologian' (comparing him with the Fourth Evangelist, or St John the Theologian), and his works were declared, by Rufinus, 'sufficient in themselves to educate believers in the catholic faith'.

Gregory tells us much about his life and times and offers many close details of his family in his voluminous writings. He is the first Christian (long before Augustine wrote his *Confessions*) to use extensively the genre of autobiography. It was his belief that this scrutiny of the soul revealed to the careful observer the secret marks of God's providence as written in the life of creatures. Gregory studied the works of Origen closely and with the Cappadocian Christian friend he met and greatly admired in his time at Athens, the young student Basil, he would later collaborate to produce an edition of Origen's writings, known as the *Philocalia of Origen* – one that removed all 'objectionable elements'[10] and established the old master as one of the church's perennial exemplars of how to read the scriptures.

Gregory's three great contributions to Christian doctrinal history were: first that he secured the opinion that to be truly open to the Spirit of God, one had to cultivate the life of the mind. Before him, there had been a great temptation to regard the pious uneducated rustic (the village martyr-zealot, or the cave-dwelling illiterate hermit) as one of the highest levels attainable of Christian sanctity. In his writings about his family Gregory set before the church the example of domestic good nature and reliability as something even more admirable than such stark zealotry. More than this he celebrated the life of the mind as equivalent to a *katharsis* of soul – a cleansing preparation to receive the inspirations of the Spirit of God.[11] Before him (and indeed at many times after) it has been a temptation among the higher ranks of clergy to regard education as a dispensable factor in the processes of clerical education and evangelization. For Gregory, when the uneducated come to be in charge of church affairs, lamentable decline is always the result, and he excoriates many of his contemporary bishops for being blind guides who lead their charges into the ditch.[12]

This insistence on the life of the mind as inseparable from the life of the Spirit (true holiness must always be allied with reflective intelligence) has not always been high on the horizons of ecclesiastical thinking, but in the life of the Eastern church, the memory of the Cappadocian Fathers became a kind of talisman that this was an unbreakable law of spirituality: and it has saved Eastern Christianity through many long generations of times when, faced with financial ruin and political oppression,

---

[10]Later generations, generally mis-reading Origen's intent, and often his explicit text, suspected him of teaching the pre-existence of souls, their fall to the earth as punishment, the non-eternity of the after-death punishment of the wicked, the on-divinity of the Spirit and other doctrines which, by the fourth century, were not acceptable to the established Orthodoxy of the day. Further, see H. Ramelli, *A Larger Hope: Universal Salvation from Christian Beginnings to Julian of Norwich* (Eugene, OR: Cascade Books, 2019).

[11]In this argument he took up and refined classical Hellenistic arguments about the status of poetry and inspiration. Further, see: J. A. McGuckin, 'Gregory of Nazianzus: The Rhetorician as Poet', in *Gregory of Nazianzus: Images and Reflections*, eds T. Hagg and J. Bortnes (Copenhagen: Museum Tusculanum Press, 2005), pp. 193–212.

[12]See, for example, his castigation of the majority of bishops at the Council of Constantinople 381 in his autobiographical poem *De Vita Sua*. English version in: C. White, *Gregory of Nazianzus: Autobiographical Poems* (Cambridge: Cambridge University Press, 1996).

the temptation to dismiss the costly demands of educating clergy and people looked very appealing to indigent church leaders.

Gregory's second great contribution to the church was his almost instinctive reaction to the theology that he found the disciples of Apollinaris propagating in his Cappadocian diocese. Before his priest Cledonius alerted him to the work of a group of zealous Apollinarian ascetics making preaching tours among his churches, Gregory had been of the opinion that Apollinaris was a friend of Athanasius the Great, and that this association therefore made him an ally of the Nicene cause. When Cledonius forwarded to him the closer detail of what they were saying, he realized that this was a mistake. Considering what was at stake, long before anyone else had seen the implications, Gregory sat down in 383 to compose a small dossier of letters that came to be given the highest status in the church's understanding of Christology: Letters 101 and 102 to the Priest Cledonius, Letter 202 to Nektarios of Constantinople,[13] and Letter 125 to his friend Olympios the aristocratic governor of the Province of Cappadocia Secunda. This small library of texts came, in retrospect, to be seen as quintessentially important to the Christian tradition about the person of Christ. Apollinaris, wishing to fight against Arian statements that if Christ had a mortal body like ours, he could not be fully divine, decided to stress an opposite viewpoint: chiefly out of misguided piety rather than having any biblical or theological precedent. He taught that Christ's body was not the same as ours at all. It was, in fact, a body that the Eternal Word had selected before time and had joined himself to it intimately. When he descended to earth, he brought this heavenly body with him and through its instrumentation performed divine works on earth.

Apollinaris answered the critiques of Arians by saying that the Word of God is the supreme Mind or reason within creation; so, when he joined a heavenly body to himself that would become his earthly vehicle, he did not need any bodily consciousness in it (for this would only confuse the issues of personhood and choice): and so dispensed with the bodily mind, substituting his own eternal and infinite consciousness in its place (a much better solution as far as Apollinaris was concerned) and dispensed with the human soul, having his own divine person as the replacement for a human, fallible, soul.

Gregory was appalled by this movement, knowing that while it has often been a temptation among the pious throughout Christian history, it falsifies the Gospel records and ultimately denies that Christ was a human being. Someone who looks and talks like a human being but has no mortal mind, or soul, or personality, is – simply put – not human. Gregory insisted that Apollinaris had destroyed the true scandal of the Incarnation, namely that God had not simply assumed an 'apparent human form', but had actually 'become Man', for the salvation of Mankind. This, Gregory said, was what Apollinaris had failed to appreciate. The Word did not descend to earth like one of the Olympian gods, for a visit or for some mischief; rather, he came to save and rebuild a fallen race. If he did not have a human soul, or

---

[13]Sometimes classified as *Orat. 46*.

a truly human body (weakness and all), he could not be said to have entered into the heart of our race. For Gregory, the entering into the very heart of humanity, to leave there the divine power (energy or grace) of immortality, was all that the Incarnation was about.

In addition, if he did not have a human soul (which was the seat of moral choice for Gregory, and thus also the seat of sin and disobedience), how could he enter into the very fabric of that inherent weakness and leave there the divine grace of healing and forgiveness? Gregory had the ability and skill to sum up these complex and involved theological arguments in scintillating catchphrases. In this case he came up, in the Cledonius letters, with the axiom[14] that was repeated ever afterwards in the eastern church: 'What [the Word] did not assume, he did not heal.'

This insists that the Incarnation be seen as the intimate transference, within the single life of the Word of God made Man and thus truly human, of the divine grace and energy to the fallible forms of creaturehood. What happened in the life of Christ, therefore, as a natural condition (God-Manhood) becomes given to the entire human race as a grace of salvation; life enters back into mortality and reconciliation is effected in what was formerly alienation.

Because of Gregory's intervention, the Eastern church tradition has always afterwards combined the highest sense of mystical reverence for the Incarnate Lord and, at the same time, confessed his closeness to all human sorrows and joys. This Christology has coloured all of the Eastern church's spirituality and theology to this day: a culture in which Gregory is still regarded as one of the greatest theologians of the church, even though his name is not nearly so well known in the West.

Gregory's third great contribution to the eastern Christian culture was so important that, because of it, the Council of Chalcedon posthumously awarded him the title of 'Gregory the Theologian': implying that he stood on a height of theological insight comparable to St John, the author of the Fourth Gospel. He has been known by this name ever since in the Eastern churches, while the Western churches usually call him St Gregory of Nazianzus. Three years before the Cledonius letters, in 380, Gregory had been called by the leading Nicene bishops in exile, to go to Constantinople (after the death of the pro-Arian emperor Valens) and preach there the Nicene faith. When he arrived in the capital, the Arian clergy dominated the scene and he was subjected to much abuse from their hands as a dissident. He converted a cousin's villa near the great cathedral as a house-church which he called 'The Resurrection Church' (*Anastasia*) and began there a series of evening Orations, speaking down to the inner courtyard from an internal balcony.

These not only expounded the Nicene faith but went forward in many important respects and explained the essence of the Christian faith as the Trinity that saves Mankind. Arianism, of course, denied the fundamental divine status of the Word of God, so introducing the Trinity of three co-equal and divine persons proved anathema to the resident clergy. Riots broke out, stones were thrown and attempts

---

[14]He borrowed it from Origen, but sharpened the point: *Heracl.*, 7; *Comm.Matt.*, 12.29; *Cels.*, 4.19.

were made to prosecute Gregory to stop his preaching. But he first of all hired a bodyguard of Egyptian sailors (once they heard he stood for the faith of their own Athanasius of Alexandria they would do anything for him) and soon his enemies drew back, afraid because they had heard rumours that a new emperor of the Nicene faith had been appointed in the West and was moving eastwards to take command of his capital.

When Emperor Theodosius arrived, he acknowledged Gregory as the Nicene bishop of the capital and instructed him to arrange a great synod to be gathered the following year. In the interim Gregory finished his set of sermons on the Trinity. They are numbers 27 to 31 and collectively became known as the *Theological Orations*. Gregory coalesced the many disparate strands of Trinitarian thinking that had preceded him and supplied the necessary infrastructure of logic, demonstrating that faith in the Trinity is a metaphysical way of expressing the church's salvation in Christ and stands as the core insight of all Christianity's vision of God. Gregory did not believe that God had a 'being' in the sense of constitutive 'stuff' (in other words a bounded nature) since He was both utterly transcendent and spiritual. Nor did he teach that the Trinity was three aspects of the self-same thing (merely a disguised monism) all sharing the same characters or substance. These were common ideas available at the time, but few had taken the trouble to pursue the concepts deeply; and as a result there did not exist any widely agreed syntax or semantics to approach this core theological issue. Gregory, however, insisted that the Alexandrian tradition that described Father, Son and Spirit as distinct *hypostases* was correct. The term 'hypostasis' meant 'concrete instantiation of something'. It is usually translated in English as 'Person', but that term carries psychological weight it did not necessarily have in Greek. It certainly meant 'individually existent reality', and so, for Gregory it meant an insistence that Father, Son and Spirit were not merely different aspects or titles of the same underlying reality but were each in their own distinct way existents. He went on to insist that all three were God. Not one-third of God each, or one supreme God (The Father) with two lesser deities (Son and Spirit), but rather each one was fully and totally God: since divinity is a concept that cannot be divided, or diminished by definition.

He puzzled many people of the time and outraged his Arian enemies: For how could this be confessed without falling into the profession that there were three Gods, which is a major contradiction of Monotheism? Gregory answered that while all three *hypostases* were fully and coequally God (or we could say 'divine'), there was only One God. This was because God the Father, the One God, before all time and all creation, eternally gifted his own being to the Son (or the Word); and gifted his own being to the Holy Spirit; each of them commissioned for distinct purposes in the formation, regulation and preservation of the Creation. Because the Son and Spirit each had the Father's being – now as their own being – they were not separate in essence, although they were uniquely distinct. They were each bound to one another and to the Father by the inseparable bond of having the self-same essential being. In that case how could one make any distinction? Gregory said: by *hypostasis* not by essence (*ousia*). This meant sameness in being but distinctness in relationship. They were three yet at the same time they were one: and to this end he invented the word 'Trinity' – meaning a 'threefold unity'.

What Gregory had insisted on was that Unity in respect to God did not have to be a simple monism (that of Judaism or Islam, for example) but could be a complex unity: truly one since there was only a singularity of being; but also distinctly nuanced in internal relations because each of the Trinity served a different (but intimately related) purpose in expressing that self-same being. The Father is the Progenitor of Godhead (the *Arche*) and is Ineffable and Inconceivable. The Son is the Word and Creative rational power in the Universe who makes the Father known and serves as the High Priest of All Creation in allowing creatures to approach the Unapproachable. The Holy Spirit is the sanctifying energy of the Father and the Son, healing and fortifying everything that is good, and lifting up all sentient life to the Knowledge of the Son and to life in the Son. The shorthand, for Gregory, was: 'Light through light in light.' Liturgically, the church generally expressed this dynamic (for the Trinity in the Eastern church amounts to a highly dynamic spirituality): 'To the Father through the Son, in the Holy Spirit.'

Gregory's close friend in his decade-long studies at Athens was a compatriot from Cappadocia named Basil of Caesarea. Basil grew tired of the life of a student before Gregory and left to explore the growing monastic movement in Egypt and Cappadocia. For a time he and his sister Macrina were disciples of the zealous ascetic Eustathius of Sebaste and took from him a lifelong love of the monastic life. Basil began his ecclesiastical career as one of Eustathius' orators and preachers but soon afterwards parted from him because of the latter's unease with the Nicene formulae and because of his reluctance to affirm the deity of the Holy Spirit. Basil became of high importance for the Nicene cause after serving the bishop of Cappadocian Caesarea as resident theologian and administrator. He eventually succeeded in the episcopate at Caesarea and was chiefly responsible for leading the majority of bishops of the entire region into a caucus that affirmed and accepted the Nicene faith.

His treatise *On the Holy Spirit*[15] is a classic statement of the deity of the Spirit and explains His sanctifying presence in the world and the church. Basil Collaborated with Gregory the Theologian to make an edition of the 'best of' Origen of Alexandria and shared with Gregory the renown for having saved Origen for posterity, when later generations were willing to jettison him for his occasional lapses. To his pen is also attributed the set of ascetical advices and scripture reflections[16] that served as one of the very earliest 'Guides for a new monk'. This became an immense bestseller that formed the fundamental character of eastern Christian monasticism ever afterwards. It gave a highly inflected stress to personal development and mystical prayer, and, in this, it diverged significantly from the much more regulated character of Western monasticism that would rise up with the Benedictine Rule.

---

[15] English translation: *St. Basil on the Holy Spirit*, trans. D. Anderson (New York: St. Vladimir's Seminary Press, 1980).

[16] He is traditionally seen as the author of the 'Longer Rules' and 'Shorter Rules'. Further, see E. F. Morison, *St. Basil and His Rule: A Study in Early Monasticism* (Oxford: Oxford University Press, 1912); P. Rousseau, *Basil of Caesarea* (Berkeley: University of California Press, 1998).

Basil was above all else an intellectual who was also a man of action. In the long centuries following his death, he rose to be one of the most honoured saints of the Eastern church. Generations of Orthodox bishops have ever afterwards taken him as a model for their vocations: combining a deep and ascetical life of prayer with energetic action on behalf of the Christian mission. Basil was one of the first to suggest that monks should prefer working for the poor in the city suburbs to living in isolation in desert regions. He is truly the father of all Christian institutions of mercy: hospitals, schools and orphanages, and these envisaged as aspects of the church's philanthropic mission, staffed by professed monastics. Until the rise of the modern welfare state, this legacy had a major impact modelling the development of civilization.

Basil's younger brother, named Gregory,[17] was educated on the family's monastically organized country estates, by his sister the Abbess Macrina.[18] Like his brother, he too was a powerful intellect and a devoted churchman. As a young man he and his friend Evagrius went to Nazianzus in order to study rhetoric for a while with their family friend Gregory the Theologian. Both the younger Gregory and Evagrius (of Pontus) would become internationally renowned theologians in their maturity, Evagrius becoming one of the world's leading monastic theorists on prayer.[19]

After Basil became Archbishop of Caesarea he called on the young Gregory to assist him as a bishop of the country town of Nyssa (Nevsehir in modern Turkey). In this way Gregory was thrust into the very midst of the strong conflicts that were going on in the eastern empire over the fate of the Nicene Creed. Alongside his brother, Gregory of Nyssa's labours and scintillating orations were immensely important in securing the ultimate victory of the Nicene cause. After Basil's death in 379, Gregory heard that his former teacher, Gregory of Nazianzus, had gone to Constantinople to rally the Nicene cause there, and he sent his friend, now his episcopal deacon Evagrius, to assist the old man in preparing his famous Theological Orations. Gregory of Nyssa joined them just before the great council of 381 opened, and the three collaborated in preparing many texts concerned with refuting Arian claims to be the only logical version of Christianity possible.

Gregory the Theologian became president of the council after the unexpected death of Meletius of Antioch but was more or less forced to resign because his eirenic church polity (leaving dissident bishops in office if they agreed to profess the Nicene faith) did not please the many eastern bishops who had suffered under Arian oppression and wanted imperial punishments to follow. The older Gregory returned home to write in retirement, and the younger Gregory remained to become a great imperial favourite and was appointed by the emperor to be the supervisor (and

---

[17]The Church of Cappadocia had close Armenian and Syrian links. The word 'Gregorios' means 'Watcher' and was a title of 'Angel'.

[18]Further, see A. M. Silvas, *Macrina the Younger: Philosopher of God* (Turnhout: Brepols, 2008).

[19]Further, see J. Kalvesmaki and R. D. Young (eds), *Evagrius and His Legacy* (South Bend, IN: University of Notre Dame Press, 2016).

standard) of Orthodox teaching in Cappadocia. His writings range over matters of fundamental catechesis, profoundly symbolic exegesis of scriptures and mystical theology. As was his mentor, the older Gregory, the Nyssen too is one of the most learned and profound of all the Greek Fathers, but his theological insights remained more obscure, less approachable, until modern times when, with new editions of his complete works made available to a much wider audience, his real power as a theologian was once more revealed. Immense interest has been attracted to his theology throughout the twentieth century and beyond. In a nutshell, Gregory of Nyssa is a perfect representative of the manner in which eastern Christian theology prefers the mystical, intuitive and so-called 'apophatic'[20] modalities of doing theology to the more rational and deductive spirit that often characterized medieval and early modern Western Christian thinking.

THE BYZANTINE FATHERS: MAXIMUS AND JOHN DAMASCENE

The Byzantines prided themselves on making no changes in the churchly customs they had inherited from their fathers, and the theological tradition throughout the long Byzantine centuries is indeed remarkably slow-moving and only develops by nuanced clarification on the authorities received by the great councils of the patristic age. The Byzantines saw church affairs as they saw their own 'Roman' heritage (albeit they now spoke Greek not Latin). They could see that great monuments of Roman civilization ('their' civilization) were decaying (one thinks of architecture as well as heritage – such as the law codes), but this did not mean they should be demolished and replaced, rather that the process of repair should be considered a 'Renovation' (*enkainismos*). The two most outstanding Byzantine theologians, Maximus the Confessor (ca. 580–662) and John of Damascus (ca. 675–749), both show this aspect of trying to renovate the patristic tradition, but also being careful to synthesize and re-present it in a faithful consonance with patristic thought.

Maximus is the most impressive of all the Byzantine-era theologians. His mind is acute and merges philosophy with theology in a confident and deeply mystical manner. He is the Christian writer who most successfully synthesizes Platonic and Aristotelian methodologies so as to place them in the service of scriptural and mystical theology. Maximus values Origen's thought but understood how the uncritical adoption of everything he said had led to much disruption in Eastern church affairs (the so-called Origenistic crises); but he also regarded the attitude that wished to ban Origen from all future consideration was both futile (Origen's approach to the scriptures had become constitutive of how most of Christendom read the Bible by then) and wooden-headed (he did not wish to see fundamentalistic and non-intellectual trends elevate the closure of the Christian mind as a virtue). And so he took for his model and mentor the great fourth-century Father, Gregory

---

[20]So named from the Greek: 'turning away from speech'.

the Theologian, and used his theological commentaries (by then they had become difficult to interpret) as a source from which to mount his own commentary and explications on how the world worked.

Just as Gregory, in his own day, had revised and moderated Origen's work, and advanced upon it, so too did Maximus. He saw the Logos of God as the creative underpinning of all that exists. The notion of Logos means not only Word but also rationale or plan. Maximus placed as central to his view of the sacrality of all creation, that the divine Word was immanent in all things, but the believer who realized this and conformed mind and heart and soul to the emergence of divine Logos through the sacrament of materiality realized the inherent destiny of created things,[21] thus becoming the 'priest' of creation. This fulfilment of the highest consciousness (the sense and veneration of the divine presence) gave the world its meaning, and the believer who understood the presence entered into the salvific dynamic and, in this way, offered the created order back to God its maker as a priestly offering.[22] To synopsize this mystically capacious theology, and also to pin it in to the Alexandrian patristic tradition, thus making its connection to the doctrine of salvation abundantly clear, Maximus prioritized the concept of salvation as the believer's deification (*theiopoiesis*): the entry by divine grace into communion with God. After Maximus the concept became the primary way all subsequent eastern Christian theology envisaged the transformative effects of the Incarnation on humanity.

John of Damascus is called in the eastern tradition, *Chrysorrhoas*, or 'streaming with gold': a sign of the immensely high opinion the Byzantines had of both his style and his teaching content. John was not possessed of the same subtle acuity of Maximus, but his great clarity of expression, and his ability to sum up the central aspects of the earlier thinkers, while adding his own incisive comment, made his body of work much more approachable by larger numbers of people. And so it was that his work, deliberately composed as a kind of 'summing up' or compendium of Orthodox theology, and titled *The Fount of Knowledge*, became the standard textbook of theologians in the late Byzantine period and held its reputation even into modern times.[23]

It is divided into three sections. The first is the *Philosophical Chapters* (a student primer of logic meant to prepare the mind for discussing theology). The second is: *Concerning the Heresies* (a catalogue and digest of all the heresies the church had hitherto condemned). It makes massive simplifications and lists Islam as the latest heretical deviation (not approaching it as a new religion). The last part was his dogmatics: *An Exact Exposition of the Orthodox Faith*.

---

[21]See Hans Urs von Balthasar, *Cosmic Liturgy: The Universe According to Maximus the Confessor* (San Francisco, CA: Ignatius Press, 2003).

[22]Further, see P. M. Blowers, *Maximus the Confessor: Jesus Christ and the Transfiguration of the World* (Oxford: Oxford University Press, 2016).

[23]For a more detailed consideration, see A. Louth, *St John Damascene: Tradition and Originality in Byzantine Theology* (Oxford: Oxford University Press, 2005).

It was particularly this part which had a very wide circulation and standardized much of later eastern Christian thinking, as it was widely used as the prime teaching aid in seminaries and monasteries. John wrote at a time when the Byzantine culture was waning under relentless external pressures. His work is in the manner of a life raft, preserving the best of the past. It is itself a sign of the decline when the higher schools and highly learned bishops of classical antiquity can no longer be counted on: but it was prescient, for the political disasters that would overtake Byzantine Christianity increasingly after the eleventh century made this little 'compendium' a veritable treasure house. Its reputation also rose high in the West where it became one of the major sources that impressed Thomas Aquinas and is regularly cited as an authority in his own *Summa Theologiae*.

John, who ended his life as a monk and priest of Mar Saba monastery in the Holy Land, also produced many works on the liturgy, as well as numerous elegant hymns that are used to this day in the services of many churches and the Orthodox East. He wrote against the imperial policy of Iconoclasm (being safe enough distant from the imperial court), and his work had a considerable impact, both in his own day where it was received as a welcome answer to Iconoclastic charges that Icon veneration was tantamount to idolatry and also in a later generation, when it was used as an important source and authority in the pro-Icon theology endorsed by the Seventh Oecumenical Council in 787.

The clear desire of all these major thinkers to stand together in a received tradition that they creatively nuance among themselves gives a dominant voice to eastern Christian theology that clearly shapes a consonance and coherence within it. This can best be summarized as a form of Christianity centred around a mystical understanding of the Incarnation which sees it as a sacrament[24] of transformation: the lifting up of humanity into the communion of divine life. It also marks Greek Christian thought, however advanced and philosophical it became, as a system determined to keep in touch with common piety. It makes its advance as much through teachings on prayer and liturgy, through hymns and icons and cultic practices, as ever it does through syllogism and discourse.

BIBLIOGRAPHY

Balthasar, H. Urs von. *Cosmic Liturgy: The Universe According to Maximus the Confessor.* San Francisco, CA: Ignatius Press, 2003.

Blowers, P. M. *Maximus the Confessor: Jesus Christ and the Transfiguration of the World.* Oxford: Oxford University Press, 2016.

Drobner, H. *The Fathers of the Church: A Comprehensive Introduction.* Ada, MI: Baker Academic, 2016.

Frend, W. H. C. *The Rise of Christianity.* Minneapolis, MN: Augsburg Fortress Press, 1984.

---

[24]The Greek term is *Mysterion.*

Grillmeier, A. *Christ in Christian Tradition*, vol. 1, 2nd edn. London: Mowbrays, 1975.

Hanson, R. P. C. *The Search for the Christian Doctrine of God*. Edinburgh: T&T Clark, 1988.

Kalvesmaki, J. and Young, R. D. (eds). *Evagrius and His Legacy*. South Bend, IN: University of Notre Dame Press, 2016.

Kelly, J. N. D. *Early Christian Doctrines*, Fifth edn. London: Bloomsbury, 1977.

Kelly, J. N. D. *Golden Mouth: The Story of John Chrysostom: Ascetic, Preacher, Bishop*. London: Duckworth, 1996.

Louth, A. *St John Damascene: Tradition and Originality in Byzantine Theology*. Oxford: Oxford University Press, 2005.

McGuckin, J. A. 'Gregory of Nazianzus: The Rhetorician as Poet'. In T. Hagg and J. Bortnes (eds), *Gregory of Nazianzus: Images and Reflections*, 193–212. Copenhagen: Museum Tusculanum Press, 2005.

McGuckin, J. A. *The Path of Christianity: The First Thousand Years*. Downer's Grove, IL: IVP Academic, 2017.

Meyendorff, J. *Byzantine Theology*. New York: Fordham University Press, 1975.

Meyendorff, J. *Imperial Unity and Christian Divisions*. New York: St. Vladimir's Seminary Press, 1989.

Morison, E. F. *St. Basil and His Rule: A Study in Early Monasticism*. Oxford: Oxford University Press, 1912.

Norris, F. W. *Faith Gives Fullness to Reasoning: The Five Theological Orations of Gregory Nazianzen*. Leiden: E.J. Brill, 2015.

Pelikan, J. *The Christian Tradition: vol. 1. The Emergence of the Classical Tradition*. Chicago: University of Chicago Press, 1975.

Pelikan, J. *Christianity and Classical Culture*. New Haven, CT: Yale University Press, 1993.

Ramelli, H. *A Larger Hope? Universal Salvation from Christian Beginnings to Julian of Norwich*. Eugene, OR: Cascade Books, 2019.

Rousseau, P. *Basil of Caesarea*. Berkeley: University of California Press, 1998.

Shapland C. R. B. *The Letters of St. Athanasius Concerning the Holy Spirit to Bishop Serapion*. London: Epworth Press, 1951.

Silvas, A. M. *Macrina the Younger: Philosopher of God*. Turnhout: Brepols, 2008.

White, C. *Gregory of Nazianzus: Autobiographical Poems*. Cambridge: Cambridge University Press, 1996.

CHAPTER 28

The Coptic church

Faithful to its roots

MARK SHERIDAN

COPTIC ORIGINS

The words 'Copt' and 'Coptic', derived from the Arabic *qibṭ*, which is in turn derived from the Greek word for Egypt (*Aigyptos*), have been used in Latin and modern European languages since the sixteenth century to designate the modern Christian inhabitants of Egypt and also the language used by them in their liturgy. The Arabs used the word of the native Christian inhabitants of Egypt, and it was also used in late medieval Egypt, especially in the Mamluk period (1249–1517) to designate Muslims of Coptic (as distinguished from Arabic) descent. Westerners have used it, inaccurately, to designate the church in Ethiopia, which, prior to 1959, was dependent on the church in Egypt. The Arabic word *qibṭ* is used by the Coptic (Egyptian) Christians as the equivalent of the Coptic word for Egypt (*cheme*). With the increased flow of Coptic manuscripts into Europe in the eighteenth and nineteenth centuries and the more scientific study of the language, the word 'Coptic' came to be applied to the Egyptian language in all its dialects as spoken and written from the third century of the present era onwards, independently of the religious association.

According to the church historian Eusebius,[1] reflecting the traditions of his own time in the early fourth century, the evangelist Mark first preached the gospel in Alexandria, and the Coptic church claims an unbroken succession of patriarchs from that time to the present. Although manuscript evidence reveals that Christianity was firmly established in Egypt in the early second century, it is only in the last quarter of that century that it emerges into the full light of history with the figures of the catechists Pantaenus, Clement of Alexandria and Origen, and the bishop Demetrius I (188–230), as well as with heretics such as Basileides. By the time of the Peace of the church under Constantine and the Council of Nicaea (325), the number of bishops had notably increased. Under Athanasius another diocese was established

---

[1] Eusebius, *HE.*, 2. 16, 24.

at Philae in southern Egypt. The Egyptian church was unique among the oriental churches in the highly monarchical structure that it developed under the bishop of Alexandria.[2] From the third century onwards it was the custom of the bishops of Alexandria to send a circular letter to all the bishops of Egypt announcing the date of Easter and dealing with other doctrinal and disciplinary matters.[3] Tension caused by this structure may have contributed to the Meletian schism that began during the reign of Alexander I (312–26) when the bishop of Lycopolis, Meletius, ordained other bishops. By long-established tradition all the bishops in Egypt are ordained by the bishop of Alexandria. Since the fourth century the church in Egypt has dated events from the accession of Diocletion as emperor in 284, heralding a period later referred to as the age of the martyrs because of the numerous victims of persecution, including the Alexandrian patriarch Peter (d. 311), at the beginning of the fourth century.

Greek had been spoken in Egypt since the conquest of the country by Alexander the Great in 332 BC and the foundation, the following year, of the city of Alexandria, which soon became one of the principal cities of the Hellenistic world. Greek-speaking communities were to be found in towns throughout the Nile Valley, and Christianity seems to have spread first among the Greek-speaking population in these towns. There is reason to believe that, at least by the second and third century, there was a fairly large and prosperous bilingual population of native Egyptian origin.[4] The older forms of writing the Egyptian language, hieroglyphic and hieratic, had long since given way to the demotic script for practical purposes, but it too had given way to Greek for most administrative purposes. The creation of the Coptic script in the middle or second half of the third century seems to have been a deliberate attempt on the part of a bilingual educated elite to revive the Egyptian language as a literary medium.[5] This script made use of the Greek alphabet together with several letters borrowed from the demotic tongue to represent sounds not found in the Greek alphabet. Documents using this script exist from the fourth century in a variety of Coptic dialects including Fayumic, Achmimic and Sahidic. The last of these quickly became the standard literary dialect, and the first major literary work to have been produced in this language appears to have been the translation of the Christian Scriptures. This form of writing was also employed by others besides orthodox Christians, as Manichaean, gnostic and other documents testify. Most of the early Coptic literature consists of translations from Greek works but some early Christian apocryphal writings may have been originally composed

---

[2] A. Martin, *Athanase d'Alexandrie et l'église d'Égypte au IVe siècle: (328-373)* (Rome: École française de Rome, 1996).

[3] A. Camplani, *Le lettere festali di Atanasio di Alessandria: studio storico-critico* (Rome: Centro Italiano Microfiches, 1989); idem, *Athanasius, Lettere festali* (Milan: Paoline, 2003).

[4] R. S. Bagnall and B. W. Frier, *The Demography of Roman Egypt* (Cambridge: Cambridge University Press, 1994).

[5] T. Orlandi, 'Letteratura copta e cristianesimo nazionale egiziano', in *L'Egitto cristiano. Aspetti e problemi in età tardo-antica*, ed. A. Camplani, SEA vol. 56 (Rome: Institutum Augustinianum, 1997), pp. 39–120.

in Coptic.[6] Original Christian literature in Sahidic dating from the fourth to the seventh centuries includes many lives of saints, encomia, homilies, catecheses, monastic rules and letters.[7]

COPTIC MONASTICISM

From at least the first part of the fourth century an extensive monastic movement became an important feature of the life of the Egyptian church and has remained such throughout its history. The monastic movement assumed a variety of external forms ranging from the solitary hermit to the highly organized cenobitic communities, and this variety is found throughout the Nile Valley and in delta from the beginning of this period.[8] Two names, in particular, are associated with the rise of monasticism: those of Antony (d. 356) and Pachomius (d. 346) who became the patrons of the eremitical and cenobitical forms of monasticism respectively. Letters attributed to them and to the successors of Pachomius, Theodore and Horsiesius, are among the earliest items of Coptic literature.[9]

By the middle of the fourth century many thousands had taken up the monastic life, and the fame of the monks spread beyond Egypt, attracting many recruits from other parts of the Roman Empire. Soon after the death of Antony, Athanasius wrote his *Life of Antony*, which became the first great classic of monastic literature and was quickly translated into many other languages.[10] Works like the *Life of Antony* and the various *Lives* of Pachomius cannot be taken at face value as descriptions of the historical reality, but through the ideal they presented and promoted, they contributed to the growth of the historical phenomenon. Egyptian monasticism began and spread as a popular movement, but successive generations of theologians

---

[6]See: D. Frankfurter, *Elijah in Upper Egypt: Studies in the History and Composition of the Coptic Elijah Apocalypse* (Minneapolis, MN: Fortress Press, 1990); J.-C. Haelewyck, *Clavis apocryphorum Veteris Testamenti* (Turnhout: Brepols, 1998); M. Geerard, *Clavis apocryphorum Novi Testamenti* (Turnhout: Brepols, 1992).

[7]M. Sheridan, 'Rhetorical Structure in Coptic Sermons', in *The World of Early Egyptian Christianity: Language, Literature, and Social Context (In honor of D. W. Johnson)*, eds J. E. Goering and J. A. Timbie (Washington, DC: Catholic University of America Press, 2007), pp. 25–48; idem, 'The Encomium in the Coptic Literature of the Late Sixth Century', in *ICCoptS* 9, pp. 443–64; idem, *Rufus of Shotep: Homilies on the Gospels of Matthew and Luke. Introduction, Text, Translation, Commentary*, Unione Accademica Nazionale, Corpus dei Manoscritti Copti Letterari (Rome: Centro Italiano Microfiches, 1998).

[8]M. Sheridan, 'The Spiritual and Intellectual World of Early Egyptian Monasticism', *C* 1, (2002): 2–51; idem, 'The Modern Historiography of Early Egyptian Monasticism', in *Il Monachesimo tra Eredità e Aperture. Atti del simposio 'Testi e temi nella tradizione del monachesimo cristiano' per il 50° anniversario dell'Istituto Monastico di Sant'Anselmo*, eds M. Bielawski and D. Hombergen, SA, vol. 140 (Rome: Institutum Anselmianum, 2004), pp. 197–220.

[9]S. Rubenson, *The Letters of St. Antony: Monasticism and the Making of a Saint* (Minneapolis, MN: Fortress Press, 1997); H. Quecke, *Die Briefe Pachoms: griechischer Text der Handschrift W. 145 der Chester Beatty Library* (Regensburg: F. Pustet, 1975).

[10]G. J. M. Bartelink (ed.), *Athanase: Vie d'Antoine* (Paris: Editions du Cerf, 2011); M. Sheridan, 'Early Egyptian Monasticism: Ideals and Reality, or: The Shaping of the Monastic Ideal', *JCSCopS* 7 (2015): 9–22.

attempted to give it coherence and consistency. Even if we can engage in well-founded speculation, we shall never know what inspired or motivated the many thousands who took up the monastic life in Egypt at the end of the third century and the early fourth century to do so. They did not leave any written testimony. Our literary sources come later and are clearly aimed at creating an ideal of the monastic life.

The monks of Scetis and Cellia[11] became particularly famous outside of Egypt because of the accounts of foreigners such as Rufinus of Aquileia, who wrote a continuation of the *Ecclesiastical History* of Eusebius[12] and Palladius of Helenopolis.[13] However, the most important Coptic monastic writer was undoubtedly Shenoute of Atripe, who, however, remained unknown outside of Egypt until modern times.

SHENOUTE OF ATRIPE

Shenoute's works, along with those of many others, were preserved in the White Monastery in Upper Egypt near Akhmim. Beginning in the sixteenth century the manuscripts of the White Monastery came to be dispersed across many countries and libraries in Europe and the United States.[14] Only recently has it been possible to understand the nature and organization of the works of Shenoute.[15] The publication of the complete surviving works of Shenoute is still in progress.[16]

Shenoute was born in the middle of the AD fourth century (the date AD 348, often mentioned but not universally accepted, is based on an inscription in his monastery, dating from the twelfth or thirteen century). Around AD 385, Shenoute became the father of the White Monastery in Upper Egypt near Akhmim. It has often been assumed that Shenoute was the immediate successor of the White Monastery's

---

[11]H. G. Evelyn-White and W. Hauser, *The Monasteries of the Wadi 'n Natrûn: Part II, the History of the Monasteries of Nitria and Scetis* (New York: The Metropolitan Museum of Art, 1932); R. Kasser, *Kellia 1. Topographie générale. - 1967. - 62 S. : Ill., Kt. 1. Topographie générale. - 1967. - 62 S. : Ill., Kt.* (Genève: Georg, 1967); F. Daumas, N. H. Henein and P. Ballet, *Kellia 2, L'ermitage copte QR 195 1, Archéologie et architecture [1] 2, L'ermitage copte QR 195 1, Archéologie et architecture [1]* (Cairo: IFAO, 2000); D. Weidmann, *Kellia kôm Qouçoûr 'Îsa' 1 ; fouilles de 1965 à 1978* (Louvain: Peeters, 2013).

[12]P. R. Amidon, *Rufinus, Eusebius, and the History of the Church* (Washington, DC: Catholic University of America Press, 2016).

[13]C. Butler, *The Lausiac History of Palladius. Vols. 1-2* (Hildesheim: Olms, 1967).

[14]O. V. Volkoff, *A la recherche de manuscrits en Egypte* (Cairo: Institut français d'archéologie orientale, 1970). In the process of dispersion many manuscripts or parts of manuscripts have been lost. For example, the homilies of Rufus of Shotep originally extended to about 2,000 pages, of which only about 120 have survived.

[15]S. Emmel, *Shenoute's Literary Corpus*, 2 vols, CSCO, vols. 599–600, also: CSCO Subsidia, vols. 111–12 (Leuven: Peeters, 2004), with an extensive bibliography on Shenoute up to 2004; idem. 'Shenoute's Place in the History of Monasticism', in *Christianity and Monasticism in Upper Egypt*, vol. 1: *Akhmim and Sohag*, eds G. Gabra and H. N. Takla (Cairo and New York: The American University in Cairo Press, 2008), pp. 31–46; (with useful bibliography on pp. 321–50).

[16]Recent publications include B. Layton, *The Canons of Our Fathers: Monastic Rules of Shenoute* (Oxford: Oxford University Press, 2014); A. Boud'hors, *Le canon 8 de Chénouté d'après le manuscrit Ifao Copte 2 et les fragments complémentaires* (Cairo: Institut français d'archéologie orientale, 2013).

founder, Pigol. However, the reconstruction of Shenoute's literary corpus made it possible to realize that Pigol died in the 370s and was then succeeded not by Shenoute but by another father, Ebonh, and that a spiritual crisis during Ebonh's tenure as head of the White Monastery, a crisis which seems to have involved carnal sin, enabled Shenoute to come to prominence and to become Ebonh's immediate successor.[17]

Because of his popularity in Upper Egypt and his zeal for Orthodoxy, Shenoute was chosen by the Patriarch Cyril to accompany him in representing the Church of Alexandria at the Council of Ephesus in AD 431.[18] There he provided the moral support that Cyril needed to defeat the heresy of Nestorius, bishop of Constantinople. The eventual exile of the latter to Akhmim, across the river from Atripe, was a testimony to the impression that Shenoute had made upon the attendees of this council and upon the court.

On 7 Epip (14 July) AD 466, following a short illness possibly brought on by advanced age, Shenoute died in the presence of his monks.[19] From Pigol, who was his uncle, Shenoute had inherited a monastery based on the Pachomian system, though much more austere and stringent. This made its followers few in number and probably promoted decline rather than growth. Shenoute implemented a more comprehensive system that was less stringent and more suitable to the surroundings and the background of the people. This new system had an unusual component, which was a covenant (*diatheke*) to be recited and adhered to literally by the new novices. It read as follows:

> I vow before God in His Holy Place, the word which I have spoken with my mouth being my witness; I will not defile my body in any way, I will not steal, I will not bear false witness, I will not lie, I will not do anything deceitful secretly. If I transgressed what I have vowed, I will see the Kingdom of Heaven, but will not enter it. God before whom I made the covenant will destroy my soul and my body in the fiery Hell because I transgressed the covenant I made.[20]

Transgressors of that covenant were expelled from the monastery altogether. This was considered a near death sentence for those peasant monks.

Another interesting feature of Shenoute's monastic system was the requirement for the new novices to live outside the monastery for a period of time before they were deemed worthy to be consecrated as monks. This seemed to be at odds with the Nitrian monastic system, which allowed the monks to live away from the monastic settlements only after they became proficient in the monastic life. Shenoute also utilized the time of the monks, outside prayer and worship, in more varied tasks within the monastery than the Nitrian monks were exposed to. Aside from the traditional trades of rope and basket weaving, Shenoute's monks engaged in weaving

---

[17]Emmel, *Shenoute's Literary Corpus*, pp. 9–10, and pp. 558–64.
[18]Ibid., p. 8.
[19]Ibid., pp. 11–12.
[20]D. N. Bell, *Besa: The Life of Shenoute* (Kalamazoo, MI: Cistercian Publications, 1989), pp. 9–10.

and tailoring linen, cultivation of flax, leather work and shoe-making, writing and book-binding, carpentry, and metal and pottery-making. All in all, Shenoute tried as much as possible to employ the monks in their old professions. Such activities made the monastery a vast self-supporting complex, which occupied some 20 square miles of land.

As a monastic leader, Shenoute recognized the need for literacy among the community. So he required all his monks and nuns to learn to read and encouraged more of them to pursue the art of writing manuscripts. This made the monastery more and more appealing to belong to and consequently made the threat of expulsion more painful. In his laudatory *Life of Saint Shenoute*,[21] his disciple Besa recounts several incidents of Shenoute coming to the aid of poor Coptic peasants. One time he went to Akhmim to chastise a pagan because of the oppression he was inflicting on the poor.[22] Another time he acted to eliminate a grievance of the peasants whom the pagan landlords of Paneleou had forced to buy their spoiled wine.[23] On a third occasion he risked his life to ask, successfully, for the freedom of the captives at Psoi from the hands of the Blemmyes warriors.[24] At times he also appealed on behalf of the peasants to those in power, including the Emperor Theodosius I. In summary, Shenoute fully recognized the misery of his people and emerged as their sincere advocate and popular leader.

Shenoute wrote in a style that was essentially his own, with writings based on a careful study of the scholastic rhetoric of his time, which displayed the wide and deep range of knowledge he possessed. They were adorned with endless quotations from the Holy Scriptures, a typical feature of patristic writings. The scriptures were quoted whenever a presented argument needed support. In doing so, Shenoute also displayed an astonishing memory as he rendered these passages with amazing accuracy. But Shenoute's knowledge was not confined to the Bible, as was the case for the majority of the monks in Egypt. He was fluent in both Coptic and Greek and was fairly well acquainted with Greek thought and theology. The sprinkling of Greek loanwords in his writings was both extensive and sophisticated, and it was definitely not a product of his living environment. He also expressed knowledge of the works of Aristotle, Aristophanes, the Platonic school and even some of the Greek legends. He certainly read some of the works of Athanasius such as the *Life of Antony* and some of the latter's homiletic works. Shenoute also knew the *Letters of Antony*, some of the *Letters of Pachomius* and most likely some of the works of Evagrius of Pontus. His knowledge further extended to such popular non-canonical texts as the *Acts of Archelaus*[25] and the *Gospel of Thomas*.[26]

---

[21]N. Lubomierski, *Die Vita Sinuthii: Form- und Überlieferungsgeschichte der hagiographischen Texte über Schenute den Archimandriten* (Tübingen: Mohr Siebeck, 2007).

[22]Ibid., chs. 81–2.

[23]Ibid., chs. 85–6.

[24]Ibid., ch. 89.

[25]See, J. BeDuhn and P. A. Mirecki, *Frontiers of Faith: The Christian Encounter with Manichaeism in the Acts of Archelaus* (Leiden: E.J. Brill, 2007).

[26]B. Layton, *The Gnostic Scriptures* (New York: Doubleday, 2015).

According to Emmel's reconstruction of Shenoute's works, his corpus consists of two main components: the *Canons* and the *Discourses*.[27] The designation *canon* seems to reflect Shenoute's own terminology and refers to monastic rules. The *Discourses* include works such as letters, sermons and tracts (treatises or discourses). This category includes the richest collection that has survived from Shenoute's writings. The whole dossier is organized by Emmel[28] in eight volumes. Some of his notable compositions are: *The Lord Thundered, Since It Is Necessary to Pursue the Devil, A Beloved Asked Me Years Ago, Because of You Too, O Prince of Evil, Not because a Fox Barks, As We Began to Preach, I Have Heard about Your Wisdom, God Is Blessed, The Idolatrous Pagans* and *I am Amazed*.

One of Shenoute's longest works, which was probably written as a treatise rather than just a sermon, is the work against the Origenists and the Gnostics: *Contra Origenistas et Gnosticos*.[29] The aim of this work was to oppose heretics in general and Origenists in particular, regarding the apocryphal books that they used and circulated. He also touches upon the subjects of the plurality of the worlds, the position and the work of the Saviour, and the meaning of Easter. Other subjects mentioned in the treatise included the relationship between the Father and the Son, the origin of souls, Christ's conception, the Eucharist, the resurrection of the body and the four elements.

As more and more identifications of Shenoute's literary works are made, his contribution to Coptic literature appears to be even greater than previously assumed. On the one hand, it is becoming clear that he treated a wide range of subjects (not only monastic issues), which suggests a more favourable assessment of the theological character of his writing, his spirituality and his moral and nationalistic behaviour. On the other hand, he accepted the inclusion of literary activity in the religious field. This sets him apart from the Pachomian system that tended to treat religious literature as mere written instructions with no regard being given to stylistic concerns. Shenoute further developed a personal style that is clearly a product of careful study of the scholastic Greek rhetoric of his time.

THE CHURCH OF ALEXANDRIA

Due partly to the strategic importance of the city of Alexandria, but also to the vigour of the literary tradition of the Egyptian church, the patriarchs of Alexandria played an important role in church affairs throughout the fourth and fifth centuries – outside as well as inside of Egypt. This is particularly true of Athanasius whose long reign (326–73) established him as the champion of the orthodox faith of

---

[27]Emmel, *Shenoute's Literary Corpus*, vol. 1, pp. 3–5.

[28]These volumes are essential for understanding the works of Shenoute. The *Discourses* are listed according to the *Incipits* in English. The Vienna *Incipit* list contains ninety-one works. See Emmel, *Shenoute's Literary Corpus*, pp. 238–41.

[29]H. J. Cristea (ed.), *Schenute Von Atripe: Contra Origenistas: Edition Des Koptischen Textes Mit Annotierter Übersetzung Und Indizes Einschließlich Einer Übersetzung Des 16. Osterfestbriefs Des Theophilus in Der Fassung Des Hieronymus (Ep. 96)* (Tubingen: Mohr Siebeck, 2012).

Nicaea against the Arian heresy. Theophilus (385–412) is known chiefly for his role in the Origenist controversy and in the deposition of John Chrysostom, the bishop of Constantinople.[30] His nephew Cyril of Alexandria (patriarch, 412–44) became a principal protagonist in the conflict over Nestorius and a dominant figure at the Council of Ephesus (431), which he attended with an entourage of fifty bishops. His theological writings were an important factor in the refusal of the Egyptian church under Patriarch Dioscorus (451–4) to accept the innovative language of the Council of Chalcedon and the *Tome of Leo*. Athanasius, Cyril and Dioscurus are revered as saints by the Coptic church.

The Council of Chalcedon (451) proved to be a turning point in the relationship of the Egyptian church with the other churches. From the point of view of the Alexandrian Christology loyal to Cyril's formulation, the Chalcedonian definition of the two enduring natures of Christ after the Union was tantamount to the adoption of the Nestorian heresy, and therefore a denial of the full reality of the Incarnate Union. From the point of view of the defenders of Chalcedon, however, the Alexandrian-Egyptian theology was 'Monophysite'; that is, it did not sufficiently distinguish the two natures of Christ, divine and human but recognized only a single nature (*mia physis* in Cyril's terminology). The dispute revolved around the sense of the word *physis* (nature), and neither side was able to recognize that the other was using the term in a different sense. In the course of the century and more that followed, various attempts were made to preserve the unity of the church (and the empire), by devising compromise formulae, by controlling the appointment of the patriarch of Alexandria or by force.[31] The Egyptian church was not alone in refusing to accept Chalcedon, and the long exile of the most important literary exponent of the monophysite theology, the patriarch Severus of Antioch, spent in Egypt (518–38), helped to reinforce the resistance of the Egyptian church.[32] Severus is revered as a saint by the Coptic church and is mentioned in the liturgy together with Athanasius, Cyril and Dioscurus, among others.

The patriarchate of Theodosius I (536–67) was particularly decisive for the formation of the Coptic church. When he refused to subscribe to the formula of Chalcedon, Theodosius was brought to Constantinople by the Emperor Justinian and kept under house arrest for over thirty years. The Egyptian church did not recognize the validity of sacraments administered by those who subscribed to the formula of Chalcedon, whom they regarded as heretics. Therefore, they would not

---

[30]A. M. Malingrey and P. Leclercq (eds), *[Palladius Helenopolitanus]: Dialogue sur la vie de Jean Chrysostome* (Paris: Cerf, 1988); N. Russell, *Theophilus of Alexandria* (London: Routledge, 2007).

[31]The literature concerning the controversy is very extensive. See especially: P. B. Clayton, Jr., *The Christology of Theodoret of Cyrus: Antiochene Christology from the Council of Ephesus (431) to the Council of Chalcedon (451)* (Oxford: Oxford University Press, 2007); A. Grillmeier and T. Hainthaler, *Christ in Christian tradition*, vol. 2, Pt. 4 (London: Mowbray, 1996); J. Roldanus and J. Van Oort, *Chalkedon: Geschichte und Aktualität : Studien zur Rezeption der christologischen Formel von Chalkedon* (Louvain: Peeters, 1998); J. E. Steppa, *John Rufus and the World Vision of Anti-Chalcedonian Culture*, Second Revised edn (Piscataway, NJ: Gorgias Press, 2019).

[32]I. R. Torrance, *Christology after Chalcedon* (London: Canterbury Press, 1988).

accept ordination from the patriarch imposed by Constantinople. This caused the gradual depletion of the hierarchy, and the resulting crisis led to establishment of a separate hierarchy and patriarch through the intervention of Jacob Baradaeus (consecrated bishop by Patriarch Theodosius in 543), whose missionary journeys throughout the Middle East were so extensive that these churches became known as the Jacobites. From the time of Patriarch Peter IV (576–8) there existed in Egypt two competing patriarchs and hierarchies, the Chalcedonian (or Melchite) and the non-Chalcedonian or Jacobite. The vast majority of the people in the Egyptian church recognized only the latter, while the former was maintained in power only in the city of Alexandria with the aid of the civil and military authority. The non-Chalcedonian patriarch had to take refuge in one of the monasteries outside of Alexandria. The long patriarchate of Damian (578–605), a Syrian by birth, was particularly important for consolidating the non-Chalcedonian hierarchy. In the *History of the Patriarchs*, we find the following passage:

> And Damian, the blessed patriarch, remained all his days composing letters and homilies and treatises, in which he refuted the heretics. And there were in his days certain bishops whom he admired, marveling at their purity and excellence; and among them was John of Burlus, and John his disciple, and Constantine the bishop, and Cleistus, and many others who tended the vineyard of the Lord of Sabaoth.[33]

A last, but futile, attempt to force the Egyptian church to accept Chalcedon was made with the appointment of the Melchite patriarch Cyrus al-Muqawqas ('the Caucasian', 631–41) endowed with full civil and military, as well as religious, power. The Arab conquest of Egypt in 641–2 finally put an end to the Byzantine efforts to control the church and opened up a new era in the history of the Egyptian church.[34] There has continued to be a Melchite (Greek Orthodox) patriarch of Alexandria to the present day, although under Turkish rule he was obliged to live in Constantinople. It is important to emphasize that the original division was not along the lines of Greek versus Copt: all of the original champions of the monophysite cause, for example, were speakers and writers of Greek.

THE LANGUAGE OF THE EGYPTIAN CHRISTIANS

It is estimated that at the time of the Arab invasion two-thirds at least of the Egyptian population was Christian, but the pressure exerted to convert to Islam in

---

[33]B. Evetts, *History of the Patriarchs of Alexandria* (Severus of Ashmunein). *Patrologia Orientalis*, vol. 1 (Turnhout: Brepols, 1904), p. 477. Although the author of the *History* probably had in mind the ecclesiastical achievements of these bishops, each of them also engaged in literary activity. See T. Orlandi, 'La patrologia copta', in *Complementi Interdisciplinari di Patrologia*, ed. A. Quacquarelli (Rome: Citta Nuova, 1989), pp. 497–502. To these must be added also the bishop Rufus of Shotep. See Sheridan, *Rufus of Shotep: Homilies on the Gospels of Matthew and Luke.*

[34]A. J. Butler and P. M. Fraser, *The Arab Conquest of Egypt and the Last Thirty Years of the Romans Dominion* (Oxford: Clarendon Press, 1978).

the subsequent centuries resulted in the Coptic church being reduced to a minority status in the country. It also resulted in the gradual disappearance of Greek as a spoken language and even as a liturgical language and the substitution of the Bohairic dialect of Coptic as the liturgical language, and eventually of Arabic as the spoken language of the Christian population.

In the 300 years between the death of the Prophet and the appearance of the first Egyptian Christian works in Arabic, Arabic had become a highly developed literary and scientific language. Arabic replaced Greek first, not just as the administrative language of Egypt but as the language of prestige and learning. It was also, like Greek, an international language, which Coptic had never been. Even for Naṣṭās ibn Jurayj (mid-tenth century), Sa'īd ibn al'Baṭrīq (or Eutychius 877–940), and for Severus Ibn al-Muqaffaʿ (d. 987), it had become more important to write in Arabic. The Coptic Bohairic dialect, because of the connection with the patriarchate in the ninth and tenth centuries,[35] took on a role that it had not enjoyed in the pre-conquest period, serving as the link with the tradition, even though it was not the traditional literary dialect. It had never served as a literary language for original compositions. The one example that is cited as evidence to the contrary, the *Life of John of Phanijoit*, is rather the exception that proves the rule.[36] One is compelled to observe that the reasons why a language becomes and functions as a literary and/or sacred language are not the same as why it ceases or continues to be spoken.

Although Greek remained a source of inspiration for Sahidic, numerous Egyptian writers produced new works in Sahidic often following Greek models. That was not the case with Bohairic, which did not and could not retain the link with Greek *paideia*. As a literary phenomenon there is no evidence that it ever had such a link. Bohairic became a literary phenomenon within the context of a process of Arabization that had already begun. It came to be substituted as the link of honour with the past, taking the place, in this respect, of Greek. It had never served as a real literary language in the same sense as Sahidic nor as a vehicle for business purposes. And yet, Coptic did not die out, first as a literary medium and then later as a spoken medium, because of repression.[37] Nor was it a case of literary suicide versus literary genocide as has been suggested recently.[38] It was rather a question of conscious

---

[35]For details, see Evelyn-White, *The Monasteries of the Wadi 'n Natruîn: Part II*, pp. 322–41.

[36]J. R. Zaborowski, *The Coptic Martyrdom of John of Phanijoit: Assimilation and Conversion to Islam in Thirteenth-Century Egypt* (Leiden: E.J. Brill, 2005).

[37]This is not to say that the periodic persecution and repression of the Egyptian Christians did not have an effect on the preservation of the language but, rather, that the language as such was not the object of repression. For the question of persecution and repression of the Christians, see: M. N. Swanson, *The Coptic Papacy in Islamic Egypt: 641-1517*, The Popes of Egypt. Vol. 2 (Cairo: American University in Cairo Press, 2007); and A. Elli, *Storia della chiesa copta* (Cairo and Jerusalem: Franciscan Centre of Christian Oriental Studies, 2003).

[38]T. S. Richter, *Greek, Coptic and the Language of the Hijra: The Rise and Decline of the Coptic Language in Late Antique and Medieval Egypt. From Hellenism to Islam: Cultural and Linguistic Change in The Roman Near East. 401-446* (Cambridge: Cambridge University Press, 2009), p. 430. Richter cites Maccoull as does Papconstantinou for this idea: L. S. B. Maccoull, 'Three Cultures under Arab Rule: The Fate of

adaptation to the new sociopolitical reality. For writers such as Naṣṭās ibn Jurayj, Sa'īd ibn al'Baṭrīq (Eutychius) and Severus of Ashmunein, it made no sense to write about medicine or even world history in Bohairic, which had never been a language of secular learning, nor even in Greek, which had once been the language of the erudite. The language of higher learning was now Arabic. Their choice stands at the beginning of the creation of a new Christian literature in Arabic in Egypt, somewhat later than in Syria-Palestine.[39]

At the beginning of Islamic rule, despite the imposition of the poll tax (ji- zyah) levied on non-Muslims ('The people of the book' ahl-al-kitab) the Christians enjoyed religious freedom, and the Patriarch Benjamin was received with honour by the conqueror 'Amr ibn al-'Āṣ. However, in 706 a series of laws was introduced to encourage Arabization and the Islamization of the population, including a law requiring the use of Arabic in public documents and a decree ordering the destruction of Christian icons. The latter led to revolt, which was repressed with bloodshed. In 750 Egypt passed from Umayyad rule (Damascus) to that of the Abbasids (Baghdad). A series of Coptic revolts led to waves of repression which in turn led to numerous conversions to Islam, with the result that by the middle of the ninth century the Coptic Christians had become a minority. Although the rule of the Fatimids (969–1171) as such was not hostile towards the Copts, one of the most serious persecutions took place under Caliph Al-Hakim (996–1021), who ordered the destruction of the churches and the confiscation of their property. The Coptic population continued to decrease and the language itself began to die out.

In this situation the monasteries, particularly those of the Wādī-al-Naṭrūn, the Red Sea monasteries of Antony and Paul, and the White Monastery near Panopolis (modern Akhmim), played an important role in the preservation of the Coptic heritage. Here the earlier literature was collected and copied for preservation. From the ninth to the eleventh centuries the majority of the patriarchs came from the monastery of Abu-Makar in the Wādī-al-Naṭrūn. It was this predominance that led to the adoption, noted earlier, of the Bohairic dialect of the region as the liturgical language of the Coptic church. This period also saw the beginning of Arabic Coptic literature, of which one of the earliest and most important works is the *History of the Patriarchs* associated with the name of Sawirus ibn al-Muqaffa', which represents a tradition of historical writing continued by later authors that is now our main source for Coptic history. Another important monument of Coptic literature in Arabic is the work on *The Churches and Monasteries of Egypt* by Abu al-Makarim (but attributed erroneously in the English translation to Abu Salih the Armenian). In this period also, Arabic was introduced into the liturgy and from the late medieval period onwards the liturgical manuscripts tend to be in both Arabic and Coptic

---

Coptic', *BSAC* 27 (1985): 61–70; idem, 'The Strange Death of Coptic Culture', *Coptic Church Review* 10 (1989): 34–45.

[39]M. Sheridan, 'The Mystery of Bohairic', in *Coping with Religious Change in the Late-Antique Eastern Mediterranean*, eds E. Iricinschi and C. Kotsifou (Tübingen: Mohr Siebeck, 2021).

(Bohairic). The situation of the Copts in Egypt did not change significantly in the subsequent periods of Muslim rule (under the Ayyubids, Mamluks and Ottomans), throughout which, despite sporadic waves of persecution, Copts often held important administrative posts.

MODERN FREEDOMS AND DEVELOPMENTS

The modern era for the Copts began with the French invasion under Bonaparte in 1798, and the rule of Mohammed Ali permitted them to be reintegrated into the national life of the country and eventually to receive equal recognition before the law. The patriarchate of Cyril IV (1854–61) marked an important step in the revival of Coptic institutions and the promotion of education. More recently the revival in the Coptic monasteries during the last thirty years has had important effects throughout the life of the Coptic church, though in recent years the rise of Islamic fundamentalism has caused tensions and even led to the house arrest of the patriarch, Pope Shenouda III, from 1981 to 1985.

The history of the Coptic liturgy (especially the surviving manuscripts) is insufficiently studied to give a clear account of the stages of its development. The liturgical language of the Egyptian church had been Greek from the beginning and Greek continued to be used in the liturgy, at least in part, long after the Arab invasion. In the eighth century the patriarchs were still sending their festal letters in Greek to other parts of Egypt. But there is also evidence that Coptic (Sahidic) was being introduced into the liturgy in the seventh century. It is not clear that there was ever a completely Sahidic liturgy or that there was uniform liturgical practice in the Coptic church before the time of the patriarch Gabriel II (1130–44), who made Bohairic the liturgical language and forbade the use of anaphoras other than those transmitted under the names of Basil, Gregory and Mark/Cyril. By this time Arabic was already entering into the celebration of the liturgy. The decree of Gabriel V in 1411 seems to have given a definitive form to the Coptic liturgy; by this time it had already undergone certain Syrian and even Byzantine influences despite the separation from Constantinople. In addition to the Eucharist, the Coptic church knows the sacraments of baptism, chrism, penance, marriage, orders and anointing of the sick. The liturgical books include the *Euchologion* (Altar book), the *Katameros* (Lectionary), the *Synaxary* (Lives of the saints), the *Horologion/Agpeia* (Canonical hours), the *Difnar* (Antiphonal), as well as the Sacramentary and the Pontifical, among others.

The Coptic calendar is punctuated by a number of periods of fasting. The church celebrates fourteen feasts of the Lord, seven major and seven minor, and five major feasts of the Virgin Mary, as well as feasts of the saints and angels. From ancient times pilgrimages, often lasting as long as a week and connected with a fair, have been an important feature of popular religious culture in the Coptic church. In ancient times the most important pilgrimage centre was that of St Menas at Maryut near Alexandria. More than sixty pilgrimage centres exist, including that of St Menas, that of the Virgin Mary at Musturud, Mar Jirjis at Mit Damsis, Sitt Dimyanah near

Bilgas and Deir el-Muharraq. Some sites are identified with the sojourn of the Holy Family in Egypt, a source of popular devotion already in antiquity.[40]

Estimates of the number of members of the Coptic Orthodox Church vary considerably (from fifteen to twenty million in Egypt alone) because of the inexact population figures for Egypt. There is also a large diaspora of up to three million. It is undoubtedly the largest Christian community in the Middle East. The church organization includes some forty-one dioceses in Egypt with diaspora dioceses in North America, East Africa, France, Jerusalem, Nubia and Khartoum. Because of the large number of Copts who have emigrated since the 1970s, there are now thirteen diocesan bishops in Europe, seven in North America, two in South America, two in Sudan and two in Australia. There are also Coptic communities with resident priests in several other European countries including Austria, Italy, England and Switzerland. The bishops by ancient tradition are not married and are usually drawn from the monks. In addition to the diocesan bishops and their auxiliaries, there are also a number of bishops with special responsibilities such as ecumenical affairs, youth and higher education. The church maintains schools and seminaries in Egypt and conducts an extensive Sunday school programme. The patriarch is chosen from one of three candidates selected by an assembly composed of the bishops, representatives of the clergy, the monks and laymen. The final selection is made by a child who draws the name of one of the shortlisted three candidates.

Ecumenical dialogue has been carried on with the Roman Catholic Church since 2004, and at times with the Greek Orthodox Church, the Anglican communion, and the Evangelical and Reformed churches. The Coptic church belongs to the group of seven churches now known as the Oriental Orthodox Churches. In Egypt, in addition to the Coptic Orthodox Church, there is a relatively small body of Coptic rites united with the Roman Catholic Church. Although Franciscans are known to have been in Egypt earlier, the continuous presence of the Catholics in Egypt in modern times dates to the Franciscan mission in Cairo in 1630, followed by the Jesuits in 1697. Vicars-apostolic have been appointed since 1741 for Catholics of the Coptic rite which at that time numbered about 2,000.[41] Pope Leo XII erected a Coptic patriarchate in 1824 but did not name a patriarch. Leo XIII named the first Catholic patriarch, Cyril Makarios, in 1899; he was deposed in 1910, but a second was not named until 1947. Today this church has 6 dioceses and about 200 priests with 100 Coptic parishes and a total membership of about 150,000 members.

Although numerous Protestant bodies are represented in Egypt, the only one that defines itself as 'Coptic' is the Coptic Evangelical Church, founded by the United Presbyterian Church in North America in 1854 and completely independent since 1957. The church has about 250 church buildings and another 250 prayer centres

---

[40]G. Viaud, *Les pelerinages coptes en Egypte d'apres les notes du Qommos Jacob Muyser* (Cairo: Imprimerie de l'Institut Francais d'Archeologie Orientale, 1979); O. F. A. Meinardus, *The Holy Family in Egypt* (Cairo: American University in Cairo Press, 2000).

[41]A. Colombo, *La nascita della chiesa copto-cattolica nella prima metà del 1700*. OCA., 250 (Rome: Pontifical Oriental Institute, 1996).

and an overall community of about 250,000 with about 340 pastors. It maintains the Evangelical Theological Seminary in Cairo and runs a large publishing house.

BIBLIOGRAPHY

Butler, C. *The Lausiac History of Palladius*, vols. 1–2. Hildesheim: Olms, 1967.

Camplani, A. *Le lettere festali di Atanasio di Alessandria: studio storico-critico. (Corpus dei manoscritti copti letterari / Unione accademica nazionale).* Rome: Centro Italiano Microfiches, 1989.

Camplani, A. *Athanasius, Lettere festali.* Milan: Paoline, 2003.

Bagnall, R. S. and Frier, B. W. *The Demography of Roman Egypt.* Cambridge: Cambridge University Press, 1994.

Bartelink, G. J. M. (ed.). *Athanase: Vie d'Antoine.* Paris: Editions du Cerf, 2011.

BeDuhn, J. and Mirecki, P. A. *Frontiers of Faith: The Christian Encounter with Manichaeism in the Acts of Archelaus.* Leiden: E.J. Brill, 2007.

Bell, D. N. *Besa: The Life of Shenoute.* Kalamazoo, MI: Cistercian Publications, 1989.

Boud'hors, A. *Le canon 8 de Chénouté d'après le manuscrit Ifao Copte 2 et les fragments complémentaires.* Cairo: Institut français d'archéologie orientale, 2013.

Butler, A. J. and Fraser, P. M. *The Arab Conquest of Egypt and the Last Thirty Years of the Roman Dominion.* Oxford: Clarendon Press, 1978.

Clayton, P. B., Jr. *The Christology of Theodoret of Cyrus: Antiochene Christology from the Council of Ephesus (431) to the Council of Chalcedon (451).* Oxford: Oxford University Press, 2007.

Colombo, A. *La nascita della chiesa copto-cattolica nella prima metà del 1700.* OCA., 250; Rome: Pontifical Oriental Institute, 1996.

Cristea, H. J. (ed.). *Schenute Von Atripe: Contra Origenistas: Edition Des Koptischen Textes Mit Annotierter Übersetzung Und Indizes Einschließlich Einer Übersetzung Des 16. Osterfestbriefs Des Theophilus in Der Fassung Des Hieronymus (Ep. 96).* Tubingen: Mohr Siebeck, 2012.

Daumas, F., Henein, N. H. and Ballet, P. *Kellia 2, L'ermitage copte QR 195 1, Archéologie et architecture [1] 2, L'ermitage copte QR 195 1, Archéologie et architecture [1].* Cairo: IFAO, 2000.

Elli, A. *Storia della chiesa copta.* Cairo and Jerusalem: Franciscan Centre of Christian Oriental Studies, 2003.

Emmel, S. *Shenoute's Literary Corpus.* 2 vols. Corpus Scriptorum Christianorum Orientalium, vols. 599–600, also: CSCO Subsidia, vols. 111–112. Leuven: Peeters, 2004.

Emmel, S. 'Shenoute's Place in the History of Monasticism'. in G. Gabra and H. N. Takla, (eds). *Christianity and Monasticism in Upper Egypt*, vol. 1: *Akhmim and Sohag*, 31–46. Cairo and New York: The American University in Cairo Press, 2008.

Evelyn-White, H. G. and Hauser, W. *The Monasteries of the Wadi 'n Natrûn : Part II, the History of the Monasteries of Nitria and Scetis.* New York: The Metropolitan Museum of Art, 1932.

Evetts, B. *History of the Patriarchs of Alexandria (Severus of Ashmunein). Patrologia Orientalis*, vol. 1. Turnhout: Brepols, 1904.

Frankfurter, D. *Elijah in Upper Egypt: Studies in the History and Composition of the Coptic Elijah Apocalypse.* Minneapolis, MN: Fortress Press, 1990.

Grillmeier, A. and Hainthaler, T. *Christ in Christian Tradition. Vol. 2, Pt. 4.* London: Mowbray, 1996.

Kasser, R. *Kellia 1. Topographie générale. - 1967. - 62 S. : Ill., Kt. 1. Topographie générale. - 1967. - 62 S.: Ill., Kt.* Geneva: Georg, 1967.

Layton, B. *The Canons of Our Fathers: Monastic Rules of Shenoute.* Oxford: Oxford University Press, 2014.

Layton, B. *The Gnostic Scriptures.* New York: Doubleday, 2015.

Martin, A. *Athanase d'Alexandrie et l'église d'Égypte au IVe siècle: (328–373).* Rome: École française de Rome, 1996.

Geerard, M. *Clavis apocryphorum Novi Testamenti.* Turnhout: Brepols, 1992.

Haelewyck, J. C. *Clavis apocryphorum Veteris Testamenti.* Turnhout: Brepols, 1998.

Lubomierski, N. *Die Vita Sinuthii: Form- und Überlieferungsgeschichte der hagiographischen Texte über Schenute den Archimandriten.* Tübingen: Mohr Siebeck, 2007.

Maccoull, L. S. B. 'Three Cultures under Arab Rule: The Fate of Coptic', *BSAC* 27 (1985): 61–70.

Malingrey, A. M. and Leclercq, P. (eds). *[Palladius Helenopolitanus]: Dialogue sur la vie de Jean Chrysostome.* Paris: Editions du Cerf, 1988.

Meinardus, O. F. A. *The Holy Family in Egypt.* Cairo: American University in Cairo Press, 2000.

Orlandi, T. 'La patrologia copta', in A. Quacquarelli (ed.), *Complementi Interdisciplinari di Patrologia,* 497–502. Rome: Citta Nuova, 1989.

Orlandi, T. 'Letteratura copta e cristianesimo nazionale egiziano', in A. Camplani (ed.), *L'Egitto cristiano. Aspetti e problemi in età tardo-antica,* 39–120. Rome: Institutum Patristicum Augustinianum, 1997.

Quecke, H. *Die Briefe Pachoms: griechischer Text der Handschrift W. 145 der Chester Beatty Library.* Regensburg: F. Pustet, 1975.

Richter, T. S. *Greek, Coptic and the Language of the Hijra: The Rise and Decline of the Coptic Language in Late Antique and Medieval Egypt. From Hellenism to Islam: Cultural and Linguistic Change in The Roman Near East,* 401–46. Cambridge: Cambridge University Press, 2009.

Roldanus, J. and van Oort, J. *Chalkedon: Geschichte und Aktualität: Studien zur Rezeption der christologischen Formel von Chalkedon.* Louvain: Peeters, 1998.

Rubenson, S. *The Letters of St. Antony: Monasticism and the Making of a Saint.* Minneapolis, MN: Fortress Press, 1997.

Russell, N. *Theophilus of Alexandria.* London: Routledge, 2007.

Sheridan, M. *Rufus of Shotep. Homilies on the Gospels of Matthew and Luke. Introduction, Text, Translation, Commentary.* Rome: Unione Accademica Nazionale, Corpus dei Manoscritti Copti Letterar, 1988.

Sheridan, M. 'The Spiritual and Intellectual World of Early Egyptian Monasticism', *Coptica* 1 (2002): 2–51.

Sheridan, M. 'The Modern Historiography of Early Egyptian Monasticism'. In M. Bielawski, and D. Hombergen (eds). *Il Monachesimo tra Eredità e Aperture. Atti*

*del simposio 'Testi e temi nella tradizione del monachesimo cristiano' per il 50°
anniversario dell'Istituto Monastico di Sant'Anselmo*, Rome: Studia Anselmiana 140,
2004.

Sheridan, M. 'Rhetorical Structure in Coptic Sermons', in J. E. Goering and J. A. Timbie
(eds), *The World of Early Egyptian Christianity: Language, Literature, and Social
Context (In honor of D. W. Johnson)*. Washington, DC: Catholic University of America
Press, 2007.

Sheridan, M. 'The Encomium in the Coptic Literature of the Late Sixth Century', in P.
Buzi and A. Camplani, *Christianity in Egypt: Literary Production and Intellectual
Trends: Studies in Honor of Tito Orlandi*, 443–64. Roma: Institutum Patristicum
Augustinianum, 2011.

Sheridan, M. 'Early Egyptian Monasticism: Ideals and Reality, or: The Shaping of the
Monastic Ideal', *Journal of the Canadian Society for Coptic Studies* 7 (2015): 9–22.

Sheridan, M. 'The Mystery of Bohairic'. In E. Iricinschi and C. Kotsifou (eds), *Coping
with Religious Change in the Late-Antique Eastern Mediterranean*. Tübingen: Mohr
Siebeck, 2020.

Steppa, J. E. *John Rufus and the World Vision of Anti-Chalcedonian Culture*. Second
Revised edn. Piscataway, NJ: Gorgias Press, 2019.

Swanson, M. N. *The Coptic Papacy in Islamic Egypt: 641–1517*. The Popes of Egypt.
Vol.2. Cairo: American University in Cairo Press, 2007.

Torrance I. R. *Christology After Chalcedon*. London: Canterbury Press, 1988.

Viaud, G. *Les pelerinages coptes en Egypte d'apres les notes du Qommos Jacob Muyser*.
Cairo: Institut français d'archéologie orientale, 1979.

Volkoff, O. V. *A la recherche de manuscrits en Egypte*. Cairo: Institut français d'archéologie
orientale, 1970.

Weidmann, D. *Kellia kôm Qouçoûr 'Îsâ 1 ; fouilles de 1965 à 1978*. Louvain: Peeters,
2013.

Zaborowski, J. R. *The Coptic Martyrdom of John of Phanijoit: Assimilation and
Conversion to Islam in Thirteenth-Century Egypt*. Leiden: E.J. Brill, 2005.

CHAPTER 29

The Syriac Orthodox Church

SALIBA ER

INTRODUCTION: SYRIAC CHRISTIANITY

Early Syriac Christianity expanded into the eastern Roman Empire frontiers, but little is known about its history in the second and third centuries. Early Syriac Christianity is rooted first of all in Antioch, according to the Acts of the Apostles where the first followers of Christ after Jerusalem were called 'Christian' in Antioch (11.26). Antioch was the capital of Syria at that time and from there Christianity spread into the Near East, in particular, to Mesopotamia.[1] As Baumstark states, Antioch, Jerusalem and Edessa played a significant role in Syriac Christianity, especially in its liturgy.[2] Besides the biblical traces that there were Christians in the region of Antioch, there is other evidence that attests the existence of Christianity in this area, for instance, the story of Addai the Apostle and Tatian's *Gospel Harmony* (*Diatessaron*), which we will discuss in due course. In particular, the Tatian's work from the historical and academic point of view is a sign that Jesus' followers were in Syria as early as the second century.[3] This plainly hints that after Jerusalem, early Syriac Christianity originated in Antioch and flourished across the entire region, from where the Syriac Church is originated.

Nevertheless, we cannot argue that the early Christians in Antioch were a pure Aramaic or Syriac-speaking community, or as it is called today 'Syriac Christianity'. In this section, we will attempt to shed light on these historical developments, regarding the early Syriac Christianity, the work of the early Syriac Fathers and their contributions to the liturgy. Sebastian Brock allocates early Syriac Christianity to three main cultural traditions – Mesopotamian, Jewish and Greek.[4] This diversity

---

[1]D. G. K. Taylor, 'The Syriac Tradition', in *The First Christian Theologians*, ed. G. R. Evans (Oxford: Blackwell Publishing, 2004), pp. 201–24, here, p. 201.
[2]A. Baumstark, *On the Historical Development of the Liturgy*, trans. F. West (Collegeville, MN: Pueblo Books, 2011), p. 117.
[3]See J. Lössl, *The Early Church: History and Memory* (London: T&T Clark, 2010), p. 61.
[4]S. Brock, *Studies in Syriac Christianity: History Literature and Theology* (Aldershot: Ashgate, 1992), p. 212.

demonstrates the richness of the Syriac Christian tradition, derived from these three cosmopolitical backgrounds, expanding into western Mesopotamia. Hence, in this section, we will attempt to glimpse briefly the importance of early Syriac Christianity and its role in liturgy of the early church, in particular the contribution of the Syriac Fathers in the field of liturgy.

SYRIAC LANGUAGE AND EARLY SYRIAC LITERATURE

The credibility of early Syriac Christianity is intimately connected with the Syriac or Aramaic language in ancient Syria. The Syriac language, originating in Edessa (Syriac ܐܘܪܗܝ *Orhoy*, Urfa Southeast Turkey), is a branch of Aramaic that expanded throughout the Near East region.[5] Sebastian Brock confirms the historical details that Syriac is known as the language of Edessa (ܠܫܢܐ ܐܘܪܗܝܐ), Aramaic in its origin, and the language of Jesus in which first the Gospel was orally preached before it was written in Greek.[6] John Healey provides essential details about how the Syriac language and the spread of Christianity in the Near East frontiers were vital elements for missionary work.[7] Edessa was touted as the birthplace of Syriac Christianity and flourished throughout the region, thus the Syriac language is always identified with Edessa.[8] In Syriac tradition, the earliest text is the *Teaching of Addai* that reputedly goes back to the time of Jesus and Abgar V (the Black), the king of Edessa.[9]

When Christianity spread across the Near East, the Syriac/Aramaic language was prevailing in the region.[10] Healey attempts to explain the influential reason that the Syriac language had on Syriac Christianity was its existence prior to the arrival of Christianity in Edessa, which was already an imperial language in the Dynasty of Edessa during the Abgaric reign,[11] and so became a significant vehicle for early eastern Christian authors in spreading Christianity.[12] Klaus Beyer observes that there

---

[5]R. Murray, *Symbols of Church and Kingdom: A Study in Early Syriac Tradition* (Cambridge: Cambridge University Press, 1975), p. 2.

[6]S. Brock, *The Luminous Eye: The Spiritual World Vision of Saint Ephrem the Syrian* (Kalamazoo, MI: Cistercian Publications, 1992), p. 14.

[7]See J. F. Healey, 'The Edessan Milieu and the Birth of Syriac', *JSS* 10 (2007): 115–27, here, p. 115.

[8]See S. Brock, 'The Greek Language in Late Antique Syria', in *Literacy and Power in the Ancient World*, eds A. Bowman and G. Woolf (Cambridge: Cambridge University Press, 1940), pp. 149–60, here, p. 150.

[9]See Taylor, 'The Syriac Tradition', p. 202. It must be stated that the Teaching of Addai has been a critical matter among the scholars due to its authenticity, while many of them classify it as a legend but traditionally is accepted a first Syriac text in Syriac Christianity.

[10]See N. Macabasag, *The Annunciation (LK 1:26-38) in the Writings of Jacob of Serugh and Early Syriac Fathers*, Mōran Ethō 34 (Kottayam and Kerala: St. Joseph Press, 2015), p. 22.

[11]See Healey, 'The Edessan Milieu', p. 116.

[12]See Macabasag, *The Annunciation (LK 1:26-38)*, p. 24. It should be noted that the Syriac language was used in Edessa before spreading of Christianity. As the recent excavations show that the Aramaic/Syriac script use goes back to the fifth milieu BCE, especially in Sogmatar and Çineköy in the vicinity of Adana (historically Cilicia region). See for further details J. W. Drijvers, *Old Syriac (Edessan) Inscriptions* (Leiden: E.J. Brill 1972), p. 14.

were several dialects in Aramaic spoken in ancient Syria, but all could understand each other.[13] Opinions about the Edessan language vary, as Edessa in this era was a multicultural city, with remnant of Greek and Persian cultures, but with Syriac or Semitic influence as dominant.[14] The Syriac language paved the way for the disciples of Christ to communicate easily with local people and preach the Gospel, as they had Palestinian or Galilean Aramaic background. Brock observes that the Syriac language emerged within Christianity as a solid bridge not only for religious spaces but also for philosophical literature in competing with Greek, like Bardaisan, although he was familiar with Greek, but wrote in Syriac.[15]

Reputedly, the first text written in Syriac is believed to be the story of Addai the apostle, or the *Teaching of Addai*.[16] Brock has thoroughly investigated the details of this story and made a comparison analysis between Eusebius' *Ecclesiastical History* and a separate manuscript dated back to 500 CE (British Library, Add. 14618), and he concludes that this manuscript could have been written before Eusebius account.[17] However, a number of scholars are uncertain about the authenticity of the story of Addai and the Abgar, the king of Edessa. One of the scholars Han J. Drijvers is dubious about the actuality of the story and calls it a legend, claiming that it may have been written by Bishop Qune of Edessa as early as fourth century in order to associate Edessan Christianity with apostolic origins.[18] Hence, some scholars also see it as a reliable source to trace the origin of Edessan Christianity to the apostolic era and suggest that the *Teaching of Addai* expresses an embryonic portrait of early Christian missionary work in Edessa in the imperial court by Addai, the disciple of Thomas.[19]

Brock's judgement about this historical document is different from other scholars who mostly deny its authentication, but he argues that it 'might contain some grains of historical value'.[20] For this reason, Addai's story has been a polemical point among the scholars and its authenticity questioned by a number of scholars. This has led some scholars to be cautious in relating Syriac Christianity to the first and second century, due to lack of sufficient evidence. Drijvers linked the beginning of Syriac Christianity with the philosophical writings of Bardaisan in Edessa who wrote in pure Syriac and not in Greek.[21] Taylor also suggests that the *Teaching of Addai* has been a leading point in the history of the early ages of Syriac Christianity.[22] This can

---

[13]See B. Klaus, *The Aramaic Language: Its Distribution and Subdivision* (Göttingen: Vandenhoeck & Ruprecht 1986), p. 38.

[14]See Healey, 'The Edessan Milieu', p. 117.

[15]See S. Brock, *Greek into Syriac and Syriac into Greek: Syriac Perspectives on Late Antiquity* (London Variorum, 1984), p. 155.

[16]P. George (ed. and trans.), *The Doctrine of Addai the Apostle* (London: Trübner & Co, 1876).

[17]See S. Brock, 'Eusebius and Syriac Christianity', in *Eusebius Christianity and Judaism*, eds H. W. Attridge and G. Hata (Detroit, MI: Wayne State University Press, 1992), pp. 212–34, here: p. 213.

[18]See D. J. William, 'Early Syriac Christianity', *VChr* 19 (1996): 159–77, here: p. 164.

[19]See M. S. Jeanne-Nicole, *Missionary Stories and the Formation of the Syriac Churches* (Milwaukee: University of California Press, 2015), p. 40.

[20]Brock, 'Eusebius and Syriac Christianity', p. 221.

[21]See H. J. W. Drijvers, 'Early Syriac Christianity: Some Recent Publications', *Vigiliae Christianae* 50, no. 2 (1966): 159–77, here: p. 162.

[22]See Taylor, 'The Syriac Tradition', p. 202.

be easily observed how deeply it is reflected in the Syriac liturgy, which has a memorial feast in the middle of the Lent, commemorated together with the elevation of the Cross. The entire story of Addai and the healing of Abgar through the mandilion is well reflected in the liturgical texts.

[1] The just king Abgar sent to Christ in true faith and said: I have heard about You that You are a good physician, You heal sickness without medicine and I have learned the truth that You are God Who came down from the heights to the depths to heal the sick, Hallelujah.[23]

[1] ܐܝܟܢܐ ܟܬܒ ܐܒܓܪ ܡܠܟܐ ܙܕܝܩܐ ܠܘܬ ܡܫܝܚܐ ܒܗܝܡܢܘܬܐ

Other Apocryphal Acts of the Apostles, including the *Acts of Thomas*, are assumed to have been composed originally in Syriac and later translated into Greek.[25] The evidence about Edessa is shrouded, and it is almost impossible to state whether there were Christians from the first century, but the narrative of the *Teaching of Addai* may contain a grain of evidence. Edessa like Antioch was from the very beginning of Christianity not only an important centre for Christians but also a cosmopolitan and commercial centre in the Osrhoene kingdom. As early as the second century, Christians played an important role in Edessa and its vicinities. The very early Syriac Christian literature that has survived, such as the *Odes of Solomon* and, later, the writings of Bardaisan, such as his *Book of the Law of Countries*, all indicate the existence of Christians in Edessa.[26]

Similarly, among early Syriac Christian literature comes also the *Diatessaron* of Tatian, the harmony of the four Gospels, witnessing to the existence of Christians in the region in the second century.[27] The origin of the Diatessaron is lost and whether it was written in Greek or Syriac, but most scholars are in agreement that it was written in Syriac, presumably in Edessa. McCarthy suggests that the Diatessaron was the main Bible in Edessa until the fifth century, and it is also mentioned being used in the Doctrine of Addai for liturgical readings and was called 'the Gospel of the mixed' (ܐܘܢܓܠܝܘܢ ܕܡܚܠܛܐ).[28] The Diatessaron is perceived to be the first version of

---

[23] My own translation.

[24] S. M. Gabriel (ed.), *The Breviary of the Syriac Church for the Lent* (Damascus: Bap Tuma Press, 1982), p. 212.

[25] See S. Brock, 'The Earliest Syriac Literature', in *The Cambridge History of Early Christian Literature*, eds F. Young, L. Ayres and A. Louth (Cambridge: Cambridge University Press, 2004), pp. 161–171, here: p. 164.

[26] See Murray, *Symbols of Church*, p. 4.

[27] See U. Schmid, 'The Diatessaron of Tatian', in *The Text of the New Testament in Contemporary Research*, eds B. Ehrman and M. Holmes (Leiden: E.J. Brill, 2013), pp. 115–42, here: 123f. In this study Schmid is sceptical that the Diatessaron originally was written in Syriac. He is reluctant about the origin language of the Diatessaron, and therefore, he does not exclude the idea that it could have been written in Greek.

[28] See Carmel McCarthy (ed. and trans.), *Saint Ephrem's Commentary on Tatian's Diatessaron* (Oxford: Oxford University Press, 1993), p. 2. Tatian was born in Syria or Mesopotamia and was a native Syriac speaker, but he studied in Rome, where he became a pupil of Justin the Martyr and was converted to Christianity.

the New Testament in Syria and is used in the works of the early Syriac writers, such as Aphrahat the Persian Sage and Ephrem the Syrian who has a commentary on it.[29]

Consequently, Tatian's Diatessaron is believed to be the oldest Syriac Gospel, which became a foundation for the *Peshitta* version during Rabbula's episcopacy in Edessa. Drijvers provides significant details about the date of the Diatessaron that existed sometime before (AD) 180 and was available for Syriac-speaking community in Syria.[30] This suggests that Tatian played a significant role in the early Christian era, having access to existing Graeco-Roman literature and providing the Gospel (Diatessaron) to those who were far from the Greek language.

EARLY SYRIAC FATHERS

Before examining the main subject of this study, an overview about the Syriac Fathers and writers who contributed immensely to Syriac Christianity and literature is required. Brock notes that 'the first Syriac writers who do come down to us in any extensive way, the fourth-century Aphrahat and Ephrem, both represent Syriac Christianity in a pure Semitic, and as yet unhellenized form'.[31] Both authors were among the founders of Syriac Christianity, and their writings that have survived consist of the earliest systematic Syriac literature – the twenty-three *Demonstrations* of Aphrahat the Persian Sage, and the *madroše* (ܡܕܪ̈ܫܐ) or *Hymns* (ܐܝܡܢܐ) of Ephrem the Syrian. Both figures appear to have emerged from the same ascetic circle known as ܩܝܡܐ ܒܢܝ (*bnay qyomō*) 'the sons/children of the covenant'.[32] Syriac Christianity inherited a significant body of work from this period, written in pure Syriac style, leading to the suggestion that fourth-century Syriac Christianity was an indigenous Semitic development, not effected by the Greek culture and language as it was in the west. That is to say, the Syriac theology and literature seem to have been distilled from other cultural sources, outside of Greek or Latin influences until the late fourth century, an almost purely Mesopotamian background virtually untouched by Greek influence.[33] Thus, both Syriac writers are important to be considered in the context of the early Syriac Christianity.

Aphrahat the Persian sage

Aphrahat is listed in the first stage among early Syriac writers of the middle fourth century. He wrote in an authentic Syriac style and became a prominent and respected theologian in eastern Mesopotamia by his writings and ecclesial position, whose

---

[29]See S. Brock, 'The Use of the Syriac Fathers for New Testament Textual Criticism', in *The Text of the New Testament in Contemporary Research*, eds B. Ehrman and M. Holmes (Leiden: E.J. Brill, 2013), pp. 407–28, here: p. 407.

[30]See Drijvers, 'Early Syriac Christianity', p. 163.

[31]S. Brock, *Syriac Perspectives on Late Antiquity* (Aldershot: Ashgate, 1984), p. 406.

[32]See J. Wickes, 'Between Liturgy and School: Reassessing the Performative Context of Ephrem's Madrašē', *JECS* 26, no. 1 (2018): 25–51, here: p. 44.

[33]See Brock, *The Luminous Eye*, p. 15.

writings involve various theological themes, among them Christological and ascetical themes.[34] Aphrahat's aim in writing his *Demonstrations* can be considered under two categories, namely pedagogy and apology, as clear from the first ten *Demonstrations*, which he wrote in a catechetical context upon request of one of his pupils, presumably from the monastic order. The other *Demonstrations* are apologetic works, possibly against Jews or pagans.[35] Although nothing is known about his life or where he studied, we can deduce from his writings that he was a learned man, and possibly an abbot or teacher for the *bnay qyomō* order. It has been also gleaned from his writings that he used Tatian's Diatessaron as the New Testament.[36]

It is claimed by some scholars that Aphrahat was an abbot of the famous monastery of Mor Matai on the outskirts of Mosul, but Ephrem Barsoum refutes this claim, for the mentioned monastery was not yet founded in his time.[37] Aphrahat's writings are packed with biblical references and so are valuable for theological studies generally, as the earliest commentary in Syriac studies. Aphrahat's writings are in prose style rather than poetic, in contrast to Ephrem's approach, who expressed his theology in poetry, or metrical homilies.

Ephrem the Syrian

Saint Ephrem the Syrian is considered the icon of Syriac Christianity, due to his extensive works and active role as a catechetical teacher and deacon.[38] Ephrem the Syrian is highly venerated in the entire Christian church, but in a particular way in the Syriac Church, as he is described 'The Prophet of the Syrian', 'The Sun of the Syrian' and 'The Harp of the Holy Spirit'.[39] Ephrem's contribution to early Syriac Christianity lies in his poetic writings in Syriac that presents true Semitic Christianity as a whole, in addition to his persistent teaching, first in the school of Nisibis under the supervision of Bishop Jacob of Nisibis (d. 338) and later in the Edessan school. Nisibis was a strategic town on the eastern Roman Empire border, which was ceded

---

[34]See S. Brock (ed. and trans.), *The Syriac Fathers on Prayer and the Spiritual Life* (Kalamazoo, MI: Cistercian Publications, 1987), p. 2. See also W. Petersen, 'The Christology of Aphrahat the Persian Sage: An Excursus on the 17th Demonstration', *VChr* 46 (1992): 241–56, here: p. 242.

[35]See W. Wright (ed.), *The Homilies Aphraates the Persian Sage* (London: William and Norgate, 1869). See also, S. K. Jarkins-Skoyles, *Aphrahat the Persian Sage and the Temple of God: A Study of Early Syriac Theological Anthropology* (Piscataway, NY: Gorgias Press, 2014), p. 3.

[36]See M. Lattke, 'Einsetzung und Vollzug der christlichen Paschafeier bei Aphrahat', in *The Eucharist - Its Origins and Context*, vol. 2: Patristic Traditions, Iconography, eds D. Hellholm and D. Sänger, WUNT 376 (Tübingen: Mohr Siebeck, 2017), pp. 1091–119, here: p. 1094.

[37]See E. Barsoum, *The Scattered Pearls: The History of Syriac Sciences and Literature*, trans. Matti Moosa, 2nd edn (Piscataway, NY: Gorgias Press, 2003), p. 228f.

[38]See Brock, *The Luminous Eye*, p. 16. Brock in this masterpiece has devoted a comprehensive introductory on St Ephrem's biography. In addition, under the following link, http://syri.ac/ephrem (accessed 27 February 2019), it is possible to find numerous references on Ephrem's writings, including main and second literature. Especially Edmund Beck's contribution on Ephrem's works is highly significant, in editing and translating numerous writings of Ephrem into German.

[39]See Barsoum, *The Scattered Pearls*, p. 229f.

to the Persian rule in an agreement between both sides, as part of the peace treaty.[40] Ostensibly, this agreement caused many Christians to immigrate to Edessa, among them Ephrem the Syrian who did not want to be ruled by a pagan ruler. Ephrem's last years in Edessa were involved in numerous struggles. The challenges that he faced in Edessa included straggling with famine, helping poor people and confrontations with various heretical groups, namely Marcianism, Bardaisanism, Arianism, Manicheanism, etc.[41] These controversies did not prevent Ephrem from teaching and writing; in contrast, Ephrem's engagement with these groups caused him to produce more effective work, to refute energetically their tendentious thoughts and claims.

Ephrem's writings can be categorized under two headings, namely prose works (metrical treatises ܡܕܪ̈ܫܐ *madrošē*) and poetry (ܡܐܡܖ̈ܐ *mimrē*). His poetical *mimrē* could also be called Hymns, for these were used to express a particular event or narrative in a musical way, likely for ecclesial choirs to sing during the liturgy, and were structured in a stanzaic form, in seven-syllable metre. *Madrošē* are also written in stanzas, but in different syllabic metres, in which Ephrem freely expressed his theology and exegetical work in a wider context, like biblical commentaries, especially on Genesis and polemical texts. *Madrošē* can also be characterized under two headings: first, liturgical, such as clarifications on the Nativity, fasting and Easter events; and second, theological discourse against the above-mentioned heresies.[42] Ephrem's surviving works according to Brock number about 400 *madrošē*, some of which survived in the Armenian language. In addition, there are some *mimrē* attributed to him, but scholars doubt that these were originally written by Ephrem. Brock emphasizes that Ephrem's theological works to some extent involve Mesopotamian and Jewish background, due to his Semitic mind as an Aramaic speaker and reading Jewish biblical literature.[43] To suggest that Ephrem may have been able to read the Old Testament in Hebrew directly would not be far off. Although Ephrem wrote and spoke in Syriac and not in Greek, Possekel argues, however, that is not accurate to confine Ephrem's thoughts to the Semitic mind only, as he lived inside Roman territory where the Greek language and culture was prevalent. She claims that Ephrem's writings reveal Greek philosophical knowledge too.[44] Ephrem not only became a fundamental figure for Syriac-speaking community, but his influence on Syriac Christianity in later centuries remained significant in a multitude of theological perspectives. He was a conscientious man who would

---

[40]S. Brock, 'Ephrem and the Syriac Tradition', in Young, Ayres and Louth (eds), *The Cambridge History of Early Christian Literature*, pp. 362–72, here: p. 363. Nisibis (today Nusaybin in southeast Turkey on the North Syrian border) is about hundred miles distance from Edessa which was a leading centre of Syriac Christianity before Edessa.

[41]See Brock, *The Luminous Eye*, p. 17.

[42]See U. Possekel, 'Ephrem's Doctrine of God', in *God in Early Christian Thought*, eds A. B. McGowan, B. E. Daley and T. J. Gaden (Leiden: E.J. Brill, 2009), pp. 195–237, here: p. 197.

[43]See Brock, *The Luminous Eye*, p. 19f.

[44]See U. Possekel, *Evidence of Greek Philosophical Concepts in the Writings of Ephrem the Syrian*, CSCO 580, Subsidia 102 (Leuven: Peeters, 1999), p. 54.

candidly express the events of the Holy Scriptures in his works and teaching.[45] Syriac Christianity is indebted immensely to St Ephrem, due to his spectacular writings, which became a profound source of inspiration for various theological aspects, but particularly for the liturgy and monasticism, providing a solid path for later Syriac writers.

Jacob of Serugh

Another prolific Syriac author is St Jacob of Serugh (ca. 451–521, today Serugh is known as Suruç in southeast Turkey), who was born in Curtam (a town near Edessa) and studied in the school of Edessa, where his fame spread in that region, due to his poetic writings and metrical homilies, but in twelve syllable metre, not seven like Ephrem.[46] Jacob was a proficient and sophisticated author and an influential teacher (ܡܠܦܢܐ *malphōnō*) who wrote around 400 homilies on various themes according to the liturgical cycle of the year, numerous explanations of biblical passages, sacramental interpretations and on the apostles' acts and martyrs.[47] Thomas Kollamparampil states that Jacob's work is highly valuable covering various fields, namely exegesis, sacramental theology, and in particular baptism and the Eucharist, and penitence.[48] Susan A. Harvey has thoroughly examined Jacob's homilies and concludes that he was actively engaged in writing catechetical poets for teaching and preaching in various places in the vicinity of Edessa.[49] Barsoum has provided a wide range of details about Jacob's bibliography that he was a well-known teacher in his time, especially in the monastic tradition where his expertise emerged, and due to his effort was selected first as a local bishop of Hawra, and in the last couple of years he was elevated to the diocesan bishop of Batnan/Serugh near Edessa, from which he was called ܣܘܪܓ ܕ (of Serugh).[50] Kilian McDonnell describes Jacob as one of the greatest doctors of the Syriac Church; although he knew Greek from the school of Edessa, he wrote his whole works in pure Syriac style, like his predecessors namely Aphrahat and Ephrem.[51] Sidney Griffith noted that Jacob in his writings reminds his

---

[45]See Barsoum, *The Scattered Pearls*, 30.

[46]See S. Brock, 'Ya'qub of Serugh', in *GEDSH*, eds S. Brock, A. M. Butts, G. A. Kiraz and L. V. Rompay (Piscataway, NY: Gorgias Press, 2011), pp. 433–5, here: p. 433. See also P. Bruns, 'Jacob of Serugh', in *DECL*, ed. S. Döpp, W. Geerlings (New York: Crossroad, 2000), pp. 315–16, here: p. 315.

[47]P. Bedjan (ed.), *Homiliae Selectae Mar-Jacobi Sarugensis*, vol. 5 (Paris: Harrasowitz, 1905-1910). These volumes are reprinted in 2006, P. Bedjan and S. Brock (eds), *Homilies of Mar Jacob of Sarugh*, 6 vols (Piscataway, NY: Gorgias, 2006). It is added an extra volume to those previously edited by Bedjan, which includes four Homilies that accumulated by the effort of Sebastian Brock.

[48]See T. Kollamparampil, *Salvation in Christ According to Jacob of Serugh* (Piscataway, NY: Gorgias Press, 2001), p. 29.

[49]S. A. Harvey, 'To Whom Did Jacob Preach?', in *Jacob of Serugh and His Time*, ed. George A. Kiraz (Piscataway, NY: Georgia Press, 2010), pp. 115–31, here: p. 116.

[50]See Barsoum, *The Scattered Pearls*, p. 57.

[51]See K. McDonnell, *The Baptism of Jesus in the Jordan* (Collegeville, MN: Michael Glazier, 1996), p. 210.

readers of the writings of St Ephrem, due to their style and contents.[52] In recent studies by Robert Kitchen on Jacob's biography written by Sa'īd Bar Ṣabūnī who calls Jacob 'the harp of the words', because of his numerous works and pastoral administration, who is considered as a superior to all fathers (ܐܒܗܬܐ) and teachers (ܡܠܦܢܐ).[53] Jacob lived in a polemical period, when the common era of Christian unity had collapsed due to diverse Christological views among Christians. Nevertheless, he is still well received among some Chalcedonian churches, like the Maronite Church, whose baptismal rite is attributed to Jacob and which also had integrated numerous of his *mimrē* into its liturgy.[54] For this reason, some Western scholars via Maronite sources label Jacob as a pro-Chalcedonian, although this claim is rejected by eastern and a majority of Western scholars too.[55] One of the scholars who dealt with this matter significantly is Paul Krüger, who held the notion initially that Jacob had a pro-Chalcedonian tendency but later reached the conclusion that Jacob remained a 'Miaphysite' throughout his life.[56] Jacob did write a homily on the Nativity addressed against Chalcedon, where he firmly expressed his understanding of Christology that Christ after the union had one nature, in other words, as it is interpreted in the modern era 'Miaphysite' dogma, as follows:

In the bosom of Mary, He brought the natures into unity and made the two of them one as it is written.[57]

ܡܚܕ ܕܩܕܡ ܐܟܪ ܗܘܝ̈ܬ ܟܢ̈ܫܐ ܠܟܝܢ̈ܐ ܘܥܒܕ ܐܟܪ
ܠܬܪ̈ܝܗܘܢ ܚܕ ܐܟܪ ܕܟܬܝܒ.[58]

Jacob left a remarkable literature of theology behind, in addition to his *mimrē* (Metrical Homilies) and Letters. He wrote an Anaphora which is still in use in the Syriac Church. For this reason, he is called in the Syriac Church the 'flute of the Holy Spirit'.[59] Jacob played a prominent role in the growth of Syriac theology, his wide range of writings remain significant not only for liturgical studies but for

---

[52]See S. H. Griffith, 'Mar Jacob of Serugh on Monks and Monasticism', in *Jacob of Serugh and His Time*, eds G. A. Kiraz (Piscataway, NY: Georgia Press, 2010), pp. 71–89, here: p. 72.

[53]See R. Kitchen, 'A Poetic Life: Metrical Vita of Jacob of Serugh by Sa'īd Bar Ṣabūnī', in *Syriac Encounters: Papers from the Sixth North American Syriac Symposium Duke University, 26-29 June 2011*, ed. M. Doerfler et al., ECS 20 (Leuven: Peeters, 2015), pp. 65–75, here: p. 68f.

[54]See Brock, 'Ya'qub of Serugh', p. 434.

[55]See Ph. M. Forness, 'Cultural Exchange and Scholarship on Eastern Christianity: An Early Modern Debate over Jacob of Serugh's Christology', *JECS* 70 (2018): 257–84, here: p. 260. Recently Forness has published a significant monograph on Jacob's Christological understanding, which is an essential as a secondary references on Jacob's works, as follows: Forness, M. Philip, *Preaching Christology in the Roman Near East: A Study of Jacob of Serugh* (Oxford: Oxford University Press: 2018). Another important work on Jacob's view of Christology is the following one: R. Chesnut, *Three Monophysite Christologies* (Oxford: Oxford University Press, 1976).

[56]P. Krüger, 'Das Problem der Rechtgläubigkeit Jakobs von Serugh und seine Lösung', in *OS*, 23 (1974): 188–96, here p. 195.

[57]My own translation

[58]R. Akhrass, and I. Syryany (eds), *160 Unpublished Homilies of Jacob of Serugh*, vol. 1 (Beirut: Zakaria Press, 2017), p. 9.

[59]See Griffith, 'Mar Jacob of Serugh on Monks', p. 73.

multifarious use in theology and worship generally. His *95th mimrō* on the Eucharist can be reckoned as a proto-eucharistic commentary.[60] In this *mimrō* Jacob provides an outline of the eucharistic liturgy, according to his era. There will be considerable analysis concerning this *mimrō* in due course.

SYRIAC FATHERS' APPROACH TO THEOLOGY

The Syriac liturgical tradition was instituted in the late antique era and enriched enormously by the Syriac Fathers through their hymns, poems, exegesis and commentaries. The Eucharist was their central point, and they endeavoured to adorn it with the most valuable texts, expressing its theological, spiritual and mystical perspectives. The Syriac liturgy is often abandoned by Western theologians and scholars, which is immensely rich and historic in terms of tradition and heritage. It is therefore important to pay attention to the approach of the Syriac Fathers, which is described through the types and symbols. This became a practised method, a foundation of the liturgy in the West Syriac tradition, which is rooted in the biblical text. The Antiochene tradition seems to be attentive in interpreting the literal sense of scripture. They used a typological method that expounded the liturgical mysteries as an explanation of the historical mysteries of salvation.[61] This section will attest to the contributions of the Syriac writers on the Eucharist as the central and climax mystery of the church.

Early Syriac writers, such as Ephrem the Syrian and his contemporary Aphrahat the Persian, used symbolic theology rather than systematic theology, expressing their thoughts entirely through symbols, signs and types, either traditional or freely invented, an Eastern or Semitic way of discerning theology. Symbolism is broadly connected with early Syriac Christianity and developed expansively later within the Syriac writers, in particular, Jacob of Serugh, who imitated Ephrem the Syrian in his homilies and hymns. Murray underlines that Syriac usage of symbolism is the most common exegetical methodology, which allows the writer to encapsulate his thought symbolically, particularly if his purpose is didactic.[62] In fact, Syriac writers intended to interpret theological matters through types and imaginations, in order to reveal invisible divine mysteries through visible and imaginative symbols. As attested by Brock reflecting on Syriac writers concerning the operation of symbolism that is clarified at different levels, between the Old and New Testaments, world and heaven, sacrament and eschaton, in every case they 'reveal' something of what must remain 'hidden'.[63] The uniqueness of the Semitic mind seems to be naturally conversant

---

[60]P. Bedjan (ed.), *Homiliae Selectae Mar-Jacobi Sarugensis*, vol. 3 (Paris: Harrasowitz, 1905), pp. 646–63. See also A. Harrak, 'The Syriac Orthodox Celebration of the Eucharist in Light of Jacob of Serugh's Mimro 95', in *Jacob of Serugh and His Time*, ed. George A. Kiraz (Piscataway, NY: Georgia Press, 2010), pp. 91–113.

[61]See R. Taft, *Liturgy in Byzantium and Beyond* (Aldershot: Ashgate, 1995), p. 61.

[62]See Murray, *Symbols of Church*, p. 1.

[63]See S. Brock (ed.), *St Ephrem the Syrian Hymns on Paradise* (New York: St Vladimir Press, 1990), p. 42.

with types and symbols, which Syriac writers inherited from Judaism and developed this methodology through Christian understanding.

In fact, this is what distinguishes the Syriac tradition from other traditions, namely the Greek and Persians, as poetry and hymns are the usual way of carrying out theological enquiry. Brock argues that one may explain the two methods, 'systematic and symbolic', simply as approaching theology from two directions: systematic is the philosophical approach with its search for definitions, a heritage from Greek philosophy; the symbolic one is the typological approach, using such an approach reveals God's plan of salvation for humanity and discerning God's purpose in light of the incarnation by illustrating different paradoxical themes.[64] These expressed profound aspects of the incarnation in a straightforward manner: 'the Great One who became Small', 'the Rich One who became poor', 'the Hidden One who revealed himself'.[65] It is clear from these examples that Ephrem is reflecting on Paul's language concerning the incarnation:

> For you know the grace of our Lord Jesus Christ that though he was rich, yet for your sakes he became poor, so that by his poverty you might become rich. (2 Cor. 8.9)

The crucial point in Ephrem's vision is to make approachable the divine matter in a luminous understanding, to reach the divine reality, in order to avoid investigating the One Who is beyond the human perception.[66] Kees den Biesen reasons that in Ephrem's thought it was convenient to explain the divine matters through the symbolic notion.[67]

The usage of symbolic theology clarifies the significance of the incarnation and provides different examples of its understanding in a symbolic approach, in order to emphasize the union of divinity with humanity as a key point in salvation history. Brock observes that the aim of symbolism is to persuade humanity back from its fallen state by offering a variety of glimpses of the glorious divine reality and salvation's history, particularly to raise awareness that through these images humanity is granted access into the growth of spiritual life.[68] The aspect of symbolism that Brock relies on is deeply inspired by different hymns of Ephrem, in particular the Hymns on Faith, such imagery is boldly highlighted, 'Lord, You bent down and put on humanity's types so that humanity might grow through Your self-abasement'. The poems' use of symbolism aims at portraying the relationship of God with humanity through such symbols and signs, establishing communion between Creator and creatures.[69] It is realized that Ephrem's insight in using symbolism is to create a

---

[64]See Brock, *The Luminous Eye*, p. 24.

[65]Ibid., 27.

[66]Ibid., p. 28.

[67]See K. d. Biesen, *Simple and Bold Ephrem's Art of Symbolic Thought* (Piscataway, NY: Georgia Press, 2006), p. 37.

[68]Ibid., 54.

[69]See J. Wickes, 'The Poetics of Self-Presentation in Ephrem's Hymns on Faith 10', in *Syriac Encounters: Papers from the Sixth North American Syriac Symposium Duke University, 26-29 June 2011*, eds. M. Doerfler et al., ECS 20 (Leuven: Peeters, 2015), pp. 51–63, here: p. 53.

special method of language providing real access to the mystical dimension, a creative approach that is artistic, intellectual and religious at the same time. Such a symbolic language allows its readers to explore precisely the reality of the mystery in a spiritual understanding.

Furthermore, Brock observes the Syriac Fathers' approach in his wide-range analysis after the fourth century and notes that Jacob of Serugh also applied the same methodology of symbolic theology which became an essential instrument for his writings, especially concerning baptism and the Eucharist, which is important for the modern mind and scholarly work.[70] Kollamparampil has also widely examined Jacob's writings and points out that one can glimpse the scriptural depth in the works of Jacob, illustrating the biblical text in various images.[71] This resulted in Syriac Christianity occupying a significant role in the history of the Christendom, due to its rich theological literature and equally important language Greek and Latin for studying Christianity in late antiquity. It is possible to perceive the tendency of symbolism in the Catechetical Homilies of Theodore of Mopsuestia (d. 428). Although he wrote in Greek, he still sees symbols and types instrumental in expressing his theology. Thomas Finn sums up Theodore's symbolic understanding regarding sacramental theology and salvation history as having two stages: the first stage is temporal, which is subjected to the present life; the second stage is the invisible and immutable future that is regained by the resurrection of Christ, which is imbued with the mystical union and is enacted through signs and symbols.[72]

Such a figurative language is not merely to explain and explore, but to deepen the understanding of salvation that is embodied in the theology of sacraments, mainly in baptism and the Eucharist. The context of symbolism demonstrates the significance of the authors' theological background. They engaged with such an application in order to signify symbolically the indispensable spirituality of sacraments. At all levels, the types and symbols are a standing invitation to the understanding of their actualization in Christ and the realization in the eschatological context. As a whole, one could say that Syriac theology is a distinctive tradition, set apart from the rest of early Christian thought. While in its early stages it developed quite distantly from the Hellenistic cultural tradition, in later centuries one can easily observe that the Syriac Fathers adopted some Greek patterns in order to compete with the complex theological discussions.

GREEK CROSSROADS IN SYRIAC CHRISTIANITY

Brock argues that from the fifth century onwards due to the steady globalization of Christendom, the Greek language played a crucial and influential role in writing

---

[70]S. Brock, *Baptismal Themes in the Writings of Jacob of Serugh*, OCA 205 (Rome: Pontificium Institutum Orientalium Studiorum, 1978), pp. 324–47, here: p. 326.

[71]See Kollamparampil, *Salvation in Christ*, p. 78.

[72]See T. Finn, *Early Christian Baptism and the Catechumenate* (Collegeville, MN: The Liturgical Press, 1992), p. 9.

apologetic treatises and catechetical documents against various heresies.[73] Brock has noted that generally Syriac Christianity was influenced by Jewish, Mesopotamian and Greek cultures, a fundamental starting point for our current study. In urban centres such as the city of Antioch, the Greek language was already prevailing. Syriac still was predominant in Mesopotamia, in Central Asia and in China, which became a bridge for Armenian Christianity to translate the Bible and other Syriac literature into the Armenian Church.[74] Early Syriac Christianity seemed confined to the ancient Mesopotamian culture as purely Semitic-minded until the end of the fourth century. However, this Semitic trend in early Syriac Christianity was experiencing a dramatic change at the turn of the fifth century.

The Greek language became a significant channel of communication in exchanging discussions and producing writings between Greek and Syriac readers. The influence of Greek Christianity on Syriac Christianity is readily noticed through the lectionaries and Greek expressions in the Syriac liturgy. One aspect of this phenomenon was the dynamic increase in most Christianized regions, Syria being no exception. Such influence is well exhibited in the first quarter of the fifth century, where Rabbula, bishop of Edessa (d. 435), played a vital role in translating various Greek texts, especially the writings of Cyril of Alexandria into Syriac.[75] Rabbula's influence on Syriac literature is counted highly among the early Syriac writers after Ephrem the Syrian and Aphrahat the Persian Sage. Brock concludes his analysis on Rabbula's role on the *Peshitta* (ܦܫܝܛܬܐ Pšiṭṭō) version, whether he was the first writer of the *Peshitta* or not, stating that this is an open question which is hard to verify, but undoubtedly, he provoked the enhancement of its revision.[76] This demonstrates the importance of the school of Edessa, which was a vital platform for both Greek and Syriac cultures. The school of Edessa at the same time was called 'the school of the Persians', which ostensibly was founded by Ephrem when he immigrated from Nisibis to Edessa in 363, and where he spent the last decade of his life.[77] The school of Edessa, as Vaschalde notes, not only was a centre of learning for the Syriac-

---

[73]See Brock, *Studies in Syriac Christianity*, p. 212.

[74]See P. J. Williams, 'The Syriac Versions of the New Testament', in *The Text of the New Testament in Contemporary Research*, eds B. D. Ehrman M. W. Holmes (Leiden: E.J. Brill, 2013), pp. 143–66, here: p. 143.

[75]See J. W. Drijvers, 'Rabula Bishop of Edessa: Spiritual Authority and Secular Power', in *Portraits of Spiritual Authority: Religious Power in Early Christianity Byzantium and the Christian Orient*, eds. J. W. Drijvers and J. W. Watt (Leiden: E.J. Brill, 1999), pp. 139–4, here: p. 149f. It is worth mentioning that Drijvers points out that the Nestorian crises soured relations between Rabbula and Hiba who was the head of the Persian school and as a sign of his adherents to Nestorius, Hiba translated Theodore of Mopsuestia's works from Greek into Syriac.

[76]See Brock, 'The Use of the Syriac Fathers', p. 413. In this piece of research Brock concludes that the *Peshitta* preceded Rabbula. In this case, it was available before Rabbula.

[77]See A. Becker, *Fear of God and the Beginning of Wisdom: The School of Nisibis and Christian Scholastic Culture in Late Antique Mesopotamia* (Philadelphia: University of Pennsylvania Press, 2006), p. 41.

speaking community but also became the scene of theological polemics after the Nestorian schism.[78]

According to Vaschalde, the leading West Syriac figure to dominate the life of this school until its closure was Philoxenos of Mabbûg (d. 523), who endeavoured to combat both Nestorianism and Chalcedonianism for a long period, approximately a half-century.[79] This proves that Philoxenos was involved vigorously in the theological polemics of the time, as he studied and lived most of his time in Edessa and Mabbûg's region (Menbij today in northern Syria). The Persian school of Edessa had become a hotbed, placed between the West and East Syriac Churches, and each side attempted to strengthen its position against the other. Ostensibly, Philoxenos' concern was to defend the Miaphysite theology against various theological debates, first Nestorianism and later Chalcedonianism.[80] Philoxenos' attitude towards Ephrem the Syrian seems to be critical, due to the lack of terminological precision, particularly regarding the Incarnation expression ܠܒܫ ܦܓܪܐ *lbeš pagrō* ('clothed himself with the body').[81] Ultimately, Philoxenos turned to embrace the Greek tradition in order to strengthen his argument against his opponents.[82] Regarding this phraseology in early Syriac theology was a common understanding for the Incarnation, as Brock points out in his analysis of the historical developments of Syriac Christology that 'put on the body' became a standard term for the Incarnation in early Syriac Christianity.[83] Consequently, the school of Edessa was closed in 489 by the order of King Zeno, due to the polemical situation among the students and masters, mainly about Nestorianism.[84]

This phraseology accords with the *Acts of Thomas*, indicating the Incarnation of Christ that became a man, 'put on a body and became a man ܦܓܪܐ ܘܗܘܐ ܒܪܢܫܐ'.[85] Murray points out that this phrase was a favourite expression for early Syriac writers, in which they describe the doctrine of the Incarnation.[86] Nevertheless, as Gabriele Winkler has discussed this matter and emphasized that after the fifth century, during the flowering of Christological debate, the Syriac writers preferred using the term ܐܬܓܫܡ *eṭgašam* ('He was incarnate') rather than ܦܓܪܐ ܠܒܫ, to express

---

[78]A. A. Vaschalde, *Three Letters of Philoxenus Bishop of Mabbôgh* (Rome: Tipografia Della R. Accademia Dei Linchi, 1902), p. 8.

[79]Ibid., p. 9.

[80]See D. Michelson, *The Practical Christology of Philoxenos of Mabbug* (Oxford: Oxford University Press, 2014), p. 3.

[81]My own translation.

[82]L. V. Rompay, 'Malphana Dilan Suryaya. Ephrem in the Works of Philoxenos of Mabbug', *JSS* 7 (2004): 83–105, here: p. 93.

[83]See S. Brock, 'Clothing Metaphors as a Means of Theological Expression in Syriac Tradition', in *Typus, Symbol, Allegorie bei den östlichen Vätern und ihre Parallelen im Mittelalter*, eds M. Schmidt and G. Carl-Friedrich, Eichstätter Beiträge 4 (Eichstätt: F. Pustet Regensburg, 1982), pp. 11–38, here: 15.

[84]See Backer, *Fear of God*, p. 43.

[85]W. Wright (ed.), *Apocryphal Acts of the Apostles: The Syriac Text 1*, 2nd edn (Piscataway, NY: Gorgias Press, 2005), p. 210. See also S. Brock, 'Some Early Witnesses to the East Syriac Liturgical Tradition', *JAAS* 18 (2004): 19–38.

[86]See Murray, *Symbols of Church*, 69.

precisely the Nicene term, and in the sixth century they began to use ܐܬܒܪܢܫ *eṯbarnaš* ('became man') to reflect on the Nicene Creed accurately.[87] The reason for such a rapid development in the Syriac Christological understanding seems to be the Nestorian conflict, as Brock reports that after the fifth century this phrase seems to be rarely used by the Syriac writers, for the non-Chalcedonian writers, like Philoxenus and Severus, assumed that the term ܒܪܐ ܢܫܐ expresses the Nestorian opinion hence was replaced by ܐܬ ܒܪܢܫ to convey the Christological understanding accurately.[88] This shows that Syriac theology and literature of the sixth century were influenced by the Greek culture, but Philoxenos' role in this development cannot be excluded.[89] In other words, Philoxenos turned to embrace the Greek language in order to strengthen his argument against his opponents, who saw the usefulness of Greek terminology for his discourses.[90]

   These theological polemics prompted ecclesial leaders to express their dogma and defend their positions. For this reason, the Syriac authors eagerly used the Greek language to have access to the political and ecclesial spheres. Consequently, the Greek language gained acceptance among Syriac theologians, in order to negotiate polemical matters of the time, especially right after the split of the councils of Ephesus (431) and Chalcedon (451). This new development brought a tremendous shift into the Syriac tradition, for there was a series of scholastic translations of various theological books from Greek into Syriac, in particular the Cappadocian Fathers' works.[91] The Qennešrē (ܩܢܫܪܝ) monastery played a fundamental role in this development in which Greek and Syriac were prevailing in an advanced level.[92] The Qennešrē monastery founded by John Bar Aphtonia (d. 537) became an educational hotspot for Syriac Church clergy and nurtured prominent teachers, ecclesial leaders and outstanding scholars such as Severus Sabokht (d. 667), Jacob of Edessa (d. 708), Athanasius of Balad (d. ca. 687) and George bishop of the Arabs (725).[93] Consequently, in the seventh and eighth centuries Qennešrē became one of the main centres of Greek studies along with Syriac, where the Syriac Bible was

---

[87]G. Winkler, *Die Jakobus-Liturgie in ihren Überlieferungssträngen. Edition des Cod. arm. 17 von Lyon, Übersetzung und Liturgievergleich*, Anaphorae Orientales 4, Anaphorae Armeniacae 4 (Rome: Pontifical Oriental Institute, 2013), p. 281.

[88]See S. Brock, *Fire from Heaven: Studies in Syriac Theology and Liturgy* (Aldershot: Ashgate, 2006), p. 83.

[89]See S. Ruzer and A. Kofsky, *Syriac Idiosyncrasies: Theology and Hermeneutics in Early Syriac Literature* (Leiden: E.J. Brill, 2010), p. 5.

[90]For more details about Philoxenos' Christological understanding, see André De Halleux, *La Philoxénienne du symbole*, OCA 205 (Rome: Pontifical Oriental Institute, 1978).

[91]See A. Rigolio, 'Some Syriac Monastic Encounters with Greek Literature', in *Syriac Encounters. Papers from the Sixth North American Syriac Symposium Duke University, 26-29 June 2011*, eds M. Doerfler et al., ECS 20 (Leuven: Peeters, 2015), pp. 295–304. here: p. 298.

[92]See A. Palmer, R. Hoyland and S. Brock, *The Seventh Century in the West-Syrian Chronicles* (Liverpool: Liverpool University Press, 1993), p.11.

[93]See J. Tannous, *The Making of the Medieval Middle East: Religion Society and Simple Believers* (Princeton, NJ: Princeton University Press, 2018), p. 172. The monastery also was a home to the Syriac patriarchs after Severus of Antioch (d. 538).

revised and compared with the Greek LXX version, by Thomas of Harkel (d. ca640) and Athanasius Gamolō (d. 631).[94]

Some of the earliest Syriac liturgical commentators graduated from this monastery, and so, it occupied a vast space in the history of the Syriac Church, due to its prominent school. To conclude, one can suggest that after the fifth century Syriac writers tend to draw closer to Greek culture, employing Greek terms rather than Syriac terms in order to be effective in their writings, as they faced various challenges of the time about the Christological and political polemics. Those who trained in this monastery, like Jacob of Edessa and George the bishop of Arab tribes today, are counted among the earliest liturgical commentators. It could be in this monastery Jacob revised the Anaphora of James, comparing it with the Greek text, which is an interesting point to be touched briefly, in the following section.

ST JAMES'S ANAPHORA IN SYRIAC TRADITION

The Anaphora of St James according to the Syriac version is the chief Anaphora used in the Syriac Church. It is believed that the first version of the Anaphora of James was in Greek, which was used in Jerusalem and later in the Antioch region around the fourth or early fifth century.[95] However, the translation of the Syriac version from Greek into Syriac is believed to be after the fifth century. Bryan Spinks notices that James's Anaphora was translated word by word from the Greek version either by John of Tella (d. 538) or by Jacob of Baradaeus (d. 578) around the first half of the sixth century, before the Justinian persecution of the non-Chalcedonian Churches.[96] Similarly, Varghese also suggests that the Syriac text of the Anaphora goes back to the early sixth century, during the Justinian persecutions on the non-Chalcedonian.[97] One of the most characteristic features of James's Anaphora is the concentration on the trinitarian formula throughout the prayers. Such formulation in the Anaphora of James is thought to be the product of the fourth century after the Councils of Nicaea 325 and Constantinople 382.

The Anaphora of St James historically has two versions: one is the Greek believed to be the original language, and the other is the Syriac version, translated from Greek into Syriac. The Syriac version would play an important role in transmitting James's Anaphora to other traditions, namely Armenian, Ethiopian and Maronite.[98] The Syriac version underwent critical changes, first by Jacob of Edessa and second

---

[94]Ibid., 172.
[95]See J. D. Witvliet, 'The Anaphora of St. James', in *Essays on Early Eastern Eucharistic Prayers*, eds P. F. Bradshaw and F. Kacmarcik (Collegeville, MN: Pueblo Books, 1997), pp. 153–72, here: p. 153.
[96]See B. Spinks, *Do This in Remembrance of Me: The Eucharist from the Early Church to the Present Day* (London: SCM Press, 2013), p. 160.
[97]See B. Varghese, *The Syriac Version of the Liturgy of James: A Brief History for Students*, Alcuin/Joint Liturgical Studies, 49 (Cambridge: Cambridge University Press, 2001), p. 6.
[98]See Winkler, *Die Jakobus-Liturgie*, p. 13.

by Bar 'Ebroyō.[99] Recent studies also show that Jacob of Edessa revised the James's Anaphora in order to agree with the Greek version,[100] as he illustrates its structure in his *Letter* to Thomas the presbyter. Likewise, Fenwick believes that Jacob played an important role in the recension of the Anaphora of James, comparing it with the Greek version.[101] Some manuscripts contain James's Anaphora in their titles as written 'according to the correction of Jacob of Edessa'.

The Anaphora of St James, the Brother of our Lord, according to a new and authentic correction of Jacob of Edessa.[102]	ܐܘܣܝܐ ܕܩܕܝܫܐ ܝܥܩܘܒ ܐܚܘܗܝ ܕܡܪܢ ܐܝܟ ܬܘܪܨܐ ܚܕܬܐ ܘܫܪܝܪܐ ܕܝܥܩܘܒ ܐܘܪܗܝܐ.[103]

The second stage of the recension of the Anaphora of James was reputedly made by Bar 'Ebroyō, although there is no strong evidence to support this idea. It is supposed that he revised the Anaphora of James, in the thirteenth century and shortened it to be more efficient.[104] Ironically, he does not record this reduction in his writings, yet incorporated the *Letter* of Jacob of Edessa to Thomas the presbyter in his book *Nomo-Canon*, where the whole structure of the Anaphora is provided, but he did not comment on any revisions that he made or it should be made.[105] Nevertheless, in the last century the Western scholars argue that it was revised and shortened by Bar 'Ebroyō. This opinion is initially supported by Baumstark, as suggests that the short version of James's Anaphora is redacted by Bar 'Ebroyō, and further states that the Armenian version of James seems to have emerged from the Syriac original.[106] Therefore, today the Anaphora of James is known in two forms, the longer and shorter version. The Anaphora of James has been the fundamental eucharistic structure throughout history for the composition of an anaphora or writing a commentary on the Eucharist. Most Syriac commentators followed its structure in interpreting the eucharistic prayers, which is to say, if James's Anaphora is not the oldest, it definitely is counted as one of the oldest Anaphoras of Early Christendom, derived from Jerusalem and adopted in Antioch before the Synod of Chalcedon.[107] The Syriac Church considers the Anaphora of James as the main one which can be used in any eucharistic celebration, but it is mandatory to be used on the occasions

---

[99]See P. D. Day, *Eastern Christian Liturgies: The Armenian Coptic Ethiopian and Syrian Rites* (Shannon: Irish University Press, 1972), p. 154.

[100]See Witvliet, 'The Anaphora of St James', p. 154.

[101]See J. R. K. Fenwick, *The Anaphoras of St Basil and St James. An Investigation into their Common Origin*, OCA 240 (Rome: Pontifucum Institutum Orientale, 1992), p. 48.

[102]My own translation.

[103]British Library MS Add. 14691, fol. 3. Also, Add. 14695, fol. 25.

[104]See B. Varghese, *West Syrian Liturgical Theology: Liturgy, Worship and Society* (Aldershot: Ashgate, 2004), p. 2.

[105]See J. I. Cicek (ed.), *Nomo-Canon of Bar Hebraeus* (Losser: Bar Hebraeus Verlag, 1986), p. 30.

[106]See A. Baumstark, *Geschichte der syrischen Literatur, mit Ausschluss der christlich-palästinensischen Texte* (Bonn: Weber, 1922), p. 312.

[107]See G. Dix, *The Shape of the Liturgy* (London: Continuum Press, 2005), p. 176.

of all feasts of Christ like the Nativity, Theophany, Easter, etc. and festivals of the church, such as the ordination of deacons, priests and the consecration of a bishop or patriarch, as well as the consecration of churches and altars. It is also obligatory that the newly ordained person, priest or bishop celebrate the first Eucharist according to James's Anaphora.[108]

SYRIAC LITURGICAL COMMENTATORS AND THE SO-CALLED RENAISSANCE

The Syriac liturgy is rich in commentaries that come down to us from different church fathers in different centuries. Among the earliest Syriac commentators were Jacob of Edessa (d. 708) and George of the Arab tribes (d. 725), who wrote extensive commentaries on various sacraments. Brock has thoroughly investigated the early Syriac commentaries and notes that George of the Arabs considerably applied previous church fathers' liturgical commentaries into his commentary, on baptism and the Eucharist, which became an important source for later Syriac commentators who considered his commentaries as a reliable source.[109] The second important Syriac commentator is Jacob of Edessa, a vital Syriac author of the seventh and early eighth centuries. Alison Salvesen has widely studied Jacob's works in the last few decades and suggests that Jacob engaged himself with various subjects, namely biblical exegesis, Syriac orthography, liturgy, chronology and cannon law.[110] Jacob of Edessa's name is found in numerous manuscripts that he edited or corrected liturgical rites, namely the Anaphora of James and the rite of Baptism.[111] Hence, the later Syriac writers are indebted to Jacob and George' writings for their valuable resources.

Later Syriac commentators, specifically Bar Kephō (d. 903) and Bar Ṣalībī (d. 1171), inevitably benefited from the writings of Jacob and George. Varghese's analysis of the Syriac commentators is significant, in which he argues that the majority of Syriac commentaries follow the same methodology by interpreting theological subjects through typological understanding, except for the commentary of John of Dara (d. 825).[112] This period between late antiquity and middle ages is a crucial time in the history of Syriac Christianity, seeing the developments of the liturgy and literature in the West Syriac tradition, when many Anaphoras were

---

[108]See A. Y. Samuel (ed.), *Anaphoras the Book of the Divine Liturgies According to the Rite of the Syrian Orthodox Church of Antioch* (Lodi, CA: Syriac Orthodox Church Press, 1991), p. 96.

[109]S. Brock, 'An Early Syriac Commentary on the Liturgy', *Journal of the Theological Studies* 37 (1986): 387–403, here: 387. This commentary was published by Rahmani in 1920 and reedited by Brock together with a slightly later and more developed form. It is very clear from the context that this commentary was known to George bishop of the Arabs tribes, as there are plenty of parallel references in both commentaries.

[110]See A. Salvesen, 'Jacob of Edessa's Life and Work: A Biographical Sketch', in *Jacob of Edessa and the Syriac Culture of His Day*, ed Bas T. H. Romeny (Leiden: E.J. Brill, 2008), pp. 1–10, here: p. 5.

[111]The manuscript at the British Library cod. MS Add. 14496 witnesses to his contribution on the liturgies of baptism and the Eucharist.

[112]See Varghese, *West Syrian Liturgical Theology*, p. 27.

written by different ecclesial figures, mainly bishops, patriarchs and monks, as Barsoum provides in his list of seventy-nine Syriac Anaphoras.[113] In recent research scholars suggest that the number of the Syriac Anaphoras is eighty, the majority in disuse, but still some are used.[114] Much of our knowledge concerning the development of the Syriac liturgy is based on the sixth and thirteenth centuries, for the Syriac tradition is highly indebted to the vast commentaries of George of the Arabs and Jacob of Edessa, Bar Kephō, Bar Ṣalībī and Bar 'Ebroyō who immensely contributed to the Syriac liturgy and provided considerable interpretations on various liturgical aspects, in particular on the Eucharist. This paved the way in developing the liturgy to make it effective for the faithful, focusing on the liturgical commentaries, providing clarifications for the prayers and elements used in the liturgy.

Although the Syriac Christianity had experienced a short renaissance between the tenth and thirteenth centuries, where a significant literature was produced, such as the well-known Chronicle of Michael the Great (d. 1199), Bar Ṣalībī's invaluable liturgical, exegetical and apologetical works and similarly Bar 'Ebroyō's scientific writings. This revival unluckily could not survive for a long time, in the thirteenth century already the Syriac Church began to suffer from various surrounding powers, Arabs, Crusaders and finally from the Mongols, who destroyed a vast part of the heritage of the Syriac community.[115]

CONCLUSION

The Syriac Church was under Ottoman rule for more than six centuries, and finally, this rule ended with the devastating trauma in the First World War. This period is known in Syriac as the 'Year of the Sword' (ܣܝܦܐ ܫܢܬ), where hundreds of thousands of Syriacs Christians along with other Christians under the Ottoman rule were massacred. This tragedy caused the Syriac Christians to scatter around the world. Today, the Syriac-speaking community lives in different continents, mainly in Europe, the United States, Australia and the Middle East. In the last decade the strongest Syriacs populated country was Syria, where about 250,000 people lived, just before the current war began. Unfortunately, the majority of the Syriacs left their homeland, especially after the abduction of the top clergy, Gregorios Yuhanna Abraham and Paul Yazigi. The Syriac Church today has four million population around the world. Finally, although the Syriac Church has clearly passed through periods of sever persecution, it still retains the ancient heritage it accumulated through history, and even now the Syriac language is alive and the hymns of St Ephrem and Jacob of Serugh are sung in Syriac.

---

[113]See Barsoum, The Scattered Pearls, pp. 65–7.

[114]See H. J. Feulner, '"Ex Oriente Lux" – Die Ostkirchen und Ihre Liturgien. Ein liturgie-wissenschaftlicher Beitrag zum ökumenischen Dialog', OS 61 (2012): 10–42, here: 23. The particular list of the Anaphoras can be found here: H. J. Feulner, 'Zu den Editionen orientalischer Anaphoren', in Crossroad of Cultures: Studies in Liturgy and Patristics in Honor of Gabriele Winkler, OCA 260 (Rome: Pontifical Oriental Institute, 2000), pp. 251–82.

[115]See H. Teule, 'The Syriac Renaissance', in The Syriac Renaissance. Eastern Christian Studies 9 (Leuven: Peeters, 2010), pp. 1–30, here: p. 1f.

BIBLIOGRAPHY
ANCIENT SOURCES
Manuscripts at the British Library

MS Add. 14691.
MS Add. 14695.
MS Add. 14496.

MODERN SOURCES

Anaphoras the Book of the Divine Liturgies According to the Rite of the Syrian Orthodox Church of Antioch, ed. Samuel, A. Y. Lodi, CA: Syriac Orthodox Church Press, 1991.

Akhrass, R. and Syryany, I. (eds), *160 Unpublished Homilies of Jacob of Serugh*, vol. 2. Beirut: Zakaria Press, 2017.

Apocryphal Acts of the Apostles: The Syriac Text 1, ed. Wright, W., 2nd edn. Piscataway, NY: Gorgias Press, 2005.

Barsoum, E. *The Scattered Pearls: The History of Syriac Sciences and Literature*, trans. M. Moosa, 2nd edn. Piscataway NY: Gorgias Press, 2003.

Baumstark, A. *Geschichte der syrischen Literatur, mit Ausschluss der christlich-palästinensischen Texte*. Bonn: Weber, 1922.

Baumstark, A. *On the Historical Development of the Liturgy*, trans. F. West. Collegeville, MN: Pueblo Books, 2011.

Becker, A. *Fear of God and the Beginning of Wisdom. The School of Nisibis and Christian Scholastic Culture in Late Antique Mesopotamia*. Philadelphia: University of Pennsylvania Press, 2006).

Beyer, K. *The Aramaic Language: Its Distribution and Subdivision*. Göttingen: Vandenhoeck & Ruprecht, 1986.

Biesen, d. K. *Simple and Bold Ephrem's Art of Symbolic Thought*. Piscataway, NY: Georgia Press, 2006.

Brock, S. *Baptismal Themes in the Writings of Jacob of Serugh*, 324–47. OCA 205. Rome: Pontificium Institutum Orientalium Studiorum, 1978.

Brock, S. 'Clothing Metaphors as a Means of Theological Expression in Syriac Tradition', in M. Schmidt and G. Carl-Friedrich (eds), *Typus, Symbol, Allegorie bei den östlichen Vätern und ihre Parallelen im Mittelalter*, 11–38. Eichstätter Beiträge 4. Eichstätt: F. Pustet Regensburg, 1982.

Brock, S. *Greek into Syriac and Syriac into Greek: Syriac Perspectives on Late Antiquity*. London: Variorum, 1984.

Brock, S. *Syriac Perspectives on Late Antiquity*. Aldershot: Ashgate, 1984.

Brock, S. 'An Early Syriac Commentary on the Liturgy', *JTS* 37 (1986): 387–403.

Brock, S. (ed. and trans.). *The Syriac Fathers on Prayer and the Spiritual Life*. Kalamazoo, MI: Cistercian Publications, 1987.

Brock, S. (ed.). *St Ephrem the Syrian Hymns on Paradise*. New York: St Vladimir Press, 1990.

Brock, S. (eds). 'Eusebius and Syriac Christianity', in H. W. Attridge and G. Hata (eds), *Eusebius Christianity and Judaism*, 212–34. Detroit, MI: Wayne State University Press, 1992.

Brock, S. *Studies in Syriac Christianity: History Literature and Theology*. Aldershot: Ashgate, 1992.

Brock, S. *The Luminous Eye: The Spiritual World Vision of Saint Ephrem the Syrian*. Kalamazoo, MI: Cistercian Publications, 1992.

Brock, S. 'The Greek Language in Late Antique Syria', in A. Bowman and G. Woolf (eds), *Literacy and Power in the Ancient World*, 149–60. Cambridge: Cambridge University Press, 1994.

Brock, S. 'The Earliest Syriac Literature', in F. Young, L. Ayres and A. Louth (eds), *CHECL*, 161–71. Cambridge: Cambridge University Press, 2004.

Brock, S. 'Ephrem and the Syriac Tradition', in F. Young, L. Ayres and A. Louth (eds), *CHECL*, 362–72. Cambridge: Cambridge University Press, 2004.

Brock, S. 'Some Early Witnesses to the East Syriac Liturgical Tradition', *JAAS* 18 (2004): 19–38.

Brock, S. *Fire from Heaven: Studies in Syriac Theology and Liturgy*. Aldershot: Ashgate, 2006.

Brock, S. 'Ya'qub of Serugh', in S. Brock, A. M. Butts, G. A. Kiraz and L. V. Rompay (eds), *GEDSH*, 433–5, Piscataway, NY: Gorgias Press, 2011.

Brock, S. 'The Use of the Syriac Fathers for New Testament Textual Criticism', in B. Ehrman and M. Holmes (eds), *The Text of the New Testament in Contemporary Research*, 407–28. Leiden: E.J. Brill, 2013.

Bruns, P. 'Jacob of Serugh', in S. Döpp and W. Geerlings (eds), *DECL*, 315–16. New York: Crossroad, 2000.

Chesnut, R. *Three Monophysite Christologies*. Oxford: Oxford University Press, 1976.

Cicek J. I. (ed.). *Nomo-Canon of Bar Hebraeus*. Losser: Bar Hebraeus Verlag, 1986.

Day, P. D. *Eastern Christian Liturgies: The Armenian Coptic Ethiopian and Syrian Rites*. Shannon: Irish University Press, 1972.

De Halleux, A. *La Philoxénienne du symbole*. OCA 205. Rome: Pontifical Oriental Institute, 1978.

Dix, G. *The Shape of the Liturgy*. London: Continuum Press, 2005.

Drijvers, J. W. *Old Syriac (Edessan) Inscriptions*. Leiden: E.J. Brill, 1972.

Drijvers, J. W. 'Rabula Bishop of Edessa. Spiritual Authority and Secular Power', in J. W. Drijvers and J. W. Watt (eds), *Portraits of Spiritual Authority: Religious Power in Early Christianity Byzantium and the Christian Orient*, 139–54. Leiden: E.J. Brill, 1999.

Fenwick, J. R. K. *The Anaphoras of St Basil and St James: An Investigation into their Common Origin*. OCA 240. Rome: Pontifucum Institutum Orientale, 1992.

Feulner, H. J. '„Ex Oriente Lux" –Die Ostkirchen und Ihre Liturgien. Ein liturgie-wissenschaftlicher Beitrag zum ökumenischen Dialog', *OS* 61 (2012): 10–42.

Feulner, H. J. 'Zu den Editionen orientalischer Anaphoren', in H. J. Feulner and R. Taft (eds), *Crossroad of Cultures: Studies in Liturgy and Patristics in Honor of Gabriele Winkler*, 251–82. OCA 260. Rome: Pontifical Oriental Institute, 2000.

Finn, T. *Early Christian Baptism and the Catechumenate*. Collegeville, MN: The Liturgical Press, 1992.

Forness, M. Ph. 'Cultural Exchange and Scholarship on Eastern Christianity: An Early Modern Debate over Jacob of Serugh's Christology', *JECS* 70 (2018): 257–84.

Forness, M. Ph. *Preaching Christology in the Roman Near East: A Study of Jacob of Serugh*. Oxford: Oxford University Press, 2018.

Gabriel, S. M. (ed.). *The Breviary of the Syriac Church for the Lent*. Damascus: Bap Tuma Press, 1982.

George, P. (ed. and trans.). *The Doctrine of Addai the Apostle*. London: Trübner & Co, 1876.

Griffith, S. H. 'Mar Jacob of Serugh on Monks and Monasticism', in G. A. Kiraz (ed.), *Jacob of Serugh and His Time*, 71–89. Piscataway, NY: Georgia Press, 2010.

Harrak, A. 'The Syriac Orthodox Celebration of the Eucharist in Light of Jacob of Serugh's Mimro 95', in George A. Kiraz (ed.), *Jacob of Serugh and His Time*, 91–113. Piscataway, NY: Georgia Press, 2010.

Harvey, S. A. 'To Whom Did Jacob Preach?', in G. A. Kiraz (ed.), *Jacob of Serugh and His Time*, 115–31. Piscataway, NY: Georgia Press, 2010.

Healey, J. F. 'The Edessan Milieu and the Birth of Syriac', *JSS* 10 (2007): 115–27.

Homiliae Selectae Mar-Jacobi Sarugensis, ed. P. Bedjan, vol. 5. Paris: Harrasowitz, 1905–1910.

Jarkins-Skoyles, S. K. *Aphrahat the Persian Sage and the Temple of God: A Study of Early Syriac Theological Anthropology*. Piscataway, NY: Gorgias Press, 2014.

Jeanne, M. S. N. *Missionary Stories and the Formation of the Syriac Churches*. Milwaukee: University of California Press, 2015.

Lattke, M. 'Einsetzung und Vollzug der christlichen Paschafeier bei Aphrahat', in D. Hellholm and D. Sänger (eds), *The Eucharist - Its Origins and Context*, *vol.* 2: *Patristic Traditions, Iconography*, 1091–119. WUNT 376. Tübingen: Mohr Siebeck, 2017.

Kitchen, R. 'A Poetic Life: Metrical Vita of Jacob of Serugh by Saʿīd Bar Ṣabūnī', in M. Doerfler et al. (eds), *Syriac Encounters: Papers from the Sixth North American Syriac Symposium Duke University, 26–29 June 2011*, 65–75. ECS 20. Leuven: Peeters, 2015.

Kollamparampil, T. *Salvation in Christ According to Jacob of Serugh*. Piscataway, NY: Gorgias Press, 2001.

Krüger, P. 'Das Problem der Rechtgläubigkeit Jakobs von Serugh und seine Lösung', *OS* 23 (1974): 188–96.

Lössl, J. *The Early Church: History and Memory*. London: T&T Clark, 2010.

Macabasag, N. *The Annunciation (LK 1:26-38) in the Writings of Jacob of Serugh and Early Syriac Fathers*. Mōran Ethō 34. Kottayam and Kerala: St. Joseph Press, 2015.

Mansour, T. B. 'The Christology of Jacob of Sarug', in Th. Hainthaler and M. Ehrhardt (eds and trans.), *CCT 2*, 434–56. Oxford: Oxford University Press, 2013.

McCarthy, C. C. (ed. and trans.). *Saint Ephrem's Commentary on Tatian's Diatessaron*. Oxford: Oxford University Press, 1993.

McDonnell, K. *The Baptism of Jesus in the Jordan*. Collegeville, MN: Michael Glazier, 1996.

Michelson, D. *The Practical Christology of Philoxenos of Mabbug*. Oxford: Oxford University Press, 2014.

Murray, R. *Symbols of Church and Kingdom: A Study in Early Syriac Tradition*. Cambridge: Cambridge University Press, 1975.

Palmer, A. R. and Hoyland, S. B. *The Seventh Century in the West-Syrian Chronicles*. Liverpool: Liverpool University Press, 1993.

Petersen, W. 'The Christology of Aphrahat the Persian Sage. An Excursus on the 17th Demonstration', *VCh* 46 (1992): 241–56.

Possekel, U. *Evidence of Greek Philosophical Concepts in the Writings of Ephrem the Syrian*. CSCO 580 Subsidia 102. Leuven: Peeters, 1999.

Possekel, U. 'Ephrem's Doctrine of God', in A. B. McGowan, B. E. Daley and T. J. Gaden (eds), *God in Early Christian Thought*, 195–237. Leiden: E.J. Brill, 2009.

Rigolio, A. 'Some Syriac Monastic Encounters with Greek Literature', in M. Doerfler et al (eds), *Syriac Encounters. Papers from the Sixth North American Syriac Symposium Duke University, 26–29 June 2011*, 295–304. ECS 20. Leuven: Peeters, 2015.

Rompay, V. L. 'Malphana Dilan Suryaya. Ephrem in the Works of Philoxenos of Mabbug', *JSS* 7 (2004): 83–105.

Ruzer, S. and Kofsky, A., *Syriac Idiosyncrasies: Theology and Hermeneutics in Early Syriac Literature*. Leiden: E.J. Brill, 2010.

Salvesen, A. 'Jacob of Edessa's Life and Work: A Biographical Sketch', in Bas T. H. Romeny (ed.), *Jacob of Edessa and the Syriac Culture of His Day*, 1–10. Leiden: E.J. Brill, 2008.

Schmid, U. 'The Diatessaron of Tatian', in B. Ehrman and M. Holmes (eds), *The Text of the New Testament in Contemporary Research*, 115–42. Leiden: E.J. Brill, 2013.

Spinks B., *Do This in Remembrance of Me: The Eucharist from the Early Church to the Present Day*. London: SCM Press, 2013.

Taft, R. *Liturgy in Byzantium and Beyond*. Aldershot: Ashgate, 1995.

Tannous, J. *The Making of the Medieval Middle East: Religion Society and Simple Believers*. Princeton: NJ, Princeton University Press, 2018.

Taylor, D. G. K. 'The Syriac Tradition', in G. R. Evans (ed.), *The First Christian Theologians*, 201–24. Oxford: Blackwell Publishing, 2004.

Teule, H. 'The Syriac Renaissance', in H. Teule et al. (eds), *The Syriac Renaissance*, 1–30. ECS 9. Leuven: Peeters, 2010.

Varghese, B. *The Syriac Version of the Liturgy of James: A Brief History for Students*. Alcuin / GJLS 49. Cambridge: Cambridge University Press, 2001.

Varghese, B. *West Syrian Liturgical Theology: Liturgy, Worship and Society*. Aldershot: Ashgate, 2004.

Vaschalde, A. A. *Three Letters of Philoxenus Bishop of Mabbôgh*. Rome: Tipografia Della R. Accademia Dei Linchi, 1902.

Wickes, J. 'Between Liturgy and School. Reassessing the Performative Context of Ephrem's Madrašĕ', *JECS* 26, no. 1 (2018): 25–51.

Wickes, J. 'The Poetics of Self-Presentation in Ephrem's Hymns on Faith 10', in M. Doerfler et al. (eds), *Syriac Encounters: Papers from the Sixth North American Syriac Symposium Duke University, 26–29 June 2011*, 51–63. ECS 20. Leuven: Peeters, 2015.

William, D. J. 'Early Syriac Christianity', *VCh* 19 (1996): 159–77.

Williams, P. J. 'The Syriac Versions of the New Testament', in B. D. Ehrman and M. W. Holmes (eds), *The Text of the New Testament in Contemporary Research*, 143–66. Leiden: E.J. Brill, 2013.

Winkler, G. *Die Jakobus-Liturgie in ihren Überlieferungssträngen. Edition des Cod. arm. 17 von Lyon, Übersetzung und Liturgievergleich*. Anaphorae Orientales 4, Anaphorae Armeniacae 4. Rome: Pontifical Oriental Institute, 2013.

Witvliet, J. D. 'The Anaphora of St. James', in P. F. Bradshaw and F. Kacmarcik (eds), *Essays on Early Eastern Eucharistic Prayers*, 153–72. Collegeville, MN: Pueblo Books, 1997.

Wright, W. (ed.), *The Homilies Aphraates the Persian Sage*. London: William and Norgate, 1869.

PART V

The early church and systematic theology

CHAPTER 30

Does Jerusalem still need Athens?[1]

GYÖRGY GERÉBY

FIRST REFLECTIONS

Responding to this question is a tall order. The formulation hearkens back to a rhetorical catchword of Tertullian, the great Christian theologian from the early AD third century. As a timeless formula, however, it prompts an answer from us today. While Tertullian addressed the relationship between Christianity and the philosophy of his days, a modern answer would have to carry the heavy weight of a love–hate relationship evolving throughout the following two millennia. The symbolic opposition between 'Jerusalem' and 'Athens' is well alive. On the one hand, it survives as the 'conflict thesis' between 'science' and 'religion' and, on the other, as repeated attempts to 'liberate' Christianity from the pernicious external influence of philosophy.[2] While there are theistic philosophers who try to substantiate Christian claims, the debates between creationists and radical atheists witness to a continuing tension.[3] This chapter cannot do justice to all facets of this relationship. It will have

---

[1]This chapter was written during the Covid-19 pandemic, which affected access to library holdings. The author, therefore, had to rely on available digitial editions, and in some cases Hungarian translations of the originals. If otherwise not indicated all translations are mine. For biblical quotations I use the *New King James* translation, but for the Old Testament I consulted (2nd edn.) A. Piertsma and B. G. Wright (eds), *A New English Translation of the Septuagint* (Oxford: Oxford University Press, 2007). I owe special thanks to Ilaria Ramelli and John A. McGuckin for their trust in, and patience towards, the author's snailpace writing.

[2]The classic presentation of the 'conflict thesis' is by John William Draper (1811–82), *History of the Conflict Between Religion and Science* (New York: D. Appleton, 1874), and Andrew Dickson White (1832–1918), *A History of the Warfare of Science with Theology in Christendom*, 2 vols (London, 1896). The largely Protestant paradigm about the corruption of the original Christian message through the influence of Hellenism is discussed and modified in Christoph Markschies, *Hellenisierung des Christentums. Geschichte und Bedeutung eines umstrittenen Konzepts* (Berlin: Evangelische Verlagsanstalt, 2012).

[3]From the abundant recent controversy literature I only mention two characteristic books, that of the atheist Richard Dawkins, *The God Delusion* (London: Bantam, 2006), and one by the apologist Henry Morris (Ada, MI: Baker Books, 1989).

to leave many branchings of the labyrinthine relation uncharted and will have to be content emerging with only a meagre collection of hints and fragments of reflection.

Tertullian's rhetorical juxtaposition of Jerusalem and Athens is obviously meant in a figurative sense. Jerusalem stands for Christianity, being its birthplace while Athens, as the proverbial centre of ancient rationalism, stands for philosophy. (It is important to stress that it is Athens and not Rome which is contrasted to Jerusalem in the adage, the intellectual centre and not the power centre of the gentile world.) The catchy phrase became a symbolic summary of the opposition between philosophy, the pinnacle of rational thought and Christianity. It was quoted innumerable times by posterity either to justify an exclusive reliance on 'blind faith' or to discredit unenlightened fideism.[4] As Tertullian raised the question: *What indeed has Athens to do with Jerusalem? What concord is there between the Academy and the Church?*[5] More will be said about the complexities involved in this problem later in the chapter, but three points can be stated right now.

First, we see that Tertullian's question is a specific Christian query. It is not a question of Judaism, even if Jerusalem is both her symbolic and at the same time historic centre. For Judaism, Tertullian's juxtaposition is of little significance. Even for the more philosophical branches of rabbinic Judaism, which follow the inspiration of Maimonides, the primacy of the *Halacha*, the Law is absolute. The Law does not require the reasons of Athens. The TaNaCh (the Jewish Bible), neither in terms of its commandments in the Torah nor in terms of its historical accounts, requires philosophical justification. Reason can help or support the interpretation of the letter of the Covenant, but neither the events of Biblical history nor the *mitzvot* (the 613 commandments) ought to rely on external support. Nor is philosophy an indispensable element in Islam. In Islam, *falsafa* (philosophy) might attract the occasional thinker, but again, in the face of the Holy *Qur'an* and the *hadith* philosophy is of marginal significance. The *Qu'ran* always trumps rational arguments, whether for or against it. Hence, both Judaism and Islam philosophy plays a secondary role against the explicit rulings of the sacred laws.[6] Going further away, for other religions, such as Hinduism, neither of these cities carry any symbolic significance.[7]

Second, as will be discussed later, the issues between the Christianity of the Great Church (setting aside the different alternative Christianties of the period)

[4]Jaroslav Pelikan, *What Has Athens to Do with Jerusalem? Timaeus and Genesis in Counterpoint* (Ann Arbor: University of Michigan Press, 1997).

[5]Tertullian, *Prescr.*, 7, 9.

[6]As pointed out by Erik Peterson, 'Was ist Theologie?' in Erik Peterson, *Theologische Traktate*, Hrsg. Barbara Nichtweiss (Würzburg: Echter, 1994), pp. 3–22. Ausgewählte Schriften 1. English translation: *Theological Tractates*, tranze. Michael Hollerich (Stanford, CA: Stanford University Press, 2011). Also, Peter Hünermann, 'Ort und Wesen theologischen Denken', in Bernhard Casper, Klaus Hemmerle and Peter Hünermann, *Theologie als Wissenschaft* (Freiburg, Basel and Wien: Herder, 1970), pp. 88–9.

[7]These remarks are not meant to say that there can be no rationality in other religions in the form of explanatory digressions, as exegesis or mythological, even metaphysical explanations. The stress is on the difference in the specific significance of philosophy.

and philosophy were relatively well defined in the early centuries.[8] Since then, however, a barrage of issues has emerged, not least because the two parties have branched into distinct labyrinths. Over long centuries there evolved a plethora of 'Jerusalems', that is, many varieties and forms of competing or even mutually exclusive Christianities. Again, partly independently, partly motivated by the conflicts with Christianity, there arose a rich and diverse group of the many 'Athens', that is, various and mutually incompatible schools of philosophy. In both cases the various branches often display only a 'family resemblance'. The various trends are connected by not much more than historical lineage. They have developed their own arguments and positions about the relationship of the two cities, an abundance which cannot be covered in all detail, except some of the central issues. By our modern era both 'cities' had become 'blanket terms' standing for a bewildering variety of different traditions.

In many cases these family branches cannot share a greatest common denominator, having developed into 'relative primes' so to say. To put it simply: Which 'Athens' should be referred to which 'Jerusalem' and about which problem? Consequently, there is a main obstacle for an answer to the title question: How to bring the many different 'Jerusalems' in connection with the many and hugely diverse 'Athens'?

Third, the question requires clarification on a closer investigation, since it can be read in various ways. Let us settle that the question addresses the issue of whether Christianity needs philosophy anymore. Then, however, comes the difficulty. The formulation can be understood in the sense that Jerusalem had needed Athens until recently. Such a reading implies that Athens had provided good service for 'Jerusalem' for a while, but (as the modifier 'still' indicates) their once abiding relation has lately become problematic. Hence, the formulation implies that something has changed. Since there are two parties to an alliance, an alienation can work both ways. Either party or both could have changed. Has Jerusalem become more self-reliant and independent than it used to be? How did it happen, and why only now? Alternatively, has Athens given up her support for some reason? Why did 'Athens' change her attitude towards Jerusalem? Has she forfeited this connection because of some failure on her side? Or has Athens discovered that providing help to Jerusalem was a mistake? How did their relationship come under stress? Is this a new issue or has some tension characterized their relationship all along? But then why and how could Athens become an ally of Jerusalem at all? Why did this need for Athens arise in Jerusalem at all? Was Tertullian's observation mistaken?

These reasons explain why I will try to answer the title question in three steps. First, I will attempt to clarify the specific meaning of Tertullian's position. Then I'll try to explain the paradoxical relation of Christianity to philosophy. Third, I'll try to address specific issues of the present-day situation. Finally, I will suggest some conclusions.

---

[8]The criticism of Christianity by the philosopher Celsus (around 175 CE) neatly summarizes the main problems. His arguments survive in the rejoinder of Origen's treatise *Cels.*

THE MEANING OF TERTULLIAN'S ADAGE[9]

As was said earlier, the title refers back to a rhetorical question of Tertullian, clearly implying a negative answer. Hence, it seems to be a straight refusal of any connection of Christianity to philosophy. However, did Tertullian really exclude all forms of philosophy? Was he only a champion of 'simple faith'?[10] Did he really, as a representative of 'Christian anti-intellectualism', 'excoriate philosophy in the name of the gospel'?[11] While Tertullian clearly denied that Athens would be of any use for Jerusalem, the interpreter shouldn't be too rash in declaring him an obstinate fideist, in the sense that he rejected *all* forms of reason. The meaning of the adage is more complex than this somewhat reductive understanding.

For Tertullian, Athens was not only a symbol but also a living centre of powerful rivals. Athens's glory derived from the fact that all major schools of ancient philosophical thought originated there: the schools of Plato (the Academy, and the later Platonists), of Aristotle (the Peripatetics), of Epicurus (and his 'garden') and of Zeno (the Stoa). This historical role certainly justified Athens fame as the centre of philosophy representing reason, human knowledge or scientific thought in general. On the other hand, Athens was also the city where the above schools actually resided in Tertullian's times, since at the end of the second century Emperor Marcus Aurelius honoured the Athenian legacy by founding there four chairs for the four great schools of thought that originated there, thereby reestablishing Athens once again as the home of philosophy.[12] I suggest, therefore, that Tertullian's rhetorical question is best understood as being directed against definite targets. Rejecting 'Athens' meant for Tertullian that he dismissed the dominant rivals who were now being officially supported by Rome.

Their variety notwithstanding, the philosophies of his day dealt also with theology, beyond logic, physics or ethics. Aristotle explicitly included theology among the theoretical sciences.[13] This 'natural philosophy', *philosophia naturalis* (θεολογία φυσική), aimed at investigating the existence and the nature of the divine.[14] Their views were justly jettisoned by Tertullian, since all four of them proposed theologies incompatible with the basic doctrines of Christianity, from the point of view of both theology and ethical teaching.

---

[9]Justo L. González, 'Athens and Jerusalem Revisited: Reason and Authority in Tertullian', *Church History* 43 (1974): 17–25; Robert D. Sider, 'Credo Quia Absurdum?' *Church History* 73 (1980): 417–19; Robert M. Grant, 'Two Notes on Tertullian', *VChr* 5 (1951): 113–15.

[10]Charles Norris Cochrane, *Christianity and Classical Culture: A Study of Thought and Action from Augustus to Augustine* (London: Oxford University Press, 1944), pp. 222–5.

[11]Scott Macdonald, 'The Christian Contribution to Medieval Philosophical Theology', in *A Companion to the Philosophy of Religion*, eds Charles Taliaferro, Paul Draper and Philip L. Quinn (Chichester: Wiley-Blackwell, 2010), p. 92.

[12]Emperor Marcus Aurelius founded chairs in Athens for the four most important schools of philosophy in 176 CE. See Cassius Dio 71.31.3; Philostratus, *Vitae* 2, 566,8–567,7.

[13]Aristotle, *Metaph.*, 1000a9 f., 1071b2 ff, 1075b26 and 1091a33 ff.

[14]Jean Pépin, 'La thologie tripertite de Varron. Essai de reconstition et recherche des sources', *Revue des Études Augustiniennes et Patristiques* 2 (1956): 265–94.

Let us start with the Epicureans. It is easy to see that their gods were as if non-existent. They are strictly confined to the Elysian fields from where they conduct no business whatsoever with a world ruled by the chance configuration of the atoms. This world of the Epicureans was not even a cosmos, since the falling atoms were guided only by unpredictable swerve, resulting in a world of pure contingency. Epicureans were therefore labelled as atheists and could lend no support to Christianity. In ethics, the Epicurean ideal of pleasure left no room for a divine reward and could not accommodate happiness as a return to God in any way.

The Stoics were also in the wrong because of their assertion of the materiality of divinity.[15] They were therefore charged with 'making matter equal to god'.[16] What is more, the Stoic divinity was an impersonal force, the *pneuma*, the fiery material force cementing and guiding the *cosmos*, and hence they did not allow for a transcendent and personal deity. Their ethical doctrine was based on the use of reason, which was a sufficient capability endowed by nature, and allowed – in the normative sense – individuals to attain virtue which was the ultimate happiness. The divine transcendence and God as the supreme legislator could not possibly be fitted into the Stoic way.

The Peripatetics maintained the existence of a transcendent Prime Mover or First Cause, but this strange, impersonal entity was only concerned with its own perfection and had no inclination to exercise providence, that is, care for the cosmos. The Prime Mover moved the heavens by attraction, but without direct interference, a relation which precludes active providence. It motivated the cosmos to imitate its perfection, but this continuous 'pull' was like a gravitational force, nothing more. Besides, the Peripatetics consistently maintained the eternity of the world, excluding a possible temporal creation, and they also assumed the perishable nature of the soul. Its 'ethics of the mean' were hardly able to accommodate unconditional faith and love.

Finally, the Platonists couldn't offer much better service, either, because of their 'three-principled creation' (i.e. the master artisan, the *demiurge* imprinted independently existing ideas on the pre-existent matter). While the independent existence of the ideas was largely given up by the Neoplatonists (attributing them to the divine mind), the concept of an emanation from the One or the Supreme Being was certainly not compatible with the Christian sense of *creatio ex nihilo* by divine will, a firm view which emerged relatively early in the second century.[17] What is more, the Platonic Demiurge was only responsible for the basic structure of the cosmos, and the rest was entrusted to a densely populated divine hierarchy, the

---

[15]Here I set aside the problem of Tertullian's 'material' interpretation of the divinity. I suspect that his less fortunate pronouncements were due to his uncompromising insistence on the absolute reality of God. He certainly rejected Stoicism in general, when he contrasts the Porch with the Porch of Solomon in *Prescr.*, 7, 10.

[16]Cf. Hippolytus, *Haer.*, 1, 21, 1.

[17]Gerhard May, *Creatio ex Nihilo: The Doctrine of 'Creation Out of Nothing' in Early Christian Thought*, trans. A. S. Worrall (Edinburgh: T&T Clark, 1994).

Generated Gods,[18] plainly accommodating the multitude of the traditional Greek deities, as pointed out later by Augustine.[19] (Augustine, on the other hand, admitted that Plato glimpsed a morsel of truth that there is a higher divinity. Hence, from among the gentile philosophers, his views were the closest to Christianity. Closest, indeed, but only from among the thoroughly gentile fold.)[20]

Hence, these gentile philosophies were not only unhelpful, but also, in fact, antagonistic to the Christian teaching. In a chapter against the heretics, Tertullian reproaches them precisely because of their allure leading to heresy. The heresiarchs of his times based their teaching on 'miserable Aristotle' and his ilk, Plato, the Stoics or Heraclitus.[21] In an even more sweeping formulation, Tertullian repeated his position:

> Furthermore, what likeness is there between the philosopher and the Christian, the disciple of Greece and the disciple of heaven, the trader in reputation and the trader in salvation, the doer of words and the worker of deeds, the builder up and the destroyer of things, the friend and the enemy of error, the corrupter and the restorer and exponent of truth, its thief and its guardian?[22]

These lines again ought to be interpreted in the context of his times. 'Greece' certainly plays here the same role as 'Athens', as a *synecdoche*. 'Trader in reputation' can be understood from the satires of Lucian (ca. 125–ca. 180) ridiculing the greedy, ostentatious philosophers of his times.[23] Empty verbosity was (and is) a standard charge against debating philosophers, and a sceptic or critical philosopher is a 'destroyer', juxtaposed to the builder, probably an allusion to the Christian principle that 'love edifies' (1 Cor. 8.1). It is also an allusion to the endless debates of the schools. The sceptical argument from disagreement, or *diaphonia*, used to be a standard charge against the multiplicity of philosophical schools putting forward diametrically opposed teachings about truth.

Tertullian clearly perceived the noxious attraction and the corrosive effect of the gentile philosophies of his age on Christianity. He realized that these were the (current) philosophical ideas which provided the tools for the heresies of Valentinus, Marcion and other sects of mainstream Christianity. The scholarly trend of revisionism charges Tertullian with malice, although he was not alone in identifying the influence of gentile philosophy in the heretical doctrines. In the same period, Irenaeus' great work against the heresies or the *Philosophoumena* (once attributed to Hippolytus, now to Pseudo-Origen) shared the opinion that the various philosophical schools infected Christianity and seduced their followers into doctrinal aberrations.

---

[18]Plato, *Ti* 40d4 – 41a8.

[19]Augustine, *Civ.*, 8, 12.

[20]Augustine, *Civ.*, 8, 9.

[21]Ps-Tertullian, *Haer.* c. 7, 9.

[22]Tertullian, *Apol.*, 46.

[23]For example, Lucian, *Vitarum auctio*, a viciously amusing text.

On the other hand, Tertullian was not averse to reason when arguments were required to support his exposition of Christianity. There is no room here for a detailed analysis, but his complex arguments against Marcion or the Valentinians testify to his proficient debating skills.[24] To sum up, Tertullian's position was not a rejection of 'philosophy' *tout court*, so to say, that is, he did not jettison reasoned thought as such in the service of Christianity but rejected specific kinds of antagonistic and incompatible schools of thought.

BEYOND TERTULLIAN

The broader background shows the same complications. Tertullian and the apologists dismissed gentile philosophy, but on the other hand, they were intimately associated with philosophy on various levels.

First of all, in antiquity in a general and practical sense, philosophy was supposed to offer guidance for a reasoned way of life by setting out the theoretical foundations for an understanding of the world and man's place in it.[25] Ancient collections listed as many as 288 possible ways for leading a meaningful and happy life.[26] Philosophical doctrines were supposed to have practical consequences. Adopting a philosophy entailed an effect on one's lifestyle. As Aristotle pointed out, 'the syllogisms imply the principle of actions'.[27]

In this broad sense, even a Jew or a Christian could claim to follow a particular philosophy since both adhered to a specific type of conduct, manifested in consistent religious observation, diet, ethical and political habits.[28] These habits followed their respective religious principles, and in this, they were supported by reasons. Before Tertullian Justin Martyr could call his Christianity 'divine philosophy'[29] and his discussion partner, Trypho, could claim his philosophy to be Judaism.[30] They both agree then that the primary task of philosophy is the investigation of the divine, especially the nature of the monarchy and of providence.[31] In the same period, Clement of Alexandria called Christianity 'the true gnosis', the valid and real knowledge of the things divine. According to Clement, Christianity carried the

---

[24]The issues are analysed in more detail by González, 'Athens and Jerusalem Revisited', 17–25, and Robert H. Ayers, *Language, Logic, and Reason in the Church Fathers: A Study of Tertullian, Augustine, and Aquinas* (Hildesheim and New York: Georg Olms, 1979), pp. 24–60.

[25]Philosophy was meant to answer the problem 'How to live?' (πῶς βιωτέον) Plato, *Gorg.* 492d. According to Albinus' *Epitome* 1, 1, philosophy is 'the knowledge of things divine and human', which was a standard rendering of the period, for example, Sextus *adv. math.* IX 13 or Augustine *Trin* 14, 1, 3.

[26]The collection of Marcus Terentius Varro (ca. 116–ca. 27 BCE) about the *summum bonum*, as reported by Augustine, *Civ.*, 19, 1-3.

[27]Aristotle, *EN* 1144a31-2.

[28]Pierre Hadot, *Philosophy as a Way of Life: Spiritual Exercises from Socrates to Foucault*, trans. Michael Chase (Oxford: Blackwell, 1995).

[29]φιλοσοφία θεία, Justin, *2 Apol.*, 12, 5.

[30]Justin, *Dial.*, 8.1.

[31]Justin, *Dial.*, 1.3.

ideal guidance for life as compared to her alternatives. Christ is a teacher of how to live well in the eyes of God.[32] The teaching role of Christ is attested often in early iconography.

From the Apologists onward, therefore, Christianity had a dual approach to 'Athens'.[33] On the one hand, it rejected the gentile guides to life. Had philosophy been a purely speculative metaphysical enterprise, it wouldn't have presented much concern. As ideals, however, gentile philosophies were competitors in the 'religious market' of the day.[34] Since from the Christian point of view these ways could be classified either as atheistic (the Epicureans) or as polytheistic theologies (the other schools), these had to be refuted and their falsity had to be spelled out against the truth of Christianity, which in turn had to be demonstrated. Neither refutations nor demonstrations can be made without arguments, and the church fathers always insisted that they did not accept Christianity on the basis of blind faith but by reason and demonstration.[35]

There is also another fundamental reason why Christianity accommodated philosophy. The universal mission of Christianity (Matt. 28.19-20) required a message which could not rely solely on the Scriptures. Christianity had a common basis with Judaism since it had not denied the validity of the Old Law. Such a common (although contested) platform was denied to her when taking the gospel tidings to the gentile nations. For the *nations* the Old Law was unknown or unaccepted (such as in the case of educated Hellenists). The preaching of the New Law to the gentiles, therefore, had to rely on the assumption of Reason common to all humanity (Rom. 1.20). The universality of the intellect was guaranteed first by the common sharing of the 'image and likeness' received in the creation (Gen. 1.26), by which humanity is endowed with reason, but also by the gospel of the Divine Word, the *Logos*, who is the Creator of everything 'from the beginning'. In this task, the idea of the *praeparatio evangelica* offered great help. By pursuing philosophy, relying on the divine gift of reason, if used in the right way, by the greatest of the gentile wise men, like Socrates, Plato or Seneca, it leads them to anticipate fragments of the truth. This idea offered legitimacy for the acceptance of the best parts of the gentile philosophies. Augustine rightfully compared this to the 'Despoiling of the Egyptians'.[36]

Hence, it was the reason which provided the common conceptual frame of reference for preaching the gospel to the nations. Since the tidings had to be formulated in a great variety of languages, it could not be secured by relying on the letter. The 'letter' is always the letters of an alphabet and spelled out by a particular

---

[32]Clement of Alexandria, *Protrep.*, 1, 7, 4, 1. or Ps-Hippolytus, *De consummatione mundi* ὁ διδάσκαλος τῆς ἐκκλησίας.

[33]References to Clement, Origen, Hilarius in: Michael Fiederowicz, *Theologie der Kirchenväter* (Freiburg, Basel and Wien: Herder, 2007), pp. 28–34.

[34]For example, Eusebius, *Praep.Ev.*, 1, 5, 6.

[35]Eusebius, *Praep.Ev.*, 1, 2, 4 – 4, 10.

[36]Augustine, *Doc.*, 2. 40. 60-1. (Based on Exod. 3.21-22, 11.2-3 and 12-35-36.)

language (Jn 14.10 and Jn 1.1).[37] The identity of the gospel message required other means of securing like-mindedness (ὁμόνοια), as happened at the first Pentecost. The universal task then could only be accomplished by the presence of the Spirit of Truth (Jn 15.26).

Christianity has faith in the Incarnate Word of God. This faith, however, according to Heb. 11.1, is not founded on the written law, but on 'the reality of things hoped for, the evidence of things not seen'.[38] How to understand this enigmatic definition? It was Martin Buber who pointed out that the Christian history of salvation relies on the pillars of two historical events: the promised Second Coming of Christ, which is 'hoped for', and His Resurrection, which was 'not seen' since nobody was present at that. The risen Christ appeared to the apostles, but their witness also belongs to a distant past.[39] No metaphysics can offer proof for these events.

These events are about the relationship between the Father, the Son and the Spirit. The Son, who glorified the Name of the Father (Jn 13.31-32), and the Father, who will seat Christ on His right hand (Lk. 20.42; Eph. 1.20) and who will send His Spirit to guide the church, the 'people of God' (λαὸς τοῦ θεοῦ) whose pilgrimage 'begins here at the earthly Jerusalem and rejoices in God in that heavenly city', as Augustine poignantly formulated it.[40] Neither of the foundational events of faith, however, can be presented to the gentile nations as evidence. For Jews, the Torah contains the Law as a written document to which the people testified at the mountain of Sinai, and it can be presented to every interested person. Christianity does not have the privilege of a similar written covenant. The guarantees of the new covenant are the reality of the two events: the Resurrection and the promise of the Second Coming. 'If Christ is not risen, then our preaching is empty, and your faith is also empty' (1 Cor. 15.14).

Tertullian's other famous adage highlights a problem of the Christian mission. Since Christianity does not have the privilege of inheriting religion by lineage, someone can only *become* a Christian, and not *born* into it. 'Christians are made, not born.'[41] The principle is well manifested from the earliest times by the practice of the required doctrinal preparations for adult conversion.[42] Christ teaches according to the Gospels, and the Christian message is called a *doctrine* in the Epistles.[43]

---

[37]Erik Peterson, 'Was ist Theologie?' in *Erik Peterson. Theologische Traktate*, ed. Barbara Nichtweiß, Ausgewählte Schriften 1 (Würzburg: Echter, 1994), 3–22.

[38]I have changed the NKJ 'substance' to 'reality', since *hypostasis* means rather a subsistent reality. 'Substance' would guide the attention too much towards a philosophical terminology, while here the stress is on the present reality of the event hoped for.

[39]Martin Buber, *Two Types of Faith* (New York: Macmillan, 1951), p. 10. An argument for the eyewitness account: Richard Bauckham, *Jesus and the Eyewitnesses* (Grand Rapids, MI: Eerdmans, 2006).

[40]*Coepit enim haec Ecclesia ab Jerusalem ista terrena, ut gaudeat inde Deo in illa Jerusalem coelesti. Ab hac enim incipit, ad illam terminat.* Augustine, *In psalmum cxlvii enarratio*. PL. 37:1929a.

[41]*Fiunt non nascuntur Christiani.* Tertullian, *Apol.*, 18, 4. Also in *An* 1, 7. Also Augustine, *Pecc. Merit.* I.3, 9.

[42]Arthur D. Nock, *Conversion: The Old and the New in Religion from Alexander the Great to Augustine of Hippo* (Lanham, MD: Univseristy Press of America, 1988).

[43]In the Greek διδάσκειν or διδαχή, except in 1-2 Tim and Tit, where it is called διδασκαλία.

Hence, the gospel message ought to be explained and has to be 'taught'. Every candidate for baptism had to start with the *catechumenate*; that is, he or she was required to participate in doctrinal instruction first. Only after the instruction could the candidates receive baptism and join the faithful, that is, the people of God, the Body of Christ, the church.

While in the gospels Christ speaks the words of God (Jn 14.24), the gospel message can only be accepted on the authority of its custodian, the Church of Christ which is sustained by the presence of the Spirit. As Augustine confessed: 'I would not believe the gospel unless the authority of the Church moved me to do so.'[44] Authority can be rationalized, but reason cannot establish it.

If, however, Christianity relies on authoritative doctrine and teaching, how much room does authority allow for reasoning? Authority depends on acceptance, while reason depends on investigation and analysis. At this junction, serious objections can be raised against a significant role of rational investigation for Christianity. One objection can refer to an event reported by the gospels. At a certain point, Jesus asks his disciples: 'What do people say who am I?' They reply that some say he is Elijah, some that he is Jeremiah or John the Baptist. 'But what do you say?', insists Jesus. To which Peter answers: 'You are the Christ, the Son of the living God.' A powerful statement, indeed, especially for someone raised in Judaism. Declaring someone to be the Messiah is brave but not unheard of in the period. To state, however, that there is a Son to God is beyond the pale, so to say. Now there is no hint in the gospels that Peter would have arrived in this confession by analytical reflection, as it is acknowledged by Jesus himself: 'Blessed are you, Simon Bar-Jonah, for flesh and blood has not revealed this to you, but my Father who is in heaven.'[45]

For the contemporaries, Jesus is just an ordinary human being, even if an exceptional one. Isn't Jesus the 'carpenter's son', well known to his community? (Matt 13.55; cf. Mk 6.3). He is too familiar with the people of his village. Familiarity implies the experience of the ordinary, and it imposes limitations on perception. The guesses of strangers don't go much further either. Peter, however, does not rely on his senses which would only present him a human person. Neither does he try to fit Jesus into the religious framework of his environment. Peter understands something that is beyond the bodily appearance and the expectations of his times. It is not the flesh and blood human person which shows Jesus' divinity. It ought to be something that is way beyond the material presence.

The certainty of Peter's confession points to epistemological problems. How did he arrive at this recognition? How could he perceive what is not manifest to the senses? Of course, he was witness to many miracles performed by Jesus, but miracles on their own are not enough to account for such an avowal. There were countless 'miracle workers' around, tricksters and frauds, as was well known to the educated

---

[44]*Ego vero Evangelio non crederem, nisi me catholicae Ecclesiae commoveret auctoritas.* Augustinus, *c. Ep. Man*, c. 5. PL. 42:176.
[45]Matt. 16.13-16; cf. the shortened version in Lk. 9.18-20.

gentiles, such as Celsus and Lucian. Besides, Peter, being an observant Jew, must have been aware of the theological weight of his confession.

Peter's avowal recalls Abraham's when he was approached by God or Moses when he was addressed by God from the burning bush. Their responses, like all major actions of the scriptural heroes, resulted from faith, as pointed out by the Epistle to the Hebrews (11.4-40). None of these great heroes of faith of the past acted on deliberation. The model case of Abraham shows that he was responding to the command of God against every maxim of reason.

György Tatár called attention to the conflict between Abraham's gesture to sacrifice Isaac and Kant's categorical imperative. According to Kant, the philosophically justifiable supreme command of reason is to act 'according to that maxim whereby you can, at the same time, will that it should become a universal law'.[46] Now it clearly cannot be a supreme command of reason, a 'universal maxim' to sacrifice one's son on the command of a being hardly known. This voice, if it is a voice audible to human ears at all, must be like any other earthly voice, points out Kant. Hence, it is impossible to know who is speaking: God or an ordinary human being, or Satan himself. Kant goes further: 'But in some cases, a man can be sure that the voice he hears is not God's; for if the voice commands him to do something contrary to the moral law, then no matter how majestic the apparition may be, and no matter how it may seem to surpass the whole of nature, he must consider it an illusion.'[47] Therefore, Abraham's trust is not only not 'reasonable' in the slightest degree, but on Kant's terms, Abraham acts immorally.

While Abraham's acceptance of the divine call was independent of reason, even so, his faith cannot be rationalized as a 'wager'. He was not a naked soul desperately exposed to an alien world. Hence, the odds of betting on God's command being just would have been absurdly high. Risking his fatherland, his only son and thereby his whole progeny would have been a foolhardy venture. Abraham does not wager all this. He knows whom to trust, and this is fundamentally different from Pascal's thought experiment.

Faith preceded Abraham's actions. The important textual variant of Isa. 7.9 (the reading of the LXX) spells out this kind of relationship between faith and reason: 'If you do not believe, neither shall you understand.'[48] The Hebrew version is an address to the people of Israel reminding them to adhere to the Covenant of Sinai and threatening them with the abandonment of divine protection: 'If you will not believe, surely you shall not be established.' Jerome's Latin translation returned

---

[46]Immanuel Kant, *Grounding for the Metaphysics of Morals*, trans. James W. Ellington, 3rd edn (Indianapolis and Cambridge: Hackett, 1993), p. 30. (Kant, GA, vol. IV, p. 421.)

[47]Tatár, Gy. *Viharra várva*. [Waiting for the storm] in *A 'másik oldal'* (Kalligram, 2014). The reference is to a passage in Kant's *Streit der Fakultäten,* I. Kant, *Conflict of the Faculties* (New York: Abaris, 1979), p. 115.

[48]Also used by Tertullian in *Bapt.* 10, 1-2: *utpote non intelligentes quia nec credentes. nos quidem quantula fide sumus tantulo et intellectu possumus aestimare.*

to the Hebrew (following Symmachus), but the Septuagint reading continued to command authority for the patristic and medieval theologians.[49]

It is a telling sign of the methodological importance of the LXX reading for the Christian theologians that while Jerome's rendering was well known, even in the Latin realm the LXX version was used again and again as guidance. It was the Septuagint text which offered the correct meaning for the Christians. Jn 6.69 also seems to point in the same direction: 'Also we have come to believe and know that you are the Christ, the Son of the living God.' The order of the key terms is the same: first 'believe' (πεπιστεύκαμεν) and then 'know' (ἐγνώκαμεν).

Thomas Aquinas is often attributed with the saying that 'For those with faith, no evidence is necessary; for those without it, no evidence will suffice'. Aquinas' actual formulation was different, but the adage captures his point. According to Aquinas, the opponents of Christianity neither see nor know what is acceptable as knowable or perceivable for the faithful. What is more, the opponents consider these as utterly beyond the knowable or the credible. Aquinas acknowledges the difference between the believers and their opponents and points to the difference which consists in faith. What is known is not belief, and what is believed to be the case is not known.[50] The believers do not accept the truth of Christianity on the grounds of proofs or demonstrations but 'by the light of faith, which makes them see what they ought to believe'.[51]

The first paradox of Christianity, then, is that faith has to pass through the obstacle of reason in order to be justified by reason. One might use here a similarly paradoxical analogy from quantum physics. In the case of the 'quantum tunnelling', a particle as a wave passes through the obstacle of a potential barrier without going over it. On this image, if allowed, faith seems to behave in a similar way. Faith is not 'bypassing' reason, but passes through the barrier of ordinary rationality without a confrontation or clash.

TALES OF THE TWO CITIES[52]

Another formulation of the paradox, then, is the following: Christianity relies on doctrine and teaching, but the acceptance of the teaching depends on antecedent faith. Faith denies the role of reason, but teaching requires reason and argument.

---

[49]The LXX version was adopted, for example, by John Chrysostom, Augustine and even Aquinas (who was, of course, aware of Jerome's version, too).

[50]*Non autem est possibile quod idem ab eodem sit creditum et visum.* Thomas Aquinas, STh II[a]-IIae q. 1 a. 5 co. https://www.corpusthomisticum.org/sth3001.html English: *The Summa Theologiæ of St. Thomas Aquinas* Second and Revised Edition, 1920. Literally translated by Fathers of the English Dominican Province. At: https://www.newadvent.org/summa/3001.htm#article5 (accessed 20 November 2020).

[51]Thomas Aquinas, STh II[a]-IIae q. 1 a. 5 ad 1.

[52]Wolfhart Pannenberg, *Theologie und Philosophie. Ihr Verhältnis im Lichte ihrer gemeinsamen Geschichte* (Göttingen: Vandenhoeck & Ruprecht, 1996). After treating Christian Late Antiquity Pannenberg concentrates on the Continental and especially the German tradition up until the nineteenth century. It should be supplemented by accounts of twentieth-century thinkers: Graham Oppy and N. N. Trakakis

The first horn of the dilemma is manifested first of all in an adage by Ambrose of Milan: 'It did not please God to save his people with dialectics. The kingdom of God dwells in the simplicity of faith and not in the rivalry of words.'[53] In contrast, the second horn is formulated by the fourteenth-century scholastic theologian John Lutterell: 'a theologian ignorant of logic is a monstrous heretic'[54] – only to be angrily rejected by Luther, who abhorred the adage and called this out as precisely a monstrous heresy.[55]

Luther's Jerusalem, however, cannot dismiss Athens entirely, as an extreme version of Tertullian's principle. The Scriptures on their own support the ambiguity. Wisdom indeed surpasses reason, since wisdom is imparted by the 'fear of the Lord' (Ps. 111.10 (LXX, 110,10)).[56] Without the fear of the Lord secular reason cannot claim true wisdom. The limitation of the secular compared to the sacred is an idea carried on by the New Testament, too. 'For the wisdom of this world is foolishness with God. For it is written, 'He catches the wise in their own craftiness' (1 Cor. 3.19 quoting Job 5.13). Again, there are strictures on the possibilities of humanly attainable insights, too. 'Do not try to understand things that are too difficult for you or try to discover what is beyond your powers' (Sirach 3.22, Vulg.). The injunction clearly alludes to the things divine. The human condition is under explicit constraint by the admonition 'For my thoughts are not your thoughts, nor are your ways my ways, says the Lord' (Isa. 55.8).

On the other hand, 'this is your wisdom and your understanding in the sight of the peoples' (Deut. 4.6)[57] because wisdom 'taught him the knowledge of holy things' (Wis. 10.10 LXX, Vulg.). In the New Testament, the Apostle encourages knowledge since 'all scripture is given by inspiration of God, and is profitable for doctrine, for reproof, for correction, for instruction in righteousness' (2 Tim. 3.16).[58] In a similar vein he sets out the proper uses of knowledge: 'holding fast the faithful word as he has been taught, that he may be able, by sound doctrine, both to exhort and convict those who contradict' (Tit. 1.9). Rom. 1.20 has been understood, generation after generation, as a support for natural theology. This famous verse probably alludes to the psalms that reflections on the cosmos signal the works of God (Ps. 8.3), His 'invisible things', such as His justice (Ps. 50.6) or His glory (Ps. 19.1). The biblical injunctions, however, assume faith, either in the sense of keeping or being faithful to the Covenant (the meaning of *emuna* in the Jewish case) or holding to the two great events foundational to Christianity (Heb. 11.1).

(eds.), *Twentieth-Century Philosophy of Religion*, The History of Western Philosophy of Religion, vol. 5 (London and New York: Routledge, 2009).

[53]*Non in dialectica complacuit deo salvum facere populum suum*. Ambrose, *Fid* 1, 5. PL 16:536C.

[54]*Theologus non loycus est monstruosus hereticus*. Johannes Lutterell, *Epistola de visione beatifica* 20.

[55]'Theologus non logicus est monstruosus haereticus' est monstruosa et haeretica oratio. Contra dictum commune. Martin Luther, *Disputatio contra scholasticam theologiam* (1517), Prop. 45.

[56]Also in Prov. 1.7 and ibid., 9. 10.

[57]Quoted by Aquinas *Summa Th* 1a.q1.a6. sc 2.

[58]Quoted by Aquinas *Summa Th* 1a.q.1.a1.sc.

If secular wisdom cannot have priority, the relationship implies subordination. In the form of one-way traffic, the philosophical schools can be considered as 'service providers'. Philosophy provides and theology makes fair use of it. Although this 'service' might be imagined as the 'servant' going *in front of* the 'mistress', showing her the way, the formula of the 'handmaid' was rather taken as expressing the status of the captive.[59] Too much emphasis on this servant role lead to repercussions, and the emancipation from the 'tyranny' of theology was hailed as a great success in the history of modern philosophy.

Emancipated philosophy, then, jettisoned its ancient interest in theology. A trenchant – albeit probably Apocryphal – anecdote attributed to Pierre-Simon Laplace (1749–1827), the French mathematician, highlights the point. When Laplace presented his work on the solar system to Napoleon, the emperor supposedly challenged the mathematician with the question where is the Creator's place in his system? Laplace was attributed with the crisp answer: 'Sir, I had no need of that hypothesis.' This often-quoted quip was most probably not a witticism denying the existence of God, but a proud declaration that his equations improved on Newton's. Laplace's method excluded the instability in Newton's system, which theoretically did require an adjustment by God's occasional interference.

Whatever the original intent of Laplace's adage, it shows two significant issues. On the one hand, it shows that 'god' is not an operational term. A 'god' variable cannot be required in the equations, since 'god' has no measurable dimensions, that is, no mass or charge or whichever physical dimension one could assign to it. God cannot be quantified; hence, the 'god' variable or constant cannot affect the results of the equations. Therefore, it can be left out of consideration, and then, by Occam's razor, this superfluous entity can be discarded. A transcendent entity (an entity beyond the purview of physical thought) can be relegated to the realm of the human psyche or social conventions and traditions.

The other issue is the flip side of the Laplace adage. The equations of the celestial mechanics might work without any reference to an external element, but then by the same token, neither can 'god' be disproved by the formulae. From the fact that the equations of science are restricted to quantifiable operational elements, it follows that neither can God's existence be refuted by them. Science, being confined to its domain of interpretation, turns neutral in questions beyond its territory, such as those in theology. Such questions become *interpretations* of science when they try to have a say in matters theological.

In a fragment preserved by Sextus Empericus, Aristotle identifies two reasons for humanity to believe in the gods. The first is psychological. In extreme situations, the soul returns to itself and anticipates the future, seeing it as the gods. The second reason is the regular movement of the heavens which raises the question as to the cause of their movements and the source of their regular arrangement.[60] We have

---

[59]Malcolm De Mowbray, 'Philosophy as Handmaid of Theology: Biblical Exegesis in the Service of Scholarship', *Traditio* 59 (2004): 1–37.
[60]Aristotle, frg. 947 Gigon (= 10 Rose).

seen that the second is solved by the equations of Laplace. Sigmund Freud and modern psychology promise to explain the first on immanent grounds. Finally, evolutionary theory renders superfluous teleology or final causation.

In this way, the Laplace adage could become the characteristic position of the modern period. Athens does not have a mistress. Philosophy does not need theology. Modernity, mainly speaking, has arrived at what Aristotle pointed out long ago that 'if there is no separate and unmoving entity', that is, a different nature, then physics is the supreme form of knowledge.[61]

There were also historical issues at play. In the early modern period, in the context of religious controversies and wars, philosophers were advised to keep aloof from the far too sensitive, even dangerous, waters of theology. An alternative was offered to the new successes of science, which could provide philosophy with an empiricist ideal. This method came to dominate most philosophy during the last centuries. The enormous strides in the understanding of nature and the concomitant robust technological developments raised great expectations for a comprehensive and exhaustive understanding of nature in an immanentist way. The method relied on naturalist and verificationist principles. Truth came to mean experimental verifiability, which can only admit operational variables. The successes in the study of natural processes pushed the possibility of non-physical, or non-observable, truth to the margins or even beyond.

Therefore, much of modern philosophy began to possess little in common with pre-modern philosophy, which is thereby relegated to antiquarian interests. While in antiquity atheism was in the minority and was derided and even detested by most schools (as we have seen they differed only about the number and the nature of the gods), most modern philosophy has become either openly atheistic or decidedly agnostic.[62]

Philosophy also resigned the task or duty of being a guide to life. There is no 'philosopher's garb' any more.[63] Philosophers look like and behave like everybody else. Their speciality is that they think *ex professo* about particular things. They are expected to 'solve problems', whatever problems science leaves for them to be solved, like the 'last enigma' of human knowledge, the problem of the mind and its relation to the body. Others branches of philosophy specialize in analysing the phenomena of the social realm. The explanations, however, do not offer normative guidance any more, as ethical theory is mostly about abstract analysis of ethical statements.

Little surprise, then, that Rom. 1.20, gradually lost its importance for natural philosophy. Nature does not declare being creation any more than it reveals the 'eternal power and divinity' of God. It can only be discovered by the *intellect*, which is a problematic concept, after all. The *intellectually* attainable, the νοούμενα,

---

[61]Aristotles, *Metaph.*, 1064b 9-14.

[62]A good overview of the atheistic positions is in Kai Nielsen, *Contemporary Critiques of Religion* (London and Basingstoke: Macmillan, 1971).

[63]Justin Martyr was noticed by Trypho because of the philosophers' toga. *Dial.*, 1.2.

however, are obscure things, unsubstantiated by modern physics and psychology.[64] How could psychology make sense of a 'higher faculty' of non-discursive character, grasping the intellectibles directly if it cannot be identified with the help of experimental methods? Where would this faculty be in the human psyche if only personal experience can exemplify it? The naturalist approach disregards the possible object of such a mystical faculty. Hence, it will be another candidate for Occam's razor.

The great expectations that were directed towards science, however, have not yielded the ultimate results. It has certainly not provided the 'Theory of Everything'. It has not solved the issues of the Grand Unified Theory, the unification of quantum mechanics and relativity. The problems of dark matter and dark energy, the existence of multiversums, remain hanging. Physics-based cosmology has developed a standard view about the origin of the expanding universe, but it hasn't managed to prove it beyond doubt, as the representatives of the 'steady-state' position have pointed out. The unsolved issues haunt the scientists, but even more importantly, there remain great problems of a different kind for humanity. Poverty, persistent political oppression, population growth, environmental degradation, the lack of ethical control over technological civilization and a throng of other problems are affecting human society that have become even more urgent priorities.[65]

Of course, no one would question the tremendous advancements humanity has witnessed, but the exaggerated triumph of science seems to have led to something of a backlash. The optimism of the positivist approach has waned as the very nature of the scientific method has been questioned by Paul Feyerabend and others.[66] Beyond the unsolved problems, which should indicate some modesty should be observed concerning the general claims of science, a basic problem affects both science and scientifically minded philosophy. This methodological aspect was pointed out by Plato in the *Republic*.[67]

In the epistemological context of the *Simile of the Line*, Plato distinguished various forms of knowledge: first imagination, then belief, finally thought and then understanding.[68] Here I am not concerned about the precise exegesis of the simile but will only summarize the main points. After discussing imagination and belief as

---

[64]In fact, *intellectus* present in the Neoplatonic and Patristic authors had gradually lost its epistemological significance already in the Later Middle Ages. Endre von Ivanka, *Plato Christianus. Übernahme und Umgestaltung des Platonismus durch die Väter* (Einsiedeln: Johannes Verlag, 1964).

[65]The ambiguous consequences of technological development can be summarized by the parable of Goethe's *The sorcerer's apprentice* (*Der Zauberlehrling*), a modern version of Lucian's story in the *Incredulus* (*The lover of lies*, 36).

[66]A good colletion of important studies is Hans Lenk (ed.), *Zur Kritik der wissenschaftlichen Rationalität* (Freiburg and München: Karl Alber, 1986).

[67]For details of the role of Plato's theory of knowledge in late antiquity and Middle Ages, see the brilliant paper of Charles H. Lohr, 'The Pseudo-Aristotelian Liber de causis and Latin Theories of Science in the Twelfth and Thirteenth Centuries', in *Pseudo-Aristotle in the Middle Ages: The Theology and Other Texts*, ed. Jill Kraye, W. F. Ryan and Charles B. Schmitt (London: The Warburg Institute, 1986), pp. 53–62.

[68]Plato, *Rep.*, 509d6–511e3. For the English translation I used *Plato. Republic*. Translated from the New Standard Greek Text by C. D. C. Reeve (Indianapolis and Cambridge: Hackett, 2004).

to the less critical forms of knowledge, Plato explains the reasoned knowledge or thought (διάνοια) of the geometers. Here the paradigm is axiomatized geometry. Thought (διάνοια) is a form of knowledge that cannot achieve more than what is granted by its axioms.[69] It proceeds step by step from the axioms as hypotheses towards the conclusion. This conclusion, however, cannot be the first principle, since it depends on the choice of the hypotheses.[70] The realm of discursive, or hypothetical, reason is staked out by the chosen starting points.[71] According to Plato, however, hypothetical knowledge is surpassed by the next level, thought or intellect (νόησις), which approaches the first principle without hypotheses.[72] The unhypothetic science is dialectics, which, after attaining the first principle, 'reverses itself' and concludes step by step what follows from it.[73] This kind of knowledge proceeds without the images provided by the senses, and thereby it is a purely intellectual approach.[74]

Reflections on the natural sciences prove Plato's insight correct. In the case of physics, natural events are represented by mathematical objects, such as points, waves, fields, vectors, tensors and various types of space (Euclidean, Rieman, Hilbert spaces). These objects are described by equations, themselves well-defined, specific abstract constructs based on axiomatic structures. Their success depends on their capability to predict observational data. The same task was set to the astronomers by Plato, charging them with saving observational data with the help of well-defined geometrical theory (of the day), σώζειν τὰ φαινόμενα. What is more, the observational data themselves depend on observational strategies, such as the measuring instruments and other detection devices. Measurements depend on preset scales and intervals. Hence, the simple expression 'observational data' breaks down into a complex matrix of measurement strategies and mathematical structures.

At rare moments even physicists will confess that 'The ones that may long elude us are in some sense ultimate questions: why the physical laws are the way they are, where the matter of the universe came from "in the first place", and what was there before the universe existed. But these questions may not be real questions, operationally defined.'[75] To put it in another way: the question of why the fundamental constants of physics are of a particular value is not a physical question.

Plato's observation about the nature of hypostasized knowledge applies to philosophy, too. Being honest to the philosophers with the best intentions to prove the existence of God, one would have to say that it is by no chance that none of

---

[69]Plato, *Rep.*, 511a3-5. *The soul is forced to use hypotheses* in the investigation of it, not travelling up to a first principle, since *it cannot escape or get above its hypotheses*, but using as images those very things of which images were made by the things below them . . . trans. C. D. C. Reeve (My emphases.)

[70]Plato, *Rep.*, 510b3-8.

[71]Plato, *Rep.*, 510c1-d2.

[72]Plato, *Rep.*, 533b7-d7.

[73]Plato, *Rep.*, 511b5-c1.

[74]Plato, *Rep.*, 511a3-5.

[75]Carl Sagan in his preface to Timothy Ferris, *The Red Limit: The Search for the Edge of the Universe*, Second edn (London: Harper-Collins, 1983), p. 15.

the many proposed proofs succeeded in convincing the critiques. From Aristotle to the Stoics, from Anselm of Canterbury to Descartes and Kurt Gödel, from Thomas Aquinas to Richard Swinburne highly sophisticated attempts ran aground on Plato's problem. Any apodictic proof, even ones establishing a certain level of plausibility, requires discursive reasoning which is then bound by the inexorable methodological problem of proof itself: it cannot but start from assumptions and proceed via agreed steps of inference to the establishment of conclusions. For first, the hypotheses can be false, as when Aristotle fails when he assumes the false principle of 'one cannot go to infinity', or when Aquinas fails by assuming a defective principle of motion. Descartes' ontological proof runs into problems because of his practice of using existence as a first-order predicate. Second, the rules of inference can prove to be problematic, as in the case of Anselm's proof because of the semantic closedness of his logical language.[76] Here we have, of course, no room for engaging with the various types of arguments in detail. However, one can always choose a different system of modal logic, or an alternative interpretation of a scientific theory, such as opposing the cosmological theory of the Steady State Universe to the Standard Model, which, for a while, promised a proof for the temporal beginning of the world. The systematic causes of the failure of such arguments need to be pointed out. But the challenge remains, since the methodological limitations do not, of course, disprove the existence of God.

Science is a meticulously built edifice sanding upon complex hypotheses and presuppositions and tested against experience. The unavoidable structural character of science, however, always leaves open the possibility of a change in the fundamental hypotheses. For such changes, serious reasons are required, but it does happen, as is shown by the well-known cases of Copernicus, Galileo or twentieth-century physics. Plato's epistemological observation helps to understand why the recurring optimism that philosophy or science would, in some way, justify faith, is doomed to frustration.

Instead, it seems that philosophy in this respect can help the Christian theologian to develop a healthy scepticism towards philosophical claims which rely on scientific tropes. These might want to support faith, but with weak arguments, or criticize faith with flawed conclusions. These arguments might be called 'tropes' since as a consequence of the Laplace principle, no *properly scientific* proof has ever been produced either for or against the existence of God.

Finally, we should not bypass Plato's highest form of knowledge, νόησις, intellection (or 'thought' in Reeve's terminology).[77] This kind of knowledge is the way to access the intelligible realm of the ideas. Plato's complicated theory of the ideas does not concern us here, since, for the church fathers, the ideas were those of the Divine Mind. The role of the intellect, however, plays an essential role for the church fathers. Intellect, νοῦς, is the vehicle by which the human mind can

---

[76]For the details, see György Geréby, 'What Anselm and Gaunilo Told Each Other', *Przegląd Tomistyczny* 15 (2009): 1–22.
[77]Plato himself does not insist on the terminology, *Rep.*, 553d9.

gain access to the realm of the intelligible things beyond the empirical world. If the intellect does have this capability, then the question arises as to what extent is this realm accessible. Plato allows going very far. In the *Republic*, he not only speaks about the access to the first principle but then in the *Simile of the Cave* he explicitly assigns to the last stage of the philosopher's journey the gazing into the Sun 'as it is'. Regarding the Sun of the 'upper realm directly' expresses the ultimate epistemological optimism of classical Greek thought.[78]

It is at this point that Plato is abandoned by the church fathers since the vision of God is explicitly denied by many scriptural verses. God dwells 'in unapproachable light whom no man has seen or can see' (1 Tim. 6.16). Moreover, 'No one has seen God at any time' (1 Jn 4.12). This is why Gregory Nazianzen rejects the Platonic consummation of vision since the 'purity of the light [of the Sun],[79] defeats the senses'.[80]

The same can be found in the Gospel of John: 'No one has seen God at any time,' but then it continues: 'The only-begotten Son, who is in the bosom of the Father, he has declared him' (Jn 1.18). It was a common insight of the fathers of the church that solely by natural reason, God remains strictly inaccessible. There is, however, another way, namely the self-manifestation of God.[81] Origen made a rejoinder to Celsus who propounded the sceptical Platonic adage of the unknowability of God, that Christianity stands for a very different situation:[82] 'We for our part declare that human nature is not sufficient to seek out God in any way and to arrive at a pure apprehension of him unless it is assisted by the One whom it is seeking.'[83] Independently or not, Marius Victorinus says very similar things in Rome.

> Know this: it is difficult to know God, but it is not hopeless, for on this account he wanted to be known, on this account he created the world and established his divine works, in order that by all this we should comprehend him. The Word for sure, who is His Son, His image and manifestation, granted access to the Father by means of Himself.[84]

While, indeed, there is no possibility to ascend, there is another way, the condescension (συγκατάβασις) of God (Jn 3.13). Indeed, the descent of the Son, the

---

[78]Plato, *Rep.*, 514a–516c. The key phrase is Τελευταῖον δὴ οἶμαι τὸν ἥλιον, οὐκ ἐν ὕδασιν οὐδ' ἐν ἀλλοτρίᾳ ἕδρᾳ φαντάσματα αὐτοῦ, ἀλλ' αὐτὸν καθ' αὑτὸν ἐν τῇ αὑτοῦ χώρᾳ δύναιτ' ἂν κατιδεῖν καὶ θεάσασθαι οἷός ἐστιν.
[79]The 'divine light' we might say.
[80]Gregory Nazianzen, *Or.*, 28, 3, 15-18.
[81]A historical study of the problem is the still valuable book of Vladimir Lossky, *The Vision of God*, tran Asheleigh Moorhouse (Crestwood, NY: St Vladimir's Seminary Press, 1983).
[82]Celsus refers to Plato, *Tim.*, 28c3-4, 'The maker and father and maker of the all is a hard task to find, and having found him, it would be impossible to declare him to mankind.' trans. F. Cornford, slightly modified.
[83]Origen, *Cels.*, 7, 42.
[84]Marius Victorinus, *Adv. Arium* III, 6. PL. 8:1102-1103.

divine *economy* is the surest sign of the divine philanthropy, and it depends on the divine initiative.[85]

CONCLUDING SUMMARY

In this chapter, I hope to have touched upon a few key aspects of the relation between the two great cities Tertullian mentioned. First, I tried to show that what Tertullian rejected was the 'Athens' of the contemporary theological alternatives to Christianity. Then I argued that while Christianity is based on faith, philosophy is in a sense an indispensable requirement for her, too, which involves a paradoxical relationship. As a third move, I tried to sketch out certain vital issues in the conflict of faith with science, which characterized their inseparable duality, a veritable *syzygia*, over the centuries, despite all the changes occurring in both. It seems, then, that Jerusalem cannot discard the role of faith, while Athens must accept the methodological constraints upon it identified by Plato. Hence, Christianity has to continue to live with an uneasy paradox. Philosophy, human reason, is not going to take away the burden of faith, but it may help to explain, correct and suggest.

One could, half-jokingly, offer an answer to the initial question by a *consequentia mirabilis*: even if Christianity does not need philosophy, she needs philosophy, since the argument, by which the need is discarded, must need be posed in the form of a philosophical argument. Such an argument would be an easy way out, though. There are serious tasks still waiting for rational arguments. There are many challenges to Jerusalem arising from interpretations of science on a whole range from astrophysics to evolutionary biology, from neurology to the social sciences. If our argument sketchily presented earlier is correct, all these interpretations urgently need to be answered, which means, of course, that they have to be assessed on their own ground.

There is, however, no such thing as a specific 'Christian philosophy', as rationality is as neutral to faith as it is to logic or mathematics. The hypotheses, the premises or the conceptual frameworks might be different, but it is the same reason which leads the argumentation. It is Reason only that might help to criticize false premises or overblown interpretations of science. Again, these are arguments which can be used to justify or differentiate doctrinal points, highlight contrasts or show deeper implications; and it is Reason that helps to argue for probable positions. In rare moments philosophy can even point beyond reason, but it is, more accurately speaking, reflection and analysis which takes the mind to this point. Finally, Christianity cannot discard the fact that she is offering a 'rational service' to God (Rom. 12.1).

The lead of reason, however, should be followed out. To illustrate the point let me finish this chapter with a famous remark of Franz Rosenzweig's in his letter to Gertrud Oppenheimer, 30 May 1917:

---

[85]Gregory of Nyssa, *Cant.*, vol. 6. 304, 16-17.

With the knowledge of the mere *createdness* of things, nothing is really known; there is no paganism, from the Babylonian priests to the Jena Monists, that doesn't have its creation myths. But rather only that the created . . . things are 'created' for the sake of the End and He, who is first, is also the Last (as *Yesayahu* 44:6 and 48:12) or the Alpha *and* the Omega (as John says)[86] – only this gives knowledge.[87]

BIBLIOGRAPHY

Assmann, J. *The Price of Monotheism*, trans. Robert Savage. Stanford, CA: Stanford University Press, 2010.

Ayers, R. H. *Language, Logic, and Reason in the Church Fathers: A Study of Tertullian, Augustine, and Aquinas*. Hildesheim and New York: Georg Olms, 1979.

Barth, K. 'Kirche und Theologie', in Gerhard Sauter (ed.), *Theologie als Wissenschaft. Afsätze und Thesen*, 152–75. München: Chr.Kaiser, 1971.

Bauckham, R. *Jesus and the Eyewitnesses*. Grand Rapids, MI: Eerdmans, 2006.

Brown, C. *Philosophy and the Christian Faith: A Historical Sketch from the Middle Ages to the Present Day*. London: Tyndale Press, 1968.

Buber, M. *Two Types of Faith*, trans. Norman P. Goldhawk. New York: Macmillan, 1951.

Casper, B. et al. (eds). *Theologie als Wissenschaft*. Freiburg, Basel and Wien: Herder, 1970.

Cochrane, C. N. *Christianity and Classical Culture: A Study of Thought and Action from Augustus to Augustine*. London: Oxford University Press, 1944.

Crane, T. *The Meaning of Belief: Religion from an Atheist's Point of View*. Cambridge, MA: Harvard University Press, 2017.

Dawkins, R. *The God Delusion*. London: Bantam, 2006.

Draper, J. W. *History of the Conflict Between Religion and Science*. New York: D. Appleton, 1874.

Duhem, P. 'Letter to Father Bulliot, on Science and Religion', in *Essays in History and Philosophy of Science*, 157–62. Indianapolis and Cambridge: Hackett, 1996.

Fiederowicz, M. *Theologie der Kirchenväter*. Freiburg, Basel and Wien: Herder, 2007.

Geréby, G. 'Theistic Fallacies', in Péter Losonczi and Géza Xeravits (eds), *Reflecting Diversity*, 166–90. Wien and Berlin: Lit, 2007.

Geréby, G. 'What Anselm and Gaunilo Told Each Other', *Przegląd Tomistyczny* 15 (2009): 1–22.

González, J. L. 'Athens and Jerusalem Revisited: Reason and Authority in Tertullian', *Church History* 43, no. 1 (1974): 17–25.

Grant, R. M. 'Two Notes on Tertullian', *VChr* 5 (1951): 113–15.

---

[86]Rev. 1.18, 21.6, 22.13.

[87]Franz Rosenzweig, *Der Mensch und sein Werk. Gesammelte Schriften vol. 1. Briefe und Tagebücher*. Hrsg. Rachel Rosenzweig und Edith Rosenzweig- Scheinmann unter Mitwirkung von Bernhard Casper. I. Band 1900-1918 (Dondrecht: Springer, 1979), 412. trans. B. Pollock.

Hadot, P. *Philosophy as a Way of Life: Spiritual Exercises from Socrates to Foucault*, trans. M. Chase. Oxford: Blackwell, 1995.

Hoffmann, F. (ed.). 'Lutterell, Johannes, *Epistola de visione beatifica*', in *Die Schriften des Oxforder Kanzlers Iohannes Lutterell. Texte zur Theologie des vierzehnten Jahrhunderts*. Leipzig: Benno, 1959.

Hünermann, P. 'Ort und Wesen theologischen Denken', in B. Casper, K. Hemmerle and P. Hünermann, *Theologie als Wissenschaft*, 88–9, 73–123. Questiones Disputatae 45. Freiburg, Basel and Wien: Herder, 1970.

Ivanka, E. von. *Plato Christianus. Übernahme und Umgestaltung des Platonismus durch die Väter*. Einsiedln: Johannes Verlag, 1964.

Jaroszińsky, P. *Science in Culture*, trans. Hugh McDonald. Amsterdam and New York: Editions Rodopi, 2007.

Kant, I. *Conflict of the Faculties*, trans. Mary J. Gregor. New York: Abaris, 1979.

Kant, I. *Grounding for the Metaphysics of Morals*, 3rd edn, trans. James W. Ellington. Indianapolis and Cambridge: Hackett, 1993.

Kolakowski, L. *Religion*. London: Fontana, 1982.

Lenk, H. *Zur Kritik der wissenschaftlichen Rationalität*. Freiburg and München: Karl Alber, 1986.

Lohr, C. H. 'The Pseudo-Aristotelian Liber de causis and Latin Theories of Science in the Twelfth and Thirteenth Centuries', in Jill Kraye, W. F. Ryan and Charles B. Schmitt (eds), *Pseudo-Aristotle in the Middle Ages: The Theology and Other Texts*, 53–62. London: The Warburg Institute, 1986.

Löhr, W. 'Christianity as Philosophy: Problems and Perspectives of an Ancient Intellectual Project', *VChr* 64, no. 2 (2010): 160–88.

Macdonald, S. 'The Christian Contribution to Medieval Philosophical Theology', in C. Taliaferro, P. Draper and P. L. Quinn (eds), *A Companion to the Philosophy of Religion*. Chichester: Wiley–Blackwell, 2010.

Mann, W. E. (ed.). *The Blackwell Guide to the Philosophy of Religion*. Malden, Oxford and Carlton: Blackwell, 2005.

Markschies, C. *Hellenisierung des Christentums. Geschichte und Bedeutung eines umstrittenen Konzepts*. Berlin: Evangelische Verlagsanstalt, 2012.

May, G. *Creatio ex Nihilo: The Doctrine of 'Creation out of Nothing' in Early Christian Thought*, trans. A. S. Worrall. Edinburgh: T&T Clark, 1994.

Morris, H. *The Long War Against God: The History and Impact of the Creation/Evolution Conflict*. New York: Baker Books, 1989.

Mowbray, M. De. 'Philosophy as Handmaid of Theology: Biblical Exegesis in the Service of Scholarship', *Traditio* 59 (2004): 1–37.

Nielsen, K. *Contemporary Critiques of Religion*. London and Basingstoke: Macmillan, 1971.

Nock, A. D. *Conversion: The Old and the New in Religion from Alexander the Great to Augustine of Hippo*. Lanham, MD: University Press of America, 1988.

Oppy, G. and Trakakis, N. N. (eds). *Twentieth-Century Philosophy of Religion*. The History of Western Philosophy of Religion 5. London and New York: Routledge, 2009.

Pannenberg, W. *Theologie und Philosophie. Ihr Verhältnis im Lichte ihrer gemeinsamen Geschichte*. Göttingen: Vandenhoeck & Ruprecht, 1996.

Pelikan, J. *What Has Athens to Do with Jerusalem?* Timaeus *and* Genesis *in Counterpoint*. Ann Arbor: University of Michigan Press, 1997.

Peterson, E. 'Was ist Theologie?' in Erik Peterson, *Theologische Traktate Hrsg. Barbara Nichtweiss*, 3–22. Würzburg: Echter, 1994. Ausgewählte Schriften 1. English translation: *Theological Tractates*, trans. Michael Hollerich. Stanford, CA: Stanford University Press, 2011.

Piertsma, A. and Wright, B. G. (eds). *A New English Translation of the Septuagint and the Other Greek Translations Traditionally Included under that Title*, 2nd edn. Oxford: Oxford University Press, 2007.

Rosenzweig, Franz. *Der Mensch und sein Werk. Gesammelte Schriften, Vol. 1. Briefe und Tagebücher*. Hrsg. Rachel Rosenzweig und Edith Rosenzweig Scheinmann unter Mitwirkung von Bernhard Casper. I. Band 1900–1918. Dondrecht: Springer, 1979.

Sauter, G. (ed.). *Theologie als Wissenschaft*. München: Chr. Kaiser, 1971.

Sider, R. D. 'Credo Quia Absurdum?' *The Classical World* 73 (1980): 417–19.

Swinburne, R. *Faith and Reason*. Second edn. Oxford: Clarendon, 2005.

Taliaferro, C., Draper, P. and Quinn, P. L. (eds). *A Companion to Philosophy of Religion*. Malden, Oxford and Carlton: Blackwell, 2010.

Tatár, G. 'Viharra várva [Waiting for the storm]', in *A „másik oldal"* [The other side]. Budapest: Kalligram, 2014. Available Online: https://www.holmi.org/2010/02/tatar -gyorgy-viharra-varva

White, A. D. *A History of the Warfare of Science with Theology in Christendom*, 2 vols. London: Macmillan and Co., 1896.

Yandell, K. E. *Philosophy of Religion: A Contemporary Introduction*. London and New York: Routledge, 1999.

CHAPTER 31

Is the Canon of the Scriptures closed?

Recent interest in the Nag Hammadi Codices

PAULA TUTTY

INTRODUCTION

In December 1945, a group of labourers from the village of Hamra Dum in Upper Egypt were digging for fertilizer when they found a large earthenware jar buried close to the cliffs of the Jabal al-Ṭārif.[1] The twelve leather-bound books, plus the remains of a thirteenth found within the jar, are now better known to the world under the title of the 'Nag Hammadi Codices'.[2] The codices are written in Coptic, the last stage of the ancient Egyptian language, and they contain an astonishing array of early Christian texts, including a collection of previously unknown gospels. Palaeographical studies of the handwriting of the scribes who created the codices demonstrate that they worked in groups, with the scribe who copied Codices XI and I also working alongside the writer of Codex VII.[3] A second group of scribes created

---

[1] For detailed accounts of the discovery of the codices, see J. Doresse, *Les livres secrets des gnostiques d'Égypte* (Paris: Plon, 1958). J. M. Robinson, *The Nag Hammadi Story*, NHMS, vols. 86.2 (Leiden: E.J. Brill, 2014); Robinson, 'The Discovery of the Nag Hammadi Codices', *BibA* 42, no. 4 (1979): 206–24; Robinson, 'From the Cliff to Cairo: The Story of the Discoverers and the Middlemen of the Nag Hammadi Codices', in *Colloque International sur le textes de Nag Hammadi (Québec, 22-25 août 1978)*, ed. Bernard Barc, BCNH.É, vol. 1 (Québec: Les Presses de l'Université Laval, 1981), pp. 21–58; Robinson, 'The Discovering and Marketing of Coptic Manuscripts: The Nag Hammadi Codices and the Bodmer Papyri', in *The Roots of Egyptian Christianity*, eds B. A. Pearson and J. E. Goehring, STAC (Philadelphia, PA: Fortress Press, 1986), pp. 2–25; Robinson, 'The Discovery of the Nag Hammadi Codices', *JCoptS* 11 (2009): 1–21.

[2] The town of Nag Hammadi, which lies on the railway line that runs from Cairo to Luxor, is approximately 11 kilometres from the find site of the Nag Hammadi Codices.

[3] For Robinson's description of these groups, see the section 'construction' in J. M. Robinson, *The Facsimile Edition of the Nag Hammadi Codices: Introduction* (Leiden: E.J. Brill, 1984), pp. 71–86. See also the comments on subgroups in H. Lundhaug and L. Jenott, *The Monastic Origins of the Nag Hammadi Codices*, STAC, vol. 97 (Tübingen: Mohr Siebeck, 2015), pp. 208–14.

Codices VIII, IV and V, a grouping that was extended by Michael Williams to include codices IV, V, VI and IX on account of the similarities apparent in the scribal hands.[4] The relationships that are apparent between the codices, including similarities in their size and construction techniques, would suggest that whole collection was written within a reasonably short timeframe, perhaps of no more than fifty years or so. Dates found on the papyri used to stiffen the covers of Codex VII, taken along with considerable amounts of money mentioned in documents from the covers of Codex V, further indicate that the codices were written no earlier than the second half of the fourth century, a time when rampant inflation was present in the Roman economy.[5] Taking into consideration all the available evidence, it seems likely that all the codices were completed at some point after mid-fourth century, up to perhaps the early fifth century CE.[6]

The texts, numbering fifty-two in total, have their origins in diverse set of traditions, and they are a testament to the wide variety of religious works that were in circulation in late antique Upper Egypt. The majority of texts are unique, although some of their titles were previously known to scholars through lists provided by second- and third-century heresiologists. To what extent these titles reflect the content of these earlier works is hard to judge, and it should be assumed that they had a long history of transmission and adaptation before they were selected, translated and copied into these particular volumes. Some texts, such as the *Apocryphon of John*, are duplicated in several versions.[7] This may indicate that the editors did not necessarily see these codices as forming a single 'library' but rather that each separate volume was planned out individually. These books are thus the products of an ongoing process of acquisition, translation and manuscript creation, a process in which several editors, translators and copyists took part, perhaps over several decades. They are significant in that not only have they revolutionized our understanding of the development of early Christian thought, but they have sparked controversy and speculation among both scholars and the public at large. In this chapter, I shall examine the scholarly debates that have arisen over the codices over recent years regarding their significance as examples of early Christian literature

---

[4]M. A. Williams, *Rethinking Gnosticism: An Argument for Dismantling a Dubious Category* (Princeton, NJ: Princeton University Press, 1996), pp. 242–3.

[5]Three documents found within the covers of Codex VII are dated November 341, November 346 and October 348 CE, respectively. See J. Shelton, 'Introduction', in J. W. B. Barns, G. M. Browne, and J. C. Shelton, *Nag Hammadi Codices: Greek and Coptic Papyri from the Cartonnage of the Covers*, NHS, vol. 16 (Leiden: E.J. Brill, 1981), pp. 4–5. For a discussion of the sums of money written on fragments of papyri from the covers of Codex V, see Lundhaug and Jenott, *Monastic Origins*, pp. 117–23.

[6]Disagreements still remain regarding the exact relationships between the codices, but the connections between the main subgroups are accepted by the majority of Nag Hammadi scholars. For a summary of the different positions taken on the question of the scribes who worked on these two codices, see Lundhaug and Jenott, *Monastic Origins*, pp. 209 n.11. Also, M. A. Williams and D. Coblentz, 'A Reexamination of the Articulation Marks in Nag Hammadi Codices II and XIII', in *The Nag Hammadi Codices and Late Antique Egypt*, eds Hugo Lundhaug and Lance Jenott, STAC, vol. 110 (Tübingen: Mohr Siebeck, 2018), pp. 427–56.

[7]NHC II, IV and III. A further version exists in *P.Berol.* 8502.

and their disputed origins. What do we know of the people who created and/or read these books? What status would these books have had within the Christian community when placed alongside the recognized Christian canon? What can their contents tell us about the development of religious movements in late antique Egypt and the existence of localized influences that might have left their mark on this diverse set of works? In order to attempt to find an answer to these questions, I shall outline the recent discussions that have taken place within scholarly communities concerning the contents of the codices and those who potentially created and read them. The Nag Hammadi Codices have found a modern audience that extends far beyond the narrow confines of academia, so I shall also explore the impact they have had on modern religious thought and practice, as well as on popular culture.

THE DISCOVERY

In describing the story of the discovery of the Nag Hammadi Codices, we soon encounter details that have significant bearing on the actions that led to their disposal and their motivations. Jean Doresse, who visited the find site in 1950, took several brief statements on the matter from local inhabitants and photographed the approximate place where the jar containing the codices was found.[8] James Robinson later went to strenuous lengths to conduct his own in-depth investigations into the background story during the early 1970s, leading to the publication of several versions of his findings over the decades.[9] His investigations were not without their critics and, following a rather bitter disagreement, two prominent Coptologists, Rodolphe Kasser and Martin Krause, even issued a disclaimer concerning everything except 'the core of the story (the general location and approximate date of the discovery)'.[10] The inconsistencies and ambiguities to be found in the accounts given by Robinson have led certain scholars in recent years to jettison the find story in its entirety, with the suggestion that the more, to Western eyes at least, fantastic sections of the tale were fabricated for a colonialist audience. Instead, according to arguments made in particular by Nicola Denzey Lewis and Mark Goodacre, the codices were the possessions of a group of affluent individuals who commissioned them for private study or as potent grave goods.[11] This argument gained several

---

[8]Doresse wrote a letter to his colleague H-Ch. Puech on the subject of the location which is published and translated in Robinson, *The Nag Hammadi Story*, pp. 1:1–2. For Doresse's description of the find site, see Doresse, *Les livres secrets*, pp. 133–59. For photographs, sketches of sections of the cliff face and a map of the area, see Lundhaug and Jenott, *Monastic Origins*, pp. 12–15.

[9]See note 1.

[10]Robinson, *The Nag Hammadi Story*, p. 3.

[11]See, in particular, N. Denzey Lewis, 'Death on the Nile: Egyptian Codices, Gnosticism, and Early Christian Books of the Dead', in *Practicing Gnosis: Ritual, Magic, Theurgy and Liturgy in Nag Hammadi, Manichaean and Other Ancient Literature. Essays in Honor of Birger A. Pearson*, eds A. D. DeConick, G. Shaw and J. D. Turner, NHMS, vol. 85 (Leiden: E.J. Brill, 2013), pp. 161–80. N. Denzey Lewis and J. Ariel Blount, 'Rethinking the Origins of the Nag Hammadi Codices', *JBL* 133, no. 2 (2014): 399–419. M. Goodacre, 'How Reliable Is the Story of the Nag Hammadi Discovery?' *JSNT* 35 (2013): 303–22.

adherents among religious scholars, and the discussions that followed did much to stimulate a reconsideration about how Western academics should tell the story of the discovery of the Nag Hammadi Codices. However, the several counterarguments and articles that have since followed, while accepting that inconsistencies are present in Robinson's retelling, are fairly unanimous in reiterating the essential elements of a find story in which the codices remain firmly lodged within their storage jar.[12] Like so many elements of Nag Hammadi scholarship, this one has proved highly controversial, exposing as it does the fault lines that lie between the competing understandings of the people who created and read the codices. Consensus remains elusive as scholars continue to expand their understanding of the complexities of the development of early Christianity when posed against the manicured accounts of early writers.

Following the discovery, the codices made a somewhat convoluted journey to their present home in the Coptic Museum in Cairo, passing through the hands of several dealers including Phokion J. Tano who made various attempts to sell the codices internationally. Following the 1952 revolution, they were proclaimed national property and placed in the Coptic Museum in Cairo for safekeeping under the aegis of its director, Pahor Labib. Only one volume, Nag Hammadi Codex 1, travelled a different route. Bought by the dealer Albert Eid, the bulk of the codex was sold to the Jung Institute of Zurich in May 1952 before it too was transferred to the Coptic Museum in 1975. The leather cover of the Jung Codex, and the bowl apparently used as the lid of the jar, found their way instead to the Institute for antiquity and Christianity in Claremont before eventually joining the Schøyen Collection in Oslo.

EARLIEST CHRISTIAN TEXTS?

Scholars studying the codices soon came across a dazzling array of titles. Besides the *Gospel of Thomas* and the *Gospel of Philip*, the find included the so-called *Gospel of Truth* and the *Gospel to the Egyptians*, which identifies itself as 'the [sacred book] of the Great Invisible [Spirit]'. Another group of texts consists of writings attributed to Jesus' followers, such as the *Secret Book of James*, the *Apocalypse of Paul*, the *Letter of Peter to Philip* and the *Apocalypse of Peter*. Similar works had been discovered previously; the fifth-century *Codex Berolinensis* (*P.Berol.* 8502), for example, which was discovered in the late nineteenth century, apart from containing a well-known fragment of the *Gospel of Mary*, also contains two versions of books found at Nag Hammadi, the *Apocryphon of John* and the *Wisdom of Jesus Christ*. In addition, the *Hermetic Prayer of Thanksgiving*, which appears in Codex VI as an epilogue to the *Discourse on the Eighth and Ninth*, appears as a conclusion to both a fourth-century Greek collection of magical texts (PGM III) and *Asclepius*, a Latin adaptation of the

---

[12]Lundhaug and Jenott, *Monastic Origins,* pp. 11–21. B. Nongbri, 'Finding Early Christian Books at Nag Hammadi and Beyond', *BSR* 45, no. 2 (2016): 11–19. D. Burns, 'Telling Nag Hammadi's Egyptian Stories', *BSR* 45, no. 2 (2016): 5–11.

Greek *Perfect Discourse of Hermes Trismegistus*.[13] The indications therefore are that the works collected in the Nag Hammadi Codices are but a small representation of the many various types of religious and esoteric texts that were in vogue in Christian circles throughout Egypt and the Roman Empire in the late antique period.

For those seeking insight into the formation of Christian doctrine, the question of the date of composition of the Nag Hammadi gospels in relation to other NT materials soon became an issue of paramount importance, impacting as it does on our understanding of early Jesus traditions. Helmut Koester, for example, in his discussion of the collection of sayings found within the *Gospel of Thomas*, suggested that they might include some traditions that were even older than those found in the canon of the New Testament, citing a relationship with the hypothetical Q document among other reasons for such an early dating.[14] Quispel, in his turn, suggested a date of composition of ca. 140 CE, while Nicholas Perrin, in contrast, argued that the *Gospel of Thomas* is dependent on the *Diatessaron*, which was composed shortly after 172 CE by Tatian in Syria.[15] The publication of a select number of parallel sayings from the Coptic version of the *Gospel of Thomas* retroverted into Greek is one product of this scholarly speculation.[16] The arguments for and against an early date are complex and beyond the scope of this chapter, reliant as they are on a variety of factors such as communal memory, ancient literacy, oral transmission and other correlating evidence, but, in any event, this argument has been superseded in recent years by new discussions regarding textual fluidity and transmission which lay an emphasis on the fourth- or fifth-century manuscripts rather than any hypothetical original text.

DIVERGENT GROUPS

The possible relationship of the texts found at Nag Hammadi to other early Christian works created a dilemma for the first Nag Hammadi scholars who struggled to create a typology in which to place this dazzling array of new works. There were few parallels with other known works beyond some small fragments of early codices discovered in Oxyrhynchus and manuscripts such as *Codex Berolinensis*, mentioned earlier. It was known that Greek gospels bearing titles similar to those found within the Nag Hammadi Codices were condemned as heretical by second- and

[13]*Papyrus Mimaut* (*P. Louvre Papyrus* N 2391= PGM III) col. XVIII and Asclepius 41b. See, P. A. Dirkse and J. Brashler, 'The Prayer of Thanksgiving', in *Nag Hammadi Codices V, 2-5 and VI, with Papyrus Belolinensis 8502*, ed. D. Parrott, NHS, vol. 11 (Leiden: E.J. Brill, 1979), pp. 375–88.

[14]H. Koester, 'Introduction to the Gospel of Thomas', in *The Nag Hammadi Library in English*, ed. J. M. Robinson, 3rd edn (San Francisco, CA: HarperSanFrancisco, 1990), pp. 124–6.

[15]N. Perrin, 'Recent Trends in Gospel of Thomas Research (1991-2006): Part I, The Historical Jesus and the Synoptic Gospels', *Currents in Biblical Research 5*, no. 2 (2007): 183–206.

[16]Published in K. Aland (ed.), *Synopsis Quattuor Evangeliorum: Locis parallelis evangeliorum apocryphorum et partum adhibitis*, 15th edn (Stuttgart: Deutsche Bibelgesellschaft, 1996), pp. 517–46. Cf. S. Emmel, 'Religious Tradition, Textual Transmission, and the Nag Hammadi Codices', in *The Nag Hammadi Library after Fifty Years*, eds J. D. Turner and A. McGuire (Leiden: E.J. Brill, 1997), pp. 39–40.

third-century Christian apologists. Irenaeus, for example, writing in the late second century about the followers of Valentinus complained that 'Indeed they have arrived at such a pitch of audacity as to entitle their comparatively recent writing "the Gospel of Truth", although it agrees in nothing with the Gospels of the Apostles' (*Haer.* 3.11.9). The fact that an untitled Gospel was discovered to bear the incipit, 'The Gospel of Truth is joy for those who have received from the Father of truth the grace of knowing him' (*Gos. Truth* I.16.31-33), excited many scholarly imaginations with the thought that this was indeed the very same Gospel. A total of eight works found within the Nag Hammadi Codices are widely considered to be the products of the Valentinian schools.[17] These have inspired a number of important recent studies on Valentinianism that explore their writings and their ritual practices.[18] Even so, serious questions remain regarding the identification of texts as Valentinian, particularly when we consider that the extent to which it can be claimed that a Valentinian school existed at all remains a matter of some debate.[19] In the case of so-called *Gospel of Truth*, for example, the original editor, Gilles Quispel, was in little doubt that this was indeed the work referred to by Irenaeus.[20] However, as Dunn noted, 'great edifices of fancy have been built upon the words of Irenaeus.'[21] There are many elements in so-called Nag Hammadi 'Valentinian' texts that stand in contradiction to any accepted understanding of what constituted Valentinian teaching. In relation, for example, to a text often associated with Valentinianism, the *Gospel of Philip*, Hugo Lundhaug makes the point that 'In much of what has been written concerning *Gos.Phil.*, evidence from the early heresiologists has taken precedence over *Gos.Phil.'s* own internal logic.'[22] Further, he makes the point that 'one might reply that *Gos.Phil.* indeed only takes on a specifically 'Valentinian' colour by reading it in the light of 'Valentinian' theologoumena'.[23] Even if it is

---

[17]Including, in particular, *Gospel of Truth (NHC 1,3), Tripartite Tractate (NHC 1, 5), Gospel of Philip (NHC II,3)* and *A Valentinian Exposition (NHC, XI, 2)*. For a complete list, see I. Dunderberg, 'The School of Valentinus', in *A Companion to Second-Century Christian 'Heretics'*, eds A. Marjanen and P. Luomanen, SupVCh, 76 (Leiden: E.J. Brill, 2005), p. 84. Also, E. Thomassen, 'Notes pour la délimitation d'un corpus valentinien à Nag Hammadi', in *Les textes de Nag Hammadi et le* problème *de leur classification. Actes du colloque tenu à. Québec du 15 au 19 septembre 1993*, eds L. Panchaud and A. Pasquier, BCNH.É, vol. 3 (Québec: Les Presses de l'Université Laval, 1995), pp. 243–63.

[18]Including E. Thomassen, *The Spiritual Seed: The Church of the 'Valentinians*, NHMS, vol. 60 (Leiden: E.J. Brill, 2006). P. L. Tite, *Valentinian Ethics and Paraenetic Discourse: Determining the Social Function of Moral Exhortation in Valentinian Christianity*, NHMS, vol. 67 (Leiden: E.J. Brill, 2009). P. Linjamaa, *The Tripartite Tractae (NHC 1, 5): A Study of Determinism and Early Christian Philosophy of Ethics*, NHMS, vol. 95 (Leiden: E.J. Brill, 2019).

[19]For an affirmative view of the existence of a Valentinian 'school', see I. Dunderberg, *Beyond Gnosticism, Myth, Lifestyle, and Society in the School of Valentinus* (New York: Columbia University Press, 2008). In contrast, see G. S. Smith, *Guilt by Association: Heresy Catalogues in Early Christianity* (Oxford: Oxford University Press, 2015), pp. 146–72.

[20]G. Quispel, 'Note on an Unknown Gnostic Codex', *VChr* 7 (1953): 193.

[21]W. Dunn, 'What does "Gospel of Truth Mean?"' *VChr* 15, no. 3 (1961): 161.

[22]H. Lundhaug, *Images of Rebirth: Cognitive Poetics and Transformational Soteriology in the Gospel of Philip and the Exegesis on the Soul*, NHMS, vol. 73 (Leiden: E.J. Brill, 2001), p. 349.

[23]Ibid., p. 356.

accepted that the texts in question do spring for a Valentinian source, it cannot be assumed that the editions found in the Nag Hammadi Codices bear any resemblance to their second- or third-century predecessors.

Martin Schenke noticed that several texts from Nag Hammadi shared a preoccupation with the character Seth and several also spoke of God's elect as the 'seed of Seth'.[24] Irenaeus (*Haer.* 1.30) referred to a group known as 'Sethians' (alternately, 'Sethian-Ophites') who, we are told, essentially identified Christ with Seth and viewed themselves as his offspring or 'seeds'.[25] Jean Doresse even suggested that the Nag Hammadi Codices were the creations of a 'Sethian' sect,[26] an idea that was revived more recently by Alastair Logan who maintains that Sethian Gnostic communities persisted in Egypt as late as the fifth century.[27] Epiphanius of Salamis, writing in the fourth century, was uncertain as to whether he had met this group or not, noting that his evidence came mainly from his enquiries (*Pan.* I, 39.1-2). Whatever the actual history of this group, and the evidence is exceedingly sparse, nearly all scholars have recognized the utility of the term 'Sethianism' when describing certain mythological details found within individual works. Debates continue, however, as to whether specific Nag Hammadi texts should be labelled as Sethian or not.[28]

While it might be accepted that a certain proportion of the texts in the NHC collection contain elements that are deserving of the 'Sethian' or 'Valentinian', it does not account for the diverse range of typologies that can be identified within even single codices. Jean-Pierre Mahé, for example, considered that translators and the scribe of Codex VI to be some form of Gnostics with a particular interest in Hermes Trismegistos.[29] Bentley Layton, in his description of Codex II, noted the inclusion of 'at least three distinct ancient currents' to wit, Sethianism, a parody or

---

[24]H.-M. Schenke, 'Das sethianische System nach Nag-Hammadi-Handschriften', in *Studia Coptica*, ed. Peter Nagel, Berliner byzantinische Arbeiten, vol. 45 (Berlin: Akademie, 1974), pp. 165–72.

[25]Hippolytus, *Haer.*, 5.19.1-22.1. See M. A. Williams, 'Sethianism', in Marjanen and Luomanen (eds), *A Companion to Second-Century Christian 'Heretics'*, pp. 32–63.

[26]Doresse, *Les livres secrets*, pp. 281–2. The relationship between the Sethians and the Ophites is explored in T. Rasimus, *Paradise Reconsidered in Gnostic Mythmaking: Rethinking Sethianism in Light of the Ophite Evidence* NHMS, vol. 68 (Leiden: E.J. Brill, 2009). Rasimus, 'Ophite Gnosticism, Sethianism and the Nag Hammadi Library', *VChr* 59, no. 3 (2005): 235–63.

[27]A. H. B. Logan, *The Gnostics: Identifying an Early Christian Cult* (London: T&T Clark, 2006).

[28]For example, B. Layton argued for labelling *Thunder: Perfect Mind* as Sethian, see Layton, 'The Riddle of the Thunder [NHC VI,2]: The Function of Paradox in a Gnostic Text from Nag Hammadi', in *Nag Hammadi, Gnosticism, and Early Christianity*, eds Ch. W. Hedrick and R. Hodgson, Jr. (Peabody, MA: Hendrickson, 1986), pp. 37–54. P.-H. Poirier disagrees in his 'Introduction to Thunder', in M. Meyer (ed.), *The Nag Hammadi Scriptures: The International Version* (New York: HarperOne, 2007), pp. 367–71.

[29]J.-P. Mahé, *Hermès en Haute-Égypte*, 2 vols, BCNH.T vols. 3 & 7 (Québec: Les Presses de l'Université Laval, 1978–1982), pp. 1:26-8, 2:114-20. Cf. Ch. H. Bull, 'Hermes between Pagans and Christians: The Nag Hammadi Hermetica in Context', in Lundhaug and Jenott (eds), *The Nag Hammadi Codices*, pp. 207–60.

inversion of elements from Judaism, Valentinianism and what he describes as 'yet another kind of Christian spirituality' that was focused on twinship and unity.[30]

More recent approaches to the study of texts labelled as 'Sethian' or 'Valentinian' have acknowledged dynamic elements at work that can reflect more than one early train of thought. For John Turner, the relationship between the Sethian texts *Zostrianos, Marsanes, The Three Steles of Seth* and *Allogenes* to Platonic thought proved particularly intriguing and led to the production of his major work, *Sethian Gnosticism and the Platonic Tradition*.[31] As he noted, the texts reveal important diversities which would suggest that they are 'indices to a series of related religious innovations.'[32] Following on from this, Karen King's 1997 study of the variants of the *Apocryphon of John* viewed them as evidence for a changing Sethian tradition rather than products of a static belief system.[33]

Within the last decade, the greater attention paid to the complex transmission histories of the Nag Hammadi texts has demanded a reassessment of the codices and their various attributions. Recent scholarship by Dylan Burns, for example, reinterprets recognized Sethian works found within the Nag Hammadi Codices by placing them firmly within the context of Judeo-Christian authorship rather than ascribing them to a pagan offshoot of Gnosticism.[34] According to Burns, this Sethian literature emerged from an interplay between Judaism and Christianity and while also imbibing the Platonic philosophic ideals that were current in late antique thinking. The resultant admixture still retains elements that are familiar to us from earlier descriptions, but now recast for a fourth-century audience. The significance of characters and rituals alluded to in the Nag Hammadi texts certainly changed over the centuries as they were adapted into their new context. A good example of this is the character 'Eleleth', one of four Luminaries who appear in various Nag Hammadi texts. It was the appearance of this character that led Schenke to label certain Nag Hammadi texts as 'Sethian' yet, as Dylan Burns points out, the character Eleleth also appears in texts that are very un-Sethian in their nature. Furthermore, the name Eleleth continues to appear in Coptic literature, including the ninth century *Investiture of the Archangel Gabriel*, a work that was composed at a time when any supposed Sethian connection would have long been forgotten.[35]

---

[30]B. Layton, 'Preface', in *Nag Hammadi Codex II, 2-7, together with XIII, 2* Brit. Lib. Or.4926(1) and P.Oxy. 1,654, 655*, ed. Bentley Layton, 2 vols, NHS, vols. 20–21 (Leiden: E.J. Brill, 1989), p. xiii.

[31]J. D. Turner, *Sethian Gnosticism and the Platonic Tradition*, BCNH.É, vol. 6 (Leuven: Peeters, 2001). See also, J. D. Turner and R. Majercik (eds), *Gnosticism and Later Platonism: Themes, Figures, and Texts*, SBL Symp. Series, vol. 12 (Atlanta, GA: Society of Biblical Literature, 2000).

[32]Williams, *Rethinking Gnosticism*, pp. 91–3.

[33]K. King, 'Approaching the Variants of the Apocryphon of John', in *The Nag Hammadi Library after Fifty Years: Proceedings of the 1995 Society of Biblical Literature Commemoration*, eds J. D. Turner and A. McGuire, NHMS vol. 44 (Leiden: E.J. Brill, 1997), pp. 105–37. Williams, *Rethinking Gnosticism*, pp. 91–3.

[34]D. Burns, *Apocalypse of the Alien God: Platonism and the Exile of Sethian Gnosticism* (Philadelphia: University of Pennsylvania Press, 2014).

[35]D. Burns, 'Magical, Coptic, Christian: The Great Angel Eleleth and the "Four Luminaries" in Egyptian Literature of the First Millenium CE', in *The Nag Hammadi Codices in the Context of Fourth- and Fifth-*

'GNOSTIC' TEXTS?

During his attempted purchase of several Nag Hammadi Codices in 1946, Jacques Schwartz wrote that his superior, the Director of IFAO, Charles Kuentz 'understands quite well the importance of these documents, which can only be "Gnostic"'.[36] The application of the rather loaded term 'Gnostic' to the Nag Hammadi Codices has significantly influenced the direction taken by Nag Hammadi research over the decades – Doresse's 1960 book on the codices and their discovery was entitled in English *The Secret Books of the Egyptian Gnostics*, a clear signal to its readers that the Nag Hammadi texts that did not emanate from mainstream thinking but were, rather, products of a Christianity that might be considered esoteric and somewhat deviant. This understanding, that Egyptian Christianity was somehow peculiar, had earlier found its reflection in the writings of Walter Bauer among others.[37] Maia Kotrosits reflects that, 'Not just for history of religions scholars, but for much modern scholarly and popular consciousness, "Gnosticism" and even "Nag Hammadi" have functioned largely as oriental foils to European Christianity and the biblical canon'.[38] It is undeniably the case that the works found within the Nag Hammadi Codices have often been dismissed as standing in opposition from other forms of early Christian literature and the application of the term 'Gnostic' to the Nag Hammadi texts has done much to reinforce this sense of apartness and alienation from works that considered to belong to 'mainstream' Christianity.

A major problem with the application of the term 'Gnostic' to any ancient work is that there is little consensus over what its defining traits actually are, despite the several colloquia and conferences have taken place on the subject.[39] To what extent what might be termed a 'Gnostic school' even existed is hard to know, reliant as we are on second-hand descriptions from antagonistic sources.[40] Should we for example, label Sethians and Valentinians as 'Gnostic' or are they merely localized groupings that lay outside the jurisdiction of the mainstream church authorities? Michael Williams struck a grave blow against the use of the term in his 1996 monograph *Rethinking Gnosticism. An Argument for Dismantling a Dubious Category* in which he demonstrated how early Christian writings labelled

---

Century Christianity in Egypt, eds H. Lundhaug and L. Jenott, STAC, vol. 110 (Tübingen: Mohr Siebeck, 2018), pp. 141–62.

[36]From a written report by Schwartz, quoted in Robinson, *The Nag Hammadi Story*, 47.

[37]W. Bauer, *Orthodoxy and Heresy in Earliest Christianity*, trans. Robert A. Kraft (Philadelphia, PA: Fortress Press, 1934), pp. 47–53.

[38]Maia Kotrosits, 'Romance and Danger at Nag Hammadi', *The Bible and Critical Theory* 8, no. 1 (2012): 47.

[39]In particular the 1996 colloquium in Messina which unsuccessfully attempted to define Gnosticism. The proceedings are published in U. Bianchi (ed.), *Le origini dello Gnosticismo: Colloquio di Messina, 13-18 Aprile 1966*, SHR, vol. 12 (Leiden: E.J. Brill, 1967).

[40]On this point, see D. Brakke, 'Prolegomena to the Study of Ancient Gnosticism', in *The Social World of the First Christians: Essays in Honor of Wayne A. Meeks*, eds M. L. White and L. O. Yarbrough (Minneapolis, MN: Fortress Press, 1995), 334–50. For an overview of recent discussions, see Smith, *Guilt by Association*, pp. 131–76.

'Gnostic' reveal many diversities of thought but that these are often obscured through the judgements made by modern scholars when using terms associated with Gnostic thinking.[41] Karen King too, writing in *What is Gnosticsm?* (2003), criticized the use of typologies associated with heresies on the grounds that they do not reveal the complexities of thought that existed within the early Christian church. Moreover, they reinforce the idea that one set of norms was extant within the whole of Christianity rather than allowing for the likelihood that local variations and anomalies would have been present within individual Christian communities, even those that lay within a reasonably close geographical proximity.[42] Majella Franzmann reinforces this point by reminding us that by the time the ideas of the founders of the early Christian movement were written down, they had been reshaped and allocated new meaning as rifts grew within the growing church in response to a copious flow of doctrinal and theological debates.[43] Despite these criticisms, terms coined by ancient heresiologists continue to be popular with a significant proportion of Nag Hammadi scholars, who, while acknowledging the difficulties inherent in their use, plead their usefulness for a variety of self-professed reasons.[44] April DeConick, for example, suggests the term 'Gnostic' should be used positively in order to describe an alternative, or countercultural, Christianity rather than one that is merely deviant.[45]

Even if the several texts that are found in the Nag Hammadi Codices contain elements that might be seen as deserving of the label 'Gnostic', it does not mean that the fourth- or fifth-century readers of these works considered themselves as belonging to any particular group or sect. What is clear, however, is that the creators of the codices viewed themselves as 'Christian' as evidenced by the use of various Christian symbols throughout the codices and the wording of the colophons.[46] In his discussion of the use of the term 'Gnostic', Burns notes how this term is often misleadingly used to cover a wide range of often conflicting traditions that have become incorporated into later works. One suitable alternative, he suggests, is the term 'ancient esoteric traditions' in order to encompass a prominent group of early religious writings which include references to hidden knowledge.[47] While such a term may not necessarily be viewed as applying to all the works found in the Nag Hammadi Codices, it is useful in that it is not specific to any one tradition.

---

[41]Also, M. A. Williams, 'Was there a Gnostic Religion?', in *Was there a Gnostic Religion?*, ed. A. Marjanen (Göttingen: Vandenhoeck & Ruprecht, 2005), pp. 55–79.

[42]K. King, *What Is Gnosticism?* (Cambridge: Cambridge University Press, 2003), pp. 189–90.

[43]M. Franzmann, 'A Complete History of Early Christianity: Taking the "Heretics" Seriously', *JRH* 29, no. 2 (2005): 117–18.

[44]See, for example, B. Pearson, *Gnosticism and Christianity in Roman and Coptic Egypt* (New York: T&T Clark International, 2004), pp. 201–3.

[45]A. DeConick, *The Gnostic New Age: How a Countercultural Spirituality Revolutionized Religion from Antiquity to Today* (New York: Columbia University Press, 2016), pp. 5–9.

[46]See 'Chapter 7: The Colophons' in Lundhaug and Jenott, *Monastic Origins*, pp. 178–206.

[47]D. Burns, 'Ancient Esoteric Tradition: Mystery, Revelation, Gnosis', in *The Occult World*, ed. Christopher Partridge (London: Routledge, 2014), pp. 17–33.

The term 'non-canonical' is also commonly used in discussions of works such as those located within the Nag Hammadi Codices. This term, while not as laden with negative connotations as 'Gnostic', is problematical to some extent in that, while the Nag Hammadi texts will not be discovered located in any late antique list of canonical books, we cannot assume that, at the time when the Nag Hammadi Codices were created, very clear boundaries existed between works considered canonical and those that might be placed on some form of speculative *Index Librorum Prohibitorum*. Numerous works still retained an authority that is now lacking, such as, for example, the extremely popular *Shepherd of Hermas*.[48] Furthermore, even when books were openly condemned, as was the case with an apocryphal work entitled the *Investiture of Michael*, there is clear evidence to show that a number of such texts were still being copied and read in monastic libraries centuries later.[49] It should be acknowledged therefore that while the works found within the Nag Hammadi Codices could hardly be described as 'canonical', it cannot be taken for granted that their readers necessarily perceived them as being 'forbidden'. The same can be said for the extremely large collection of works labelled as *apocrypha* that were written and reworked well into the medieval period. A recent article by François Bovon puts forward the argument for the need for a new categorization for works that were neither apocryphal nor canonical but were rather 'Books useful for the soul'.[50] The works found in the Nag Hammadi Codices may well have functioned in this way for their collators as we must assume that the texts within them were considered useful as some form of devotional readings even if we cannot know their specific import for their individual readers.

TEXTS IN THEIR CONTEXT

While the bulk of early Nag Hammadi scholars focused on the hypothetical origins of the Nag Hammadi texts, several observations were made regarding how such books may have functioned within their fourth- or fifth-century context. Torgny Säve-Söderbergh, for example, writing in 1974, argued that the codices were created as fourth-century reference books for Christians who wished to refute heresy.[51] It was not until the late 1990s, however, that the issue of the late antique became particularly pertinent when Stephen Emmel suggested that the texts should be read,

---

[48]This work is the best attested outside of the texts that became part of the NT canon. It was copied well into the fourth century and beyond.

[49]For example, the *Investiture of Michael*, a work that was condemned as blasphemous in a sixth-century sermon by Bishop John of Parallos (*On Heretical Books*, 48). It continued to be copied in various languages including a codex produced in an Egyptian monastery in 892/893 CE (Pierpont Morgan Codex M593 [folios 31r–50r]).

[50]F. Bovon, 'Beyond the Canonical and the Apocryphal Books, the Presence of a Third Category: The Books Useful for the Soul', *HTR* 105 (2012): 125–37.

[51]T. Säve-Söderbergh, 'Holy Scriptures or Apologetic Documentations? The *Sitz im Leben* of the Nag Hammadi Library', in *Les textes de Nag Hammadi*, ed. J. É. Ménard, NHS 7 (Leiden: E.J. Brill, 1975), pp. 3–14.

not merely to access hypothetical second- or third-century Greek originals, but as Coptic literature produced for a late antique audience that was located in Upper Egypt.[52] In a similar vein, Alberto Camplani argued against using the fourth-century texts in order to reconstruct the doctrinal debates of the second century noting that texts which have undergone constant textual revisions would also have been subject to theological corrections.[53] The complex nature of textual transmission is particularly highlighted in cases where earlier copies of texts are available for comparison. In the case of the Nag Hammadi Codices, the radically revised passage from Plato's *Republic* (588a–589b) found in Codex VI provides an excellent example of the ways in which a traditional text might be adapted for a late antique Christian audience.[54]

Within the last decade, Nag Hammadi scholars have increasingly turned to what is often termed 'New' or 'Material' Philology in order to gain a greater understanding of the Nag Hammadi Codices as products of a fourth-century Coptic manuscript culture.[55] One scholar at the forefront of this research is Hugo Lundhaug who suggests that, rather than becoming involved in discussions of orthodoxy versus Gnosticism or looking for an 'original text' by attempting to get back to hypothetical Greek originals, we ought rather to endeavour to understand the transmission and use of such texts within the social, historical and theological context in which they have been preserved in order to understand the significance of these works for those who created the codices and their intended readership.[56] This approach lays an emphasis on the fluidity of textual transmission in a manuscript culture with the understanding that instability in textual transmission leads to the production of variants in cases where more than one text is preserved.[57] It demands that we explore the texts as they were understood within their fourth- or fifth-century context as products of a Coptic-speaking community with their own particular

---

[52]Emmel, 'Religious Tradition, Textual Transmission', pp. 34–43. Also, L. Jenott, 'Recovering Adam's Lost Glory: Nag Hammadi Codex II in Its Egyptian Monastic Environment', in *Jewish and Christian Cosmogony in Late Antiquity*, eds L. Jenott and S. Kattan Gribetz, TSAJ, vol. 155 (Tübingen: Mohr Seibeck, 2013), pp. 1–22.

[53]A. Camplani, 'Per la cronologia di testi valentiniani: il *Trattato Tripartito* e la crisi ariana', *Cassiodorus* 1 (1995): 171–95.

[54]This passage does not carry the name of Plato but was identified as such by H. M. Schenke's review of Codex VI, 'Zur Faksimile-Ausgabe der Nag-Hammadi-Schriften', *OLZ* 69 (1974): 236–41.

[55]For an introduction to New Philology, see S. G. Nicols, 'Introduction: Philology in a Manuscript Culture', *Speculum* 65, no. 1 (1990): 1–10. M. J. Driscoll, 'The Words on the Page: Thoughts on Philology, Old and New', in *Creating the Medieval Saga: Versions and Editoria Interpretations of Old Norse Saga Literature*, eds J. Quinn and E. Lethbridge (Odense: University Press of Southern Denmark, 2010), pp. 87–104.

[56]See H. Lundhaug, 'The Nag Hammadi Codices: Textual Fluidity in Coptic', in *Comparative Oriental Manuscript Studies: An Introduction*, ed. A. Bausi (Hamburg: COMSt, 2015), pp. 419–23.

[57]See H. Lundhaug and L. Ingeborg Lied, 'Studying Snapshots: On Manuscript Culture, Textual Fluidity, and New Philology', in *Snapshots of Evolving Traditions: Jewish and Christian Manuscript Culture, Textual Fluidity, and New Philology*, eds L. Ingeborg Lied and H. Lundhaug, TUGAL, vol. 175 (Berlin: W. de Gruyter, 2017), 1–19.

social, theological and political preoccupations.[58] Several important analyses of works found in the Nag Hammadi Codices have now appeared that explore the texts as they appear in the manuscripts, taking into consideration the important features of the material evidence and their socio-economic contexts.[59]

MONASTIC MANUSCRIPTS?

As recent research has continued to emphasize the need to understand the circumstances in which ancient books were created, the question of context has become ever more pertinent. As Jenott and Pagels remind us, 'few have asked what *appeal* these codices held for fourth-century readers'.[60] Who then were the people for whom the Nag Hammadi Codices were created? We know that this was a group of people who preferred to read texts in Coptic rather than Greek and, as the colophons tell us, were part of a network of people who were able to call on others to send them diverse texts that could then be selected and copied for each individual volume.[61] The fact that these works were copied onto papyrus and bound in leather indicates a group of people who were able to fund what was an extremely costly undertaking at this period in time. Who then were these people who had the wealth to commission such works or the leisure time and skills to create these works for themselves? The close proximity of the find site to several early monastic sites quickly led to the suggestion that the Nag Hammadi Codices were the works of monks.[62] As doubt was expressed that monks would have been involved in such a venture, several alternative suggestions for the ownership of the codices soon followed, including that they belonged to members of a gnostic cult (Doresse) or to a cultured military officer posted to the Thebaid (Guillaumont).[63] John Barns, who

---

[58]On this point, see also H. Lundhaug, 'The Nag Hammadi Codices in the Complex World of the 4th- and 5th-Cent. Egypt', in *Beyond Conflicts: Cultural and Religious Cohabitations in Alexandria and Egypt between the 1st and the 6th Century* CE, ed. L. Arcari, STAC, vol. 103 (Tübingen: Mohr Siebeck, 2017), pp. 339–60.

[59]Including, Lundhaug, *Images of Rebirth*; L. Jenott, 'Reading Variants in James and the Apocalypse of James: A Perspective from New Philology', in Lundhaug and Jenott (eds), *The Nag Hammadi Codices and Late Antique Egypt*, pp. 55–84; R. Falkenberg, 'The Making of a Secret Book of John: Nag Hammadi Codex III in Light of New Philology', in idem, pp. 85–125.

[60]L. Jenott, 'Antony's Letters and Nag Hammadi Codex I: Sources of Religious Conflict in Fourth-Century Egypt', *JECS* 18, no. 4 (2010): 557–58.

[61]See, in particular, the colophon following the *Prayer of Thanksgiving* in Codex VI which discusses the acquisition and copying of texts; see Lundhaug and Jenott, *Monastic Origins*, pp. 197–206.

[62]Notably, F. Wisse, 'Gnosticism and Early Monasticism in Egypt', in *Gnosis, Festschrift für Hans Jonas*, ed. B. Aland (Göttingen: Vandenhoeck & Ruprecht, i978), pp. 431–40; Robinson, *The Nag Hammadi Library in English*, pp. 14–21; Ch. Hedrick, 'Gnostic Proclivities in the Greek *Life of Pachomius* and the *Sitz im Leben* of the Nag Hammadi Library', *NovT* 22 (l980): 78–94.

[63]Doresse, *Les livres secrets*, p. 155. A. Guillaumont, 'Gnose et monachisme', in *Gnosticisme et monde hellénistique: actes du colloque de Louvain-la-Neuve 911-14 mars 1980*, eds J. Ries et al., Publications de l'Institut orientaliste de Louvain, vol. 27 (Louvain-la-Neuve: Institut orientaliste de l'Université catholique de Louvain, 1982), pp. 97–100.

worked on the cartonnage materials found within the covers of the codices until his death in 1974, hypothesized a Pachomian monastic connection in his preliminary report on the cartonnage materials, prompted in particular by the correlation that exists between several names that appear in letters found within the cartonnage with those that appear in the Pachomian *Vitae*, including most prominently, a Coptic letter written to a 'Pachome' (*P.Nag.Hamm.Copt* 6).[64] Following Barnes's sudden death, his work on the cartonnage material was completed by John Shelton who pointedly rejected the concept of a monastic in the introduction he wrote for the final publication.[65] His pronouncement that the documentation in the cartonnage may all have just come from a 'town rubbish heap' played a significant role in shaping scholarly thinking on the contents of the cartonnage and their seeming irrelevance to the study of the codices.[66] A decade later (1995), Alexandr Khosroyev produced a book that many scholars at the time felt provided compelling arguments to prove that the codices could not have had a monastic origin but belonged to a group of urban literati, in particular because of what he describes as their 'bizarre' and 'philosophizing' teaching.[67] Stephen Emmel, an eminent authority on Coptic manuscripts, went so far as to state that Khosroyev had 'effectively demolished the edifice of the 'Pachomian monastic hypothesis'.[68] This, in turn, was followed by an influential article written by Ewa Wipszycka who reopened the debate on the cartonnage materials and their relation to the creators of the codices in 2000. Her endorsement of the views put forward previously by Shelton likewise played an important role in discrediting the argument for a monastic provenance.[69]

In the last decade, however, the suggestion of a monastic provenance has gained new strength, particularly as scholars interested in New Philology have added to our understanding of the codices as material artefacts and have attempted to interpret the Nag Hammadi texts as being read within such a context.[70] Lundhaug and Jenott's highly influential work, *The Monastic Origins of the Nag Hammadi Codices* (2015), was written not only as a response to the arguments made by Khosroyev and others but in order to demonstrate how a detailed examination of the codices could, in itself, provide a compelling argument for a monastic origin. The revised view of Egyptian

---

[64]Barns's report was published posthumously in 1975, see J. W. B. Barns, 'Greek and Coptic Papyri from the Covers of the Nag Hammadi Codices: A Preliminary Report', in *Essays on the Nag Hammadi Texts: In Honour of Pahor Labib*, ed. M. Krause, NHS, vol. 6 (Leiden: E.J. Brill, 1975), pp. 9–18.

[65]Shelton, *Greek and Coptic Papyri*, pp. 1–11.

[66]Ibid., p. 11.

[67]A. Khosroyev, *Die Bibliothek von Nag Hammadi: Einige Probleme des Christenturns in Agypten wahrend der ersten Jahrhunderte*, ASKA, vol. 7 (Altenberge: Oros Verlag, 1995).

[68]S. Emmel, 'The Coptic Gnostic Texts as Witnesses to the Production and Transmission of Gnostic (and Other) Traditions', in *Das Thomasevangelium: Entstehung- Rezeption- Theologie*, eds J. Frey, E. E. Popkes and J. Schröter, BZNW, vol. 157 (Berlin: W. de Gruyter, 2008), p. 36.

[69]E. Wipszycka, 'The Nag Hammadi Library and the Monks: Papyrologist's Point of View', *JJP* 30 (2000): 179–91.

[70]See for example, H. Lundhaug, 'The Dialogue of the Savior (NHC III,5) as a Monastic Text', in *Studia Patristica XCIII: The First Two Centuries – Apocrypha and Gnostica SP*, ed. M. Vinzent, vol. 93 (Leuven: Peeters, 2017), pp. 335–46.

monastics presented by scholars such as James Goehring and Samuel Rubenson has also played a substantial role in developing our understanding of late antique monastics and the highly diverse nature of Egyptian monasticism. As their research has demonstrated, it cannot be assumed that all the Egyptian monks were incapable of reading a sophisticated range of reading materials or that they would not have had access to them.[71] Accounts written by late antique monks such as Epiphanius of Salamis and Shenoute would certainly seem to suggest that literature condemned as heretical was indeed circulating in fourth-century monasteries, as seems to have been the case with the *Investiture of Michael* mentioned earlier.[72] Prohibitions set forth by various church authorities also demonstrate their awareness that these materials were proving popular among a proportion of their flock.[73] The debate concerning the people who created and owned the Nag Hammadi Codices continues to rage, and there remains some resistance to the theory that the Nag Hammadi Codices could have been produced and read in a monastic setting, particularly a Pachomian one.[74] New evidence for or against this theory is still forthcoming.

FURTHER DEVELOPMENTS

Over recent years, a number of innovative studies have appeared that have called for a reappraisal of hitherto neglected aspects of the Nag Hammadi texts and their import for the study of late antique religion and society. A significant number of works have focused on the role played by female characters in the Nag Hammadi texts and the complex relationship that existed between the gendered imagery to be found within the texts and the social roles allotted to women in the late antique period.[75] The use of gender imagery in a literary context and the ways in which gender and sexuality are portrayed have also inspired scholars to re-examine texts

---

[71]Notably, S. Rubenson, *The Letters of St. Antony: Monasticism and the Making of a Saint* SAC (Minneapolis, MN: Fortress Press, 1995). J. E. Goehring, *Ascetics, Society, and the Desert: Studies in Early Egyptian Monasticism*, SAC (Harrisburg, PA: Trinity Press, 1999).

[72]For the descriptions given by Epiphanius, see E. Iricinschi, '"They fabricate books in Ialdabaoth's name" (Pan. 25, 3). Threatening Religious Books in Epiphanius of Cyprus' Heresiology and in the Nag Hammadi Writings', in F. Ruani and J. Sanzo (eds), *Dangerous Books: Scribal Activity and Religious Boundaries in Late Antiquity and Beyond: Henoch* 39, no. 2 (2017): 271. On the Egyptian monk Shenoute, see T. Orlandi, 'A Catechesis against Apocryphal Texts by Shenute and the Gnostic Texts of Nag Hammadi', *HTR* 75, no. 1 (1982): 85–95.

[73]Including Athanasius' famous *Festal Letter of 367*, in which the archbishop defined the biblical canon and prohibited the reading of apocrypha.

[74]One brief response to Lundhaug and Jenott can be found in, P. Piwowarczyk and E. Wipszycka, 'A Monastic Origin of the Nag Hammadi Codices?' *Adamantius* 23 (2017): 432–58.

[75]K. L. King (ed.), *Images of the Feminine in Gnosticism*, Studies in Antiquity and Christianity (Harrisburg, PA: Trinity Press Int., 2000); idem, 'The Book of Norea Titled Hypostasis of the Archons', in *Searching the Scriptures. Vol. 2 A Feminist Commentary*, ed. E. Schüssler (New York: Crossroads Press, 1994), pp. 66–85; King, 'Reading Sex and Gender in the Secret Revelation of John', *JECS* 19, no. 4 (2011): 519–38. A. Marjanen, *The Woman Jesus Loved: Mary Magdalene in the Nag Hammadi Library and Related Documents*, NHMS, vol. 40 (Leiden: E.J. Brill, 1996).

from the codices.[76] Other studies have included investigations into the role of women as readers of religious materials in late antique society.[77] A greater cognizance of the role played by Eastern religious movements in the Graeco-Roman world has also led to a reconsideration of the ways in which these religions may have influenced the writings found within the codices. The Egyptian roots of certain Nag Hammadi texts have proved a particularly fruitful area of study. The inclusion of Hermetic literature in Codex VI for example is just one indicator of how the creators of the Nag Hammadi Codices could have been linked to local religious traditions in which Hermetic literature was particularly valued.[78]

MODERN CULTURE

Growing accessibility to the Nag Hammadi texts played a significant role in inspiring several thinkers and writers including such notables as the philosopher Hans Jonas, the literary scholar Harold Bloom and the poet Allan Ginsberg.[79] Perhaps the writer most associated with Gnostic thought is the sci-fi author Philip K Dick, who was profoundly affected by the Nag Hammadi Codices which he perceived as both a source of information and a sacred artefact.[80] In more recent times, Dan Brown has attracted millions of readers with novels that allude to the secrets that might be revealed within such works as the *Gospel of Philip*. Various musicians have also found their inspirations within the pages of the Nag Hammadi Codices. In particular, David Tibet, founder of the group Current 93, has used his extensive knowledge of Coptic and apocryphal literature as a source for numerous albums and art works.[81] Other modern musicians who have turned to the Nag Hammadi Codices include the Columbian band Imperium des Tenebras who inserted an English translation of *The Gospel of the Egyptians* into the track 'Nag Hammadi Gnosis Arcanus on their album *Absconditus Umbrae*'.[82] *Thunder Perfect Mind* is a work that has attracted attention from several writers and artists. Toni Morrison includes excerpts from the text in her novels *Jazz and Paradise*, and it features in Umberto Eco's book *Foucault's Pendulum*. Julie Dash's 1991 feature film *Daughters of the Dust* opens with an extensive voice-over of *Thunder Perfect Mind*, and a reading of the text

---

[76]Including, J. Cahana, 'Gnostically Queer: Gender Trouble in Gnosticism', *Biblical Theology Bulletin: Journal of Bible and Culture* 41, no. 1 (2010): 24–35; B. Dunning, 'What Sort of Thing Is this Luminous Woman? Thinking Sexual Difference in *On the Origin of the World*', *JECS* 17 (2009): 55–84.

[77]S. Kattan Gribetz, 'Women as Readers of the Nag Hammadi Codices', *JECS* 26, no. 3 (2018): 463–94.

[78]On this point, see Bull, 'Hermes between Pagans and Christians', pp. 243–60.

[79]See, R. Smith, 'Afterword: The Modern Relevance of Gnosticism', in *The Nag Hammadi Library in English: The Definitive New Translation of the Gnostic Scriptures Compete in One Volume*, ed. J. M. Robinson, 3rd edn (Leiden: E.J. Brill, 1988), pp. 532–49.

[80]L. Kucukalic, *Philip K. Dick: Canonical Writer of the Digital Age* (New York: Routledge, 2009), p. 145.

[81]The album *Thunder Perfect Mind*, for example, contains two tracks based on the NHC text of the same name.

[82]Track 6 on the CD *Absconditus Umbrae* (Cvlminis label, 2012).

also made its way onto the small screen as an advertisement for a Prada fragrance produced by the director Ridley Scott and his daughter Jordan.

NEW GNOSTICISM

The Nag Hammadi Codices have not only created intrigue and debate among academics but have also inspired large numbers of people looking for some form of modern spiritual insight.[83] At the time that the codices were discovered, several scholars self-identified as 'Gnostics', including perhaps most notably Carl Gustave Jung. The phenomenon of Neo-Gnosticism owes a large debt to the recent publication of modern language translations of the Nag Hammadi texts. Popular works, such as *The Allure of Gnosticism* (1995), were published that drew largely on the works to be found within the Nag Hammadi Codices.[84] Marvin Meyer, who popularized the Nag Hammadi texts in several books and articles, created a 'Gnostic Bible' in which works from the codices were placed alongside other significant texts from a variety of Christian and non-Christian traditions.[85] Links to religious movements that were even further afield have also been suggested; the existence of trade routes between the Roman world and South India, for example, has led some scholars to discern a Buddhist influence on 'Gnostic' thought.[86]

In 2013, Harold Haussig, working alongside a council of biblical scholars and religious leaders, incorporated seven texts from Nag Hammadi Codices into the canon of the New Testament along with other significant texts such as the *Acts of Paul and Thecla* and the fragmentary *Gospel of Mary*. This *New New Testament*, as it was called, was subtitled by its editor as, 'A Bible for the 21st Century Combining Traditional and Newly Discovered Texts'.[87] While Karen King, who worked with Taussig on the panel, considered the inclusion of these texts added historical depth to the New Testament, the relevance of this particular book in relation to any discussion of canon has to a large extent been dismissed by most religious scholars who raise questions regarding the relevance of texts that cannot with any certainty be dated to the earliest centuries of Christianity.[88] Even so, the texts found within the

---

[83]On modern Gnostic movements, see D. M. Burns, 'Seeking Ancient Wisdom in the New Age: New Age and Neo-Gnostic Commentators on the Gospel of Thomas', in *Polemical Encounters: Esoteric Discourse and Its Others*, eds K. von Stuckrad and O. Hammer (Leiden: E.J. Brill, 2007), pp. 252–89.
[84]R. Segal et al. (eds), *The Allure of Gnosticism: The Gnostic Experience in Jungian Psychology and Contemporary Culture* (Chicago: Open Court, 1995).
[85]W. Barnstone and M. Meyer, *The Gnostic Bible* (Boston, MA: Shambhala, 2003).
[86]Burns, 'Telling Nag Hammadi's Egyptian Stories', pp. 9–10. See also, R. Powell, *Christian Zen: The Essential Teachings of Jesus Christ: The Secret Sayings of Jesus as Related in the Gospel of Thomas* (Berkeley, CA: North Atlantic Books, 2003).
[87]H. Taussig (ed.), *A New New Testament: A Bible for the Twenty-First Century Combining Traditional and Newly Discovered Texts* (Boston, MA: Houghton Mifflin Harcourt, 2013).
[88]See, for example, R. W. L. Moberly, 'Canon and Religious Truth: An Appraisal of *A New New Testament*', in *When Texts Are Canonized*, ed. T. H. Lim. Brown Judaic Studies, vol. 359 (Providence, RI: Brown Judaic Studies, 2017), pp. 108–36.

volume provoked great interest among readers looking to expand their knowledge of early Christian readings. Taussig describes, for example, the rapturous reception given to a reading of the *Gospel of Thomas* in a Baptist church in New York.[89] The responses of modern readers to such late antique materials are extremely subjective, and as Kirsten Grimstad comments, 'modern readers have projected a wide variety of contradictory meaning onto Gnosticism that cannot be reconciled into a unified picture.'[90] This may not be surprising when we reflect not just on the heterogeneous nature of the Nag Hammadi Codices but the fact that such texts are reinterpreted, not according to their late antique status but for what people living in our modern, diverse, society feel they can gain as personal insight. One consequence has been the establishment of new religious movements that proclaim themselves to be modern Gnostics, and self-proclaimed Gnostic churches can now be found in hundreds of locations across the globe. Other modern Gnostics disseminate their knowledge through the internet, making available translations of Nag Hammadi texts to a new audience through blogs and vlogs. It is this rising interest in 'Gnosticism', induced in part by exposure to texts from the Nag Hammadi Codices and works that reference them, that prompt scholars such as April DeConick to write for a public in ways that juxtapose both ancient and modern movements. Such activities have ensured that the Nag Hammadi Codices will continue to find new, highly diverse, audiences among people with an appetite for literature that is not directly associated with any mainstream church or religious movement.

CONCLUSION

For over fifty years the Nag Hammadi Codices have provoked discussion and controversy for not only are they vital witnesses to the development of early Christianity, but they are also a testament to the dynamic and syncretic nature of late antique Egyptian religious thought. Within their pages are to be found texts originating from a diverse range of traditions, including as they do concepts and characters that are associated with many different movements and philosophies. The question of how these texts fit into the Christian landscape has been answered variously and their relationship to the authorized Christian canon is a matter of some dispute. None of the tractates within the Nag Hammadi Codices form part of any authorized Christian canon, and the very fact of their disappearance reminds us that the reception history of early Christianity involves marginalization, conflict and controversy as much as it reflects any early form of consensus. However, it might be argued that renewed interest in the works found within the codices has prompted the creation of a new canon, one that admits into its fold books that have long disappeared from any mainstream Christian reading list.

---

[89]Taussig, *The New New Testament*, p. xvi.
[90]K. J. Grimstad, *The Modern Revival of Gnosticism and Thomas Mann's Doktor Faustus* SGLLC (Rochester, NY: Camden House, 2002), p. 35.

For many early scholars, the principal importance of the texts within the Nag Hammadi Codices was in their value as potential witnesses to second- or third-century heretical movements. The texts were analysed and discussed on the assumption of textual stability as well as a reliance on the writings of early Christian polemicists in regard to authorship. As a result, the texts were variously labelled using terms such as 'Valentinian' and 'Sethian'. Additionally, the whole collection was then placed neatly under the umbrella term 'Gnostic'. The work of scholars such as Michael Williams, Karen King and Elaine Pagels has played a major role in challenging the neat dichotomy that appeared to exist between heretical texts that were 'Gnostic' and mainstream Christian writings. We are now more aware than ever of the complex nature of these texts and their multiplex relationships to various strands of religious belief.

What then can be said of the status of the works found within the Nag Hammadi Codices? We know that many late antique works that would be considered outlandish or unusual by a modern audience were accepted as 'authoritative' by those early Christians who had access to them, and several works viewed by leading church figures as apocryphal or doctrinally incorrect were copied and read in Egypt well into the ninth century and beyond. This in itself raises the question of what could be considered 'normative' Christianity in the late antique period, a time when numerous conflicts were taking place over fundamental questions of theological and doctrinal significance. Whatever modern or ancient typologies might be applied to the wide variety of texts that can be found in the Nag Hammadi Codices, the people who produced them certainly perceived themselves to be 'Christian' as can be attested through an examination of the codices themselves and the symbols that were written within the margins and among the texts. We do not have to assume that the scribes who copied these works intended to discard the accepted Christian canon, but rather, it would seem that they were collecting works valued for their spiritual and/or theological significance, works that could be read as a supplement to canonical literature rather than as a replacement. Whatever the origin of such works, either as writings associated with cults or movements that existed in earlier centuries or as syncretic writings that reinterpreted earlier Egyptian traditions and pagan cosmologies within a Christian world view, their import to those who incorporated them into the Nag Hammadi Codices is less clear. We do not necessarily have to assume that those who read such works viewed them as particularly unwholesome reading for Christians, even if their readership may have been restricted. The fact that these volumes were hidden away at some stage would suggest, however, that some person in authority raised questions over their authenticity and permitted rights of access.

Debates continue to rage over both the origins of the Nag Hammadi Codices and their significance to late antique Christians, but increasingly they are viewed not merely as the obsolete creations of heretical cults and sects, but they are reframed as alternative Christian works that could just as likely be read by devout monks and nuns as by esoteric individuals in search of hidden knowledge. In our modern society, the works found within the codices continue to be foci of attention, making their appearance in popular culture as well as inspiring a renewed interest in forgotten spiritual texts. Their influence as works of religious literature thus continues to be felt as later generations search their pages for new answers to old questions.

BIBLIOGRAPHY

Aland, K. (ed.). *Synopsis Quattuor Evangeliorum: Locis parallelis evangeliorum apocryphorum et partum adhibitis*, 15th edn. Stuttgart: Deutsche Bibelgesellschaft, 1996.

Barns, J. W. B. 'Greek and Coptic Papyri from the Covers of the Nag Hammadi Codices: A Preliminary Report', in M. Krause (ed.), *Essays on the Nag Hammadi Texts: In Honour of Pahor Labib*, 9–18. NHS 6. Leiden: E.J. Brill, 1975.

Barns, J. W. B., Browne, G. M. and Shelton, J. C. *Nag Hammadi Codices: Greek and Coptic papyri from the Cartonnage of the Covers*. NHS 16. Leiden: E.J. Brill, 1981.

Barnstone, W. and Meyer, M. W. (eds). *The Gnostic Bible*. Boston, MA: Shambhala, 2003.

Bauer, W. *Orthodoxy and Heresy in Earliest Christianity*, trans. R. A. Kraft. Philadelphia, PA: Fortress Press, 1934.

Bianchi, U. (ed.). *Le origini dello Gnosticismo: Colloquio di Messina, 13–18 Aprile 1966*. SHR 12. Leiden: E.J. Brill, 1967.

Bovon, F. 'Beyond the Canonical and the Apocryphal Books, the Presence of a Third Category: The Books Useful for the Soul', *HTR* 105 (2012): 125–37.

Brakke, D. 'Prolegomena to the Study of Ancient Gnosticism', in L. M. White and L. O. Yarbrough (eds), *The Social World of the First Christians: Essays in Honor of Wayne A. Meeks*, 334–50. Minneapolis, MN: Fortress Press, 1995.

Bull, C. H. 'Hermes between Pagans and Christians: The Nag Hammadi Hermetica in Context', in H. Lundhaug and L. Jenott (eds), *The Nag Hammadi Codices and Late Antique Egypt*, 207–60. STAC 110. Tübingen: Mohr Siebeck, 2018.

Burns, D. M. 'Seeking Ancient Wisdom in the New Age: New Age and Neo-Gnostic Commentators on the Gospel of Thomas', in K. von Stuckrad and O. Hammer (eds), *Polemical Encounters: Esoteric Discourse and Its Others*, 252–89. Leiden: E.J. Brill, 2007.

Burns, D. M. 'Ancient Esoteric Tradition: Mystery, Revelation, Gnosis', in C. Partridge (ed.), *The Occult World*, 17–33. London: Routledge, 2014.

Burns, D. M. *Apocalypse of the Alien God: Platonism and the Exile of Sethian Gnosticism*. Philadelphia: University of Pennsylvania Press, 2014.

Burns, D. M. 'Telling Nag Hammadi's Egyptian Stories', *BSR* 45, no. 2 (2016): 5–11.

Burns, D. M. 'Magical, Coptic, Christian: The Great Angel Eleleth and the "Four Luminaries" in Egyptian Literature of the First Millenium CE', in H. Lundhaug and L. Jenott (eds), *The Nag Hammadi Codices in the Context of Fourth- and Fifth-Century Christianity in Egypt*, 141–62. STAC 110. Tübingen: Mohr Siebeck, 2018.

Cahana, J. 'Gnostically Queer: Gender Trouble in Gnosticism', *Biblical Theology Bulletin: Journal of Bible and Culture* 41, no. 1 (2010): 24–35.

Camplani, A. 'Per la cronologia di testi valentiniani: il Trattato Tripartito e la crisi ariana', *Cassiodorus* 1 (1995): 171–95.

DeConick, A. *The Gnostic New Age: How a Countercultural Spirituality Revolutionized Religion from Antiquity to Today*. New York: Columbia University Press, 2016.

Denzey Lewis, N. 'Death on the Nile: Egyptian Codices, Gnosticism, and Early Christian Books of the Dead', in A. D. DeConick, G. Shaw and J. D. Turner (eds), *Practicing Gnosis: Ritual, Magic, Theurgy and Liturgy in Nag Hammadi, Manichaean and Other Ancient Literature. Essays in Honor of Birger A. Pearson*, 161–80. NHMS 85. Leiden: E.J. Brill, 2013.

Denzey Lewis, N. and Blount, J. A. 'Rethinking the Origins of the Nag Hammadi Codices', *JBL* 133, no. 2 (2014): 399–419.

Dirkse, P. A. and Brashler, J. 'The Prayer of Thanksgiving', in D. Parrott (ed.), *Nag Hammadi Codices V, 2–5 and VI, with Papyrus Belolinensis 8502*, 375–88. NHS 11. Leiden: E.J. Brill, 1979.

Doresse, J. *Les Livres secrets des gnostiques d'Égypte*. Paris: Plon, 1958.

Driscoll, M. J. 'The Words on the Page: Thoughts on Philology, Old and New', in J. Quinn and E. Lethbridge (eds), *Creating the Medieval Saga: Versions and Editoria Interpretations of Old Norse Saga Literature*, 87–104. Odense: University Press of Southern Denmark, 2010.

Dunderberg, I. 'The School of Valentinus', in A. Marjanen and P. Luomanen (eds), *A Companion to Second-Century Christian 'Heretics'*, 64–99. Vigiliae Christianae, Suppl. 76. Leiden: E.J. Brill, 2005.

Dunderberg, I. *Beyond Gnosticism, Myth, Lifestyle, and Society in the School of Valentinus*. New York: Columbia University Press, 2008.

Dunn, W. 'What does "Gospel of Truth Mean?"' *VChr* 15, no. 3 (1961): 160–4.

Dunning, B. 'What Sort of Thing Is this Luminous Woman? Thinking Sexual Difference in *On the Origin of the World*', *JECS* 17 (2009): 55–84.

Emmel, S. 'Religious Tradition, Textual Transmission, and the Nag Hammadi Codices', in J. D. Turner and A. McGuire (eds), *The Nag Hammadi Library after Fifty Years*, 34–43. Leiden: E.J. Brill, 1997.

Emmel, S. 'The Coptic Gnostic Texts as Witnesses to the Production and Transmission of Gnostic (and Other) Traditions', in Jörg Frey, Enno E. Popkes and Jens Schröter (eds), *Das Thomasevangelium: Entstehung- Rezeption- Theologie*, 33–49. BZNW 157. Berlin: W. de Gruyter, 2008.

Falkenberg, R. 'The Making of a Secret Book of John: Nag Hammadi Codex III in Light of New Philology', in H. Lundhaug and L. Jenott (eds), *The Nag Hammadi Codices and Late Antique Egypt*, 85–125. STAC 110. Tübingen: Mohr Siebeck, 2018.

Franzmann, M. 'A Complete History of Early Christianity: Taking the "Heretics" Seriously', *JRH* 29, no. 2 (2005): 117–28.

Goehring, J. E. *Ascetics, Society, and the Desert: Studies in Early Egyptian Monasticism SAC*. Harrisburg, PA: Trinity Press, 1999.

Goodacre, M. 'How Reliable Is the Story of the Nag Hammadi Discovery?' *JSNT* 35 (2013): 303–22.

Grimstad, K. J. *The Modern Revival of Gnosticism and Thomas Mann's Doktor Faustus*. Studies in German Literature, Linguistics and Culture. Rochester, NY: Camden House, 2002.

Guillaumont, A. 'Gnose et monachisme', in J. Ries et al. (ed.), *Gnosticisme et monde hellénistique: actes du colloque de Louvain-la-Neuve 911-14 mars 1980*, 97–100. Publications de l'Institut orientaliste de Louvain 27. Louvain-la-Neuve: Institut orientaliste de l'Université catholique de Louvain, 1982.

Hedrick, C. 'Gnostic Proclivities in the Greek *Life of Pachomius* and the *Sitz im Leben* of the Nag Hammadi Library', *NovT* 22 (1980): 78–94.

Iricinschi, E. '"They Fabricate Books in Ialdabaoth's Name" (Pan. 25, 3). Threatening Religious Books in Epiphanius of Cyprus' Heresiology and in the Nag Hammadi Writings', in F. Ruani and J. Sanzo (eds), *Dangerous Books: Scribal Activity and Religious Boundaries in Late Antiquity and Beyond: Henoch* 39, no. 2 (2017): 247–69.

Jenott, L. 'Antony's Letters and Nag Hammadi Codex I: Sources of Religious Conflict in Fourth-Century Egypt', *JECS* 18, no. 4 (2010): 557–8.

Jenott, L. 'Recovering Adam's Lost Glory: Nag Hammadi Codex II in Its Egyptian Monastic Environment', in L. Jenott and S. Kattan Gribetz (eds), *Jewish and Christian Cosmogony in Late Antiquity*, 1–22. TSAJ 155. Tübingen: Mohr Seibeck, 2013.

Jenott, L. 'Reading Variants in James and the Apocalypse of James: A Perspective from New Philology', in H. Lundhaug and L. Jenott (eds), *The Nag Hammadi Codices and Late Antique Egypt*, 55–84. STAC 110. Tübingen: Mohr Siebeck, 2018.

Kattan Gribetz, S. 'Women as Readers of the Nag Hammadi Codices', *JECS* 26, no. 3 (2018): 463–94.

Khosroyev, A. *Die Bibliothek von Nag Hammadi: Einige Probleme des Christenturns in Agypten wahrend der ersten Jahrhunderte*. Arbeiten zum spatantiken und koptischen Agypten 7. Altenberge: Oros Verlag, 1995.

King, K. L. 'The Book of Norea Titled Hypostasis of the Archons', in E. Schüssler (ed.), *Searching the Scriptures: Vol. 2 A Feminist Commentary*, 66–85. New York: Crossroads Press, 1994.

King, K. L. 'Approaching the Variants of the Apocryphon of John', in J. D. Turner and A. McGuire (eds), *The Nag Hammadi Library after Fifty Years: Proceedings of the 1995 Society of Biblical Literature Commemoration*, 105–37. NHMS 44. Leiden: E.J. Brill, 1997.

King, K. L. (ed.). *Images of the Feminine in Gnosticism Studies in Antiquity and Christianity*. Harrisburg, PA: Trinity Press Int., 2000.

King, K. L. *What Is Gnosticism?* Cambridge: Cambridge University Press, 2003.

King, K. L. 'Reading Sex and Gender in the Secret Revelation of John', *JECS* 19, no. 4 (2011): 519–38.

Koester, H. 'Introduction to the Gospel of Thomas', in J. M. Robinson (ed.), *The Nag Hammadi Library in English*, 3rd edn, 124–6. San Francisco, CA: HarperSanFrancisco, 1990.

Kotrosits, M. 'Romance and Danger at Nag Hammadi', *The Bible and Critical Theory* 8, no. 1 (2012): 39–52.

Kucukalic, L. *Philip K. Dick: Canonical Writer of the Digital Age*. New York: Routledge, 2009.

Layton, B. 'The Riddle of the Thunder [NHC VI,2]: The Function of Paradox in a Gnostic Text from Nag Hammadi', in C. W. Hedrick and R. Hodgson, Jr (eds), *Nag*

Hammadi, Gnosticism, and Early Christianity, 37–54. Peabody, MA: Hendrickson, 1986.

Layton, B. (ed.). *Nag Hammadi Codex II, 2–7, together with XIII, 2* Brit. Lib. Or.4926(1) and P.Oxy. 1,654, 655*, 2 vols. NHS 20-21. Leiden: E.J. Brill, 1989.

Linjamaa P. *The Tripartite Tractae (NHC 1, 5): A Study of Determinism and Early Christian Philosophy of Ethics*. NHMS 95. Leiden: E.J. Brill, 2019.

Logan, A. H. B. *The Gnostics: Identifying an Early Christian Cult*. London: T&T Clark, 2006.

Lundhaug, H. *Images of Rebirth: Cognitive Poetics and Transformational Soteriology in the Gospel of Philip and the Exegesis on the Soul*. NHMS 73. Leiden: E.J. Brill, 2001.

Lundhaug, H. 'The Nag Hammadi Codices: Textual Fluidity in Coptic', in A. Bausi (ed.), *Comparative Oriental Manuscript Studies: An Introduction*, 419–23. Hamburg: COMSt, 2015.

Lundhaug, H. 'The Dialogue of the Savior (NHC III,5) as a Monastic Text', in M. Vinzent (ed.), *Studia Patristica XCIII: The First Two Centuries – Apocrypha and Gnostica*, 335–46. Studia Patristica 93. Leuven: Peeters, 2017.

Lundhaug, H. 'The Nag Hammadi Codices in the Complex World of the 4th- and 5th-Cent. Egypt', in L. Arcari (ed.), *Beyond Conflicts: Cultural and Religious Cohabitations in Alexandria and Egypt between the 1st and the 6th Century* CE, 339–60. STAC 103. Tübingen: Mohr Siebeck, 2017.

Lundhaug, H. and Jenott, L. *The Monastic Origins of the Nag Hammadi Codices*. STAC 97. Tübingen: Mohr Siebeck, 2015.

Lundhaug, H. and Lied, L. I. 'Studying Snapshots: On Manuscript Culture, Textual Fluidity, and New Philology', in L. I. Lied and H. Lundhaug (eds), *Snapshots of Evolving Traditions: Jewish and Christian Manuscript Culture, Textual Fluidity, and New Philology*, 1–19. TUGAL 175. Berlin: W. de Gruyter, 2017.

Mahé, J.-P. *Hermès en Haute-Égypte*, 2 vols. BCNH.T 3 & 7. Québec: Les Presses de l'Université Laval, 1978–1982.

Marjanen, A. *The Woman Jesus Loved: Mary Magdalene in the Nag Hammadi Library and Related Documents*. NHMS, vol. 40. Leiden: E.J. Brill, 1996.

Moberly, R. W. L. 'Canon and Religious Truth: An Appraisal of *A New New Testament*', in T. H. Lim (ed.), *When Texts are Canonized*, 108–36. Brown Judaic Studies 359. Providence, RI: Brown Judaic Studies, 2017.

Nicols, S. G. 'Introduction: Philology in a Manuscript Culture', *Speculum* 65, no. 1 (1990): 1–10.

Nongbri, B. 'Finding Early Christian Books at Nag Hammadi and Beyond', *BSR* 45, no. 2 (2016): 11–19.

Orlandi, T. 'A Catechesis against Apocryphal Texts by Shenute and the Gnostic Texts of Nag Hammadi', *HTR* 75, no. 1 (1982): 85–95.

Pearson, B. *Gnosticism and Christianity in Roman and Coptic Egypt*. New York: T&T Clark International, 2004.

Perrin, N. 'Recent Trends in Gospel of Thomas Research (1991-2006): Part I, The Historical Jesus and the Synoptic Gospels', *Currents in Biblical Research* 5, no. 2 (2007): 183–206.

Poirier, P. 'Introduction to Thunder', in M. Meyer (ed.), *The Nag Hammadi Scriptures: The International Version*, 367–71. New York: HarperOne, 2007.

Powell, R. *Christian Zen: The Essential Teachings of Jesus Christ: The Secret Sayings of Jesus as Related in the Gospel of Thomas*. Berkeley, CA: North Atlantic Books, 2003.

Przemysław, P. and Wipszycka, E. 'A Monastic Origin of the Nag Hammadi Codices?' *Adamantius* 23 (2017): 432–58.

Quispel G. 'Note on an Unknown Gnostic Codex', *VChr* 7 (1953): 193.

Rasimus, T. 'Ophite Gnosticism, Sethianism and the Nag Hammadi Library', *VChr* 59, no. 3 (2005): 235–63.

Rasimus, T. *Paradise Reconsidered in Gnostic Mythmaking: Rethinking Sethianism in Light of the Ophite Evidence*. NHMS 68. Leiden: E.J. Brill, 2009.

Robinson J. M. 'The Discovery of the Nag Hammadi Codices', *BibA* 42, no. 4 (1979): 206–24.

Robinson J. M. 'From the Cliff to Cairo: The Story of the Discoverers and the Middlemen of the Nag Hammadi Codices', in B. Barc (ed.), *Colloque International sur le textes de Nag Hammadi (Québec, 22–25 août 1978)*, 21–58. BCNH.É 1. Québec: Les Presses de l'Université Laval, 1981.

Robinson J. M. *The Facsimile Edition of the Nag Hammadi Codices: Introduction*. Leiden: E.J. Brill, 1984.

Robinson J. M. 'The Discovering and Marketing of Coptic Manuscripts: The Nag Hammadi Codices and the Bodmer Papyri', in B. A. Pearson and J. E. Goehring (eds), *The Roots of Egyptian Christianity*, 2–25. STAC. Philadelphia, PA: Fortress Press, 1986.

Robinson J. M. (ed.). *The Nag Hammadi Library in English*, 4th edn. Leiden: E.J. Brill, 1996.

Robinson J. M. 'The Discovery of the Nag Hammadi Codices', *JCoptS* 11 (2009): 1–21.

Robinson J. M. *The Nag Hammadi Story*, 2 vols. NHMS 86. Leiden: E.J. Brill, 2014.

Rubenson, S. *The Letters of St. Antony: Monasticism and the Making of a Saint*. SAC. Minneapolis, MN: Fortress Press, 1995.

Säve-Söderbergh, T. 'Holy Scriptures or Apologetic Documentations? The "Sitz im Leben" of the Nag Hammadi Library', in Jacque É. Ménard (ed.), *Les textes de Nag Hammadi NHS*, vol. 7, 3–14. Leiden: E.J. Brill, 1975.

Schenke, H.-M. 'Das sethianische System nach Nag-Hammadi-Handschriften', in P. Nagel (ed.), *Studia Coptica*, 165–72. Berliner byzantinische Arbeiten 45. Berlin: Akademie, 1974.

Schenke, H.-M. 'Zur Faksimile-Ausgabe der Nag-Hammadi-Schriften', *OLZ* 69 (1974): 236–41.

Segal, R. et al. (eds). *The Allure of Gnosticism: The Gnostic Experience in Jungian Psychology and Contemporary Culture*. Chicago: Open Court, 1995.

Smith, G. S. *Guilt by Association: Heresy Catalogues in Early Christianity*. Oxford: Oxford University Press, 2015.

Taussig, H. (ed.). *A New New Testament: A Bible for the Twenty-First Century Combining Traditional and Newly Discovered Texts*. Boston, MA: Houghton Mifflin Harcourt, 2013.

Thomassen, E. 'Notes pour la délimitation d'un corpus valentinien à Nag Hammadi', in
    L. Panchaud and A. Pasquier (eds), *Les textes de Nag Hammadi et le problème de leur
    classification. Actes du colloque tenu à. Québec du 15 au 19 septembre 1993*, 243–59.
    BCNH.É 3. Québec: Les Presses de l'Université Laval, 1995.
Thomassen, E. *The Spiritual Seed: The Church of the 'Valentinians*. NHMS 60. Leiden:
    E.J. Brill, 2006.
Tite, P. L. *Valentinian Ethics and Paraenetic Discourse: Determining the Social Function of
    Moral Exhortation in Valentinian Christianity*. NHMS 67. Leiden: E.J. Brill, 2009.
Turner, J. D. *Sethian Gnosticism and the Platonic Tradition*. BCNH.É 6. Leuven: Peeters,
    2001.
Turner, John D. and Majercik, R. (eds). *Gnosticism and Later Platonism: Themes, Figures,
    and Texts*. SBL Symp. Series 12. Atlanta: Society of Biblical Literature, 2000.
Williams, M. A. *Rethinking 'Gnosticism': An Argument for Dismantling a Dubious
    Category*. Princeton, NJ: Princeton University Press, 1996.
Williams, M. A. 'Sethianism', in A. Marjanen and P. Luomanen (eds), *A Companion to
    Second-Century Christian 'Heretics'*, 32–63. Vigiliae Christianae, Suppl. 76. Leiden:
    E.J. Brill, 2005.
Williams, M. A. 'Was there a Gnostic Religion?' in Antti Marjanen (ed.), *Was there a
    Gnostic Religion?* 55–79. Göttingen: Vandenhoeck & Ruprecht, 2005.
Williams, M. A. and Coblentz, D. 'A Reexamination of the Articulation Marks in
    Nag Hammadi Codices II and XIII', in H. Lundhaug and L. Jenott (eds), *The Nag
    Hammadi Codices and Late Antique Egypt*, 427–56. STAC 110. Tübingen: Mohr
    Siebeck, 2018.
Wipszycka, E. 'The Nag Hammadi Library and the Monks: A Papyrologist's Point of
    View', *JJP* 30 (2000): 179–91.
Wisse, F. 'Gnosticism and Early Monasticism in Egypt', in B. Aland (ed.), *Gnosis,
    Festschrift für Hans Jonas*, 431–40. Göttingen: Vandenhoeck & Ruprecht, 1978.

CHAPTER 32

The early church's developing theology of (new) creation

PAUL M. BLOWERS

INTRODUCTION

The philosophical culture in which early Christian theologians began the arduous task of articulating a distinctively Christian doctrine of the origins, nature and destiny of the universe was one that was already saturated with cosmogonic and cosmological speculations that were intellectually funded by interpretation of classical sources extending all the way back to the Pre-Socratic philosophers. Unfortunately, historical theologians have all too often generalized that Graeco-Roman philosophy had no serious conceptions of divine creation of the world and no genuine analogues of the biblical vision of Creator and creation, a vision assumed to be uniquely grounded in Genesis 1–2, revised intermittently across the Hebrew scriptures, reworked in the New Testament and elucidated by numerous early Christian commentators. The actual picture, however, is much more complex. There was a tremendously broad spectrum of Graeco-Roman cosmological perspectives that endured well into the Christian era, complicating but also prompting and energizing the responses of Christian theologians who were anxious to stake Christianity's unique claims concerning divine creation of the world.

In contrast with 'infinite world' models wherewith certain classical thinkers (most famously Aristotle) saw no beginning or end per se of the world that we know,[1] there also unfolded in Graeco-Roman philosophical cosmology, as David Sedley has demonstrated, a 'creationist' tradition of relatively sophisticated and variegated form. It was already nascent in the Pre-Socratics Anaxagoras of Clazomenae, who posited an infinite (divine) Mind ordering the elements of the world, and Empedocles of Acragas, who conceived two divine first principles, Love and Strife, interacting with the four cosmic elements and each of the two working in its turn

---

[1] See especially Aristotle, *Ph.*, *lib.* 8; much later Proclus, *ET.*, 53–55; *in Ti.*, 1.252–254.

to pave the way ontologically for earthly life forms.[2] This emerging philosophical creationism took on a whole new dimension, however, with Plato's *Timaeus*, which contains the intricately developed myth of a subsidiary divine Demiurge who fashioned the cosmos according to the pattern of transcendent Ideas.[3] The figure of the Demiurge was destined to be reimagined in other sources as well before and during the Christian era.[4] If, as seems appropriate, Plato's story is interpreted in a philosophically literal way, such that this Demiurge was a figure truly separate from the world that he formed, rather than an immanent intelligence emerging within it,[5] then the stage was set not only for later Platonic commentators to give their respective interpretations of this creation myth but also for Christian theologians to counter it with a sophisticated rival form of the biblical narrative. That rivalry was heightened by the fact that cosmogony and cosmology were intrinsically tied up with a religious world view that shaped the understanding of humanity's nature and destiny, the contours of human community and the norms of morality and ethics.

Meanwhile, the early churches had their hands full with the Genesis creation narrative itself, which, by the second and third centuries, had become subject not only to dismissive or tendentious renderings by Marcionite and Gnostic interpreters but also to pagan critics who lampooned the foolishness of Jewish and Christian 'fables'. The second-century pagan intellectual Celsus, an eclectic Platonist, enjoyed a knowledge of details of the Mosaic cosmogony but also perceived Christianity's embarrassing vulnerability to novel versions of the story, including Marcion's pitting of the vindictive Old Testament Creator against the benevolent God worshipped by Jesus and his followers.[6] Beginning with Theophilus of Antioch in the second century, the first formal Christian commentator on the six-day creation story in Genesis 1[7] and a writer fully aware of the attractiveness and plausibility of a rival cosmogony like that of Plato, patristic interpreters, both in apologetic and expository modes, sifted through the details of the narrative for clues to its full philosophical and theological riches. From the more abbreviated treatments like that of Theophilus to advanced and heuristically styled commentaries such as Augustine's *De Genesi ad Litteram* (*On the Literal Interpretation of Genesis*) in the early fifth century, early Christian interpreters deployed the tools of philology, grammar, rhetoric and natural philosophy to support their exegetical work of investigating Genesis 1 in conjunction with the larger primeval history of Genesis and with other relevant creation texts throughout the Bible. Along the way they engaged old and new

---

[2]Anaxagoras, *Ph.*, (Diels-Kranz edition), frg. 59 B12; Empedocles, *Nat.*, (Dielz-Kranz edition), frgs. 31 B17, 21, 26, 27, 35, 59. See also D. Sedley, *Creationism and Its Critics in Antiquity.* (Berkeley: University of California Press, 2007).

[3]*Ti*, 27C–69A.

[4]See C. S. O'Brien, *The Demiurge in Ancient Thought: Secondary Gods and Divine Mediators* (Cambridge: Cambridge University Press, 2015).

[5]See S. Broadie, *Nature and Divinity in Plato's Timaeus* (Cambridge: Cambridge University Press, 2011), pp. 7–26.

[6]Origen, *Cels.*, 6.49-53.

[7]Theophilus, *Autol.*, 2.10-19.

questions not just of the origins and constitution of spiritual and material creation but of the identity and freedom of the Creator, the Creator's providence and judgement, the contamination of the cosmos with moral evil, the perceived fallenness of the world and the possibility of a renewal and transformation of creation through the Creator's ongoing interventions in history.

In what follows in this chapter, I will forego a detailed examination of the philosophical cosmology that preceded and affected Christian thinking on creation and instead will concentrate on certain archetypal themes in the development of a Christian 'theology of creation' which prioritized the biblical witnesses while nonetheless addressing those cosmological questions deemed most relevant to creation's 'sacred history'. Sacred history in the Bible, after all, was not restricted solely to the destinies of individual peoples, even the elect people of Israel or the newly graced Gentiles after Christ. In early Christian understanding, sacred history comprehended the drama of the origins and destiny of *all* – even non-human and inanimate – creation, which, as the Apostle Paul intimated in Rom. 8.19-23, was implicated in the tragic consequences of human sin and in the adoption and bodily redemption of the human race.

GENESIS 1 AS TELEOLOGY

While references and allusions to the creation story of Genesis 1 are common in the New Testament, interest specifically in its cosmogonic or cosmological significance is minimal and often oblique. Earliest Christianity inherited from the Hebrew and Jewish scriptures a perspective in which the creation narrative did not stand alone but belonged to the larger history of salvation. Much of the New Testament language of Creator and creation is doxological, as in praising the Maker of 'heaven and earth' (cf. Acts 4.24, 17.24; Rev. 14.7) or the Son or Word through whom and for whom all things were made (cf. Jn 1.3, 1.10; Eph. 3.9; Col. 1.16; Heb. 1.2). But even this worshipful stance is aimed not merely at celebrating the divine initiative in creating the world but at reframing the Creator's original and ongoing activity of creation in seamless connection with his redemptive and salvific work. Already the Gospels capitalize on Gen. 1.1 ('in the beginning God created') to project the new age begun in Jesus the Christ. John the Evangelist accentuates this in his Prologue when he states that 'in the beginning was the Word' (Jn 1.1-3), the Word destined to take flesh and to illumine cosmic darkness (1.4-14). Matthew begins his gospel as the 'book of the genealogy (βίβλος γενέσεως) of Jesus Christ', clearly paralleling Gen. 2.4, which announces the (second) creation narrative in Genesis 2 as the 'book of the origins (βίβλος γενέσεως) of heaven and earth'.

This primitive Christocentric appropriation of the Genesis creation story stimulated patristic commentators on the Hexameron (the six-day creation narrative in Gen. 1.1-2.3, for which Gen. 2.4-25 was a putative supplement) to rethink the original horizon of the primeval history. It was not enough to view the Hexaemeron as just a distant precursor of the new 'beginning' of the world in Jesus Christ. The Christian gospel warranted a thoroughgoing reinterpretation of Genesis 1 itself, all the more so in the light of the intermittent bid of Marcion and his disciples fully to dissociate the allegedly capricious creator-god of the Hebrew scriptures from the benevolent Father of Jesus Christ. Accordingly, the Hexaemeron demanded to be treated literally – and *teleologically* – as a prophecy of the 'new' creation inaugurated in Christ. Accordingly, its narrative details contained crucial pointers to the work of Christ as the transcendent and universal Logos, the Creator's primary agent in creating the very world that, as the New Adam, he would eventually renew and transform from out of its fallen, atrophying state. Genesis 1 was not, then, purely protological, preoccupied with cosmic origins; it was *eschatological*, a witness to the Creator's ultimate purpose in creating the world and guiding it to perfection.

A strong indicator of this trend was Christian commentators' early fixation on the fuller meaning of 'in the beginning' (ἐν ἀρχῇ; *in principio*) in Gen. 1.1. They were acutely aware of the pregnancy of the word *archē* in Greek, such as could denote not only a temporal beginning but also the richly philosophical notion of a causal foundation, or an ontological or epistemological 'first principle'.[8] Treatments of the hotly contested 'first principles' (ἀρχαί) of things were common in Hellenistic philosophy and, in part, inspired Christian interpreters to rethink the 'beginning' designated in the very first line of canonical scripture. Theophilus of Antioch, in his late second-century apology *To Autolycus*, is one of the first Christian authors to collapse Jn 1.1-3 and Gen. 1.1 in order to identify the true *archē* as the divine Logos himself, the beginning of all beginnings.[9] An entire train of subsequent patristic commentators would follow exegetical suit.[10] Ultimately, 'In the beginning God created' could very well suggest that the timeless God created the universe and time along with it (a chronological meaning); but it could also be the equivalent of affirming that 'in' or 'through' the Son/Word/Christ, God created all things. Creation was imbued with the Creator's Christocentric intentions from the outset. Indeed, for Irenaeus of Lyons, the Creator originally revealed his plan for creation only to the 'Lamb who was slain', suggesting that the very rationale for creating the world (having foreknowledge of the Adamic fall) was to reveal the depth of his love in sacrificing his own Son for it.[11] Clement of Alexandria envisions the Son as the true *archē* in Gen. 1.1, insofar as he was the very Wisdom of God whose role was to serve as Pedagogue of all creation (i.e. before, during and after his incarnation).[12]

Reading Genesis 1 as prophecy, as a testament to God's future plan in Jesus Christ, freed patristic exegetes to see manifold signals of his providence and salvific economy throughout the Hexaemeron, some more latent than others. For example, amid the extensive patristic interpretation of 'heaven and earth' (Gen. 1.1) that previewed the detailed account of the six days, Origen posits that 'heaven and

---

[8]See, for example, Aristotle, *Metaph.*, 1012B-1013A.
[9]*Autol.*, 2.10.
[10]Cf. Tatian, *Or.*, 5; Irenaeus, *Haer.*, 2.2.5; Tertullian, *Hermog.*, 18-20; Origen, *Hom.Gen.*, *Com.Joh*, 1.17.101-1.19.116; 1.22.132; Ambrose, *Hex.*, 1.4.15; Augustine, *Conf.*, 11.9.11.
[11]Irenaeus, *Haer.*, 3.22.3; 4.20.2; cf. much later Maximus the Confessor, *Ambig.Io.*, 60.
[12]Clement, *Strom.*, 6.7.58.

earth' projected something else besides the 'firmament' and 'dry land' (Gen. 1.6), that it pointed ahead to the ultimate translation of creation from a corruptible to an incorruptible state.[13] The profuse speculations on the 'spirit' that 'hovered over the waters' (Gen. 1.2) split between identifying the spirit as an animating wind bringing life to the lifeless abyss[14] and as the Holy Spirit completing the work of creation as a Trinitarian action. Tertullian and other interpreters see the Holy Spirit sanctifying the element of water itself to become life-giving and efficacious for eventually cleansing sinners through Christian baptism.[15] And while some patristic commentators attended substantially to whether the primordial light (Gen.1.3) was corporeal and how it related to the luminaries created on the fourth day, Origen led the way in speculating that it was to Christ, as co-Creator and eternal Wisdom, that the Father said 'Let there be light', pointing to Christ's work of illuminating darkness in his incarnate ministry.[16]

These are merely a few examples of the early Christian rereading of Genesis 1 as a proto-evangelium and as a vector of the destiny of creation within the divine economy. Some interpretations were more adventurous than others, but most followed the pattern of a theologically 'literal' rendering of the Hexaemeral events that substantiated the Creator's future plan centred in Jesus Christ. Augustine's influential *On the Literal Interpretation of Genesis* pioneered a way towards maintaining multiple legitimate interpretations of the Hexaemeral events. This by no means precluded figurative and allegorical interpretations under the canopy of 'literal' meaning, such as when Augustine revisits Genesis 1 in his *Confessions* and finds there a rich tableau of the creation and mission of the church,[17] or when the far less known monastic author Anastasius of Sinai (seventh century) ascertains that the Spirit's work in ordering the creation out of chaos (Gen. 1.2) pointed to the Spirit's role in commanding the church itself out of its disorderliness.[18]

CREATION *EX NIHILO*: DIVINE FREEDOM AND RESOURCEFULNESS

Christian claims about the Creator making the world 'from nothing' were among the most audacious in the context of long-standing Graeco-Roman cosmological convictions. Over and beyond philosophical denials of a real 'beginning' or 'end' of the world were strong assertions, most famous that of the Epicurean Lucretius, that 'nothing can be created from nothing'.[19] And indeed, Plato's creation myth in the *Timaeus*, again the most serious rival to the biblical cosmogony in late antiquity,

---

[13]Origen, *Princ.*, 2.3.6.
[14]Theophilus of Antioch, *Autol.*, 2.13; Eusebius of Emesa, *ComGen.*, frg. 3; Ephrem Syrus, *Com.Gen.*, 1.7.
[15]See Tertullian, *Bapt.*, 3–4.
[16]Origen, *Com. Joh.*, 1.19.110-111; 2.23.148-154.
[17]Augustine, *Conf.*, *lib.* 13 (CCSL 242-273).
[18]Anastasius of Sinai, *Hex.*, 1.7.4–5.
[19]Lucretius, *Rerum*, ll. 155-156.

assumed that there was a 'material' substratum coeternal with the Divine. Plato called it the 'receptacle' or 'space' (χώρα), an enigmatic and functional notion for which he used multiple analogies, including the malleable stuff (τὸ διασχηματιζόμενον) of all things.[20] Christian rejection of the coeternity of matter with the Creator, however, was rather swift in coming. For one thing, the text of Gen. 1.2 was clearly vulnerable to the perception of a pre-existing, albeit formless, mass awaiting the Creator's intervention; and certain Christian authors – including Justin Martyr, Athenagoras, Clement of Alexandria and Hermogenes – happily conceded that God shaped a pre-existent matter.[21] A strong patristic consensus nonetheless developed in opposition to matter being an eternal substratum, principally because any breach of the Creator's own pure transcendence and eternity, or any constraint on his freedom, omnipotence and resourcefulness in giving being to 'what was not',[22] was untenable.

Theophilus and Irenaeus led the way, both of them quoting Jesus' words: 'What is impossible with human beings is possible with God' (Lk. 18.27).[23] The Creator created matter itself *ex nihilo* before he formed it into a cosmos; and yet the 'nothing' from which he formed it admitted of multiple plausible meanings. At the bottom, it could mean the sheer vacuum or absence of being that the Creator graciously filled with matter that he subsequently fashioned into a world.[24] It could instead mean the primordially 'formless' state of matter to which the Creator generously gave form,[25] or even matter already formed but given greater definition and order.[26] Some later interpreters, sensing that the notion of an absolute ontological or dimensionless void appeared philosophically incomprehensible, proposed that the 'nothing' from which God created the world was in fact God himself, in the (apophatic) sense that God is *no-thing* from which another might be made, but is rather the infinitely free, loving, gracious source of all that is or ever will be.[27] In Maximus the Confessor's words, he is the ineffable author of creatures' 'being' (τὸ εἶναι), 'well-being' (τὸ εὖ εἶναι) and 'eternal-well-being' (τὸ ἀεὶ εὖ εἶναι) alike.[28]

All this is to say that the doctrine of creation *ex nihilo* was the intersection of theological nuances extending well beyond the issue of cosmic beginnings per se. As noted, it signalled the freedom and power of the Creator, but also the sheer

---

[20]Plato, *Ti.*, 50C.

[21]Cf. Justin, *1 Apol.*, 10, 59; Athenagoras, *Leg.*,15.1–3; Clement, *Strom.*, 5.14.90. 92; Hermogenes, as cited in Tertullian, *Hermog.*

[22]See, for example, 2 Macc. 7.28 (τὰ οὐκ ἐξ ὄντα); Rom. 4.17 (τὰ μὴ ὄντα).

[23]Theophilus of Antioch, *Autol.*, 2.13; Irenaeus, *Haer.*, 2.10.4.

[24]See Irenaeus, *Haer.*, 2.9.1-4.

[25]Augustine, *Conf.*, 12.13.16; *Gn. litt.*, 1.1.3.

[26]Cf. Tertullian, *Hermog.*, 29.1-6; 33.1; Basil of Caesarea, *Hom. in hexaemeron*, 1.5-7; Gregory Nazianzen, *Poema arcana*, 4 (*de Mundo*).

[27]Ps-Dionysius the Areopagite, *DN.*, 7.3; Maximus the Confessor, *Mystagog.*, *prooemium*; John Scotus Eriugena, *Periph.*, 3.5.

[28]Maximus the Confessor, *Ambig.Io.*, 7 (PG 91:1073C, 1084B); ibid., 10 (1116B-C, 1204D); ibid., 42 (1325B-C, 1329A-B, 1348D); and esp. ibid., 65 (1392A-C).

dependence of the creature on the Creator. In the Platonic idiom that numerous patristic thinkers appropriated and modified, matter was ontologically impoverished on its own terms – Augustine calls it 'practically nothing' (*prope nihil*).[29] And yet matter gained a whole new dignity in the hands of the biblical Creator. Athanasius capitalizes on Plato's striking reflection that the creator, being free of envy, did not begrudge any creature a likeness to himself and the prospect of being good.[30] In his own words, the Creator 'envies nothing its existence but rather wishes all creatures to exist, in order to manifest his loving-kindness'.[31] Nothing was more vulnerable and contingent than created, material nature, which the Creator redeemed from reversion, from lapsing back into nothingness, by labouring to nurture and stabilize it through the divine Logos.[32] Athanasius' particular interest is materially embodied human beings, whose sin has jeopardized their continuing existence, setting them into a fateful trajectory of dissolving again into nothing, a threatening reversal of the Creator's gracious action of creation *ex nihilo*.[33] The divine wisdom of creation and salvation is one and the same, strategically aimed at consummating the creative grace that has been invested in human nature in the first place. God not only gave human beings, like all creatures, the 'strength' to exist[34] but also endowed them with his very image as a shield against corruptibility.[35] With the incarnation of Christ the New Adam, Athanasius believes, the impending cosmic reversal has itself been reversed once for all, corruptibility and mortality vanquished, and the ultimate goal for humankind, deification, fully realized.[36] The benefits extend to all of creation. Citing Eph. 3.17-19, where Paul calls believers to fathom 'what is the breadth and length and height and depth', Athanasius affirms that 'the Word spread himself everywhere, above and below and in the depth and in the breadth; above, in creation; below, in the incarnation; in the depth, in hell; in breadth, in the world'.[37]

CREATION, EVIL AND PROVIDENCE

Creation *ex nihilo*, as an assertion of the Creator's freedom and resourcefulness in early Christian thought, also elicited a certain sense of *creatio continua*. God's original work of creation was already itself a *new* creation, and a work of 'salvation' from chaos and nonbeing, and so too the commencement of a covenantal bond with the creature enduring to the consummation of the world. As we have already observed, the Hexaemeron for many of its Christian exegetes prophetically indicated

---

[29]Augustine, *Conf.*, 12.6.6.
[30]Plato, *Ti.*, 29E-30A.
[31]Athanasius, *Gent.*, 41, Greek text ed. R. Thomson (Oxford: Oxford University Press, 1971), p. 114. My translation.
[32]Athanasius, *Gent.*, 41.
[33]Athanasius, *Incar.*, 6.
[34]Athanasius, *Gent.*, 46.
[35]Athanasius, *Inc.*, 3, 5.
[36]Athanasius, *Inc.*, 13, 20, 54.
[37]Athanasius, *Inc.*, 16 (ed. and trans. Thomson, 172, 173).

an eschatological pledge to bring all things to perfection and transformation. Creative grace was also providential grace.

An early challenge, nevertheless, was the collective impact of various Gnostic and Marcionite reconstructions of creation and providence, which early polemicists like Irenaeus caricatured as myths which thoroughly deviated from the coherent plot (ὑπόθεσις) of scriptural revelation and the church's Rule of Faith.[38] Rather than viewing creation as a free and gracious divine act prior to the entrance of moral evil into the world through angelic and human dereliction, Irenaeus targeted myths like that in the Sethian *Apocryphon of John*, where moral evil already erupted within the spiritual realm among subsidiary divine beings, leading eventually to a demented demiurge creating the material world.[39] Gnostic systems differed in their theories of just how far this world and its creator were alienated from the Divine, and the extent to which material creation ontologically hosted moral evil. But for Irenaeus and other critics, the overall upshot was a distorted and aberrant representation of the pattern of the divine *oikonomia*, replete with deterministic scenarios that seemed to obliterate the dynamic interplay of divine grace and creaturely freedom.

Early Christian theologians developed various models for explicating how the divine *oikonomia* (or active plan of salvation) sustains itself amid the vicissitudes of creatures' concrete history in time and space, including the domino effect of the Adamic fall. Irenaeus for his part reasons that the *oikonomia* was itself key to the doctrine of divine providence. The Creator, through his Logos, has set forth the pre-eminently self-consistent plan to educate humanity from an immature and inchoate state at the beginning to a thoroughly mature and perfect condition at the end.[40] Accordingly, the fall has frustrated but not derailed the *oikonomia*, the encounter with evil being a learning experience for the human race. The Alexandrians Clement and Origen, while echoing Irenaeus' connection between divine providence and the mission of the Logos-Pedagogue to instruct rational beings towards perfection through their earthly experience,[41] also explored the metaphysical groundwork of the *oikonomia*, deciding to improvise on Philo's theory of a dual-phased creation.

'Double-creation' theory, as it so happens, took on a life of its own in early Christian cosmology as a means to tie together the beginning and final goal of creation, and the divine providence operative in the whole scheme. Although there were interpretive variations, the basic concept was that God in his eternity had 'simultaneously' or ideally projected the plan of all intelligible and sensible creation, a creation-in-potency as it were, before actualizing that plan in time and space.[42] Origen's construction was one version, and a controversial one at that, since he envisioned a sequence, beginning with the spiritual creation, coeternal with the

---

[38]Irenaeus, *Haer.*, 1.8.1; 1.9.4.
[39]Irenaeus, *Haer.*, 1.4.1–1.5.6.
[40]Irenaeus, *Haer.*, 4.38.1–4.39.4.
[41]Cf. Clement, *Strom.*, 6.7.58; *Paed.* (passim); Origen, *Com.Joh*, *lib.* 1 and 2.
[42]For an overview, see P. Blowers, *Drama of the Divine Economy: Creator and Creation in Early Christian Theology and Piety* (Oxford: Oxford University Press, 2012), pp. 54–8, 91–3, 145–66.

Creator and yet ontologically inferior to him, followed by the creation of material bodies to host spiritual beings fallen to varying degrees from union with God.[43]

Subsequent versions of 'double creation' clearly sought to revise or correct Origen's perspective (which Origen himself conceded was speculation rather than dogma). Gregory of Nyssa rejects Origen's thesis of a spiritual creation pre-existing the material one, insisting in the case of human creatures that (spiritual) soul and (material) body were co-created while nonetheless affirming the former's ontological priority.[44] In a simultaneous, non-temporal instant, the Creator, like a transcendent Sower, threw down the seeds of all created things, being their 'starting-points' (ἀφορμάς), 'causes' (αἰτίας) and 'potencies' (δυνάμεις), the teleological keys to creatures' fulfilment and perfection.[45] Similarly, Augustine proposes that the Creator simultaneously pre-planted in the recesses of the world the 'causal' or 'seminal' reasons (*rationes causales*; *rationes seminales*) that encode individual creatures' emergence and existential flourishing.[46] Rather than being purely deterministic, these *rationes* lay the providential groundwork for the dynamic historical relation of Creator and creation.[47] Indeed, the simultaneous causation (*conditio*) of the world already assumes the divine *administratio* even before that stewardship is carried out by the Creator within the *oikonomia*.[48] Much later, in the early seventh century, another patristic luminary, Maximus the Confessor, reaffirms the idea of a simultaneous creation[49] but also extensively develops the notion of the *logoi* (or *rationes*) not only as the teleological principles embedded in individual creatures but also as the staging points for the continuing presence, movement and activity of the Creator-Logos within all created beings.[50] Maximus, moreover, reworks Evagrius Ponticus' notion of the '*logoi* of providence and judgment'. Evagrius, the prolific monastic theologian of the fourth century, had deployed this idea in espousing an essentially Origenist cosmology, wherein 'judgement' had to do with the Creator's diversification of bodies specifically suited to the degree of spiritual beings' fall from heavenly paradise, and 'providence' the Creator's guidance of those fallen beings from differentiation back into pure union with him.[51] Maximus instead sees the divine providence and judgement as seamlessly intertwined, bespeaking the Creator's wise governance of the intended (not punitive) diversity of embodied creatures whom he is drawing into an eschatological unity-in-diversity.[52]

---

[43]Origen, *Princ.*, 1.4.1, 1.4.4-5, 1.5.1-5, 1.8.1-4, 1.6.2, 2.1.1-5, 2.9.1-8.

[44]*De hom opif.*, 28–29.

[45]*Expl.hex.*, 7–9.

[46]*Gn.litt.*, 4.33.51; 6.10.17–6.11.19; 6.14.25–6.18.29.

[47]See R. Williams, '"Good for Nothing?" Augustine on Creation', *AS* 25 (1994): 9–24.

[48]Augustine, *Trin.*, 3.9.16.

[49]*QTh.*, 2.

[50]*Ambig. Io.*, 7.

[51]*Gnosticus*, 48 (*Sources Chrétiennes*, vol 356); *Kephalaia gnostica* (Syriac version) 1.27, 2.59, 5.23-24, 6.43, 6.75.

[52]*ExOr,* (*prologus*); *Ambig.Io.*, 32.

Meanwhile, early Christian articulation of a doctrine of divine providence not only addressed intramural concerns for a consistent theological cosmology but also answered long-standing Graeco-Roman philosophical perspectives on providence, a theme still very much in play among pagan intellectuals during the early Christian era. Seneca in his treatise *On Providence* (ca. 64), or the peripatetic Alexander of Aphrodisias in his work *On Fate* (ca. 200), or the Neoplatonist Plotinus in *Ennead* 3.2-3 (Περὶ Προνοίας, pub. ca. 270), or later still the Neoplatonists Hierocles of Alexandria (fifth century) and Proclus (d. 485) in their writings on providence, fate and free will were seen as philosophically correcting the capriciousness, ineptitude or even vice of the gods often depicted in ancient epic and tragedy. Though such sources were scarcely normative for patristic theologians, there was sometimes common ground. Seneca, for example, indicated 'Nature', 'Fate' and 'Fortune' all as legitimate names of the provident God who ultimately benefits the human race.[53] Both Hierocles and Proclus upheld the reality of divine providence, although Hierocles saw 'fate' too as a lower providence that rendered persons their moral due,[54] while Proclus considered fate 'something divine, but not god'.[55] Christian thinkers knew very well the appeal of the idea of fate at the level of people's experience of life's vagaries, and at least one Christian author, Boethius, rhetorically entertained Fortuna as a serious conversation partner in the discussion of divine providence.[56] And yet an early consensus had appeared in patristic theology that providence had nothing to do with fate. We see this in Origen's strong rebuke of the fatalism of pagan astrology,[57] and again in Gregory of Nyssa's strongly philosophical treatise *Against Fate*.[58] In the long run, many patristic thinkers concurred, in their respective ways, with Irenaeus' original vision of providence as a divine 'pedagogy' guiding rational creatures through the experience of evil to an unprecedented maturity and perfection. The vision of providence in terms of the Creator constantly seizing order from chaos, and ushering in 'new' creation from out of the old, resonated theologically and rhetorically in early Christian doctrine, but also in liturgy, sacramental practice and ethics.[59]

SUBJECTION TO VANITY AND THE RENEWAL OF CREATION IN CHRIST AND THE SPIRIT

We have already touched briefly on the deadening, corrupting impact of human sin on the integrity of creation. Various patristic authors subscribed to the image of the

---

[53]*Ben.*, 4.8.

[54]*De Providentia* extracts from Photius trans. H. Schibli, *Hierocles of Alexandria* (Oxford: Oxford University Press, 2002), p. 342 (codex 251 § 9), 351 (ibid., § 20).

[55]*De providentia* 14.

[56]*DeCon.*, 2.2.12; 4.6.1-57.

[57]*Comm.Gen.*, lib. 3, in *Origenis Philokalia* (SC 226:130–66).

[58]In GNO, 3/2:31-63.

[59]See Blowers, *Drama of the Divine Economy*, pp. 313–72.

senectus mundi, the cosmos as an ageing and increasingly decrepit old man desperate for rejuvenation.[60] Many more, however, gravitated to Qoheleth's depiction of the world's 'vanity' (Eccl. 1.2 et al.) and Paul's own teaching on the Creator's subjection of all creation to 'vanity' or 'futility' (ματαιότης), its 'groaning' along with humanity in advance of adoption and bodily redemption (Rom. 8:19-23). Paul's language in this passage has always raised questions about the *non-human* 'creation' designated as sharing in this subjection to vanity. Irenaeus and a fairly long train of interpreters after him played up the fact that the whole creation must participate in the liberation of humanity from vanity and corruption in the dawn of a new creation.[61] Theodoret of Cyrus, for example, avers that all creatures, from the inanimate ones to the archangels, groan with humanity to this end.[62] Because Paul says that the whole creation 'groans *together*' (συστενάζει) and 'travails together' (συνωδίνει), Theodore of Mopsuestia argues that the solidarity and fellowship (κοινωνια) of creatures, their sympathy with each other in this condition of vanity, is precisely the Apostle's emphasis.[63] But earlier Origen had taken quite a different tack, insisting that the groaning 'creation' is really only the *higher* creatures – the heavenly bodies and the angels or 'ministering spirits' (Heb. 1.14) – setting an example of eschatological longing for the lower creatures and tutoring them in the worship of their shared Creator.[64]

In the West, however, both Ambrosiaster and Augustine, in their unique ways, focused on the weight of human guilt born by all creation. Ambrosiaster points to the laborious movement of the planetary bodies and the loud moaning of servile livestock as evidence of all creation languishing in advance of redemption. Subhuman creation merely echoes back to humanity the universal effects of its sinfulness, and, unlike Origen, Ambrosiaster places the responsibility on human beings to be morally exemplary for their fellow creatures as creation waits out this subjugation.[65] Augustine, on the other hand, is even more anthropocentric, positing that subhuman creatures cannot truly 'groan in travail' and that 'every creature' who has been groaning until now (Rom. 8.22) is humanity itself, which, because it is a microcosm of the larger creation, extends its vanity to the whole.[66] More specifically, this groaning everyman represents all those who have not yet come to faith but who, by divine election, will be revealed in the end as true 'sons of God' (Rom. 8.19, 23).[67]

Patristic interpreters were nonetheless attentive to Paul's caveat that the Creator had subjected creation to vanity *in hope* (Rom. 8.20). This decidedly did *not* mean

---

[60]For exemplary texts, see B. Daley, *The Hope of the Early Church: A Handbook of Patristic Eschatology* (Cambridge: Cambridge University Press, 1991), pp. 41, 48, 67, 98, 101–2, 133, 211.
[61]See Irenaeus, *Haer.*, 5.36.3.
[62]Theodoret, *Comm.Rom.*, 8.19-21.
[63]*Comm.Rom.*, 8.22.
[64]*Princ.*, 1.7.5; *Ex.M.*, 7; *Comm.Rom.*, 7.2.
[65]*Comm.Rom* (CSEL 81.1, 279-83).
[66]*Ex. Prop. Rom.*, 53.1-6.
[67]Ibid., 53.13-21.

that the redemption of creation was to be indefinitely deferred, or to be an outcome purely at the end of cosmic history. Just as the original creation had been 'new' in its own way, salvation of the world was to take the form of ever 'new' creation. For just this reason, Tertullian repudiated the claims of Marcionite interpreters that the ancient Demiurge of the Old Testament had to be displaced right along with what he created. The Creator renewed rather than destroyed his handiwork.[68] And while later Manichaean interpreters tried to drive a wedge between old and new creation, lampooning the Old Testament creator for 'resting' from his work of creation as if fatigued (Gen. 2.2), respondent patristic exegetes cited Jesus' words in Jn 5.17: 'My Father is working even until now (ἕως ἄρτι), and I am working.' They understood this to mean that the Creator had never really rested as such, and that the work of renewing what he created had been, and would always be, relentless.[69] But it also set in bold relief the work of Jesus Christ as Creator in his own right. He who has been the divine Wisdom from before all ages – the one 'from' whom (1 Cor. 8.6; Rom. 11.36), 'in' whom (Col. 1.16, 17), 'through' whom (Jn 1.3, 10; Rom. 11.36; Heb. 1.2), and 'for' whom (1 Cor. 8.6; Rom. 11.36; Col. 1.16) God made the world[70] – is also the one who, in his incarnation, and in concert with the Holy Spirit, decisively carries forward the Father's creative purposes. Even though scripture can speak of each of the three persons as having initiative in creation, they share a common *energeia*.[71] Or as Gregory of Nyssa summarizes it, creation is a will, an impulse, a transmission of power 'beginning from the Father, advancing through the Son, and completed in the Holy Spirit'.[72]

For early Christian interpreters, the redemptive labour of the incarnate Son was also, intrinsically, a *creative* and *re-creative* labour. It focused not only on rectifying the legacy of the Adamic fall but also on introducing new riches and horizons in God's creative project, suppressing the idea that humanity's fall had defeated that project. Christ makes us 'greater (*amplius*) than we were in the beginning', says the Latin writer Marius Victorinus.[73] It was not enough for Christ simply to correct Adam's fall and restore Adam's prelapsarian state. The New Adam inaugurated a *new* creation that began with his very conception in the virgin's womb – the womb which, as Basil of Caesarea described it, was the 'workshop (ἐργαστήριον) of the economy',[74] the matrix of an unprecedented renewal and transformation of human nature not available even before the fall. Athanasius proposes that Christ, as Creator

---

[68]*Marc*, 4.1.6–10; 5.2.1-3; 5.19.11. For further analysis of Rom. 8.19-23 in patristic commentary, see P. Blowers, 'The Groaning and Longing of Creation: Variant Patterns of Patristic Interpretation of Romans 8:19–23', in *SP* 63 (Leuven: Peeters, 2013), pp. 45–54.

[69]Cf. Origen, *Hom.Num*, 23.4; Ps-Archelaeus, *Acta*, 31; Gregory Nazianzen, *Or.*, 30.11; Augustine, *Adv. Man.*, 1.22.33; *c.Adim.*, 2; *Gen.litt*, 4.11.21–4.12.23; *Jo.Tr*, 20.2; Maximus the Confessor, *QTh.*, 2.

[70]On patristic interpretation of these phrases, see Blowers, *Drama of the Divine Economy*, pp. 222–34.

[71]Gregory Nazianzen, *Or.*, 34.15.

[72]*Maced.* (GNO 3.1:99-100).

[73]*Comm.Eph.* 1.1.8.

[74]*Hom.* 27 (*in sanctam Christi generationem*).

in his own right, created his own flesh;[75] but later in the development of patristic Christology, Leontius of Byzantium further claims that the Son created his own unique human nature, thoroughly deified, such as could unite with the divine nature in Christ's hypostatic union.[76] This is the new, eschatological 'mode' (τρόπος) or 'regimen' (πολιτεία) of human nature of which human beings are beneficiaries and prospective participants.[77]

In his carnal birth itself, free from postlapsarian sexual procreation, Christ was already healing the possibility and desire associated with sexual passion, commencing his transformation of human possibility as a whole.[78] Christ's further incarnate acts were also interpreted as gestures towards, and embodiments of, the 'new creation' that he was inaugurating in and beyond human nature itself. Even his baptism, for example, had cosmic repercussions. Irenaeus surmises that Christ was already anointed by the Father before his incarnation and that he in turn 'anointed and adorned' all creation, whereas at his baptism, the Father anointed Jesus' humanity with the Spirit.[79] Origen claims, moreover, that Jesus' 'exaltation' over all creatures (Phil. 2.9-11) begins precisely at his baptism.[80] All of creation from that point forward is being drawn towards his final glorification as Lord of creation. Various patristic authors, especially in the East, also mythologized the interconnections between the waters of creation (Gen. 1.2), the rivers of paradise (Gen. 2.10-14), the Jordan River sanctified by Jesus' baptism and the future waters of baptismal 'new creation' within the church.[81] In his miracles, Jesus demonstrated his authority over the elements of creation, as in calming a storm at sea (Matt. 8.24-27),[82] or walking on water (Matt. 14.26; Mark 6.48-49; Jn 6.19);[83] but he also revealed his creative capacity to do new things with what, as God, he created, such as when he made wine not *ex nihilo* but out of water already created (Jn 2.1-11)[84] and mixed old soil with his own spittle to form a healing, even deifying salve for a man born blind (Jn 9.6).[85]

Modern readers may find it difficult to grasp the fact that, very early on, patristic theologians focused on the passion and death of Jesus Christ as profoundly instrumental to the realization of a new creation. I already briefly noted Irenaeus' extraordinary claim that God's original rationale in creation was to reveal the depths of his love through Christ the Paschal Lamb. 'Insofar as [the Creator] preexisted as

---

[75]*Inc.*, 8, 18.

[76]*Nes.*, 1.20; 2.1; cf. also Maximus the Confessor, *Ambig. Th.*, 5.

[77]Maximus the Confessor, *QTh.*, 21; *Ambig.Th.*, 5.

[78]Maximus the Confessor, *QTh.* 21, 61.

[79]*Dem, 53; Haer.* 3.9.3.

[80]*Hom.Jos.* 4.2.

[81]For key sources and analysis, see K. McDonnell, *The Baptism of Jesus in the Jordan: The Trinitarian and Cosmic Order of Salvation* (Collegeville, MN: Liturgical Press, 1996), pp. 10–68, 101–55; Blowers, *Drama of the Divine Economy*, pp. 251–7.

[82]Ambrose of Milan, *Ex.Luc.*, 4.68-69; *Fid.*, 4.4.43–4.5.47; Peter Chrysologus, *Serm.*, 20.

[83]Maximus, *Ambig.Th.*, 5.

[84]Irenaeus, *Haer.*, 3.11.5.

[85]Cf. Irenaeus, *Haer.*, 5.15.2-4; Cyril of Alexandria, *Comm.Jo, lib.* 6.

the one who saves, it was necessary that what would be saved should also come into existence, so that the Savior should not exist in vain.'[86] As John Behr has pointed out in his extensive studies of Irenaeus, 'death' did not serve the divine *oikonomia* merely as a punishment for sin, but as a mysterious instrument of new life.[87] Christ was crucified on the 'sixth day' just as humanity was created on the original 'sixth day', thus granting humankind 'a second creation by means of his passion, which is a recreation from out of his death (*a morte*)'.[88] The image of the 'cosmic cross', with its arms extended vertically and horizontally to gather all of creation in its redemptive and transformative embrace, consistently appeared in Greek patristic theology,[89] as did the connection between the cross and the 'tree of life' (Gen. 2.9, 3.22, 24) in both Greek and Syriac writers.

Christ's resurrection and ascension in turn completed the transformation of human nature and renewal of all corporeal creation begun in the incarnation proper. In his writings on the Paschal Triduum, Gregory of Nyssa speaks of the fullness of the 'Paschal Day' that bridged Christ's death and resurrection and was 'the beginning of a new creation' and 'a new heaven and new earth' (2 Pet. 3.13; Rev. 21.1). As 'firstborn from the dead' (Col. 1.18) and 'first-fruits' of the resurrection (1 Cor. 15.20, 23), Christ fulfils his work as Firstborn of the new creation, which for his ecclesial body is realized first in baptism and later in resurrection from the dead.[90] Theodore of Mopsuestia and Maximus the Confessor alike play up how, when Christ's resurrected body and 'new' humanity ascended towards session at the right hand of the Father, all creation behind him participated in the renewal. Maximus projects an entire scheme of how, in all his incarnate acts, but lastly in the ascension and session, Christ finalized the recapitulation of God's creative purposes, healing and uniting the polarities of creation: male and female; paradise and inhabited earth; heaven and earth, intelligible and sensible creation, and at last uncreated and created nature.[91]

Not surprisingly, patristic theology of the 'new creation' in Christ also consistently attended to the role of the Holy Spirit. Indeed, in the later stages of the fourth-century Trinitarian controversies, when the divinity of the Spirit had been called into question by some critics, one of the strongest claims for the Spirit's divinity was that the Spirit too was Creator (or as the revised Nicene Creed says, 'Lord, the Giver of Life').[92] While, as we have seen, disagreement arose over whether the 'spirit' hovering over the waters of creation (Gen. 1.2) was in fact the Holy Spirit, even some of the commentators who denied this, notably Ephrem Syrus, still

---

[86]*Haer.*, 3.22.3 (SCh 211:438).
[87]*The Mystery of Christ: Life in Death* (Crestwood, NY: St. Vladimir's Seminary Press, 2006), pp. 73–114.
[88]Irenaeus, *Haer.*, 5.23.2.
[89]Cf. Irenaeus, *Dem*, 34; *Haer.*, 5.17.4; Gregory of Nyssa, *Contra Eunom.*, lib. 3; *Or. Catech.*, 32; John Damascene, *Fide*, 4.11.
[90]Gregory of Nyssa, *Contra Eunom.*, 2.81; cf. Theodore of Mopsuestia, *Comm.Eph.*, 1.10, 23; 4.16; Augustine, *En.Ps.*, 3.9.
[91]*Ambig.Io.*, 41.
[92]See, for example, Basil of Caesarea, *Spir*, 13.29; 16.38); Ambrose, *De Spiritu Sancto*, 1.2.27-31.

affirmed that the Spirit, as the very 'breath of God' (Ps. 33.6), had played a role in the original work of creation.[93] As Origen recognized early on, the Holy Spirit is not to be confused merely as a divine 'activity' (ἐνέργεια) but is a Person operative in cooperation with the Father and the Son.[94] Extensive attention was given by Christian exponents, especially from the fourth century on, to the precise roles of the Holy Spirit in realizing the new creation: animating, sanctifying, beautifying, perfecting.[95]

CONCLUSION: PROJECTING THE CONSUMMATION OF CREATION

By now it should be clear that the theology of creation that took shape in the early church, notwithstanding variations in representative patristic writers, was as much a Christian teleology (and eschatology) as a cosmology. It aimed not just to explain the world's beginning but to contemplate the Creator's original pre-creation plan as pointed towards a final, glorious, *Christocentric* end. This goal was projected to culminate a single divine economy, a providentially staged cosmic drama, enfolding two seamlessly intertwined subplots: the redemption of the creation as compromised by creaturely sin; and the inauguration of a new, transformed state of all creation, albeit with humankind as the primary beneficiary.

That said, the *final* destiny of creation, and the continuity between 'old' and 'new' creation, inevitably prompted considerable speculation in early Christian thought. Some, like Justin, Irenaeus, Tertullian and Lactantius, entertained some form of chiliastic (millenarian) hope for a final physical paradise on earth. Irenaeus for his part focused not on a 'thousand-year' reign of Christ on earth (Rev. 20.1-7) but on a final physical transformation of material creation capping Christ's incarnate work.[96] Others, like Augustine, approached more dialectically the relation between material history and the arrival of a new order transcending or displacing the old. In the *City of God*, he interprets the millennium spoken of in Revelation 20 merely as a symbol of the whole age between Christ's first and second advents, when the faithful reign with Christ until he arrives to judge the world.[97] But he is at one with Irenaeus that with the appearance of a 'new heavens and new earth' (Rev. 21.1), the material creation is destined not for annihilation but for a glorious transmutation, since only its 'outward form' (σχῆμα; *figura*) will pass away (1 Cor. 7.31).[98] The sixth-century Greek commentator Oecumenius, citing Paul's vision of all creation being released from vanity (Rom. 8.19-21), confirms that the 'new heavens and new earth' will

---

[93]*Comm.Gen.* 1.7; *Hym.* 3.11; cf. Jacob of Sarug, *Hom. in Hex.* 1.
[94]Origen, Frg. 37, on Jn 3.8.
[95]For illustrative patristic texts and analysis, see Blowers, *Drama of the Divine Economy*, pp. 286–307.
[96]*Haer.*, 5.36.1.
[97]*De Civitate Dei*, 20.7–9.
[98]Irenaeus, *Haer.*, 5.36.1; Augustine, *De Civitate Dei*, 20.14.

see the physical creation released from decay, an all-out renewal.[99] The upshot was a fairly strong patristic consensus that the creation was neither to be returned to nothingness nor replaced by an altogether transcendent order, since the work of the triune Creator remained ever resourceful, ever true to purpose and ever free, even beyond the 'present age'.

BIBLIOGRAPHY

Anderson, G. and Bockmuehl, M. (eds). *Creation ex nihilo: Origins, Development, Contemporary Challenges*. Notre Dame, IN: University of Notre Dame Press, 2018.

Behr, J. *The Mystery of Christ: Life in Death*. Crestwood, NY: St. Vladimir's Seminary Press, 2006.

Blowers, P. *Drama of the Divine Economy: Creator and Creation in Early Christian Theology and Piety*. Oxford: Oxford University Press, 2012.

Blowers, P. 'The Groaning and Longing of Creation: Variant Patterns of Patristic Interpretation of Romans 8:19–23', in *SP* 63, 45–54. Leuven: Peeters, 2013.

Blowers, P. 'Beauty, Tragedy, and New Creation: Theology and Contemplation in Cappadocian Cosmology', *IJST* 18 (2016): 7–29.

Broadie, S. *Nature and Divinity in Plato's Timaeus*. Cambridge: Cambridge University Press, 2011.

Daley, B. *The Hope of the Early Church: A Handbook of Patristic Eschatology*. Cambridge: Cambridge University Press, 1991.

Köckert, C. *Christliche Kosmologie und kaiserzeitliche Philosophie: Die Auslegung des Schöpfungsberichtes bei Origenes, Basilius und Gregor von Nyssa vor dem Hintergrund kaiserzeitlicher Timaeus-Interpretationen*. Tübingen: Mohr Siebeck, 2009.

May, G. *Creatio ex Nihilo: The Doctrine of 'Creation Out of Nothing' in Early Christian Thought*, trans. A. S. Worrall. London: T&T Clark, 2004.

McDonnell, K. *The Baptism of Jesus in the Jordan: The Trinitarian and Cosmic Order of Salvation*. Collegeville, MN: Liturgical Press, 1996.

McDonough, S. *Christ as Creator: Origins of a New Testament Doctrine*. Oxford: Oxford University Press, 2009.

Norris, R. *God and World in Early Christian Theology: A Study in Justin, Irenaeus, Tertullian, and Origen*. New York: Seabury Press, 1965.

O'Brien, C. S. *The Demiurge in Ancient Thought: Secondary Gods and Divine Mediators*. Cambridge: Cambridge University Press, 2015.

Sedley, D. *Creationism and Its Critics in Antiquity*. Berkeley: University of California Press, 2007.

---

[99] *Comm. in Apocalypsin,* 11.10.13–14; cf. Andrew of Caesarea, *Comm. in Apoc.,* 65.

CHAPTER 33

Suffering of Christ

Suffering of people

STEFANO SALEMI

INTRODUCTION

Generally, both the New Testament and the early church understood suffering as a human experience somehow shared by both Christ and his people, the believers. In 1 Pet. 4.12-19, suffering is considered part of the Christian life. At the same time, it is described as a means through which God sanctifies the believers. In Rom. 8.15–11.35 suffering precedes future glory.[1] Suffering, intended in its broad spectrum of sense,[2] is both physical and psychological, human and not. It may affect in a negative way, with various degrees of intensity, several areas of human existence. Early Christians were aware that suffering could be experienced in several ways.[3]

The Bible ascribes the origin and causes of suffering to the entrance of evil into the world, through the transgression of God's command in Eden, and therefore the violation of his law, which is called 'sin' (Rom. 5.12; 1 Jn 3.4). Suffering occurs in numerous and often dramatical manners, but the Bible and its early Christian exegetes have tried to analyse its nature, processes, meaning and impact in Christian life. Most of all, all agreed that only in Christ there may be a remedy and a way

---

[1]Jewett argues that Paul's discourse highlights, among many others, the concepts of hope and glory within the frame of the restoration of a suffering world, 'Overcoming ecological disorder is depicted here as a divine gift enacted as a result of God's restoration of humanity to its position of rightful dominion, reflecting God's intended glory,' p. 515; 'The content of the future hope is that the full and undistorted dominion of God's children will one day manifest itself in the context of a restored creation,' p. 519, R. Jewett, *Romans: A Commentary*, *Hermeneia* (Minneapolis, MN: Augsburg Fortress, 2007), p. 519; see also R. N. Longenecker, *The Epistle to Romans*, NIGTC (Grand Rapids, MI: Eerdmans, 2016), pp. 866–906; D. J. Moo, *The Epistle to the Romans*, NICNT (Grand Rapids, MI: Eerdmans, 1996), pp. 295–315.
[2]Selling argues that there is a difference between suffering and pain, as 'pain demands a response, while suffering demands an interpretation', Joseph Selling, 'A Credible Response to the Meaning of Suffering', in *God and Human Suffering*, eds Jan Lambrecht and Raymond Collins (Louvain: Peeters, 1990), p. 181.
[3]'Living in a society of dramatic inequality, early Christians were acutely aware of the suffering caused by poverty, greed and the abuse of wealth. Sickness was a constant threat, and devastating plagues periodically inflicted widespread suffering, dramatically demonstrating the transience of human life,' in L. D. Lefebure, 'The Understanding of Suffering in the Early Christian Church', CLARITAS, *JDC* 4, no. 2 (2015): 28–37.

to manage suffering. Since early times in Christian history, one of the moments of Christ's suffering that has attracted the greatest attention, emblem of pain and sorrow, has been the Passion on the cross. Several interpreters of the first centuries have read it as an anticipation of the suffering of the believers in Christ. Thus, the suffering of Christ may be perceived as the true suffering of people.[4] This, as we can see in the following sections, has been at the centre of early Christian theology and its systematic developments.

IMITATIO CHRISTI AND *PREFIGURATIO MORTIS*

In Rom. 8.17 the text says that the believers are heirs of God (κληρονόμοι) and joint-heirs with Christ (συγκληρονόμοι) through sufferings. In addition, if they suffer with (συμπάσχομεν) Christ, they will also be glorified with (συνδοξασθῶμεν) him. The verbs used in the verse, in reference to suffering and glory, are constructed with the preposition prefix σύν which denotes union. Sufferings, therefore, unite the believers with Christ and are an integral part of the Christian experience. They are intended to be a form of participation to the sufferings of Christ. Moreover, paradoxically, the future glory will be proportional to the number of sufferings lived in life (1 Pet. 4.13). This is why sufferings should not cause surprise. In fact, in 1 Pet. 4.12 the text says, 'do not be surprised' (μὴ ξενίζεσθε), as if something strange (ξένου) happened. According to what 1 Peter mentions (4.14), to be reviled (ὀνειδίζεσθε) for Christ is a beatitude, not a shame. Rather, God is glorified in suffering. It is a privilege and an honour to be able to suffer for the name of Christ, because when one suffers for Christ, he participates in God's work in the world. In a sense, suffering 'according to the will of God' (1 Pet. 4.19, πάσχοντες κατὰ τὸ θέλημα τοῦ θεοῦ) means suffering any kind of pain because of Christian faith. As suffering is therefore also the result of faith in Christ, certainly martyrdom constitutes one of the most emblematic examples. Martyrdom must be understood in a broader sense including not only death and torture purposely inflicted to followers of Christ but also any other form of pain produced because of faith in Christ.

For instance, Polycarp (69–155 CE), bishop of Smyrna, who according to Irenaeus and Eusebius of Caesarea, was educated by the apostles and in particular by John, connects the sufferings of Christ to those of the martyrs. In his *Letter to the Philippians* (9.2), he writes regarding some martyrs (Ignatius, Zosimus and Rufus) as an example of faith and righteousness because they died for the Lord 'with whom they also suffered'[5] (ᾧ καὶ συνέπαθον) and they did not love the world. Therefore,

---

[4]All Scripture quotations are taken from the New Revised Standard Version, unless otherwise noted.

The Greek or Latin text of primary sources is provided according to the purposes of the argumentation. All translations into English, when necessary, are personal and intended to offer an easy reading, otherwise noted.

[5]Michael W. Holmes, *The Apostolic Fathers: Greek Texts and English Translations* (Grand Rapids, MI: Baker Books, 2007), p. 291, see also pp. 272–97; see, P. Hartog (ed.), *Polycarp's Epistle to the Philippians and the Martyrdom of Polycarp* (Oxford: Oxford University Press, 2013), pp. 7–9.

the parallelism between Christ's suffering and that of his followers, especially the martyrs, already emerges in the apostolic era. The experience of Christ in his suffering is not simply conceived as a sharable one but as a true form of imitation.

In fact, if credit is given to a fragment attributed, not without problems, to Polycarp, on the ground of Jn 19.34 about the pierced side of Jesus and a biblical comparison of Adam with Christ, all those who suffer and die for Christ are included in the path of the *imitatio* of the suffering and Passion of Christ. In this text, the blood of Christ receives the ecclesiological value of symbolizing the blood of martyrs, thus through suffering the followers of Christ imitate him.[6]

Focusing our attention mainly on the content of this fragment, the text prefigures, in the blood of Christ, the blood of the martyrs. From the pierced side of Christ, the blood of martyrdom (*sanguis martyrii*) flows. Thus, in this sense, the death of Christ, being a martyr's death, is a *prefiguratio mortis*, a prefiguration of the death of the believers, and at the same time, the death of the martyrs is an *imitatio Christi*, an imitation of the suffering and death of Christ.

This exegetical reading, based on only one element of the Passion – Christ's pierced side – as the culmination of a series of painful sufferings, portrays suffering as intimately uniting Christ's people with him. What Christ lives corresponds to what his people live. The experience of suffering becomes a moment to share, something in common to Christ and to his followers. In addition, as the Passion has been reported in the Gospels so 'that you may believe that Jesus is the Christ, the Son of God, and that believing you may have life in his name' (Jn 20.31), then the suffering of Christ is also ultimately an instrument to believe, to remember and on which to meditate.

SHARING THE SUFFERING OF CHRIST

Sharing suffering finds its central theme in the scene of the Passion of Christ. Early Christian exegetes have generally considered the pain of Christ on the cross rich of deep meaning and have drawn out of it different interpretations. Their hermeneutics has often ranged from soteriological to ecclesiological and sacramental readings. For example, the wounded side of Jesus on the cross, reported only in Jn 19.34, has been

---

[6]The text is extant in a Latin translation and inserted in a *catena* on the fourth Gospel probably by Victor, bishop of Capua. The text informs that human creation is based on the conjunction of three elements, dust, semen and rib, and that because of his wife, as his rib or side, Adam lost paradise. Following this exegetical development, the church receives paradise through the blood of the martyrs and the water of baptism that flowed from the wounded and sacramental side of Christ. Polycarp, *Frag.*, 7 (PG 5, 1028B), 'We are born, since indeed produced by other nature; a woman from the rib of a man already made; but we are out of a seed. Because three may be the principles of the creation of man: dust, rib and seed (*pulvis, costa et semen*). And because of his side, that is the wife, Adam was cast out of paradise. And the sacrament of the side of Christ (*sacramento lateris Christi*), from which flowed the blood of martyrdom (*sanguis martyrii*) and the water of baptism (*aqua baptism*), the Church receives (*recipit*) the paradise.'

interpreted as the place of origin for the church (as Eve from the side of Adam),[7] and his flowing of water and blood, respectively, as the purifying streams of baptism and Eucharist,[8] and more. Besides these hermeneutical approaches, patristic writers have generally thought of the suffering of Christ as a way of sharing human fate with his people. It seems proper to remember that elevating the suffering of Christ to the level of a divine revelation seems to be part of the theological project of the Gospels. Christ hanging from the cross is the visible emblem of how through sufferings one may be victorious. It is, especially in John, another sign of his divinity. Therefore, incarnation and sacrifice emphasize the salvific value of Christ's earthly life and suffering but, at the same time, incorporate humanity in the common experience of sorrow. This perspective animates the whole story of the Passion.

The scene of the Passion is rich in describing Christ's sufferings in all the four gospels. Even the spear wound appears to be the ultimate act of cruelty;[9] it is not certainly a coup de grâce, even if it would have put an end in a more honourable and compassionate way to the torment of the cross, instead of the ignominious and painful method used with the two criminals[10] hanging together with Christ. The Passion is precisely what allows one to perceive a sense of suffering, and it is as well an invitation to contemplate Christ hanging on the cross. This view is not a mere vision,[11] but it is rather a theologically framed revelation of the meaning of the suffering of Christ. Many early Christian writers[12] saw the suffering of Christ essentially as an indication of God's love towards humanity and in a certain sense as a tangible sign of the result of sin. Thus, through undeserved suffering, Christ saves humanity from sin. As M. B. Dinkler states,

---

[7]Methodius of Olympus, *Symp.*, III.8; Augustine, *In Io.Ev.tr*, IX.10, XV.8; Augustine, *En. Ps.*, 40.10; John Chrysostom, *Catech.*, III.17; and others. For further study, see Stefano Salemi, 'Sacramenti tra anamnesi e pictura verbi,' in *O 'Odigos*, Centre P.Salvatore Manna (Bari, 2012), pp. 15–18; Idem, 'Esegesi Ecclesiologica della morte di Cristo', in *Il Sangue della Redenzione*, ed. Michele Colagiovanni, Unione del Prez.issimo Sangue, XII.n.2 (Rome, 2014), pp. 23–59; Idem, 'Aspetti Sacramentali e Aspetti Soteriologici', in *Il Sangue della Redenzione*, X.n.1 (Rome, 2012), pp. 21–15.

[8]Hippolytus of Rome, *Antichr.* XI (also in *De Benedictione Jacobi*); Chrysostom, *Catech.* III.16; Cyril of Alexandria, *Jo.* XII, 19.32-37; Theodore of Mopsuestia, *Jo.* XIX,28-35; and others. See also Manlio Simonetti, *Note su antichi commenti alle Benedizioni dei Patriarchi* (Cagliari: Università di Cagliari, 1961).

[9]A tradition, also reported in the apocryphal Greek 'Acts of Pilate' (16.4) written between the II-III centuries, and then merged as the first eleven chapters of the apocryphal Gospel of Nicodemus in the V century, tells that the soldier Longinus pierced the side of the Lord. Having a disability in his eyes, he was immediately healed with the drops of blood that flowed from Christ's side. Longinus, who looks like a transformation of the Greek word λόγχη (spear), according to tradition, was converted. It is said that he travelled to Cappadocia and preached the Gospel, dying as a martyr.

[10]The *crurifragium* (*crura*= knees; *fragium* = to break) is the breaking of the legs of the condemned to crucifixion, to cause the loss of any foothold resulting in a suffocating hyperextension of the chest (you cannot exhale completely and there is a lack of supply of oxygenated air at the organism).

[11]See Jn 19.35: A.) He who saw this has testified; B.) his testimony is true; C) he knows that he tells the truth.

[12]Ambrose, *Exp. ps.118*. 1; Eusebius, *ComPss* CI.7; John Chrysostom, *Hom.*, LXXXVIII. 1.

just as the ancient Israelite prophets suffered for the benefit of their people, [. . .] Jesus suffers in service to others. This is true in two senses: Jesus suffers, like the Hebrew prophets generally, so that God's people will become aware of and repent from their sin; Jesus also suffers vicariously, like the so-called Suffering Servant of Second Isaiah, suffering though he does not deserve it.[13]

In this line, the writings of Clement of Alexandria (ca.150–ca. 215 CE), around the end of the second century, offer a valid contribution. Among his writings, a text called the *Instructor* (*Paedagogus*) (ca. 190) deals with questions related to the practical and daily moral life. The ethical focus of this writing constitutes the ground to develop an exegesis around the sufferings of Christ. In Book two, elaborating Paul's advice to Timothy 'No longer drink only water, but take a little wine for the sake of your stomach and your frequent ailments' (1 Tim. 5.23), Clements writes,

> The same way, therefore, wine is indeed mixed with water, so it is the spirit with man; as the mixture, nourishes faith, so the Spirit leads into immortality (ἀφθαρσίαν), and the drink of the blended mixture is called Eucharist, called laudable and good grace, and those who partake in faith are sanctified body and soul, that is in the divine mixture, which is man, and that the Father wanted mystically united with the Spirit and the Logos, and verily the spirit is joined to the soul, but the flesh to the Logos, for that the Logos became flesh.[14]

Clement sees the wine mixed with the water of the Eucharist pointing both to the suffering of Christ and to what constitutes a human being, man plus spirit. In this sense, through the Spirit, man can share divine incorruptibility and immortality. The whole image is linked to that of blood and water and strongly oriented towards salvific imagery, while the mixture of these elements leads to eternal life. Therefore, if it is true that Christians may share the sufferings of Christ, it is also true that they share immortality and salvation. Another passage of the same work expands the concept of Clement:

> Then the holy vine brought forth the prophetic cluster (Ἔπειτα ἡ ἄμπελος ἡ ἁγία τὸν βότρυν ἐβλάστησεν τὸν προφητικόν). This is a sign for those who are trained from error to rest, the great cluster (ὁ μέγας βότρυς), the Logos, bruised for us, the blood of grapes, wanted to be mixed with water, as his blood is mixed with salvation (καὶ τὸ αἷμα αὐτοῦ σωτηρίᾳ κίρναται). The blood of the Lord is twofold, for there is his carnal blood that redeems us from destruction, and the spiritual one that anoints us. And, by drinking of the blood of Jesus, we partake of the Lord's

---

[13]M. B. Dinkler, 'Suffering, Misunderstanding, and Suffering Misunderstanding: The Markan Misunderstanding Motif as a Form of Jesus' Suffering', *JSNT* 38, no. 3 (2016): 316–38 (327).

[14]For Clement of Alexandria, see *Clément d'Alexandrie: Le Pédagogue, Livre II*, trans. C. Mondésert, notes H.-I. Marrou, SCh. 108 (Paris: Les Éditions du Cerf, 1965), *Paed.*, 2.20.1-2. (As stated in n.4, all translations into English, when necessary, are personal and intended to offer an easy reading, otherwise noted.)

incorruptibility (Καὶ τοῦτ' ἔστι πιεῖν τὸ αἷμα τοῦ Ἰησοῦ, τῆς κυριακῆς μεταλαβεῖν ἀφθαρσίας), this is for the Logos to the Spirit as the blood to the flesh.[15]

Christ has been bruised, as a cluster of grapes, to offer salvation and to redeem from destruction. Then, suffering is remarked as being integral to salvation. Moreover, partaking of the blood of Jesus means sharing with him. This is possible through a form of assimilation, incorporation or even 'ingestion' of Christ's suffering through the wine of the Lord's Supper, as by drinking Jesus' blood. As Jesus has been bruised for humankind, his blood redeems the believer once he partakes of the wine of the Supper. In this reading, the sacramental moment of the Lord's Supper becomes the hour of sharing the suffering of Christ. Clements connects the suffering of Christ to the Lord's Supper as another most sublime way of understanding how to partake with Christ. Certainly, one of the most common ways of thinking how the believers may share the suffering of Christ is that of martyrdom.

BLOOD-BAPTISM

Ignace De La Potterie recognizes that these elements of the Passion of Christ, blood and water flowing from the side of Jesus 'certainly have a profound symbolic significance'.[16] Therefore, after a long discussion about the prophetical quotations of John, he places the suffering of Christ in the context of the Feast of Tabernacles and the celebrations related to water. In this development, he refers to Hippolytus of Rome (ca. 170–235 CE) for a summary of his exegesis.

Actually, in the *Apostolic Tradition (Traditio Apostolica)*, traditionally ascribed to Hippolytus but not without problems,[17] we find a text where the idea that the two elements, water and blood, have a symbolic meaning is strongly supported. However, differently from the sacramental reading of Clement, according to the *Apostolic Tradition*, through the blood of Christ, the believers receive the water of the Spirit and the outward sign of Christ's death becomes a manifestation of God's self-sacrifice. This creates a strong link between the sufferings of Jesus and those of the martyrs on the level of the common experience. By stating that the martyrdom should not be a hindrance to faith, this early Christian treatise claims that when the martyrs suffer violence, then their sins are removed because 'they have received the baptism in their own blood'.[18]

---

[15]Ibid., *Paed.*, 2.19.3-4–2.20.1.

[16]I. De La Potterie, *Il Mistero del cuore trafitto* (Bologna: Edizioni Dehoniane, 1988), p. 37, 'hanno certamente una profonda portata simbolica'.

[17]The authorship is object of discussion. See, A. Brent, *Hippolytus and the Roman Church in the Third Century: Communities in Tension before the Emergence of a Monarch-Bishop*, SupVCh 31 (Leiden: E.J. Brill, 1995).

[18]*Trad. Ap.*, 19.2. The *Apostolic Tradition* is partly preserved in Latin and in several oriental versions (Coptic, Arab, Ethiopic and others), though the original Greek is lost (fragments are present in the heavily edited excerpts in the Apostolic Constitutions). My translation here is based on the one of G. Dix in *The*

This concept becomes stronger in Hyppolitus' *On Christ and Antichrist (Demonstratio de Christo et antichristo)* where he turns to a typological reading of the wounded side of Jesus as a squeezed bunch of grapes, highlighting visually the value of blood, 'He will wash his garment in wine, the paternal gift of the Holy Spirit, descended on him at the Jordan . . . in the blood therefore of which grape if not of its holy flesh pressed on wood like a bunch? From whose side flowed two sources of blood and water from which the people are purified.[19]

The text presents a theological framework composed of many biblical references that form a very solid plot where the gush of water mixed with blood points first to the suffering of Christ as a means of purification. Then, the image of Christ as a bunch of grapes, hanging from the cross, is rendered more concrete and vivid with the addition of the action of being pressed on the wood, which should be identified with the spear blow. This evocative image of suffering, even if not developed extensively around the concept of blood-baptism, still conveys an important concept which is more articulated in other early Christian writers such as Cyril, and which, therefore, requires much attention.

Cyril of Jerusalem, to a certain degree routed in the Antiochene tradition, active in Palestine in the fourth century CE (ca. 315–387), exerts particularly tense preaching to fight Docetism, in order to affirm the reality of Incarnation. His *Catechetical Lectures*[20] propose a synthesis of Christian doctrine in a Christocentric key, with a focus on the Passion. Among the most precious memories of Christian antiquity, the Catecheses offer a clear view of the life of the communities of the fourth century, in places close to the origin of Christianity. The main important topic of these catechetical lectures is the mystagogical initiation to the Christian life, highlighting particularly the meaning of baptism and then of the other sacraments. In exposing the reality of the sacraments, Cyril implements an exegetical method that is functional to pastoral purposes. More than allegory, typology prevails to show the unity of Scriptures and especially the convergence of them into the living reality of the sacraments.

In his third catechetical lecture on baptism, Cyril writes:

Whoever does not receive baptism, he is not saved. Only the martyrs reach the kingdom without the baptism of water, because when the Saviour on the Cross redeemed the world, pierced in his side, he shed forth blood and water; that men living in times of peace might be baptized in water, and in times of persecution in their own blood. Martyrdom is what the Saviour intended to mention by

---

Treatise on the Apostolic Tradition of St. Hippolytus of Rome, Bishop and Martyr (London: Alban Press, 1992), and on that of B. Botte in *La Tradition Apostolique*, SCh 11 bis (Paris: Les Éditions du Cerf, 1984).
[19]For Hippolytus, see G. Garitte, *Traités d'Hippolyte sur David et Goliath, sur le Cantique des Cantiques et sur l'Antéchrist*, CSCO 263 (Peeters Publishers, 1965), *Antichr.* XI.
[20]Collection of twenty-three lectures given to catechumens in Jerusalem, recorded by stenographers. There is a current debate about the attribution of all or part of the catechesis to Cyril, or to his successor in Jerusalem (John 386–417). See, J. Quaster, *Patrology*, vol. 1 (Utrecht: Spectrum Publishers, 1950).

using baptism in that expression 'Can you drink the cup that I must drink and be baptized of the baptism with which I must be baptized?' (Mk 10.38) Yes, even the martyrs, making themselves objects of admiration before the angels and men (1Cor. 4.9), they profess the faith that you soon will profess. But, it is not yet the time for you to hear of this.[21]

Only through baptism, there is salvation. Nevertheless, baptism is not only the one performed in water. Martyrs can be baptized in blood. Cyril intends the two distinct streams of liquids, from the pierced side of Jesus, as a prefiguration of these two separate baptisms. Therefore, while water baptism is what the believer receives in times of peace, the baptism of blood is for the martyrs in times of persecution. Cyril paired the words of Jesus in Mark to his concept of blood-baptism, 'Can you drink the cup that I must drink and be baptized of the baptism with which I must be baptized?' He does it in order to support the sacramental–baptismal reading of the Passion and to establish the suffering of Christ as prophetically pointing to all the sufferings of martyrs. According to Cyril, God made water mixed with blood coming out to indicate this double baptismal dimension. This makes the suffering of Christ the suffering of people. Martyrdom, in times of persecution, can be considered in light of the words of Jesus in Mk 10.38 where Jesus' suffering and death are called a 'baptism'. All those who are persecuted share with Christ his baptism of blood. The bishop of Jerusalem is one of the few who have seen a relation between the two types of baptism as prefigured in the dual flow of blood and water from Christ's side.

In the thirteenth catechesis, Cyril continues highlighting the parallelism between the suffering of Christ and that of the martyrs but diverging from the soteriological approach of the third catechesis in order to introduce a sacramental reading based, as he claims, on the Fathers. He says,

> Our Fathers, as exegetes, have provided also another reason for this reality. In fact, since in the Gospels the power of salvific baptism is double, one is given to the baptized ones through the water, the second to the martyrs who are in persecution by their own shed blood, there came out of that saving Side blood and water, one for the confession in favour of Christ, while in the mystery of baptism the grace of martyrdom is confirmed.[22]

In the previous paragraph (20) of this catechesis, Cyril speaks of the cross. He presents thematic parallelisms between Moses and Christ. The serpent elevated by Moses in the wilderness appears as a figure of Christ. His 'symmetrical' typological interpretation allows Cyril to establish, once more, that baptism is as well a figure of the sufferings of Christ and of the martyrs, a blood-baptism.

---

[21]For Cyril of Jerusalem, see *Cyrille de Jérusalem: Catéchèses mystagogiques*, ed. A. Piédagnel, trans. P. Paris, SCh 126bis (Paris: Les Éditions du Cerf, 1966, reprinted 2009), pp. 82–174; *Catech.* III.10; my translation is here based on Edward Hamilton Gifford (trans.), *The Catechetical Lectures of St. Cyril*, ed. Philip Schaff (New York: Christian Literature Publishing Co., 1893; reprint, Peabody, MA: Hendrickson, 1994).

[22]Cyril of Jerusalem, *Catech.* XIII.21.

As it is written in 2 Tim. 3.12, 'Indeed, all who want to live a godly life in Christ Jesus will be persecuted', those who experience persecution for their faith in Christ may draw a lesson of strength and comfort from these words. God does not prevent sufferings, but he shares them and he works them out for good to those who maintain their faith in trials and conflicts. Cyril sees in blood-baptism not only a form of sharing the same experience of Christ but also the salvific value of this experience. Unity with Christ in suffering means unity with Christ in glory. Through faith, the martyrs rest in God in their darkest hour. Faith alone can look beyond the persecution to estimate aright the worth of salvation. Even in the Gospel, Christ does not present to his followers the hope of earthly riches or a life free of trials. In Jn 16.33, Jesus says that 'in the world you face persecution. But take courage; I have conquered the world.'

Cyril's words are a call to follow Christ in the path of self-denial and reproach. Christ himself, in order to save the world, was opposed by any form of suffering. Therefore, persecution and pains await all who are imbued with the Spirit of Christ. In all ages, martyrs had to pass through the baptism of blood. They have been tortured and put to death, but in dying, they became conquerors as Christ conquered. Even if they had been incarcerated in prison walls, their spirit could not be imprisoned. Through trial and persecution, the character of Christ is revealed in his people. They follow Christ through sore conflicts and endure self-denial and bitter disappointments. Being partakers of Christ's suffering, they look beyond the gloom to the glory, joining the words of Paul, 'I consider that the sufferings of this present time are not worth comparing with the glory about to be revealed to us' (Rom. 8.18).

CHRIST'S SUFFERING, A FORM OF FELLOWSHIP (ΚΟΙΝΩΝΙΑ): ΜΙΜΗΣΙΣ, ΕἸΚΌΝΙ, ἈΛΗΘΕΙΑ, ὉΜΟΙΩΜΑ

In his catechetical lectures, Cyril talks of the experience of all who share the sufferings of Christ as a form of fellowship:

O strange and inconceivable thing! We did not really die, we were not really buried, we were not really crucified and raised again; but while our imitation was in a figure (ἐν εἰκόνι ἡ μίμησις), our salvation is in reality. Christ was indeed crucified and indeed buried, and actually rose again. He has freely bestowed upon us all these things, so that we, by imitation, communicating in his sufferings, might truly gain salvation. O surpassing loving-kindness! Christ suffered anguish and received nails in His undefiled hands and feet. While he freely bestows salvation on me without pain or toil by the fellowship of His pain. (καὶ ἀπονητὶ χαρίζεται διὰ τῆς κοινωνίας τὴν σωτηρίαν).[23]

---

[23]Cyril of Jerusalem, *Catech.*, XX.5 (*Mystagogical Catechesis* 2).

Baptism is certainly seen as an antitype of the Passion of Christ in Cyril (τοῦ Χριστοῦ παθημάτων ἀντίτυπον)[24] in the previous paragraphs of this catechesis. He advances a doctrine of baptism as conformity to the Passion and death of Christ, then ultimately to his suffering. Cyril uses the term 'similitude' (μίμησις) and 'participation' (κοινωνία) in reference to Christ's Passion. In this sense, blood-baptism or martyrdom is participation (κοινωνία) to the sufferings of Christ through similitude (μίμησις). Paul, quoted by Cyril in this catechesis, confirms it in Rom. 6.5, 'For if we have been united with him in a death like his, we will certainly be united with him in a resurrection like his.' Cyril understands that this death implies the imitation of Christ's sufferings and, much more, a form of fellowship with him. Paradoxically, if, on the one hand, there is the imitation of the sufferings, on the other, there is also the reality of salvation. In effect, baptism is both a figure of the Passion and of the resurrection. In fact, the development and enrichment given to this concept are worthy of notice. When Cyril explains it, he clearly states that the imitation is effected in an image (ἐν εἰκόνι) while salvation in reality (ἐν ἀλήθεια). While sharing by imitation in Christ's sufferings, one might truly obtain salvation; by communion in/with his sufferings, Christ imparts the grace of salvation.

Cyril continues, in the following paragraphs (6–7), by saying that baptism constitutes the fellowship by the representation of Christ's true sufferings (ἔτι δὲ καὶ τῶν ἀληθινῶν τοῦ Χριστοῦ παθημάτων ἐν μιμήσει ἔχον τὴν κοινωνίαν).[25] He says that we may learn that all the pain Christ suffered, he endured it for our salvation in reality, and not in appearance, and that we are partakers in His sufferings. In fact, everything 'happened really to Him; but in your case, there was only a likeness (ὁμοίωμα) of death and sufferings, whereas of salvation there was not a likeness but a reality'.[26]

Following this concept, water baptism symbolizes the suffering of Christ (τοῦ Χριστοῦ παθημάτων ἀντίτυπον), as well as blood-baptism, and unites in a κοινωνία by imitation of the real sufferings of Christ. What the believers live in a figurative way through baptism, mirroring what Christ truly lived is in a certain sense a 'likeness' (ὁμοίωμα) of Christ's suffering. This is here presented as in comparison and contrast with the reality (ἀλήθεια) of what Christ suffered. This particular form of typological language is open to a sacramental realism constituted by the use of μίμησις, εἰκόνι, ἀλήθεια, ὁμοίωμα, to describe the symbiotic experience of Christ and his people in suffering as a form of κοινωνία. This concept acquires a more articulated nature in the writings of Eusebius of Caesarea.

CHRIST RELIVES IN THE MARTYRS: LOCUS REVELATIONI

Eusebius of Caesarea (ca. 265–ca. 340) was a prolific writer with various interests (theological, philosophical, apologetic and exegetical). Not immune to the Aryan

---

[24]Ibid., *Catech.*, XX.6.
[25]Ibid., *Catech.*, XX.6.
[26]Ibid., *Catech.*, XX.7.

tendencies, he is led to the condemnation of the Council of Antioch. Eventually, he surrenders to Christian orthodoxy in the next Council of Nicaea (325). He devoted himself to investigate the difference between the persons of the Trinity with a subordinate vision of the Son to the Father. Among his greatest works, worthy of mention is the 'Historia Ecclesiastica'.[27] In this text, a letter about the martyrs of Lyon is recorded. This anonymous document, sent by a witness to his brothers of Asia, is the testimony of the persecution of 177 CE. In the letter, the sad account of the persecution is inserted into the background of the Passion of Christ. The redeeming death of the Lord is presented as evidence of the faith of the martyrs. After a discourse around a deacon of Vienne and his Christian testimony (I am a Christian! Χριστιανός εἰμι), while tortured by incandescent bronze, Eusebius writes that he[28]

> remained unbending and unyielding, firm in his confession of faith, sprinkled and refreshed by the heavenly source of the water of life (ὕδατος τῆς ζωῆς) that flows from the belly (νηδύος) of Christ. His poor flesh, however, bore witness to that which was inflicted, all one wound, all a clot, all wrinkled and unrecognizable in his human form. And Christ, suffering in him, obtained great glory (ἐν ᾧ πάσχων Χριστὸς μεγάλας ἐπετέλει δόξας), annihilating the adversary and showing, as an example for everyone else, that nothing is fearful where there is the love of the Father, that nothing is painful where there is the glory of Christ.[29]

The water gushed from the bowels of Christ is the water of life that soothes the pain of martyrdom, because Christ relives in the martyr. The martyr, suffering in the flesh, obtains with Christ great glory. The sacrifice of the martyr becomes the opportunity for the Passion to be revived. Therefore, if Cyril developed the idea of a κοινωνία of suffering, in the text of Eusebius suffering is, to a certain degree, a form of embodiment of Christ in the life of the martyr. The martyr becomes the place of a special revelation of the suffering Christ and ultimately of a divine revelation. He is indeed *locus revelationi* of a true *theologia crucis*. And, where Christ's glory is, there is no pain (μηδὲ ἀλγεινὸν ὅπου Χριστοῦ δόξα). As Randazzo articulates, suffering is

---

[27]Written in the early fourth century and consisting of ten books about the period between the birth of the church and Licinius' defeat by Constantine (324); a valuable source of information on many different writings and excerpts otherwise lost.

[28]In reference to the Passion or Perpetua, martyrdom and related arguments, see also Judith Perkins, 'Perpetua's *vas*: Asserting Christian Identity', in *Group Identity and Religious Individuality in Late Antiquity*, eds É. Rebillard and J. Rüpke (Washington, DC: The Catholic University of America Press, 2015), pp. 129–65.

[29]For Eusebius, see *Eusèbe de Césarée: Histoire ecclésiastique*, ed. F. Richard, trans. G. Bardy, rev. L. Neyrand, Sagesses chrétiennes (Paris: Les Éditions du Cerf, 2003), and *Eusèbe de Césarée: Histoire ecclésiastique, Livres V-VII*, ed. G. Bardy, SCh 41 (Paris: Les Éditions du Cerf, 1984, reprinted, 1995); *HE.*, V.1,22–23. For another English translation, see *Eusebius: The History of the Church*, ed. A. Louth, trans. Williamson (London and New York: Penguin Classics, 1989).

a gift of both the Father and the Son, and when the believer relies on them, he will receive the strength to bear physical and spiritual suffering.[30]

SUFFERING OF CHRIST: LIFE TO DYING PEOPLE

In his Commentary on the Psalms, Eusebius evokes a striking image from Ps. 102.7-9, which sees a flow of life-giving blood falling from the pierced side of Jesus over his people. Eusebius attributes the remarkable story of the lonely pelican cited in the Psalm to the Lord Jesus himself. This is because of the great love[31] that the pelican has in feeding its 'children', and for its spirit of protection towards them. The pelican, flying up, shakes its wings with great force, from which drops of blood ooze cut through the clouds and give back life to those who have been killed by the snake attacking the nest. He says,

> For pelican, therefore, it is meant the Lord, and his little ones are the first men formed, the nest is the paradise, and the serpent is the apostate devil. The latter has blown through the transgression of those first men placed in paradise, and brought in them mortality, but Christ, in His love for us, lifted up on the cross and pierced in his side, from there he has made oozing the blood that gives life, and through the cloud of the Holy Spirit, he has given life to us who were dead.[32]

The life-giving blood oozed through the cloud of the Holy Spirit is undoubtedly among the most beautiful and poetic descriptions that may be encountered in the patristic interpretations of the suffering of Christ as a symbol of life for his dying people. The event described emphasizes the love of Christ, his paternal protection, his victory over the devil and the offer of paradise. All this is implied, for Eusebius, in the exalted suffering Christ on the cross. The sufferings of Christ are a source of life and love. The believers may receive life and be nourished. Finally, what Christ has suffered on the cross constitutes the defeat of the serpent, the apostate devil. Sanctified by the cloud of the Spirit, the blood of Christ, emblem of his suffering, anoints the people and brings them back from death to life. Paradoxically, suffering and death are the means to obtain true life and peace.

CONCLUSION

Suffering is a human and Christian experience. Christ and his people, as both the New Testament and the early church highlighted, share the same experience. The sufferings that human beings live are both instruments of sanctification and prelude of

---

[30]'la sofferenza figura come dono di Dio e del Figlio e, conseguentemente, l'uomo che si rivolge a loro e li segue diviene sopportatore della sofferenza fisica e spirituale,' Cinzia Randazzo, *Il senso della sofferenza e della morte ai primissimi esordi del cristianesimo* (Tricase, IT: Youcanprint, 2017), 'Conclusion.'

[31]About the question of suffering as expression of love, see also J. M. Hallman, 'Divine Suffering and Change in Origen and *Ad Theopompum*', *SC/JECS* 7, no. 2 (1989–90): 85–98.

[32]Eusebius of Cesarea, *ComPss,* Ps. CI.7 (PG 23, 1256AB).

future glory. In addition, the early church developed a theological framework rich in insights regarding the sufferings of the believers as a reflection of Christ's sufferings. The Passion on the cross has remained at the centre of many interpretations. Six main lines of hermeneutics have been here analysed.

1. While the suffering of Christ's people has been perceived as an *imitatio Christi*, Christ's suffering has been seen as a *prefiguratio mortis* for his people. Suffering is, therefore, an element of union between Christ and the Christians. The believers may take part in Christ's suffering as a form of imitation, while what Christ has lived on the cross foreshadows the experiences of physical and mental sufferings that Christians may live because of their faith. Suffering intimately unites Christ's people to him and this becomes a sharable moment and a common experience.

2. Sharing Christ's suffering has been at the centre of many exegetical developments of sacramental and soteriological nuance. Often, the sharing of the Lord's Supper has been interpreted as to have a meaning for the community in reference to the suffering of Christ. By partaking of the wine, the believers recall, share and incorporate the suffering of Christ as well as the promise of salvation and immortality. Drinking of the cup is a form of assimilation of the suffering of Christ.

3. The Passion of Christ, as the most emblematic moment of the suffering of the Lord, has attracted the attention of the early church in developing a systematic theology centred on the idea of Christ as the proto-martyr. In this argumentation, the blood of Christ and the experience of the martyrs have offered the perfect ground to advance the concept of blood-baptism as the encounter of Christ's and people's suffering. According to authors like Cyril, the mixing of water and blood flowing from Christ's pierced side are purposely pointing to the experience of all those who will pass persecution and will be baptized in the blood of martyrdom.

4. Christian suffering creates fellowship, the κοινωνία of Christ's suffering. The baptism in water is both a figure of the Passion and of the resurrection. In baptism, the believer imitates the suffering of Christ but also he truly obtains salvation. By communion with Christ, the people receive the grace of life. Baptism constitutes a lesson regarding the suffering Christ had to live in order to save humanity. Therefore, water baptism is a symbol of the sufferings of Christ. The believers in a figurative way, through baptism, live Christ's suffering and enter in his communion.

5. The sufferings of the martyrs are the time and space in which Christ's suffering may be revived. The martyr is truly a *locus revelationi* of God and of the real meaning of suffering. At the centre of this *theologia crucis* there is Christ's suffering renewed in people's suffering. In all of this, God's glory is manifested. Therefore, martyrdom becomes the moment and the place of a special divine revelation.

6. When believers suffer, the suffering of Christ offers comfort. His sacrifice is evidence of his paternal love and care for his people, and assurance of victory over pain, sorrow and the devil. Paradoxically, only through suffering and death, sanctified by the Spirit, there is true life, peace and salvation.

The theological frame resulted from the few examples here taken in examination from early Christian theologies clearly portrays suffering as part of a journey towards salvation in its broader sense. The exegetical passages here considered show the importance of understanding that suffering is part of Christian life. Suffering is God's work to sanctify the believers, and vice-versa it is also a way through which believers can glorify God in the world. When one suffers for the name of Christ, he can rejoice, knowing that suffering for Christ brings great joy in the promise of salvation. Even Girardi, elaborating on the reflections of Basil of Cesarea, explains that Christian joy is intertwined with the most frequent antithesis represented by pain, suffering, persecution and death. The problem of evil and its origin is the cause of anguish for a Christian who holds firm to the dogma of a good God. The answer does not presume to explain the mystery. Suffering and evil call into question human freedom and the intrinsic limit of creation. According to Girardi, Basil sees suffering as a joyful response of love and service based essentially on Pauline texts, configuring the suffering joy of the Christian on the model of Paul as a form of identification with Christ and his death.[33]

Remembering this may transform the way Christians face and understand the sufferings of this life. Christ is present in suffering; everyone who suffers is part of Christ's κοινωνία of suffering. Suffering is an elected form of divine revelation, a special *locus revelationi* and a *memento* of Christ's love and offer of grace. The early church imbued its systematic theology of Christ's suffering as the element par excellence to share fully with Christ. It is indeed *theologia crucis*. True communion with Christ is a symbiotic relationship where the suffering of Christ is indeed the suffering of people in its fullest sense.

BIBLIOGRAPHY

Bardy, G. *Eusèbe de Césarée: Histoire ecclésiastique, Livres V-VII*. SCh 41. Paris: Les Éditions du Cerf, 1984, reprinted, 1995.
Botte, B. *La Tradition Apostolique*. SCh 11 bis. Paris: Les Éditions du Cerf, 1984.
Brent, A. *Hippolytus and the Roman Church in the Third Century: Communities in Tension before the Emergence of a Monarch-Bishop*. SupVCh, 31. Leiden: E.J. Brill, 1995.
De La Potterie, I. *Il Mistero del cuore trafitto*. Bologna: Edizioni Dehoniane, 1988.
Dinkler, M. B. 'Suffering, Misunderstanding, and Suffering Misunderstanding: The Markan Misunderstanding Motif as a Form of Jesus' Suffering', *JSNT* 38, no. 3 (2016): 316–38.

[33]M. Girardi, 'Gioia, dolere, persecuzione in Basilio di Cesarea', in *Gioia, sofferenza, persecuzione nei Padri della Chiesa*, ed. S. A. Panimolle, Dizionario di spiritualità biblico-patristica 27 (Roma: Borla, 2000), pp. 168–98. See all the volume for further study.

Dix, G. (ed.). *The Treatise on the Apostolic Tradition of St. Hippolytus of Rome, Bishop and Martyr*. London: Alban Press, 1992.

Garitte, G. *Traités d'Hippolyte sur David et Goliath, sur le Cantique des Cantiques et sur l'Antéchrist*. CSCO 263. Leuven: Peeters Publishers, 1965.

Girardi, M. 'Gioia, dolere, persecuzione in Basilio di Cesarea', in S. A. Panimolle (ed.), *Gioia, sofferenza, persecuzione nei Padri della Chiesa*, 168–98. Dizionario di spiritualità biblico-patristica 27. Roma: Borla, 2000.

Hallman, J. M. 'Divine Suffering and Change in Origen and *Ad Theopompum*', *SC/JECS* 7, no. 2 (1989–1990): 85–98.

Hamilton Gifford, E. (trans.). *The Catechetical Lectures of St. Cyril*, ed. Philip Schaff. New York: Christian Literature Publishing Co., 1893; reprint, Peabody, MA: Hendrickson, 1994.

Hartog, P. (ed.). *Polycarp's Epistle to the Philippians and the Martyrdom of Polycarp*. Oxford: Oxford University Press, 2013.

Holmes, M. W. *The Apostolic Fathers: Greek Texts and English Translations*, 3rd edn. Grand Rapids, MI: Baker Books, 2007.

Jewett, R. *Romans: A Commentary*. 'Hermeneia'. Minneapolis, MN: Augsburg Fortress, 2007.

Lefebure, L. D. 'The Understanding of Suffering in the Early Christian Church', CLARITAS, *JDC* 4, no. 2 (2015): 28–37.

Longenecker, R. N. *The Epistle to Romans*. 'NIGTC'. Grand Rapids, MI: Eerdmans, 2016.

Marrou, H.-I. (ed.). *Clément d'Alexandrie: Le Pédagogue, Livre II*, trans. C. Mondésert. SCh 108. Paris: Les Éditions du Cerf, 1965.

Moo, D. J. *The Epistle to the Romans*. 'NICNT'. Grand Rapids, MI: Eerdmans, 1996.

Perkins, J. 'Perpetua's *vas*: Asserting Christian Identity', in É. Rebillard and J. Rüpke (eds), *Group Identity and Religious Individuality in Late Antiquity*, 129–65. Washington, DC: The Catholic University of America Press, 2015.

Piédagnel, A. (ed.). *Cyrille de Jérusalem. Catéchèses mystagogiques*, trans. P. Paris. SCh, 126. Paris: Les Éditions du Cerf, 1966.

Quaster, J. *Patrology*, vol. 1. Utrecht: Spectrum Publishers, 1950.

Randazzo, C. *Il senso della sofferenza e della morte ai primissimi esordi del cristianesimo*. Tricase: Youcanprint, 2017.

Richard, F. (ed.). *Eusèbe de Césarée: Histoire ecclésiastique*, trans. G. Bardy, rev. L. Neyrand. Sagesses Chrétiennes. Paris: Les Éditions du Cerf, 2003.

Salemi, S. 'Aspetti Sacramentali e Aspetti Soteriologici', in Michele Colagiovanni (ed.), *Il Sangue della Redenzione*, 21–115. Unione del Prez.issimo Sangue, X.n.1. Roma: Sanguis Editrice, 2012.

Salemi, S. 'Sacramenti tra anamnesi e pictura verbi', in O 'Odigos, 15–18. Centre P.Salvatore Manna. Bari: Centro P. Salvatore Manna, 2012.

Salemi, S. 'Esegesi Ecclesiologica della morte di Cristo', in Michele Colagiovanni (ed.), *Il Sangue della Redenzione*, 23–59. Unione del Prez.issimo Sangue, XII.n.2. Roma: Sanguis Editrice, 2014.

Selling, J. 'A Credible Response to the Meaning of Suffering', in J. Lambrecht and R. Collins (eds), *God and Human Suffering*. Louvain: Peeters, 1990.

Simonetti, M. *Note su antichi commenti alle Benedizioni dei Patriarchi*. Cagliari: Università di Cagliari, 1961.

CHAPTER 34

The Church

One, holy, catholic, apostolic

NICHOLAS SAGOVSKY

INTRODUCTION: FROM THE EARLIEST CHURCHES TO THE COUNCIL OF CONSTANTINOPLE (381)

The overwhelming preoccupation of the early Christians was the attainment of salvation. The Christian Faith was a lived response to the question, 'What must I do to be saved?' (cf. Acts 16.30). 'Being saved' was both an event and a practice. In baptism there was a new beginning; through baptism converts passed from death to life; in a proleptic sense they were at that point 'raised with Christ' (Col 2.12-13). But in a physical sense they were not yet 'raised' (cf. 2 Tim. 2.18): in this world, they had to 'lead lives worthy of the Lord' (Col. 1.10). Many early Christian texts characterize the sort of behaviour to be expected from the members of God's holy people ('saints') whom the Spirit is assuredly guiding towards life in the world to come.

The oldest professions of faith by Christians say nothing about the church.[1] They are focused, first, on Jesus Christ as Lord (1 Cor. 12.3) or Son of God (Jn 11.27); then on God, Father, Son and Holy Spirit (cf. Matt. 28.19). Public profession of faith was the pre-requisite for baptism into Christ and for further instruction in the faith. Those who confessed with their lips that 'Jesus is Lord' and believed in their hearts that he had been raised from the dead (cf. Rom. 10.9; Acts 8.37-38; Mk 16.16) were numbered among the saved.

It was not until controversies arose about the nature and boundaries of the church that the 'marks' (*notae*) of the church – that it is 'one, holy, catholic and apostolic' – were sifted from experience of life – especially from worship – in the church and made explicit. In the earliest years, it was enough for baptized Christians to profess their belief in God, Father, Son and Holy Spirit and share in the Eucharist with other Christians, but from the second century on, as broadly Christian groups

---

[1]See J. N. D. Kelly, *Early Christian Creeds*, 3rd edn (Harlow: Longman, 1972), pp. 1–29.

proliferated, the question was asked with increasing urgency, 'Which purportedly Christian religious or philosophical group should I belong to and why?'

The church of the second century was increasingly aware of its far-flung reach. It consistently claimed that the Eucharist offers to believers a pledge (sacrament) of their salvation, 'of immortality'. It maintained the discipline that only its own, baptized members could participate in the Eucharist (cf. *Didache* 9:5). Sharing in the Eucharist was seen as 'a taste' of the world to come. The gathered eucharistic body is characterized by a 'sharing' (*koinonia*) in the very life of God. This 'sharing' is guided and sustained by the ministry of recognized leaders (*episkopoi, presbuteroi*) whose responsibility, individually and corporately, is to ensure that the whole body, the whole 'communion of local communities' which constitutes the Catholic Church, remains faithful to the apostolic witness that has been passed down to them.[2]

When Hippolytus expounded what he called 'The Apostolic Tradition' about the year 215, he described the threefold baptismal interrogation of catechumens in Rome. First, they were asked, 'Dost thou believe in God the Father Almighty?', to which they responded, 'I believe' and were submerged for the first time. Then they were asked, 'Dost thou believe in Christ Jesus, the Son of God?', to which they replied, 'I believe' and were submerged a second time. Finally, they were asked, 'Dost thou believe in the Holy Spirit, in the holy Church, and the resurrection of the flesh?', to which they responded, 'I believe' and were submerged for the third time.[3] The third article of the creed used by the Church of Rome (from which the Apostles' Creed was later developed) included by this time belief in 'the Holy Spirit, the holy Church, the remission of sins, the resurrection of the flesh'.[4]

From the second century, the bishops of the local churches began to meet in synods to resolve conflicts and to discuss matters of common interest.[5] The scale of such synods, which usually met in great cities, grew, until, in 325, with the active support of the Emperor Constantine, the first synod which brought together bishops from the whole Empire met at Nicaea, near Constantinople. Christianity had recently been given a privileged position, though the emperor himself was not yet a baptized Christian.[6] Later synods recognized the Council of Nicaea as the first ecumenical Council. A further major council, with little representation from the West but recognized by later councils as ecumenical, met at Constantinople in 381. The bishops who met at the First Council of Constantinople formally 'received' the creed of the Council of Nicaea as an expression of the church's faith. In the face of the violent controversy there was at that time about the identity of the Holy Spirit, these bishops accepted as an expression of 'the Nicene faith' a credal text which

---

[2]See J.-M. R. Tillard, *Église d'Églises, L'ecclésiologie de communion* (Paris: Éditions du Cerf, 1987).
[3]*Ap.Trad.*, pp. 36–7. In a footnote, Dix gives later variants of these questions, which, for the third question, include 'Dost thou believe . . . in one Baptism in the Holy Catholic Apostolic Church for life eternal?'
[4]Kelly, *Early Christian Creeds*, pp. 100–30, 152.
[5]See R. MacMullen, *Voting about God in Early Church Councils* (New Haven, CT and London: Yale University Press, 2006).
[6]Eusebius, *V. C.* in eds A. Cameron and S. G. Hall (Oxford: Clarendon Press, 1999), pp. 122–7, 177–8.

enlarged on the third article of the Nicene Creed. The phrase 'one holy, catholic, and apostolic Church' was thus incorporated into the credal teaching received by the Council.[7] In affirming their faith in the church, the bishops also affirmed their faith in 'one baptism to [for] the remission of sins . . . the resurrection of the dead and the life of the world to come'.

THE CHURCH IN THE EARLIEST CHRISTIAN WRITINGS

Only after considerable reflection by those who participated in the life of the church had certain central themes – unity, holiness, catholicity and apostolicity – emerged. In the second and third centuries these are so closely interwoven that it would be artificial to tease them out too sharply as distinct strands. The *unity* that should be experienced by the disciples of Christ goes back to the prayer of Jesus himself (cf. Jn 17.20ff.). This unity is just one aspect of the *holiness* of the church (cf. Eph. 5.26-27). This united and holy church is to be open to all throughout the world; it is to be all-inclusive (Gal. 3.27-29). The word that came to be used, borrowed from contemporary Greek thought, was *catholic*. The church was seen as a building, securely founded on Jesus Christ and the witness of the *apostles* (Eph. 2.20). In the earliest Christian writers these four interwoven themes are developed richly.

The first letter of Clement

The first letter of Clement, which reflects the preoccupations of the Church of Rome, was written towards the end of the first century in an attempt to restore order to the church of Corinth. The deposition of certain presbyters had split the church. Clement weighed in in their favour as he believed them to have been appointed by the apostles and to be beyond reproach:

> The apostles received the gospel for us from the Lord Jesus Christ: Jesus the Christ was sent forth from God. So then Christ is from God, and the apostles are from Christ. Both, therefore, came of the will of God in good order. . . . So, preaching both in the country and in the towns, [the apostles] appointed their first fruits, when they had tested them by the Spirit, to be bishops and deacons for the future believers. (42)[8]

Clement saw a direct line of succession from the apostles to the leaders of the church in Corinth who, he says, had 'ministered to the flock of Christ blamelessly, humbly, peaceably, and unselfishly' and had 'offered the gifts (led the church's eucharistic

---

[7]Kelly notes (*Early Christian Creeds*, p. 331) that there is no contemporary account of the precise credal text that was received, in addition to that of Nicaea, at the Council of Constantinople: we only have the text of the Niceno-Constantinopolitan Creed as reported to the Council of Chalcedon in 451.

[8]For translations from The Apostolic Fathers, including Ignatius and *The Shepherd of Hermas*, I have used M. W. Holmes (eds), *The Apostolic Fathers*, 3rd edn (Grand Rapids, MI: Baker Academic, 2007).

worship) blamelessly and in holiness' (44). In arguing strongly against the ministers' deposition, he was concerned that the bitterly divided church in Corinth should be united, holy *and* apostolic.

Ignatius of Antioch

It is now generally accepted that we have seven genuine letters from Ignatius, six to churches and one to Polycarp, bishop of Smyrna (whose death is described in the *Church History* of Eusebius). These letters were written as Ignatius travelled from Antioch, where he was bishop, to Rome, where he expected to be put to death. He is thought to have died in Rome, perhaps in the Colosseum, about 107. Like Paul, and 'John', author of the book of Revelation, Ignatius wrote letters of encouragement to the churches of Asia Minor, urging them to remain faithful in their commitment to Christ. Unlike Paul and 'John', he is preoccupied with the structure of authority within the churches, focusing on the bishop and the presbyters, together with the deacons, a ministerial body that together serves the unity of the whole church. To the Philadelphians he wrote,

> I called out when I was with you; I was speaking with a loud voice, God's voice: 'Pay attention to the bishop, the council of presbyters, and the deacons.' . . . The Spirit itself was preaching, saying the words: 'Do nothing without the bishop. . . . Love unity. Flee from divisions. Become imitators of Jesus Christ, just as he is of his Father.' (7)

To the Smyrnaeans he wrote,

> Flee from divisions, as the beginning of evils. . . . Let no one do anything that has to do with the church without the bishop. Only that Eucharist which is under the authority of the bishop (or whomever he himself designates) is to be considered valid. Wherever the bishop appears, there let the congregation be; just as wherever Jesus Christ is, there is the catholic Church. (8)

This is the first known use of 'catholic' to describe the universal church.[9] As with the Fourth Gospel, Ignatius is writing against Docetists who claimed that Jesus only appeared to be human, that he had not really died and that the Eucharist was not really a participation in his flesh and blood. He passionately wanted the churches to which he wrote to remain united as they followed the teaching they had received from the first, apostolic generation of Christians about Jesus Christ 'son of man and son of God'. They are to share in the 'harmony' that exists between the bishop, the council of presbyters and Jesus Christ, for 'in your unanimity and harmonious love Jesus Christ is sung' (Ignatius, *Eph.* 4). He believed that the bishops had a crucial, representative role to play in the maintenance of unity. The bishop of the local

---

[9] Cf. *The Martyrdom of St Polycarp* 8.1; 19.2. The Muratorian Canon, which dates from the later second century, twice uses the phrase 'the catholic church' in listing the writings to be received as Scripture by the Church of Rome – and some not to be received.

church represented Christ to the church: 'We must regard the bishop as the Lord himself' (Ignatius, *Eph.* 6). To share in this one Eucharist, over which the bishop or his delegate presided, was to be on the path to salvation, for the Eucharist is 'the medicine of immortality, the antidote we take in order not to die but to live forever in Jesus Christ' (Ignatius, *Eph.* 20). To be separated from the one, holy, apostolic church, guided, instructed and served by the bishops, presbyters and deacons, and united in the Eucharist, is to be separated from Christ and to lose the God-given gift of salvation. 'The one who is within the sanctuary is clean, but the one who is outside the sanctuary is not clean. That is, whoever does anything without the bishop and council of presbyters and deacons does not have a clean conscience' (Ignatius, *Trallians* 7).

The Shepherd of Hermas

The Shepherd of Hermas was composed in Rome after 1 Clement but before the time of Irenaeus. It was probably written because of conflicts in the church, especially over the forgiveness of post-baptismal sin and the behaviour of rich believers towards the poor. The first part depicts the church as an elderly woman, aged and weakened by the sins of the baptized. Later, Hermas is taught by the shepherd, 'the angel of repentance'. In the first part, the woman teaches Hermas about his urgent need for repentance and the right way for him and his family to lead a Christian life. Hermas is told that the woman (the church) is elderly 'because she was created before all things; . . . and for her sake the world was formed' (8). He is given a vision of a tower which is being built by the angels of God. In response to a question about the stones being used for the building, he is told:

> The stones that are square and white and fit at their joints, these are the apostles and bishops and teachers and deacons who have walked according to the holiness of God and have ministered to the elect of God as bishops and teachers and deacons with purity and reverence. . . . And they always agreed with one another, and so they had peace with one another and listened to one another. (13)

Later in the text, the elderly woman is, in two stages, depicted as younger and stronger as she responds to the repentance of Christians like Hermas, who have sinned. Finally, she appears in her youthful beauty. It is especially striking that in the situations of sin and failure to which the text alludes, it is the figure of *the church* that indicates the right way forward for the baptized, the way in accord with apostolic teaching.

THE CHURCH IN THE WRITING OF IRENAEUS

Irenaeus was born in Asia Minor about AD 130. As a young man, he met and listened to Polycarp, bishop of Smyrna. He records with admiration that Polycarp 'departed this life (as a martyr), having always taught the things which he had learned from the apostles, and which the Church has handed down, and which alone are true' (*Haer.*, 3.4). As a mature Christian, Irenaeus moved to Gaul, where there was a substantial

Greek-speaking community. Eusebius records that in 177 Irenaeus, having become a presbyter, brought to Pope Eleutherus a letter written from prison by some of the Gallic martyrs who were pleading for peace in the divided churches. In this letter Irenaeus was himself commended, and later in the same year, he became Bishop of Lyons.

Irenaeus is known for his rambling text entitled *The Refutation of False Gnosis*, or *Adversus Haereses*.[10] At this time, the catholic churches were embroiled in a series of debates with teachers like Valentinus, Basilides and Marcion, who claimed a 'gnostic' – or esoteric – way of interpreting the Jewish Scriptures and the Christian teaching. Irenaeus was acutely conscious that the gnostic teaching in its variety ran counter to the treasured witness of the apostles which was foundational for all the churches, so he set out to describe and refute these misleading teachings in detail. His central concern was for the church's fidelity to the apostolic *tradition*, handed down by those who had been taught by Jesus and guided by the Holy Spirit to communicate his message of salvation throughout the world: 'For where the Church is, there is the Spirit of God; and where the Spirit of God is, there is the Church and every kind of grace. The Spirit is truth' (*Haer.*, 3.24.1).

The truth that guides the churches is summed up in a 'rule of faith'. Irenaeus draws out from the tradition that has been passed down to his generation more than one summary of the truths that are contained in this oral teaching and which act as a yardstick in the recognition of written Scripture. In his *Demonstration of the Apostolic Preaching*, he says:

> This then is the order of the *rule of our faith*, and the foundation of the building, and the stability of our conversation: God, the Father, not made, not material, invisible; one God, the creator of all things: this is the first point of our faith. The second point is: The Word of God, Son of God, Christ Jesus our Lord, who was manifested to the prophets according to the form of their prophesying and according to the method of the dispensation of the Father: through whom all things were made; who also at the end of the times, to complete and gather up all things, was made man among men, visible and tangible, in order to abolish death and show forth life and produce a community of union between God and man. And the third point is: The Holy Spirit, through whom the prophets prophesied, and the fathers learned the things of God, and the righteous were led forth into the way of righteousness; and who in the end of the times was poured out in a new way upon mankind in all the earth, renewing man unto God. (6)[11]

---

[10]Irenaeus wrote in Greek, but *Adversus Haereses* survives only in inelegant, Latin translation. I have used the most widely available English translation, *The Ante-Nicene Fathers*, vol. 1, in eds A. Roberts and J. Donaldson, rev. A. Cleveland Coxe (reprinted Grand Rapids, MI: William B. Eerdmans Publishing Company, 1981).

[11]See, *St Irenaeus, The Demonstration of the Apostolic Preaching*, trans. J. Armitage Robinson (London: SPCK, 1920), pp. 74–5.

Commenting on a similar summary of 'the faith' which the church has received 'from the apostles and from their disciples', Irenaeus affirms that

> the Church . . . although scattered throughout the whole world, yet, as if occupying but one house, carefully preserves it. She also believes these points [of doctrine] just as if she had but one soul, and one and the same heart, and she proclaims them and teaches them, and hands them down, with perfect harmony, as if she possessed only one mouth. (*Haer.*, 1.10.1-2)

This ideal of unanimity can be traced back to the account of the Jerusalem consultation in Acts 15 and forward to the deliberation of the ecumenical councils of the fourth and fifth centuries. Irenaeus claims, 'Although the languages of the world are dissimilar, yet the import of the tradition is one and the same' (*Haer.*, 1.10.2).

Those who have the primary responsibility for maintaining the church in the truth it has received are the bishops. It was to the bishops of the church and to their successors that the apostles 'handed on' the faith that they had received from the Lord. Irenaeus is at pains to demonstrate this succession in the major apostolic sees, and especially Rome, because the unbroken succession of those who have taught the same faith bears witness to its trustworthiness in and for the present generation. The bishops, guided by the Holy Spirit, have a special responsibility to pass on this faith intact, neither adding to it nor taking anything away. Their unity (demonstrated and deepened by their sharing in the one communion of the church) is essential to their authority and the authenticity of their teaching. The threat of gnostic teaching is a threat to this unity.

Irenaeus is himself a creative exponent of Scripture, but in service to the truths that are summed up in the 'rule of faith'. He reads the Jewish Scriptures in the light of the Trinitarian faith that is now taught by the church. Thus, the church does not, like Marcion, reject the Jewish Scriptures as teaching falsehood but reinterprets them in the light of deeper truths. The story of the Fall is reversed and transcended in the story of the crucifixion. Adam's loss of Paradise is reversed in the victory of the Second Adam, Jesus Christ. Eve, by her disobedience, brought death upon herself and the human race; Mary, by her obedience, brought salvation. In Jesus Christ, the history of humanity was triumphantly 'recapitulated' as one of fulfilment rather than loss.

It is clear that for Irenaeus the church must be one. He confidently contrasts the unity of Christian tradition with the chaotic diversity of gnostic teaching. It must be holy because in all its doings it is inspired by the Holy Spirit. It is catholic because it extends throughout the known world. Above all, it must be apostolic because it owes its very existence and its claim to truth not to philosophical speculation of any kind but to the faithful witness of the apostles by which its own identity is constituted. It is clear that for Irenaeus, 'that tradition derived from the apostles, of the very great, the very ancient, and universally known Church founded and organized at Rome by the two most glorious apostles Peter and Paul', has a special place to play in the whole church – 'For it is a matter of necessity that every Church should agree with this Church, on account of its pre-eminent authority' (*propter potiorem principalitatem*) (*Haer.*, 3.3.2).[12]

THE CHURCH IN THE WRITING OF CYPRIAN

The writings of Cyprian are of outstanding significance for the Christian understanding of the church, especially in the West. He lived through extraordinarily difficult times of intermittent, widespread persecution. As bishop of Carthage in the mid-third century, he was forced to confront the central questions about the unity, the holiness, the catholicity and the apostolicity of the church. In doing so, he drew on a clear, analytical mind (his approach is characteristically firm but judicious), a humane intelligence and a knowledge of the Christian tradition passed on through the brilliant but less measured writings of Tertullian, whom he called 'The Master'. Faced with the task of guiding his flock through extreme peril, he proved an outstanding pastoral theologian.

Cyprian was converted about the year 246 and within two years he was elected bishop of Carthage. Only months later, the church faced a crisis after an edict in 250 of the Emperor Decius who, to promote the unity of the Empire, required that all should publicly reverence the pagan deities. Not for fifty years had there been sustained or widespread persecution and the church had become somnolent. Many baptized Christians opted for the quiet life and did as the authorities required. Some evaded punishment by buying certificates that they had offered incense at pagan shrines. Others, like Cyprian himself, went into hiding. A minority refused to compromise and were imprisoned, tortured and, in some cases, martyred. After about a year, the persecution abated and Cyprian was able to emerge from hiding. The situation that he faced and the way he approached it is evident in *De Lapsis* ('On those who have fallen'), a treatise written shortly after the end of the persecution. What was relatively new was the scale of the problem. There were many who acknowledged that they had committed the sin of apostasy but now sought readmission to the church. The question that faced pastors like Cyprian was one that engaged both the apostolicity and the holiness of the church. The apostolic precedent, to which texts like *The Shepherd of Hermas* bore witness, was that Christians who had fallen badly but confessed their sins and did public penance could be readmitted to the church – after all, the disciples (who became apostles) had been given authority to 'forgive' and to 'retain' sins (Jn 20.23). The situation was complicated for Cyprian because some even had written notes from those who had subsequently been martyred, pleading, with all the spiritual authority attributed to the martyrs who died, and to the confessors who survived, for the lapsed to

---

[12]'*Ad hanc enim ecclesiam propter potiorem principalitatem necesse est omnem convenire ecclesiam.*' Irenaeus' meaning here is much disputed. From an ecumenical point of view, it is important to note that he speaks of the role of Peter *and* Paul in the founding and nurture of the Roman church, and his focus on the position of the church precedes his genealogy of the bishops. On the issues raised, see J.-M. R. Tillard, *The Bishop of Rome* (London: SPCK, 1983), pp. 74–86.

be forgiven and embraced once more by the church. Cyprian well knew that if reintegration of the lapsed was made too easy, the church's authority as a witness to salvation in Christ – its holiness – would be compromised, but if it was made too difficult, the church would no longer be faithful to the apostolic witness that it indeed embraced sinners. He believed that 'the duty of a bishop of the Lord is, not to deceive with false flatteries, but to provide the remedies needed for salvation' (*Laps.* 14). His solution was to say that those who had fallen and wished to be reintegrated with the church should do penance for a time that depended on the gravity of their sin. The bishops would consult about policy concerning the path to readmission to the Eucharist, which they did at the Council of Carthage in 251. It was agreed that the readmission of baptized penitents could readily be granted if there was a danger of death (as when plague struck Carthage in the following year). When widespread persecution was renewed under the Emperor Gallus, Cyprian speedily admitted to communion, without fear of compromising the church's holiness, those who had been doing penance.

Cyprian's treatise 'On the unity of the Catholic Church' (*De unitate ecclesiae*) contains the seeds of his mature thought about the unity of the church. Much of Cyprian's thinking is, however, contained in some eighty-two surviving letters, which often discuss matters of practical ecclesiology.[13] When Cyprian wrote *De unitate*, two schisms had broken out. The first was associated with the rigorism of Novatian, a Roman presbyter who, having once been an advocate of leniency, now opposed the forgiveness of those who had committed apostasy. As a candidate to be the bishop of Rome, he set himself against the more lenient position of Cornelius, who was chosen by a clear majority. Cyprian saw in Novatian and his rigorist stand against the legitimate bishop of Rome, which had attracted a considerable following, a serious threat to the unity of the church. His public opposition to Novatian helped to bolster the position of Cornelius, and so the unity of the church.

However, on another church-defining issue, Cyprian found himself at odds with the teaching of Cornelius' successor as bishop of Rome, Stephen. A number of Christians had been baptized by those who followed Novatian and others adjudged to be schismatic, or heretical, or both. Cyprian took the line that only the church could minister salvation: 'You cannot have God for your Father if you have not the Church for your mother' (*Unit. Eccl.*, 6). Baptism in the name of the Trinity, when administered by heretics, counted for nothing. Catechumens baptized by heretics should be baptized properly (it was not a matter of *re*-baptism as the first, pretended baptism was completely ineffective). Stephen, however, believed that baptism, as an act of the Holy Spirit, even when administered by heretics, did potentially admit

---

[13]A useful compendium is *St Cyprian of Carthage, On the Church, Select Letters*, in A. Brent (Crestwood, NY: St Vladimir's Seminary Press, 2006). For the letters of Cyprian, I have used the numbering of *The Ante-Nicene Fathers*, vol. V, eds A. Roberts and J. Donaldson, rev. A. Cleveland Coxe (reprinted Grand Rapids, MI: William B. Eerdmans Publishing Company, 1995). P. Hinchliff, *Cyprian of Carthage and the Unity of the Christian Church* (London: Geoffrey Chapman, 1974), pp. 131–3, provides a helpful chart to guide the reader through the confusing numbering of Cyprian's letters in the main sources.

the baptized to the church and all that was needed for them to be admitted to communion was the laying on of hands. God could use those who were in error to bring salvation to those who offered themselves in good faith for baptism. This was the position later taken by Augustine when he opposed the re-baptism of those baptized by Donatists (whose error was a new form of rigorism). Cyprian's motives were clear – to preserve the unity and the holiness of the church – but it was Stephen who was found by posterity to have the better understanding of all-embracing catholicity.

Perhaps the most important contributions made by Cyprian lay in his understanding of episcopal authority. For him, as for Ignatius and Irenaeus before him, the bishops were in a direct line of succession from the apostles, and they carried responsibility not only for their own church but, corporately, for all the churches (cf. 2 Cor. 11.28). Without the church within which they ministered by their apostolic leadership they were nothing: 'The bishop is in the church, and the church is in the bishop' (*Ep.*, LXVIII). Cyprian was keen to preserve for each bishop the maximum personal responsibility for the spiritual health of their churches, but he also stressed the overlapping responsibility ('solidarity') of the bishops, so that where bishops went astray it was the responsibility of others to correct them. The mutual love and the unanimity of the college of bishops as a decision-making body were of the greatest importance for him: 'The authority of the bishops forms a unity of which each holds his part in its totality' (*Unit. Eccl.*, 5). The authority of the bishops was, for him, ultimately, Petrine. Peter was the rock on which the Church of Christ was built, but what that meant for Cyprian is a matter of dispute. On this issue, we have two versions of a key section (paras 4–5) in *Unit. Eccl.* The first 'primacy' text is more affirmative of the unique authority of the bishop of Rome: 'No doubt the other [Apostles] were all that Peter was, but a primacy is given to Peter.' The second 'received' text sets Petrine authority in the context of the college of bishops: 'No doubt the other Apostles were all that Peter was, endowed with equal dignity and power, but the start comes from him alone.'

It is not clear to what extent Cyprian acknowledged a unique and determinative authority in the ministry of the bishop of Rome. He undoubtedly saw the ministry of the bishop of Rome as of great significance, but he was himself prepared to oppose the bishop of Rome – though remaining in communion with him – when he thought he was wrong.

One significant advance made by Cyprian was to affirm the importance of church synods – by which he meant synods of bishops, at which presbyters and laity might be present – in achieving unanimity. He expected to act responsibly in his diocese, but he did not expect, as a bishop, to act alone. He passionately believed that bishops should act in a mutually consultative manner and with a passion for unity. Only in unity could the church remain faithful to apostolic tradition; only in unity could it endure the persecutions and pressures to which it was subject. Cyprian was found by posterity to have been absolutely right in his concern that the church should be catholic: it should indeed be one, with one message of salvation for all the world. He was found to be right in his conviction that the church should be holy (not offering what Bonhoeffer called 'cheap grace'), but should also be a church that truly welcomed repentant sinners. Similarly, he was found to be right in his concern for fidelity to the tradition which the church had inherited from the apostles. His most important heir in these convictions was another North African, Augustine, who could look back to the witness of Cyprian and see a church *in via*, a pilgrim church travelling through the wilderness of this world towards the fullness of its salvation in the heavenly City of God.

EUSEBIUS OF CAESAREA

What we have followed so far is a trajectory in the self-understanding of the church. The first historian known to trace this trajectory was Eusebius of Caesarea, who wrote his *History of the Church*[14] early in the fourth century, concluding it with the glorious reign of Constantine and the Peace of the church. The story as he tells it, beginning with the life of Jesus Christ, brings out the identity of the church under the guidance of the Holy Spirit. The church Eusebius described is the continuation of the church described in the Acts of the Apostles.[15]

Eusebius begins by setting out his prospectus. He aims to trace 'the lines of succession from the holy apostles'; the errors of those who 'through a passion for innovation' divided the flock of Christ; 'the martyrdoms of later days down to my own time' (*HE*.1.1). Strikingly, he lays out a Christology of Jesus Christ as 'the sole High Priest of the universe, the sole King of all creation, and of prophets the sole Archprophet of the Father' (1.3). What Eusebius does not do is to bring out the relation between Christ as prophet, priest and king and the church, which, through the Spirit, participates in him. Furthermore, Eusebius is so preoccupied with the sufferings of the Jews as punishment for the way that they treated Christ that he does not see any continuity between the Jews as 'people of God', to which the Old Testament bears witness, and the church as the new people of God. In commending the writing of Hegesippus and Irenaeus, he speaks of 'the splendour of the Catholic and only true Church, always remaining the same and unchanged' over against a succession of new heresies (4.7). When he writes about the development of synods to resolve controverted issues, as with the Quartodeciman controversy over the precise date for the celebration of Easter, he stresses the unanimity with which the bishops settled conflicts (*HE*. 5.23). In describing the Peace of the church under Constantine, he writes euphorically, 'There was one power of the divine Spirit coursing through all the members, one soul in them all, the same enthusiasm for the faith, one hymn of praise on all their lips' (*HE*. 10.3). The church as described at the beginning of the Acts of the Apostles (4.32) has been restored. Eusebius reproduces an extraordinary meditation on the newly dedicated cathedral at Tyre,

---

[14]I have used the admirably clear translation, Eusebius, *The History of the Church from Christ to Constantine*, trans. G. A. Williamson (Harmondsworth: Penguin, 1965).

[15]This is made explicit in Eusebius' description of the gathering of bishops from every part of the known world at the Council of Nicaea as a 'new Pentecost' (cf. Acts 2.5, 9-11) in V. C., p. 124.

which becomes a meditation on the nature of the church itself and the trials through which it has been, now to emerge in its pristine beauty. He concludes:

> Such is the great cathedral which throughout the whole world under the sun the great Creator of the universe, the Word, has built, Himself again fashioning this spiritual image on earth of the vaults beyond the skies, so that by the whole creation and by rational beings His Father might be honoured and worshipped. (*HE*. 10.4)

ONE, HOLY, CATHOLIC AND APOSTOLIC – AN ECUMENICAL VISION

Eusebius died about 340, when, despite the clear teaching of the Council of Nicaea, the Catholic Church remained deeply divided over Arianism. As the crisis was eventually resolved in favour of the 'Nicene faith' with respect to the full deity of Jesus, the focus shifted towards the deity of the Holy Spirit within a Trinitarian account of God. The Council of Constantinople was convened in 381 to address, among other things, the status of the Holy Spirit. In doing so, it also received teaching concerning the church, adding to the Creed of Nicaea the phrase that the church was 'one, holy, catholic and apostolic'.[16]

These 'notes' of the church have proved both divisive and uniting. They have proved divisive for those who, like Cyprian, discerned no saving action of the Holy Spirit outside the boundaries of the visible Catholic Church. Cyprian's 'Outside the Church there is no salvation' (*'Salus extra ecclesiam non est'*, *Letter* LXXII) was for many centuries taken by the Catholic Church to mean 'Outside the (visible, Catholic) Church there is no salvation', so that, from the Catholic point of view, ecumenism could only ever be an ecumenism of return to Rome – while, from a Protestant point of view, according to the Augsburg Confession VII (1530), the 'one holy Christian church' is 'the assembly of all believers among whom the Gospel is preached in its purity and the holy sacraments are administered according to the Gospel'. The beginnings of a shift in the Catholic position can be seen in the seminal work of J. A Möhler, *Unity in the Church* (1825).[17] Möhler's emphasis on the spirit of the church fathers of the first three centuries took the emphasis off the juridical, institutional criteria for membership of the Tridentine Church, placing it on participation in the spiritual community of those who are being saved, on *communion*. There has been

---

[16]This wording was probably indebted to the creed of the Church of Jerusalem, which spoke of 'one holy catholic Church'. Cyril of Jerusalem, who played a prominent role at the Council of Constantinople, reflects on this phrase in his *Catechetical Lecture* XVIII, 'On the Words, And in One Holy Catholic Church', written about 348. See *The Ante-Nicene and Post-Nicene Fathers*, second series, vol. VII (S. Cyril of Jerusalem et al.), eds P. Schaff and H. Wace (reprinted Grand Rapids, MI: Eerdmans, 1996), pp. xlvii, 139–41.

[17]J. A. Möhler, *Die Einheit in der Kirche, oder das Prinzip des Katholizismus, Dargestellt im Geiste der Kirchenväter der drei ersten Jahrhunderte*, ed. J. R. Geiselmann (Köln: Jakob Hegner, 1956).

much debate as to whether J. H. Newman read Möhler,[18] but Newman's *Essay on the Development of Christian Doctrine* (1845) similarly stressed the spirit-led dynamism of the church, whereby it maintained its identity through centuries of change. The emphases of both Möhler and Newman were taken up in the twentieth-century movement referred to as *Ressourcement*,[19] which, with the help of Catholic scholars such as G. Bardy and Y. Congar OP, explored the life of the church as a communion and played a key role in the transformation of the self-understanding of the Roman Catholic Church at Vatican II (1962–5). Two key Conciliar texts signal this transformation: *Lumen Gentium* (The Dogmatic Constitution on the Church) and *Unitatis Redintegratio* (The Decree on Ecumenism). Both were promulgated on the same day, 21 November 1964, and both use the same, novel language of 'subsistence' to describe an understanding of the Catholic Church which is open to enrichment through dialogue with Christians of other traditions.[20] *Lumen Gentium* claims, 'The sole Church of Christ, which in the Creed we profess to be one, holy, catholic and apostolic . . . *subsists* in the Catholic Church, which is governed by the successor of Peter and by the bishops in communion with him.' It goes on to say, 'Nevertheless, many elements of sanctification and of truth are found outside its visible confines' (*LG* 8). In similar words, *Unitatis Redintegratio* spoke of the conviction that 'All Christians will be gathered, in a common celebration of the Eucharist, into the unity of the one and only Church, which Christ bestowed on his Church from the beginning', adding, 'This unity, we believe, *subsists* in the Catholic Church as something she can never lose' (*UR* 4). By speaking of 'separated Churches' and 'separated brethren', and by speaking of those who 'believe in Christ and have been properly baptized' as in 'some, though imperfect, communion with the Catholic Church' (*UR* 3), the Catholic Church signalled a new openness to the experience of Christians of other traditions. It was this transformation which opened the way for the Catholic Church to participate in the ecumenical movement of the last fifty years, and for churches of various traditions to find a meeting point in the ecclesiology of the first four Christian centuries. The Orthodox scholar John Zizioulas summed this up when, about 1965, he wrote:

> The gradual abandonment of the confessional mentality of past generations and the recognition of the need for our theology to be an expression not of one confession but of the one, holy, catholic and apostolic Church herself, now directs

---

[18]For a discussion which takes this unproven idea seriously, see O. Chadwick, *From Bossuet to Newman, The Idea of Doctrinal Development* (Cambridge: University Press, 1957), pp. 111–14.

[19]For a fine introduction, see G. Flynn and P. Murray (eds), *Ressourcement* (Oxford: Oxford University Press, 2011).

[20]There has been much scholarly discussion of the term *'subsistit in'*. According to the Congregation for the Doctrine of the Faith, 'In number 8 of the Dogmatic Constitution *Lumen gentium* "subsistence" means [the] perduring, historical continuity and the permanence of all the elements instituted by Christ in the Catholic Church' ('Responses to some Questions regarding the Doctrine of the Church', 29 June 2007). Though other historic Christian traditions do not use the same language, they make substantially the same claim, hence the need for dialogue.

the course of theological study towards the sources of the ancient undivided Church.[21]

CONCLUSION: ONE, HOLY, CATHOLIC AND APOSTOLIC – ECUMENICAL CONVERGENCE

The fruit of the ecumenical movement is evident in the convergence text of the World Council of Churches, *The Church, Towards a Common Vision* (2013). In a key section on 'The Church of the Triune God as *Koinonia*', the 'One, Holy, Catholic and Apostolic Church' is discussed. Four crisp paragraphs explore the following ecumenical claims:

The church is one because God is one.

The church is holy because God is holy.

The church is catholic because of the abundant goodness of God 'who desires everyone to be saved and come to the knowledge of the truth' (1 Tim. 2.4).

The church is apostolic because the Father sent the Son to establish it. The Son, in turn, chose and sent the apostles and prophets, empowered with the gifts of the Holy Spirit at Pentecost, to serve as its foundation and to oversee its mission (22).

For the ecumenical movement, there is nothing arbitrary or adventitious about the *notae* of the church. It is because the church is constituted by its participation in the triune God that, in its deepest identity, it can never be other than 'one, holy, catholic and apostolic'.

BIBLIOGRAPHY

The Ante-Nicene Fathers, vol. I (The Apostolic Fathers, Justin Martyr, Irenaeus), eds A. Roberts and J. Donaldson, rev. A. Cleveland Coxe. reprinted Grand Rapids, MI: William B. Eerdmans Publishing Company, 1981.

The Ante-Nicene Fathers, vol. V (Hippolytus, Cyprian et al.), eds A. Roberts and J. Donaldson, rev. A. Cleveland Coxe. reprinted Grand Rapids, MI: William B. Eerdmans Publishing Company, 1995.

The Apostolic Fathers, ed. and trans. M. W. Holmes. Grand Rapids, MI: Baker Academic, 2007.

Augustine. *The City of God against the Pagans*, ed. R. W. Dyson. Cambridge Texts in the History of Political Thought Series. Cambridge: Cambridge University Press, 1998.

Bardy, G. *La Théologie de l'Église de saint Clément de Rome à saint Irenée*. Paris: Éditions du Cerf, 1945.

---

[21]J. Zizioulas, Preface to *Eucharist, Bishop, Church: The Unity of the Church in the Divine Eucharist and the Bishop during the First Three Centuries* (Brookline, MA: Holy Cross Orthodox Press, 2001), p. 1.

St Cyprian, The Lapsed, The Unity of the Catholic Church, trans. M. Bévenot. London: Longmans, Green and Co., 1957.

St Cyprian of Carthage: On the Church, Select Letters, trans. A. Brent. Popular Patristics Series, Volume 33. Crestwood, NY: St Vladimir's Seminary Press, 2006.

Eusebius. *The History of the Church from Christ to Constantine*, trans. G. A. Williamson. Harmondsworth: Penguin, 1965.

Hinchliff, P. *Cyprian of Carthage and the Unity of the Christian Church*. London: Geoffrey Chapman, 1974.

St Irenaeus, The Demonstration of the Apostolic Preaching, trans. J. Armitage Robinson. London: SPCK, 1920.

Kelly, J. N. D. *Early Christian Creeds*, 3d edn. Harlow: Longman, 1972.

MacMullen, R. *Voting about God in Early Church Councils*. New Haven, CT and London: Yale University Press, 2006.

Möhler, J. A. *Die Einheit in der Kirche, oder das Prinzip des Katholizismus, Dargestellt im Geiste der Kirchenväter der drei ersten Jahrhunderte*, ed. J. R. Geiselmann. Köln: Jakob Hegner, 1956.

Newman, J. H. *An Essay on the Development of Christian Doctrine*, ed. J. M. Cameron. Harmondsworth: Penguin, 1974.

Tillard, J.-M. R. *The Bishop of Rome*. London: SPCK, 1983.

Tillard, J.-M. R. *Église d'Églises, L'ecclésiologie de communion*. Paris: Éditions du Cerf, 1987.

The Treatise on the Apostolic Tradition of St Hippolytus of Rome, ed. G. Dix, rev. H. Chadwick. London: SPCK, 1968.

Vatican Council II, The Conciliar and Post Conciliar Documents, ed. Austin Flannery O.P. Dublin: Dominican Publications, 1975.

World Council of Churches. *The Church, Towards a Common Vision*. Faith and Order Paper 214. Geneva: WCC Publications, 2013.

Zizioulas, J. D. *Eucharist, Bishop, Church*. Brookline, MA: Holy Cross Orthodox Press, 2001.

INDEX

9 780567 700582